# BOOKS FOR COLLEGE LIBRARIES

# BOOKS FOR COLLEGE LIBRARIES

A CORE COLLECTION OF 50,000 TITLES

*Third edition*

A project of the Association of College and Research Libraries

Volume 1
Humanities

American Library Association
*Chicago and London 1988*

Preliminary pages composed by Impressions, Inc.,
    in Times Roman on a Penta-driven
    Autologic APS-$\mu$5
    Phototypesetting system

Text pages composed by Logidec, Inc., in Times Roman on an
    APS-5 digital typesetter

Printed on 50 lb. Glatfelter B-16, a pH neutral stock,
    and bound in Roxite B-grade cloth by
    Edwards Brothers.

The paper used in this publication meets the minimum
requirements of American National Standard for Information
Sciences—Permanence of Paper for Printed Library Materials,
ANSI Z39.48-1984.

**Library of Congress Cataloging-in-Publication Data**

Books for college libraries.

    "A project of the Association of College and Research
Libraries."

    Contents: v. 1.   Humanities—v. 2.   Language
and literature—v. 3.   History—[etc.]
    1.  Libraries, University and college—Book
lists.  2.  Bibliography—Best books.  I.  Association of
College and Research Libraries.
Z1039.C65B67   1988        025.2′1877        88-16714
ISBN 0-8389-3357-2 (v. 1)
ISBN 0-8389-3356-4 (v. 2)
ISBN 0-8389-3355-6 (v. 3)
ISBN 0-8389-3354-8 (v. 4)
ISBN 0-8389-3358-0 (v. 5)
ISBN 0-8389-3359-9 (v. 6)

BOOKS FOR COLLEGE LIBRARIES

# Volumes 1–6    Contents

*Biology*
*physics*
*Nursing*

# Volume 1   Contents

# Introduction

BOOKS FOR COLLEGE LIBRARIES (BCL3) presents a third recommended core collection for undergraduate libraries in full awareness of the tensions and paradoxes implicit in such list making. There is the pull between ideals of excellence and sufficient coverage of all subjects. There is the balance to be weighed among subjects. There are the rival temptations to identify the basic with the time tested and to equate the important with the new. There is the risk of ranking with the obsolete the merely temporary victims of scholarly fashion. There is the certainty that new definitive works will be published just as the selection closes.

That BCL3 exists supposes some resolution of these problems. A final paradox remains: BCL3 can fully succeed only by failing. It would be disastrous should the collection it suggests serve perfectly to ratify the finished work of the book selection in any library. Some inclusions and some omissions should displease everyone; for on-going professional questioning and the search for individual library answers remain as basic to collection development as basic book lists.

In overall plan and appearance, BCL3 is much the same as BCL2 (1975). The division into five volumes takes the same liberties with Library of Congress classification to provide coherent subject groups and volumes similar in size. Individual entries contain the same elements of full cataloging and classification information; and within volumes, entries are arranged in exact call number order.

BCL3 also exists as a database to allow further development of formats alternative to print. An electronic tape version will be made available. Since BCL2, online catalogs and reference databases have become familiar library tools. The provision of BCL3 in searchable form is thus important; and it may add possible uses of the list within larger libraries—easy identification of key titles in very large online catalogs, for instance.

## HISTORY

The first bibliography to bear this title was published in 1967 as a replacement for Charles B. Shaw's *List of Books for College Libraries* (1931). The origin of BCL1 was in the University of California's New Campuses Program (1961–1964), which also made use of other compilations such as the published catalog of Harvard's Lamont Library (1953) and the shelflist of the undergraduate library of the University of Mich-

igan. The 1963 cut-off date for BCL1 titles deliberately coincided with the 1964 beginning of *Choice*, whose current reviews for academic libraries were foreseen as a complementary, on-going revision and supplement. Such a role proved impossible, however, even for so comprehensive a journal as *Choice* with its 6,600 reviews a year and its retrospective evaluation of perhaps another 1,000 titles in topical monthly bibliographic essays. Periodic reassessments that could include categories of material not usually reviewed by *Choice* (revisions, fiction, works published abroad, for instance) seemed still an essential aid in college library collection development. BCL2 appeared in 1975; work on BCL3 began in late 1985.

## SIZE AND SCOPE: STANDARDS, LIBRARIES AND BOOK LISTS

The number of books of which college libraries need potentially to be aware continues its relentless growth. In the years from the Shaw list to BCL1, total annual United States book output averaged slightly more than 11,500 volumes. Between the cut-off dates for BCL1 and BCL2, that figure (revised to show titles, a lesser number) was just under 32,000. Since the 1973 BCL2 cut-off, the annual average has been 41,000.[1] Given such increase, the task of book selectors would be challenging enough, even had the growth of buildings and book budgets characteristic of the late 1960s and early 1970s continued. By the time BCL2 was published, however, the rate of academic library book acquisitions had begun to fall. This downward trend continues, and it makes careful title selection ever more vital, especially for the small library.[2]

When BCL1 was published, the already outdated 1959 standards for college libraries called for a minimum undergraduate collection of only 50,000 titles; BCL1 recommended 53,400. BCL2 and the 1975 revision of those standards appeared in the same year. The new standards set out a formula whose add-on stipulations plus a starting figure of 85,000 raised basic requirements for even very small institutions to 100,000. The 1970 proposal for BCL2 called for a list of 40,000 titles. The thinking behind this lower figure may be explained by a published study of 1977 library

[1]*Bowker Annual of Library & Book Trade Information.* New York: Bowker. 26th ed., 1981; 32nd ed., 1987.
[2]"Three Years of Change in College and University Libraries, Prepared by the National Center for Education Statistics, Washington, D.C." *College & Research Libraries News* 45 (July/August 1984): 359–361.

statistics against the 1975 standards. This analysis found that 52 percent of all undergraduate libraries still reported fewer than 100,000 volumes and that 55 percent of private undergraduate libraries held even fewer than the "starter" figure of 85,000.[3] A very brief basic list might thus serve rather than intimidate the many libraries still far below standard.

The college library standards were revised again in 1985, just as work on BCL3 began.[4] The same formula (Standard 2.2, Formula A) was recommended. Applying it to a very small hypothetical college of 100 faculty and 1,000 students pursuing majors in only 10 fields of study yields a basic book requirement of 104,000 volumes. BCL3 suggests about half that number, hoping again to pause somewhere between usefulness and utopia. Very recent figures show that the average book expenditures for academic libraries in 26 U.S. states fall below the figure that would be necessary to meet the median annual growth rate of our hypothetical library, also set by the 1985 standards.[5]

In scope, the focus of BCL3 remains the traditionally book-using disciplines. Contributors were asked to keep in mind an imaginary college or small university that concentrates on the customary liberal arts and sciences curriculum but also offers work at the undergraduate level in business, computer science, engineering, and the health sciences. The proportions of the broad subject groupings by volume have remained roughly constant through the three BCL editions. (See Table 1.) There have been steady decreases in the humanities and literature allocations, however, very slightly offset by increased use of single-entry "complete works" citations that include large numbers of titles.

These changes have come about despite editorial quotas candidly designed to minimize them. Sharp

[3]Ray L. Carpenter, "College Libraries: A Comparative Analysis in Terms of the ACRL Standards," *College and Research Libraries* 42 (January 1981): 7–18.

[4]"Standards for College Libraries, 1986, Prepared by the College Library Standards Committee, Jacquelyn M. Morris, chair," *College & Research Libraries News* 47 (March 1986): 189–200.

[5]*Bowker Annual of Library & Book Trade Information.* 32nd ed. New York: Bowker, 1987. The preceding calculation by the BCL editor is based on figures given in the *Bowker Annual* using the formula in the standards cited in note 4.

difficulties confront both BCL editors and librarians juggling hopes for lasting value, necessities for current coverage, and the certainties of obsolescence. Some of the growth in Volume 5 is attributable to a marked increase in its bibliography component, which serves all subjects; but it may be well to repeat, with reference both to Volume 4 and to Volume 5, a statement from my BCL2 introduction that "Perhaps only those works already sufficiently outdated to be ranked as history may safely be included in a 'basic' collection." Despite their increases, both volumes remain brief in comparison with the volume of publication.

As to those titles constituting the rest of the minimal 104,000 requirement but not named in BCL3, much of any collection must respond uniquely to the demands of individual and current curricula. But some, it is to be hoped, will continue to consist of those works, especially belles lettres, not subject to cumulation and replacement by current scholarship. These are often difficult to continue to justify in lists which though "basic" cannot remain immune to shifts in academic enthusiasms.

Across these proportionate subject representations, the focus remains the undergraduate user of the undergraduate library. Both are protean concepts, but they permit some limitation, for instance almost wholly to works in English except for dictionaries and editions chosen to support foreign-language study. With the exception of some of the more basic surveys among "annual reviews" and some serial reference works, the limitation is not only to print but, further, to monographs. There is a need for college-level model collections of periodicals and of nonprint material, but this project does not address it. Still further to define the print universe, BCL3 contributors were asked not to recommend classroom texts unless exceptional, especially for their bibliographies. Volumes of previously published works are seldom listed except for literary anthologies which, together with their indexes, received special consideration in this edition. In-print availability was not considered an important factor.

## CONTRIBUTORS AND WORKING MATERIALS

BCL3 was from the beginning designed as a two-stage selection process and there were two distinct sets

**Table 1. Distribution of Titles by Volume. (In percentages.)**

| Volumes & Subjects | BCL1 | BCL2 | BCL3 |
|---|---|---|---|
| v. 1 (Humanities) | 16.4 | 15.1 | 13.6 |
| v. 2 (Language & Literature) | 32.2 | 30.0 | 28.4 |
| v. 3 (History) | 18.7 | 19.7 | 18.8 |
| v. 4 (Social Sciences) | 20.8 | 21.2 | 22.2 |
| v. 5 (Psychology, Science, Technology, Bibliography) | 11.9 | 14.0 | 17.0 |

of contributors. The first-round team numbered more than 400 college faculty members and about 50 academic reference librarians who made the reference selections. The second group consisted of 64 academic librarian referees, picked for their combination of subject specialization and collection development skills. The librarian referees were asked to review broader subject areas than their faculty counterparts with the intent of adding a wider perspective to help assure the overall coverage and balance to the collection.

Virtually all of the first-round contributors and about half of the second-round referees are *Choice* reviewers. They were selected for excellence, needed subject coverage, altruism (all served unpaid), and availability at the crucial time. (A few sabbaticals were much regretted in the BCL office.) Contributors were not selected with statistical games in mind, but it is an interesting if incidental function of the nature of the *Choice* reviewer pool that they prove a nationally representative lot. They come from 265 institutions in 44 states. The 10 states with the most academic institutions provide 8 of the 10 largest contributor groups. Institutions are divided between public, including federal (145) and private (120), with a mix of small and large from each sector. There are 10 representatives of 2-year campuses. There are 134 women. There are 15 Canadian and 2 British contributors.

As working materials, the round-one contributors received pages from BCL2 (latest titles 1973) and selected *Choice* review cards (1972 through 1985). Approximately 60,000 of some 85,000 reviews published in those years were distributed. Contributors were asked to assign one of four rankings to each title; they were also urged to recommend any other titles they felt essential to undergraduate work in their fields. Many did so. Assignments, some of which overlapped, ranged from 25 to 600 titles.

Preparation of 450 packets of working lists involved the fascinating task of reconciling various assumptions about the organization of knowledge. It was necessary to "deconstruct" and rearrange the LC-classed BCL2 and the subject organization of *Choice* to match the convictions of academics as to just what constituted the definitions and boundaries of their subjects.

## COMPILATION AND REVIEW

Working list packets came back displaying varying neatness, erudition, zeal, and attention to editorial instructions and deadlines. A very few were reassigned; most were extremely well done and miraculously on time. All titles rated "essential" (and some lesser ratings, depending on subject coverage and the rigor of contributor selectivity) were requested, by LC card number if possible, from the Utlas database. (Utlas, the Canadian bibliographic utility, had previously been

selected as the vendor to house the BCL3 database while the collection was being compiled.)

As lists came in and major blocks of LC classification were judged to be reasonably complete, Utlas was asked to produce provisional catalogs in LC class order, showing complete catalog records. These catalogs, after review by the editor, were divided among the second-round referees, whose assignments typically included the work of several first-round contributors. Referees were asked to assess overall quality and suitability of the selections, coverage of the various aspects of a field, and compliance with numerical quotas. The editor's review included the making and insertion of page headings and further observations of (and occasional interventions in) rival views of knowledge as the academic visions of round one were once more refracted through the prism, the worldview of LC classification. A second set of provisional catalogs, reviewed by the editor's assistant, incorporated referee suggestions and the page headings for a final check before typesetting.

## PRESENTATION: HEADINGS, ENTRIES, AND ARRANGEMENT

Page headings are phrased to outline LC classification, to gloss the sometimes very miscellaneous contents of the sections they head, and to indicate the method of arrangement of some special sequences. The printed BCL3 entries contain conventionally complete cataloging and classification information, but not every element of a full LC MARC record. Among notes, only the general (MARC tag 500) are printed; cross-reference and authority information tagged in the 800s is omitted. Those entries for items retained from BCL2 in exactly the same version carry a special symbol, a heavy dot (.) preceding the item number. Entries are sequentially numbered within each volume. The cataloging in some of the entries made by contributors to the Utlas database is less full than the original LC cataloging; some entries vary in other ways.

Database response to titles requested for the collection displayed significant changes since the compilation of BCL2. During that project, both LC MARC and electronic cataloging and bibliographic utilities were new. Nearly two-thirds of BCL2 entries had to be converted especially for that project. BCL3 is in some ways the victim of the success of such cataloging enterprises. There are now many versions of catalog records, especially for pre-1968 titles. These offer varying degrees of adoption of AACR2 and equally various and often unsignalled states of adherence to LC classification, to say nothing of the range of simple cataloging and typing skills. It is therefore impossible to repeat here the certainties of the BCL2 Introduction about the use of LC cataloging and classification, although preference was certainly for LC records. Call numbers completed or assigned by BCL are identified with "x" as the final character, but there are numbers not so flagged that are not LC assignments. BCL3 is designed as a book selection guide, however, not as an exemplar of either cataloging or classification.

Arrangement has been stated to be by LC call number; but some catalog records carry more than one number, some sections of LC classification are being redeveloped, and some allow alternate treatments. BCL3's editor, therefore, had decisions to make. In all volumes, the existence of new LC sequences is signposted with cross-references. Individual subject classification of titles published in series was preferred to numerical gatherings within series. For Volume 2, alternate national literature numbers were selected or created in preference to PZ3 and PZ4 for fiction. Works by and about individual Canadian, Caribbean, African, South Asian, and Australasian authors writing in English have been pulled from the PR4000–6076 sequence and united with the general historical and critical material on those literatures in the PR9000s. Volume 5 displays the decision to keep most subject bibliography in class Z.

## INDEXES

The computer-made Author Index lists personal and institutional names of writers, editors, compilers, translators, sponsoring bodies, and others identified in the numbered "tracings" that bear roman numerals at the ends of entries. The Title Index, also machine generated, lists both uniform and title page titles from the printed entries, including nondistinctive titles and adding variant titles if traced. Because of the use of many "complete works" entries, many famous and highly recommended titles, especially novels, are absent from this index though present by implication in the list. References in the Author and Title indexes are to the sequential numbers, within volume, as-signed to each entry. The Subject Index is a handmade guide to classification. It has its own brief explanatory introduction.

## LACUNAE, ERRORS AND REVISIONS

The virtual absence of serials and the exclusion of formats other than print have been noted under Size and Scope. Additionally, although undergraduate study ranges ever wider, student information needs outside fairly "academic" disciplines and some traditional sporting activities are not fulfilled here; users are referred to college bookstores and recommended lists for public libraries for titles in many craft, technical, and recreational subjects.

Errors of cataloging and questionable classifications will, as it has been stated, be noted. They are present in the database used and though many were corrected, others as surely remain. Reports of errors, expressions of opinion about favorite titles missing and abhorrences present, and general suggestions for future revisions are sincerely sought. They may be addressed to: Editor, Books for College Libraries, c/o *Choice*, 100 Riverview Center, Middletown, CT 06457–3467.

With the breakup of BCL1 into the individual volumes of BCL2, separate revision in an on-going project was predicted. That did not happen, and it would offer some difficulties in indexing and the handling of subjects split among volumes. It is a challenge to assemble the mix of organization to command the seemingly more and more specialized contributors required, the technology to facilitate presentation, and the finance to enable the whole. But it is to be hoped that the even greater challenges college libraries face in collection development will continue to find *Choice* and its reviewers, ACRL, and ALA ready with the help future circumstances require.

VIRGINIA CLARK, *Editor*

# Acknowledgments

Without the contributors and referees of the many subject lists, BCL3 would not exist. They are named in the appropriate volumes and identified by academic or other professional institution and by subject field. To enable the calling together of this team, however, and the presentation of its work took vision, planning, determination, and much help from many groups and individuals.

Both the users and the editorial staff of BCL3 owe thanks to the staff and two successive Executive Directors of the Association of College and Research Libraries (ACRL). Julie Virgo and JoAn S. Segal convened a preliminary investigative committee and commissioned a request for proposal (RFP) that established the first outline of the project for the revised edition. Patricia Sabosik, newly appointed Editor and Publisher of *Choice*, encompassed in her initial plans for the magazine the BCL project. Her response to ACRL's RFP involved the *Choice* staff in the editorial work and the Canadian bibliographic utility Utlas in the technical construction of the database. The staffs of *Choice* and BCL3 are grateful to ACRL for accepting this proposal and to Publishing Services of the American Library Association for co-funding the project with ACRL. Patricia Sabosik served as Project Manager. Liaison with ALA Books was Managing Editor Helen Cline.

An editorial advisory committee, chaired by Richard D. Johnson, SUNY College at Oneonta, was selected to allow the BCL3 Editor to draw advice from representatives of academic libraries of different types, sizes, and locales. Stephen L. Gerhardt, Cerritos College; Michael Haeuser, Gustavus Adolphus College; Barbara M. Hirsh, formerly Marist College; Thomas Kirk, Berea College; Craig S. Likness, Trinity University; and Mary K. Sellen, Spring Valley College, served the project well. Special thanks are due Richard D. Johnson and Craig S. Likness, each of whom also contributed subject lists, and Michael Haeuser, who spent several days as a volunteer in the BCL office and served as committee secretary.

The BCL project was housed in space in the *Choice* office and enjoyed a unique member/guest relationship that involved virtually every member of the *Choice* staff in some work for BCL. The subject editors—Robert Balay, Claire C. Dudley, Ronald H. Epp, Francine Graf, Helen MacLam, and Kenneth McLintock—suggested from their reviewer lists most of the BCL contributors and several referees. Claire C. Dudley and Helen MacLam served as referees; Claire C. Dudley

and Francine Graf gave much other valuable help. Library Technical Assistant Nancy Sbona, Systems Manager Lisa Gross, Office Assistant Mary Brooks, and Administrative Assistant Lucille Calarco deserve special mention for extraordinary assistance.

In addition to using the bibliographic and personnel resources of *Choice*, the Editor of BCL relied for vital support on the collections, equipment, and staffs of five very gracious institutions. Particular thanks go to the libraries of Kenyon College, Wesleyan University, and the Library Association, London, for use of behind-the-scenes cataloging and classification tools in addition to reference sources publicly available; to Trinity University, San Antonio, for tapés of BCL2; and to Trinity College, Hartford, for outstanding help from George R. Graf on preliminary aspects of the project in addition to those for which he is named in the contributor lists.

For work without regard for office hours or job description the Editor would particularly like to thank Judith Douville. She edited the science sections of Volume 5 in addition to assisting the Editor with some parts of Volume 4. She coordinated the corrections to the BCL3 computer file and reviewed the final page proofs. Her enthusiasm and dedication were vital in bringing the project to completion.

BCL3 secretary Anna Barron worked throughout the project. Special thanks are also owed to short-term staff members Alison Johnson and Virginia Carrington.

## CONTRIBUTORS

Title selection for BCL3 reflects three types of expert opinion: from scholars teaching in the field, from reference librarians, and from special referees chosen for their combination of subject and collection-development knowledge. Names appear in the approximate order of contributions in the volume, but Library of Congress classification will have scattered many titles selected by those named here into other sections of the list. The topical labels try to suggest both the depth of specialization required of some contributors and the broad knowledge and responsibility demanded of others; but no list such as this can do more than hint at the nature and amount of work for which these contributors are most gratefully thanked.

GENERAL WORKS: *General Reference*: Reference contributors are named with subjects. *Periodical In-*

*dexes*: George R. Graf, Trinity College, Conn. *Foundations & Grants*: Agnes Haigh Widder, Michigan State University. *Reference Referee*: Byron Anderson, Northern Illinois University.

PHILOSOPHY: *Oriental*: Jane Cauvel, Colorado College; Fred Gillette Sturm, University of New Mexico. *Classical*: Nathan A. Greenberg, Oberlin College; Robert H. Grimm, Oberlin College. *American*: Darnell Rucker, Skidmore College. *Latin American*: Fred Gillette Sturm, University of New Mexico. *European*: Martin A. Bertman, SUNY College at Potsdam; Sister Dorothy A. Haney, Marywood College; Walter G. Moss, Eastern Michigan University; Victor Nuovo, Middlebury College; Howard N. Tuttle, University of New Mexico; Daniel Williman, SUNY at Binghamton; Fred Wilson, University of Toronto. *Special Fields*: Daniel D. Merrill, Oberlin College (Logic); Shane Andre, California State University, Long Beach (Metaphysics); Jane Cauvel, Colorado College, and Albert W. Hayward, Southeast Missouri State University (Aesthetics); John H. Riker, Colorado College (Ethics); Helen James John, S.N.D., Trinity College, DC, and Kathryn Russell, SUNY College at Cortland (Women). *Referee*: Karin Sandvik, University of Wisconsin–LaCrosse.

RELIGION: *Philosophy*: Robert L. Perkins, Stetson University. *Classical Religion & Mythology*: Z. Philip Ambrose, University of Vermont. *Oriental*: Thomas B. Coburn, St. Lawrence University; James P. McDermott, Canisius College; Hall Peebles, Wabash College. *African*: Newell S. Booth, Jr., Miami University, Ohio. *Judaism*: Robert Goldenberg, SUNY at Stony Brook. *Islam*: J. W. Fiegenbaum, Mt. Holyoke College. *Christianity*: Robert F. Berkey, Mt. Holyoke College; Dennis Linehan, S.J., headed a group of consultants at the University of Scranton; Carter Lindberg, Boston University; Paul Mojzes, Rosemont College; Samuel C. Pearson, Southern Illinois University at Edwardsville; William L. Pitts, Jr., Baylor University; Daniel Williman, SUNY at Binghamton. *Special Fields*: Robert F. Berkey, Mt. Holyoke College; Lloyd Gaston, Vancouver School of Theology; and J. Kenneth Kuntz, University of Iowa (Biblical Studies). Sharon Propas, University of Cincinnati (Bible as Literature). William C. Placher, Wabash College (Theology). Chalmers MacCormick, Wells College, and Alice McDowell, Ithaca College (Mysticism). Harold W. Melvin, Jr., Fitchburg State College (Sociology of Religion). Alice McDowell, Ithaca College; Anne E. Patrick, S.N.J.M., Carleton College; and Jenny Yates-Hammett, Wells College (Women). *Reference & Referees*: David Kranzler, Queensborough Community College, CUNY (Judaism); Elaine Peterson, Gonzaga University.

MUSIC: *History*: Jane P. Ambrose, University of Vermont; William E. Grim, Howard Payne University; Clayton W. Henderson, St. Mary's College, Ind.; Cecil Isaac, Austin College; Raymond Stahura, Ripon College. *Instruments*: William Bigham, Morehead State University; Douglas G. Engelhardt, University of Hawaii at Manoa; Sylvia Glickman, Franklin & Marshall College; Kathleen Thomerson, Southern Illinois University at Edwardsville and St. Louis Conservatory of Music; Edgar M. Turrentine, University of Minnesota. *Special Fields*: Jane P. Ambrose, University of Vermont (Women); William H. Baxter, Jr., Birmingham-Southern College (Church Music, Sociology of Music); William M. Bigham, Morehead State University (Psychology); Newel K. Brown, North Texas State University (Music Education, Conducting, Theory); Douglas G. Engelhardt, University of Hawaii at Manoa (Conducting); A. David Franklin, Winthrop College (Jazz); William E. Grim, Howard Payne University (Rock); David P. McAllester, Wesleyan University, emeritus (Ethnomusicology); Richard Miller, Oberlin College (Vocal Music, Opera); Raymond Stahura, Ripon College (Theory). *Reference*: Clifford Haka, Michigan State University (Popular, Rock, Jazz); Guy A. Marco, U.S. Army Libraries, Fort Dix; Sister Louise Smith, University of Western Ontario. *Referees*: D. W. Krummel, University of Illinois at Urbana-Champaign, with assistance from Calvin Elliker, University of Illinois at Urbana-Champaign, and Thomas D. Walker, University of Illinois at Urbana-Champaign.

ART: *Aesthetics & Philosophy*: Jane Cauvel, Colorado College; Albert W. Hayward, Southeast Missouri State University; Wendy B. Holmes, University of Rhode Island. *Art History—Classical*: Richard Brilliant, Columbia University. *American*: William B. Miller, Colby College; Gerald Eager, Bucknell University. *Canadian*: R. W. Liscombe, University of British Columbia. *Latin American*: Carl Coker, University of Tulsa; Humberto Rodriguez-Camilloni, Virginia Polytechnic Institute and State University. *European*: Gretel Chapman, Southern Illinois University at Carbondale; Amy Golahny, Lycoming College; Mary Hamel-Schwulst, Maryland Institute, College of Art; Robert E. McVaugh, Colgate University; Lynn Robert Matteson, University of Southern California; John R. Spencer, Duke University; Damie Stillman, University of Delaware; Charles W. Talbot, Trinity University. *Oriental*: Ülkü Ü. Bates, Hunter College, CUNY; James O. Caswell, University of British Columbia; Mary Morehart, University of British Columbia. *African, Oceanian, Primitive*: Christopher D. Roy, University of Iowa. *Special Fields*: Frederick Koeper, California State Polytechnic University, Pomona, and H. W. Liscombe, University of British Columbia (Architecture); Peter Kaufman, Suffolk County Community College (City Planning); John Albert Day, University of South Dakota (Sculpture); Karen F. Beall, Carleton College (Drawings & Prints); Mel Casas, San Antonio College (Painting); Virginia M. Juergensen, Mohawk Valley Community College, and Ronald M. Labuz, Mohawk Valley Community College (Design; Graphics); Judith A. Barter, Amherst College (Decorative Arts); William L. Whitwell, Hollins College (Furniture); Barbara A. Schreier, University of Massachusetts at Amherst (Textiles); William B. Miller, Colby College (Calligraphy); Dale K. Haworth, Carleton College (Ceramics); Elliott Pujol, Kansas State University (Metals). *Reference*: Patricia Brauch, Brooklyn College, CUNY. *Referees*: Donald L. Ehresmann, University of Illinois at Chicago; Peter Kaufman, Suffolk County Community College (Architecture).

# A  General Works

## AC Collections

**Great books of the Western World / Encyclopaedia Britannica, inc., in collaboration with the University of Chicago; [Robert Maynard Hutchins, editor in chief.**  • 1.1
Founders' ed. Chicago]: W. Benton [1952] 54 v.: ill., maps; 25 cm. General t.p. in vol. 1 only: each vol. has special t.p. 'Limited to 500 numbered copies signed by the editor.' L.C. copy neither numbered nor signed. 1. Literature — Collections 2. Literature — Indexes. I. Hutchins, Robert Maynard, 1899- ed. II. University of Chicago. III. Encyclopaedia Britannica.
AC1.G7    082    *LC* 52-2133

**Priestley, Joseph.**  • 1.2
Joseph Priestley, selections from his writings. Edited by Ira V. Brown. Pennsylvania: Pennsylvania State University Press, 1962. 343p.,port. I. Brown, Ira Vernon, ed. II. T.
AC7 P68    081    *LC* 62-14946

**Smith, Adam, 1723-1790.**  1.3
[Works. 1986] The Glasgow edition of the works and correspondence of Adam Smith. — 2nd ed. — Oxford; New York: Clarendon Press, 1986- , c1977-. v. Includes indexes. I. T.
AC7.S59 1986    330.15/3 19    *LC* 86-12680    *ISBN* 0198285701

**Barfield, Owen, 1898-.**  1.4
History, guilt, and habit / Owen Barfield. — Middletown, Conn.: Wesleyan University Press, c1979. xx, 97 p.; 21 cm. I. T.
AC8.B4247    081    *LC* 79-65333    *ISBN* 0819550388

**Buckley, William F. (William Frank), 1925-.**  1.5
Execution eve, and other contemporary ballads / William F. Buckley, Jr. — New York: Putnam, [1975] 512 p.; 22 cm. Includes index. I. T.
AC8.B732 1975    973.924    *LC* 75-17593    *ISBN* 0399115315

**Shils, Edward Albert, 1911-.**  1.6
Selected papers of Edward Shils. — [Chicago: University of Chicago Press, 1972- <80 >. v. <1-3 >; 25 cm. I. T.
AC8.S5337    082    *LC* 72-172381

**Barthes, Roland.**  1.7
[Mythologies. English] Mythologies. Selected and translated from the French by Annette Lavers. New York, Hill and Wang [1972] 158 p. 21 cm. I. T.
AC25.B3132 1972b    081    *LC* 75-185427    *ISBN* 0809071932 *ISBN* 080901369X

**Derrida, Jacques.**  1.8
[Dissémination. English] Dissemination / Jacques Derrida; translated, with an introduction and additional notes, by Barbara Johnson. — Chicago: University Press, 1981. xxxiii, 366 p.; 24 cm. Translation of: La dissémination. I. T.
AC25.D45513    808/.00141 19    *LC* 81-3359    *ISBN* 0226143279

**Pisarev, D. I. (Dmitriĭ Ivanovich), 1840-1868.**  • 1.9
[Selected works. English] Selected philosophical, social, and political essays. Moscow, Foreign Languages Pub. House, 1958. 711 p. illus. 23 cm. I. T.
AC65.P5213 1958    087/.1 19    *LC* 59-528

## AE–AG Encyclopedias. General Reference Books

**Academic American encyclopedia.**  • 1.10
Danbury, Conn.: Grolier, c1985. 21 v.: ill. (some col.); 26 cm. 1. Encyclopedias and dictionaries I. Grolier Incorporated.
AE5.A23 1985    031 19    *LC* 84-25128    *ISBN* 0717220087

**The Americana annual; an encyclopedia of current events.**  • 1.11
1923-. New York, Chicago, Americana corporation [etc.] v. ill., plates, ports., maps. 26 cm. Annual. Subtitle varies. 1. Encyclopedias and dictionaries I. McDannald, Alexander Hopkins, 1877- ed.
AE5.A55    031    *LC* 23-10041

**The Encyclopedia Americana.**  • 1.12
International ed. — Danbury, Conn.: Grolier, 1983. 30 v.: ill.; 27 cm. 1. Encyclopedias and dictionaries
AE5.E333 1983    031 19    *LC* 82-24191    *ISBN* 0717201147

**The New Encyclopaedia Britannica.**  • 1.13
15th ed. — Chicago: Encyclopaedia Britannica, c1985. 32 v.: ill. (some col.); 29 cm. Spine title: Britannica. 1. Encyclopedias and dictionaries I. Title: Encyclopaedia Britannica. II. Title: Britannica.
AE5.E363 1985    031 19    *LC* 83-83118    *ISBN* 0852294239

**Britannica book of the year.**  • 1.14
1938-. Chicago, Encyclopaedia Britannica, inc. v. front., ill. (incl. ports.) diagrs. 29 cm. Annual. 'The Britannica book of the year bridges the gap between editions [of the Encyclopaedia Britannica].' — Introd. With supplements. 1. Encyclopedias and dictionaries I. Hooper, Franklin Henry, 1862-1940, ed. II. Yust, Walter, 1894- ed. III. Encyclopaedia Britannica.
AE5.E364    030.2    *LC* 38-12082

**Encyclopédie, ou Dictionnaire raisonné des sciences, des arts et des métiers / par une société des gens de lettres; mis en ordre & publié par m. Diderot, & quant à la partie mathématique, par m. d'Alembert.**  1.15
Stuttgart: F. Frommann Verlag, 1969. 35 v. Originally published Paris: Briasson, 1751-1765. Includes Supplément à l'Encyclopédie, originally published Amsterdam: M. M. Rey, 1776-1777. 4 v. Includes Recueil de planches, sur les sciences, les arts libéraux, et les arts méchaniques, avec leur explication, originally published Paris: Briasson, 1762-1772. 11 v. Includes Suite du Recueil des planches, originally published Paris: Panckoucke, 1777. Includes Table analytique et raisonnée des matieres contenues dans les XXXIII volumes in-folio du Dictionnaire ... et dans son supplément, originally published Paris: Panckoucke, 1780. 2 v.
AE25.E53

**Lough, John.**  1.16
The Encyclopédie. — New York: D. McKay Co., [1971] xii, 430 p.: illus.; 23 cm. 1. Encyclopédie, ou, Dictionnaire raisonné des sciences, des arts et des métiers. I. T.
AE25.E6 L64 1971b    034/.1    *LC* 77-142343

**La Grande encyclopédie ...**  1.17
Paris: Larousse, 1971-76. 60 v. (12931 p.): illus. (part col.); 30 cm. 1. Encyclopedias and dictionaries, French
AE25.G69    034.1    *LC* 72-334017    *ISBN* 203000930X

**Brockhaus Enzyklopädie in zwanzig Bänden.**  • 1.18
Siebzehnte völlig neu bearb. Aufl. des Grossen Brockhaus. — Wiesbaden: Brockhaus; 1966-1974. 20 v.: ill., plates (part col.) maps; 25 cm. — Earlier editions published under titles: Allgemeine deutsche Real-Encyklopädie für die gebildeten Stände; Brockhaus' Konversations- Lexikon, und Der Grosse Brockhaus. - Vol.21- issued as supplements. - 1. Encyclopedias and dictionaries, German I. F.A. Brockhaus Wiesbaden (Firm)
AE27.G672    033.1    *LC* 66-68667    *ISBN* 3765300004

**Gran enciclopedia Rialp, G E R.**  1.19
Madrid: Ediciones Rialp, 1971-1976. 24 v.: ill., ports.; 28 cm. On cover:G E R. I. Title: G E R.
AE61.G75    *LC* 72-300734    *ISBN* 843219011X

**The Canadian encyclopedia.**  1.20
Edmonton: Hurtig Publishers, c1985. 3 v. (xxxv, 2089 p.): ill. (some col.); 29 cm. Editor in chief: James H. Marsh. Col. ill. on lining papers. Includes index. 1. Encyclopedias and dictionaries I. Marsh, James H.
AG5.C27 1985    971/.00321 19    *LC* 84-243080    *ISBN* 088830269X

**The New Columbia encyclopedia / edited by William H. Harris and Judith S. Levey.**  • 1.21
4th ed. — New York: Columbia University Press: distributed by Lippincott, 1975. xiii, 3052 p.: ill.; 32 cm. Previous editions published under title: The Columbia encyclopedia. 1. Encyclopedias and dictionaries I. Harris, William H., 1927- ed. II. Levey, Judith S., 1936- ed. III. Columbia University.
AG5.C725 1975    031    *LC* 74-26686    *ISBN* 0231035721

**Kane, Joseph Nathan, 1899-.**  • 1.22
Famous first facts: a record of first happenings, discoveries, and inventions in American history / Joseph Nathan Kane. — 4th ed., expanded and rev. — New York: H.W. Wilson, 1981. 1350 p.; 26 cm. Includes indexes. 1. Encyclopedias and dictionaries I. T.
AG5.K315 1981    031/.02 19    *LC* 81-3395    *ISBN* 0824206614

**Petit Larousse illustré 1985.** **1.23**
Ed. rev. et corr. Paris: Larousse, 1984, c1980. xxxi, 1798, xvi p., [52] p. de pl.: ill. (certaines en coul.), cartes, graph., portr.; 21 cm. En tête du titre: Dictionnaire encyclopédique pour tous
AG25.P43    034.1 P489    *ISBN* 2033013855

**Guinness book of world records.** **• 1.24**
New York: Sterling Pub. Co. v.: ill.; 22 cm. Annual. Description based on: 1980 ed. 1. Curiosities and wonders — Periodicals. I. McWhirter, Ross. II. McWhirter, Norris, 1925-
AG243.G87    031/.02 19    *LC* 64-4984

**Educators grade guide to free teaching aids.** **1.25**
1955-. Randolph, Wisconsin, Educators Progress Service. v. 29 cm. Annual. Supplements accompany some issues. 1. Free material — Periodicals. 2. Teaching — Audio-visual aids — Catalogs. I. Educators' Progress Service.
AG600.E3    016.3713    *LC* 56-2444

# AI Indexes

**Baer, Eleanora A.** **1.26**
Titles in series: a handbook for librarians and students / Eleanora A. Baer. — 3d ed. — Metuchen, N.J.: Scarecrow Press, 1978. 4 v. (vii, 3318 p.); 23 cm. Includes indexes. 1. Indexes I. T.
AI3.B3 1978    011    *LC* 78-14452    *ISBN* 0810810433

**Bloomfield, B. C. (Barry Cambray)** **1.27**
An author index to selected British 'little magazines,' 1930–1939 / B. C. Bloomfield. — London: Mansell, 1976. xiii, 153 p.; 26 cm. Label mounted on t.p.: Exclusive distributor in the U.S. and Canada, ISBS, Forest Grove, Or. 1. Little magazines — Great Britain — Indexes. 2. English periodicals — Indexes. I. T.
AI3.B56    052    *LC* 77-353190    *ISBN* 0720105420

**British humanities index.** **• 1.28**
1962-. London, The Library Association. v. 25-32 cm. Annual. Cumulation of the quarterly publication. 1. Periodicals — Indexes I. Library Association.
AI3.B7    011/.34    *LC* 63-24940

**The Catholic periodical and literature index.** **• 1.29**
Haverford, Pa., Catholic Library Association. 29 cm. Bimonthly. Began with July/Aug. 1968 issue. Cf. New serial titles. 1. Catholic Church — Periodicals — Indexes. 2. Periodicals — Indexes 3. Catholic literature — Bio-bibliography. I. Catholic Library Association.
AI3.C32    011    *LC* 70-649588

**Humanities index.** **• 1.30**
v. 1- 1974/75-. [New York] H. W. Wilson Co. v. 26 cm. Annual. Cumulation of the quarterly publication. 1. Periodicals — Indexes 2. Humanities — Periodicals — Indexes.
AI3.H85    016.0013    *LC* 75-648836

**IAC magazine index: microform.** **1.31**
1977-    . — [Menlo Park, Calif.: Information Access Corp.] c1982-. microfiches; 11 x 15 cm. Annual. Indexes over 370 popular American periodicals. Each issue contains a full retrospective cumulation. Also available online through Lockheed Information Systems' Dialog. 1. Periodicals — Indexes I. Information Access Corporation.
AI3.I2x    *LC* sn 85-10113

**Index to Commonwealth little magazines.** **1.32**
1964/65-. Troy, N.Y. [etc.]: Whitson Pub. Co. [etc.] v.; 23 cm. Biennial. Retrospective indexes to 1900 will also be published. Vol. for 1970/73 combined in one issue. 1. English periodicals — Indexes. I. Goode, Stephen H., 1925- comp.
AI3.I48    051    *LC* 66-28796

**Index to American little magazines.** **• 1.33**
1900/1919-1920/39. — Troy, N.Y., Whitston. — 2 v. in 4 24 cm. Irregular. Vols. for 1900/1919 have subtitle: To which is added a selected list of British and continental titles for the years, 1900-1950, together with addenda and corrigenda to previous indexes. Issued retrospectively as a supplement to Index to little magazines. 1. Periodicals — Indexes I. Goode, Stephen H., 1925-
AI3.I54

**Index to little magazines.** **• 1.34**
Denver, A. Swallow, 19 –. v. 23cm. Began publication with vol. for 1948 but after vol. for 1962/63 was issued started retrospective as well as current publication. Vol. for 1948 'published also as special issue for 1949 of the Advance guard.' 1. Little magazines — Indexes.
AI3.I54    *LC* a 51-4490

**The New periodicals index.** **1.35**
Vol. 1, no. 1 (Jan.-June 1977)-v. 4 (Jan.-Dec. 1980) — Boulder, Colo.: Mediaworks Ltd., 1977-1983. 4 v.; 26-28 cm. Annual. 1. Periodicals — Indexes — Periodicals.
AI3.N49    051 19    *LC* 86-647327

**Poole's index to periodical literature, by William Frederick** **• 1.36**
**Poole, with the assistance as associate editor of William I.**
**Fletcher, and the coöperation of the American Library**
**Association and the Library Association of the United Kingdom.**
Rev. ed. — Gloucester, Mass.: P. Smith, 1938. 1 v. in 2; 27 cm. 1. Periodicals — Indexes I. Poole, William Frederick, 1821-1894. II. Fletcher, William Isaac, 1844-1917.
AI3 P7    *LC* 38-32445

**Popular periodical index.** **1.37**
no. 1- Jan./June 1973-. [Camden, N.J.: Rutgers University, Camden Library] v.; 25 cm. — 1. Periodicals — Indexes 2. American periodicals — Indexes.
AI3.P76    016.05    *LC* 74-640955

**Social sciences and humanities index.** **• 1.38**
Vol. 19 (1965/1966)-v. 27 (1973/1974). — New York, N.Y.: H. W. Wilson Co., 1966-1974. 43 v. 25-27 cm. Quarterly. An author and subject index to publications in fields of anthropology, archeology and classical studies, economics, folklore, geography, history, language and literature, music, philosophy, political science, religion and theology, sociology and theatre arts. 1. Periodicals — Indexes
AI3.R28x    *LC* sn78-1588

**Readers' guide to periodical literature.** **• 1.39**
v. 1- 1900/04-. New York [etc.] H. W. Wilson Co. v. 26 cm. Annual. Cumulation of the semimonthly publication. Vols. 1-24, 1900/04-Mar. 1963/Feb. 1965, issued also in biennial or longer cumulations. 1. Periodicals — Indexes I. Guthrie, Anna Lorraine, ed. II. Tannehill, Bertha, ed. III. Shimer, Neltje Marie Tannehill, ed. IV. American Library Association. A.L.A. index. An index to general literature. 2d ed.
AI3.R48    051    *LC* 06-8232

**Nineteenth century readers' guide to periodical literature,** **• 1.40**
**1890–1899: with supplementary indexing, 1900–1922 / edited by**
**Helen Grant Cushing and Adah V. Morris.**
New York: H.W. Wilson, 1944. 2 v.; 26 cm. 1. Periodicals — Indexes I. Cushing, Helen Grant, 1896- II. Morris, Adah Vivian, 1895-1944. III. Title: Readers' guide to periodical literature,1890-1899.
AI3.R496    050    *LC* a 44-5439

**Social sciences index.** **• 1.41**
v. 1- 1974/75-. New York, H. W. Wilson Co. v. 26 cm. Annual. Cumulation of the quarterly publication. 1. Periodicals — Indexes 2. Social sciences — Periodicals — Indexes.
AI3.S62    016.3    *LC* 75-649443

**Sutton, Roberta Briggs.** **• 1.42**
Speech index: an index to 259 collections of world famous orations and speeches for various occasions. — 4th ed., rev. and enl. — Metuchen, N.J.: Scarecrow Press, 1966-. vii, 947 p.; 21 cm. Includes indexes. 'Incorporates all the materials in the three previous Speech indexes: 1935, 1935-55, and 1956-1961, and augments it [sic] with ... new publications ...through 1965.' 1. Speeches, addresses, etc — Indexes. 2. Speeches, addresses, etc — Indexes. 3. Speeches, addresses, etc., American — Indexes. I. Mitchell, Charity. joint author. II. T.
AI3.S85 1966 suppl    AI3 S85 1966.    016.80885    *LC* 66-13749

**French periodical index 1973–1974 / compiled by Jean–Pierre** **1.43**
**Ponchie.**
Westwood, Mass: Faxon, c1976. 606 p. (Useful reference series; no.106) I. Ponchie, Jean-Pierre
AI7.F7x    *LC* 75-28987    *ISBN* 0873051068

**National newspaper index (Monthly)** **1.44**
The National newspaper index [microform]. — Apr. 1979-    . — Belmont, Calif.: Information Access Co., c1979-. microfilm reels; 16 mm. Monthly. For use on an IAC Index microfilm reader. Index to: New York times (late ed. and national ed.), Wall Street journal (Eastern ed. and Western ed.), Christian science monitor (Western ed.), Los Angeles times (from Sept. 22, 1982), and: Washington post (from Nov. 1, 1982). Also available online through DIALOG. 1. American newspapers — Indexes — Periodicals. I. T.
AI21.N36    *LC* sn 86-23093

**The New York times index.** **• 1.45**
v. 1- Jan./Mar. 1913-. New York, New York Times Co. v. 26-31 cm. Semimonthly. 'Master-Key to the news since 1851.' Title varies slightly. 1. New York times — Indexes
AI21.N45    071/.47/1    *LC* 13-13458

## AM–AS Museums. Academies. Learned Societies. Foundations

**Museums of the world.**                                                    **1.46**
3rd rev. ed. — München; New York: Saur; Detroit, Mich.: Distributed by Gale Research, 1981. viii, 623 p.; 31 cm. — (Handbook of international documentation and information. v. 16) Distributor label mounted on t.p. Includes indexes. 1. Museums — Directories. I. Series.
AM1.M76 1981    069/.025 19    *LC* 81-198337    *ISBN* 359810118X

**The Official museum directory.**                                           **1.47**
Washington, D.C.: American Association of Museums. v.; 28 cm. Annual. Began in 1971. Description based on: 1983 issue. 1. Museums — North America — Directories. 2. Museums — Canada — directories. 3. Museums — United States — directories. I. American Association of Museums.
AM10.A2 O4    069/.025/7 19    *LC* 79-144808

**Sellers, Charles Coleman, 1903-.**                                         **1.48**
Mr. Peale's Museum: Charles Willson Peale and the first popular museum of natural science and art / Charles Coleman Sellers. — 1st ed. — New York: Norton, 1980 (c1979). xiv, 370 p.: ill.; 24 cm. 'A Barra Foundation book.' 1. Peale, Charles Willson, 1741-1827. 2. Peale family 3. Peale's Museum (Philadelphia, Pa.) 4. Museum directors — United States — Biography. I. T.
AM101.P496 S44    069/.09748/11 19    *LC* 80-139055    *ISBN* 0393057003

**The New York times book review index 1896–1970 / ed. by**                  **1.49**
Wingate Froscher.
New York: Arno Press, 1973. 5 v. 1. The New York times book review — Indexes 2. New York times — Indexes 3. Books — Reviews — Indexes
AP2 N6582    REF028.1N567

**The World of learning.**                                                 ● **1.50**
[1st ed. (1947)]-          . — London: Allen & Unwin, 1947- v.; 26 cm. Annual. Published: London: Europa Publications, 1948- First ed. lacks numeric and chronological designations. 1. Learned institutions and societies — Directories.
AS2.W6    060.25 19    *LC* 47-30172

**Awards, honors & prizes: an international directory of awards**          ● **1.51**
**and their donors ... transportation / Gita Siegman, editor.**
6th ed. — Detroit, Mich.: Gale Research Co., c1985. — 2 v.;29 cm. Includes indexes. First-5th eds. were edited by Paul Wasserman. 1. Rewards (Prizes, etc.) — Directories. 2. Rewards (Prizes, etc.) — United States — Directories. 3. Rewards (Prizes, etc.) — Canada — Directories. I. Siegman, Gita.
AS8.A9    011.4/4 19    *LC* 85-70620    *ISBN* 0810304457

**Walter, Claire.**                                                          **1.52**
Winners, the blue ribbon encyclopedia of awards / by Claire Walter; indexed by Felice D. Levy and Cynthia Crippen. — Rev. ed. — New York, NY: Facts on File Inc., c1982. ix, 916 p.; 29 cm. Includes index. 1. Rewards (Prizes, etc.) — Directories. I. Facts on File, Inc. II. T.
AS8.W34 1982    929.8/1 19    *LC* 80-22177    0871963688

**Scientific and technical societies of the United States and**            ● **1.53**
**Canada.**
6th-7th ed.; 19 -1961. Washington: National Academy of Sciences, National Research Council. 2 v. (Publication - National Research Council; 369,900) 1. Technical societies — Directories. 2. United States — Learned institutions and societies — Directories. 3. Canada — Learned institutions and societies — Directories. I. National Research Council (U.S.) II. National Research Council of Canada.
AS15.H3    *LC* 27-21604

**Encyclopedia of associations.**                                            **1.54**
3rd- ed. Detroit, Gale Research Co., 1961-. v. 29 cm. Annual. Issued in 2 vols. 1961; in 3 vols. 1964-83; in 4 vols. 1984-      : v. 1, National organizations of the U.S.; v. 2, Geographic and executive index; v. 3, 4th-5th eds., New associations; 6th-    ed., New associations and projects; v. 4, 18th-    ed., International organizations. Beginning with the 4th ed., a 3d vol. (called New associations and projects (varies)) and, with the 18th ed., a 4th vol. (called International organizations) are issued periodically in parts as inter-edition supplements. Vol. 3 is cumulative supplement to each edition. 1. Associations, institutions, etc — Directories. I. Ruffner, Frederick G. ed. II. Fisk, Margaret. ed. III. Gale Research Company.
AS22.E5    060    *LC* 76-46129

**Research centers directory.**                                            ● **1.55**
Detroit, Mich.: Gale Research Co. v.; 29 cm. Irregular. Began with 2nd ed. Description based on: 6th ed. 1. Research — United States — Directories.

2. United States — Learned institutions and societies — Periodicals. I. Gale Research Company.
AS25.D5    *LC* 60-14807

**Who's who in European institutions, organizations and**                    **1.56**
**enterprises.**
[2nd ed.]-. Bresso (Milano): Who's Who in Italy S.r.l., 1985-. v. — (Sutter's international red series) Triennial. 1. Associations, institutions, etc — Europe — Officials and employees — Biography 2. Associations, institutions, etc — Europe — Directories
AS98 W52

**Vucinich, Alexander, 1914-.**                                              **1.57**
Empire of knowledge: the Academy of Sciences of the USSR (1917–1970) / Alexander Vucinich. — Berkeley: University of California Press, c1984. x, 484 p.; 24 cm. Includes index. 1. Akademiia nauk SSSR — History. I. T.
AS262.A68 V79 1984    354.470085/5 19    *LC* 83-3484    *ISBN* 0520048717

**Annual register of grant support.**                                      ● **1.58**
1969-. Chicago [etc.] Marquis Academic Media, Marquis Who's Who [etc.] v. 29 cm. Annual. 1. Endowments — Directories.
AS911.A2 A67    001.4/4    *LC* 69-18307

**The Foundation Center national data book.**                                **1.59**
-4th ed. (1979). — New York, N.Y.: The Center, -1979. v.; 21 x 27 cm. Began with: 2nd ed., 1974/76. Description based on: 4th ed. (1979). Issued in 2 vols.: v. 1: Alphabetical listing by foundation name; v. 2, State listing with foundations in descending grant order. 1. Endowments — United States — Directories. I. Foundation Center.
AS 911.A2 F64    001.4/4/02573    *LC* 77-86479

**The Foundation directory.**                                              ● **1.60**
1st- ed.; 1960-. New York, Foundation Center; distributed by Columbia University Press. v. ill. 25-29 cm. Kept up to date between editions by supplements. 1. Endowments — Directories. I. Foundation Center. II. Foundation Library Center. III. Russell Sage Foundation.
AS911.A2 F65    061 060    *LC* 60-13807

**The Foundation grants index.**                                           ● **1.61**
[1st]- ; 1970/71-. New York: Foundation Center; distributed by Columbia University Press. v.; 29 cm. Annual. 1. Endowments — Directories. I. Noe, Lee. II. Foundation Center.
AS911.A2 F66    001.4/4    *LC* 72-76018

**Nobelstiftelsen.**                                                       ● **1.62**
Nobel, the man and his prizes. Edited by the Nobel Foundation and W. Odelberg. Individual sections written by H. Schück [and others] 3d ed. New York, American Elsevier Pub. Co. [1972] x, 659 p. port. 25 cm. First ed. (1950) originally published in Swedish under title: Nobelprisen 50 år; forskare, diktare, fredskämpar. 1. Nobel prizes I. Odelberg, Wilhelm. ed. II. T.
AS911.N7553 1972    001.4/4    *LC* 77-169840    *ISBN* 0444001174

**Opfell, Olga S.**                                                          **1.63**
The lady laureates: women who have won the Nobel Prize / by Olga S. Opfell. — 2nd ed. — Metuchen, N.J.: Scarecrow Press, 1986. xviii, 316 p.: ill.; 23 cm. Includes index. 1. Nobel prizes 2. Women — Biography 3. Women authors — Biography 4. Women scientists — Biography. I. T.
AS911.N9 O63 1986    001.4/4 19    *LC* 85-19670    *ISBN* 0810818515

## AY Yearbooks. Almanacs

**Information please almanac, atlas and yearbook.**                        ● **1.64**
1947-. New York, Simon & Schuster. v. ill., maps. Annual. 'Planned and supervised by Dan Golenpaul Associates,' 1947- Editors: 1947-53, J. Kieran. - 1954- D. Golenpaul. 1. Almanacs, American I. Kieran, John, 1892- II. Golenpaul, Dan. III. Dan Golenpaul Associates. IV. Title: Information please almanac.
AY64.I55    *LC* 47-845

**The World almanac and book of facts.**                                   ● **1.65**
New York, Newspaper Enterprise Association [etc.] v. ill. (maps) tables. 19-22 cm. Annual. 1. Almanacs, American 2. Statistics — Yearbooks.
AY67.N5 W7    317.3    *LC* 04-3781

**The National Catholic almanac.**                                         ● **1.66**
Paterson, N.J., St. Anthony's guild [c1903-] v. illus. (incl. ports., maps, music) plates (part col.) tables. 20-27 cm. 1. Catholic Church — Year-books. 2. Almanacs, American I. Franciscans. Province of the most holy name of

Jesus. II. Washington, D.C. Holy name college. III. St. Anthony's guild, Paterson, N.J.
AY81.R6 N3      *LC* a 43-2500

**Canadian almanac and directory.**                                      • **1.67**
v. 1-   1848-. Vancouver: Copp Clark. v.: ill. Annual. Publisher varies. 'Including a complete directory of municipal, provincial and federal governments.' 1. Almanacs, Canadian 2. Canada — Yearbooks. 3. Canada — Directories. I. Title: Scobie & Balfour's Canadian almanac, and repository of useful knowledge. II. Title: Scobie's Canadian almanac. III. Title: Maclear & Co.'s Canadian almanac. IV. Title: The Canadian almanac and miscellaneous directory. V. Title: The Canadian almanac and legal and court directory.
AY414.C2      FC2.C2.      *LC* 07-24314

**Whitaker's almanack.**                                      • **1.68**
1st (1869)- . — London: Whitaker, 1869-    . — Annual. 1. Almanacs, English 2. Statistics — Yearbooks. I. Whitaker, Joseph, 1820-1895.
AY754.W5      *LC* 04-3780

# AZ Scholarship. Learning

**Bird, Otto A., 1914-.**                                      **1.69**
Cultures in conflict: an essay in the philosophy of the humanities / Otto A. Bird. — Notre Dame, Ind.: University of Notre Dame Press, c1976. xii, 220 p.; 24 cm. Includes index. 1. Humanities 2. Science and the humanities 3. Learning and scholarship 4. Civilization — Philosophy I. T.
AZ101.B57      001.3      *LC* 76-638      *ISBN* 0268007136

**Foucault, Michel.**                                      **1.70**
[Mots et les choses. English] The order of things: an archaeology of the human sciences. New York: Random House, 1970. xxiv, 387 p. 25 cm. (World of man) Translation of Les mots et les choses. 1. Learning and scholarship 2. Civilization — History I. T.
AZ101.F6913 1971      901.9      *LC* 68-10251

**Pelikan, Jaroslav Jan, 1923-.**                                      **1.71**
The vindication of tradition / Jaroslav Pelikan. — New Haven: Yale University Press, c1984. x, 93 p.; 22 cm. (The 1983 Jefferson lecture in the humanities) 1. Learning and scholarship — Addresses, essays, lectures. 2. Tradition (Philosophy) — Addresses, essays, lectures. I. T.
AZ103.P44 1984      001.2 19      *LC* 84-5132      *ISBN* 0300031548

**International Conference on Computers and the Humanities.**      **1.72**
**(6th: 1983: North Carolina State University)**
Sixth International Conference on Computers and the Humanities / Sarah K. Burton and Douglas D. Short, editors. — Rockville, Md.: Computer Science Press, c1983. x, 782 p.: ill.; 28 cm. 1. Humanities — Data processing — Congresses. I. Burton, Sarah K. II. Short, Douglas D. III. T.
AZ105.I56 1983      001.3/028/54 19      *LC* 83-7479      *ISBN* 091489496X

**A Casebook of grant proposals in the humanities / edited by**      **1.73**
**William Coleman, David Keller, and Arthur Pfeffer.**
New York: Neal-Schuman Publishers, c1982. xvii, 248 p.; 22 x 28 cm. Includes index. 1. Humanities — Research grants — United States. I. Coleman, William Emmet, 1942- II. Keller, David (David Mathias) III. Pfeffer, Arthur.
AZ188.U5 C37 1982      001.3 19      *LC* 81-18859      *ISBN* 0918212456

**Margolin, Judith B.**                                      **1.74**
The individual's guide to grants / Judith B. Margolin. — New York: Plenum Press, c1983. xvii, 295 p.; 22 cm. Includes index. 1. Research grants — United States — Handbooks, manuals, etc. I. T.
AZ188.U5 M37 1983      001.4/4 19      *LC* 83-2252      *ISBN* 0306413094

**Pfeiffer, Rudolf, 1889-.**                                      • **1.75**
History of classical scholarship from the beginnings to the end of the Hellenistic age. — Oxford: Clarendon P., 1968. xviii, 311 p.; 24 cm. 1. Learning and scholarship — Greece. I. T.
AZ301.P4      001.2/0938      *LC* 68-112031      *ISBN* 0198143427

**Pfeiffer, Rudolf.**                                      **1.76**
History of classical scholarship from 1300 to 1850 / [by] Rudolf Pfeiffer. Oxford: Clarendon Press, 1976. ix, 214 p.; 24 cm. 1. Classical philology — History. I. T.
AZ301.P4x      938/.007      *ISBN* 0198143648

**Snow, C. P. (Charles Percy), 1905-.**                                      • **1.77**
[Two cultures and the scientific revolution] The two cultures; and, A second look: an expanded version of 'The two cultures and the scientific revolution', by C. P. Snow. London, Cambridge U.P., 1969. iv, 107 p. 19 cm. 1. Science and the humanities I. T.
AZ361.S56 1969      001      *LC* 70-442528      *ISBN* 052109576X

**Leavis, F. R. (Frank Raymond), 1895-.**                                      • **1.78**
Two cultures? The significance of C. P. Snow. Being the Richmond lecture, 1962. With a new pref. for the American reader. And an essay on Sir Charles Snow's Rede lecture, by Michael Yudkin. New York, Pantheon Books [1963] 64 p. 20 cm. 1. Snow, C. P. (Charles Percy), 1905- Two cultures and the scientific revolution. 2. Science and the humanitites. I. Yudkin, Michael. II. T.
AZ361.S57L4      001      *LC* 63-11775

**Unesco.**                                      • **1.79**
Statistical Yearbook. Annuaire statistique. — 1963-. Paris: Unesco. v. — 1. Intellectual life — Statistics. I. United Nations Educational, Scientific and Cultural Organization. Annuaire statistique. II. T. III. Title: Annuaire statistique. IV. Title: Unesco statistical yearbook. V. Title: Unesco annuaire statistique.
AZ361.U45      *LC* 65-3517

**Machlup, Fritz, 1902-.**                                      **1.80**
Knowledge, its creation, distribution, and economic significance / by Fritz Machlup. — Princeton, N.J.: Princeton University Press, c1980-c1984. 3 v.; 25 cm. 1. Learning and scholarship — United States — Collected works. 2. Knowledge, Theory of — Collected works. I. T.
AZ505.M28      001 19      *LC* 80-7544      *ISBN* 0691042268

**The Organization of knowledge in modern America, 1860–1920**      **1.81**
**/ edited by Alexandra Oleson and John Voss.**
Baltimore: Johns Hopkins University Press, c1979. xxi, 478 p.; 24 cm. 1. Learning and scholarship — United States. I. Oleson, Alexandra, 1939- II. Voss, John, 1917-
AZ505.O73      001.2      *LC* 78-20521      *ISBN* 0801821088

**Directory of American scholars.**                                      **1.82**
8th ed. / edited by Jaques Cattel Press. — New York; London: Bowker, 1982. 4 v.; 29 cm. 1. Humanities — United States — Biography. I. Jaques Cattell Press.
AZ507.Dx      001.3/092/2 19      *LC* 57-9125      *ISBN* 0835214761

## B1–67 GENERAL AND REFERENCE WORKS

### B11–29 Congresses. Collections

**Arendt, Hannah.** **1.83**
The life of the mind / Hannah Arendt. — 1st ed. — New York: Harcourt Brace Jovanovich, c1978. 2 v.; 25 cm. 1. Philosophy — Collected works. I. T.
B29.A73    110 19    *LC* 77-1162    *ISBN* 0151518955

**Dummett, Michael A. E.** **1.84**
Truth and other enigmas / Michael Dummett. — Cambridge: Harvard University Press, 1978. lviii, 470 p.; 24 cm. 1. Frege, Gottlob, 1848-1925 — Addresses, essays, lectures. 2. Philosophy — Addresses, essays, lectures. 3. Logic — Addresses, essays, lectures. 4. Time — Addresses, essays, lectures. I. T.
B29.D85    192    *LC* 77-12777    *ISBN* 0674910753

**Gadamer, Hans Georg, 1900-.** **1.85**
Reason in the age of science / Hans–Georg Gadamer; translated by Frederick G. Lawrence. — Cambridge, Mass.: MIT Press, 1982, c1981. xxxiii, 179 p.; 21 cm. — (Studies in contemporary German social thought. 2) Selected essays from author's Vernunft im Zeitalter der Wissenschaft, and two others. 1. Philosophy — Addresses, essays, lectures. I. T. II. Series.
B29.G17 1982    100 19    *LC* 81-20911    *ISBN* 0262070855

**Gardner, Martin, 1914-.** **1.86**
The whys of a philosophical scrivener / by Martin Gardner. — New York: Quill, 1983. 453 p. 1. Philosophy — Addresses, essays, lectures I. T.
B29.G253 1983b    191 19    *LC* 83-4474    *ISBN* 068802064X

**Goodman, Nelson.** **1.87**
Of mind and other matters / Nelson Goodman. — Cambridge, Mass.: Harvard University Press, 1984. 210 p.: ill.; 25 cm. 1. Philosophy — Addresses, essays, lectures. I. T.
B29.G619 1984    191 19    *LC* 83-12868    *ISBN* 0674631250

**Hanson, Norwood Russell.** **1.88**
What I do not believe, and other essays. Ed. by Stephen Toulmin and Harry Woolf. — Dordrecht: Reidel, [1972] xii, 390 p.; 23 cm. — (Synthese library) 1. Philosophy — Addresses, essays, lectures. I. Toulmin, Stephen Edelston. ed. II. Woolf, Harry. ed. III. T.
B29.H326    100    *LC* 74-154738

**Kallen, Horace Meyer, 1882-.** **1.89**
Creativity, imagination, logic; meditations for the eleventh hour, by Horace M. Kallen. New York, Gordon and Breach [1973] x, 212 p. 24 cm. (Current topics of contemporary thought, v. 12) 1. Philosophy — Collected works. I. T.
B29.K296    100    *LC* 73-81073    *ISBN* 0677049404

**Margolis, Joseph Zalman, 1924-.** **1.90**
Culture and cultural entities: toward a new unity of science / Joseph Margolis. — Dordrecht; Boston: D. Reidel Pub.Co.; Hingham, MA, U.S.A.: Sold and distributed in the U.S.A. and Canada by Kluwer Academic Publishers, c1984. xiii, 170 p.; 23 cm. — (City College studies in the history and philosophy of science and technology.) (Synthese library; v. 170) 1. Philosophy — Addresses, essays, lectures. I. T. II. Series.
B29.M3673 1984    110 19    *LC* 83-4635    *ISBN* 9027715742

**Mehta, J. L. (Jaswant Lal), 1931-.** **1.91**
India and the West, the problem of understanding: selected essays / of J.L. Mehta; [with an introduction by Wilfred Cantwell Smith]. — Chico, Calif.: Scholars Press, c1985. xvii, 268 p.; 23 cm. (Studies in world religions. no. 4) 1. Philosophy — Addresses, essays, lectures. I. T. II. Series.
B29.M453 1985    100 19    *LC* 85-2050    *ISBN* 089130827X

**Miller, John William.** **1.92**
The paradox of cause and other essays / John William Miller. — New York: Norton, c1978. 192 p.; 22 cm. 1. Philosophy — Addresses, essays, lectures. I. T.
B29.M533 1978    191    *LC* 78-5998    *ISBN* 0393011720

**Philosophy in France today / edited by Alan Montefiore.** **1.93**
Cambridge [Cambridgeshire]; New York: Cambridge University Press, 1983. xxvi, 201 p.; 23 cm. 1. Philosophy — Addresses, essays, lectures. 2. Philosophy, French — 20th century — Addresses, essays, lectures. I. Montefiore, Alan.
B29.P5248 1983    194 19    *LC* 82-9730    *ISBN* 0521228387

**Sellars, Wilfrid.** **1.94**
Science, perception, and reality. — New York, Humanities Press [1963] viii, 366 p. diagrs. 23 cm. — (International library of philosophy and scientific method.) Bibliographical footnotes. 1. Philosophy — Addresses, essays, lectures. I. T. II. Series.
B29.S49    110.81    *LC* 63-17056

**Strawson, P. F.** **1.95**
Freedom and resentment, and other essays [by] P. F. Strawson. — [London]: Methuen [distributed in the USA by Harper & Row, Barnes & Noble Import Division, 1974] viii, 214 p.; 22 cm. 1. Philosophy — Addresses, essays, lectures. I. T.
B29.S8217    192    *LC* 74-176629    *ISBN* 0416799507

**Weinberg, Julius Rudolph, 1908-1971.** **1.96**
Ockham, Descartes, and Hume: self–knowledge, substance, and causality / Julius R. Weinberg. — Madison: University of Wisconsin Press, 1977. ix, 179 p.; 23 cm. Includes index. 1. William, of Ockham, ca. 1285-ca. 1349 — Addresses, essays, lectures. 2. Descartes, René, 1596-1650 — Addresses, essays, lectures. 3. Hume, David, 1711-1776 — Addresses, essays, lectures. 4. Philosophy — Addresses, essays, lectures. I. T.
B29.W4145    190    *LC* 76-11315    *ISBN* 0299071200

**Woodbridge, Frederick James Eugene, 1867-1940.** **• 1.97**
Nature and mind: selected essays / of Frederick J. E. Woodbridge; presented to him on the occasion of his seventieth birthday by Amherst College, the University of Minnesota, Columbia University; with a bibliography of his writings. — New York: Russell & Russell, 1965 [i.e. 1966, c1937]. 509 p.: port.; 23 cm. 1. Philosophy — Addresses, essays, lectures I. Amherst College. II. University of Minnesota (Minneapolis-St. Paul campus) III. Columbia University. IV. T.
B29.W66 1966    191    *LC* 65-18839

**Tragesser, Robert S., 1943-.** **1.98**
Phenomenology and logic / Robert S. Tragesser. — Ithaca, N.Y.: Cornell University Press, 1977. 138 p.; 22 cm. 1. Husserl, Edmund, 1859-1938. 2. Phenomenology. 3. Logic I. T.
B29.5.T66    B29.5 T66.    142/.7    *LC* 76-28025    *ISBN* 0801410681

### B41–51 Dictionaries. Encyclopedic Works

**Baldwin, James Mark, 1861-1934. ed.** **1.99**
Dictionary of philosophy and psychology, including many of the principal conceptions of ethics, logic, aesthetics, philosophy of religion, mental pathology, anthropology, biology, neurology, physiology, economics, political and social philosophy, philology, physical science, and education, and giving a terminology in English, French, German, and Italian / written by many hands and edited by James Mark Baldwin ... with the co–operation and assistance of an international board of consulting editors ... with ... extensive bibliographies. — New ed., with corrections. — New York: P. Smith, 1940. 3 v. in 4 pts.: ill., plates (part col.) diagrs.; 26 cm. 'New edition with corrections printed 1925, reprinted 1940 by Peter Smith.' 1. Philosophy — Dictionaries. 2. Philosophy — Bibliography. 3. Psychology — Dictionaries. 4. Psychology — Bibliography. I. T.
B41.B3 1940    103    *LC* 40-27299

A Dictionary of philosophy / editorial consultant, Antony Flew. **1.100**
Rev. 2nd ed. — New York: St. Martin's Press, 1984, c1979. xi, 380 p.; 21 cm. 1. Philosophy — Dictionaries. I. Flew, Antony, 1923-
B41.D52 1984    103/.21 19    LC 78-68699    ISBN 031220924X

The Encyclopedia of philosophy. Paul Edwards, editor in chief.    • **1.101**
New York: Macmillan, [1967] 8 v.; 29 cm. 1. Philosophy — Dictionaries. I. Edwards, Paul, 1923- ed.
B41.E5    103    LC 67-10059

Lacey, A. R. (Alan Robert)    **1.102**
A dictionary of philosophy / A. R. Lacey. — London; Boston: Routledge & K. Paul, 1976. vii, 239 p.; 23 cm. 1. Philosophy — Dictionaries. I. T.
B41.L32 1976    103    LC 76-378097    ISBN 0710083610

Tice, Terrence N.    **1.103**
Research guide to philosophy / Terrence N. Tice and Thomas P. Slavens. — Chicago: American Library Association, 1983. xii, 608 p.; 24 cm. — (Sources of information in the humanities. no. 3) Includes indexes. 1. Philosophy — Study and teaching — History. 2. Philosophy — Historiography. I. Slavens, Thomas P., 1928- II. T. III. Series.
B52.T5 1983    107 19    LC 83-11834    ISBN 0838903339

## B53–67 Theory. Scope. Relations

Abel, Reuben, 1911-.    **1.104**
Man is the measure: a cordial invitation to the central problems of philosophy / Reuben Abel. — New York: Free Press, c1976. xxiv, 296 p.; 21 cm. Includes index. 1. Philosophy 2. Man 3. Cosmology I. T.
B53.A23    B53 A23.    128    LC 75-16646    ISBN 0029001404

Ayer, A. J. (Alfred Jules), 1910-.    • **1.105**
Language, truth and logic / by Alfred Jules Ayer. — 2nd ed., rev. and reset. — London: V. Gollancz, 1946. 160 p. 1. Experience 2. Philosophy 3. Knowledge, Theory of 4. Language and languages I. T.
B53.A9 1946    LC 46-8544

Bontempo, Charles J.    **1.106**
The owl of Minerva: philosophers on philosophy / edited and with an introd. by Charles J. Bontempo and S. Jack Odell. — New York: McGraw-Hill, [1975] xiii, 264 p.; 21 cm. Includes index. 1. Philosophy — Addresses, essays, lectures. I. Odell, S. Jack, 1933- joint author. II. T.
B53.B578    B53 B578.    190    LC 74-31440    ISBN 0070064806

Kekes, John.    **1.107**
The nature of philosophy / John Kekes. — Totowa, N.J.: Rowman and Littlefield, 1980. xiv, 226 p.; 23 cm. — (APQ library of philosophy.) 1. Philosophy 2. Ideology I. T. II. Series.
B53.K38    100    LC 80-111351    ISBN 0847662470

Lacey, A. R. (Alan Robert)    **1.108**
Modern philosophy, an introduction / A.R. Lacey. — Boston: Routledge & K. Paul, 1982. 246 p.; 22 cm. Includes index. 1. Philosophy 2. Philosophy, Modern — 20th century I. T.
B53.L29 1982    190 19    LC 81-8710    ISBN 0710009356

Lazerowitz, Morris, 1909-.    **1.109**
Philosophical theories / Morris Lazerowitz and Alice Ambrose. — The Hague: Mouton, [1976] 304 p.; 24 cm. Includes index. 1. Philosophy — Addresses, essays, lectures. 2. Theory (Philosophy) — Addresses, essays, lectures. I. Ambrose, Alice, 1906- joint author. II. T.
B53.L388    B53 L388.    100    LC 76-379136    ISBN 9027975019

Nozick, Robert.    **1.110**
Philosophical explanations / Robert Nozick. — Cambridge, Mass.: Harvard University Press, 1981. xii, 764 p. 1. Philosophy 2. Knowledge, Theory of 3. Values I. T.
B53.N7    B53 N7.    191 19    LC 81-1369    ISBN 0674664485

Reichenbach, Hans, 1891-1953.    • **1.111**
The Rise of scientific philosophy / Hans Reichenbach. — 1st paperbound ed. — Berkeley; Los Angeles: University of California Press, 1964, c1951. ix, 333 p.; 19 cm. 1. Philosophy I. T.
B53.R4 1964

Rorty, Richard.    **1.112**
Philosophy and the mirror of nature / Richard Rorty. — Princeton: Princeton University Press, c1979. xv, 401 p.; 22 cm. 1. Philosophy 2. Philosophy, Modern 3. Mind and body 4. Representation (Philosophy) 5. Analysis (Philosophy) 6. Civilization — Philosophy I. T.
B53.R68    190    LC 79-84013    ISBN 0691072361

Wisdom, John Oulton.    **1.113**
Philosophy and its place in our culture / J. O. Wisdom. — New York: Gordon and Breach, [1975] x, 270 p.; 24 cm. (Current topics of contemporary thought; v. 13) 1. Philosophy 2. Ideology I. T.
B53.W57    B53 W57.    100    LC 74-79475    ISBN 0677051506

Stace, W. T. (Walter Terence), 1886-.    • **1.114**
Mysticism and philosophy. [1st ed.] Philadelphia, Lippincott [1960] 349 p. 22 cm. 1. Mysticism 2. Philosophy 3. Philosophy and religion I. T.
B56.S8    LC 60-13581

Addis, Laird.    **1.115**
The logic of society: a philosophical study / by Laird Addis. — Minneapolis: University of Minnesota Press, [1975] ix, 226 p.; 24 cm. Includes index. 1. Philosophy 2. Social sciences — Philosophy 3. History — Philosophy 4. Science — Philosophy I. T.
B63.A3    146/.4    LC 74-83131    ISBN 0816607338

Dewey, John, 1859-1952.    **1.116**
Lectures in China, 1919–1920. Translated from the Chinese and edited by Robert W. Clopton [and] Tsuin–chen Ou. — Honolulu: University Press of Hawaii, [1973] vi, 337 p.; 24 cm. 'An East-West Center book.' Originally delivered in English. 1. Philosophy — Addresses, essays, lectures. 2. Social sciences — Addresses, essays, lectures. 3. Education — Philosophy — Addresses, essays, lectures. I. T.
B63.D47 1972    300/.1    LC 72-84061    ISBN 0824802128

Marković, Mihailo, 1923-.    **1.117**
From affluence to praxis: philosophy and social criticism. — Ann Arbor: University of Michigan Press, [1974] xiv, 265 p.; 22 cm. 1. Marx, Karl, 1818-1883. 2. Philosophy 3. Sociology 4. Social change I. T.
B63.M37 1974    300/.1    LC 72-94763    ISBN 04726400003

Popper, Karl Raimund, Sir, 1902-.    • **1.118**
The open society and its enemies. [4th ed. rev.] Princeton, N.J., Princeton University Press, 1963. 2 v. diagrs. 21 cm. 1. Philosophy 2. Social sciences — Philosophy I. T.
B63.P6 1963    301    LC 63-18324

Maistre, Joseph Marie, comte de, 1753-1821.    • **1.119**
On God and society: essay on the generative principle of political constitutions and other human institutions / edited by Elisha Greifer. — Chicago: Regnery, c1959. xxxiii, 92 p.; 17 cm. — (A Gateway edition) 1. Political science I. T.
B65.M3    LC 63-6801

Burtt, Edwin A. (Edwin Arthur), 1892-.    • **1.120**
[Metaphysics of Sir Isaac Newton] The metaphysical foundations of modern physical science. Rev. ed. Garden City, N.Y., Doubleday, 1954. 352 p. 19 cm. (Doubleday anchor books, A41) 1. Newton, Isaac, Sir, 1642-1727. 2. Metaphysics 3. Physics 4. Science — Philosophy I. T.
B67.B8 1954    501    LC 54-4532

Quine, W. V. (Willard Van Orman)    **1.121**
Theories and things / W.V. Quine. — Cambridge, Mass.: Harvard University Press, 1981. 219 p.; 22 cm. Includes index. 1. Philosophy — Miscellanea. I. T.
B68.Q56    191 19    LC 81-4517    ISBN 0674879252

## B69–4695 HISTORY

Copleston, Frederick Charles.    • **1.122**
A history of philosophy. Westminster, Md.: Newman Bookshop, 1946-[75] 9 v.; 22 cm. Vols. 2-9 have imprint: Westminster, Md., Newman Press. Vols. 5-7 issued as Bellarmine series, 16-18. 1. Philosophy — History I. T.
B72.C62    109    LC 47-875

Fuller, Benjamin Apthorp Gould, 1879-1956.    • **1.123**
A history of philosophy. — 3d ed., rev. by Sterling M. McMurrin. — New York: Holt, [1955] 2 v.; 22 cm. Vol. 2 has title: A history of modern philosophy; general title on cover. 1. Philosophy — History I. McMurrin, Sterling M. II. T.
B72.F8 1955    109    LC 55-6044

Gilson, Etienne, 1884-1978.    • **1.124**
History of Christian philosophy in the Middle Ages. New York, Random House [c1955] 829 p. 24 cm. (A History of philosophy, v. 1) 1. Philosophy — History 2. Philosophy, Medieval 3. Christianity — Philosophy I. T.
B72.G48    189.09    LC 54-7802

**Levi, Albert William, 1911-.** **1.125**
Philosophy as social expression / Albert William Levi. — Chicago; London: The University of Chicago Press, [1974]. –. xii, 328 p.; 22 cm. — 1. Philosophy — History I. T.
B72.L47    B72 L4.    *LC* 73-84191    *ISBN* 0226473899

**Radhakrishnan, S. (Sarvepalli), 1888-1975. ed.** • **1.126**
History of philosophy, eastern and western. Sponsored by the Ministry of Education, Government of India. Editorial board: Sarvepalli Radhakrishnan [and others] London, Allen & Unwin [1952-53] 2 v. 24 cm. 1. Philosophy — History I. T.
B72.R3    109    *LC* 53-9287

**Bréhier, Émile, 1876-1952.** • **1.127**
[Histoire de la philosophie. English] The history of philosophy. Translated by Joseph Thomas. Chicago, University of Chicago Press [1963-69] 7 v. 23 cm. Vols. 2-7 translated by Wade Baskin. 1. Philosophy — History I. T.
B77.B723    109    *LC* 63-20912

**Heer, Friedrich, 1916-.** • **1.128**
[Europäische Geistesgeschichte. English] The intellectual history of Europe. Translation by Jonathan Steinberg. [1st ed.] Cleveland, World Pub. Co. [1966] viii, 558 p. 25 cm. 1. Philosophy — History 2. Religious thought — Europe. 3. Europe — Intellectual life I. T.
B82.H413 1966a    914.03    *LC* 66-23090

**Hirschberger, Johannes.** **1.129**
[Kleine Philosophiegeschichte. English] A short history of Western philosophy / by Johannes Hirschberger; translated from the German of Jeremy Moiser. — Boulder, Colo.: Westview Press, 1977, c1976. xi, 218 p.; 22 cm. Translation of Kleine Philosophiegeschichte. Includes indexes. 1. Philosophy — History I. T.
B82.H5613 1976b    190    *LC* 76-25125    *ISBN* 0891586423

**Jaspers, Karl.** • **1.130**
The great philosophers / Karl Jaspers; edited by Hannah Arendt; translated by Ralph Manheim. — New York: Harcourt, Brace & World, 1962-1966. 2v. — (A Helen and Kurt Wolff book.) 1. Philosophy — History 2. Philosophers I. T.
B82.J313    *LC* 62-9436

**Windelband, W. (Wilhelm), 1848-1915.** • **1.131**
[Geschichte der Philosophie. English] A history of philosophy. New York, Harper [1958] 2 v. 21 cm. (Harper torchbooks, TB38-39) 'Reprinted ... from the revised edition of 1901, translated by James H. Tufts.' 1. Philosophy — History I. T.
B82.W53 1958    180.9    *LC* 58-7114

**Marías, Julián, 1914-.** **1.132**
[Biografia de la filosofia. English] A biography of philosophy / Julian Marías; translated by Harold C. Raley. — University, Ala.: University of Alabama Press, c1984. xii, 255 p.; 25 cm. Translation of: Biografia de la filosofia. 1. Philosophy — History I. T.
B92.M2813 1984    190 19    *LC* 83-6939    *ISBN* 0817301801

**Wedberg, Anders, 1913-1978.** **1.133**
[Filosofins historia. English] A history of philosophy / Anders Wedberg. — Oxford: Clarendon Press, 1982-1984. 3 v.: ill.; 23 cm. Translation of: Filosofins historia. 1. Philosophy — History I. T. II. Title: Antiquity and the middle ages. III. Title: The Modern age to romanticism. IV. Title: From Bolzano to Wittgenstein.
B99.S82 W413 1982    190 19    *LC* 81-22418    *ISBN* 0198246390

## B105 Special Topics, A–Z

**Brand, Myles.** **1.134**
Intending and acting: toward a naturalized action theory / Myles Brand. — Cambridge, Mass.: MIT Press, c1984. xiii, 296 p.: ill.; 24 cm. 'A Bradford book.' Includes index. 1. Act (Philosophy) 2. Intentionality (Philosophy) I. T.
B105.A35 B73 1984    128/.4 19    *LC* 83-24817    *ISBN* 0262022028

**Davidson, Donald, 1917-.** **1.135**
Essays on actions and events / Donald Davidson. — Oxford: Clarendon Press; New York: Oxford University Press, 1980. xvi, 304 p.; 23 cm. Includes index. 1. Act (Philosophy) — Collected works. 2. Events (Philosophy) — Collected works. I. T.
B105.A35 D37    128/.4    *LC* 80-40064    *ISBN* 0198245297

**Lovejoy, Arthur O. (Arthur Oncken), 1873-1962.** • **1.136**
The great chain of being; a study of the history of an idea. The William James lectures delivered at Harvard university, 1933, by Arthur O. Lovejoy.

Cambridge, Mass., Harvard university press, 1936. ix p., 2 l., [3]-382. 23 cm. 1. Continuity 2. Chain of being (Philosophy) I. T. II. Title: Chain of being.
B105.C5 L6    119    *LC* 36-14264

**Thomson, Judith Jarvis.** **1.137**
Acts and other events / Judith Jarvis Thomson. — Ithaca, N.Y.: Cornell University Press, 1977. 274 p. — (Contemporary philosophy) 1. Events (Philosophy) 2. Act (Philosophy) 3. Agent (Philosophy) 4. Causation I. T.
B105.E7 T47    B105E7 T47.    122    *LC* 77-4791    *ISBN* 0801410509

**Searle, John R.** **1.138**
Intentionality, an essay in the philosophy of mind / John R. Searle. — Cambridge [Cambridgeshire]; New York: Cambridge University Press, 1983. x, 278 p.: ill.; 22 cm. 1. Intentionality (Philosophy) I. T.
B105.I56 S43 1983    128/.2 19    *LC* 82-19849    *ISBN* 0521228956

**Adler, Mortimer Jerome, 1902-.** • **1.139**
The idea of freedom / by Mortimer J. Adler, for the Institute for Philosophical Research. Garden City, N.Y.: Doubleday, 1958-61. 2 v.; 25 cm. 1. Liberty. I. San Francisco. Institute for Philosophical Research. II. T.
B105.L45 A3    323.44    *LC* 58-7348

**Polanyi, Michael, 1891-.** **1.140**
Meaning / Michael Polanyi and Harry Prosch. — Chicago: University of Chicago Press, 1975. xiv, 246 p.; 21 cm. 1. Meaning (Philosophy) — Addresses, essays, lectures. I. Prosch, Harry, 1917- joint author. II. T.
B105.M4 P64    B105M4 P64.    111.8/3    *LC* 75-5067    *ISBN* 0226672948

**Schiffer, Stephen R.** **1.141**
Meaning, by Stephen R. Schiffer. — Oxford: Clarendon Press, 1972. x, 170 p.; 23 cm. 1. Meaning (Philosophy) 2. Languages — Philosophy I. T.
B105.M4 S34 1972    149/.94    *LC* 73-155691    *ISBN* 0198243677

**Linsky, Leonard.** **1.142**
Names and descriptions / Leonard Linsky. — Chicago: University of Chicago Press, 1977. xxi, 184 p. Includes index. 1. Reference (Philosophy) 2. Names 3. Description (Philosophy) 4. Modality (Logic) 5. Semantics (Philosophy) I. T.
B105.R25 L56    B105R25 L56.    110    *LC* 76-8093    *ISBN* 0226484416

**Sober, Elliott.** **1.143**
Simplicity / Elliott Sober. — Oxford: Clarendon Press, 1975. x, 189 p.: ill.; 23 cm. (Clarendon library of logic and philosophy) Includes index. 1. Simplicity (Philosophy) I. T.
B105.S55 S6    121    *LC* 76-359016    *ISBN* 019824407X

**Shils, Edward Albert, 1911-.** **1.144**
Tradition / Edward Shils. — Chicago: University of Chicago Press, c1981. viii, 334 p.; 24 cm. 1. Tradition (Philosophy) 2. Progress 3. History — Philosophy 4. Civilization — Philosophy 5. Social change I. T.
B105.T7 S5    306/.4 19    *LC* 80-21643    *ISBN* 0226753255

**Armstrong, D. M. (David Malet), 1926-.** **1.145**
Universals and scientific realism / D. M. Armstrong. — Cambridge; New York: Cambridge University Press, 1978. 2 v.; 23 cm. 1. Universals (Philosophy) 2. Realism 3. Nominalism I. T.
B105.U5 A75    111    *LC* 77-80824    *ISBN* 0521217415

**Landesman, Charles. comp.** • **1.146**
The problem of universals. Edited and with an introd. by Charles Landesman. — New York: Basic Books, [1971] vi, 314 p.; 24 cm. 1. Universals (Philosophy) — Addresses, essays, lectures. I. T.
B105.U5 L35    101    *LC* 72-158443    *ISBN* 0465063616

# B108–708 Ancient Philosophy

## B121–162 Oriental Philosophy

**Koller, John M.** **1.147**
Oriental philosophies / John M. Koller. — 2nd ed. — New York: Scribner, c1985. xi, 369 p.: ill.; 24 cm. 1. Philosophy, Oriental I. T.
B121.K56 1985    181 19    *LC* 84-20300    *ISBN* 0684181452

**Reyna, Ruth.**                                                              **1.148**
Dictionary of oriental philosophy / edited and collated by Ruth Reyna; with a foreword by Moni Bagchi. — New Delhi: Munshiram Manoharlal, 1984. xx, 419 p.: ill.; 25 cm. 1. Philosophy, Oriental — Dictionaries — Polyglot. 2. Dictionaries, Polyglot I. T.
B121.R46 1984      181/.003/21 19      *LC* 84-902365

# B125–128 Chinese Philosophy

**Chan, Wing-tsit, 1901- comp. and tr.**                                      • **1.149**
A source book in Chinese philosophy. — Princeton, N.J.: Princeton University Press, 1963. xxv, 856 p.; 25 cm. 1. Philosophy, Chinese — Collections. 2. Philosophy — China — History — Sources. I. T.
B125.C45      181.11082      *LC* 62-7398

**Reflections on things at hand: the neo–Confucian anthology /**              • **1.150**
**compiled by Chu Hsi and Lü Tsu-ch'ien; translated, with notes,**
**by Wing–tsit Chan.**
New York: Columbia University Press, 1967. xli, 441 p. — (UNESCO collection of representative works. Chinese series.) Records of civilization; sources and studies, no.75. 'Prepared for the Columbia College program of translations from the oriental classics.' Translation of Chin ssü lu I. Lü, Tsu-ch'ien, 1137-1181. II. Chu, Hsi, 1130-1200. III. Chan, Wing-tsit, 1901- IV. Series.
B125.C513      180/.11      *LC* 65-22548

**Creel, Herrlee Glessner, 1905-.**                                           • **1.151**
Chinese thought, from Confucius to Mao Tsê-tung. — [Chicago]: University of Chicago Press, [1953] ix, 292 p.; 22 cm. 1. Philosophy, Chinese I. T.
B126.C67      181.1      *LC* 53-10054

**Feng, Yu-lan, 1895-.**                                                      • **1.152**
A history of Chinese philosophy / by Fung Yu-lan; translated by Derk Bodde, with introd., notes, bibliography and index. — Princeton: Princeton University Press, 1952-1953. 2 v.: fold. map, diagrs.; 25 cm. 1. Philosophy, Chinese I. Bodde, Derk, 1909- II. T.
B126.F38      181.11      *LC* 52-9807      *ISBN* 0691071144

**Feng, Yu-lan, 1895-.**                                                      • **1.153**
A short history of Chinese philosophy, edited by Derk Bodde. — New York: Macmillan Co., 1948. xx, 368 p.; 22 cm. A shorter version of the author's A history of Chinese philosophy. 1. Philosophy, Chinese I. Bodde, Derk, 1909- ed. II. T.
B126.F42      181.1      *LC* 48-9573

**Feng, Yu-lan, 1895-.**                                                      • **1.154**
The spirit of Chinese philosophy, by Fung Yu-lan. Translated by E. R. Hughes. — Westport, Conn.: Greenwood Press, [1970] xiv, 224 p.; 23 cm. Reprint of the 1947 ed. Translation of Hsin yüan tao (romanized form) 1. Philosophy, Chinese I. T.
B126.F43 1970      181/.1      *LC* 71-98757      *ISBN* 0837128161

**Hughes, E. R. (Ernest Richard), 1883-1956.**                                • **1.155**
Chinese philosophy in classical times. — London: Dent; New York: Dutton, 1966. xiv, 336 p. (Everyman's library, 973. Philosophy) 1. Philosophy, Chinese I. T.
B126.H84 1960

**Hu, Shih, 1891-1962.**                                                      • **1.156**
The development of the logical method in ancient China / by Shih Hu. — 2d ed.; with introd. by Hyman Kublin. — New York, Paragon Book Reprint Corp., 1963. 2, 187 p. 1. Philosophy, Chinese 2. Logic — History I. T.
B 126 H87 1968      181.11      *LC* 63-21053

**Waley, Arthur.**                                                            • **1.157**
Three ways of thought in ancient China. — Garden City, N.Y.: Doubleday, 1956. 216 p.; 18 cm. — (Doubleday anchor books, A75) 'Consists chiefly of extracts from Chuang Tzu, Mencius and Han Fei Tzu.' 1. Philosophy, Chinese I. T.
B126.W3x      181.1      *LC* 56-5973

**Wright, Arthur F., 1913-1976, ed.**                                         • **1.158**
Studies in Chinese thought. With contributions by Derk Bodde [and others. — Chicago]: University of Chicago Press, [1953] xiv, 317 p.; illus.; 25 cm. — (Comparative studies in cultures and civilizations) Based on papers presented at a conference held by a subcommittee on Chinese thought attached to the Committee on Far Eastern Studies jointly sponsored by the American Council of Learned Societies and the Far Eastern Association. 1. Philosophy, Chinese 2. Chinese language — Translating 3. China — Civilization I. T. II. Series.
B126.W7      181.1      *LC* 53-13533

**Chang, Chün-mai, 1886-1969.**                                               **1.159**
The development of Neo–Confucian thought / by Carsun Chang. — Westport, Conn.: Greenwood Press, 1977, c1957. 376 p.; 23 cm. Reprint of the ed.

published by Bookman Associates, New York. Includes index. 1. Neo-Confucianism I. T.
B127.N4 C46 1977      181/.11      *LC* 77-8338      *ISBN* 0837196930

**Conference on Seventeenth-Century Chinese Thought, Bellagio,**              **1.160**
**Italy, 1970.**
The unfolding of Neo–Confucianism, by Wm. Theodore de Bary and the Conference on Seventeenth–Century Chinese Thought. New York, Columbia University Press, 1975. xiv, 593 p. 23 cm. (Studies in Oriental culture. no. 10) 'This volume is the product of a Conference on Seventeenth-Century Chinese Thought, held at the Villa Serbelloni in September 1970, under the sponsorship of the Committee on the Study of Chinese Civilization of the American Council of Learned Societies.' 1. Neo-Confucianism — Congresses. 2. Confucianism — Relations — Buddhism — Congresses. 3. Buddhism — Relations — Confucianism — Congresses. I. De Bary, William Theodore, 1918- ed. II. American Council of Learned Societies. Committee on Studies of Chinese Civilization. III. T. IV. Series.
B127.N4 C66 1970      181/.09/512      *LC* 74-10929      *ISBN* 0231038283
*ISBN* 0231038291

**Principle and practicality: essays in Neo–Confucianism and**                **1.161**
**practical learning / Wm. Theodore de Bary and Irene Bloom,**
**editors.**
New York: Columbia University Press, 1979. xvi, 543 p.; 24 cm. — (Neo-Confucian studies.) 1. Neo-Confucianism — Addresses, essays, lectures. 2. Practice (Philosophy) — Addresses, essays, lectures. 3. China — History — Ming dynasty, 1368-1644 — Addresses, essays, lectures. 4. Japan — History — Tokugawa period, 1600-1868 — Addresses, essays, lectures. I. De Bary, William Theodore, 1918- II. Bloom, Irene. III. Series.
B127.N4 P74      181/.09/512      *LC* 78-11530      *ISBN* 023104612X

## B128 PHILOSOPHERS, A–Z

**Chu, Hsi, 1130-1200.**                                                      • **1.162**
[Hsing li. English] The philosophy of human nature. Translated from the Chinese, with notes, by J. Percy Bruce. London, Probsthain, 1922. [New York, AMS Press, 1973] xvi, 444 p. 19 cm. Original ed. issued as v. 10 of the Probsthain's oriental series. 'The work here translated forms a part of the imperial edition of Chu Hsi's complete works ... published in ... 1713 ... The title of the present work, which is complete in itself, is Hsing li.' I. T.
B128.C53 H7413 1973      128/.3      *LC* 73-38057      *ISBN* 0404569137

**Bruce, Joseph Percy, 1861-.**                                               • **1.163**
Chu Hsi and his masters; an introduction to Chu Hsi and the Sung School of Chinese Philosophy, by J. Percy Bruce. London, Probsthain, 1923. — [New York: AMS Press, 1973] xvi, 336 p.; 19 cm. Originally presented as the author's thesis. London. Original ed. issued as v. 11 of Probsthain's oriental series. 1. Chu, Hsi, 1130-1200. 2. Philosophy, Chinese I. T.
B128.C54 B78 1973      181/.11 B      *LC* 78-38050      *ISBN* 0404569048

**Chan, Wing-tsit, 1901-.**                                                   **1.164**
Chu Hsi, life and thought / Wing–tsit Chan. — Hong Kong: Chinese University Press; New York: St. Martin's Press, 1986. p. cm. Includes index. 1. Chu, Hsi, 1130-1200. 2. Philosophers — China — Biography. I. T.
B128.C54 C4 1986      181/.11 19      *LC* 86-6683      *ISBN* 0312134703

**Confucius.**                                                                • **1.165**
The sayings of Confucius; a new translation by James R. Ware. — New York: New American Library, 1955. 125 p. A Mentor religious classic. 1. Philosophy, Chinese 2. Ethics, Chinese I. Ware, James Roland. tr. II. T.
B128.C7W33      181.1

**Smith, D. Howard (David Howard), b. 1900.**                                 **1.166**
Confucius, by D. Howard Smith. — New York: Scribner, [1973] 240 p.: map.; 25 cm. — (Makers of new worlds) 1. Confucius. I. T.
B128.C8 S56 1973b      181/.095/12      *LC* 72-9821      *ISBN* 0684132575

**Han, Fei, d. 233 B.C.**                                                     • **1.167**
The complete works of Han Fei tzu ... London, A. Probsthain, 1939-59. 2 v. 20 cm. I. Ssu-ma, Ch'ien, ca. 145-ca. 86 B.C. II. T.
B128.H32 E55      *LC* 41-11756

**Hsün-tzu, 340-245 B.C.**                                                    **1.168**
[Hsün-tzu English] The works of Hsüntze / translated from the Chinese, with notes, by Homer H. Dubs. — New York: AMS Press, 1977. 336 p.; 18 cm. — Reprint of the 1928 ed. published by A. Probsthain, London, which was issued as v. 16 of Probsthain's oriental series. I. Dubs, Homer Hasenpflug, 1892- II. T.
B128.H66 E5 1977      181/.09/512      *LC* 75-41145      *ISBN* 0404147544

**Hsün-tzu, 340-245 B.C.**                                                    • **1.169**
Basic writings / Hsün Tzu; translated by Burton Watson. — New York: Columbia University Press, 1963. vi, 177 p.; 21 cm. (UNESCO collection of representative works. Chinese series.) Prepared for the Columbia College

program of translations from the Oriental classics. I. Watson, Burton, 1925-
II. T. III. Series.
B128.H66 E55      LC 63-20340      ISBN 0231086075

**Mencius.**                                                      • **1.170**
Mencius: a new translation arranged and annotated for the general reader / by
W.A.C.H. Dobson. Toronto: University Press, 1963. xviii, 215 p. — (UNESCO
collection of representative works. Chinese series.) 1. Conduct of life —
Quotations, maxims, etc. I. Dobson, William Arthur Charles Harvey, 1913-
II. T. III. Series.
B128.M33 E54 1963      LC 63-23889

**Mo, Ti, fl. 400 B.C.**                                          • **1.171**
Mo Tzu; basic writings. Translated by Burton Watson. New York, Columbia
University Press, 1963. vi, 140 p. 21 cm. (UNESCO collection of representative
works: Chinese series) I. Watson, Burton, 1925- tr. II. T.
B128.M6W3      LC 63-20339

**Mo, Ti, fl. 400 B.C.**                                          • **1.172**
The ethical and political works of Motse, translated from the original Chinese
text by Yi–Pao Mei, PH. D. London, A. Probsthain, 1929. xiv, 275 p.; 20 cm.
(Probsthain's Oriental series, vol. XIX) The translator's thesis, University of
Chicago, 1927. I. Mei, I-pao, 1900- II. T.
B128.M7 E5      LC 30-4133

**Liu, James T.C.**                                               **1.173**
Ou–Yang Hsiu, an eleventh–century Neo–Confucianist / James T.C. Liu. —
Stanford, Calif.: Stanford University Press, 1967. viii, 227 p.: ill.; 23 cm. —
(Stanford studies in the civilizations of Eastern Asia.) 'Originally published in
Hong Kong in 1963, under the title Ou-yang Hsiu ti chih-hsüeh yü ts'ung-
cheng.' 1. Ou-yang, Hsiu, 1007-1072. 2. Neo-Confucianism I. T. II. Series.
B128.O84 L5      LC 67-13660

**Wang, Yang-ming, 1472-1529.**                                   • **1.174**
Instructions for practical living and other Neo–Confucian writing / by Wang
Yang–ming; translated, with notes by Wing–Tsit Chan. — New York:
Columbia University Press, 1963. xli, 358 p.: port. — (Records of civilization,
sources and studies. no. 68) (UNESCO collection of representative works.
Chinese series.) 1. Philosophy, Chinese 2. Neo-Confucianism I. Chan, Wing-
tsit, 1901- II. T. III. Series. IV. Series: UNESCO collection of representative
works. Chinese series.
B128.W4 E47      181.11      LC 62-16688

**Wang, Yang-ming, 1472-1529.**                                   **1.175**
The philosophy of Wang Yang–ming / translated from the Chinese by
Frederick Goodrich Henke; introd. by James H. Tufts. — 2d ed. — New York:
Paragon Book Reprint Corp., 1964. xvii, 512 p.: ports. — (Paragon reprint
Oriental series; no. 25) 1. Philosophy, Chinese I. Henke, Frederick Goodrich,
1876- II. T.
B128.W4 E5 1964      LC 64-18447

# B130–133 Indian Philosophy

**A Source book in Indian philosophy / edited by Sarvepalli**     • **1.176**
**Radhakrishnan and Charles A. Moore.**
Princeton, N.J.: Princeton University Press, c1957. xxxi, [684] p. (Princeton
paperbacks) 1. Philosophy, Hindu I. Moore, Charles Alexander.
II. Radhakrishnan, S. (Sarvepalli), 1888-1975. III. Title: Indian philosophy.
IV. Title: A sourcebook in Indian philosophy.
B130.R3      LC 55-6698      ISBN 0691019584

**Singh, Balbir.**                                                **1.177**
The philosophy of Upanishads / Balbir Singh. — Atlantic Highlands, N.J.:
Humanities Press, c1983. 150 p.; 23 cm. 1. Philosophy, Indic 2. Upanishads.
3. Philosophy, Hindu I. T.
B130.S617      ISBN 0391029355

**Dasgupta, Surendranath, 1885-1952.**                            • **1.178**
A history of Indian philosophy / by the late Surendranath Dasgupta. —
Cambridge: University Press, 1922-1955. 5 v. 'Surendranath Dasgupta, a
memoir [by Surama Dasgupta]': v. 5, p. [v]-xii. 1. Philosophy, Hindu 2. India
— Religion I. Dasgupta, Surama. II. T.
B131.D3      LC 22-18463      ISBN 0521047781

**The Encyclopedia of Indian philosophies [by] Sibajiban**       • **1.179**
**Bhattacharya [and others.**
1st ed. — Delhi: Published for American Institute of Indian Studies by Motilal
Banarsidass, 1970-. v.      ; 25 cm. Vol. 1 has separate title page. 1. Philosophy,
Indic — Dictionaries. 2. Philosophy, Indic — Bibliography. I. Bhattacharya,
Sibajiban. II. Potter, Karl H. comp. III. American Institute of Indian Studies.
B131.E5      181/.4      LC 70-911664

**Gupta, Shanti Nath, 1929-.**                                    **1.180**
The Indian concept of values / Shanti Nath Gupta. — Columbia, Mo.: South
Asia Books, c1978. x, 197 p.; 23 cm. Originally presented as the author's thesis,
Punjab University. 1. Philosophy, India. 2. Values I. T.
B 131 G885 1978      ISBN 0836400702

**Hiriyanna, Mysore, 1871-1950.**                                 • **1.181**
The essentials of Indian philosophy / by M. Hiriyanna. — Bombay: Allen &
Unwin, 1973. 216 p. 1. Philosophy, Hindu 2. India — Religion I. T.
B131.H48 1973

**Indian philosophy: past and future / edited by S.S. Rama Rao**  **1.182**
**Pappu and R. Puligandla.**
1st ed. — [s.l.]: South Asia Books, 1983. xvii, 434 p.; 22 cm. 1. Philosophy,
Indic — Addresses, essays, lectures. I. Rama Rao Pappu, S. S. II. Puligandla,
R., 1930-
B131.I48 1983      181/.4 19      LC 82-901541      ISBN 0836406702

**Organ, Troy Wilson.**                                           **1.183**
Western approaches to eastern philosophy / Troy Wilson Organ. Athens: Ohio
University Press, c1975. 282 p.; 22 cm. 1. Philosophy, Indic — Addresses,
essays, lectures. 2. Philosophy, Comparative — Addresses, essays, lectures.
I. T.
B131.O73      181      LC 75-14554      ISBN 0821401947

**Potter, Karl H.**                                               • **1.184**
Presuppositions of India's philosophies [by] Karl H. Potter. — Westport,
Conn.: Greenwood Press, [1972, c1963] xi, 276 p.; 22 cm. Original ed. issued in
series: Prentice-Hall philosophy series. 1. Philosophy, Indic I. T.
B131.P6 1972      181/.4      LC 72-6843      ISBN 0837164974

**Radhakrishnan, S. (Sarvepalli), 1888-1975. ed.**                • **1.185**
Contemporary Indian philosophy, by M. K. Gandhi [and others] edited by S.
Radhakrishnan and J. H. Muirhead. — [Rev. 2d and enl. ed.]. — London, G.
Allen & Unwin [1952] 648 p. 23 cm. — (The Muirhead library of philosophy)
Includes bibliographies. 1. Philosophy, Hindu I. Muirhead, John H. (John
Henry), 1855-1940. joint ed. II. T.
B131.R25 1952      181.4      LC 52-10717

**Radhakrishnan, S. (Sarvepalli), 1888-1975.**                    • **1.186**
The Hindu view of life; Upton lectures delivered at Manchester college, Oxford,
1926 / by S. Radhakrishnan. — London: G. Allen & Unwin, ltd.; New York:
The Macmillan company, [1927] 133, [1] p.: 21 cm. 'First published in 1927.'
1. Hinduism I. Martha Upton lectures, 1926. II. T.
B131.R28      LC 27-26906

**Radhakrishnan, S. (Sarvepalli), 1888-1975.**                    • **1.187**
Indian philosophy, by Radhakrishnan. London, Allen & Unwin; New York,
Humanities Press [1966] 2 v. 22 cm. (The Muirhead library of philosophy)
'Second edition, 1929 ... eighth impression, 1966.' 1. Vedas. 2. Upanishads.
3. Philosophy, Indic I. T.
B131.R3212      LC 79-23612

**Raju, P. T. (Poolla Tirupati), 1904-.**                         **1.188**
The philosophical traditions of India [by] P. T. Raju. [Pittsburgh] University of
Pittsburgh Press [1972] 256 p. 23 cm. 1. Philosophy, Indic I. T.
B131.R345 1972      181/.4      LC 70-189859      ISBN 0822911051

**Sharma, Chandradhar.**                                          • **1.189**
Indian philosophy: a critical survey. — [New York]: Barnes & Noble, [1962]
405 p.; 21 cm. — I. T.
B131.S48 1962      LC 62-18222

**Zimmer, Heinrich Robert, 1890-1943.**                           • **1.190**
Philosophies of India; edited by Joseph Campbell. [New York] Pantheon Books
[1951] xvii, 687 p. ill. 24 cm. (Bollingen series, 26) 1. Philosophy, Hindu I. T.
B131.Z52      LC 51-13167

## B132 SPECIAL TOPICS, A–Z

**Sharma, B. N. Krishnamurti, 1909-.**                            **1.191**
History of the Dvaita school of Vedānta and its literature: from the earliest
beginnings to our own time / B.N.K. Sharma. — 2nd rev. ed. — Delhi: Motilal
Banarsidass, 1981. xxxii, 618 p., [4] leaves of plates: ill.; 25 cm. 1. Dvaita
(Vedanta) I. T.
B132.D8 S5 1981      181/.4841 19      LC 81-903270

**Sastri, P. S.**                                                 **1.192**
Indian idealism: epistemology & ontology / P. S. Sastri. Delhi: Bharatiya Vidya
Prakashan, 1975-. v.; 22 cm. 1. Śaṅkarācārya. 2. Idealism 3. Philosophy,
Indic I. T.
B132.I3 S27      181/.4      LC 75-908409

**Mittal, Kewal Krishan, 1931-.**                                                    **1.193**
Materialism in Indian thought. — [New Delhi]: Munshiram Manoharlal
Publishers, [1974] xii, 336 p.; 22 cm. Running title: Role of materialism in
Indian thought. Originally presented as the author's thesis, University of Delhi,
1967. 1. Lokāyata 2. Philosophy, Indic I. T. II. Title: Role of materialism in
Indian thought.
B132.L6 M57 1974      146/.3      LC 74-901145

**Riepe, Dale Maurice, 1918-.**                                                    • **1.194**
The naturalistic tradition in Indian thought. — Seattle: University of
Washington Press, 1961. xi, 308 p.: illus.; 23 cm. 1. Philosophy, Indic
2. Naturalism I. T.
B132.N3 R5      181.4      LC 61-7157

**Indian metaphysics and epistemology: the tradition of Nyāya–**      **1.195**
**Vaiśe–sika up to Gaṅgeśa / edited by Karl H. Potter.**
Princeton, N.J.: Princeton University Press, c1977. xiii, 744 p.; 24 cm. At head
of title: Encyclopedia of Indian philosophies. 1. Nyaya — Addresses, essays,
lectures. 2. Vaiśesika — Addresses, essays, lectures. I. Potter, Karl H.
II. Title: Encyclopedia of Indian philosophies.
B132.N8 I48      181/.43      LC 78-306563

**Jayanta Bhatta, fl. 850-910.**                                                    **1.196**
[Nyāyamañjari. English] Jayanta Bhatta's Nyāya–mañjarī: the compendium of
Indian speculative logic / translated into English by Janaki Vallabha
Bhattacharyya. — 1st ed. — Delhi: Motilal Banarsidass, 1978-. v.; 22 cm.
Includes index. 1. Nyaya 2. Hindu logic I. T. II. Title: Nyāya-mañjari.
B132.N8 J3813      181/.43      LC 78-904754

**Keith, Arthur Berriedale, 1879-1944.**                                          • **1.197**
Indian logic and atomism; an exposition of the Nyāya and Vaiçesika systems. —
New York: Greenwood Press, 1968. 291 p.; 20 cm. Reprint of the 1921 ed.
1. Nyaya 2. Vaiśesika I. T.
B132.N8 K4 1968      181/.43      LC 68-54422

**Beidler, William, 1928-.**                                                    **1.198**
The vision of self in early Vedānta / William Beidler. — 1st ed. — Delhi:
Motilal Banarsidass, 1975. xii, x, 266 p.; 22 cm. A revision of the author's thesis,
Osmania University. Includes index. 1. Vedanta 2. Self (Philosophy)
3. Ātman I. T.
B132.V3 B42 1975      126      LC 76-900890      ISBN 0842609903

**Deutsch, Eliot.**                                                    • **1.199**
A source book of Advaita Vedānta [by] Eliot Deutsch [and] J. A. B. van
Buitenen. Honolulu, University Press of Hawaii, 1971. ix, 335 p. 25 cm.
Includes English translations of the major Sanskrit writings of the most
important Vedāntic philosophers. 1. Vedanta — Collections. 2. Advaita —
Collections. I. Buitenen, J. A. B. van (Johannes Adrianus Bernardus van) joint
author. II. T.
B132.V3 D542      181/.482      LC 75-148944      ISBN 0870221892

**Lott, Eric J.**                                                    **1.200**
Vedantic approaches to God / Eric Lott; foreword by John Hick. — Totowa,
N.J.: Barnes & Noble, 1980. xii, 214 p.; 23 cm. (Library of philosophy and
religion) Originally presented as the author's thesis, Liverpool, 1977. Publishers
from label on t.p. Includes index. 1. Śaṅkarācārya. 2. Rāmānuja, 1017-1137.
3. Madhva, 13th cent. 4. Vedanta I. T.
B132.V3 L62 1980      181/.48 19      LC 78-17886      ISBN 0064943658

**Vedanta and the West.**                                                    **1.201**
Vedanta for modern man / edited and with an introduction by Christopher
Isherwood. — 1st ed. — New York: Harper, 1951. xvi, 410 p.; 22 cm.
1. Vedanta I. Isherwood, Christopher, 1904- II. T.
B132.V3 V38      LC 51-11293

**Dasgupta, Surendranath, 1885-1952.**                                          **1.202**
Yoga as philosophy and religion / Surendranath Dasgupta. — Delhi: Motilal
Banarsidass, 1973, 1978 printing. x, 200 p.; 22 cm. Reprint of the 1924 ed.
published by Kegan Paul, London. 1. Yoga 2. Philosophy, Hindu 3. Patañjalī.
I. T.
B132.Y6 D27 1973      181/.452      LC 78-913009

**Eliade, Mircea, 1907-.**                                                    **1.203**
[Yoga: immortalité et liberté. English] Yoga; immortality and freedom.
Translated from the French by Willard R. Trask. [New York] Pantheon Books
[1958] xxii, 529 p. 25 cm. (Bollingen series. 56) 1. Yoga I. T. II. Series.
B132.Y6 E523      181.45      LC 58-8986

**Patañjali.**                                                    • **1.204**
The Yoga–system of Patañjali; or, The ancient Hindu doctrine of concentration
of mind, embracing the mnemonic rules, called Yoga–sūtras, of Patañjali and
the comment, called Yoga–bhāshya, attributed to Veda–Vyāsa and the
explanation, called Tattva–vācāradī, of Vachaspati–Miçra. Translated from the
original Sanskrit by James Haughton Woods. [3d ed.] Delhi Motilal
Banarsidass [1966] 381p. (Harvard oriental series, v. 17) 1. Yoga — Early
works to 1800 I. Vyāsa. Yogabhāṣya II. Vācaspatimiśra, fl. 976-1000.

Yogatattvavaisāradī III. Woods, James Haughton, 1864-1935, tr. IV. T.
V. Series.
B132 Y6 P267 1966

**Patañjali.**                                                    **1.205**
[Yogasūtra. English & Sanskrit] Yoga philosophy of Patañjali: containing his
Yoga aphorisms with Vyāsa's commentary in Sanskrit and a translation with
annotations including many suggestions for the practice of Yoga / [annotated]
by Swāmi Hariharānanda Āranya; rendered into English by P.N. Mukerji;
foreword by Swāmi Gopalananda. — Albany: State University of New York
Press, c1983. xix, 483 p.; 24 cm. Includes index. 1. Yoga I. Hariharānanda
Āranya, Swami. II. Mukerji, Paresh Nath, 1882- III. Vyāsa. Yogabhāsya.
English & Sanskrit. 1983. IV. T.
B132.Y6 P267 1983      181/.45 19      LC 83-4944      ISBN 0873957288

**Varenne, Jean.**                                                    **1.206**
[Yoga et la tradition hindoue. English] Yoga and the Hindu tradition / Jean
Varenne; translated from the French by Derek Coltman. — Chicago:
University of Chicago Press, 1976. x, 253 p.; 23 cm. Translation of Le yoga et la
tradition hindoue. 'Yoga Darshana Upanishad': p. 200-222. Includes index.
1. Yoga I. Upanishads. Darśanopaniṣad. English. Selections. II. T.
B132.Y6 V2913      181/.45      LC 75-19506      ISBN 0226851141

## B133 PHILOSOPHERS, A–Z

**Gandhi, Mahatma, 1869-1948.**                                          • **1.207**
All men are brothers: life and thoughts of Mahatma Gandhi as told in his own
words. — Paris: UNESCO, 1958. 196 p.: ill.,; 20 cm. I. T.
B133.G4 A3      923.254      LC 59-426

**Richards, Glyn.**                                                    **1.208**
The philosophy of Gandhi: a study of his basic ideas / Glyn Richards. —
London: Curzon Press; Totowa, N.J.: Barnes & Noble, 1982. ix, 178 p.; 23 cm.
Includes index. 1. Gandhi, Mahatma, 1869-1948. I. T.
B133.G4 R52 1982      181/.4 19      LC 81-14859      ISBN 0389202479

**Schilpp, Paul Arthur, 1897- ed.**                                          • **1.209**
The philosophy of Sarvepalli Radhakrishnan. — New York: Tudor Pub. Co.,
1952. 883 p.: port., facsim. (Library of living philosophers.) 1. Radhakrishnan,
Sarvepalli, Sir, 1888-. I. T. II. Series.
B133.R16 S4

**Ramakrishna, 1836-1886.**                                                    • **1.210**
The gospel of Sri Ramakhrishna / translated into English with an introd. by
Swami Nikhilananda. — Abridged ed. — New York: Ramakrishna-
Vivekananda Center, c1958. xiv, 615 p.: port. 'Originally recorded in Bengali by
M., a disciple of the Master.' 1. Philosophy, Hindu I. T.
B133.R2G74 1958      181.4      LC 58-8948

**Bhatt, Siddheshwar Rameshwar, 1939-.**                                          **1.211**
Studies in Rāmānuja Vedānta / S. R. Bhatt. — 1st ed. — New Delhi: Heritage
Publishers, 1975. x, 200 p.; 22 cm. 'A revised form of ... thesis submitted to the
M. S. University of Baroda'. Includes index. 1. Rāmānuja, 1017-1137.
2. Vedanta 3. Advaita I. T.
B133.R366 B45      181/.48      LC 75-908081

## B135–138 Japanese Philosophy

**Fujisawa, Chikao, 1893-.**                                                    • **1.212**
Zen and Shinto; the story of Japanese philosophy. — Westport, Conn.:
Greenwood Press, [1971, c1959] 92 p.; 23 cm. 1. Philosophy, Japanese 2. Zen
Buddhism — Japan. 3. Shinto I. T.
B136.F83 1971      181/.12      LC 78-139133      ISBN 0837157498

**Nakamura, Hajime, 1912-.**                                                    • **1.213**
A history of the development of Japanese thought from A.D. 592 to 1868. —
[2d ed.]. — Tokyo: Kokusai Bunka Shinkokai, 1969. 2 v.; 24 cm. — (Japanese
life and culture series) 1. Philosophy — Japan — History. I. Kokusai Bunka
Shinkōkai. II. T.
B136.N3 1969      LC 74-97242

## B162–162.5 Buddhism. Jainism

**Buddhism and American thinkers / edited by Kenneth K. Inada**      **1.214**
**& Nolan P. Jacobson.**
Albany: State University of New York Press, 1984. xviii, 180 p.; 24 cm.
Includes index. 1. Philosophy, Buddhist — Addresses, essays, lectures.
2. Philosophy, American — 20th century — Addresses, essays, lectures.
3. Philosophy, Comparative — Addresses, essays, lectures. 4. Buddhism —

Doctrines — Addresses, essays, lectures. I. Inada, Kenneth K. II. Jacobson, Nolan Pliny.
B162.B83 1984      181/.043/0973 19      *LC* 83-409      *ISBN* 0873957539

**Keith, Arthur Berriedale, 1879-1944.**                                    • **1.215**
Buddhist philosophy in India and Ceylon / by A. Berriedale Keith. — 4th ed. — Varanasi: Chowkhamba Sanskrit Series Office, 1963. 339 p.; 20 cm. — (The Chowkhamba Sanskrit studies; v. 26) 1. Philosophy, Buddhist 2. Hinayana Buddhism 3. Mahayana Buddhism I. T. II. Series.
B162.K4 1963      *LC* 64-1387

**Mookerjee, Satkari.**                                    **1.216**
The Buddhist philosophy of universal flux: an exposition of the philosophy of critical realism as expounded by the school of Dignāga / by Satkari Mookerjee. — 1st ed. — Delhi: Motilal Banarsidass, 1975. xlvii, 448 p.; 25 cm. Reprint of the 1935 ed. published by University of Calcutta, Calcutta. 'Substantially based upon ... [the author's] thesis which was approved for the degree of doctorate in philosophy by the University of Calcutta in 1932.' 1. Dignāga, 5th cent. 2. Philosophy, Buddhist I. T.
B162.M65 1975      181/.043      *LC* 75-907666

**Bhattacharyya, Narendra Nath, 1934-.**                                    **1.217**
Jain philosophy: historical outline / by Narendra Nath Bhattacharyya. New Delhi: Munshiram Manoharlal Publishers, 1976. xix, 220 p.; 23 cm. Running title: Jain philosophy in historical outline. Includes index. 1. Philosophy, Jaina I. T.
B162.5.B483      181/.04/4      *LC* 76-902152

# B165–708 WESTERN PHILOSOPHY

## B165–491 Greek Philosophy

**Diels, Hermann, 1848-1922, ed.**                                    **1.218**
[Fragmente der Vorsokratiker. 4. Ältere Sophistik. English] The older Sophists; a complete translation by several hands of the fragments in Die Fragmente der Vorsokratiker, edited by Diels–Kranz ... with a new edition of Antiphon and Euthydemus. Edited by Rosamond Kent Sprague. [1st ed.] Columbia, University of South Carolina Press [1972] x, 347 p. 24 cm. Translation of pt. 4, Ältere Sophistik, of Diels' Die Fragmente der Vorsokratiker, 7th ed., with a regrouping of the Antiphon and Euthydemus fragments. 1. Philosophy, Ancient — Collections. 2. Sophists (Greek philosophy) I. Sprague, Rosamond Kent. ed. II. T.
B165.D4213      183/.1      *LC* 71-120587      *ISBN* 0872491927

**Ancilla to The pre–Socratic philosophers: a complete translation**                                    **1.219**
**of the fragment in Diels Fragmente der Vorsokratiker / by**
**Kathleen Freeman.**
Cambridge, Harvard University Press, 1983. ix, 162 p.; 23 cm. 'This book is a complete translation of the fragments of the Pre-Socratic philosphers given in Diels' Fragmente der Vorsokratiker, 5th ed. (B-section)'- Foreword. 1. Philosophy, Ancient I. Fitt, Mary, 1897-1959. II. Title: Pre-Socratic philosophers.
B165.D423 1956      182      *LC* A 48-9987      *ISBN* 0674035011

**Freeman, Kathleen, 1897-1959.**                                    • **1.220**
The pre–Socratic philosophers; a companion to Diels' Fragmente der Vorsokratiker. 2d. ed. Cambridge, Mass. Harvard University Press 1959. 486p. 1. Philosophy, Ancient I. T. Diels, Hermann, 1848-1922. Die Fragmente der Vorsokratiker II. T. III. Title: Companion to the pre-Socratic philosophers
B165 D43 F7 1959A

**Armstrong, A. H. (Arthur Hilary).**                                    • **1.221**
The Cambridge history of later Greek and early medieval philosophy; edited by A. H. Armstrong. London, Cambridge U.P., 1967. xiv, 711 p. 24 cm. 1. Philosophy, Ancient — Addresses, essays, lectures. 2. Philosophy, Medieval — Addresses, essays, lectures. I. T.
B171.A79      182      *LC* 66-12305

**Burnet, John, 1863-1928.**                                    • **1.222**
Greek philosophy, Thales to Plato, by John Burnet. London, Macmillan and co., limited, 1950. x, 360 p. incl. illus., geneal. tab. 22 cm. 1. Philosophy, Ancient I. T.
B171.B85 1950      *LC* 39-7819

**Cornford, Francis Macdonald, 1874-1943.**                                    • **1.223**
Before and after Socrates / by Francis MacDonald Cornford. — Cambridge: University Press, 1960. x, 113 p. 'The four lectures contained in the book were delivered ... at Cambridge in August, 1932.' 1. Philosophy, Ancient. 2. Socrates. 3. Plato. 4. Aristotle. I. T.
B171.C7 1960

**Cornford, Francis Macdonald, 1874-1943.**                                    • **1.224**
Principium sapientiae: the origins of Greek philosophical thought / by F. M. Cornford; [edited by W.K.C. Guthrie]. — London: Cambridge University Press, 1952. vii, 270 p. 1. Philosophy, Ancient I. Guthrie, W. K. C. (William Keith Chambers), 1906- II. T.
B171.C72      *LC* 52-14534

**Guthrie, W. K. C. (William Keith Chambers), 1906-.**                                    • **1.225**
The Greek philosophers, from Thales to Aristotle. London, Methuen [1950] 168 p. 18 cm. (Home study books [9]) 1. Philosophers, Greek 2. Philosophy, Ancient I. T.
B171.G8 1950a      *LC* 50-36839

**Guthrie, W. K. C. (William Keith Chambers), 1906-.**                                    • **1.226**
A history of Greek philosophy / by W. K. C. Guthrie. — Cambridge: University Press, 1962-. v. 1. Philosophy, Ancient I. T.
B171.G83      *LC* 62-52735      *ISBN* 0521051592

**Guthrie, W. K. C. (William Keith Chambers), 1906-.**                                    • **1.227**
In the beginning: some Greek views on the origins of life and the early state of man / W.K.C. Guthrie. — Ithaca, N. Y.: Cornell University Press, 1957. 151 p. 1. Philosophy, Ancient 2. Mythology, Greek I. T.
B171.G84      182      *LC* 58-2176

**Vlastos, Gregory.**                                    **1.228**
Plato's universe / Gregory Vlastos. — Seattle: University of Washington Press, [1975] xiii, 130 p.: ill.; 23 cm. (Jessie and John Danz lectures.) Includes indexes. 1. Plato. 2. Cosmology — History. 3. Philosophy, Ancient I. T. II. Series.
B187.C7 V55      113      *LC* 75-4548      *ISBN* 0295953888

*(handwritten: B 187 C7 V55)*

**Baldry, H. C.**                                    **1.229**
The unity of mankind in Greek thought, by H. C. Baldry. — Cambridge [Eng.] University Press, 1965. vii, 223 p. 23 cm. 'Notes and references': p. 204-212. 1. Philosophy, Ancient 2. Philosophical anthropology — Hist. I. T.
B187.M25B3      128      *LC* 65-14356

## B188–258 FIRST PERIOD

**Barnes, Jonathan.**                                    **1.230**
The Presocratic philosophers / Jonathan Barnes. — Rev. ed. — London; Boston, Mass.: Routledge & Kegan Paul, 1982. xxiii, 703 p.: ill.; 24 cm. — (Arguments of the philosophers.) 1. Philosophy, Ancient I. T. II. Series.
B188.B34 1982      182 19      *LC* 81-23465      *ISBN* 0710092008

**Burnet, John, 1863-1928.**                                    • **1.231**
Early Greek philosophy. — [4th ed.]. — New York: Meridian Books, 1957. vii, 375 p.; 21 cm. — (Meridian library, ML5) 1. Philosophy, Ancient I. T.
B188.B9 1957      182      *LC* 57-10842

**Cornford, Francis Macdonald, 1874-1943.**                                    • **1.232**
From religion to philosophy; a study in the origins of western speculation. — New York, Harper [1957] 275 p. 21 cm. — (Harper torchbooks, TB20) The Library of religion and culture. 1. Philosophy, Ancient 2. Greece — Religion I. T.
B188.C6 1957      180      *LC* 57-10120

**Kirk, G. S. (Geoffrey Stephen), 1921-.**                                    • **1.233**
The presocratic philosophers: a critical history with a selection of texts. — 2nd ed. / by G.S. Kirk, J.E. Raven, M. Schofield. — Cambridge [Cambridgeshire]; New York: Cambridge University Press, 1983. xiii, 501 p.; 24 cm. Includes indexes. 1. Philosophy, Ancient I. Raven, J. E. (John Earle) II. Schofield, Malcolm. III. T.
B188.K5 1983      182 19      *LC* 82-23505      *ISBN* 0521254442

*(handwritten: B 188 K59)*

**Mourelatos, Alexander P. D., 1936- comp.**                                    **1.234**
The Pre–Socratics; a collection of critical essays. Edited by Alexander P. D. Mourelatos. — [1st ed.]. — Garden City, N.Y.: Anchor Press, 1974. xiv, 559 p.; 21 cm. — (Modern studies in philosophy, APO-21) 1. Philosophy, Ancient — Addresses, essays, lectures. I. T.
B188.M64      182      *LC* 73-11729      *ISBN* 0385054807

**Schofield, Malcolm.**                                    **1.235**
An essay on Anaxagoras / Malcolm Schofield. — Cambridge [Eng.]; New York: Cambridge University Press, 1980. xi, 187 p.; 22 cm. (Cambridge classical studies.) Includes indexes. 1. Anaxagoras. 2. Aristotle. I. T. II. Series.
B205.Z7 S36      182/.8      *LC* 79-10348      *ISBN* 0521227224

**Kahn, Charles H.**                                    **1.236**
The art and thought of Heraclitus: an edition of the fragments with translation and commentary / Charles H. Kahn. — Cambridge, [Eng.]; New York: Cambridge University Press, 1979. xiv, 354 p.; 24 cm. Includes Greek original and English translation of the fragments. Includes indexes. 1. Heraclitus, of Ephesus. I. Heraclitus, of Ephesus. II. T.
B223.K3      182/.4      *LC* 77-82499      *ISBN* 0521218837

**Heraclitus, of Ephesus.**                                   • **1.237**
The cosmic fragments / edited with an introd. and commentary by G.S. Kirk.
— Cambridge [Eng.]: University Press, 1962. xv, 423 p.; 25 cm. I. Kirk, G. S.
(Geoffrey Stephen), 1921- II. T.
B223.K48 1962        182.4      *LC* 54-2967

**Parmenides.**                                               **1.238**
Fragments, a text and translation / Parmenides of Elea; with an introduction by
David Gallop. — Toronto; Buffalo: University of Toronto Press, c1984. x,
144 p.; 24 cm. (Phoenix pre-Socratics; v. 1 = Les Pré-socratiques Phoenix; t. 1)
(Phoenix. Supplementary volume; v. 18 = Phoenix. Tome supplémentaire; t.
18) Text in English and Greek. Includes index. 1. Philosophy — Addresses,
essays, lectures. I. T.
B235.P23 F7 1984      182/.3 19      *LC* 85-123404      *ISBN* 0802024432

**Burkert, Walter, 1931-.**                                   **1.239**
[Weisheit und Wissenschaft. English] Lore and science in ancient
Pythagoreanism. Translated by Edwin L. Minar, Jr. Cambridge, Mass.,
Harvard University Press, 1972. 535 p. 25 cm. Translation of Weisheit und
Wissenschaft; Studien zu Pythagoras, Philolaos und Platon. 1. Plato.
2. Philolaus. 3. Pythagoras and Pythagorean school I. T.
B243.B813        182/.2      *LC* 70-162856      *ISBN* 0674539184

## B265–491 SECOND–THIRD PERIODS

**Kerferd, G. B.**                                            **1.240**
The sophistic movement / G.B. Kerferd. — Cambridge; New York: Cambridge
University Press, 1981. vii, 184 p.; 23 cm. Includes index. 1. Sophists (Greek
philosophy) I. T.
B288.K47        183/.1 19      *LC* 80-41934      *ISBN* 0521239362

**Xenophon.**                                                 **1.241**
Recollections of Socrates, and Socrates' defense before the jury / Xenophon;
translated, with an introd., by Anna S. Benjamin. — Indianapolis: Bobbs-
Merrill, [1965] xxv, 157 p.; 21 cm. — (Library of liberal arts. 205.) Includes
index. I. Socrates. I. Xenophon. Socrates' defense before the jury. II. T.
III. Series.
B316.X2 B4      *LC* 64-66080

**Santas, Gerasimos Xenophon.**                               **1.242**
Socrates, philosophy in Plato's early dialogues / Gerasimos Xenophon Santas.
— London; Boston: Routledge & K. Paul, 1979. viii, 343 p.; 24 cm. — (The
Arguments of the philosophers) Includes indexes. 1. Socrates. 2. Plato.
Dialogues 3. Questioning I. T.
B317.S28 1979      183/.2      *LC* 78-40735      *ISBN* 0710089996

## B350–398 Plato

**Brandwood, Leonard.**                                       **1.243**
A word index to Plato / by Leonard Brandwood. — Leeds: W. S. Maney and
Son, 1976. xxxi, 1003 p.; 29 cm. — (Compendia, computer-generated aids to
literary and linguistic research; v. 8) 1. Plato — Concordances. I. T.
B351.B72        184      *LC* 76-380277      *ISBN* 0901286095

**Allen, Reginald E., 1931-.**                                **1.244**
Socrates and legal obligation / R.E. Allen. — Minneapolis: University of
Minnesota Press, c1980. ix, 148 p.; 24 cm. Includes the author's translations of
Plato's Apology and Crito. Includes indexes. 1. Plato. Apology 2. Plato. Crito
3. Socrates. 4. Law — Philosophy. I. Plato. Apologia. English. 1980.
II. Plato. Crito. English. 1980. III. T.
B365.A95        184      *LC* 80-18193      *ISBN* 0816609624

**Woozley, A. D. (Anthony Douglas)**                          **1.245**
Law and obedience: the arguments of Plato's Crito / A. D. Woozley. — Chapel
Hill: University of North Carolina Press, c1979. 160 p.; 23 cm. Errata slip
inserted. 1. Plato. Crito 2. Socrates. 3. Law — Philosophy. 4. Obedience
I. T.
B368.W66 1979      172/.1      *LC* 79-456      *ISBN* 0807813664

**Sprague, Rosamond Kent.**                                   • **1.246**
Plato's use of fallacy: a study of the Euthydemus and some other dialogues /
Rosamond K. Sprague. — New York: Barnes & Noble, [1963, c1962] xv,
106 p.; 23 cm. 1. Plato. Euthydemus 2. Logic I. T.
B369.S6 1963        184      *LC* 63-484

**Plato.**                                                    **1.247**
[Gorgias. English] Gorgias / Plato; translated with notes by Terence Irwin. —
Oxford: Clarendon Press; New York: Oxford University Press, 1979. ix, 268 p.;
21 cm. — (Clarendon Plato series) Includes index. 1. Ethics 2. Political science
— Early works to 1800 I. Irwin, Terence. II. T.
B371.A5 I78        170      *LC* 79-40477      *ISBN* 0198720874

**Plato.**                                                    • **1.248**
Plato and Parmenides: Parmenides' Way of truth and Plato's Parmenides /
translated, with an introduction and running commentary by Francis
MacDonald Cornford. — London: Routledge & K. Paul, 1939. xvii, 251 p. —
(International library of psychology, philosophy, and scientific method.)
1. Parmenides. I. Cornford, Francis Macdonald, 1874-1943. II. Parmenides.
Way of truth. III. T. IV. Title: Way of truth. V. Title: Parmenides. VI. Series.
B378.A2 C6      *LC* 40-4021

**Plato.**                                                    **1.249**
[Parmenides English] Plato's Parmenides / translation and analysis, R.E.
Allen. — Minneapolis: University of Minnesota Press, c1983. xv, 329 p.; 24 cm.
1. Socrates. 2. Zeno, of Elea. 3. Reasoning I. Allen, Reginald E., 1931- II. T.
B378.A5 A44 1983      184 19      *LC* 82-7051      *ISBN* 0816610703

**Plato.**                                                    **1.250**
[Phaedo. English] Phaedo / Plato; translated with notes by David Gallop. —
Oxford [Eng.]: Clarendon Press, 1975. vi, 245 p.; 21 cm. — (Clarendon Plato
series) Translation of Phaedo. Includes index. 1. Immortality (Philosophy)
I. Gallop, David. II. T.
B379.A5 G34        184      *LC* 76-355935      *ISBN* 0198720475

**Plato.**                                                    **1.251**
[Philebus. English] Philebus / [by] Plato; translated [from the Greek] with
notes and commentary by J. C. B. Gosling. — Oxford: Clarendon Press, 1975.
xxi, 238 p.; 21 cm. — (Clarendon Plato series) Translation of Philebus. Includes
index. 1. Pleasure I. Gosling, J. C. B. (Justin Cyril Bertrand) II. T.
B381.A5 G67      171/.4 19      *LC* 76-371243      *ISBN* 0198720440

**Plato.**                                                    **1.252**
[Protagoras. English] Protagoras / Plato; translated with notes by C. C. W.
Taylor. — Oxford: Clarendon Press, 1976. vi, 230 p.; 21 cm. (Clarendon Plato
series) Includes indexes. 1. Protagoras. 2. Socrates. 3. Sophists (Greek
philosophy) 4. Ethics I. Taylor, C. C. W. (Christopher Charles Whiston),
1936- II. T.
B382.A5 T39 1976        170      *LC* 76-379216      *ISBN* 0198720459

**Plato.**                                                    • **1.253**
Plato's theory of knowledge: the Theaetetus and the Sophist of Plato /
translated with a running commentary by Francis Macdonald Cornford. —
New York: Liberal Arts Press, 1957. 336 p. — (The Library of liberal arts; no.
100) 1. Plato. I. Cornford, Francis Macdonald, 1874-1943. II. Plato.
Theaetetus III. Plato. Sophist IV. T.
B386.A5 C6 1957      *LC* 57-4254

**Plato.**                                                    **1.254**
[Theaetetus English] Theaetetus; translated with notes by John McDowell.
Oxford, Clarendon Press, 1973. 264 p. 21 cm. (Clarendon Plato series)
1. Knowledge, Theory of I. McDowell, John Henry. II. T.
B386.A5 M32        121      *LC* 74-164763      *ISBN* 0198720432 *ISBN*
0198720831

**Plato.**                                                    • **1.255**
Plato's cosmology: the Timaeus of Plato, translated with a running commentary
/ by Francis Macdonald Cornford. — London: Routledge & Kegan Paul, 1937.
376 p.: front., illus., (incl. music) (International library of psychology,
philosophy, and scientific method.) I. Cornford, Francis Macdonald,
1874-1943. II. T. III. Series.
B387.A5 C65      *LC* 37-15188

**Plato. Spurious and doubtful works.**                       • **1.256**
Plato's epistles; a translation, with critical essays and notes, by Glenn R.
Morrow. — Indianapolis, Bobbs-Merrill [1962] 282 p. geneal. table. 21 cm. —
(The Library of liberal arts) 'A revised edition of Studies in the Platonic epistles,
published ... in 1935.' 1. Sicily — Hist. — To 800. I. Morrow, Glenn R. (Glenn
Raymond), 1895-1973. ed. and tr. II. T.
B391.E8M6 1962        184      *LC* 61-18063

**Plato.**                                                    **1.257**
[Hippias major. English] Hippias major / Plato; translated, with commentary
and essay, by Paul Woodruff. — Indianapolis: Hackett Pub. Co., c1982. xvi,
211 p.; 24 cm. Includes indexes. 1. Values I. Woodruff, Paul, 1943- II. T.
B391.H42 E5 1982      184 19      *LC* 81-7027      *ISBN* 0915145251

### B393–395 Criticism. Interpretation

**Burnet, John, 1863-1928.**                                  • **1.258**
Platonism. Berkeley, Calif., University of California Press, 1928. 130 p. 24 cm.
(Sather classical lectures. 5.) 1. Plato. I. T. II. Series.
B 393 B96 1928      *LC* 29-941

**Bambrough, Renford. ed.**                                   • **1.259**
New essays on Plato and Aristotle, by G. E. M. Anscombe [and others]. — New
York, Humanities Press [1965] viii, 176 p. 23 cm. — (International library of
philosophy and scientific method.) Bibliographical footnotes. 1. Plato —

Addresses, essays, lectures. 2. Aristoteles — Addresses, essays, lectures. I. Anscombe, G. E. M. II. T. III. Series.
B395.B28 1965        185.08        *LC* 65-17418

**Crombie, I. M.**                                                      • **1.260**
An examination of Plato's doctrines / by I. M. Crombie. — New York: Humanities Press, 1962-1963. 2 v. — (International library of philosophy and scientific method.) Vol. 2, with series statement, has imprint: London, Routledge & Paul; New York, Humanities Press. 1. Plato. I. T. II. Title: Plato's doctrines. III. Series.
B395.C7        *LC* 62-6238

**Crombie, I. M.**                                                      • **1.261**
Plato: the midwife's apprentice / I.M. Crombie. — New York: Barnes & Noble, [1965, c1964] viii, 195 p.; 22 cm. 1. Plato. I. T.
B395.C72 1964        *LC* 65-7748

**Gosling, J. C. B. (Justin Cyril Bertrand)**                            **1.262**
Plato [by] J. C. B. Gosling. London, Boston, Routledge and Kegan Paul, 1973. viii, 319 p. 24 cm. (The Arguments of the philosophers) Includes index. 1. Plato. I. T.
B395.G46        184        *LC* 73-83075        *ISBN* 0710076649

**Grube, G. M. A. (George Maximilian Anthony)**                          • **1.263**
Plato's thought. — Boston, Beacon Press [1958] 320 p. 21 cm. — (Beacon paperback no. 60) Includes bibliography. 1. Plato. I. T.
B395.G67 1958        184        *LC* 59-1672

**Levinson, Ronald Bartlett, 1896- .**                                  • **1.264**
In defense of Plato. — Cambridge: Harvard University Press, 1953. xii, 674 p. 1. Plato. I. T.
B395.L38

**Raven, J. E.**                                                        • **1.265**
Plato's thought in the making: a study of the development of his metaphysics / by J. E. Raven. — Cambridge [Eng.]: University Press, 1965. xi, 256 p. 1. Plato. I. T.
B395.R37        110        *LC* 65-25585        423

**Shorey, Paul, 1857-1934.**                                            • **1.266**
The unity of Plato's thought. — [Hamden, Conn.]: Archon Books, 1968. 88 p.; 26 cm. 1. Plato. I. T.
B395.S5 1968        184        *LC* 68-12527

**Taylor, A. E. (Alfred Edward), 1869-1945.**                           • **1.267**
Plato: the man and his work / A. E. Taylor. — 7th ed. — London: Methuen, 1960. xi, 562 p. 1. Plato. I. T.
B395.T25 1960a        *LC* 63-5138        *ISBN* 0416675905

**Vlastos, Gregory. comp.**                                             • **1.268**
Plato: a collection of critical essays. — [1st ed.]. — Garden City, N.Y.: Anchor Books, 1971. 2 v.; 18 cm. — (Modern studies in philosophy) 1. Plato — Addresses, essays, lectures. I. T.
B395.V57        184/.08        *LC* 69-11014

## *B398 Special Topics, A–Z*

**Murdoch, Iris.**                                                      **1.269**
The fire & the sun: why Plato banished the artists / Iris Murdoch. — Oxford [Eng.]: Clarendon Press, 1977. 89 p.; 23 cm. Based upon the Romanes lecture, 1976. 1. Plato — Aesthetics — Addresses, essays, lectures. I. T.
B398.A4 M87        111.8/5        *LC* 77-5827        *ISBN* 0198245807

**Plato on beauty, wisdom, and the arts / edited by Julius**             **1.270**
**Moravcsik and Philip Temko.**
Totowa, N.J.: Rowman and Littlefield, 1982. x, 150 p.; 22 cm. — (APQ library of philosophy.) 1. Plato — Aesthetics — Congresses. 2. Aesthetics — History — Congresses. I. Moravcsik, J. M. E. II. Temko, Philip, 1924- III. Title: On beauty, wisdom, and the arts. IV. Series.
B398.A4 P55 1982        111/.85 19        *LC* 81-23434        *ISBN* 0847670309

**Sayre, Kenneth M., 1928- .**                                          • **1.271**
Plato's analytic method [by] Kenneth M. Sayre. — Chicago: University of Chicago Press, [1969] xi, 250 p.; 23 cm. 1. Plato. 2. Analysis (Philosophy) I. T.
B398.A6 S28        184        *LC* 69-15496

**Gould, John, 1927- .**                                                • **1.272**
The development of Plato's ethics. New York, Russell & Russell [1972] xiii, 240 p. 23 cm. Reprint of the 1955 ed., which is a revision of the author's thesis, Cambridge, College 1952. 1. Plato — Ethics. 2. Ethics, Ancient I. T.
B398.E8 G6 1972        184        *LC* 70-180609

**Irwin, Terence.**                                                     **1.273**
Plato's moral theory: the early and middle dialogues / Terence Irwin. — Oxford [Eng.]; New York: Clarendon Press, 1977. xvii, 376 p.; 23 cm. Includes indexes. 1. Plato — Ethics. 2. Ethics, Ancient I. T.
B398.E8 I78        170/.92/4        *LC* 78-300940        *ISBN* 019824567X

**Mackenzie, Mary Margaret.**                                           **1.274**
Plato on punishment / Mary Margaret Mackenzie. — Berkeley: University of California Press, c1981. 278 p.; 24 cm. A revision of the author's thesis, Cambridge. Includes indexes. 1. Plato — Ethics. 2. Punishment 3. Values 4. Ethics, Ancient I. T.
B398.E8 M3 1981        364.6/01 19        *LC* 80-6065        *ISBN* 0520041690

**Wild, John Daniel, 1902-1972.**                                       • **1.275**
Plato's modern enemies and the theory of natural law. — [Chicago] University of Chicago Press [1953] xi, 259 p. 24 cm. Bibliographical references included in 'Notes' (p. 235-251) 1. Plato. 2. Ethics 3. Natural law I. T.
B398.E8W5        184.1        *LC* 53-2434

**Cherniss, Harold F. (Harold Fredrik), 1904-1987.**                     • **1.276**
The riddle of the early Academy. — New York, Russell & Russell, 1962 [c1945] 103 p. 1. Plato. 2. Aristoteles. I. T.
B398.I3C5 1962        184        *LC* 62-13832

**Ross, W. D. (William David), 1877- .**                                • **1.277**
Plato's theory of ideas / by Sir David Ross. — Oxford: Clarendon Press, 1951. 250 p. 1. Plato. I. T.
B398.I3 R6        *LC* 52-1984

**Gulley, Norman.**                                                     • **1.278**
Plato's theory of knowledge. — London, Methuen; New York, Barnes & Noble [1962] 203 p. 23 cm. 1. Plato. 2. Knowledge, Theory of I. T.
B398.K7G8        184        *LC* 62-5885

**Moline, Jon, 1937- .**                                                **1.279**
Plato's theory of understanding / Jon Moline. — Madison, Wis.: University of Wisconsin Press, 1981. xv, 255 p.; 24 cm. 1. Plato — Knowledge, Theory of. 2. Knowledge, Theory of 3. Comprehension I. T.
B398.K7 M64        121 19        *LC* 81-50826        *ISBN* 0299086607

**Robinson, Richard, 1902- .**                                          • **1.280**
Plato's earlier dialectic. — 2d ed. — Oxford: Clarendon Press, [1962] x, 286 p. 1. Plato. 2. Logic I. T.
B398.L8 R6 1962

**Wedberg, Anders, 1913-1978.**                                         • **1.281**
Plato's philosophy of mathematics / by Anders Wedberg. — Stockholm: Almqvist & Wiksell, 1955. 154 p.; 23 cm. 1. Plato. 2. Mathematics — Philosophy I. T.
B398.M3 W4        *LC* a 56-5574

## B400–491 Aristotle

**Aristotle.**                                                          • **1.282**
The basic works of Aristotle / edited and with an introd. by Richard McKeon. — New York: Random House, 1941. xxxix, 1487 p.: ill.; 24 cm. I. McKeon, Richard Peter, 1900- II. McKeon, Richard Peter. III. T.
B407.M2        888.5        *LC* 41-51734

**Aristotle.**                                                          • **1.283**
Works translated into English under the editorship of W. D. Ross. — Oxford: Clarendon Press, 1908-52. 12 v.: illus.; 23 cm. Vols. 4-5 and 8, those first published, edited by J. A. Smith and W. D. Ross. Each work in v. 1-11 has special t.p. or half title, and many were issued separately, as printed, in boards or paper covers. The volumes and paging correspond to the Oxford ed. of Bekker's Greek text. 1. Philosophy — Collected works. I. Ross, W. D. (William David), 1877- II. Smith, J. A. (John Alexander), 1863-1939. III. T. IV. Title: The works of Aristotle translated into English ...
B407.S6 1908        185.1        *LC* 09-16369

**Aristotle.**                                                          **1.284**
[Works. English. 1984] The complete works of Aristotle: the revised Oxford translation / edited by Jonathan Barnes. — Princeton, N.J.: Princeton University Press, 1984. 2 v. (xi, 2487 p.); 23 cm. — (Bollingen series. 71:2) Includes indexes. 1. Philosophy — Collected works. I. Barnes, Jonathan. II. T. III. Series.
B407.S6 1984        185 19        *LC* 82-5317        *ISBN* 0691099502

**Aristotle.**                                                          **1.285**
Aristotle's Eudemian ethics, books I, II, and VIII / translated with a commentary by Michael Woods. — Oxford: Clarendon Press; Toronto: Oxford University Press, 1982. xii, 234 p. — (Clarendon Aristotle series) 1. Aristotle. Ethica Eudemia. I. Woods, Michael. II. T. III. Title: Eudemian ethics.
B422.A5 W896 1982        170        *ISBN* 0198720602

**Aristotle.**      • **1.286**
[De republica Atheniensium. English] Aristotle's Constitution of Athens and related texts / translated with an introd. and notes by Kurt von Fritz and Ernst Kapp. — New York: Hafner, c1950. xii, 233 p.; 21 cm. — (The Hafner library of classics; 13) Also issued in 1966. 1. Athens (Greece) Constitution 2. Athens (Greece) — Politics and government I. Fritz, Kurt von, 1900- tr. II. Kapp, Ernst, 1863-    tr. III. T.
B426.5.A5 F7      *LC* A 50-9754

**Essays on Aristotle's ethics / edited by Amélie Oksenberg**     **1.287**
**Rorty.**
Berkeley: University of California Press, c1980. viii, 438 p.; 24 cm. (Major thinkers series. 2) 1. Aristotle Nicomachean ethics — Addresses, essays, lectures. 2. Ethics — Addresses, essays, lectures. I. Rorty, Amélie. II. Series.
B430.A5 R66     171/.3 19     *LC* 78-62858     *ISBN* 0520037731

**Aristotle.**      **1.288**
[Metaphysics. Book 13-14. English] Aristotle's Metaphysics: Books [mu] and [nu] / translated with introd. and notes by Julia Annas. — Oxford [Eng.]: Clarendon Press, 1976. 227 p.; 21 cm. (Clarendon Aristotle series) Includes indexes. 1. Metaphysics — Early works to 1800. I. Annas, Julia. II. T. III. Title: Metaphysics.
B434.A5 A66     110     *LC* 77-353536     *ISBN* 0198720858

**Aristotle.**      • **1.289**
[Metaphysics English. 1952] Metaphysics; newly translated as a postscript to natural science, with an analytical index of technical terms, by Richard Hope. New York Columbia University Press 1952. 394p. 1. Metaphysics I. Hope, Richard, 1895-1955, tr. II. T.
B434 A5 H6

**Owens, Joseph.**      • **1.290**
The doctrine of being in the Aristotelian Metaphysics; a study in the Greek background of mediaeval thought. With a pref. by Étienne Gilson. [2d ed., rev.] Toronto, Pontifical Institute of Mediaeval Studies [1963, c1951] 535 p. 26 cm. 1. Aristotle. Metaphysics 2. Ontology I. T.
B 434 O97 1963     185     *LC* 66-36313

**Aristotle.**      **1.291**
[Organon English. 1853] The Organon, or Logical treatises, of Aristotle. With the introd. of Porphyry. Literally translated, with notes, syllogistic examples, analysis, and introd. by Octavius Freire Owen. London H.G. Bohn 1853. (Bohn's classical library. [v. 11-12]) I. Owen, Octavius Freire, 1816?-1873, tr. II. Porphyry, ca. 234-ca. 305. III. T.
B437 A5 O84 1853

**Aristotle.**      **1.292**
[Posterior analytics English] Aristotle's Posterior analytics / translated [from the Greek] with notes by Jonathan Barnes. — Oxford: Clarendon Press, 1975 [i.e. 1976]. xix, 277 p.; 21 cm. — (Clarendon Aristotle series) Includes index. 1. Logic — Early works to 1800. 2. Knowledge, Theory of 3. Definition (Logic) I. Barnes, Jonathan. II. T. III. Title: Posterior analytics.
B441.A5 B37     160     *LC* 76-365351     *ISBN* 0198720661

## B481–485 Criticism. Interpretation

**Chroust, Anton-Hermann, 1907-.**      **1.293**
Some novel interpretations of the man and his life. [Notre Dame, Ind.] University of Notre Dame Press [1973] xxvi, 437 p. 23 cm. (His Aristotle: new light on his life and on some of his lost works, v. 1) 1. Aristotle. I. T. II. Series.
B481.C56 vol. 1     185 s 185 B     *LC* 73-8892     *ISBN* 0268005176

**Chroust, Anton-Hermann, 1907-.**      **1.294**
Observations on some of Aristotle's lost works. [Notre Dame, Ind.] University of Notre Dame Press [1973] xx, 500 p. 23 cm. (His Aristotle: new light on his life and on some of his lost works, v. 2) 1. Aristotle. I. T. II. Series.
B481.C56 vol. 2     185 s B 185     *LC* 73-8895     *ISBN* 0268005184

**Ackrill, J. L.**      **1.295**
Aristotle the philosopher / J.L. Ackrill. — Oxford; New York: Oxford University Press, 1981. 160 p.; 20 cm. — (OPUS) Includes index. 1. Aristotle. I. T. II. Series.
B485.A3     185 19     *LC* 82-103501     *ISBN* 0192891189

**Anscombe, G. E. M. (Gertrude Elizabeth Margaret)**     • **1.296**
Three philosophers / by G. E. M. Anscombe and P. T. Geach. — Ithaca, N.Y.: Cornell University Press, 1961. 162 p. 1. Aristotle. 2. Thomas, Aquinas, Saint, 1225?-1274. 3. Frege, Gottlob, 1848-1925. I. Geach, P. T. (Peter Thomas), 1916- II. T.
B485.A48

**Articles on Aristotle / ed. by Jonathan Barnes, Malcolm**     **1.297**
**Schofield, Richard Sorabji.**
New York: St. Martin's Press, 1978-     , c1977-. v. 1. Aristotle — Addresses, essays, lectures. I. Barnes, Jonathan. II. Schofield, Malcolm. III. Sorabji, Richard.
B485.A7x     *LC* 77-20604     *ISBN* 0312054785

**Barnes, Jonathan.**      **1.298**
Aristotle / Jonathan Barnes. — Oxford; New York: Oxford University Press, 1982. 101 p.; 23 cm. — (Past masters.) Includes index. 1. Aristotle. I. T. II. Series.
B485.B35 1982     185 19     *LC* 83-159918     *ISBN* 0192875825

**Cherniss, Harold F. (Harold Fredrik), 1904-1987.**     • **1.299**
Aristotle's criticism of Plato and the Academy. New York, Russell & Russell, 1962 [c1944] 610 p. 23 cm. 1. Aristotle. 2. Plato. I. T.
B485.C48 1962     185     *LC* 62-13831

**Cherniss, Harold F. (Harold Fredrik), 1904-1987.**     • **1.300**
Aristotle's criticism of presocratic philosophy. Baltimore Johns Hopkins Press 1935. 418p. 1. Aristotle. 2. Philosophy, Ancient I. T. II. Title: Presocratic philosophy
B485 C55

**Wolfson, Harry Austryn, 1887-1974.**     • **1.301**
Crescas' critique of Aristotle: problems of Aristotle's Physics in Jewish and Arabic philosophy / by Harry Austryn Wolfson. — Cambridge: Harvard university press, 1929. 759 p. (Harvard Semitic series; vol. VI) 1. Chasdai ben Abraham Crescas, 1340-1410. 2. Aristotle. 3. Philosophy, Jewish 4. Philosophy, Arabic. I. Chasdai ben Abraham Crescas, 1340-1410. Or Adonai. II. T. III. Series.
B485.C7 W6

**Düring, Ingemar, 1903-.**     • **1.302**
Aristotle in the ancient biographical tradition. Göteborg [Distr.: Almqvist & Wiksell, Stockholm] 1957. 490p. (Studia Graeca et Latina Gothoburgensia. 5) 1. Aristotle. I. T. II. Series.
B485 D84

**Edel, Abraham, 1908-.**      **1.303**
Aristotle and his philosophy / Abraham Edel. — Chapel Hill, N.C.: University of North Carolina Press, c1982. xii, 479 p.; 24 cm. Includes index. 1. Aristotle. I. T.
B485.E33 1982     185 19     *LC* 81-7561     *ISBN* 0807814938

**Ferguson, John, 1921-.**      **1.304**
Aristotle. New York, Twayne Publishers [1972] 195 p. 21 cm. (Twayne's world authors series, TWAS 211. Greece) 1. Aristotle. I. T.
B485.F47     185 B     *LC* 70-186637

**Jaeger, Werner Wilhelm, 1888-1961.**     • **1.305**
Aristotle: fundamentals of the history of his development / translated with the author's corrections and additions, by Richard Robinson. — 2d ed. — Oxford: Clarendon Press, 1948. 475 p. 1. Aristotle. 2. Philosophy, Ancient I. Robinson, Richard, 1902- II. T.
B485.J33 1948     *LC* 49-1973

**Moravcsik, J. M. E. comp.**     • **1.306**
Aristotle; a collection of critical essays, edited by J. M. E. Moravcsik. [1st ed.] Garden City, N.Y., Anchor Books, 1967. 341 p. 18 cm. (Modern studies in philosophy) 1. Aristotle. I. T.
B485.M6     185/.08     *LC* 66-24304

**Mure, G. R. G. (Geoffrey Reginald Gilchrist), 1893-.**     • **1.307**
Aristotle / G. R. G. Mure. — New York: Oxford University Press, 1964. vii, 280 p. — (A Galaxy book) 1. Aristotle. I. T.
B485.M8 1964     *LC* 64-1534

**Ross, W. D. (William David), 1877-.**     • **1.308**
Aristotle. [Rev. and enl. ed.] London, Methuen; New York, Barnes & Noble [1964] xi, 300 p. front. 21 cm. (University paperbacks) 'UP-50.' 1. Aristotle. I. T.
B485.R6 1964     185     *LC* 64-754

**Studies in Aristotle / edited by Dominic J. O'Meara.**     **1.309**
Washington, D.C.: Catholic University of America Press, c1981. 313 p.; 24 cm. — (Studies in philosophy and the history of philosophy. v. 9) 'The majority of the papers contained in this volume was delivered in the fall of 1978 at the Catholic University of America as part of the Machette series of lectures on Aristotle.' 1. Aristotle — Addresses, essays, lectures. I. O'Meara, Dominic J. II. Series.
B21.S78 vol. 9 B485.S8x     100 s 185 19     *LC* 81-4381     *ISBN* 081320559X

## B491 Special Topics, A–Z

**Charles, David (David Owain Maurice)**   **1.310**
Aristotle's philosophy of action / David Charles. — Ithaca, N.Y.: Cornell University Press, 1984. xi, 282 p.; 24 cm. Includes indexes. 1. Aristotle. 2. Act (Philosophy) — History. I. T.
B491.A27 C43 1984    128/.4 19    LC 83-73068    ISBN 0801417082

**Cooper, John M. (John Madison), 1939-.**   **1.311**
Reason and human good in Aristotle / John M. Cooper. — Cambridge, Mass.: Harvard University Press, 1975. xii, 192 p.; 22 cm. 1. Aristotle — Ethics. 2. Reason 3. Ethics, Ancient I. T.
B491.E7 C66    121    LC 74-30852    ISBN 0674749529

**Hardie, William Francis Ross.**   **1.312**
Aristotle's ethical theory / by W. F. R. Hardie. — 2d ed. — Oxford; Clarendon Press; New York: Oxford University Press, 1980. x, 448 p.; 23 cm.. Includes indexes. 1. Aristotle — Ethics. 2. Ethics, Ancient I. T.
B491.E7 H3 1980    171/.3    LC 79-41243    ISBN 0198246323

**Kenny, Anthony John Patrick.**   **1.313**
The Aristotelian ethics: a study of the relationship between the Eudemian and Nicomachean ethics of Aristotle / Anthony Kenny. — Oxford [Eng.]: Clarendon Press, 1978. xi, 250 p.; 23 cm. Includes index. 1. Aristotle — Ethics. 2. Ethics, Ancient I. T.
B491.E7 K46    171/.3    LC 77-30640    ISBN 0198245548

**Kenny, Anthony John Patrick.**   **1.314**
Aristotle's theory of the will / Anthony Kenny. — New Haven: Yale University Press, 1979. x, 181 p.; 23 cm. Includes indexes. 1. Aristotle — Ethics. 2. Ethics, Ancient 3. Free will and determinism 4. Will I. T.
B491.E7 K47    171/.3    LC 79-426    ISBN 0300023952

**Sorabji, Richard.**   **1.315**
Necessity, cause, and blame: perspectives on Aristotle's theory / by Richard Sorabji. — Ithaca, N.Y.: Cornell University Press, 1980. xv, 326 p., [1] leaf of plates: ill.; 24 cm. Includes index. 1. Aristotle — Ethics. 2. Ethics, Ancient 3. Free will and determinism 4. Necessity (Philosophy) 5. Causation I. T.
B491.E7 S67    185    LC 79-2449    ISBN 0801411629

**Lear, Jonathan.**   **1.316**
Aristotle and logical theory / Jonathan Lear. — Cambridge; New York: Cambridge University Press, 1980. xi, 123 p.; 23 cm. Based on the author's thesis, Rockefeller University. Includes indexes. 1. Aristotle — Contributions in logic. 2. Logic — History. I. T.
B491.L8 L38 1980    160/.92/4    LC 79-20273    ISBN 0521230314

**Łukasiewicz, Jan.**   • **1.317**
Aristotle's syllogistic from the standpoint of modern formal logic / by Jan Lukasiewicz. — 2d ed., enl. — Oxford: Clarendon Press, 1967. xiii, 222 p.: ill. 1. Aristotle. Organon 2. Syllogism 3. Logic I. T.
B491.L8 L8 1967    185.1

## B505–626 Greco–Roman Philosophy

**Clarke, M. L. (Martin Lowther)**   • **1.318**
The Roman mind; studies in the history of thought from Cicero to Marcus Aurelius, by M. L. Clarke. New York, Norton [1968] 172 p. 20 cm. (The Norton library) 1. Philosophy, Ancient I. T.
B505.C58 1968    187    LC 68-7693

**Oates, Whitney Jennings, 1904- ed.**   • **1.319**
The Stoic and Epicurean philosophers; the complete extant writings of Epicurus, Epictetus, Lucretius, Marcus Aurelius. Edited and with an introd. — New York: Modern Library, [1957] xxvi, 627 p.; 21 cm. — (The Modern library of the world's best books. Modern library giants, G45) 1. Philosophy, Ancient I. T.
B505.O3 1957    187    LC 57-6494

**Zeller, Eduard, 1814-1908.**   • **1.320**
The Stoics, Epicureans, and Sceptics. Translated from the German of E. Zeller by Oswald J. Reichel. — A new and rev. ed. — New York: Russell & Russell, 1962. xvi, 585 p.; 22 cm. Translation of a part of the author's Die Philosophie der Griechen in ihrer geschichtlichen Entwicklung. 1. Epicurus. 2. Philosophy, Ancient 3. Stoics 4. Skeptics (Greek philosophy) I. T.
B505.Z413 1962    188    LC 62-10701

**Dudley, Donald Reynolds.**   • **1.321**
A history of cynicism from Diogenes to the 6th century A. D., by Donald R. Dudley ... London, Methuen & co., ltd. [1937] 224 p. 1. Cynicism I. T.
B508.D8    183.4    LC 38-617

**Dillon, John M.**   **1.322**
The middle Platonists, 80 B.C. to A.D. 220 / John Dillon. Ithaca, N.Y.: Cornell University Press, 1977. xvi, 427 p.; 22 cm. Includes indexes. 1. Platonists I. T.
B517.D54 1977b    141    LC 76-48382    ISBN 0801410835

**Whittaker, Thomas, 1856-1935.**   • **1.323**
The Neo–Platonists, a study in the history of Hellenism. — 2d ed., with a supplement on the commentaries of Proclus. — Freeport, N.Y.: Books for Libraries Press, [1970] xv, 318 p.; 23 cm. Reprint of the 1918 ed. 1. Proclus, ca. 410-485. Commentarii. 2. Neoplatonism I. T.
B517.W5 1970    141    LC 76-114901    ISBN 0836953053

**Doubt and dogmatism: studies in Hellenistic epistemology /**   **1.324**
edited by Malcolm Schofield, Myles Burnyeat, Jonathan Barnes.
Oxford: Clarendon Press; New York: Oxford University Press, 1980. xii, 342 p.; 23 cm. Selected papers presented at a conference held at Oriel College in 1978. Includes indexes. 1. Skeptics (Greek philosophy) — Congresses. 2. Dogmatism — Congresses. 3. Hellenism — Congresses. 4. Knowledge, Theory of — History — Congresses. 5. Philosophy, Ancient — Congresses. I. Schofield, Malcolm. II. Burnyeat, Myles. III. Barnes, Jonathan.
B525.D68    121/.0938    LC 79-41044    ISBN 0198246013

**Long, A. A.**   **1.325**
Hellenistic philosophy; Stoics, Epicureans, Sceptics [by] A. A. Long. — New York: Scribner, [1974] x, 262 p.: ports.; 23 cm. — (Classical life and letters) 1. Epicurus. 2. Stoics 3. Skeptics (Greek philosophy) I. T.
B525.L66 1974b    180    LC 73-14393    ISBN 0684136678

**Arnold, Edward Vernon, 1857-1926.**   • **1.326**
Roman Stoicism; being lectures on the history of the Stoic philosophy with special reference to its development within the Roman Empire. — Freeport, N.Y.: Books for Libraries Press, [1971] ix, 468 p.; 23 cm. Reprint of the 1911 ed. 1. Stoics I. T.
B528.A7 1971    188/.09    LC 76-169750    ISBN 0836959701

**Sandbach, F. H.**   **1.327**
The stoics / F. H. Sandbach. — New York: Norton, [1975] 190 p.; 20 cm. (Ancient culture and society) Includes index. 1. Stoics I. T.
B528.S27 1975    188    LC 74-23247    ISBN 0393044114

**The Stoics / edited by John M. Rist.**   **1.328**
Berkeley: University of California Press, c1978. viii, 295 p.; 24 cm. — (Major thinkers series. 1) 1. Stoics — Addresses, essays, lectures. I. Rist, John M. II. Series.
B528.S68    188    LC 75-27932    ISBN 0520031350

**Verbeke, Gérard.**   **1.329**
The presence of Stoicism in medieval thought / by Gerard Verbeke. — Washington, D.C.: Catholic University of America Press, [1983] viii, 101 p.; 21 cm. 1. Stoics — History — Addresses, essays, lectures. 2. Philosophy, Medieval — Addresses, essays, lectures. I. T.
B528.V4 1983    188 19    LC 82-4134    ISBN 0813205735

**De Witt, Norman Wentworth.**   • **1.330**
Epicurus and his philosophy / by Norman Wentworth De Witt. — Minneapolis: University of Minnesota Press, 1954. 388 p.; 24 cm. 1. Epicurus. I. T.
B 573 D52 1954    187    LC 54-6368

**Rist, John M.**   **1.331**
Epicurus; an introduction [by] J. M. Rist. — Cambridge [Eng.]: University Press, 1972. xiv, 185 p.; 23 cm. 1. Epicurus. I. T.
B573.R57    187    LC 70-177939    ISBN 0521084261

**Clay, Diskin.**   **1.332**
Lucretius and Epicurus / Diskin Clay. — Ithaca: Cornell University Press, 1983. 361 p.; 24 cm. Includes indexes. 1. Lucretius Carus, Titus. 2. Epicurus. I. T.
B577.L64 C58 1983    187 19    LC 83-45142    ISBN 0801415594

## B630–708 Alexandrian and Early Christian Philosophy

**Gilson, Etienne, 1884-1978.**   • **1.333**
[Introduction à l'étude de saint Augustin. English] The Christian philosophy of Saint Augustine. Translated by L. E. M. Lynch. New York, Random House [1960] xii, 398 p. 24 cm. (The Random House lifetime library) Translation of Introduction à l'étude de saint Augustin. 1. Augustine, Saint, Bishop of Hippo. 2. God — Knowableness — History of doctrines — Early church, ca. 30-600. I. T.
B655.Z7 G52    189.2    LC 60-12121

**Nash, Ronald H.**                                                                    • **1.334**
The light of the mind; St. Augustine's theory of knowledge [by] Ronald H. Nash. [Lexington] University Press of Kentucky [1969] viii, 146 p. 23 cm. 1. Augustine, Saint, Bishop of Hippo — Knowledge, Theory of. I. T.
B655.Z7 N37       121       LC 69-19765       *ISBN* 0813111757

**Boethius, d. 524.**                                                                  • **1.335**
The consolation of philosophy / translated, with introd. and notes, by Richard Green. — Indianapolis: Bobbs-Merrill, [c1962] 134 p. 21 cm. — (The Library of liberal arts,; 86) 1. Philosophy and religion 2. Happiness I. T.
B659.C2E59       189.4       *LC* 62-11788

**Boethius, d. 524.**                                                                  **1.336**
[De topicis differentiis. English] Boethius's De topicis differentiis / translated, with notes and essays on the text, by Eleonore Stump. — Ithaca: Cornell University Press, 1978. 287 p.; 24 cm. Includes indexes. 1. Aristotle. Topics 2. John XXI, Pope, d. 1277. Summulae logicales. 3. Dialectic 4. Logic — Early works to 1800. I. Stump, Eleonore, 1947- II. T. III. Title: De topicis differentiis.
B659.D582 E5 1978       180       *LC* 77-17275       *ISBN* 0801410673

**Chadwick, Henry, 1920-.**                                                            **1.337**
Boethius, the consolations of music, logic, theology, and philosophy / Henry Chadwick. — Oxford: Clarendon Press; New York: Oxford University Press, 1981. xv, 313 p.; 23 cm. Includes index. 1. Boethius, d. 524. I. T.
B659.Z7 C45       189 19       *LC* 82-115955       *ISBN* 019826447X

**Philo, of Alexandria.**                                                              **1.338**
[Selections. English. 1981] The contemplative life; The giants; and, Selections / Philo of Alexandria; translation and introduction by David Winston; preface by John Dillon; [cover art, Liam Roberts]. — New York: Paulist Press, c1981. xxi, 425 p.; 23 cm. (Classics of Western spirituality.) 1. Philosophy — Collected works. I. Winston, David. II. T. III. Series.
B689.A4 E5 1981       296.3 19       *LC* 80-84499       *ISBN* 0809123339

**Wolfson, Harry Austryn, 1887-1974.**                                                 • **1.339**
Philo: foundations of religious philosophy in Judaism, Christianity, and Islam. — Cambridge: Harvard University Press, 1947. 2 v. (His. Structure and growth of philosophic systems from Plato to Spinoza; 2) 1. Philo, of Alexandria. I. T. II. Series.
B689.Z7 W83

**Plotinus.**                                                                          • **1.340**
The essence of Plotinus; extracts from the six Enneads and Porphyry's life of Plotinus, based on the translation by Stephen Mackenna; with an appendix giving some of the most important Platonic and Aristotelian sources on which Plotinus drew, and an annotated bibliography, compiled by Grace H. Turnbull; foreword by the Very Reverend W. R. Inge, D.D. New York, Oxford university press, 1934. xx, 303 p. 20 cm. 'First edition.' I. Turnbull, Grace Hill, 1880- ed. II. Mackenna, Stephen, 1872-1934. tr. III. Porphyry, ca. 234-ca. 305. IV. T.
B693.E5E5 1934       *LC* 34-39732

**Plotinus.**                                                                          • **1.341**
[Enneades. English. 1947] The Enneads. Translated by Stephen MacKenna. 2d ed. rev. by B. S. Page, with a foreword by E. R. Dodds and an introd. by Paul Henry. New York, Pantheon Books [1957] ii, 635 p. 26 cm. I. Mackenna, Stephen, 1872-1934. tr. II. Page, B. S. (Bertram Samuel) tr. III. T.
B693.E53 M3 1957       186.4       *LC* 56-10418

**Bréhier, Émile, 1876-1952.**                                                         • **1.342**
[Philosophie de Plotin. English] The philosophy of Plotinus / translated by Joseph Thomas. — [Chicago]: University of Chicago Press [1958] 204 p.; 23 cm. 1. Plotinus. I. T.
B693.Z7 B713       186.4       *LC* 58-11946

**Rist, John M.**                                                                      **1.343**
Plotinus: the road to reality, by J. M. Rist. — Cambridge: Cambridge U.P., 1967. vii, 280 p.; 23 cm. 1. Plotinus. I. T.
B693.Z7 R5       186/.4       *LC* 67-17009

# B720–765 Medieval Philosophy

**Fremantle, Anne Jackson, 1909-.**                                                    • **1.344**
The age of belief; the medieval philosophers. Selected, with introd. and interpretive commentary by Anne Fremantle. — Freeport, N.Y.: Books for Libraries Press, [1970, c1954] 218 p.; 23 cm. — (The Great ages of Western philosophy 1) (Essay index reprint series.) 1. Philosophy, Medieval I. T. II. Series.
B720.F7 1970       189       *LC* 75-117793       *ISBN* 0836918290

**Philosophy in the Middle Ages: the Christian, Islamic, and**                          **1.345**
**Jewish traditions / edited by Arthur Hyman, James J. Walsh.**
2nd ed. — Indianapolis: Hackett Pub. Co., 1983, c1973. x, 805 p.; 24 cm. Includes index. 1. Philosophy, Medieval — Addresses, essays, lectures. I. Hyman, Arthur, 1921- II. Walsh, James J. (James Jerome), 1924-
B720.P5 1983       189 19       *LC* 82-23337       *ISBN* 0915145804

**Shapiro, Herman, 1922- ed.**                                                         • **1.346**
Medieval philosophy; selected readings from Augustine to Buridan. New York, Modern Library [1964] xiv, 547 p. 19 cm. (The Modern library of the world's best books, 344) 1. Philosophy — Collections. 2. Theology — Collections. I. T.
B720.S5       189.4082       *LC* 64-11996

**The Cambridge history of later medieval philosophy: from the**                        **1.347**
**rediscovery of Aristotle to the disintegration of scholasticism,**
**1100–1600 / editors, Norman Kretzmann, Anthony Kenny, Jan**
**Pinborg; associate editor, Eleonore Stump.**
Cambridge [Cambridgeshire]; New York: Cambridge University Press, c1982. xiv, 1035 p.; 24 cm. Includes index. 1. Aristotle — Addresses, essays, lectures. 2. Philosophy, Medieval — History — Addresses, essays, lectures. 3. Scholasticism — History — Addresses, essays, lectures. I. Kretzmann, Norman. II. Kenny, Anthony John Patrick. III. Pinborg, Jan.
B721.C35 1982       189 19       *LC* 81-10086       *ISBN* 0521226058

**Copleston, Frederick Charles.**                                                      **1.348**
A history of medieval philosophy [by] F. C. Copleston. — New York: Harper & Row, [1972] 399 p.; 23 cm. — (A Torchbook library edition) 'Revision and enlargement of Medieval philosophy ... published in 1952.' 1. Philosophy, Medieval I. T.
B721.C57 1972b       189/.09       *LC* 71-181837       *ISBN* 0061360732

**Gilson, Etienne, 1884-1978.**                                                        • **1.349**
The spirit of mediaeval philosophy / by Étienne Gilson; translated by A. H. C. Downes. — New York: C. Scribner's sons, 1936. ix, 490 p.; 23 cm. (Gifford lectures, 1931-1932) 1. Philosophy, Medieval 2. Christianity — Philosophy 3. Religion — Philosophy 4. Scholasticism I. Downes, Alfred Howard Campbell, 1882- tr. II. T.
B721.G433 1936a       189       *LC* 36-16204

**Gilson, Etienne, 1884-1978.**                                                        • **1.350**
Reason and revelation in the middle ages, by Etienne Gilson. New York, C. Scribner's sons, 1938. 6 p. l., 3-114 p. 20 cm. (The Richards lectures in the University of Virginia [1937]) 1. Philosophy and religion 2. Philosophy, Medieval I. T.
B721.G53       189       *LC* 38-38645

**Haren, Michael.**                                                                    **1.351**
Medieval thought: the Western intellectual tradition from antiquity to the thirteenth century / Michael Haren. — New York: St. Martin's Press, c1985. x, 269 p., [4] p. of plates: ill.; 23 cm. Includes index. 1. Philosophy, Medieval 2. Philosophy, Ancient I. T.
B721.H34 1985       189 19       *LC* 84-24773       *ISBN* 0312528167

**Knowles, David, 1896-.**                                                             • **1.352**
The evolution of medieval thought. — Baltimore: Helicon Press, [1962] 356 p.; 23 cm. 1. Philosophy, Medieval I. T.
B721.K6       189       *LC* 62-18776

**Leff, Gordon.**                                                                      **1.353**
The dissolution of the medieval outlook: an essay on intellectual and spiritual change in the fourteenth century / Gordon Leff. — New York: New York University Press, 1976. 154 p.; 21 cm. 1. William, of Ockham, ca. 1285-ca. 1349. 2. Philosophy, Medieval 3. Religious thought — Middle Ages, 600-1500 4. Fourteenth century I. T.
B721.L38 1976b       B721 L38 1976b.       189       *LC* 76-48865       *ISBN* 0814749747

**Marenbon, John.**                                                                    **1.354**
Early medieval philosophy (480–1150): an introduction / John Marenbon. — London; Boston: Routledge & K. Paul, 1983. ix, 190 p.; 23 cm. Includes index. 1. Philosophy, Medieval 2. Philosophy, Ancient I. T.
B721.M338 1983       189 19       *LC* 82-23046       *ISBN* 0710094051

**Maurer, Armand A. (Armand Augustine), 1915-.**                                       • **1.355**
Medieval philosophy / [by] Armand A. Maurer. New York: Random House [1962] xviii, 435 p.; 24 cm. (A History of philosophy, v. 2) 1. Philosophy, Medieval 2. Philosophy, Renaissance I. T.
B721.M37       189       *LC* 62-10783

**Steenberghen, Fernand van, 1904-.**                                                  • **1.356**
The philosophical movement in the thirteenth century. — [Edinburgh] Nelson, 1955. ix, 115 p. 23 cm. 'Lectures given under the auspices of the Department of Scholastic Philosophy, the Queen's University, Belfast.' Includes bibliographies. 1. Philosophy, Medieval I. T.
B721.S65       189       *LC* A 56-1259

**Weinberg, Julius Rudolph.**    • **1.357**
A short history of medieval philosophy / by Julius R. Weinberg. — 1st Princeton Paperback ed. Princeton, N.J.: Princeton University Press, 1964. — ix, 304 p.; 23 cm. — 1. Philosophy, Medieval I. T.
B721.W4 1964   189   *LC* 63-18652   *ISBN* 0691019568

**Wulf, Maurice Marie Charles Joseph de, 1867-1947.**   • **1.358**
History of media eval philosophy. Translated by Ernest C. Messenger. [Definitive translation of the 6th French ed.] London, New York, Nelson [1952-. v. port. 23 cm. 1. Philosophy, Medieval I. T.
B721.W942   *LC* 55-21007

**Steenberghen, Fernand van, 1904-.**   • **1.359**
Aristotle in the West: the origins of Latin Aristotelianism / translated by Leonard Johnston. Louvain: E. Nauwelaerts, 1955. 244 p. 1. Aristotle. 2. Thomas, Aquinas, Saint, 1225?-1274. 3. Philosophy, Medieval I. T.
B725.S753   *LC* 56-5742

## B728–738 Special Topics

**Fairweather, Eugene Rathbone. ed. and tr.**   • **1.360**
A scholastic miscellany: Anselm to Ockham. — Philadelphia, Westminster Press [1956] 457 p. 24 cm. — (The Library of Christian classics, v. 10) Includes bibliographies. 1. Scholasticism I. T. II. Series.
B734.F3   189.4   *LC* 56-5104

**Pieper, Josef, 1904-.**   • **1.361**
Scholasticism: personalities and problems of medieval philosophy / [translated by Richard and Clara Winston]. — New York: Pantheon Books, [1960]. 192 p.; 21 cm. 1. Scholasticism I. T.
B734.P513   *LC* 60-11766

**Wulf, Maurice Marie Charles Joseph de, 1867-1947.**   • **1.362**
An introduction to scholastic philosophy, medieval and modern. Scholasticism old and new. Translated by P. Coffey. New York, Dover Publications [1956] 327 p. 21 cm. Unabridged republication of the English edition published as: Scholasticism old and new. 1. Scholasticism 2. Neo-Scholasticism I. T.
B734.W78 1956   189.4   *LC* 57-3219

**Conscience in medieval philosophy / [edited by] Timothy C. Potts.**   **1.363**
Cambridge; New York: Cambridge University Press, 1980. xiii, 152 p.; 23 cm. Includes indexes. 1. Conscience — Religious aspects — Christianity 2. Conscience — Addresses, essays, lectures. 3. Philosophy, Medieval — Addresses, essays, lectures. I. Potts, Timothy C.
B738.C65 C66   170   *LC* 80-40380   *ISBN* 0521232872

## B741–759 Arabic, Moorish, Islamic, Jewish Philosophers

**Boer, Tjitze J. de, 1866-.**   • **1.364**
[Geschichte der Philosophie im Islam. English] The history of philosophy in Islam, by T. J. de Boer. Translated by Edward R. Jones. New York, Dover Publications [1967] xiii, 216 p. 22 cm. 'Unabridged and unaltered republication of the work originally published ... in 1903.' Translation of Geschichte der Philosophie im Islam. 1. Philosophy, Islamic — History. I. T.
B741.B7 1967   181/.07   *LC* 66-30424

**Fakhry, Majid.**   **1.365**
A history of Islamic philosophy / Majid Fakhry. — 2nd ed. — New York: Columbia University Press: Longman, 1983. xxiv, 394 p.; 22 cm. — (Studies in Oriental culture. no. 5) Includes index. 1. Philosophy, Islamic — History. I. T. II. Series.
B741.F23 1983   181/.07 19   *LC* 81-21781   *ISBN* 0231055323

**O'Leary, De Lacy Evans, 1872-.**   • **1.366**
Arabic thought and its place in history. London: K. Paul, Trench, Trubner, 1939. 327p. 1. Philosophy,Arabic. I. T.
B741.O4 1939   *ISBN* 0710019041

**Netton, Ian Richard.**   **1.367**
Muslim neoplatonists: an introduction to the thought of the Brethren of Purity, Ikhwān al-Safā' / Ian Richard Netton. — London; Boston: G. Allen & Unwin, 1982. x, 146 p.; 23 cm. Includes index. 1. Ikhwān al-Safā'. I. Ikhwān al-Safā'. II. T.
B746.N47 1982   181/.9 19   *LC* 83-131009   *ISBN* 0042970431

**Averroës, 1126-1198.**   • **1.368**
Tahafut al-tahafut (The incoherence of the incoherence) Translated from the Arabic with introd. and notes by Simon van den Bergh. London, Luzac, 1954. 2

v. 25 cm. ('E.J.W. Gibb memorial.' New series, 19) (UNESCO collection of great works. Arabic series) 1. Ghazzālī, 1058-1111. Tahāfut al-falāsifah. I. Bergh, Simon van den, 1882- II. T. III. Series.
B753.G33 T32   B749.A5 E3x.   *LC* 55-4157

**Avicenna, 980-1037.**   • **1.369**
Avcienna on theology. [1st ed.] London: Murray [1951] vi, 82 p.; 18 cm. 1. Islam I. T.
B751.A4 E5   *LC* 51-11811

**Avicenna, 980-1037.**   **1.370**
[Sīrat al-Shaykh al-Ra'īs. English & Arabic] The life of Ibn Sina; a critical edition and annotated translation, by William E. Gohlman. [1st ed.] Albany, State University of New York Press, 1974. 163 p. 24 cm. (Studies in Islamic philosophy and science.) Arabic text and English translation of the author's autobiography, Sīrat al-Shaykh al-Ra'īs, which was completed by al-Jūzajānī. Originally presented as the editor's thesis, University of Michigan. 1. Avicenna, 980-1037. I. Jūzajānī, 'Abd al-Wāhid ibn Muhammad, 11th cent. II. Gohlman, William E., ed. III. T. IV. Series.
B751.A5 S5 1974   189/.5   *LC* 73-6793   *ISBN* 087395226X *ISBN* 0873952278

**Afnan, Soheil Muhsin.**   • **1.371**
Avicenna, his life and works. — London: G. Allen & Unwin, 1958. 298 p. 1. Avicenna, 980?-1037. I. T.
B751.Z7 A6

**Fārābī.**   • **1.372**
[Selected works. English. 1962] Philosophy of Plato and Aristotle / Translated with an introd. by Muhsin Mahdi. [New York]: Free Press of Glencoe [1962] 158 p. 22 cm. (Agora editions) 1. Philosophy, Ancient I. Mahdi, Muhsin. ed. and tr. II. T.
B753.F33 P53   180   *LC* 62-11856

**al-Ghazzali, 1058-1111.**   • **1.373**
The faith and practice of al-Ghazzali / [translated] by W. Montgomery Watt. — London: Allen and Unwin, 1953. 155 p. (Ethical and religious classics of East and West; no. 8) I. Watt, William Montgomery, tr. II. T. III. Series.
B753 G33M83   *LC* 53-8071

**Ghazzālī, 1058-1111.**   • **1.374**
al-Ghazali's Tahafut al'falasifah; incoherence of the philosophers. Translated into English by Sabih Ahmad Kamali. Lahore, Pakistan Philosophical Congress, 1963. 267 p. (Publications / Pakistan Philosophical Congress; no.3) Thesis (M.A.)—McGill University. 1. Islam and philosophy I. Kamali, Sabih Ahmad. II. Pakistan Philosophical Congress. III. T.
B753.G33 T33 1963   181.07

**Kindī, d. ca. 873.**   **1.375**
[Falsafah al-ūlā. English] al-Kindī's Metaphysics; a translation of Ya'qub ibn Ishāq al-Kindī's treatise 'On first philosophy' (fi al-Falsafah al-ūlā) with introd. and commentary by Alfred L. Ivry. [1st ed.] Albany, State University of New York Press, 1974. ix, 207 p. 24 cm. (Studies in Islamic philosophy and science.) A revised version of the editor's doctoral dissertation, Oxford University. 1. Philosophy, Islamic I. Ivry, Alfred L., 1935- ed. II. T. III. Title: On first philosophy. IV. Series.
B753.K53 F3513 1974   181/.07   *LC* 70-171182   *ISBN* 0873950925

**Israeli, Isaac, ca. 832-ca. 932.**   • **1.376**
Isaac Israeli: a Neoplatonic philosopher of the early tenth century, his works translated with comments and on outline of his philosophy / by A. Altmann and S.M. Stern. — [London]: Oxford University Press, 1958. xxiii, 226 p.: facsim.; 22 cm. (Scripta Judaica. 1) 1. Philosophy — Collected works. I. Altmann, Alexander, 1906- ed. II. Stern, S. M. (Samuel Miklos), 1920-1969. ed. III. T. IV. Series.
B759.I82 E5

**Maimonides, Moses, 1135-1204.**   **1.377**
[Dalālat al-hā'irīn. English. Selections] Rambam: readings in the philosophy of Moses Maimonides / selected and translated, with introd. and commentary by Lenn Evan Goodman. — New York: Viking Press, 1976. xvi, 444 p.; 22 cm. (The Jewish heritage classics) Selections from the author's Dalālat al-hā'irīn and Thamāniyat fuṣūl. Includes index. 1. Maimonides, Moses, 1135-1204. 2. Philosophy, Jewish 3. Philosophy, Medieval 4. Ethics, Jewish I. Maimonides, Moses, 1135-1204. Thamāniyat fuṣūl. English. Selections. 1976. II. Goodman, Lenn Evan, 1944- III. T. IV. Title: Readings in the philosophy of Moses Maimonides. V. Series.
B759.M33 D3132 1976   181/.3   *LC* 75-14476

# B765 EUROPEAN PHILOSOPHERS

**Abelard, Peter, 1079-1142.**     • **1.378**
[Ethica. English & Latin] Peter Abelard's Ethics: an edition with introduction, English translation and notes by D. E. Luscombe. Oxford, Clarendon Press, 1971. lxi, 144 p. facsim. 22 cm. (Oxford medieval texts.) Abailard's text in English and Latin. 1. Christian ethics I. Luscombe, David Edward, ed. II. T. III. Series.
B765.A23 E82 1971     241/.04/2     LC 70-885574     ISBN 0198222173

**Anselm, Saint, Archbishop of Canterbury, 1033-1109.**     • **1.379**
[Selected works. English] Basic writings: Proslogium; Monologium; Gaunilon's on behalf of the fool; Cur deus homo. Translated by S. W. [i.e. N.] Deane, with an introd. by Charles Hartshorne. 2d ed. La Salle, Ill., Open Court Pub. Co., 1962. 19, xxxv, 288 p. 22 cm. I. Deanne, Sidney Norton, 1878-1943, tr. II. T.
B765.A82 E54 1962     189.4     LC 62-6955

**Anselm, Saint, Archbishop of Canterbury, 1033-1109.**     • **1.380**
[Selected works. English] Truth, freedom, and evil: three philosophical dialogues / edited and translated by Jasper Hopkins & Herbert Richardson. — [1st ed.] New York: Harper & Row [1967] 196 p.; 21 cm. (Harper torchbooks. The Cathedral library, TB317) This translation first published in 1965 as v. 1 of the author's Theological treatises. 1. Philosophy — Collected works. I. Hopkins, Jasper. ed. II. Richardson, Herbert Warren. ed. III. T.
B765.A82 E58     189/.4     LC 67-10679

**Barth, Karl, 1886-1968.**     • **1.381**
Anselm: Fides quaerens intellectum; Anselm's proff of the existence of God in the context of his theological scheme; translated by Ian W. Robertson from the German. — Richmond, Va.: John Knox Press, c1960. 173 p. 1. Anselm, Saint, 1033-1109. Prosologuim 2. God — Proof, Ontological I. T. II. Title: Fides quaerens intellectum
B765.A83 P833     LC 61-5569

**Bacon, Roger, 1214?-1294.**     • **1.382**
Opus majus / a translation by Robert Belle Burke. New York: Russell & Russell, 1962. 2 v. (xiii, 840 p.) I. T.
B765.B23 O23 1962     LC 62-10702

**Gilson, Etienne, 1884-1978.**     • **1.383**
The philosophy of St. Bonaventure / by Étienne Gilson; translated by Dom Illtyd Trethowan & F. J. Sheed. — New York: Sheed & Ward, 1938. xiii, 551 p.; 22.5 cm. 'Printed in Great Britain.' 'Pages 139-403, with the relevant notes, were translated by Dom Illtyd Trethowan (permissu superiorum), the remainder by F. J. Sheed.'—p. [v] 1. Bonaventure, Saint, Cardinal, ca. 1217-1274. I. Trethowan, Illtyd, 1907- tr. II. Sheed, F. J. (Francis Joseph), 1897- tr. III. T.
B765.B74G52     189.4     LC 38-12735

**Duns Scotus, John, ça. 1266-1308.**     • **1.384**
Philosophical writings; a selection edited and translated by Allan Wolter. — [Edinburgh] Nelson, 1962. xxiii, 162, 162, [163]-198 facsim. 19 cm. — (The Nelson philosophical texts) Latin and English on opposite pages, numbered in duplicate. 'Taken from Scotus's ... Ordinatio (called more frequently ... Oxford commentary on the Sentences of Peter Lombard)' The Latin text is taken from the manuscript Codex Assisii, bibliotheca communalis 137. Bibliography: p. xxii-xxiii. 1. Petrus Lombardus, Bp. of Paris, 12th cent. Sententiarum libri quattuor. 2. Metaphysics I. Wolter, Allan Bernard, 1913- ed. and tr. II. T.
B765.D7W6     110     LC 62-6266

**McEvoy, J. J.**     **1.385**
The philosophy of Robert Grosseteste / James McEvoy. — Oxford: Clarendon Press; New York: Oxford University Press, 1982. xvii, 560 p., [1] leaf of plates: ill.; 23 cm. Includes indexes. 1. Grosseteste, Robert, 1175?-1253. I. T.
B765.G74 M38 1982     192 19     LC 81-22438     ISBN 0198246455

**Marrone, Steven P., 1947-.**     **1.386**
William of Auvergne and Robert Grosseteste: new ideas of truth in the early thirteenth century / Steven P. Marrone. — Princeton, N.J.: Princeton University Press, c1983. x, 318 p.; 23 cm. Includes index. 1. William, of Auvergne, Bishop of Paris, d. 1249 — Knowledge, Theory of. 2. Grosseteste, Robert, 1175?-1253 — Knowledge, Theory of. 3. Knowledge, Theory of — History. 4. Truth — History. I. T.
B765.G824 M37 1983     121/.09/022 19     LC 82-61375     ISBN 0691053839

**John, of Salisbury, Bishop of Chartres, d. 1180.**     • **1.387**
The metalogicon of John of Salisbury: a twelfth–century defense of the verbal and logical arts of the trivium / translated with an introd. & notes by Daniel D. McGarry. — Berkeley: University of California Press, 1962. xxvii, 305 p.: facsims. I. McGarry, Daniel D. II. T.
B765.J43 M43 1962

**Nicholas, of Cusa, Cardinal, 1401-1464.**     • **1.388**
Of learned ignorance / by Nicolas Cusanus; translated by Germain Heron; with an introd. by D.J.B. Hawkins. — New Haven: Yale University Press, 1954.

xxviii, 174 p.: ill.; 23 cm. — (Rare masterpieces of philosophy and science) Translation of De docta ignorantia. 1. Mysticism — History — Middle Ages, 600-1500 I. T. II. Series.
B765.N53 D6313

**William, of Ockham, ca. 1285-ca. 1349.**     • **1.389**
Philosophical writings; a selection edited and translated by Philotheus Boehner. — [London] Nelson, 1957. lix, 154 p. facsim. 19 cm. Latin and English. Bibliography: p. lii-lix. 1. Philosophy — Collected works. I. Boehner, Philotheus, Father, ed. and tr. II. T.
B765.O3P45

## B765.T5 Thomas Aquinas

**Thomas, Aquinas, Saint, 1225?-1274.**     • **1.390**
Philosophical texts / St. Thomas Aquinas; selected and translated with notes and an introd. by Thomas Gilby. — London: Oxford University Press, 1951. xxii, 405 p.; 21 cm. — 1. Thomas, Aquinas, Saint, 1225?-1274 — Philosophy. I. Gilby, Thomas. II. T.
B765.T52 E48 1951     189/.4     LC 52-9228

**Ullmann, Walter, 1910-.**     • **1.391**
The medieval papacy, St. Thomas and beyond. [London] Aquin Press [1960] 31 p. 22 cm. 1. Papacy — History 2. Church and state — Catholic Church I. T.
B765.T54 A22 no. 35     LC 60-51796

**Gilson, Etienne, 1884-1978.**     • **1.392**
Elements of Christian philosophy. Garden City, N.Y., Doubleday, Catholic Textbook Division [1960] 358 p. 24 cm. 1. Thomas, Aquinas, Saint, 1225?-1274 — Contributions in theology I. T. II. Title: Christian philosophy.
B765.T54 G47     189.4     LC 60-6405

**Gilson, Etienne, 1884-1978.**     • **1.393**
The philosophy of St. Thomas Aquinas. St. Louis, Mo., and London, B. Herder book co., 1937. xv, 372 p. 19 cm. 1. Thomas, Aquinas, Saint, 1225?-1274. 2. Philosophy, Medieval I. Bullough, Edward, 1880-1934, tr. II. Elrington, G. Aidan, ed. III. T.
B765.T54 G5 1937     LC 39-4162

**Gilson, Etienne, 1884-1978.**     • **1.394**
[Thomisme. English] The Christian philosophy of St. Thomas Aquinas. With A catalog of St. Thomas's works, by I.T. Eschmann. Translated by L.K. Shook. New York, Random House [1956] x, 502 p. 24 cm. Translation of Le thomisme. 1. Thomas, Aquinas, Saint, 1225?-1274. I. T.
B765.T54 G52     189.4     LC 56-8813

**McInerny, Ralph M.**     **1.395**
St. Thomas Aquinas / by Ralph McInerny. — Boston: Twayne Publishers, c1977. 197 p.: port.; 21 cm. (Twayne's world authors series; TWAS 408: Italy) Includes index. 1. Thomas, Aquinas, Saint, 1225?-1274. I. T.
B765.T54 M244     230/.2/0924     LC 76-25959     ISBN 0805762485

**Reith, Herman R.**     • **1.396**
The metaphysics of St. Thomas Aquinas / Herman Reith. — Milwaukee: Bruce Pub., [1958] xvii, 403 p. 1. Thomas, Aquinas, Saint, 1225?-1274 — Contributions in metaphysics I. T.
B765.T54 R44 1958     LC 58-12070 rev

# B770–785 Renaissance Philosophy

**Fallico, Arturo B., comp.**     • **1.397**
Renaissance philosophy, edited, translated, and introduced by Arturo B. Fallico and Herman Shapiro. — New York: [Random House, 1967-69] 2 v.; 19 cm. — (The Modern library of the World's best books. [376], [301]) Shapiro's name appears first on the t.p. of v. 2. 1. Philosophy — Collections. 2. Philosophy, Renaissance I. Shapiro, Herman, 1922- joint comp. II. T.
B770.F313     108     LC 67-11590

**Popkin, Richard Henry, 1923- ed.**     • **1.398**
The philosophy of the sixteenth and seventeenth centuries / edited and with an introd. by Richard H. Popkin. — New York: Free Press [1966] ix, 365 p.; 21 cm. — (Readings in the history of philosophy) Bibliography: p. 357-360. 1. Philosophy — Collections. I. T.
B770.P6     108     LC 66-10365

**Cassirer, Ernst, 1874-1945.**     • **1.399**
The individual and the cosmos in Renaissance philosophy / translated with an introd. by Mario Domandi. — New York: Barnes & Noble, 1964, c1963. xvi,

199 p. 1. Philosophy, Renaissance 2. Individualism 3. Cosmology 4. Free will and determinism 5. Knowledge, Theory of I. T.
B775.C313 1964

**Koenigsberger, Dorothy.**                                              **1.400**
Renaissance man and creative thinking: a history of concepts of harmony, 1400–1700 / Dorothy Koenigsberger. — Atlantic Highlands, N.J.: Humanities Press, 1979. xiii, 282 p.; 23 cm. Includes index. 1. Philosophy, Renaissance 2. Renaissance 3. Harmony (Aesthetics) 4. Nature 5. Analogy 6. Europe — Intellectual life I. T.
B775.K6 1979        190        LC 78-956        ISBN 039100851X

**Kristeller, Paul Oskar, 1905-.**                                     **• 1.401**
Renaissance thought: the classic, scholastic, and humanistic strains. A rev. and enl. ed. of 'The classics and Renaissance thought.' A rev. and enl. ed. New York Harper & Row [1961] 169p. (Harper torchbooks) 1. Renaissance 2. Humanism I. T.
B775.K7 1961

**Winny, James. ed.**                                                  **• 1.402**
The frame of order: an outline of Elizabethan belief taken from treatises of the late sixteenth century. — London: Allen & Unwin [1957] 224 p.: ill.; 23 cm. 1. Philosophy, English I. T.
B776.E5W5        192.082        LC 57-4365

**Kristeller, Paul Oskar, 1905-.**                                     **• 1.403**
Eight philosophers of the Italian Renaissance. — Stanford, Calif.: Stanford University Press, 1964. ix, 194 p. 23 cm. 'Bibliographical survey': p. 181-188. 1. Philosophers, Italian. 2. Philosophers, Renaissance. I. T.
B776.I8K7        195        LC 64-17002

**Noreña, Carlos G.**                                                  **1.404**
Studies in Spanish renaissance thought / by Carlos G. Noreña. — The Hague: Nijhoff, 1975. ix, 277 p.; 23 cm. — (International archives of the history of ideas; 82) Includes index. 1. Philosophy, Renaissance 2. Renaissance — Spain. 3. Spain — Intellectual life I. T.
B776.S7 N67        196/.1        LC 76-357166        ISBN 9024717272

**Bush, Douglas, 1896-.**                                              **• 1.405**
The renaissance and English humanism, by Douglas Bush. — [Toronto] The Unversity of Toronto press, 1939. 139 p. 21 cm. 'The Alexander lectures in English at the University of Toronto, 1939.' 1. Milton, John, 1608-1674. 2. Humanism 3. Renaissance I. T.
B778.B8        144        LC 40-11006

**Caspari, Fritz, 1914-.**                                             **• 1.406**
Humanism and the social order in Tudor England. — New York: Teachers College Press, [1968, c1954] xii, 400 p.; 20 cm. — (Classics in education, no. 34) 1. Humanism 2. Philosophy, English 3. Great Britain — Social conditions I. T.
B778.C35 1968        144        LC 68-29071

**Hadas, Moses, 1900-1966.**                                           **• 1.407**
Humanism: the Greek ideal and its survival. — [1st ed.]. — New York, Harper [1960] 132 p. 20 cm. — (World perspectives, v. 24) 1. Humanism I. T.
B778.H3        144        LC 60-7525

**Popkin, Richard Henry, 1923-.**                                      **1.408**
The history of scepticism from Erasmus to Spinoza / Richard H. Popkin. — Rev. and expanded ed. — Berkeley: University of California Press, c1979. xxii, 333 p.; 22 cm. Rev. ed. published in 1964 under title: The history of scepticism from Erasmus to Descartes. Includes index. 1. Descartes, René, 1596-1650. 2. Spinoza, Benedictus de, 1632-1677. 3. Skepticism — History. 4. Philosophy, Renaissance I. T.
B779.P65 1979        149/.73        LC 79-126126

**Cassirer, Ernst, 1874-1945.**                                        **• 1.409**
The Renaissance philosophy of man: selections in translation / edited by Ernst Cassirer, Paul Oskar Kristeller, John Herman Randall, jr. — Chicago: University of Chicago Press, 1956, c1948. viii, 405 p. — (Phoenix books; P1) 1. Philosophy, Renaissance 2. Man I. Kristeller, Paul Oskar, 1905- II. Randall, John Herman, 1899- III. Petrarca, Francesco, 1304-1374. IV. T.
B780.M3 R4 1956.        128        LC 56-184

**Rice, Eugene F.**                                                    **• 1.410**
The Renaissance idea of wisdom / by Eugene F. Rice, Jr. — Cambridge, Mass.: Harvard University Press, 1958. ix, 220 p.: ill.; 21 cm. (Harvard historical monographs. 37) Based on the author's thesis, Harvard, 1953. 1. Wisdom 2. Philosophy, Renaissance I. T. II. Series.
B780.W5 R5        190        LC 58-12973

## B781–785 PHILOSOPHERS

**Michel, Paul-Henri.**                                                **1.411**
The cosmology of Giordano Bruno. Translated [from the French] by R. E. W. Maddison. — Paris: Hermann; Ithaca, N.Y.: Cornell University Press, [1973] 306 p.; 22 cm. Translation of La cosmologie de Giordano Bruno. 1. Bruno, Giordano, 1548-1600. 2. Cosmology — History. I. T.
B783.Z7 M513        195        LC 71-87006        ISBN 0801405092

**Singer, Dorothea (Waley) 1884-.**                                    **• 1.412**
Giordano Bruno; his life and thought. With annotated translation of his work, On the infinite universe and worlds. — New York: Greenwood Press, 1968 [c1950] xi, 389 p.: illus., charts, maps, ports.; 24 cm. Appendices (p. 203-224): List of Bruno's writings.—Printers of Bruno.—Surviving manuscripts of Bruno's works.—Select bibliography of Bruno's philosophy. 1. Bruno, Giordano, 1548-1600. 2. Infinite I. Bruno, Giordano, 1548-1600. On the infinite universe and worlds. II. T.
B783.Z7 S45 1968        195        LC 68-23329

**Yates, Frances Amelia.**                                             **1.413**
Giordano Bruno and the Hermetic tradition / Frances A. Yates. — Chicago: University of Chicago Press, 1964. xiv, 466 p.: ill.; 23 cm. 1. Bruno, Giordano, 1548-1600. 2. Occultism — History I. T.
B783.Z7 Y3        133        LC 64-10094

**Bainton, Roland Herbert, 1894-.**                                    **1.414**
Erasmus of Christendom [by] Roland H. Bainton. New York, Scribner [1969] xii, 308 p. illus., facsims., ports. 24 cm. 1. Erasmus, Desiderius, d. 1536. I. T.
B785.E64 B3        199/.492        LC 68-27788        6.95

**Kristeller, Paul Oskar, 1905-.**                                     **• 1.415**
The philosophy of Marsilio Ficino, by Paul Oskar Kristeller ... Translated into English by Virginia Conant. New York Columbia University Press 1943. 441p. (Columbia studies in philosophy, ed. under the Dept. of philosophy, Columbia university. No. 6) 1. Ficino, Marsilio, 1433-1499. I. T.
B785 F44 K713        LC 43-7253

**Finocchiaro, Maurice A., 1942-.**                                    **1.416**
Galileo and the art of reasoning: rhetorical foundations of logic and scientific method / Maurice A. Finocchiaro. — Dordrecht, Holland; Boston: D. Reidel Pub. Co.; Hingham, MA: sold and distributed in the U.S.A. by Kluwer Boston, c1980. xx, 478 p.; 23 cm. (Boston studies in the philosophy of science. v. 61) Includes index. 1. Galilei, Galileo, 1564-1642 — Logic. 2. Galilei, Galileo, 1564-1642. Dialogo dei massimi sistemi 3. Logic, Modern — History. 4. Reasoning 5. Science — Methodology — History. 6. Solar system — Early works to 1800 7. Astronomy — Early works to 1800. I. T. II. Series.
B785.G24 F56        160        LC 80-15232        ISBN 9027710945

**Kautsky, Karl, 1854-1938.**                                          **• 1.417**
Thomas More and his Utopia / Karl Kautsky; with a foreword by Russell Ames. — New York: Russell & Russell, 1959. 250 p.; 21 cm. 1. More, Thomas, Sir, Saint, 1478-1535. 2. More, Thomas, Sir, Saint, 1478-1535. Utopia I. T.
B785.M84 K4 1959        LC 59-10095        ISBN 084620214X

**Pico della Mirandola, Giovanni, 1463-1494.**                         **• 1.418**
[De hominis dignitate. English] On the dignity of man / translated by Charles Glenn Wallis; On being and the one, translated by Paul J. W. Miller; Heptaplus, translated by Douglas Carmichael; with an introd. by Paul J. W. Miller. — Indianapolis: Bobbs-Merrill [1965] xxxiii, 174 p.; 21 cm. (The Library of liberal arts, 227) 1. Bible. O.T. Genesis I, 1-27 — Criticism, interpretation, etc. 2. Ontology 3. Man I. Pico della Mirandola, Giovanni, 1463-1494. On being and the one. II. Pico della Mirandola, Giovanni, 1463-1494. Heptaplus. III. Wallis, Charles Glenn, tr. IV. Miller, Paul J. W., tr. V. Carmichael, Douglas, 1923- tr. VI. T. VII. Title: On being and the one. VIII. Title: Heptaplus.
B785.P53 D443 1965        195        LC 65-26540

## B790–5739 Modern Philosophy

**Beardsley, Monroe C. ed.**                                           **• 1.419**
The European philosophers from Descartes to Nietzsche. — New York: Modern Library, [1960] 870 p.; 21 cm. — (The Modern library of the world's best books. [A Modern library giant, G-16]) 1. Philosophers, Modern 2. Philosophy, Modern I. T.
B790.B4        190        LC 60-10004

**Bronowski, Jacob, 1908-1974.**                                       **• 1.420**
The Western intellectual tradition, from Leonardo to Hegel [by] J. Bronowski [and] Bruce Mazlish. — New York: Harper, [1960] 522 p.; 22 cm.

1. Philosophy, Modern 2. Civilization, Modern I. Mazlish, Bruce, 1923- joint author. II. T.
B791.B75      190      *LC* 59-12671

**Collins, James Daniel.**      • **1.421**
Interpreting modern philosophy, by James Collins. — Princeton, N.J.: Princeton University Press, 1972. xii, 463 p.; 23 cm. 1. Kant, Immanuel, 1724-1804. 2. Philosophy, Modern 3. Teleology I. T.
B791.C582      190      *LC* 70-160259      *ISBN* 0691071799

**Gilson, Etienne, 1884-1978.**      • **1.422**
Modern philosophy: Descartes to Kant [by] Etienne Gilson [and] Thomas Langan. New York, Random House [1963] 570 p. 25 cm. (A History of philosophy, v. 3) 1. Philosophy, Modern I. Langan, Thomas. joint author. II. T.
B791.G5      190      *LC* 62-16201

**Randall, John Herman, 1899-.**      • **1.423**
The career of philosophy. — New York: Columbia University Press, 1962-65. 2 v.; 24 cm. 1. Philosophy, Modern — History. I. T.
B791.R25      190.9      *LC* 62-10454

**Royce, Josiah, 1855-1916.**      • **1.424**
The spirit of modern philosophy; an essay in the form of lectures. Introd. by Ralph Barton Perry. New York, G. Braziller, 1955. xix, 519 p. 21 cm. 1. Philosophy, Modern I. T.
B791.R8 1955      190      *LC* 55-37385

**Scruton, Roger.**      **1.425**
From Descartes to Wittgenstein: a short history of modern philosophy / Roger Scruton. — London; Boston: Routledge & Kegan Paul, 1981. vi, 298 p.: 23 cm. Includes index. 1. Philosophy, Modern I. T.
B791.S28      190 19      *LC* 80-42352      *ISBN* 0710007981

**Høffding, Harald, 1843-1931.**      • **1.426**
[Den nyere filosofis historie. English] A history of modern philosophy; a sketch of the history of philosophy from the close of the Renaissance to our own day. Translated from the German ed. by B. E. Meyer. Authorised translation. [New York] Dover Publications [1955] 2 v. 21 cm. 'An unabridged republication of the English translation originally published by Macmillan and Company.' 1. Philosophy, Modern — History. I. T.
B798.D3 H7 1955      190.9      *LC* 57-4728

**Bahm, Archie J.**      **1.427**
Comparative philosophy: Western, Indian, and Chinese philosophies compared / Archie J. Bahm. Albuquerque, N.M.: Universal Publications, c1977. xiii, 98 p.; 23 cm. Publisher covered by label: World Books. 1. Philosophy, Comparative I. T.
B799.B34      100      *LC* 76-10406      *ISBN* 0911714073

**Philosophy East/philosophy West: a critical comparison of**      **1.428**
**Indian, Chinese, Islamic, and European philosophy / Ben–Ami Scharfstein ... [et al.].**
New York: Oxford University Press, 1978. viii, 359 p.; 22 cm. Includes index. 1. Philosophy, Comparative — Addresses, essays, lectures. I. Scharfstein, Ben-Ami, 1919-
B799.P47 1978      109      *LC* 78-18473      *ISBN* 0195200640

**Raju, P. T. (Poolla Tirupati), 1904-.**      **1.429**
Introduction to comparative philosophy / by P.T. Raju. — Carbondale: Southern Illinois University Press, 1970, c1962. xii, 364 p.; 20 cm. — (Arcturus books; AB73) 1. Philosophy, Comparative I. T.
B799.R3      109      *LC* 62-7870      *ISBN* 0809304198

**Saher, P. J.**      • **1.430**
Eastern wisdom and Western thought; a comparative study in the modern philosophy of religion, by P. J. Saher. — New York, N.Y.: Barnes and Noble, [1970] 292 p.; 23 cm. 1. Philosophy, Comparative 2. Religion — Philosophy I. T.
B799.S32 1970      200/.1      *LC* 73-16605

## B801–802 17th–18th Centuries

**Leyden, W. von (Wolfgang von), 1911-.**      • **1.431**
Seventeenth–century metaphysics; an examination of some main concepts and theories, by W. von Leyden. New York, Barnes & Noble [1968] xvi, 316 p. 23 cm. 1. Philosophy, Modern — 17th century 2. Metaphysics — History. I. T.
B801.L44 1968b      190      *LC* 74-1299

**Becker, Carl Lotus, 1873-1945.**      • **1.432**
The heavenly city of the eighteenth century philosophers, by Carl L. Becker. — New Haven: Yale university press, 1932. 5 p., l., 168 p.; 21 cm. 'Lectures delivered in the School of law in Yale university on the Storrs foundation ... April, 1931.'—Pref. 'Published on the Mary Cady Tew memorial fund.'—1st

prelim. leaf. 1. Philosophy and religion 2. Philosophy, Modern 3. Eighteenth century 4. History — Philosophy I. Yale University. Mary Cady Tew fund. II. T.
B802.B4      190      *LC* 32-31169

**Cassirer, Ernst, 1874-1945.**      • **1.433**
[Philosophie der Aufklärung. English] The philosophy of the enlightenment. Translated by Fritz C. A. Koelln and James P. Pettegrove. Boston, Beacon Press [1955, c1951] xiii, 366 p. 21 cm. (Humanitas: toward the study of man) Beacon paperbacks, 7. 1. Enlightenment 2. Philosophy, Modern I. T.
B802.C33x      190      *LC* 55-13561

**Gay, Peter, 1923- comp.**      **1.434**
The Enlightenment; a comprehensive anthology. — New York: Simon and Schuster, [1973] 829 p.; 23 cm. 1. Enlightenment — Addresses, essays, lectures. 2. Philosophy, Modern — 18th century — Addresses, essays, lectures. I. T.
B802.G29      190      *LC* 72-87947      *ISBN* 0671214659

**Gay, Peter, 1923-.**      • **1.435**
The Enlightenment, an interpretation. — [1st ed.]. — New York: Knopf, 1966-69. 2 v.; 22 cm. 1. Enlightenment 2. Philosophy — History 3. Europe — Intellectual life I. T.
B802.G3      190      *LC* 66-10740

**Hazard, Paul, 1878-1944.**      • **1.436**
[Pensée européenne au XVIIIème siècle. English] European thought in the eighteenth century, from Montesquieu to Lessing. [Translation from the original French by J. Lewis May] New Haven, Yale University Press, 1954. xx, 477 p. 22 cm. Companion volume to the author's The European mind, 1680-1715. 1. Philosophy — History 2. Eighteenth century 3. Religious thought — 18th century I. T.
B802.H313      901      *LC* a 54-10078

**Schlereth, Thomas J.**      **1.437**
The cosmopolitan ideal in Enlightenment thought, its form and function in the ideas of Franklin, Hume, and Voltaire, 1694–1790 / Thomas J. Schlereth. — Notre Dame, Ind.: University of Notre Dame Press, c1977. xxv, 230 p.; 24 cm. Includes index. 1. Franklin, Benjamin, 1706-1790. 2. Hume, David, 1711-1776. 3. Voltaire, 1694-1778. 4. Enlightenment 5. Philosophy, Modern — 18th century 6. Internationalism I. T. II. Title: Cosmopolitan ideal in Enlightenment thought ...
B802.S34      190/.9/033      *LC* 76-22405      *ISBN* 0268007209

## B803 19th Century

**Gilson, Etienne, 1884-1978.**      • **1.438**
Recent philosophy: Hegel to the present [by] Étienne Gilson, Thomas Langan [and] Armand A. Maurer. New York, Random House [1966] xv, 876 p. 24 cm. (A History of philosophy [v. 4]) 1. Philosophy, Modern — 19th century — Addresses, essays, lectures. 2. Philosophy, Modern — 20th century — Addresses, essays, lectures. I. Langan, Thomas. joint author. II. Maurer, Armand A. (Armand Augustine), 1915- joint author. III. T. IV. Series.
B803.G5      190.9      *LC* 66-12388

**Landgrebe, Ludwig.**      • **1.439**
Major problems in contemporary European philosophy, from Dilthey to Heidegger. Translated from the German by Kurt F. Reinhardt. — New York, F. Ungar Pub. Co. [1966] vi, 227 p. 22 cm. Translation of Philosophie der Gegenwart. Bibliography: p. 196-209. 1. Philosophy, Modern — 19th cent. — Addresses, essays, lectures. 2. Philosophy, Modern — 20th cent. — Addresses, essays, lectures. I. T.
B803.L3413      190.8      *LC* 64-25558

**Levi, Albert William, 1911-.**      • **1.440**
Philosophy and the modern world. — Bloomington: Indiana University Press, [1959] 591 p.; 25 cm. 1. Philosophy, Modern 2. Civilization, Modern I. T.
B803.L45      190      *LC* 59-13532

**Löwith, Karl, 1897-1973.**      • **1.441**
[Von Hegel zu Nietzsche. English] From Hegel to Nietzsche: the revolution in nineteenth–century thought. Translated from the German by David E. Green. [1st ed.] New York, Holt, Rinehart and Winston [1964] xiii, 464 p. 24 cm. 1. Hegel, Georg Wilhelm Friedrich, 1770-1831. 2. Philosophy, Modern 3. Sociology 4. Religious thought — 19th century I. T. II. Title: Revolution in nineteenth-century thought.
B803.L623      190/.9/034 19      *LC* 64-11274

**Mead, George Herbert, 1863-1931.**      • **1.442**
Movements of thought in the nineteenth century / George H. Mead; edited by Merritt H. Moore. — Chicago, Ill.: The University of Chicago Press, [1936]. xxxix, 518, p. 'Appendix. French philosophy in the nineteenth century': p. 418-510. 1. Philosophy, Modern — History. 2. Science — Philosophy

3. Philosophy, French I. Moore, Merritt Hadden. II. T. III. Title: Thought in the nineteenth century.
B803.M4    *LC* 36-9407    *ISBN* 0226536386

**Merz, John Theodore, 1840-1922.**       • **1.443**
A history of European thought in the nineteenth century. New York, Dover Publications [1965] 4 v. 21 cm. 'Unabridged and unaltered republication of the work first published by William Blackwood & Sons, between 1904 and 1912.' 1. Philosophy, Modern — 19th century 2. Science — History I. T.
B803.M54    190    *LC* 64-18363

**Peckham, Morse.**       **1.444**
Beyond the tragic vision; the quest for identity in the nineteenth century. — New York: G. Braziller, 1962. 380 p.; 24 cm. 1. Philosophy, Modern 2. Civilization, Modern — 19th century 3. Self I. T.
B803.P4    171.3    *LC* 62-9932

**Randall, John Herman, 1899-.**       **1.445**
Philosophy after Darwin: chapters for The career of philosophy, volume III, and other essays / John Herman Randall, Jr.; edited by Beth J. Singer. — New York: Columbia University Press, 1977. x, 352 p.; 24 cm. 1. Philosophy, Modern — 19th century I. Randall, John Herman, 1899- The career of philosophy. II. T.
B803.R25    190/.9    *LC* 76-30897    *ISBN* 0231041144

**Schacht, Richard, 1941-.**       **1.446**
Hegel and after; studies in continental philosophy between Kant and Sartre. — [Pittsburgh]: University of Pittsburgh Press, [1975] xviii, 297 p.; 24 cm. 1. Hegel, Georg Wilhelm Friedrich, 1770-1831 — Influence. 2. Philosophy, Modern — 19th century 3. Philosophy, Modern — 20th century I. T.
B803.S328    190    *LC* 74-4526    *ISBN* 0822932873

**Tatarkiewicz, Władysław, 1886-.**       **1.447**
Nineteenth century philosophy [by] Wladyslaw Tatarkiewicz. Translated by Chester A. Kisiel. — Belmont, Calif.: Wadsworth Pub. Co., [c1973] 250 p.; 24 cm. Translation of v. 3 of the author's Historia filozofii. 1. Philosophy, Modern — 19th century I. T.
B803.T3813    190/.9/034    *LC* 72-93474    *ISBN* 0534001408

# B804 20th Century

**Handbook of world philosophy: contemporary developments**    **1.448**
**since 1945 / edited by John R. Burr.**
Westport, Conn.: Greenwood Press, 1980. xxii, 641 p.; 24 cm. 1. Philosophy, Modern — 20th century — Addresses, essays, lectures. I. Burr, John Roy, 1933-
B804.A1 H36    190/.904    *LC* 80-539    *ISBN* 0313223815

**Ayer, A. J. (Alfred Jules), 1910-.**       **1.449**
Philosophy in the twentieth century / A.J. Ayer. — 1st ed. — New York: Random House, c1982. x, 283 p.; 25 cm. 1. Philosophy, Modern — 20th century I. T. II. Title: Philosophy in the 20th century.
B804.A818 1982    190/.9/04 19    *LC* 82-40131    *ISBN* 0394504542

**Barrett, William, 1913-.**       **1.450**
The illusion of technique: a search for meaning in a technological civilization / William Barrett. — 1st ed. — Garden City, N.Y.: Anchor Press, 1978. xx, 359 p.; 24 cm. Includes index. 1. Wittgenstein, Ludwig, 1889-1951. 2. Heidegger, Martin, 1889-1976. 3. James, William, 1842-1910. 4. Philosophy, Modern — 20th century 5. Technology and civilization 6. Liberty. I. T.
B804.B358    190    *LC* 77-27765    *ISBN* 0385112017

**Contemporary philosophy: a new survey / edited by Guttorm**    **1.451**
**Fløistad.**
The Hague; Boston: M. Nijhoff; Hingham, MA: Distributors for the U.S. and Canada, Kluwer Boston, 1983 (c1982) 550 p.; 25 cm. Added t.p.: La philosophie contemporaine. Half-title: International Institute of Philosophy. Institut international de philosophie. English or French. 'A continuation of two earlier series of chronicles, Philosophy in the mid-century (Firenze 1958/59) and Contemporary philosophy (Firenze 1968)'—Pref. 1. Philosophy, Modern — 20th century — Addresses, essays, lectures. I. Fløistad, Guttorm. II. Wright, G. H. von (Georg Henrik), 1916- III. International Institute of Philosophy. IV. Title: Philosophie contemporaine.
B804.C573    190/.9/047 19    *LC* 81-3972    *ISBN* 9024724368

**James, William, 1842-1910.**       **1.452**
A pluralistic universe / William James. Cambridge, Mass.: Harvard University Press, 1977. xxix, 488 p.: ill.; 24 cm. (The works of William James) 1. Philosophy, Modern — Addresses, essays, lectures. I. T.
B804.J2 1977    191    *LC* 76-45464    *ISBN* 0674673913

**Kearney, Richard.**       **1.453**
Dialogues with contemporary continental thinkers: the phenomenological heritage: Paul Ricoeur, Emmanuel Levinas, Herbert Marcuse, Stanislas Breton, Jacques Derrida / Richard Kearney. — Manchester, UK; Dover, N.H., USA: Manchester University Press, c1984. vi, 133 p.; 23 cm. 1. Philosophy, Modern — 20th century — Addresses, essays, lectures. I. Ricoeur, Paul. II. T.
B804.K36 1984    190 19    *LC* 84-17162    *ISBN* 071901087X

**Krutch, Joseph Wood, 1893-1970.**       • **1.454**
The measure of man: on freedom, human values, survival, and the modern temper. — [1st ed.]. — Indianapolis: Bobbs-Merrill, [1954] 261 p.; 23 cm. 1. Philosophy, Modern 2. Civilization, Modern — 20th century I. T.
B804.K68    190    *LC* 54-6504

**Krutch, Joseph Wood, 1893-1970.**       • **1.455**
The modern temper: a study and a confession / by Joseph Wood Krutch. — New York: Harcourt, Brace, 1956,1929. xviii, 160 p.; 19 cm. — (Harvest books; 20) 1. Philosophy, Modern 2. Civilization I. T.
B804.K7 1956    190    *LC* 56-58376    *ISBN* 015661579

**Macquarrie, John.**       • **1.456**
Twentieth–century religious thought: the frontiers of philosophy and theology, 1900–1970. — Revised ed. — London: S.C.M. Press, 1971. 408 p.; 23 cm. 1. Philosophy, Modern — 20th century 2. Religious thought — 20th century I. T.
B804.M25 1971    200/.9/04    *LC* 72-176158    *ISBN* 0334017025

**Magee, Bryan.**       **1.457**
Men of ideas / Bryan Magee. — New York: Viking Press, 1979, c1978. 314 p.: ports.; 25 cm. Interviews with Isaiah Berlin and others. Includes index. 1. Philosophy, Modern — 20th century 2. Philosophers — Interviews. I. Berlin, Isaiah, Sir. II. T.
B804.M257 1979    190    *LC* 78-27263    *ISBN* 0670468886

**Perry, Ralph Barton, 1876-1957.**       **1.458**
Present philosophical tendencies; a critical survey of naturalism, idealism, pragmatism, and realism, together with a synopsis of the philosophy of William James. — New York: Greenwood Press, 1968. xv, 383 p.; 23 cm. Reprint of 1955 edition. 1. Philosophy, Modern — 20th century I. T.
B804.P3 1968    140    *LC* 68-21328

**Theunissen, Michael.**       **1.459**
[Andere. English] The other: studies in the social ontology of Husserl, Heidegger, Sartre, and Buber / Michael Theunissen; translated by Christopher Macann; with an introduction by Fred R. Dallmayr. — Cambridge, Mass.: MIT Press, c1984. xxv, 451 p.; 24 cm. — (Studies in contemporary German social thought.) Translation of: Der Andere. Includes index. 1. Husserl, Edmund, 1859-1938. 2. Heidegger, Martin, 1889-1976. 3. Sartre, Jean Paul, 1905- 4. Buber, Martin, 1878-1965. 5. Ontology — History — 20th century. 6. Transcendentalism — History — 20th century. I. T. II. Series.
B804.T4513 1984    111 19    *LC* 83-16267    *ISBN* 0262200481

**Urmson, J. O.**       • **1.460**
Philosophical analysis; its development between the two World Wars. — Oxford: Clarendon Press, 1956. 202 p.; 19 cm. 1. Analysis (Philosophy) I. T.
B804.U7    190    *LC* 56-13682

**White, Morton Gabriel, 1917-.**       • **1.461**
Toward reunion in philosophy / Morton White. Cambridge, [Mass.]: Harvard University Press, 1956. 304p. 1. Philosophy, Modern I. T.
B804.W48 1956    190    *LC* 56-6527

# B808–840 SPECIAL TOPICS

## B808.5 Analysis

**Analytic philosophy and phenomenology / edited by Harold A.**    **1.462**
**Durfee.**
The Hague: Nijhoff, 1976. viii, 277 p.; 24 cm. — (American University publications in philosophy. 2) Includes index. 1. Analysis (Philosophy) — Addresses, essays, lectures. 2. Phenomenology — Addresses, essays, lectures. I. Durfee, Harold Allen, 1920- II. Series.
B808.5.A53    B808.5 A53.    149/.94    *LC* 77-352564    *ISBN* 9024718805

**Black, Max, 1909-.**       **1.463**
Caveats and critiques: philosophical essays in language, logic, and art / Max Black. — Ithaca [N.Y.]: Cornell University Press, 1975. 274 p.; 23 cm. Includes index. 1. Analysis (Philosophy) — Addresses, essays, lectures. 2. Logic — Addresses, essays, lectures. I. T.
B808.5.B525    B808.5 B525.    160    *LC* 74-25365    *ISBN* 0801409586

**Black, Max, 1909-.** • **1.464**
Philosophical analysis: a collection of essays / edited by Max Black. — Englewood Cliffs, N.J.: Prentice-Hall, 1963, c1950. viii, 401 p.; 22 cm. 1. Analysis (Philosophy) — Addresses, essays, lectures. I. T.
B808.5.B53 1963    *LC* 63-13299

**Black, Max, 1909-.** • **1.465**
Problems of analysis; philosophical essays. — Westport, Conn.: Greenwood Press, [1971, c1954] xi, 304 p.; 23 cm. 1. Analysis (Philosophy) — Addresses, essays, lectures. I. T.
B808.5.B55 1971    160    *LC* 74-139124    *ISBN* 0837157404

**Cooper, David Edward.** **1.466**
Philosophy and the nature of language / [by] David E. Cooper. — London: Longman, 1973. x, 222 p.; 23 cm. — (Longman linguistics library; v. 14) Includes index. 1. Analysis (Philosophy) 2. Languages — Philosophy 3. Meaning (Philosophy) I. T.
B808.5.C57 1973   B808.5 C57 1973.    149/.94    *LC* 74-190164    *ISBN* 0582550513

**Contemporary perspectives in the philosophy of language /** **1.467**
**edited by Peter A. French, Theodore E. Uehling, Jr., Howard K. Wettstein.**
Minneapolis: University of Minnesota Press, c1979. viii, 417 p.; 24 cm. A rev. and enl. ed. of Studies in the philosophy of language published in 1977. 1. Analysis (Philosophy) — Addresses, essays, lectures. I. French, Peter A. II. Uehling, Theodore Edward. III. Wettstein, Howard K.
B808.5.S85 1979    147/.94    *LC* 78-18463    *ISBN* 0816608652

**Vendler, Zeno.** **1.468**
Res cogitans: an essay in rational psychology. — Ithaca [N.Y.] Cornell University Press [1972] ix, 225 p. 22 cm. — (Contemporary philosophy) 1. Descartes, René, 1596-1650. 2. Analysis (Philosophy) 3. Thought and thinking 4. Speech 5. Meaning (Philosophy) I. T.
B808.5.V45    153.4    *LC* 72-3182    *ISBN* 0801407435

## B809.15 Convention

**Lewis, David K.** • **1.469**
Convention: a philosophical study, by David K. Lewis. — Cambridge: Harvard University Press, 1969. xii, 213 p.: illus.; 22 cm. 1. Convention (Philosophy) 2. Languages — Philosophy I. T.
B809.15.L47    149/.94    *LC* 69-12727

## B809.8 Dialectical Materialism

**Bochenski, Joseph M., 1902-.** **1.470**
Soviet Russian dialectical materialism (Diamat) / J.M. Bocheński. — Dordrecht, Holland: D. Reidel, 1963. vii, 185 p.; 23 cm. 'Translated from the German by Nicolas Sollohub and revised after the third German edition by Thomas J. Blakeley.' 1. Dialectical materialism I. T.
B809.8.B613    *LC* 64-1535

**Garaudy, Roger.** • **1.471**
Marxism in the twentieth century / translated by René Hague. — New York: Scribner, [1970] 224 p.; 22 cm. Translation of Marisme du XXe siècle. I. Marx, Karl, 1818-1883. II. T.
B809.8.G29913 1970b    146.3    *LC* 70-106527

**Lefebvre, Henri, 1901-.** • **1.472**
Dialectical materialism / translated from the French by John Sturrock. — London: Cape, 1968. 171 p.; 19 cm. — (Cape editions; 27) Translation of Le matérialisme dialectique. I. T.
B809.8 L3413    146.3    *LC* 79-411276    *ISBN* 0224615076

**Lichtheim, George, 1912-.** • **1.473**
From Marx to Hegel. — [New York]: Herder and Herder, [1971] viii, 248 p.; 22 cm. Essays. I. T.
B809.8.L499    146.3    *LC* 70-167871

**Lunn, Eugene.** **1.474**
Marxism and modernism: an historical study of Lukács, Brecht, Benjamin, and Adorno / Eugene Lunn. — Berkeley: University of California Press, c1982. 330 p.; 24 cm. Includes index. 1. Dialectical materialism — History. 2. Modernism (Aesthetics) — History. I. T.
B809.8.L84 1982    335.4/1 19    *LC* 81-23169    *ISBN* 0520045254

**Merleau-Ponty, Maurice, 1908-1961.** **1.475**
Adventures of the dialectic / translated by Joseph Bien. — Evanston [Ill.]: Northwestern University Press, 1973. xxix, 237 p.; 24 cm. — (Northwestern University studies in phenomenology & existential philosophy) 1. Sartre, Jean Paul, 1905- 2. Dialectical materialism I. T. II. Series.
B809.8.M4413    335.4/11    *LC* 72-96697    *ISBN* 0810104040

**Sartre, Jean Paul, 1905-.** **1.476**
[Critique de la raison dialectique. v. 1. Théorie des ensembles pratiques. English] Critique of dialectical reason, theory of practical ensembles / Jean-Paul Sartre; translated by Alan Sheridan-Smith; edited by Jonathan Rée. — London: NLB; Atlantic Highlands, N.J.: Humanities Press, 1976. 835 p.; 22 cm. Translation of Critique de la raison dialectique. v. 1. Théorie des ensembles pratiques. Includes index. 1. Dialectical materialism 2. Existentialism I. T.
B809.8.S324913    142/.7    *LC* 76-15680

**Schaff, Adam.** • **1.477**
Marxism and the human individual / introd. by Erich Fromm; edited by Robert S. Cohen, based on a translation by Olgierd Wojtasiewicz. — New York: McGraw-Hill, [1970] xii, 268 p.; 21 cm. Translation of Marksizm a jednostka ludzka. I. T.
B809.8.S34713    *LC* 68-58510

**Sheehan, Helena.** **1.478**
Marxism and the philosophy of science: a critical history / Helena Sheehan. — Atlantic Highlands, NJ: Humanities Press, 1985-. v. <1 >; 24 cm. 1. Philosophy, Marxist — History. 2. Science — Philosophy — History. I. T.
B809.8.S4324 1985    146/.32 19    *LC* 83-18603    *ISBN* 0391029983

**Society for the Philosophical Study of Dialectical Materialism.** **1.479**
Dialogues on the philosophy of Marxism, from the proceedings of the Society for the Philosophical Study of Dialectical Materialism / Edited by John Somerville and Howard L. Parsons. — Westport, Conn.: Greenwood Press, [1974]. -. xvi, 420 p.; 23 cm. — (Contributions in philosophy; no. 6) 1. Dialectical materialism — Addresses, essays, lectures. I. Somerville, John, 1905- ed. II. Parsons, Howard L. ed. III. T.
B809.8.S557 1974   B809.8 S63 1974.    335.4/11    *LC* 77-149963    *ISBN* 0837160626

## B812 Dualism

**Lovejoy, Arthur O. (Arthur Oncken), 1873-1962.** • **1.480**
The revolt against dualism; an inquiry concerning the existance of ideas. — 2d ed. — La Salle: Ill., Open Court Pub. Co., 1960. xiii, 405 p.; 21 cm. — (The Paul Carus lectures; series 2.) (Open Court classics; P79) 1. Dualism 2. Knowledge, Theory of 3. Mind and body I. T.
B812.L6 1960    *LC* 60-53406

## B818 Evolution

**Maxwell, Mary.** **1.481**
Human evolution: a philosophical anthropology / Mary Maxwell. — New York: Columbia University Press, 1984. 374 p.: ill.; 23 cm. Includes index. 1. Evolution 2. Philosophical theology I. T.
B818.M43 1984    128 19    *LC* 83-24005    *ISBN* 0231059469

**Sober, Elliott.** **1.482**
The nature of selection: evolutionary theory in philosophical focus / Elliott Sober. — Cambridge, Mass.: MIT Press, c1984. x, 383 p.: ill.; 24 cm. 'A Bradford book.' Includes index. 1. Evolution I. T.
B818.S66 1984    575.01 19    *LC* 84-19470    *ISBN* 0262192322

**Wiener, Philip Paul, 1905-.** • **1.483**
Evolution and the founders of pragmatism [by] Philip P. Wiener. With a foreword by John Dewey. — Gloucester, Mass.: P. Smith, 1969 [c1949] xii, 288 p.; 21 cm. 1. Evolution 2. Pragmatism I. T.
B818.W63 1969    144/.3    *LC* 70-7772

## B819 Existentialism

**Barrett, William, 1913-.** • **1.484**
Irrational man; a study in existential philosophy. — [1st ed.]. — Garden City, N.Y.: Doubleday, 1958. 278 p.; 22 cm. — (Doubleday Anchor books) 1. Existentialism I. T.
B819.B34    111    *LC* 58-8081

**Blackham, H. J. (Harold John), 1903-.** • **1.485**
Six existentialist thinkers. — New York: Macmillan, 1952. vii, 173 p.; 22 cm. 1. Existentialism 2. Philosophers, Modern I. T.
B819.B58 1961    111    *LC* 53-4309

**Collins, James Daniel.** • **1.486**
The existentialists, a critical study. — Chicago: H. Regnery Co., 1952. xi, 268 p.; 22 cm. 1. Existentialism I. T.
B819.C6    111    *LC* 52-8886

**Grene, Marjorie Glicksman, 1910-.** • **1.487**
[Dreadful freedom] Introduction to existentialism. [Chicago] University of Chicago Press [1959] 149 p. 21 cm. (Phoenix books, P34) First published in 1948 under title: Dreadful freedom, a critique of existentialism. 1. Sartre, Jean

Paul, 1905- 2. Heidegger, Martin, 1889-1976. 3. Kierkegaard, Søren, 1813-1855. 4. Marcel, Gabriel, 1889-1973. 5. Jaspers, Karl, 1883-1969. 6. Existentialism I. T.
B819.G68 1959    111.1    *LC* 59-1934

**Kaufmann, Walter Arnold. ed.**        • **1.488**
Existentialism from Dostoevsky to Sartre, edited, with an introd., prefaces, and new translations. — New York: Meridian Books, 1956. 319 p.; 19 cm. — (Meridian books, M39) 1. Existentialism 2. Existentialism in literature I. T.
B819.K3    111.1    *LC* 56-10018

**Maritain, Jacques, 1882-1973.**        • **1.489**
Existence and the existent; English version by Lewis Galantière and Gerald B. Phelan. — [New York] Pantheon [1948] 148 p. 21 cm. Translation of Court traité de l'existence et de l'existant. 1. Existentialism I. Galantière, Lewis, 1893- tr. II. T.
B819.M314    111    *LC* 49-7062 *

**Marcel, Gabriel, 1889-1973.**        • **1.490**
The philosophy of existence. London Harvill Press [1948] 96p. (The Changing world series, No. 3) 1. Existentialism I. T.
B819 M353

**Sartre, Jean Paul, 1905-.**        • **1.491**
[Être et le néant. English] Being and nothingness; an essay on phenomenological ontology. Translated and with an introd. by Hazel E. Barnes. New York, Philosophical Library [1956] 638 p. 23 cm. 1. Existentialism I. T.
B819.S272    111    *LC* 56-13912

**Sartre, Jean Paul, 1905-.**        • **1.492**
Existentialism and humanism / Jean–Paul Sartre; translation [from the French] and introduction by Philip Mairet. — 1st English ed. — London: Methuen, 1948. 70 p.; 19 cm. Translation of L'existentialisme est un humanisme. 1. Existentialism I. Mairet, Philip, 1886- tr. II. T.
B819.S273213 1948    142/.7    *LC* 49-61    *ISBN* 0416509207

**Sartre, Jean Paul, 1905-.**        • **1.493**
[Transcendence de l'ego. English] The transcendence of the ego; an existentialist theory of consciousness. Translated and annotated with an introd. by Forrest Williams and Robert Kirkpatrick. New York, Noonday Press [1957] 119 p. 21 cm. 1. Existentialism 2. Phenomenology 3. Consciousness I. T.
B819.S2743    111    *LC* 57-14171

**Desan, Wilfrid.**        • **1.494**
The tragic finale: an essay on the philosophy of Jean–Paul Sartre / by Wilfrid Desan. — Cambridge: Harvard University Press, 1954. xiv, 220 p.; 22 cm. Deals with Sartre's philosophy as it appears principally in his L'être et le néant. 1. Sartre, Jean Paul, 1905- Être et le néant. 2. Existentialism I. T.
B819.S275D4    B819.S2738 D4.    111    *LC* 53-10473

**Sartre, Jean Paul, 1905-.**        • **1.495**
[Existentialisme et marxisme. English] Search for a method. Translated from the French and with an introd. by Hazel E. Barnes. [1st American ed.] New York, Knopf, 1963. 181 p. 22 cm. Translation of Existentialisme et marxisme. 1. Existentialism 2. Dialectical materialism I. T.
B819.S3363 1963    111    *LC* 63-9135

## B820 General Semantics

**Hayakawa, S. I. (Samuel Ichiyé), 1906-.**        • **1.496**
Symbol, status, and personality. [1st ed.] New York, Harcourt, Brace & World [1963] vii, 188 p. 21 cm. 1. General semantics I. T.
B820.H3    149.94    *LC* 63-17772

**Rapoport, Anatol, 1911-.**        • **1.497**
Operational philosophy; integrating knowledge and action. [1st ed.] New York, Harper [1953] 258 p. 22 cm. 1. General semantics I. T.
B820.R38    149.9    *LC* 53-8550

**Rapoport, Anatol, 1911-.**        • **1.498**
Science and the goals of man; a study in semantic orientation. Foreword by S. I. Hayakawa. — Westport, Conn.: Greenwood Press, [1971, c1950] xxxii, 262 p.; 23 cm. 1. General semantics I. T.
B820.R4 1971    149/.94    *LC* 70-138126    *ISBN* 0837141427

## B821 Humanism

**Ehrenfeld, David W.**        1.499
The arrogance of humanism / David Ehrenfeld. — New York: Oxford University Press, 1978. ix, 286 p.; 22 cm. Includes index. 1. Humanism — 20th century I. T.
B821.E35    144    *LC* 78-1664    *ISBN* 019502415X

**Hoeveler, J. David, 1943-.**        1.500
The new humanism: a critique of modern America, 1900–1940 / J. David Hoeveler, Jr. Charlottesville: University Press of Virginia, 1977. ix, 207 p.: ports.; 24 cm. Includes index. 1. Babbitt, Irving, 1865-1933. 2. More, Paul Elmer, 1864-1937. 3. Humanism — 20th century 4. United States — Intellectual life — 20th century I. T.
B821.H59    144    *LC* 76-25168    *ISBN* 081390658X

**Lamont, Corliss, 1902-.**        • **1.501**
Humanism as a philosophy / by Corliss Lamont. — New York: Philosophical Library, 1949. 368 p. 'An expansion and revision of a lecture course entitled 'The philosophy of naturalistic humanism' given ... at Columbia University, 1946-1949.' 1. Humanism I. T.
B821.L3    *LC* 49-7777

## B823 Idealism

**Brightman, Edgar Sheffield, 1884-1953.**        1.502
A Philosophy of ideals. — New York, H. Holt and company [c1928] vii, 243 p. 22 cm. A revision of seven of the author's addresses and essays. 1. Idealism 2. Philosophy, Modern I. T.
B823.B7    *LC* 28-14913

**Ewing, A.C. (Alfred Cyril), 1899- ed.**        • **1.503**
The idealist tradition: from Berkeley to Blanshard. Glencoe, Ill., Free Press [1957] 369 p. 22 cm. (The Library of philosophical movements) 1. Idealism I. T.
B823.E82    141 190*    *LC* 57-6753

## B823.3 Ideology

**Earle, William, 1919-.**        1.504
Public sorrows and private pleasures / William Earle. — Bloomington: Indiana University Press, c1976. xiii, 175 p.; 24 cm. (Studies in phenomenology and existential philosophy) 1. Hegel, Georg Wilhelm Friedrich, 1770-1831. Phänomenologie des Geistes. 2. Ideology — Addresses, essays, lectures. 3. Philosophy — Addresses, essays, lectures. 4. Self (Philosophy) — Addresses, essays, lectures. I. T.
B823.3.E2 1976    B823.3 E2 1976.    191    *LC* 75-28911    *ISBN* 0253346789

**Seliger, M.**        1.505
Ideology and politics / M. Seliger. — New York: Free Press, 1976. 352 p.; 24 cm. Includes index. 1. Ideology 2. Political science I. T.
B823.3.S43 1976    301.2/1

**Drucker, H. M. (Henry Matthew)**        1.506
The political uses of ideology [by] H. M. Drucker. [London] Macmillan [for] the London School of Economics and Political Science [1974] xiii, 170 p. 22 cm. 1. Marx, Karl, 1818-1883. 2. Political sociology 3. Ideology I. T.
B823.5.D78    301.5/92    *LC* 74-164485    *ISBN* 0333154819

## B824.6 Logical Positivism

**Ayer, A. J. (Alfred Jules), 1910- ed.**        • **1.507**
Logical positivism. Glencoe, Ill., Free Press [c1959] viii, 455 p. 22 cm. (The Library of philosophical movements) 1. Logical positivism I. T.
B824.6.A9    146.4    *LC* 58-6479

**Bergmann, Gustav, 1906-.**        1.508
Meaning and existence. — Madison, University of Wisconsin Press, 1960 [c1959] 274 p. 25 cm. Includes bibliography. 1. Logical positivism 2. Analysis (Philosophy) I. T.
B824.6.B398    111.1    *LC* 60-5036

**Bergmann, Gustav, 1906-.**        • **1.509**
The metaphysics of logical positivism; [papers]. — [2d ed.]. — Madison: University of Wisconsin Press, 1967. xii, 340 p.; 22 cm. 1. Logical positivism I. T.
B824.6.B4 1967    146/.4    *LC* 67-4145

**Blanshard, Brand, 1892-1987.**        • **1.510**
Reason and analysis. — La Salle, Ill., Open Court Pub. Co. [1962] 505 p. 24 cm. — (The Paul Carus lectures, 12th ser.) 'First in a sequence of three volumes...[the other two have titles] Reason and goodness, and Reason and belief.' Bibliography: p. [494]-499. 1. Reason 2. Logical positivism 3. Knowledge, Theory of I. T.
B824.6.B57 1962a    146.4    *LC* 62-9576

**Carnap, Rudolf, 1891-1970.**        • **1.511**
Philosophy and logical syntax / by Rudolf Carnap. — London: K. Paul, Trench, Trubner, 1935. 100 p.; 19 cm. — (Psyche miniatures: General series; no. 70.) 1. Logical positivism — Addresses, essays, lectures. 2. Logic,

Symbolic and mathematical — Addresses, essays, lectures. 3. Philosophy — Addresses, essays, lectures. I. T. II. Series.
B824.6.C28    146/.4    *LC* 35-8828

**Hanfling, Oswald.**    **1.512**
Logical positivism / Oswald Hanfling. — New York: Columbia University Press, 1981. 181 p.; 23 cm. Includes index. 1. Logical positivism I. T.
B824.6.H26    146/.42 19    *LC* 81-6175    *ISBN* 023105386X

**The Legacy of logical positivism; studies in the philosophy of**    • **1.513**
**science. Edited by Peter Achinstein and Stephen F. Barker.**
Baltimore: Johns Hopkins Press, [1969] x, 300 p.; 24 cm. — (Johns Hopkins seminars in philosophy) 1. Logical positivism — Addresses, essays, lectures. 2. Science — Philosophy — Addresses, essays, lectures. I. Achinstein, Peter. ed. II. Barker, Stephen Francis. ed. III. Series.
B824.6.L4    146/.4    *LC* 69-15396    *ISBN* 0801810140

**Von Mises, Richard, 1883-1953.**    • **1.514**
[Kleines Lehrbuch des Positivismus. English] Positivism; a study in human understanding. New York, Dover Publications [1968, c1951] xi, 404 p. 22 cm. Translation of Kleines Lehrbuch des Positivismus. 1. Science — Philosophy 2. Languages — Philosophy 3. Logical positivism I. T.
B824.6.V613 1968    146/.4    *LC* 67-18741

## B825 Materialism

**Engels, Friedrich, 1820-1895.**    • **1.515**
On historical materialism / by Frederick Engels. — New York: International publishers, 1940. 30 p. (Little Marx library) 1. Materialism I. T. II. Series.
B825.E5

**Matson, Wallace I.**    **1.516**
Sentience / by Wallace I. Matson. — Berkeley: University of California Press, c1976. 190 p.; 22 cm. 1. Materialism 2. Mind and body 3. Senses and sensation I. T.
B825.M35    B825 M35.    120    *LC* 75-3774    *ISBN* 0520095383

## B829.5 Phenomenology

**Goodman, Nelson.**    **1.517**
The structure of appearance. — [2d ed.]. — Indianapolis: Bobbs-Merrill, [c1966] xix, 392 p.; 21 cm. 1. Phenomenology 2. Structuralism 3. System theory 4. Science — Philosophy I. T.
B829.5.G6 1966    142/.7    *LC* 65-26543

**Gurwitsch, Aron.**    • **1.518**
Studies in phenomenology and psychology / Aron Gurwitsch. — Evanston: Northwestern University Press, 1966. xxv, 452 p.; 24 cm. — (Northwestern University studies in phenomenology & existential philosophy) 1. Husserl, Edmund, 1859-1938. 2. Phenomenology — Addresses, essays, lectures 3. Consciousness — Addresses, essays, lectures I. T. II. Series.
B829.5.G83    142.7    *LC* 65-24664    *ISBN* 0810101106

**Merleau-Ponty, Maurice, 1908-1961.**    • **1.519**
[Phénoménologie de la perception. English] Phenomenology of perception. Translated from the French by Colin Smith. New York, Humanities Press [1962] 466 p. illus. 23 cm. (International library of philosophy and scientific method) 1. Phenomenology I. T.
B829.5.M413    142.7    *LC* 63-4378

**Natanson, Maurice Alexander, 1924-.**    **1.520**
Phenomenology and the social sciences. Edited by Maurice Natanson. — Evanston [Ill.]: Northwestern University Press, 1973. 2 v.; 24 cm. — (Northwestern University studies in phenomenology & existential philosophy) 1. Phenomenology — Collected works. 2. Humanities — Collected works. I. T. II. Series.
B829.5.N32    B829.5 N32.    142/.7/08    *LC* 72-91001    *ISBN* 0810104024

**Peursen, Cornelis Anthonie van, 1920-.**    **1.521**
[Fenomenologie en analytische filosofie. English] Phenomenology and analytical philosophy, by Cornelis A. van Peursen. Pittsburgh, Duquesne University Press [1972] 190 p. 24 cm. (Duquesne studies. Philosophical series. 28) Translation of Fenomenologie en analytische filosofie. 1. Phenomenology 2. Analysis (Philosophy) 3. Logical positivism I. T. II. Series.
B829.5.P393 1972    142/.7    *LC* 79-176037    *ISBN* 0820701394

**Phenomenology and natural existence; essays in honor of**    **1.522**
**Marvin Farber. Edited by Dale Riepe.**
[1st ed.]. — Albany: State University of New York Press, 1973. viii, 408 p.; port.; 24 cm. 1. Farber, Marvin, 1901- 2. Husserl, Edmund, 1859-1938. 3. Phenomenology — Addresses, essays, lectures. 4. Naturalism — Addresses, essays, lectures. I. Farber, Marvin, 1901- II. Riepe, Dale Maurice, 1918- ed.
B829.5.P445    142/.7    *LC* 71-171185    *ISBN* 0873950992

**Sallis, John, 1938-.**    **1.523**
Phenomenology and the return to beginnings. — Pittsburgh: Duquesne University Press; distributed by Humanities Press, New York, [1973] 120 p.; 23 cm. — (Duquesne studies. Philosophical series. v. 32) 1. Phenomenology I. T. II. Series.
B829.5.S23    142/.7    *LC* 72-97470    *ISBN* 0391003127

**Spiegelberg, Herbert, 1904-.**    **1.524**
The Phenomenological Movement: a historical introduction / Herbert Spiegelberg. — 3rd rev. and enl. ed. / with the collaboration of Karl Schuhmann. — The Hague; London: Nijhoff, 1982. xlviii, 768 p., [19] leaves of plates: facsims., ports.; 25 cm. — (Phaenomenologica. 5-6) 1. Phenomenology — History. I. Schuhmann, Karl. II. T. III. Series.
B829.5.S64 1982    142/.7/09 18    142/.7/09 19    *ISBN* 9024725771

**Zaner, Richard M. comp.**    **1.525**
Phenomenology and existentialism [by] Richard M. Zaner and Don Ihde. — New York, Putnam [1973] 374 p. 22 cm. — (Capricorn books) 1. Phenomenology — Addresses, essays, lectures. 2. Existentialism — Addresses, essays, lectures. I. Ihde, Don, 1934- joint comp. II. T.
B829.5.Z33 1973    142/.7/08    *LC* 78-163421    *ISBN* 039910951X
*ISBN* 0399502866

## B832 Pragmatism

**James, William, 1842-1910.**    **1.526**
Pragmatism / William James; [Fredson Bowers, textual editor, Ignas K. Skrupskelis, associate editor; introd. by H. S. Thayer]. Cambridge, Mass.: Harvard University Press, 1975. xxxviii, 316 p.: ill.; 24 cm. (The works of William James) 1. Pragmatism I. T.
B832.J2 1975    144/.3    *LC* 74-84089    *ISBN* 0674697359

**James, William, 1842-1910.**    **1.527**
The meaning of truth / William James; [edited by Fredson Bowers, textual editor, Ignas K. Skrupskelis, associate editor; introd. by H. S. Thayer]. — Cambridge, Mass.: Harvard University Press, 1975. xlvi, 328 p.: port.; 24 cm. (The works of William James) 1. Truth 2. Pragmatism I. Bowers, Fredson Thayer 1905- II. Skrupskelis, Ignas K., 1938- III. T.
B832.J4 1975    144/.3    *LC* 75-30758    *ISBN* 0674558618

**Konvitz, Milton Ridvas, 1908- ed.**    • **1.528**
The American pragmatists; selected writings. Edited by Milton R. Konvitz and Gail Kennedy. — New York: Meridian Books, [1960] 413 p.; 18 cm. — (Meridian books, M105) 1. Pragmatism I. Kennedy, Gail, 1900- joint ed. II. T.
B832.K6    144.3    *LC* 60-12329

**Lovejoy, Arthur O. (Arthur Oncken), 1873-1962.**    • **1.529**
The thirteen pragmatisms, and other essays. — Baltimore, Johns Hopkins Press [1963] 290 p. 19 cm. 1. Pragmatism I. T.
B832.L6    144.3081    *LC* 63-11890

**Moore, Edward C. (Edward Carter), 1917-.**    • **1.530**
American pragmatism: Peirce, James and Dewey, / by Edward C. Moore. — New York: Columbia University Press, 1961. xii, 285 p. 1. Peirce, Charles S. (Charles Sanders), 1839-1914. 2. James, William, 1842-1910. 3. Dewey, John, 1859-1952. 4. Pragmatism I. T.
B832.M812 1961    *LC* 61-5244

**Rucker, Darnell, 1921-.**    • **1.531**
The Chicago pragmatists, by Darnell Rucker. — Minneapolis: University of Minnesota Press, [1969] ix, 200 p.; 23 cm. 1. Pragmatism I. T.
B832.R77    144/.3    *LC* 69-13188

**Smith, John Edwin.**    **1.532**
Purpose and thought: the meaning of pragmatism / John E. Smith. — New Haven: Yale University Press, 1978. 236 p.; 24 cm. 1. Pragmatism I. T.
B832.S6 1978    144/.3    *LC* 78-399    *ISBN* 0300021712

**Thayer, H. S. (Horace Standish), 1923-.**    **1.533**
Meaning and action: a critical history of pragmatism / H. S. Thayer. — 2d ed. — Indianapolis: Hackett Pub. Co., c1981. xxii, 616 p.; 23 cm. Includes index. 1. Pragmatism I. T.
B832.T48 1981    144/.3/09 19    *LC* 80-20890    *ISBN* 0915144735

## B835 Realism

**Chisholm, Roderick M. ed.**    • **1.534**
Realism and the background of phenomenology. — Glencoe, Ill., Free Press [1961, c1960] viii, 308 p. 22 cm. — (The Library of philosophical movements) Bibliography: p. 283-304. 1. Realism 2. Phenomenology I. T.
B835.C5    149.2    *LC* 60-10891

## B837 Scepticism

**Penelhum, Terence, 1929-.**      **1.535**
God and skepticism: a study in skepticism and fideism / Terence Penelhum. — Dordrecht; Boston: D. Reidel Pub. Co.; Hingham, MA: Sold and distributed in the U.S.A. and Canada by Kluwer Boston, c1983. xii, 186 p.; 23 cm. — (Philosophical studies series in philosophy. v. 28) 1. Skepticism 2. Faith 3. Faith and reason I. T. II. Series.
B837.P45 1983    149/.73 19    *LC* 83-6791    *ISBN* 9027715505

**Stroud, Barry.**      **1.536**
The significance of philosophical scepticism / Barry Stroud. — Oxford [Oxfordshire]: Clarendon Press; New York: Oxford University Press, 1984. xiv, 277 p.; 22 cm. 1. Skepticism 2. Knowledge, Theory of I. T.
B837.S87 1984    121 19    *LC* 83-25244    *ISBN* 0198247303

## B840 Semantics

**Black, Max, 1909-.**      • **1.537**
The Labyrinth of language / Max Black. — New York: Praeger, 1968. vii, 178 p.; 25 cm. — (Britannica perspective) 1. Languages — Philosophy 2. Semantics (Philosophy) I. T.
B840.B57    149/.94    *LC* 68-19506

**Black, Max, 1909-.**      • **1.538**
Language and philosophy: studies in method / Max Black. — Ithaca, N.Y.: Cornell University Press, c1949. xiii, 264 p. 1. Semantics (Philosophy) 2. Logical positivism 3. General semantics I. T.
B840.B58    *LC* 49-11624

**Burke, Kenneth, 1897-.**      • **1.539**
A rhetoric of motives. — Berkeley: University of California Press, 1969. xv, 340 p.; 24 cm. 1. Semantics (Philosophy) 2. Rhetoric I. T.
B840.B8 1969    149/.94    *LC* 69-16742    8.50

**Carnap, Rudolf, 1891-1970.**      • **1.540**
Meaning and necessity: a study in semantics and modal logic / by Rudolph Carnap. — 2d ed., enl. Chicago: Univ. of Chicago P., 1956. 258 p. 1. Semantics (Philosophy) 2. Logic, Symbolic and mathematical I. T.
B840.C3 1956    164    *LC* 56-9132    *ISBN* 0226093468

**Fogelin, Robert J.**      • **1.541**
Evidence and meaning; studies in analytic philosophy, by Robert J. Fogelin. — New York: Humanities Press, [1967] xi, 187 p.: illus.; 22 cm. — (International library of philosophy and scientific method.) 1. Semantics (Philosophy) 2. Evidence 3. Analysis (Philosophy) I. T. II. Series.
B840.F6 1967b    149/.94    *LC* 67-21587

**Lyas, Colin, comp.**      **1.542**
Philosophy and linguistics. — London: Macmillan; New York: St Martin's Press, 1971. 332 p.; 23 cm. — (Controversies in philosophy) 1. Semantics (Philosophy) — Addresses, essays, lectures. 2. Analysis (Philosophy) — Addresses, essays, lectures. 3. Languages — Philosophy — Addresses, essays, lectures. I. T.
B840.L9    149/.94    *LC* 76-147781    *ISBN* 0333105133

**Morris, Charles William, 1901-.**      • **1.543**
Signs, language, and behavior. — New York, G. Braziller, 1955 [c1946] xii, 365 p. 23 cm. Bibliography: p. 311-343. 1. Semantics (Philosophy) I. T.
B840.M6 1955    422    *LC* 56-1550

**Osgood, Charles Egerton.**      **1.544**
The measurement of meaning / [by] Charles E. Osgood, George J. Suci [and] Percy H. Tannenbaum. — Urbana: University of Illinois Press, 1957. 342 p.: ill.; 24 cm. 1. Semantics (Philosophy) 2. Meaning (Psychology) I. T.
B840.O7    153.1    *LC* 56-5684

**Quine, W. V. (Willard Van Orman)**      • **1.545**
Ontological relativity, and other essays, by W. V. Quine. New York, Columbia University Press, 1969. viii, 165 p. 21 cm. (The John Dewey essays in philosophy, no. 1) 1. Semantics (Philosophy) 2. Ontology 3. Knowledge, Theory of 4. Relativity I. T. II. Series.
B840.Q49    110    *LC* 72-91121    *ISBN* 0231033079

**Quine, W. V. (Willard Van Orman)**      • **1.546**
Word and object. [Cambridge] Technology Press of the Massachusetts Institute of Technology [1960] 294 p. 24 cm. (Studies in communication) 1. Semantics (Philosophy) 2. Logic, Symbolic and mathematical 3. Languages — Philosophy I. T.
B840.Q5    149.94    *LC* 60-9621

**Rorty, Richard. ed.**      • **1.547**
The linguistic turn; recent essays in philosophical method, edited and with an introd. by Richard Rorty. Chicago, University of Chicago Press [1967] 393 p. 1. Semantics (Philosophy) — Addresses, essays, lectures 2. Languages —

Philosophy — Addresses, essays, lectures 3. Analysis (Philosophy) — Addresses, essays, lectures I. T.
B840 R6    *LC* 67-13811

**Searle, John R. comp.**      • **1.548**
The philosophy of language; edited by J. R. Searle. — London: Oxford University Press, 1971. [5], 149 p.: illus.; 21 cm. — (Oxford readings in philosophy) 1. Languages — Philosophy 2. Semantics (Philosophy) 3. Analysis (Philosophy) I. T.
B840.S38    401    *LC* 70-27065    *ISBN* 0198750153

**Searle, John R.**      • **1.549**
Speech acts: an essay in the philosophy of language [by] John R. Searle. — London: Cambridge U.P., 1969. vii, 203 p.; 23 cm. 1. Speech acts (Linguistics) 2. Semantics (Philosophy) I. T.
B840.S4    401    *LC* 68-24484    *ISBN* 0521071844

**Zabeeh, Farhang. comp.**      **1.550**
Readings in semantics. Edited by Farhang Zabeeh, E. D. Klemke, and Arthur Jacobson. — Urbana: University of Illinois Press, [1974] 853 p.; 26 cm. 1. Semantics (Philosophy) — Addresses, essays, lectures. 2. Modality (Logic) — Addresses, essays, lectures. I. Klemke, E. D., 1928- joint comp. II. Jacobson, Arthur, 1929- joint comp. III. T.
B840.Z32    B840 Z32.    149/.94    *LC* 74-639    *ISBN* 0252001966

**Structuralism: an introduction / edited by David Robey.**      **1.551**
Oxford: Clarendon Press, 1973. [6], 154 p.: ill.; 23 cm. (Wolfson College lectures, 1972) 1. Structuralism — Addresses, essays, lectures. I. Robey, David. ed.
B841.4.S85    149/.96 19    *LC* 73-173608    *ISBN* 0198740123

**Aronson, Jerrold L., 1940-.**      **1.552**
A realist philosophy of science / Jerrold L. Aronson. — New York: St. Martin's Press, 1984. x, 278 p.: ill.; 23 cm. 1. Theory (Philosophy) 2. Science — Philosophy I. T.
B842.A76 1984    121 19    *LC* 82-22956    *ISBN* 0312664745

# B850–5739 By Country

# B850–945 United States

**Kurtz, Paul W.**      • **1.553**
American thought before 1900; a sourcebook from puritanism to Darwinism. New York, Macmillan, 1966. 448 p. 1. Philosophy — Collections 2. Philosophy, American I. T.
B850.K8    *LC* 65-24106    660

**Blau, Joseph L. (Joseph Leon), 1909-1986.**      • **1.554**
Men and movements in American philosophy. — New York, Prentice-Hall, 1952. xi, 403 p. 22 cm. — (Prentice-Hall philosophy series) 'Footnotes and suggested reading': p. 357-383. 1. Philosophy, American 2. Philosophers, American. I. T.
B851.B52    191    *LC* 52-8596

**Cohen, Morris Raphael, 1880-1947.**      • **1.555**
American thought; a critical sketch. Edited and with a foreword by Felix S. Cohen. — Glencoe, Ill.: Free Press, [1954] 360 p.; 24 cm. 1. Philosophy, American 2. United States — Intellectual life I. T.
B851.C6    191    *LC* 54-10667

**Flower, Elizabeth.**      **1.556**
A history of philosophy in America / by Elizabeth Flower and Murray Murphey. — New York: Putnam, c1977. 2 v.; 24 cm. 1. Philosophy, American — History. I. Murphey, Murray G., joint author. II. T.
B851.F56 1977    191    *LC* 75-40254    *ISBN* 0399116508

**Schneider, Herbert W.**      • **1.557**
A history of American philosophy / Herbert W. Schneider. — 2d ed. — New York: Columbia University Press, 1963. 590 p. 1. Philosophy, American 2. Philosophy — History — United States 3. United States — Civilization I. T.
B851.S4 1963    191    *LC* 63-14114    *ISBN* 0231026455

**Smith, John Edwin.**      • **1.558**
The spirit of American philosophy. — New York, Oxford University Press, 1963. 219 p. 21 cm. 1. Philosophy, American I. T.
B851.S48    191    *LC* 63-12553

**White, Morton Gabriel, 1917-.** • **1.559**
Science and sentiment in America; philosophical thought from Jonathan Edwards to John Dewey [by] Morton White. — New York: Oxford University Press, 1972. viii, 358 p.; 22 cm. 1. Philosophy, American — History. I. T.
B851.W46      191      *LC* 73-177996      *ISBN* 0195015193

**Townsend, Harvey Gates, 1885-1948.** **1.560**
Philosophical ideas in the United States. New York, Octagon Books, 1968 [c1934] v, 293 p. 22 cm. 1. Philosophy, American 2. Philosophy — United States — History. I. T.
B858.T6 1968      191      *LC* 68-23128

**Boller, Paul F.** **1.561**
Freedom and fate in American thought: from Edwards to Dewey / Paul F. Boller, Jr. — Dallas: SMU Press, c1978. xiv, 300 p.; 24 cm. — (Bicentennial series in American studies; 7) Includes index. 1. Liberty. 2. Free will and determinism 3. Philosophy, American I. T.
B861.L52 B64      123      *LC* 78-5813      *ISBN* 0870741691

**Edwards, Jonathan, 1703-1758.** • **1.562**
The philosophy of Jonathan Edwards from his private notebooks. Edited by Harvey G. Townsend. — Westport, Conn.: Greenwood Press, [1972] xxii, 270 p.; 24 cm. Reprint of the 1955 ed., issued in series: University of Oregon monographs. Studies in philosophy, no. 2. 1. Philosophy I. T.
B870.A5 1972      191      *LC* 72-7503      *ISBN* 0837165113

## B893–945 19TH–20TH CENTURIES

**Reck, Andrew J.** • **1.563**
Recent American philosophy; studies of ten representative thinkers / by Andrew J. Reck. Pantheon Books, 1964. xxiii, 343 p., bibl. 1. Philosophy, American — 20th century 2. Philosophers, American. I. T.
B893.R4 1964      191.0904      *LC* 64-13268

**Boller, Paul F.** **1.564**
American transcendentalism, 1830–1860: an intellectual inquiry / by Paul F. Boller, Jr. — New York: Putnam, [1974] xxiii, 227 p.; 22 cm. Includes index. 1. Transcendentalism (New England) 2. Philosophy, American — 19th century I. T.
B905.B64 1974      141/.3/0974      *LC* 73-78616      *ISBN* 0399111638

**Frothingham, Octavius Brooks, 1822-1895.** • **1.565**
Transcendentalism in New England: a history / Octavius B. Frothingham. — New York: Harper, 1959. xxix, 386 p.; 21 cm. (Harper torchbooks,TB59) Includes index. 1. Transcendentalism (New England) I. T.
B905.F7 1965      *LC* 59-10346

**Goddard, Harold Clarke, 1878-1950.** • **1.566**
Studies in New England transcendentalism / Harold Clarke Goddard. — New York: Hilliary House Publishers, 1960. 217 p.: 24 cm. 1. Transcendentalism (New England) I. T.
B905.G5 1960      *LC* a 62-5518

**Miller, Perry, 1905-1963.** • **1.567**
The transcendentalists: an anthology / Perry Miller. — Cambridge, Mass.: Harvard University Press, 1950. xvii, 521 p. 1. Transcendentalism (New England) I. T.
B905 M5      *LC* 50-7360

**Rose, Anne C., 1950-.** **1.568**
Transcendentalism as a social movement, 1830–1850 / Anne C. Rose. — New Haven: Yale University Press, c1981. xii, 269 p.; 24 cm. Based on the author's thesis (Ph.D.)—Yale University. Includes index. 1. Transcendentalism (New England) 2. Social movements — New England. I. T.
B905.R67      974/.03 19      *LC* 81-3340      *ISBN* 0300025874

**Contemporary American philosophy; personal statements, by G.** • **1.569**
**H. Palmer [and others] Edited by George P. Adams and Wm.**
**Pepperell Montague.**
New York, Russell & Russell, 1962. 2 v. illus. 23 cm. 1. Philosophy, American — Collections. I. Adams, George Plimpton, 1882-1961. ed. II. Montague, William Pepperell, 1873-1953, ed.
B934.C6 1962      191      *LC* 62-20304

**Kurtz, Paul W., 1925- ed.** • **1.570**
American philosophy in the twentieth century; a sourcebook from pragmatism to philosophical analysis, edited, with an introductory survey, notes, and bibliographies, by Paul Kurtz. — [1st ed.]. — New York: Macmillan, [1966] 573 p.; 22 cm. — (Classics in the history of thought) 1. Philosophy — Collections. 2. Philosophy, American — 20th century I. T.
B934.K8 1966      191.08      *LC* 65-24107

**Bertocci, Peter Anthony.** **1.571**
Mid–twentieth century American philosophy: personal statements. Edited by Peter A. Bertocci. — New York: Humanities Press, 1974. xvi, 251 p.; 25 cm. 1. Philosophy, American — 20th century — Addresses, essays, lectures. I. T.
B935.B47      191      *LC* 73-18467      *ISBN* 0391003402

**Reck, Andrew J., 1927-.** **1.572**
The new American philosophers; an exploration of thought since World War II [by] Andrew J. Reck. — Baton Rouge: Louisiana State University Press, [1968] xxi, 362 p.; 24 cm. 1. Philosophers, American. 2. Philosophy, American — 20th century I. T.
B935.R4      191      *LC* 68-21807

**Eames, Samuel Morris, 1916-.** **1.573**
Pragmatic naturalism: an introduction / S. Morris Eames. — Carbondale: Southern Illinois University Press, c1977. xxvii, 242 p.; 22 cm. 1. Naturalism 2. Pragmatism 3. Philosophy, American — 19th century 4. Philosophy, American — 20th century I. T.
B944.N3 E2      146      *LC* 76-58441      *ISBN* 0809308029

## B945 PHILOSOPHERS

### B945.A–.C

**Adler, Mortimer Jerome, 1902-.** **1.574**
Philosopher at large: an intellectual autobiography / by Mortimer J. Adler. New York: Macmillan, c1977. xii, 349 p., [16] leaves of plates: ill.; 24 cm. Includes index. 1. Adler, Mortimer Jerome, 1902- 2. Philosophers — United States — Biography. I. T.
B945.A2864 A35      191 B      *LC* 77-1383      *ISBN* 0025004905

**The Philosophy of Brand Blanshard / edited by Paul Arthur** **1.575**
**Schilpp.**
1st ed. — La Salle, Ill.: Open Court, c1980. xviii, 1142 p.: port.; 24 cm. — (The Library of Living philosophers; v. 15) Includes index. 1. Blanshard, Brand, 1892-1987 — Addresses, essays, lectures. I. Blanshard, Brand, 1892-1987. II. Schilpp, Paul Arthur, 1897-
B945.B564 P46      191      *LC* 79-20754      *ISBN* 0875483496

**Burke, Kenneth, 1897-.** • **1.576**
A grammar of motives. — Berkeley: University of California Press, 1969. xxiii, 530 p.; 24 cm. 1. Reasoning 2. Knowledge, Theory of 3. Thought and thinking 4. Semantics I. T.
B945.B773 G7 1969      191      *LC* 69-16741

**Burke, Kenneth, 1897-.** • **1.577**
Permanence & change: an anatomy of purpose / by Kenneth Burke. — 2d. rev. ed. — Los Altos, Calif.: Hermes, 1954. xxiv, 294 p.; 22 cm. 1. Ethics, Evolutionary 2. Motivation (Psychology) 3. Change I. T.
B945.B773 P4 1954      *LC* 53-11195

**The philosophy of Rudolf Carnap / edited by Paul Arthur** • **1.578**
**Schilpp.**
1st ed. — La Salle, Ill.: Open Court, 1963. xvi, 1088 p.: facsim., port. — (Library of living philosophers. v.11) 'Bibliography of the writings of Rudolf Carnap, compiled by Arthur J. Benson.': p.1015-1070. Includes index. 1. Carnap, Rudolf, 1891-1970. I. Schilpp, Paul Arthur, 1897- II. Carnap, Rudolf, 1891-1970. III. Series.
B945.C164 S3      193      *LC* 62-9577

**Cohen, Morris Raphael, 1880-1947.** • **1.579**
The faith of a liberal; selected essays. — Freeport, N.Y.: Books for Libraries Press, [1970, c1946] ix, 497 p.; 23 cm. — (Essay index reprint series) 1. Liberalism I. T.
B945.C53F3 1970      191      *LC* 76-111820      *ISBN* 0836915984

**Cohen, Morris Raphael, 1880-1947.** • **1.580**
Reason and nature; an essay on the meaning of scientific method. — Glencoe, Ill., Free Press [1964, c1959] xxiv, 470 p. 21 cm. — (Free Press paperback edition) Bibliographical footnotes. 1. Methodology 2. Science — Philosophy 3. Social sciences I. T.
B945.C53R4 1964      112      *LC* 53-13311

**Cohen, Morris Raphael, 1880-1947.** • **1.581**
A dreamer's journey; the autobiography of Morris Raphael Cohen. Boston, Beacon Press, 1949. xii, 318 p. ports. 24 cm. I. T.
B945.C54 A3 1949      *LC* 49-7881

**Creighton, James Edwin, 1861-1924.** **1.582**
Studies in speculative philosophy / by James Edwin Creighton; edited, with a select bibliography, by Harold R. Smart. — New York: Kraus Reprint, 1970. 290 p. 1. Philosophy — Addresses, essays, lectures. I. T.
B945.C8 1970

## B945.D4 Dewey

**Dewey, John, 1859-1952.**         **1.583**
The middle works, 1899–1924. — Carbondale: Southern Illinois University Press, 1976-1983. 15 v. — For full information see entry classified at LB875.D34 1976. I. T.

**Dewey, John, 1859-1952.**         **1.584**
The later works, 1925–1953 / John Dewey; edited by Jo Ann Boydston, associate textual editors, Patricia Baysinger, Barbara Levine; with an introd. by Sidney Hook, with a new introd. by John Dewey, edited by Joseph Ratner. — Carbondale: Southern Illinois University Press; London: Feffer & Simons, c1981-<c1984 >. v. <1-5 >; 22 cm. Textual editors and writers of introductions vary from volume to volume. Continues The middle works, 1899-1924. Vol. 4-<5 > have imprint: Carbondale: Southern Illinois University Press. 1. Philosophy — Collected works. I. Boydston, Jo Ann, 1924- II. T.
B945.D41 1981     191 19     *LC* 80-27285     *ISBN* 0809309866

**Dewey, John, 1859-1952.**         • **1.585**
The early works, 1882–1898. Carbondale, Southern Illinois University Press [1967-72. v. 1, 1969] 5 v. port. 21 cm. Continued by: The middle works, 1899-1924. 'Result of a cooperative research project at Southern Illinois University.' I. Southern Illinois University (System) II. T.
B945.D41 I4     150     *LC* 67-13938     *ISBN* 0809304961

**Dewey, John, 1859-1952.**         • **1.586**
Intelligence in the modern world; John Dewey's philosophy, edited, and with an introduction by Joseph Ratner. — New York, The Modern library [1939] xv, 1077 p. 21 cm. — (Half-title: The modern library of the world's best books) 'First Modern library giant edition 1939.' 1. Dewey, John, 1859-1952. I. Ratner, Joseph, 1901- ed. II. T.
B945.D41R17     191.9     *LC* 39-27121

**Bernstein, Richard J.**         • **1.587**
John Dewey [by] Richard J. Bernstein. — New York: Washington Square Press, 1966. ix, 213 p.; 22 cm. — (The Great American thinkers series) 1. Dewey, John, 1859-1952. I. T.
B945.D44 B43     191     *LC* 66-16176

**Dykhuizen, George, 1899-.**         **1.588**
The life and mind of John Dewey. Introd. by Harold Taylor. Edited by Jo Ann Boydston. — Carbondale: Southern Illinois University Press, [1973] xxv, 429 p.: illus.; 25 cm. 1. Dewey, John, 1859-1952. I. T.
B945.D44 D94     191 B     *LC* 73-4602     *ISBN* 0809306166

**Geiger, George Raymond, 1903-.**         • **1.589**
John Dewey in perspective / George R. Geiger. — New York: Oxford University Press, 1958. vi, 248 p. Includes index. 1. Dewey, John, 1859-1952. I. T.
B945D44 G4     B945D44 G4.     191.9     *LC* 58-9463

**Hook, Sidney, 1902-.**         • **1.590**
John Dewey, philosopher of science and freedom; a symposium. New York, Dial Press, 1950. vi, 383 p. 22 cm. W. Sellars.—The analytic and the synthetic; an untenable dualism, by M. G. White.—John Dewey and Karl Marx, by J. Cork,—Dewey in Mexico, by J. T. Farrell.—A selected bibliography of publications by John Dewey (p. 381-382)—Some publications about John Dewey (p. 383) 1. Dewey, John, 1859-1952. I. T.
B945.D44 H473     191.9     *LC* 50-7272

**Dialogue on John Dewey / James T. Farrell...[et al.]; edited by**     • **1.591**
**Corliss Lamont with the assistance of Mary Redmer.**
New York: Horizon Press, 1959. 155 p. 1. Dewey, John, 1859-1952. I. Farrell, James T. (James Thomas), 1904-1979. II. Lamont, Corliss, 1902-
B945.D44 L3     *LC* 59-14697

**Nathanson, Jerome.**         • **1.592**
John Dewey: the reconstruction of the democratic life / Jerome Nathanson. — New York: Scribner, 1951. ix, 127 p. — (Twentieth century library) 1. Dewey, John, 1859-1952. 2. Philosophy, American I. T.
B945.D44N3     191     *LC* 51-6859

**Schilpp, Paul Arthur, 1897- ed.**         • **1.593**
The philosophy of John Dewey. — [2d ed.]. — New York, Tudor Pub. Co. [1951] 718 p. illus. 25 cm. — (Library of living philosophers.) 1. Dewey, John, 1859-1952. I. T. II. Series.
B945.D44S35 1951     191.9     *LC* 51-6324

## B945.E–.I

**Funk, Rainer.**         **1.594**
[Mut zum Menschen. English] Erich Fromm: the courage to be human / Rainer Funk; with a postscript by Erich Fromm; [translated by Michael Shaw]. — New York: Continuum, 1982. xvi, 424 p.; 24 cm. Translation of: Mut zum Menschen. Includes index. 1. Fromm, Erich, 1900- 2. Humanism — History — 20th century. I. T.
B945.F754 F8613 1982     191 19     *LC* 81-22186     *ISBN* 0826400612

**Hook, Sidney, 1902-.**         • **1.595**
The quest for being, and other studies in naturalism and humanism. Westport, Conn., Greenwood Press [1971] 254 p. 23 cm. Reprint of the 1961 ed. 1. Philosophy, Modern — Addresses, essays, lectures. I. T.
B945.H68 1971     191     *LC* 79-139136     *ISBN* 0837157528

## B945.J2 James

**James, William, 1842-1910.**         **1.596**
Essays in philosophy / William James; [edited by Frederick H. Burkhardt, Fredson Bowers, Ignas K. Skrupskelis; introd. by John J. McDermott]. — Cambridge, Mass.: Harvard University Press, 1978. xxxv, 410 p.; 25 cm. — (The works of William James) 1. Philosophy — Addresses, essays, lectures. I. Burkhardt, Frederick, 1912- II. Bowers, Fredson Thayer. III. Skrupskelis, Ignas K., 1938- IV. T.
B945.J23 E66     100     *LC* 77-27361     *ISBN* 0674267125

**James, William, 1842-1910.**         **1.597**
Essays in radical empiricism / William James; [Fredson Bowers, textual editor, Ignas K. Skrupskelis, associate editor; introd. by John J. McDermott]. Cambridge: Harvard University Press, 1976. xlviii, 318 p.: port.; 24 cm. (The works of William James) 1. Experience 2. Pragmatism 3. Philosophy, Modern I. T.
B945.J23 E7 1976     191     *LC* 76-4937     *ISBN* 0674267176

**James, William, 1842-1910.**         **1.598**
The will to believe and other essays in popular philosophy / William James; [edited by Frederick H. Burkhardt, Fredson Bowers, Ignas K. Skrupskelis; introd. by Edward H. Madden]. — Cambridge, Mass.: Harvard University Press, 1979. xxxviii, 490 p.; 24 cm. — (The works of William James) 1. Philosophy — Addresses, essays, lectures. 2. Belief and doubt — Addresses, essays, lectures. I. Burkhardt, Frederick, 1912- II. Bowers, Fredson Thayer. III. Skrupskelis, Ignas K., 1938- IV. T.
B945.J23 W5 1979     100     *LC* 78-5315     *ISBN* 0674952812

**James, William, 1842-1910.**         • **1.599**
The letters of William James, edited by his son, Henry James. Boston, Atlantic Monthly Press [c1920] 2 v. illus., ports., facsim. 25 cm. I. James, Henry, 1879-1947, ed. II. T.
B945.J24 A3 1920     *LC* 20-23198

**Allen, Gay Wilson, 1903-.**         • **1.600**
William James; a biography. — New York: Viking Press, [1967] xx, 556 p.: illus., facsims., geneal. table, ports.; 25 cm. 1. James, William, 1842-1910. I. T.
B945.J24 A63     B945J24 A63.     191 B     *LC* 67-10217

**Levinson, Henry S.**         **1.601**
The religious investigations of William James / Henry Samuel Levinson. — Chapel Hill: University of North Carolina Press, c1981. xii, 311 p.; 24 cm. — (Studies in religion) Includes index. 1. James, William, 1842-1910 — Religion. 2. Religion — Philosophy 3. Experience (Religion) I. T.
B945.J24 L437     201 19     *LC* 80-26109     0807814687

**Moore, Edward C. (Edward Carter), 1917-.**         • **1.602**
William James. — New York: Washington Square Press; [distributed in the U.S. by Affiliated Publishers, 1965] 194 p.; 18 cm. — (The Great American thinkers series) 1. James, William, 1842-1910. I. T.
B945.J24 M57     191     *LC* 65-2183

**Perry, Ralph Barton, 1876-1957.**         • **1.603**
The thought and character of William James, as revealed in unpublished correspondence and notes, together with his published writings, by Ralph Barton Perry. Boston, Little, Brown, and Company, 1935. 2 v. illus. 25 cm. 1. James, William, 1842-1910. I. T.
B945.J24P4     *LC* 35-25802

**Wild, John Daniel, 1902-1972.**         • **1.604**
The radical empiricism of William James [by] John Wild. — [1st ed.]. — Garden City, N.Y.: Doubleday, 1969. xiv, 430 p.; 22 cm. 1. James, William, 1842-1910. 2. Empiricism I. T.
B945.J24 W47     191 19     *LC* 68-27140

## B945.K–.M

**Langer, Susanne Katherina Knauth, 1895-.**         • **1.605**
Philosophical sketches. — [Baltimore]: Johns Hopkins Press, [1962] 190 p.; 22 cm. — I. T.
B945.L273 P45     191     *LC* 62-12570

**Lewis, Clarence Irving, 1883-1964.**                                    • 1.606
Collected papers. Edited by John D. Goheen and John L. Mothershead, Jr. —
Stanford, Calif.: Stanford University Press, 1970. x, 444 p.; 24 cm.
1. Philosophy — Collected works. I. T.
B945.L451G6        108        LC 73-97913        *ISBN* 0804707170

**The Philosophy of C. I. Lewis. Edited by Paul Arthur Schilpp.**        • 1.607
[1st ed.]. — La Salle, Ill., Open Court [1968] xiv, 709 p. facsim., port. 25 cm. —
(Library of living philosophers. v. 13) 1. Lewis, Clarence Irving, 1883-1964 —
Addresses, essays, lectures. I. Lewis, Clarence Irving, 1883-1964. II. Schilpp,
Paul Arthur, 1897- ed. III. Series.
B945.L454 P5        191        LC 67-10007

**Lovejoy, Arthur O. (Arthur Oncken), 1873-1962.**                        • 1.608
Essays in the history of ideas. — Baltimore, Johns Hopkins Press, 1948. xvii,
359 p. 24 cm. 'Published for the History of Ideas Club of the Johns Hopkins
University.' 'Bibliography of the published writings of Arthur O. Lovejoy,
1898-1948': p. 339-344. 1. Philosophy — Addresses, essays, lectures.
2. Literature — Addresses, essays, lectures. I. Johns Hopkins University.
History of Ideas Club. II. T.
B945.L583E7        104        LC 48-8055 *

**McKeon, Richard Peter, 1900-.**                                        1.609
Thought, action, and passion. [Essays. — Chicago] University of Chicago Press
[1954] 304 p. 23 cm. 1. Mann, Thomas, 1875-1955. 2. Philosophy —
Addresses, essays, lectures. I. T.
B945.M287T5        104        LC 54-9579

**Marcuse, Herbert, 1898-.**                                             • 1.610
Negations; essays in critical theory. With translations from the German by
Jeremy J. Shapiro. — Boston: Beacon Press, [1968] xx, 290 p.; 24 cm.
1. Philosophy — Addresses, essays, lectures. 2. Liberalism 3. Industry —
Social aspects I. T.
B945.M2982 E5        191        LC 68-12842

**Kellner, Douglas, 1943-.**                                             1.611
Herbert Marcuse and the crisis of Marxism / Douglas Kellner. — Berkeley:
University of California Press, 1985 (c1984). x, 505 p.: port.; 23 cm. Includes
index. 1. Marcuse, Herbert, 1898- 2. Philosophy, Marxist 3. Fascism
4. Communism I. T.
B945.M2984 K44 1984        335.4/1 19        LC 84-69        *ISBN* 0520051769

**Mead, George Herbert.**                                                • 1.612
Selected writings. Ed. with an introd. by Andrew J. Reck. Indianapolis, Bobbs-
Merrill, c1964. 416 p. (Library of liberal arts, no.177) 1. Philosophers,
American 2. Philosophy — Collected works I. T.
B945.M461R4        LC 64-16708

**Mead, George Herbert, 1863-1931.**                                     • 1.613
The philosophy of the act, by George Herbert Mead, edited, with introduction,
by Charles W. Morris, in collaboration with John M. Brewster, Albert M.
Dunham [and] David L. Miller. — Chicago, Ill.: The University of Chicago
press, [1938] lxxxiv, 696 p.: front. (port.); 24 cm. 'This volume consists almost
entirely of unpublished papers which George H. Mead left at his death in
1931.'—Pref. 1. Knowledge, Theory of 2. Science — Philosophy
3. Cosmology 4. Values 5. Act (Philosophy) I. Morris, Charles William,
1901- ed. II. Brewster, John Monroe, 1904- joint ed. III. Dunham, Albert
Millard, 1906- joint ed. IV. Miller, David L., 1903- joint ed. V. T.
B945.M463 P4        191.9        LC 38-15971

**Mead, George Herbert, 1863-1931.**                                     • 1.614
The philosophy of the present / by George Herbert Mead; edited by Arthur E.
Murphy, with prefatory remarks by John Dewey. — Chicago: Open Court,
1932. xl, 199 p.: ill.; 24 cm. — (Lectures upon the Paul Carus foundation.)
1. Philosophy — Addresses, essays, lectures. I. Murphy, Arthur E. II. T.
B945.M463 P5        LC 32-19616

**Mead, George Herbert, 1863-1931.**                                     • 1.615
[Social psychology of George Herbert Mead] On social psychology; selected
papers. Edited and with an introd. by Anselm Strauss. [Rev. ed] Chicago,
University of Chicago Press [1964] xxv, 358 p. 21 cm. (The Heritage of
sociology) First published in 1956 under title: the social psychology of George
Herbert Mead. I. T.
B945.M463 S6 1964        301.15        LC 64-23419

**Miller, David L., 1903-.**                                            1.616
George Herbert Mead: self, language, and the world, by David L. Miller. —
Austin: University of Texas Press, [1973] xxxviii, 280 p.: illus.; 23 cm. 1. Mead,
George Herbert, 1863-1931. I. T.
B945.M464 M53 1973        191 19        LC 72-3098        *ISBN* 0292727003

**Otto, Max Carl, 1876-.**                                              1.617
The human enterprise; an attempt to relate philosophy to daily life. New York,
F. S. Crofts & co., 1940. ix p., l., 385 p. 21 cm. I. T.
B945.O73 H8        LC 40-6898

**Otto, Max Carl, 1876-.**                                              1.618
Things and ideals, essays in functional philosophy, by M. C. Otto. New York,
Kraus Reprint, 1970. xi, [1], 320 p. 21 cm. Reprint of New York, Holt [c1924]
edition 1. Philosophy, Modern 2. Idealism 3. Ethics 4. Science — Philosophy
I. T.
B945.O73 T5 1970

## B945.P4 Peirce

**Peirce, Charles S. (Charles Sanders), 1839-1914.**                    1.619
[Works. 1982] Writings of Charles S. Peirce: a chronological edition / Max H.
Fisch, general editor. — Bloomington: Indiana University Press,
c1982- <c1984 > . v. <1-2 > : ill.; 24 cm. Includes indexes. 1. Philosophy —
Collected works. I. Fisch, Max Harold, 1900- II. T.
B945.P4 1982        191 19        LC 79-1993        *ISBN* 0253372011

**Knight, Thomas Stanley, 1921-.**                                      1.620
Charles Peirce [by] Thomas S. Knight. New York, Washington Square Press
[1965] vi, 200 p. illus. 18 cm. (The Great American thinkers series) 'W885.'
Bibliography: p. 192-194. 1. Peirce, Charles S. (Charles Sanders), 1839-1914.
I. T.
B945.P4K6        191        LC 65-2960

**Peirce, Charles S. (Charles Sanders), 1839-1914.**                    1.621
Charles Sanders Peirce: contributions to The Nation / compiled and annotated
by Kenneth Laine Ketner and James Edward Cook. — Lubbock: Texas Tech
Press, 1975-. v.; 26 cm. (Graduate studies - Texas Tech University; no. 10, 16
0082-3198) I. Nation. II. T.
B945.P41 1975        191        LC 76-621710

**Peirce, Charles S. (Charles Sanders), 1839-1914.**                    • 1.622
[Philosophy of Peirce] Philosophical writings of Peirce, selected and edited with
an introd. by Justus Buchler. New York, Dover Publications [1955] 386 p. illus.
21 cm. 'An unabridged and unaltered republication of the book first published
in 1940 under the title 'The philosophy of Peirce: selected writings." I. T.
B945.P41 B8 1955        191.9        LC 56-13549

**Peirce, Charles S. (Charles Sanders), 1839-1914.**                    • 1.623
Essays in the philosophy of science. Edited with an introd. by Vincent Tomas.
— New York, Liberal Arts Press [1957] 271 p. 21 cm. — (The American
heritage series, no. 17) Includes bibliography. 1. Philosophy — Collected
works. I. T.
B945.P41T6        191.9        LC 57-2087

**Peirce, Charles S. (Charles Sanders), 1839-1914.**                    • 1.624
Values in a universe of chance; selected writings of Charles S. Peirce ... Edited,
with an introd. and notes, by Philip P. Wiener. — [1st ed.]. — Garden City, N.
Y., Doubleday, 1958. 446 p. illus. 18 cm. Includes bibliography. I. T.
B945.P41W5        191.9        LC 58-5585

**Peirce, Charles S. (Charles Sanders), 1839-1914.**                    • 1.625
Chance, love, and logic; philosophical essays. Edited with an introd. by Morris
R. Cohen. With a supplementary essay on the pragmatism of Peirce by John
Dewey. New York, Barnes & Noble [1968, c1923] xxxiii, 318 p. 22 cm.
1. Peirce, Charles S. (Charles Sanders), 1839-1914 — Bibliography.
2. Philosophy — Addresses, essays, lectures. I. T.
B945.P43 C5 1968        191        LC 68-23762

**Bernstein, Richard J. ed.**                                           • 1.626
Perspectives on Peirce; critical essays on Charles Sanders Peirce, edited by
Richard J. Bernstein. — New Haven, Yale University Press, 1965. ix, 148 p. 23
cm. Bibliographical footnotes. 1. Peirce, Charles S. (Charles Sanders),
1839-1914. I. T.
B945.P44B4        191        LC 65-12539

**Buchler, Justus, 1914-.**                                             • 1.627
Charles Peirce's empiricism; by Justus Buchler with a foreword by Ernest
Nagel. New York, Harcourt, Brace and company; London, K. Paul, Trench,
Trubner & co. ltd., 1939. viii, 275 p. (International library of psychology,
philosophy, and scientific method.) I. T. II. Series.
B945.P44 B8 1939        LC 40-4294

**Feibleman, James Kern, 1904-.**                                       1.628
[Introduction to Peirce's philosophy] An introduction to the philosophy of
Charles S. Peirce, interpreted as a system, by James K. Feibleman. Cambridge,
Mass., M.I.T. Press [1970, c1946] xxiv, 503 p. 21 cm. First published in 1946
under title: An introduction to Peirce's philosophy. 1. Peirce, Charles S.
(Charles Sanders), 1839-1914. I. T.
B945.P44 F4 1970        191        LC 71-97496        *ISBN* 0262060353

**Gallie, W. B., 1912-.**                                               • 1.629
Peirce and pragmatism / W. B. Gallie. — Harmondsworth, Middlesex: Penguin
Books, 1952. 247 p.; 18 cm. — (Pelican books; A254) (Pelican philosophy
series) 1. Peirce, Charles S. (Charles Sanders), 1839-1914. 2. Pragmatism I. T.
B945.P44 G3        191.9        LC 53-3033

Wiener, Philip Paul, 1905- ed.                • 1.630
Studies in the philosophy of Charles Sanders Peirce, edited by Philip P. Wiener and Frederic H. Young. — Cambridge, Harvard University Press, 1952-[64] 2 v. ports. 25 cm. Vol. 2 edited by Edward C. Moore and Richard S. Robin, has imprint: Amherst, University of Massachusetts Press. Includes bibliographical references. 1. Peirce, Charles S. (Charles Sanders), 1839-1914. I. Young, Frederic Harold, 1905- ed. II. Moore, Edward C. (Edward Carter), 1917- ed. III. Robin, Richard S., ed. IV. T.
B945.P44W5    191.9    LC 52-5411

## B945.Q–.R

Quine, W. V. (Willard Van Orman)              1.631
The ways of paradox, and other essays / W. V. Quine. — Rev. and enl. ed. — Cambridge, Mass.: Harvard University Press, 1976. x, 335 p.; 22 cm. Includes index. 1. Philosophy — Addresses, essays, lectures. I. T.
B945.Q51 1976    191    LC 76-4200    ISBN 0674948351. ISBN 0674948378 pbk

Davidson, Donald, 1917-.                      • 1.632
Words and objections. Essays on the work of W. V. Quine. Edited by Donald Davidson and Jaakko Hintikka. Dordrecht, D. Reidel [1969] vii, 366 p. 23 cm. (Synthese library) 'Publications of W. V. Quine': p. 353-366. First appeared in Synthese, vol. 19, nos. 1-2. 1. Quine, W. V. (Willard Van Orman) Word and object. I. Quine, W. V. (Willard Van Orman) Word and object. II. Hintikka, Jaakko, 1929- joint author. III. Synthese. IV. T.
B945.Q54 D38 1969    149/.94/0924    LC 79-495176

Gibson, Roger F.                              1.633
The philosophy of W.V. Quine: an expository essay / Roger F. Gibson, Jr.; with a foreword by W.V. Quine. — Tampa: University Presses of Florida, c1982. xx, 218 p.: port.; 24 cm. 'A University of South Florida book.' Includes index. 1. Quine, W. V. (Willard Van Orman) I. T.
B945.Q54 G5 1982    191 19    LC 81-16338    ISBN 0813007070

Randall, John Herman, 1899-.                  • 1.634
Nature and historical experience: essays in naturalism and in the theory of history. — New York: Columbia University Press, 1958. viii, 308 p. 25 cm. 1. History — Philosophy 2. Naturalism I. T.
B945.R253 N3    901    LC 57-11694

## B945.R6 Royce

Royce, Josiah, 1855-1916.                     • 1.635
The religious philosophy of Josiah Royce; edited, with an introductory essay, by Stuart Gerry Brown. [Syracuse, N.Y.] Syracuse University Press, 1952. 239 p. 1. Religion — Philosophy 2. Philosophy, American — 19th century I. Brown, Stuart Gerry, 1911-, ed. II. T.
B945.R61 B7    LC 52-41521

Royce, Josiah, 1855-1916.                     1.636
The philosophy of Josiah Royce. Edited and with an introd. by John K. Roth. — New York: Crowell, [1971] viii, 421 p.; 22 cm. 1. Philosophy — Addresses, essays, lectures. 2. Religion — Philosophy — Addresses, essays, lectures. 3. Ethics — Addresses, essays, lectures. I. Roth, John K. ed. II. T.
B945.R61 R67 1971    191    LC 76-146287    ISBN 0690618395

Royce, Josiah, 1855-1916.                     1.637
William James and other essays on the philosophy of life, by Josiah Royce. New York, The Macmillan company, 1911. xi, 301 p. 20 cm. 1. James, William, 1842-1910. 2. Ethics 3. Christianity 4. Truth 5. Immortality I. T.
B945.R63 W5    LC 11-28098

Royce, Josiah, 1855-1916.                     • 1.638
The world and the individual. With an introd. by John E. Smith. — New York: Dover Publications, [1959] 2 v.; 21 cm. 1. Natural theology 2. Ontology 3. Reality I. T.
B945.R63 W7 1959    111    LC 59-14226

Fuss, Peter Lawrence, 1932-.                  • 1.639
The moral philosophy of Josiah Royce [by] Peter Fuss. — Cambridge, Mass., Harvard University Press, 1965. xv, 272 p. 22 cm. 'Revised version of [the author's] doctoral dissertation at Harvard University in 1962.' Bibliography: p. [265]-268. 1. Royce, Josiah, 1855-1916. I. T.
B945.R64F8    171    LC 65-11590

Marcel, Gabriel, 1889-1973.                   • 1.640
Royce's metaphysics. Translated by Virginia and Gordon Ringer. — Chicago, H. Regnery Co., 1956. 180 p. 22 cm. 1. Royce, Josiah, 1855-1916. 2. Metaphysics I. T.
B945.R64M33    191.9    LC 56-11854 rev

Powell, Thomas F.                             • 1.641
Josiah Royce [by] Thomas F. Powell. — New York: Washington Square Press, [1967] 260 p.; 18 cm. — (The Great American thinkers series) 1. Royce, Josiah, 1855-1916. I. T.
B945.R64 P6    191    LC 68-1862

Royce, Josiah, 1855-1916.                     1.642
The religious aspect of philosophy; a critique of the bases of conduct and of faith, by Josiah Royce ... Gloucester, Mass., Peter Smith, 1965. xix, 484 p. 19.5 cm. 'Reprint of the 1885 edition.' 1. Philosophy and religion I. T.
B945.R83R3 1965    LC 10-29062

## B945.S2 Santayana

Santayana, George, 1863-1952.                 • 1.643
The philosophy of Santayana, edited, with an introductory essay, by Irwin Edman. [New York] The Modern Library [1942] lvi, 596 p. 19 cm. (The Modern Library of the world's best books) I. Edman, Irwin, 1896-1954. II. T.
B945.S21 1942    LC 42-36370

Santayana, George, 1863-1952.                 • 1.644
Character and opinion in the United States. — Garden City, N.Y.: Doubleday, 1956. 144 p. — (Doubleday anchor books; A73) 1. James, William, 1842-1910. 2. Royce, Josiah, 1855-1916. 3. United States — Civilization I. T.
B945.S23 C5

Santayana, George, 1863-1952.                 • 1.645
Dialogues in limbo, with three new dialogues. — [Ann Arbor] University of Michigan Press [1957, c1948] 248 p. 21 cm. I. T.
B945.S23 D5x    191.9    LC 57-687

Santayana, George, 1863-1952.                 • 1.646
The life of reason; or, The phases of human progress. — One-volume ed., rev. by the author in collaboration with Daniel Cory. — [New York, Scribner, 1954 [i. e. 1953] 504 p. 24 cm. 1. Philosophy I. T.
B945.S23L7 1953    191.9    LC 54-477

Santayana, George, 1863-1952.                 • 1.647
Realms of being. — One-volume ed., with a new introd. by the author. — New York: Cooper Square Publishers, 1972 [c1942] xxxii, 862 p.; 24 cm. 'Compact edition ... originally issued in four separate volumes at intervals of years.' 1. Ontology 2. Matter 3. Truth 4. Consciousness I. T.
B945.S23 R42 1972    111    LC 72-79638    ISBN 0815404255

Santayana, George, 1863-1952.                 • 1.648
Scepticism and animal faith; introduction to a system of philosophy. — [New York]: Dover Publications, [1955] xii, 314 p.; 21 cm. 1. Skepticism 2. Belief and doubt I. T.
B945.S23 S3 1955    191.9    LC 55-14672

Santayana, George, 1863-1952.                 • 1.649
Winds of doctrine, and Platonism and the spiritual life. — New York, Harper [1957] 312 p. 21 cm. 1. Philosophy, Modern 2. Spiritual life I. T. II. Title: Platonism and the spiritual life.
B945.S23W7 1957    191.9    LC 57-10533

Cory, Daniel, 1904-.                          • 1.650
Santayana; the later years: a portrait with letters. — New York: G. Braziller, 1963. 330 p.; 24 cm. 1. Santayana, George, 1863-1952. 2. Philosophers — United States — Biography. I. T.
B945.S24 C65    LC 63-19573

Schilpp, Paul Arthur, 1897- ed.               • 1.651
The philosophy of George Santayana. [2d ed.] New York, Tudor Pub. Co. [1951] 710 p. illus. 25 cm. (The Library of living philosophers) 1. Santayana, George, 1863-1952. I. T.
B945.S24 S35 1951    191.9    LC 51-6325

## B945.T–.Z

Weiss, Paul, 1901-.                           • 1.652
Modes of being. — Carbondale: Southern Illinois University Press, 1958. xi, 617 p.; 24 cm. 1. Philosophy I. T.
B945.W396 M6 1958    191.9    LC 57-11877

Woodbridge, Frederick James Eugene, 1867-1940.    • 1.653
An essay on nature, by Frederick J. E. Woodbridge. New York, Columbia University Press, 1940. x p., 2β., [3]-351p. 23cm. I. T.
B945.W63E7    113    LC 40-36191

Jones, William Frank.                         1.654
Nature and natural science: the philosophy of Frederick J.E. Woodbridge / by William Frank Jones. — Buffalo, N.Y.: Prometheus Books, 1983. 197 p., [1]

leaf of plates: ill.; 22 cm. Includes index. 1. Woodbridge, Frederick James Eugene, 1867-1940. I. T.
B945.W64 J66 1983     191 19     *LC* 82-48969     *ISBN* 0879751835

**Wright, Chauncey, 1830-1875.**               **1.655**
Philosophical writings; representative selections. Edited with an introd., by Edward H. Madden. New York, Liberal Arts Press [1958] 145 p. 21 cm. (American heritage series; 23) 1. Philosophy — Collected works. I. T. II. Series.
B 945 W71 M17 1958     *LC* 58-9962

**Madden, Edward H.**               • **1.656**
Chauncey Wright. New York, Washington Square Press [1964] 170 p. 18 cm. (The Great American thinkers series) 'W878.' 'Annotated bibliography': p. 149-164. 1. Wright-Chauncey, 1830-1875. I. T.
B945.W74M29     191     *LC* 64-2594

**Madden, Edward H.**               • **1.657**
Chauncey Wright and the foundations of pragmatism. Seattle, University of Washington Press, 1963. vii, 203 p. illus. 23 cm. Includes bibliography. 1. Wright, Chauncey, 1830-1875. I. T.
B945.W74M3     191     *LC* 63-9939

# B1001–1084 Latin America

**Davis, Harold Eugene, 1902-.**          **1.658**
Latin American thought; a historical introduction. — Baton Rouge: Louisiana State University Press, [1972] ix, 269 p.; 24 cm. 1. Philosophy, Latin American I. T.
B1001.D38     199/.8     *LC* 78-181564     *ISBN* 0807102490

**Stabb, Martin S.**               **1.659**
In quest of identity; patterns in the Spanish American essay of ideas, 1890–1960 [by] Martin S. Stabb. — Chapel Hill: University of North Carolina Press, 1967. 244 p.; 24 cm. 1. Philosophy, Latin American 2. Latin America in literature. 3. Spanish American essays — History and criticism. I. T.
B1001.S65     199/.8     *LC* 67-27160

**Zea, Leopoldo, 1912-.**             • **1.660**
[Dos etapas del pensamiento en Hispanoamérica. English] The Latin–American mind. Translated from the Spanish by James H. Abbott and Lowell Dunham. [1st ed.] Norman, University of Oklahoma Press [1963] 308 p. 24 cm. Translation of Dos etapas del pensamiento en Hispanoamérica. 1. Philosophy, Spanish American. 2. Positivism I. T.
B1001.Z423     199.8     *LC* 63-9955

**Mexico (City). Universidad Nacional. Consejo Técnico de**   **1.661**
**Humanidades.**
Major trends in Mexican philosophy. [Pref. by] Mario de la Cueva. [Contributors]: Miguel Léon–Portilla [and others] Translated by A. Robert Caponigri. — Notre Dame, University of Notre Dame Press [1966] x, 328 p. 23 cm. Translation of Estudios de historia de la filosofia en México. Studies prepared on the occasion of the Thirteenth International Congress of Philosophy at the invitation of the Consejo Técnico de Humanidades. 1. Philosophy, Mexican I. León Portilla, Miguel. II. Caponigri, Aloysius Robert, 1913- tr. III. International Congress of Philosophy, 13th, Mexico, 1963. IV. T.
B1016.M413     199.72     *LC* 66-14624

**Zea, Leopoldo, 1912-.**             **1.662**
[Positivismo en México. English] Positivism in Mexico. Translated by Josephine H. Schulte. Austin, University of Texas Press [1974] xxiii, 241 p. 23 cm. (Texas pan-American series) 1. Positivism 2. Philosophy, Mexican 3. Mexico — Intellectual life I. T.
B1018.P6 Z413     199/72     *LC* 74-549     *ISBN* 0292764138

**Cruz Costa, João.**               **1.663**
[Desenvolvimento da filosofia no Brasil. English] A history of ideas in Brazil; the development of philosophy in Brazil and the evolution of national history. Translated from the Portuguese by Suzette Macedo. Berkeley, University of California Press, 1964. x, 427 p. 25 cm. Translation of Contribuição a história das idéias no Brasil: o desenvolvimento da filosofia no Brasil e a evolução historica nacional, published as no. 86 of the collection of Documentos Brasileiros. 1. Philosophy, Brazilian I. T.
B1041.C693     199.81     *LC* 64-16081

# B1111–1674 Great Britain

**Mehta, Ved, 1934-.**              **1.664**
Fly and the fly-bottle. [1st ed.] Boston, Little, Brown [1962] 269 p. 21 cm. 1. Philosophers — Great Britain 2. Historians, British. I. T.
B1111.M4     *LC* 63-12097

# B1131–1299 17TH CENTURY

## B1150–1199 Bacon

**Bacon, Francis, viscount St. Albans.**        • **1.665**
Essays; Advancement of learning, New Atlantis, and other pieces; as selected and edited by Richard Foster Jones. 1st ed., Garden City, New York: Doubleday-Doran, 1937. xxxiv, 491 p., 19 cm. (Doubleday-Doran series in literature.) 1. Science — Methodology 2. Logic 3. Utopias I. Jones, Richard Foster, ed. II. T. III. Series.
B1155 1937a     192.1     *LC* 37-27481

**Bacon, Francis, 1561-1626.**           • **1.666**
Selected writings. With an introd. and notes by Hugh G. Dick. New York, Modern Library [1955] xxxii, 604 p. 19 cm. (The Modern library of the world's best books [256]) 1. Philosophy — Collected works. I. T.
B1155 1955     192.1     *LC* 55-6393

**Bacon, Francis, 1561-1626.**           • **1.667**
The New organon, and related writings. Edited with an introd. by Fulton H. Anderson. — New York, Liberal Arts Press [1960] 292 p. 21 cm. — (The Library of liberal arts, no. 97) 1. Science — Methodology I. Anderson, Fulton Henry, 1895- ed. II. T.
B1168.E5A5     112     *LC* 59-11682 rev 2

**Bacon, Francis, 1561-1626.**           **1.668**
[Advancement of learning. Book 1] The advancement of learning: book 1 / [by] Francis Bacon; edited by William A. Armstrong. — London: Athlone Press, 1975. [6], 153 p.; 21 cm. — (Athlone Renaissance library) Distributed in the U.S.A. by Humanities Press, Atlantic Highlands, N.J. 1. Science — Methodology 2. Logic — Early works to 1800. I. Armstrong, William A. II. T.
B1190 1975     121     *LC* 79-322749     *ISBN* 0485136058

**Anderson, Fulton Henry, 1895-.**         • **1.669**
Francis Bacon: his career and his thought. — [Los Angeles] University of Southern California Press [1962] 367 p. 22 cm. — (The Arensberg lectures, 1957) 'An enlargement of a series of lectures delivered at the University of Southern California.' 1. Bacon, Francis, 1561-1626. I. T. II. Series.
B1197.A5     *LC* 61-14339

## B1203–1248 Hobbes

**Hobbes, Thomas, 1588-1679.**          • **1.670**
The English works of Thomas Hobbes of Malmesbury / now first collected and edited by Sir William Molesworth, Bart. — London: J. Bohn, 1839-1845. 11 v.: ill., port. 1. Philosophy — Collected works. 2. Political science — Collected works. I. Molesworth, William, Sir, 1810-1855. II. T.
B1203 1839     *LC* 10-29074

**Hobbes, Thomas, 1588-1679.**          • **1.671**
Selections. Edited by Frederick J.E.Woodbridge. New York Chicago [etc.] Scribner, [c1930]. xxx,418p.,bibl. (Modern student's library. Philosophy series.) At head of title: Hobbes. I. Woodbridge, Frederick James Eugene, 1867-1940. ed. II. T. III. Series.
B1205 1930     192.9     *LC* 30-14676

**Cranston, Maurice William, 1920- comp.**     **1.672**
Hobbes and Rousseau: a collection of critical essays. Edited by Maurice Cranston and Richard S. Peters. [1st ed.] Garden City, N.Y., Anchor Books, 1972. ix, 505 p. 18 cm. (Modern studies in philosophy) 1. Hobbes, Thomas, 1588-1679 — Addresses, essays, lectures. 2. Rousseau, Jean-Jacques, 1712-1778 — Addresses, essays, lectures. I. Peters, R. S. (Richard Stanley), 1919- joint comp. II. T.
B1247.C7     192     *LC* 77-168283

## B1253–1298 Locke

**Locke, John, 1632-1704.**           • **1.673**
Essays on the law of nature. The Latin text, with a translation, introd. and notes, together with transcripts of Locke's shorthand in his journal for 1676. Edited by W. von Leyden. Oxford Clarendon Press [1965] 292p. 1. Natural law — Addresses, essays, lectures I. T.
B1255 L4 1965

**Locke, John, 1632-1704.**           **1.674**
An essay concerning human understanding / John Locke; edited with an introd., critical apparatus and glossary by Peter H. Nidditch. — Oxford: Clarendon Press, 1975. liv, 867 p.: port.; 23 cm. (The Clarendon edition of the works of John Locke) Includes index. 1. Knowledge, Theory of I. Nidditch, P. H. II. T.
B1290 1975     121     *LC* 75-316096

**Jenkins, John J.**                                                    **1.675**
Understanding Locke: an introduction to philosophy through John Locke's Essay / John J. Jenkins. — Edinburgh: University Press, c1983. xviii, 256 p.; 20 cm. Includes index. 1. Locke, John, 1632-1704. Essay concerning human understanding 2. Knowledge, Theory of — Early works to 1800. I. T.
B1294.J46 1983          121 19          LC 83-151780          ISBN 0852244495

**Mackie, J. L. (John Leslie)**                                        **1.676**
Problems from Locke / by J. L. Mackie. — Oxford [Eng.]: Clarendon Press, 1976. ix, 237 p.; 23 cm. Includes index. 1. Locke, John, 1632-1704. An essay concerning human understanding. 2. Knowledge, Theory of 3. Perception 4. Substance (Philosophy) I. T.
B1294.M18          121          LC 76-365002          ISBN 0198245556

**Yolton, John W.**                                                  **• 1.677**
Locke and the compass of human understanding; a selective commentary on the Essay [by] John W. Yolton. — Cambridge [Eng.]: University Press, 1970. x, 234 p.; 22 cm. 1. Locke, John, 1632-1704. An essay concerning human understanding. I. Locke, John, 1632-1704. An essay concerning human understanding. II. T.
B1294.Y64 1970          121          LC 76-112477          ISBN 0521078385

**Aaron, Richard Ithamar, 1901-.**                                   **• 1.678**
John Locke, by Richard I. Aaron. — 3rd ed. — Oxford: Clarendon Press, 1971. xiv, 383 p.; 23 cm. 1. Locke, John, 1632-1704. I. T.
B1296.A62 1971          192          LC 79-586664          ISBN 0198243553

**Dunn, John, 1940-.**                                                  **1.679**
Locke / John Dunn. — Oxford [Oxfordshire]; New York: Oxford University Press, 1984. xii, 97 p.; 18 cm. (Past masters.) Includes index. 1. Locke, John, 1632-1704. I. T. II. Series.
B1297.D86 1984          192 19          LC 83-13169          ISBN 0192875604

**Woolhouse, R. S.**                                                    **1.680**
Locke / R.S. Woolhouse. — Minneapolis: University of Minnesota Press, c1983. 198 p.; 23 cm. — (Philosophers in context. [no 1]) 1. Locke, John, 1632-1704. I. T. II. Series.
B1297.W66 1983          121 19          LC 84-114699          ISBN 0816612498

**Yolton, John W.**                                                  **• 1.681**
John Locke and the way of ideas, by John W. Yolton. — Oxford: Clarendon Press, 1968. x, 235 p.; 23 cm. Bibliography: p. [209]-232. 1. Locke, John, 1632-1704. I. T.
B1297.Y6 1968          121          LC 76-389586          ISBN 0198243316

**Yolton, John W.**                                                  **• 1.682**
John Locke: problems and perspectives; a collection of new essays; edited by John W. Yolton. — London: Cambridge U.P., 1969. vii, 278 p.; 24 cm. 1. Locke, John, 1632-1704 — Addresses, essays, lectures. I. T.
B1297.Y63          192          LC 69-10435          ISBN 0521073499

## B1300–1559 18TH CENTURY

**Stephen, Leslie, Sir, 1832-1904.**                                 **• 1.683**
History of English thought in the eighteenth century. With a new pref. by Crane Brinton. — New York, Harcourt, Brace & World [1963, c1962] 2 v. 21 cm. 1. Philosophy, English I. T.
B1301.S8 1963          192          LC 62-20104

**Willey, Basil, 1897-.**                                            **• 1.684**
The eighteenth century background: studies on the idea of nature in the thought of the period / by Basil Willey. — New York: Columbia University Press, 1977. viii, 301, [1] p., 1 l.; 23 cm. Includes index. 1. Eighteenth century 2. Natural theology 3. Natural law 4. Naturalism in literature 5. English literature — 18th century — History and criticism. I. T.
B1301.W5 1977          192          LC 43-7255

**Yolton, John W.**                                                    **1.685**
Thinking matter: materialism in eighteenth–century Britain / by John W. Yolton. — Minneapolis: University of Minnesota Press, c1983. xiv, 238 p.; 24 cm. Includes index. 1. Materialism — History — Addresses, essays, lectures. 2. Philosophy, English — 18th century — Addresses, essays, lectures. I. T.
B1302.M37 Y64 1983          146/.3/0941 19          LC 83-6507          ISBN 0816611602

## B1303–1385 Berkeley. Shaftesbury

**Berkeley, George, 1685-1753.**                                     **• 1.686**
Berkeley's Philosophical writings. Edited with an introd. by David M. Armstrong. — 1st ed. — New York, Collier Books 1965. 384 p. illus. 18 cm. — (Collier classics in the history of thought) A Collier books original. 1. Philosophy — Collected works. I. Armstrong, D. M. (David Malet), 1926- ed. II. T.
B1303 1965          192          LC 64-22680

**Berkeley, George, 1685-1753.**                                     **• 1.687**
Works on vision. Edited, with a commentary, by Colin Murray Turbayne. — Indianapolis, Bobbs-Merrill [1963] lii, 158 p. illus. 21 cm. — (The Library of liberal arts, 83) Bibliography: p. xlvii—l. 1. Vision — Collected works. 2. Knowledge, Theory of — Collected works. I. T.
B1305.T8          192          LC 62-11787

**Berkeley, George, 1685-1753.**                                     **• 1.688**
Three dialogues between Hylas and Philonous; edited with an introd. by Colin M. Turbayne. New York, Liberal Arts Press [1954] 113 p. 21 cm. (Library of liberal arts, no. 39) 1. Idealism 2. Soul I. T.
B1325 1954          192.3          LC 55-35831

**Berkeley, George, 1685-1753.**                                     **• 1.689**
A treatise concerning the principles of human knowledge. Edited with an introd. by Colin M. Turbayne. — New York, Liberal Arts Press [1957] xxiv, 104 p. 21 cm. — (The Library of liberal arts, no. 53) Bibliography: p. xxiii-xxiv. 1. Knowledge, Theory of 2. Idealism I. T.
B1331.T8          192.3          LC 57-1290

**Gaustad, Edwin Scott.**                                              **1.690**
George Berkeley in America / Edwin S. Gaustad. — New Haven: Yale University Press, 1979. xi, 225 p., [1] leaf of plates: ill.; 22 cm. 1. Berkeley, George, 1685-1753 — Homes and haunts — Rhode Island — Newport. 2. Philosophers — England — Biography. 3. United States — Civilization — To 1783 I. T.
B1347.G38 1979          192 B          LC 79-64076          ISBN 0300023944

**Berkeley: critical and interpretive essays / Colin M. Turbayne,**    **1.691**
**editor.**
Minneapolis: University of Minnesota Press, c1982. xii, 340 p.; 24 cm. 'Some of the papers delivered at the Berkeley Commemorative Conference held at Newport, Rhode Island, from September 27 to 30, 1979'—P. xi. Includes index. 1. Berkeley, George, 1685-1753 — Addresses, essays, lectures. I. Turbayne, Colin Murray.
B1348.B44 1982          192 19          LC 82-1967          ISBN 0816610657

**Bracken, Harry McFarland, 1926-.**                                   **1.692**
Berkeley / Harry M. Bracken. — New York: St. Martin's Press, 1974. 173 p.; 21 cm. 1. Berkeley, George, 1685-1753. I. T.
B1348.B7 1974          192          LC 74-15569

**Urmson, J. O.**                                                      **1.693**
Berkeley / J.O. Urmson. — Oxford; New York: Oxford University Press, 1982. 90 p.; 18 cm. — (Past masters.) Includes index. 1. Berkeley, George, 1685-1753. I. T. II. Series.
B1348.U75 1982          192 19          LC 82-203281          ISBN 0192875469

**Pitcher, George.**                                                   **1.694**
Berkeley / George Pitcher. — London; Boston: Routledge & Kegan Paul, 1977. xi, 277 p.: ill.; 24 cm. — (The Arguments of the philosophers) Includes index. 1. Berkeley, George, 1685-1753 — Metaphysics. 2. Mind and body 3. Obedience I. T.
B1349.M47 P57          192          LC 77-30062          ISBN 0710086857

**Shaftesbury, Anthony Ashley Cooper, Earl of, 1671-1713.**          **• 1.695**
Characteristics of men, manners, opinions, times. Edited, with notes, by John M. Robertson. With an introd. by Stanley Green. Indianapolis, Bobbs-Merrill [1964] 2v. in 1 21 cm. (Library of liberal arts. 179) Cover title: Characteristics. 1. Ethics 2. Characters and characteristics I. Robertson, J. M. (John Mackinnon), 1856-1933. ed. II. T. III. Title: Characteristics. IV. Series.
B1385.A3 R6          LC 64-16707

## B1401–1559 SCOTTISH PHILOSOPHY

**The Origins of the Scottish enlightenment / [compiled by] Jane**     **1.696**
**Randall.**
New York: St. Martin's Press, 1979 (c1978). vii, 257 p.; 23 cm. Includes index. 1. Philosophy, Scottish — 18th century 2. Enlightenment — History. 3. Scotland — Intellectual life. I. Rendall, Jane, 1945-
B1402.E55 O74          941.107          LC 78-16552          ISBN 0312588666

## B1450–1499 Hume

**Hume, David, 1711-1776.**                                            **1.697**
[Philosophical essays concerning human understanding] Enquiries concerning human understanding and concerning the principles of morals / by David Hume; reprinted from the posthumous edition of 1777 and edited with introd., comparative table of contents, and analytical index by L. A. Selby-Bigge. — 3d ed. / with text revised and notes by P. H. Nidditch. — Oxford: Clarendon Press, 1975. xl, 417 p.; 19 cm. Reprint of the 2d volume of Essays and treatises on several subjects. 1. Knowledge, Theory of 2. Ethics I. Selby-Bigge, L. A.

(Lewis Amherst), Sir, 1860-1951. II. Nidditch, P. H. III. Hume, David, 1711-1776. Enquiry concerning the principles of morals. 1975. IV. T.
B1455.A5 1975    192    *LC* 75-327338    *ISBN* 0198245351. *ISBN* 019824536X pbk

**Hume, David, 1711-1776.**      • **1.698**
Of the standard of taste and other essays / David Hume; edited, with an introd., by John W. Lenz. — Indianapolis: Bobbs-Merrill, c1965. xxviii, 183 p.; 21 cm. — (The Library of liberal arts) 1. Philosophy — Collected works. 2. Aesthetics — Early works to 1800. 3. Taste I. Lenz, John W. II. T.
B1455.L4    192    *LC* 64-66070

**Flew, Antony, 1923-.**      • **1.699**
Hume's philosophy of belief; a study of his first Inquiry. London, Routledge & Paul; New York, Humanities Press [1961] 286 p. 23 cm. (International library of philosophy and scientific method) 1. Hume, David, 1711-1776. Philosophical essays concerning human understanding I. T.
B1484.F5 1961a    *LC* 62-51959

**Hume, David, 1711-1776.**      • **1.700**
A treatise of human nature / by David Hume; edited with an analytical index by L. A. Selby-Bigge. — 2d ed. / with text rev. and variant readings by P. H. Nidditch. — Oxford: Clarendon Press; New York: Oxford University Press, 1978. xix, 743 p.; 20 cm. Includes original t.p. Includes index. 1. Knowledge, Theory of I. Selby-Bigge, L. A. (Lewis Amherst), Sir, 1860-1951. II. Nidditch, P. H. III. T.
B1485 1978    128    *LC* 77-30415    *ISBN* 0198245874. *ISBN* 0198245882 pbk

**Mossner, Ernest Campbell, 1907-.**      **1.701**
The life of David Hume / Ernest Campbell Mossner. — 2d ed. — Oxford: Clarendon Press; New York: Oxford University Press, 1980. xx, 709 p., [1] leaf of plates: ill.; 23 cm. Includes index. 1. Hume, David, 1711-1776. 2. Philosophers — Scotland — Biography. I. T.
B1497.M65 1980    192 B 19    *LC* 78-41137    *ISBN* 0198243812

**Hendel, Charles William, 1890-.**      • **1.702**
Studies in the philosophy of David Hume / Charles W. Hendel. — Indianapolis: Bobbs-Merrill, 1963. li, 516 p. — (Library of liberal arts) 1. Hume, David, 1711-1776. I. T.
B1498.H4    192 19    *LC* 62-18220

**Hume: a re–evaluation / edited by Donald W. Livingston & James T. King.**      **1.703**
New York: Fordham University Press, 1976. x, 421 p.; 24 cm. 1. Hume, David, 1711-1776 — Addresses, essays, lectures. I. Livingston, Donald W. II. King, James T.
B1498.H87    192    *LC* 76-13968    *ISBN* 0823210073

**Livingston, Donald W.**      **1.704**
Hume's philosophy of common life / Donald W. Livingston. — Chicago: University of Chicago Press, 1984. xiv, 371 p.; 24 cm. Includes index. 1. Hume, David, 1711-1776. I. T.
B1498.L58 1984    192 19    *LC* 83-18227    *ISBN* 0226487148

**Noxon, James H.**      **1.705**
Hume's philosophical development; a study of his methods by James Noxon. — Oxford; New York: Clarendon Press, 1973. xiv, 197 p.; 23 cm. 1. Hume, David, 1711-1776. I. T.
B1498.N68    192    *LC* 73-159942    *ISBN* 0198243987

**Smith, Norman Kemp, 1872-1958.**      • **1.706**
The philosophy of David Hume: a critical study of its origins and central doctrines / by Norman Kemp Smith. — London: Macmillan, 1949. xxiv, 568 p. 1. Hume, David, 1711-1776. I. T.
B1498.S5 1949

**Stroud, Barry.**      **1.707**
Hume / Barry Stroud. — London: Routledge and Kegan Paul, 1977. xii, 280 p.; 24 cm. — (The Arguments of the philosophers) Includes index. 1. Hume, David, 1711-1776. I. T.
B1498.S85    192    *LC* 77-374283    *ISBN* 0710086016

**Wright, John P.**      **1.708**
The sceptical realism of David Hume / John P. Wright. — Minneapolis: University of Minnesota Press, c1983. x, 269 p.; 23 cm. Includes index. 1. Hume, David, 1711-1776. I. T.
B1498.W74 1983    192 19    *LC* 83-187173    *ISBN* 0816612234

**Beauchamp, Tom L.**      **1.709**
Hume and the problem of causation / Tom L. Beauchamp, Alexander Rosenberg. — New York: Oxford University Press, 1981. xxiv, 340 p.; 23 cm. 1. Hume, David, 1711-1776. 2. Causation I. Rosenberg, Alexander, 1946- joint author. II. T.
B1499.C38 B4    122 19    *LC* 80-20259    *ISBN* 0195202368

**Harrison, Jonathan.**      **1.710**
Hume's moral epistemology / Jonathan Harrison. — Oxford [Eng.]: Clarendon Press, 1976. 131 p.; 21 cm. Includes index. 1. Hume, David, 1711-1776 — Ethics. 2. Hume, David, 1711-1776. A treatise of human nature. 3. Hume, David, 1711-1776. An enquiry concerning the principles of morals. 4. Knowledge, Theory of 5. Ethics I. T.
B1499.E8 H37    170/.92/4    *LC* 76-365003    *ISBN* 0198245661

**Mackie, J. L. (John Leslie)**      **1.711**
Hume's moral theory / J.L. Mackie. — London; Boston: Routledge & K. Paul, 1980. viii, 166 p.; 23 cm. — (International library of philosophy.) 1. Hume, David, 1711-1776 — Ethics. 2. Ethics I. T. II. Series.
B1499.E8 H855    170/.92/4 19    *LC* 79-41565    *ISBN* 0710005245

## B1504–1538 Hutcheson. Reid

**Kivy, Peter.**      **1.712**
The seventh sense: a study of Francis Hutcheson's aesthetics and its influence in eighteenth–century Britain / by Peter Kivy. New York: B. Franklin, c1976. ii, 268 p.: port.; 24 cm. Includes index. 1. Hutcheson, Francis, 1694-1746. 2. Aesthetics, British I. T.
B1504.A33 K58    111.8/5    *LC* 75-28447    *ISBN* 0891020446

**Reid, Thomas, 1710-1796.**      **1.713**
Thomas Reid's inquiry and essays / edited by Keith Lehrer and Ronald E. Beanblossom; introd. by Ronald E. Beanblossom. — 1st ed. — Indianapolis: Bobbs-Merrill, 1975. lxi, 368 p.; 21 cm. (Library of liberal arts; 156) Selected from the 6th ed. of the Works of Thomas Reid, edited by W. Hamilton, and published in 1863 by Maclachlen and Stewart, Edinburgh. 1. Philosophy I. Lehrer, Keith. ed. II. Beanblossom, Ronald E., 1941- ed. III. T. IV. Title: Inquiry and essays.
B1532.A3 L43 1975    192    *LC* 75-1197    *ISBN* 0672611732

**Daniels, Norman, 1942-.**      **1.714**
Thomas Reid's Inquiry: the geometry of visibles and the case for realism. Foreword by Hilary Putnam. — New York: B. Franklin, [1974] xix, 147 p.: port.; 24 cm. A revision of the author's thesis, Harvard. 1. Reid, Thomas, 1710-1796. An inquiry into the human mind. 2. Geometry, Non-Euclidean 3. Mind and body I. T.
B1533.I24 D36 1974    128/.2    *LC* 74-1478    *ISBN* 0833754823

**Reid, Thomas, 1710-1796.**      **1.715**
[Lectures on the fine arts] Thomas Reid's Lectures on the fine arts. Transcribed from the original manuscript, with an introd. and notes by Peter Kivy. The Hague, M. Nijhoff, 1973. viii, 57 p. 24 cm. (International archives of the history of ideas. Series minor, 7) 1. Aesthetics 2. Art I. Kivy, Peter. II. T. III. Title: Lectures on the fine arts.
B1533.L4 1973    111.8/5    *LC* 73-177893    *ISBN* 9024715393

## B1561–1674 19TH–20TH CENTURIES

**Willey, Basil, 1897-.**      • **1.716**
More nineteenth century studies; a group of honest doubters. — New York: Columbia University Press, 1956. 304 p.; 23 cm. 1. Nineteenth century 2. Philosophy, Modern — History. 3. English literature — 19th century. — History and criticism. 4. Religious thought — 19th century I. T.
B1561.W5    192    *LC* 57-13564

**Willey, Basil, 1897-.**      • **1.717**
Nineteenth century studies; Coleridge to Matthew Arnold. New York, Columbia University Press, 1949. v, 287 p. 23 cm. 1. Nineteenth century — Addresses, essays, lectures. 2. Philosophy, Modern — 19th century — Addresses, essays, lectures. 3. English literature — 19th century — History and criticism — Addresses, essays, lectures. 4. Religious thought — 19th century — Addresses, essays, lectures. I. T.
B1561.W52    192    *LC* 49-50265

**Halévy, Elie, 1870-1937.**      • **1.718**
The growth of philosophic radicalism / by Elie Halévy; translated by Mary Morris; with a preface by A.D. Lindsay. — Boston: Beacon Press, c1955. 554 p.; 21 cm. (Beacon paperbacks; 17) Beacon studies in the history of ideas. Includes index. 1. Bentham, Jeremy, 1748-1832. 2. Utilitarianism 3. France — History — Revolution — Causes and character. I. T.
B1571.H33 1955    *LC* 55-13792

**Mill, John Stuart, 1806-1873.**      **1.719**
Utilitarianism. With critical essays, edited by Samuel Gorovitz. — Indianapolis: Bobbs-Merrill, [1971] xxv, 410 p.; 24 cm. — (The Bobbs-Merrill text and commentary series, 7) 1. Utilitarianism I. Gorovitz, Samuel. ed., comp. II. T.
B1571.M6 1971    144/.6    *LC* 70-132934

**Plamenatz, J. p.**     • **1.720**
The English utilitarians. — 2d rev. ed. — Oxford: Blackwell, c1958. 192 p.
1. Utilitarianism I. T.
B1571.P56 1958     *LC* 58-4489     189

**Stephen, Leslie, Sir, 1832-1904.**     • **1.721**
The English utilitarians. New York, A. M. Kelley, 1968. 3 v. 22 cm. (Reprints of economic classics) Sequel to the author's History of English thought in the eighteenth century. Reprint of the 1900 ed. 1. Bentham, Jeremy, 1748-1832. 2. Mill, James, 1773-1836. 3. Mill, John Stuart, 1806-1873. 4. Utilitarianism — Great Britain — History. I. T.
B1571.S85 1968     144/.6     *LC* 67-29517

**Bentham, Jeremy, 1748-1832.**     • **1.722**
An introduction to the principles of morals and legislation; with an introd. by Laurence J. Lafleur. — New York: Hafner Pub. Co., 1948. lii, 378 p.; 21 cm. — (The Hafner library of classics, no. 6) 'A reprint of the edition of 1823, which contains the author's final corrections.' 1. Ethics 2. Criminal law 3. Utilitarianism I. Lafleur, Laurence Julien, 1907-1966, ed. II. T.
B1574.B33 I5 1948     340/.112 19     *LC* 48-8231

**Bentham, Jeremy, 1748-1832.**     • **1.723**
Bentham's Theory of fictions / by C.K. Ogden. — London: Kegan Paul: Trench, Trubner & Co., 1932. 161 p.: 2 port. (incl. front.) facsim. (International library of psychology, philosophy, and scientific method.) 1. Fictions, Theory of I. Ogden, Charles Kay, 1880- II. T. III. Series.
B1574.B33 T5

**Harrison, Ross.**     **1.724**
Bentham / Ross Harrison. — London; Boston: Routledge & Kegan Paul, 1983. xxv, 286 p.; 24 cm. — (Arguments of the philosophers.) Includes index. 1. Bentham, Jeremy, 1748-1832. I. T. II. Series.
B1574.B34 H37 1983     192 19     *LC* 83-9543     *ISBN* 0710095260

**Mack, Mary Peter, 1927-.**     • **1.725**
Jeremy Bentham; an odyssey of ideas [1748-1792]. — New York, Columbia University Press, 1963. 482 p. illus. 22 cm. Includes bibliography. 1. Bentham, Jeremy, 1748-1832. I. T.
B1574.B34M3     921.2     *LC* 62-19900

**Mill, John Stuart, 1806-1873.**     • **1.726**
On Bentham and Coleridge / [with an] introd. by F.R. Leavis. — New York: G.W. Stewart, [1962, c1950] 168 p. (Harper torchbooks. The Academy Library) 1. Bentham, Jeremy, 1748-1832. 2. Coleridge, Samuel Taylor, 1772-1834. I. T.
B1574.B34 M5 1962

**Tjoa, Hock Guan, 1943-.**     **1.727**
George Henry Lewes: a Victorian mind / Hock Guan Tjoa. — Cambridge, Mass.: Harvard University Press, 1978 (c1977). vii, 172 p.; 21 cm. — (Harvard historical monographs. 70) Includes index. 1. Lewes, George Henry, 1817-1878. 2. Philosophers — England — Biography. I. T. II. Series.
B1593.Z7 T59     192     *LC* 77-8610     *ISBN* 0674348745

**Mill, John Stuart, 1806-1873.**     • **1.728**
[Works. 1963] Collected works. [Toronto, University of Toronto Press, 1963- <c1985 > v. <1-5, 7-8, 10-19, 21-22 > illus. 25 cm. Half title; each vol. has special t.p. 1. Philosophy — Collected works. 2. Political science — Collected works. 3. Economics — Collected works. I. T.
B1602.A2 1963     192 19     *LC* 63-25976

**Mill, John Stuart, 1806-1873.**     • **1.729**
John Stuart Mill and Harriet Taylor: their correspondence [i. e. friendship] and subsequent marriage / by F. A. Hayek. — Chicago: University of Chicago Press, [1951]. 320 p.: ports., facsim., general, tables. Errata slip (inserted) indicates correct title. I. Mill, Harriet Hardy Taylor, 1807-1858. II. Hayek, Friedrich A. von (Friedrich August), 1899- ed. III. T.
B1606.A28

**Anschutz, Richard Paul, 1902-.**     • **1.730**
The philosophy of J.S. Mill / by R.P. Anschutz. — Oxford: Clarendon Press, 1953. 184 p.: port. 1. Mill, John Stuart, 1806-1873. I. T.
B1607.A57     *LC* 53-8183

**August, Eugene R., 1935-.**     **1.731**
John Stuart Mill: a mind at large / Eugene August. — New York: Scribner, [1975] xii, 276 p.: ill.; 23 cm. Includes index. 1. Mill, John Stuart, 1806-1873. I. T.
B1607.A95     192     *LC* 75-12649     *ISBN* 0684142325

**Semmel, Bernard.**     **1.732**
John Stuart Mill and the pursuit of virtue / Bernard Semmel. — New Haven: Yale University Press, c1984. xi, 212 p.; 22 cm. Includes index. 1. Mill, John Stuart, 1806-1873. I. T.
B1607.S44 1984     192 19     *LC* 83-10215     *ISBN* 0300030061

**Berger, Fred R., 1937-.**     **1.733**
Happiness, justice, and freedom: the moral and political philosophy of John Stuart Mill / Fred R. Berger. — Berkeley: University of California Press, c1984. x, 363 p.; 24 cm. Includes index. 1. Mill, John Stuart, 1806-1873 — Ethics. 2. Mill, John Stuart, 1806-1873 — Political and social views. 3. Ethics — History — 19th century. 4. Political science — History — 19th century. I. T.
B1608.E8 B47 1984     171/.5 19     *LC* 83-6502     *ISBN* 0520048679

**Williams, Bernard Arthur Owen.**     • **1.734**
British analytical philosophy, edited by Bernard Williams and Alan Montefiore. New York, Humanities Press [1966] v, 346 p. 23 cm. (International library of philosophy and scientific method.) 1. Analysis (Philosophy) — Collections. I. Montefiore, Alan. II. T. III. Series.
B1614.W5 1966     192     *LC* 65-28185

### B1615–1674 20TH CENTURY

**Contemporary British philosophy; personal statements. 1st–4th**     **1.735**
**ser. / by J. B. Baillie [and others].**
London, Allen & Unwin; New York, Macmillan [1924-77] 4 v. 23 cm. — (Library of philosophy.) (The Muirhead library of philosophy.) First-second ser. edited by J. H. Muirhead; third-fourth ser. edited by H. D. Lewis. 1. Philosphy, English — 20th century — Addresses, essays, lectures. I. Muirhead, John H. (John Henry), 1855-1940. II. Lewis, Hywel David. III. Series.
B1615.C62     192     *LC* 24-26491

**Passmore, John Arthur.**     • **1.736**
A hundred years of philosophy / John Passmore. — 2nd ed. — London: Duckworth, c1966. 574 p.; 23 cm. 1. Philosophy, English 2. Philosophy — History I. T.
B1615.P3 1966     109     *LC* 66-67868     *ISBN* 0715601768

**Warnock G.J. (Geoffrey James), 1923-.**     • **1.737**
English philosophy since 1900 [by] G. J. Warnock. 2nd ed. London, New York, Oxford U.P., 1969. ix, 126 p. 21 cm. (A Galaxy book, GB 153) 1. Philosophy, English — 20th century I. T.
B1615.W3 1969     192     *LC* 73-435708

### B1618–1646 Philosophers, A–L

**Austin, J. L. (John Langshaw), 1911-1960.**     • **1.738**
Philosophical papers. Edited by J. O. Urmson and G. J. Warnock. 2d ed. Oxford, Clarendon Press, 1970. vii, 290 p. 21 cm. 1. Philosophy — Addresses, essays, lectures. I. Urmson, J. O. ed. II. Warnock G.J. (Geoffrey James), 1923- ed. III. T.
B1618.A8 1970     192     *LC* 70-19274     *ISBN* 0198243464

**Austin, J. L. (John Langshaw), 1911-1960.**     • **1.739**
How to do things with words. — Cambridge, Harvard University Press, 1962. 166 p. 19 cm. — (The William James lectures 1955) 1. Languages — Philosophy 2. Semantics I. T.
B1618.A83H6     149.94     *LC* 62-52034

**Fann, K. T., 1937- comp.**     • **1.740**
Symposium on J. L. Austin, edited by K. T. Fann. London, Routledge & K. Paul; New York, Humanities P., 1969. xii, 486 p. plate, port. 23 cm. (International library of philosophy and scientific method.) 1. Austin, J. L. (John Langshaw), 1911-1960 — Addresses, essays, lectures. I. T. II. Series.
B1618.A84 F36     192     *LC* 70-441745     *ISBN* 0710064861

**Graham, Keith.**     **1.741**
J. L. Austin: a critique of ordinary language philosophy / Keith Graham. — Atlantic Highlands, N.J.: Humanities Press, c1977. 281 p.; 23 cm. Includes index. 1. Austin, J. L. (John Langshaw), 1911-1960. 2. Ordinary-language philosophy I. T.
B1618.A84 G72 1977b     192     *LC* 77-22624     *ISBN* 0391007475

**Ayer, A. J. (Alfred Jules), 1910-.**     **1.742**
The central questions of philosophy / A. J. Ayer. — New York: Holt, Rinehart and Winston, 1974, c1973. x, 243 p.; 22 cm. 'Reproduces the series of Gifford lectures ... delivered at the University of St. Andrews in 1972-3.' 1. Philosophy — Collected works. I. T.
B1618.A91 1974     192     *LC* 74-4407     *ISBN* 0030131162

**Ayer, A. J. (Alfred Jules), 1910-.**     • **1.743**
The concept of a person; and other essays. — London, Macmillan; New York, St. Martin's Press, 1963. vii, 272 p. 23 cm. I. T.
B1618.A93C6 1963     192     *LC* 63-18763

**Berlin, Isaiah, Sir.**      **1.744**
Selected writings / Isaiah Berlin; edited by Henry Hardy. — New York: Viking Press, 1978-[1981] 4 v. 1. Philosophy — Collected works. I. Hardy, Henry. II. T.
B1618.B45 A1 1978b     192 19     *LC* 80-19336

**The Philosophy of F.H. Bradley / edited by Anthony Manser**      **1.745**
**and Guy Stock.**
Oxford [Oxfordshire]; New York: Clarendon Press, 1984. viii, 321 p.; 23 cm. 1. Bradley, F. H. (Francis Herbert), 1846-1924 — Addresses, essays, lectures. I. Manser, Anthony Richards. II. Stock, Guy.
B1618.B74 P47 1984     192 19     *LC* 83-23918     *ISBN* 0198246889

**Broad, C. D. (Charlie Dunbar), 1887-1971.**      • **1.746**
Induction, probability, and causation. Selected papers. By C. D. Broad. — Dordrecht: D. Reidel, [1968] xi, 297 p.; 23 cm. — (Synthese library) 1. Logic — Addresses, essays, lectures. 2. Probabilities — Addresses, essays, lectures. 3. Causation — Addresses, essays, lectures. I. T.
B1618.B75I5     160     *LC* 74-355561

**Collingwood, R. G. (Robin George), 1889-1943.**      • **1.747**
Speculum mentis; or, The map of knowledge, by R. G. Collingwood ... — Oxford, The Clarendon press, 1924. 327, [1] p. 23 cm. I. T. II. Title: The map of knowledge.
B1618.C73S6     *LC* 25-4224

**Collingwood, R. G. (Robin George), 1889-1943.**      • **1.748**
An autobiography, by R. G. Collingwood ... — [London, New York, etc.] Oxford university press, 1939. 4 p. l., 167, [1] p. 22.5 cm. I. T.
B1618.C74A3     921.2     *LC* 40-5733

**Fowles, John, 1926-.**      **1.749**
The aristos. Rev. ed. Boston: Little, Brown [1970] 224 p. 21 cm. I. T.
B1626.F63 A7 1970     192     *LC* 74-126905

## B1647.M7 Moore

**Moore, G. E. (George Edward), 1873-1958.**      • **1.750**
Philosophical papers. — London: Allen & Unwin; New York: Macmillan, [1959] 324 p. — (The Muirhead library of philosophy) 1. Philosophy — Addresses, essays, lectures. I. T.
B1647.M73 P38     *LC* 62-52780

**Moore, G. E. (George Edward), 1873-1958.**      • **1.751**
Philosophical studies. Paterson,N.J., Littlefield, Adams, 1959. 342 p.; 21 cm. (International library of psychology, philosophy, and scientific method) 1. Philosophy, Modern I. T.
B 1647 M73 P5 1959     *LC* 59-3192

**Moore, G. E. (George Edward), 1873-1958.**      • **1.752**
Some main problems of philosophy. — London, Allen & Unwin; New York, Macmillan [1953] xii, 380 p. 22 cm. — (The Muirhead library of philosophy) 1. Philosophy — Addresses, essays, lectures. I. T.
B1647.M73S6     104     *LC* 53-12843

**Ambrose, Alice, 1906- comp.**      • **1.753**
G. E. Moore: essays in retrospect; edited by Alice Ambrose and Morris Lazerowitz. — London, Allen & Unwin; New York, Humanities P., 1970. 3-376 p. 23 cm. index. — (Muirhead library of philosophy) Includes bibliographical references. 1. Moore, G. E. (George Edward), 1873-1958. I. Lazerowitz, Morris, 1909- joint comp. II. T.
B1647.M74A65     192     *LC* 70-478308     *ISBN* 041920236

**Hill, John.**      **1.754**
The ethics of G. E. Moore: a new interpretation. — Amsterdam: Van Gorum, 1976. 144 p. 1. Moore, G. E. (George Edward), 1873-1958. I. T.
B1647.M74 H54     *ISBN* 9023213274

**Klemke, E. D., 1926- comp.**      • **1.755**
Studies in the philosophy of G. E. Moore. Edited with an introd. by E. D. Klemke. Chicago, Quadrangle Books, 1969. viii, 306 p. 21 cm. (A Quadrangle paperback original, QP115) 1. Moore, G. E. (George Edward), 1873-1958. I. T.
B1647.M74 K54 1969     192     *LC* 74-78311

**Schilpp, Paul Arthur, 1897- ed.**      • **1.756**
The philosophy of G. E. Moore. [3d ed.] La Salle, Ill., Open Court [1968] xv, 727 p. ports. 25 cm. (Library of living philosophers. v. 4) 1. Moore, G. E. (George Edward), 1873-1958. I. Moore, G. E. (George Edward), 1873-1958. II. T. III. Series.
B1647.M74S35 1968     192     *LC* 68-57206

## B1649.P6 Popper

**Burke, T. E.**      **1.757**
The philosophy of Popper / T.E. Burke. — Manchester, UK; Dover, N.H., USA: Manchester University Press, c1983. ix, 222 p.; 23 cm. Includes index. 1. Popper, Karl Raimund, Sir, 1902- I. T.
B1649.P64 B87 1983     192 19     *LC* 83-80361     *ISBN* 0719009049

**The Philosophy of Karl Popper / edited by Paul Arthur**      **1.758**
**Schilpp.**
1st ed. — La Salle, Ill.: Open Court, c1974. 2 v. (xvi, 1323 p.): port.; 24 cm. — (Library of living philosophers. v. 14) 1. Popper, Karl Raimund, Sir, 1902- — Addresses, essays, lectures. I. Popper, Karl Raimund, Sir, 1902- II. Schilpp, Paul Arthur, 1897- III. Series.
B1649.P64 P48     192     *LC* 76-186983     *ISBN* 0875481418

## B1649.R9 Russell

**Russell, Bertrand, 1872-1970.**      **1.759**
Cambridge essays, 1888-99 / Bertrand Russell; edited by Kenneth Blackwell ... [et al.]. — McMaster University ed. — London; Boston: G. Allen & Unwin, 1983. xxxiv, 554 p.: port. — (The Collected papers of Bertrand Russell) Includes indexes. 1. Philosophy — Addresses, essays, lectures. I. Blackwell, Kenneth. II. T.
B1649.R91 1983     192 19     *LC* 83-15865     *ISBN* 004920095X

**Russell, Bertrand, 1872-1970.**      **1.760**
Bertrand Russell: an introduction / edited selections from his writings [by] Brian Carr. — London: International Publications Service, 1975. 3-149 p.; 23 cm. 1. Philosophy — Collected works. I. Carr, Brian. II. T.
B1649.R91 C37     192     *LC* 75-327863     *ISBN* 0041920325

**Russell, Bertrand, 1872-1970.**      • **1.761**
Basic writings, 1903-1959. Edited by Robert E. Egner and Lester E. Denonn. New York, Simon and Schuster [1961] 736 p. 25 cm. 'Chronological list of Russell's principal works': p. [17]-19. I. T.
B1649.R91 E38     192     *LC* 61-3396

**Russell, Bertrand, 1872-1970.**      • **1.762**
An inquiry into meaning and truth / by Bertrand Russell. — London: G. Allen and Unwin, 1940. 352 p.; 22 cm. The William James lectures for 1940 delivered at Harvard University. 'These lectures formed the basis for seminar courses at the University of Chicago in 1938-9 and the University of California at Los Angeles in 1930-40.' -Pref. 1. Knowledge, Theory of 2. Meaning (Psychology) 3. Truth I. T.
B 1649 R93 I5 1940a     *LC* 41-15571

**Russell, Bertrand, 1872-1970.**      • **1.763**
Logic and knowledge: essays, 1901-1950 / Bertrand Russell; edited by Robert Charles Marsh. — London: Allen and Unwin, 1956. xi, 382 p.; 23 cm. 1. Philosophy — Addresses, essays, lectures. 2. Logic, Symbolic and mathematical — Addresses, essays, lectures. I. T.
B1649.R93 L6     192.9     *LC* 56-14393     *ISBN* 0041640012

**Russell, Bertrand, 1872-1970.**      • **1.764**
Our knowledge of the external world / by Bertrand Russell. — New York: W.W. Norton, c1929. ix, 268 p.; 22 cm. 'Second edition.' 'Delivered as Lowell Lectures in Boston, in March and April 1914.'—p. vii 1. Knowledge, Theory of 2. Philosophy I. T.
B1649.R93 O8 1929     *LC* 29-7231

**Russell, Bertrand, 1872-1970.**      • **1.765**
Mysticism and logic / by Bertrand Russell. — 1st ed. — New York: W.W. Norton, 1929. vi, 234 p. First published in London, 1910, under title: Philosophical essays. 1. Philosophy 2. Science — Philosophy I. T.
B1649.R93 P5     *LC* 29-19713

**Russell, Bertrand, 1872-1970.**      • **1.766**
The autobiography of Bertrand Russell. [1st American ed.] Boston, Little, Brown [1967- v. illus., facsim., ports. 24 cm. 'An Atlantic Monthly Press book.' I. T.
B1649.R94 A33     828/.9/1203     *LC* 67-14453

**Ayer, A. J. (Alfred Jules), 1910-.**      **1.767**
Bertrand Russell [by] A. J. Ayer. New York, Viking Press [1972] xii, 168 p. 19 cm. (Modern masters) 1. Russell, Bertrand, 1872-1970. I. T.
B1649.R94 A86     192 B     *LC* 76-181979     *ISBN* 0670158992 *ISBN* 067001950X

**Ayer, A. J. (Alfred Jules), 1910-.**      • **1.768**
Russell and Moore; the analytical heritage [by] A. J. Ayer. Cambridge, Harvard University Press, 1971. x, 254 p. 23 cm. (William James lectures. 1970]) 1. Russell, Bertrand, 1872-1970. 2. Moore, G. E. (George Edward), 1873-1958. 3. Analysis (Philosophy) I. T. II. Series.
B1649.R94 A9     192     *LC* 77-133216     *ISBN* 0674781031

**Bertrand Russell; a collection of critical essays. Edited by D. F.    1.769
Pears.**
[1st ed.] Garden City, N.Y., Anchor Books, 1972. x, 387 p. 18 cm. (Modern
studies in philosophy, AP 15) 1. Russell, Bertrand, 1872-1970 — Addresses,
essays, lectures. I. Pears, David Francis. ed.
B1649.R94 B33      192      LC 76-171339

**Clark, Ronald William.**                                        1.770
The life of Bertrand Russell / Ronald W. Clark. — 1st American ed. — New
York: Knopf, 1976, c1975. 766 p., [16] leaves of plates: ports.; 25 cm. Includes
index. 1. Russell, Bertrand, 1872-1970. I. T.
B1649.R94 C55 1976      192 B      LC 75-8226      ISBN 0394490592

**Schilpp, Paul Arthur, 1897- ed.**                              • 1.771
The philosophy of Bertrand Russell, edited by Paul Arthur Schilpp. [2d ed.]
New York: Tudor Pub. Co., [1952] xv, [1], 829 p. incl. front. (port.) illus.
(facsim.) (Library of living philosophers.) 1. Russell, Bertrand Russell, 3rd
Earl, 1872- I. Russell, Bertrand Russell, 3rd Earl, 1872- II. T. III. Series.
B1649.R94S35 1952

**Tait, Katharine, 1923-.**                                        1.772
My Father, Bertrand Russell / Katharine Tait. — 1st ed. — New York:
Harcourt Brace Jovanovich, [1975] xii, 211 p., [4] leaves of plates: ill; 22 cm.
1. Russell, Bertrand, 1872-1970. I. T.
B1649.R94 T34      192      LC 75-15719      ISBN 0151304327

### B1649.R96 Ryle

**Ryle, Gilbert, 1900-1976.**                                      • 1.773
Collected papers. — New York: Barnes & Noble, [1971] 2 v.; 24 cm.
1. Philosophy — Collected works. I. T.
B1649.R961 1971      108      LC 70-28252      ISBN 0389041122

### B1674.W35 Whitehead

**Whitehead, Alfred North, 1861-1947.**                           • 1.774
Alfred North Whitehead: an anthology; selected by F. S. C. Northrop and
Mason W. Gross. Introductions and a note on Whitehead's terminology, by
Mason W. Gross. New York, Macmillan, 1953. 928 p. 22 cm. I. Northrop, F.
S. C. (Filmer Stuart Cuckow), 1893- comp. II. Gross, Mason W., comp. III. T.
B 1674 W351 N87 1953      LC 53-12112

**Whitehead, Alfred North, 1861-1947.**                           • 1.775
Dialogues of Alfred North Whitehead / as recorded by Lucien Price. — [1st
ed.] Boston: Little, Brown, 1954. 396 p.; 23 cm. (Atlantic Monthly Press book.)
Includes index. 1. Whitehead, Alfred North, 1861-1947 — Addresses, essays,
lectures. 2. Philosophy — Addresses, essays, lectures 3. Philosophers —
England — Biography — Addresses, essays, lectures. I. Price, Lucien, 1883-
II. T. III. Series.
B1674.W353 D5      192      LC 54-6869

**Christian, William A., 1905-.**                                 • 1.776
An interpretation of Whitehead's metaphysics / by William A. Christian. —
New Haven: Yale University Press, 1967. xii, 419 p.; 24 cm. 1. Whitehead,
Alfred North, 1861-1947. 2. Metaphysics I. T.
B1674.W354 C5 1967      110

**Kuntz, Paul Grimley, 1915-.**                                    1.777
Alfred North Whitehead / by Paul Grimley Kuntz. — Boston: Twayne, c1984.
160 p.: port.; 23 cm. — (Twayne's English authors series. TEAS 374) Includes
index. 1. Whitehead, Alfred North, 1861-1947. I. T. II. Series.
B1674.W354 K86 1984      192 19      LC 83-12999      ISBN 0805768602

**Leclerc, Ivor. ed.**                                            • 1.778
The relevance of Whitehead: philosophical essays in commemoration of the
centenary of the birth of Alfred North Whitehead / edited by Ivor Leclerc. —
London: Allen & Unwin; New York, Macmillan, [1961] 383 p.; 23 cm. — (The
Muirhead library of philosophy) 1. Whitehead, Alfred North, 1861-1947.
2. Philosophy — Addresses, essays, lectures. I. Whitehead, Alfred North,
1861-1947. II. Leclerc, Ivor. III. T.
B1674.W354L38 1961      108.2      LC 61-3432

**Leclerc, Ivor.**                                                 1.779
Whitehead's metaphysics: an introductory exposition / Ivor Leclerc. —
Bloomington: Indiana University Press, [1975] c1958. xiii, 233 p.; 21 cm.
Reprint of the 1958 ed. published by Allen and Unwin, London. 1. Whitehead,
Alfred North, 1861-1947 — Metaphysics. I. T.
B1674.W354 L4 1975      110      LC 74-23296      ISBN 0253201810

**Lowe, Victor, 1907-.**                                           1.780
Alfred North Whitehead: the man and his work / Victor Lowe. — Baltimore,
Md.: Johns Hopkins University Press, c1985-. xi, 351 p.; 24 cm. Includes index.

1. Whitehead, Alfred North, 1861-1947. 2. Philosophers — England —
Biography. 3. Mathematicians — England — Biography. I. T.
B1674.W354 L57 1985      192 B 19      LC 84-15467      ISBN
0801824885

**Lowe, Victor, 1907-.**                                           • 1.781
Understanding Whitehead. — Baltimore: Johns Hopkins Press, 1962. 398 p.:
illus.; 22 cm. 1. Whitehead, Alfred North, 1861-1947. I. T.
B1674.W354 L6      192      LC 62-15312

**Sherburne, Donald W.**                                           • 1.782
A Whiteheadian aesthetic; some implications of Whitehead's metaphysical
speculation, by Donald W. Sherburne. With a foreword by F. S. C. Northrop.
— [Hamden, Conn.]: Archon Books, 1970 [c1961] xxix, 219 p.: illus.; 22 cm.
'With the exception of one added chapter and minor revisions, this book is the
dissertation submitted in September of 1959 to Yale University ... for the degree
of doctor of philosophy.' 1. Whitehead, Alfred North, 1861-1947 —
Aesthetics. I. T.
B1674.W354 S45 1970      111.8/5      LC 70-103997      ISBN 0208008195

**Whitehead, Alfred North, 1861-1947.**                           • 1.783
Modes of thought / by Alfred North Whitehead. — New York: MacMillan,
1938. viii, 241 p.; 19 cm. 'First printing' 'Six lectures delivered in Wellesley
College, Massachusetts, and Two lectures in the University of Chicago.'
Includes index. 1. Philosophy — Addresses, essays, lectures I. T.
B1674.W37 M6      LC 38-33184

**Schilpp, Paul Arthur, 1897- ed.**                               • 1.784
The philosophy of Alfred North Whitehead. — [2d ed.]. — New York: Tudor
Pub. Co., [1951] 797 p.: illus.; 25 cm. — (The Library of living philosophers)
1. Whitehead, Alfred North, 1861-1947. I. T.
B1674.W38 S35 1951      192.9      LC 51-6323

## B1801–2430 France

### B1815–1907 17TH CENTURY

**Labrousse, Elisabeth.**                                          1.785
Bayle / Elisabeth Labrousse; translated by Denys Potts. — Oxford; New York:
Oxford University Press, 1983. 97 p.; 23 cm. — (Past masters.) Includes index.
1. Bayle, Pierre, 1647-1706. I. T. II. Series.
B1825.Z7 L28 1983      194 19      LC 83-177870      ISBN 0192875418

### B1837–1875 Descartes

**Beck, L. J. (Leslie John)**                                     • 1.786
The metaphysics of Descartes; a study of the Meditations, by L. J. Beck. —
Oxford, Clarendon Press, 1965. xi, 307 p. 22 cm. Bibliographical footnotes.
1. Descartes, René, 1596-1650. Meditationes de prima philosophia I. T.
B1854.B4      194      LC 66-1407

**Descartes, René, 1596-1650.**                                   1.787
[Principia philosophiae. English] Principles of philosophy / René Descartes;
translated, with explanatory notes by Valentine Rodger Miller and Reese P.
Miller. — Dordrecht, Holland; Boston, U.S.A.: Reidel; Hingham, Mass.:
Distributed by Kluwer Boston, c1983. xxviii, 325 p.: ill.; 23 cm. — (Synthese
historical library: texts and studies in the history of logic and philosophy; v. 24)
Translation of: Principia philosophiae. 1644. With additional material from the
French translation of 1647. 1. Philosophy I. Miller, Valentine Rodger, 1939-
II. Miller, Reese P., 1934- III. T.
B1863.E53 M54 1983      100 19      LC 82-18111      ISBN 9027714517

**Descartes, René, 1596-1650.**                                   • 1.788
Rules for the direction of the mind. Translated with an introd. by Laurence J.
Lafleur. Indianapolis, Liberal Arts Press [1961] 92 p. illus. (Library of liberal
arts. no. 129) 1. Reasoning 2. Logic, Symbolic and mathematical I. T.
II. Series.
B1868.R42.4 E5

**Beck, L. J. (Leslie John)**                                     • 1.789
The method of Descartes; a study of the Regulae. Oxford, Clarendon Press,
1952. x, 316 p. 23 cm. 1. Descartes, René, 1596-1650. Regulae ad directionem
ingenii. 2. Descartes, René, 1596-1650. Discours de la méthode. I. T.
B1868.R43 B4      194.1      LC 53-1799

**Joachim, Harold H. (Harold Henry), 1868-1938.**                 • 1.790
Descartes's Rules for the direction of the mind. London, Allen & Unwin [1957]
122 p. 19 cm. 1. Descartes, René, 1596-1650. Regulae ad directionem ingenii.
I. T.
B1868.R43 J6      LC a 57-5261

**Descartes, René, 1596-1650.**      **1.791**
[Responsiones ad quasdam difficultates ex Meditationibus. English] Descartes' Conversation with Burman / translated with introd. and commentary by John Cottingham. — Oxford: Clarendon Press, 1976. xl, 133 p.; 23 cm. Translation of: Responsiones ad quasdam difficultates ex Meditationibus. Spine title: Conversation with Burman. Includes index. 1. Descartes, René, 1596-1650. 2. Burman, Frans, 1628-1679. 3. Philosophy I. Burman, Frans, 1628-1679. II. T. III. Title: Conversation with Burman.
B1868.R462 E5 1976      194      *LC* 76-363862      *ISBN* 0198245289

**Descartes, René, 1596-1650.**      • **1.792**
Descartes: philosophical letters; translated and edited by Anthony Kenny. Oxford, Clarendon Press, 1970. xiii, 270 p. 22 cm. 1. Philosophers, French — Correspondence, reminiscences, etc. I. Kenny, Anthony John Patrick. ed. II. T.
B1873.A29      194      *LC* 79-459631

**Guéroult, Martial.**      **1.793**
[Descartes selon l'ordre des raisons. English] Descartes' philosophy interpreted according to the order of reasons / Martial Guéroult; translated by Roger Ariew with the assistance of Robert Ariew and Alan Donagan. — Minneapolis: University of Minnesota Press, c1984-c1985. 2 v.; 24 cm. Translation of: Descartes selon l'ordre des raisons. 1. Descartes, René, 1596-1650. I. T.
B1875.G813 1984      194 19      *LC* 83-21771      *ISBN* 0816612595

**Kenny, Anthony John Patrick.**      • **1.794**
Descartes; a study of his philosophy. New York, Random House [1968] vii, 242 p. 19 cm. (Studies in philosophy, SPH15) (A Random House study in the history of philosophy.) 1. Descartes, René, 1596-1650. I. T.
B1875.K43      194      *LC* 68-13164

**Smith, Norman Kemp, 1872-1958.**      • **1.795**
New studies in the philosophy of Descartes; Descartes as pioneer. New York, Russell & Russell, 1963. xii, 369 p. port. 23 cm. 1. Descartes, René, 1596-1650. I. T.
B1875.S58 1963      *LC* 63-15181

**Spinoza, Benedictus de, 1632-1677.**      • **1.796**
The principles of Descartes' philosophy / by Benedictus de Spinoza; translated from the Latin by Halbert Hains Britan. — La Salle, Ill.: Open court, 1961. lxxxi, 177 p.: ill. 'Appendix, containing Cogitata metaphysica ...' p. 113-177. 1. Descartes, René, 1596-1650. I. Britan, Halbert Hains 1874- II. T.
B1875.S713 1961a      *LC* 61-65110

**Williams, Bernard Arthur Owen.**      **1.797**
Descartes: the project of pure enquiry / Bernard Williams. — Atlantic Highlands, N.J.: Humanities Press, 1978. 320 p.; 23 cm. Includes index. 1. Descartes, René, 1596-1650. I. T.
B1875.W56 1978      194      *LC* 78-5023      *ISBN* 0391005634

**Curley, E. M. (Edwin M.), 1937-.**      **1.798**
Descartes against the skeptics / E. M. Curley. — Cambridge: Harvard University Press, 1978. xvii, 242 p.; 24 cm. Includes index. 1. Descartes, René, 1596-1650. 2. Skepticism I. T.
B1878.S55 C87      194      *LC* 77-14366      *ISBN* 0674198263

**Malebranche, Nicolas, 1638-1715.**      **1.799**
[Entretiens sur la métaphysique & sur la religion. English & French] Entretiens sur la métaphysique = Dialogues on metaphysics / Nicolas Malebranche; translation and introduction by Willis Doney. — New York: Abaris Books, 1980. 359 p.; 24 cm. (Janus series 13) English and French texts of: Entretiens sur la métaphysique & sur la religion. 1. Metaphysics — Early works to 1800. 2. Religion — Philosophy — Early works to 1800. 3. God — Early works to 1800. I. Doney, Willis. II. T. III. Title: Dialogues on metaphysics. IV. Series.
B1893.E63 E5 1980      110 19      *LC* 77-86229      *ISBN* 0913870579

**Malebranche, Nicolas, 1638-1715.**      **1.800**
[Recherche de la vérité. English] The search after truth: translated from the French by Thomas M. Lennon and Paul J. Olscamp; Elucidations of the Search after truth: translated from the French by Thomas M. Lennon / Nicolas Malebranche. Philosophical commentary / by Thomas M. Lennon. — Columbus: Ohio State University Press, c1980. xxxii, 861 p.: ill.; 24 cm. Translation of De la recherche de la vérité. 1. Knowledge, Theory of I. Lennon, Thomas M. II. T.
B1893.R33 E5 1980      121      *LC* 79-23881

## B1897 Malebranche

**Radner, Daisie.**      **1.801**
Malebranche: a study of a Cartesian system / Daisie Radner. — Assen: Van Gorcum, 1978. ix, 150 p.; 25 cm. Includes index. 1. Malebranche, Nicolas, 1638-1715. I. T.
B1897.R3      *LC* 78-318208      *ISBN* 9023215885

## B1900–1903 Pascal

**Pascal, Blaise, 1623-1662.**      • **1.802**
Oeuvres complètes. Texte établi et annoté par Jacques Chevalier. [Paris, Gallimard, c1954) xxviii, 1529 p. illus. 18 cm. (Bibliothèque de la Pléiade, v. 34) 'Note bibliographique': p. [xxv]-xxviii. Bibliographical references included in 'Notes' (p. [1359]-1517) I. Chevalier, Jacques, 1882-1962, ed. II. T.
B1900.A2 1954      194      *LC* 73-5792

**Davidson, Hugh McCullough, 1918-.**      **1.803**
The origins of certainty: means and meanings in Pascal's Pensées / Hugh M. Davidson. — Chicago: University of Chicago Press, 1979. xi, 158 p.; 22 cm. 1. Pascal, Blaise, 1623-1662. Pensées 2. Catholic Church — Doctrinal and controversial works. 3. Apologetics — 17th century 4. Certainty 5. Belief and doubt I. T.
B1901.P43 D38      239/.7      *LC* 78-12768      *ISBN* 0226137163

**Pascal, Blaise, 1623-1662.**      • **1.804**
Pensées. Harmondsworth, Penguin, 1966. 359 p. 18 cm. 1. Catholic Church — Doctrinal and controversial works — Catholic authors. 2. Apologetics — 17th century I. T.
B1901.P43 K7 1966      *LC* 66-72858

**Pascal, Blaise, 1623-1662.**      • **1.805**
Pensées. The provincial letters. By Blaise Pascal. New York, The Modern library [1941] xvi, 620 p. 19 cm. (The Modern library of the world's best books) 'First Modern library edition.' 'Pensées translated by W. F. Trotter. The provincial letters translated by Thomas M'Crie.' 1. Catholic Church — Doctrines 2. Apologetics — 17th century I. Trotter, William Finlayson, 1871-tr. II. McCrie, Thomas, 1797-1875, tr. III. T. IV. Title: The provincial letters.
B1901.P43 T68      194.9      *LC* 41-24292

**Cailliet, Émile, 1894-.**      • **1.806**
Pascal; the emergence of genius. — 2d., with an appendix on recent research. Introd. by C. S. Duthie. — New York: Greenwood Press, [1969, c1961] 383 p.; 23 cm. 1. Pascal, Blaise, 1623-1662. I. T.
B1903.C34 1969      194      *LC* 75-94602      *ISBN* 0837125375

**Davidson, Hugh McCullough, 1918-.**      **1.807**
Blaise Pascal / by Hugh M. Davidson. — Boston: Twayne, c1983. 150 p.: port.; 23 cm. — (Twayne's world authors series. TWAS 701) Includes index. 1. Pascal, Blaise, 1623-1662. I. T. II. Series.
B1903.D35 1983      230/.2 19      *LC* 83-8438      *ISBN* 0805765484

**Nelson, Robert James, 1925-.**      **1.808**
Pascal, adversary and advocate / Robert J. Nelson. Cambridge, Mass.: Harvard University Press, 1982. vi, 286 p.; 24 cm. Includes index. 1. Pascal, Blaise, 1623-1662. I. T.
B1903.N46      230/.2/0924 B 19      *LC* 81-6330      *ISBN* 0674005775

## B1911–2178 18TH CENTURY. DIDEROT. ROUSSEAU

**Crocker, Lester G.**      • **1.809**
An age of crisis; man and world in eighteenth century French thought. — Baltimore, Johns Hopkins Press [1959] xx, 496 p. 24 cm. — (The Goucher College series) Bibliography: p. 474-488. 1. Philosophy, French, 18th cent. 2. Ethics — Hist. — France. 3. Enlightenment I. T. II. Series.
B1911.C7      194.0903      *LC* 59-14233

**Manuel, Frank Edward.**      • **1.810**
The prophets of Paris. Cambridge, Harvard University Press, 1962. x, 349 p. ports. 24 cm. 1. Philosophers — France I. T.
B1911.M3      194      *LC* 62-8182

**Vartanian, Aram, 1922-.**      • **1.811**
Diderot and Descartes. Princeton, Princeton University Press, 1953. vi, 336 p. 23 cm. 1. Descartes, René, 1596-1650. 2. Diderot, Denis, 1713-1784. 3. Materialism 4. Philosophy, French — History. 5. Science — Philosophy I. T.
B1911.V25 1953      *LC* 52-8781

**Wade, Ira Owen, 1896-.**      **1.812**
The intellectual origins of the French enlightenment [by] Ira O. Wade. Princeton, N.J., Princeton University Press, 1971. xxi, 677 p. 25 cm. 1. Enlightenment — History. 2. Philosophy, French — 18th century 3. France — Intellectual life — History — 18th century. I. T.
B1925.E5 W3      914.4/03      *LC* 70-132244      *ISBN* 0691060525

**Diderot, Denis, 1713-1784.**      • **1.813**
Selected philosophical writings / edited by J. Lough. — Cambridge [Eng.]: University Press, 1953. vii, 222 p.; 19 cm. 1. Philosophy — Collected works. I. Lough, John, 1913- II. T.
B2012.L6      *LC* a54-8987

**Crocker, Lester G.** • 1.814
Diderot, the embattled philosopher [by] Lester G. Crocker. New York, Free Press [c1966] 420 p. 21 cm. First published in 1954 under title: The embattled philosopher. 1. Diderot, Denis, 1713-1784. I. T. II. Title: The embattled philosopher.
B2016.C68 1966     194     *LC* 66-22213

**Mornet, Daniel, 1878-.** • 1.815
Diderot, l'homme et l'oeuvre. Paris, Boivin, [c1941] 208 p. 17 cm. (Le Livre de l'étudiant, 7) I. T.
B2016.M63     *LC* 49-38566

**Cassirer, Ernst, 1874-1945.** • 1.816
The question of Jean–Jacques Rousseau / Ernst Cassirer; translated and edited with an introd. and additional notes by Peter Gay. — Midland book ed. — Bloomington, Ind.: Indiana University Press, 1963. vi, 129 p.; 20 cm. — (A Midland book: philosophy; MB 48) 1. Rousseau, Jean-Jacques, 1712-1778. I. T.
B2137.C32 1963     *LC* 63-16576     *ISBN* 0253200482

**Grimsley, Ronald.** 1.817
Jean–Jacques Rousseau / Ronald Grimsley. — Brighton, Sussex: Harvester Press; Totowa, N.J.: Barnes & Noble Books, 1983. 193 p.; 23 cm. Includes index. 1. Rousseau, Jean-Jacques, 1712-1778. I. T.
B2137.G69 1983     194 19     *LC* 82-24409     *ISBN* 0710800517

**Grimsley, Ronald.** 1.818
The philosophy of Rousseau. — London; New York: Oxford University Press, 1973. 175 p.; 21 cm. — (Oxford paperbacks University series, 61) 1. Rousseau, Jean-Jacques, 1712-1778. I. T.
B2137.G73     194     *LC* 73-161157     *ISBN* 0198880626

### B2185–2430 19TH–20TH CENTURIES

### B2200–2408 Comte. Taine

**Comte, Auguste, 1798-1857.** 1.819
[Cours de philosophie positive. English. Selections] The essential Comte; selected from Cours de philosophie positive. Edited and with an introduction by Stanislav Andreski. Translated and annotated by Margaret Clarke. London, Croom Helm; New York, Barnes & Noble [1974] 252 p. 23 cm. 1. Positivism I. Andreski, Stanislav. ed. II. T.
B2223.E5 C55     194     *LC* 74-176149     *ISBN* 0064901815

**Comte, Auguste, 1798-1857.** 1.820
[Cours de philosophie positive. English] The positive philosophy / with a new introd. by Abraham S. Blumberg. — New York: AMS Press, 1974. xi, 838 p.; 23 cm. (Language, man, and society: foundations of the behavioral sciences) 'Freely translated and condensed by Harriet Martineau.' Reprint of the 1855 translation of Cours de philosophie positive published by C. Blanchard, New York. 1. Positivism I. Martineau, Harriet, 1802-1876. tr. II. T.
B2223.E5 M3 1974     146/.4     *LC* 70-147959     *ISBN* 0404082092

**Comte, Auguste, 1798-1857.** • 1.821
[Discours sur l'ensemble du positivisme. English] A general view of positivism. Official centenary ed. of the International Auguste Comte Centenary Committee. [Translated from the French by J. H. Bridges] New York, R. Speller, 1957. 444 p. port 22 cm. Translation of Discours sur l'ensemble du positivisme. 1. Positivism I. T.
B2228.E5 B7 1957     146     *LC* 57-3453

**Weinstein, Leo.** 1.822
Hippolyte Taine. New York, Twayne [1972] 186 p. 21 cm. (Twayne's world authors series, TWAS 139. France) 1. Taine, Hippolyte, 1828-1893. I. T.
B2408.W45     194     *LC* 79-120511

### B2421–2424 20TH CENTURY

**Descombes, Vincent.** 1.823
[Même et l'autre. English] Modern French philosophy / Vincent Descombes; translated by L. Scott–Fox and J. M. Harding. — Cambridge [Eng.]; New York: Cambridge University Press, 1980. xii, 192 p.; 22 cm. Translation of Le Même et l'autre. Includes index. 1. Philosophy, French — 20th century I. T.
B2421.D4413     194 19     *LC* 80-40768     *ISBN* 0521228379

**Poster, Mark.** 1.824
Existential Marxism in postwar France: from Sartre to Althusser / Mark Poster. — Princeton, N.J.: Princeton University Press, c1975. xii, 415 p.; 23 cm. Includes index. 1. Sartre, Jean Paul, 1905- 2. Philosophy, French — 20th century 3. Dialectical materialism 4. Existentialism 5. Sociology — France — History. I. T.
B2424.D5 P68     194     *LC* 75-3471     *ISBN* 0691072124

### B2430–B2 Bachelard

**Bachelard, Gaston, 1884-1962.** 1.825
The poetics of space. Translated from the French by Maria Jolas. Foreword by Étienne Gilson. New York, Orion Press [1964] xxxv, 240 p. 22 cm. Bibliographical footnotes. 1. Space and time 2. Imagination 3. Poetry I. T.
B2430.B253P63     194     *LC* 62-15019

**Tiles, Mary.** 1.826
Bachelard, science and objectivity / Mary Tiles. — Cambridge [Cambridgeshire]; New York: Cambridge University Press, 1985 (c1984). xxii, 242 p.; 23 cm. (Modern European philosophy.) Includes index. 1. Bachelard, Gaston, 1884-1962. I. T. II. Series.
B2430.B254 T55 1984     121 19     *LC* 84-5001     *ISBN* 0521248035

### B2430.B4 Bergson

**Bergson, Henri, 1859-1941.** • 1.827
The two sources of morality and religion, by Henri Bergson; translated by R. Ashley Audra and Cloudesley Brereton, with the assistance of W. Horsfall Carter. New York, H. Holt and company [c1935] viii, 308 p. 22 cm. 1. Ethics 2. Religion — Philosophy 3. Mysticism I. Audra, Ruth Ashley, 1888- tr. II. Brereton, Cloudesley Shovell Henry, 1863- joint tr. III. Carter, William Horsfall, 1900- joint tr. IV. T.
B2430.B4 D42 1935a     194.9     *LC* 35-5957

**Bergson, Henri, 1859-1941.** • 1.828
[Evolution créatrice. English] Creative evolution, by Henri Bergson; in the authorized translation by Arthur Mitchell, with a foreword by Irwin Edman. New York, The Modern library [1944] xxv, 453 p. 19 cm. (The Modern library of the world's best books) 1. Metaphysics 2. Life 3. Evolution I. Mitchell, Arthur, 1872- tr. II. T.
B2430.B4 E72 1944     113     *LC* 44-40113

**Bergson, Henri, 1859-1941.** • 1.829
Matter and memory / Henri Bergson; authorized translation by Nancy Margaret Paul and W. Scott Palmer. — London: Allen; New York: Macmillan, 1912. xx, 339 p.; 23 cm. — (Library of philosophy) 1. Mind and body 2. Memory I. T.
B2430.B4 M32     *LC* 13-10884

### B2430.F7 Foucault

**Smart, Barry.** 1.830
Michel Foucault / Barry Smart. — Chichester: Ellis Horwood, 1985. 150 p.; 20 cm. — (Ellis Horwood series in key sociologists) 1. Foucault, Michel, 1926-1984. I. T.
B2430.F724     194 19     *ISBN* 0853128820

**Lemert, Charles C., 1937-.** 1.831
Michel Foucault: social theory as transgression / Charles C. Lemert and Garth Gillan. — New York: Columbia University Press, 1982. xv, 169 p.; 24 cm. Includes index. 1. Foucault, Michel. I. Gillan, Garth, 1939- II. T.
B2430.F724 L45 1982     303.3/092/4 19     *LC* 82-4276     *ISBN* 0231051905

### B2430.M25 Marcel

**Marcel, Gabriel, 1889-1973.** • 1.832
Searchings. New York, Newman Press [1967] 118 p. 22 cm. 1. Philosophy — Addresses, essays, lectures. I. T.
B2430.M253 A93     *LC* 67-15716

**Marcel, Gabriel, 1889-1973.** • 1.833
Being and having: an existentialist diary / by Gabriel Marcel; translated by Katherine Farrer. — New York: Harper & Row, 1965. 236p. xvii, 9-236 p. 'Harper torchbooks,TB1002.Cathedral library.' Translation of Être et avoir. 1. Consciousness 2. Ontology 3. Faith I. T.
B2430.M253.E85 1965     110     *LC* 65-9149

**Marcel, Gabriel, 1889-1973.** • 1.834
Man against mass society / Foreword by Donald MacKinnon. [Translated from the French by G. S. Fraser] Chicago: Regnery, [1962] 273 p.; 18 cm. (A Gateway edition, 6077) Translation of Les hommes contre l'humain. 1. Philosophical anthropology I. T.
B2430.M253 H583 1962     194     *LC* 63-1430

**Marcel, Gabriel, 1889-1973.** • 1.835
Homo viator; introduction to a metaphysic of hope. London, Gollancz, 1951. 270 p. 20 cm. 1. Philosophy — Addresses, essays, lectures. I. T.
B2430.M253 H63     *LC* 52-4179

**The Philosophy of Gabriel Marcel / edited by Paul Arthur**　**1.836**
**Schilpp and Lewis Edwin Hahn.**
1st ed. — La Salle, Ill.: Open Court Pub. Co., c1984. xviii, 624 p.; 24 cm. (Library of living philosophers. v. 17) Includes index. 1. Marcel, Gabriel, 1889-1973 — Addresses, essays, lectures. I. Marcel, Gabriel, 1889-1973. II. Schilpp, Paul Arthur, 1897- III. Hahn, Lewis Edwin, 1908- IV. Series.
B2430.M254 P47 1984　　194 19　　LC 83-4063　　ISBN 0875483690

## B2430.M3 Maritain

**Maritain, Jacques, 1882-1973.**　• **1.837**
The social and political philosophy of Jacques Maritain; selected readings by Joseph W. Evans and Leo R. Ward. — New York: Scribner, 1955. 348 p.; 22 cm. 1. Philosophy — Collected works. I. T.
B2430.M32 E5　　194.9　　LC 55-7199

## B2430.M37 Merleau–Ponty

**Madison, Gary Brent.**　**1.838**
[Phénoménologie de Merleau-Ponty. English] The phenomenology of Merleau–Ponty: a search for the limits of consciousness / by Gary Brent Madison; foreword by Paul Ricoeur; translated from the French by the author. — Athens: Ohio University Press, c1981. xxxii, 345 p.; 24 cm. — (Series in continental thought. 3) Translation of: La phénoménologie de Merleau-Ponty. 1. Merleau-Ponty, Maurice, 1908-1961. 2. Phenomenology I. T. II. Series.
B2430.M3764 M3213　　194 19　　LC 81-4026　　ISBN 0821404482

**Merleau-Ponty, Maurice, 1908-1961.**　• **1.839**
The primacy of perception, and other essays on phenomenological psychology, the philosophy of art, history, and politics. Edited, with an introd. by James M. Edie. [Evanston, Ill.] Northwestern University Press, 1964. xix, 228 p. 24 cm. (Northwestern University studies in phenomenology & existential philosophy) 1. Phenomenology — Addresses, essays, lectures I. T. II. Series.
B2430.M378 E5 1964　　194　　LC 64-22712

**Merleau-Ponty, Maurice, 1908-1961.**　• **1.840**
[Selections. English] The essential writings of Merleau–Ponty. Edited by Alden L. Fisher. New York, Harcourt, Brace & World [1969] viii, 383 p. 21 cm. 1. Philosophy — Collected works. I. Fisher, Alden L., 1928- ed. II. T.
B2430.M378 F53　　194　　LC 69-17417

**Merleau-Ponty, Maurice, 1908-1961.**　• **1.841**
Sense and non–sense. [Evanston, Ill.] Northwestern University Press, 1964. xxvii, 193 p. 24 cm. 1. Phenomenology I. T.
B2430.M379 S43　　LC 64-23443

**Merleau-Ponty, Maurice, 1908-1961.**　• **1.842**
Signs. Translated, with an introd. by Richard C. McCleary. — [Evanston, Ill.] Northwestern University Press, 1964. xxxiv, 355 p. 24 cm. — (Northwestern University studies in phenomenology & existential philosophy) Bibliographical footnotes. 1. Semantics (Philosophy) I. T.
B2430.M379S53 1964　　194　　LC 64-19455

**Merleau-Ponty, Maurice, 1908-1961.**　• **1.843**
[Visible et l'invisible. English] The visible and the invisible; followed by working notes. Edited by Claude Lefort. Translated by Alphonso Lingis. Evanston [Ill.] Northwestern University Press, 1968. lvi, 282 p. 24 cm. (Northwestern University studies in phenomenology & existential philosophy) 1. Ontology 2. Knowledge, Theory of I. Lefort, Claude. ed. II. T. III. Series.
B2430.M379 V513　　111　　LC 68-31025

**Mallin, Samuel B.**　**1.844**
Merleau–Ponty's philosophy / Samuel B. Mallin. — New Haven: Yale University Press, 1979. xi, 302 p.; 24 cm. Includes index. 1. Merleau-Ponty, Maurice, 1908-1961. I. T.
B2430.M38 M34　　194　　LC 79-64078　　ISBN 0300022751

**Spurling, Laurie.**　**1.845**
Phenomenology and the social world: the philosophy of Merleau–Ponty and its relation to the social sciences / Laurie Spurling. — London; Boston: Routledge and K. Paul, 1977. xiii, 208, 15 p.: ill.; 23 cm. — (Routledge social science series) (International library of sociology) Includes index. 1. Merleau-Ponty, Maurice, 1908-1961. 2. Phenomenology 3. Social sciences I. T.
B2430.M38 S68　　300/.1　　LC 77-30141　　ISBN 0710087128

## B2430.R5 Ricoeur

**Ihde, Don, 1934-.**　**1.846**
Hermeneutic phenomenology; the philosophy of Paul Ricoeur. Foreword by Paul Ricoeur. — Evanston: Northwestern University Press, 1971. xx, 192 p.; 24 cm. — (Northwestern University studies in phenomenology and existential

philosophy) 1. Rico eur, Paul. 2. Hermeneutics 3. Phenomenology I. T. II. Series.
B2430.R554 I43　　194　　LC 71-138922　　ISBN 0810103478

**Studies in the philosophy of Paul Ricoeur / edited by Charles**　**1.847**
**E. Reagan.**
Athens: Ohio University Press, c1979. 194 p.; 24 cm. 1. Rico eur, Paul — Addresses, essays, lectures. I. Reagan, Charles E.
B2430.R554 S78　　194　　LC 79-10343　　ISBN 0821402234

## B2430.S3 Sartre

**Sartre, Jean Paul, 1905-.**　• **1.848**
The philosophy of Jean–Paul Sartre. Edited by Robert Denoon Cumming. New York, Random House [1965] xii, 491 p. 22 cm. Translations of extracts from the author's works. 1. Philosophy — Collected works. I. Cumming, Robert Denoon, 1916- ed. II. T.
B2430.S32 E53　　194　　LC 65-11282

**Aron, Raymond, 1905-.**　**1.849**
[Histoire et dialectique de la violence. English] History and the dialectic of violence: an analysis of Sartre's Critique de la raison dialectique / Raymond Aron; translated by Barry Cooper. — New York: Harper & Row, c1975. xxv, 241 p.; 23 cm. — (Explorations in interpretative sociology) Translation of Histoire et dialectique de la violence. 1. Sartre, Jean Paul, 1905- 2. Dialectic 3. Violence I. T.
B2430.S34 A7813 1975b　　194　　LC 75-331089　　ISBN 0061361704

**Charlesworth, M. J. (Maxwell John), 1925-.**　**1.850**
The existentialists and Jean–Paul Sartre / Max Charlesworth. — New York: St. Martin's Press, 1976, c1975. x, 158 p.; 23 cm. Contains the text of 2 programs broadcast on the Australian Broadcasting Commission's Radio 2 in 1975. 1. Sartre, Jean Paul, 1905- — Addresses, essays, lectures. 2. Existentialism — Addresses, essays, lectures. I. T.
B2430.S34 C52 1976　　142/.7　　LC 75-37424

**Chiodi, Pietro.**　**1.851**
[Sartre e il marxismo. English] Sartre and Marxism / Pietro Chiodi; translated from the Italian by Kate Soper. — Atlantic Highlands, N.J.: Humanities Press, 1976. xiv, 162 p.; 23 cm. — (European philosophy and the human sciences) Translation of Sartre e il marxismo. 1. Sartre, Jean Paul, 1905- 2. Existentialism 3. Dialectical materialism I. T.
B2430.S34 C5313 1976　　194　　LC 76-3778　　ISBN 0391005901

**Hayim, Gila J., 1938-.**　**1.852**
The existential sociology of Jean–Paul Sartre / Gila J. Hayim. — Amherst: University of Massachusetts Press, 1980. xviii, 157 p.; 22 cm. 1. Sartre, Jean Paul, 1905- 2. Existentialism 3. Sociology I. T.
B2430.S34 H384　　194　　LC 80-10131　　ISBN 0870232983

**LaCapra, Dominick, 1939-.**　**1.853**
A preface to Sartre / Dominick La Capra. — Ithaca: Cornell University Press, 1978. 250 p.; 22 cm. Errata slip inserted. 1. Sartre, Jean Paul, 1905- I. T.
B2430.S34 L24　　848/.9/1409　　LC 78-58022　　ISBN 0801411750

**Murdoch, Iris.**　**1.854**
Sartre, romantic rationalist / Iris Murdoch. — New Haven: Yale University Press, 1953. 114 p.; 22 cm. (Studies in modern European literature and thought) 1. Sartre, Jean Paul, 1905- 2. Existentialism I. T.
B2430.S34 M8

**Thompson, Kenneth A.**　**1.855**
Sartre, life and works / Kenneth and Margaret Thompson. — New York, N.Y.; Bicester, England: Facts on File, c1984. xv, 227 p.; 23 cm. (Facts on File chronology series.) Includes indexes. 1. Sartre, Jean Paul, 1905- 2. Philosophers — France — Biography. 3. Authors, French — 20th century — Biography. I. Thompson, Margaret. II. T. III. Series.
B2430.S34 T52 1984　　848/.91409 B 19　　LC 82-15585　　ISBN 0871967197

## B2430.T37 Teilhard de Chardin

**Teilhard de Chardin, Pierre.**　**1.856**
[Hymne de l'univers. English] Hymn of the universe. [Translated by Gerald Vann] New York, Harper & Row [1969, c1965] 157 p. 21 cm. (Harper colophon books, CN 173) 1. Mysticism — Catholic Church. 2. Cosmology 3. Creation I. T.
B2430.T373　　248.2/2　　LC 78-8361

## B2430.W4 Weil

**Weil, Simone, 1909-1943.**    **1.857**
On science, necessity, and the love of God; essays collected, translated, and edited by Richard Rees. London, New York [etc.] Oxford U.P., 1968. ix, 201 p. 22 cm. 1. Science — Addresses, essays, lectures. 2. God — Addresses, essays, lectures. I. Rees, Richard. ed. II. T.
B2430.W472E56    194    *LC* 79-359730    *ISBN* 019213941X

**Weil, Simone, 1909-1943.**    **1.858**
[Leçons de philosophie. English] Lectures on philosophy / Simone Weil; translated by Hugh Price; with an introd. by Peter Winch. — Cambridge [Eng.]; New York: Cambridge University Press, 1978. vii, 232 p.; 21 cm. Translation of Leçons de philosophie. 1. Philosophy — Addresses, essays, lectures. I. T.
B2430.W473 L3513    194    *LC* 77-26735    *ISBN* 052122005X. *ISBN* 0521293332 pbk

**Weil, Simone, 1909-1943.**    **1.859**
Gravity and grace; with an introd. by Gustave Thibon. Translated by Arthur Wills. New York, Putnam [1952] 236 p. 21 cm. I. T.
B2430.W473.P4 E5    *LC* 52-9847

**Pétrement, Simone.**    **1.860**
[Vie de Simone Weil. English] Simone Weil: a life / Simone Pétrement; translated from the French by Raymond Rosenthal. — 1st American ed. — New York: Pantheon Books, c1976. xiv, 576 p., [12] leaves of plates: ill.; 24 cm. Translation of La vie de Simone Weil. 1. Weil, Simone, 1909-1943. 2. Philosophers — France — Biography. I. T.
B2430.W474 P4613    194 B    *LC* 76-9576    *ISBN* 0394498151

# B2521–3396 Germany. Austria

**Beck, Lewis White.**    • **1.861**
Early German philosophy; Kant and his predecessors. — Cambridge, Mass.: Belknap Press of Harvard University Press, 1969. xi, 556 p.; 25 cm. 1. Kant, Immanuel, 1724-1804. 2. Philosophy, German — History. I. T.
B2521.B4    193    *LC* 79-75427    *ISBN* 0674221257

### B2535–2729 17TH–18TH CENTURIES

### B2558–2598 Leibniz

**Leibniz, Gottfried Wilhelm, Freiherr von, 1646-1716.**    • **1.862**
[Prose works. English. Selections] The monadology and other philosophical writings, translated with introduction and notes by Robert Latta. [London, New York, etc.] Oxford University Press, H. Milford [1925] x p., 1 l., 437 p. 20 cm. At head of title: Leibniz. 'Parts II and III of the introduction were accepted by the University of Edinburgh as a thesis for the degree of doctor of philosophy.'—Pref. 'Second impression 1925; first edition 1898.' I. Latta, Robert, 1865- ed. and tr. II. T.
B2558.L3 1925    *LC* 25-20516

**Leibniz, Gottfried Wilhelm, Freiherr von, 1646-1716.**    • **1.863**
[Selected works. English] Philosophical papers and letters. A selection translated and edited, with an introd. by Leroy E. Loemker. 2d ed. Dordrecht, D. Reidel [1970] xii, 736 p. port. 23 cm. (Synthese historical library.) Distributed in the U.S.A. by Humanities Press, New York. 1. Philosophy — Collected works. I. Loemker, Leroy E. ed. II. T. III. Series.
B2558.L62 1970    193    *LC* 70-484386    *ISBN* 0391000306

**Leibniz, Gottfried Wilhelm, Freiherr von, 1646-1716.**    **1.864**
[Nouveaux essais sur l'entendement humain. English] New essays on human understanding / G. W. Leibniz; translated and edited by Peter Remnant and Jonathan Bennett. — Cambridge [Eng.]; New York: Cambridge University Press, 1981. xxii, 527, xcvi p.: ill.; 24 cm. Translation of Nouveaux essais sur l'entendement humain. Includes indexes. 1. Locke, John, 1632-1704. Essay concerning human understanding 2. Knowledge, Theory of I. Remnant, Peter. II. Bennett, Jonathan Francis. III. T.
B2581.E5 R45 1981    121    *LC* 79-42668    *ISBN* 0521231477

**Leibniz, Gottfried Wilhelm, von, Freiherr, 1646-1716.**    • **1.865**
[Essais de théodicée. English] Theodicy, abridged. Edited, abridged, and with an introd. by Diogenes Allen. [Translated by E. M. Huggard.] Indianapolis, Bobbs-Merrill, 1966. xx, 176 p. 21 cm. (The Library of liberal arts, 121) Translation of Essais de théodicée sur la bonté de Dieu, la liberté de l'homme et l'origine du mal. 1. Theodicy — Early works to 1800. 2. Free will and determinism I. Allen, Diogenes. ed. II. T.
B2590.E5 1966    231/.8    *LC* 67-4155

**Brown, Stuart C.**    **1.866**
Leibniz / Stuart Brown. — Minneapolis: University of Minnesota Press, c1984. xii, 223 p.; 23 cm. (Philosophers in context.) Includes index. 1. Leibniz, Gottfried Wilhelm, Freiherr von, 1646-1716. I. T. II. Series.
B2598.B74 1984    193 19    *LC* 84-13205    *ISBN* 0816613907

**Leibniz: critical and interpretive essays / Michael Hooker, editor.**    **1.867**
Minneapolis: University of Minnesota Press, c1982. 373 p.; 24 cm. Includes indexes. 1. Leibniz, Gottfried Wilhelm, Freiherr von, 1646-1716 — Addresses, essays, lectures. I. Hooker, Michael.
B2598.L435 1982    193 19    *LC* 82-7010    *ISBN* 0816610207

**Loemker, Leroy E.**    **1.868**
Struggle for synthesis; the seventeenth century background of Leibniz's synthesis of order and freedom [by] Leroy E. Loemker. — Cambridge, Mass.: Harvard University Press, 1972. xi, 318 p.; 24 cm. 1. Leibniz, Gottfried Wilhelm, Freiherr von, 1646-1716. 2. Order (Philosophy) 3. Liberty. I. T.
B2598.L6    190/.9/032    *LC* 72-79308    *ISBN* 0674845455

**MacDonald Ross, G. (George)**    **1.869**
Leibniz / G. MacDonald Ross. — Oxford [Oxfordshire]; New York: Oxford University Press, 1984. 121 p.; 23 cm. — (Past masters.) Includes index. 1. Leibniz, Gottfried Wilhelm, Freiherr von, 1646-1716. I. T. II. Series.
B2598.M24 1984    193 B 19    *LC* 83-25131    *ISBN* 019287621X

**Martin, Gottfried, 1901-.**    • **1.870**
Leibniz: logic and metaphysics. Translated from the German by K. J. Northcott and P. G. Lucas. — [Manchester, Eng.] Manchester University Press [1964] viii, 195 p. 23 cm. 1. Leibniz, Gottfried Wilhelm, Freiherr von, 1646-1716. I. T.
B2598.M273 1964a    *LC* 64-7223 rev

**Rescher, Nicholas.**    • **1.871**
The philosophy of Leibniz. — Englewood Cliffs, N.J.: Prentice-Hall, [1967] viii, 168 p.; 22 cm. 'The Leibniz literature': p. 7-10. 1. Leibniz, Gottfried Wilhelm, Freiherr von, 1646-1716. I. T.
B2598.R46    193    *LC* 66-29698

**Russell, Bertrand, 1872-1970.**    • **1.872**
A critical exposition of the philosophy of Leibniz; with an appendix of leading passages. — [2d ed.]. — London, Allen & Unwin [1958] xxii, 311 p. 23 cm. 1. Leibniz, Gottfried Wilhelm, Freiherr von, 1646-1716. I. T.
B2598.Rx    193    *LC* 63-6754

**McRae, Robert F.**    **1.873**
Leibniz: perception, apperception, and thought / Robert McRae. — Toronto; Buffalo: University of Toronto Press, c1976. x, 148 p.; 24 cm. 1. Leibniz, Gottfried Wilhelm, Freiherr von, 1646-1716 — Knowledge, Theory of. 2. Perception I. T.
B2599.K7 M3    121    *LC* 76-6084    *ISBN* 0802053491

**Ishiguro, Hidé.**    **1.874**
Leibniz's philosophy of logic and language. — Ithaca, N.Y.: Cornell University Press, [1972] viii, 157 p.; 23 cm. 1. Leibniz, Gottfried Wilhelm, Freiherr von, 1646-1716 — Logic. 2. Languages — Philosophy I. T.
B2599.L8 I83 1972    160    *LC* 72-2357    *ISBN* 0801407370

### B2690–2963 Mendelssohn

**Mendelssohn, Moses, 1729-1786.**    **1.875**
[Selections. English. 1975] Moses Mendelssohn: selections from his writings / edited and translated by Eva Jospe; with an introd. by Alfred Jospe. — New York: Viking Press, [1975] xiv, 210 p.; 22 cm. — (The Jewish heritage classics) Includes index. 1. Mendelssohn, Moses, 1729-1786. 2. Jews — Emancipation 3. Judaism — Apologetic works 4. Immortality I. T. II. Series.
B2690.E5 J67 1975    193    *LC* 74-34046    *ISBN* 067048993X

**Altmann, Alexander, 1906-.**    **1.876**
Moses Mendelssohn: a biographical study. — University: University of Alabama Press, [1973] xvi, 900 p.: ill.; 25 cm. 1. Mendelssohn, Moses, 1729-1786. I. T.
B2693.A64    193 B    *LC* 72-12430    *ISBN* 0817368604

### B2741–3177 18TH–19TH CENTURIES

**Royce, Josiah, 1855-1916.**    **1.877**
Lectures on modern idealism. New foreword by John E. Smith. — New Haven, Yale University Press [1964, c1919] xvi, 266 p. 21 cm. — (A Yale paperbound, Y-107) 'The lectures here published were first delivered at the Johns Hopkins University in 1906 under the title 'Aspects of post-Kantian idealism.'' 1. Idealism 2. Philosophy, German I. T.
B2745.R8 1964    141    *LC* 64-3803

## B2750–2799 Kant

**Kant, Immanuel, 1724-1804.**                                        • **1.878**
The fundamental principles of the metaphysic of ethics / Translated by Thomas
Kingsmill Abbott. — 3rd ed. — London: Longmans, Green, 1907. 102 p.
1. Ethics I. Abbott, Thomas Kingsmill. II. T.
B2766.E6 M3 1916        *LC* a 14-1199

**Kant, Immanuel, 1724-1804.**                                        • **1.879**
[Grundlegung zur Metaphysik der Sitten. English] The moral law; Kant's
Groundwork of the metaphysic of morals. Translated and analysed by H. J.
Paton. New York, Barnes & Noble [1967] 142 p. 22 cm. Translation of
Grundlegung zur Metaphysik der Sitten. 1. Ethics I. Paton, Herbert James,
1887- ed. and tr. II. T.
B2766.E6 P3 1967        171        *LC* 67-4642

**Ross, W. D. (William David), 1877-.**                                        • **1.880**
Kant's ethical theory; a commentary on the Grundlegung zur Metaphysik der
Sitten. Oxford: Clarendon P. 1954. 96p. 1. Kant,Immanuel,
1724-1804.Grundlegung zur Metaphysik der Sitten. 2. Ethics I. T.
B2769.R6        *LC* A55-4769

**Kant, Immanuel, 1724-1804.**                                        • **1.881**
[Kritik der praktischen Vernunft. English] Critique of practical reason;
translated, with an introd., by Lewis White Beck. New York, Liberal Arts Press
[1956] 168 p. 21 cm. (The Library of liberal arts, no. 52) 1. Ethics I. T.
B2773.E5 B4        193.2        *LC* 56-2993

**Beck, Lewis White.**                                        • **1.882**
A commentary on Kant's Critique of practical reason. — [Chicago, University
of Chicago Press [1960] xvi, 308 p. front. 24 cm. Bibliography: p. 287-293.
1. Kant, Immanuel, 1724-1804. Kritik der praktischen Vernunft. I. T.
B2774.B4        121        *LC* 60-5464

**Kant, Immanuel, 1724-1804.**                                        • **1.883**
[Kritik der reinen Vernunft. English] Critique of pure reason. Unabridged ed.
New York, St. Martin's Press [1965, c1929] xii, 681 p. facsims. 19 cm.
1. Knowledge, Theory of 2. Causation 3. Reason I. T.
B2778.E5 S6 1965        *LC* 65-15126

**Cassirer, H. W. (Heinrich Walter), 1903-.**                                        • **1.884**
Kant's first critique; an appraisal of the permanent significance of Kant's
Critique of pure reason. London, Allen & Unwin [1955] 367 p. 22 cm. (The
Muirhead library of Philosophy) 1. Kant, Immanuel, 1724-1804. Kritik der
reinen Vernunft. I. T.
B2779.C3        *LC* 55-3481

**Paton, Herbert James, 1887-.**                                        • **1.885**
Kant's metaphysic of experience. London, G. Allen & Unwin, ltd. [1936] 2 v. 22
cm. 1. Kant, Immanuel, 1724-1804. Kritik der reinen vernunft. I. T.
B2779.P3        *LC* 36-35593

**Smith, Norman Kemp, 1872-1958.**                                        • **1.886**
A commentary to Kant's Critique of pure reason / by Norman Kemp Smith. —
2d ed., rev. and enl. — New York: Humanities Press, 1962. lxi, 651 p; 24 cm.
1. Kant, Immanuel, 1724-1804. Kritik der reinen Vernunft. I. T.
B2779.S5 1962        121        *LC* 63-3781

**Strawson, P. F.**                                        • **1.887**
The bounds of sense: an essay on Kant's 'Critique of pure reason' [by] P. F.
Strawson. — London: Methuen, 1966. 3-296 p.; 22 1/2 cm. Label mounted on
t.p.: New York, Barnes & Noble. 1. Kant, Immanuel, 1724-1804. Immanuel,
Kritik der reinen Vernunft. I. T.
B2779.S8        121        *LC* 66-69909

**Walsh, William Henry.**                                        **1.888**
Kant's criticism of metaphysics / W. H. Walsh. — Edinburgh: University
Press, c1975. viii, 265 p.; 23 cm. Includes index. 1. Kant, Immanuel,
1724-1804. Kritik der reinen Vernunft. 2. Metaphysics. I. T.
B2779.W32        110        *LC* 75-330253        *ISBN* 0852242832

**Weldon, Thomas Dewar.**                                        • **1.889**
Kant's Critique of pure reason. 2d ed. Oxford, Clarendon Press, 1958. 331 p. 23
cm. 1. Kant, Immanuel, 1724-1804. Kritik der reinen Vernunft. I. T.
B2779.W4 1958        *LC* 58-4404

**Kant, Immanuel, 1724-1804.**                                        **1.890**
The critique of judgement / Immanuel Kant; translated with analytical indexes
by James Creed Meredith. — Oxford: Clarendon Press, 1952. 246, 180 p.; 19
cm. Originally published in 2 v. under titles: Critique of aesthetic judgement
and Critique of teleological judgement. 1. Judgment (Logic) I. Meredith,
James Creed. II. T. III. Title: Critique of aesthetic judgement. IV. Title:
Critique of teleological judgement.
B2783.E5 M4 1952        *ISBN* 0198245890

**Kant, Immanuel, 1724-1804.**                                        • **1.891**
[Metaphysische Anfangsgründe der Naturwissenschaft. English] Metaphysical
foundations of natural science. Translated, with introd. and essay, by James
Ellington. Indianapolis, Bobbs-Merrill [1970] xxxi, 230 p. 21 cm. (The Library
of liberal arts, LLA 108) Translation of Metaphysische Anfangsgründe der
Naturwissenschaft. 1. Science — Philosophy I. T.
B2786.E5E43        501        *LC* 76-103934

**Kant, Immanuel, 1724-1804.**                                        • **1.892**
Religion within the limits of reason alone. 2d ed. La Salle, Ill., Open Court Pub.
Co., 1960. cliv, 190 p 21 cm. 1. Philosophy and religion I. T.
B2791.E5 G7 1960a        *LC* 61-1013

**Kant, Immanuel, 1724-1804.**                                        • **1.893**
Prolegomena to any future metaphysics that will be able to present itself as a
science. A translation from the German based on the original editions, with an
introd. and notes by Peter G. Lucas. [Manchester] Manchester University Press
[1953] 155p. (Philosophical classics; 1) 1. Metaphysics 2. Knowledge, Theory
of I. T. II. Series.
B2792.E5Lx        *LC* a 53-7069

**Kant, Immanuel, 1724-1804.**                                        **1.894**
[Anthropologie in pragmatischer Hinsicht. English] Anthropology from a
pragmatic point of view / Immanuel Kant; translated by Victor Lyle Dowdell;
rev. and edited by Hans H. Rudnick; with an introd. by Frederick P. Van De
Pitte. — Carbondale: Southern Illinois University Press, c1978. xxii, 298 p.; 22
cm. Translation of Anthropologie in pragmatischer Hinsicht. 1. Man
2. Psychology — Early works to 1850 I. T.
B2794.A572 E5 1978        150        *LC* 77-10819        *ISBN* 0809306239

**Kant, Immanuel, 1724-1804.**                                        • **1.895**
Kant's inaugural dissertation and early writings on space, translated by John
Handyside. Chicago, London, The Open court publishing company, 1929. xii,
85 p. 20 cm. Published 1928. Contains reproduction of original t.-p. of the
dissertation: De mundi sensibilis atque intelligibilis forma et principiis ... 1770.
Preface signed: Norman Kemp Smith. 1. Reality 2. Space and time
I. Handyside, John, 1883-1916 II. Smith, Norman Kemp, 1872-1958. III. T.
B2794.D4 E5 1929        *LC* 28-23812

**Kant, Immanuel, 1724-1804.**                                        • **1.896**
First introduction to the Critique of judgment. Translated by James Haden. —
Indianapolis, Bobbs-Merrill [c1965] xv, 55 p. 21 cm. — (The Library of liberal
arts) Translation of the introduction to Kant's Kritik der Urtheilskraft. This
introduction was first published in English in 1935 under title: On philosophy in
general. Bibliography: p. xv. 1. Judgment (Logic) I. T.
B2794.E73E5 1965        153.46        *LC* 64-66071

**Kant, Immanuel, 1724-1804.**                                        **1.897**
[Vorlesungen über die philosophische Religionslehre. English] Lectures on
philosophical theology / Immanuel Kant; translated by Allen W. Wood and
Gertrude M. Clark; with introd. and notes by Allen W. Wood. — Ithaca:
Cornell University Press, 1978. 175 p.; 23 cm. Translation of Vorlesungen über
die philosophische Religionslehre. 1. Philosophical theology — Addresses,
essays, lectures. I. Wood, Allen W. II. Clark, Gertrude M. III. T.
B2794.V642 E54 1978        200/.1        *LC* 78-58034        *ISBN* 0801411998

**Kant, Immanuel, 1724-1804.**                                        **1.898**
[Welches sind die wirklichen Fortschritte, die die Metaphysik seit Leibnitzens
und Wolfs Zeiten in Deutschland gemacht hat? English & German] What real
progress has metaphysics made in Germany since the time of Leibniz and
Wolff? / Immanuel Kant; translation and introduction by Ted Humphrey. —
New York: Abaris Books, 1983. 206 p.; 24 cm. — (Janus library. 4) German
text and English translation of: Welches sind die wirklichen Fortschritte die die
Metaphysik seit Leibnitzens und Wolfs Zeiten in Deutschland gemacht hat?
1. Leibniz, Gottfried Wilhelm, Freiherr von, 1646-1716 — Metaphysics.
2. Wolff, Christian, Freiherr von, 1679-1754 — Metaphysics. 3. Metaphysics
— History — 18th century. 4. Philosophy, German — 18th century I. T.
II. Series.
B2794.W52 E5 1983        110/.943 19        *LC* 83-71751        *ISBN*
0913870560

### B2797–2799 General Criticism

**Cassirer, Ernst, 1874-1945.**                                        **1.899**
[Kants Leben und Lehre. English] Kant's life and thought / Ernst Cassirer;
translated by James Haden; introduction by Stephan Körner. — New Haven:
Yale University Press, 1982, c1981. xxiii, 429 p.; 25 cm. Translation of: Kants
Leben und Lehre, 2nd ed. Berlin: B. Cassirer, 1921. Includes index. 1. Kant,
Immanuel, 1724-1804. I. T.
B2797.C313 1982        193 19        *LC* 81-3354        *ISBN* 0300023588

**Körner, Stephan, 1913-.**                                        • **1.900**
Kant. [Harmondsworth, Middlesex] Penguin Books [1955] 230 p. 18 cm.
1. Kant, Immanuel, 1724-1804. I. T.
B2798.K6        *LC* 56-257

**Sherover, Charles M.** **1.901**
Heidegger, Kant & time [by] Charles M. Sherover. With an introd. by William Barrett. Bloomington, Indiana University Press [1971] xvii, 322 p. 25 cm. 1. Heidegger, Martin, 1889-1976. 2. Kant, Immanuel, 1724-1804. 3. Time I. T.
B2798.S54 1971   115   *LC* 74-135011   *ISBN* 0253327202

**Walker, Ralph Charles Sutherland.** **1.902**
Kant: the arguments of the philosophers / Ralph C. S. Walker. — London; Boston: Routledge & Kegan Paul, 1978. xii, 201 p.; 24 cm. — (The Arguments of the philosophers) Includes index. 1. Kant, Immanuel, 1724-1804. I. T.
B2798.W23   193   *LC* 78-40585   *ISBN* 0710089945

**Coleman, Francis X. J.** **1.903**
The harmony of reason: a study in Kant's aesthetics / Francis X. J. Coleman. — [Pittsburg]: University of Pittsburgh Press, [1974] xv, 221 p.; 22 cm. Includes index. 1. Kant, Immanuel, 1724-1804 Immanuel, — Aesthetics. I. T.
B2799.A4 C63   111.8/5   *LC* 74-4520   *ISBN* 0822932822

**Crawford, Donald W., 1938-.** **1.904**
Kant's aesthetic theory [by] Donald W. Crawford. — [Madison]: University of Wisconsin Press, [1974] ix, 189 p.; 24 cm. 1. Kant, Immanuel, 1724-1804 Immanuel, — Aesthetics. I. T.
B2799.A4 C7   111.8/5   *LC* 73-15259   *ISBN* 0299065103

**Essays in Kant's aesthetics / edited and introduced by Ted** **1.905**
**Cohen & Paul Guyer.**
Chicago: University of Chicago Press, c1982. x, 323 p.; 24 cm. 1. Kant, Immanuel, 1724-1804 — Aesthetics — Addresses, essays, lectures. 2. Aesthetics — Addresses, essays, lectures. I. Cohen, Ted. II. Guyer, Paul, 1948-
B2799.A4 E87   111/.85/0924 19   *LC* 81-13091   *ISBN* 0226112268

**Bennett, Jonathan Francis.** **1.906**
Kant's Dialectic [by] Jonathan Bennett. — [London; New York]: Cambridge University Press, [1974] xi, 291 p.; 23 cm. 1. Kant, Immanuel, 1724-1804. 2. Dialectic I. T.
B2799.D47 B4   193   *LC* 73-89762   *ISBN* 0521204208

**Knox, Israel, 1904-.** • **1.907**
The aesthetic theories of Kant, Hegel, and Schopenhauer. — New York, Humanities Press, 1958. 219 p. 23 cm. Issued in 1936 as thesis, Columbia University. 1. Hegel, Georg Wilhelm Friedrich, 1770-1831. 2. Schopenhauer, Arthur, 1788-1860. 3. Kant, Immanuel — Aesthetics. 4. Aesthetics I. T.
B2799.E7 K6x   701   *LC* A 63-5065

**Bernstein, John Andrew, 1944-.** **1.908**
Shaftesbury, Rousseau, and Kant: an introduction to the conflict between aesthetic and moral values in modern thought / John Andrew Bernstein. — Rutherford [N.J.]: Fairleigh Dickinson University Press, c1980. 190 p.; 22 cm. Based on the author's thesis. Includes index. 1. Kant, Immanuel, 1724-1804 — Ethics. 2. Shaftesbury, Anthony Ashley Cooper, Earl of, 1671-1713 — Ethics. 3. Rousseau, Jean-Jacques, 1712-1778 — Ethics. 4. Ethics — History. 5. Aesthetics — History. 6. Values — History. I. T.
B2799.E8 B39   170   *LC* 78-75190   *ISBN* 0838623514

**Murphy, Jeffrie G.** • **1.909**
Kant: the philosophy of right [by] Jeffrie G. Murphy. — London: Macmillan; New York: St. Martin's P., 1970. 186 p.; 19 cm. — (Philosophers in perspective) 1. Kant, Immanuel, 1724-1804 — Ethics. 2. Law — Philosophy. I. T.
B2799.E8 M85 1970   170/.924   *LC* 75-108406   *ISBN* 0333074602

**Paton, Herbert James, 1887-.** • **1.910**
The categorical imperative; a study in Kant's moral philosophy [by] H. J. Paton. New York, Harper & Row [1967] 283 p. 21 cm. (Harper torchbooks, TB1325) 'Originally published in 1947.' 1. Kant, Immanuel, 1724-1804 — Ethics. I. T.
B2799.E8 P3 1967   170/.924   *LC* 68-794

**Schilpp, Paul Arthur, 1897-.** • **1.911**
Kant's pre-critical ethics / by Paul Arthur Schilpp; with a foreword by H.J. Paton. — 2d. ed. — Evanston: Northwestern University Press, 1960. xviii, 199 p.; 24 cm. 1. Kant, Immanuel, 1724-1804 — Ethics. I. T.
B2799.E8 S35 1960   *LC* 60-7102   *ISBN* 081010217X

**Kant, Immanuel, 1724-1804.** **1.912**
[Einzig mögliche Beweisgrund zu einer Demonstration des Daseins Gottes. English & German] Der einzig mögliche Beweisgrund = The one possible basis for a demonstration of the existence of God / Immanuel Kant; translation and introduction by Gordon Treash. — New York, N.Y.: Abaris Books, 1979. 247 p.; 24 cm. — (The Janus library; 5) English and German; introd. and notes in English. 'The German text of this edition is that of the [Prussian] Academy edition'—P. 32. 1. God — Proof I. Treash, Gordon. II. T. III. Title: One possible basis for a demonstration of the existence of God.
B2799.G6 K3613   212/.1 19   *LC* 77-86227   *ISBN* 0913870374

**Kant, Immanuel, 1724-1804.** • **1.913**
On history. Edited, with an introd. by Lewis White Beck. Translated by Lewis White Beck, Robert E. Anchor and Emil L. Fackenheim. — Indianapolis, Bobbs-Merrill [1963] xxxi, 154 p. 21 cm. — (The Library of liberal arts) '162.' Bibliography: p. xxix—xxx. Bibliographical footnotes. 1. History — Philosophy I. Beck, Lewis White. ed. and tr. II. T.
B2799.H7B43   901   *LC* 62-22315

**Findlay, J. N. (John Niemeyer), 1903-.** **1.914**
Kant and the transcendental object: a hermeneutic study / by J.N. Findlay. — Oxford: Clarendon Press; New York: Oxford University Press, 1981. xxiv, 392 p.; 22 cm. Includes index. 1. Kant, Immanuel, 1724-1804 — Metaphysics. 2. Metaphysics 3. Transcendentalism 4. Object (Philosophy) 5. Idealism I. T.
B2799.M5 F56 1981   110 19   *LC* 80-41782   *ISBN* 0198246382

**Heidegger, Martin, 1889-1976.** • **1.915**
Kant and the problem of metaphysics. Translated by James S. Churchill. Foreword by Thomas Langen. Bloomington, Indiana University Press [1962] xxv, 255 p. 22 cm. 1. Kant, Immanuel, 1724-1804. 2. Metaphysics I. T.
B2799.M5H43   *LC* 62-8974

**Gram, Moltke S.** • **1.916**
Kant, ontology & the a priori [by] Moltke S. Gram. — Evanston [Ill.]: Northwestern University Press, 1968. x, 194 p.; 25 cm. 1. Kant, Immanuel, 1724-1804 — Ontology. I. T.
B2799.O5 G7   111   *LC* 68-29324

**Saner, Hans, 1934-.** **1.917**
Kant's political thought: its origins and development/ Hans Saner. Translated by E.B. Ashton. — Chicago: University of Chicago Press, 1973. 374 p.; 22 cm. 1. Kant, Immanuel, 1724-1804 — Political science. I. T.
B2799.P6 S2613   *LC* 73-77627   *ISBN* 0226734757

**Ameriks, Karl, 1947-.** **1.918**
Kant's theory of mind: an analysis of the paralogisms of pure reason / Karl Ameriks. — Oxford: Clarendon Press; New York: Oxford University Press, 1982. ix, 314 p.; 22 cm. Includes index. 1. Kant, Immanuel, 1724-1804 — Psychology. 2. Mind and body I. T.
B2799.P7 A53 1982   128/.2 19   *LC* 81-18670   *ISBN* 0198246617

**Despland, Michel.** **1.919**
Kant on history and religion, with a translation of Kant's 'On the failure of all attempted philosophical theodicies'. — Montreal: McGill-Queen's University Press, 1973. 355 p.; 24 cm. 1. Kant, Immanuel, 1724-1804. 2. Religion — Philosophy 3. History — Philosophy I. Kant, Immanuel, 1724-1804, Über das misslingen aller philosophischen versuche in der theodizee. English. 1973. II. T.
B2799.R4 D47   193   *LC* 73-79094   *ISBN* 0773501258

**Wood, Allen W.** **1.920**
Kant's rational theology / Allen W. Wood. — Ithaca, N.Y.: Cornell University Press, 1978. 156 p.; 23 cm. 1. Kant, Immanuel, 1724-1804. 2. Religion — Philosophy I. T.
B2799.R4 W66   200/.1   *LC* 78-58059   *ISBN* 0801412005

## B2800–2898 Fichte. Schelling

**Fichte, Johann Gottlieb, 1762-1814.** • **1.921**
The vocation of man / Johann Gottlieb Fichte; edited, with an introd. by Roderick M. Chisholm. — New York: Liberal Arts, c1956. xx, 154 p.; 21 cm. — (Library of liberal arts. no. 50) Translation of Die Bestimmung des Menschen. Translation also under title: The destination of man. 1. Man 2. Faith I. T. II. Title: The destination of man. III. Series.
B2844.B53 E54   *LC* 56-44104

**Schelling, Friedrich Wilhelm Joseph von, 1775-1854.** **1.922**
[Bruno. English] Bruno, or, On the natural and the divine principle of things / F.W.J. Schelling; edited and translated, with an introduction, by Michael G. Vater. — Albany: State University of New York Press, c1984. xiv, 269 p.; 24 cm. (SUNY series in Hegelian studies.) 1. Metaphysics I. Vater, Michael G., 1944- II. T. III. Title: On the natural and the divine principle of things. IV. Series.
B2864.E5 V37 1984   110 19   *LC* 83-5101   *ISBN* 0873957938

**Schelling, Friedrich Wilhelm Joseph von, 1775-1854.** **1.923**
[System des transzendentalen Idealismus. English] System of transcendental idealism (1800) / by F. W. J. Schelling; translated by Peter Heath; with an introd. by Michael Vater. — Charlottesville: University Press of Virginia, 1978. xxxvi, 248 p.; 24 cm. Translation of System des transzendentalen Idealismus. 1. Idealism 2. Transcendentalism I. Heath, Peter Lauchlan, 1922- II. T.
B2883.E5 H4   141/.3   *LC* 78-6638   *ISBN* 0813907802

**White, Alan, 1951-.**     **1.924**
Schelling: an introduction to the system of freedom / Alan White. — New Haven: Yale University Press, c1983. xii, 201 p.; 22 cm. Includes index. 1. Schelling, Friedrich Wilhelm Joseph von, 1775-1854. I. T.
B2898.W46 1983     193 19     *LC* 82-16034     *ISBN* 0300028962

## B2900–2949 Hegel

**Hegel, Georg Wilhelm Friedrich, 1770-1831.**     • **1.925**
Hegel on tragedy / edited, with an introd., by Anne and Henry Paolucci. — Garden City, N.Y.: Anchor Books, 1962. xxxi, 404 p. (Anchor [books] A276) 1. Tragedy I. T.
B2905.P3

**Hegel, Georg Wilhelm Friedrich, 1770-1831.**     • **1.926**
The philosophy of Hegel; edited, with an introd., by Carl J. Friedrich. — New York: Modern Library, [c1954] lxiv, 552 p.; 19 cm. — (The Modern library college editions.) I. Friedrich, Carl J. (Carl Joachim), 1901- ed. II. T.
B2908.F7 1954     193.5     *LC* 54-13055

**Hegel, Georg Wilhelm Friedrich, 1770-1831.**     • **1.927**
[Selections. English. 1970] On art, religion, philosophy; introductory lectures to the realm of absolute spirit. Edited and with an introd. by J. Glenn Gray. [1st ed.] New York, Harper & Row [1970] 324 p. 21 cm. (Harper torchbooks, 1463) Translation of the author's introductions to his Ästhetik; Vorlesungen über die Philosophie der Religion, 1. Bd.; and, Vorlesungen über die Geschichte der Philosophie. 1. Philosophy — Collected works. I. Gray, J. Glenn (Jesse Glenn), 1913-1977. ed. II. T.
B2908.G7     193     *LC* 70-10295

**Hegel, Georg Wilhelm Friedrich, 1770-1831.**     • **1.928**
On Christianity; early theological writings. Translated by T. M. Knox. With an introd. and fragments translated by Richard Kroner. — New York, Harper [1961, c1948] xi, 339 p. 21 cm. — (Harper torchbooks. The Cloister library) 'With the exception of On classical studies, the Hegel texts have been translated from Hegel's theological Jugendschriften, edited by Herman Nohl and published ... in 1907.' First published in 1948 under title: Early theological writings. 'Bibliographical note': p. 331-334. I. T.
B2908.K5x     193     *LC* 64-9054

**Hegel, Georg Wilhelm Friedrich, 1770-1831.**     • **1.929**
Hegel's philosophy of nature; edited and translated [from the German] with an introduction and explanatory notes by M. J. Petry. — London, Allen & Unwin; New York, Humanities Press, 1970. 3 v. 25 cm. — ([Muirhead library of philosophy]) Translation of Naturphilosophie, Teil 2 of Encyclopädie der philosophischen Wissenschaften. 1. Philosophy of nature I. Petry, Michael John. tr. II. T.
B2918.E5P4 1970     113     *LC* 68-55234     *ISBN* 0041000218

**Hegel, Georg Wilhelm Friedrich, 1770-1831.**     • **1.930**
[Philosophie des Geistes. English] Hegel's Philosophy of mind: being part three of the 'Encyclopaedia of the philosophical sciences' (1830), translated [from the German] by William Wallace, together with the Zusätze' in Boumann's text (1845); translated by A. V. Miller; with foreword by J. N. Findlay. Oxford, Clarendon Press, 1971. xxii, 320 p. 21 cm. Translation of Philosophie des Geistes, Teil 3 of Encyklopädie der philosophischen Wissenschaften. 1. Mind and body I. Wallace, William, 1844-1897. II. Miller, Arnold V. III. Boumann, Ludwig, 1801-1871. IV. T.
B2918.E5 W315     128/.2     *LC* 78-22856     *ISBN* 0198243456

**Marx, Karl, 1818-1883.**     • **1.931**
[Kritik des Hegelschen Staatsrechts. English] Critique of Hegel's 'Philosophy of right'. Translated from the German by Annette Jolin and Joseph O'Malley. Edited with an introd. and notes by Joseph O'Malley. Cambridge [Eng.] University Press, 1970. lxvii, 151 p. 23 cm. (Cambridge studies in the history and theory of politics) Translation of Marx's Kritik des Hegelschen Staatsrechts. 1. Hegel, Georg Wilhelm Friedrich, 1770-1831. Grundlinien der Philosophie des Rechts I. O'Malley, Joseph J. ed. II. T.
B2923.Z7 M313 1970     320.1/01 19     *LC* 74-112471     *ISBN* 0521078369

**Hegel, Georg Wilhelm Friedrich, 1770-1831.**     **1.932**
Phenomenology of spirit / by G. W. F. Hegel; translated by A. V. Miller; with analysis of the text and foreword by J. N. Findlay. — Oxford: Oxford University Press, 1977. xxxv, 595 p.; 22 cm. Translation of Phänomenologie des Geistes. 1. Spirit 2. Conscience 3. Truth I. Findlay, J. N. (John Niemeyer), 1903- II. T.
B2928.E5 M54     193     *LC* 77-483437     *ISBN* 0198245300

**Hyppolite, Jean.**     **1.933**
[Genèse et structure de la Phénoménologie de l'esprit de Hegel. English] Genesis and structure of Hegel's Phenomenology of spirit / Jean Hyppolite; translated by Samuel Cherniak and John Heckman. — Evanston: Northwestern University Press, 1974. xli, 608 p.; 24 cm. — (Northwestern University studies in phenomenology & existential philosophy) Translation of Genèse et structure

de la Phénoménologie de l'esprit de Hegel. 1. Hegel, Georg Wilhelm Friedrich, 1770-1831. Phänomenologie des Geistes. I. T. II. Series.
B2929.H913     193     *LC* 73-94431     *ISBN* 0810104474

**Kainz, Howard P.**     **1.934**
Hegel's Phenomenology part I: analysis and commentary / Howard P. Kainz. — University [Ala.]: University of Alabama Press, 1976. 218 p.: ill. — (Studies in the humanities; no. 12: Philosophy) 1. Hegel, Georg Wilhelm Friedrich, 1770-1831. Phänomenologie des Geistes 2. Phenomenology I. T.
B2929.K35     B2929 K35.     *ISBN* 0817366172

**Kojève, Alexandre, 1902-1968.**     • **1.935**
[Introduction à la lecture de Hegel. English] Introduction to the reading of Hegel, by Alexandre Kojève. Lectures on the phenomenology of spirit assembled by Raymond Queneau. Edited by Allan Bloom. Translated from the French by James H. Nichols, Jr. New York, Basic Books [1969] xiv, 287 p. 25 cm. Abridged translation of Introduction à la lecture de Hegel. 1. Hegel, Georg Wilhelm Friedrich, 1770-1831 Phaenomenologie des Geistes — Addresses, essays, lectures. I. Queneau, Raymond, 1903-1976. II. T.
B2929.K613     193     *LC* 70-78467

**Lauer, Quentin.**     **1.936**
A reading of Hegel's Phenomenology of spirit / Quentin Lauer. — New York: Fordham University Press, 1976. vii, 303 p.; 23 cm. (A Rose Hill book) 1. Hegel, Georg Wilhelm Friedrich, 1770-1831. Phänomenologie des Geistes. 2. Spirit 3. Conscience 4. Truth I. T.
B2929.L38     193     *LC* 75-41657     *ISBN* 0823210006

**Loewenberg, Jacob.**     • **1.937**
Hegel's Phenomenology: dialogues on the life of the mind [by] J. Loewenberg. — La Salle, Ill., Open Court Pub. Co., 1965. xv, 377 p. 24 cm. — (The Open Court library of philosophy) 1. Hegel, Georg Wilhelm Friedrich, 1770-1831. Phänomenologie des Geistes. I. T.
B2929.L6     193     *LC* 65-15621

**Westphal, Merold.**     **1.938**
History and truth in Hegel's Phenomenology / Merold Westphal. — Atlantic Highlands, N.J.: Humanities Press, 1979, c1978. ii, 233 p.; 24 cm. 1. Hegel, Georg Wilhelm Friedrich, 1770-1831. Phänomenologie des Geistes. 2. Spirit 3. Conscience 4. Truth 5. Knowledge, Theory of 6. History — Philosophy I. T.
B2929.W47 1979     193     *LC* 78-3490     *ISBN* 039100557X

**Hegel, Georg Wilhelm Friedrich, 1770-1831.**     • **1.939**
Hegel's lectures on the history of philosophy / translated from the German by E.S. Haldane and Frances H. Simson. New York; Humanities Press, 1955. 3 v. Vol. 1 translated by E.S. Haldane; v.2-3 translated by E.S. Haldane and Frances H. Simson. 1. Philosophy — History I. T.
B2936.E5 H2     *LC* 56-1144

**Lauer, Quentin.**     • **1.940**
Hegel's idea of philosophy. With a new translation of Hegel's Introduction to the history of philosophy. — New York: Fordham University Press, 1971. x, 159 p.; 22 cm. 'The present translation ... [of Einleitung in die Geschichte der Philosophie] is the translation of a text ... [which] can be found, along with five other versions, in the Hoffmeister edition [of Vorlesungen über die Geschichte der Philosophie] of 1940 or in the Nicolin revised edition of 1959.' 1. Philosophy — History I. Hegel, Georg Wilhelm Friedrich, 1770-1831. Einleitung in die Geschichte der Philosophie. English. 1971. II. T.
B2936.Z7 L37     193     *LC* 74-152244     *ISBN* 0823209253

**Hegel, Georg Wilhelm Friedrich, 1770-1831.**     • **1.941**
[Wissenschaft der Logik. English] Hegel's Science of logic; translated [from the German] by A. V. Miller, foreword by J. N. Findlay. London, Allen & Unwin; New York, Humanities Press, 1969. 5-845 p. 23 cm. (Muirhead library of philosophy.) Translation of Wissenschaft der Logik. 1. Logic I. T. II. Series.
B2942.A313     160     *LC* 75-390294     *ISBN* 0041930134

### B2947–2949 General Criticism

**Caird, Edward, 1835-1908.**     **1.942**
Hegel. Edinburgh, W. Blackwood, 1883. — [New York: AMS Press, 1972] viii, 224 p.: port.; 19 cm. Original ed. issued as v. 7 of Philosophical classics for English readers. 1. Hegel, Georg Wilhelm Friedrich, 1770-1831. I. T.
B2947.C3 1972     193     *LC* 71-181924     *ISBN* 0404013627

**Harris, H. S. (Henry Silton), 1926-.**     **1.943**
Hegel's development, night thoughts (Jena 1801–1806) / by H.S. Harris. — Oxford [Oxfordshire]: Clarendon Press; New York: Oxford University Press, 1983. lxx, 627 p.; 23 cm. Includes index. 1. Hegel, Georg Wilhelm Friedrich, 1770-1831. I. T.
B2947.H34 1983     193 19     *LC* 82-3550     *ISBN* 0198246544

**Harris, H. S. (Henry Silton), 1926-.**    **1.944**
Hegel's development: toward the sunlight, 1770 – 1801, by H. S. Harris. Oxford, Clarendon Press, 1972. xxxii, 574 p. 22 cm. 1. Hegel, Georg Wilhelm Friedrich, 1770-1831. I. T.
B2947.H35 1972    193 B    *LC* 72-179181    *ISBN* 0198243588

**Findlay, J. N. (John Niemeyer), 1903-.**    ● **1.945**
Hegel, a re-examination / J. N. Findlay. — London: Allen & Unwin; New York: Macmillan, [1958] 372 p.; 23 cm. (Muirhead library of philosophy) 1. Hegel, Georg Wilhelm Friedrich, 1770-1831. I. T.
B2948.F47    193    *LC* 59-1917

**Kaufmann, Walter Arnold.**    ● **1.946**
Hegel: reinterpretation, texts, and commentary / Walter Kaufmann. — 1st ed. — Garden City, N. Y.: Doubleday, 1965. 498 p. 1. Hegel, Georg Wilhelm Friedrich, 1770-1831. I. T.
B2948.K3    193    *LC* 65-13982

**Lauer, Quentin.**    **1.947**
Essays in Hegelian dialectic / Quentin Lauer. — New York: Fordham University Press, 1977. 208 p.; 23 cm. (A Rose Hill book) 1. Hegel, Georg Wilhelm Friedrich, 1770-1831 — Addresses, essays, lectures. I. T.
B2948.L33    193    *LC* 76-18465    *ISBN* 0823210219

**MacIntyre, Alasdair C. comp.**    ● **1.948**
Hegel; a collection of critical essays, edited by Alasdair MacIntyre. — [1st ed.]. — Garden City, N.Y.: Anchor Books, 1972. viii, 350 p.; 19 cm. — (Modern studies in philosophy) 1. Hegel, Georg Wilhelm Friedrich, 1770-1831 — Addresses, essays, lectures. I. T.
B2948.M18    193    *LC* 71-171335

**Marquette Hegel Symposium, 1970.**    **1.949**
The legacy of Hegel. Proceedings of the Marquette Hegel Symposium 1970. Ed. by J. J. O'Malley [and others] The Hague, Nijhoff, 1973. viii, 308 p. 24 cm. 'The symposium, celebrating the two-hundredth anniversary of Hegel's birth, was presented under the combined sponsorship of the Philosophy Department of Marquette University, the American Council of Learned Societies, and the Johnson Foundation of Racine, Wisconsin.' 1. Hegel, Georg Wilhelm Friedrich, 1770-1831 — Influence — Congresses. I. O'Malley, Joseph J. ed. II. Marquette University. Dept. of Philosophy. III. American Council of Learned Societies. IV. Johnson Foundation (Racine, Wis.) V. T.
B2948.M27 1970    193    *LC* 73-178430    *ISBN* 9024715288

**Mure, G. R. G. (Geoffrey Reginald Gilchrist), 1893-.**    ● **1.950**
An introduction to Hegel, by G. R. G. Mure ... — Oxford, The Clarendon press, 1940. xx, [2], 180 p. 23 cm. 1. Hegel, Georg Wilhelm Friedrich, 1770-1831. 2. Kant, Immanuel, 1724-1804. 3. Aristoteles. I. T.
B2948.M8    193.5    *LC* 40-33478

**Singer, Peter.**    **1.951**
Hegel / Peter Singer. — Oxford; New York: Oxford University Press, 1983. ix, 97 p.; 23 cm. — (Past masters.) Includes index. 1. Hegel, Georg Wilhelm Friedrich, 1770-1831. I. T. II. Series.
B2948.S56 1983    193 19    *LC* 82-14240    *ISBN* 0192875655

**Art and logic in Hegel's philosophy / edited by Warren E.**    **1.952**
**Steinkraus and Kenneth I. [i.e. L.] Schmitz.**
Atlantic Highlands, N.J.: Humanities Press; [Brighton], Sussex: Harvester Press, 1980. 274 p.; 24 cm. 'Papers presented at the 1974 meeting of the Society which was held at Georgetown University.' Includes indexes. 1. Hegel, Georg Wilhelm Friedrich, 1770-1831 — Aesthetics — Congresses. 2. Hegel, Georg Wilhelm Friedrich, 1770-1831 — Logic — Congresses. I. Steinkraus, Warren E. II. Schmitz, Kenneth L. III. Hegel Society of America.
B2949.A4 A7 1980    193    *LC* 77-25081    *ISBN* 0391005421

**Harris, Errol E.**    **1.953**
An interpretation of the logic of Hegel / Errol E. Harris. — Lanham: University Press of America, c1983. xiii, 346 p.; 24 cm. Includes index. 1. Hegel, Georg Wilhelm Friedrich, 1770-1831. Wissenschaft der Logik. English 2. Logic, Modern — 19th century I. T.
B2949.L8 H29 1983    160/.92/4 19    *LC* 83-17112    *ISBN* 0819135437

**Fackenheim, Emil L.**    ● **1.954**
The religious dimension in Hegel's thought [by] Emil L. Fackenheim. — Bloomington: Indiana University Press, [1968, c1967] xiii, 274 p.; 22 cm. 1. Hegel, Georg Wilhelm Friedrich, 1770-1831 — Religion. I. T.
B2949.R3 F3    193    *LC* 68-14601

## B2970–3098 Feuerbach. Schleiermacher

**Feuerbach, Ludwig, 1804-1872.**    **1.955**
[Gedanken über Tod und Unsterblichkeit. English] Thoughts on death and immortality: from the papers of a thinker, along with an appendix of theological-satirical epigrams / Ludwig Feuerbach; edited by one of his friends; translated, with introd. and notes, by James A. Massey. — Berkeley: University of California Press, c1980. xliii, 261 p.; 23 cm. Translation of Gedanken über Tod und Unsterblichkeit. 1. Death 2. Immortality (Philosophy) I. T.
B2971.G392 E5 1980    218 19    *LC* 80-25259    *ISBN* 0520040511

**Feuerbach, Ludwig, 1804-1872.**    ● **1.956**
Principles of the philosophy of the future / Ludwig Feuerbach; translated, with an introd., by Manfred H. Vogel. — Indianapolis: Bobbs-Merrill, 1966. lxxxiii, 85 p. — (The library of liberal arts; 197) Translation of Grundsatze der philosophie der zukunft. 1. Philosophy 2. Religion — Philosophy I. Vogel, Manfred H. II. T.
B2971.G7 E52    193    *LC* 64-66068

**Schleiermacher, Friedrich, 1768-1834.**    ● **1.957**
Schleiermacher's soliloquies, an English translation of the Monologen, with a critical introduction and appendix. Chicago, The Open court publishing company, 1926. 3 p.l., [v]-lx, 176 p. 20 cm. I. Friess, Horace Leland II. T.
B3093.M63    *LC* 27-5043

## B3100–3149 Schopenhauer

**Schopenhauer, Arthur, 1788-1860.**    ● **1.958**
[Works. English] The works of Schopenhauer, abridged, edited by Will Durant, PH.D. New York, Simon and Schuster, 1928. xx, 539 p. 20 cm. (The Philosophers' library) The translations of the Essays are by T. Bailey Saunders, the selections from The world as will and idea are taken from the translation by R. B. Haldane and J. Kemp. I. Saunders, Thomas Bailey, 1860-1928. tr. II. Haldane, R. B. Haldane (Richard Burdon Haldane), Viscount, 1856-1928. tr. III. Kemp, John, joint tr. IV. Durant, Will, 1885- ed. V. T. VI. Series.
B3108.S35    193.7    *LC* 28-9139

**Schopenhauer, Arthur, 1788-1860.**    ● **1.959**
On the basis of morality / translated by E. F. J. Payne; with an introduction by Richard Taylor. — Indianapolis: Bobbs-Merrill, 1965. xxviii, 226 p.; 21 cm. — (The Library of liberal arts) 'First published in 1841 as part of The two fundamental problems of ethics.' 1. Ethics I. T.
B3114.E5 P3    170    *LC* 65-26525

**Schopenhauer, Arthur, 1785-1860.**    ● **1.960**
Religion: a dialogue, and other essays, / selected and tr. by T. Bailey Saunders. — London: S. Sonnenschein; New York: Macmillan, 1899. 140 p.; 20 cm. (The philosophy at home series) 1. Religion — Addresses, essays, lectures. 2. Philosophy I. Saunders, Thomas Bailey, 1860-1928. II. T.
B3118.E5 S413 1891 v.3

**Schopenhauer, Arthur, 1788-1860.**    ● **1.961**
[Parerga und Paralipomena. Selections. English] Studies in pessimism; a series of essays. Selected and translated by T. Bailey Saunders. 4th ed. London, S. Sonnenschein, 1893. St. Clair Shores, Mich., Scholarly Press [1970?] 142 p. 23 cm. Translation of selections from Parerga und Paralipomena. 1. Pessimism I. Saunders, Thomas Bailey, 1860-1928. tr. II. T.
B3118.E5 S492 1970    083/.1    *LC* 73-121311    *ISBN* 0403000440

**Schopenhauer, Arthur, 1788-1860.**    ● **1.962**
The world as will and idea. Translated from the German by R.B. Haldane and J. Kemp. 6th ed. London Paul, Trench, Trübner 1909. (English and foreign philosophical library) I. T.
B3138 E5 H2 1909

**Magee, Bryan.**    **1.963**
The philosophy of Schopenhauer / by Bryan Magee. — Oxford: Clarendon Press; New York: Oxford University Press, 1983. 400 p.; 25 cm. 1. Schopenhauer, Arthur, 1788-1860. I. T.
B3148.M27 1983    193 19    *LC* 82-22523    *ISBN* 0198246730

## B3180–3396 19TH–20TH CENTURIES

**Bubner, Rüdiger, 1941-.**    **1.964**
Modern German philosophy / Rüdiger Bubner; translated by Eric Matthews. — Cambridge [Cambridgeshire]; New York: Cambridge University Press, 1981. xi, 223 p.; 23 cm. Translated from the author's unpublished manuscript. 1. Philosophy, German — 20th century 2. Phenomenology — History. 3. Hermeneutics — History. 4. Languages — Philosophy I. T.
B3181.B813    193 19    *LC* 81-3901    *ISBN* 0521229081

**Schnädelbach, Herbert, 1936-.**    **1.965**
Philosophy in Germany, 1831–1933 / Herbert Schnädelbach; translated by Eric Matthews. — Cambridge; New York: Cambridge University Press, 1984. x, 265 p.; 22 cm. Includes index. 1. Philosophy, German — 19th century 2. Philosophy, German — 20th century I. T.
B3181.S47 1984    193 19    *LC* 83-20944    *ISBN* 0521227933

## B3199.A3 Adorno

**Adorno, Theodor W., 1903-1969.**                                    **1.966**
[Ästhetische Theorie. English] Aesthetic theory / T.W. Adorno; translated by
C. Lenhardt; edited by Gretel Adorno and Rolf Tiedemann. — London;
Boston: Routledge & K. Paul, 1984. x, 526 p.; 22 cm. (International library of
phenomenology and moral sciences.) Translation of: Ästhetische Theorie.
1. Aesthetics I. Adorno, Gretel. II. Tiedemann, Rolf. III. T. IV. Series.
B3199.A33 A813 1984      111/.85 19      LC 82-12195      *ISBN*
0710092040

**Adorno, Theodor W., 1903-1969.**                                    **1.967**
Minima moralia: reflections from damaged life / Theodor Adorno; translated
from the German by E. F. N. Jephcott. 1st U.S. ed. London: NLB; New York:
Distributed in the U. S. and Canada by Schocken Books, 1978, [c1974] 251 p.;
21 cm. This translation first published 1974. 1. Philosophy, Modern —
Collected works. I. T.
B3199.A33 M513 1978      *ISBN* 902308955

**Adorno, Theodor W., 1903-1969.**                                    **1.968**
[Negative Dialektik. English] Negative dialectics. Translated by E. B. Ashton.
New York, Seabury Press [1973] xxi, 416 p. 22 cm. (A Continuum book)
1. Philosophy — Addresses, essays, lectures. 2. Dialectic — Addresses, essays,
lectures. I. T.
B3199.A33 N413 1973      193      LC 72-11720      *ISBN* 0816491291

## B3213.B8 Buber

**Buber, Martin, 1878-1965.**                                    • **1.969**
[Selected works. English] Writings. Selected, edited, and introduced by Will
Herberg. New York, Meridian Books, 1956. 351 p. 19 cm. (Meridian books,
M29) 1. Philosophy — Collected works. I. T.
B3213.B82 E53      181.3      LC 56-6573

**Buber, Martin, 1878-1965.**                                    • **1.970**
[Ich und du. English] I and Thou. A new translation with a prologue 'I and
You' and notes by Walter Kaufmann. New York, Scribner [1970] 185 p. 21 cm.
Translation of Ich und du. 1. Life 2. Relationism 3. God — Knowableness
I. Kaufmann, Walter Arnold. ed. II. T.
B3213.B83I1213 1970      181/.3      LC 72-123845

**Diamond, Malcolm Luria.**                                    • **1.971**
Martin Buber, Jewish existentialist / by Malcolm L. Diamond. — New York:
Oxford University Press, 1960. ix, 240 p. 1. Buber, Martin, 1878-1965. I. T.
B3213.B84 D48      LC 60-7059

**Friedman, Maurice S.**                                    **1.972**
Martin Buber's life and work: the early years, 1878–1923 / Maurice Friedman.
— 1st ed. — New York: Dutton, c1981. xxiii, 455 p., [4] leaves of plates: ill.; 25
cm. 1. Buber, Martin, 1878-1965. 2. Philosophers, Jewish — Germany —
Biography. 3. Philosophers — Germany — Biography. 4. Zionists —
Germany — Biography. I. T.
B3213.B84 F69 1981      296.3/092/4 B 19      LC 79-17868      *ISBN*
052515325X

**Friedman, Maurice S.**                                    **1.973**
Martin Buber: the life of dialogue / Maurice S. Friedman. — [3d ed.]. —
Chicago: University of Chicago Press, 1976. xvii, 322 p.; 21 cm. Includes index.
1. Buber, Martin, 1878-1965. I. T.
B3213.B84 F7 1976      296.3/092/4      LC 76-369402      *ISBN*
0226263568

**Friedman, Maurice S.**                                    **1.974**
Martin Buber's life and work: the later years, 1945–1965 / Maurice Friedman.
— 1st ed. — New York: Dutton, c1983. xviii, 493 p., [8] p. of plates: ill.; 25 cm.
Includes index. 1. Buber, Martin, 1878-1965. 2. Philosophers, Jewish —
Germany — Biography. 3. Philosophers — Germany — Biography. 4. Jews
— Germany — Biography. I. T.
B3213.B84 F73 1983      296.3/092/4 B 19      LC 83-1946      *ISBN*
0525242120

**Friedman, Maurice S.**                                    **1.975**
Martin Buber's life and work: the middle years, 1923–1945 / Maurice
Friedman. — 1st ed. — New York: Dutton, c1983. xviii, 398 p., [8] p. of plates:
ill.; 25 cm. 1. Buber, Martin, 1878-1965. 2. Philosophers, Jewish — Germany
— Biography. 3. Philosophers — Germany — Biography. 4. Jews —
Germany — Biography. I. T.
B3213.B84 F733 1983      296.3/092/4 B 19      LC 82-73072      *ISBN*
0525241760

**Schilpp, Paul Arthur, 1897-.**                                    • **1.976**
The Philosophy of Martin Buber / edited by Paul Arthur Schilpp and Maurice
Friedman. — [1st ed.]. — La Salle, Ill.: Open Court, [1967] xx, 811 p.: portr.; 25
cm. — (Library of living philosophers. v. 12) 1. Buber, Martin, 1878-1965.

I. Friedman, Maurice S. joint author. II. Buber, Martin, 1878-1965. III. T.
IV. Series.
B3213.B84 S3      193      LC 65-14535

## B3216.C3 Cassirer

**Cassirer, Ernst, 1874-1945.**                                    **1.977**
Symbol, myth, and culture: essays and lectures of Ernst Cassirer, 1935–1945 /
edited by Donald Phillip Verene. — New Haven: Yale University Press, 1979.
xii, 304 p.; 25 cm. 1. Philosophy — Addresses, essays, lectures. 2. Civilization
— Philosophy — Addresses, essays, lectures. 3. Aesthetics — Addresses,
essays, lectures. 4. Political science — Addresses, essays, lectures. I. Verene,
Donald Phillip, 1937- II. T.
B3216.C31 V47 1979      193      LC 78-9887      *ISBN* 0300023065

**Cassirer, Ernst, 1874-1945.**                                    • **1.978**
An essay on man; an introduction to the philosophy of human culture, by Ernst
Cassirer. — New Haven: Yale university press; London: H. Milford, Oxford
university press, 1944. ix p., 1 l., 237, [1] p.; 24 cm. 'Published on the Louis
Stern memorial fund.' 1. Philosophical anthropology 2. Knowledge, Theory of
3. Civilization — Philosophy 4. Symbolism I. Yale university. Louis Stern
memorial fund. II. T.
B3216.C33 E8      901      LC a 44-5386

**Cassirer, Ernst, 1874-1945.**                                    • **1.979**
[Logik der Kulturwissenschaften. English] The logic of the humanities.
Translated by Clarence Smith Howe. New Haven, Yale University Press, 1961.
217 p. 21 cm. Translation of Logik der Kulturwissenschaften. 1. Humanities
I. T.
B3216.C33 L63      193      LC 61-6311

**Cassirer, Ernst, 1874-1945.**                                    • **1.980**
[Philosophie der symbolischen Formen. English] The philosophy of symbolic
forms; translated by Ralph Manheim. Pref. and introd. by Charles W. Hendel.
New Haven, Yale University Press, 1953-57. 3 v. 24 cm. 1. Languages —
Philosophy 2. Knowledge, Theory of 3. Symbolism 4. Mythology I. T.
B3216.C33 P513      193.9      LC 52-13969

**Schilpp, Paul Arthur, 1897- ed.**                                    • **1.981**
The philosophy of Ernst Cassirer. [1st ed., 2d print.] New York, Tudor Pub. Co.
[1958, c1949] xviii, 936 p. port. 25 cm. (Library of living philosophers. [6])
1. Cassirer, Ernst, 1874-1945. I. Cassirer, Ernst, 1874-1945. II. T. III. Series.
B3216.C34S3 1958      193      LC 58-9554

## B3216.D8 Dilthey

**Dilthey, Wilhelm, 1833-1911.**                                    **1.982**
Selected writings / W. Dilthey; edited, translated, and introduced by H. P.
Rickman. — Cambridge [Eng.]; New York: Cambridge University Press, 1976.
268 p.; 24 cm. Includes index. 1. Schleiermacher, Friedrich, 1768-1834.
2. Philosophy — Collected works. I. Rickman, H. P. (Hans Peter). II. T.
B3216.D82 E57      193      LC 75-23530      *ISBN* 0521209668

**Ermarth, Michael.**                                    **1.983**
Wilhelm Dilthey: the critique of historical reason / Michael Ermarth. —
Chicago: University of Chicago Press, 1978. xiv, 414 p.; 24 cm. Based on the
author's thesis, University of Chicago, 1975. Includes index. 1. Dilthey,
Wilhelm, 1833-1911. I. T.
B3216.D84 E67      193      LC 77-16223      *ISBN* 0226217426

**Hodges, Herbert Arthur, 1905-.**                                    **1.984**
The philosophy of Wilhelm Dilthey, by H. A. Hodges. — Westport, Conn.:
Greenwood Press, [1974] xxvi, 368 p.; 22 cm. Reprint of the 1952 ed. published
by Routledge & Kegan Paul, London, in series: International library of
sociology and social reconstruction. 1. Dilthey, Wilhelm, 1833-1911. I. T.
B3216.D84 H57 1974      193      LC 73-13024      *ISBN* 0837171121

**Plantinga, Theodore, 1947-.**                                    **1.985**
Historical understanding in the thought of Wilhelm Dilthey / Theodore
Plantinga. — Toronto; Buffalo: University of Toronto Press, c1980. x, 205 p.;
24 cm. Includes index. 1. Dilthey, Wilhelm, 1833-1911. 2. History —
Philosophy I. T.
B3216.D84 P55      193      LC 79-19240      *ISBN* 0802054757

## B3258.H3 Habermas

**Habermas, Jürgen.**                                    **1.986**
[Philosophisch-politische Profile. English] Philosophical–political profiles /
Jürgen Habermas; translated by Frederick G. Lawrence. — Cambridge, Mass.:
MIT Press, c1983. xxv, 211 p.; 24 cm. — (Studies in contemporary German
social thought.) Rev. translation of: Philosophisch-politische Profile.
1. Philosophy — Addresses, essays, lectures. I. T. II. Series.
B3258.H32113 1983      193 19      LC 83-42517      *ISBN* 0262081334

**McCarthy, Thomas A.**                                                    **1.987**
The critical theory of Jürgen Habermas / Thomas McCarthy. — Cambridge:
MIT Press, c1978. xiii, 466 p.; 24 cm. 1. Habermas, Jürgen. 2. Criticism
(Philosophy) 3. Theory (Philosophy) 4. Social evolution 5. Communication
— Social aspects 6. System theory I. T.
B3258.H324 M32       193       *LC* 78-4540       *ISBN* 0262131382

## 3279.H4 Heidegger

**Heidegger, Martin, 1889-1976.**                                          **1.988**
Basic writings from Being and time (1927) to The task of thinking (1964) /
Martin Heidegger; edited, with general introd. and introductions to each
selection by David Farrell Krell. 1st ed. — New York: Harper & Row, c1977.
xvi, 397 p.; 21 cm. (His Works) 1. Philosophy — Collected works. I. T.
B3279.H47 E5 1977     193       *LC* 76-9957       *ISBN* 006063846X

**Heidegger, Martin, 1889-1976.**                                        • **1.989**
[Über die Linie. English] The question of being / translated with an introd. by
William Kluback and Jean T. Wilde. — New York: Twayne, 1958. 109 p.; 23
cm. German text and translation of the author's Über die Linie, an article
contributed to the publication issued in honor of Ernst Jünger (1955).
1. Ontology I. T. II. Title: Über die Linie. English
B3279.H47 E56 1958     111       *LC* 59-382

**Heidegger, Martin, 1889-1976.**                                        • **1.990**
[Frage nach dem Ding. English] What is a thing? Translated by W. B. Barton,
Jr., and Vera Deutsch, with an analysis by Eugene T. Gendlin. Chicago, H.
Regnery Co. [1968, c1967] vii, 310 p. 21 cm. Translation of Die Frage nach dem
Ding. 1. Kant, Immanuel, 1724-1804 — Addresses, essays, lectures. 2. Ding
an sich — Addresses, essays, lectures. 3. Metaphysics — Addresses, essays,
lectures. I. T.
B3279.H48 F7313 1967      141/.3       *LC* 67-31050

**Heidegger, Martin, 1889-1976.**                                          **1.991**
[Grundprobleme der Phänomenologie. English] The basic problems of
phenomenology / Martin Heidegger; translation, introduction, and lexicon by
Albert Hofstadter. — Bloomington: Indiana University Press, c1982. xxxi,
396 p.; 25 cm. — (Studies in phenomenology and existential philosophy.)
Translation of: Die Grundprobleme der Phänomenologie. 1. Phenomenology
— Addresses, essays, lectures. I. T. II. Series.
B3279.H48 G7813      142/.7 19       *LC* 80-8379       *ISBN* 0253176867

**Heidegger, Martin, 1889-1976.**                                        • **1.992**
[Hegels Begriff der Erfahrung. English] Hegel's concept of experience. [1st ed.]
New York, Harper & Row [c1970] 155 p. 22 cm. 'With a section from Hegel's
Phenomenology of spirit, in the Kenley Royce Dove translation.' Translation of
the author's Hegels Begriff der Erfahrung. 1. Hegel, Georg Wilhelm Friedrich,
1770-1831. 2. Experience — History — 19th century. I. Hegel, Georg
Wilhelm Friedrich, 1770-1831. Phänomenologie des Geistes. Vorrede. English.
1970. II. T.
B3279.H48 H43 1970       121       *LC* 71-85060

**Heidegger, Martin, 1889-1976.**                                          **1.993**
The question concerning technology, and other essays / Martin Heidegger;
translated and with an introd. by William Lovitt. — New York: Garland Pub.,
1977. xxxix, 182 p.; 23 cm. Translations of essays which originally appeared in
Die Technik und die Kehre, Holzwege, and Vorträge und Aufsätze.
1. Ontology — Addresses, essays, lectures. 2. Technology — Addresses,
essays, lectures. I. T.
B3279.H48 Q47 1977       193       *LC* 77-87181       *ISBN* 0824024273

**Heidegger, Martin, 1889-1976.**                                        • **1.994**
[Sein und Zeit. English] Being and time. Translated by John Macquarrie &
Edward Robinson. New York, Harper [1962] 589 p. 23 cm. 1. Ontology
2. Space and time I. T.
B3279.H48 S43 1962a       111.1       *LC* 62-7289

**Gelven, Michael.**                                                      • **1.995**
A commentary on Heidegger's Being and time; a section–by–section
interpretation. — New York: Harper & Row, [1970] xv, 234 p.; 21 cm. —
(Harper torchbooks, TB 1464) 1. Heidegger, Martin, 1889-1976. Sein und Zeit.
I. T.
B3279.H48 S465       111.1       *LC* 76-112895

**Heidegger, Martin, 1889-1976.**                                        • **1.996**
The essence of reasons. Translated by Terrence Malick. — A bilingual ed.
incorporating the German text of Vom Wesen des Grundes. — Evanston [Ill.]:
Northwestern University Press, 1969. xviii, 144 p.; 20 cm. — (Northwestern
University studies in phenomenology & existential philosophy) 1. Ontology
2. Reason 3. Cosmology I. T. II. Series.
B3279.H48V63       193       *LC* 69-12849

**Demske, James M.**                                                     • **1.997**
[Sein, Mensch, und Tod. English] Being, man, & death: a key to Heidegger [by]
James M. Demske. [Lexington] University Press of Kentucky, 1970. vii, 233 p.

25 cm. Translation of Sein, Mensch, und Tod. 1. Heidegger, Martin,
1889-1976. 2. Death I. T.
B3279.H49 D4513       193       *LC* 70-94065       *ISBN* 0813111943

**Heidegger, the man and the thinker / edited by Thomas**                  **1.998**
**Sheehan.**
Chicago: Precedent Publishing, c1981. xx, 347 p.; 24 cm. 1. Heidegger, Martin,
1889-1976. I. Sheehan, Thomas F.
B3279.H49 H348       *LC* 77-82476       *ISBN* 0913750166

**Heidegger and the quest for truth. Edited with an introd. by**         • **1.999**
**Manfred S. Frings.**
Chicago: Quadrangle Books, 1968. 205 p.; 22 cm. Six of the papers were
originally delivered during the Heidegger symposium at De Paul Univ.,
Chicago, Nov. 11-12, 1966. 1. Heidegger, Martin, 1889-1976 — Addresses,
essays, lectures. I. Frings, Manfred S. ed.
B3279.H49 H35       193       *LC* 67-21643

**Langan, Thomas.**                                                      • **1.1000**
The meaning of Heidegger; a critical study of an existentialist phenomenology.
— New York, Columbia University Press [1959] ix, 246 p. 23 cm.
Bibliography: p. 239-240. 1. Heidegger, Martin, 1889-1976. I. T.
B3279.H49L3 1959       193       *LC* 59-9976

**Macomber, William B.**                                                 • **1.1001**
The anatomy of disillusion: Martin Heidegger's notion of truth / [by] W. B.
Macomber. — Evanston: Northwestern University Press, 1967. xvi, 227 p. —
(Northwestern University studies in phenomenology & existential philosophy)
1. Heidegger, Martin, 1889-1976. I. T. II. Series.
B3279.H49 M25       *LC* 67-27474

**Macquarrie, John.**                                                    • **1.1002**
Martin Heidegger. [American ed.] Richmond, John Knox Press [1968] 62 p. 19
cm. (Makers of contemporary theology) 1. Heidegger, Martin, 1889-1976.
I. T.
B3279.H49 M26 1968b       111       *LC* 68-11970

**Naess, Arne.**                                                         • **1.1003**
[Moderne filosofer. English] Four modern philosophers: Carnap, Wittgenstein,
Heidegger, Sartre. Translated by Alastair Hannay. Chicago, University of
Chicago Press [1968] xiii, 367 p. 21 cm. Translation of Moderne filosofer.
1. Heidegger, Martin, 1889-1976. 2. Wittgenstein, Ludwig, 1889-1951.
3. Sartre, Jean Paul, 1905- 4. Carnap, Rudolf, 1891-1970. I. T.
B3279.H49 N33       190       *LC* 68-14011

**Richardson, William J.**                                               • **1.1004**
Heidegger: through phenomenology to thought / by William J. Richardson;
preface by Martin Heidegger. — The Hague: M. Nijhoff, 1963. xxix, 764 p.:
port.; 25 cm. — (Phaenomenologica. 13) 1. Heidegger, Martin, 1889-1976.
I. T. II. Series.
B3279.H49 R5       *LC* 64-54746

**Robinson, James McConkey, 1924- ed.**                                  • **1.1005**
The later Heidegger and theology, edited by James M. Robinson [and] John B.
Cobb, Jr. — [1st ed.]. — New York, Harper & Row [1963] xii, 212 p. 22 cm. —
(New Frontiers in theology: discussions among German and American
theologians, v. 1) Bibliographical footnotes. 1. Heidegger, Martin, 1889-1976.
2. Theology, Doctrinal — 20th cent. — Addresses, essays, lectures. I. Cobb,
John B. joint ed. II. T. III. Series.
B3279.H49R6       230.82       *LC* 63-10506

**Waterhouse, Roger.**                                                     **1.1006**
A Heidegger critique: a critical examination of the existential phenomenology
of Martin Heidegger / Roger Waterhouse. — Brighton, Sussex: Harvester
Press; Atlantic Highlands, N.J.: Humanities Press, 1981. xi, 239 p.; 23 cm. —
(Harvester philosophy now. 15) 1. Heidegger, Martin, 1889-1976. I. T.
II. Series.
B3279.H49 W38 1981       193 19       *LC* 82-119431       *ISBN* 0391022253

## B3279.H8 Horkheimer

**Horkheimer, Max, 1895-1973.**                                            **1.1007**
Eclipse of reason / Max Horkheimer. — New York: Continuum, [1985], c1974.
vii, 191 p.; 20 cm. 1. Reason 2. Civilization I. T.
B3279.H8473 E3 1985       193 19       *LC* 83-20866       *ISBN* 0826400094

## B3279.H9 Husserl

**Husserl, Edmund, 1859-1938.**                                          • **1.1008**
The Paris lectures. Translated by Peter Koestenbaum, with an introductory
essay. The Hague, M. Nijhoff, 1964. lxxvi, 39 p. 22 cm. Imprint covered by
label: New York, Humanities Press. Two lectures delivered in 1929 at the
Sorbonne and later expanded into the author's Cartesianische Meditationen.
The translation is based on the German original as reconstructed by E. Strasser

and published in Husserl's Gesammelte Werke, Bd. 1, 1950. 1. Phenomenology I. Koestenbaum, Peter, 1928- II. T.
B3279.H91 1964     *LC* 66-1825

**Husserl, Edmund, 1859-1938.**     • **1.1009**
The phenomenology of internal time–consciousness / edited by Martin Heidegger; translated by James S. Churchill; introd. by Calvin O. Schrag. — Bloomington: Indiana University Press, [1964] 188 p; 21 cm. Translation of Vorlesungen zur Phänomenologie des innern Zeitbewusstseins. 1. Time perception 2. Knowledge, Theory of 3. Phenomenology I. T.
B3279.H91H43     152.753     *LC* 64-10829

**Husserl, Edmund, 1859-1938.**     • **1.1010**
Phenomenology and the crisis of philosophy: Philosophy as rigorous science, and Philosophy and the crisis of European man. Translated with notes and an introd. by Quentin Lauer. — New York, Harper & Row [1965] 192 p. 21 cm. — (Harper torchbooks. The Academy library, TB1170) Bibliographical footnotes. 1. Phenomenology I. Husserl, Edmund, 1859-1938. Philosophy as a rigorous science. II. Husserl, Edmund, 1859-1938. Philosophy and the crisis of European man. III. T.
B3279.H92E5     193     *LC* 64-8794

**Husserl, Edmund, 1859-1938.**     **1.1011**
Husserl, shorter works / edited by Peter McCormick and Frederick A. Elliston. — Notre Dame, Ind.: University of Notre Dame Press; Brighton, Sussex: Harvester Press, c1981. xix, 440 p.; 25 cm. 'NDP-266'–p. 4 cover. Includes index. 1. Philosophy — Collected works. 2. Phenomenology — Collected works. I. McCormick, Peter (Peter J.) II. Elliston, Frederick. III. T.
B3279.H92 E5 1981     193 19     *LC* 80-53178     *ISBN* 0268017034

**Husserl, Edmund, 1859-1938.**     • **1.1012**
Cartesian meditations: an introduction to phenomenology. Translated by Dorion Cairns. [The Hague] M. Nijhoff, 1966 [c1964] xii, 157 p. 22 cm. Imprint covered by label: Humanities Press, New York. Based on 2 lectures delivered at the Sorbonne in 1929 under title: Einleitung in die transzendentale Phänomenologie. 1. Phenomenology I. T.
B3279.H93 C3     *LC* 66-4973

**Husserl, Edmund, 1859-1938.**     **1.1013**
[Erfahrung und Urteil. English] Experience and judgment; investigations in a genealogy of logic. Rev. and edited by Ludwig Landgrebe. Translated by James S. Churchill and Karl Ameriks. Evanston, Northwestern University Press, 1973. xxxi, 443 p. 24 cm. (Northwestern University studies in phenomenology & existential philosophy) Translation of Erfahrung und Urteil. 1. Judgment (Logic) 2. Experience I. Landgrebe, Ludwig, ed. II. T. III. Series.
B3279.H93 E7313     160     *LC* 72-80566

**Husserl, Edmund, 1859-1938.**     • **1.1014**
[Ideen zur einer reinen Phänomenologie. English] Ideas; general introduction to pure phenomenology. Translated by W. R. Boyce Gibson. London, Allen & Unwin; New York, Humanities P., 1969. 465 p. 23 cm. (The Muirhead library of philosophy) Translation of Ideen zu einer reinen Phänomenologie. 1. Phenomenology I. T.
B3279.H93I33 1969     142/.7     *LC* 66-28240     *ISBN* 0041100050

**Kohák, Erazim V.**     **1.1015**
Idea & experience: Edmund Husserl's project of phenomenology in Ideas I / Erazim Kohák. — Chicago: University of Chicago Press, c1978. xiv, 249 p.; 24 cm. Includes index. 1. Husserl, Edmund, 1859-1938. Ideen zu einer reinen Phänomenologie. 2. Phenomenology I. T.
B3279.H93 I343     142/.7 19     *LC* 78-661

**Husserl, Edmund, 1859-1938.**     • **1.1016**
[Krisis der europäischen Wissenschaften und die transzendentale Phänomenologie. English] The crisis of European sciences and transcendental phenomenology; an introduction to phenomenological philosophy. Translated, with an introd., by David Carr. Evanston, Northwestern University Press, 1970. xliii, 405 p. 24 cm. (Northwestern University Studies in phenomenology & existential philosophy) Translation of Die Krisis der europäischen Wissenschaften und die transzendentale Phänomenologie; eine Einleitung in die phänomenologische Philosophie, which was posthumously edited by Walter Biemel and published in 1954. 1. Philosophy, Modern 2. Science — Philosophy 3. Transcendentalism 4. Psychology 5. Phenomenology I. T. II. Series.
B3279.H93K73     142/.7     *LC* 77-82511     *ISBN* 0810102552

**Berger, Gaston.**     **1.1017**
[Cogito dans la philosophie de Husserl. English] The cogito in Husserl's philosophy. Translated by Kathleen McLaughlin. With an introd. by James M. Edie. Evanston [Ill.] Northwestern University Press, 1972. xxvii, 159 p. 24 cm. (Northwestern University studies in phenomenology & existential philosophy) 1. Husserl, Edmund, 1859-1938. 2. Phenomenology I. T. II. Series.
B3279.H94 B413     193     *LC* 75-186546     *ISBN* 0810103753

**Derrida, Jacques.**     **1.1018**
Speech and phenomena, and other essays on Husserl's theory of signs. Translated, with an introd., by David B. Allison. Pref. by Newton Garver. — Evanston: Northwestern University Press, 1973. xlii, 166 p.; 24 cm. — (Northwestern University studies in phenomenology & existential philosophy) 1. Husserl, Edmund, 1859-1938. 2. Phenomenology 3. Signs and symbols 4. Meaning (Philosophy) 5. Difference (Philosophy) I. T. II. Series.
B3279.H94 D382     142/.7     *LC* 72-80565     *ISBN* 0810103974

**Kołakowski, Leszek.**     **1.1019**
Husserl and the search for certitude / Leszek Kolakowski. — New Haven: Yale University Press, 1975. 85 p.; 22 cm. (The Cassirer lectures) 1. Husserl, Edmund, 1859-1938 — Addresses, essays, lectures. 2. Certainty — Addresses, essays, lectures. I. T.
B3279.H94 K64     193     *LC* 74-29724     *ISBN* 0300018584

**Lévinas, Emmanuel.**     **1.1020**
[Théorie de l'intuition dans la phénoménologie de Husserl. English] The theory of intuition in Husserl's phenomenology. Translated by André Orianne. Evanston [Ill.] Northwestern University Press, 1973. xxxvi, 163 p. 24 cm. (Northwestern University studies in phenomenology & existential philosophy) Translation of Théorie de l'intuition dans la phénoménologie de Husserl. 1. Husserl, Edmund, 1859-1938. 2. Phenomenology 3. Intuition I. T. II. Series.
B3279.H94 L413     111     *LC* 72-96698     *ISBN* 081010413X

**Mohanty, Jitendranath, 1928-.**     **1.1021**
Husserl and Frege / J.N. Mohanty. — Bloomington: Indiana University Press, c1982. vii, 147 p.; 25 cm. — (Studies in phenomenology and existential philosophy) 1. Husserl, Edmund, 1859-1938 — Addresses, essays, lectures. 2. Frege, Gottlob, 1848-1925 — Addresses, essays, lectures. 3. Phenomenology — Addresses, essays, lectures. 4. Analysis (Philosophy) — Addresses, essays, lectures. I. T. II. Series.
B3279.H94 M563 1982     193 19     *LC* 81-48554     *ISBN* 0253328780

**Ricoeur, Paul.**     • **1.1022**
Husserl: an analysis of his phenomenology. Translated by Edward G. Ballard and Lester E. Embree. Evanston, Northwestern University Press, 1967. xxii, 238 p. 24 cm. (Northwestern University studies in phenomenology & existential philosophy) 1. Husserl, Edmund, 1859-1938. 2. Phenomenology I. T. II. Series.
B3279.H94 R5     142/.7     *LC* 67-12676

**Sokolowski, Robert.**     **1.1023**
Husserlian meditations; how words present things. — Evanston, Ill.: Northwestern University Press, 1974. xix, 296 p.; 24 cm. — (Northwestern University studies in phenomenology & existential philosophy) 1. Husserl, Edmund, 1859-1938. I. T. II. Series.
B3279.H94 S624     193     *LC* 73-91312     *ISBN* 0810104407

## B3279.J3 Jaspers

**Jaspers, Karl, 1883-1969.**     • **1.1024**
Philosophy and the world: selected essays and lectures / Karl Jaspers; translated by E.B. Ashton. — Chicago: H. Regnery, 1963. 314 p. — (A Gateway edition; 6083) 1. Philosophy — Addresses, essays, lectures. I. T.
B3279.J32 E52     191     *LC* 63-14897

**Jaspers, Karl, 1883-1969.**     • **1.1025**
[Existenzphilosophie. English] Philosophy of existence. Translated and an introd. by Richard F. Grabau. Philadelphia, University of Pennsylvania Press [1971] xxvii, 99 p. 23 cm. (Works in continental philosophy) 1. Existentialism I. T.
B3279.J33E83     142/.7     *LC* 79-133203     *ISBN* 0812276299

**Jaspers, Karl, 1883-1969.**     • **1.1026**
Philosophy. Translated by E. B. Ashton. — Chicago: University of Chicago Press, [1969-71] 3 v.; 24 cm. Translation of Philosophie. 1. Philosophy I. T.
B3279.J33P513     193     *LC* 69-19922     *ISBN* 0226394913

**Jaspers, Karl, 1883-1969.**     • **1.1027**
[Philosophische Glaube. English] The perennial scope of philosophy. Translated by Ralph Manheim. [Hamden, Conn.] Archon Books, 1968. 188 p. 22 cm. Translation of Der philosophische Glaube. Reprint of the 1949 ed. 1. Philosophy I. T.
B3279.J33 P533 1968     193     *LC* 68-12525

**Jaspers, Karl, 1883-1969.**     • **1.1028**
[Vernunft und Existenz. English] Reason and Existenz; five lectures. Translated with an introd. by William Earle. [New York, Noonday Press, 1955] 157 p. 22 cm. 1. Kierkegaard, Søren, 1813-1855. 2. Nietzsche, Friedrich Wilhelm, 1844-1900. 3. Reason 4. Existentialism I. T.
B3279.J33 V414     193.9     *LC* 55-8231

**Jaspers, Karl, 1883-1969.** • 1.1029
[Von der Wahrheit. Selections. English] Tragedy is not enough. Translated by Harald A. T. Reiche, Harry T. Moore, and Karl W. Deutsch. [Hamden, Conn.] Archon Books, 1969 [c1952] 123 p. 19 cm. Translation of a section of Von der Wahrheit. 1. Tragic, The I. T.
B3279.J33 V653 1969    193    *LC* 69-13628    *ISBN* 020800730X

**Schilpp, Paul Arthur, 1897- ed.** • 1.1030
The philosophy of Karl Jaspers. — [1st ed.]. — New York: Tudor Pub. Co., [c1957] xxvi, 918 p.: port., facsim.; 25 cm. — (Library of living philosophers.) 1. Jaspers, Karl, 1883-1969. 2. Jaspers, Karl, 1883- — Bibliography. I. Jaspers, Karl, 1883-1969. II. T. III. Series.
B3279.J34 S3    193.9    *LC* 57-14578

**Wallraff, Charles F.** • 1.1031
Karl Jaspers; an introduction to his philosophy, by Charles F. Wallraff. — Princeton, N.J.: Princeton University Press, 1970. xvii, 232 p.; 23 cm. 1. Jaspers, Karl, 1883-1969. I. T.
B3279.J34 W3    193    *LC* 74-100996    *ISBN* 0691071640

## B3305.M74 Marx
### (see also: HX39.5, HX276.M)

**Althusser, Louis.** • 1.1032
For Marx / translated [from the French] by Ben Brewster. — London: Allen Lane, 1969. 272 p.; 23 m. Originally published as Pour Marx. Paris, F. Maspero, 1965. I. Marx, Karl, 1818-1883. II. T.
B3305.M74 A533 1969    *LC* 76-476141    *ISBN* 713901098

**Dupré, Louis K., 1925-.** 1.1033
The philosophical foundations of Marxism [by] Louis Dupré. — New York: Harcourt, Brace & World, [1966] xiv, 240 p.; 22 cm. 1. Marx, Karl, 1818-1883. 2. Hegel, Georg Wilhelm Friedrich, 1770-1831 — Influence. 3. Dialectical materialism I. T.
B3305.M74 D8    335.411    *LC* 66-17348

**Hook, Sidney, 1902-.** • 1.1034
From Hegel to Marx: studies in the intellectual development of Karl Marx. — [Ann Arbor]: University of Michigan Press, [1962] 335 p.; 21 cm. — (Ann Arbor paperbacks for the study of communism and Marxism; AA66) I. T.
B3305.M74 H6 1962    320.15    *LC* 62-2978

**Hyppolite, Jean.** • 1.1035
Studies on Marx and Hegel / translated with an introd., notes, and bibliography, by John O'Neill. — New York: Basic Books, [1969] xxii, 202 p.; 22 cm. Translation of Études sur Marx et Hegel. I. T.
B3305.M74 H913    193    *LC* 70-77231

**Kamenka, Eugene.** • 1.1036
The ethical foundations of Marxism. — 2nd ed. — London; Boston: Routledge and Kegan Paul, 1972. xxii, 208 p.; 23 am. I. T.
B3305.M74K3 1972    172    *LC* 73-157233    *ISBN* 0710073607

**McLellan, David.** • 1.1037
The young Hegelians and Karl Marx. — New York: F. A. Praeger, [1969] ix, 170 p.; 23 cm. I. T.
B3305.M74M3 1969b    193    *LC* 76-90413

**Marcuse, Herbert, 1898-.** 1.1038
The aesthetic dimension: toward a critique of Marxist aesthetics / Herbert Marcuse. — Boston: Beacon Press, c1978. xiii, 88 p.; 21 cm. Revised translation of Die Permanenz der Kunst. Includes index. 1. Marx, Karl, 1818-1883 — Aesthetics — Addresses, essays, lectures. 2. Aesthetics — Addresses, essays, lectures. I. T.
B3305.M74 M3513 1978    335.4/11    *LC* 76-9001    *ISBN* 0807015180

**Miller, Richard W., 1945-.** 1.1039
Analyzing Marx: morality, power, and history / Richard W. Miller. — Princeton, N.J.: Princeton University Press, c1984. xi, 319 p.; 23 cm. 1. Marx, Karl, 1818-1883. 2. Ethics, Modern — 19th century 3. Elite (Social sciences) — History — 19th century. 4. Power (Social sciences) — History — 19th century. 5. History — Philosophy — History — 19th century. 6. Economic history — 1750-1918 7. Positivism — History — 19th century. I. T.
B3305.M74 M55 1984    193 19    *LC* 84-42571    *ISBN* 0691066132

**Plamenatz, John Petrov.** 1.1040
Karl Marx's philosophy of man / by John Plamenatz. — Oxford [Eng.]: Clarendon Press, 1975. x, 484 p.; 25 cm. 1. Marx, Karl, 1818-1883. 2. Man I. T.
B3305.M74 P5    128    *LC* 76-350225    *ISBN* 0198245513

**Rader, Melvin Miller, 1903-.** 1.1041
Marx's interpretation of history / Melvin Rader. — New York: Oxford University Press, 1979. xxiii, 242 p.; 22 cm. 1. Marx, Karl, 1818-1883. 2. History — Philosophy I. T.
B3305.M74 R32    901    *LC* 78-14851    *ISBN* 0195024755

**Tucker, Robert C.** • 1.1042
Philosophy and myth in Karl Marx / byRobert C. Tucker. — 2d ed. — Cambridge, [Eng.]: University Press, 1972. 263 p.; 21 cm. I. T.
B3305.M74 T8 1972    193    *LC* 70-180022    *ISBN* 0521084555

**Wood, Allen W.** 1.1043
Karl Marx / Allen W. Wood. — London; Boston: Routledge & Kegan Paul, 1981. xviii, 282 p.; 24 cm. — (Arguments of the philosophers.) Includes index. 1. Marx, Karl, 1818-1883. I. T. II. Series.
B3305.M74 W63    193 19    *LC* 80-41119    *ISBN* 0710006721

B 3305 M74 W63

## B3310–3318 Nietzsche

**Nietzsche, Friedrich Wilhelm, 1844-1900.** • 1.1044
[Selections. English] The portable Nietzsche; selected and translated, with an introd., prefaces, and notes, by Walter Kaufmann. New York, Viking Press, 1954. 687 p. 17 cm. (The Viking portable library [62]) 1. Nietzsche, Friedrich Wilhelm, 1844-1900. I. T.
B3312.E52 K3    193.9    *LC* 54-7985

**Nietzsche, Friedrich Wilhelm, 1844-1900.** • 1.1045
The philosophy of Nietzsche ... — New York: The Modern library, [1937] [1146] p.; 21 cm. — (The Modern library of the world's best books) Various pagings. 'First modern library giant edition 1937.' I. Common, Thomas, tr. II. Zimmern, Helen, 1846-1934, tr. III. Samuel, Horace Barnett, 1883- tr. IV. Kennedy, John McFarland. tr. V. Fadiman, Clifton, 1904- tr. VI. T.
B3312.E52 W67    193.9    *LC* 37-27408

**Nietzsche, Friedrich Wilhelm, 1844-1900.** 1.1046
[Fröhliche Wissenschaft. English] The gay science; with a prelude in rhymes and an appendix of songs. Translated, with commentary, by Walter Kaufmann. [1st ed.] New York, Random House [1974] 396 p. 22 cm. 'This translation is based on the second edition of Die fröhliche Wissenschaft, published in 1887.' 1. Philosophy 2. Man 3. Religion — Philosophy 4. Power (Philosophy) 5. Ethics I. Kaufmann, Walter Arnold. tr. II. T.
B3313.F72 E5 1974    193    *LC* 73-10477    *ISBN* 0394482069

**Nietzsche, Friedrich Wilhelm, 1844-1900.** 1.1047
[Geburt der Tragödie. English] The birth of tragedy, and The case of Wagner. Translated, with commentary, by Walter Kaufmann. [1st Vintage ed.] New York, Vintage Books [1967] 223 p. 19 cm. Translation of Die Geburt der Tragödie, and Der Fall Wagner. 1. Wagner, Richard, 1813-1883. 2. Music — Philosophy and aesthetics 3. Tragedy 4. Greek drama (Tragedy) — History and criticism. 5. Tragic, The 6. Aesthetics I. Nietzsche, Friedrich Wilhelm, 1844-1900. Der Fall Wagner. English. 1967. II. T.
B3313.G42 E55    111.8/5    *LC* 67-11589

**Nietzsche, Friedrich Wilhelm, 1844-1900.** 1.1048
[Jenseits von Gut und Böse. English] Beyond good and evil: prelude to a philosophy of the future; translated [from the German], with an introduction and commentary, by R. J. Hollingdale. Harmondsworth, Penguin, 1973. 238 p. 18 cm. (Penguin classics) Translation of Jenseits von Gut und Böse. I. T.
B3313.J43 E5 1973    193    *LC* 73-330985    *ISBN* 0140442677

B 3313 B57

**Nietzsche, Friedrich Wilhelm, 1844-1900.** 1.1049
[Menschliches, Allzumenschliches. English] Human, all too human: a book for free spirits / Friedrich Nietzsche; translated by Marion Faber, with Stephen Lehmann; introduction and notes by Marion Faber. — Lincoln: University of Nebraska Press, c1984. xxvii, 275 p.; 21 cm. Translation of: Menschliches, Allzumenschliches. Includes index. 1. Man I. T.
B3313.M52 E5 1984    128 19    *LC* 83-25955    *ISBN* 0803283539

**Nietzsche, Friedrich Wilhelm, 1844-1900.** • 1.1050
[Wille zur Macht. English] The will to power. A new translation by Walter Kaufmann and R. J. Hollingdale. Edited, with commentary, by Walter Kaufmann, with facsims. of the original manuscript. New York, Random House [1967] xxxii, 576 p. facsims. 22 cm. Translation of Der Wille zur Macht. I. Kaufmann, Walter Arnold. tr. II. Hollingdale, R. J. tr. III. T.
B3313.N5    193    *LC* 66-21465

**Nietzsche, Friedrich Wilhelm, 1844-1900.** 1.1051
Untimely meditations / Friedrich Nietzsche; translated by R.J. Hollingdale; with an introduction by J.P. Stern. Cambridge [Cambridgeshire]; New York: Cambridge University Press, 1984. xxxii, 256 p.; 23 cm. (Texts in German philosophy) Translation of: Unzeitgemässe Betrachtungen. Includes index. 1. Strauss, David Friedrich, 1808-1874. 2. Schopenhauer, Arthur, 1788-1860. 3. Wagner, Richard, 1813-1883. 4. History — Study and teaching I. Hollingdale, R. J. II. T.
B3313.U52 E5 1984    *LC* 83-6609    *ISBN* 0521247403

**Hayman, Ronald, 1932-.**      **1.1052**
Nietzsche, a critical life / Ronald Hayman. — New York: Oxford University Press, 1980. xxiii, 424 p., [4] leaves of plates: ill.; 22 cm. Includes index. 1. Nietzsche, Friedrich Wilhelm, 1844-1900. 2. Philosophers — Germany — Biography. I. T.
B3316.H44    193 B     *LC* 80-14218     *ISBN* 019520204X

**Hollingdale, R. J.**      **1.1053**
Nietzsche: the man and his philosophy, by R. J. Hollingdale. — Baton Rouge, Louisiana State University Press [1965] xvi, 326 p. 23 cm. Bibliography: p. 314-320. 1. Nietzsche, Friedrich Wilhelm, 1844-1900. I. T.
B3316.H64 1965a    193 (B)     *LC* 65-17723

**Jaspers, Karl, 1883-1969.**      • **1.1054**
Nietzsche: an introduction to the understanding of his philosophical activity. Translated by Charles F. Wallraff and Frederick J. Schmitz. — Tucson, University of Arizona Press [1965] xiv, 496 p. 24 cm. Bibliography: p. 464-470. 1. Nietzsche, Friedrich Wilhelm, 1844-1900. I. T.
B3316.J313    193     *LC* 65-12660

**Kaufmann, Walter Arnold.**      • **1.1055**
Nietzsche: philosopher, psychologist, antichrist, by Walter Kaufmann. — 3d ed. — Princeton, N.J.: Princeton University Press, 1968. xviii, 524 p.: facsims.; 25 cm. 1. Nietzsche, Friedrich Wilhelm, 1844-1900. I. T.
B3316.K3 1968b    193     *LC* 68-29389

**Deleuze, Gilles.**      **1.1056**
[Nietzsche et la philosophie. English] Nietzsche and philosophy / Gille Deleuze; translated by Hugh Tomlinson. — New York: Columbia University Press, 1983. xiv, 221 p.; 22 cm. — (European perspectives) Translation of: Nietzsche et la philosophie. 1. Nietzsche, Friedrich Wilhelm, 1844-1900. I. T. II. Series.
B3317.D413 1983    193 19     *LC* 82-17676     *ISBN* 0231056680

**Heidegger, Martin, 1889-1976.**      **1.1057**
[Nietzsche. English] Nietzsche / Martin Heidegger; translated from the German with notes and an analysis by David Farrell Krell. — 1st ed. — San Francisco: Harper & Row, c1979- <c1984 >. v. <1-2, 4 >; 22 cm. Translation of: Nietzsche. Vol. 4: Translated from the German by Frank A. Capuzzi. 1. Nietzsche, Friedrich Wilhelm, 1844-1900. I. Krell, David Farrell. II. T.
B3317.H3713 1979    193     *LC* 78-19509     *ISBN* 0060638478

**Stern, J. P. (Joseph Peter).**      **1.1058**
A study of Nietzsche / J. P. Stern. — Cambridge; New York: Cambridge University Press, 1979. xi, 220 p.; 22 cm. (Major European authors) Includes index. 1. Nietzsche, Friedrich Wilhelm, 1844-1900. I. T.
B3317.S69    193     *LC* 78-54328     *ISBN* 0521221269

## B3329.S4 Scheler

**Scheler, Max, 1874-1928.**      **1.1059**
[Selected works. English] Selected philosophical essays. Translated, with an introd., by David R. Lachterman. Evanston, Northwestern University Press, 1973. xli, 359 p. 24 cm. (Northwestern University studies in phenomenology & existential philosophy) 1. Philosophy — Collected works. I. T. II. Series.
B3329.S482 E5 1973    193     *LC* 70-186550     *ISBN* 0810103796

**Scheler, Max, 1874-1928.**      **1.1060**
[Formalismus in der Ethik und die materiale Wertethik. English] Formalism in ethics and non–formal ethics of values; a new attempt toward the foundation of an ethical personalism [by] Max Scheler. [5th rev. ed.] Translated by Manfred S. Frings and Roger L. Funk. Evanston, Northwestern University Press, 1973. xxxiv, 620 p. 24 cm. (Northwestern University studies in phenomenology & existential philosophy) Translation of Der Formalismus in der Ethik und die materiale Wertethik. 1. Kant, Immanuel, 1724-1804. 2. Ethics 3. Values I. T. II. Series.
B3329.S483 F622 1973    170     *LC* 72-97416     *ISBN* 0810104156

## B3329.S5 Schweitzer

**Schweitzer, Albert, 1875-1965.**      • **1.1061**
Albert Schweitzer: an anthology. Edited by Charles R. Joy. — Rev. and enl., in honor of Albert Schweitzer's ninetieth birthday. — Boston, Beacon Press [1967, c1947] xxv, 367 p. port. 22 cm. — (Beacon paperback, BP-1) 'Bibliography of the writings of Albert Schweitzer': p. [346]-353. I. Joy, Charles Rhind, 1885- ed. II. T.
B3329.S52E5 1965    193     *LC* 65-12499

**Schweitzer, Albert, 1875-1965.**      • **1.1062**
The teaching of reverence for life. Translated from the German by Richard and Clara Winston. — [1st ed.]. — New York: Holt, Rinehart and Winston, [1965] 63 p.: port.; 21 cm. Essays. 1. Philosophical anthropology 2. Life 3. Nuclear warfare — Moral and ethical aspects. I. Winston, Richard. tr. II. Winston, Clara. tr. III. T. IV. Title: Reverence for life.
B3329.S53 T43    179.7     *LC* 65-11472

## B3354.V Vaihinger. Vogelin

**Vaihinger, Hans, 1852-1933.**      • **1.1063**
The philosophy of 'As if': a system of the theoretical, practical and religious fictions of mankind, by H. Vaihinger; translated [from the 6th German ed.] by C. K. Ogden. — 2nd ed. reprinted. — London, Routledge & K. Paul [1965] xlviii, 368 p. diagr. 22 1/2 cm. — (International library of psychology, philosophy, and scientific method.) Bibliographical footnotes. 1. Kant, Immanuel, 1724-1804. 2. Nietzsche, Friedrich Wilhelm, 1844-1900. 3. Positivism 4. Pragmatism 5. Fictions, Theory of I. T. II. Series.
B3354.V5P6 1965    *LC* 67-79188

**Eric Voegelin's thought: a critical appraisal / edited with an introduction by Ellis Sandoz.**      **1.1064**
Durham, N.C.: Duke University Press, 1982. xv, 208 p.; 25 cm. 1. Voegelin, Eric, 1901- — Addresses, essays, lectures. I. Sandoz, Ellis, 1931-
B3354.V884 E74 1982    193 19     *LC* 81-43591     *ISBN* 0822304651

## B3376.W5 Wittgenstein

**Wittgenstein, Ludwig, 1889-1951.**      **1.1065**
Wittgenstein's Lectures, Cambridge, 1932–1935: from the notes of Alice Ambrose and Margaret Macdonald / edited by Alice Ambrose. — Totowa, N.J.: Rowman and Littlefield, 1979. xi, 225 p.; 22 cm. 1. Wittgenstein, Ludwig, 1889-1951. 2. Philosophy 3. Mathematics — Philosophy I. Ambrose, Alice, 1906- II. Macdonald, Margaret. III. T.
B3376.W561 1979    192     *LC* 78-26909     *ISBN* 0847661512

**Wittgenstein, Ludwig, 1889-1951.**      **1.1066**
Wittgenstein's Lectures, Cambridge, 1930–1932: from the notes of John King and Desmond Lee / edited by Desmond Lee. — Totowa, N.J.: Rowman and Littlefield, 1980. xvii, 124 p.; 22 cm. Includes index. 1. Wittgenstein, Ludwig, 1889-1951 — Addresses, essays, lectures. 2. Philosophy — Addresses, essays, lectures. 3. Mathematics — Philosophy — Addresses, essays, lectures. I. King, John, 1909- II. Lee, Henry Desmond Pritchard, Sir, 1908- III. T.
B3376.W561 1980    192     *LC* 79-17052     *ISBN* 0847662012

**Wittgenstein, Ludwig, 1889-1951.**      • **1.1067**
Zettel. Edited by G. E. M. Anscombe and G. H. vonn Wright. Translated by G. E. M. Anscombe. Berkeley, University of California Press, 1967. v, v, 124, 124 p. 23 cm. Opposite pages numbered in duplicate. English and German. 1. Philosophy — Collected works. I. Anscombe, G. E. M., ed. II. Wright, G. H. von (Georg Henrik), 1916- ed. III. T.
B3376.W561 A6    *LC* 67-17113     *ISBN* 0520016351

**Wittgenstein, Ludwig, 1889-1951.**      **1.1068**
Culture and value / Ludwig Wittgenstein; edited by G.H. von Wright, in collaboration with Heikki Nyman; translated by Peter Winch. — Chicago: University of Chicago Press, 1980. 94, 87 p.; 23 cm. Parallel texts in English and German, which consists of a revision of Vermischte Bermerkungen and its English translation. Pages 1-87 numbered in duplicate. Includes index. 1. Philosophy — Collected works. I. Wright, G. H. von (Georg Henrik von), 1916- II. Nyman, Heikki. III. Wittgenstein, Ludwig, 1889-1951. Vermischte Bemerkungen.1980. IV. T.
B3376.W561 W7413    192     *LC* 80-15234     *ISBN* 0226904326

**Engel, S. Morris, 1931-.**      **1.1069**
Wittgenstein's doctrine of the tyranny of language; an historical and critical examination of his blue book. [By] S. Morris Engel. With an introduction by Stephen Toulmin. — The Hague: Nijhoff, 1971. xvii, 147 p.; 24 cm. 1. Wittgenstein, Ludwig, 1889-1951. Blue book. I. T.
B3376.W563 B534    149/.94     *LC* 72-177280     *ISBN* 9024711851

**Wittgenstein, Ludwig, 1889-1951.**      • **1.1070**
Notebooks, 1914–1916. Edited by G. H. von Wright and G. E. M. Anscombe, with an English translation by G. E. M. Anscombe. — New York, Harper [1961] vi, 91, 91e, 93-131 p. illus. 23 cm. German and English on opposite pages numbered in duplicate. I. T.
B3376.W563N6    193     *LC* 61-1235

**Wittgenstein, Ludwig, 1889-1951.**      • **1.1071**
On certainty, edited by G. E. M. Anscombe and G. H. von Wright. Translated by Denis Paul and G. E. M. Anscombe. Oxford, Blackwell, 1969. vii, 90, 90e p. 23 cm. Added t.p. in German: Über Gewissheit. Parallel German and English texts, each paged separately. 1. Certainty I. Anscombe, G. E. M. (Gertrude Elizabeth Margaret) ed. II. Wright, G. H. von (Georg Henrik von), 1916- ed. III. T. IV. Title: Über Gewissheit.
B3376.W563 O5    121/.6     *LC* 69-20428     *ISBN* 0631120009

**Wittgenstein, Ludwig, 1889-1951.** **1.1072**
[Philosophische Grammatik. English] Philosophical grammar: part I, The proposition, and its sense, part II, On logic and mathematics / Ludwig Wittgenstein; edited by Rush Rhees; translated by Anthony Kenny. — Berkeley: University of California Press, 1974. 495 p.: diagrs.; 23 cm. 1. Grammar, Comparative and general 2. Logic, Symbolic and mathematical 3. Inference 4. Mathematics — Philosophy I. T.
B3376.W563 P52613 1974b 160 *LC* 73-89389 *ISBN* 0520026640

**Wittgenstein, Ludwig, 1889-1951.** • **1.1073**
[Philosophische Untersuchungen. English and German] Philosophical investigations. Translated by G. E. M. Anscombe. With English and German indexes. 3d ed. New York, Macmillan [1968, c1958] x, xe, 232e, 272 p. illus. (part col.) 22 cm. Opposite pages numbered in duplicate. German and English; added t.p. in German. I. T.
B3376.W563 P53 1968 192 *LC* 68-3691

**Baker, Gordon P.** **1.1074**
Wittgenstein, understanding and meaning / G.P. Baker & P.M.S. Hacker. — Chicago: University of Chicago Press, 1980. ix, 692 p.; 24 cm. (An analytical commentary on the Philosophical investigations; v. 1) 1. Wittgenstein, Ludwig, 1889-1951. Philosophische Untersuchungen. 2. Philosophy 3. Languages — Philosophy 4. Semantics (Philosophy) I. Hacker, P. M. S. (Peter Michael Stephan) joint author. II. T.
B3376.W563 P5323 1980 vol. 1 192 *LC* 79-15740 *ISBN* 0226035263

**Hallett, Garth.** **1.1075**
A companion to Wittgenstein's 'Philosophical investigations' / Garth Hallett. — Ithaca: Cornell University Press, 1977. 801 p. Includes index. 1. Wittgenstein, Ludwig, 1889-1951. Philosophische Untersuchungen. I. Wittgenstein, Ludwig, 1889-1951. Philosophische Untersuchungen. II. T.
B3376.W563 P5325 B3376W563 P5325. 192 *LC* 76-28014 *ISBN* 0801409977

**Wittgenstein, Ludwig, 1889-1951.** • **1.1076**
Preliminary studies for the 'Philosophical investigations': generally known as the Blue and Brown books. — New York: Harper, [1958] xvi, 185 p.: ill. , 21 cm. — (Harper Torchbook: The Academy library.) I. T. II. Title: The Blue and Brown books.
B3376.W563 P6 1965 *LC* 58-4522

**Mounce, H. O.** **1.1077**
Wittgenstein's Tractatus: an introduction / H.O. Mounce. — Chicago: University of Chicago Press, 1981. 136 p.; 22 cm. 1. Wittgenstein, Ludwig, 1889-1951. Tractatus logico-philosophicus. 2. Logic, Symbolic and mathematical 3. Languages — Philosophy I. T.
B3376.W563 T7346 192 19 *LC* 81-40474 *ISBN* 0226543188

**Wittgenstein, Ludwig, 1889-1951.** **1.1078**
Letters to Russell, Keynes, and Moore / Ludwig Wittgenstein; edited with an introd. by G. H. von Wright, assisted by B. F. McGuinness. — Ithaca, N.Y.: Cornell University Press, 1974. 190 p.: ill.; 23 cm. English or German with English translation. 1. Philosophers — Germany — Correspondence, reminiscences, etc. I. Russell, Bertrand, 1872-1970. II. Keynes, John Maynard, 1883-1946. III. Moore, G. E. (George Edward), 1873-1958. IV. Wright, G. H. von (Georg Henrik von), 1916- ed. V. T.
B3376.W564 A4 1974 192 *LC* 73-18518 *ISBN* 0801408229

**Ambrose, Alice, 1906-.** • **1.1079**
Ludwig Wittgenstein, philosophy and language; edited by Alice Ambrose and Morris Lazerowitz. — London: Allen and Unwin; New York: Humanities Press, 1972. 325 p.; 23 cm. — (Muirhead library of philosophy) 1. Wittgenstein, Ludwig, 1889-1951 — Addresses, essays, lectures. 2. Languages — Philosophy — Addresses, essays, lectures. I. Lazerowitz, Morris, 1909- joint author. II. T.
B3376.W564 A8 1972 192 *LC* 72-179685 *ISBN* 0391001906

**Ayer, A. J. (Alfred Jules), 1910-.** **1.1080**
Wittgenstein / A.J. Ayer. — 1st ed. — New York: Random House, c1985. 155 p.; 25 cm. Includes index. 1. Wittgenstein, Ludwig, 1889-1951. I. T.
B3376.W564 A94 1985 192 19 *LC* 84-43000 *ISBN* 0394543475

**Fogelin, Robert J.** **1.1081**
Wittgenstein / Robert J. Fogelin. — London; Boston: Routledge & K. Paul, 1976. ix, 223 p.: ill.; 24 cm. — (The Arguments of the philosophers) Includes index. 1. Wittgenstein, Ludwig, 1889-1951. I. T.
B3376.W564 F63 1976 B3376W564 F63 1976. 192 *LC* 76-378611 *ISBN* 0710084269

**Kenny, Anthony John Patrick.** **1.1082**
Wittgenstein [by] Anthony Kenny. — Cambridge, Mass.: Harvard University Press, 1973. ix, 240 p.; 22 cm. 1. Wittgenstein, Ludwig, 1889-1951. I. T.
B3376.W564 K4 1973b 192 *LC* 73-81671 *ISBN* 0674953908

**Kripke, Saul A., 1940-.** **1.1083**
Wittgenstein on rules and private language: an elementary exposition / Saul A. Kripke. — Cambridge, Mass.: Harvard University Press, 1982. x, 150 p.; 22 cm. 1. Wittgenstein, Ludwig, 1889-1951. I. T.
B3376.W564 K74 1982 192 19 *LC* 81-20070 *ISBN* 0674954009

**Phillips, Derek L.** **1.1084**
Wittgenstein and scientific knowledge: a sociological perspective / Derek L. Phillips. — Totowa, N.J.: Rowman and Littlefield, 1977. xiv, 248 p.; 23 cm. 1. Wittgenstein, Ludwig, 1889-1951 — Knowledge, Theory of. 2. Knowledge, Sociology of 3. Relativity 4. Science — Philosophy I. T.
B3376.W564 P46 1977b 121/.092/4 *LC* 77-375532 *ISBN* 0874719763

**Pitcher, George.** • **1.1085**
The philosophy of Wittgenstein / George Pitcher. — Englewood Cliffs, N. J.: Prentice-Hall, 1964. xi, 340 p. 1. Wittgenstein, Ludwig, 1889-1951. I. T.
B3376.W564 P5 193 *LC* 64-12550

**Pitcher, George. comp.** **1.1086**
Wittgenstein: the Philosophical Investigations. — London; Melbourne: Macmillan, 1968. x, 510 p.; 18 cm. — (Modern studies in philosophy) 1. Wittgenstein, Ludwig, 1889-1951. I. T.
B3376.W564 P52 1968 193 *LC* 77-367183

**Waismann, Friedrich.** **1.1087**
[Wittgenstein und der Wiener Kreis. English] Wittgenstein and the Vienna Circle: conversations / recorded by Friedrich Waismann; edited by Brian McGuinness; translated by Joachim Schulte and Brian McGuinness. — New York: Barnes & Noble, c1979. 266 p.: ill.; 23 cm. Translation of Wittgenstein und der Wiener Kreis. Discussions by Wittgenstein, Schlick and Waismann. 1. Wittgenstein, Ludwig, 1889-1951. 2. Logical positivism I. Wittgenstein, Ludwig, 1889-1951. II. Schlick, Moritz, 1882-1936. III. McGuinness, Brian. IV. T.
B3376.W564 W213 146/.4 *LC* 78-6452 *ISBN* 0064973107

**Wright, G. H. von (Georg Henrik), 1916-.** **1.1088**
Wittgenstein / Georg Henrik von Wright. — Minneapolis: University of Minnesota Press, [1982?] 218 p.; 22 cm. 1. Wittgenstein, Ludwig, 1889-1951. I. T.
B3376.W564 W74 1982b 192 19 *LC* 82-143577 *ISBN* 0816612102

**Malcolm, Norman, 1911-.** • **1.1089**
Ludwig Wittgenstein: a memoir / by Norman Malcolm; with a biographical sketch by Georg Henrik von Wright. — 1st ed. — London; Toronto: Oxford University Press, 1958. 99 p. 1. Philosophers — Great Britain — Biography. I. T.
B3376.W567 M2 1958 921.3 *LC* 58-4281

# B3551–3656 Italy. Vico

**Vico, Giambattista, 1668-1744.** **1.1090**
Vico: selected writings / edited and translated by Leon Pompa. — Cambridge [Cambridgeshire]; New York: Cambridge University Press, 1982. xvii, 279 p.; 24 cm. 1. Philosophy — Addresses, essays, lectures. I. Pompa, Leon. II. T.
B3580.A5 1982 195 19 *LC* 81-12215 *ISBN* 0521235146

**Pompa, Leon.** **1.1091**
Vico: a study of the new science / Leon Pompa. — London; New York: Cambridge University Press, 1975. xii, 194 p.; 23 cm. 1. Vico, Giambattista, 1668-1744. Principi di una scienza nuova. I. T.
B3581.P74 P65 195 *LC* 74-79140 *ISBN* 0521205840

**Berlin, Isaiah, Sir.** **1.1092**
Vico and Herder: two studies in the history of ideas / Isaiah Berlin. — New York: Viking Press, 1976. xxvii, 228 p.; 22 cm. 1. Vico, Giambattista, 1668-1744. 2. Herder, Johann Gottfried, 1744-1803. I. T.
B3583.B46 901 *LC* 75-33299 *ISBN* 0670745855

**Giambattista Vico's science of humanity / edited by Giorgio** **1.1093**
**Tagliacozzo and Donald Phillip Verene; consulting editors,**
**Isaiah Berlin ... [et al.]; special advisors, Ernesto Grassi ... [et al.].**
Baltimore: Johns Hopkins University Press, c1976. xxix, 496 p. 1. Vico, Giambattista, 1668-1744 — Addresses, essays, lectures. I. Tagliacozzo, Giorgio. II. Verene, Donald Phillip, 1937-
B3583.G48 195 *LC* 75-26753 *ISBN* 080181720X

**Verene, Donald Phillip, 1937-.** **1.1094**
Vico's science of imagination / Donald Phillip Verene. — Ithaca: Cornell University Press, 1981. 227 p.; 22 cm. Includes index. 1. Vico, Giambattista, 1668-1744. I. T.
B3583.V45 195 19 *LC* 80-69828 *ISBN* 0801413915

## B3801–4175 Netherlands. Spinoza

**Spinoza, Benedictus de, 1632-1677.**　　　　　　• 1.1095
[Works. English. 1984] The collected works of Spinoza / edited and translated by Edwin Curley. — Princeton, N.J.: Princeton University Press, c1985-. v. < 1 >; 25 cm. Includes indexes. 1. Philosophy — Collected works. I. Curley, E. M. (Edwin M.), 1937- II. T.
B3958 1985　　　199/.492 19　　*LC* 84-11716　　*ISBN* 0691072221

**Spinoza, Benedictus de, 1632-1677.**　　　　　　• 1.1096
The correspondence of Spinoza, translated and edited with introd. and annotations by A. Wolf. New York, Russell & Russell, 1966. 502 p. illus., facsim., ports. 22 cm. A reissue of the 1928 ed. 1. Philosophers — Correspondence, reminiscences, etc. I. Wolf, A. (Abraham), 1876-1948. ed. II. T.
B3964.E5W6 1966a　　*LC* 66-15948

**Spinoza, Benedictus de, 1632-1677.**　　　　　　1.1097
[Ethica. English] The ethics and selected letters / Baruch Spinoza; translated by Samuel Shirley; edited, with introduction, by Seymour Feldman. — 1st ed. — Indianapolis: Hackett Pub. Co., c1982. 262 p.; 23 cm. Translation of: Ethica. 1. Ethics 2. Philosophers — Netherlands — Correspondence. I. Spinoza, Benedictus de, 1632-1677. Correspondence. Selections. English. II. Shirley, Samuel, 1912- III. Feldman, Seymour. IV. T.
B3973.E5 S47　　170 19　　*LC* 81-7199　　*ISBN* 0915145189

**Bennett, Jonathan Francis.**　　　　　　　　1.1098
A study of Spinoza's Ethics / Jonathan Bennett. — [Indianapolis, IN]: Hackett Pub. Co., c1984. ix, 396 p.; 23 cm. Includes indexes. 1. Spinoza, Benedictus de, 1632-1677. Ethica. 2. Ethics — Early works to 1800. I. T.
B3974.B46 1984　　170 19　　*LC* 83-18568　　*ISBN* 0915145839

**Hampshire, Stuart, 1914-.**　　　　　　　　• 1.1099
Spinoza. — London, Faber and Faber [1956] 176 p. 23 cm. 1. Spinoza, Benedictus de, 1632-1677. I. T.
B3998.H16 1956　　199.492　　*LC* 56-43325

**Harris, Errol E.**　　　　　　　　　　　1.1100
Salvation from despair; a reappraisal of Spinoza's philosophy [by] Errol E. Harris. The Hague, Martinus Nijhoff, 1973. xix, 270 p. 24 cm. (International archives of the history of ideas, 59) 1. Spinoza, Benedictus de, 1632-1677. I. T.
B3998.H27　　199/.492　　*LC* 73-179004　　*ISBN* 9024751586

**Wienpahl, Paul.**　　　　　　　　　　　1.1101
The radical Spinoza / Paul Wienpahl. — New York: New York University Press, 1979. xiii, 281 p.; 24 cm. 1. Spinoza, Benedictus de, 1632-1677. I. T.
B3998.W63　　199/.492　　*LC* 78-65448　　*ISBN* 0814791867

**Wolfson, Harry Austryn, 1887-1974.**　　　　　• 1.1102
The philosophy of Spinoza; unfolding the latent processes of his reasoning. New York, Schocken Books [1969, c1934] 2 v. 21 cm. 1. Spinoza, Benedictus de, 1632-1677. 2. Spinoza, Benedictus de, 1632-1677. Ethica. 3. Ethics — History — 17th century. I. T.
B3998.W65 1969　　199/.492　　*LC* 70-83674

## B4201–4279 Russia

**Edie, James M. ed.**　　　　　　　　　　• 1.1103
Russian philosophy. Edited by James M. Edie, James P. Scanlan [and] Mary-Barbara Zeldin, with the collaboration of George L. Kline. [1st ed.] Chicago, Quadrangle Books [1965] 3 v. 22 cm. 1. Philosophy, Russian — Addresses, essays, lectures. 2. Philosophers — Soviet Union — Biography. I. Scanlan, James P. (James Patrick), 1927- joint ed. II. Zeldin, Mary-Barbara. joint ed. III. T.
B4201.E3　　197.2　　*LC* 64-10928

**Losskiĭ, N. O. (Nikolaĭ Onufrievich), 1870-1965.**　• 1.1104
History of Russian philosophy. — New York, International Universities Press [1951] 416 p. 24 cm. Includes bibliographical references. 1. Philosophy, Russian I. T.
B4201.L6　　197　　*LC* 51-11822

**Zen'kovskiĭ, V. V. (Vasiliĭ Vasil'evich), 1881-1962.**　• 1.1105
A history of Russian philosophy. Authorized translation from the Russian by George L. Kline. — New York, Columbia University Press, 1953. 2 v. (xiv, 947 p.) 23 cm. — (Columbia Slavic studies) 1. Philosophy, Russian I. T. II. Series.
B4201.Z413　　197　　*LC* 53-12113

**Scanlan, James P. (James Patrick), 1927-.**　　　1.1106
Marxism in the USSR: a critical survey of current Soviet thought / James P. Scanlan. — Ithaca: Cornell University Press, 1985. 362 p.; 24 cm. Includes index. 1. Philosophy, Marxist — Soviet Union. 2. Philosophy, Russian — 20th century I. T. II. Title: Marxism in the U.S.S.R.
B4231.S32 1985　　335.43/01 19　　*LC* 84-45802　　*ISBN* 0801416493

**Somerville, John, 1905-.**　　　　　　　　• 1.1107
Soviet philosophy: a study of theory and practice / by John Somerville. — New York: Philosophical library, 1946. xi, 269 p. 1. Philosophy, Russian I. T.
B4231.S6　　*LC* 47-3367

**Zen'kovskiĭ, V. V. (Vasiliĭ Vasil'evich), 1881-1962.**　• 1.1108
Russian thinkers and Europe / by V. V. Zenkovskii; translated from the Russian by Galia S. Bodde. — Ann Arbor, Mich.: Published for American Council of Learned Societies by J. W. Edwards, c1953. iii, 199 p.; 22 cm. — (Russian translation project series of the American Council of Learned Societies; 21) Translation of Russkie mysliteli i Evropa. 1. Philosophy, Russian 2. Soviet Union — Civilization 3. Europe — Civilization I. T.
B4231.Z514 1953　　*LC* 53-1905

**Belinsky, Vissarion Grigoryevich, 1811-1848.**　　• 1.1109
Selected philosophical works / V. G. Belinsky. — Moscow: Foreign Languages Publishing House, 1948. li, 552 p.: port. I. T.
B4238.B32 E5　　*LC* 49-22990

**Berdiaev, Nikolaĭ, 1874-1948.**　　　　　　• 1.1110
The destiny of man. New York, C. Scribner's sons, 1937. vi, 377 p. 23 cm. At head of title: Nicolas Berdyaev. 'Translated from the Russian by Natalie Duddington, M. A.' 'Printed in Great Britain.' 1. Ethics 2. Christian ethics 3. Man 4. Eschatology 5. Philosophy and religion I. Duddington, Nataliia Aleksandrovna Ērtel'. tr. II. T.
B4238.B43 O23　　197　　*LC* 38-4683

**Berdiaev, Nikolaĭ, 1874-1948.**　　　　　　• 1.1111
Dream and reality: an essay in autobiography / Nikolaĭ Aleksandrovich Berdiaev; [translated by Katharine Lampert]. — New York: Macmillan, 1951, [c1950]. xv, 332 p.: port.; 24 cm. Translation of Samopoznanie. 'Principal works by Nicolas Berdyaev': p. 327-328. I. T.
B4238.B43 S314 1950a　　921.7　　*LC* 51-1608

**Lowrie, Donald Alexander.**　　　　　　　• 1.1112
Rebellious prophet; a life of Nicolai Berdiaev. New York Harper [1960] 310p. 1. Berdiaev, Nikolaĭ, 1874-1948. I. T.
B4238 B44 L6

**Chernyshevsky, Nikolay Gavrilovich, 1828-1889.**　• 1.1113
Selected philosophical essays / N. G. Chernyshevsky. — Moscow: Foreign Languages Publishing House, 1953. 610 p.: port. 1. Philosophy — Collected works. I. T.
B4238.C62 E5　　*LC* 55-17182

**Koehler, Ludmilla, 1917-.**　　　　　　　1.1114
N.F. Fedorov: the philosophy of action / by Ludmila Koehler. — Pittsburgh, Pa.: Institute for the Human Sciences, c1979. 164 p.; 23 cm. 1. Fedorov, Nikolai Federovich, 1828-1903 2. Philosophy — Soviet Union I. T. II. Title: The philosophy of action.
B4238F44 K627

**Althusser, Louis.**　　　　　　　　　　• 1.1115
Lenin and philosophy, and other essays. Translated from the French by Ben Brewster. — New York: Monthly Review Press, [1972, c1971] 253 p.; 21 cm. — (Modern reader, PB-213) 1. Lenin, Vladimir Il'ich, 1870-1924. 2. Marx, Karl, 1818-1883. Das Kapital. I. T.
B4249.L384 A69 1972　　335.43　　*LC* 78-178710　　*ISBN* 085345213X

**Lukashevich, Stephen.**　　　　　　　　• 1.1116
Konstantin Leontev, 1831–1891: a study in Russian 'heroic vitalism.'. — [1st ed.]. — New York, Pageant Press [1967] xvii, 235 p. 21 cm. Includes bibliographical references. 1. Leont'ev, Konstantin Nikolaevich, 1831-1891. I. T.
B4249.L44L8　　197/.2 (B)　　*LC* 67-28981

**Strémooukhoff, D.**　　　　　　　　　　1.1117
[Vladimir Soloviev et son oeuvre messianique. English] Vladimir Soloviev and his messianic work / D. Strémooukhoff; translated from the French by Elizabeth Meyendorff; edited by Phillip Guilbeau and Heather Elise MacGregor. — Belmont, Mass.: Nordland Pub. Co., 1980, c1979. 394 p.; 22 cm. Translation of Vladimir Soloviev et son oeuvre messianique. Includes index. 1. Solovyov, Vladimir Sergeyevich, 1853-1900. I. Guilbeau, Phillip. II. MacGregor, Heather Elise. III. T.
B4267.S813　　230 19　　*LC* 78-78264　　*ISBN* 0913124362

## B4301–4495 Scandinavia. Kierkegaard

**Kierkegaard, Søren, 1813-1855.**      **1.1118**
[Selected works. English. 1967] Søren Kierkegaard's journals and papers. Edited and translated by Howard V. Hong and Edna H. Hong, assisted by Gregor Malantschuk. Bloomington, Indiana University Press [1967-78] 7 v. 24 cm. 1. Philosophy — Collected works. I. Hong, Howard Vincent, 1912- ed. II. Hong, Edna Hatlestad, 1913- ed. III. Malantschuk, Gregor. IV. T.
B4372.E5 1967      198/.9      *LC* 67-13025      *ISBN* 0253182395

**Kierkegaard, Søren, 1813-1855.**      • **1.1119**
[Selections. English] A Kierkegaard anthology. Edited by Robert Bretall. New York, Modern Library [1959] xxv, 494 p. 19 cm. (The Modern library of the world's best books [no. 303]) I. T.
B4372.E5 B7 1959      198.9      *LC* 59-9955

**Kierkegaard, Søren, 1813-1855.**      • **1.1120**
[Stadier paa livets vej. English] Stages on life's way. Translated by Walter Lowrie. Introd. by Paul Sponheim. New York, Schocken Books [1967] 472 p. facsim. 21 cm. Reprint of the 1940 ed. I. Lowrie, Walter, 1868-1959, tr. II. T.
B4373.S83 E55 1967      198.9      *LC* 66-14875

**Kierkegaard, Søren, 1813-1855.**      • **1.1121**
[Breve og aktstykker. English] Letters and documents / Kierkegaard; translated by Henrik Rosenmeier, with introd. and notes. — Princeton, N.J.: Princeton University Press, c1978. xxviii, 518 p.: maps; 23 cm. (His Kierkegaard's writings; 25) Translation of Breve og aktstykker. Includes index. 1. Kierkegaard, Søren, 1813-1855. 2. Philosophers — Denmark — Correspondence. 3. Philosophers — Denmark — Biography. I. Rosenmeier, Henrik, 1931- II. T.
B4376.A413 1978      198/.9 B      *LC* 77-85897      *ISBN* 0691072280

**Collins, James Daniel.**      • **1.1122**
The mind of Kierkegaard / by James Collins. — Chicago: H. Regnery, 1953. xiv, 304 p. 1. Kierkegaard, Søren, 1813-1855. I. T.
B4377.C63      *LC* 53-10152

**Mackey, Louis.**      **1.1123**
Kierkegaard: a kind of poet. Philadelphia, University of Pennsylvania Press [c1971] xiii, 327 p. 24 cm. 1. Kierkegaard, Søren, 1813-1855. I. T.
B4377.M26      198/.9      *LC* 75-157050      *ISBN* 0812276418

**Malantschuk, Gregor.**      **1.1124**
[Dialektik og Eksistens hos Søren Kierkegaard. English] Kierkegaard's thought. Edited and translated by Howard V. Hong and Edna H. Hong. [Princeton, N.J.] Princeton University Press, 1971. x, 388 p. 23 cm. Translation of Dialektik og Eksistens hos Søren Kierkegaard. 1. Kierkegaard, Søren, 1813-1855. 2. Dialectic I. T.
B4377.M3213      198.9      *LC* 77-155000      *ISBN* 0691071667

**Elrod, John W., 1940-.**      **1.1125**
Kierkegaard and Christendom / John W. Elrod. — Princeton, N.J.: Princeton University Press, c1981. xxiv, 320 p.; 22 cm. 1. Kierkegaard, Søren, 1813-1855. 2. Christianity — Philosophy 3. Self (Philosophy) I. T.
B4378.C5 E45      230/.044 19      *LC* 80-8547      *ISBN* 0691072612

**Evans, C. Stephen.**      **1.1126**
Kierkegaard's 'Fragments' and 'Postscript': the religious philosophy of Johannes Climacus / by C. Stephen Evans. — Atlantic Highlands, N.J.: Humanities Press, 1983. xiv, 304 p.; 24 cm. Includes index. 1. Kierkegaard, Søren, 1813-1855 — Religion. 2. Religion — Philosophy — History — 19th century. I. T.
B4378.R44 E83 1983      200/.1 19      *LC* 82-23329      *ISBN* 0391027379

## B4511–4568 Spain. Ortega. Unamuno

**Ortega y Gasset, José, 1883-1955.**      **1.1127**
[Sobre la razón histórica. English] Historical reason / José Ortega y Gasset; translated by Philip W. Silver. — 1st ed. — New York: Norton, c1984. 223 p.; 21 cm. Translation of: Sobre la razón histórica. 1. Rationalism I. T.
B4568.O73 S6213 1984      196/.1 19      *LC* 83-13139      *ISBN* 0393018318

**Ortega y Gasset, José, 1883-1955.**      • **1.1128**
The modern theme. Translated from the Spanish by James Cleugh. Introd. by José Ferrater Mora. — New York, Harper [1961] 152 p. 21 cm. — (Harper torchbooks, TB1038. The Academy library) Translation of El tema de nuestro tiempo. 1. Philosophy — Addresses, essays, lectures. 2. Revolutions 3. Relativity (Physics) I. T.
B4568.O73T43 1961      196      *LC* 61-1591

**Ferrater Mora, José, 1912-.**      • **1.1129**
Ortega y Gasset, an outline of his philosophy. New rev. ed. New Haven, Yale University Press [1963] 103 p. 21 cm. 1. Ortega y Gasset, José, 1883-1955. I. T.
B4568.O74 F4 1963      *LC* 63-6198

**Holmes, Oliver W., 1938-.**      **1.1130**
Human reality and the social world: Ortega's philosophy of history / Oliver W. Holmes. — Amherst: University of Massachusetts Press, 1975. xi, 175 p.; 24 cm. Includes index. 1. Ortega y Gasset, José, 1883-1955. 2. History — Philosophy I. T.
B4568.O74 H63      901      *LC* 74-21238      *ISBN* 0870231731

**Ouimette, Victor.**      **1.1131**
José Ortega y Gasset / by Victor Ouimette. — Boston: Twayne Publishers, 1982. 176 p.: port.; 21 cm. — (Twayne's world authors series; TWAS 624. Spain) Includes index. 1. Ortega y Gasset, José, 1883-1955. I. T.
B4568.O74 O84 1982      196/.1 19      *LC* 81-6266      *ISBN* 0805764666

**Silver, Philip.**      **1.1132**
Ortega as phenomenologist: the genesis of Meditations on Quixote / Philip W. Silver. — New York: Columbia University Press, 1978. xi, 175 p.; 22 cm. Includes index. 1. Ortega y Gasset, José, 1883-1955. 2. Ortega y Gasset, José, 1883-1955. Meditaciones del Quijote. 3. Phenomenology 4. Aesthetics I. T.
B4568.O74 S56      196/.1      *LC* 78-667      *ISBN* 0231045441

**Unamuno, Miguel de, 1864-1936.**      **1.1133**
Del sentimiento trágico de la vida en los hombres y en los pueblos. New York, Las Américas Pub. Co. [1964] 236 p. 22 cm. 1. Immortality 2. Philosophy and religion 3. Pessimism I. T.
B4568.U53 D48 1964a      196.1

**Unamuno, Miguel de, 1864-1936.**      **1.1134**
The Tragic sense of life in men and nations / Miguel de Unamuno; translated by Anthony Kerrigan; with an introd. by Salvador de Madariaga and an afterword by William Barret; edited and annotated by Anthony Kerrigan and Martin Nozick. — Princeton, N.J.: Princeton University Press, 1977, c1972. xlvi, 528 p.; 21 cm. — (Bollingen series. 85) (The Selected works of Miguel de Unamuno; v. 4) (Princeton/Bollingen paperbacks) Translation of Del sentimiento trágico de la vida en los hombres y en los pueblos. 1. Immortality (Philosophy) 2. Philosophy and religion 3. Pessimism I. T. II. Series.
B4568.U53 D5 1977      *ISBN* 0691018200

**Ferrater Mora, José, 1912-.**      • **1.1135**
Unamuno, a philosophy of tragedy. Translated by Philip Silver. — Berkeley, University of California Press, 1962. 136 p. 21 cm. Includes bibliography. 1. Unamuno, Miguel de, 1864-1936. I. T.
B4568.U54F43      196      *LC* 62-7437

## B4811–4815 Hungary

**Parkinson, G. H. R. (George Henry Radcliffe)**      **1.1136**
Georg Lukács / by G. H. R. Parkinson. — London; Boston: Routledge and Kegan Paul, 1977. vii, 205 p.; 22 cm. Includes index. 1. Lukács, György, 1885-1971. I. T.
B4815.L84 P3      199/.439      *LC* 77-30010      *ISBN* 0710086784

## B5000–5289 Asia

**Indian philosophy today / edited by N. K. Devaraja.**      **1.1137**
Delhi: Macmillan Co. of India, 1975. xxiii, 286 p.; 22 cm. Includes index. 1. Philosophy, Indic — 20th century — Addresses, essays, lectures. I. Devaraja, N. K. (Nand Kishore), 1917-
B5131.I5      181/.4      *LC* 75-908522

**Brière, O.**      • **1.1138**
Fifty years of Chinese philosophy, 1898–1948 / O. Brière; translated from the French by Laurence G. Thompson; edited, with an introd. by Dennis J. Doolin. — New York: Praeger, 1965. 159 p.; 23 cm. Translation of Les courants philosophiques en Chine depuis 50 ans. 1. Philosophy, Chinese — 20th century 2. Philosophy, Chinese — Bibliography. I. T.
B5231.B713 1965      181/.11      *LC* 65-21106

**Alitto, Guy.**      **1.1139**
The last Confucian: Liang Shu–ming and the Chinese dilemma of modernity / Guy S. Alitto. — Berkeley: University of California Press, c1979. xvii, 396 p.: ill.; 24 cm. 'Sponsored by the Center for Chinese Studies, University of California, Berkeley.' Includes index. 1. Liang, Shu-ming, 1893- 2. Philosophers — China — Biography. I. University of California, Berkeley. Center for Chinese Studies. II. T.
B5234.L52 A44      181/.09/512 B      *LC* 75-27920      *ISBN* 0520031237

**Ching, Julia.** • 1.1140
To acquire wisdom: the way of Wang Yang–ming / Julia Ching. — New York: Columbia University Press, 1976. xxvi, 373 p.: ill.; 24 cm. (Studies in Oriental culture. no. 11) (Oriental monograph series; no. 16) Includes selected essays and poems by Wang Yang-ming in English translation. Includes index. 1. Wang, Yang-ming, 1472-1529. I. Wang, Yang-ming, 1472-1529. Selected works. English. 1976. II. T. III. Series. IV. Series: Oriental monograph series; no. 16
B5234.W35 C49 181/.11 *LC* 75-20038 *ISBN* 0231039387

**East-West Philosophers' Conference.** • 1.1141
Japanese mind; essentials of Japanese philosophy and culture / Charles A.Moore,editor, with the assistance of Aldyth V. Morris. Honolulu: East-West Center Press 1967. 357p.; 24 cm. "Consists exclusively of papers taken from the books resulting from the four East-West Philosophers' Conferences held at the University of Hawaii in 1939,1949,1959 and 1964." 1. Philosophy, Japanese I. Moore,Charles Alexander, ed. II. University of Hawaii (Honolulu) III. T.
B5241.E2 199.52 *LC* 67-16704

**Piovesana, Gino K.** • 1.1142
Recent Japanese philosophical thought, 1862–1962 [by] Gino K. Piovesana. — Revised ed. — Tokyo: Enderle Bookstore, 1968. vi, 296 p.; 22 cm. 1. Philosophy, Japanese — 19th century 2. Philosophy, Japanese — 20th century I. T.
B5241.P5 1968 181/.12 *LC* 77-460083

**Spae, Joseph John, 1913-.** • 1.1143
Itô Jinsai: a philosopher, educator, and sociologist of the Tokugawa period / by Joseph John Spae. — New York: Paragon Book Reprint Corp., 1967. xv, 278 p., [1] leaf of plates: ill.; 24 cm. Reprint of the 1948 ed. published by the Catholic University of Peking, Peking, which was issued as Monograph 12 of Monumenta serica. Includes index. 1. Itô, Jinsai, 1627-1705. 2. Philosophy, Confucian — Japan. I. T.
B5244.Ix *LC* 67-20720/CD

**Nishida, Kitarō, 1870-1945.** • 1.1144
[Tetsugaku no kompon mondai. English] Fundamental problems of philosophy; the world of action and the dialectical world. Translated with an introduction by David A. Dilworth. Tokyo, Sophia University [1970] 258 p. illus. 27 cm. (A Monumenta Nipponica monograph) Translation of Tetsugaku no kompon mondai. I. Jōchi Daigaku. II. T. III. Series.
B5244.N55 A463 100 *LC* 73-97720

## B5300–5320 Africa

**Hountondji, Paulin J., 1942-.** 1.1145
[Sur la philosophie africaine. English] African philosophy: myth and reality / Paulin J. Hountondji; translated by Henri Evans with the collaboration of Jonathan Rée; Introduction by Abiola Irele. — Bloomington: Indiana University Press, 1983. 221 p.; 23 cm. — (African systems of thought.) Translation of: Sur la philosophie africaine. 1. Philosophy, African I. T. II. Series.
B5305.H6813 1983 199/.6 19 *LC* 83-47508 *ISBN* 0253302706

**African philosophy: an introduction / edited by Richard A. Wright.** 1.1146
2nd ed. — Washington: University Press of America, 1977. xv, 273 p.; 23 cm. Includes indexes. 1. Philosophy, African I. Wright, Richard A.
B5305.W753 199.6 *ISBN* 0819105058 pa

# BC Logic

## BC6 Collections

**Copi, Irving M.** • 1.1147
Contemporary readings in logical theory / Irving M. Copi, James A. Gould. — New York: Macmillan, 1967. 342 p.: ill. 1. Logic — Addresses, essays, lectures. I. Gould, James Adams, 1922- II. T.
BC6.C58 *LC* 67-15535

**Flew, Antony, 1923- ed.** • 1.1148
Essays in conceptual analysis, by H. Brotman [and others]. — London, Macmillan, 1966. xi, 265 p. diagrs. 23 cm. Bibliographical footnotes. 1. Logic — Addresses, essays, lectures. I. T.
BC6.F58 160.4 *LC* 56-4230

**Flew, Antony, 1923- ed.** • 1.1149
Essays on logic and language / [by] Gilbert Ryle [and others]; edited with an introd. by Antony Flew. — Oxford, Eng.: Blackwell, 1951. vii, 206 p.; 23 cm. Second series of essays published in 1953 under title: Logic and language. 1. Logic — Addresses, essays, lectures. 2. Language and languages 3. Meaning (Psychology) I. T.
BC6.F6 1951 160.4 *LC* 51-5542

**Flew, Antony, 1923- ed.** • 1.1150
Logic and language (second series) Essays by J. L. Austin [and others] Oxford, Blackwell, 1953. vii, 242 p. diagrs. 23 cm. First series published in 1951 under title: Essays on logic and language. 1. Logic — Addresses, essays, lectures. 2. Language and languages I. T.
BC6.F63 1953a 160.4 *LC* 53-2749 rev

**Iseminger, Gary. comp.** • 1.1151
Logic and philosophy; selected readings. New York, Appleton-Century-Crofts [1968] viii, 248 p. 21 cm. (The Century philosophy series) 1. Logic — Addresses, essays, lectures. I. T.
BC6.I8 160/.8 *LC* 68-15407

**Strawson, P. F.** • 1.1152
Philosophical logic / edited by P. F. Strawson. — London: Oxford U.P., 1967. [5], 177 p.: diagrs.; 21 cm. — (Oxford readings in philosophy) 1. Logic — Collections. I. T.
BC6.S8 160/.8 *LC* 68-72121

**Wright, G. H. von (Georg Henrik), 1916-.** • 1.1153
Logical studies. — London, Routledge and K. Paul [1957] 195 p. illus. 23 cm. — (International library of psychology, philosophy, and scientific method) 1. Logic — Addresses, essays, lectures. I. T.
BC6.W7 160.4 *LC* 58-732

## BC11–57 History. Theory

**Bochenski, Joseph M., 1902-.** • 1.1154
[Formale Logik. English] A history of formal logic, by I. M. Bochenski. Translated and edited by Ivo Thomas. [2d ed.] New York, Chelsea Pub. Co. [1970] xxii, 567 p. illus. 21 cm. Translation of Formale Logik. 1. Logic — History. I. T. II. Title: Formal logic.
BC15.B643 1970 160/.9 *LC* 72-113118 *ISBN* 0828402388

**Kneale, W. C. (William Calvert)** • 1.1155
The development of logic / by William Kneale and Martha Kneale. — Oxford [Eng.]: Clarendon Press, 1962. 761 p.: ill.; 22 cm. Includes bibliography. 1. Logic — Hist. I. Kneale, Martha. II. T.
BC15.K55 160.9 *LC* 62-1892

**Bocheński, Innocentius Maria, 1902-.** • 1.1156
Ancient formal logic. Amsterdam, North-Holland Pub. Co., 1951. vi, 122 p. illus. fold. table. 22 cm. (Studies in logic and the foundations of mathematics.) 1. Logic I. T. II. Series.
BC 28 B66 1951

**Mates, Benson, 1919-.** • 1.1157
Stoic logic. — Berkeley: University of California Press, 1953. — 148 p.; 24 cm. — (University of California publications in philosophy. v. 26) Based on the author's thesis, University of California. 1. Stoics 2. Logic, Ancient I. T. II. Series.
BC28.M37 1973 188 *LC* 53-9918

**Böhner, Philotheus, Father.** • 1.1158
Medieval logic: an outline of its development from 1250 to c.1400 / by Philotheus Boehner. — [Manchester, Eng.]: Manchester University Press, 1952. xvii, 130 p. 1. Logic — History. I. T.
BC34.B6 *LC* 52-3201

**Henry, Desmond Paul.** 1.1159
Medieval logic and metaphysics: a modern introduction [by] D. P. Henry. — London: Humanities, 1972. xiii, 133 p.; 23 cm. — (Hutchinson University Library) 1. Logic, Medieval 2. Ontology. I. T.
BC34.H45 160/.94 *LC* 72-196775 *ISBN* 0091108306

**Howell, Wilbur Samuel, 1904-.** 1.1160
Eighteenth–century British logic and rhetoric. Princeton, Princeton University Press, 1971. xii, 742 p. 25 cm. 1. Aristotle — Contributions in logic. 2. Logic, Modern — History. 3. Rhetoric — 1500-1800 4. Logic — Great Britain — History — 18th century. I. T.
BC38.H59 160/.942 *LC* 70-151531 *ISBN* 069106203X

**Dewey, John, 1859-1952.**     • 1.1161
Logic, the theory of inquiry / by John Dewey. — New York: H. Holt and company, c1938. viii, 546 p. 'This book is a development of ideas regarding the nature of logical theory that were first presented ... in Studies in logical theory; that were somewhat expanded in Essays in experimental logic and were briefly summarized with special references to education in How we think.' - Pref. 1. Logic 2. Thought and thinking I. T.
BC50.D43     *LC* 38-27918

**Fogelin, Robert J.**     1.1162
Understanding arguments: an introduction to informal logic / Robert J. Fogelin. — 2nd ed. — New York: Harcourt Brace Jovanovich, c1982. x, 430 p.: ill.; 24 cm. 1. Logic I. T.
BC50.F63 1982     160 19     *LC* 81-85590     *ISBN* 0155928589

**Hintikka, Jaakko, 1929-.**     1.1163
The intentions of intentionality and other new models for modalities / Jaakko Hintikka. — Dordrecht; Boston: D. Reidel Pub. Co., c1975. xviii, 262 p.: ill.; 23 cm. — (Synthese library; v. 90) 1. Logic — Addresses, essays, lectures. 2. Semantics (Philosophy) — Addresses, essays, lectures. 3. Modality (Logic) — Addresses, essays, lectures. 4. Knowledge, Theory of — Addresses, essays, lectures. I. T.
BC50.H55     160     *LC* 75-31698     *ISBN* 9027705836

**Nagel, Ernest, 1901-.**     • 1.1164
Logic without metaphysics, and other essays in the philosophy of science. — Glencoe, Ill., Free Press [c1956] 433 p. 22 cm. 1. Logic I. T.
BC50.N23     160     *LC* 56-10582

**Contemporary philosophical logic / Irving M. Copi, James A.**     1.1165
**Gould, editors.**
New York: St. Martin's Press, c1978. x, 334 p.; 23 cm. 1. Logic 2. Philosophy I. Copi, Irving M. II. Gould, James A., 1922-
BC51.C7     160     *LC* 77-85986     *ISBN* 0312167865

**Haack, Susan.**     1.1166
Deviant logic: some philosophical issues / Susan Haack. — London; New York: Cambridge University Press, 1975 (c1974) xii, 191 p.; 23 cm. Includes index. 1. Logic 2. Philosophy 3. Intuition 4. Quantum theory I. T.
BC51.H3     160     *LC* 74-76949     *ISBN* 052120500X

**Putnam, Hilary.**     • 1.1167
Philosophy of logic. — New York: Harper & Row, [1971] 76 p.; 21 cm. — (Harper essays in philosophy) (Harper torchbooks, TB1544) 1. Logic I. T.
BC51.P88 1971     160     *LC* 71-149364     *ISBN* 0061360422(pbk)

**Quine, W. V. (Willard Van Orman)**     1.1168
Philosophy of logic / W.V. Quine. — 2nd ed. — Cambridge, Mass.: Harvard University Press, 1986. ix, 109 p.; 23 cm. Includes index. 1. Logic 2. Philosophy I. T.
BC51.Q5 1986     160 19     *LC* 85-24734     *ISBN* 0674665635

**Hintikka, Jaakko, 1929-.**     1.1169
Logic, language–games and information: Kantian themes in the philosophy of logic, by Jaakko Hintikka. Oxford, Clarendon Press, 1973. x, 291 p. 23 cm. 'Based on the John Locke lectures ... delivered at Oxford University in 1964. 1. Kant, Immanuel, 1724-1804 — Logic. 2. Languages — Philosophy 3. Logic 4. Inference 5. First-order logic I. T.
BC57.H55 1973     160     *LC* 73-156486     *ISBN* 0198243642

## BC60–78 Deductive Logic

**Kant, Immanuel, 1724-1804.**     1.1170
[Logik. English] Logic. Translated, with an introd., by Robert S. Hartman and Wolfgang Schwarz. Indianapolis, Bobbs-Merrill [1974] cxv, 164 p. 21 cm. (The Library of liberal arts, LLA 189) 1. Logic — Early works to 1800. I. T.
BC63.K3 1974     160     *LC* 72-10560     *ISBN* 0672514346 *ISBN* 0672612283

**Bradley, F. H. (Francis Herbert), 1846-1924.**     • 1.1171
The principles of logic / by F.H. Bradley. — 2d ed., rev., with commentary and terminal essays ... — London: Oxford University Press, 1950, [c1922] 2 v. Paged continuously. 1. Logic I. T.
BC71.B8 1922     *LC* 22-23132

**Davies, Martin.**     1.1172
Meaning, quantification, necessity: themes in philosophical logic / Martin Davies. — London; Boston: Routledge & Kegan Paul, 1981. xii, 282 p.; 23 cm. — (International library of philosophy.) Includes index. 1. Logic I. T. II. Series.
BC71.D25 1981     160 19     *LC* 81-201700     *ISBN* 0710007590

**Geach, P. T. (Peter Thomas), 1916-.**     • 1.1173
Reference and generality: an examination of some medieval and modern theories. — Emended ed. Ithaca, N.Y.: Cornell University Press [1968, c1962] xx, 202 p.; 22 cm. (Contemporary philosophy) 1. Logic 2. Languages — Philosophy 3. Reference (Philosophy) I. T. II. Series.
BC71.G34 1968     160     *LC* 68-7084

**Grayling, A. C.**     1.1174
An introduction to philosophical logic / A.C. Grayling. — Totowa, N.J.: Barnes & Noble Books, c1982. 300 p.; 23 cm. 1. Logic 2. Languages — Philosophy I. T.
BC71.G7 1982     160 19     *LC* 82-6854     *ISBN* 0389202991

**Haack, Susan.**     1.1175
Philosophy of logics / Susan Haack. — Cambridge [Eng.]; New York: Cambridge University Press, 1978. xvi, 276 p.: ill.; 24 cm. Includes index. 1. Logic I. T.
BC71.H15     160     *LC* 77-17071     *ISBN* 0521219884

**Jeffrey, Richard C.**     • 1.1176
Formal logic: its scope and limits / [by] Richard C. Jeffrey. — New York: McGraw-Hill, [1967] xii, 238 p.: ill. 1. Logic I. T.
BC71.J38

**Leblanc, Hugues, 1924-.**     1.1177
Deductive logic / Hugues Leblanc and William A. Wisdom. 2d ed. — Boston: Allyn and Bacon, c1976. xiv, 443 p.: ill.; 24 cm. Includes index. 1. Logic I. Wisdom, William A., joint author. II. T.
BC71.L38 1976     160     *LC* 75-42443     *ISBN* 020505496X

**Quine, Willard Van Orman, 1908-.**     • 1.1178
From a logical point of view: 9 logico–philosophical essays / Willard Van Orman Quine. — 2 ed. rev. — Cambridge, Mass.: Harvard University Press, c1961. vi, 184 p. 1. Logic — Addresses, essays, lectures. I. T.
BC71.Q48 1961     *LC* 61-15277     *ISBN* 0674323505

**Quine, W. V. (Willard Van Orman)**     1.1179
Methods of logic / W.V. Quine. — 4th ed. — Cambridge, Mass.: Harvard University Press, 1982. x, 333 p.: ill.; 24 cm. Includes index. 1. Logic I. T.
BC71.Q5 1982     160 19     *LC* 81-22929     *ISBN* 0674571754

**Shcherbatskoĭ, Fedor Ippolitovich, 1866-1942.**     • 1.1180
Buddhist logic / by Th. Stcherbatsky. — New York: Dover Publications, 1962. 2 v.; 22 cm. Vol. 2 includes 'A short treatise of logic (Nyāya-bindu) by Dharmakīrti with its commentary (Nyāya-bindu-tīkā) by Dharmottara, translated from the Sanscrit text.' 1. Buddhism 2. Logic 3. Philosophy, Hindu I. Dharmakīrti, 7th cent. Nyāyahindu. English. 1962. II. Dharmottara. Nyāyabindutīkā. English. 1962. III. T.
BC71.S45 1962     160     *LC* 62-52862     Pbk

**Sommers, Frederic Tamler, 1923-.**     1.1181
The logic of natural language / Fred Sommers. — Oxford: Clarendon Press; New York: Oxford University Press, 1982. xvii, 469 p.; 22 cm. — (Clarendon library of logic and philosophy.) Includes index. 1. Logic I. T. II. Series.
BC71.S715 1982     160 19     *LC* 81-14199     *ISBN* 0198244258

## BC80–99 Inductive Logic

**Applications of inductive logic: proceedings of a conference at**     1.1182
**the Queen's College, Oxford 21–24, August 1978 / edited by L.**
**Jonathan Cohen and Mary Hesse.**
Oxford: Clarendon Press; New York: Oxford University Press, 1980. xiv, 432 p.; 24 cm. 1. Induction (Logic) — Congresses. 2. Reasoning — Congresses. I. Cohen, L. Jonathan (Laurence Jonathan) II. Hesse, Mary B.
BC91.A66     161     *LC* 79-41126     *ISBN* 019824584X

**Goodman, Nelson.**     1.1183
Fact, fiction, and forecast / Nelson Goodman. — 4th ed. — Cambridge, Mass.: Harvard University Press, 1983. xxv, 131 p.; 21 cm. 1. Induction (Logic) — Addresses, essays, lectures. 2. Conditionals (Logic) — Addresses, essays, lectures. 3. Possibility — Addresses, essays, lectures. 4. Forecasting — Addresses, essays, lectures. 5. Science — Philosophy — Addresses, essays, lectures. I. T.
BC91.G66 1983     161 19     *LC* 82-15764     *ISBN* 0674290712

**Harrod, Roy Forbes, Sir, 1900-.**     1.1184
Foundations of inductive logic / by Roy Harrod. — London; New York: Macmillan, 1974. xix, 290 p.; 23 cm. Includes index. 1. Induction (Logic) I. T.
BC91.H3 1974b     161     *LC* 74-195175     *ISBN* 0333169514

**Kyburg, Henry Ely, 1928-.**     • **1.1185**
Probability and inductive logic [by] Henry E. Kyburg, Jr. — [New York]: Macmillan, [1970] x, 272 p.; 24 cm. 1. Probabilities 2. Induction (Logic) I. T.
BC91.K9 1970     161     *LC* 71-85793

**Mill, John Stuart, 1806-1873.**     • **1.1186**
A system of logic, ratiocinative and inductive, being a connected view of the principles of evidence and the methods of scientific investigation. People's ed. London, Longmans, Green, and co., 1884. xvi, 622 p. 20 cm. 1. Logic 2. Science — Methodology 3. Knowledge, Theory of I. T.
BC91.M5 1884     *LC* 10-7122

**Skyrms, Brian.**     **1.1187**
Choice and chance: an introduction to inductive logic / Brian Skyrms. — 3rd ed. — Belmont, Calif: Wadsworth Pub. Co., c1986. vi, 218 p.; 23 cm. 1. Induction (Logic) 2. Probabilities I. T.
BC91.S5 1986     161 19     *LC* 85-7137     *ISBN* 0534051901

**Swinburne, Richard. comp.**     **1.1188**
The justification of induction. — [London; New York]: Oxford University Press, 1974. 179 p.; 21 cm. — (Oxford readings in philosophy) 1. Induction (Logic) — Addresses, essays, lectures. I. T.
BC91.S96     161     *LC* 74-158460     *ISBN* 0198570293

**Wright, G. H. von (Georg Henrik), 1916-.**     • **1.1189**
A treatise on induction and probability. New York Harcourt, Brace 1951. 310p. (International library of psychology, philosophy and scientific method) 1. Logic 2. Probabilities I. T.
BC91 W72 1951

# BC101–117 Textbooks

**Cohen, Morris Raphael, 1880-1947.**     • **1.1190**
An introduction to logic and scientific method, by Morris R. Cohen and Ernest Nagel. — New York: Harcourt, Brace and company, [c1934] xii, 467 p.: diagrs.; 22 cm. 'First edition.' 1. Logic 2. Methodology I. Nagel, Ernest, 1901- joint author. II. T.
BC108.C67     160     *LC* 34-2513

**Copi, Irving M.**     **1.1191**
Introduction to logic / Irving M. Copi. — 7th ed. — New York: Macmillan; London: Collier Macmillan, c1986. xiv, 617 p.: ill; 24 cm. Includes index. 1. Logic I. T.
BC108.C69 1986     160 19     *LC* 85-13751     *ISBN* 0023250208

**Prior, Arthur N.**     • **1.1192**
Formal logic. — 2d ed. — Oxford, Clarendon Press, 1962. 341 p. illus. 23 cm. 1. Logic I. T.
BC108.P8 1962     160     *LC* 62-3329

**Salmon, Wesley C.**     **1.1193**
Logic / Wesley C. Salmon. — 3rd ed. — Englewood Cliffs, N.J.: Prentice-Hall, c1984. xii, 180 p.: ill; 23 cm. — (Prentice-Hall foundations of philosophy series.) Includes index. 1. Logic I. T. II. Series.
BC108.S2 1984     160 19     *LC* 83-13924     *ISBN* 013540021X

**Strawson, P. F.**     • **1.1194**
Introduction to logical theory / by P. F. Strawson. — London: Methuen, 1952. x, 266 p. 1. Logic I. T.
BC108.S8

**Suppes, Patrick, 1922-.**     • **1.1195**
Introduction to logic. Princeton, N.J., D. Van Nostrand Co. [1957] 312 p. illus. 24 cm. (The University series in undergraduate mathematics) 1. Logic I. T.
BC108.S85     160     *LC* 57-8153

# BC121–128 Special Types

**Rescher, Nicholas.**     • **1.1196**
Many–valued logic. — New York: McGraw-Hill, [1969] xv, 359 p.; 23 cm. 1. Many-valued logic I. T.
BC126.R4     164     *LC* 69-11708

**Hunter, Geoffrey.**     **1.1197**
Metalogic: an introduction to the metatheory of standard first order logic. — Berkeley: University of California Press, 1971. xiii, 288 p.: illus.; 23 cm. 1. First-order logic I. T.
BC128.H85 1971     511/.3     *LC* 71-131195     *ISBN* 0520018222

# BC131–135 Symbolic and Mathematical Logic

(see also: QA9-10.3)

**Bergmann, Merrie.**     **1.1198**
The logic book / Merrie Bergmann, James Moor, Jack Nelson. — 1st ed. — New York: Random House, c1980. ix, 459 p.; 24 cm. Includes indexes. 1. Logic, Symbolic and mathematical 2. Predicate (Logic) I. Moor, James, 1942- joint author. II. Nelson, Jack, 1944- joint author. III. T.
BC135.B435     511/.3     *LC* 79-16459     *ISBN* 0394323238

**Boole, George, 1815-1864.**     • **1.1199**
Collected logical works. La Salle, Ill.: Open Court Pub. Co., 1952. 2 v.; 22 cm. 1. Logic, Symbolic and mathematical 2. Probabilities I. T.
BC135.B7x     *LC* a 62-5673

**Carnap, Rudolf, 1891-1970.**     • **1.1200**
The continuum of inductive methods / by Rudolf Carnap. — Chicago: University of Chicago Press, 1952. v, 92 p. 1. Logic, Symbolic and mathematical I. T.
BC135.C312

**Carnap, Rudolf, 1891-1970.**     • **1.1201**
Introduction to symbolic logic and its applications / Translated by William H. Meyer and John Wilkinson. — New York: Dover Publications, [1958] 241 p.; 21 cm. 1. Logic, Symbolic and mathematical I. T.
BC135.C3142     164     *LC* 58-12611

**Carnap, Rudolf, 1891-1970.**     • **1.1202**
Introduction to semantics, and Formalization of logic. Cambridge, Harvard University Press, 1959. 259, 159 p. 22 cm. (His Studies in semantics, v. 1-2) Includes bibliography. 1. Semantics (Philosophy) 2. Logic, Symbolic and mathematical I. T. II. Title: Formalization of logic.
BC135.C316 1959     149.94     *LC* 58-13846

**Carnap, Rudolf, 1891-1970.**     • **1.1203**
The logical syntax of language / by Rufolf Carnap. — London: K. Paul, Trench, Trubner, 1937. xvi, 352 p. — (International library of psychology, philosophy, and scientific method.) 1. Logic, Symbolic and mathematical 2. Language and languages I. T. II. Series.
BC135.C323     *LC* 37-7689

**Church, Alonzo, 1903-.**     • **1.1204**
Introduction to mathematical logic. — Princeton: Princeton University Press, 1956-. v.    ; 24 cm. — (Princeton mathematical series, 17) Vol. 1, 'A revised and much enlarged edition of Introduction to mathematical logic ... which was published in 1944 as one of the Annals of mathematics studies.' 1. Logic, Symbolic and mathematical I. T.
BC135.C42     164     *LC* 53-10150

**Copi, Irving M.**     **1.1205**
Symbolic logic / by Irving M. Copi. — 5th ed. — New York: Macmillan, c1979. xiii, 398 p.; 24 cm. 1. Logic, Symbolic and mathematical I. T.
BC135.C58 1979     511/.3     *LC* 78-15671     *ISBN* 0023249803

**De Morgan, Augustus, 1806-1871.**     • **1.1206**
On the syllogism, and other logical writings / edited with an introd. by Peter Heath. New Haven: Yale University Press, 1966. xxxi, 355 p. 1. Logic, Symbolic and mathematical 2. Syllogism I. Heath, Peter Lauchlan, 1922- II. T.
BC135.D4 1966     164     *LC* 66-3469

**Fitch, Frederic B. (Frederic Brenton), 1908-1987.**     • **1.1207**
Symbolic logic: an introduction / by Frederic Brenton Fitch. — New York: Ronald Press, 1952. x, 238 p.: ill. 1. Logic, Symbolic and mathematical I. T.
BC135.F48     *LC* 52-6196

**Frege, Gottlob, 1848-1925.**     • **1.1208**
The basic laws of arithmetic; exposition of the system. Translated and edited, with an introd., by Montgomery Furth. — Berkeley: University of California Press, 1964. lxiii, 142 p.; 24 cm. 'Translation of ... the introductory portions of the first volume and an epilogue appended to the second.' 1. Logic, Symbolic and mathematical I. Furth, Montgomery. ed. and tr. II. T.
BC135.F6813 1964     164     *LC* 64-23479

**Frege, Gottlob, 1848-1925.**                                          **1.1209**
Translations from the philosophical writings of Gottlob Frege / edited Peter
Geach and Max Black; index prepared by E.D. Klemke. — 3rd ed. — Oxford,
England: Blackwell, 1980. x, 228 p.; 23 cm. 1. Logic, Symbolic and
mathematical — Addresses, essays, lectures. 2. Mathematics — Philosophy —
Addresses, essays, lectures. I. Geach, P. T. (Peter Thomas), 1916- II. Black,
Max, 1909- III. T.
BC135.F7 1980        160 19        *LC* 82-124415      *ISBN* 0631129014

**Grandy, Richard E.**                                                  **1.1210**
Advanced logic for applications / Richard E. Grandy. — Dordrecht, Holland;
Boston: D. Reidel Pub. Co., c1977. xi, 167 p.: ill.; 23 cm. — (Synthese library; v.
110) Includes indexes. 1. Logic, Symbolic and mathematical I. T.
BC135.G7      511/.3      *LC* 77-3046      *ISBN* 9027707812

**Hilbert, David, 1862-1943.**                                        • **1.1211**
Principles of mathematical logic / by D. Hilbert and W. Ackermann; translated
from the German by Lewis M. Hammond, George G. Leckie [and] F.
Steinhardt. Edited and with notes by Robert E. Luce. — New York: Chelsea
Pub. Co., 1950. xii, 172 p.; 24 cm. Translation of the 2d ed. of the author's
Grundzüge der theoretischen Logik, Published in 1938. 1. Logic, Symbolic and
mathematical I. Ackermann, Wilhelm, 1896- II. T.
BC135.H514        164        *LC* 50-4784

**Kalish, Donald.**                                                   • **1.1212**
Logic: techniques of formal reasoning / [by] Donald Kalish [and] Richard
Montague. — New York: Harcourt, Brace & World, [1964]. –. x, 350 p.; 24 cm.
— 1. Logic, Symbolic and mathematical I. Montague, Richard, joint author.
II. T.
BC135.K18        164        *LC* 64-10046      *ISBN* 0155511807

**Lewis, Clarence Irving, 1883-1964.**                                • **1.1213**
A survey of symbolic logic / by C. I. Lewis. — New York: Dover, 1960. x,
327 p.: ill.; 22 cm. 1. Logic, Symbolical and mathematical. I. T.
BC135.L4 1960        164        *LC* 60-51510      *ISBN* 0486606430

**Lewis, Clarence Irving, 1883-1964.**                                • **1.1214**
Symbolic logic, by Clarence Irving Lewis and Cooper Harold Langford. — 2d
ed. — [New York]: Dover Publications, [1959] 518 p.: illus.; 21 cm. 1. Logic,
Symbolic and mathematical I. Langford, Cooper Harold, 1895- II. T.
BC135.L43 1959        164        *LC* 59-4164

**McCall, Storrs. comp.**                                             • **1.1215**
Polish logic, 1920–1939, papers by Ajdukiewicz [and others]; with an
introduction by Tadeusz Kotarbínski, edited by Storrs McCall, translated by B.
Gruchman [and others] Oxford, Clarendon P., 1967. [2] viii, 406 p. 1. Logic,
Symbolic and mathematical — Addresses, essays, lectures 2. Logicians, Polish
I. Ajdukiewicz, Kazimierz. II. T.
BC135 M1813        *LC* 67-106639

**Mates, Benson, 1919-.**                                             • **1.1216**
Elementary logic. — 2d ed. — New York: Oxford University Press, 1972. xii,
237 p.; 24 cm. 1. Logic, Symbolic and mathematical I. T.
BC135.M37 1972        511/.3        *LC* 74-166004      *ISBN* 019501491X

**Mostowski, Andrzej.**                                               • **1.1217**
Sentences undecidable in formalized arithmetic: an exposition of the theory of
Kurt Gödel. — Amsterdam: North-Holland Pub. Co., 1952. 117 p.; 23 cm.
(Studies in logic and the foundations of mathematics.) 1. Logic, Symbolic and
mathematical 2. Semantics (Philosophy) 3. Gödel's theorem I. T. II. Series.
BC135.M6        164        *LC* 52-2458

**Prior, Arthur N.**                                                  • **1.1218**
Past, present and future / by Arthur Prior. — Oxford: Clarendon Press, 1967.
x, 217 p.: ill.; 23 cm. 'Sequel to Time and modality'. 1. Logic, Symbolic and
mathematical 2. Time 3. Modality (Logic) I. T.
BC135.P775        164        *LC* 67-91521

**Prior, Arthur N.**                                                  • **1.1219**
Time and modality / by A. N. Prior. — Oxford: Clarendon Press, 1957. viii,
148 p. — (John Locke lectures; 1955-6) 1. Deontic logic — Addresses, essays,
lectures. 2. Logic, Symbolic and mathematical — Addresses, essays, lectures.
3. Modality (Logic) — Addresses, essays, lectures. 4. Tense (Logic) —
Addresses, essays, lectures. I. T. II. Series.
BC135.P78        *LC* 57-2267

**Quine, W. V. (Willard Van Orman)**                                  • **1.1220**
Mathematical logic. — Rev. ed. — Cambridge, Harvard University Press, 1961.
xii, 346 p. Errata slip inserted in copy 2. 1. Logic, Symbolic and mathematical
I. T.
BC135.Q48 1951        164        *LC* 51-7541

**Rosenbloom, Paul C.**                                               • **1.1221**
The elements of mathematical logic. — [1st ed. — New York]: Dover
Publications, 1950. iv, 214 p.; 20 cm. — (The Dover series in mathematics and
physics) 1. Logic, Symbolic and mathematical I. T.
BC135.R55        164        *LC* 51-2626

**Rosser, J. Barkley (John Barkley), 1907-.**                           **1.1222**
Logic for mathematicians / J. Barkley Rosser. — 2d ed. — New York: Chelsea
Pub. Co., c1978. xv, 574 p.; 24 cm. Includes index. 1. Logic, Symbolic and
mathematical I. T.
BC135.R58 1978        511/.3        *LC* 77-7663      *ISBN* 0828402949

**Tarski, Alfred.**                                                     **1.1223**
Logic, semantics, metamathematics: papers from 1923 to 1938 / by Alfred
Tarski; translated by J.H. Woodger. — 2nd ed. / edited and introduced by John
Corcoran. — Indianapolis, Ind.: Hackett Pub. Co., c1983. xxx, 506 p.; 23 cm.
Includes indexes. 1. Logic, Symbolic and mathematical — Addresses, essays,
lectures. 2. Semantics (Philosophy) — Addresses, essays, lectures.
I. Corcoran, John. II. T.
BC135.T35 1983        160 19        *LC* 83-10850      *ISBN* 0915144751

**Thomason, Richmond H.**                                             • **1.1224**
Symbolic logic; an introduction [by] Richmond H. Thomason. — [New York]:
Macmillan, [1969, c1970] xiii, 367 p.; 24 cm. 1. Logic, Symbolic and
mathematical I. T.
BC135.T48        164        *LC* 72-83069

**Wittgenstein, Ludwig, 1889-1951.**                                  • **1.1225**
Tractatus logico–philosophicus / The German text Logisch–philosophische
Abhandlung, with a new translation by D. F. Pears & B. F. McGuinness, and
with the introd. by Bertrand Russell. — New York: Humanities Press, [1961]
xxii, 166 p.: diagrs.; 23 cm. — (International library of philosophy and scientific
method.) 1. Logic, Symbolic and mathematical. 2. Languages — Philosophy
I. T. II. Title: Logisch-philosophische Abhandlung. III. Series.
BC135.W5 1961        149.94        *LC* 62-661

**Wittgenstein, Ludwig, 1889-1951.**                                  • **1.1226**
[Tractatus logico-philosophicus. English and German] Prototractatus; an early
version of Tractatus logico–philosophicus. Edited by B. F. McGuinness, T.
Nyberg [and] G. H. von Wright, with a translation by D. F. Pears [and] B. F.
McGuinness. An historical introd. by G. H. von Wright and a facsim. of the
author's manuscript. Ithaca, N.Y., Cornell University Press [1971] 256 p. 26
cm. Text in English and German. 1. Logic, Symbolic and mathematical
2. Languages — Philosophy I. T. II. Title: Tractatus logico-philosophicus.
BC135.W5 1971        192        *LC* 79-136737      *ISBN* 0801406102

**Black, Max, 1909-.**                                                • **1.1227**
A companion to Wittgenstein's Tractatus, by Max Black. — Ithaca, N. Y.,
Cornell University Press [c1964] xv, 450 p. facsim. 23 cm. Bibliography: p.
416-421. 1. Wittgenstein, Ludwig, 1889-1951. Tractatus logico-philosophicus.
I. T.
BC135.W52B6        164        *LC* 64-56501

**Copi, Irving M. ed.**                                               • **1.1228**
Essays on Wittgenstein's Tractatus. Edited by Irving M. Copi and Robert W.
Beard. — New York, Macmillan [1966] x, 414 p. 21 cm. Bibliography: p.
393-405. 1. Wittgenstein, Ludwig, 1889-1951. Tractatus logico-philosophicus.
2. Logic, Symbolic and mathematical 3. Languages — Philosophy I. Beard,
Robert W., joint ed. II. T.
BC135.W52C6        164.08        *LC* 66-25586

**Stenius, Erik.**                                                    • **1.1229**
Wittgenstein's Tractatus: a critical exposition of its main lines of thought. —
Ithaca, N. Y., Cornell University Press, 1960. 241 p. 23 cm. Includes
bibliography. 1. Wittgenstein, Ludwig, 1889-1951. Tractatus logico-
philosophicus. 2. Logic, Symbolic and mathematical 3. Language —
Philosophy. I. T.
BC135.W52S8        164        *LC* 60-50023

# BC141 Probability

**Carnap, Rudolf, 1891-1970.**                                        • **1.1230**
Logical foundations of probability. — 2d ed. — Chicago: University of Chicago
Press, 1962. 613 p. 1. Probabilities 2. Logic, Symbolic and mathematical
3. Logic 4. Semantics (Philosophy) I. T.
BC141.C3 1962        *LC* 62-52505

Keynes, John Maynard, 1883-1946.                                    • 1.1231
A treatise on probability / by John Maynard Keynes. — London: Macmillan,
1921. xi, 466 p.; 23 cm. Includes index. 1. Probabilities 2. Probabilities —
Bibliography. I. T.
BC141.K4          519.2          LC 21-20432

Leblanc, Hugues, 1924-.                                    • 1.1232
Statistical and inductive probabilities / Hugues Leblanc. — Englwood Cliffs,
N.J.: Prentice-Hall, 1962. 148 p. — (Prentice-Hall philosophy series)
1. Probabilities I. T.
BC141.L4          QA273.L44.          LC 62-20091

Weatherford, Roy, 1943-.                                    1.1233
Philosophical foundations of probability theory / Roy Weatherford. —
London; Boston: Routledge & K. Paul, 1982. xi, 282 p.; 23 cm. —
(International library of philosophy.) Includes index. 1. Probabilities I. T.
II. Series.
BC141.W4 1982          121/.63 19          LC 81-22730          ISBN 0710090021

# BC171–199 Special Topics

Mackie, J. L. (John Leslie)                                    1.1234
Truth, probability and paradox: studies in philosophical logic [by] J. L. Mackie.
Oxford, Clarendon Press, 1973. xii, 305 p. 23 cm. (Clarendon library of logic
and philosophy) 1. Truth 2. Probabilities 3. Paradox I. T.
BC171.M24          160          LC 73-157025          ISBN 0198244029

Moody, Ernest A. (Ernest Addison), 1903-.                                    • 1.1235
Truth and consequence in mediaeval logic. Amsterdam: North-Holland Pub.
Co., 1953. 113 p.; 22 cm. (Studies in logic and the foundations of mathematics.)
1. Truth 2. Logic, Medieval I. T. II. Series.
BC171.M65          160          LC 53-4268

The Concept of evidence / edited by Peter Achinstein.                                    1.1236
Oxford [Oxfordshire]; New York: Oxford University Press, 1983. 182 p.; 21 cm.
— (Oxford readings in philosophy.) Includes index. 1. Evidence — Addresses,
essays, lectures. 2. Logic — Addresses, essays, lectures. I. Achinstein, Peter.
II. Series.
BC173.C66 1983          121/.65 19          LC 83-8266          ISBN 0198750625

Advances in argumentation theory and research / edited by J.                                    1.1237
Robert Cox and Charles Arthur Willard.
Carbondale: Published for the American Forensic Association by Southern
Illinois University Press, c1982. xlvii, 421 p. Includes index. 1. Reasoning —
Addresses, essays, lectures. I. Cox, J. Robert. II. Willard, Charles Arthur.
BC177.A43          BC177 A43.          001.54 19          LC 82-5496          ISBN
0809310503

Lloyd, Genevieve.                                    1.1238
The man of reason: 'male' and 'female' in Western philosophy / Genevieve
Lloyd. — Minneapolis: University of Minnesota Press, c1984. x, 138 p.; 21 cm.
1. Reason 2. Sex differences 3. Relativity I. T.
BC177.L58 1984          128/.3 19          LC 84-10396          ISBN 0816613818

Passmore, John Arthur.                                    • 1.1239
Philosophical reasoning [by] John Passmore. — New York: Basic Books, [1969,
c1961] ix, 149 p.; 22 cm. 1. Reasoning I. T.
BC177.P3 1969          160          LC 77-93694

Toulmin, Stephen Edelston.                                    1.1240
Human understanding [by] Stephen Toulmin. — Princeton, N.J.: Princeton
University Press, [1972-. v. ; 23 cm. 1. Reason 2. Reasoning
3. Comprehension 4. Concepts I. T.
BC177.T58          160          LC 73-166391          ISBN 0691071853

Toulmin, Stephen Edelston.                                    1.1241
An introduction to reasoning / Stephen Toulmin, Richard Rieke, Allan Janik.
— 2nd ed. — New York: Macmillan; London: Collier Macmillan Publishers,
c1984. ix, 435 p.; 26 cm. Includes index. 1. Reasoning I. Rieke, Richard D.
II. Janik, Allan. III. T.
BC177.T59 1984          160 19          LC 83-16196          ISBN 0024211605

Toulmin, Stephen Edelston.                                    • 1.1242
The uses of argument. — Cambridge [Eng.] University Press, 1958. vi, 264 p. 22
cm. Bibliography: p. [260]-261. 1. Logic. 2. Reasoning. I. T.
BC177.T6 1958          160          LC A 58-2813

Ryle, Gilbert, 1900-1976.                                    • 1.1243
Dilemmas: the Tarner Lectures, 1953 / by Gilbert Ryle. Cambridge, Eng.:
University Press, 1954. 129 p. (The Tarner lectures, 1953) 1. Dilemma
2. Philosophy 3. Logic I. T.
BC185.R9

## BC199 By Topic, A–Z

Moutafakis, Nicholas J., 1941-.                                    1.1244
Imperatives and their logics / Nicholas J. Moutafakis. — 1st ed. — New Delhi:
Sterling Publishers, 1975. xiv, 216 p.; 23 cm. Includes index. 1. Commands
(Logic) I. T.
BC199.C5 M68          160          LC 75-904097

Lewis, David K.                                    1.1245
Counterfactuals [by] David K. Lewis. — Cambridge: Harvard University Press,
1973. x, 150 p.: illus.; 23 cm. 1. Counterfactuals (Logic) I. T.
BC199.C66 L48 1973b          160          LC 72-78430          ISBN 0674175409

Reichenbach, Hans, 1891-1953.                                    1.1246
[Nomological statements and admissible operations] Laws, modalities, and
counterfactuals / Hans Reichenbach; with a foreword by Wesley C. Salmon. —
Berkeley: University of California Press, [1977] xliii, 140 p.; 23 cm. — (Studies
in the logic of science; 4) Reprint of the 1954 ed. published by North-Holland
Pub. Co., Amsterdam, under title: Nomological statements and admissible
operations. Includes index. 1. Counterfactuals (Logic) 2. Modality (Logic)
3. Law (Philosophy) I. T. II. Series.
BC199.C66 R44 1977          160

Robinson, Richard, 1902-.                                    1.1247
Definition / Richard Robinson. — Oxford: Clarendon Press, 1972, 1950. viii,
207 p.; 23 cm. 'Reprinted from the corrected sheets.' 1. Definition (Logic) I. T.
BC199.D4 R6

Anscombe, G. E. M. (Gertrude Elizabeth Margaret)                                    1.1248
Intention, by G. E. M. Anscombe. [2d ed.] Oxford, Blackwell [1963, c1957] ix,
94 p. 23 cm. 1. Intention (Logic) I. T.
BC199.I5 A5 1963          LC 68-114578

Chellas, Brian F.                                    1.1249
Modal logic: an introduction / Brian F. Chellas. — Cambridge [Eng.]; New
York: Cambridge University Press, [1980] xii, 295 p.: ill.; 24 cm. Includes
indexes. 1. Modality (Logic) I. T.
BC199.M6 C47          160          LC 76-47197          ISBN 0521224764

Feys, Robert, 1889-.                                    • 1.1250
Modal logics / Robert Feys; edited with some complements by Joseph Dopp. —
Louvain: E. Nauwelaerts; Paris: Gauthier-Villars, 1965. xiv, 219 p.; 25 cm. —
(Collection de logique mathématique; Sér. B, 4) 1. Modality (Logic) 2. Logic,
Symbolic and mathematical I. Dopp, Joseph. II. T. III. Series.
BC199.M6 F4          164          LC 65-9700

Hughes, G. E. (George Edward), 1918-.                                    • 1.1251
An introduction to modal logic [by] G. E. Hughes [and] M. J. Cresswell.
London, Methuen, 1968. iii-xii, 388 p. illus. 23 cm. 1. Modality (Logic)
I. Cresswell, M. J. joint author. II. T.
BC199.M6 H8          160          LC 76-364635

Konyndyk, Kenneth.                                    1.1252
Introductory modal logic / Kenneth Konyndyk. — Notre Dame, Ind.:
University of Notre Dame Press, c1986. x, 133 p.: ill.; 23 cm. 1. Modality
(Logic) I. T.
BC199.M6 K66 1986          160 19          LC 85-41007          ISBN 0268011591

Linsky, Leonard.                                    • 1.1253
Reference and modality; edited by Leonard Linsky. — London: Oxford
University Press, 1971. [5], 177 p.; 21 cm. — (Oxford readings in philosophy)
1. Modality (Logic) — Addresses, essays, lectures. 2. Description
(Philosophy) — Addresses, essays, lectures. I. T.
BC199.M6 L54          160          LC 72-595855          ISBN 019875017X

Plantinga, Alvin.                                    1.1254
The nature of necessity. — Oxford: Clarendon Press, 1974. ix, 255 p.; 23 cm. —
(Clarendon library of logic and philosophy) 1. Modality (Logic) 2. Essence
(Philosophy) 3. Necessity (Philosophy) 4. Good and evil I. T.
BC199.M6 P55          160          LC 74-174797          ISBN 0198244045

Belnap, Nuel D., 1930-.                                    1.1255
The logic of questions and answers / Nuel D. Belnap, Jr., Thomas B. Steel, Jr.
New Haven: Yale University Press, 1976. vi, 209 p.; 22 cm. Includes index.
1. Question (Logic) 2. Question-answering systems 3. Formal languages
I. Steel, Thomas B., 1929- joint author. II. T.
BC199.Q4 B44          160          LC 75-27761          ISBN 0300019629

**Copi, Irving M.**                                                    • **1.1256**
The theory of logical types / by Irving M. Copi. — London: Routledge and K. Paul, 1971. x, 129 p.; 19 cm. — (Monographs in modern logic series) 1. Type theory I. T.
BC199.T9 C66 1971      160      *LC* 75-881300      *ISBN* 0710070268

# BD SPECULATIVE PHILOSOPHY

**Ewing, A.C. (Alfred Cyril), 1899-.**                                 • **1.1257**
The fundamental questions of philosophy. New York Macmillan, 1951. 260 p. 22 cm. 1. Philosophy I. T.
BD21.E85      *LC* 52-6296

**Hocking, William Ernest, 1873-1966.**                                **1.1258**
Types of philosophy, by William Ernest Hocking, with the collaboration of Richard Boyle O'Reilly Hocking. — 3d ed. — New York, Scribner [1959] 340 p. 24 cm. 1. Philosophy — Introductions 2. Metaphysics I. T.
BD21.H6 1959      140      *LC* 59-8019

**Russell, Bertrand, 1872-1970.**                                      • **1.1260**
The problems of philosophy. New York, Oxford University Press, 1959. 167 p. 21 cm. (A Galaxy book, GB21) 1. Philosophy — Introductions I. T.
BD21.R8 1959      110      *LC* 59-16125

**Wolff, Robert Paul.**                                                **1.1261**
About philosophy / by Robert Paul Wolff. — Englewood Cliffs, N.J.: Prentice-Hall; Toronto: Prentice-Hall of Canada, c1976. xiv, 305 p.: ill., ports. 1. Philosophy — Introductions I. T.
BD21.W64      BD21 W64.      100      *LC* 75-15739      *ISBN* 0130008362

**Heidegger, Martin, 1889-1976.**                                      • **1.1262**
What is philosophy? / Martin Heidegger; translated with an introduction by William Kluback and Jean T. Wilde. — [New York]: Twayne Publishers, c1958. 97 p. Translation of Was ist das—die Philosophie? 1. Philosophy — Introductions I. T.
BD23.H412      *LC* 58-2869

**Whitehead, Alfred North, 1861-1947.**                                • **1.1263**
The function of reason / by Alfred North Whitehead. — Princeton: Princeton University Press, 1929. 72 p. — (Louis Clark Vanuxem Foundation lectures; 1929) 1. Reason I. T.
BD41.W5      *LC* 30-2482

# BD100–131 Metaphysics

**Bowne, Borden Parker, 1847-1910.**                                   **1.1264**
Metaphysics / by Borden P. Bowne. — 1st AMS ed. — New York: AMS Press, 1979. xiv, 429 p.; 23 cm. — (Philosophy in America) Reprint of the rev. ed. of 1898 published by Harper, New York. 1. Metaphysics I. T. II. Series.
BD111.B73 1979      110      *LC* 75-948      *ISBN* 0404590721

**Bradley, F. H. (Francis Herbert), 1846-1924.**                       • **1.1265**
Appearance and reality: a metaphysical essay, by F. H. Bradley. [New ed.] with an introduction by Richard Wollheim. London, New York [etc.] Oxford U.P., 1969. xxvi, 570 p. index. 21 cm. (Oxford paperbacks, no. 150) Originally published, London, Swan Sonnenschein, 1893. 1. Metaphysics 2. Reality 3. Knowledge, Theory of I. T.
BD111.B8 1969      110      *LC* 79-405526      *ISBN* 0198811500

**Collingwood, R. G. (Robin George), 1889-1943.**                      • **1.1266**
An essay on metaphysics. Oxford Clarendon Press 1940. 354p. (Philosophical essays, v. 2) 1. Metaphysics I. T.
BD111 C6      *LC* 41-1356

**Comfort, Alex, 1920-.**                                              **1.1267**
Reality and empathy: physics, mind, and science in the 21st century / Alex Comfort. — Albany: State University of New York Press, c1984. xxi, 272 p.: ill.; 24 cm. Includes index. 1. Metaphysics 2. Science — Philosophy 3. Intuition I. T.
BD111.C624 1984      110 19      *LC* 83-9318      *ISBN* 0873957628

**Harris, Errol E.**                                                   • **1.1268**
The foundations of metaphysics in science, by Errol E. Harris. — New York, Humanities Press, 1965. 512 p. 23 cm. — (Muirhead library of philosophy.) Bibliographical footnotes. 1. Science. 2. Metaphysics I. T. II. Series.
BD111.H274      110      *LC* 65-16169

**Lazerowitz, Morris, 1909-.**                                         • **1.1269**
Studies in metaphilosophy. — New York, Humanities Press [1964] xi, 264 p. 23 cm. — (International library of philosophy and scientific method.) Bibliography: p. 257-259. 1. Metaphysics I. T. II. Series.
BD111.L35 1964      110      *LC* 63-23176

**Pears, David Francis. ed.**                                          • **1.1270**
The nature of metaphysics. London, Macmillan; New York, St. Martin's Press, 1957. vi, 163 p. 20 cm. 'The essays originated as talks in the Third programme of the B.B.C.' 1. Metaphysics — Addresses, essays, lectures. I. T.
BD111.P37      *LC* 57-13944

**Strawson, P. F.**                                                    • **1.1271**
Individuals, an essay in descriptive metaphysics. — London, Methuen [1959] 255 p. 23 cm. 1. Metaphysics I. T.
BD111.S78      110      *LC* 59-1521

**Urban, Wilbur Marshall, 1873-.**                                     • **1.1272**
The intelligible world: metaphysics and value / by Wilbur Marshall Urban. London: G. Allen and Unwin, 1929. 479 p.; 22 cm. (Library of philosophy.) 1. Metaphysics 2. Values 3. Philosophy, Modern I. T. II. Series.
BD111.U7 1929a      110

**Bergson, Henri, 1859-1941.**                                         • **1.1273**
[Introduction à la métaphysique. English.] An introduction to metaphysics / by Henri Bergson; authorized translation by T.E. Hulme; with an introd. by Thomas A. Goudge. — New York: Liberal Arts Press, 1949. 61 p. — (The Little library of liberal arts; no. 10) 1. Metaphysics I. Hulme, T. E. (Thomas Ernest), 1883-1917. II. T. III. Series.
BD112.B42 1949      *LC* 49-3135

# BD140–235 Epistemology. Theory of Knowledge

**Swartz, Robert J., ed.**                                             • **1.1274**
Perceiving, sensing, and knowing; a book of readings from twentieth–century sources in the philosophy of perception, edited, with an introd. by Robert J. Swartz. [1st ed.] Garden City, N.Y., Anchor Books, 1965. xxii, 538 p. 19 cm. 1. Knowledge, Theory of — Collected works I. T.
BD143S95      *LC* 65-14024

**Thomas, Aquinas, Saint, 1225?-1274.**                                • **1.1275**
Truth; translated from the definitive Leonine text. — Chicago, H. Regnery Co., 1952-54. 3 v. 24 cm. — (Library of living Catholic thought) Translation of Quaestiones disputatae de veritate. Includes bibliographies. 1. Knowledge, Theory of I. T.
BD150.T513      189.4      *LC* 52-12511

**Cavell, Stanley, 1926-.**                                            **1.1276**
The claim of reason: Wittgenstein, skepticism, morality and tragedy / Stanley Cavell. — Oxford: Clarendon Press; New York: Oxford University Press, 1979. xxii, 511 p.; 24 cm. Includes indexes. 1. Wittgenstein, Ludwig, 1889-1951 — Addresses, essays, lectures. 2. Skepticism — Addresses, essays, lectures. 3. Ethics — Addresses, essays, lectures. 4. Philosophy — Addresses, essays, lectures. 5. Knowledge, Theory of — Addresses, essays, lectures. I. T.
BD161.C355      121      *LC* 78-26970      *ISBN* 0195025717

**Chisholm, Roderick M.**                                              • **1.1277**
Perceiving: a philosophical study. — Ithaca, Cornell University Press [1968,c1957] 203 p. 22 cm. — (Contemporary philosophy) 1. Knowledge, Theory of I. T.
BD161.C47      121      *LC* 58-28

**Danto, Arthur Coleman, 1924-.**                                      • **1.1278**
Analytical philosophy of knowledge, by Arthur C. Danto. — London: Cambridge U.P., 1968. xiv, 270 p.; 24 cm. 1. Knowledge, Theory of I. T.
BD161.D3      121      *LC* 68-30951      *ISBN* 0521072662

**Dewey, John.**                                                       • **1.1279**
The quest for certainty: a study of the relation of knowledge and action / by John Dewey. — New York: Minton, Balch, 1929. 318 p.; 23 cm. — (Gifford lectures. 1929) 1. Knowledge, Theory of 2. Thought and thinking 3. Science — Philosophy I. T. II. Series.
BD161.D4      *LC* 29-23500

**Grene, Marjorie Glicksman, 1910-.**                          • **1.1280**
The knower and the known / Marjorie Grene. — New York: Basic Books,
c1966. 283 p.; 21 cm. 1. Knowledge, Theory of I. T.
BD161.G74 1974      121      *LC* 66-12294

**Pap, Arthur, 1921-1959.**                                   • **1.1281**
Semantics and necessary truth: an inquiry into the foundations of analytic
philosophy / by Arthur Pap. — New Haven: Yale University Press, 1958. xii,
456 p.; 25 cm. 1. Analysis (Philosophy) 2. Knowledge, Theory of 3. Semantics
(Philosophy) I. T.
BD161.P25      121      *LC* 58-6543

**Russell, Bertrand, 1872-1970.**                             • **1.1282**
Human knowledge, its scope and limits. New York, Simon and Schuster, 1948.
xvi, 524 p. 22 cm. 1. Knowledge, Theory of I. T.
BD161.R78      121      *LC* 48-11754

**Sellars, Roy Wood, 1880-.**                                 **1.1283**
Critical realism; a study of the nature and conditions of knowledge. — New
York: Russell & Russell, [1969] 283 p.; 23 cm. Reprint of the 1916 ed.
1. Knowledge, Theory of 2. Realism I. T.
BD161.S4 1969      121      *LC* 68-27086

**Maritain, Jacques, 1882-1973.**                             • **1.1284**
Distinguish to unite; or, The degrees of knowledge. — Newly translated from
the 4th French ed. under the supervision of Gerald B. Phelan. — New York,
Scribner [1959] xix, 476 p. diagrs. 25 cm. Bibliographical footnotes.
1. Knowledge, Theory of 2. Metaphysics I. T. II. Title: The degrees of
knowledge.
BD162.M273 1959      121      *LC* 59-12892

**Meyerson, Emile, 1859-1933.**                               • **1.1285**
Identity & reality. Authorized translation by Kate Loewenberg. New York,
Dover Publications [1962] 495 p. 22 cm. 1. Reality 2. Knowledge, Theory of
I. T.
BD162.M43 1962      121      *LC* 62-53523

**Cassirer, Ernst, 1874-1945.**                               • **1.1286**
[Erkenntnisproblem in der Philosophie. v. 4. English] The problem of
knowledge; philosophy, science, and history since Hegel; translated by William
H. Woglom and Charles W. Hendel. With a pref. by Charles W. Hendel. New
Haven, Yale University Press, 1950. xviii, 334 p. 25 cm. A translation from MS.
of the author's Von Hegel's Tode his zur Gegenwart, 1832-1932, to be published
as v. 4 of his Das Erkenntnisproblem in der Philosophie und Wissenschaft der
neueren Zeit. 1. Knowledge, Theory of I. T.
BD163.C35      *LC* 50-7218

**Habermas, Jürgen.**                                         **1.1287**
[Erkenntnis und Interesse. English] Knowledge and human interests.
Translated by Jeremy J. Shapiro. Boston, Beacon Press [1971] viii, 356 p. 22
cm. Translation of Erkenntnis und Interesse. 1. Knowledge, Theory of —
History. I. T.
BD163.H2213 1971      121/.09/034      *LC* 72-136230      *ISBN*
0807015407

**Reichenbach, Hans, 1891-1953.**                             • **1.1288**
Experience and prediction: an analysis of the foundations and structure of
knowledge. — [Chicago]: University of Chicago Press, 1961, c1938. x, 408 p. —
(Phoenix book; P81) 1. Experience 2. Knowledge, Theory of I. T.
BD163.R4 1961

**Berger, Peter L.**                                          • **1.1289**
The social construction of reality; a treatise in the sociology of knowledge, by
Peter L. Berger and Thomas Luckmann. — [1st ed.]. — Garden City, N.Y.:
Doubleday, 1966. vii, 203 p.; 21 cm. 1. Knowledge, Sociology of I. Luckmann,
Thomas. joint author. II. T.
BD175.B4      301.01      *LC* 66-14925

**Douglas, Mary. comp.**                                      **1.1290**
Rules and meanings; the anthropology of everyday knowledge. Selected
readings edited by Mary Douglas. [Harmondsworth, Eng.] Penguin Education
[1973] 319 p. illus. 20 cm. (Penguin modern sociology readings) 1. Knowledge,
Sociology of — Addresses, essays, lectures. 2. Meaning (Philosophy) —
Addresses, essays, lectures. 3. Moral conditions — Addresses, essays, lectures.
I. T.
BD175.D7      108      *LC* 73-173999      *ISBN* 0140807128

**Horowitz, Irving Louis.**                                   • **1.1291**
Philosophy, science and the sociology of knowledge. With a foreword by Robert
S. Cohen. Springfield, Ill., Thomas, [1961] 169 p. (American lecture series,
publication; no.442) A monograph in the Bannerstone Division of American
lectures in philosophy. 1. Knowledge, Sociology of I. T.
BD175.H65      121

**Morris, Monica B., 1928-.**                                 **1.1292**
An excursion into creative sociology / Monica B. Morris. — New York:
Columbia University Press, 1977. x, 212 p.; 24 cm. Includes index.
1. Knowledge, Sociology of 2. Phenomenology 3. Social interaction I. T.
BD175.M67 1977      301/.01      *LC* 76-19023      *ISBN* 0231039875

## BD181–235 Origin and Sources of Knowledge

**Ayer, A. J. (Alfred Jules), 1910-.**                        • **1.1293**
The foundations of empirical knowledge. London, Macmillan; New York, St.
Martin's Press, 1963. 276 p. 22 cm. Bibliographical footnotes. 1. Knowledge,
Theory of 2. Perception I. T.
BD181.B9 1963      121      *LC* 56-4948

**Lewis, Clarence Irving, 1883-1964.**                        • **1.1294**
An analysis of knowledge and valuation. — La Salle, Ill.: Open Court Pub. Co.,
[1946]. 567 p. — (The Paul Carus lectures; 7) 1. Knowledge, Theory of
2. Values I. T.
BD181.L47      *LC* 47-20878

**Price, Henry Habberley, 1899-.**                            • **1.1295**
Perception / by H.H. Price. — 2d ed., rev. — London: Methuen, 1950. ix,
332 p. 1. Perception I. T.
BD181.P7 1950

**Wisdom, John.**                                             **1.1296**
Other minds. — 2nd ed. — Oxford: Blackwell, 1965 [i.e. 1966] viii, 265 p.; 23
cm. 1. Knowledge, Theory of 2. Mind and body I. T.
BD201.W55 1966      121      *LC* 66-72161

**Ellis, B. D. (Brian David), 1929-.**                        **1.1297**
Rational belief systems / Brian Ellis. — Totowa, N.J.: Rowman and Littlefield,
1979. ix, 118 p.,; 23 cm. (APQ library of philosophy.) Includes indexes.
1. Belief and doubt 2. Logic 3. Reasoning 4. Rationalism I. T. II. Series.
BD215.E43 1979      121/.6      *LC* 78-11988      *ISBN* 0847661083

**Jaspers, Karl, 1883-1969.**                                 • **1.1298**
Philosophical faith and revelation. Translated by E. B. Ashton. — New York,
Harper & Row [1967] xxiii, 368 p. 24 cm. — (Religious perspectives, v. 18)
Translation of Der philosophische Glaube angesichts der Offenbarung.
1. Belief and doubt 2. Faith and reason 3. Revelation I. T.
BD215.J313      121      *LC* 67-14944

**Price, H. H. (Henry Habberley), 1899-.**                    • **1.1299**
Belief: the Gifford lectures delivered at the University of Aberdeen in 1960, by
H. H. Price. London, Allen & Unwin; New York, Humanities P., 1969. 3-495 p.
23 cm. (Gifford lectures. 1959-60.) (Muirhead library of philosophy) 1. Belief
and doubt — Addresses, essays, lectures. I. T. II. Series.
BD215.P7      121/.6      *LC* 76-390002      *ISBN* 0041210093

**Scheffler, Israel.**                                        • **1.1300**
Science and subjectivity. — Indianapolis: Bobbs-Merrill, [1967] v, 132 p.; 21
cm. 1. Knowledge, Theory of 2. Objectivity 3. Science — Philosophy I. T.
BD220.S2      121      *LC* 67-27839

**Aschenbrenner, Karl.**                                      • **1.1301**
The concepts of value; foundations of value theory. Dordrecht, Reidel [1971]
xvii, 462 p. 25 cm. (Foundations of language. Supplementary series, v. 12) 'Sole
distributors in the U.S.A. and Canada: Humanities Press, New York.'
1. Values I. T. II. Series.
BD232.A73      121/.8      *LC* 70-159651

**Köhler, Wolfgang, 1887-1967.**                              **1.1302**
The place of value in a world of facts / Wolfgang Köhler. — New York: New
American Library, 1966. 320 p. — (Mentor books; MQ691) The William James
lectures on philosophy and psychology, which were originally delivered at
Harvard, 1934-35. 1. Values 2. Science — Philosophy I. T.
BD232.K6 1966      *LC* 67-1672

**Perry, Ralph Barton, 1876-1957.**                           • **1.1303**
General theory of value, its meaning and basic principles construed in terms of
interest. Cambridge Harvard University Press 1967. 702p. 1. Values
2. Philosophy, Modern I. T.
BD232 P45 1967

# BD240–241 Methodology

**Bauman, Zygmunt.**                                                                 **1.1304**
Hermeneutics and social science / Zygmunt Bauman. — New York: Columbia
University Press, 1978. 263 p.; 23 cm. — (European perspectives)
1. Hermeneutics 2. Social sciences I. T.
BD241.B33 1978     300/.1     LC 78-877     ISBN 0231045468

**Collingwood, R. G. (Robin George), 1889-1943.**                          • **1.1305**
An essay on philosophical method, by R. G. Collingwood. — Oxford, The
Clarendon press, 1933. xii, 226, [2] p. 22.5 cm. 1. Methodology I. T.
BD241.C6     112     LC 34-8972

**Gadamer, Hans Georg, 1900-.**                                               **1.1306**
[Wahrheit und Methode. English] Truth and method / Hans–Georg Gadamer;
[translation edited by Garrett Barden and John Cumming]. — New York:
Seabury Press, [1975] xxvi, 551 p.; 24 cm. — (A Continuum book) Translation
of Wahrheit und Methode. 1. Humanities — Methodology. 2. Hermeneutics
3. Aesthetics I. T.
BD241.G313     111.8/3     LC 75-2053     ISBN 0816492204

**Popper, Karl Raimund, Sir, 1902-.**                                        • **1.1307**
Conjectures and refutations; the growth of scientific knowledge. — New York,
Basic Books [c1962] 412 p. 25 cm. 1. Methodology 2. Knowledge, Theory of
3. Science — Methodology I. T.
BD241.P6     112     LC 63-11566

**Ricoeur, Paul.**                                                            **1.1308**
[Conflit des interprétations. English] The conflict of interpretations: essays in
hermeneutics / Paul Ricoeur; edited by Don Ihde. — Evanston: Northwestern
University Press, 1974. xxv, 512 p.; 24 cm. (Northwestern University studies in
phenomenology & existential philosophy) Includes index. 1. Hermeneutics
I. T. II. Series.
BD241.R4813     121     LC 73-91311     ISBN 0810104423

**Rosenberg, Jay F.**                                                         **1.1309**
The practice of philosophy: a handbook for beginners / Jay F. Rosenberg. —
Englewood Cliffs, N.J.: Prentice-Hall, c1978. xii, 111 p.; 23 cm.
1. Methodology 2. Philosophy — Introductions I. T.
BD241.R65     101/.8     LC 77-13424     ISBN 013687178X

**Todorov, Tzvetan, 1939-.**                                                  **1.1310**
[Symbolisme et interprétation. English] Symbolism and interpretation /
Tzvetan Todorov; translated by Catherine Porter. — Ithaca, N.Y.: Cornell
University Press, c1982. 175 p.; 23 cm. Translation of: Symbolisme et
interprétation. Includes index. 1. Hermeneutics 2. Symbolism 3. Structural
linguistics I. T.
BD241.T5813 1982     001.54 19     LC 82-5078     ISBN 0801412692

# BD300–450 Ontology

**Ballard, Edward G.**                                                        **1.1311**
Man and technology: toward the measurement of a culture / by Edward
Goodwin Ballard. — Pittsburgh: Duquesne University Press; Atlantic
Highlands, [N.J.]: distributed by Humanities Press, c1978. x, 251 p.; 24 cm.
1. Ontology 2. Civilization, Modern — 20th century 3. Technology — Moral
and ethical aspects I. T.
BD311.B3     111     LC 77-20902     ISBN 0391007513

**Bowne, Borden Parker, 1847-1910.**                                          **1.1312**
Personalism / by Borden Parker Bowne. — Norwood, Mass.: Privately printed
by the Plimpton Press, 1936. xiii, 326 p. — (Northwestern University
(Evanston, Ill.). The Norman Walt Harris lectures; 1907) Edition in
commemoration of the twenty-fifth anniversary of his death, April 1, 1910,
foreward by Frank W. Collier. 1. Personalism I. T. II. Series.
BD311.B7 1936     B828.5.B6 1936.     LC 36-31250

**Gilson, Etienne, 1884-1978.**                                              • **1.1313**
Being and some philosophers / Étienne Gilson. — 2d ed., corr. and enl. —
Toronto: Pontifical Institute of Mediaeval Studies, 1952. xi, 235 p.; 24 cm.
1. Ontology I. T.
BD331.G495 1952     111     LC 53-7043

**Goodman, Nelson.**                                                          **1.1314**
Ways of worldmaking / Nelson Goodman. — Indianapolis,: Hackett Pub. Co.,
c1978. x, 142 p.: ill.; 22 cm. 1. Reality — Addresses, essays, lectures. 2. Style
(Philosophy) — Addresses, essays, lectures. 3. Facts (Philosophy) —

Addresses, essays, lectures. 4. Art — Philosophy — Addresses, essays,
lectures. I. T.
BD331.G65     191     LC 78-56364     ISBN 0915144522

**Heidegger, Martin, 1889-1976.**                                            • **1.1315**
[Einführung in die Metaphysik. English] An introduction to metaphysics.
Translated by Ralph Manheim. New Haven, Yale University Press, 1959. xi,
214 p. 22 cm. 1. Ontology I. T.
BD331.H4313     111     LC 59-6796     ISBN 0300017405

**Infinity and continuity in ancient and medieval thought / edited**   **1.1316**
**by Norman Kretzmann.**
Ithaca, N.Y.: Cornell University Press, 1982. 367 p.; 24 cm. Includes index.
1. Infinite — History — Addresses, essays, lectures. 2. Continuity — History
— Addresses, essays, lectures. I. Kretzmann, Norman.
BD411.I53     111/.6 19     LC 81-15209

**Baker, Herschel Clay, 1914-.**     **ISBN 080141444X**                       **1.1318**
The image of man; a study of the idea of human dignity in classical antiquity,
the Middle Ages, and the Renaissance. — New York, Harper [1961, c1947]
365 p. 21 cm. — (Harper torchbooks, TB1047. The Academy library)
'Originally published under the title: The dignity of man.' 1. Man I. T.
BD431.B24x     128     LC A 62-5612

**Jonas, Hans, 1903-.**                                                      • **1.1319**
The phenomenon of life: toward a philosophical biology;. — [essays. 1st ed.]. —
New York, Harper & Row [1966] x, 303 p. 22 cm. Bibliographical footnotes.
1. Life I. T.
BD431.J48     110     LC 66-15037

**Scheler, Max, 1874-1928.**                                                 • **1.1320**
Man's place in nature / by Max Scheler; translated with an introduction, by
Hans Meyerhoff. — Boston: Beacon Press, c1961. xxxv, 105 p.; 21 cm.
Translation of Die Stellung des Menschen im Kosmos published in 1928.
1. Man 2. Soul I. T.
BD431.S2713 1961     LC 61-6417

**Temkin, Owsei, 1902-.**                                                     **1.1321**
Respect for life in medicine, philosophy, and the law / Owsei Temkin, William
K. Frankena, Sanford H. Kadish. Baltimore: Johns Hopkins University Press,
c1977. ix, 107 p.; 21 cm. (Alvin and Fanny Blaustein Thalheimer lectures. 1975)
Lectures delivered at the Johns Hopkins University in 1975. 1. Life —
Addresses, essays, lectures. 2. Medical ethics — Addresses, essays, lectures.
I. Frankena, William K. joint author. II. Kadish, Sanford H. joint author.
III. T. IV. Series.
BD431.T19     179/.7     LC 76-47366     ISBN 0801819423

**Singer, Irving.**                                                          **1.1322**
The nature of love / Irving Singer. — Chicago: University of Chicago Press,
1984-. v. < 1-2 >; 24 cm. Vol. 1, 2nd ed. 1. Love I. T.
BD436.S5 1984     128 19     LC 84-2554     ISBN 0226760944

**Ariès, Philippe.**                                                          **1.1323**
[Essais sur l'histoire de la mort en Occident. English] Western attitudes toward
death: from the Middle Ages to the present. Translated by Patricia M. Ranum.
Baltimore, Johns Hopkins University Press, 1976. xi, 111 p. illus. 21 cm. (Johns
Hopkins symposia in comparative history. 4th) Translation of Essais sur
l'histoire de la mort en Occident. 1. Death — Addresses, essays, lectures. I. T.
II. Series.
BD444.A6713     128/.5     LC 73-19340     ISBN 0801815665

**The Meaning of death / Herman Feifel, editor.**                            • **1.1324**
New York: McGraw-Hill, 1965, c1959. xvi, 3-351 p.: ill.; 20 cm. — (McGraw-
Hill paperbacks) 1. Death I. Feifel, Herman.
BD444.F415 1965     ISBN 0070203474

**Suicide, the philosophical issues / edited by M. Pabst Battin**            **1.1325**
**and David J. Mayo.**
New York: St. Martin's Press, c1980. viii, 292 p.; 22 cm. 1. Suicide —
Addresses, essays, lectures. I. Battin, M. Pabst. II. Mayo, David J.
BD445.S93     179/.7     LC 79-27372     ISBN 0312775318

# BD450 Philosophical Anthropology

**Platt, John Rader, 1918-.**                                                • **1.1326**
Perception and change; projections for survival. Essays by John Platt. — Ann
Arbor: University of Michigan Press, [1970] 178 p.: illus.; 24 cm.
1. Philosophical anthropology 2. Change 3. Perception 4. Science and
civilization 5. Decision-making I. T.
BD450.P57 1970     301.2/4     LC 70-124450     ISBN 0472731009

**Schrag, Calvin O.**　　　　　　　　　　　　　　　　　　**1.1327**
Radical reflection and the origin of the human sciences / by Calvin O. Schrag. — West Lafayette, Ind.: Purdue University Press, 1980. xii, 134 p.; 22 cm. 1. Philosophical anthropology 2. Humanities — Philosophy. 3. Knowledge, Theory of 4. Hermeneutics I. T.
BD450.S37　　　128 19　　　*LC* 79-91085　　　*ISBN* 0911198571

**Taylor, Richard.**　　　　　　　　　　　　　　　　　• **1.1328**
Action and purpose. Englewood Cliffs, N.J.: Prentice-Hall, 1966. 269 p. 1. Act (Philosophy) 2. Agent (Philosophy) 3. Philosophical anthropology I. T.
BD450.T28　　　128.3　　　*LC* 66-13642

# BD493–708 Cosmology

**Ancient cosmologies / edited by Carmen Blacker and Michael**　　**1.1329**
**Loewe; with contributions by J. M. Plumley ... [et al.].**
London: Allen and Unwin, 1975. 3-270 p., leaf of plate, [16] p. of plates: ill. (incl. 1 col.), map; 23 cm. 1. Cosmology, Ancient — Addresses, essays, lectures. I. Blacker, Carmen. II. Loewe, Michael. III. Plumley, J. Martin.
BD495.A5　　　523.1/01　　　*LC* 76-363037　　　*ISBN* 0041000382

**Koyré, Alexandre, 1892-1964.**　　　　　　　　　　　• **1.1330**
From the closed world to the infinite universe. Baltimore, Johns Hopkins Press [1957] 313 p. 21 cm. (Publications of the Institute of the History of Medicine, the Johns Hopkins University. 3d ser.: The Hideyo Noguchi lectures, v. 7) 1. Cosmology I. T.
BD511.K67　　　113　　　*LC* 57-7080

**Whitehead, Alfred North, 1861-1947.**　　　　　　　　**1.1331**
Process and reality: an essay in cosmology / by Alfred North Whitehead. — Corrected ed. / edited by David Ray Griffin, Donald W. Sherburne. — New York: Free Press, 1978, c1929. xxxi, 413 p.; 24 cm. — (Gifford lectures. 1927-28) 1. Cosmology — Addresses, essays, lectures. 2. Science — Philosophy — Addresses, essays, lectures. 3. Organism (Philosophy) — Addresses, essays, lectures. I. Griffin, David, 1939- II. Sherburne, Donald W. III. T. IV. Series.
BD511.W5 1978　　　113　　　*LC* 77-90011　　　*ISBN* 0029345804

**Teilhard de Chardin, Pierre.**　　　　　　　　　　　• **1.1332**
[Phénomène humain English] The phenomenon of man. With an introd. by Julian Huxley. [Translation by Bernard Wall] New York, Harper [1959] 318 p. illus. 22 cm. Translation of Le phénomène humain. 1. Cosmology 2. Evolution 3. Philosophical anthropology I. T.
BD512.T413　　　113　　　*LC* 59-5154

**Wildiers, N. M., 1904-.**　　　　　　　　　　　　　　**1.1333**
The theologian and his universe: theology and cosmology from the Middle Ages to the present / N. Max Wildiers. — New York: Seabury Press, 1982. viii, 289 p. Translation of: Wereldbeeld en teologie. 1. Cosmology — History. 2. Theology — History. 3. Religion and science — History 4. Philosophy of nature — History. I. T.
BD518.D8 W5413　　　261.5/5 19　　　*LC* 82-3257　　　*ISBN* 0816424101

**Bunge, Mario Augusto.**　　　　　　　　　　　　　　**1.1334**
Causality and modern science / by Mario Bunge. — 3d rev. ed. — New York: Dover Publications, 1979. xxx, 394 p.: ill.; 21 cm. Published in 1959 under title: Causality, the place of the causal principle in modern science. 1. Causation 2. Determinism (Philosophy) 3. Science — Philosophy I. T.
BD541.B85 1979　　　122　　　*LC* 78-74117　　　*ISBN* 0486237281

**Collins, James Daniel.**　　　　　　　　　　　　　• **1.1335**
God in modern philosophy. — Chicago: H. Regnery Co., 1959. 476 p.; 25 cm. 1. God — History of doctrines 2. Philosophy, Modern I. T.
BD573.C6　　　211　　　*LC* 59-10545

**Armstrong, D. M. (David Malet), 1926-.**　　　　　　　**1.1336**
What is a law of nature? / D.M. Armstrong. — Cambridge [Cambridgeshire]; New York: Cambridge University Press, 1984. x, 180 p.; 22 cm. (Cambridge studies in philosophy.) Includes index. 1. Philosophy of nature I. T. II. Series.
BD581.A75 1984　　　113 19　　　*LC* 83-5130　　　*ISBN* 0521253438

**Kohák, Erazim V.**　　　　　　　　　　　　　　　　**1.1337**
The embers and the stars: a philosophical inquiry into the moral sense of nature / Erazim Kohák. — Chicago: University of Chicago Press, 1984. xiii, 269 p.; ill.; 24 cm. Includes index. 1. Philosophy of nature 2. Ethics 3. Philosophical anthropology I. T.
BD581.K54 1984　　　113 19　　　*LC* 83-17889　　　*ISBN* 0226450228

**Wright, G. H. von (Georg Henrik von), 1916-.**　　　　**1.1338**
Causality and determinism. New York: Columbia University Press, 1974. xxi, 143 p.: ill.; 21 cm. (Woodbridge lectures delivered at Columbia University, no. 10, 1972) 1. Causation 2. Free will and determinism I. T.
BD591.W74　　　122　　　*LC* 74-11030　　　*ISBN* 0231037589

## BD620–701 Space. Time

**Alexander, Samuel, 1859-1938.**　　　　　　　　　　• **1.1339**
Space, time, and deity: the Gifford lectures at Glasgow, 1916–1918, by S. Alexander. — 1st ed. reissued with a new foreword by Dorothy Emmet. — London, Macmillan, 1966. 2 v. 22 cm. — (Gifford lectures, 1916-1918) I. T.
BD632.A4 1966a　　　115.4　　　*LC* 67-72556

**Grünbaum, Adolf.**　　　　　　　　　　　　　　　• **1.1340**
Philosophical problems of space and time. — New York: Knopf, 1963. xi, 448 p.; 23 cm. — (Borzoi books in the philosophy of science) 1. Space and time 2. Relativity (Physics) 3. Science — Philosophy I. T.
BD632.G69　　　501 s 115/.4　　　*LC* 63-18683

**Reichenbach, Hans, 1891-1953.**　　　　　　　　　　• **1.1341**
[Philosophie der Raum-Zeit-Lehre. English] The philosophy of space & time. Translated by Maria Reichenbach and John Freund. With introductory remarks by Rudolf Carnap. New York, Dover Publications [1958] 295 p. illus. 21 cm. 1. Space and time 2. Relativity (Physics) I. T.
BD632.R413　　　113　　　*LC* 58-7082

**Sorabji, Richard.**　　　　　　　　　　　　　　　　**1.1342**
Time, creation, and the continuum: theories in antiquity and the early middle ages / Richard Sorabji. — Ithaca, N.Y.: Cornell University Press, 1983. xviii, 473 p.: ill.; 24 cm. Includes index. 1. Time 2. Creation 3. Continuity I. T.
BD638.S67 1983　　　115 19　　　*LC* 82-48714　　　*ISBN* 0801415934

**Toulmin, Stephen Edelston.**　　　　　　　　　　　• **1.1343**
The discovery of time [by] Stephen Toulmin [and] June Goodfield. New York, Harper & Row [1965] 280 p. 22 cm. (The Ancestry of science) 1. Time 2. Cosmology — History. I. Goodfield, June, 1927- joint author. II. T.
BD638.T67　　　901　　　*LC* 64-25123

**Eliade, Mircea, 1907-.**　　　　　　　　　　　　　• **1.1344**
[Mythe de l'éternel retour. English] Cosmos and history; the myth of the eternal return. Translated from the French by Willard R. Trask. New York, Harper [1959] 176 p. 21 cm. (Harper torchbooks, TB50) Translation of Le mythe de l'éternel retour. 1. Religion, Primitive 2. Religion 3. Myth 4. History (Theology) I. T.
BD701.E383 1959　　　113　　　*LC* 59-6648

BF Psychology. see vol. 5

# BH Aesthetics

**Philosophies of beauty from Socrates to Robert Bridges: being**　• **1.1345**
**the sources of aesthetic theory / selected and edited by E. F.**
**Carritt.**
Oxford: Clarendon Press, 1931. xxix, 334 p.; 23 cm. 1. Aesthetics — Collected works. I. Carritt, E. F. (Edgar Frederick), 1876-1964.
BH21.C3 1931　　　BH21.P49.　　　111.8/5　　　*ISBN* 0837188121

**Hofstadter, Albert, 1910- ed.**　　　　　　　　　　**1.1346**
Philosophies of art and beauty; selected readings in aesthetics from Plato to Heidegger. Edited by Albert Hofstadter and Richard Kuhns. — New York [Modern Library, 1964] xix, 701 p. 21 cm. — (The Modern library of the world's best books. Modern library giants, G90) 1. Aesthetics — Collections. I. Kuhns, Richard Francis, 1924- joint ed. II. T.
BH21.H6　　　111.85042　　　*LC* 64-18941

**Margolis, Joseph Zalman, 1924- ed.**　　　　　　　• **1.1347**
Philosophy looks at the arts: contemporary readings in aesthetics / edited by Joseph Margolis. — Rev. ed. — Philadelphia: Temple University Press, 1978. ix, 481 p.; 24 cm. 1. Aesthetics — Addresses, essays, lectures. 2. Art — Philosophy — Addresses, essays, lectures. 3. Analysis (Philosophy) — Addresses, essays, lectures. I. T.
BH21.M3 1978　　　111.8/5　　　*LC* 77-95028　　　´*ISBN* 0877221235

**Rader, Melvin Miller, 1903- ed.**　　　　　　　　　• **1.1347a**
A modern book of esthetics: an anthology / edited with introd. and notes by Melvin Rader. — 5th ed. — New York: Holt, Rinehart and Winston, c1979.

563 p.; 25 cm. Includes index. 1. Aesthetics — Addresses, essays, lectures.
I. T.
BH21.R3 1979      111.8/5      *LC* 78-16041

**Sesonske, Alexander. ed.**                              • **1.1348**
What is art? Aesthetic theory from Plato to Tolstoy. — New York, Oxford
University Press, 1965. xvi, 428 p. 26 cm. Bibliography: p. [419]-428.
1. Aesthetics — Collections. I. T.
BH21.S4      111.85082      *LC* 65-12469

**Vivas, Eliseo. ed.**                                    • **1.1349**
The problems of aesthetics, a book of readings, edited by Eliseo Vivas and
Murray Krieger. — New York: Rinehart, [1953] 639 p.; 24 cm. 1. Aesthetics
I. Krieger, Murray, 1923- joint ed. II. T.
BH21.V55      701.17 101      *LC* 52-14017

**Weitz, Morris, ed.**                                    • **1.1350**
Problems in aesthetics; an introductory book of readings. — 2d ed. — [New
York]: Macmillan, [1970] xiii, 927 p.: illus.; 24 cm. 1. Aesthetics — Addresses,
essays, lectures. I. T.
BH21.W4 1970      701.17      *LC* 74-85775

**Adams, Hazard, 1926- comp.**                            • **1.1351**
Critical theory since Plato. — New York: Harcourt Brace Jovanovich, [1971]
xx, 1267 p.; 24 cm. 1. Criticism — Collections. 2. Literature — Aesthetics —
Collections. 3. Aesthetics — Collections. I. T.
BH39.A23      111.8/5      *LC* 74-152575      *ISBN* 0155161423

**Art and its significance: an anthology of aesthetic theory /**     **1.1352**
**edited by Stephen David Ross.**
Albany: State University of New York Press, c1984. x, 574 p.; 24 cm. —
(SUNY series in philosophy.) 1. Aesthetics — Addresses, essays, lectures.
2. Art — Philosophy — Addresses, essays, lectures. I. Ross, Stephen David.
II. Series.
BH39.A69 1984      701/.1/7 19      *LC* 83-9683      *ISBN* 0873957644

**Culture and art: an anthology / edited by Lars Aagaard–**          **1.1353**
**Mogensen.**
Nyborg: F. Løkke; Atlantic Highlands, N.J.: Humanities Press, 1976. 211 p.; 22
cm. (Eclipse books) 1. Aesthetics — Addresses, essays, lectures. 2. Art —
Philosophy — Addresses, essays, lectures. I. Aagaard-Mogensen, Lars, 1944-
BH39.C84 1976      111.8/5      *LC* 75-45455      *ISBN* 0391005391

**Danto, Arthur Coleman, 1924-.**                         **1.1354**
The transfiguration of the commonplace: a philosophy of art / Arthur C.
Danto. — Cambridge, Mass.: Harvard University Press, 1981. x, 212 p.; 24 cm.
Includes index. 1. Aesthetics 2. Art — Philosophy I. T.
BH39.D36      700/.1      *LC* 80-18700      *ISBN* 0674903455

**Dickie, George, 1926-.**                                • **1.1355**
Aesthetics; an introduction. — [Indianapolis]: Pegasus, [c1971] x, 200 p.; 21
cm. — (Traditions in philosophy) 1. Aesthetics 2. Aesthetics, Modern — 20th
century I. T.
BH39.D48      111.8/5      *LC* 72-128659

**Dickie, George, 1926-.**                                **1.1356**
Art and the aesthetic: an institutional analysis / George Dickie. — Ithaca,
N.Y.: Cornell University Press, 1974. 204 p.; 21 cm. 1. Aesthetics 2. Art —
Philosophy I. T.
BH39.D49 1974      111.8/5      *LC* 74-7699      *ISBN* 0801408873

**Isenberg, Arnold.**                                     **1.1357**
Aesthetics and the theory of criticism; selected essays of Arnold Isenberg.
Edited by William Callaghan [and others] With an introd. by Mary Mothersill
and a biographical sketch by William Callaghan. — Chicago: University of
Chicago Press, [1973] xxxix, 322 p.: port.; 24 cm. 1. Isenberg, Arnold.
2. Aesthetics — Collected works. 3. Criticism — Collected works. I. T.
BH39.I83      111.8/5      *LC* 73-77133      *ISBN* 0226385116

**Morawski, Stefan.**                                     **1.1358**
Inquiries into the fundamentals of aesthetics. — Cambridge, Mass.: MIT Press,
[1974] xviii, 408 p.; 23 cm. 1. Aesthetics I. T.
BH39.M618      111.8/5      *LC* 74-6123      *ISBN* 0262130963

**Munro, Thomas, 1897-.**                                 • **1.1359**
Toward science in aesthetics: selected essays / by Thomas Munro. — New
York: Liberal Arts Press, 1956. xv, 371 p.: ill.; 25 cm. 1. Aesthetics 2. Art —
Philosophy I. T.
BH39.M83      *LC* 56-3418

**Sircello, Guy.**                                        **1.1360**
A new theory of beauty / Guy Sircello. — Princeton, N.J.: Princeton University
Press, [1975] vi, 141 p.; 25 cm. (Princeton essays on the arts; 1) 1. Aesthetics
I. T.
BH39.S54      111.8/5      *LC* 75-3475      *ISBN* 0691072116

**Sparshott, Francis Edward, 1926-.**                     **1.1361**
The theory of the arts / Francis Sparshott. — Princeton, N.J.: Princeton
University Press, c1982. xiii, 726 p.; 25 cm. Includes index. 1. Arts —
Philosophy. 2. Aesthetics I. T.
BH39.S634 1982      700/.1 19      *LC* 82-5333      *ISBN* 0691072663

**Wollheim, Richard, 1923-.**                             **1.1362**
Art and its objects: with six supplementary essays / Richard Wollheim. — 2d
ed. — Cambridge; New York: Cambridge University Press, 1980. xv, 270 p.; 22
cm. 1. Aesthetics — Addresses, essays, lectures. I. T.
BH39.W64 1980      700/.1      *LC* 79-20790      *ISBN* 0521228980

**Bennett, Tony.**                                        **1.1363**
Formalism and Marxism / Tony Bennett. — London: Methuen, 1979. xii,
200 p.; 20 cm. (New accents) Includes index. 1. Communist aesthetics
2. Formalism (Literary analysis) 3. Criticism 4. Literature — Aesthetics I. T.
BH41.B45      801/.95      *LC* 80-473608      *ISBN* 0416708706

**Smith, Ralph Alexander. comp.**                         **1.1364**
Aesthetics and problems of education / edited by Ralph A. Smith. — Urbana:
University of Illinois Press, 1971. xv, 581 p.; 21 cm. — (Readings in the
philosophy of education) (Illini books IB-75) 1. Aesthetics — Study and
teaching. I. T.
BH61.S6      111.8/5      *LC* 77-146011      *ISBN* 0252001656

# BH81–221 History

**Beardsley, Monroe C.**                                  • **1.1365**
Aesthetics from classical Greece to the present; a short history [by] Monroe C.
Beardsley. — [1st ed.]. — New York, Macmillan [1966] 414 p. 21 cm. Includes
bibliographies. 1. Aesthetics — Hist. I. T.
BH81.B4 1966      111.85      *LC* 65-24765

**Bosanquet, Bernard, 1848-1923.**                        • **1.1366**
A history of aesthetic. 2d ed. London, Allen & Unwin; New York, Humanities
P., 1966. xxiii, 502 p. 22 cm. (Muirhead library of philosophy) 'First published
in 1892. Second edition 1904. Reprinted ... 1966.' 1. Aesthetics — History.
I. T.
BH81.B6 1966      *LC* 66-27376

**Gilbert, Katharine (Everett) 1886-1952.**               • **1.1367**
A history of esthetics, by Katharine Everett Gilbert and Helmut Kuhn. Rev.
and enl. Bloomington, Indiana University Press, 1953. xxi, 613 p. 22 cm.
1. Aesthetics — History. I. Kuhn, Helmut, 1899- joint author. II. T.
BH81.G5 1953      701.17 101*      *LC* 53-7022

**Deutsch, Eliot.**                                       **1.1368**
Studies in comparative aesthetics / Eliot Deutsch. — [Honolulu]: University
Press of Hawaii, 1975. 95 p.: ill.; 23 cm. (Monograph of the Society for Asian
and Comparative Philosophy; no. 2) 1. Aesthetics, Comparative — Addresses,
essays, lectures. 2. Experience — Addresses, essays, lectures. I. T.
BH85.D48      111.8/5      *LC* 74-34028      *ISBN* 0824803655

**Harrison, Jane Ellen, 1850-1928.**                      • **1.1369**
Ancient art and ritual. — New York: Greenwood Press, [1969, c1951] 256 p.:
illus.; 23 cm. 1. Art, Primitive 2. Ritual 3. Aesthetics I. T.
BH91.H32 1969      291/.3      *LC* 69-13924      *ISBN* 0837119812

**Burke, Edmund, 1729-1797.**                             • **1.1370**
A philosophical enquiry into the origin of our ideas of the sublime and beautiful
/ Edmund Burke; edited with an introduction and notes by James T. Boulton.
— London: Routledge and Paul, 1958. cxxx, 197 p. 1. Aesthetics — Early
works to 1800. 2. Sublime, The I. Boulton, James T. ed. II. Boulton, James T.
III. T.
BH181.B8 1958      701      *LC* 58-9089

**Kant, Immanuel, 1724-1804.**                            • **1.1371**
Observations on the feeling of the beautiful and sublime. Translated by John T.
Goldthwait. — Berkeley, University of California Press, 1960. 124 p. 19 cm.
Published with variations in 1957 in microfilm form as the translator's thesis,
Northwestern University, under title: Kant's precritical esthetic.
Bibliographical references included in 'Translator's notes' (p. [117]-124)
1. Aesthetics I. T.
BH183.K313 1960      111.85      *LC* 60-14379

**Schiller, Friedrich, 1759-1805.**                       • **1.1372**
[Briefe über die aesthetische Erziehung des menschen. English] On the aesthetic
education of man, in a series of letters [by] Friedrich Schiller; edited and
translated [from the German] with an introduction, commentary and glossary
of terms by Elizabeth M. Wilkinson and L. A. Willoughby. Oxford, Clarendon
P., 1967 [i.e. 1968]. [2], cxcvi, 372 p. 23 cm. Translation of Briefe über die

aesthetische Erziehung des Menschen. Parallel German text, English translation. 1. Aesthetics — Early works to 1800. I. Wilkinson, Elizabeth M. (Elizabeth Mary) ed. II. Willoughby, Leonard Ashley, 1885- ed. III. T.
BH183.S25 1968     111.8/5     LC 68-80682

**Gilson, Etienne, 1884-1978.**         • **1.1373**
The arts of the beautiful [by] Etienne Gilson. — New York, Scribner [1965] 189 p. 22 cm. 1. Aesthetics I. T.
BH201.G55     111.85     LC 65-14767

**Hofstadter, Albert, 1910-.**         **1.1374**
Truth and art. New York Columbia University Press 1965. 227p. 1. Aesthetics I. T.
BH201 H6     LC 65-12521

**Kaelin, Eugene Francis, 1926-.**         **1.1375**
Art and existence: a phenomenological aesthetics [by] Eugene F. Kaelin. — Lewisburg [Pa.]: Bucknell University Press, [1971, c1970] 357 p.: col. illus.; 22 cm. 1. Husserl, Edmund, 1859-1938. 2. Heidegger, Martin, 1889-1976. 3. Aesthetics, Modern — 20th century 4. Phenomenology I. T.
BH201.K34 1971     700/.1     LC 74-101236     ISBN 0838775829

**Nahm, Milton Charles, 1903-.**         **1.1376**
The artist as creator; an essay of human freedom. Baltimore, Johns Hopkins Press, 1956. 352 p. 1. Aesthetics 2. Creation (Literary, artistics, etc.) 3. Art — Philosophy I. T.
BH201.N32     LC 56-8241

**Parker, De Witt Henry, 1885-.**         • **1.1377**
The principles of aesthetics. — 2d ed. [By] De Witt H. Parker ... — New York, Appleton-Century-Crofts, 1946. viii, 316 p. front, plates. 21 cm. Bibliography: p. 298-302. 1. Aesthetics I. T.
BH201.P35 1946     701.17     LC 46-2616

**Pepper, Stephen Coburn, 1891-.**         • **1.1378**
Aesthetic quality; a contextualistic theory of beauty, by Stephen C. Pepper. — Westport, Conn.: Greenwood Press, [1970, c1965] ix, 255 p.; 23 cm. 1. Aesthetics I. T.
BH201.P4 1970     111.8/5     LC 79-110052     ISBN 083714437X

**Pepper, Stephen Coburn, 1891-.**         • **1.1379**
The basis of criticism in the arts, by Stephen C. Pepper ... — Cambridge, Mass., Harvard university Press, 1965 [c1945] viii p., 3 l., [3]-177 p. diagrs. 22 cm. 1. Aesthetics 2. Criticism I. T.
BH201.P42 1965     701.18     LC A 45-5598

**The Quest for imagination; essays in twentieth century aesthetic**    **1.1380**
**criticism. Edited by O. B. Hardison, Jr.**
Cleveland: Press of Case Western Reserve University, 1971. xiv, 286 p.; 24 cm. 1. Aesthetics, Modern — 20th century — Addresses, essays, lectures. 2. Criticism (Philosophy) — Addresses, essays, lectures. 3. Imagination I. Hardison, O. B. ed.
BH201.Q47 1971     801     LC 70-145425     ISBN 0829502076

**Rader, Melvin Miller, 1903-.**         **1.1381**
Art and human values / Melvin Rader, Bertram Jessup; with a foreword by Virgil C. Aldrich. — Englewood Cliffs, N.J.: Prentice-Hall, c1976. x, 406 p.; 24 cm. Includes index. 1. Aesthetics 2. Values 3. Art — Philosophy I. Jessup, Bertram Emil, 1899- joint author. II. T.
BH201.R28     111.8/5     LC 75-22486     ISBN 0130468215

**Croce, Benedetto, 1866-1952.**         • **1.1382**
Aesthetic as science of expression and general linguistic. Translated from the Italian by Douglas Ainslie. [Rev. ed.] New York, Noonday [1953] xxx, 503 p. 23 cm. 1. Aesthetics 2. Language and languages I. T.
BH204.C7 1953     LC 53-9069

**Ortega y Gasset, José, 1883-1955.**         • **1.1383**
[Deshumanización del arte. English] The dehumanization of art; and other essays on art, culture, and literature. Princeton, N.J., Princeton University Press, 1968 [c1948] 204 p. 21 cm. (Princeton paperbacks, 128) Translation of La deshumanización del arte. 1. Aesthetics 2. Fiction I. T.
BH205.O713 1968     700/.1     LC 68-8963

**Anderson, Mary R., 1937-.**         **1.1384**
Art in a desacralized world: nineteenth century France and England / Mary R. Anderson. — Lanham, MD: University Press of America, c1984. x, 174 p.; 22 cm. 1. Aesthetics, French — 19th century 2. Aesthetics, British — 19th century I. T.
BH221.F8 A53 1984     801/.93 19     LC 84-13081     ISBN 081914147X

**German aesthetic and literary criticism. Kant, Fichte, Schelling,**   **1.1385**
**Schopenhauer, Hegel / edited and introduced by David**
**Simpson.**
Cambridge [Cambridgeshire]; New York: Cambridge University Press, 1984. x, 294 p.; 24 cm. Includes index. 1. Aesthetics, German — 18th century 2. Aesthetics, German — 19th century 3. Criticism — Germany — History — 18th century. 4. Criticism — Germany — History — 19th century. I. Simpson, David, 1951- II. Title: Kant, Fichte, Schelling, Schopenhauer, Hegel.
BH221.G3 G47 1984     111/.85 19     LC 83-15320     ISBN 0521236304

**Bate, Walter Jackson, 1918-.**         • **1.1386**
From classic to romantic: premises of taste in eighteenth–century England. Cambridge Harvard University Press 1946. 197p. (Lowell Institute. Lectures, 1945) 1. Aesthetics — History 2. Classicism 3. Romanticism — England I. T.
BH221 G7 B36

**Bullough, Edward, 1880-1934.**         • **1.1387**
Esthetics: lectures and essays / Edited with an introd. by Elizabeth M. Wilkinson. — Stanford, Calif.: Stanford University Press, 1957. 158 p. 1. Aesthetics I. T.
BH221.G74.B8 1957a     LC 57-12025

**Pandit, Sneh.**         **1.1388**
An approach to the Indian theory of art and aesthetics / Sneh Pandit. — New Delhi: Sterling Publishers; New York: distributed in the U.S.A. by International Publications Service, c1977. vii, 148 p.; 23 cm. A revision of the author's thesis, Punjab University, 1973. Includes index. 1. Aesthetics, Indic I. T.
BH221.I53 P33 1977     BH221I43 P33 1977.     111.8/5     LC 77-905389     ISBN 0842610057

**Harrell, Jean G. (Jean Gabbert), 1921- comp.**         **1.1389**
Aesthetics in twentieth–century Poland; selected essays. Edited by Jean G. Harrell and Alina Wierzbiańska. Lewisburg [Pa.] Bucknell University Press [1973] 285 p. 22 cm. 1. Aesthetics, Polish. 2. Aesthetics, Modern — 20th century I. Wierzbiańska, Alina, joint comp. II. T.
BH221.P63 H37     111.8/5     LC 78-38984     ISBN 0838711006

# BH301 Special Topics. Irony. Surrealism. Symbolism

**Bürger, Peter, 1936-.**         **1.1390**
[Theorie der Avantgarde. English] Theory of the avant–garde / Peter Bürger; translation from the German by Michael Shaw; foreword by Jochen Schulte–Sasse. — Minneapolis: University of Minnesota Press, c1984. lv, 135 p.: ill.; 24 cm. — (Theory and history of literature. v. 4) Translation of: Theorie der Avantgarde. Includes index. 1. Avant-garde (Aesthetics) I. T. II. Series.
BH301.A94 B8313 1984     111/.85 19     LC 83-10549     ISBN 0816610673

**McFadden, George, 1916-.**         **1.1391**
Discovering the comic / George McFadden. — Princeton, N.J.: Princeton University Press, c1982. 268 p.; 23 cm. Includes indexes. 1. Comic, The I. T.
BH301.C7 M38     809/.917 19     LC 81-15825     ISBN 0691064962

**The Concept of creativity in science and art / edited by Denis**   **1.1392**
**Dutton and Michael Krausz.**
The Hague; Boston: M. Nijhoff; Hingham, MA: Distributors for the U.S. and Canada, Kluwer Boston, 1981. 212 p.; 25 cm. — (Martinus Nijhoff philosophy library. v. 6) (American University publications in philosophy. 3) Includes index. 1. Creation (Literary, artistic, etc.) — Addresses, essays, lectures. 2. Creative ability in science — Addresses, essays, lectures. 3. Creative thinking — Addresses, essays, lectures. I. Dutton, Denis. II. Krausz, Michael. III. Series. IV. Series: American University publications in philosophy. 3
BH301.C84 C66 1981     128/.3 19     LC 81-4001     ISBN 902472418X

**Dufrenne, Mikel.**         **1.1393**
[Phénoménologie de l'experience esthétique. English] The phenomenology of aesthetic experience. Translated by Edward S. Casey [and others] Evanston [Ill.] Northwestern University Press, 1973. lxvii, 578 p. 24 cm. (Northwestern University studies in phenomenology & existential philosophy) Translation of Phénoménologie de l'experience esthétique. 1. Aesthetics 2. Experience 3. Phenomenology I. T. II. Series.
BH301.E8 D8313     111.8/5     LC 73-76806     ISBN 0810104261

**Kierkegaard, Søren, 1813-1855.**         • **1.1394**
[Om begrebet ironi. English] The concept of irony, with constant reference to Socrates. Translated and with an introd. and notes by Lee M. Capel. New York,

Harper & Row [1966, c1965] 442 p. 22 cm. 1. Socrates. 2. Irony I. Capel, Lee M. ed. and tr. II. T.
BH301.I7 K53 1966a      111.85      *LC* 66-10227

**The Anti–aesthetic: essays on postmodern culture / edited by**    **1.1395**
**Hal Foster.**
1st ed. — Port Townsend, Wash.: Bay Press, 1983. xvi, 159 p.: ill.; 23 cm. 1. Modernism (Aesthetics) — Addresses, essays, lectures. 2. Civilization, Modern — 1950- — Addresses, essays, lectures. I. Foster, Hal.
BH301.M54 A57 1983      909.82 19      *LC* 83-70650      *ISBN*
094192002X

**Megill, Allan.**      **1.1396**
Prophets of extremity: Nietzsche, Heidegger, Foucault, Derrida / Allan Megill. — Berkeley: University of California Press, c1985. xxiii, 399 p.; 24 cm. Includes index. 1. Nietzsche, Friedrich Wilhelm, 1844-1900. 2. Heidegger, Martin, 1889-1976. 3. Foucault, Michel. 4. Derrida, Jacques. 5. Modernism (Aesthetics) 6. Philosophy, Modern — 19th century 7. Philosophy, Modern — 20th century I. T.
BH301.M54 M44 1985      190 19      *LC* 84-8518      *ISBN* 0520052390

**Thacker, Christopher.**      **1.1397**
The wildness pleases: the origins of romanticism / by Christopher Thacker. — London: Croom Helm; New York: St. Martin's Press, 1983. vi, 282 p., [24] p. of plates: ill.; 22 cm. Includes index. 1. Nature (Aesthetics) I. T.
BH301.N3 T47 1983      111/.85 19      *LC* 82-10769      *ISBN* 0312879601

**Weiskel, Thomas.**      **1.1398**
The romantic sublime: studies in the structure and psychology of transcendence / Thomas Weiskel. — Baltimore: Johns Hopkins University Press, c1976. xi, 220 p.; 24 cm. 1. Sublime, The 2. Transcendence (Philosophy) I. T.
BH301.S7 W44      128/.3      *LC* 75-36932      *ISBN* 0801817706

**Breton, André, 1896-1966.**      **1.1399**
Manifestoes of surrealism / André Breton; translated from the French by Richard Seaver and Helen R. Lane. — Ann Arbor: University of Michigan Press, c1969. xi, 304 p.; 21 cm. Ann Arbor paperbacks. Translation of Les manifestes du surréalisme. 1. Surrealism I. T.
BH301.S75 B683 1972      700.1      *ISBN* 0472061828 Pbk

**Fowlie, Wallace, 1908-.**      • **1.1400**
Age of surrealism. — Bloomington: Indiana University Press, [1960] 215 p.: illus.; 21 cm. — (A Midland book, MB24) 1. Surrealism I. T.
BH301.S75 F6 1960      709.04      *LC* 60-8309

**Nadeau, Maurice.**      • **1.1401**
[Histoire du surréalisme. English] The history of surrealism. Translated from the French by Richard Howard. With an introd. by Roger Shattuck. New York, Macmillan [1965] 351 p. illus. 22 cm. 1. Surrealism 2. Arts, Modern — 20th century I. T.
BH301.S75 N33      709.04      *LC* 65-23834

**Goodman, Nelson.**      • **1.1402**
Languages of art; an approach to a theory of symbols. — Indianapolis, Bobbs-Merrill [1968] xiii, 277 p. illus. (part col.) 22 cm. 1. Symbolism 2. Signs and symbols 3. Knowledge, Theory of I. T.
BH301.S8G6      110      *LC* 68-31825

# BJ Ethics

## BJ21–28 Collections

**Foot, Philippa.**      • **1.1403**
Theories of ethics; edited by Philippa Foot. — London: Oxford U.P., 1967. [4], 188 p.; 20 1/2 cm. — (Oxford readings in philosophy) 1. Ethics — Collections. I. T.
BJ21.F6      171/.08      *LC* 68-74186

**Moral development and behavior: theory, research, and social**    **1.1404**
**issues / Thomas Lickona, editor, consulting editors, Gilbert**
**Geis, Lawrence Kohlberg.**
New York: Holt, Rinehart and Winston, c1976. xiv, 430 p.; 25 cm. Includes index. 1. Ethics — Addresses, essays, lectures. 2. Social ethics — Addresses, essays, lectures. 3. Moral education — Addresses, essays, lectures. I. Lickona, Thomas.
BJ21.M58      170      *LC* 75-29471      *ISBN* 0030028116

**Pahel, Kenneth, comp.**      • **1.1405**
Readings in contemporary ethical theory. Edited by Kenneth Pahel & Marvin Schiller. — Englewood Cliffs, N.J.: Prentice-Hall, [1970] ix, 572 p.; 24 cm. 1. Ethics — Collections. I. Schiller, Marvin, 1940- joint comp. II. T.
BJ21.P33      170/.8      *LC* 78-87265      *ISBN* 0137558198

## BJ37–57 Theory. Scope. Relations

**Brandt, Richard B.**      • **1.1406**
Ethical theory; the problems of normative and critical ethics. — Englewood Cliffs, N.J.: Prentice-Hall, 1959. 538 p.: illus.; 24 cm. — (Prentice-Hall philosophy series) 1. Ethics I. T.
BJ37.B77      170      *LC* 59-10075

**Mackie, J. L. (John Leslie)**      • **1.1407**
Ethics: inventing right and wrong / [by] J. L. Mackie. — Harmondsworth; New York: Penguin, 1977. 249 p.; 18 cm. (Pelican books: Philosophy) 1. Ethics I. T.
BJ37.M24      170      *LC* 78-300959      *ISBN* 0140219579

**Moore, G. E. (George Edward), 1873-1958.**      • **1.1408**
Principia ethica. — Cambridge [Eng.]: University Press, 1962. xxvii, 232 p.; 23 cm. 1. Ethics I. T.
BJ37.M817 1962

**Veatch, Henry Babcock.**      • **1.1409**
Rational man; a modern interpretation of Aristotelian ethics. — Bloomington, Indiana University Press [1962] 226 p. 21 cm. 1. Ethics 2. Aristoteles. I. T.
BJ37.V4      170      *LC* 62-16161

**Stevenson, Charles L. (Charles Leslie), 1908-.**      • **1.1410**
Ethics and language. — New Haven, Yale University Press [1960] xi, 338 p. 21 cm. — (Yale paperbound, Y-19) Bibliographical footnotes. 1. Ethics 2. Language and languages 3. Meaning (Psychology) 4. Judgment (Logic) I. T.
BJ43.S8 1960      *LC* A 45-1043

**Toulmin, Stephen Edelston.**      • **1.1411**
An examination of the place of reason in ethics / by Stephen Edelston Toulmin. — Cambridge, Eng.: University Press, 1968. xiv, 228 p.: ill. Title on cover: Reason in ethics. 1. Ethics 2. Reason I. T. II. Title: Reason in ethics.
BJ43.T6 1968

**Fromm, Erich, 1900-.**      • **1.1412**
Man for himself, an inquiry into the psychology of ethics. — New York: Rinehart, [1947] xiv, 254 p.; 22 cm. 1. Ethics 2. Psychology I. T.
BJ45.F7      171      *LC* 47-12365

**Lippmann, Walter, 1889-.**      • **1.1413**
A preface to morals. — New York: The Macmillan company, 1929. viii, 348 p.; 22 cm. 1. Ethics 2. Philosophy and religion I. T.
BJ47.L5      *LC* 29-10228

**Singer, Peter.**      **1.1414**
The expanding circle: ethics and sociobiology / Peter Singer. — 1st ed. — New York: Farrar, Straus & Giroux, 1981. xii, 190 p.; 22 cm. 1. Ethics 2. Sociobiology I. T.
BJ51.S57 1981      170/.42 19      *LC* 80-20718      *ISBN* 0374234965

**Lyons, David, 1935-.**      **1.1415**
Ethics and the rule of law / David Lyons. — Cambridge [Cambridgeshire]; New York: Cambridge University Press, 1984. x, 229 p.; 21 cm. Include index. 1. Law and ethics I. T.
BJ55.L95 1984      174/.3 19      *LC* 83-7687      *ISBN* 0521257859

## BJ71–944 History

**Sidgwick, Henry, 1838-1900.**      • **1.1416**
Outlines of the history of ethics for English readers. With an additional chapter by Alban G. Widgery. — Boston, Beacon Press [1960] 342 p. 21 cm. — (Beacon paperback no. 108) Includes bibliography. 1. Ethics — Hist. I. T.
BJ71.S55 1960      170.9      *LC* 60-50661

**Maritain, Jacques, 1882-1973.**                                    • 1.1417
Moral philosophy; an historical and critical survey of the great systems. — New
York, Scribner [1964] xii, 468 p. illus. 25 cm. Bibliographical footnotes.
1. Ethics — Hist. I. T.
BJ72.M313        170.9        LC 64-14663

## BJ101–285 ANCIENT. MEDIEVAL.
### RENAISSANCE

**Adkins, A. W. H. (Arthur W. H.)**                                    • 1.1418
Merit and responsibility: a study in Greek values / by Arthur W.H. Adkins. —
Oxford: Clarendon Press, 1960. xiv, 380 p.; 22 cm. — 1. Responsibility
2. Ethics, Greek I. T.
BJ171.R4 A3        LC 60-811        ISBN 0226007286

**Adkins, A. W. H. (Arthur W. H.)**                                    1.1419
Moral values and political behaviour in ancient Greece: from Homer to the end
of the fifth century / [by] A. W. H. Adkins. — New York: Norton [1972] xiv,
160 p.: map; 20 cm. (Ancient culture and society) 1. Ethics, Ancient I. T.
BJ182.A3 1973        172/.0938        LC 72-8796        ISBN 0393043673

**Dover, Kenneth James.**                                    1.1420
Greek popular morality in the time of Plato and Aristotle / K. J. Dover. —
Berkeley: University of California Press, 1974. xix, 330 p.; 25 cm. Includes
indexes. 1. Ethics, Ancient 2. Greek literature — History and criticism. I. T.
BJ182.D68        170/.938        LC 73-94451        ISBN 0520027213

## BJ301–944 MODERN

**Warnock, Mary.**                                    1.1421
Ethics since 1900 / [by] Mary Warnock. — 3rd ed. — Oxford; New York:
Oxford University Press, 1978. ix, 150 p.; 20 cm. — (Oxford paperbacks
university series) Includes index. 1. Ethics, Modern — 20th century I. T.
BJ319.W3 1978        170/.9/04        LC 79-311024        ISBN 0192891081

**Meyer, Donald Harvey, 1935-.**                                    1.1422
The instructed conscience: the shaping of the American national ethic / by D.
H. Meyer. — Philadelphia: University of Pennsylvania Press, [1972] xiv, 220 p.;
23 cm. 1. Ethics — United States — History. I. T.
BJ352.M49        170/.973        LC 76-175512        ISBN 0812276515

**Thomas, David Oswald.**                                    1.1423
The honest mind: the thought and work of Richard Price / D. O. Thomas. —
Oxford: Clarendon Press, 1977. xvi, 366 p.; 23 cm. Includes index. 1. Price,
Richard, 1723-1791. I. T.
BJ604.P7 T47        192        LC 77-374313        ISBN 0198245718

**Schneewind, J. B. (Jerome B.), 1930-.**                                    1.1424
Sidgwick's ethics and Victorian moral philosophy / by J. B. Schneewind. —
Oxford; New York: Clarendon Press, 1977. xvi, 465 p.; 22 cm. Includes index.
1. Sidgwick, Henry, 1838-1900. 2. Ethics — England — History. I. T.
BJ604.S5 S36        170/.92/4        LC 78-301054        ISBN 0198245521

**Madsen, Richard, 1941-.**                                    1.1425
Morality and power in a Chinese village / Richard Madsen. — Berkeley:
University of California Press, 1985 (c1984). xvi, 283 p.; 22 cm. 'Sponsored by
the Center for Chinese Studies, University of California, Berkeley.' 1. Ethics,
Chinese — History — 20th century. 2. Confucianism 3. China — Politics and
government — 1949- I. University of California, Berkeley. Center for Chinese
Studies. II. T.
BJ966.M3        170/.951 19        LC 83-4887        ISBN 0520047974

**Mishima, Yukio, 1925-1970.**                                    1.1426
[Hagakure nyūmon. English] The way of the samurai: Yukio Mishima on
Hagakure in modern life / [by Yukio Mishima]; translated by Kathryn N.
Sparling. — New York: Basic Books, c1977. x, 166 p.; 22 cm. Translation of
Hagakure nyūmon. 1. Yamamoto, Tsunetomo, 1659-1719. Hagakure
2. Bushido I. Yamamoto, Tsunetomo, 1659-1719. Hagakure II. T.
BJ971.B8 Y333313        170/.952        LC 75-36381        ISBN 0465090893

## BJ991–1185 General Works

**Hutcheson, Francis, 1694-1746.**                                    1.1427
Francis Hutcheson: an inquiry concerning beauty, order, harmony, design.
Edited, with an introd. and notes by Peter Kivy. — The Hague: Martinus

Nijhoff, 1973. 123 p.; 24 cm. — (Archives internationales d'histoire des idées.
Series minor, 9) An inquiry concerning beauty, order, harmony, design is the
first of two treatises which together comprise the Inquiry into the original of our
ideas of beauty and virtue, first published in 1725; the three papers which
comprise the Reflections upon laughter were previously published in 1750 as
part of a work titled Reflections upon laughter, and remarks upon the fable of
the bees. 1. Ethics 2. Aesthetics — Early works to 1800. I. Kivy, Peter. ed.
II. Hutcheson, Francis, 1694-1746. Inquiry into the original of our ideas of
beauty and virtue. III. Hutcheson, Francis, 1694-1746. Reflections upon
laughter. 1973. IV. T. V. Title: An inquiry concerning beauty, order,
harmony, design. VI. Series.
BJ1005.H87 1973        170        LC 73-179575        ISBN 9024715458

**Hutcheson, Francis, 1694-1746.**                                    1.1428
Illustrations on the moral sense [by] Francis Hutcheson. Edited by Bernard
Peach. — Cambridge, Mass.: Belknap Press of Harvard University Press, 1971.
viii, 252 p.; 21 cm. Originally published in 1728 in the author's An essay on the
nature and conduct of the passions and affections. 'Letters between the late Mr.
Gilbert Burnet, and Mr. Hutchinson [i.e. Hutcheson] concerning the true
foundation of virtue or moral goodness' (London, 1735) with special t.p. (p.
[197]-247) 1. Ethics I. Peach, Bernard, 1918- ed. II. Burnet, Gilbert,
1690-1726. Letters between the late Mr. Gilbert Burnet, and Mr. Hutcheson
concerning the true foundation of virtue or moral goodness. 1971. III. T.
BJ1005.H876 1971        170        LC 71-135545        ISBN 0674443268

**Hutcheson, Francis, 1694-1746.**                                    1.1429
An inquiry into the original of our ideas of beauty and virtue. — New York:
Garland Pub., 1971. xxvi, 304 p.; 21 cm. 'Facsimile ... made from a copy in the
Yale University Library [originally published in 1726]' 1. Ethics 2. Aesthetics
— Early works to 1800. I. T.
BJ1005.H88 1726a        170        LC 77-112157

**Smith, Adam.**                                    • 1.1430
Adam Smith's moral and political philosophy. New York: Hafner Pub. Co.,
1948. xxviii, 484 p. (Hafner library of classics; no.8.) All three works here
incorporated have been abridged. 1. Ethics 2. Economics I. T. II. Title:
Moral and political philosophy.
BJ1005 S59        170        LC 49-1022

**Bradley, Francis Herbert.**                                    • 1.1431
Ethical studies. 2d ed. rev. with additional notes by the author. With an introd.
by Richard Wollheim. — [London]: Oxford University Press, 1962. 344p.
(Oxford paperbacks, no.39.) 1. Ethics I. T.
BJ1008.B8 1962        170.81

**Green, Thomas Hill, 1836-1882.**                                    • 1.1432
Prolegomena to ethics. Edited by A. C. Bradley. New York, Crowell [1969] lvii,
427 p. 20 cm. (Apollo editions, A-232) Reprint of the 1890 ed. 1. Ethics
I. Bradley, A. C. (Andrew Cecil), 1851-1935. ed. II. T.
BJ1008.G64 1969        170        LC 71-94782

**Sidgwick, Henry, 1838-1900.**                                    • 1.1433
The methods of ethics / Henry Sidgwick. — [7th ed.]. — [Chicago]: University
of Chicago Press, 1962. xxxvi, 528 p. 1. Ethics I. T.
BJ1008.S5 1962        170 19        LC 62-15049

**Baier, Kurt.**                                    • 1.1434
The moral point of view; a rational basis of ethics. — Ithaca, Cornell University
Press [1958] 326 p. 23 cm. — (Contemporary philosophy) 1. Ethics I. T.
BJ1011.B25        170        LC 58-2113

**Edwards, Paul, 1923-.**                                    • 1.1435
The logic of moral discourse. With an introd. by Sidney Hook. — Glencoe, Ill.,
Free Press [1955] 248 p. 22 cm. 1. Ethics I. T.
BJ1011.E34        170        LC 55-7340

**Jordan, Elijah.**                                    1.1436
The good life / by E. Jordan. — [Chicago]: University of Chicago Press, 1949.
vi, 453 p. 1. Ethics I. T.
BJ1011.J6        LC 49-11893

**Moore, G. E. (George Edward), 1873-1958.**                                    • 1.1437
Ethics / G.E. Moore. — 2nd ed. — London; New York: Oxford U.P., 1966.
137 p.; 20 cm. — (Oxford paperbacks university series, opus; 10) 1. Ethics I. T.
BJ1011.M7 1966        LC 67-73816

**Nowell-Smith, Patrick Horace, 1914-.**                                    • 1.1438
Ethics. London, Baltimore, Penguin, 1954. 323 p. 19 cm. (Pelican books,
A293.) 1. Ethics I. T.
BJ1011.N68        LC 55-892

**Rashdall, Hastings, 1858-1924.**                                    • 1.1439
The theory of good and evil: a treatise on moral philosophy / by Hastings
Rashdall. — Oxford: Clarendon Press, 1907. 2 v. 1. Ethics 2. Good and evil
I. T.
BJ1011.R2

**Ross, W. D. (William David), 1877-.**    • **1.1440**
Foundations of ethics; the Gifford lectures delivered in the University of Aberdeen, 1935–6, by Sir W. David Ross ... — Oxford, The Clarendon press, 1939. xvi, 328, [2] p. 2 diagr. 23 cm. 1. Ethics I. T.
BJ1011.R75     170.4     *LC* 40-4299

**Russell, Bertrand, 1872-1970.**    • **1.1441**
Human society in ethics and politics. — London, Allen & Unwin [1954] 239 p. front. 22 cm. 1. Ethics 2. Social ethics 3. Political ethics I. T.
BJ1011.R87     *LC* 54-4060

**Singer, Marcus George, 1926-.**    • **1.1442**
Generalization in ethics; an essay in the logic of ethics, with the rudiments of a system of moral philosophy. — New York: Russell & Russell, [1971, c1961] 351, x p.; 22 cm. 1. Ethics I. T.
BJ1011.S55 1971     170     *LC* 70-152539

**Brandt, Richard B.**    **1.1443**
A theory of the good and the right / Richard B. Brandt. — Oxford: Clarendon Press; New York: Oxford University Press, 1979. xiii, 362 p.; 23 cm. Includes index. 1. Ethics I. T.
BJ1012.B63     170     *LC* 78-40647     *ISBN* 0198245505

**Campbell, Charles Arthur.**    • **1.1444**
In defence of free will, with other philosophical essays, by C. A. Campbell. — London: Allen & Unwin, 1967. 3-277 p.; 23 cm. — (Muirhead library of philosophy) 1. Ethics — Addresses, essays, lectures. 2. Knowledge, Theory of — Addresses, essays, lectures. I. T.
BJ1012.C3 1967     170     *LC* 67-91696

**Cua, A. S. (Antonio S.), 1932-.**    **1.1445**
Dimensions of moral creativity: paradigms, principles, and ideals / A. S. Cua. — University Park: Pennsylvania State University Press, c1978. 174 p.; 24 cm. Includes index. 1. Ethics I. T.
BJ1012.C8     170     *LC* 77-16169     *ISBN* 0271005408

**Donagan, Alan.**    **1.1446**
The theory of morality / Alan Donagan. — Chicago: University of Chicago Press, 1977. xvi, 278 p.; 23 cm. Includes index. 1. Ethics I. T.
BJ1012.D57     170     *LC* 76-25634     *ISBN* 0226155668

**Foot, Philippa.**    **1.1447**
Virtues and vices and other essays in moral philosophy / Philippa Foot. — Berkeley: University of California Press, 1978. xiv, 207 p.; 23 cm. 1. Ethics — Collected works. I. T.
BJ1012.F57 1978     170     *LC* 78-54794     *ISBN* 0520036867

**Frankena, William K.**    • **1.1448**
Ethics. — Englewood Cliffs, N.J.: Prentice-Hall, [1963] 109 p.; 23 cm. — (Prentice-Hall foundations of philosophy series) 1. Ethics I. T.
BJ1012.F7     170     *LC* 63-10527

**Fried, Charles, 1935-.**    **1.1449**
Right and wrong / Charles Fried. — Cambridge, Mass.: Harvard University Press, 1978. x, 226 p.; 24 cm. 1. Ethics 2. Right and wrong I. T.
BJ1012.F74     170     *LC* 77-16479     *ISBN* 0674769058

**Gewirth, Alan.**    **1.1450**
Reason and morality / Alan Gewirth. — Chicago: University of Chicago Press, 1978. xii, 393 p. ; 24 cm. 1. Ethics I. T.
BJ1012.G47     170     *LC* 77-13911     *ISBN* 0226288757

**Hare, R. M. (Richard Mervyn)**    • **1.1451**
Freedom and reason. Oxford, Clarendon Press, 1963. 228 p. 19 cm. 1. Ethics I. T.
BJ1012.H3     170     *LC* 63-1450

**Harman, Gilbert.**    **1.1452**
The nature of morality: an introduction to ethics / Gilbert Harman. New York: Oxford University Press, 1977. xiii, 165 p.; 25 cm. 1. Ethics I. T.
BJ1012.H317     160     *LC* 76-29806     *ISBN* 0195021428

**MacIntyre, Alasdair C.**    **1.1453**
After virtue: a study in moral theory / by Alasdair MacIntyre. — 2nd ed. — Notre Dame, Ind.: University of Notre Dame Press, 1984. xi, 286 p.; 24 cm. Includes index. 1. Ethics 2. Virtues 3. Virtue I. T.
BJ1012.M325 1984     170/.42 19     *LC* 83-40601     *ISBN* 0268006105

**Matters of life and death / Tom L. Beauchamp ... [et al.]; edited**    **1.1454**
**by Tom Regan.**
Philadelphia: Temple University Press, c1980. xvi, 343 p. 1. Ethics I. Beauchamp, Tom L. II. Regan, Tom.
BJ1012.M37     *LC* 79-3421     *ISBN* 0877221812

**Midgley, Mary, 1919-.**    **1.1455**
Animals and why they matter / Mary Midgley. — Athens: University of Georgia Press, 1984, c1983. 158 p.: ill.; 23 cm. 1. Ethics 2. Social ethics 3. Social contract 4. Animals I. T.
BJ1012.M5 1984     179/.3 19     *LC* 83-17933     *ISBN* 0820307041

**Midgley, Mary, 1919-.**    **1.1456**
Heart and mind: the varieties of moral experience / Mary Midgley. — New York: St. Martin's Press, c1981. x, 176 p.; 23 cm. 1. Ethics — Addresses, essays, lectures. I. T.
BJ1012.M52     170 19     *LC* 81-82751     *ISBN* 0312365888

**Murdoch, Iris.**    **1.1457**
The sovereignty of good. — New York: Schocken Books, [1971] 106 p.; 23 cm. — (Studies in ethics and the philosophy of religion) 1. Ethics — Addresses, essays, lectures. I. T.
BJ1012.M86 1971     170     *LC* 70-132197     *ISBN* 0805233857

**Murphy, Jeffrie G.**    **1.1458**
Evolution, morality, and the meaning of life / Jeffrie G. Murphy. — Totowa, N.J.: Rowman and Littlefield, 1982. xii, 158 p.; 22 cm. — (Philosophy and society.) Based on a series of lectures delivered at the University of Virginia in October 1981. 1. Ethics — Addresses, essays, lectures. 2. Evolution — Addresses, essays, lectures. 3. Sociobiology — Addresses, essays, lectures. 4. Meaning (Philosophy) — Addresses, essays, lectures. I. T. II. Series.
BJ1012.M88 1982     171 19     *LC* 82-9782     *ISBN* 084767147X

**Nielsen, Kai.**    **1.1459**
Ethics without God. — London: Pemberton; Buffalo: Prometheus Books, 1973. [7], 103 p.; 20 cm. — (The Humanist library) 1. Ethics I. T.
BJ1012.N53 1973     171     *LC* 73-179515     *ISBN* 0879750146

**Singer, Peter.**    **1.1460**
Practical ethics / Peter Singer. — Cambridge; New York: Cambridge University Press, 1979. viii, 237 p.; 21 cm. 1. Ethics 2. Social ethics I. T.
BJ1012.S49     170     *LC* 79-52328     *ISBN* 0521229200

**Stevenson, Charles L. (Charles Leslie), 1908-.**    • **1.1461**
Facts and values, studies in ethical analysis. — New Haven, Yale University Press, 1963. xi, 244 p. 21 cm. Bibliography: p. 233-235. 1. Ethics — Addresses, essays, lectures. 2. Semantics (Philosophy) — Addresses, essays, lectures. I. T.
BJ1012.S8     149.94     *LC* 63-7948

**Hare, R. M. (Richard Mervyn)**    • **1.1462**
The language of morals. Oxford [Eng.] Clarendon Press, 1952. 202 p. 20 cm. 1. Ethics I. T.
BJ1025.H3     170     *LC* 52-4801

**Wong, David B.**    **1.1463**
Moral relativity / David B. Wong. — Berkeley: University of California Press, c1984. xii, 248 p.; 24 cm. Includes index. 1. Ethical relativism I. T.
BJ1031.W65 1984     170/.42 19     *LC* 83-18073     *ISBN* 0520049764

**Walton, Craig, 1934-.**    **1.1464**
De la recherche du bien: a study of Malebranche's science of ethics. The Hague, Nijhoff, 1972. 178 p. 24 cm. (International archives of the history of ideas, 48) English text. 1. Malebranche, Nicolas, 1638-1715. Traité de morale. 2. Ethics — History. I. T.
BJ1051.M23 W33     *LC* 72-361345     *ISBN* 902471205X

**Beauvoir, Simone de, 1908-.**    • **1.1465**
The ethics of ambiguity; tr. from the French by Bernard Frechtman. New York, Philosophical Library [1949, c1948] 163 p. 23 cm. 1. Ethics I. Frechtman, Bernard, tr. II. T.
BJ1063.B382     *LC* 49-8287

**Brentano, Franz Clemens, 1838-1917.**    **1.1466**
[Grundlegung und Aufbau der Ethik. English] The foundation and construction of ethics compiled from his lectures on practical philosophy by Franziska Mayer–Hillebrand. English ed. edited and translated by Elizabeth Hughes Schneewind. New York: Humanities Press, 1973. viii, 390 p. 22 cm. (International library of philosophy and scientific method.) Translation of Grundlegung und Aufbau der Ethik. 1. Ethics I. Mayer, Franziska (von Reicher) 1885- ed. II. Schneewind, Elizabeth Hughes, ed. III. T. IV. Series.
BJ1111.B713 1973     170     *LC* 73-159255     *ISBN* 0391002546

# BJ1190–1292 Religious Ethics: Christian. Jewish. Islamic

**Long, Edward Le Roy.**     **1.1467**
A survey of recent Christian ethics / Edward LeRoy Long, Jr. — New York: Oxford University Press, 1982. xi, 215 p.; 22 cm. 1. Christian ethics — History — 20th century. I. T.
BJ1231.L66 1982     241/.09/048 19     LC 82-2099     *ISBN* 0195031598

**Ramsey, Paul.**     • **1.1468**
Nine modern moralists. Englewood Cliffs, N.J., Prentice-Hall [1962] 271 p. 20 cm. (A Spectrum book, S-36) 1. Christian ethics 2. Natural law I. T.
BJ1231.R3     241/.09/03 19     LC 62-13729

**Hauerwas, Stanley, 1940-.**     **1.1469**
Vision and virtue; essays in Christian ethical reflection. — Notre Dame, Ind.: Fides Publishers, [1974] ix, 264 p.; 22 cm. 1. Christian ethics — Addresses, essays, lectures. I. T.
BJ1241.H38     241     LC 74-9712     *ISBN* 0819004855

**Curran, Charles E.**     **1.1470**
Themes in fundamental moral theology / Charles E. Curran. — Notre Dame: University of Notre Dame Press, c1977. vii, 241 p.; 21 cm. 1. Christian ethics — Catholic authors — Addresses, essays, lectures. I. T.
BJ1249.C84     241/.04/2     LC 76-51614     *ISBN* 0268018332

**Häring, Bernhard.**     **1.1471**
Free and faithful in Christ: moral theology for clergy and laity / Bernard Häring. — New York: Crossroad, 1978-1981. 3 v.; 22 cm. 'A Crossroad book.' 1. Christian ethics — Catholic authors I. T.
BJ1249.H36     241/.042 19     LC 78-12253     *ISBN* 0816403988

**Gustafson, James M.**     **1.1472**
Ethics from a theocentric perspective / James M. Gustafson. — Chicago: University of Chicago Press, c1981-c1984. 2 v.; 24 cm. 1. Christian ethics 2. Ethics I. T.
BJ1251.G876     241 19     LC 81-11603     *ISBN* 0226311104

**Hauerwas, Stanley, 1940-.**     **1.1473**
A community of character: toward a constructive Christian social ethic / Stanley Hauerwas. — Notre Dame, Ind.: University of Notre Dame Press, c1981. x, 298 p.; 24 cm. 1. Christian ethics 2. Social ethics I. T.
BJ1251.H325     241 19     LC 80-53072     *ISBN* 0268007330

**Hauerwas, Stanley, 1940-.**     **1.1474**
Truthfulness and tragedy: further investigations in Christian ethics / Stanley Hauerwas with Richard Bondi and David B. Burrell. — Notre Dame, Ind.: University of Notre Dame Press, c1977. xii, 251 p.; 24 cm. 1. Christian ethics — Addresses, essays, lectures. 2. Social ethics — Addresses, essays, lectures. I. Bondi, Richard, joint author. II. Burrell, David B. joint author. III. T.
BJ1251.H33     241     LC 76-30425     *ISBN* 0268018316

**Niebuhr, Reinhold, 1892-1971.**     • **1.1475**
An interpretation of Christian ethics, by Reinhold Niebuhr. New York and London, Harper & brothers, 1935. 6 p. l., 3-244 p. 20 cm. 'The substance of these chapters was presented at the Rauschenbusch memorial lectures at Colgate-Rochester divinity school in the spring of 1934.'—Pref. 'First edition.' 1. Christian ethics 2. Love — Religious aspects — Christianity I. T.
BJ1251.N5     171.1     LC 35-27444

**Niebuhr, H. Richard (Helmut Richard), 1894-1962.**     • **1.1476**
The responsible self; an essay in Christian moral philosophy. With an introd. by James M. Gustafson. [1st ed.] New York, Harper & Row [1963] 183 p. 22 cm. 1. Christian ethics I. T.
BJ1251.N52 1963     171.1     LC 63-15955

**Tillich, Paul, 1886-1965.**     • **1.1477**
Morality and beyond. — [1st ed.]. — New York, Harper & Row [c1963] 95 p. 21 cm. — (Religious perspectives. v. 9) 1. Christian ethics I. T. II. Series.
BJ1251.T47     171.1     LC 63-18280

**Barth, Karl, 1886-1968.**     **1.1478**
[Christliche Leben. English] The Christian life: church dogmatics IV, 4: lecture fragments / by Karl Barth; translated by Geoffrey W. Bromiley. — Grand Rapids, Mich.: Eerdmans Pub. Co., c1981. xv, 310 p.; 24 cm. Translation of Das christliche Leben. 1. Christian ethics — Reformed authors 2. Reconciliation — Religious aspects — Christianity. I. T.
BJ1253.B3413     241 19     LC 80-39942     *ISBN* 0802835236

**Barth, Karl, 1886-1968.**     **1.1479**
[Ethik. English] Ethics / Karl Barth; edited by Dietrich Braun; translated by Geoffrey W. Bromiley. — New York: Seabury Press, 1981. x, 534 p.; 25 cm. Translation of Ethik. 1. Christian ethics — Reformed authors — Addresses, essays, lectures. I. Braun, Dietrich, 1928- II. T.
BJ1253.B3513     241 19     LC 80-29327     *ISBN* 0816404844

**Bonhoeffer, Dietrich, 1906-1945.**     • **1.1480**
Ethics. Edited by Eberhard Bethge. [Translated by Neville Horton Smith] New York, Macmillan, 1955. xii, 340 p. 22 cm. (The Library of philosophy and theology) 1. Christian ethics I. T.
BJ1253.B615 1955a     171.1     LC 55-12644

**Brunner, Emil, 1889-1966.**     • **1.1481**
The divine imperative / [by] Emil Brunner ... translated by Olive Wyon. — Philadelphia: The Westminster press, [1947] 728 p.; 23.5 cm. At head of title: A study in Christian ethics. Bibliographical references in 'Notes and appendices' (p. 569-719) 1. Christian ethics 2. Sociology, Christian 3. Social ethics I. Wyon, Olive, 1890- tr. II. T.
BJ1253.B73 1947     171.1     LC 47-2443

**Cordovero, Moses ben Jacob, 1522-1570.**     **1.1482**
[Tomer Devorah. English] The palm tree of Deborah / Moses Cordovero; translated from the Hebrew with an introd. and notes by Louis Jacobs. — New York: Hermon Press, 1974, c1960. 133 p.; 24 cm. Translation of Tomer Devorah. Reprint of the ed. published by Vallentine, Mitchell, London. 1. Ethics, Jewish — Early works to 1800. I. T.
BJ1287.C63 T63 1974     296.3/8     LC 73-93366     *ISBN* 0872030393

**Al-Tusi, Nasir al-Din Muhammad ibn Muhammad, 1201-1274.**     **1.1483**
The Nasirean ethics, by Nasir ad-Din Tusi, tr. from the Persian by G.M. Wickens. London Allen and Unwin [1964] 352p. (UNESCO collection of representative works: Persian series) I. Wickens, G. M. ed. and tr. II. T. III. Title: Akhlaq-i Nasiri IV. Series.
PK6550 T8 A163 1964     BJ1291.T7813.

# BJ1298–1388 Evolutionary and Genetic Ethics. Socialist Ethics

**Huxley, Thomas Henry, 1825-1895.**     • **1.1484**
Touchstone for ethics, 1893-1943 [by] Thomas H. Huxley and Julian Huxley. Freeport, N.Y., Books for Libraries Press [1971, c1947] viii, 257 p. 23 cm. (Essay index reprint series) 1. Ethics, Evolutionary I. Huxley, Julian, 1887-1975. II. T.
BJ1311.H8 1971     171/.7     LC 74-156661     *ISBN* 0836924029

**Fisk, Milton.**     **1.1485**
Ethics and society: a Marxist interpretation of value / Milton Fisk. — New York: New York University Press, 1980. xx, 272 p.; 25 cm. 1. Socialist ethics 2. Social ethics I. T.
BJ1388.F57 1980     170     LC 79-3513     *ISBN* 0814725643

# BJ1400–1500 Special Topics

## BJ1400–1429.5 Good and Evil. Right and Wrong. Truth and Falsehood. Lying. Secrecy

**Evans, G. R. (Gillian Rosemary)**     **1.1486**
Augustine on evil / G.R. Evans. — Cambridge [Cambridgeshire]; New York: Cambridge University Press, 1982. xiv, 198 p.; 22 cm. Includes index. 1. Augustine, Saint, Bishop of Hippo. 2. Good and evil — History. I. T.
BJ1401.E77 1982     241/.092/4 19     LC 81-21793     *ISBN* 0521245265

**Lewis, C. S. (Clive Staples), 1898-1963.**     • **1.1487**
The great divorce, by C. S. Lewis. New York, The Macmillan company, 1946. viii, 1 l., 133 p. 19 cm. 'First printing.' 1. Good and evil I. T.
BJ1401.L4     237     LC 46-1417

**Midgley, Mary, 1919-.**     **1.1488**
Wickedness: a philosophical essay / Mary Midgley. — London; Boston: Routledge & Kegan Paul, 1984. viii, 224 p.; 23 cm. 1. Good and evil — Addresses, essays, lectures. I. T.
BJ1401.M52 1984     170 19     LC 84-3257     *ISBN* 071009759X

**O'Flaherty, Wendy Doniger.**     **1.1489**
The origins of evil in Hindu mythology / Wendy Doniger O'Flaherty. Berkeley: University of California Press, c1976. xi, 411 p.; 25 cm. (Hermeneutics, studies in the history of religions; 6) Includes index. 1. Good and evil (Hinduism) I. T. II. Series.
BJ1401.O35     294.5/2     *LC* 75-40664     *ISBN* 0520031636

**Ross, W. D. (William David), 1877-.**     • **1.1490**
The right and the good [by] W. D. Ross ... — Oxford, The Clarendon press, 1930. vi p., 1 l., 176 p. 23 cm. 1. Good and evil 2. Duty I. T.
BJ1401.R6     170     *LC* 31-7002

**Buber, Martin, 1878-1965.**     • **1.1491**
[Tsedek veha-'avel 'al-pi tseror mizmore Tehilim. English] Good and evil, two interpretations: I. right and wrong. [Translated by Ronald Gregor Smith] II. Images of good and evil. [Translated by Michael Bullock] New York, Scribner, 1953. 143 p. 20 cm. A Hebrew version of the first essay was published in 1950 under title: ha-Tsedek veha-'avel 'al-pi tseror mizmore Tehilim; the second essay is a translation of Bilder von Gut und Böse. 1. Good and evil — Biblical teaching. I. Buber, Martin, 1878-1965. Bilder von Gut und Böse. English. 1953. II. T. III. Title: Right and wrong. IV. Title: Images of good and evil.
BJ1406.B7713     111.84     *LC* 53-8318

**Bok, Sissela.**     **1.1492**
Lying: moral choice in public and private life / by Sissela Bok. — 1st ed. — New York: Pantheon Books, c1978. xxii, 326 p.; 22 cm. Includes index. 1. Truthfulness and falsehood I. T.
BJ1421.B64     177/.3     *LC* 77-88779     *ISBN* 0394413700

**Bok, Sissela.**     **1.1493**
Secrets: on the ethics of concealment and revelation / Sissela Bok. — 1st ed. — New York: Pantheon Books, [1983] c1982. xviii, 332 p.; 24 cm. 1. Secrecy — Moral and ethical aspects. I. T.
BJ1429.5.B64 1983     177 19     *LC* 82-47891     *ISBN* 0394515811

## BJ1450–1468 Duty. Obligation. Responsibility. Freedom of the Will

**Ingarden, Roman, 1893-.**     **1.1494**
Man and value / Roman Ingarden; translation by Arthur Szylewicz. — Washington, D.C.: Catholic University of America Press; München: Philosophia Verlag, 1984 [c1983] 184 p.; 23 cm. — (Philosophia resources library.) Includes translation of: Książeczka o człowieku and Über die Verantwortung. 1. Responsibility — Addresses, essays, lectures. 2. Man — Addresses, essays, lectures. 3. Values — Addresses, essays, lectures. I. Ingarden, Roman, 1893- Książeczka o człowieku. English. 1983. II. Ingarden, Roman, 1893- Über die Verantwortung. English. 1983. III. T. IV. Series.
BJ1453.I49 1983     170 19     *LC* 83-15245     *ISBN* 0813205921

**Jonas, Hans, 1903-.**     **1.1495**
[Prinzip Verantwortung. English] The imperative of responsibility: in search of an ethics for the technological age / Hans Jonas; translated by Hans Jonas, with the collaboration of David Herr. — Chicago: University of Chicago Press, 1984. xii, 255 p.; 24 cm. Translation of: Das Prinzip Verantwortung. Includes index. 1. Responsibility 2. Technology — Moral and ethical aspects 3. Ethics I. T.
BJ1453.J6613 1984     170/.42 19     *LC* 83-18249     *ISBN* 0226405966

**Luther and Erasmus: Free will and salvation.**     • **1.1496**
Philadelphia: Westminster Press [1969] xiv, 348 p.; 24 cm. (The Library of Christian classics, v. 17) 'Erasmus: De libero arbitrio, translated and edited by E. Gordon Rupp, in collaboration with A. N. Marlow': p. [33]-97. 'Luther: De servo arbitrio, translated and edited by Philip S. Watson, in collaboration with B. Drewery': p. [99]-334. 1. Free will and determinism I. Luther, Martin, 1483-1546. De servo arbitrio. English. 1969. II. Erasmus, Desiderius, d. 1536. De libero arbitrio diatribē. English. 1969. III. Rupp, E. Gordon (Ernest Gordon), 1910- tr. IV. Watson, Philip S. (Philip Saville), 1909- tr. V. Series.
BJ1461.L8     234/.9     *LC* 76-79870     *ISBN* 0664220177

**Luther, Martin, 1483-1546.**     • **1.1497**
Martin Luther on the bondage of the will: a new translation of De servo arbitrio (1525), Martin Luther's reply to Erasmus of Rotterdam / by J.I. Packer and O.R. Johnston. — Westwood, N.J.: Fleming H. Revell, c1957. 322 p. 1. Free will and determinism I. Packer, J.I. II. Johnston, O.R. III. De servo arbitrio. IV. T. V. Title: Bondage of the will.
BJ1461.L88 1957     *LC* 58-8660

**Schopenhauer, Arthur, 1788-1860.**     • **1.1498**
Essay on the freedom of the will / Arthur Schopenhauer; translated with an introd. by Konstantin Kolenda. — New York: Liberal Arts Press, [1960] xx, 103 p.; 21 cm. — (The Library of liberal arts. no. 70) Translation of Ueber die Freiheit des menschlichen Willens. 1. Free will and determinism I. T. II. Title: On the freedom of the will. III. Series.
BJ1463.S37 1960     *LC* 59-11675

## BJ1470–1487 Self–realization. Conscience. Altruism. Happiness

**Norton, David L.**     **1.1499**
Personal destinies: a philosophy of ethical individualism / by David L. Norton. Princeton, N.J.: Princeton University Press, c1976. xiv, 398 p.; 22 cm. Includes index. 1. Self-realization 2. Social ethics I. T.
BJ1470.N68     170/.202     *LC* 76-3011     *ISBN* 0691072159

**Amato, Joseph Anthony.**     **1.1500**
Guilt and gratitude: a study of the origins of contemporary conscience / Joseph Anthony Amato II; foreword by Thaddeus C. Radzialowski. — Westport, Conn.: Greenwood Press, c1982. xxv, 218 p.; 22 cm. — (Contributions in philosophy. 0084-926X; no. 20) Includes index. 1. Conscience 2. Guilt 3. Gratitude I. T. II. Series.
BJ1471.A468 1982     170/.42 19     *LC* 81-6991     *ISBN* 0313229465

**Roberts, Tom Aerwyn.**     **1.1501**
The concept of benevolence: aspects of eighteenth–century moral philosophy [by] T. A. Roberts. — London: Macmillan, 1973. [7], 119 p.; 23 cm. — (New studies in practical philosophy) 1. Benevolence I. T.
BJ1474.R6     170/.1/9     *LC* 73-155652     *ISBN* 0333120558

**Noddings, Nel.**     **1.1502**
Caring, a feminine approach to ethics & moral education / Nel Noddings. — Berkeley: University of California Press, c1984. xi, 216 p.; 24 cm. Includes index. 1. Caring — Moral and ethical aspects. 2. Ethics 3. Women — Psychology 4. Moral education I. T.
BJ1475.N62 1984     170 19     *LC* 83-18223     *ISBN* 0520050436

**Gosling, J. C. B. (Justin Cyril Bertrand)**     **1.1503**
The Greeks on pleasure / J.C.B. Gosling and C.C.W. Taylor. — Oxford [Oxfordshire]: Clarendon Press; New York: Oxford University Press, 1982. xiii, 497 p.; 23 cm. Includes indexes. 1. Pleasure 2. Philosophy, Ancient I. Taylor, C. C. W. (Christopher Charles Whiston), 1936- II. T.
BJ1481.G636 1982     128 19     *LC* 82-7940     *ISBN* 0198246668

**Russell, Bertrand, 1872-1970.**     • **1.1504**
The conquest of happiness. New York, Liveright, [1971, c1930] 249 p. 21 cm. 'Liveright, L-44.' 1. Happiness I. T.
BJ1481.R75 1971     131.3     *LC* 74-149626     *ISBN* 0871400510

**Murphy, James Frederick, 1943-.**     **1.1505**
Concepts of leisure / James F. Murphy. — 2d ed. — Englewood Cliffs, NJ: Prentice-Hall, c1981. xi, 210 p.: ill.; 24 cm. 1. Leisure I. T.
BJ1498.M87 1981     790/.01/35 19     *LC* 80-22349     *ISBN* 013166512X

# BJ1518–1535 Individual Ethics. Character

**Edwards, Jonathan, 1703-1758.**     • **1.1506**
The nature of true virtue. With a foreword by William K. Frankena. — [Ann Arbor]: University of Michigan Press, [1960] xiii, 107 p.; 21 cm. — (Ann Arbor paperbacks, AA37) 1. Virtue I. T.
BJ1520.E3     170     *LC* 60-1751

**Mandeville, Bernard, 1670-1733.**     • **1.1507**
The fable of the bees: or, Private vices, publick benefits. By Bernard Mandeville. With a commentary critical, historical, and explanatory by F. B. Kaye ... — Oxford, The Clarendon press, 1924. 2 v. front., facsims., geneal. tab. 23 cm. With reproductions of original title-pages. Part I of the Fable, from the 6th edition, 1732, consists of the original poem, the 'Grumbling hive: or, Knaves turn'd honest', first published in 1705, with prose commentary: An enquiry into the origin of moral virtue; Remarks; An essay on charity and charity-schools; a Search into the nature of society; a Vindication of the book. Part II, from the first edition, 1729, consists of preface and six prose dialogues, amplifying and defending his doctrines. 1. Ethics 2. Virtue 3. Charity-schools I. Kaye, Frederick Benjamin, 1892-1930, ed. II. T.
BJ1520.M4 1924     *LC* 25-7869

**Tillich, Paul, 1886-1965.**     • **1.1508**
The courage to be. — New Haven: Yale University Press, 1952. 197 p.; 22 cm. — (The Terry lectures) 1. Courage 2. Ontology 3. Anxiety 4. Existentialism I. T.
BJ1533.C8 T5     179.6     *LC* 52-9261

**Royce, Josiah, 1855-1916.** • **1.1509**
The philosophy of loyalty. — New York: Hafner Pub. Co., 1971 [c1908] xiii, 409 p.; 23 cm. 'Facsimile of the 1924 edition.' 1. Loyalty I. T.
BJ1533.L8 R6 1908a     177    *LC* 76-153586

# BJ1545–2193 Conduct of Life. Etiquette

**Yüan, Ts'ai, chin shih 1163.**    **1.1510**
[Yüan shih shih fan. English] Family and property in Sung China: Yüan Ts'ai's Precepts for social life / translated, with annotations and introduction by Patricia Buckley Ebrey. — Princeton, N.J.: Princeton University Press, c1984. x, 367 p.; 23 cm. — (Princeton library of Asian translations.) Includes index. 1. Conduct of life — Early works to 1900 2. Family — China. 3. Property — China. 4. Upper classes — China. 5. China — Social life and customs I. Ebrey, Patricia Buckley, 1947- II. T. III. Series.
BJ1558.C5 Y8313 1984    646.7/8 19    *LC* 84-42580    *ISBN* 0691054266

**Oakeshott, Michael Joseph, 1901-.**    **1.1511**
On human conduct / by Michael Oakeshott. — Oxford [Eng.]: Clarendon Press, 1975. x, 329 p.; 23 cm. 1. Conduct of life 2. Social contract 3. Europe — Politics and government — 1492-1648 I. T.
BJ1581.2.O2    320.5    *LC* 75-323711    *ISBN* 0198271956

**Woodhouse, John Robert.**    **1.1512**
Baldesar Castiglione: a reassessment of The courtier / J. R. Woodhouse. — [Edinburgh]: Edinburgh University Press, [c1978] xi, 217 p.: port.; 22 cm. — (Writers of Italy series; 7) Includes index. 1. Castiglione, Baldassarre, conte, 1478-1529. Il libro del cortegiano. 2. Courts and courtiers 3. Courtesy I. T.
BJ1604.C33 W66    170/.44 19    *LC* 79-307263    *ISBN* 0852243464

**Castiglione, Baldassare.**    **1.1513**
The book of the courtier / [by] Baldesar Castiglione; translated [from the Italian] and with an introduction by George Bull. Harmondsworth [etc.]: Penguin, 1976. 367 p.; 19 cm. (Penguin classics.) Translation of: 'Il Libro del cortegiano'. Venice: Aldo Ramaro and Andred d'Asola, 1528. 1. Courts and courtiers I. Bull, George. II. T. III. Series.
BJ1604.C37 1976x    395    *ISBN* 0140441921 pa

**Astell, Mary, 1668-1731.**    **1.1514**
A serious proposal to the ladies. 4th ed. [New York] Source Book Press 1971 (c1970) 162p. 1. Women — Conduct of life I. T.
BJ1609 A88 1701A

**Christine, de Pisan, ca. 1364-ca. 1431.**    **1.1515**
[Trésor de la cité des dames. English] The treasure of the city of ladies, or, The book of the three virtues / Christine de Pisan; translated with an introduction by Sarah Lawson. — Harmondsworth, Middlesex, England; New York, N.Y., U.S.A.: Penguin, 1985. 179 p.; 20 cm. Translation of: Le trésor de la cité des dames. 1. Women — Conduct of life — Early works to 1800. 2. Women — Religious life — Early works to 1800. I. T. II. Title: Treasure of the city of ladies. III. Title: Book of the three virtues.
BJ1609.C4713 1985    170/.2/0244 19    *LC* 85-152226    *ISBN* 014044453X

**Simon, Sidney B.**    **1.1516**
Beginning values clarification: a guidebook for the use of values clarification in the classroom / Sidney B. Simon, Jay Clark. — San Diego, Calif.: Pennant Press, c1975. 183 p.: ill.; 22 cm. On cover: Strategies for the classroom. 1. Youth 2. Moral education I. Clark, Jay. II. T.
BJ1631.S3    370.114    *ISBN* 0913458236

**Post, Emily, 1873-1960.**    • **1.1517**
[Etiquette in society, in business, in politics, and at home] Emily Post's Etiquette. — 14th ed. / Elizabeth L. Post. — New York: Harper & Row, c1984. xiv, 1018 p.: ill.; 25 cm. First published in 1922 under title: Etiquette in society, in business, in politics, and at home. Includes index. 1. Etiquette I. Post, Elizabeth L. II. T. III. Title: Etiquette.
BJ1853.P6 1984    395 19    *LC* 83-48375    *ISBN* 0061816833

**Vanderbilt, Amy.**    • **1.1518**
[Etiquette] The Amy Vanderbilt complete book of etiquette: a guide to contemporary living / rev. and expanded by Letitia Baldrige; drawings by Mona Marks. — 1st ed. — Garden City, N.Y.: Doubleday, 1978. xxix, 879 p.; 24 cm. Includes index. 1. Etiquette I. Baldrige, Letitia. II. T. III. Title: Etiquette.
BJ1853.V27 1978    395    *LC* 77-16896    *ISBN* 0385133758

## BL RELIGIONS. MYTHOLOGY. RATIONALISM

## BL1–50 General Works

**Religion, power, and protest in local communities: the northern**  **1.1519**
**shore of the Mediterranean / edited by Eric R. Wolf.**
Berlin; New York: Mouton, c1984. vi, 275 p., [12] p. of plates: ill.; 24 cm.
(Religion and society; 24) Contributions to a conference held at the Free
University of Amsterdam, 1979. 1. Mediterranean Region — Religion —
Congresses. I. Wolf, Eric Robert, 1923-
BL21.R433 1984      306/.6/091822 19      *LC* 84-8407      *ISBN*
3110097834

**Smith, Wilfred Cantwell, 1916-.**      • **1.1520**
Questions of religious truth. New York, Scribner [1967] 127 p. 21 cm. 'The
material ... was delivered first as the Taylor lectures for 1963 at Yale Divinity
School, except the opening chapter.' 1. Religion — Addresses, essays, lectures.
2. Truth — Addresses, essays, lectures. I. T.
BL27.S45      200      *LC* 67-14494

**Stephen, Leslie, Sir, 1832-1904.**      **1.1521**
An agnostic's apology, and other essays. 2d ed. New York: Putnam; London:
Smith, Elder, 1903. 367p. 1. Agnosticism I. T.
BL27 S7 1903

## BL31 DICTIONARIES. ENCYCLOPEDIAS

**Abingdon dictionary of living religions / Keith Crim, general**      **1.1522**
**editor; Roger A. Bullard, Larry D. Shinn, associate editors.**
Nashville, Tenn.: Abingdon, c1981. xviii, 830 p., [8] leaves of plates: ill. (some
col.); 26 cm. 1. Religions — Dictionaries. I. Crim, Keith R. II. Bullard, Roger
Aubrey. III. Shinn, Larry D., 1942- IV. Title: Dictionary of living religions.
BL31.A24      291/.03/21 19      *LC* 81-1465      *ISBN* 0687004098

**A Dictionary of comparative religion. General editor: S. G. F.**      • **1.1523**
**Brandon.**
New York, Scribner [1970] 704 p. 27 cm. 1. Religions — Dictionaries.
I. Brandon, S. G. F. (Samuel George Frederick), 1907-1971. ed.
BL31.D54 1970      291/.03      *LC* 76-111390

**Hastings, James, 1852-1922.**      • **1.1524**
Encyclopoedia of religion and ethics, edited by James Hastings with the
assistance of John A. Selbie and other scholars. New York: Scribner;
Edinburgh: T.&T. Clark, 1924-1927. 13 v.: illus., plates, plans, facsims., tables,
29 cm. Vols. 6-12 'edited by James Hastings, with the assistance of John A.
Selbie and Louis H. Gray. Vols.1-2, 1926; v.3, 1924; v.4-6, 1925; v.7-8, 1926;
v.9-12, 1925; v.[13] 1927. 1. Religion — Dictionaries. 2. Ethics —
Dictionaries. 3. Theology — Dictionaries I. Selbie, John Alexander,
1856-1931, joint editor. II. Gray, Louis Herbert, 1875-1955, joint editor.
III. T.
BL31.E4 1924      203      *LC* 30-20143

**The Encyclopedia of religion / Mircea Eliade, editor in chief;**      **1.1525**
**[editors, Charles J. Adams ... et al.].**
New York, N.Y.: Macmillan, c1987. 16 v. 1. Religion — Dictionaries.
I. Eliade, Mircea, 1907- II. Adams, Charles J.
BL31.E46 1986      200/.3/21 19      *LC* 86-5432      *ISBN* 0029094801

**The Facts on File dictionary of religions / edited by John R.**      **1.1526**
**Hinnells.**
New York: Facts on File, c1984. 550 p.: ill., maps; 23 cm. Includes indexes.
1. Religions — Dictionaries. I. Hinnells, John R. II. Facts on File, Inc.
III. Title: Religions. IV. Title: Dictionary of religions.
BL31.F33 1984      291/.03/21 19      *LC* 83-20834      *ISBN* 0871968622

## BL48–50 RELIGION, GENERAL

**Chesterton, G. K. (Gilbert Keith), 1874-1936.**      • **1.1527**
The everlasting man / by G. K. Chesterton ... — New York: Dodd, Mead &
company, 1925. xxv, 344 p.; 21 cm. 1. Religion 2. Christianity and other
religions 3. Catholic Church — Apologetic works I. T.
BL48.C5 1925a      *LC* 25-23426

**Dewey, John, 1859-1952.**      • **1.1528**
A common faith [by] John Dewey ... New Haven, Yale university press [c1934]
3 p.l., 87 p. 21 cm. (Half-title: The Terry lectures) 1. Religion I. T.
BL48.D4      201      *LC* 34-27264

**Douglas, Mary.**      **1.1529**
Natural symbols; explorations in cosmology [by] Mary Douglas. [1st American
ed.] New York, Pantheon Books [1970] xvii, 177 p. 22 cm. 1. Body, Human —
Religious aspects 2. Body, Human — Mythology 3. Symbolism 4. Ritual
I. T.
BL48.D67 1970b      301.5/8      *LC* 77-110128

**Eliade, Mircea, 1907-.**      **1.1530**
[Histoire des croyances et des idées religieuses. English] A history of religious
ideas / Mircea Éliade; translated from the French by Willard R. Trask. —
Chicago: University of Chicago Press, c1978-c1985. 3 v.; 24 cm. Translation of
Histoire des croyances et des idées religieuses. Vol. 3 translated by Alf
Hiltebeitel and Diane Apostolow-Cappadona. 1. Religion — History.
2. Religions — History. I. T.
BL48.E3813      291      *LC* 77-16784      *ISBN* 0226204006

**Eliade, Mircea, 1907-.**      • **1.1531**
The sacred and the profane; the nature of religion. Translated from the French
by Willard R. Trask. — [1st American ed.]. — New York, Harcourt, Brace
[1959] 256 p. 22 cm. Includes bibliography. 1. Religion I. T.
BL48.E413      290      *LC* 58-10904 rev

**Huxley, Julian, 1887-1975.**      • **1.1532**
Religion without revelation, by Julian Huxley. New ed. London, Watts, 1967.
viii, 203 p. 19 cm. (The New thinker's library, no. 19) 1. Religion I. T.
BL48.H8 1967      210      *LC* 68-79651

**La Barre, Weston, 1911-.**      **1.1533**
The ghost dance; origins of religion. — [1st ed.]. — Garden City, N.Y.:
Doubleday, 1970. xvi, 677 p.; 24 cm. 1. Religion 2. Psychology, Religious
I. T.
BL48.L25      200      *LC* 71-89094

**Mencken, H. L. (Henry Louis), 1880-1956.**      • **1.1534**
Treatise on the gods [by] H. L. Mencken. — 2d ed.: corr. and rewritten. — New
York, A. A. Knopf, 1965[c1946] ix, 302, xvii p., 1 l. 22 cm. 'Bibliographical
note': p. 294-302. 1. Religion 2. Gods I. T.
BL48.M4 1946      290      *LC* 46-6976

**Otto, Rudolf, 1869-1937.**      • **1.1535**
The idea of the holy; an inquiry into the non–rational factor in the idea of the
divine and its relation to the rational. Translated by John W. Harvey. — New
York, Oxford University Press, 1958. xix, 232 p. 21 cm. — (A Galaxy book,
GB14) Translation of Das Heilige. Bibliographical footnotes. 1. Religion I. T.
BL48.O82 1958      201      *LC* 58-776

**Schleiermacher, Friedrich, 1768-1834.**      • **1.1536**
[Über die Religion. English] On religion: addresses in response to its cultured
critics. Translated, with introd. and notes, by Terrence N. Tice. Richmond,
John Knox Press [1969] 383 p. 21 cm. (Research in theology) Translation of
Über die Religion. 1. Religion I. Tice, Terrence N. ed. II. T.
BL48.S33 1969      200      *LC* 72-82936      *ISBN* 0804206732

**Smart, Ninian, 1927-.**      **1.1537**
The phenomenon of religion [by] Ninian Smart. — [New York]: Herder and
Herder, [1973] v, 157 p.; 22 cm. — (Philosophy of religion series) 1. Religion
I. T.
BL48.S592 1973b      200/.1      *LC* 72-8067      *ISBN* 0070737932

**Whitehead, Alfred North, 1861-1947.**      • **1.1538**
Religion in the making; Lowell lectures, 1926, by Alfred North Whitehead ...
New York, The Macmillan Company, 1926. 160 p. 20 cm. 1. Religion
I. Lowell Institute lectures, 1926. II. T.
BL48.W35      *LC* 26-15643

**Durkheim, Emile, 1858-1917.** **1.1539**
Durkheim on religion: a selection of readings with bibliographies / [compiled by] W. S. F. Pickering; new translations by Jacqueline Redding and W. S. F. Pickering. — London; Boston: Routledge & K. Paul, 1975. x, 376 p.; 23 cm. 1. Religion — Addresses, essays, lectures. I. Pickering, W. S. F. II. T.
BL50.D85 1975    200    *LC* 75-325445    *ISBN* 0710081081

**James, William, 1842-1910.** **1.1540**
Essays in religion and morality / William James; [Frederick H. Burkhardt, general editor; Fredson Bowers, textual editor; Ignas K. Skrupskelis, associate editor; introduction by John J. McDermott]. — Cambridge, Mass.: Harvard University Press, 1982. xxviii, 345 p.: port.; 24 cm. — (The works of William James) Includes index. 1. Religion — Addresses, essays, lectures. 2. Ethics — Addresses, essays, lectures. I. Burkhardt, Frederick, 1912- II. Bowers, Fredson Thayer. III. Skrupskelis, Ignas K., 1938- IV. T.
BL50.J35 1982    200 19    *LC* 81-7040    *ISBN* 0674267354

**Toynbee, Arnold Joseph, 1889-1975.** **1.1541**
An historian's approach to religion / Arnold Toynbee. — 2d ed. — Oxford; New York: Oxford University Press, 1979. xiii, 340 p.; 23 cm. Includes the author's essay Gropings in the dark. 1. Religion — Addresses, essays, lectures. 2. Civilization, Occidental — History — Addresses, essays, lectures. I. T.
BL50.T69 1979    200 19    *LC* 78-40535    *ISBN* 0192152602

# BL51 Philosophy of Religion

**Bloch, Ernst, 1885-1977.** • **1.1542**
[Religion im Erbe. English] Man on his own; essays in the philosophy of religion. Translated by E. B. Ashton. [New York] Herder and Herder [1970] 240 p. 22 cm. Translation of Religion im Erbe. 1. Religion — Philosophy — Addresses, essays, lectures. I. T.
BL51.B584513    200/.1    *LC* 79-87749

**Buber, Martin, 1878-1965.** • **1.1543**
Eclipse of God; studies in the relation between religion and philosophy. — New York, Harper [1957, c1952] 148 p. 21 cm. — (Harper torchbooks, TB12) Includes bibliography. 1. Religion — Philosophy 2. Philosophy and religion I. T.
BL51.B82 1957    201    *LC* 61-678

**Burtt, Edwin A. (Edwin Arthur), 1892-.** • **1.1544**
Types of religious philosophy. Rev. ed. New York, Harper [1951] xi, 468 p. 22 cm. Includes bibliographies. 1. Religion — Philosophy 2. Religion — Philosophy — History. I. T.
BL51.B87 1951    201    *LC* 51-11521

**Collins, James Daniel.** • **1.1545**
The emergence of philosophy of religion, by James Collins. New Haven, Yale University Press, 1967. xv, 517 p. 25 cm. (St. Thomas More lectures; 1963) Bibliography: p. [492]-506. 1. Religion — Philosophy — History. I. T. II. Series.
BL51.C62    200.1    *LC* 67-13432

**Hegel, Georg Wilhelm Friedrich, 1770-1831.** • **1.1546**
Lectures on the philosophy of religion, together with a work on the proofs of the existence of God. London, K. Paul, Trench, Trübner, & co., ltd., 1895. 3 v. 22 cm. 1. Religion — Philosophy I. Speirs, Ebenezer Brown, ed. and tr. II. Sanderson, Miss J. Burdon, joint tr. III. T.
BL51.H4    *LC* 01-6792

**Heschel, Abraham Joshua, 1907-1972.** **1.1547**
Man is not alone; a philosophy of religion. — New York: Farrar, Straus & Young, 1951. 305 p.; 22 cm. 1. Religion — Philosophy 2. Judaism I. T.
BL51.H476    201    *LC* 51-9992

**Hick, John.** • **1.1548**
Faith and knowledge. — 2d ed. — Ithaca, N.Y.: Cornell University Press, [1966] x, 268 p.; 23 cm. 1. Knowledge, Theory of (Religion) 2. Faith I. T.
BL51.H49 1966    201    *LC* 66-28018

**Hocking, William Ernest.** • **1.1549**
The meaning of God in human experience: a philosophic study of religion / by William Ernest Hocking. — New Haven: Yale University Press, 1912. xxxix, 586 p., 1 l. 23.5 cm. 1. Religion — Philosophy 2. God I. T.
BL51.H6    *LC* 12-14946

**Hügel, Friedrich, Freiherr von, 1852-1925.** • **1.1550**
Essays & addresses on the philosophy of religion, by Baron Friedrich von Hügel. London & Toronto, J. M. Dent & sons limited; New York, E. P. Dutton & co., 1921. xix, 308 p. 24 cm. 1. Jesus Christ — Messiahship 2. Troeltsch, Ernst, 1865-1923. 3. Catholic Church — Doctrinal and controversial works —

Catholic authors. 4. Religion — Philosophy 5. Theism 6. Heaven 7. Hell I. T.
BL51.H9    201/.1    *LC* a 21-1966

**Hume, David, 1711-1776.** **1.1551**
The natural history of religion / by David Hume; edited by A. Wayne Colver, and Dialogues concerning natural religion / by David Hume; edited by John Valdimir Price. — Oxford [Eng.]: Clarendon Press, 1976. 299 p.; 22 cm. The natural history of religion is from the text of the 1st ed. of 1757; Dialogues concerning natural religion is edited from the author's original manuscript. Includes index. 1. Religion — Philosophy 2. Natural theology — Early works to 1900 I. Hume, David, 1711-1776. Dialogues concerning natural religion. 1976. II. Colver, A. Wayne (Anthony Wayne) III. Price, John Valdimir. IV. T. V. Title: The natural history of religion.
BL51.H963 1976    210    *LC* 77-354407    *ISBN* 0198243790

**Jaspers, Karl, 1883-1969.** • **1.1552**
[Frage der Entmythologisierung. English] Myth and Christianity; an inquiry into the possibility of religion without myth, by Karl Jaspers and Rudolf Bultmann. New York, Noonday Press [1958] 116 p. 21 cm. Translation of Die Frage der Entmythologisierung. 1. Bultmann, Rudolf Karl, 1884-1976. 2. Demythologization I. Bultmann, Rudolf Karl, 1884-1976. II. T.
BL51.J353    201    *LC* 58-8951

**Kierkegaard, Søren, 1813-1855.** **1.1553**
[Philosophiske smuler. English] Philosophical fragments, Johannes Climacus / by Søren Kierkegaard; edited and translated with introduction and notes by Howard V. Hong and Edna H. Hong. — Princeton, N.J.: Princeton University Press, c1985. xxii, 371 p.; 23 cm. (Kierkegaard's writings; 7) Translation of: Philosophiske smuler; and of: Johannes Climacus. Includes index. 1. Religion — Philosophy I. Hong, Howard Vincent, 1912- II. Hong, Edna Hatlestad, 1913- III. Kierkegaard, Søren, 1813-1855. Johannes Climacus. English. 1985. IV. T.
BL51.K48713 1985    201 19    *LC* 85-3420    *ISBN* 0691072736

**Luijpen, W. (Wilhelmus), 1922-.** **1.1554**
[Erwtensoep is klaar! English] Theology as anthropology; philosophical reflections on religion, by William A. Luijpen. Pittsburgh, Duquesne University Press; distributed by Humanities Press, New York [1973] 148 p. 21 cm. (Duquesne studies. Theological series, 12) Translation of De erwtensoep is klaar! 1. Religion — Philosophy I. T. II. Series.
BL51.L713    200/.1    *LC* 72-90638    *ISBN* 0391003119

**Marcel, Gabriel, 1889-1973.** • **1.1555**
Creative fidelity. Translated from the French and with an introd., by Robert Rosthal. New York, Farrar, Straus [1964] xxvi, 261 p. 21 cm. Translation of Du refus à l'Invocation. Includes bibliographies. 1. Knowledge, Theory of (Religion) 2. Philosophy and religion I. T.
BL51.M343    194    *LC* 64-11453

**Mill, John Stuart, 1806-1873.** • **1.1556**
Nature, and Utility of religion. [Essays] Edited with an introd. by George Nakhnikian. New York, Liberal Arts Press [1958] xxx, 80 p. 21 cm. (The Library of liberal arts, no. 81) Bibliography: p. xxix. 1. Nature 2. Religion I. T. II. Title: Utility of religion.
BL51.M58    215    *LC* 58-59889

**Mill, John Stuart, 1806-1873.** • **1.1557**
Three essays on religion. New York, Greenwood Press [1969] xi, 302 p. 23 cm. Reprint of the 1874 ed. 1. Berkeley, George, 1685-1753. 2. Nature 3. Theism 4. Religion — Philosophy I. T.
BL51.M62 1969    200/.1    *LC* 69-13997    *ISBN* 0837119863

**Reason and religion / edited by Stuart C. Brown.** **1.1558**
Ithaca, N.Y.: Cornell University Press, c1977. 315 p.; 21 cm. — (Cornell paperbacks) Papers originated at a conference sponsored by the Royal Institute of Philosophy and held at the University of Lancaster in 1975. 1. Religion — Philosophy — Congresses. 2. Good and evil — Congresses. 3. Immortality — Congresses. I. Brown, Stuart C. II. Royal Institute of Philosophy, London BL51.R325    BL51 R325.    200/.1    *LC* 77-3115    *ISBN* 0801410258

**Scheler, Max, 1874-1928.** • **1.1559**
[Vom Ewigen im Menschen. English] On the eternal in man. Translated by Bernard Noble. [Hamden, Conn.] Archon Books, 1972 [c1960] 480 p. 23 cm. Translation of Vom Ewigen im Menschen. 1. Philosophy and religion 2. Religion — Philosophy I. T.
BL51.S423 1972    100    *LC* 72-6599    *ISBN* 020801280X

**Westphal, Merold.** **1.1560**
God, guilt, and death: an existential phenomenology of religion / Merold Westphal. — Bloomington: Indiana University Press, c1984. xiv, 305 p.; 24 cm. — (Studies in phenomenology and existential philosophy.) Includes index. 1. Religion — Philosophy 2. Guilt — Religious aspects 3. Death — Religious aspects I. T. II. Series.
BL51.W44 1984    200/.1 19    *LC* 83-48525    *ISBN* 0253325862

# BL53 Psychology of Religion

**Allport, Gordon W. (Gordon Willard), 1897-1967.**    • **1.1561**
The individual and his religion, a psychological interpretation. New York, Macmillan, 1950. xi, 147 p. 21 cm. 1. Psychology, Religious I. T.
BL53.A428    201    *LC* 50-5982

**Bourguignon, Erika, 1924-.**    **1.1562**
Religion, altered states of consciousness, and social change. Edited by Erika Bourguignon. — Columbus: Ohio State University Press, 1973. x, 389 p.: illus.; 22 cm. 1. Psychology, Religious 2. Trance 3. Sects 4. Religion and sociology I. T.
BL53.B643    200/.19    *LC* 72-8448    *ISBN* 0814201679

**The Dialogue between theology and psychology, by LeRoy Aden**    • **1.1563**
**[and others] Edited by Peter Homans.**
Chicago, University of Chicago Press [1968] x, 295 p. 24 cm. (Essays in divinity, v. 3) Many of the papers were first presented at the Alumni Conference of the Religion and Personality Field, Jan. 27-29, 1969, celebrating the 75th anniversary of the University of Chicago and the 100th anniversary of its Divinity School. 1. Psychology, Religious I. Homans, Peter. ed. II. Aden, LeRoy. III. University of Chicago. Divinity School. IV. Series.
BL53.D47    200/.19    *LC* 68-16698

**Freud, Sigmund, 1856-1939.**    **1.1564**
[Zukunft einer Illusion. English] The future of an illusion / Sigmund Freud; translated by W.D. Robson-Scott. — Rev. ed. / revised and newly edited by James Strachey. — London: Hogarth Press: Institute of Psycho-analysis, 1962. x, 59 p.; 23 cm. — (International psycho-analytical library. no. 15) Translation of: Die Zukunft einer Illusion. 'This translation first published 1928'—P. [iv] Includes index. 1. Psychology, Religious 2. Religion 3. Psychotherapy I. Robson-Scott, W. D. (William Douglas) II. Strachey, James. III. T. IV. Series.
BL53.F67 1962    201/.9 19    *LC* 82-179739

**Heisig, James W., 1944-.**    **1.1565**
Imago Dei: a study of C. G. Jung's psychology of religion / James W. Heisig. — Lewisburg [Pa.]: Bucknell University Press, c1979. 253 p. — (Studies in Jungian thought.) Includes index. 1. Jung, C. G. (Carl Gustav), 1875-1961. 2. Psychology, Religious — History. I. T. II. Series.
BL53.H378    BL53 H378.    200/.1/9    *LC* 77-74405    *ISBN* 0838720765

**Jung, C. G. (Carl Gustav), 1875-1961.**    • **1.1566**
Psychology and religion, by Carl Gustav Jung. New Haven, Yale university press; London, H. Milford, Oxford university press, 1938. 3 p. l., 131 p. 21 cm. (The Terry lectures) 'Notes': p. [115]-131. 1. Psychology, Religious 2. Symbolism I. T.
BL53.J8    201    *LC* 38-27254

**Lofland, John.**    • **1.1567**
Doomsday Cult: a study of conversion, proselytization, and maintenance of faith / John Lofland. — Enl. ed. — New York: Irvington Publishers: distributed by Halsted Press, c1977. xii, 362 p.; 22 cm. Includes index. 1. Psychology, Religious 2. Religion and sociology I. T.
BL53.L6 1977    299    *LC* 77-23028    *ISBN* 0470992492

**Thouless, Robert Henry, 1894-.**    • **1.1568**
An introduction to the psychology of religion [by] Robert H. Thouless. — 3rd ed. — London: Cambridge University Press, 1971. viii, 152 p.; 23 cm. 1. Psychology, Religious I. T.
BL53.T5 1971    200/.19    *LC* 76-184142    *ISBN* 0521081491

**Transpersonal psychologies / edited by Charles T. Tart.**    **1.1569**
1st ed. — New York: Harper & Row, [1975] 502 p.: ill.; 24 cm. Includes indexes. 1. Psychology, Religious I. Tart, Charles T., 1937-
BL53.T67 1975    291.4/2    *LC* 73-18672    *ISBN* 0060678232

**Ulanov, Ann Belford.**    **1.1570**
Religion and the unconscious / by Ann and Barry Ulanov. — Philadelphia: Westminster Press, [1975] 287 p.; 24 cm. 1. Psychology, Religious 2. Subconsciousness 3. Ethics I. Ulanov, Barry. joint author. II. T.
BL53.U45    BL53 U45.    200/.19    *LC* 75-16302    *ISBN* 0664207995

# BL54-65 Religion: Relation to Other Subjects

**Dawson, Christopher, 1889-1970.**    • **1.1571**
Religion and culture. — New York, Sheed & Ward, 1948. v, 225 p. 23 cm. — (Gifford lectures, 1947) 'Delivered in the University of Edinburgh.' Bibliographical footnotes. 1. Religion I. T. II. Series.
BL55.D32 1949    290    *LC* 49-7957

**Berger, Peter L.**    • **1.1572**
The precarious vision; a sociologist looks at social fictions and Christian faith. — [1st ed.]. — Garden City, N.Y., Doubleday, 1961. 238 p. 22 cm. 1. Religion and sociology 2. Sociology, Christian I. T.
BL60.B4    261.8    *LC* 61-12493

**Berger, Peter L.**    • **1.1573**
The sacred canopy; elements of a sociological theory of religion, by Peter L. Berger. — [1st ed.]. — Garden City, N.Y.: Doubleday, 1967. vii, 230 p.; 22 cm. 1. Religion and sociology I. T.
BL60.B42    301.5/8    *LC* 67-19805

**Brown, Peter Robert Lamont.**    **1.1574**
Religion and society in the age of Saint Augustine [by] Peter Brown. [1st U.S. ed.] New York, Harper & Row [1972] 351 p. 23 cm. 1. Augustine, Saint, Bishop of Hippo — Contributions in sociology — Addresses, essays, lectures. 2. Religion and sociology — History — Addresses, essays, lectures. I. T.
BL60.B75 1972b    270.2/08    *LC* 70-181609    *ISBN* 0060105542

**Johnstone, Ronald L.**    **1.1575**
Religion in society: a sociology of religion / by Ronald L. Johnstone. — 2nd ed. — Englewood Cliffs, N.J.: Prentice-Hall, c1983. viii, 312 p.; 24 cm. 1. Religion and sociology 2. United States — Religion I. T.
BL60.J63 1983    306/.6 19    *LC* 82-7592    *ISBN* 0137730772

**Lenski, Gerhard Emmanuel, 1924-.**    • **1.1576**
The religious factor: a sociological study of religion's impact on politics, economics, and family life. — [1st ed.] Garden City, N.Y.: Doubleday, 1961. xvi, 381 p.: forms, tables; 22 cm. 1. Religion and sociology — Case studies. 2. Detroit (Mich.) — Religion — Case studies. I. T.
BL60.L44    261.8    *LC* 61-9197

**O'Dea, Thomas F.**    • **1.1577**
Sociology and the study of religion; theory, research, interpretation [by] Thomas F. O'Dea. — New York: Basic Books, [1970] x, 307 p.; 25 cm. 1. Religion and sociology I. T.
BL60.O28 1970    301.5    *LC* 79-94307    *ISBN* 0465080030

**The Religious dimension: new directions in quantitative research**    **1.1578**
**/ edited by Robert Wuthnow.**
New York: Academic Press, c1979. xiv, 376 p.; 24 cm. 1. Religion and sociology — Addresses, essays, lectures. I. Wuthnow, Robert.
BL60.R44    301.5/8    *LC* 79-6948    *ISBN* 012766050X

**Weber, Max, 1864-1920.**    • **1.1579**
The sociology of religion / by Max Weber. — 4th ed. / revised by Johannes Winckelmann; translated by Ephraim Fischoff. — Boston: Beacon Press, [1963] lxvii, 304 p.; 22 cm. 'First published in Germany, in 1922 ... under the title 'Religionssoziologie,' from Wirtschaft und Gesellschaft.' 1. Religion and sociology I. T.
BL60.W433 1963    290    *LC* 62-16644

**Wilson, Bryan R.**    **1.1580**
Magic and the millennium; a sociological study of religious movements of protest among tribal and third-world peoples [by] Bryan R. Wilson. — [1st U.S. ed.]. — New York: Harper & Row, [1973] xi, 547 p.; 25 cm. 1. Religion and sociology 2. Cults 3. Magic I. T.
BL60.W54 1973b    301.5/8    *LC* 72-9762    *ISBN* 0060146710

**Wilson, Bryan R.**    **1.1581**
Religion in sociological perspective / Bryan Wilson. — Oxford; New York: Oxford University Press, 1982. vii, 187 p.; 22 cm. 1. Religion and sociology I. T.
BL60.W543 1982    306/.6 19    *LC* 81-16829    *ISBN* 0198266642

**Burke, Kenneth, 1897-.**    • **1.1582**
The rhetoric of religion; studies in logology. Berkeley, University of California Press, 1970. vi, 327 p. 21 cm. 'Cal 188.' 1. Augustine, Saint, Bishop of Hippo. Confessions 2. Bible. O.T. Genesis — Language, style. 3. Languages — Religious aspects 4. Semantics (Philosophy) I. T.
BL65.L2 B8 1970    201/.4    *LC* 70-89892    *ISBN* 0520016106

**Gilkey, Langdon Brown, 1919-.**     • **1.1583**
Naming the whirlwind; the renewal of God–language, by Langdon Gilkey.
Indianapolis, Bobbs-Merrill [1969] x, 483 p. 22 cm. 1. Languages — Religious
aspects — Christianity 2. Theology — 20th century I. T.
BL65.L2 G5     230/.09/04     *LC* 68-11146

**Religion and nationalism in Soviet and East European politics /**    **1.1584**
**edited by Pedro Ramet.**
Durham, N.C.: Duke University Press, 1984. 282 p.; 25 cm. (Duke Press policy
studies.) Papers presented at a conference held at the University of California,
Los Angeles and the University of California, Santa Barbara, Oct. 29-30, 1982
and sponsored by the Center for Russian and East European Studies (UCLA).
1. Nationalism — Religious aspects — Addresses, essays, lectures.
2. Nationalism — Europe, Eastern — Addresses, essays, lectures. 3. Religion
and state — Europe, Eastern — Addresses, essays, lectures. 4. Europe, Eastern
— Religion — Addresses, essays, lectures. 5. Europe, Eastern — Politics and
government — 1945- — Addresses, essays, lectures. I. Ramet, Pedro, 1949-
II. University of California, Los Angeles. Center for Russian and East
European Studies. III. Series.
BL65.N3 R45 1984     322/.1/0947 19     *LC* 84-18732

**Lewy, Guenter, 1923-.**     **1.1585**
Religion and revolution. — New York: Oxford University Press, 1974. xvii,
694 p.; 25 cm. 1. Religion and politics — Case studies. 2. Revolutions — Case
studies. I. T.
BL65.P7 L46     301.6/333     *LC* 73-87610     *ISBN* 0195017447

**Religion and political modernization / edited by Donald Eugene**   **1.1586**
**Smith.**
New Haven: Yale University Press, 1974. 340 p.; 24 cm. 1. Religion and
politics — Addresses, essays, lectures. I. Smith, Donald Eugene, 1927-
BL65.P7 R43     322/.1     *LC* 73-86917     *ISBN* 0300017308

## BL71.5–72 Biography

**Bowden, Henry Warner.**     **1.1587**
Dictionary of American religious biography / Henry Warner Bowden; Edwin
S. Gaustad, advisory editor. — Westport, Conn.: Greenwood Press, 1977. xi,
572 p.; 24 cm. 1. Religious biography — United States. 2. United States —
Biography I. T.
BL72.B68     209/.2/2 B     *LC* 76-5258     *ISBN* 0837189063

## BL74–98 Religions of the World

**Al-Faruqi, Isma'il R., 1921-.**     **1.1588**
Historical atlas of the religions of the world. Isma'īl Rāgī al Fārūqī, editor;
David E. Sopher, map editor. New York, Macmillan [1974] xviii, 346 p. illus.
29 cm. 1. Religions 2. Religions — Maps. I. Sopher, David Edward. joint
author. II. T.
BL80.2.F28     912/.1/2     *LC* 73-16583     *ISBN* 0023364009

**Ling, Trevor Oswald.**     **1.1589**
A history of religion East and West; an introduction and interpretation [by]
Trevor Ling. — New York: Harper & Row, [1970, c1968] xxix, 464 p.: maps.;
21 cm. — (Harper colophon books, CN 155) 1. Religions — History. I. T.
BL80.2.L53 1970     200/.9     *LC* 71-102219

**Smart, Ninian, 1927-.**     **1.1590**
Beyond ideology: religion and the future of Western civilization / Ninian
Smart. — 1st ed. — San Francisco: Harper & Row, c1981. 350 p.; 21 cm. —
(Gifford lectures delivered in the University of Edinburgh; 1979-1980)
1. Religions — Addresses, essays, lectures. 2. Ideology — Addresses, essays,
lectures. 3. Secularism — Addresses, essays, lectures. I. T.
BL80.2.S593 1981     291.1/7 19     *LC* 81-47429     *ISBN* 0060674024

**Frankfort, Henri, 1897-1954.**     **1.1591**
The intellectual adventure of ancient man; an essay on speculative thought in
the ancient Near East, by H. and H. A. Frankfort, John A. Wilson, Thorkild
Jacobsen [and] William A. Irwin. Chicago, The University of Chicago press
[1946] vii, 401 p. 24 cm. 'An Oriental institute essay.' 'Contains lectures given
as a public course in the Division of the humanities of the University of
Chicago.'–Pref. 1. Religious thought — To 600 2. Philosophy, Ancient
3. Middle East — Civilization — To 622. I. Frankfort, Henriette Antonia
(Groenewegen) 1896- joint author. II. Wilson, John Albert, 1899-
III. Jacobsen, Thorkild, 1904- IV. Irwin, William Andrew, 1884- V. T.
BL96.F8     290     *LC* 47-1318

## BL175–235 Natural Theology

**Hartshorne, Charles, 1897-.**     • **1.1592**
A natural theology for our time. — La Salle, Ill.: Open Court, [1967] xi, 145 p.;
22 cm. — (Morse lectures, 1964) (The Open Court library of philosophy.)
'Somewhat extended and revised versions of ... [the] lectures.' 1. Natural
theology I. T. II. Series.
BL182.H34     210     *LC* 66-14722

**Hartshorne, Charles, 1897-.**     **1.1593**
The divine relativity: a social conception of God / by Charles Hartshorne. —
New Haven: Yale University Press, 1948. xvi, 164 p. — (The Terry lectures)
I. T.
BL205 H37     B945.H335 D618 1948.     231     *LC* 48-7802

**Mbiti, John S.**     **1.1594**
Concepts of God in Africa [by] John S. Mbiti. — New York: Praeger
Publishers, [1970] xv, 348 p.; 23 cm. 1. God 2. Africa — Religion I. T.
BL205.M34 1970     299/.6     *LC* 78-95360

**Albright, William Foxwell, 1891-1971.**     **1.1595**
From stone age to Christianity. 2d ed. Baltimore, The Johns Hopkins press,
1957. 432 p. 21 cm. 1. Monotheism 2. Religion, Primitive 3. History —
Philosophy 4. History — Methodology I. T.
BL221.A47 1957a     *LC* 57-59184

## BL239–265 Religion and Science

**Bozeman, Theodore Dwight, 1942-.**     **1.1596**
Protestants in an age of science: the Baconian ideal and ante–bellum American
religious thought / by Theodore Dwight Bozeman. — Chapel Hill: University
of North Carolina Press, c1977. xv, 243 p.; 24 cm. Includes index. 1. Bacon,
Francis, 1561-1626. 2. Religion and science — History of controversy —
United States. 3. Protestantism I. T.
BL245.B7     261.5     *LC* 76-25962     *ISBN* 0807812994

**Koestler, Arthur, 1905-.**     **1.1597**
The sleep walkers: a history of man's changing vision of the universe / with an
introd. by Herbert Butterfield. — New York: Macmillan, 1959. 624 p.: ill.; 22
cm. 1. Astronomy — History. 2. Religion and science — History I. T.
BL245.K63 1959a     215     *LC* 59-7218

**Russell, Bertrand, 1872-1970.**     • **1.1598**
Religion and science / by Bertrand Russell. — London: T. Butterworth, c1935.
255 p. The Home University Library of modern knowledge. 1. Religion and
science — 1900- 2. Religion and science — History I. T.
BL245.R8     *LC* 36-18962

## BL300–325 Myth. Comparative Mythology

**Mythologies of the world: a concise encyclopedia / Max S.**    **1.1599**
**Shapiro, executive editor; compiled by Rhoda A. Hendricks,**
**research editor.**
1st ed. — Garden City, N.Y.: Doubleday, 1979. xviii, 216, [1] p.: ill.; 22 cm.
1. Mythology — Dictionaries I. Shapiro, Max S. II. Hendricks, Rhoda A.
BL303.M95     291.1/3     *LC* 78-1221     *ISBN* 0385136676

**Sykes, Egerton.**     • **1.1600**
Everyman's dictionary of non–classical mythology. [3d ed.] London, Dent;
New York, Dutton [1961] xxiii, 280 p. plates. 20 cm. (Everyman's reference
library) 1. Mythology — Dictionaries I. T.
BL303.S9x     *LC* 52-3946

**Tripp, Edward.**     • **1.1601**
Crowell's handbook of classical mythology. — New York: Crowell, [1970] ix,
631 p.: geneal. table, maps.; 24 cm. — (A Crowell reference book)
1. Mythology — Dictionaries I. T. II. Title: Handbook of classical
mythology.
BL303.T75 1970     398     *LC* 74-127614     *ISBN* 069022608X

**Sacred narrative, readings in the theory of myth** / edited by   **1.1602**
Alan Dundes.
Berkeley: University of California Press, c1984. ix, 352 p.: ill.; 24 cm. Includes index. 1. Myth — Addresses, essays, lectures. 2. Mythology — Addresses, essays, lectures. I. Dundes, Alan.
BL304.S19 1984        291.1/3 19        *LC* 83-17921        *ISBN* 0520051564

**Frazer, James George, Sir, 1854-1941.**        • **1.1603**
The golden bough: a study in magic and religion / [James George Frazer]. — 3rd ed. — London: Macmillan, 1980. 13 v. Each v. has separate t.p. Preface to 3rd ed. dated 1910 to 1915. 1. Mythology 2. Religion, Primitive 3. Magic 4. Superstition I. T.
BL310.F7 1980        *ISBN* 0333012828

**Vickery, John B.**        **1.1604**
The literary impact of The golden bough, by John B. Vickery. — Princeton: Princeton University Press, [1973] viii, 435 p.; 25 cm. 1. Frazer, James George, Sir, 1854-1941. The golden bough. I. T.
BL310.F713 V52        291        *LC* 72-4049        *ISBN* 0691062439

**Larousse encyclopedia of mythology** / with an introd. by Robert        • **1.1605**
Graves; [translated by Richard Aldington and Delano Ames, and rev. by a panel of editorial advisors from the Larousse mythologie générale edited by Felix Guirand].
New York: Prometheus Press, 1960. viii, 500 p.: ill., col. plates, maps; 30 cm. 1. Mythology 2. Folklore I. Guirand, Félix, ed. Mythologie générale.
BL310.G853        290        *LC* 59-11019

**Campbell, Joseph, 1904-.**        **1.1606**
The way of the animal powers / Joseph Campbell. — New York: A. van der Marck Editions; San Francisco: Distributed by Harper & Row, 1983. 304 p.: ill.; 36 cm. (Historical atlas of world mythology; v.1) Include index. 1. Mythology I. T. II. Series.
BL311.C26 1983        291.1/3 19        *LC* 83-80561        *ISBN* 0912383003

**Campbell, Joseph, 1904-.**        **1.1607**
The mythic image / by Joseph Campbell; assisted by M. J. Abadie. — Princeton, N.J.: Princeton University Press, c1974. xii, 552 p.: ill. (some col.); 32 cm. (Bollingen series. 100) 1. Mythology 2. Symbolism I. Abadie, M. J. II. T. III. Series.
BL311.C274        291.1/3        *LC* 79-166363        *ISBN* 0691098697

**Frankfort, Henri, 1897-1954.**        • **1.1608**
Kingship and the gods, a study of ancient Near Eastern religion as the integration of society & nature. Chicago, University of Chicago Press [1948] xxiii, 444 p. illus. 25 cm. (Oriental Institute essay) 1. Assyro-Babylonian religion 2. Egypt — Kings and rulers — Religious aspects. 3. Egypt — Religion I. T.
BL325.K5 F7        299.31        *LC* 48-5158

# BL425–619 Religious Doctrines. Worship

## BL458 WOMAN: COMPARATIVE RELIGION

**Christ, Carol P.**        **1.1609**
Diving deep and surfacing: women writers on spiritual quest / Carol P. Christ. — 2nd ed. — Boston: Beacon Press, 1986. xxxii, 159 p.; 21 cm. Includes index. 1. Women and religion 2. Spiritual life I. T.
BL458.C47 1986        291.4 19        *LC* 86-70552        *ISBN* 0807063517

**Goldenberg, Naomi R.**        **1.1610**
Changing of the gods: feminism and the end of traditional religions / Naomi R. Goldenberg. — Boston: Beacon Press, c1979. viii, 152 p.; 21 cm. 1. Women and religion 2. Religions (Proposed, universal, etc.) 3. Psychology, Religious 4. Christianity — Controversial literature 5. Judaism — Controversial literature 6. Feminism — Religious aspects I. T.
BL458.G64 1979        291.1/7834/12        *LC* 78-19602        *ISBN* 080701110X

**Immaculate & powerful: the female in sacred image and social**        **1.1611**
reality / edited by Clarissa W. Atkinson, Constance H. Buchanan, and Margaret R. Miles.
Boston: Beacon Press, c1985. viii, 330 p.; 24 cm. (Harvard women's studies in religion series.) 1. Women and religion — Addresses, essays, lectures. 2. Feminism — Religious aspects. 3. Woman

(Theology) — Addresses, essays, lectures. I. Atkinson, Clarissa W. II. Buchanan, Constance H. III. Miles, Margaret Ruth. IV. Title: Immaculate and powerful. V. Series.
BL458.I46 1985        291.1/78344 19        *LC* 85-70448        *ISBN* 0807010049

**Ochshorn, Judith, 1928-.**        **1.1612**
The female experience and the nature of the divine / Judith Ochshorn. — Bloomington: Indiana University Press, c1981. xvii, 269 p.; 24 cm. 1. Women and religion 2. Sex — Religious aspects 3. Sex in the Bible 4. Polytheism I. T.
BL458.O26        291.1/78344 19        *LC* 81-47012        *ISBN* 025331898X

**Unspoken worlds: women's religious lives in non–western**        **1.1613**
cultures / [edited by] Nancy Auer Falk, Rita M. Gross.
1st ed. — San Francisco: Harper & Row, c1980. xviii, 292 p.; 21 cm. 1. Women — Religious life — Addresses, essays, lectures. I. Falk, Nancy Auer. II. Gross, Rita M.
BL458.U57 1980        291.1/7834/12        *LC* 79-2989        *ISBN* 0060634928

**Womanguides: readings toward a feminist theology** / [compiled        **1.1614**
by] Rosemary Radford Ruether.
Boston: Beacon Press, c1985. xii, 274 p.: ill.; 24 cm. Includes index. 1. Women and religion — Addresses, essays, lectures. 2. Feminism — Religious aspects — Addresses, essays, lectures. 3. Woman (Theology) — Addresses, essays, lectures. I. Ruether, Rosemary Radford.
BL458.W63 1985        291.8/088042 19        *LC* 84-14508        *ISBN* 0807012025

**Women in ritual and symbolic roles** / edited by Judith Hoch–        **1.1615**
Smith and Anita Spring.
New York: Plenum Press, c1978. xv, 289 p.: ill.; 24 cm. 1. Women and religion — Addresses, essays, lectures. 2. Sex role — Addresses, essays, lectures. I. Hoch-Smith, Judith. II. Spring, Anita.
BL458.W65        301.41/2        *LC* 77-17448        *ISBN* 0306310678

**Womanspirit rising: a feminist reader in religion** / edited by        **1.1616**
Carol P. Christ and Judith Plaskow.
1st ed. — San Francisco: Harper & Row, c1979. xi, 287 p.; 21 cm. — (Harper forum books) 1. Woman (Theology) — Addresses, essays, lectures. I. Christ, Carol P. II. Plaskow, Judith.
BL458.W657 1979        261.8/34/12        *LC* 78-3363        *ISBN* 0060613858

## BL473–480 GODS. DEMONS

**The Book of the goddess, past and present: an introduction to**        **1.1617**
her religion / edited by Carl Olson.
New York: Crossroad, 1983. x, 261 p.; 24 cm. 1. Goddesses — Addresses, essays, lectures. I. Olson, Carl.
BL473.5.B66 1983        291.2/11 19        *LC* 82-23606        *ISBN* 0824505662

**Russell, Jeffrey Burton.**        **1.1618**
The Devil: perceptions of evil from antiquity to primitive Christianity / Jeffrey Burton Russell. — Ithaca, N.Y.: Cornell University Press, c1977. 276 p.: ill.; 24 cm. Includes index. 1. Devil — History of doctrines 2. Good and evil I. T.
BL480.R86        291.2/16        *LC* 77-3126        *ISBN* 0801409381

## BL500–547 ESCHATOLOGY

**Reincarnation: the phoenix fire mystery: an East–West dialogue**        **1.1619**
on death and rebirth from the worlds of religion, science, psychology, philosophy, art, and literature, and from great thinkers of the past and present / compiled and edited by Joseph Head and S. L. Cranston.
New York: Julian Press, c1977. xix, 620 p.; 24 cm. Includes index. 1. Reincarnation — Addresses, essays, lectures. I. Head, Joseph. II. Cranston, S. L.
BL518.R44 1977        133.9/013        *LC* 76-30439        *ISBN* 0517528932. *ISBN* 0517528940 pbk

**Royce, Josiah, 1855-1916.**        • **1.1620**
The conception of immortality. — New York: Greenwood Press, 1968 [c1900] 91 p.; 19 cm. — (The Ingersoll lecture, 1899) 1. Immortality — Addresses, essays, lectures. 2. Individuality — Addresses, essays, lectures. I. T.
BL530.R68 1968        236/.22 19        *LC* 68-19293

**Küng, Hans, 1928-.**        **1.1621**
[Ewiges Leben? English] Eternal life?: life after death as a medical, philosophical, and theological problem / Hans Küng; translated by Edward Quinn. — Garden City, N.Y.: Doubleday, 1984. xvi, 271 p.; 24 cm. Translation of: Ewiges Leben? 'Based on a nine-day course of lectures at Tübingen'—Pref. 1. Jesus Christ — Resurrection — Addresses, essays, lectures. 2. Future life — Christianity — Addresses, essays, lectures. 3. Death — Religious aspects —

Christianity — Addresses, essays, lectures. 4. Resurrection — Addresses, essays, lectures. 5. Heaven — Christianity — Addresses, essays, lectures. 6. Hell — Christianity — Addresses, essays, lectures. 7. Eschatology — Addresses, essays, lectures. I. T.
BL535.K8613 1984      236/.2 19      *LC* 82-45112      *ISBN* 0385182074

## BL600–619 Rites. Ceremonies

**Bocock, Robert.**                                                      **1.1622**
Ritual in industrial society; a sociological analysis of ritualism in modern England. — London: Allen & Unwin, [1974, i.e. 1973] 209 p.: illus.; 22 cm. 1. Ritual I. T.
BL600.B62      301.2/1/0942      *LC* 74-157285      *ISBN* 0043000444

**Firth, Raymond William, 1901-.**                                      **1.1623**
Symbols: public and private [by] Raymond Firth. — Ithaca, N.Y.: Cornell University Press, [1973] 469 p.; 23 cm. — (Symbol, myth, and ritual series) 1. Symbolism I. T.
BL600.F55 1973      301.2/1      *LC* 72-11806      *ISBN* 0801407605

**Oesterley, W. O. E. (William Oscar Emil), 1866-1950.**           • **1.1624**
The sacred dance; a study in comparative folklore. Brooklyn, Dance Horizons [1968?] x, 234 p. 21 cm. (Series in republications by Dance Horizons, no. 13) Reprint of the 1923 ed. 1. Dancing — Religious aspects 2. Religion, Primitive I. T.
BL605.O4 1968      291.3/8      *LC* 68-28047

## BL624–635 Religious Life and Organization. Mysticism

**Easwaran, Eknath.**                                                    **1.1625**
The mantram handbook: formulas for transformation / Eknath Easwaran; introd. by Richard B. Applegate. — Berkeley, Calif.: Nilgiri Press, c1977. 260 p.; 19 cm. Includes index. 1. Mantras 2. Spiritual life I. T.
BL624.E17      294.5/43 19      *LC* 77-3222      *ISBN* 0915132109

**Cheney, Sheldon, 1886-.**                                         • **1.1626**
Men who have walked with God, being the story of mysticism through the ages told in the biographies of representative seers and saints, with excerpts from their writings and sayings, by Sheldon Cheney. New York, A. A. Knopf, 1945. xiv p., 1 l., 395, viii p., 1 l. plates. 22 cm. 'First edition.' 1. Mysticism — History I. T.
BL625.C5      149.3      *LC* 45-8427

**Happold, F. Crossfield (Frederick Crossfield), 1893-.**              **1.1627**
Mysticism: a study and an anthology, [by] F. C. Happold. Revised ed. Harmondsworth, Penguin, 1970. 407 p. 18 cm. (Pelican books) 1. Mysticism I. T.
BL625.H25 1970      291.4/2      *LC* 73-159216      *ISBN* 0140205683

**Mysticism and philosophical analysis / edited by Steven T. Katz.**      **1.1628**
New York: Oxford University Press, 1978. 264 p.; 23 cm. 1. Mysticism — Addresses, essays, lectures. I. Katz, Steven T., 1944-
BL625.M89 1978      291.4/2      *LC* 78-5958      0195200276

**Mysticism and religious traditions / edited by Steven T. Katz.**      **1.1629**
New York: Oxford University Press, 1983. 279 p.; 20 cm. 1. Mysticism — Comparative studies — Addresses, essays, lectures. I. Katz, Steven T., 1944-
BL625.M894 1983      291.4/2 19      *LC* 82-22508      *ISBN* 0195033132

**Otto, Rudolf, 1869-1937.**                                            **1.1630**
Mysticism east and west: a comparative analysis of the nature of mysticism / Rudolf Otto; translated by Bertha L. Bracey, Richenda C. Payne. — New York: Macmillan, 1932. xvii, 282 p.; 22 cm. An enlarged form of the Haskell lectures delivered at Oberlin College, Oberlin, Ohio, in the winter of 1923-24. Translation of West-östliche Mystik. 1. Mysticism 2. Philosophy and religion I. T.
BL625.O73 1932

**Suzuki, Daisetz Teitaro, 1870-1966.**                             • **1.1631**
Mysticism: Christian and Buddhist. [1st ed.] New York, Harper [c1957] xix, 214 p. 20 cm. (World perspectives, v. 12) 1. Mysticism I. T.
BL625.S85      *LC* 56-11086

**Understanding mysticism / edited by Richard Woods.**                  **1.1632**
1st. ed. — Garden City, N.Y.: Image Books, 1980. xi, 586 p.; 21 cm. Includes index. 1. Mysticism — Comparative studies — Addresses, essays, lectures. 2. Mysticism — Psychology — Addresses, essays, lectures. I. Woods, Richard, 1941-
BL625.U52      291.4/2      *LC* 78-22743      *ISBN* 0385151179

**Zaehner, R. C. (Robert Charles), 1913-1974.**                     • **1.1633**
Mysticism, sacred and profane; an inquiry into some varieties of praeternatural experience. — Oxford, Clarendon Press, 1957. xviii, 256 p. 25 cm. Bibliographical footnotes. 1. Mysticism I. T.
BL625.Z18      149.3      *LC* 57-2468

**Lewis, I. M.**                                                        **1.1634**
Ecstatic religion: an anthropological study of spirit possession and Shamanism / [by] I. M. Lewis. — [Rev. ed.]. — Harmondsworth; New York: Penguin, 1978. 223 p., [16] p. of plates: ill.; 19 cm. — (Pelican anthropology library) Includes index. 1. Ecstasy 2. Spirit possession 3. Religion and sociology I. T.
BL626.L48 1978      301.5/8      *LC* 79-319634      *ISBN* 0140212779

**Carrington, Patricia.**                                               **1.1635**
Freedom in meditation / by Patricia Carrington. 1st ed. — Garden City, N.Y.: Anchor Press, 1977. xxii, 384 p.: ill.; 22 cm. 1. Meditation I. T.
BL627.C33      158/.1      *LC* 76-6240      *ISBN* 0385113927

**Johnston, William, 1925-.**                                           **1.1636**
Silent music: the science of meditation / William Johnston. — 1st U.S. ed. — New York: Harper & Row, [1974] 190 p., [2] leaves of plates: ill.; 22 cm. Includes index. 1. Meditation I. T.
BL627.J63 1974      291.4/3      *LC* 73-18688      *ISBN* 0060641932

## BL660–2630 History and Principles of Religion

**Dumézil, Georges, 1898-.**                                            **1.1637**
[Enjeu du jeu des dieux—un héros. English] The stakes of the warrior / Georges Dumézil; translated by David Weeks; edited, with an introduction, by Jaan Puhvel. — Berkeley: University of California Press, c1983. xvii, 154 p.: ill.; 23 cm. Translation of: L'enjeu du jeu des dieux—un héros (which is pt. 1 of v. 2, Types épiques indo-européens—un héros, un sorcier, un roi, of Mythe et épopée) Continued by: The plight of a sorcerer. c1986. 1. Mythology, Indo-European I. Puhvel, Jaan. II. Dumézil, Georges, 1898- Mythe et épopée. 2. Types épiques indo-européens—un héros, un sorcier, un roi. 1. Stakes of the warrior. III. T.
BL660.D793513 1983      291.1/3/089034 19      *LC* 82-13384      *ISBN* 0520048342

## BL690–980 European Religions

**McLeod, Hugh.**                                                       **1.1638**
Religion and the people of Western Europe, 1789–1970 / Hugh McLeod. — Oxford; New York: Oxford University Press, 1981. 169 p.; 20 cm. — (OPUS) Includes index. 1. Europe — Religion I. T. II. Series.
BL690.M38 1981      274/.08 19      *LC* 82-112525      *ISBN* 0192158325

## BL700–820 Classical Religion and Mythology

**Bell, Robert E.**                                                     **1.1639**
Dictionary of classical mythology: symbols, attributes & associations / by Robert E. Bell; illustrations by John Schlesinger. — Oxford, England; Santa Barbara, Calif.: ABC-Clio, c1982. xi, 390 p.; 26 cm. Includes index. 1. Mythology, Classical — Dictionaries. I. T.
BL715.B44 1982      292/.13/0321 19      *LC* 81-19141      *ISBN* 0874363055

**Grant, Michael, 1914-.**                                          • **1.1640**
Myths of the Greeks and Romans. — [1st ed.]. — Cleveland: World Pub. Co., [1962] 487 p.: illus.; 23 cm. 1. Mythology, Classical I. T.
BL722.G7      292      *LC* 62-15713

**Rose, H. J. (Herbert Jennings), 1883-1961.**                      • **1.1641**
Religion in Greece and Rome, with a new introd. by the author. — New York: Harper, [1959] 312 p.; 21 cm. — (Harper torchbooks, TB55) 'Originally

published as Ancient Greek religion (1946) and Ancient Roman religion (1948)'
1. Greece — Religion 2. Rome — Religion. I. T.
BL722.R66    292    *LC* 59-11124

**Norton, Daniel Silas, 1908-1951.**      • **1.1642**
Classical myths in English literature [by] Dan S. Norton and Peters Rushton.
With an introd. by Charles Grosvenor Osgood. — New York: Greenwood
Press, [1969, c1952] xvi, 444 p.; 22 cm. 1. Mythology, Classical 2. Mythology
in literature I. Rushton, Peters, 1915-1949. II. T.
BL727.N67 1969    292    *LC* 70-92305    *ISBN* 0837124409

**Farnell, Lewis Richard, 1856-1934.**      • **1.1643**
The cults of the Greek states / by Lewis Richard Farnell. — Oxford: Clarendon
Press, 1896-1909. 5 v.: ill. 1. Cults, Greek. 2. Greece — Religion I. T.
BL781.F4    *LC* 01-20255

**Guthrie, W. K. C. (William Keith Chambers), 1906-.**      • **1.1644**
The Greeks and their gods. — Boston: Beacon Press, 1951. xvi, 388 p.; 22 cm.
1. Greece — Religion I. T.
BL781.G8 1951    292    *LC* 51-2187

**Murray, Gilbert, 1866-1957.**      • **1.1645**
Five stages of Greek religion; studies based on a course of lectures delivered in
April 1912 at Columbia University, by Gilbert Murray. Oxford, The Clarendon
Press, 1925. 276 p. 23 cm. Second edition, enlarged, of 'Four stages of Greek
religion, New York, 1912.' 1. Greece — Religion I. Sallustius, Neoplatonist.
II. T.
BL781.M8 1925    *LC* 25-25292

**Nilsson, Martin Persson, 1874-1967.**      • **1.1646**
Greek folk religion / Martin P. Nilsson; with a foreword to the Torchbook
edition by Arthur Darby Nock. — New York: Harper, 1961. xviii, 166 p.: ill. —
(Harper Torchbooks: The Cloister library; TB 78) 1. Greece — Religion
2. Mythology, Greek I. T.
BL781.N5 1961    292    *LC* 61-594

**Nilsson, Martin Persson, 1874-1967.**      • **1.1647**
A history of Greek religion. Translated from the Swedish by F. J. Fielden. 2d
ed. Oxford, Clarendon Press, 1949. 316 p. 23 cm. Bibliographical references in
'Notes and corrections' (p. [305]-309) 1. Mythology, Greek 2. Greece —
Religion 3. Crete — Antiquities I. T.
BL781.N53 1949    *LC* A 51-5437

**Rose, H. J. (Herbert Jennings), 1883-1961.**      • **1.1648**
A handbook of Greek mythology, including its extension to Rome. — [6th ed.].
— London, Methuen [1958] ix, 363 p. 22 cm. Bibliography: p. 335-339.
1. Mythology, Greek 2. Mythology, Roman I. T.
BL781.R65 1958    292    *LC* 58-1932

**Burkert, Walter, 1931-.**      **1.1649**
[Griechische Religion der archaischen und klassischen Epoche. English] Greek
religion / by Walter Burkert; translated by John Raffan. — Cambridge, Mass.:
Harvard University Press, 1985. 493 p.; 24 cm. Translation of: Griechische
Religion der archaischen und klassischen Epoche. Includes indexes. 1. Greece
— Religion I. T.
BL782.B8313 1985    292/.08 19    *LC* 84-25209    *ISBN* 0674362802

**Kirk, G. S. (Geoffrey Stephen), 1921-.**      **1.1650**
The nature of Greek myths / G. S. Kirk. — Woodstock, N.Y.: Overlook Press,
1975, c1974. 332 p.; 24 cm. Includes index. 1. Mythology, Greek I. T.
BL782.K57 1975    292/.1/3    *LC* 74-21683    *ISBN* 0875910315

**Pinsent, John, 1922-.**      **1.1651**
Greek mythology / John Pinsent. — New York: P. Bedrick Books: Distributed
in the USA by Harper & Row, 1983, c1982. 144 p.: ill. (some col.); 29 cm. —
(Library of the world's myths and legends.) 'New revised edition'-T.p. verso.
Includes index. 1. Mythology, Greek I. T. II. Series.
BL782.P53 1983    292/.13 19    *LC* 83-71479    *ISBN* 0911745084

**Rice, David Gerard, 1945-.**      **1.1652**
Sources for the study of Greek religion / David G. Rice and John E.
Stambaugh. — Missoula, Mont.: Published by Scholars Press for the Society of
Biblical Literature, c1979. xv, 277 p.; 24 cm. — (Sources for biblical study. no.
14 0145-2762) 1. Greece — Religion — Collected works. I. Stambaugh, John
E. joint author. II. T. III. Series.
BL782.S7    292/.08    *LC* 79-18389    *ISBN* 0891303464

**Downing, Christine, 1931-.**      **1.1653**
The goddess: mythological images of the feminine / Christine Downing. —
New York: Crossroad, 1981. 250 p.: ill.; 24 cm. 1. Goddesses 2. Mythology,
Greek I. T.
BL785.D66    292/.211 19    *LC* 81-7851    *ISBN* 0824500911

**Festugière, A. J. (André Jean), 1898-1982.**      • **1.1654**
Personal religion among the Greeks / André-Jean Festugière. — Berkeley:
University of California Press, 1954. viii, 186 p.: front; 24 cm. (Sather classical
lectures. v.26) 1. Greece — Religion I. T. II. Series.
BL785.F4    292    *LC* 53-11234

**Harrison, Jane Ellen, 1850-1928.**      • **1.1655**
Themis: a study of the social origins of Greek religion / Jane Ellen Harrison;
with an excursus on the ritual forms preserved in Greek tragedy by Gilbert
Murray, and a chapter on the origin of the Olympic games by F. M. Cornford.
— Cleveland: World Publishing, 1962. xxxvi, 559 p.: ill.; 21 cm. 1. Cultus,
Greece 2. Olympic games I. T.
BL785.H45 1962    *LC* 62-18676

**Myth, religion, and society: structuralist essays / by M.**      **1.1656**
**Detienne ... [et al.]; edited by R. L. Gordon.**
Cambridge [Eng.]; New York: Cambridge University Press, 1981. xvii, 306 p.;
24 cm. English translations of essays previously published in French. Includes
index. 1. Mythology, Greek — Addresses, essays, lectures. I. Gordon, R. L.
(Raymond L.) II. Detienne, Marcel.
BL790.M95    292/.13 19    *LC* 80-40783    *ISBN* 0521227801

**Nilsson, Martin Persson, 1874-1967.**      • **1.1657**
The Mycenaean origin of Greek mythology. New York, Norton [1963, c1932]
258 p. 20 cm. (The Norton library, N234) Bibliographical footnotes.
1. Mythology, Greek 2. Civilization, Mycenaean I. T.
BL793.M8N53 1963    292    *LC* 63-23840

**Alteheim, Franz, 1898-.**      **1.1658**
A history of Roman religion. Translated by Harold Mattingly. London
Methuen [1938] 548p. 1. Rome — Religion I. T.
BL801 A513

**Grant, Frederick C. (Frederick Clifton), 1891-1974.**      • **1.1659**
Ancient Roman religion. — New York, Liberal Arts Press [1957] 252 p. 21 cm.
— (The Library of religion, no. 8) 1. Rome — Religion. I. T.
BL801.G7    *LC* 57-3661

**Dumézil, Georges, 1898-.**      • **1.1660**
[Religion romaine archaïque. English] Archaic Roman religion, with an
appendix on the religion of the Etruscans. Translated by Philip Krapp.
Foreword by Mircea Eliade. Chicago, University of Chicago Press [1970] 2 v.
(xxx, 715 p.) 24 cm. Translation of La religion romaine archaïque. 1. Rome —
Religion. I. T.
BL802.D813    292/.07    *LC* 76-116981    *ISBN* 0226169685

**Ferguson, John, 1921-.**      • **1.1661**
The religions of the Roman Empire. — Ithaca, N.Y.: Cornell University Press,
[1970] 296 p.: illus.; 23 cm. — (Aspects of Greek and Roman life) 1. Rome —
Religion. I. T. II. Series.
BL802.F45 1970    200/.937    *LC* 71-110992    *ISBN* 080140567X

**Grant, Michael, 1914-.**      • **1.1662**
Roman myths. — New York: Scribner, [1972, c1971] xviii, 293 p.: illus.; 24 cm.
1. Mythology, Roman I. T.
BL802.G7 1972    292/.07    *LC* 75-162749    *ISBN* 0684125714

**Brown, Peter Robert Lamont.**      **1.1663**
Society and the holy in late antiquity / Peter Brown. — Berkeley: University of
California Press, c1982. vii, 347 p.; 24 cm. 1. Church history — Primitive and
early Church, ca. 30-600 — Collected works. 2. Rome — Religion — Collected
works. 3. Rome — History — Empire, 284-476 — Collected works. I. T.
BL805.B74 1982    270.2 19    *LC* 80-39862    *ISBN* 0520043057

**Galinsky, Karl, 1942-.**      • **1.1664**
Aeneas, Sicily, and Rome, by G. Karl Galinsky. — Princeton, N.J.: Princeton
University Press, 1969. xxvi, 278 p., [90] p. of illus.; 25 cm. — (Princeton
monographs in art and archaeology. 40) 1. Aeneas. I. T. II. Series.
BL820.A34 G3    398.22    *LC* 69-18059    *ISBN* 0691035334

**Tyrrell, William Blake.**      **1.1665**
Amazons, a study in Athenian mythmaking / Wm. Blake Tyrrell. — Baltimore:
Johns Hopkins University Press, c1984. xix, 166 p.: ill.; 24 cm. Includes index.
1. Amazons 2. Mythology, Greek 3. Matriarchy 4. Patriarchy 5. Androgyny
(Psychology) 6. Marriage — Mythology. 7. Athens (Greece) — Social life and
customs. I. T.
BL820.A6 T95 1984    305.3 19    *LC* 83-18782    *ISBN* 0801831180

**Cook, Arthur Bernard, 1868-1952.**      • **1.1666**
Zeus: a study in ancient religion / by Arthur Bernard Cook. — New York:
Biblo and Tannen, 1964. v.: ill.,(some col.,part fold. in pocket). Reprint of the
work first published 1914-40. 1. Zeus. 2. Cults, Greek. 3. Sun worship
4. Classical antiquities 5. Folk literature — Themes, motives I. T.
BL820.J8 C6 1964    *LC* 64-25839

**Guthrie, W. K. C. (William Keith Chambers), 1906-.**          • **1.1667**
Orpheus and Greek religion; a study of the Orphic Movement [by] W. K. C. Guthrie. [Rev. ed.] New York, Norton [1966, i.e. 1967] x, 291 p. illus. 21 cm. 1. Orpheus (Greek mythology) 2. Dionysia 3. Mysteries, Religious 4. Cultus, Greek. I. T.
BL820.O7 G8 1967          292          *LC* 67-250

**Orpheus, the metamorphoses of a myth / edited by John**          ˙**1.1668**
**Warden.**
Toronto; Buffalo: University of Toronto Press, c1982. xiii, 238 p.: ill.; 24 cm. Includes index. 1. Orpheus (Greek mythology) — Addresses, essays, lectures. I. Warden, John, 1936-
BL820.O7 O76 1982          809/.93351 19          *LC* 82-189058          *ISBN* 0802055184

**Friedrich, Paul, 1927-.**          **1.1669**
The meaning of Aphrodite / Paul Friedrich. — Chicago: University of Chicago Press, 1978. xi, 243 p.: ill., map. Includes index. 1. Venus (Goddess) I. T.
BL820.V5 F74          BL820V5 F74.          291.1/3          *LC* 78-9485          *ISBN* 0226264823

# BL830–875 Germanic and Norse Mythology

**Dumézil, Georges, 1898-.**          **1.1670**
[Dieux des Germains. English] Gods of the ancient Northmen. Edited by Einar Haugen; introd. by C. Scott Littleton and Udo Strutynski. Berkeley, University of California Press, 1973. xlvi, 157 p. 24 cm. (UCLA Center for the Study of Comparative Folklore and Mythology. Publications, 3) Translation of Les dieux des Germains and 4 articles written between 1952 and 1959. 1. Mythology, Norse 2. Germanic tribes — Religion I. T.
BL860.D7813          293/.2/11          *LC* 74-157819          *ISBN* 0520020448

# BL900–910 Celtic Mythology, Druids

**Chadwick, Nora K. (Nora Kershaw), 1891-1972.**          **1.1671**
The druids. Cardiff: Wales University Press, 1966. 119p. 1. Druids and Druidism I. T.
BL910 C5

**Piggott, Stuart.**          • **1.1672**
The Druids. New York, Praeger [1968] 236 p. illus., facsims., maps, plans, ports. 22 cm. (Ancient peoples and places, v. 63) 1. Druids and Druidism I. T.
BL910.P5 1968          299/.1/6          *LC* 68-8971

# BL930–980 Other

**Aspects of religion in the Soviet Union, 1917–1967. Edited by**          • **1.1673**
**Richard H. Marshall, Jr. Associate editors: Thomas E. Bird and**
**Andrew Q. Blane.**
Chicago, University of Chicago Press [1971] xv, 489 p. port. 24 cm. 1. Soviet Union — Religion — Addresses, essays, lectures. I. Marshall, Richard H., 1897- ed.
BL980.R8 A9          200/.947          *LC* 70-115874          *ISBN* 0226507009

**Read, Christopher, 1946-.**          **1.1674**
Religion, revolution, and the Russian intelligentsia, 1900–1912: the Vekhi debate and its intellectual background / Christopher Read. — Totowa, N.J.: Barnes & Noble, c1979. ix, 221 p.; 23 cm. Includes index. 1. Revolutionists — Russia. 2. Vekhi. 3. Russia — Religion. 4. Russia — Intellectual life — 1801-1917. I. T.
BL980.R8 R4          947.08          *LC* 79-13453          *ISBN* 0064958221

# BL1000–2370 Asian Religions

**Eliot, Charles Norton Edgecumbe, Sir, 1862-1931.**          • **1.1675**
Hinduism and Buddhism; an historical sketch. New York, Barnes & Noble, 1954. 3 v. 22 cm. 1. Hinduism 2. Buddha and Buddhism. 3. Asia — Religion. I. T.
BL1031.E6 1954          *LC* 54-14201

# BL1100–1710 By Religion

## BL1100–1295 HINDUISM

**Stutley, Margaret.**          **1.1676**
Harper's dictionary of Hinduism: its mythology, folklore, philosophy, literature, and history / Margaret and James Stutley. — 1st U.S. ed. — New York: Harper & Row, 1977. xx, 372 p.; 25 cm. Published in Great Britain under title: A dictionary of Hinduism. 1. Hinduism — Dictionaries. I. T. II. Title: A dictionary of Hinduism.
BL1105.S74 1977          *LC* 76-9999          *ISBN* 0060677635

**Renou, Louis, 1896-1966. ed.**          • **1.1677**
Hinduism. — New York: G. Braziller, 1961. 255 p.; 21 cm. — (Great religions of modern man) 1. Hinduism I. T.
BL1107.R4          294.5          *LC* 61-15496

## BL1111–1146 Sacred Books. Sources

**Vedas. Rgveda. English.**          **1.1678**
The hymns of the Rgveda. Translated, with a popular commentary, by Ralph T.H. Griffith. Edited by J.L. Shastri. [New rev. ed.] Delhi, Motilal Banarsidass [1973] x, 707 p. 26 cm. 1. Griffith, Ralph T. H. (Ralph Thomas Hotchkin), 1826-1906. tr. II. Shastri, Jagdish Lal. ed. III. T.
BL1112.52.E53 1973          294.5/9212 19          *LC* 74-900532

**Vedas. Rgveda. English. Selections.**          **1.1679**
Pinnacles of India's past: selections from the Rgveda / translated and annotated by Walter H. Maurer. — Amsterdam; Philadelphia: Benjamins, 1986. p. cm. (University of Pennsylvania studies on South Asia. 0169-0361; v. 2) Translated from the Sanskrit. Includes index. I. Maurer, Walter H. II. T. III. Series.
BL1112.54.E5 1986          294.5/9212 19          *LC* 85-30784          *ISBN* 0915027623

**Bādarāyana.**          • **1.1680**
The Vedānta Sūtras of Bādarāyana / with the commentary by Saṅkara; translated by George Thibaut. — New York: Dover Publications, 1962. 2 v. — (The Sacred books of the East; v. 34, 38, 48) 1. Brahmanism I. Thibaut, G. (George), 1848-1914. II. Saṅkarācārya. III. T.
BL1115.B23 1962          294.1          *LC* 62-53242

**Gonda, J. (Jan), 1905-.**          **1.1681**
Vedic literature: (Samhitās and Brāhmanas) / Jan Gonda. — Wiesbaden: Harrassowitz, 1975. vii, 463 p.; 24 cm. — (A History of Indian literature; v. 1: Veda and Upanishads; fasc. 1) Includes index. 1. Vedas — Criticism, interpretation, etc. 2. Brahmanas — Criticism, interpretation, etc. I. T.
BL1115.G597          294/.1          *LC* 75-521350          *ISBN* 3447016035

**Upanishads.**          • **1.1682**
The principal Upanishads; edited with introd., text, translation, and notes by S. Radhakrishnan. New York, Harper [1953] 958 p. 22 cm. I. Radhakrishnan, S. (Sarvepalli), 1888-1975. II. Upanishads. English. III. T.
BL1120.A3 R32 1953a          *LC* 53-10977

**Upanishads. English. Selections.**          **1.1683**
The thirteen principal Upanishads / translated from the Sanskrit, with an outline of the philosophy of the Upanishads and an annotated bibliography by Robert Ernest Hume; with a list of recurrent and parallel passages by George C. O. Haas. — 2nd ed., rev. — London: Oxford University Press, 1931. xvi, 587 p. Includes indexes. 'Recurrent and parallel passages ...': p. 516-562. 1. Upanishads — Bibliography 2. Hinduism — Sacred books I. Hume, Robert Ernest, 1877-1948. II. Haas, George C. O. III. T.
BL1124.54 E5

**Subrahmaniam, N. S.**          **1.1684**
Encyclopaedia of the Upanisads / N.S. Subrahmanian. — New Delhi: Sterling, c1985. xii, 564 p.; 23 cm. Adaptation of: Upanishads. Includes index. 1. Upanishads — Introductions. I. Upanishads. English. II. T.
BL1124.56.S83 1985          294.539218 19          *LC* 85-903547

**Manu.**          • **1.1685**
The laws of Manu. Translated with extracts from seven commentaries by G. Bühler. — [1st AMS ed.] Delhi, Motilal Banarsidass. — [New York: AMS Press, 1971] cxxxviii, 620 p.; 23 cm. Reprint of the 1886 ed. 1. Hindu law I. Bühler, Georg, 1837-1898. ed. II. T.
BL1125.A3 B8 1971          294.5/92          *LC* 73-149682          *ISBN* 0404011489

**Mahābhārata. Bhagavadgītā. English & Sanskrit.**          **1.1686**
The Bhagavadgītā in the Mahābhārata: text and translation / J. A. B. van Buitenen. — Chicago: University of Chicago Press, c1981. xii, 176 p.; 24 cm. I. Buitenen, J. A. B. van (Johannes Adrianus Bernardus van) II. T.
BL1130.A4 B84          294/.5/924          *LC* 79-13021          *ISBN* 0226846601

**Hopkins, Edward Washburn, 1857-1932.**                          • **1.1687**
Epic mythology. — New York: Biblo and Tannen, 1969. 277 p.; 26 cm. The
mythology of the two epics of India, the Mahābhārata and the Rāmāyana.
Reprint of the 1915 ed. 1. Mahābhārata. 2. Vālmīki. Rāmāyana.
3. Mythology, Hindu I. T.
BL1130.H6 1969          294.5/922        LC 76-75358

**Puranas. English. Selections.**                                  **1.1688**
Classical Hindu mythology: a reader in the Sanskrit Purāṇas / edited and
translated by Cornelia Dimmitt and J. A. B. van Buitenen. — Philadelphia:
Temple University Press, c1978. xiii, 373 p.; 23 cm. Includes index. I. Dimmitt,
Cornelia, 1938- II. Buitenen, J. A. B. van (Johannes Adrianus Bernardus van)
III. T.
BL1135.P6213        294.5/925        LC 77-92643        ISBN 0877221170

**Mani, Vettam, 1921-.**                                            **1.1689**
[Purānanighantu. English] Purāṇic encyclopaedia: a comprehensive dictionary
with special reference to the epic and Purāṇic literature / Vettam Mani. — 1st
ed. in English. — Delhi: Motilal Banarsidass, 1975. viii, 922 p.: geneal. tables;
28 cm. Translation of the author's Purānanighantu. 1. Vālmīki Rāmāyana —
Dictionaries. 2. Puranas — Dictionaries. 3. Mahābhārata — Dictionaries.
I. T.
BL1135.P88 M3613 1975         294.5/92        LC 76-900024

**Brahmanas. Śatapathabrāhmana. English.**                         • **1.1690**
The Śatapatha–brāhmana: according to the text of the mādhyadina school /
translated by Julius Eggeling. — Delhi: M. Banarsidass, 1963. 5 v. (The Sacred
books of the East; 12, 26, 41, 43, 44) (UNESCO collection of representative
works: Indian series) 1. Sacrifice — Hinduism I. Eggeling, Julius, 1842-1918.
II. T.
BL1135.S3E54 1963          LC sa 65-4519

**Tantras. Mahānirvānatantra.**                                    **1.1691**
Tantra of the great liberation (Mahānirvāna Tantra) / a translation from the
Sanskrit, with introd. and commentary by Arthur Avalon. — New York: Dover
Publications, 1972. cxlvi, 359 p. '...republication of the work originally by
Luzac & Co., London, in 1913.' I. Woodroffe, John George, Sir, 1865-1936.
II. Avalon Arthur. III. T.
BL1135.T5 W7 1972         LC 70-186314        ISBN 0486201503 pa

**Woodroffe, John George, Sir, 1865-1936.**                        • **1.1692**
The garland of letters: studies in the mantra–śāstra / by Sir John Woodroffe. —
7th ed. — Madras: Ganesh, 1979. xiv, 318 p.: port. 1. Tantras. 2. Shaktism
I. T.
BL1135.T6 W65 1979

**Vālmīki.**                                                        **1.1693**
[Rāmāyana. English] The Rāmāyana of Vālmīki: an epic of ancient India /
introduction and translation by Robert P. Goldman; annotation by Robert
Goldman and Sally J. Sutherland. — Princeton, N.J.: Princeton University
Press, c1984-. v. <1 > : col. ill.; 25 cm. (Princeton library of Asian
translations.) Includes index. I. Goldman, Robert P., 1942- II. Sutherland,
Sally J. III. T. IV. Series.
BL1139.22.E54 1984         294.5/922 19        LC 82-61364        ISBN
0691065616

**International Seminar on the Ramayana Tradition in Asia (1975:   1.1694**
**New Delhi, India)**
The Ramayana tradition in Asia: papers presented at the International Seminar
on the Ramayana Tradition in Asia, New Delhi, December 1975 / edited by V.
Raghavan. — New Delhi: Sahitya Akademi, 1980. xvi, 727 p.; 22 cm.
1. Vālmīki Rāmāyana — Congresses. 2. Rāma (Hindu deity) — Congresses.
3. Civilization, Hindu — Congresses. I. Raghavan, V. (Venkatarama), 1908-
II. T.
BL1139.26.I57 1975         294.5/922 19        LC 81-901408

**Embree, Ainslie Thomas. comp.**                                  • **1.1695**
The Hindu tradition, edited by Ainslie T. Embree. — New York: Modern
Library, [1966] xv, 363 p.; 19 cm. — (Readings in oriental thought) (The
Modern library of the world's best books.) 1. Hindu literature I. T.
BL1145.5.E5        294.508        LC 66-13011

### BL1147–1211 History. General Works

**Babb, Lawrence A.**                                               **1.1696**
The divine hierarchy: popular Hinduism in central India / Lawrence A. Babb.
— New York: Columbia University Press, 1975. xviii, 266 p.: ill.; 23 cm.
Includes index. 1. Hinduism — Chhattisgarh, India. 2. Chhattisgarh, India —
Religious life and customs. I. T.
BL1150.B29        294.5/0954/3        LC 75-16193        ISBN 0231038828

**Eck, Diana L.**                                                   **1.1697**
Banāras, City of Light / Diana L. Eck. — 1st ed. — New York: Knopf:
Distributed by Random House, 1982. xvi, 427 p.: ill.; 25 cm. Includes index.

1. Hinduism — India — Vārānasi. 2. Vārānasi (India) — Religious life and
customs. I. T.
BL1150.E25 1982         294.5/35 19        LC 81-48134        ISBN 039451971X

**Keith, Arthur Berriedale, 1879-1944.**                           • **1.1698**
The religion and philosophy of the Veda and Upanishads. — Westport, Conn.:
Greenwood Press, [1971] 2 v. (xviii, 683 p.); 27 cm. Reprint of the 1925 ed.
1. Vedas. 2. Upanishads. 3. Philosophy, Hindu 4. India — Religion I. T.
BL1150.K43 1971         294/.1        LC 71-109969        ISBN 0837144752

**Agehananda Bharati, Swami, 1923-.**                              **1.1699**
The ochre robe: an autobiography / Agehananda Bharati. — 2d ed. — Santa
Barbara, CA: Ross-Erikson Publishers, c1980. 300 p.; 22 cm. Includes index.
1. Agehananda Bharati, Swami, 1923- 2. Hindus — Biography 3. Hinduism
I. T.
BL1175.A4 A36 1980         294.5/64 B 19        LC 80-24101        ISBN
0915220281

**The deeds of god in Rddhipur / translated from Marāthī and      1.1700**
**annotated by Anne Feldhaus; with introductory essays by Anne**
**Feldhaus and Eleanor Zelliot.**
New York: Oxford University Press, 1984. 211 p.; 25 cm. 1. Gundam Rāul,
13th cent. 2. Mahanubhava 3. Hindus — India — Biography. I. Feldhaus,
Anne.
BL1175.G775 D44 1984         294.5/95 19        LC 83-21949        ISBN
0195034384

**Bowes, Pratima.**                                                 **1.1701**
Hindu intellectual tradition / Pratima Bowes. — Columbia, Mo.: South Asia
Books, 1977. vii, 218 p. 1. Hinduism 2. Civilization, Hindu I. T.
BL1202 B66

**Hopkins, Thomas J.**                                              • **1.1702**
The Hindu religious tradition [by] Thomas J. Hopkins. — Encino, Calif.:
Dickenson Pub. Co., [c1971] ix, 156 p.: illus.; 23 cm. — (The Religious life of
man) 1. Hinduism I. T.
BL1202.H66        294.5        LC 74-158118

**Stroup, Herbert Hewitt, 1916-.**                                  **1.1703**
Like a great river; an introduction to Hinduism [by] Herbert Stroup. — [1st
ed.]. — New York: Harper & Row, [1972] viii, 200 p.; 22 cm. 1. Hinduism
I. T.
BL1202.S77        294.5        LC 72-78049        ISBN 0060677570

**Zaehner, R. C. (Robert Charles), 1913-1974.**                     • **1.1704**
Hinduism / R.C. Zaehner. — London: Oxford University Press, 1962. [vii],
272 p. (The home university library of modern knowledge; no.247)
1. Hinduism I. T.
BL1202.Z3        LC 63-347

**Eck, Diana L.**                                                   **1.1705**
Darśan, seeing the divine image in India / Diana L. Eck. — [Chambersburg,
Pa.]: Anima Books, 1981. 79 p.: ill.; 22 cm. — (Focus on Hinduism and
Buddhism.) 1. Hinduism 2. Hinduism — Study and teaching — Audio-visual
aids. 3. Hindu symbolism I. T. II. Series.
BL1205.E25        294.5 19        LC 81-12813        ISBN 0890120242

**Hinduism: new essays in the history of religions / edited by     1.1706**
**Bardwell L. Smith.**
Leiden: E. J. Brill, 1976. 231 p., [2] leaves of plates: ill; 25 cm. (Studies in the
history of religions, supplements to Numen; 33) 1. Hinduism — Addresses,
essays, lectures. I. Smith, Bardwell L., 1925-
BL1210.H49        294.5        LC 76-369439        ISBN 9004044957

### BL1212–1243 Doctrines. Worship

**Gods of flesh/gods of stone: the embodiment of divinity in India   1.1707**
**/ edited by Joanne Punzo Waghorne and Norman Cutler in**
**association with Vasudha Narayanan.**
Chambersburg, PA: Anima, c1985. 208 p.: ill.; 22 cm. Includes index. 1. God
(Hinduism) — Addresses, essays, lectures. 2. Gods, Hindu — Addresses,
essays, lectures. 3. Hinduism — Customs and practices — Addresses, essays,
lectures. I. Waghorne, Joanne Punzo. II. Cutler, Norman, 1949-
III. Narayanan, Vasudha.
BL1213.32.G63 1984         294.5/211 19        LC 84-18543        ISBN
0890120374

**Daniélou, Alain.**                                                • **1.1708**
Hindu polytheism / Alain Daniélou. — New York: Bollingen Foundation:
distributed by Pantheon Books, 1964. xxxi, 537 p., [16] leaves of plates: ill. —
(Bollingen series; 73) Appendix (p. [387]-480): Sanskrit texts. 1. Gods, Hindu
I. T. II. Series.
BL1216.D313        LC 62-18191

**O'Flaherty, Wendy Doniger.**                                    **1.1709**
Asceticism and eroticism in the mythology of Śiva. — London; New York: Oxford University Press, 1973. xii, 386 p.: illus.; 24 cm. 1. Siva (Hindu deity) 2. Mythology, Hindu I. T.
BL1218.O34        294.5/2/11        *LC* 73-180569        *ISBN* 0197135730

**Daner, Francine Jeanne.**                                      **1.1710**
The American children of Krsna: a study of the Hare Krsna movement / by Francine Jeanne Daner; [photos. by Marjorie Daner–Sós]. — New York: Holt, Rinehart and Winston, c1976. ix, 118 p.: ill.; 24 cm. (Case studies in cultural anthropology.) 1. International Society for Krishna Consciousness. 2. Krishna (Hindu deity) — Cult. I. T. II. Series.
BL1220.D35        301.5/8        *LC* 75-15616        *ISBN* 003013546X

**Hiltebeitel, Alf.**                                            **1.1711**
The ritual of battle: Krishna in the Mahābhārata / Alf Hiltebeitel. — Ithaca, N.Y.: Cornell University Press, 1976. 368 p.; 22 cm. (Symbol, myth, and ritual series) 1. Mahābhārata. 2. Krishna. I. T.
BL1220.H47        294.5/2/11        *LC* 75-18496        *ISBN* 0801409705

**Kinsley, David R.**                                            **1.1712**
The divine player: a study of Krsna līlā / David R. Kinsley. — 1st ed. — Delhi: Motilal Banarsidass, 1979. xii, 306 p.; 22 cm. Originally presented as the author's thesis, University of Chicago. Includes index. 1. Krishna. 2. Play — Religious aspects 3. Vaishnavism I. T.
BL1220.K538 1979        294.5/211 19        *LC* 79-902687        *ISBN* 0896840190

**Kinsley, David R.**                                            **1.1713**
The sword and the flute: Kālī and Krsna, dark visions of the terrible and the sublime in Hindu mythology / David R. Kinsley. — Berkeley: University of California Press, c1975. viii, 167, [1] p.; 24 cm. (Hermeneutics, studies in the history of religions; 3) Based in part on the author's thesis. 1. Krishna. 2. Kali (Hindu deity) I. T. II. Series.
BL1220.K54        294.5/2/11        *LC* 73-91669        *ISBN* 0520026756

**Singer, Milton B. ed.**                                        **1.1715**
Krishna, myths, rites, and attitudes / edited by Milton Singer; with a foreword by Daniel H. H. Ingalls. — Westport, Conn.: Greenwood Press, 1981, c1966. xvii, 277 p.; 22 cm. Reprint of the ed. published by East-West Center Press, Honolulu, Hawaii. Includes index. 1. Krishna. I. T.
BL1220.S5 1981        294.5/211 19        *LC* 80-29194        *ISBN* 0313228221

**Östör, Ákos.**                                                 **1.1716**
The play of the gods: locality, ideology, structure, and time in the festivals of a Bengali town / Ákos Östör. — Chicago: University of Chicago Press, 1980. x, 241 p.: ill.; 24 cm. A revision of the author's thesis, University of Chicago, 1971. Includes index. 1. Durgā (Hindu deity) — Cult — India — Bishnupur. 2. Siva (Hindu deity) — Cult — India — Bishnupur. 3. Bishnupur (India) — Festivals. I. T.
BL1225.D8 O34 1980        294.5/211        *LC* 79-25661        *ISBN* 0226639541

**The Divine consort: Rādhā and the goddesses of India / edited**    **1.1717**
**by John Stratton Hawley and Donna Marie Wulff.**
[Berkeley, Calif.]: Berkeley Religious Studies Series, c1982. xviii, 414, [16] p.: ill. (some col.); 24 cm. Includes index. 1. Rādhā (Hindu deity) — Congresses. 2. Goddesses, Hindu — Congresses. I. Hawley, John Stratton, 1941- II. Wulff, Donna Marie, 1943- III. Harvard University. Center for the Study of World Religions.
BL1225.R24 D58 1982        294.5/211 19        *LC* 81-18128        *ISBN* 0895811022

**Miller, David M., PhD.**                                       **1.1718**
Hindu monastic life: the monks and monasteries of Bhubaneswar / by David M. Miller and Dorothy C. Wertz. Montreal: McGill-Queen's University Press, 1976. xv, 228 p.; [10] leaves of plates: ill.; 26 cm. Includes index. 1. Monastic and religious life (Hinduism) — India — Bhubaneswar. 2. Monasteries, Hindu — India — Bhubaneswar. I. Wertz, Dorothy C., joint author. II. T.
BL1226.85.M54        294.5/6/5        *LC* 76-373803        *ISBN* 0773501908

**Tripathi, Bansi Dhar.**                                        **1.1719**
Sadhus of India: the sociological view / B. D. Tripathi; foreword by G. S. Ghurye. — Bombay: Popular Prakashan, 1978. xv, 258 p., [2] leaves of plates: ill., map; 22 cm. A revision of the author's thesis, University of Lucknow, 1966, with title: The religious mendicants of Uttar Pradesh. Includes index. 1. Sadhus — India — Uttar Pradesh. 2. Hindu sects — India. 3. Uttar Pradesh (India) — Religious life and customs. I. T.
BL1226.85.T74 1978        301.5/8        *LC* 78-904439

**Bhardwaj, Surinder Mohan.**                                    **1.1720**
Hindu places of pilgrimage in India; a study in cultural geography. — Berkeley: University of California Press, [1973] xviii, 258 p.: illus.; 24 cm. 1. Pilgrims and pilgrimages — India. 2. Hindu shrines — India. I. T.
BL1227.A1 B495        294.5/3/8        *LC* 73-174454        *ISBN* 0520021355

**Morinis, E. Alan.**                                            **1.1721**
Pilgrimage in the Hindu tradition: a case study of West Bengal / E. Alan Morinis. — Delhi: New York: Oxford University Press, 1984. viii, 346 p., 8 p. of plates: ill., maps; 22 cm. (Oxford University South Asian studies series.) Includes index. 1. Hindu pilgrims and pilgrimages — India — West Bengal. I. T. II. Series.
BL1239.36.W47 M67 1984        294.5/446 19        *LC* 84-900693        *ISBN* 0195614127

## BL1245–1295 Hindu Sects

**Woodroffe, John George, Sir, 1865-1936.**                      • **1.1722**
Śakti andŚākta: essays and addresses / Sir John Woodroffe. — 3d ed. rev. and enl. — Madras: Ganesh, 1929. xvi, 724 p.; 26 cm. — 1. Shaktism I. T.
BL1245.S4W6 1929        294.5/514        *LC* 60-56288

**Woodroffe, John George, Sir, 1865-1936.**                      • **1.1723**
The world as power; reality, life, mind, matter, causality and continuity, by Sir John Woodroffe. With an introd. by M.P. Pandit. 3d ed. Madras Ganesh 1966. 398p. 1. Shaktism I. T.
BL1245 S4 W66 1966

**Lorenzen, David N.**                                           **1.1724**
The Kāpālikas and Kālāmukhas; two lost Śaivite sects [by] David N. Lorenzen. — Berkeley: University of California Press, [1972] xiv, 214 p.; 23 cm. 1. Kāpālikas 2. Kālāmukhas I. T.
BL1245.S5 L67        294.5/5        *LC* 70-138509        *ISBN* 0520018427

**Shulman, David Dean, 1949-.**                                  **1.1725**
Tamil temple myths: sacrifice and divine marriage in the South Indian Śaiva tradition / David Dean Shulman. — Princeton, N.J.: Princeton University Press, c1980. xvi, 471 p.: ill.; 24 cm. Includes indexes. 1. Sivaism 2. Mythology, Tamil 3. Temples, Hindu — India, South. 4. Sacred marriage (Mythology) 5. Sacrifice — Hinduism 6. Hinduism — Doctrines I. T.
BL1245.S5 S53        294.5/513        *LC* 79-17051        *ISBN* 0691064156

**Sivaraman, Krishna.**                                          **1.1726**
Śaivism in philosophical perspective; a study of the formative concepts, problems, and methods of Śaiva Siddhānta [by] K. Sivaraman. — [1st ed.]. — Delhi: Motilal Banarsidass, [1973] xiv, v, 687 p.; 24 cm. 1. Sivaism I. T.
BL1245.S5 S58        181/.4        *LC* 73-91126

**Goudriaan, Teun.**                                             **1.1727**
Hindu tantric and 'Śākta literature / Teun Goudriaan and Sanjukta Gupta. — Wiesbaden: Harrassowitz, 1981. 245 p.; 24 cm. — (History of Indian literature. v. 2, fasc. 2) 1. Tantrism 2. Shaktism 3. Hindu literature — History and criticism I. Gupta, Sanjukta. II. T. III. Series.
BL1245.T3 G69        BL1245T3 G69.        *ISBN* 3447020911

**A. C. Bhaktivedanta Swami Prabhupāda, 1896-1977.**            **1.1728**
Teachings of Lord Caitanya: the Golden Avatara / A. C. Bhaktivedanta Swami. — New York: Bombay; Bhaktivedanta Book Trust, c1974. xxv, 440 p., [10] leaves of plates: ill.; 21 cm. 1. Chaitanya, 1486-1534. I. T.
BL1245.V36 B48 1974        294.5/513        *LC* 75-2060        *ISBN* 0912776072. *ISBN* 0912776080

**Jones, Kenneth W.**                                            **1.1729**
Arya dharm: Hindu consciousness in 19th–century Punjab / Kenneth W. Jones. — Berkeley: University of California Press, c1976. xvi, 343 p., [1] leaf of plates: maps; 25 cm. 1. Arya-Samaj. 2. Hindus — India — Punjab 3. Punjab — History I. T.
BL1254.5.P86 J66        294.5/0954/552        *LC* 74-27290        *ISBN* 0520029208

**Dayananda Sarasvati, Swami, 1824-1883.**                      **1.1730**
Autobiography of Swami Dayanand Saraswati / edited with an introd. and notes by K. C. Yadav. New Delhi: Manohar Book Service, 1976. 108 p.; 22 cm. 1. Dayananda Sarasvati, Swami, 1824-1883. 2. Arya-Samaj — Biography. I. T.
BL1255.D3 A32        294.5/6/4 B        *LC* 76-900170

**Jordens, J. T. F.**                                            **1.1731**
Dayānanda Sarasvatī, his life and ideas / J. T. F. Jordens. — Delhi: Oxford University Press, 1979 (c1978). xvii, 368 p.; 23 cm. Includes index. 1. Dayananda Sarasvati, Swami, 1824-1883. 2. Arya-Samaj — Biography. I. T.
BL1255.D3 J67        294.5/6/4 B        *LC* 79-111204        *ISBN* 0195609956

**Ghose, Aurobindo, 1872-1950.**                                • **1.1732**
The life divine. Pondicherry, Sri Aurobindo Ashram, 1960. iv, 1272 p. 19 cm. (Sri Aurobindo International Centre of Education collection, v.3) 1. Metaphysics 2. Knowledge, Theory of 3. Spiritual life I. T.
BL1270.G38x

**Bhattacharyya, Narendra Nath, 1934-.**                     **1.1733**
History of the tantric religion: a historical, ritualistic, and philosophical study / N.N. Bhattacharyya. — 1st ed. — New Delhi: Manohar, 1982. xviii, 507 p.; 23 cm. Includes index. 1. Tantrism — History. I. T.
BL1283.83.B46 1982      294.5/514 19      *LC* 82-904123

**Gosvāmī, Satsvarūpa Dāsa, 1939-.**                          **1.1734**
Prabhupāda: he built a house in which the whole world can live / by Satsvarūpa Dāsa Goswami. — Los Angeles: Bhaktivedanta Book Trust, c1983. 362 p., [16] p. of plates: ill., ports.; 18 cm. 1. A. C. Bhaktivedanta Swami Prabhupāda, 1896-1977. 2. Hare Krishnas — Biography 3. Hindus — Biography I. T.
BL1285.892.A28 G682 1983      294.5/512/0924 B 19      *LC* 84-194163      *ISBN* 0892131330

## BL1300–1380 JAINISM

**Jaina Āgama. Selections. English.**                         **1.1735**
Jaina Sutras. Translated from Prakrit by Hermann Jacobi. New York, Dover Publications [1968] 2 v. 22 cm. (The Sacred books of the East, v. 22, 45) I. Jacobi, Hermann Georg, 1850-1937, tr. II. T.
BL1311.S5 E5 1968      294.4/8/2      *LC* 68-9452      *ISBN* 0486211568

**Jaini, Padmanabh S.**                                       **1.1736**
The Jaina path of purification / Padmanabh S. Jaini. — Berkeley: University of California Press, c1979. xv, 374 p.: ill.; 23 cm. 'This volume is sponsored by the Center for South and Southeast Asia Studies, University of California, Berkeley.' Includes index. 1. Jainism I. University of California, Berkeley. Center for South and Southeast Asia Studies. II. T.
BL1351.2.J293      294.4      *LC* 77-73496      *ISBN* 0520034597

## BL1400–1495 BUDDHISM
(Works classified before 1972. For later works see BQ.)

## BL1410–1411 Sacred Books. Sources

**Buddhist Mahāyāna texts.**                                  **1.1737**
Delhi, Motilal Banarsidass [1965] xiii, 207, xxvi, 208 p. 23 cm. (The Sacred books of the East, v. 49) (UNESCO collection of representative works. Indian series) 1. Mahayana Buddhism — Sacred books I. Aśvaghosa. Buddhacarita. English. 1965. II. Cowell, Edward Byles, 1826-1903, ed. and tr. III. Müller, F. Max (Friedrich Max), 1823-1900. ed. and tr. IV. Takakusu, Junjirō, tr. V. Sukhāvat īvyūha. 1965. VI. Tripitaka. Sūtrapitaka. Prajñāpāramitā. Vajracchedikā. English. 1965. VII. Prajnaparamits. 1965. VIII. Kuan wu liang shou ching. 1965. IX. Title: Mahāyāna texts. X. Series.
BL1410.B87 1965      *LC* sa 66-666

**Conze, Edward, 1904-.**                                     **1.1738**
Buddhist scriptures / selected and translated by Edward Conze. — Harmondsworth, Middlesex: Penguin, 1959. 250 p.: ill. (Penguin classics; L88.) 1. Buddhism — Sacred books I. T.
BL1410.C58      294.30082      *LC* 59-2558      *ISBN* 0140440887

**Conze, Edward, 1904- comp.**                                **1.1739**
Buddhist texts through the ages. Translated from Pali, Sanskrit, Chinese, Tibetan, Japanese, and Apabhramsa. Edited by Edward Conze in collaboraton with I.B. Horner, D. Snellgrove [and] A. Waley. Oxford: B. Cassirer, [1954] 322p. 1. Buddha and Buddhism — Sacred books (Selections; Extracts, etc.) I. T.
BL1410 C6 1954      *LC* 54-3272

**Warren, Henry Clarke, 1854-1899. ed. and tr.**             **1.1740**
Buddhism in translations; passages selected from the Buddhist sacred books and translated from the original Pāli into English. New York, Atheneum, 1963 [c1896] xx, 496 p. 19 cm. 1. Buddhism — Sacred books I. T.
BL1410.W3 1963      294.3/82 19      *LC* 63-879

**Bardo thödol.**                                             **1.1741**
The Tibetan book of the dead; or, The after–death experiences on the Bardo plane, according to Lāma Kazi Dawa–Samdup's English rendering, by W. Y. Evans-Wentz. With a psychological commentary by C. G. Jung, introducing foreword by Lāma Anagarika Govinda, and foreword by John Woodruffe [i.e. Woodroffe]. — 3d ed. — London; New York: Oxford University Press, 1957. lxxxiv, 249 p.: illus., plates., group port.; 23 cm. I. Zla-ba-Bsam-'grub, Kāzī, 1868-1922, tr. II. Evans-Wentz, W. Y. (Walter Yeeling), 1878-1965. ed. III. T.
BL1411.B3 E6 1957      294.32      *LC* 57-3183

**Milindapañhā.**                                             **1.1742**
The questions of King Milinda. Translated from the Pali by T. W. Rhys Davids. New York, Dover Publications [1963] 2 v. 22 cm. (The Sacred books of the East, v. 35-6) I. Davids, T. W. Rhys (Thomas William Rhys), 1843-1922. ed. and tr. II. T.
BL1411.M5 E5 1963      294.3      *LC* 63-19514

**Suttapitaka. English. Selections.**                         **1.1743**
Buddhist suttas. Translated from Pāli by T. W. Rhys Davids. New York, Dover Publications [1969] xlviii, 320 p. 22 cm. (The Sacred books of the East, v. 11) I. Davids, T. W. Rhys (Thomas William Rhys), 1843-1922. tr. II. T.
BL1411.S83 E4 1969      294.3/823      *LC* 68-8043      *ISBN* 048622192X

**Tantras. Hevajratantrarājānāma.**                           **1.1744**
The Hevajra Tantra; a critical study, by D. L. Snellgrove. — London, New York, Oxford University Press, 1959. 2 v. illus. 26 cm. — (London oriental series. v. 6) Bibliography: v. 1, p. xiii-xv. I. Snellgrove, David L. ed. and tr. II. Krisnācāryapāda. Yogaratamālā. III. T. IV. Series.
BL1411.T3E57      294.3282      *LC* 60-282

**Aśvaghosa.**                                                **1.1745**
[Mahayanaśraddhotpadaśastra. English] The awakening of faith, attributed to Aśvaghosha. Translated, with commentary, by Yoshito S. Hakeda. New York, Columbia University Press, 1967. xi, 128 p. 24 cm. 'Prepared for the Columbia College program of translations from the oriental classics.' Translation of the Chinese version of the Sanskrit manuscript: Mahāyānaśraddhotpādaśastra. I. Hakeda, Yoshito S. tr. II. T.
BL1416.A7 M33      294.3/82      *LC* 67-13778

**Phra Thēpwisutthimēthī (Ngūam), 1906-.**                    **1.1746**
Toward the truth. Edited by Donald K. Swearer. Philadelphia, Westminster Press [1971] 189 p. 19 cm. I. T.
BL1416.B8 A33 1971      294.3/4      *LC* 72-135627      *ISBN* 066424906X

**Streng, Frederick J.**                                      **1.1747**
Emptiness; a study in religious meaning [by] Frederick J. Streng. Nashville, Abingdon Press [1967] 252 p. 24 cm. 1. Nāgārjuna, 2nd cent. 2. Sunyata. I. T.
BL1416.N33 S7      294.3/01      *LC* 67-11010

## BL1420–1448 History

**Ch'ên, Kenneth Kuan Shêng, 1907-.**                         **1.1748**
Buddhism in China, a historical survey, by Kenneth K. S. Ch'ên. Princeton, N.J., Princeton University Press, 1964. xii, 560 p. map. 25 cm. (The Virginia and Richard Stewart memorial lectures, 1961) Princeton studies in the history of religions. 1. Buddha and Buddhism — China — History. I. T.
BL1430.C486      294.320951      *LC* 63-23402

**Suzuki, Daisetz Teitaro, 1870-1966.**                       **1.1749**
Essays in Zen Buddhism (third series) / Daisetz Teitaro Suzuki; edited by Christmas Humphreys. — London: Rider, 1973, c1953. 376 p., [33] leaves of plates. 1. Zen Buddhism 2. Buddha and Buddhism — China. I. T.
BL1430.S8 3d series      *ISBN* 009048442X

**Suzuki, Daisetz Teitaro, 1870-1966.**                       **1.1750**
Zen Buddhism, selected writings. Edited by William Barrett. — [1st ed.]. — Garden City, N.Y.: Doubleday, 1956. 294 p.; 18 cm. — (Doubleday anchor books, A90) 1. Zen Buddhism — China. I. T.
BL1430.S848      294.32      *LC* 56-9406

**Welch, Holmes.**                                            **1.1751**
The practice of Chinese Buddhism. — Cambridge: Harvard University Press, 1967-. v.    : illus., maps, ports.; 25 cm. — (Harvard East Asian studies, 26) 1. Buddha and Buddhism — China. I. T.
BL1430.W4      *LC* 67-13256

**Welch, Holmes.**                                            **1.1752**
The Buddhist revival in China / Holmes Welch; with a section of photos by Henri Cartier–Bresson. — Cambridge: Harvard University Press, 1968. vi, 385 p.: ill., col. maps (on lining papers). — (Harvard East Asian series. 33) 1. Buddha and Buddhism — China — History I. T. II. Series.
BL1431.6 W4      BQ626 W4.      294/.3/0951      294/.3/0951      *LC* 68-15645

**Suzuki, Daisetz Teitaro, 1870-1966.**                       **1.1753**
Essays in Zen Buddhism (second series) London Luzac 1933. 326p. 1. Zen Buddhism 2. Buddha and Buddhism — China I. T.
BL1432 Z4 S7 1933

**Suzuki, Daisetz Teitaro, 1870-1966.**                       **1.1754**
Essays in Zen Buddhism, first series. — New York: Grove Press, [1961] 387 p.; 21 cm. — (Evergreen original,E-309) 1. Zen Buddhism — Addresses, essays, lectures. I. T.
BL1432.Z4 S8 1961      294.329      *LC* 61-11477

**Suzuki, Daisetz Teitaro, 1870-1966.**                       **1.1755**
Manual of Zen Buddhism. New York, Grove Press [1960] 192 p. illus. 21 cm. (Evergreen original, E-231) 1. Zen Buddhism 2. Buddhism — Sacred books 3. Gods, Buddhist I. T. II. Title: Zen Buddhism.
BL1432.Z4 S82 1960      294.329      *LC* 60-7637

**Watts, Alan, 1915-1973.**      • **1.1756**
The spirit of Zen; a way of life, work, and art in the Far East. New York, Grove Press [1960, c1958] 128 p. illus. 21 cm. (The Wisdom of the East) (An Evergreen book, E-219.) 1. Zen Buddhism — China. 2. Zen Buddhism — Japan. I. T.
BL1432.Z4 W28 1960     294.329     *LC* 60-7347

**Blofeld, John Eaton Calthorpe, 1913-.**      **1.1757**
The Tantric mysticism of Tibet; a practical guide, by John Blofeld. — [1st ed.]. — New York: Dutton, 1970. 257 p.: illus.; 22 cm. 1. Tantric Buddhism — Tibet. I. T.
BL1433.3.T3 B55 1970b     294.3/925 19     *LC* 76-119478     *ISBN* 0525214232

**Reischauer, August Karl, 1879-.**      • **1.1758**
Studies in Japanese Buddhism. — New York: AMS Press, [1970] xviii, 361 p.: port.; 23 cm. Reprint of the 1917 ed. 1. Buddhism — Japan I. T.
BL1440.R5 1970     294.3/92/0952     *LC* 73-107769     *ISBN* 0404052371

**Anesaki, Masaharu, 1873-1949.**      • **1.1759**
Nichiren, the Buddhist prophet. — Gloucester, Mass.: P. Smith, 1966 [c1916] viii, 160 p.; 21 cm. 1. Nichiren, 1222-1282. 2. Buddha and Buddhism — Japan. I. T.
BL1442.N53 A5 1966     294.3/92/0924 B     *LC* 67-2824

**Murata, Kiyoaki, 1922-.**      • **1.1760**
Japan's new Buddhism; an objective account of Soka Gakkai, by Kiyoaki Murata. Foreword by Daisaku Ikeda. — [1st ed.]. — New York: Walker/Weatherhill [i.e. J. Weatherhill; distributed by Walker, 1969] xii, 194 p.: illus., ports.; 24 cm. 1. Sōka Gakkai. I. T.
BL1442.S6 M87     294.3/65     *LC* 74-83640

**Dumoulin, Heinrich.**      • **1.1761**
[Zen. English] A history of Zen Buddhism. Translated from the German by Paul Peachey. New York, Pantheon Books [1963] 335 p. illus. 21 cm. Translation of Zen. 1. Zen Buddhism — History. I. T.
BL1442.Z4 D83     294.329     *LC* 62-17386

**Hakuin, 1686-1769.**      **1.1762**
The Zen Master Hakuin: selected writings. Translated by Philip B. Yampolsky. New York, Columbia University Press, 1971. xii, 253 p. 24 cm. (Records of civilization, sources and studies. no. 86) Translation of Orategama, Yabukōji, and Hebilichigo (romanized form) 1. Zen Buddhism — Early works to 1800. I. T. II. Series.
BL1442.Z4 E3613     294.3/4     *LC* 75-145390     *ISBN* 0231034636

**Suzuki, Daisetz Teitaro, 1870-1966.**      • **1.1763**
[Zen Buddhism and its influence on Japanese culture] Zen and Japanese culture. [Rev. and enl. 2d ed. New York] Pantheon Books [1959] xxiii, 478 p. 68 plates (incl. ports.) 24 cm. (Bollingen series. 64) First ed. published in 1938 under title: Zen Buddhism and its influence on Japanese culture. 1. Zen Buddhism — Japan. 2. Philosophy, Japanese 3. Japan — Civilization — Zen influences I. T. II. Series.
BL1442.Z4 S8 1959     294.329     *LC* 58-12174

**Sarkisyanz, Manuel.**      • **1.1764**
Buddhist backgrounds of the Burmese revolution / by E. Sarkisyanz; pref. by Paul Mus. — The Hague: M. Nijhoff, 1965. xxix, 248 p.; 25 cm. 1. Buddhism — Burma 2. Buddhism and state — Burma I. T.
BL1443.1.S2     BQ418.S2.     *LC* 66-81311

**Spiro, Melford E.**      • **1.1765**
Buddhism and society; a great tradition and its Burmese vicissitudes [by] Melford E. Spiro. — [1st ed.]. — New York: Harper & Row, [c1970] xiv, 510 p.; 24 cm. 1. Buddhism — Burma. I. T.
BL1443.1.S65 1970     294.3/91/09591     *LC* 70-124697

## BL1450–1475 General Works

**Conze, Edward, 1904-.**      • **1.1766**
Buddhism; its essence and development. With a pref. by Arthur Waley. — New York: Harper, [1959] 212 p.: illus.; 21 cm. — (Harper torchbooks, TB58) 1. Buddha and Buddhism. I. T.
BL1451.2.C6 1959     294.3     *LC* 59-10345

**Khantipālo, Phikkhu, 1933 or 4-.**      • **1.1767**
What is Buddhism? An introduction to the teachings of Lord Buddha with reference to the belief in and the practice of those teachings and their realization. Bangkok Social Science Association Press of Thailand 1965. 150p. 1. Buddha and Buddhism I. T.
BL1451.2 K47

**Rāhula, Walpola.**      • **1.1768**
What the Buddha taught. Foreword by Paul Demiéville. New York, Grove Press [1962, c1959] 103 p. illus. 21 cm. (Evergreen original, E-330.) 1. Buddha and Buddhism. 2. Buddhism — Doctrines I. T.
BL1451.2.R3 1962     *LC* 62-16338

**Conze, Edward, 1904- ed. and tr.**      • **1.1769**
Buddhist meditation. — London: Allen and Unwin, [1956] 183 p.; 19 cm. — (Ethical and religious classics of East and West, no. 13) 'The bulk of the selections are derived from the Old Wisdom school [i. e. of the Theravādin and Sarvastivadin schools] and in particular from Buddhaghosa's Path of purity.' Continued by Buddhist thought in India. 1. Buddhist meditations I. Buddhaghosa. Visuddimagga. II. T.
BL1453.C6     294.3     *LC* a 56-4188

**Schecter, Jerrold L.**      • **1.1770**
The new face of Buddha: Buddhism and political power in Southeast Asia / Jerrold Schecter. — New York: Coward-McCann, 1967. xix, 300 p.: ill., ports, map (on lining papers). 1. Buddhism and state I. T.
BL1459.S7S3     294.3     *LC* 67-10560

**Tao-Yüan, Shih.**      • **1.1771**
Original teachings of Ch'an Buddhism, selected from The transmission of the lamp / translated with introductions by Chang Chung–Yüan. — New York: Pantheon Books, 1969. 333p. Includes index. 1. Zen Buddhism — Biography. I. Chang, Chung-yüan. II. T.
BL1460.T3513 1969     294.3927     *LC* 75-79799     *ISBN* 0394713338

**Foucher, A. (Alfred), 1865-1952.**      **1.1772**
The life of the Buddha: according to the ancient texts and monuments of India / by A. Foucher; abridged translation by Simone Brangier Boas. 1st ed. Middletown, Conn.: Wesleyan University Press, c1963. xiv, 272 p.: ill.; 25 cm. 1. Gautama Buddha. I. T.
BL1470.F623     294.3     *LC* 63-17795

**Thomas, E. J. (Edward Joseph), 1869-.** — [3d ed.] —      • **1.1773**
The life of Buddha as legend and history. — [3d ed.] — New York: Barnes & Noble, 1952. xxiv, 297 p., 4 plates; 25 cm. — (History of civilization) 1. Buddha and Buddhism. I. T.
BL1470.T5 1949     *LC* 54-7472

**Shunshō, 1255-1335.**      • **1.1774**
Honen, the Buddhist saint; his life and teaching. Kyoto, Society for the Pub. of Sacred Books of the World, 1949. 5 v. (lxix, 955 p.) illus. 22 cm. 1. Hōnen, 1133-1212. 2. Buddha and Buddhism — Japan. 3. Japan — Religion I. Coates, Harper Havelock, 1865- tr. II. T.
BL1473.H6 S5 1949     *LC* 49-29237

**Waley, Arthur.**      • **1.1775**
The Real Tripitaka: and other pieces / Arthur Waley. — London: Allen and Unwin, 1952. 291 p.; 22 cm. Includes index. 1. Hsüan-tsang, ca. 596-664. 2. Tales — China I. T.
BL1473.H8 W3 1952     *LC* 55-18728

**Robinson, Richard H., 1926-.**      • **1.1776**
Early Mādhyamika in India and China, by Richard H. Robinson. — Madison: [University of Wisconsin Press], 1967. xi, 347 p.: geneal. table.; 25 cm. 1. Mādhyamika (Buddhism) 2. Buddha and Buddhism — China. I. T.
BL1475.M3 R6     181/.4     *LC* 66-22853

**Swearer, Donald K., 1934- comp.**      **1.1777**
Secrets of the lotus; studies in Buddhist meditation. Edited by Donald K. Swearer. — New York: Macmillan, [1971] xii, 242 p.; 21 cm. 1. Meditation — Buddhism 2. Meditation — Zen Buddhism I. T.
BL1478.6.S93     294.3/4/43     *LC* 75-150068

## BL1479–1495 Special Sects

**Bstan-'dzin-rgya-mtsho, Dalai Lama XIV, 1935-.**      • **1.1778**
My land and my people, by His Holiness, the Dalai Lama of Tibet. New York, McGraw-Hill [1962] 271 p. illus. 22 cm. 1. Bstan-'dzin-rgya-mtsho, Dalai Lama XIV, 1935- I. T.
BL1489.B78 A35     951/.5/05     *LC* 62-13808

**Chang, Ch'eng-ch'i.**      **1.1779**
The Buddhist teaching of totality; the philosophy of Hwa Yen Buddhism [by] Garma C. C. Chang. — University Park: Pennsylvania State University Press, [c1971] xxv, 270 p.; 24 cm. 1. Hua-yen Buddhism — Doctrines. I. T.
BL1495.K4 C47     294.3/927     *LC* 70-136965     *ISBN* 0271011424

**Agehananda Bharati, Swami, 1923-.**      • **1.1780**
The Tantric tradition / Agehananda Bharati. — London: Rider, 1975. 349 p.; 22 cm. 1. Tantrism I. T.
BL1495.T3 A35 1975     294     *ISBN* 0090747216 pa

## BL1500–1590 ZOROASTRIANISM (MAZDEISM). PARSEEISM. MITHRAISM

**Boyce, Mary.**      **1.1781**
A Persian stronghold of Zoroastrianism / Mary Boyce. — Oxford [Eng.]: Clarendon Press, 1977. ix, 284 p., [4] leaves of plates: ill.; 23 cm. — (Ratanbai Katrak lectures; 1975) Based on the Ratanbai Katrak lectures, 1975. Includes indexes. 1. Zoroastrianism — Addresses, essays, lectures. 2. Sharīfābād, Iran — Religious life and customs — Addresses, essays, lectures. I. T.
BL1525.B69    295/.0955    *LC* 77-7350    *ISBN* 019826531X

**Pangborn, Cyrus R.**      **1.1782**
Zoroastrianism: a beleaguered faith / Cyrus R. Pangborn. — 1st ed. — New York: Advent Books, c1983. xvi, 162 p., [4] p. of plates: ill.; 23 cm. Includes index. 1. Zoroastrianism I. T.
BL1571.P3 1983    295 19    *LC* 82-74483    *ISBN* 0898910064

**Zaehner, R. C. (Robert Charles), 1913-1974.**      **1.1783**
The dawn and twilight of Zoroastrianism. — New York: Putnam, 1961. 371p.: ill. — (The Putnam history of religion.) 1. Zoroastrianism I. T.
BL1571.Z3 1961    *LC* 61-8353    *ISBN* 0297768921 2295

## BL1600–1710 SEMITIC RELIGIONS

**Arberry, A. J. (Arthur John), 1905-1969.**      **1.1784**
Religion in the Middle East: three religions in concord and conflict; general editor A. J. Arberry. London, Cambridge U.P., 1969. 2 v. 32 plates, 41 illus., facsim., 25 maps. 24 cm. 1. Middle East — Religion. I. T.
BL1600.A7    200/.956    *LC* 68-21187    *ISBN* 0521074002

**Wolkstein, Diane.**      **1.1785**
Inanna, queen of heaven and earth: her stories and hymns from Sumer / Diane Wolkstein and Samuel Noah Kramer; art compiled by Elizabeth Williams–Forte. — 1st ed. — New York: Harper & Row, c1983. xix, 227 p.: ill.; 24 cm. Translation and retelling of the Inanna stories from the Sumerian. Includes index. 1. Inanna (Sumerian deity) 2. Mythology, Sumerian 3. Inanna (Sumerian deity) — Poetry. I. Kramer, Samuel Noah, 1897- II. T.
BL1616.I5 W64 1983    299/.92 19    *LC* 80-8690    *ISBN* 006014713X

**Makārim, Sāmī Nasīb.**      **1.1786**
The Druze faith, by Sami Nasib Makarem. — Delmar, N.Y.: Caravan Books, 1974. xi, 153 p.; 23 cm. 1. Druzes I. T.
BL1695.M33    297/.85/09    *LC* 73-19819    *ISBN* 0882060031

# BL1750–2370 Asian Religions, by Country

## BL1800–1950 CHINA

**Granet, Marcel, 1884-1940.**      **1.1787**
[Religion des Chinois. English] The religion of the Chinese people / Marcel Granet; translated, edited, and with an introd. by Maurice Freedman. — New York: Harper & Row, c1975. viii, 200 p.; 23 cm. — (Explorations in interpretative sociology) Translation of La religion des Chinois. Includes index. 1. Cults, Chinese. 2. China — Religion I. T.
BL1801.G513 1975b    200/.951    *LC* 74-33106    *ISBN* 0061361720

**Bush, Richard Clarence, 1923-.**      ● **1.1788**
Religion in Communist China [by] Richard C. Bush, Jr. — Nashville: Abingdon Press, [1970] 432 p.; 25 cm. 1. China — Religion I. T.
BL1802.B87    200.9/51    *LC* 70-109678    *ISBN* 0687360153

**Chan, Wing-tsit, 1901-.**      ● **1.1789**
Religious trends in modern China. — New York: Octagon Books, 1969 [c1953] xiii, 327 p.; 24 cm. — (Lectures on the history of religions, new ser., no. 3) (The Haskell lectures at the University of Chicago, 1950.) 1. Religious thought — China. 2. China — Religion I. T. II. Series.
BL1802.C48    200/.951    *LC* 71-96176

**Maspero, Henri, 1883-1945.**      **1.1790**
[Taoïsme et les religions chinoises. English] Taoism and Chinese religion / Henri Maspero; translated by Frank A. Kierman, Jr. — Amherst: University of Massachusetts Press, 1981. xxxiii, 578 p.: ill.; 24 cm. Translation of Le taoïsme et les religions chinoises. 1. Taoism — China. 2. China — Religion I. T.
BL1802.M3813    299/.514/0951    *LC* 80-13444    *ISBN* 0870233084

**Smith, D. Howard (David Howard), b. 1900.**      ● **1.1791**
Chinese religions [by] D. Howard Smith. — [1st ed.]. — New York: Holt, Rinehart and Winston, [1968] xiii, 221 p.: illus.; 25 cm. — (History of religion series) 1. China — Religion I. T.
BL1802.S6 1968b    200/.951    *LC* 68-12215

**Weber, Max, 1864-1920.**      ● **1.1792**
The religion of China: Confucianism and Taoism / Max Weber; translated and edited by Hans H. Gerth. — Glencoe, Ill.: Free Press, 1951. xi, 308 p. A translation of the author's essay, Konfuzianismus und Taoismus, published in v.1 of his Gesammelte Aufsätze sur Religionssoziologie in 1922. 1. Confucianism 2. Taoism 3. Religion and sociology 4. China — Religion I. T.
BL1802.W33    *LC* 51-12055

**Yang, C. K., 1910-.**      ● **1.1793**
Religion in Chinese society; a study of contemporary social functions of religion and some of their historical factors. — Berkeley: University of California Press, 1961. viii, 473 p.; 24 cm. 1. China — Religious life and customs. 2. China — Social conditions I. T.
BL1802.Y3 1961    209.51    *LC* 61-7520

**Chai, Ch'u.**      ● **1.1794**
The sacred books of Confucius: and other Confucian classics / ed. and tr. by Ch'u Chai and Winberg Chai; introd. by Ch'u Chai. — New Hyde Park, N.Y.: University Bks, [1965] 384 p. 1. Confucianism — Sacred books. I. Chai, Winberg. II. T.
BL1829.C5    181.0951    *LC* 65-22805

## BL1830–1870 Confucianism

**I ching.**      ● **1.1795**
I Ching: Book of changes / translated by James Legge; edited with introduction and study guide by Ch'u Chai with Winberg Chai. — New Hyde Park, N.Y.: University Books, 1964. ci, 448 p.: ill.; 25 cm. 'Except for the new material added by the editors, the text ... is that published in a second edition of 1899 ... as volume XVI of 'The sacred books of the East' and also designated as part II of 'The texts of Confucianism." I. Legge, James, 1815-1897. II. Chai, Ch'u. III. Chai, Winberg. IV. T. V. Title: Book of changes.
BL1830.I23 L4 1964    *LC* 64-25866

**Chang, Chün-mai, 1886-1969.**      ● **1.1796**
The Development of Neo–Confucian thought / by Carsun Chang. — New York: Bookman Associates, 1957. 376 p.; 23 cm. 1. Confucianism 2. Neo-Confucianism I. T.
BL1851.C5    *LC* 58-177

**Shryock, John Knight, 1890-.**      **1.1797**
The origin and development of the state cult of Confucius: an introductory study / by John K. Shryock. — New York: Paragon Book Reprint, 1966. xiii, 298 p. At head of title: The American historical association. 1. Confucius and Confucianism. 2. Cultus, Chinese. 3. China — Religion I. American Historical Association. II. T.
BL1851.S5

## BL1900–1940 Taoism

**Chuang-tzu.**      ● **1.1798**
[Nan-hua ching English] The complete works of Chuang Tzu. Translated by Burton Watson. New York, Columbia University Press, 1968. 397 p. 21 cm. (UNESCO collection of representative works. Chinese series.) (Records of civilization, sources and studies. no. 80.) 'Prepared for the Columbia College program of translations from the Oriental classics.' Translation of Nan-hua ching (romanized form) I. Columbia College (Columbia University) II. T. III. Series. IV. Series: Records of civilization, sources and studies. no. 80.
BL1900.C5 W34    181/.09514    *LC* 68-19000

**Lao-tzu.**      **1.1799**
[Tao te ching. English] Commentary on the Lao Tzu / by Wang Pi; translated by Ariane Rump in collaboration with Wing-tsit Chan. — [Honolulu]: University Press of Hawaii, 1979. xxxvii, 219 p.; 23 cm. — (Monograph of the Society for Asian and Comparative Philosophy; no. 6) I. Wang, Pi, 226-249. II. Rump, Ariane. III. Chan, Wing-tsit, 1901- IV. T.
BL1900.L26 E5 1979b    299/.5148/2    *LC* 79-11212    *ISBN* 0824806778

**I ching. English.**      ● **1.1800**
The book of change; a new translation of the ancient Chinese I ching (Yi king) with detailed instruction for its practical use in divination, by John Blofeld. New York, Dutton [1966, c1965] 228 p. 23 cm. I. Blofeld, John Eton Calthorpe, 1913- ed. and tr. II. T.
BL1900.L3C44    *LC* 66-2160

**Lao-tzu.**      ● **1.1801**
[Tao te ching. English. 1963] The way of Lao Tzu (Tao-tê ching) Translated with introductory essays, comments, and notes by Wing–tsit Chan. Indianapolis, Bobbs-Merrill [c1963] viii, 285 p. 21 cm. (The Library of liberal arts, 139) I. Chan, Wing-tsit, 1901- tr. II. T.
BL1900.L3 C44    *LC* 62-21266

**Lao-tzu.** • **1.1802**
The way and its power; a study of the Tao tê ching and its place in Chinese thought, by Arthur Waley. — New York: Grove Press, [1958] 262 p.; 21 cm. — (UNESCO collection of representative works. Chinese series.) An Evergreen book, E-84. 1. Philosophy, Chinese I. Waley, Arthur. ed. and tr. II. T. III. Series.
BL1900.L3 W3 1958      299.51482      *LC* 58-5092

**Ch'en, Ku-ying.** **1.1803**
[Lao-tzu chin chu chin i chi p'ing chieh. English] Lao Tzu: text, notes, and comments / by Ch'en Kuying; translated and adapted by Rhett Y. W. Young, Roger T. Ames. — San Francisco: Chinese Materials Center, 1977. viii, 341 p.; 22 cm. — (Occasional series - Chinese Materials and Research Aids Service Center; no. 27) Translation of Lao-tzu chin chu chin i chi p'ing chieh. Includes index. 1. Lao-tzu. I. Young, Rhett, Y. W. II. Ames, Roger T. III. T.
BL1900.L35 C543313     181/.09/514    *LC* 78-101098

**Lieh-tzŭ, 4th cent. B.C.** • **1.1804**
The book of Lieh–tzŭ. A new translation by A. C. Graham. — London, Murray [c1960] xi, 183 p. 20 cm. — (The Wisdom of the East) Bibliography: p. 182. Bibliographical references included in 'Textual notes' (p. 183) I. Graham, A. C. (Angus Charles) tr. II. T.
BL1900.L5G7 1961     *LC* 62-51659

**Blofeld, John Eaton Calthorpe, 1913-.** **1.1805**
Taoism: the road to immortality / John Blofeld. — Boulder, Colo.: Shambhala, 1978. ix, 195 p., [2] leaves of plates: ill.; 22 cm. 1. Taoism I. T.
BL1920.B57     299/.514     *LC* 77-90882     *ISBN* 0877731160

**Welch, Holmes.** **1.1806**
Taoism: the parting of the way / by Holmes Welch. — Rev. ed. — Boston: Beacon Press, 1965. 196 p., 1 leaf of plates: ill. — (Beacon paperbacks; BP224) First ed. published under title: The parting of the way. 1. Lao-tzu. 2. Taoism I. T. II. Title: The parting of the way
BL1930.W4 1965     *ISBN* 0807059730

**Saso, Michael R.** **1.1807**
The teachings of Taoist Master Chuang / Michael Saso. — New Haven: Yale University Press, 1978. xiii, 317 p.: ill.; 22 cm. Includes index. 1. Chuang, Ch'en Teng-yün, 1911-1976. 2. Taoism I. T.
BL1940.C47 S27     299/.514/0924 B     *LC* 76-58919     *ISBN* 0300020805

## BL1943–1950 Other

**Gzi brjid. English & Tibetan. Selections.** • **1.1808**
The nine ways of bon; excerpts from gZi–brjid, edited and translated by David L. Snellgrove. — London; New York [etc.]: Oxford U.P., 1967. vii, 312 p.: front., illus., 12 plates (incl. facsims.), diagrs.; 26 cm. — (London oriental series. v. 18) English and Tibetan on facing pages. I. Snellgrove, David L. ed. II. T. III. Series.
BL1943.B6 G9213 1967     299/.54 19     *LC* 68-87999

**Tucci, Giuseppe, 1894-.** **1.1809**
The religions of Tibet / Giuseppe Tucci; translated from the German and Italian by Geoffrey Samuel. — Berkeley: University of California Press, c1980. xii, 340 p., [2] leaves of plates: ill.; 23 cm. A translation of the author's Die Religionen Tibets, published in 1970 in Tucci & Heissig's Die Religionen Tibets und der Mongolei; with additions and changes made for the 1976 Italian ed. and this ed. 1. Tibet (China) — Religion. I. T.
BL1945.T5 T815     294.3/923     *LC* 80-110768     *ISBN* 0520038568

**Jordan, David K.** **1.1810**
Gods, ghosts, and ancestors: the folk religion of a Taiwanese village / [by] David K. Jordan. — Berkeley: University of California Press, 1973 (c1972) xviii, 197 p.: ill.; 24 cm. Based on the author's thesis, University of Chicago, 1969. 1. Taiwan — Religion I. T.
BL1975.J67 1972     299/.51/0951249     *LC* 70-149945     *ISBN* 0520019628

## BL2000–2130 INDIA. SOUTHEAST ASIA

**Farquhar, J. N. (John Nicol), 1861-1929.** • **1.1811**
Modern religious movements in India, by J. N. Farquhar. [1st Indian ed.] Delhi, Munshiram Manoharlal [1967] xv, 471 p. illus., ports., palns. 23 cm. (The Hartford-Lamson lectures on the religions of the world) 1. India — Religion I. T.
BL2001.F3 1967     *LC* sa 67-7609

**Farquhar, J. N. (John Nicol), 1861-1929.** • **1.1812**
An outline of the religious literature of India / by J. N. Farquhar. — 1st Indian reprint. — Delhi: Motilal Banarsidass, 1967. xxviii, 451 p.; 23 cm. Includes

index. 1. Religious literature, Hindi — India. 2. Buddhist literature, Indian. 3. India — Religion I. T.
BL2001 F32 1967     BL2003.F32 1967.     *LC* 67-7844

**Nivedita, Sister, 1867-1911.** • **1.1813**
Myths of the Hindus & Buddhists, by Ananda K. Coomaraswamy and Sister Nivedita (Margaret E. Noble) With 32 illus. by Indian artists under the supervision of Abanindro Nāth Tagore. — New York: Dover Publicatons, [1967] xii, 399 p.: illus.; 22 cm. Author's names in reverse order in other editions. 'An unabridged republication of the work originally published ... in 1913.' 1. Mythology, Hindu 2. Buddha and Buddhism. I. Coomaraswamy, Ananda Kentish, 1877-1947. joint author. II. T.
BL2001.N6 1967     294.5/1/3     *LC* 67-14131

**Weber, Max, 1864-1920.** • **1.1814**
[Hinduismus und Buddhismus. English] The religion of India; the sociology of Hinduism and Buddhism. Translated and edited by Hans H. Gerth and Don Martindale. Glencoe, Ill., Free Press [1958] 392 p. 21 cm. Translation of Hinduismus and Buddhismus, published as v. 2 of the author's Gesammelte Aufsätze zur Religionssoziologie. 1. India — Religion 2. India — Social conditions I. T.
BL2001.W443     294     *LC* 58-6491

**Renou, Louis, 1896-1966.** • **1.1815**
Religions of ancient India. — New York: Schocken Books, [1968, c1953] viii, 139 p.; 21 cm. — (Jordan lectures in comparative religion, 1) 1. India — Religion I. T. II. Series.
BL2001.2.R4 1968     294/.0954     *LC* 68-16660

**Boyd, Doug.** **1.1816**
Swami / Douglas Boyd. — 1st ed. — New York: Random House, c1976. xx, 330 p.; 22 cm. 1. Rama, Swami, 1925- 2. Boyd, Doug. 3. Sadhus — India. 4. India — Religion I. T.
BL2003.B6     181/.4     *LC* 75-40566     *ISBN* 0394496035

**Dumézil, Georges, 1898-.** **1.1817**
[Entre les dieux et les hommes—un roi (Yayāti, Yima, Eochaid Feidlech). English] The destiny of a king. Translated by Alf Hiltebeitel. Chicago, University of Chicago Press [1973] 155 p. 24 cm. Translation of: Entre les dieux et les hommes—un roi (Yayāti, Yima, Eochaid Feidlech), pt. 3 of Types épiques indo-européens—un héros, un sorcier, un roi, which is v. 2 of Mythe et épopée) Continues: The plight of a sorcerer. c1986. 1. Mythology, Indic I. T.
BL2003.D8513 1973     294.5/1/3     *LC* 73-75311     *ISBN* 0226169758

**Radhakrishnan, S. (Sarvepalli), 1888-1975.** • **1.1818**
Eastern religions and western thought. Oxford: The Clarendon Press, 1939. 396 p. 'Lectures... given in the years 1936-38 ... revised and slightly expanded.' 1. Religions 2. India — Religion 3. Philosophy, Comparative I. T.
BL2003.R3 1940     *LC* 39-8335

**Zimmer, Heinrich Robert, 1890-1943.** • **1.1819**
Myths and symbols in Indian art and civilization. Edited by Joseph Campbell. — [New York]: Pantheon books, [1946] xiii, 248 p., 1 l.: plates.; 24 cm. — (The Bollingen series, VI) At head of title: Heinrich Zimmer. 'Lecture course delivered at Columbia university the winter term of 1942.' 1. Mythology, India. 2. Symbolism 3. Art, Hindu 4. India — Civilization I. Campbell, Joseph, 1904- ed. II. T.
BL2003.Z5     294.5     *LC* 46-7144

**Anand, Kewal Krishna.** **1.1820**
Indian philosophy: (The concept of karma) / Kewal Krishna Anand. — Delhi: Bharatiya Vidya Prakashan; Queens Village, N.Y.: Dist. by Asia Book Corp. of America, 1982. xix, 396 p.: 23 cm. Includes index. 1. Karma I. T.
BL2015.K3 A53

**Argüelles, José, 1939-.** **1.1821**
Mandala [by] José and Miriam Argüelles. Foreword by Chögyam Trungpa. — Berkeley, [Calif.]: Shambala, 1972. 140 p.: illus. (part col.); 28 cm. 1. Mandala I. Argüelles, Miriam, 1943- joint author. II. T.
BL2015.M3 A73     294.3/4/2     *LC* 70-189856     *ISBN* 0877730334

**Tucci, Giuseppe, 1894-.** • **1.1822**
[Teoria e pratica del mandala. English] The theory and practice of the Mandala, with special reference to the modern psychology of the subconscious; translated from the Italian by Alan Houghton Brodrick. London, Rider, 1969. ix, 147 p. 4 plates, 4 illus. 21 cm. Translation of Teoria e pratica del mandala. 1. Mandala 2. Subconsciousness I. T.
BL2015.M3 T83 1969     294.5/4/2     *LC* 79-408351     *ISBN* 0090619315

**Ādi-Granth. English. Selections.** **1.1823**
The Jap-ji / Transcreated from the Panjabi by P. Lal. — 2d ed. — Calcutta: Writers Workshop; Thompson, Conn.: distributed by Inter Culture Associates, 1971-. v.; 23 cm. — (A Writers workshop redbird book) 1. Sikhism — Prayer-books and devotions. I. Lal, P. II. T.
BL2017.422.A3     294.6

**Kohli, Surindar Singh, 1920-.**     **1.1824**
A critical study of Ādi Granth, being a comprehensive and scientific study of Guru Granth Sahib, the scripture of the Sikhs / Surindar Singh Kohli. — [2d ed.]. — Delhi: Motilal Banarsidass, 1976. xxii, 391 p.; 22 cm. Includes selections in Gurumukhi script. Originally presented as the author's thesis, University of Delhi. Includes index. 1. Ādi-Granth — Criticism, interpretation, etc. I. T.
BL2017.45.K63 1976    294.6/8/2     *LC* 76-901503

**Banerjee, Anil Chandra.**     **1.1825**
Guru Nanak and his times. — [1st ed.]. — Patiala: Punjabi University, [1971] 245 p.; 23 cm. 'Expanded version of Sitaram Kohli lectures delivered by [the author] at Punjabi University, Patiala, in March 1970, under the auspices of the Department of Punjab Historical Studies.' 1. Nānak, Guru, 1469-1538. I. T.
BL2017.9.N3 B35    294.6/6/3 B     *LC* 72-902581

**McLeod, W. H.**     • **1.1826**
Gurū Nānak and the Sikh religion [by] W. H. McLeod. — Oxford: Clarendon P., 1968. xii, 259 p.; 24 cm. 1. Nānak, Guru, 1469-1538. 2. Sikhism I. T.
BL2017.9.N3 M27    294.5/53/0924 B     *LC* 74-373992     *ISBN* 0198265212

**Cole, W. Owen (William Owen)**     **1.1827**
The Sikhs: their religious beliefs and practices / W. Owen Cole and Piara Singh Sambhi. — London; Boston: Routledge & K. Paul, 1978. xxvii, 210 p., [4] leaves of plates: ill.; 23 cm. — (Library of beliefs and practices.) Includes index. 1. Sikhism I. Sambhi, Piara Singh, joint author. II. T. III. Series.
BL2018.C65    294.6     *LC* 78-315607     *ISBN* 0710088426

**Archer, John Clark, 1881-1957.**     • **1.1828**
The Sikhs in relation to Hindus, Moslems, Christians, and Ahmadiyyas; a study in comparative religion. — New York: Russell & Russell, [1971, c1946] xi, 353 p.: illus.; 23 cm. 1. Sikhism 2. India — Religion I. T.
BL2018.15.A72 1971    294.6/172     *LC* 76-139895

**Nānak, Guru, 1469-1538.**     • **1.1829**
Hymns of Guru Nanak. Translated by Khushwant Singh. [New Delhi] Orient Longmans [1969] xv, 193 p. 22 cm. (UNESCO collection of representative works. Indian series) 1. Sikh hymns, English. I. Singh, Khushwant, tr. II. T.
BL2018.32.N3513    294.6/6/3     *LC* 74-908960

**Ortner, Sherry B., 1941-.**     **1.1830**
Sherpas through their rituals / Sherry B. Ortner. — Cambridge; New York: Cambridge University Press, 1978. xii, 195 p.: ill.; 24 cm. — (Cambridge studies in cultural systems. 2) (Anthropological studies of systems of meaning; 2) Includes index. 1. Sherpas — Religion. 2. Buddhism — Doctrines — Himalaya Mountains Region. I. T. II. Series. III. Series: Anthropological studies of systems of meaning; 2
BL2032.S45 O77    294.3/4/3     *LC* 76-62582     *ISBN* 0521215366. *ISBN* 0521292166 pbk

**Geertz, Clifford.**     • **1.1831**
The religion of Java. — Glencoe, Ill.: Free Press, [1960] xv, 392 p.: maps.; 25 cm. Part of the material issued in 1958 under title: Modjokuto, religion in Java. 1. Java (Indonesia) — Religion. I. T.
BL2120.J3 G42    299.9222     *LC* 59-13863

## BL2200–2222 JAPAN

**Hori, Ichirō, 1910-1974.**     **1.1832**
Folk religion in Japan; continuity and change. Edited by Joseph M. Kitagawa and Alan L. Miller. — Tokyo: University of Tokyo Press, [1968] xv, 278 p.: illus.; 22 cm. — (Haskell lectures on history of religions. New ser., no. 1) 1. Japan — Religion I. Kitagawa, Joseph Mitsuo, 1915- ed. II. Miller, Alan L., ed. III. T. IV. Series.
BL2202.H58 1968b    299/.56     *LC* 74-443952

**Kitagawa, Joseph Mitsuo, 1915-.**     • **1.1833**
Religion in Japanese history [by] Joseph M. Kitagawa. — New York: Columbia University Press, 1966. x, 475 p.; 22 cm. — (Lectures on the history of religions, new series, no. 7) 1. Japan — Religion I. T. II. Series.
BL2202.K5    200.952     *LC* 65-23669

**McFarland, Horace Neill, 1923-.**     • **1.1834**
The rush hour of the gods; a study of new religious movements in Japan [by] H. Neill McFarland. — New York: Macmillan, [c1967] xvi, 267 p.; 21 cm. 1. Japan — Religion — 20th century I. T.
BL2202.M25    209.52     *LC* 67-10576

**Murakami, Shigeyoshi, 1928-.**     **1.1835**
[Nihon hyakunen no shūkyō. English] Japanese religion in the modern century / Shigeyoshi Murakami; translated by H. Byron Earhart. — [Tokyo]: University of Tokyo Press, c1980. xvii, 186 p., [3] leaves of plates: ill.; 24 cm. Includes index. 1. Japan — Religion — 1868- I. T.
BL2207.5.M8813    291/.0952     *LC* 80-670074     *ISBN* 0860082601

**Bellah, Robert Neelly, 1927-.**     • **1.1836**
Tokugawa religion; the values of pre–industrial Japan. Glencoe, Ill., Free Press [1957] 249 p. 22 cm. 1. Religion and sociology 2. Japan — Religion — 1600-1868 3. Japan — Social conditions — 1600-1868 I. T.
BL2210.B4    275.2     *LC* 57-6748

**Herbert, Jean, 1897-.**     • **1.1837**
Shintô; at the fountain–head of Japan. With a pref. by Yukitada Sasaki. — New York: Stein and Day, [1967] 622 p.: illus., geneal. table, map.; 25 cm. Translation of Aux sources du Japon. 1. Shinto I. T.
BL2220.H413 1967    299/.561     *LC* 66-24531

**Ono, Motonori, 1904-.**     **1.1838**
Shinto, the Kami Way, by Sokyo Ono in collaboration with William P. Woodward. Sketches by Sadao Sakamoto. [Tokyo Rutland, Vt.]: Bridgeway Press, [1961, c1962] xii, 116 p. illus. 22 cm. 'First published in 1960, under the title: The Kami Way; an introduction to Shrine Shinto.' 1. Shinto I. T. II. Title: The Kami Way.
BL2220.O5 1962    *LC* 61-14033

**Ponsonby-Fane, Richard Arthur Brabazon, 1878-1937.**     • **1.1839**
Studies in Shintô and shrines: papers selected from the works of the late R.A.B. Ponsonby–Fane, LL.D. — Rev. ed. — Kyoto: Ponsonby Memorial Society, 1954, t.p. 1962. vi, 575 p., [36] leaves of plates (1 fold.): ill., facsims., geneal. tables, plans, ports.; 22 cm. 1. Shinto 2. Shrines — Japan. I. T.
BL2220.P6 1954

**The Sacred scriptures of the Japanese / with all authoritative variants chronologically arranged ... by Post Wheeler.**     • **1.1840**
New York: H. Schuman, 1952. xlvi, 562 p. Translations of the Kojiki and the Nihongi, supplemented and amplified by translations of a number of lesser works, collated and combined in a connected narrative. 1. Shinto 2. Mythology, Japanese 3. Japan — Kings and rulers I. Yarumaro, d. 723. Kojiki. II. Wheeler, Post, 1869- III. Nihon shoki. English.
BL2220 W45    *LC* 52-14316

## BL2350 OTHER COUNTRIES, A–Z

**Jacobsen, Thorkild, 1904-.**     **1.1841**
The treasures of darkness: a history of Mesopotamian religion / Thorkild Jacobsen. — New Haven: Yale University Press, 1976. 273 p.: ill.; 25 cm. 1. Iraq — Religion. I. T.
BL2350.I7 J3    299/.1/5     *LC* 75-27576     *ISBN* 0300018444

## BL2370 SHAMANISM

**Eliade, Mircea, 1907-.**     • **1.1842**
Shamanism: archaic techniques of ecstasy. Translated from the French by Willard R. Trask. — [Rev. and enl. — New York, Bollingen Foundation; distributed by] Pantheon Books [1964], 610 p. 25 cm. — (Bollingen series. 76) Translation of Le chamanisme et les techniques archaïques de l'extase. Bibliography: p. [513]-569. 1. Shamanism I. T. II. Series.
BL2370.S5E413 1964    291.62     *LC* 63-10339

## BL2400–2490 AFRICAN AND EGYPTIAN RELIGIONS

**Smith, Edwin William, 1876-1957.**     • **1.1843**
African ideas of God: a symposium / editor and contributor, Edwin W. Smith; other contributors, T. Cullen Young ... [et al.]. — London: Edinburgh House Press, 1950. ix, 308 p.: map; 23 cm. Includes indexes. 1. God 2. Africa — Religion I. Young, T. Cullen. II. Parrinder, Edward Geoffrey. III. T.
BL2400.A42 1950

**The Historical study of African religion. Edited by T. O. Ranger and I. N. Kimambo.**     **1.1844**
Berkeley, University of California Press, 1972. ix, 307 p. maps. 26 cm. Papers presented at a conference sponsored by the University of Dar es Salaam and the African Studies Center of the University of California, Los Angeles, and held in Dar es Salaam in June 1970. 1. Africa — Religion — Congresses. I. Ranger, T. O. (Terence O.) ed. II. Kimambo, Isaria N. ed. III. Chuo Kikuu cha Dar es Salaam. IV. University of California, Los Angeles. African Studies Center.
BL2400.H53 1972    200/.967     *LC* 76-186104     *ISBN* 0520022068

**Idowu, E. Bolaji.**     **1.1845**
African traditional religion: a definition [by] E. Bolaji Idowu. — Maryknoll, N.Y.: Orbis Books, [1973] xii, 228 p.; 23 cm. 1. Africa — Religion I. T.
BL2400.I3    299/.6     *LC* 72-96951     *ISBN* 0883440059

**Mbiti, John S.**    • **1.1846**
African religions & philosophy [by] John S. Mbiti. — New York: Praeger, [1969] xiii, 290 p.: map (on lining papers); 23 cm. 1. Philosophy, African 2. Africa — Religion I. T.
BL2400.M38 1969    200/.96    LC 70-76092

**The New religions of Africa / Bennetta Jules–Rosette, editor.**    **1.1847**
Norwood, N.J.: Ablex Pub. Corp., c1979. xxii, 248 p.: ill.; 24 cm. (Modern sociology.) Includes indexes. 1. Cults — Africa — Addresses, essays, lectures. 2. Africa — Religion — Addresses, essays, lectures. I. Jules-Rosette, Bennetta. II. Series.
BL2400.N48    301.5/8    LC 78-16925    ISBN 0893910147

**Ray, Benjamin Caleb.**    **1.1848**
African religions: symbol, ritual and community / [by] Benjamin C. Ray. Englewood Cliffs; London [etc.]: Prentice-Hall, 1975. xii, 239 p.: ill., map; 24 cm. (Prentice-Hall studies in religion) Index. ISBN 0-13-018622-8. 1. Blacks in Africa — Religion. 2. Africa — Religion I. T. II. Series.
BL2400.R34    299/.6    LC 75-17519    ISBN 0130186309

**Shorter, Aylward.**    **1.1849**
African Christian theology: adaptation or incarnation? / Aylward Shorter. — Maryknoll, N.Y.: Orbis Books, 1977, c1975. viii, 167 p.; 22 cm. 1. Christianity — Africa. 2. Theology, Doctrinal — Africa — History. 3. Africa — Religion I. T.
BL2400.S42 1977    230/.096    LC 77-23325    ISBN 0883440024

**Zahan, Dominique.**    **1.1850**
[Religion, spiritualité, et pensée africaines. English] The religion, spirituality, and thought of traditional Africa / Dominique Zahan; translated by Kate Ezra Martin and Lawrence M. Martin. — Chicago: University of Chicago Press, 1979. 180 p.; 24 cm. Translation of Religion, spiritualité, et pensée africaines. Includes index. 1. Africa — Religion I. T.
BL2400.Z2813    299/.6    LC 78-23525    ISBN 0226977773

**Zuesse, Evan M.**    **1.1851**
Ritual cosmos: the sanctification of life in African religions / Evan M. Zuesse. — Athens: Ohio University Press, c1979. x, 256 p.; 24 cm. Includes index. 1. Ritual 2. Occultism — Africa. 3. Africa — Religion I. T.
BL2400.Z83    299/.6    LC 79-13454    ISBN 0821403982

**Frankfort, Henri, 1897-1954.**    • **1.1852**
Ancient Egyptian religion: an interpretation / by H. Frankfort. — New York: Harper, 1961. x, 172 p.: ill.; 21 cm. — (Harper torchbooks; TB77) 1. Egypt — Religion I. T.
BL2441.Fx    299/.31 19    LC 63-258    ISBN 0061300772

**Parrinder, Edward Geoffrey.**    • **1.1853**
West African religion: a study of the beliefs and practices of Akan, Ewe, Yoruba, Ibo, and kindred peoples / [by] Geoffrey Parrinder; with a foreword by Edwin Smith. — New York: Barnes & Noble, [1970] xv, 203 p.: map.; 23 cm. Reprint of the 1961 ed. A revision of the author's thesis, University of London. 1. Africa, West — Religion. I. T.
BL2465.P3 1970    299/.6    LC 75-20695    ISBN 0389040401

**Baëta, C. G.**    • **1.1854**
Prophetism in Ghana, a study of some 'spiritual' churches. — London, SCM Press [1962] xiii, 169 p. 23 cm. — (World mission studies) Revised version of a thesis for the doctor of philosophy degree in the Divinity Faculty of the University of London. Bibliography: p. [149]-150. Includes bibliographical references. 1. Nativistic movements — Ghana. 2. Sects — Ghana. 3. Ghana — Religion. I. T.
BL2470.G6B3 1962    LC 63-6337

**Wipper, Audrey.**    **1.1855**
Rural rebels: a study of two protest movements in Kenya / Audrey Wipper. — Nairobi; New York: Oxford University Press, 1978 (c1977). xiv, 363 p.: map; 22 cm. Includes index. 1. Dini ya Msambwa. 2. Mumbo (Cult) I. T.
BL2470.K4 W56    299/.6    LC 78-106261    ISBN 0195724305

**Setiloane, Gabriel M.**    **1.1856**
The image of God among the Sotho–Tswana / Gabriel M. Setiloane. — Rotterdam: Balkema, 1976. x, 298 p.; 23 cm. 1. Sotho (Bantu people) — Religion. 2. Tswana (African people) — Religion. 3. Sotho (Bantu people) 4. Tswana (African people) I. T.
BL2480.B35 S47    299/.6    LC 76-362408    ISBN 9061910072

**Griaule, Marcel, 1898-1956.**    **1.1857**
Conversations with Ogotemmêli: an introduction to Dogon religious ideas / by Marcel Griaule; with an introd. by Germaine Dieterlen. — London: Published for the International African Institute by the Oxford University Press, 1965. xvii, 230 p.: ill., map, port.; 21 cm. 1. Dogons (African people) 2. Nommo (African diety) I. T.
DT530.G753 1970    BL2480.D6 G7x.    299.65    LC 65-3614    ISBN 0195198212

**Ilogu, Edmund.**    **1.1858**
[Christianity and Ibo culture] Christianity and Igbo culture: a study of the interaction of Christianity and Igbo culture / by Edmund Ilogu; with a foreword by M. A. C. Warren. — New York: NOK Publishers, 1974. xvi, 262 p., [2] leaves of plates: ill.; 25 cm. Originally presented as the author's thesis, Leiden University, 1974, under title: Christian ethics in an African background. Published in 1974 by Brill, Leiden, under title: Christianity and Ibo culture. Includes index. 1. Ibo tribe — Religion. I. T.
BL2480.I2 I42 1974c    301.5/8    LC 76-152139    ISBN 0883570300. ISBN 0883570319 pbk

**Buxton, Jean Carlile, 1921-.**    **1.1859**
Religion and healing in Mandari [by] Jean Buxton. — Oxford: Clarendon Press, 1973. xiv, 443 p.: illus.; 22 cm. 1. Mandari (African people) — Religion. I. T.
BL2480.M28 B89    301.5/8/09629    LC 73-180545    ISBN 0198231741

**Murphree, Marshall W.**    **1.1860**
Christianity and the Shona / by Marshall W. Murphree. — [London]: University of London, Athlone Press; New York: Humanities Press, 1969. viii, 200 p.: maps.; 23 cm. — (London School of Economics. Monographs on social anthropology, no. 36) 'This book is a condensation of a Ph.D. thesis submitted to the University of London in November 1965.' 1. Mashona — Religion. I. T.
BL2480.M3 M8    301.5/8/096891    LC 68-18053

**Evans-Pritchard, Edward Evan.**    • **1.1861**
Nuer religion. Oxford, Clarendon Press, 1956. 335 p., illus. 1. Nuer (African tribe) — Religion. I. T.
BL2480.N7 E9    LC 56-58065

**Harris, Grace Gredys, 1926-.**    **1.1862**
Casting out anger: religion among the Taita of Kenya / Grace Gredys Harris. — Cambridge; New York: Cambridge University Press, 1978. xi, 193 p., [4] leaves of plates: ill.; 24 cm. — (Cambridge studies in social anthropology; 21) Includes index. 1. Taita (Bantu tribe) — Religion. I. T.
BL2480.T27 H37    BL2480T27 H37.    299/.6    LC 77-80837    ISBN 0521217296

**Awolalu, J. Omosade.**    **1.1863**
Yoruba beliefs and sacrificial rites / J. Omosade Awolalu. — London: Longman, 1979. xvi, 203 p., [4] leaves of plates: ill.; 22 cm. 1. Yorubas — Religion 2. Sacrifice — Nigeria. 3. Rites and ceremonies — Nigeria. I. T.
BL2480.Y6 A96    299/.683    LC 79-670588    ISBN 0582642035

**Idowu, E. Bolaji.**    • **1.1864**
Olódùmarè; God in Yoruba belief. — [London]: Longmans [1962] 222 p.: ill.; 23 cm. 1. Yorubas — Religion I. T. II. Title: God in Yoruba belief.
BL2480.Y6I3    LC 62-52364

# BL2500–2599 RELIGIONS OF THE AMERICAS

**Simpson, George Eaton, 1904-.**    **1.1865**
Black religions in the new world / George Eaton Simpson. — New York: Columbia University Press, 1978. ix, 415 p.: ill.; 24 cm. Includes indexes. 1. Blacks — America — Religion 2. Afro-Americans — Religion 3. Cults — America. I. T.
BL2500.S55    291/.097    LC 78-16892    ISBN 0231045409

**Religion in America: 50 years, 1935–1985.**    **1.1866**
Princeton, N.J.: The Gallup Report, 1985. 56 p.: ill.; 28 cm. 1. Religion — Statistics. 2. Religion — Public opinion. 3. Public opinion — United States. 4. United States — Religion — Public opinion. 5. United States — Religion — Statistics. I. Gallup, George, 1930- II. Gallup Organization. III. The Gallup report (Princeton, N.J.); no. 236
BL2520.R452 1985

**Herberg, Will.**    **1.1867**
Protestant, Catholic, Jew: an essay in American religious sociology / Will Herberg; with a new introduction by Martin E. Marty. — Chicago: University of Chicago Press, 1983, c1960. xvi, 309 p.; 21 cm. Originally published: Garden City, N.Y.: Anchor Books, 1960. Includes index. 1. United States — Religion — 1945-1960 2. United States — Civilization — 1945- I. T.
BL2525.H47 1983    306.6 19    LC 83-9120    ISBN 0226327345

**Appel, Willa.**    **1.1868**
Cults in America: programmed for paradise / Willa Appel. — 1st ed. — New York: Holt, Rinehart, and Winston, c1983. 200 p.; 22 cm. Includes index. 1. Cults — United States 2. United States — Religion — 1960- I. T.
BL2530.U6 A66 1983    291/.0973 19    LC 82-15538    ISBN 0030548365

**Bromley, David G.**　　　　　　　　　　　**1.1869**
Strange gods: the great American cult scare / David G. Bromley and Anson D. Shupe, Jr. — Boston: Beacon Press, c1981. xvii, 249 p. Includes index. 1. Christian sects — United States 2. Cults — United States 3. United States — Religion — 1960- I. Shupe, Anson D. II. T.
BL2530.U6 B76 1981　　BL2530U6 B76 1981.　　291/.0973 19　　*LC*
81-65763　　*ISBN* 0807032565

**Chalfant, H. Paul, 1929-.**　　　　　　　　　**1.1870**
Religion in contemporary society / H. Paul Chalfant, Robert E. Beckley, C. Eddie Palmer. — 2nd ed.— [S.l.]: Mayfield, 1987. xiii, 490 p.: graphs; 24 cm. 1. Religion and sociology 2. United States — Religion — 1960- I. Beckley, Robert E. II. Palmer, C. Eddie. III. T.
BL2530.U6 C47　　261.8/0973 19　　*LC* 80-27999　　*ISBN* 0882841262

**A documentary history of religion in America, to the Civil War　1.1871
/ edited by Edwin S. Gaustad.**
Grand Rapids: Eerdmans, c1982. xx, 535 p.: ill.; 23 cm. 1. United States — Religion — Sources. I. Gaustad, Edwin Scott.
BL2530.U6 D6　　291/.0973 19

**Melton, J. Gordon.**　　　　　　　　　　　**1.1872**
The cult experience: responding to the new religious pluralism / J. Gordon Melton and Robert L. Moore. — New York: Pilgrim Press, c1982. x, 180 p.; 21 cm. Includes index. 1. Cults — United States 2. Conversion — Psychological aspects. 3. Deprogramming — United States. 4. Religious pluralism 5. United States — Religion I. Moore, Robert L. II. T.
BL2530.U6 M43 1982　　291/.0973 19　　*LC* 82-16136　　*ISBN* 0829806199

**Melton, J. Gordon.**　　　　　　　　　　　**1.1873**
The encyclopedia of American religions / J. Gordon Melton. — 2d. ed. — Detroit: Gale Research, c1987. xv, 899 p.; 29 cm. 1. Sects — United States — Dictionaries. 2. Cults — United States — Dictionaries. I. T.
BL2530.U6 M443 1987　　200/.973　　*ISBN* 0810321335

**Piepkorn, Arthur Carl.**　　　　　　　　　**1.1874**
Profiles in belief: the religious bodies of the United States and Canada / by Arthur Carl Piepkorn. — New York [etc.]; London: Harper and Row, 1977-1979. 4 v. in 3; 24 cm. Index. 1. United States — Religion. — History 2. Canada — Religion. — History I. T.
BL2530.U6.P53 1977　　200/.973 200/.971　　*LC* 76-9971　　*ISBN* 0060665807

**Shupe, Anson D.**　　　　　　　　　　　**1.1875**
The new vigilantes: deprogrammers, anti–cultists, and the new religions / Anson D. Shupe, Jr. and David G. Bromley; foreword by Joseph R. Gusfield. — Beverly Hills: Sage Publications, c1980. 267 p.; 23 cm. — (Sage library of social research; v. 113) Includes index. 1. Cults — United States 2. Deprogramming — United States. I. Bromley, David G. II. T. III. Title: Deprogrammers, anti–cultists, and the new religions.
BL2530.U6 S53　　306/.6 19　　*LC* 80-23276　　*ISBN* 080391542X

**Understanding the new religions / edited by Jacob Needleman　1.1876
and George Baker.**
New York: Seabury Press, 1978. xxi, 314 p. 'A Crossroad book.' 1. Cults — United States — Addresses, essays, lectures. 2. United States — Religion — 1945- — Addresses, essays, lectures. I. Needleman, Jacob. II. Baker, George, 1941-
BL2530.U6 U5　　BL2530U6 U5.　　200/.973　　*LC* 78-14997　　*ISBN* 0816404038

**Williams, Peter W.**　　　　　　　　　　　**1.1877**
Popular religion in America: symbolic change and the modernization process in historical perspective / Peter W. Williams. — Englewood Cliffs, N.J.: Prentice-Hall, c1980. xiv, 244 p.; 23 cm. — (Prentice-Hall studies in religion series) 1. United States — Religion I. T.
BL2530.U6 W54　　200/.973　　*LC* 79-22986

**Wuthnow, Robert.**　　　　　　　　　　　**1.1878**
Experimentation in American religion: the new mysticisms and their implications for the churches / Robert Wuthnow. — Berkeley: University of California Press, c1978. x, 221 p.: ill.; 25 cm. 1. Cults — United States — Addresses, essays, lectures. 2. Christianity and other religions — Addresses, essays, lectures. 3. United States — Religion — 1945-1960 — Addresses, essays, lectures. 4. United States — Religion — 1960- — Addresses, essays, lectures. I. T.
BL2530.U6 W87　　200/.973　　*LC* 77-71068　　*ISBN* 0520034465

**Bastide, Roger, 1898-1974.**　　　　　　　　**1.1879**
[Religions afro-brésiliennes. English] The African religions of Brazil: toward a sociology of the interpenetration of civilizations / Roger Bastide; translated by Helen Sebba. — Baltimore: Johns Hopkins University Press, c1978. xxviii, 494 p.; 23 cm. — (Johns Hopkins studies in Atlantic history and culture.)

Translation of Les religions afro-brésiliennes. 1. Blacks — Brazil — Religion. 2. Religion, Primitive 3. Brazil — Religion. I. T. II. Series.
BL2590.B7 B3713　　299/.6/0981　　*LC* 78-5421　　*ISBN* 0801820561. *ISBN* 0801821304 pbk

## BL2600–2630 PACIFIC RELIGIONS

**Worsley, Peter.**　　　　　　　　　　　● **1.1880**
The trumpet shall sound; a study of 'cargo' cults in Melanesia. — 2d augmented ed. — New York: Schocken Books, [1968] lxix, 300 p.: illus., maps.; 21 cm. 'SB 156.' 1. Cargo movement 2. Melanesia — Religion. I. T. II. Title: 'Cargo' cults in Melanesia.
BL2620.M4 W6 1968　　299/.9　　*LC* 67-26995

*[handwritten margin note: BL 2620 M4 W6 1968]*

**Keesing, Roger M., 1935-.**　　　　　　　　**1.1881**
Kwaio religion: the living and the dead in a Solomon Island society / Roger M. Keesing. — New York: Columbia University Press, 1982. xi, 257 p.: ill.; 24 cm. Includes index. 1. Kwaio (Melanesian people) — Religion. 2. Solomon Islands — Religion. I. T.
BL2630.K85 K43 1982　　299/.92 19　　*LC* 82-4122　　*ISBN* 0231053401

## BL2700–2790 Rationalism

**Darrow, Clarence, 1857-1938.**　　　　　　　● **1.1882**
Infidels and heretics: an agnostic's anthology by Clarence Darrow and Wallace Rice. Boston, Mass. The Stratford Company. [c1929] 8p. l., x 293 p. 23 cm. 1. Agnosticism I. Rice, Wallace, 1859-1939. II. T.
BL2710.D25　　*LC* 29-15054

**Paine, Thomas, 1737-1809.**　　　　　　　● **1.1883**
Age of reason: being an investigation of true and fabulous theology / by Thomas Paine. Baltimore: Ottenheimer, [1956] 2 pts. in 1; 22 cm. 1. Bible — Criticism, interpretation, etc. 2. Christianity — Controversial literature 3. Judaism — Controversial literature I. T. '
BL2740. Px　　*LC* 57-2505

**Ellul, Jacques.**　　　　　　　　　　　**1.1884**
[Nouveaux possédés. English] The new demons / Jacques Ellul; translated by C. Edward Hopkin. — New York: Seabury Press, [1975] viii, 228 p.; 22 cm. 'A Crossroad book.' Translation of Les nouveaux possédés. 1. Secularism 2. Christianity — 20th century 3. Mythology I. T.
BL2747.8.E4313　　211/.6　　*LC* 75-6969　　*ISBN* 0816402663

**Glasner, Peter E.**　　　　　　　　　　　**1.1885**
The sociology of secularisation: a critique of a concept / Peter E. Glasner. — London; Boston: Routledge & K. Paul, 1977. viii, 137 p.; 22 cm. — (International library of sociology) Includes index. 1. Secularism 2. Sociology — Methodolog. I. T.
BL2747.8.G445　　301.5/8　　*LC* 77-368411　　*ISBN* 0710084552

**Turner, James, 1946-.**　　　　　　　　　**1.1886**
Without God, without creed: the origins of unbelief in America / James Turner. — Baltimore: Johns Hopkins University Press, c1985. xviii, 316 p.; 24 cm. (New studies in American intellectual and cultural history.) Includes index. 1. Irreligion — History. 2. Irreligion — United States — History. I. T. II. Series.
BL2757.T87 1985　　211/.8/0973 19　　*LC* 84-15397　　*ISBN* 080182494X

*[handwritten margin note: — O —]*

**Chadwick, Owen.**　　　　　　　　　　　**1.1887**
The secularization of the European mind in the nineteenth century: the Gifford lectures in the University of Edinburgh for 1973-4 / Owen Chadwick. — Cambridge [Eng.]; New York: Cambridge University Press, 1975. 286 p.; 22 cm. (Gifford lectures. 1973-74) 1. Secularism — Europe. 2. Europe — Intellectual life — 19th century I. T. II. Series.
BL2765.E85 C48　　190　　*LC* 75-16870　　*ISBN* 0521208920

**Budd, Susan.**　　　　　　　　　　　**1.1888**
Varieties of unbelief: atheists and agnostics in English society, 1850–1960 / Susan Budd. — London: Heinemann Educational Books, 1977. vii, 307 p.; 22 cm. Imprint covered by label which reads: Holmes & Meier Publishers, New York. Bibliography: p. [282]-299. Includes index. 1. Rationalism — History. 2. Religious thought — England. I. T.
BL2765.G7 B83　　211　　*LC* 77-363322　　*ISBN* 0435821008

**Allen, Ethan, 1738-1789.**      • 1.1889
Reason, the only oracle of man, or, A compendious system of natural religion. — Boston, J. P. Mendum, 1854. 171 p. 19 cm. 1. Rationalism I. T.
BL2773.A5 1854     LC 48-42275

**Marx, Karl, 1818-1883.**      • 1.1890
[Selections. English] On religion [by] Karl Marx and Friedrich Engels. Introd. by Reinhold Niebuhr. New York, Schocken Books [1964] 382 p. 21 cm. (Schocken paperbacks) 'SB67.' 1. Religion — Controversial literature I. Engels, Friedrich, 1820-1895. II. T.
BL2775.M3983 1964    201    LC 64-15219

**Sinclair, Upton, 1878-1968.**      • 1.1891
The profits of religion; an essay in economic interpretation. New York, AMS Press [1970] 315 p. 23 cm. Reprint of the 1918 ed. 1. Christianity — Controversial literature I. T.
BL2775.S54 1970    200    LC 73-120566    ISBN 0404060935

# BM JUDAISM

**Cohen, Arthur Allen, 1928- comp.**      • 1.1892
Arguments and doctrines; a reader of Jewish thinking in the aftermath of the holocaust. Selected with introductory essays by Arthur A. Cohen. — [1st ed.]. — New York: Harper & Row, [1970] xviii, 541 p.; 22 cm. 1. Judaism — 20th century — Collections. I. T.
BM40.C54 1970    296/.08    LC 78-83589

**Hirsch, Samson Raphael, 1808-1888.**      • 1.1893
Judaism eternal; selected essays from the writings of Samson Raphael Hirsch. Translated from the German original and annotated with an introd. and a short biography by I. Grunfeld. London, Soncino Press, 1956. 2 v. illus. 23 cm. 1. Judaism — Addresses, essays, lectures I. T.
BM45.H4822 1956    LC 58-171

**Kook, Abraham Isaac, 1865-1935.**      1.1894
[Works. English] Abraham Isaac Kook: The lights of penitence, The moral principles, Lights of holiness, essays, letters, and poems / translation and introd. by Ben Zion Bokser; pref. by Jacob Agus and Rivka Schatz. — New York: Paulist Press, c1978. xxviii, 415 p., [1] leaf of plates: port.; 23 cm. — (Classics of Western spirituality.) Includes indexes. 1. Judaism — Addresses, essays, lectures. 2. Repentance — Judaism — Addresses, essays, lectures. 3. Ethics, Jewish — Addresses, essays, lectures. 4. Mysticism — Judaism — Addresses, essays, lectures. I. Bokser, Ben Zion, 1907- II. T. III. Series.
BM45.K65413 1978    296.3    LC 78-70465    ISBN 0809102781. ISBN 080912159X pbk

**Jacobs, Louis.**      1.1895
What does Judaism say about? [New York] Quadrangle [c1973] vi, 346 p. illus. (The New York times library of Jewish knowledge) 1. Judaism — Dictionaries I. T.
BM50.J3    LC 73-77032    ISBN 0812903498

**Werblowsky, R. J. Zwi (Raphael Jehudah Zwi), 1924-.**      1.1896
The encyclopedia of the Jewish religion / edited by R.J. Zwi Werblowsky and Geoffrey Wigoder. — New rev. ed. — New York: Adama Books, c1986. 415, [48] p. of plates: ill., ports.; 28 cm. 1. Judaism — Dictionaries I. Wigoder, Geoffrey, 1922- II. T.
BM50.W45 1986    296/.03/21 19    LC 86-10932    ISBN 0915361531

# BM150–449 History

**Epstein, Isidore, 1894-1962.**      • 1.1897
Judaism: a historical presentation / Isidore Epstein. — [Harmondsworth, Middlesex, Baltimore]: Penguin Books, 1959. 348 p. (Pelican books; A440) 1. Judaism — History I. T.
BM155.E58 1959    LC 59-1669

**Kaufmann, Yehezkel, 1889-1963.**      • 1.1898
[Toldot ha-emunah ha-Yiśre'elit. English] The religion of Israel, from its beginnings to the Babylonian exile. Translated and abridged by Moshe Greenberg. [Chicago] University of Chicago Press [1960] 486 p. 25 cm. Abridgement and translation of Toldot ha-emunah ha-Yiśre'elit. 1. Judaism — History — To 70 A.D. I. T.
BM155.K3743    296.09    LC 60-5466

**The Cambridge history of Judaism / edited by W.D. Davies, Louis Finkelstein.**      1.1899
Cambridge; New York: Cambridge University Press, <1984 >. v. <1 >: ill.; 24 cm. Includes index. 1. Judaism — History I. Davies, William David, 1911- II. Finkelstein, Louis, 1895-
BM155.2.C35 1984    296 19    LC 77-85704    ISBN 0521218802

**Silver, Daniel Jeremy. From Abraham to Maimonides. 1974.**      1.1900
A History of Judaism. — New York: Basic Books, [1974] 2 v.: ill.; 25 cm. Issued in a case. 1. Judaism — History I. Martin, Bernard, 1928- Europe and the New World. 1974. II. T.
BM155.2.H57    296/.09    LC 73-90131    ISBN 0465030084

**Seltzer, Robert M.**      1.1901
Jewish people, Jewish thought: the Jewish experience in history / Robert M. Seltzer. — New York: Macmillan, c1980. xxi, 874 p.: ill.; 24 cm. 1. Judaism — History I. T.
BM155.2.S43 1980    296/.09    LC 78-19102    ISBN 0024089508

**Glatzer, Nahum Norbert, 1903-.**      1.1902
Essays in Jewish thought / Nahum N. Glatzer. — University: University of Alabama Press, c1978. 295 p.; 25 cm. (Judaic studies; 8) 1. Zunz, Leopold, 1794-1886 — Addresses, essays, lectures. 2. Buber, Martin, 1878-1965 — Addresses, essays, lectures. 3. Rosenzweig, Franz, 1886-1929 — Addresses, essays, lectures. 4. Judaism — History — Addresses, essays, lectures. I. T.
BM157.G58    296.3    LC 76-51044    ISBN 081736904X

**Peters, F. E. (Francis E.)**      1.1903
Children of Abraham: Judaism, Christianity, Islam / F.E. Peters. — Princeton, N.J.: Princeton University Press, c1982. xi, 225 p.; 23 cm. 1. Judaism — History 2. Christianity 3. Islam — History. I. T.
BM157.P47 1982    291 19    LC 81-47941    ISBN 0691072671

**Schechter, Solomon, 1847-1915.**      • 1.1904
Studies in Judaism. — Freeport, N.Y.: Books for Libraries Press, [1972] xxv, 366 p.; 23 cm. — (Essay index reprint series) Reprint of the 1896 ed. 1. Judaism — History — Addresses, essays, lectures. I. T.
BM160.S3 1972    296    LC 78-38775    ISBN 0836926706

**Cross, Frank Moore.**      • 1.1905
The ancient library of Qumrân and modern Biblical studies. — [1st ed.]. — Garden City, N.Y.: Doubleday, 1958. 196 p.: illus.; 22 cm. — (The Haskell lectures, 1956-1957) 1. Dead Sea scrolls. 2. Dead Sea scrolls — Relation to the New Testament 3. Qumran community I. T.
BM175.Q6 C7    296    LC 58-5933

**Vermès, Géza, 1924-.**      1.1906
The Dead Sea Scrolls: Qumran in perspective / Geza Vermes, with the collaboration of Pamela Vermes. — London: Collins, 1977. 238 p.; 22 cm. Includes index. 1. Dead Sea scrolls — Criticism, interpretation, etc. 2. Qumran community I. Vermes, Pamela. joint author. II. T.
BM175.Q6 V47    296.8/1    LC 78-301620    ISBN 0002161427

**Sandmel, Samuel.**      1.1907
Judaism and Christian beginnings / Samuel Sandmel. — New York: Oxford University Press, 1978. xvii, 510 p.; 22 cm. Includes index. 1. Bible. N.T. — Criticism, interpretation, etc. 2. Judaism — History — Post-exilic period, 586 B.C.-210 A.D. 3. Christianity — Origin I. T.
BM176.S26    296/.09    LC 77-77609    ISBN 0195022815

**Stone, Michael E., 1938-.**      1.1908
Scriptures, sects, and visions: a profile of Judaism from Ezra to the Jewish revolts / Michael Edward Stone. — Philadelphia: Fortress Press, 1980. viii, 150 p.; 23 cm. Imprint from label on t.p. Imprint under label reads: Collins. Includes index. 1. Judaism — History — Post-exilic period, 586 B.C.-210 A.D. — Addresses, essays, lectures. I. T.
BM176.S84 1980    296/.09/014 19    LC 79-54151    ISBN 0529057115

**Moore, George Foot, 1851-1931.**      • 1.1909
Judaism in the first centuries of the Christian era: the age of the Tannaim / by George Foot Moore. — Cambridge: Harvard University Press, 1927-30. v. 1. Tannaim 2. Judaism I. T.
BM177.M62    296/.09/015    LC 27-8215

**Neusner, Jacob, 1932-.**      1.1910
Judaism in the beginning of Christianity / Jacob Neusner. — Philadelphia: Fortress Press, c1984. 112 p.; 22 cm. Includes index. 1. Hillel, 1st cent. B.C./1st cent. 2. Judaism — Relations — Christianity 3. Christianity and other religions — Judaism 4. Judaism — History — Post-exilic period, 586 B.C.-210 A.D. I. T.
BM177.N475 1984    296/.09 19    LC 83-48000    ISBN 0800617509

**Neusner, Jacob, 1932-.** • **1.1911**
There we sat down: Talmudic Judaism in the making. — Nashville: Abingdon Press, [1971, c1972] 158 p.: maps.; 23 cm. 1. Judaism — History — Talmudic period, 10-425 I. T.
BM177.N48     296/.09     *LC* 78-172812     *ISBN* 0687416310

**Sanders, E. P.**     **1.1912**
Paul and Palestinian Judaism: a comparison of patterns of religion / E. P. Sanders. — 1st American ed. — Philadelphia: Fortress Press, 1977. xviii, 627 p.; 24 cm. Includes indexes. 1. Dead Sea scrolls — Criticism, interpretation, etc. 2. Bible. O.T. Apocrypha — Criticism, interpretation, etc. 3. Bible. N.T. Epistles of Paul — Theology. 4. Tannaim 5. Apocryphal books (Old Testament) — Criticism, interpretation, etc. I. T.
BM177.S2 1977     296.3     *LC* 76-62612     *ISBN* 0800604997

**The Study of ancient Judaism / edited by Jacob Neusner.**     **1.1913**
[New York, N.Y.]: Ktav, 1982, c1981. 2 v.; 24 cm. 1. Mishnah — Study — History. 2. Midrash — Study and teaching — History. 3. Talmud Yerushalmi — Study — Bibliography. 4. Talmud — Study — Bibliography. 5. Judaism — History — Talmudic period, 10-425 — Historiography. 6. Judaism — Liturgy — Study and teaching — History. I. Neusner, Jacob, 1932-
BM177.S76     296.1/206 19     *LC* 81-5979     *ISBN* 0870688928

**Cohen, Arthur Allen, 1928-.**     **1.1914**
The natural and the supernatural Jew: an historical and theological introduction / Arthur A. Cohen. — 2d rev. ed. — New York: Behrman House, c1979. xvi, 334 p.; 22 cm. Includes index. 1. Judaism — History — Modern period, 1750- — Addresses, essays, lectures. 2. Judaism — Germany — Addresses, essays, lectures. 3. Judaism — United States — Addresses, essays, lectures. I. T.
BM195.C63 1979     296     *LC* 79-13038     *ISBN* 0874412919

**Rotenstreich, Nathan, 1914-.**     **1.1915**
Tradition and reality; the impact of history on modern Jewish thought. — [1st ed.]. — New York: Random House, [c1972] xii, 145 p.; 22 cm. — (Contemporary Jewish civilization series) 1. Judaism — History — Modern period, 1750- I. T.
BM195.R64     296/.09/03     *LC* 71-159369     *ISBN* 0394464257

**Blau, Joseph L. (Joseph Leon), 1909-1986. comp.**     **1.1916**
Reform Judaism: a historical perspective; essays from the Yearbook of the Central Conference of American Rabbis. Selected, edited, and with an introd. by Joseph L. Blau. — New York: Ktav Pub. House, 1973. viii, 529 p.; 24 cm. 1. Reform Judaism — Addresses, essays, lectures. 2. Judaism — United States — Addresses, essays, lectures. I. Yearbook (Central Conference of American Rabbis) II. T.
BM197.B55     296.8/346     *LC* 72-428     *ISBN* 0870681915

**Borowitz, Eugene B.**     **1.1917**
Reform Judaism today / Eugene B. Borowitz. — New York: Behrman House, c1978-. v.; 19 cm.. 1. Central Conference of American Rabbis. Reform Judaism, a centenary perspective. 2. Reform Judaism — United States. I. T.
BM197.B67     296.8/346     *LC* 77-24676     *ISBN* 0874412714

**Plaut, W. Gunther, 1912- ed.** • **1.1918**
The rise of Reform Judaism. Pref. by Solomon B. Freehof. New York, World Union for Progressive Judaism [1963-65] 2 v. 25 cm. Vol. 2. with foreword by Jacob K. Shankman, has title: The growth of Reform Judaism. 1. Reform Judaism — Collected works. I. T. II. Title: The growth of Reform Judaism. BM 197 P72 1963     *LC* 65-18555     *ISBN* 6518555

**Davis, Moshe.** • **1.1919**
The emergence of Conservative Judaism; the historical school in 19th century America. — [1st ed.]. — Philadelphia, Jewish Publication Society of America, 1963. xiv, 527 p. illus., ports., facsims. 22 cm. — (The Jacob R. Schiff library of Jewish contributions to American democracy, no. 15) Bibliography: p. 465-505. 1. Conservative Judaism — Hist. 2. Judaism — U.S. — Hist. I. T. II. Series.
BM197.5.D3     296.834     *LC* 63-21805

**Sklare, Marshall, 1921-.** • **1.1920**
Conservative Judaism; an American religious movement. New augm. ed. New York, Schocken Books [1972] 330 p. 21 cm. 1. Conservative Judaism — United States. I. T.
BM197.5.S45 1972     296.8/342     *LC* 76-183618

**Buber, Martin, 1878-1965.** • **1.1921**
[Erzählungen der Chassidim. English] Tales of the Hasidim [tr. by Olga Marx] New York, Schocken Books [1947-48] 2 v. 21 cm. Translation of Die Erzählungen der Chassidim. 1. Parables, Hasidic I. Marx, Olga, 1894- tr. II. T.
BM198.B7783     296     *LC* 47-2952

**Buber, Martin, 1878-1965.** • **1.1922**
The origin and meaning of Hasidism / Martin Buber; edited and translated by Maurice Friedman. — New York: Horizon Press, 1960. 254 p. 'The second volume of ... [the author's] two-volume comprehensive interpretation, Hasidism

and the way of man. The ... first volume [was published in 1958 under title] Hasidism and modern man.' 1. Hasidism I. T.
BM198.B843     *LC* 60-8161     *ISBN* 0818013168 cloth

**Mintz, Jerome R.** • **1.1923**
Legends of the Hasidim; an introduction to Hasidic culture and oral tradition in the New World [by] Jerome R. Mintz. Photos. by the author. — Chicago: University of Chicago Press, [1968] 462 p.: illus.; 24 cm. 1. Hasidism 2. Tales, Hasidic. I. T.
BM198.M52     296.8/33     *LC* 68-16707

**Newman, Louis Israel, 1893-.** • **1.1924**
The Hasidic anthology: tales and teachings of the Hasidim / Translated from the Hebrew, Yiddish, and German, selected, compiled and arranged by Louis I. Newman, in collaboration with Samuel Spitz. — New York: Schocken Books [1972, c1963] 556 p. 21 cm. 'SB46.' 1. Hasidism — Collected works. 2. Jewish literature 3. Homiletical illustrations I. T.
BM198.N4 1963     296.833082     *LC* 63-11041

**Scholem, Gershom Gerhard, 1897-.**     **1.1925**
Sabbatai Sevi; the mystical Messiah, 1626–1676. [Translated by R. J. Zwi Werblowsky. Princeton, N.J.] Princeton University Press [1973] xxvii, 1000 p. illus. 24 cm. (Bollingen series. 93) Rev. and augm. translation of Shabtai Tsevi veha-tenu'ah ha-shabta'it bi-yeme hayav. 1. Shabbethai Tzevi, 1626-1676. 2. Sabbathaians I. T. II. Series.
BM199.S3 S3713 1973     296.6/1 B     *LC* 75-166389     *ISBN* 0691099162

**Blau, Joseph L. (Joseph Leon), 1909-1986.**     **1.1926**
Judaism in America: from curiosity to third faith / Joseph L. Blau. — Chicago: University of Chicago Press, 1976. xiv, 156 p.; 21 cm. (Chicago history of American religion) 1. Judaism — United States — History. 2. Jews — United States 3. Zionism — United States. I. T.
BM205.B55     296/.0973     *LC* 75-5069     *ISBN* 0226057275

**Glazer, Nathan.**     **1.1927**
American Judaism / Nathan Glazer. — 2d ed. — Chicago: University of Chicago Press, c1972. xi, 210 p.; 21 cm. — (The Chicago history of American civilization) 1. Judaism — United States. 2. Jews in the United States. I. T.
BM205.G5 1972     296/.0973     *LC* 72-85433     *ISBN* 0226298418

**Jick, Leon A.**     **1.1928**
The Americanization of the Synagogue, 1820–1870 / by Leon A. Jick. — Hanover, N.H.: Published for Brandeis University Press by the University Press of New England, 1976. xi, 247 p., [6] leaves of plates: ill.; 23 cm. Includes index. 1. Judaism — United States — History. 2. Jews — United States — History. I. T.
BM205.J52     296/.073     *LC* 75-18213     *ISBN* 0874511194

**Movements and issues in American Judaism: an analysis and sourcebook of developments since 1945 / edited, with an introd., by Bernard Martin.**     **1.1929**
Westport, Conn.: Greenwood Press, 1978. vi, 350 p.; 24 cm. Includes index. 1. Judaism — United States — History — Addresses, essays, lectures. 2. Jews — United States — History — Addresses, essays, lectures. I. Martin, Bernard, 1928-
BM205.M67     296/.0973     *LC* 77-87971     *ISBN* 0313200440

**Neusner, Jacob, 1932-.** • **1.1930**
American Judaism: adventure in modernity. — Englewood Cliffs, N.J.: Prentice-Hall, [1972] xv, 170 p.; 23 cm. 1. Judaism — United States. I. T.
BM205.N48     296/.0973     *LC* 70-161677     *ISBN* 013027870X

**Meyer, Michael A.** • **1.1931**
The origins of the modern Jew: Jewish identity and European culture in Germany. 1749–1824 [by] Michael A. Meyer. — Detroit, Wayne State University Press, 1967. 249 p. 24 cm. Bibliography: p. 220-243. 1. Judaism — Germany 2. Jews in Germany — Intellectual life. I. T.
BM316.M4     910.03/174/924     *LC* 67-12384

**Rothenberg, Joshua.**     **1.1932**
The Jewish religion in the Soviet Union. — New York: Ktav Pub. House, [1972, c1971] viii, 242 p.; 24 cm. 1. Judaism — Russia. 2. Jews in Russia — History — 1917- 3. Religion and state — Russia. I. T.
BM331.R68     914.7/06/924     *LC* 75-149602     *ISBN* 0870681567

**Abramov, S. Zalman, 1908-.**     **1.1933**
Perpetual dilemma: Jewish religion in the Jewish State / S. Zalman Abramov; foreword by W. Gunther Plaut. — Rutherford, N.J.: Fairleigh Dickinson University Press, c1976. 459 p.; 24 cm. Includes index. 1. Jews — Identity 2. Judaism — Israel — History. 3. Judaism and state — Israel — History. 4. Israel — Politics and government I. T.
BM390.A4     296/.095694     *LC* 74-5897     *ISBN* 0838616879

# BM480–488 Pre–Talmudic Jewish Literature

**Jewish writings of the Second Temple period: Apocrypha, Pseudepigrapha, Qumran, sectarian writings, Philo, Josephus /** 1.1934
**edited by Michael E. Stone.**
Assen, Netherlands: Van Gorcum; Philadelphia: Fortress Press, 1984. xxiii, 697 p.; 25 cm. — (The Literature of the Jewish people in the period of the Second Temple and the Talmud; 2) (Compendia rerum Iudaicarum ad Novum Testamentum; section 2) Includes index. 1. Jewish religious literature — History and criticism. I. Stone, Michael E., 1938- II. Series.
BM485.L57 vol. 2    296.1 s 296.1 19    LC 83-48926    *ISBN* 0800606035

## BM487–488 DEAD SEA SCROLLS

**Dead Sea scrolls. English.** 1.1935
The Dead Sea Scrolls in English [translated from the Hebrew and Aramaic and edited by] G. Vermes. — 2nd ed. — Harmondsworth: Penguin, 1975. 281 p.; 19 cm. I. Vermès, Géza, 1924- ed. and tr. II. T.
BM487.A3 V4 1975    221.4    *ISBN* 0140205519

**Yadin, Yigael, 1917-1984.** 1.1936
The Temple scroll: the hidden law of the Dead Sea sect / Yigael Yadin. — 1st ed. — New York: Random House, c1985. 261 p.: ill. (some col.); 26 cm. Includes index. 1. Temple of Jerusalem (Jerusalem) 2. Temple scroll — Criticism, interpretation, etc. 3. Fasts and feasts — Judaism I. T.
BM488.T44 Y33 1985    296.1/55 19    LC 84-45773    *ISBN* 0394544986

# BM495–532 Sources of Judaism. Talmud

**Back to the sources: reading the classic Jewish texts / edited by** 1.1937
**Barry W. Holtz.**
New York: Summit Books, c1984. 448 p.: ill.; 25 cm. 1. Judaism — History — Sources — Addresses, essays, lectures. I. Holtz, Barry W.
BM496.5.B33 1984    296.1 19    LC 84-8452    *ISBN* 0671454676

**Mishnah.** 1.1938
Mishnayot: Ha–Mishnayot be–ivrit menukedet, ha–kademut, targum angli, perush angli, hosafot, luhot ha–maftehot, tosefet, tekunim. — Hotsa'ah 2 / Mugeh, metukenet u-megudelet me'et Shalom Seraga Blakman. — New York: Yudaikah Press, 724 [1963-1964; v. 1 1964] 7 v.; 23 cm. Added t. p.:Mishnayoth. Ponted Hebrew text, English translation, introductions, notes, supplement, appendix, indexes, addenda, corrigenda. 2d ed., rev., corr., enl. by Philip Blackman. Each tractate has special t. p. Vocalized. 1. Mishnah — Commentaries. I. Blackman, Philip, 1881- ed. and tr. II. T. III. Title: Mishnah.
BM497 1964    LC 64-3472

**Strack, Hermann Leberecht, 1848-1922.** 1.1939
Introduction to the Talmud and Midrash / Hermann L. Strack. — New York: Meridian Books; Philadelphia: Jewish Publication Society of America, 1959. xvii, 372 p. 'This English translation ... was prepared ... from a copy of the fifth German ed., revised by the author.' 1. Talmud — Introductions 2. Midrash I. T.
BM503.5 S8513 1959

**Mishnah. English.** 1.1940
The Mishnah / translated from the Hebrew with introduction and brief explanatory notes by Herbert Danby. — Oxford: Oxford University Press, 1933 (1983 printing)..050. xxxii, 844 p. 1. Mishnah. English. I. Danby, Herbert, 1889-1953. II. T.
BM505.A3 D3    LC 34-13008

**Montefiore, C. G. (Claude Goldsmid), 1858-1938. ed. and tr.** 1.1941
A rabbinic anthology, selected and arranged with comments and introductions by C. G. Montefiore and H. Loewe, with a prolegomenon by Raphael Loewe. New York: Schocken Books [1974] cviii, 853 p. 24 cm. Reprint of the 1938 ed. published by Macmillan, London; with new prolegomenon. 1. Midrash —

Translations into English. 2. Aggada — Translations into English. 3. Ethics, Jewish I. Loewe, Herbert Martin James, 1882-1940, joint ed. and tr. II. T.
BM516.M58 1974    296.1/42    LC 73-91340    *ISBN* 0805235396

**Pesikta rabbati. English.** • 1.1942
Pesikta rabbati; discourses for feasts, fasts, and special Sabbaths. Translated from the Hebrew by William G. Braude. — New Haven: Yale University Press, 1968. 2 v. (xi, 995 p.); 22 cm. — (Yale Judaica series. v. 18) The translation is based on an eclectic text made up in the main of the 1st ed., Prague 1654, Codex Parma 1240, and Codex Casanata 3324. I. Braude, William Gordon, 1907- tr. II. T. III. Series.
BM517.P4 E5    296.1/4    LC 68-27748

**Midrash rabbah. English.** • 1.1943
Midrash Rabbah / translated into English with notes, glossary and indices under the editorship of Rabbi H. Freedman and Maurice Simon; with a foreword by Rabbi I. Epstein. — London: Soncino Press, 1939. 13 v. in 10; 24 cm. Each part has a special title page. Volumes 1-2, 5-6 paged continuously. I. T.
BM517.R3A3 1939

**Midrash. Tehillim.** • 1.1944
The Midrash on Psalms. Translated from the Hebrew and Aramaic by William G. Braude. — New Haven: Yale University Press, 1959. 2 v. 22 cm. — (Yale Judaica series. v. 13) I. Braude, William Gordon, 1907- tr. II. T. III. Series.
BM517.T52E5    296.14    LC 58-6535 rev

**Maimonides, Moses, 1135-1204.** • 1.1945
[Mishneh Torah. English] The code of Maimonides. New Haven, Yale University Press, 1949-. v. in 22 cm. (Yale Judaica series, v. 2-5, 8-9, 11-12, 14-16, 19, 21) Translation of Mishneh Torah. 1. Jewish law I. T.
BM520.84.A213 1949    296.1/72    LC 49-9495

**Twersky, Isadore.** 1.1946
Introduction to the Code of Maimonides (Mishneh Torah) / by Isadore Twersky. — New Haven: Yale University Press, 1980. xvi, 641 p.; 23 cm. — (Yale Judaica series. v. 22) Includes index. 1. Maimonides, Moses, 1135-1204. Mishneh Torah. 2. Jewish law 3. Philosophy, Jewish I. T. II. Series.
BM520.84.T83 1980    296.1/72    LC 79-10347    *ISBN* 0300023197

**Freehof, Solomon Bennett, 1892-.** • 1.1947
[Responsa literature] A treasury of responsa. — [1st ed.] — Philadelphia: Jewish Publication Society of America, 1963. 313 p.; 22 cm. — 1. Responsa — History and criticism 2. Responsa — Collections. I. T.
BM523.F72    296.1/79    LC 62-12951

**Safed spirituality: rules of mystical piety, the beginning of** 1.1948
**wisdom / translation and introduction by Lawrence Fine;**
**preface by Louis Jacobs.**
New York: Paulist Press, c1984. xvi, 205 p.: ill.; 23 cm. (Classics of Western spirituality.) Includes indexes. 1. Cabala — Addresses, essays, lectures. 2. Judaism — Israel — Tsefat — Customs and practices — Addresses, essays, lectures. 3. Ethics, Jewish — Addresses, essays, lectures. I. Fine, Lawrence. II. Series.
BM525.A2 S24 1984    296.8/33 19    LC 84-60735    *ISBN* 0809126125

**Zohar. English. Selections.** 1.1949
Zohar, the book of enlightenment / translation and introduction by Daniel Chanan Matt; preface by Arthur Green. — New York: Paulist Press, c1983. xvi, 320 p.; 24 cm. (Classics of Western spirituality.) Includes index. 1. Bible. O.T. Pentateuch — Commentaries. 2. Cabala I. Matt, Daniel Chanan. II. T. III. Title: Book of enlightenment. IV. Series.
BM525.A52 M37 1983    296.1/6 19    LC 83-82145    *ISBN* 0809103206

**Scholem, Gershom Gerhard, 1897-.** • 1.1950
[Zur Kabbala und ihrer Symbolik. English] On the Kabbalah and its symbolism, by Gershom G. Scholem. Translated by Ralph Manheim. New York, Schocken Books [1965] v, 216 p. 24 cm. 1. Cabala — History. I. T.
BM525.S3753    296.16    LC 65-11575

**Scholem, Gershom Gerhard, 1897-.** 1.1951
Kabbalah [by] Gershom Scholem. [New York] Quadrangle/New York Times Book Co. [1974] 492 p. illus. 25 cm. (Library of Jewish knowledge) 1. Cabala — History and criticism. I. T.
BM526.S35 1974    296.1/6    LC 73-77035    *ISBN* 0812903528

**Ginzberg, Louis, 1873-1953.** • 1.1952
The legends of the Jews / by Louis Ginzberg; translated from the German manuscript by Henrietta Szold. — Philadelphia: Jewish Publication Society of America, 1909-1938. 7 v. 1. Legends, Jewish I. T.
BM530.G5    LC 09-14182

**Patai, Raphael, 1910-.**    **1.1953**
The Hebrew goddess. [New York] Ktav Pub. House [1967] 349p. 1. Mother-goddesses 2. Mythology, Jewish I. T.
BM530 P28    *LC* 67-22753

# BM535 Judaism and Christianity

**Buber, Martin, 1878-1965.**    • **1.1954**
Two types of faith; translated by Norman P. Goldhawk. London, Routledge & Paul [1951] 177 p. 23 cm. 1. Jesus Christ — Jewish interpretations 2. Judaism — Relations — Christianity 3. Christianity and other religions — Judaism 4. Belief and doubt I. T.
BM535.B813 1951    *LC* 51-7706

**Cohen, Arthur Allen, 1928-.**    • **1.1955**
The myth of the Judeo–Christian tradition, and other dissenting essays [by] Arthur A. Cohen. — New York: Schocken Books, [1971] xx, 223 p.; 21 cm. 1. Judaism — Relations — Christianity 2. Christianity and other religions — Judaism I. T.
BM535.C6 1971    296.3/87/2    *LC* 77-152766    *ISBN* 0805202935

**Gager, John G.**    **1.1956**
The origins of anti–semitism: attitudes toward Judaism in pagan and Christian antiquity / John G. Gager. — New York: Oxford University Press, 1983. viii, 312 p.; 23 cm. 1. Paul, the Apostle, Saint — Views on Judaism 2. Christianity and antisemitism 3. Judaism — Relations — Christianity 4. Christianity and other religions — Judaism 5. Philosemitism — Rome. I. T.
BM535.G33 1983    296.3/872 19    *LC* 82-24523    *ISBN* 0195033167

**Katz, Jacob, 1904-.**    • **1.1957**
Exclusiveness and tolerance; studies in Jewish–Gentile relations in medieval and modern times. — [London] Oxford University Press, 1961. xv, 200 p. 23 cm. — (Scripta Judaica. 3) Bibliography: p. [197]-198. Bibliographical footnotes. 1. Judaism — Relations — Christianity 2. Christianity and other religions — Judaism 3. Jewish question — Hist. I. T. II. Series.
BM535.K37 1962    296    *LC* 61-19429

**Oberman, Heiko Augustinus.**    **1.1958**
[Wurzeln des Antisemitismus. English] The roots of anti–Semitism in the age of Renaissance and Reformation / Heiko A. Oberman; translated by James I. Porter. — Philadelphia: Fortress Press, c1984. xi, 163 p.; 22 cm. Translation of: Wurzeln des Antisemitismus. 1. Luther, Martin, 1483-1546 — Views on Judaism. 2. Christianity and antisemitism — History — 16th century. 3. Reformation 4. Judaism I. T.
BM535.O2413 1984    261.2/6 19    *LC* 83-5695    *ISBN* 0800607090

**Parkes, James William, 1896-.**    **1.1959**
The conflict of the church and the synagogue: a study of the origins of antisemitism / James Parkes. — New York: Hermon Press, 1974. xxiv, 430 p.; 24 cm. Reprint of the 1934 ed. published by the Soncino Press, London. Originally presented as the author's thesis, Oxford. 1. Christianity and antisemitism 2. Judaism — Relations — Christianity 3. Christianity and other religions — Judaism I. T.
BM535.P195 1974    261.8/34/51924    *LC* 74-78327

**Ruether, Rosemary Radford.**    **1.1960**
Faith and fratricide: the theological roots of anti–Semitism. New York, Seabury Press [1974] ix, 294 p. 22 cm. 'A Crossroad book.' 1. Christianity and antisemitism — History. I. T.
BM535.R8    261.8/34/51924    *LC* 74-11341

# BM545–582 Principles of Judaism

**Maimonides, Moses, 1135-1204.**    • **1.1961**
A Maimonides reader, edited, with introductions and notes, by Isadore Twersky. — New York: Behrman House, [1972] xvii, 494 p.; 24 cm. — (Library of Jewish studies) 1. Judaism — Works to 1900 I. Twersky, Isadore. ed. II. T.
BM545.A45T9 1972    296.3    *LC* 76-160818    *ISBN* 0874412005

**Maimonides, Moses, 1135-1204.**    **1.1962**
[Dalālat al-hā'irīn. English] The guide of the perplexed. Translated with an introd. and notes by Shlomo Pines. With an introductory essay by Leo Strauss. [Chicago] University of Chicago Press [1963] cxxxiv, 658 p. 26 cm. 1. Philosophy, Jewish 2. Philosophy, Medieval 3. Judaism — Works to 1900 I. Pines, Shlomo, 1908- ed. and tr. II. T.
BM545.D33 P5    181.3    *LC* 62-18113

**Baeck, Leo, 1873-1956.**    • **1.1963**
[Wesen des Judentums. English] The essence of Judaism. New York, Schocken Books (1961, c1948] 287 p. 21 cm. (Schocken paperbacks, SB6) 'This rendition by Irving Howe is based on the translation from the German by Victor Grubenwieser [sic] and Leonard Pearl (Macmillan ... London, 1936) The text of the 1948 edition has been corrected.' 1. Judaism I. Howe, Irving. II. Grubwieser, Victor, tr. III. T.
BM560.B32 1961    296    *LC* 61-8992

**Herberg, Will.**    • **1.1964**
Judaism and modern man; an interpretation of Jewish religion. New York: Farrar, Straus and Young [c1951] 313 p.; 21 cm. 1. Judaism I. T.
BM560.H44    *LC* 51-13107    *[handwritten: BM 560. H44]*

**Steinberg, Milton, 1903-1950.**    • **1.1965**
Basic Judaism. — [1st ed.]. — New York: Harcourt, Brace, [1947] ix, 172 p.; 21 cm. 1. Judaism I. T.
BM560.S8    296    *LC* 47-30768

**Heschel, Abraham Joshua, 1907-1972.**    • **1.1966**
God in search of man; a philosophy of Judaism. — New York: Meridian Books, [1961, c1955] 437 p.; 21 cm. 1. Judaism I. T.
BM561.H46 1961    296.01    *LC* 59-7935

**Kaplan, Mordecai Menahem, 1881-.**    **1.1967**
If not now, when? Toward a reconstitution of the Jewish people; conversations between Mordecai M. Kaplan and Arthur A. Cohen. — New York: Schocken Books, [1973] 134 p.; 21 cm. 1. Judaism — 20th century — Addresses, essays, lectures. I. Cohen, Arthur Allen, 1928- II. T.
BM565.K27    296    *LC* 72-95901    *ISBN* 0805234977

**Mendelssohn, Moses, 1729-1786.**    **1.1968**
[Jerusalem. English] Jerusalem, or, On religious power and Judaism / Moses Mendelssohn; translated by Allan Arkush; introduction and commentary by Alexander Altmann. — Hanover: Published for Brandeis University Press by University Press of New England, c1983. vii, 254 p.; 22 cm. Title on spine: Jerusalem. 1. Judaism — Works to 1900 2. Church and state — Early works to 1800. 3. Freedom of religion — Early works to 1800. I. Arkush, Allan, 1949- II. T. III. Title: On religious power and Judaism.
BM565.M413 1983    296 19    *LC* 83-40015    *ISBN* 0874512638

**Rosenzweig, Franz, 1886-1929.**    • **1.1969**
[Stern der Erlösung. English] The star of redemption. Translated from the 2d ed. of 1930 by William W. Hallo. [1st ed.] New York, Holt, Rinehart and Winston [1971] xviii, 445 p. 24 cm. Translation of Der Stern der Erlösung. 1. Judaism 2. Cosmology 3. Religion — Philosophy 4. Philosophy, Jewish I. T.
BM565.R613    296.3    *LC* 71-118091    *ISBN* 0030850770

# BM600–648 Dogmatic Judaism. Apologetics

**Fackenheim, Emil L.**    • **1.1970**
Quest for past and future; essays in Jewish theology [by] Emil L. Fackenheim. — Bloomington: Indiana University Press, [1968] ix, 336 p.; 22 cm. 1. Judaism — Doctrines — Addresses, essays, lectures. I. T.
BM601.F3 1968    296.3    *LC* 68-27346    *[handwritten: BM 601 F3 1968]*

**Katz, Steven T., 1944-.**    **1.1971**
Jewish ideas and concepts / Steven T. Katz. — New York: Schocken Books, 1978, c1977. xiv, 326 p.; 24 cm. Includes index. 1. Judaism — Doctrines 2. God (Judaism) 3. Ethics, Jewish I. T.
BM601.K37    296.3    *LC* 77-75285    *ISBN* 0805236643

**Wyschogrod, Michael, 1928-.**    **1.1972**
The body of faith: Judaism as corporeal election / Michael Wyschogrod. — New York: Seabury Press, 1983. xviii, 265 p.; 24 cm. 1. Judaism — Essence, genius, nature. 2. Jews — Election, Doctrine of — History of doctrines. 3. God (Judaism) 4. Ethics, Jewish I. T.
BM601.W96 1983    296.3 19    *LC* 83-4776    *ISBN* 0816405492

**Eisen, Arnold M., 1951-.**    **1.1973**
The chosen people in America: a study in Jewish religious ideology / Arnold M. Eisen. — Bloomington: Indiana University Press, c1983. x, 237 p.; 25 cm. — (The Modern Jewish experience) Includes index. 1. Jews — Election, Doctrine of — History of doctrines — 20th century. 2. Judaism — United States — History — 20th century. I. T.
BM613.E37 1983    296.3/11 19    *LC* 82-49296    *ISBN* 0253313651

**Klausner, Joseph, 1874-1958.**      • **1.1974**
The messianic idea in Israel, from its beginning to the completion of the Mishnah. Translated from the 3d Hebrew ed. by W. F. Stinespring. New York, Macmillan, 1955. 543 p. 22 cm. 1. Messiah I. T.
BM615.K563     296.3     *LC* 55-14239

**Scholem, Gershom Gerhard, 1897-.**      • **1.1975**
The Messianic idea in Judaism and other essays on Jewish spirituality [by] Gershom Scholem. — New York: Schocken Books, [1971] viii, 376 p.; 24 cm. Ten of the seventeen essays translated from German and one from Hebrew. 1. Messiah 2. Judaism — History — Addresses, essays, lectures. I. T.
BM615.S33     296     *LC* 70-130212

**International Symposium on the Holocaust, Cathedral of St. John the Divine, 1974.**      **1.1976**
Auschwitz, beginning of a new era?: Reflections on the holocaust: papers given at the International Symposium on the Holocaust, held at the Cathedral of Saint John the Divine, New York City, June 3 to 6, 1974 / edited by Eva Fleischner. — New York: Ktav Pub. Co., 1977. xix, 469 p. 1. Holocaust (Jewish theology) — Congresses. 2. Christianity and antisemitism — Congresses. 3. Judaism — Relations — Christianity — Congresses. 4. Christianity and other religions — Judaism — Congresses. I. Fleischner, Eva, 1925- II. Cathedral of St. John the Divine (New York, N.Y.) III. T.
BM645.H6 I57 1974     BM645H6 I57 1974.     296.3/87     *LC* 76-53809     *ISBN* 087068499X

# BM650–747 Practical Judaism

**Millgram, Abraham Ezra, 1901-.**      **1.1977**
Jewish worship, by Abraham E. Millgram. [1st ed.] Philadelphia, Jewish Publication Society of America [c1971] 673p. illus. 1. Jews Liturgy and ritual — History. I. T.
BM660.M55     *LC* 77-151316

**Jacobs, Louis.**      **1.1978**
Hasidic prayer. — New York: Schocken Books, [1973, c1972] ix, 195 p.; 22 cm. — (The Littman library of Jewish civilization) 1. Prayer — Judaism 2. Hasidism I. T.
BM669.J3 1973     296.7/2     *LC* 72-86765     *ISBN* 0805234772

**Siddur.**      **1.1979**
The authorised daily prayer book. Rev. ed. Hebrew text, English translation, with commentary and notes, by Joseph H. Hertz. New York, Bloch Pub. Co., 1948. xxiii, 1119 p. 24 cm. I. Hertz, Joseph H. (Joseph Herman), 1872-1946. II. T.
BM675.D3H4 1948     296     *LC* 48-24170 *

**Heschel, Abraham Joshua, 1907-1972.**      • **1.1980**
The sabbath: its meaning for modern man / Abraham Joshua Heschel; with wood engravings by Ilya Schor. — New York: Farrar, Straus and Giroux, c1951. 118 p.: ill. 1. Sabbath I. Schor, Ilya. II. T.
BM685.H4     *LC* 51-8400     *ISBN* 0374512671

**Gaster, Theodor Herzl, 1906-.**      • **1.1981**
Festivals of the Jewish year; a modern interpretation and guide. — New York, Sloane [1953] 308 p. 22 cm. Includes bibliography. 1. Fasts and feasts — Judaism I. T.
BM690.G33     *296.4     *LC* 53-9341

**Donin, Hayim.**      **1.1982**
To be a Jew; a guide to Jewish observance in contemporary life. Selected and compiled from the Shulhan arukh and Responsa literature, and providing a rationale for the laws and the traditions [by] Hayim Halevy Donin. New York, Basic Books [1972] xv, 336 p. 25 cm. 1. Judaism — Customs and practices 2. Jewish way of life I. T.
BM700.D58     296.4     *LC* 72-89175     *ISBN* 0465086241

**Klein, Isaac.**      **1.1983**
A guide to Jewish religious practice / by Isaac Klein. — New York: Jewish Theological Seminary of America; distributed by Ktav Pub. House, c1979. xxvii, 588 p.; 24 cm. (The Moreshet series; 6) Includes index. 1. Judaism — Customs and practices 2. Judaism — Liturgy 3. Jews — Dietary laws 4. Jewish law 5. Conservative Judaism I. T.
BM700.K54     296.4     *LC* 78-12159     *ISBN* 0873340043

**Jewish mystical testimonies / [edited by] Louis Jacobs.**      **1.1984**
New York: Schocken Books, 1977, c1976. ix, 270 p.; 21 cm. 1. Mysticism — Judaism — History — Sources. I. Jacobs, Louis.
BM723.J48 1977     296.7/1     *LC* 76-46644     *ISBN* 0805236414

**Scholem, Gershom Gerhard, 1897-.**      • **1.1985**
Major trends in Jewish mysticism. New York, Schocken Books [1961, c1954] 460 p. illus. 21 cm. (Schocken paperbacks, SB5) 'Reprinted from the third revised edition.' 1. Mysticism — Judaism 2. Cabala — History. I. T.
BM723.S35 1961     296.833     *LC* 61-8991

**Greenberg, Blu, 1936-.**      **1.1986**
On women & Judaism: a view from tradition / Blu Greenberg. — 1st ed. — Philadelphia: Jewish Publication Society of America, 1981. xi, 178 p.; 24 cm. 1. Women in Judaism — Addresses, essays, lectures. I. T.
BM729.W6 G73     296.3/878344 19     *LC* 81-11779     *ISBN* 0827601956

**On being a Jewish feminist: a reader / edited and with introductions by Susannah Heschel.**      **1.1987**
New York: Schocken Books, 1983. xxxvi, 288 p.; 21 cm. 1. Women in Judaism — Addresses, essays, lectures. 2. Feminism — Addresses, essays, lectures. I. Heschel, Susannah.
BM729.W6 O6 1983     296.3/878344 19     *LC* 81-16543     *ISBN* 0805238379

**Heschel, Abraham Joshua, 1907-1972.**      **1.1988**
The circle of the Baal Shem Tov: studies in Hasidism / Abraham J. Heschel; edited by Samuel H. Dresner. — Chicago: University of Chicago Press, c1985. xlv, 213 p.; 24 cm. Includes index. 1. Hasidim — Biography 2. Hasidism — History. I. Dresner, Samuel H. II. T.
BM750.H48 1985     296.8/33/0922 B 19     *LC* 84-16340     *ISBN* 0226329607

**Rosenzweig, Franz, 1886-1929.**      • **1.1989**
Franz Rosenzweig: his life and thought / presented by Nahum N. Glatzer. — 2nd ed. — New York, Schocken Books, c1961. xxxviii, 406 p.: 21 cm. (Schocken paperbacks, SB21) Includes index 1. Rosenzweig, Franz, 1886-1929. 2. Jews — Biography I. Glatzer, Nahum Norbert, 1903- II. T.
BM 755 R6 A4 1961     *LC* 62-4143

**Biale, David, 1949-.**      **1.1990**
Gershom Scholem: Kabbalah and counter–history / David Biale. — Cambridge, Mass.: Harvard University Press, 1979. vi, 279 p.: port.; 25 cm. Includes index. 1. Scholem, Gershom Gerhard, 1897- 2. Scholars, Jewish — Germany — Biography. 3. Scholars, Jewish — Israel — Biography. 4. Mysticism — Judaism — Historiography. I. T.
BM755.S295 B5     296.7/1 B     *LC* 78-23620     *ISBN* 0674363302

# BP Islam

**Williams, John Alden. comp.**      • **1.1991**
Themes of Islamic civilization. — Berkeley: University of California Press, 1971. viii, 382 p.; 24 cm. 1. Islam — Collections. I. T.
BP20.W53     910.03/176/71     *LC* 78-107659     *ISBN* 0520016858

**Goldziher, Ignác, 1850-1921.**      • **1.1992**
Muslim studies. Edited by S. M. Stern. Translated from the German by C. R. Barber and S. M. Stern. Chicago, Aldine Pub. Co. 1968-. v. 23 cm. 1. Islam — Addresses, essays, lectures. I. T.
BP25.G614     297     *LC* 67-20745

**Smith, Wilfred Cantwell, 1916-.**      **1.1993**
On understanding Islam: selected studies / Wilfred Cantwell Smith. — The Hague; New York: Mouton, c1981. xiii, 351 p.; 24 cm. — (Religion and reason; 19) 1. Islam — Collected works. I. T. II. Series.
BP25.S6 1981     297 19     *LC* 81-871     *ISBN* 9027934487

**Hughes, Thomas Patrick, 1838-1911.**      **1.1994**
A dictionary of Islam; being a cyclopaedia of the doctrines, rites, ceremonies, and customs, together with the technical and theological terms, of the Muhammadan religion. Delhi Oriental Publishers 1973. 750p. 1. Islam — Dictionaries I. T.
BP40 H8 1973

**Gibb, Hamilton Alexander Rosskeen.**      • **1.1995**
Mohammedanism: an historical survey / H.R. Gibb. — 2nd ed. — London: Oxford University Press, 1953. ix, 206 p. 1. Islam — History. I. T.
BP50.G5 1953     297.09     *LC* 53-8324

**Peters, F. E. (Francis E.)**      **1.1996**
Allah's Commonwealth; a history of Islam in the Near East, 600–1100 A.D. [by] F. E. Peters. New York, Simon and Schuster [c1973] 800 p. 23 cm.

1. Islam — History. 2. Civilization, Islamic 3. Civilization, Islamic — Greek influences I. T.
BP55.P47        910/.031/7671      *LC* 73-18733      *ISBN* 0671215647

**Voices of resurgent Islam / edited by John L. Esposito.**          **1.1997**
New York: Oxford University Press, 1983. x, 294 p.; 25 cm. 1. Islam — 20th century — Addresses, essays, lectures. I. Esposito, John L.
BP60.V62 1983      297/.09/04 19      *LC* 82-24544      *ISBN* 0195033396

**Voll, John Obert, 1936-.**          **1.1998**
Islam, continuity and change in the modern world / John Obert Voll. — Boulder, Colo.: Westview Press; Essex, England: Longman, 1982. xii, 397 p.: map; 24 cm. Includes index. 1. Islam — History. 2. Islam — 20th century I. T.
BP60.V64 1982      297/.09/03 19      *LC* 82-2829      *ISBN* 0891589317

**Gilsenan, Michael.**          **1.1999**
Recognizing Islam: religion and society in the modern Arab world / Michael Gilsenan. — 1st ed. — New York: Pantheon Books, [1983] c1982. 287 p.; 22 cm. Includes index. 1. Gilsenan, Michael. 2. Islam — Arab countries. 3. Arab countries — Description and travel. I. T.
BP63.A4 A725 1983      306/.6 19      *LC* 82-47867      *ISBN* 0394521137

**Dekmejian, R. Hrair, 1933-.**          **1.2000**
Islam in revolution: fundamentalism in the Arab world / R. Hrair Dekmejian. — 1st ed. — Syracuse, N.Y.: Syracuse University Press, 1985. 249 p.: ill.; 23 cm. (Contemporary issues in the Middle East.) Includes index. 1. Islam — Arab countries — History. 2. Islam — 20th century I. T. II. Series.
BP63.A4 D45 1985      322/.1/09174927 19      *LC* 84-26766      *ISBN* 0815623291

**Esposito, John L.**          **1.2001**
Islam and politics / John L. Esposito. — 1st ed. — Syracuse, N.Y.: Syracuse University Press, 1984. xviii, 273 p.; 24 cm. (Contemporary issues in the Middle East.) Includes index. 1. Islam and politics — Near East. 2. Islam and politics — Africa, North. 3. Political science — Near East — History. 4. Political science — Africa, North — History. 5. Middle East — Politics and government. 6. Africa, North — Politics and government. I. T. II. Series.
BP63.A4 N423 1984      320.917/671 19      *LC* 84-16135      *ISBN* 0815623224

**Islam in South–East Asia / edited by M.B. Hooker.**          **1.2002**
Leiden: Brill, 1983. viii, 262 p.; 25 cm. Based on courses and seminars at the University of Kent at Canterbury, 1978-79. Includes index. 1. Islam — Asia, Southeastern — History. I. Hooker, M. B. II. University of Kent at Canterbury.
BP63.A4 S653 1983      297/.0959 19      *LC* 84-102654      *ISBN* 9004068449

**Aziz Ahmad.**          **1.2003**
An intellectual history of Islam in India. — Edinburgh: Edinburgh U.P., 1969. x, 226 p.: 14 plates.; 21 cm. — (Islamic surveys, 7) 1. Civilization, Islamic. 2. Muslims — India. 3. India — Civilization. I. T. II. Series.
BP63.I4A9x DS36.85.I8 no. 7      915.4/0976/7      *LC* 69-16010      *ISBN* 0852240570

**Ritual and religion among Muslims in India / edited by Imtiaz Ahmad.**          **1.2004**
New Delhi: Manohar, 1981. xv, 246 p.: ill., geneal. tables; 22 cm. 1. Islam — India — Addresses, essays, lectures. I. Ahmad, Imtiaz, 1940-
BP63.I4 R48      306/.6/0954 19      *LC* 81-901398

**Noer, Deliar.**          **1.2005**
The modernist Muslim movement in Indonesia, 1900–1942. — Singapore; New York: Oxford Univesrity Press, 1973. x, 390 p.; 23 cm. — (East Asian historical monographs) A revision of the author's thesis, Cornell University. 1. Islam — Indonesia — History. 2. Indonesia — Politics and government — 1798-1942 I. T.
BP63.I5 N6      297/.09598      *LC* 73-169361

**Trimingham, J. Spencer (John Spencer), 1904-.**          **1.2006**
The influence of Islam upon Africa / J. Spencer Trimingham. — 2d ed. — London; New York: Longman; Beirut: Librairie du Liban, 1980. x, 182 p.: maps; 23 cm. (Arab background series) Includes index. 1. Islam — Africa. 2. Africa — Religious life and customs. I. T.
BP64.A1 T7 1980      297/.096      *LC* 79-42873      *ISBN* 0582784999

**Trimingham, J. Spencer (John Spencer), 1904-.**          **• 1.2007**
Islam in east Africa / by J. Spencer Trimingham. — Oxford: Clarendon Press, 1964. xii, 198 p.: maps (1 fold.); 23 cm. Bibliographical footnotes. 1. Islam — Africa, East. 2. Africa, East — Religious life and customs. I. T.
BP64.A4E27      297.09676      *LC* 64-6991

**Hiskett, M.**          **1.2008**
The development of Islam in West Africa / Mervyn Hiskett. — London; New York: Longman, 1984. xi, 353 p.: ill.; 23 cm. (Longman studies in African history.) Includes index. 1. Islam — Africa, West — History. I. T. II. Series.
BP64.A4 W354 1984      297/.0966 19      *LC* 82-6545      *ISBN* 0582646944

**Kaba, Lansiné.**          **1.2009**
The Wahhabiyya: Islamic reform and politics in French West Africa. — Evanston, Ill.: Northwestern University Press, 1974. xv, 285 p.: map; 24 cm. — (Studies in African religion) 1. Wahhābīyah — Africa, French-speaking West. I. T. II. Series.
BP64.A4 W357      297/.8      *LC* 73-85874      *ISBN* 081010427X

**Geertz, Clifford.**          **• 1.2010**
Islam observed; religious development in Morocco and Indonesia. — New Haven: Yale University Press, 1968. xii, 136 p.: maps.; 23 cm. — (The Terry lectures, v. 37) 1. Islam — Morocco. 2. Islam — Indonesia. I. T. II. Title: Religious development in Morocco and Indonesia.
BP64.M6 G4      297/.0964      *LC* 68-27753

**Eickelman, Dale F., 1942-.**          **1.2011**
Moroccan Islam: tradition and society in a pilgrimage center / by Dale F. Eickelman. Austin: University of Texas Press, c1976. xx, 303 p.: ill.; 24 cm. (Modern Middle East series; no. 1) Includes index. 1. Muslim saints — Morocco — Boujad. 2. Islam — Morocco. 3. Boujad, Morocco — Social life and customs. 4. Morocco — Social life and customs. I. T.
BP64.M62 B653      297/.0964      *LC* 75-45136      *ISBN* 0292750250

# BP70–80 Biography. Muhammad

**Andrae, Tor, 1885-1947.**          **• 1.2012**
[Mohammed, sein Leben und sein Glaube. English] Mohammed; the man and his faith. Translated by Theophil Menzel. Freeport, N.Y., Books for Libraries Press [1971] 274 p. facsim. 23 cm. Reprint of the 1936 ed. 1. Moehammad. I. T.
BP75.A57 1971      297/.63 B      *LC* 79-160954      *ISBN* 0836958217

*BP 75 A57 1960*

**Haykal, Muhammad Husayn, 1888-1956.**          **1.2013**
The life of Muhammad / by Muhammad Husayn Haykal; translated from the 8th ed. by Isma'īl Rāgī A. al Fārūqī. — [Indianapolis, IN]: American Trust Publications, c1976. xcvii, 640 p. Translation of Hayāt Muhammad. 1. Moehammad.
BP75.H3x      297.63 B      *LC* 76-4661

**Ibn Hishām, 'Abd al-Malik, d. 834.**          **• 1.2014**
The life of Muhammad; a translation of Ishāq's Sirat rasūl Allāh, with introd. and notes by A. Guillaume. Lahore, Oxford University Press, 1955. 813 p. 1. Moehammad. I. Ibn Isbāk, Muhammad, d. ca. 768. II. Guillaume, Alfred. III. T. IV. Title: Sirat rasūl Allāh.
BP75.I25 1955      297.63      *LC* 55-12845

**Lings, Martin.**          **1.2015**
Muhammad: his life based on the earliest sources / by Martin Lings. — London: Islamic Texts Society: Allen & Unwin, 1983. viii, 359 p.: map, geneal. table; 24 cm. Errata slip inserted. 1. Moehammad — Biography. 2. Muslims — Saudi Arabia — Biography. I. T.
BP75.L56x 1983b      *LC* 84-672353      *ISBN* 0042970423

**Muir, William, Sir, 1819-1905.**          **1.2016**
The life of Mohammad / [by Sir William Muir]. New York: AMS Press, [1975] cxix, 556 p. [7] leaves of plates: ill.; 23 cm. Reprint of the 1923 ed., rev. by T. H. Weir; edited by J. Grant, Edinburgh. 1. Mohammad, the prophet. I. Weir, T. H. (Thomas Hunter) ed. II. T.
BP75.M8 1975      297/.63 B      *LC* 78-180366      *ISBN* 0404563066

**Watt, W. Montgomery (William Montgomery)**          **• 1.2017**
Muhammad at Mecca / by W. Montgomery Watt. — Oxford: Clarendon Press, 1953, printing 1968. xvi, 192 p. Sequel: Muhammad at Medina. 1. Muhammad, Prophet, d. 632. I. T.
BP75 W3      BP75 W3.      *LC* 53-13179

**Watt, W. Montgomery (William Montgomery)**          **• 1.2018**
Muhammad at Medina / by W. Montgomery Watt. — Oxford: Clarendon Press, 1968. xiv, 418 p. 'Sequel to Muhammad at Mecca.' 1. Muhammad, Prophet, d. 632. I. T.
BP75 W32      BP75 W32 1968.      922.97

**Rodinson, Maxime.**          **1.2019**
[Mahomet. English] Muhammad / Maxime Rodinson; translated from the French by Anne Carter; [new introd. and foreword by the author]. — New

York: Pantheon Books, c1980. li, 362 p.: ill.; 21 cm. Translation of Mahomet. Reprint of the 1971 ed. published by Pantheon Books, New York. Includes index. 1. Moehammad — Biography. 2. Muslims — Saudi Arabia — Biography. I. T.
BP75.13.R613 1980      297/.63 B      *LC* 79-17158      *ISBN* 0394509080

**Keddie, Nikki R.**                                                              • **1.2020**
Sayyid Jamāl ad–Dīn 'al–Afghānī; a political biography, by Nikki R. Keddie. Berkeley, University of California Press, 1972. xvii, 479 p. port. 24 cm. 1. Afghānī, Jamāl al-Dīn, 1838-1897. I. T.
BP80.A45 K43      297/.092/4 B      *LC* 74-159671      *ISBN* 0520019865

**Troll, Christian W., 1937-.**                                                  **1.2021**
Sayyid Ahmad Khan: a reinterpretation of Muslim theology / Christian W. Troll. — New Delhi: Vikas Publ. House, c1978. xxii, 384 p., [1] leaf of plates: ill.; 23 cm. Includes index. 1. Ahmad Khān, Sayyid, Sir, 1817-1898. 2. Muslims — India — Biography. I. T.
BP80.A485 T76      297/.2/0924      *LC* 78-905652

**Abbott, Nabia, 1897-.**                                                        • **1.2022**
Aishah, the beloved of Mohammed. Chicago, Univ. Press [1942] xiii, 230 p. front., map, genea. table. 1. Aisha. I. T.
BP80.A52A2

**Massignon, Louis, 1883-1962.**                                                 **1.2023**
[Passion de Husayn Ibn Mansûr Hallâj. English] The passion of al–Hallāj: mystic and martyr of Islam / Louis Massignon; translated from the French with a biographical foreword by Herbert Mason. — Princeton, N.J.: Princeton University Press, c1982. 4 v.: ill., maps; 24 cm. — (Bollingen series. 98) Translation of La Passion de Husayn Ibn Mansûr Hallâj. 1. Hallāj, al-Husayn ibn Mansûr, 858 or 9-922. 2. Sufis — Biography. 3. Sufism I. T. II. Series.
BP80.H27 M3713 1982      297/.6 B      *LC* 80-11085      *ISBN* 0691099103

**Smith, Margaret, 1884-.**                                                      **1.2024**
Rābi'a the mystic & her fellow–saints in Islām: being the life and teachings of Rābi'a al-'Adawiyya Al–Qaysiyya of Bas₂ra together with some account of the place of the women saints in Islām / by Margaret Smith; with a new introduction by Annemarie Schimmel. — Cambridge [Cambridgeshire]; New York: Cambridge University Press, 1984. xxxv, 219 p.; 23 cm. Originally published: London: Cambridge University Press, 1928. Includes indexes. 1. Rābi'ah al-'Adawīyah, d. 801? 2. Sufism 3. Sufis — Biography. I. T. II. Title: Rābi'a the mystic and her fellow-saints in Islām.
BP80.R3 S6 1984      297/.4/0924 B 19      *LC* 84-7655      *ISBN* 052126779X

# BP86–89 Islamic Civilization

**Ghazzālī, 1058-1111.**                                                         **1.2025**
[Munqidh min al-dalāl. English] Freedom and fulfillment: an annotated translation of Al–Ghazālī's al–Munqidh min al–dalāl and other relevant works of al–Ghazālī / by Richard Joseph McCarthy. — Boston: Twayne Publishers, c1980. 420 p.: ill.; 21 cm. — (Library of classical Arabic literature; v. 4) Includes indexes. 1. Ghazzālī, 1058-1111. 2. Islam — Doctrines — Early works to 1800. 3. Muslims — Islamic Empire — Biography. I. McCarthy, Richard Joseph. II. T.
BP88.G47 E5 1980      297/.2      *LC* 79-27100      *ISBN* 0805781676

**Arberry, A. J. (Arthur John), 1905-1969.**                                     • **1.2026**
Aspects of Islamic civilization, as depicted in the original texts, by A. J. Arberry. New York, A.S. Barnes [c1964] 408 p. 22 cm. Includes selections from original texts in English translation. 1. Islamic literature — History & criticism. 2. Civilization, Islamic — History. I. T.
BP89.A7 1964b      910.03/176/7      *LC* 65-24575

# BP100–137 Sacred Books. Koran

**Koran. English.**                                                              • **1.2027**
The Koran interpreted, by Arthur J. Arberry. Combined in one volume. New York, Macmillan [c1955] 350, 358 p. 23 cm. I. Arberry, A. J. (Arthur John), 1905-1969. tr. II. T.
BP109.A7 1955a      297.12      *LC* 64-9828

**Bosworth, Clifford Edmund.**                                                   **1.2028**
The Islamic dynasties: a chronological and genealogical handbook / Clifford Edmund Bosworth. — [Rev. ed.]. — Edinburgh: Edinburgh University Press,

1980 (c1967). xviii, 245 p.; 18 cm. (Islamic surveys; 5) 1. Islamic countries — Kings and rulers. 2. Islamic countries — History. I. T. II. Series.
BP130.B4x      909.091767      *ISBN* 0852244029

**Cragg, Kenneth.**                                                              **1.2029**
The event of the Qu'rān; Islam in its scripture. — London: Allen & Unwin, [1971] 208 p.; 22 cm. 1. Koran. I. T.
BP130.C67      297/.1226/6      *LC* 72-179748      *ISBN* 0042970245

**Ayoub, Mahmoud.**                                                              **1.2030**
The Qur'an and its interpreters, volume 1 / Mahmoud Ayoub. — Albany: State University of New York Press, c1984-. xii, 290 p.; 24 cm. 1. Koran — Commentaries. I. T.
BP130.4.A835 1984      297/.1226 19      *LC* 82-21713      *ISBN* 087395727X

**Cragg, Kenneth.**                                                              **1.2031**
The mind of the Qur'ān: chapters in reflection. — London: Allen and Unwin, 1973. 3-209 p.; 23 cm. 1. Koran — Criticism, interpretation, etc. I. T.
BP130.4.C7      297/.1226      *LC* 73-160303      *ISBN* 004297030X

**Rahman, Fazlur, 1919-.**                                                       **1.2032**
Major themes of the Qur'ān / by Fazlur Rahman. — Minneapolis, MN: Bibliotheca Islamica, 1980. xvi, 180 p.; 24 cm. 1. Koran — Theology I. T.
BP132.R33      297/.2 19      *LC* 79-54189      *ISBN* 0882970267

**Kassis, Hanna E.**                                                             **1.2033**
A concordance of the Qur'an / Hanna E. Kassis; foreword by Fazlur Rahman. — Berkeley: University of California Press, 1984, c1983. xxxix, 1444 p.; 29 cm. Includes indexes. 1. Koran — Concordances. I. Koran. II. T.
BP133.K37 1984      297/.1225/21 19      *LC* 82-40100      *ISBN* 0520043278

**Izutsu, Toshihiko, 1914-.**                                                    • **1.2034**
God and man in the Koran; semantics of the Koranic Weltanschauung. Tokyo Keio Institute of Cultural and Linguistic Studies 1964. 242,2,4p. (Studies in the humanities and social relations. v. 5) 1. Koran — Language, style 2. Cosmology, Islamic I. T. II. Series.
BP134 C6 I9

**Izutsu, Toshihiko, 1914-.**                                                    **1.2035**
[Structure of the ethical terms in the Koran] Ethico–religious concepts in the Qur'ān. [Rev. ed.] Montreal, McGill University, Institute of Islamic Studies, McGill University Press, 1966. ix, 284 p. 26 cm. (McGill Islamic studies 1) First published in 1959 under title: The structure of the ethical terms in the Koran. 1. Koran — Ethics I. T. II. Series.
BP134.E8 I9 1966      297.1228      *LC* 66-16860

**Wagtendonk, K.**                                                               **1.2036**
Fasting in the Koran. By K. Wagtendonk. — Leiden: E. J. Brill, 1968. 164 p.; 25 cm. — (Dissertationes ad historiam religionum pertinentes, v. 2. Supplementa ad Nvmen, altera series) 1. Fasting (Islam) — Koranic teaching 2. Ramadan I. T.
BP134.F3 W3      297/.1228      *LC* 68-111734

**Al-Khatib al-Tibrizi, Muhammad ibn Abd Allah, fl. 1337.**                      **1.2037**
Mishkat al–masabih. English translation with explanatory notes, by James Robson. [1st ed.] Lahore M. Ashraf [1960-65] 4 v. in 5 (xx, 1453 p.); 25 cm. A commentry on the hadith collected by al-Baghawī under title: Masābīh al-sunnah. 1. al-Baghawī, al-Husayn ibn Mas'ūd, d. 1117 or 1122. Masābīh al-sunnah 2. Hadith (Collections) I. Robson, James, 1890-, ed. II. T.
BP135 A2 K433 1960      BP135.A2 K435.

**Guillaume, Alfred, 1888-.**                                                    • **1.2038**
The traditions of Islam; an introduction to the study of the hadith literautre. Beirut Khayats 1966. 184p. (Khayats oriental reprint, no. 13) 1. Hadith I. T.
BP135 G8 1966

# BP141–144 Islamic Law

**Anderson, James Norman Dalrymple.**                                            **1.2039**
Islamic law in the modern world. — [New York] New York University Press, 1959. 106 p. 21 cm. Includes bibliography. 1. Mohammedan law. I. T.
BP141.A31      *LC* 59-13110

**Coulson, Noel J. (Noel James)**                                                **1.2040**
A history of Islamic law, by N.J. Coulson. Edinburgh, University Press [1964] viii, 264 p. (Islamic surveys, no. 2) 1. Islamic law — History I. T. II. Title: Islamic law III. Series.
BP144.C6x      *LC* 64-14916

**Khadduri, Majid, 1909-.**              **1.2041**
Law in the Middle East / edited by Majid Khadduri and Herbert J. Liebesny; with a foreword by Robert H. Jackson.— Washington, D.C.: Middle East Institute 1955. 1. Islamic law — History and criticism 2. Law — Near East — History and criticism I. Liebesny, Herbert, 1911- II. T.
BP144.K5x

**Schacht, Joseph, 1902-1969.**          **1.2042**
The origins of Muhammadan jurisprudence / by Joseph Schacht. — Oxford: Clarendon Press, 1950. xii, 348 p. 1. Islamic law — History. I. T.
BP144.S3x      340.5/9

---

# BP160–165 Islam: General Works

**Ali, Syed Ameer, 1849-1928.**        ● **1.2043**
The spirit of Islam; a history of the evolution and ideals of Islam with a life of the Prophet. London, Methuen [1967] lxxi, 515 p. 22 cm. (University paperbacks, UP107) 1. Moehammad. 2. Islam I. T.
BP161.A335 1967     297     *LC* 68-97979

**al-Ash‘arī, ‘Alī ibn Ismā‘īl, 873?-935?**    **1.2044**
The theology of al-Ash‘arī; the Arabic texts of al-Ash‘arī's Kitāb al-Luma‘ and Risālat Istihsān al-khawd fī ‘ilm al-kalām, with briefly annotated translations, and appendices containing material pertinent to the study of al-Ash‘arī. [By] Richard J. McCarthy. Beyrouth, Impr. catholique, 1953. xxviii, 275 p., 109 p. 25 cm. Added t.p. in arabic: Kitāb al-Luma‘. 1. Islam I. McCarthy, Richard Joseph. II. T. III. Title: Kitāb al-Luma‘. IV. Title: Istihsān al-khawd fī ‘ilm al-kalām.
BP 161 A82 1953     *LC* 58-42943

**Goldziher, Ignác, 1850-1921.**          **1.2045**
[Vorlesungen über den Islam. English] Introduction to Islamic theology and law / by Ignaz Goldziher; translated by Andras and Ruth Hamori; with an introd. and additional notes by Bernard Lewis. — Princeton, N.J.: Princeton University Press, c1981. xv, 302 p.; 25 cm. — (Modern classics in Near Eastern studies.) Translation of Vorlesungen über den Islam. Includes index. 1. Islam I. Lewis, Bernard. II. T. III. Series.
BP161.G5713    297 19    *LC* 80-7523    *ISBN* 0691072574

**Mas ‘ūd ibn ‘Umar, Sa‘d al-Dīn, al-Taftāzānī, 1322-1389.**   ● **1.2046**
A commentary on the creed of Islam; Sa‘d al-Dīn al-Taftāzānī on the creed of Najm al-Dīn al-Nasafī. Translated with introd. and notes by Earl Edgar Elder. New York, Columbia University Press, 1950. xxxii, 187 p. 24 cm. (Records of civilization, sources and studies. no. 43) ‘The translation was first made as a part of the requirements for the degree of doctor of philosophy a the Kennedy School of Missions of the Hartford Seminary Foundation.‘ 1. ‘Umar ibn Muhammad, al-Nassafi, al-Akā’id. 2. Islam I. Elder, Earl Edgar, 1887- II. T. III. Series.
BP161.U55 M32    297    *LC* 50-5160

**Wensinck, Arent Jan, 1882-1939.**        **1.2047**
The Muslim creed: its genesis and historical development / by A.J. Wensinck. — Cambridge: University Press, 1932. vii, 304 p. ‘This book [consists of] ... for the most part ... translations of, and commentaries upon, the creed in its various forms.‘ - Preface. 1. Islam — History. I. T.
BP161.W4    297

**Cragg, Kenneth.**            **1.2048**
The house of Islam / Kenneth Cragg. — 2d ed. — Encino, Calif.: Dickenson Pub. Co., [1975] xiii, 145 p.; 23 cm. (The Religious life of man) Includes index. 1. Islam I. T.
BP161.2.C72 1975    297    *LC* 74-83949    *ISBN* 0822101394

**Islam from within: anthology of a religion / [compiled by]**  **1.2049**
**Kenneth Cragg, R. Marston Speight.**
Belmont, Calif.: Wadsworth Pub. Co., c1980. xv, 253 p.: ill.; 24 cm. — (The Religious life of man) 1. Islam I. Cragg, Kenneth. II. Speight, R. Marston, 1924-
BP161.2.I85    297    *LC* 78-24004    *ISBN* 0878722122

**Islam: the religious and political life of a world community /**  **1.2050**
**edited by Marjorie Kelly.**
New York: Praeger, 1984. xii, 321 p.: maps; 24 cm. ‘Published for the Foreign Policy Association.‘ Includes index. 1. Islam 2. Islam and politics 3. Islamic countries — History. I. Kelly, Marjorie. II. Foreign Policy Association.
BP161.2.I882 1984    909/.097671 19    *LC* 84-13307    *ISBN* 0030010888

**Rahman, Fazlur, 1919-.**         ● **1.2051**
Islam. — [1st ed.]. — New York: Holt, Rinehart and Winston, [c1966] xi, 271 p.: illus.; 25 cm. — (History of religion series) 1. Islam I. T.
BP161.2.R29    297    *LC* 66-13499

**Williams, John Alden. ed.**       ● **1.2052**
Islam. — New York: G. Braziller, 1961. 256 p.; 21 cm. — (Great religions of modern man) 1. Islam I. T.
BP161.2.W5    297.082    *LC* 61-15500

**Cragg, Kenneth.**         **1.2053**
Counsels in contemporary Islam. Edinburgh, University Press [1965] xiv, 255 p. 22 cm. (Islamic surveys, 3) Bibliography: p. 219-238. 1. Islam — 20th century 2. Islam — Essence, genius, nature I. T. II. Series.
BP163.C7x    *LC* 65-4825

**Schacht, Joseph.**         **1.2054**
Introduction to Islamic law. — Oxford: Clarendon Press, 1964. 304 p. 1. Islamic law I. T.
BP163.S29 1964    347.97    *LC* 64-6944

**Macdonald, Duncan Black, 1863-1943.**    ● **1.2055**
The religious attitude and life in Islam. — New York: AMS Press, [1970] xvii, 317 p.; 23 cm. — (Haskell lectures on comparative religion, University of Chicago, 1906) Reprint of the 1909 ed. 1. Islam — Addresses, essays, lectures. I. T.
BP165.M23 1970    297    *LC* 70-121277    *ISBN* 0404041256

**Nasr, Seyyed Hossein.**        **1.2056**
Ideals and realities of Islam. — New York: Praeger, [1967, c1966] 184 p.; 23 cm. 1. Islam — Addresses, essays, lectures. I. T.
BP165.N28 1967    297    *LC* 67-22242

---

# BP166 Theology

**Muhammad ‘Abduh, 1849-1905.**       ● **1.2057**
The Theology of unity: translated from the Arabic by Ishaq Musa‘ad and Kenneth Cragg. London: Allen and Unwin, 1966. 164p.; 23 cm. Originally published as Risalat al-Tauhid. 1. Islam — Doctrines I. T.
BP166.M7513    297.2    *LC* 66-70498

**Watt, W. Montgomery (William Montgomery)**    **1.2058**
The formative period of Islamic thought [by] W. Montgomery Watt. [s.l.]: Aldine, 1973. vi, 424 p. 23 cm. 1. Islam — Doctrines — History. I. T.
BP166.1.W3    297/.2/09    *LC* 73-79266    *ISBN* 085224245X

**Watt, W. Montgomery (William Montgomery)**    **1.2059**
Islamic philosophy and theology: an extended survey / W. Montgomery Watt. — 2nd ed. — Edinburgh: University Press, 1985. vii, 175 p.; 23 cm. Includes index. 1. Islam — Doctrines — History. 2. Philosophy, Islamic. I. T.
BP166.1.W33 1985    297/.2 19    *LC* 85-199504    *ISBN* 0852244878

**Wensinck, Arent Jan, 1882-1939.**       ● **1.2060**
The Muslim creed, its genesis and historical development. — New York: Barnes & Noble, [1965, i.e. 1966] vii, 304 p.; 21 cm. ‘First published 1932.‘ Bibliography: p. [281]-285. 1. Islam — Doctrines — History. I. T.
BP166.1.W4    297.2    *LC* 66-1494

**Jāmī, 1414-1492.**         **1.2061**
[Durrah al-fākhirah. English] The precious pearl = al-Jamīs' al-Durrah al-fākhirah: together with his glosses and the commentary of ‘Abd al-Ghafūr al-Lārī / translated with an introd., notes, and glossary by Nicholas Heer. — Albany: State University of New York Press, 1979. ix, 237 p.; 25 cm. (Studies in Islamic philosophy and science.) ‘Glossary of terms': p. 171-237. 1. God (Islam) 2. Sufism — Early works to 1800. I. al-Lārī, ‘Abd al-Ghafūr, d. 1506. II. Heer, Nicholas. III. T. IV. Title: Durrah al-fākhirah. V. Series.
BP166.2.J3513    297/.211    *LC* 78-12607

**Ormsby, Eric L. (Eric Linn), 1941-.**    **1.2062**
Theodicy in Islamic thought: the dispute over al-Ghazālī's ‘best of all possible worlds‘ / Eric L. Ormsby. — Princeton, N.J.: Princeton University Press, c1984. xv, 309 p.; 23 cm. Revision of thesis (Ph. D.)—Princeton University, 1981. Includes index. 1. Ghazzālī, 1058-1111 — Metaphysics. 2. God (Islam) — History of doctrines. I. T.
BP166.2.O76 1984    297/.211 19    *LC* 84-3396    *ISBN* 0691072787

**Rahman, Fazlur.**        ● **1.2063**
Prophecy in Islam: philosophy and orthodoxy / Fazlur Rahman. — Midway reprint. Chicago; London: University of Chicago Press, 1979, c1958. 118 p.; 23 cm. (Islamic studies) 1. Prophecy (Islam). I. T. II. Series.
BP166.4.R34 1979    *LC* 78-66082    *ISBN* 0226702820

**Arberry, A. J. (Arthur John), 1905-1969.**                    • 1.2064
Revelation and reason in Islam. London, Allen & Unwin [1957] 122 p. 19 cm.
(Forwood lectures, 1956) 1. Revelation (Islam) I. T. II. Series.
BP166.6.A7x        LC a 57-5022

**Crone, Patricia, 1940-.**                                        1.2065
God's caliph: religious authority in the first centuries of Islam / Patricia Crone
and Martin Hinds. — Cambridge [Cambridgeshire]; New York: Cambridge
University Press, 1986. v, 157 p.; 23 cm. — (University of Cambridge oriental
publications; no. 37) Includes index. 1. Caliphate 2. Islam and state 3. Islamic
Empire — Politics and government. I. Hinds, Martin. II. T.
BP166.9.C76 1986        297/.65 19        LC 85-26992        ISBN 0521321859

**Sachedina, Abdulaziz Abdulhussein, 1952-.**                      1.2066
Islamic messianism: the idea of Mahdī in twelver Shīʿism / Abdulaziz
Abdulhussein Sachedina. — Albany: State University of New York Press,
c1981. x, 230 p.; 24 cm. Includes index. 1. Mahdism 2. Shīʿah — Doctrines
I. T.
BP166.93.S22        297/.23        LC 80-16767        ISBN 0873954424

**Ibn Taymīyah, Ahmad ibn ʿAbd al-Halīm, 1263-1328.**             1.2067
[Jawāb al-sahīh li-man baddala dīn al-Masīh. English] A Muslim theologian's
response to Christianity: Ibn Taymiyya's al-Jawab al-sahih / edited and
translated by Thomas F. Michel. — Delmar, N.Y.: Caravan Books, 1984. ix,
465 p.; 24 cm. (Studies in Islamic philosophy and science.) Translation of:
Jawāb al-sahīh li-man baddala dīn al-Masīh. 1. Christianity — Controversial
literature 2. Islam — Apologetic works I. Michel, Thomas F., 1941- II. T.
III. Series.
BP170.I18913 1984        297/.293 19        LC 83-15430        ISBN 0882060589

# BP171-173 Islam and Other Religions

**Kritzeck, James.**                                              • 1.2068
Sons of Abraham: Jews, Christians, and Moslems. — Baltimore, Helicon [1965]
126 p. 21 cm. Bibliographical references included in 'Notes' (p. 97-116)
Bibliography: p. 117-126. 1. Islam — Relations — Christianity 2. Islam —
Relations — Judaism. 3. Christianity and other religions — Islam 4. Judaism
— Relations — Islam. I. T.
BP171.K7        290        LC 65-15039

**Cragg, Kenneth.**                                               1.2069
Muhammad and the Christian: a question of response / Kenneth Cragg. —
London: Darton, Longman, and Todd; Maryknoll, N.Y.: Orbis Books, 1984.
xii, 180 p.; 21 cm. Includes indexes. 1. Moehammad — Appreciation. 2. Islam
— Relations — Christianity 3. Christianity and other religions — Islam I. T.
BP172.C656 1984        261.2/7 19        LC 84-100894        ISBN 088344349X

**Daniel, Norman.**                                               • 1.2070
Islam and the West; the making of an image. — Edinburgh: University Press,
[1960] ix, 443 p.: illus.; 23 cm. 1. Christianity and other religions — Islam
2. Islam — Relations — Christianity I. T.
BP172.D3        297        LC 60-4951

**Parrinder, Edward Geoffrey.**                                   • 1.2071
Jesus in the Qur'An. New York: Barnes and Noble, 1965. 187 p.; 23 cm. —
Bibliography. 1. Jesus Christ — Islamic interpretations 2. Koran — Relations
to the Bible. I. T.
BP172 P3        297.1228232        LC 65-29535

**Southern, R. W. (Richard William), 1912-.**                     • 1.2072
Western views of Islam in the Middle Ages. — Cambridge: Harvard University
Press, 1962. 114 p.; 22 cm. 1. Christianity and other religions — Islam 2. Islam
— Relations — Christianity 3. Islam — Historiography I. T.
BP172.S67        297.0902        LC 62-13270

**Lewis, Bernard.**                                               1.2073
The Jews of Islam / Bernard Lewis. — Princeton, N.J.: Princeton University
Press, c1984. xii, 245 p.; [16] p. of plates: ill.; 23 cm. Includes index. 1. Judaism
— Relations — Islam. 2. Islam — Relations — Judaism. 3. Jews — Islamic
countries 4. Islamic countries — Ethnic relations. I. T.
BP173.J8 L48 1984        297/.1972 19        LC 84-42575        ISBN
0691054193

**Gellner, Ernest.**                                              1.2074
Muslim society / Ernest Gellner. — Cambridge; New York: Cambridge
University Press, 1981. ix, 267 p.; 24 cm. — (Cambridge studies in social
anthropology. 0068-6794; 32) 1. Sociology, Islamic 2. Islam — Africa, North.
3. Africa, North — Social conditions. I. T. II. Series.
BP173.25.G44        909/.097671 19        LC 80-41103        ISBN 0521221609

**Turner, Bryan S.**                                              1.2075
Weber and Islam: a critical study / [by] Bryan S. Turner. — London; Boston:
Routledge & Kegan Paul, 1974. ix, 212 p.; 23 cm. (International library of
sociology) 1. Weber, Max, 1864-1920. 2. Sociology, Islamic I. T.
BP173.25.W4 T87        301.5/8/0917671        LC 74-77201        ISBN
071007848X

**Islam in the political process / edited by James P. Piscatori.**   1.2076
[London]: Royal Institute of International Affairs; Cambridge; New York:
Cambridge University Press, 1983. ix, 239 p.; 24 cm. 1. Islam and politics —
Congresses. 2. Islamic countries — Politics and government — Congresses.
I. Piscatori, James P. II. Royal Institute of International Affairs.
BP173.7.I85 1983        320.917/671 19        LC 82-9745        ISBN
0521249414

# BP174-190 The Practice of Islam

**Khadduri, Majid, 1909-.**                                       • 1.2077
War and peace in the law of Islam. — Baltimore, Johns Hopkins Press
[1962,c1955] x, 321 p. 23 cm. Revision of the 1st ed. published in London in
1940 under title: The law of war and peace in Islam. Bibliography: p. 301-307.
Bibliographical footnotes. 1. Jihad 2. Mohammedan law. 3. International law
I. T.
BP175.J5K45 1955        297        LC 55-8427

**Kalābādhī, Muhammad ibn Ibrāhīm, 10th cent.**                   • 1.2078
The doctrine of the Sūfis (Kitāb al-Taʿarruf li-madhhab ahl al-tasawwuf);
translated from the Arabic by Arthur John Arberry. Cambridge, Univ. Press,
1935. xviii, 173 p. 1. Sufism I. Arberry, Arthur John, tr. II. T.
BP175.M9A3

**Watt, W. Montgomery (William Montgomery)**                      1.2079
Free will and predestination in early Islam. London, Luzac, 1948. 181 p. 22 cm.
Xerox reprint; Ann Arbor, Mich., University Microfilms, 1973. 1. Free will
and determinism (Islam) 2. Predestination (Islam) I. T.
BP 175 P7 W34 1948        LC 50-20361 rev

**Izutsu, Toshihiko, 1914-.**                                     • 1.2080
The concept of belief in Islamic theology; a semantic analysis of îmân and islâm.
Tokyo Keio Institute of Cultural and Linguistic Studies 1965. 250,10p. (Studies
in the humanities and social relations, v. 6) 1. Faith (Islam) I. T.
BP177 I9

**Martin, Bradford G.**                                           1.2081
Muslim brotherhoods in nineteenth century Africa / B. G. Martin. Cambridge,
[Eng.]; New York: Cambridge University Press, 1977 (c1976). xiii, 267 p.; 24
cm. (African studies series. 18) Includes index. 1. Sufism — Africa — History.
2. Africa — History — 19th century I. T. II. Series.
BP188.8.A44 M37        297/.4        LC 75-35451        ISBN 0521210623

**Najm al-Dīn Rāzī, ʿAbd Allāh ibn Muhammad, d. 1256 or 7.**     1.2082
[Mirsād al-ʿibād min al-mabdaʾ ilā al-maʿād. English] The path of God's
bondsmen from origin to return = (Mersād al-ʿebād men al-mabdā' elā'l-
maʿād): a Sufi compendium / by Najm al-Dīn Rāzī, known as Dāya; translated
from the Persian, with introduction and annotation by Hamid Algar. —
Delmar, N.Y.: Caravan Books, 1982. 537 p.; 24 cm. — (Persian heritage series.
no. 35) Translation of: Mirsād al-ʿibād min al-mabdaʾ ilā al-maʿād. Includes
indexes. 1. Sufism — Early works to 1800. I. Algar, Hamid. II. T. III. Title:
Mersād al-ʿebād men al-mabdā' elā'l-maʿād. IV. Series.
BP188.9.N25413 1982        297/.4 19        LC 81-21780        ISBN
088206052X

**Arberry, A. J. (Arthur John), 1905-1969.**                     • 1.2083
Sufism: an account of the mystics of Islam / A.J. Arberry. — London: Allen &
Unwin, c1950. 141 p.; 20 cm. 1. Sufism I. T.
BP189.A7        LC 51-11267

**Hujvīrī, ʿAlī ibn ʿUsmān, d. ca. 1072.**                       1.2084
The Kashf al-mahjúb; the oldest Persian treatise on Súfism, by ʿAlí b. ʿUthmán
al-Jullábí al-Hujwírí. Translated from the text of the Lahore edition, compared
with mss. in the India Office and British Museum. New ed., by Reynold A.
Nicholson. New ed. London Luzac 1970. 443p. 1. Sufism — Early works to
1800 I. Nicholson, Reynold Alleyne, 1868-1945. II. T.
BP189 H783 1970

**Schimmel, Annemarie.**                                          1.2085
Mystical dimensions of Islam. — Chapel Hill: University of North Carolina
Press, [1975] xxi, 506 p.: illus.; 25 cm. 1. Sufism I. T.
BP189.2.S34        297/.4        LC 73-16112        ISBN 0807812234

**Ibn 'Atā' Allāh, Ahmad ibn Muhammad, d. 1309.**     **1.2086**
[Hikam al-'Atā'īyah. English] The book of wisdom / Ibn 'Ata' Illah. Intimate conversations / K[h]waja Abdullah Ansari; introd., translation, and notes of The book of wisdom by Victor Danner and of Intimate conversations by Wheeler M. Thackston; pref. by Annemarie Schimmel. — New York: Paulist Press, c1978. xvii, 233 p.; 23 cm. — (Classics of Western spirituality.) Translation of Ibn 'Atā' Allāh's al-Hikam al-'Atā'īyah and of al-Ansārī's Munājāt. 1. Sufism — Early works to 1800. I. Ansārī al-Harawī, 'Abd Allāh ibn Muhammad, 1006-1089. Munājāt. English. c1978. II. Danner, Victor, 1926- III. Thackston, W. M. (Wheeler McIntosh), 1944- IV. T. V. Title: Intimate conversations. VI. Series.
BP189.62.I2613 1978    297/.4    *LC* 79-101197    *ISBN* 080910279X

**Bouhdiba, Abdelwahab.**     **1.2087**
[Sexualité en Islam. English] Sexuality in Islam / Abdelwahab Bouhdiba; translated from the French by Alan Sheridan. — London; Boston: Routledge & Kegan Paul, 1985. viii, 288 p.; 22 cm. 1. Sex — Religious aspects — Islam 2. Sex customs — Arab countries. 3. Arab countries — Social life and customs. I. T.
BP190.5.S4 B6813 1985    297/.1978357 19    *LC* 84-18273    *ISBN* 0710096089

# BP191–223 Branches. Sects

**Jafri, Syed Husain M.**     **1.2088**
Origins and early development of Shi'a Islam / S. Husain M. Jafri. — London; New York: Longman, 1979. xii, 332 p.; 23 cm. Includes index. 1. Shī'ah — History. I. T.
BP192.4.J33    297/.82/09021    *LC* 78-40611    *ISBN* 0582780802

**Shi'ism and social protest** / edited by Juan R.I. Cole and Nikki    **1.2089**
**R. Keddie.**
New Haven: Yale University Press, c1986. x, 325 p.; 24 cm. 1. Shī'ah — History — 20th century — Addresses, essays, lectures. 2. Islam and politics — Near East — Addresses, essays, lectures. 3. Middle East — Politics and government — 1945- — Addresses, essays, lectures. I. Cole, Juan Ricardo. II. Keddie, Nikki R.
BP192.7.N33 S54 1986    322/.1 19    *LC* 85-22780    *ISBN* 0300035500

**Ibn Bābūyah, Abu Ja'far Muhammad ibn 'Ali al-Qummi al-**    **1.2090**
**Sadūq, d. 991.**
A Shi'ite creed: a translation of Risālatu'l–I'tiqādāt of Mohammad b. 'Alī Ibn Bābawayhi al–Qummī known as Shaykh Sadūq / by Asaf A. A. Fyzee. — London: H. Milford: Oxford University Press, 1942. xiii, 144 p.; 23 cm. — (Islamic research association series; 9) 1. Shiites I. Fyzee, Asaf Ali Asghar. II. T. III. Series.
BP193.I213    297

**Momen, Moojan.**     **1.2091**
An introduction to Shi'i Islam: the history and doctrines of Twelver Shi'ism / by Moojan Momen. — New Haven: Yale University Press, c1985. xxii, 397 p., [40] p. of plates: ill.; 25 cm. Includes index. 1. Shī'ah I. T.
BP193.5.M66 1985    297/.821 19    *LC* 85-40438    *ISBN* 0300034997

**Tabātabā'ī, Muhammad Husayn.**     **1.2092**
[Shī'ah dar Islām. English] Shi'ite Islam, by 'Allāmah Sayyid Muhammad Husayn Tabātabā'ī. Translated from the Persian and edited with an introd. and notes by Seyyed Hossein Nasr. [1st ed.] Albany, State University of New York Press, 1975. xiv, 253 p. 24 cm. (Persian studies series, no. 5) Translation of Shī'ah dar Islām. 1. Shī'ah I. T.
BP193.5.T3213    297/.82    *LC* 74-8289    *ISBN* 0873952723 *ISBN* 0873952731

**Ivanow, Wladimir.**     **1.2093**
Studies in early Persian Ismailism / by W. Ivanow. — 2d rev. ed. — Bombay: Ismaili Society, 1955. 157 p., [1] leaf of plates: facsim.; 22 cm. — (The Ismaili Society series; A, no. 8) 1. Ismailites — Iran — Addresses, essays, lectures. I. T.
BP195.I8 I9 1955    297/.822/0955    *LC* 77-350424

**Kalami pir: a treatise on Ismaili doctrine also (wrongly) called**    **1.2094**
**Haft babi Shah Sayyid Nasir / edited in original Persian and**
**translated into English by W. Ivanow.**
Bombay: [Islamic Research Association] 1935. lxviii, 146, 117 p. (Islamic Research Association series, no. 4) In English and Persian. 1. Ismailites I. Ivanow, Wladimir. II. Quhistani, Abu Ashaq. Haft bab III. Haft bab-ī Shah Sayyid Nāsir IV. Series.
BP195.I8 K3x

## BP300–600 BAHAISM. OTHER ORIENTAL RELIGIONS

**Bahā' Allāh, 1817-1892.**     • **1.2095**
[Selections. English. 1956] Bahá'í world faith; selected writings of Bahá'u'lláh and 'Abdu'l–Bahá. [2d ed.] Wilmette, Ill., Bahá'í Pub. Trust [1956] 465 p. 21 cm. 'Approved by the Reviewing Committee of the National Spiritual Assembly.' 1. Bahai Faith I. 'Abdu'l-Bahá, 1844-1921. II. T.
BP360.B135 1956    297.8*    *LC* 56-8259

**Hatcher, William S.**     **1.2096**
The Bahā'í faith: the emerging global religion / William S. Hatcher and J. Douglas Martin. — 1st ed. — San Francisco: Harper & Row, c1984. xvii, 226 p.; 22 cm. Includes index. 1. Bahai Faith I. Martin, J. Douglas (James Douglas) II. T.
BP365.H335 1984    297/.89 19    *LC* 84-42743    *ISBN* 0060654414

**Campbell, Bruce F.**     **1.2097**
Ancient wisdom revived: a history of the Theosophical movement / Bruce F. Campbell. — Berkeley: University of California Press, c1980. x, 249 p., [1] leaf of plates: ill.; 23 cm. Includes index. 1. Theosophy — History. I. T.
BP530.C35    299/.934/09 19    *LC* 79-64664    *ISBN* 0520039688

**Steiner, Rudolf, 1861-1925.**     **1.2098**
[Wie erlangt man Erkenntnisse der höheren Welten? English] Knowledge of the higher worlds and its attainment. [Rendered into English by George Metaxa with revisions by Henry B. and Lisa D. Monges. 3d ed.] New York, Anthroposophic Press [1970? c1947] xv, 272 p. 19 cm. Translation of Wie erlangt man Erkenntnisse der höheren Welten? 1. Anthroposophy I. T.
BP595.W8938513 1970    149/.3    *LC* 79-101595

**Ellwood, Robert S., 1933-.**     **1.2099**
Religious and spiritual groups in modern America [by] Robert S. Ellwood, Jr. — Englewood Cliffs, N.J.: Prentice-Hall, [c1973] xvi, 334 p.; 24 cm. 1. Cults — United States 2. Religions I. T.
BP603.E55 1973    200/.973    *LC* 72-4371    *ISBN* 0137733178

**Downton, James V.**     **1.2100**
Sacred journeys: the conversion of young Americans to Divine Light Mission / James V. Downton, Jr. — New York: Columbia University Press, 1979. ix, 245 p., [4] leaves of plates: ill.; 24 cm. Includes index. 1. Guru Maharaj Ji, 1957- 2. Divine Light Mission. 3. Conversion — Case studies. I. T.
BP605.D58 D69    294 19    *LC* 79-546    *ISBN* 0231041985

**Reiterman, Tim.**     **1.2101**
Raven; the untold story of the Rev. Jim Jones and his people / Tim Reiterman, with John Jacobs. — New York: Dutton, c1982. xvii, 622 p., [32] p. of plates: ill.; 25 cm. Includes index. 1. Jones, Jim, 1931-1978. 2. Peoples Temple. I. Jacobs, John, 1950- II. T.
BP605.P46 R44 1982    BP605P46 R44 1982.    289.9 19    *LC* 81-15223    *ISBN* 0525241361

**Reston, James, 1941-.**     **1.2102**
Our father who art in hell / by James Reston, Jr. — New York: Times Books, c1981. xiii, 338 p.; 25 cm. 1. Jones, Jim, 1931-1978. 2. Peoples Temple — Biography. 3. Mass suicide — Guyana. I. T.
BP605.P46 R47 1981    289.9 B 19    *LC* 80-25510    *ISBN* 0812909631

**Wallis, Roy.**     **1.2103**
The road to total freedom: a sociological analysis of scientology / Roy Wallis. — New York: Columbia University Press, 1977, c1976. xiv, 282 p.; 24 cm. Includes index. 1. Scientology I. T.
BP605.S2 W34 1977    131/.35    *LC* 76-27273    *ISBN* 0231042000

## BQ BUDDHISM
(Works classified after 1972. For earlier works see BL1400-1495.)

## BQ120–999 Collected Works. History. Biography

**The Tibetan book of the great liberation; or, The method of** • **1.2104**
realizing nirvāna through knowing the mind, preceded by an
epitome of Padma–Sambbava's biography and followed by Guru
Phadampa Sangay's teaching. According to English Renderings
by Sardar Bahadur S. W. Laden La [et al.] Intro., annotations,
and editing by W. Y. Evans–Wentz. With psychological
commentary by C. G. Jung.
London, Oxford University Press [1954] lxiv, 261 p. ill. (part col.) 23 cm.
1. Buddhism — Collected works. 2. Nirvana 3. Yoga I. Padma Sambhava,
ca. 717-ca. 762. II. Phadampa Sangay, fl. 1100 III. Jung, C. G. (Carl Gustav),
1875-1961. IV. Evans-Wentz, W. Y. (Walter Yeeling), 1878-1965. V. Title:
The method of realizing nirvāna knowing the mind.
BQ 120 T55 1954     *LC* 56-58518

**Warder, Anthony Kennedy.**                                              **1.2105**
Indian Buddhism / A.K. Warder. — 2d rev. ed. — Delhi: Motilal Banarsidass,
1980. xv, 627 p.: 2 maps; 22 cm. Includes index. 1. Buddhism — India —
History. I. T.
BQ286.W36 1980     294.3/0954 19     *LC* 80-901628

**Pande, Govind Chandra, 1923-.**                                        **1.2106**
Studies in the origins of Buddhism / Govind Chandra Pande. — 2d rev. ed. —
Delhi: Motilal Banarsidass, 1974. ix, 606 p.; 23 cm. Includes index.
1. Buddhism — Origin. I. T.
BQ288.P36 1974     294.3     *LC* 75-928043

**Conze, Edward, 1904-.**                                              • **1.2107**
Buddhist thought in India: three phases of Buddhist philosophy / by Edward
Conze. — Repr. with corrections, 1983. — London; Boston: Allen & Unwin,
1983. 302 p.; 23 cm. 'First published in 1962'—T.p. verso. Includes index.
1. Buddhism — India. 2. Philosophy, Buddhist 3. Mahayana Buddhism I. T.
BQ336.C66x 1983     *LC* 84-673618     *ISBN* 0042941288

**Obeyesekere, Gananath.**                                              **1.2108**
The two wheels of dhamma; essays on the Theravada tradition in India and
Ceylon, by Gananath Obeyesekere, Frank Reynolds [and] Bardwell L. Smith,
editor. Chambersburg, Pa., American Academy of Religion, 1972. 121 p. 24
cm. (AAR studies in religion, no. 3) 1. Theravāda Buddhism — Sri Lanka —
Addresses, essays, lectures. 2. Buddhism — History — To ca. 100 A.D. —
Addresses, essays, lectures. I. Reynolds, Frank, 1930- II. Smith, Bardwell L.,
1925- III. T.
BQ356.O2     294.3/91     *LC* 70-188906

**Religion and legitimation of power in Sri Lanka / Bardwell L.** **1.2109**
**Smith.**
Chambersburg, PA: ANIMA Books, c1978. x, 244 p. ; 22 cm. — (Religion and
legitimation of power) (South and Southeast Asia studies) 1. Buddhism and
state — Sri Lanka — Addresses, essays, lectures. 2. Buddhism and politics —
Addresses, essays, lectures. 3. Buddhism — Sri Lanka — History —
Addresses, essays, lectures. I. Smith, Bardwell L., 1925- II. Series. III. Series:
South and Southeast Asia studies
BQ359.R44     294.3/3/77095493     *LC* 77-7449

**Spiro, Melford E.**                                              **1.2110**
Buddhism and society: a great tradition and its Burmese vicissitudes / Melford
E. Spiro. — 2nd, expanded ed. — Berkeley: University of California Press,
c1982. xxiv, 510 p.; 23 cm. Includes index. 1. Buddhism — Burma.
2. Sociology, Buddhist — Burma. I. T.
BQ418.S65 1982     294.3/91/09591 19     *LC* 81-18522     *ISBN*
0520046714

**Religion and legitimation of power in Thailand, Laos, and** **1.2111**
**Burma / Bardwell L. Smith, editor.**
Chambersburg, PA: ANIMA Books, c1978. ix, 231 p.; 22 cm. — (Religion and
legitimation of power) (South and Southeast Asia studies) 1. Buddhism and
state — Thailand — Addresses, essays, lectures. 2. Buddhism and state — Laos
— Addresses, essays, lectures. 3. Buddhism and state — Burma — Addresses,
essays, lectures. 4. Buddhism and politics — Addresses, essays, lectures.

I. Smith, Bardwell L., 1925- II. Series. III. Series: South and Southeast Asia
studies
BQ554.R44     294.3/3/770959     *LC* 77-7444     *ISBN* 0890120099

**Tambiah, Stanley Jeyaraja, 1929-.**                                   **1.2112**
World conqueror and world renouncer: a study of Buddhism and polity in
Thailand against a historical background / S. J. Tambiah. — Cambridge [Eng.];
New York: Cambridge University Press, 1976. viii, 557p.: ill.; 23 cm.
(Cambridge Studies in social anthropology; 15) Includes index. 1. Buddhism
and state — Thailand. 2. Buddhism — Thailand — History. I. T.
BQ554.T35     294.3/3/77     *LC* 76-8290     *ISBN* 0521211409

**Wells, Kenneth Elmer, 1896-.**                                   • **1.2113**
Thai Buddhism, its rites and activities. Bangkok, Distributors: Christian
Bookstore, 1960. 320 p. ill. 22 cm. 1. Buddhism — Thailand. I. T.
BQ 566 W4 1960     *LC* 60-15751

**Ch'en, Kenneth Kuan Sheng, 1907-.**                              **1.2114**
The Chinese transformation of Buddhism [by] Kenneth K. S. Ch'en. —
Princeton, N.J.: Princeton University Press, [1973] ix, 345 p.; 23 cm.
1. Buddhism — China I. T.
BQ626.C52     294.3/0951     *LC* 75-39782     *ISBN* 069107187X

**Wright, Arthur F., 1913-1976.**                                  • **1.2115**
Buddhism in Chinese history. Stanford, Calif., Stanford University Press, 1959.
144 p. ill. 21 cm. (Stanford studies in the civilizations of eastern Asia)
1. Buddhism — China I. T.
BQ 626 W94 1959     *LC* 59-7432

**Overmyer, Daniel L., 1935-.**                                    **1.2116**
Folk Buddhist religion: dissenting sects in late traditional China / Daniel L.
Overmyer. — Cambridge, Mass.: Harvard University Press, 1976. xi, 295 p.; 24
cm. (Harvard East Asian series. 83) Includes index. 1. Buddhism — China —
History 2. China — Religion — History. I. T. II. Series.
BQ628.O9 1976     294.3/0951     *LC* 75-23467     *ISBN* 0674307054

**Tsukamoto, Zenryū, 1898-.**                                      **1.2117**
[Chūgoku Bukkyō tsūshi. English] A history of early Chinese Buddhism: from
its introduction to the death of Hui–yüan / by Zenryū Tsukamoto; translated
from the Japanese by Leon Hurvitz. — 1st English ed. — Tokyo; New York:
Kodansha International: Distributed in the U.S. by Kodansha International/
USA Ltd. through Harper & Row, 1985. 2 v. (1305 p.); 27 cm. Translation of:
Chūgoku Bukkyō tsūshi. Includes index. 1. Buddhism — China — History —
To 581 A.D. I. T.
BQ636.T75713 1985     294.3/0931 19     *LC* 83-48873     *ISBN*
0870116355

**Zürcher, Erik.**                                                 **1.2118**
The Buddhist conquest of China. The spread and adaptation of Buddhism in
early medieval China. By E. Zürcher. — Reprint, with additions and
corrections. — Leiden: Brill, 1972. 2 v.; 25 cm. — (Sinica Leidensia. v. 11) 'First
published 1959.' 1. Buddhism — China — History I. T. II. Series.
BQ636.Z84 1972     294.3/0951     *LC* 72-192783

**Welch, Holmes.**                                                 • **1.2119**
Buddhism under Mao. Cambridge, Mass., Harvard University Press, 1972.
xviii, 666 p. illus., maps (on lining papers) 25 cm. (Harvard East Asian series.
69) 1. Buddhism — China I. T. II. Series.
BQ647.W44     294.3/0951     *LC* 72-78428     *ISBN* 0674085655

**Nichiren, 1222-1282.**                                           • **1.2120**
The awakening to the truth; or, 'Kaimokushō' / Nichiren; translated by N. R.
M. Ehara, assisted by Bhikkhu Soma & Bhikkhu Kheminda. — Tokyo:
International Buddhist Society, 1941. 121 p.: ill. Colophon in English and
Japanese on last leaf. 1. Buddhism — Japan I. T. II. Title: Kaimokushō.
BQ672.N54     *LC* a 47-1143

**Eliot, Charles Norton Edgecumbe, Sir, 1862-1931.**              • **1.2121**
Japanese Buddhism. With a memoir of the author by Sir Harold Parlett. New
York, Barnes & Noble, 1959 [i.e.1960] 449 p. 23 cm. 'Complementary to Sir
Charles Eliot's earlier work, Hinduism and Buddhism, which appeared in
1921.' 1. Nichiren, 1222-1282. 2. Buddha and Buddhism — Japan. I. T.
BQ674.E58 1960     294.32     *LC* 60-341

**McMullin, Neil, 1940-.**                                         **1.2122**
Buddhism and the state in sixteenth–century Japan / Neil McMullin. —
Princeton, N.J.: Princeton University Press, c1984. ix, 441 p.; 23 cm. Includes
index. 1. Oda, Nobunaga, 1534-1582. 2. Buddhism and state — Japan.
3. Japan — History — Azuchi Momoyama period, 1568-1603 I. T.
BQ687.M4 1984     322/.1/0952 19     *LC* 84-42572     *ISBN*
0691072914

The Life of the Buddha, as it appears in the Pali canon, the **1.2123**
oldest authentic record / translation from the Pali, selection of
material, and arrangement, by Bhikkhu Ñānamoli.
2nd ed. — Kandy [Sri Lanka]: Buddhist Publication Society, 1978. vi, 369 p.:
map.; 23 cm. 1. Gautama Buddha. I. Ñānamoli, Bhikkhu.
BQ882.N36      294.3/63 B      *LC* 73-906958

**Saddhatissa, H.**                                                **1.2124**
The life of the Buddha / [by] H. Saddhatissa. — New York: Harper & Row,
c1976. 89 p., 2 leaves of plates: ill., map, ports.; 21 cm. 1. Gautama Buddha.
I. T.
BQ882.S22 1976a      294.3/63 B      *LC* 76-62927      *ISBN* 0060670265

**Blofeld, John Eaton Calthorpe, 1913-.**                          **1.2125**
The wheel of life; the autobiography of a Western Buddhist [by] John Blofeld.
— 2d ed. — Berkeley [Calif.]: Shambala, 1972. 291 p.: illus.; 22 cm. —
1. Blofeld, John Eaton Calthorpe, 1913- I. T.
BQ942.L64 A3 1972      294.3/63 B      *LC* 72-189854

---

# BQ1100-3300 Buddhist Literature: Tripitaka (Canonical Literature)

**De Bary, William Theodore, 1918- comp.**                         **1.2126**
The Buddhist tradition in India, China & Japan. Edited by Wm. Theodore De
Bary. With the collaboration of Yoshito Hakeda and Philip Yampolsky and
with contributions by A. L. Basham, Leon Hurvitz, and Ryusaku Tsunoda. —
New York: Modern Library, [1969] xxii, 417 p.; 20 cm. — (Readings in
Oriental thought) (The Modern library of the world's best books [205])
1. Buddhism — Sacred books I. T.
BQ1138.D4      294.3      *LC* 68-29391

**Aśvaghosa.**                                                     **1.2127**
The Buddhacarita: or, Acts of the Buddha / by E. H. Johnston. — 1st ed. —
Delhi: Motilal Banarsidass, 1972. 2 v. in 1.; 25 cm. English and Sanskrit; critical
apparatus in English. 1. Gautama Buddha — Poetry. I. Johnston, E. H.
(Edward Hamilton), 1885-1942. ed. and tr. II. T. III. Title: Acts of the
Buddha.
BQ1606.B8322 E54 1972a

**Tripitaka. Sūtrapitaka. Lankāvatārasūtra.**                    • **1.2128**
The Lankavatara sutra: a Mahayana text / translated for the first time from the
original Sanskrit by Daisetz Teitaro Suzuki. — London: Routledge K. Paul,
1978. xlix, 300 p. [7 fold.]: port. First published 1932. 1. Mahayana Buddhism
— Sacred books I. Suzuki, Daisetz Teitaro, 1870-1966. II. T. III. Title: A
Mahayana text.
BQ1722.E5 1978      294.32      *ISBN* 0710021658

**Śrīmālāsūtra. English.**                                         **1.2129**
The lion's roar of Queen Śrīmālā; a Buddhist scripture on the Tathāgatagarbha
theory. Translated, with introd. and notes by Alex Wayman and Hideko
Wayman. — New York: Columbia University Press, 1974. xv, 142 p.: port.; 23
cm. Translation of the lost Sanskrit work made from a collation of the Chinese,
Japanese, and Tibetan versions. I. Wayman, Alex, tr. II. Wayman, Hideko, tr.
III. T.
BQ1792.E5 W394      294.3/82      *LC* 73-9673      *ISBN* 0231037260

**Prajnaparamitas. Astasāhasrikā. English.**                       **1.2130**
The perfection of wisdom in eight thousand lines & its verse summary.
Translated by Edward Conze. — Bolinas: Four Seasons Foundation;
distributed by Book People, Berkeley, 1973. xxii, 325 p.; 23 cm. — (Wheel
series. 1) Contains some sections of the Ratnagunasañcayagāthā. I. Conze,
Edward, 1904- tr. II. Prajnaparamitas. Sancayagatha English. III. T.
IV. Series.
BQ1912.E5 C66 1973      294.3/8      *LC* 72-76540      *ISBN* 0877040486

**Tripitaka. Sūtrapitaka. Prajñāpāramitā. Pañcavimśatisāhasrikā.** **1.2131**
The large sutra on perfect wisdom, with the divisions of the Abhisamayālankāra
/ translated by Edward Conze. — Berkeley: University of California Press,
[1975] xviii, 679 p.; 24 cm. Includes index. I. Maitreyanātha.
Abhisamayālankāra. 1975. II. Conze, Edward, 1904- III. T.
BQ1952.E5 C66      294.3/8      *LC* 71-189224      *ISBN* 0520022408

**Prajnaparamitas. Vajracchedika. English.**                     • **1.2132**
Buddhist wisdom books, containing The diamond Sutra and The heart Sutra.
Translated and explained, by Edward Conze. — London: G. Allen & Unwin,
[1958] 110 p.: illus.; 23 cm. Includes original Sanskrit text of the Heart Sutra.
I. Conze, Edward, 1904- tr. and ed. II. T. III. Title: The heart Sutra.
BQ1992.E5 C66 1958      294.3/85 19      *LC* 60-36296

**Tripitaka. Sūtrapitaka. Saddharmapundarīkasūtra.**             • **1.2133**
The Saddharma-pundarīka: or, The lotus of the true law / translated by H.
Kern. — Delhi: M. Banarsidass, 1965. xiii, 454 p. — (The Sacred books of the
East; v. 21) (UNESCO collection of representative works: Indian series)
Translation based on a Sanskrit palm leaf ms. in the D. Wright Collection,
University of Cambridge Library. I. Kern, H. (Hendrik), 1833-1917.
II. Cambridge University Library. MSS. (Add. 1682). III. T. IV. Title: The
lotus of the true law.
BQ2052.E5 1965      *LC* sa 66-313

**Tripitaka. Sūtrapitaka. Saddharmapundarīkasūtra. English.**       **1.2134**
Scripture of the lotus blossom of the fine dharma / translated from the Chinese
of Kumarajiva by Leon Hurvitz. — New York: Columbia University Press,
1976. xxviii, 421 p.; 24 cm. — (Buddhist studies and translations.) (Translations
from the Oriental classics.) (Records of civilization, sources and studies. no. 94)
I. Hurvitz, Leon, 1923- II. T. III. Series. IV. Series: Translations from the
Oriental classics. V. Series: Records of civilization, sources and studies. no. 94
BQ2052.E5 H87      294.3/82      *LC* 75-45381      *ISBN* 0231037899.
*ISBN* 0231039204 pbk

**Vimalakīrtinirdeśa. English.**                                   **1.2135**
The Vimalakīrti nirdeśa sūtra (Wei mo chieh so shuo ching) Translated by Lu
K'uan Yü (Charles Luk). — Berkeley: Shambala, [1972] xviii, 157 p.; 23 cm. —
(The Clear light series) I. Lu, K'uan Yü, 1898- tr. II. T.
BQ2212.E5 L8 1972      294.3/82      *LC* 71-189851      *ISBN* 0877730350

**Vimalakīrtinirdeśa. English.**                                   **1.2136**
The holy teaching of Vimalakīrti: a Mahāyāna scripture / translated by Robert
A. F. Thurman. — University Park: Pennsylvania State University Press,
c1976. 166 p. I. Thurman, Robert A. F. II. T.
BQ2212.E5 T47      294.3/8      *LC* 75-29070      *ISBN* 0271012090

**Tripitaka. Vinayapitaka. Pratimoksasūtra. English.**             **1.2137**
Buddhist monastic discipline: the Sanskrit Prātimoksa sūtras of the
Mahāsāmghikas and Mūlasarvāstivādins. [Edited by] Charles S. Prebish.
University Park, Pennsylvania State University Press [1975] 156 p. 24 cm. 'The
Mahāsāmghika and Mūlasarvāstivādin Prātimoksa sūtras presented face to face
for easy comparison.' 1. Sarvāstivādins. 2. Mahāsānghikas. 3. Monasticism
and religious orders, Buddhist — Rules I. Prebish, Charles S. ed. II. T.
BQ2272.E5 P73      294.3/822      *LC* 74-10743      *ISBN* 0271011718

**Buddhaghosa.**                                                   **1.2138**
The path of purification: Visuddhimagga / Bhadantācariya Buddhaghosa;
translated from the Pali by Bhikkhu Ñānamoli. Berkeley, Calif.: Shambhala
Publications: distributed in the United States by Random House, 1976. 2 v.; 22
cm. Includes index. I. Ñānamoli, Bhikkhu, d. 1960. II. T.
BQ2632.E5 N36 1976      294.3/82      *LC* 75-40258      *ISBN* 0877730792

**Nāgārjuna, 2nd cent.**                                           **1.2139**
[Rājaparikathāratnamālā. English] The precious garland and The song of the
four mindfulnesses / Nāgārjuna and Kaysang Gyatso, Seventh Dalai Lama;
translated and edited by Jeffrey Hopkins and Lati Rimpoche, with Anne Klein;
foreword by Tenzin Gyatso, Fourteenth Dalai Lama. — 1st U.S. ed. — New
York: Harper & Row, [1975] 119 p.; 21 cm. (The Wisdom of Tibet series; 2)
Translation of Rājaparikathāratnamālā by Nāgārjuna and a poem by the
Seventh Dalai Lama. I. Bskal-bzań-rgya-mtsho, Dalai Lama VII, 1708-1757.
The song of the four mindfulnesses causing the rain of achievements to fall.
English. 1975. II. T.
BQ2872.E5 1975      294.3/4      *LC* 74-25688      *ISBN* 006063541X

---

# BQ4000-4060 Buddism: General Works

**Prebish, Charles S.**                                            **1.2140**
Buddhism—a modern perspective / edited by Charles S. Prebish. — University
Park: Pennsylvania State University Press, [1975] xv, 330 p.; 23 cm. Includes
index. 1. Buddhism I. T.
BQ4012.P73      294.3      *LC* 74-26706      *ISBN* 0271011858

**Robinson, Richard H., 1926-.**                                   **1.2141**
The Buddhist religion: a historical introduction / Richard H. Robinson,
Willard L. Johnson. 2d ed. — Encino, Calif.: Dickenson Pub. Co., c1977. xi,
243 p.: ill.; 23 cm. (The Religious life of man series) Includes index.
1. Buddhism I. Johnson, Willard L. joint author. II. T.
BQ4012.R6 1977      294.3      *LC* 76-49233      *ISBN* 0822101939

**The World of Buddhism: Buddhist monks and nuns in society**    **1.2142**
**and culture / texts by Richard Gombrich ... [et al.]; edited by**
**Heinz Bechert and Richard Gombrich.**
New York, N.Y.: Facts on File, c1984. 308 p.: ill. (some col.); 31 cm. Includes index. 1. Buddhism I. Bechert, Heinz, 1932- II. Gombrich, Richard Francis. III. Facts on File, Inc. IV. Title: Buddhism.
BQ4012.W67 1984     294.3 19     LC 84-8125     ISBN 0871969823

**Dumoulin, Heinrich.**                      **1.2143**
Buddhism in the modern world / Heinrich Dumoulin, editor, John C. Maraldo, associate editor. — New York: Macmillan, c1976. xii, 368 p.; 24 cm. Newly rev. English translation of the work originally published in German in 1970 under title: Buddhismus der Gegenwart. Includes index. 1. Buddhism I. Maraldo, John C., joint author. II. T.
BQ4015.D8513     294.3     LC 75-42342     ISBN 0025337904

**Bstan-'dzin-rgya-mtsho, Dalai Lama XIV, 1935-.**    **1.2144**
The Buddhism of Tibet and The key to the middle way / Tenzin Gyatso, the Fourteenth Dalai Lama; translated in the main by Jeffrey Hopkins and Lati Rimpoche. — 1st U.S. ed. — New York: Harper & Row, [1975] 104 p.; 21 cm. (The Wisdom of Tibet series; 1) Includes index. 1. Buddhism — Tibet. I. Bstan-'dzin-rgya-mtsho, XIV, Dalai Lama, 1935- The key to the middle way. 1975. II. T. III. Title: Buddhism of Tibet.
BQ4022.B75 1975     294.3/923     LC 74-25686     ISBN 0060648317

# BQ4061–4570 Doctrinal and Systematic Buddhism

**The path of the Buddha: Buddhism interpreted by Buddhists /**    • **1.2145**
**edited by Kenneth W. Morgan.**
New York: Ronald Press Co., 1956. x, 432 p.: maps (on lining papers) 1. Buddhism — History I. Morgan, Kenneth William
BQ4090.P37     LC 56-9981

**Kalupahana, David J., 1933-.**                **1.2146**
Buddhist philosophy: a historical analysis / David J. Kalupahana; foreword by G. P. Malalasekera. — Honolulu: University Press of Hawaii, c1976. xxi, 189 p.; 22 cm. 'An East-West Center book.' 1. Buddhism — Doctrines 2. Philosophy, Buddhist I. T.
BQ4150.K34     181/.04/3     LC 75-20040     ISBN 0824803604

**Guenther, Herbert V.**                    **1.2147**
Philosophy and psychology in the Abhidharma / Herbert V. Guenther. — [3d ed.]. — Berkeley, Calif.: Shambhala; [New York]: distributed by Random House, 1976. viii, 270 p.: ill.; 22 cm. 1. Abhidharma 2. Philosophy, Buddhist 3. Buddhism — Philosophy. I. T.
BQ4200.G83 1976     181/.04/3     LC 75-40259     ISBN 0877730814

**The Threefold refuge in the Theravāda Buddhist tradition /**    **1.2148**
**edited by John Ross Carter with George Doherty Bond ... [et al.].**
Chambersburg, Pa.: Anima Books, 1982. vi, 89 p.; 22 cm. Includes index. 1. Threefold refuge — Addresses, essays, lectures. 2. Theravāda Buddhism — Addresses, essays, lectures. I. Carter, John Ross. II. Bond, George Doherty, 1903-
BQ4350.T47 1982     294.3/42 19     LC 82-16467     ISBN 0890120307

**Karma-gliṅ-pa, 14th cent.**               **1.2149**
[Bar do thos grol. English] The Tibetan book of the dead: the great liberation through hearing in the Bardo / by Guru Rinpoche according to Karma Lingpa; a new translation with commentary by Francesca Fremantle and Chögyam Trungpa. — Berkeley: Shambhala, 1975. xx, 119 p.: ill.; 24 cm. — (The Clear light series) Translation of the author's Bar do thos grol. Includes index. 1. Intermediate state — Buddhism. 2. Funeral rites and ceremonies, Buddhist — Tibet. 3. Death — Religious aspects — Buddhism I. Fremantle, Francesca. II. Chögyam Trungpa, Trungpa Tulku, 1939- III. T.
BQ4490.K3713     294.3/423     LC 74-29615     087773741

# BQ4695–6388 Deities. Rituals. Folklore. Shrines

**Beyer, Stephan.**                      **1.2150**
The cult of Tārā; magic and ritual in Tibet. — Berkeley: University of California Press, [c1973] xxi, 542 p.; 25 cm. — (Hermeneutics: studies in the history of religions, 1) 1. Tārā (Goddess) — Cult — Tibet. 2. Buddha and Buddhism — Rituals. I. T. II. Series.
BQ4710.T34 T53     294.3/4/38     LC 74-186109     ISBN 0520021924

**Seneviratne, H. L., 1934-.**              **1.2151**
Rituals of the Kandyan state / H. L. Seneviratne. — Cambridge; New York: Cambridge University Press, 1978. 190 p.: ill.; 24 cm. — (Cambridge studies in social anthropology; 22) Includes index. 1. Kandy, Sri Lanka. Dalada Maligava. 2. Buddhism — Customs and practices — Sri Lanka — Kandy. I. T.
BQ4990.S742 K367     294.3/4/38095493     LC 77-80842     ISBN 0521217369

**Keikai, 8th/9th cent. comp.**            **1.2152**
Miraculous stories from the Japanese Buddhist tradition; the Nihon ryōiki of the monk Kyōkai. Translated and annotated with an introd. by Kyoko Motomochi Nakamura. Cambridge, Harvard University Press, 1973. xii, 322 p. 25 cm. (Harvard-Yenching Institute. Monograph series, v. 20) 1. Legends, Buddhist I. Nakamura, Kyōko, 1932- tr. II. T.
BQ5775.J3 K4313     294.3/8     LC 72-87773     ISBN 0674576357

**Covell, Jon Etta Hastings Carter, 1910-.**     **1.2153**
Zen at Daitoku-ji / Jon Covell, Yamada Sōbin. — [1st ed.]. — Tokyo; New York: Kodansha International; [New York: distributed by Harper & Row, 1974] 203 p.: ill. (some col.); 29 cm. Includes index. 1. Daitokuji (Kyoto, Japan) 2. Art, Zen — Japan — Kyoto. I. Yamada, Sōbin. joint author. II. T.
BQ6353.K82 D3634     LC 74-77956     ISBN 0870112279

# BQ7300–9800 Modifications of Buddhism

## BQ7300–7522 MAHAYANA BUDDHISM

**Dutt, Nalinaksha.**                  **1.2154**
Mahāyāna Buddhism. — Calcutta: Firma K. L. Mukhopadhyay, 1973. vi, 304 p.; 22 cm. Revised ed. of the author's Aspects of Mahāyāna Buddhism and its relation to Hīnayāna. 1. Mahayana Buddhism I. T.
BQ7374.D87 1973     294.3/92     LC 73-905181

**Mahāyāna Buddhist meditation: theory and practice / edited by**    **1.2155**
**Minoru Kiyota, assisted by Elvin W. Jones.**
Honolulu: University Press of Hawaii, c1978. xv, 312 p. 1. Mahayana Buddhism — Doctrines — Addresses, essays, lectures. 2. Meditation — Buddhism — Addresses, essays, lectures. I. Kiyota, Minoru, 1923- II. Jones, Elvin W.
BQ7405.M34     294.3/4/43     LC 78-60744     ISBN 0824805569

**Suzuki, Beatrice Lane.**             • **1.2156**
Mahayana Buddhism / Beatrice Suzuki; with an introd. by D. T. Suzuki and a foreword by Christmas Humphreys. — 3rd ed. London: Albert & Unwin, 1959. xxxx, 146 p.; 19 cm. 1. Mahayana Buddhism I. T.
BQ7405.S8x     LC 61-3991

**Takakusu, Junjirō.**                 **1.2158**
The essentials of Buddhist philosophy. Edited by Wing-tsit Chan and Charles A. Moore. — Westport, Conn.: Greenwood Press, [1973] 221 p.; 22 cm. Reprint of the 1956 ed. 1. Mahayana Buddhism. 2. Buddhist doctrines — East (Far East) 3. Buddhist sects — East (Far East) I. T.
BQ7405.T35 1973     181/.04/3     LC 72-10701     ISBN 0837166195

**Murti, T. R. V. (Tirupattur Ramaseshayyer Venkatachala)**    **1.2159**
The central philosophy of Buddhism: a study of the Mādhyamika system / T. R. V. Murti. — London; Boston: Unwin Paperbacks, 1980. xi, 372 p.; 20 cm. 'A Mandala book.' 1. Mādhyamika (Buddhism) 2. Philosophy, Buddhist I. T.
BQ7457.M87 1980     181/.04392 19     LC 80-504231     ISBN 0042941083

## BQ7530–7950 LAMAISM

**Hoffmann, Helmut, 1912-.**            • **1.2160**
The religions of Tibet / Helmut Hoffmann; translated by Edward Fitzgerald. — New York: MacMillan, 1961. 199 p.: ill.; 23 cm. Translation of Die Religionen Tibets. Includes index. 1. Lamaism — History. 2. Bonpo (Sect) — History. I. T.
BQ7576.H6313 1979     294.3/0951/5     LC 61-4236

**Kongtrul, Jamgon.**      **1.2161**
The torch of certainty / [by] Jamgon Kongtrul; translated from the Tibetan by Judith Hanson; foreword by Chögyam Trungpa. Boulder; London: Shambhala; London [etc.]: Distributed by Routledge and Kegan Paul, 1977. xix, 161 p.: ill.; 22 cm. (Clear light series.) Index. ISBN 0-87773-101-2. 1. Buddha and Buddhism. — Tibet. I. Hanson, Judith. II. T. III. Series.
BQ7602.K6x      294.3/923      *LC 76-53359*      *ISBN* 0877731004

**Kloṅ-chen-pa Dri-med-'od-zer, 1308-1363.**      **1.2162**
[Nal gso skor gsum. English] Kindly bent to ease us: from the Trilogy of finding comfort and ease = Ngal–gso skor–gsum / Klong–chen rab–'byams–pa; translated from the Tibetan and annotated by Herbert V. Guenther. — Emeryville, Calif.: Dharma Pub., c1976-. v.: ill.; 22 cm. — (Tibetan translation series.) 1. Rdzogs-chen (Rñiṅ-ma-pa) I. Guenther, Herbert V. II. T. III. Series.
BQ7662.4.K543513      294.3/4      *LC 75-29959*      *ISBN* 0913546429

**Women of wisdom / Tsultrim Allione; foreword by Chögyam**      **1.2163**
**Trungpa.**
London; Boston: Routledge & Kegan Paul, 1984 (1985 printing) xxxviii, 282 p., [16] p. of plates: ill.; 22 cm. Includes index. 1. Women, Buddhist — China — Tibet — Biography. I. Allione, Tsultrim, 1947-
BQ7920.W65 1985      294.3/923/0922 B 19      *LC 84-11440*      *ISBN* 0710202407

**Bstan-'dzin-rgya-mtsho, Dalai Lama XIV, 1935-.**      **1.2164**
Kindness, clarity, and insight / the Fourteenth Dalai Lama, his Holiness Tenzin Gyatso; translated and edited by Jeffrey Hopkins; co–edited by Elizabeth Napper. — Ithaca, N.Y., USA: Snow Lion Publications, [1984] 232 p., [12] p. of plates: ill.; 22 cm. 1. Buddhism — Doctrines — Addresses, essays, lectures. 2. Buddhism — China — Tibet — Addresses, essays, lectures. I. Hopkins, Jeffrey. II. Napper, Elizabeth. III. T.
BQ7935.B774 K56 1984      294.3/4 19      *LC 84-51198*      *ISBN* 0937938181

**Bstan-pa'i-ñi-ma, 4th Panchen Lama of Tashilhunpo, 1781-1854.**      **1.2165**
Practice and theory of Tibetan Buddhism / [translated from the Tibetan and with an introd. and notes by] Lhundup Sopa and Jeffrey Hopkins; with a foreword by the Dalai Lama. — New York: Grove Press, c1976. xxviii, 164 p. 1. Buddhism — China — Tibet II. Dkon-mchog-'jigs-med-dbaṅ-po, Jam-dbyaṅs-bźad-pa II, 1728-1791. Precious garland of tenets. II. T. III. Title: Precious garland of tenets.
BQ7945.B784 P73    BQ7945B787 P73 1976.      *LC 75-42898*      *ISBN* 0394179056

## BQ8200–8279 Hua–yen Buddhism

**Cook, Francis Dojun, 1930-.**      **1.2166**
Hua–yen Buddhism: the jewel net of Indra / Francis H. Cook. — University Park: Pennsylvania State University Press, c1977. xiv, 146 p.; 24 cm. 'Published in cooperation with the Institute for Advanced Studies of World Religions New York, N.Y.' 1. Tripitaka. Sūtrapitaka. Buddhāvatamsakamah āvaipulyasūtra — Criticism, interpretation, etc. 2. Hua-yen Buddhism — Doctrines. I. Institute for Advanced Studies of World Religions. II. T.
BQ8218.C66      294.3/92      *LC 76-43288*      *ISBN* 0271012455

## BQ8300–8459 Nichiren

**Hardacre, Helen, 1949-.**      **1.2167**
Lay Buddhism in contemporary Japan: Reiyūkai Kyōdan / Helen Hardacre. — Princeton, N.J.: Princeton University Press, c1984. xviii, 267 p., [8] p. of plates: ill.; 23 cm. Includes index. 1. Reiyūkai. I. T.
BQ8372.H37 1984      294.3/9 19      *LC 83-43075*      *ISBN* 0691072841

## BQ8500–8779 Pure Land Buddhism

**Kashima, Tetsuden.**      **1.2168**
Buddhism in America: the social organization of an ethnic religious institution / by Tetsuden Kashima. — Westport, Conn.: Greenwood Press, 1977. xvii, 272 p., [1] leaf of plates: ill.; 22 cm. — (Contributions in sociology; no. 26) Includes index. 1. Buddhist Churches of America. 2. Sociology, Buddhist — United States. 3. Japanese in the United States. I. T.
BQ8712.9.U6 K37      301.5/8      *LC 76-57837*      *ISBN* 0837195349

**Bloom, Alfred.**      • **1.2169**
Shinran's gospel of pure grace / by Alfred Bloom. — Tucson: Published for the Association for Asian Studies by the University of Arizona Press, 1965. xiv, 97 p. — (Monographs and papers / Association for Asian Studies; no. 20) Includes index. 1. Shinran, 1173-1263. 2. Pure Land Buddhism — Doctrines I. Association for Asian Studies. II. T.
BQ8749 S557B5      *LC 64-8757*

## BQ8900–8921 Tantric Buddhism

**Dasgupta, Shashi Bhushan, 1912-1964.**      **1.2170**
An introduction to Tantric Buddhism / Shashi Bhushan Dasgupta; foreword by Herbert V. Guenther. — Berkeley, Calif.: Shambhala, 1974. xi, 211 p.; 22 cm. Reprint of the 1958 ed. published by Calcutta University Press, Calcutta. Includes index. 1. Tantric Buddhism I. T.
BQ8915.4.D37 1974      294.3/92      *LC 74-75094*      *ISBN* 0877730520

**Guenther, Herbert V.**      • **1.2171**
Treasures on the Tibetan middle way. A newly revised ed. of Tibetan Buddhism without mystification. By Herbert V. Guenther. — [2d ed.]. — Leiden: Brill, 1969. viii, 150 p.; 22 cm. 1. Tantric Buddhism — Essence, genius, nature 2. Lamaist doctrines — Essence, genius, nature. I. Guenther, Herbert V. Tibetan Buddhism without mystification. II. T.
BQ8915.9.G83 1969      294.3/92      *LC 76-480911*

**Guenther, Herbert V.**      **1.2172**
The dawn of tantra / by Herbert V. Guenther and Chögyam Trungpa; edited by Michael Kohn; illustrated by Glen Eddy and Terris Temple. — Berkeley, Calif.: Shambhala; [New York]: distributed by Random House, 1975. viii, 92 p.: ill.; 22 cm. (The Clear light series) 1. Tantric Buddhism — Addresses, essays, lectures. I. Trungpa, Chogyam, 1939- Trungpa Tulku, II. T.
BQ8916.G83      294.5/92      *LC 74-10250*      *ISBN* 087773058X

## BQ9250–9800 Zen Buddhism

**Dumoulin, Heinrich.**      **1.2173**
[Erleuchtungsweg des Zen im Buddhismus. English] Zen enlightenment: origins and meaning / by Heinrich Dumoulin; translated from the German by John C. Maraldo. — 1st English ed. — New York: Westherhill, 1979. xii, 175 p.; 21 cm. Translation of Der Erleuchtungsweg des Zen im Buddhismus. Includes index. 1. Zen Buddhism — History. I. T.
BQ9262.3.D8513      294.3/927/09      *LC 78-27310*      *ISBN* 0834801418

**Early Ch'an in China and Tibet / edited by Whalen Lai and**      **1.2174**
**Lewis R. Lancaster.**
Berkeley, Ca.: Asian Humanities Press, 1983. xvii, 450 p.; 24 cm. — (Berkeley Buddhist studies series. 5) 1. Zen Buddhism — China — History — Addresses, essays, lectures. 2. Meditation — Buddhism — History — Addresses, essays, lectures. 3. Zen Buddhism — China — Tibet — History — Addresses, essays, lectures. I. Lai, Whalen. II. Lancaster, Lewis R. III. Series.
BQ9262.9.C5 E27 1983      294.3/927/0951 19      *LC 79-66989*      *ISBN* 0895811529

**Kapleau, Philip, 1912- ed.**      **1.2175**
The three pillars of Zen: teaching, practice, and enlightenment / compiled & edited, with translations, introductions & notes, by Philip Kapleau; foreword by Huston Smith. — Rev. and expanded ed. — Garden City, N.Y.: Anchor Press, 1980. xxii, 400 p.: ill.; 21 cm. 1. Zen Buddhism I. T.
BQ9265.4.K36 1980      294.3/927      *LC 78-22794*      *ISBN* 0385147864

**Kennett, Jiyu, 1924-.**      • **1.2176**
Selling water by the river: a manual of Zen training. — New York: Pantheon Books, [1972] xxv, 317 p.; 25 cm. Ed. for 1976 published under title: Zen is eternal life. 1. Sōtōshū. I. T.
BQ9415.4.K45      294.3/927      *LC 70-38836*      *ISBN* 0394467434

**Yokoi, Yūhō, 1918-.**      **1.2177**
Zen Master Dōgen: an introduction with selected writings / by Yūhō Yokoi, with the assistance of Daizen Victoria; and with a foreword by Minoru Kiyota. — 1st ed. — New York: Weatherhill, 1976. 217 p.; 23 cm. 1. Dōgen, 1200-1253. 2. Sōtōshū — Collected works. I. Dōgen, 1200-1253. Selected works. 1976. II. Victoria, Daizen, 1939- joint author. III. T.
BQ9449.D652 Y63      294.3/927      *LC 75-33200*      *ISBN* 0834801124

**Tai, Hue-Tam Ho, 1948-.**      **1.2178**
Millenarianism and peasant politics in Vietnam / Hue-Tam Ho Tai. — Cambridge, Mass.: Harvard University Press, 1983. xii, 220 p.: maps; 25 cm. — (Harvard East Asian series. 99) Includes index. 1. Huỳnh, Phú So, d. 1947. 2. Phat-giáo Hòa-Hao. 3. Millennialism — Vietnam. 4. Vietnam — History — 20th century I. T. II. Series.
BQ9800.P452 T34 1983      299/.592 19      *LC 82-11798*      *ISBN* 0674575555

# BR-BX CHRISTIANITY

Christian history and interpretation: studies presented to John                    • 1.2179
Knox / edited by W. R. Farmer, C. F. D. Moule, and R. R.
Niebuhr.
Cambridge [Eng.]: University Press, 1967. xxxv, 428 p.: port.; 24 cm. 1. Knox,
John, 1900- 2. Theology — Addresses, essays, lectures. I. Knox, John, 1900-
II. Farmer, William Reuben. III. Moule, C. F. D. (Charles Francis Digby),
1908- IV. Niebuhr, Richard R.
BR50.C52        230        LC 67-15306

[REF]
BQ
25
L69
v.9

McCracken, George Englert, 1904- ed.                                              • 1.2180
Early medieval theology. Newly translated and edited by George E. McCracken
in collaboration with Allen Cabaniss. — Philadelphia, Westminster Press
[1957] 430 p. 24 cm. — (The Library of Christian classics, v. 9) Includes
bibliographies. 1. Theology — Middle Ages. I. T. II. Series.
BR50.M18 1957 ,    230.082    LC 57-5015

# BR60-67 Early Christian Literature

Teaching of the Twelve apostles. English.                                         • 1.2181
The Didache, The epistle of Barnabas, The epistles and The martyrdom of St.
Polycarp, The fragments of Papias, The epistle to Diognetus. Newly tr. and
annotated by James A. Kleist. — Westminster, Md., Newman Press, 1948. vi,
235 p. 23 cm. — (Ancient Christian writers. no. 6) Other modern translations
listed at the end of the introd. to each work. Bibliographical references included
in 'Notes' (p. [149]-221) 1. Christian literature, Early (Collections) I. Kleist,
James Aloysius, 1873- ed. and tr. II. Polycarpus, Saint, Bp. of Smyrna. Epistola
ad Philippenses. III. Papias, Saint, Bp. of Hierapolis, 2d cent. v. Epistle to
Diognetus. IV. Bible. N. T. Apocryphal books. Epistle of Barnabas. English.
1948. V. Martyrdom of Polycarp. VI. T. VII. Series.
BR60.A35 no. 6      229.95      LC 48-11315 *

Augustine, Saint, Bishop of Hippo.                                                • 1.2182
The greatness of the soul [and] The teacher; translated and annotated by Joseph
M. Colleran. — Westminster, Md., Newman Press, 1950. 255 p. 22 cm. —
(Ancient Christian writers. no. 9) Bibliographical references included in 'Notes'
(p. [187]-239) 1. Soul 2. Knowledge, Theory of (Religion) 3. Signs and
symbols 4. Inner Light I. T. II. Title: The teacher. III. Series.
BR60.A35 no. 9      233.5      LC 50-6436

Athanasius, Saint, Patriarch of Alexandria, d. 373.                               • 1.2183
The life of Saint Antony / newly translated and annotated by Robert T. Meyer.
— Westminster, Md.,: Newman Press, 1950. 154 p.; 23 cm. — (Ancient
Christian writers. no. 10) Bibliographical references included in 'Notes' (p.
[99]-136) 1. Antonius, Saint, the Great. I. Meyer, Robert T., 1911-1987. ed.
and tr. II. T. III. Series.
BR60.A35 no. 10      922.1      LC 50-3967

Gregory I, Pope, ca. 540-604.                                                     • 1.2184
Pastoral care; translated and annotated by Henry Davis. Westminster, Md.,
Newman Press, 1950. 281 p. 23 cm. (Ancient Christian writers. no. 11)
1. Pastoral theology — Catholic Church I. Davis, Henry, 1866- II. T.
III. Series.
BR60.A35 no. 11      250      LC 50-10904

Augustine, Saint, Bishop of Hippo.                                                • 1.2185
Against the Academics; translated and annotated by John J. O'Meara. —
Westminster, Md., Newman Press, 1950 [ie. 1951] vi, 213 p. 23 cm. — (Ancient
Christian writers. no. 12) Bibliographical references included in 'Notes' (p.
[153]-199) 1. Skepticism — Controversial literature. I. O'Meara, John Joseph.
ed. and tr. II. T. III. Series.
BR60.A35 no. 12      189.2      LC 51-2548

Tertullian, ca. 160-ca. 230.                                                      • 1.2186
Treatises on marriage and remarriage: To his wife, An exhortation to chastity,
Monogamy. Translated and annotated by William P. Le Saint. — Westminster,
Md., Newman Press, 1951. vii, 196 p. 23 cm. — (Ancient Christian writers. no.
13) Bibliographical references included in 'Notes' (p. [109]-170) 1. Marriage —
Catholic Church. 2. Chastity I. T. II. Series.
BR60.A35 no. 13      265.5      LC 51-14743

Irenaeus, Saint, Bishop of Lyon.                                                  • 1.2187
Proof of the apostolic preaching; translated and annotated by Joseph P. Smith.
— Westminster, Md., Newman Press, 1952. viii, 233 p. 23 cm. — (Ancient
Christian writers. no. 16) Bibliographical references included in 'Notes' (p.
[111]-219) 1. Apologetics — Early church. I. T. II. Series.
BR60.A35 no. 16      281.3      LC 52-14882

Origen.                                                                           • 1.2188
Prayer. Exhortation to martyrdom. Translated and annotated by John J.
O'Meara. — Westminster, Md., Newman Press, 1954. vii, 253 p. 23 cm. —
(Ancient Christian writers. no. 19) Bibliographical references included in
'Notes' (p. [197]-240) 1. Prayer — Early works to 1800. 2. Prayer — Hist.
3. Martyrdom I. O'Meara, John Joseph. ed. and tr. II. T. III. Title:
Exhortation to martyrdom. IV. Series.
BR60.A35 no. 19      264.1      LC 54-13520

Rufinus Tyrannius, Aquileiensis, 345 (ca.)-410.                                   • 1.2189
A commentary on the Apostles' Creed. Translated and annotated by J. N. D.
Kelly. — Westminster, Md., Newman Press, 1955. 166 p. 23 cm. — (Ancient
Christian writers. no. 20) Translation of Commentarius in symbolum
apostolorum (otherwise described as Expositio symboli apostolorum), based on
the Latin text of D. Vallarsi. 1. Apostles' Creed. I. T. II. Series.
BR60.A35 no. 20      238.1      LC 55-7040

Athenagoras, 2d cent.                                                             • 1.2190
Embassy for the Christians. The resurrection of the dead. Translated and
annotated by Joseph Hugh Crehan. — Westminster, Md., Newman Press, 1956.
193 p. 23 cm. — (Ancient Christian writers. no. 23) Bibliographical references
included in 'Notes' (p. [117]-182) 1. Apologetics — Early church.
2. Resurrection — Early works to 1800. I. Athenagoras, 2d cent. The
resurrection of the dead. II. T. III. Title: The resurrection of the dead.
IV. Series.
BR60.A35 no. 23      239.1      LC 56-11421

Cyprian, Saint, Bishop of Carthage.                                               • 1.2191
The lapsed. The unity of the Catholic Church. Translated and annotated by
Maurice Bévenot. — Westminster, Md., Newman Press, 1957. 133 p. 23 cm. —
(Ancient Christian writers. no. 25) Bibliographical references included in
'Notes' (p. [69]-124) 1. Church discipline — Early church. 2. Church —
Unity. I. Bévenot, Maurice, ed. and tr. II. T. III. Title: The unity of the
Catholic Church. IV. Series.
BR60.A35 no. 25      281.3      LC 57-7364

Origen.                                                                           • 1.2192
[Commentarium in Canticum canticorum. English] The Song of songs:
Commentary and Homilies. Translated and annotated by R. P. Lawson. —
Westminster, Md., Newman Press, 1957. 385 p. 23 cm. — (Ancient Christian
writers; the works of the Fathers in translation, no. 26) 1. Bible. O.T. Song of
Solomon — Commentaries. I. Origen. The Song of songs: Homilies.
II. Lawson, R. P., ed. and tr. III. T.
BR60.A35 no. 26      223.9      LC 57-11826

Minucius Felix, Marcus.                                                           1.2193
[Octavius English] The Octavius of Marcus Minucius Felix. Translated and
annotated by G. W. Clarke. New York, Newman Press, 1974. v, 414 p. 22 cm.
(Ancient Christian writers; the works of the Fathers in translation, no. 39)
1. Apologetics — Early church, ca. 30-600. I. Clarke, G. W. (Graeme Wilber),
1934- ed. II. T.
BR60.A35 no. 39 BT1116.M7      281/.08 s 239/.1      LC 74-75994

The Ante-Nicene fathers. Translations of the writings of the                      • 1.2194
fathers down to A.D. 325. The Rev. Alexander Roberts, D.D.,
and James Donaldson, LL.D., editors. American reprint of the
Edinburgh edition. Revised and chronologically arranged, with
brief prefaces and occasional notes, by A. Cleveland Coxe, D.D.
Grand Rapids: Eerdmans, 1951-1962. 10 v.: ports.; 26 cm. Vol. [10] has also
special title-pages. Vols. 4-8: Authorized edition. First published under title:
Ante-Nicene Christian library. Vol. 9, edited by Allan Menzies, is 4th ed. Vols.
9-10: Original supplement to the American ed. 1. Christian literature, Early
2. Christian literature, Early — Bibliography. 3. Fathers of the church
(Collections) 4. Christian literature, Early (Collections) 5. Fathers of the
church — Bibliography. 6. Christian literature, Early — Bibliography.
I. Roberts, Alexander, 1826-1901, ed. II. Donaldson, James, Sir, 1831-1915,
joint ed. III. Coxe, A Cleveland (Arthur Cleveland), 1818-1896. ed.
IV. Menzies, Allan, ⸺5-1916, ed. V. Richardson, Ernest Cushing,
1860-1939. VI. Pick, Bernhard, 1842-1917.
BR60.A52

The Apostolic Fathers; a new translation and commentary.                          • 1.2195
[Edited by Robert M. Grant]
New York, T. Nelson [1964-68] 6 v. 22cm. Vols. 4-6 have imprint: Camden,
N.J., T. Nelson. 1. Christian literature, Early I. Grant, Robert McQueen,
1917- ed.
BR60.A62 G7      281.1      LC 64-11546

**The Fathers of the Church: a new translation.**          **1.2196**
[New York: Cima Pub. Co., 1947- <81 >. v. < >; 22 cm. Published: New York: Fathers of the Church, Inc., 1949-1960; Washington: Catholic University of America Press, 1962- < > 1. Christian literature, Early — Collected works.
BR60.F3 A-Z      270 19      *LC* 48-14069      *ISBN* 0813200709

**Greenslade, S. L. (Stanley Lawrence), 1905- ed. and tr.**          • **1.2197**
Early Latin theology; selections from Tertullian, Cyprian, Ambrose, and Jerome. Philadelphia, Westminster Press [1956] 415 p. 24 cm. (The Library of Christian classics, v. 5) 1. Christian literature, Early — Latin authors. 2. Theology — History — Early church, ca. 30-600 I. T. II. Series.
BR60.G64      281.3      *LC* 56-5229      *ISBN* 0664220053

**Richardson, Cyril Charles, 1909- ed. and tr.**          • **1.2198**
Early Christian fathers; newly translated and edited by Cyril C. Richardson, in collaboration with Eugene R. Fairweather, Edward Rochie Hardy [and] Massey Hamilton Shepherd, Jr. — Philadelphia, Westminster Press [1953] 415 p. 24 cm. — (The Library of Christian classics, v. 1) Includes bibliographies. 1. Christian literature (Collections) I. T. II. Series.
BR60.R5      281.1082      *LC* 53-8963

**The early Christian fathers: a selection from the writings of the**          • **1.2199**
**fathers from St. Clement of Rome to St. Athanasius / edited and trans. by Henry Bettenson.**
Oxford: Oxford Univ. Pr., c1956. vii, 424 p.; 18 cm. 1. Christian literature, Early (Selections: Extracts, etc.). I. Bettenson, Henry Scowcroft.
BR63.B4

**Documents in early Christian thought / Maurice Wiles, Mark**          **1.2200**
**Santer.**
Cambridge; New York: Cambridge University Press, 1975. 268 p.; 23 cm. 1. Christian literature, Early — Collected works. 2. Theology — Collected works — Early church, ca. 30-600 I. Wiles, Maurice F. II. Santer, Mark.
BR60.A62 D62      BR63 D637 1975.      281/.1      *LC* 74-31807
*ISBN* 0521206693

## BR65.A Augustine

**Augustine, Saint, Bishop of Hippo.**          • **1.2201**
[Selected works. English] Earlier writings; selected and translated with introductions by John H. S. Burleigh. Philadelphia, Westminister Press [1953] 413 p. 24 cm. (The Library of Christian classics, v. 6) 1. Theology — Collected works — Early church, ca. 30-600 I. T.
BR65.A52 E6 1953      281.4      *LC* 53-13043

**Augustine, Saint, Bishop of Hippo.**          • **1.2202**
Later works / Selected and translated with introductions by John Burnaby. Philadelphia: Westminster Press, [1955] 359 p. (Library of Christian classics; v.8) 1. Theology — Collected works — Early church. I. Burnaby, John II. T. III. Series.
BR65.A52E6 1955      230.14      *LC* 55-5022

**Augustine, Saint, Bishop of Hippo.**          • **1.2203**
Confessions and Enchiridion / Augustine; newly translated and edited by Albert C. Outler. — Philadelphia: Westminster Press, 1955. 423 p. — (The Library of Christian classics; v. 7) 1. Theology — History — Early church, ca. 30-600 I. Outler, Albert Cook, 1908- II. T. III. Series.
BR65.A6E5 1955      *LC* 55-5021

**Augustine, Saint, Bishop of Hippo.**          • **1.2204**
[De civitate Dei. English] Concerning the city of God against the pagans. A new translation by Henry Bettenson, with an introd. by David Knowles. Harmondsworth, Penguin Books [1972] 1097 p. 20 cm. (Pelican classics) Translation of De civitate Dei. 1. Kingdom of God 2. Apologetics — Early church, ca. 30-600. I. Bettenson, Henry Scowcroft. tr. II. T. III. Title: City of God against the pagans.
BR65.A64 E5 1972      239/.3      *LC* 72-197308

**Augustine, Saint, Bishop of Hippo.**          • **1.2205**
On Christian doctrine. Translated with an introd., by D. W. Robertson, Jr. — New York, Liberal Arts Press [1958] xxii, 169 p. 21 cm. — (The Library of liberal arts, no. 80) Bibliography: p. xxi—xxii. 1. Bible — Hermeneutics 2. Preaching I. Robertson, D. W. (Durant Waite), 1914- tr. II. T.
BR65.A655E5      281.4      *LC* 58-9956

**Augustine, Saint, Bishop of Hippo.**          • **1.2206**
[De libero arbitrio] On free choice of the will / Saint Augustine; translated by Anna S. Benjamin and L.H. Hackstaff; with an introd. by L.H. Hackstaff. — 1st. ed. — Indianapolis: Bobbs-Merrill, c1964, 1981 printing. xxxi, 162 p. — (Library of liberal arts. 150) 1. Free will and determinism 2. Good and evil I. Benjamin, Anna S. II. Hackstaff, L. H. III. T. IV. Series.
BR65 A66431964      BR65A664 E5 1981.      233/.7      *LC* 63-16932
*ISBN* 0672603683

**Augustine, Saint, Bishop of Hippo.**          • **1.2207**
Faith, hope and charity, tr. and annotated by Louis A. Arand. — Westminster, Md., Newman Bookshop, 1947. [4] l., 3-165 p. 23 cm. — (Ancient Christian writers. no. 3) Bibliographical references included in 'Notes' (p. [113]-147) 1. Theology — Early church. I. Arand, Louis A., 1892- ed. and tr. II. T. III. Series.
BR65.A7E5 1947      230.11      *LC* 47-5546 *

### BR65.C–BR67 Others

**Clement I, Pope.**          • **1.2208**
The epistles of St. Clement of Rome and St. Ignatius of Antioch / newly translated and annotated by James A. Kleist.— Westminster, Md.: Newman Press; London: Longmans, Green, 1961, c1946. ix, 162 p.; 22 cm. (Ancient Christian writers; the works of the Fathers in translation; no. 1) 1. Christianity — Early church, ca. 30-600 I. Kleist, James A. (James Aloysius), 1873- II. Clement I, Pope. Epistolae. English. III. T.
BR65.C54 C713 1961      *LC* NUC65-45613

**Oulton, John Ernest Leonard, 1886- ed.**          • **1.2209**
Alexandrian Christianity; selected translations of Clement and Origen with introductions and notes by John Ernest Leonard Oulton and Henry Chadwick. Philadelphia, Westminster Press [1954] 475 p. 24 cm. (The Library of Christian classics. v. 2) 1. Christian literature, Early (Selections: Extracts, etc.) I. Clement, of Alexandria, Saint, ca. 150-ca. 215. Stromateis. Stromata. English. 1954. II. Origen. Selections. English. 1954. III. Chadwick, Henry, 1920- joint ed. IV. T. V. Series.
BR65.C65 S8 1954      281.3      *LC* 54-10257

**Telfer, William, 1886- ed. and tr.**          • **1.2210**
Cyril of Jerusalem and Nemesius of Emesa. — Philadelphia, Westminster Press [1955] 466 p. plans. 24 cm. — (The Library of Christian classics, v. 4) 1. Catechetics 2. Psychology — Early works to 1850 I. Nemesius, Bp. of Emesa. On the nature of man II. Cyrillus, Saint, Bp. of Jerusalem, 315 (ca.)-396. Catechetical lectures. III. T. IV. Series.
BR65.C93C45      281.4      *LC* 55-7709

**Origen.**          **1.2211**
[Contra Celsum. English] Contra Celsum / Origen; translated with an introd. & notes by Henry Chadwick. — Cambridge [Eng.]; New York; Cambridge University Press, 1980. xl, 530 p.; 24 cm. Reprint, with additions and corrections, of the 1965 ed. Includes indexes. 1. Celsus, Platonic philosopher, fl. 180. I. Chadwick, Henry, 1920- ed. and tr. II. T.
BR65.O55 E6 1980      230/.13 19      *LC* 80-495226      *ISBN* 052105866X

**Trigg, Joseph Wilson, 1949-.**          **1.2212**
Origen: the Bible and philosophy in the third–century church / Joseph Wilson Trigg. — Atlanta, Ga.: J. Knox, c1983. 300 p.: map; 21 cm. Includes index. 1. Origen. I. T.
BR65.O68 T74 1983      230/.13/0924 19      *LC* 83-48182      *ISBN* 0804209456

**Barnes, Timothy David.**          **1.2213**
Tertullian: a historical and literary study / Timothy David Barnes. — Reissued with corrections and a postscript, 1985. — Oxford [Oxfordshire]: Clarendon Press; New York: Oxford University Press, 1985, c1971. viii, 339 p.; 22 cm. 1. Tertullian, ca. 160-ca. 230. I. T.
BR65.T7 B36 1985      230/.13/0924 19      *LC* 85-3000      *ISBN* 0198143621

# BR75–85 Later Periods

**Bunyan, John, 1628-1688.**          **1.2214**
[Selections. 1980] The poems / John Bunyan; edited by Graham Midgley. — Oxford: Clarendon Press; New York: Oxford University Press, 1980. lxii, 345 p.: ill.; 23 cm. — (The miscellaneous works of John Bunyan; v. 6) (Oxford English texts) I. Midgley, Graham. II. T.
BR75.B73 1976 vol. 6      230/.08 s 821/.4      *LC* 79-40422      *ISBN* 0198127340

**Bunyan, John, 1628-1688.**          **1.2215**
[Doctrine of the law and grace unfolded] The doctrine of the law and grace unfolded and I will pray with the Spirit / [by] John Bunyan; edited by Richard L. Greaves. — Oxford: Clarendon Press, 1976. xliv, 303 p., plate: facsims.; 23 cm. — (The miscellaneous works of John Bunyan; v. 2) 1. Grace (Theology) — Early works to 1800. 2. Law and gospel I. Greaves, Richard L. II. Bunyan, John, 1628-1688. I will pray with the Spirit and with the understanding also.

1976. III. T. IV. Title: Doctrine of the law and grace unfolded. V. Title: I will pray with the Spirit and with the understanding also.
BR75.B73 1976 vol. 2 BT760     230/.08 s 234/.1     *LC* 77-351855
   *ISBN* 0198118716

**Flew, Antony, 1923-.**                       **1.2216**

The presumption of atheism and other philosophical essays on God, freedom, and immortality / Antony Flew. — New York: Barnes & Noble, 1976. 183 p.; 23 cm. Includes index. 1. Theology — Addresses, essays, lectures. 2. Immortality — Addresses, essays, lectures. I. T. II. Title: The presumption of atheism ...
BR85.F54 1976b     210     *LC* 76-361131     *ISBN* 0064921190

**Kierkegaard, Søren, 1813-1855.**           • **1.2217**
Attack upon 'Christendom,' 1854–1855; translated, with an introduction, by Walter Lowrie. — Princeton, N. J., Princeton university press, 1944. xviii, 303 p. 22.5 cm. Bibliographical references included in 'Notes' (p. [295]-300) 1. Christianity — 19th cent. I. Lowrie, Walter, 1868-1959, tr. II. T.
BR85.K456     260     *LC* A 45-726

**Kierkegaard, Søren, 1813-1855.**           • **1.2218**
Christian discourses, and The lilies of the field and the birds of the air, and Three discourses at the communion on Fridays, by Søren Kierkegaard; translated, with an introduction, by Walter Lowrie, D. D. — London, New York [etc.] Oxford university press, 1940. xviii, 389 p. 24 cm. 1. Christianity — Addresses, essays, lectures. I. Lowrie, Walter, 1868-1959, tr. II. T.
BR85.K457     208.1     *LC* 41-1735

**Kierkegaard, Søren, 1813-1855.**           • **1.2219**
The present age, and Of the difference between a genius and an apostle. Translated by Alexander Dru. Introd. by Walter Kaufmann. — New York, Harper & Row [1962] 108 p. 21 cm. — (Harper torchbooks. The Cloister library, TB94) 'Originally published ... with a third essay ... under the title The present age and two minor ethico-religious treaties in 1940.' I. T.
BR85.K4578     208.1     *LC* 62-51867

## BR95–96.5 Dictionaries. Encyclopedias

**The Dictionary of Bible and religion / William H. Gentz,**     **1.2220**
**editor.**
Nashville: Abingdon, 1986. p. cm. 1. Bible — Dictionaries 2. Theology — Dictionaries 3. Religion — Dictionaries. 4. Religions — Dictionaries. I. Gentz, William H., 1918-
BR95.D46 1986     203/.21 19     *LC* 85-15011     *ISBN* 0687107571

**The Oxford dictionary of the Christian Church, edited by F. L.**     **1.2221**
**Cross.**
2d ed., edited by F. L. Cross and E. A. Livingstone. — London; New York: Oxford University Press, 1974. xxxi, 1518 p.; 24 cm. 1. Christianity — Dictionaries I. Cross, F. L. (Frank Leslie), 1900-1968. ed. II. Livingstone, Elizabeth A. ed.
BR95.O8 1974     203     *LC* 74-163871     *ISBN* 0192115456

**Rahner, Karl, 1904-.**                       **1.2222**
[Kleines theologisches Wörterbuch. English] Dictionary of theology / Karl Rahner, Herbert Vorgrimler; translated by Richard Strachan ... [et al.]. — 2nd ed. — New York: Crossroad, 1981. 541 p.; 22 cm. Translation of: Kleines theologisches Wörterbuch. 1. Catholic Church — Dictionaries 2. Theology — Dictionaries I. Vorgrimler, Herbert. II. Strachan, Richard. III. T.
BR95.R313 1981     230/.2/0321 19     *LC* 81-5492     *ISBN* 0824500407

**Schaff-Herzog encyclopedia.**               • **1.2223**
The new Schaff–Herzog encyclopedia of religious knowledge, embracing Biblical, historical, doctrinal, and practical theology, and Biblical, theological, and ecclesiastical biography from the earliest times to the present day; based on the 3d ed. of the Realencyklopädie founded by J. J. Herzog, and edited by Albert Hauck, prepared by more than six hundred scholars and specialists under the supervision of Samuel Macauley Jackson (editor–in–chief) with the assistance of Charles Colebrook Sherman and George William Gilmore (associate editors) and [others] Grand Rapids, Mich., Baker, 1949-50. 13 v. 25 cm. Vols. 2-12 have abbreviated title which varies slightly: v. 13: Index by George William Gilmore. Twentieth century encyclopedia of religious knowledge. An extension of The new Schaff-Herzog encyclopedia of religious knowledge. Editor-in-chief: Lefferts A. Loetscher. Grand Rapids, Mich., Baker, 1955. 2v. (xxi, 1205 p.) 25 cm. Includes bibliographies. 1. Schaff-Herzog encyclopedia. 2. Theology — Dictionaries I. Jackson, Samuel Macauley, 1851-1912. ed. II. Loetscher, Lefferts Augustine, 1904- ed. III. T. IV. Title: Twentieth century encyclopedia of religious knowledge.
BR95.S435     *LC* a 51-9847 REV

**The Westminster dictionary of Christian theology / edited by**     **1.2224**
**Alan Richardson and John S. Bowden.**
Philadelphia: Westminster Press, c1983. xvi, 614 p.; 25 cm. Published simultaneously under title: A New dictionary of Christian theology. 1. Theology — Dictionaries I. Richardson, Alan, 1905-1975. II. Bowden, John Stephen.
BR95.W494 1983     230/.03 19     *LC* 83-14521     *ISBN* 0664213987

**Gay, John Dennis.**                       **1.2225**
The geography of religion in England [by] John D. Gay. London: Duckworth, 1971. xviii, 334 p.: 1 illus., maps.; 23 cm. 1. Ecclesiastical geography — England. I. T.
BR97.G38     301.5/8/0942     *LC* 75-594210     *ISBN* 0715605577

## BR100–114 Philosophy and Psychology

**Guardini, Romano, 1885-1968.**           • **1.2226**
Freedom, grace, and destiny: three chapters in the interpretation of existence / Romano Guardini; translated by John Murray. — [New York] Pantheon Books [1961] 251 p.; 21 cm. Translation of Freiheit, Gnade, Schicksal. Reprint of the ed. published by Pantheon Books, New York. 1. Christianity — Philosophy 2. Freedom (Theology) 3. Grace (Theology) 4. Fate and fatalism I. T.
BR100.G7713 1975     233     *LC* 75-8786

**Joad, Cyril Edwin Mitchinson, 1891-1953.**        • **1.2227**
Recovery of belief: a restatement of Christian philosophy / by C. E. M. Joad. — London: Faber, 1952. 250 p.; 21 cm. Includes index. 1. Christianity — Philosophy I. T.
BR100.J6     201     *LC* 52-67063

**Kierkegaard, Søren, 1813-1855.**           • **1.2228**
[Afsluttende uvidenskabelig efterskrift. English] Kierkegaard's Concluding unscientific postscript; translated from the Danish by David F. Swenson, completed after his death and provided with introduction and notes by Walter Lowrie. Princeton, Princeton university press, for American Scandinavian foundation, 1941. xxi, 579 p. 24 cm. 1. Christianity — Philosophy 2. Apologetics — 19th century I. Swenson, David F.(David Ferdinand), 1876-1940, tr. II. Lowrie, Walter, 1868- ed. and tr. III. American-Scandinavian Foundation. IV. T. V. Title: Concluding unscientific postscript.
BR100.K47     201     *LC* 41-19350

**Kierkegaard's Fear and trembling: critical appraisals / edited by**     **1.2229**
**Robert L. Perkins.**
University: University of Alabama Press, c1981. xii, 251 p.; 25 cm. 1. Kierkegaard, Søren, 1813-1855 Frygt og ba even — Addresses, essays, lectures. 2. Christianity — Philosophy — Addresses, essays, lectures. 3. Sin — Addresses, essays, lectures. I. Perkins, Robert L., 1930-
BR100.K5216 K53     230     *LC* 79-16984     *ISBN* 0817300287

**Kierkegaard, Søren, 1813-1855.**           • **1.2230**
Fear and trembling, and The sickness unto death. Translated with introductions and notes by Walter Lowrie. [New ed.] Princeton, N. J. Princeton University Press [1968] 278p. 1. Christianity — Philosophy 2. Sin I. Kierkegaard, Søren, 1813-1855. Sygdommen til døden. English. II. T. III. Title: The sickness unto death
BR100 K523 1968

**Newman, John Henry, 1801-1890.**           • **1.2231**
An essay in aid of a grammar of assent. New ed., ed. with a pref. and introd. by Charles Frederick Harrold. New York, Longmans, Green, 1947. xxii, 394 p. 21 cm. 'A select bibliography': p. xxi-xxii. 1. Theism 2. Faith I. Harrold, Charles Frederick, 1897-1948, ed. II. T. III. Title: Grammar of assent.
BR100.N4 1947     201     *LC* 47-11560 *

**Niebuhr, Reinhold, 1892-1971.**           • **1.2232**
Beyond tragedy; essays on the Christian interpretation of history, by Reinhold Niebuhr. — New York, C. Scribner's sons, 1937. xi, 306 p. 21 cm. 1. Christianity — Philosophy 2. History — Philosophy I. T.
BR100.N55     201     *LC* 37-37824

**Rahner, Karl, 1904-.**                 • **1.2233**
[Geist in Welt. English] Spirit in the world. Translated by William Dych. [New York] Herder and Herder [1968] lv, 408 p. 22 cm. Translation of the 2d edition, published in 1957 under title: Geist in Welt. 1. Christianity — Philosophy 2. Philosophical theology I. T.
BR100.R313     121     *LC* 67-29676

**Sayers, Dorothy L. (Dorothy Leigh), 1893-1957.** • **1.2234**
The mind of the Maker. Westport, Conn., Greenwood Press [1970, c1941] xiv, 229 p. 23 cm. 1. Christianity — Philosophy I. T.
BR100.S3 1970     201     LC 72-106698     ISBN 0837133726

**Teilhard de Chardin, Pierre.** • **1.2235**
[Milieu divin. English] The divine milieu; an essay on the interior life. [1st ed.] New York, Harper [1960] 144 p. 22 cm. 1. Christianity — Philosophy I. T.
BR100.T373 1960     201     LC 60-11787

**Dunn, James D. G., 1939-.** **1.2236**
Jesus and the spirit: a study of the religious and charismatic experience of Jesus and the first Christians as reflected in the New Testament / by James D. G. Dunn. — Philadelphia: Westminster Press, [1975] xii, 515 p.; 24 cm. Includes indexes. 1. Jesus Christ — Spiritual life 2. Experience (Religion) — History. 3. Spiritual life — History of doctrines I. T.
BR110.D86     248/.2     LC 75-9802     ISBN 0664208045

**James, William, 1842-1910.** • **1.2237**
The varieties of religious experience; a study in human nature. New Hyde Park, N.Y. University Books [1963] 626p. (Gifford lectures on natural religion, 1901-02) 1. Religion 2. Philosophy and religion 3. Psychology, Religious I. T.
BR110 J3 1963

**Knox, Ronald Arbuthnott, 1888-1957.** **1.2238**
Enthusiasm: a chapter in the history of religion with special reference to the XVII and XVIII centuries / R.A. Knox. — Westminster, Md.: Christian Classics, 1983, c1950. viii, 622 p.; 22 cm. Reprint. Originally published: New York: Oxford University Press, 1950. Includes index. 1. Enthusiasm — Religious aspects — Christianity 2. Church history — 17th century 3. Church history — 18th century I. T.
BR112.K5 1983     270.7 19     LC 83-71392     ISBN 0870610805

# BR115 Christianity: Relation to Other Topics

**Ethics and nuclear deterrence / edited by Geoffrey Goodwin.** **1.2239**
New York: St. Martin's Press, 1982. 199 p.: ill.; 23 cm. 1. Nuclear warfare — Religious aspects — Christianity — Addresses, essays, lectures. 2. Nuclear warfare — Moral and ethical aspects — Addresses, essays, lectures. 3. Deterrence (Strategy) — Addresses, essays, lectures. I. Goodwin, Geoffrey L.
BR115.A85 E86 1982     261.8/73 19     LC 81-21449     ISBN 0312265557

**Dawson, Christopher, 1889-1970.** • **1.2240**
Religion and the rise of Western culture. — New York, Sheed & Ward, 1950. xvi, 286 p. illus., ports. 22 cm. — (Gifford lectures, 1948-1949) Bibliographical footnotes. 1. Civilization, Christian 2. Civilization, Occidental I. T. II. Series.
BR115.C5D37     270     LC 50-6539

**Dawson, Christopher, 1889-1970.** • **1.2241**
The historic reality of Christian culture; a way to the renewal of human life. New York, Harper [1960] 124 p. 22 cm. (Religious perspectives. v. 1) 1. Christianity and culture 2. Civilization, Christian I. T. II. Series.
BR115.C8 D3     261     LC 60-5291

**Niebuhr, H. Richard (Helmut Richard), 1894-1962.** **1.2242**
Christ and culture / H. Richard Niebuhr. — 1st ed. — New York: Harper, 1951. x, 259 p. 1. Culture 2. Christianity — 20th century I. T.
BR115.C8 N5     LC 51-11010

**Tawney, R. H. (Richard Henry), 1880-1962.** • **1.2243**
Religion and the rise of capitalism; a historical study ... by R. H. Tawney. — Gloucester, Mass.: P. Smith, 1962. xix, 337 p.; 21 cm. — (Holland memorial lectures; 1922) 1. Religious thought — History. 2. Economics — Religious aspects — Christianity — History. 3. Capitalism 4. Great Britain — Social conditions I. T. II. Series.
BR115.E3 T3 1962     LC 63-1429

**Weber, Max, 1864-1920.** • **1.2244**
[Protestantische Ethik und der Geist des Kapitalismus English] The Protestant ethic and the spirit of capitalism. Translated by Talcott Parsons. With a foreword by R. H. Tawney. [Student's ed.] New York, Scribner [1958] xvii, 292 p. 21 cm. 1. Religion and sociology 2. Christian ethics 3. Capitalism — Religious aspects — Protestant churches I. T.
BR115.E3 W4 1958     306/.6 19     LC 58-4170

**Balthasar, Hans Urs von, 1905-.** • **1.2245**
[Ganze im Fragment. English] A theological anthropology. New York, Sheed and Ward [1968, c1967] x, 341 p. 22 cm. Translation of Das Ganze im Fragment. 1. History (Theology) 2. Man (Christian theology) I. T.
BR115.H5 B283     233     LC 67-29289

**Butterfield, Herbert, Sir, 1900-.** • **1.2246**
Christianity and history. — New York, Scribner, 1950. vi, 146 p. 22 cm. 1. History — Philosophy 2. Christianity — Philosophy I. T.
BR115.H5B8 1950     901     LC 50-6450

**Cullmann, Oscar.** • **1.2247**
Salvation in history. [English translation drafted by Sidney G. Sowers and afterwards completed by the editorial staff of the SCM Press. 1st American ed.] New York, Harper & Row [1967] 352 p. 22 cm. Translation of Heil als Geschichte. 1. History (Theology) I. T.
BR115.H5 C83 1967b     234     LC 67-21545

**God, history, and historians: an anthology of modern Christian views of history / edited by C. T. McIntire.** **1.2248**
New York: Oxford University Press, 1977. 477 p.; 22 cm. Includes index. 1. History (Theology) — Addresses, essays, lectures. I. McIntire, C. T.
BR115.H5 G63     901     LC 76-47428     ISBN 0195022033

**Harvey, Van Austin.** **1.2249**
The historian and the believer: the morality of historical knowledge and Christian belief / Van A. Harvey. — Philadelphia: Westminster Press, [1981] c1966. xvii, 301 p.; 21 cm. Reprint of the ed. published by Macmillan, New York. 1. Bible — Criticism, interpretation, etc. — History — 19th century 2. Bible — Criticism, interpretation, etc. — History — 20th century 3. History (Theology) I. T.
BR115.H5 H44 1981     230/.044/0904 19     LC 80-27941     ISBN 0664243673

**Patrides, C. A.** **1.2250**
The grand design of God: the literary form of the Christian view of history, [by] C. A. Patrides. — Toronto: London: University of Toronto Press: Routledge & Kegan Paul, 1972. xvii, 157 p.: ill. — (Ideas and forms in English literature) 1. History (Theology) — History of doctrines 2. Historiography I. T.
BR115.H5 P28 1972     230     ISBN 0802019323

**Brown, Robert McAfee, 1920-.** **1.2251**
Theology in a new key: responding to liberation themes / Robert McAfee Brown. — 1st ed. — Philadelphia: Westminster Press, c1978. 212 p.; 21 cm. Includes index. 1. Christianity and justice 2. Mission of the church 3. Liberation theology I. T.
BR115.J8 B76     261.8     LC 78-6494     ISBN 0664242049

**McFague, Sallie.** **1.2252**
Speaking in parables; a study in metaphor and theology. Philadelphia, Fortress Press [1975] 186 p. 22 cm. 1. Languages — Religious aspects 2. Parables I. T.
BR 115 L2 T33 1975     LC 74-26338     ISBN 0800610970

**Niebuhr, Reinhold, 1892-1971.** • **1.2253**
Christian realism and political problems. — New York, Scribner, 1953. 203 p. 21 cm. 1. Christianity and politics I. T.
BR115.P7N54     261.7     LC 53-12785

**Religion in West European politics / edited by Suzanne Berger.** **1.2254**
London; Totowa, N.J.: Frank Cass, c1982. 191 p.: ill.; 23 cm. 1. Christianity and politics — History — 20th century — Addresses, essays, lectures. 2. Europe — Politics and government — 1945- — Addresses, essays, lectures. 3. Europe — Church history — 20th century — Addresses, essays, lectures. I. Berger, Suzanne.
BR115.P7 R4345 1982     322/.1/094 19     LC 82-238749     ISBN 071463218X

**Niebuhr, H. Richard (Helmut Richard), 1894-1962.** • **1.2255**
The social sources of denominationalism. — New York: Meridian Books, 1957. 304 p.; 18 cm. — (Living age books, LA11) 1. Sociology, Christian 2. Sects I. T.
BR115.S6 Nx     280     LC 57-6685

**Ames, William, 1576-1633.** **1.2256**
[Technometria. English] Technometry / William Ames; translated, with introd. and commentary, by Lee W. Gibbs. — Philadelphia: University of Pennsylvania Press, 1979. xii, 202 p.; 24 cm. — (The Twenty-fourth publication in the Haney Foundation series, University of Pennsylvania) Translation of Guilielmi Amesii Technometria. A revision of the translator's thesis, Harvard. 1. Theology 2. Philosophy I. Gibbs, Lee W. II. T.
BR118.A4513 1979     191     LC 78-65117     ISBN 0812277562

## BR120–126 Christianity: General Works

**Locke, John, 1632-1704.**     • **1.2257**
The reasonableness of Christianity, with A discourse of miracles, and part of A third letter concerning toleration. Edited, abridged, and introduced by I. T. Ramsey. Stanford, Calif., Stanford University Press [1958] 102 p. 22 cm. (A Library of modern religious thought) 1. Christianity — 17th century 2. Philosophy and religion I. Ramsey, Ian T. II. T. III. Series.
BR120.L62     *LC* 58-8595

**Barth, Karl, 1886-1968.**     • **1.2258**
The word of God and the word of man. Translated with a new foreword by Douglas Horton. — New York, Harper [1957] vii, 327 p. 21 cm. — (Harper torchbooks, TB13) Translation of Das Wort Gottes und die Theologie. 1. Christianity — Addresses, essays, lectures. 2. Christianity — 20th cent. I. T.
BR121.B2455 1957     230.04     *LC* 57-7531

**Chesterton, G. K. (Gilbert Keith), 1874-1936.**     • **1.2259**
Orthodoxy, by Gilbert K. Chesterton. London, John Lane; New York, John Lane company, 1909. vii p., 1 l., 11-297 p. 20 cm. A companion volume to the author's Heretics. 1. Apologetics — 20th century I. T.
BR121.C5 1909a     *LC* 44-32773

**Harnack, Adolf von, 1851-1930.**     • **1.2260**
[Wesen des Christentums. English] What is Christianity? Translated by Thomas Bailey Saunders. Introd. by Rudolf Bultmann. [1st Harper torchbook ed.] New York, Harper [1957] 301 p. 21 cm. (The Library of religion and culture) (Harper torchbooks, TB17) Translation of Das Wesen des Christentums. 1. Christianity — Essence, genius, nature I. T.
BR121.H3 1957     230     *LC* 57-7534

**Unamuno, Miguel de, 1864-1936.**     **1.2261**
The agony of Christianity and Essays on faith / Miguel de Unamuno; translated by Anthony Kerrigan; annotated by Martin Nozick and Anthony Kerrigan. — Princeton, N.J.: Princeton University press, 1974. xi, 302 p. — (Bollingen series;d 85) (Selected works of Miguel du Unamuno; v. 5) 1. Christianity — 20th century I. Nozick, Martin. II. Kerrigan, Anthony. III. T. IV. Title: Essays on faith. V. Series.
BR121.U48 1974b     204

**Van Buren, Paul Matthews, 1924-.**     • **1.2262**
The secular meaning of the gospel, based on an analysis of its language. — New York: Macmillan, [1963] 205 p.; 22 cm. 1. Christianity — 20th century I. T.
BR121.2.V3 1963     230     *LC* 63-15701

**Lewis, C. S. (Clive Staples), 1898-1963.**     • **1.2263**
Mere Christianity; a revised and enlarged edition, with a new introduction of the three books, The case for christianity, Christian behaviour, and Beyond personality. New York, Macmillan, 1952. 175 p. 21 cm. 1. Christianity — Addresses, essays, lectures. I. T.
BR123.L484 1952     230 19     *LC* 52-14321

**Lewis, C. S. (Clive Staples), 1898-1963.**     • **1.2264**
The Screwtape letters, by C. S. Lewis ... New York, The Macmillan company, 1947. 160 p. 21 cm. 'Reprinted with some alterations by ... permission of 'The Guardian' ... September, 1947.' 1. Christianity — 20th century I. T.
BR125.L67 1947     244     *LC* 44-4408

## BR127–129 Christianity and Other Religions. Origins

**Tillich, Paul, 1886-1965.**     • **1.2265**
Christianity and the encounter of the world religions. — New York: Columbia University Press, 1963. viii, 97 p.; 21 cm. — (Bampton lectures in America. no. 14) 1. Christianity and other religions I. T. II. Series.
BR127.T56     290     *LC* 63-7508

**Toynbee, Arnold, 1889-**      .     • **1.2266**
Christianity among the religions of the world / Arnold Toynbee. — New York: Scribner, 1957. 116 p. — (Hewett lectures; 1956) Includes index. 1. Christianity and other religions 2. Religions I. T.
BR127.T6     *LC* 57-12066

**Bultmann, Rudolf Karl, 1884-1976.**     • **1.2267**
[Urchristentum im Rahmen der antiken Religionen. English] Primitive Christianity in its contemporary setting. Translated by R. H. Fuller. New York, Meridian Books, 1956. 240 p. 18 cm. (Living age books, LA 4) Translation of Das Urchristentum im Rahmen der antiken Religionen. 1. Christianity and other religions I. T.
BR128.A2 B83     270.1 19     *LC* 56-9240

**Gollwitzer, Helmut.**     • **1.2268**
[Marxistische Religionskritik und der christliche Glaube. English] The Christian faith and the Marxist criticism of religion. [Translated by David Cairns] New York, Scribner [1970] ix, 173 p. 20 cm. Translation of Die marxistiche Religionskritik und der christliche Glaube. 1. Communism and Christianity I. T.
BR128.A8 G613 1970b     261     *LC* 69-17055

**Jaeger, Werner Wilhelm, 1888-1961.**     • **1.2269**
Early Christianity and Greek paideia. Cambridge, Belknap Press of Harvard University Press, 1961. 154 p. 22 cm. 1. Christianity and other religions — Greek — Addresses, essays, lectures. 2. Hellenism — Addresses, essays, lectures. 3. Education, Greek — Addresses, essays, lectures. 4. Greece — Religion — Addresses, essays, lectures. I. T.
BR128.G8 J3     209.38     *LC* 61-15275

**Fiorenza, Elisabeth Schüssler, 1938-.**     **1.2270**
In memory of her: a feminist theological reconstruction of Christian origins / Elisabeth Schüssler Fiorenza. — New York: Crossroad, 1983. xxv, 351 p.; 24 cm. 1. Bible. N.T. — Criticism, interpretation, etc. 2. Women in Christianity — History — Early church, ca. 30-600 3. Christianity — Origin I. T.
BR129.F56 1983     270.1/088042 19     *LC* 82-19896     *ISBN* 0824504933

## BR138–1500 Church History

### BR138–157 HISTORIOGRAPHY. HISTORY. CHRISTIAN DENOMINATIONS, GENERAL

**Bowden, Henry Warner.**     • **1.2271**
Church history in the age of science; historiographical patterns in the United States, 1876–1918. Chapel Hill: University of North Carolina Press, [1971] xvi, 269 p.; 24 cm. 1. Church history — Historiography 2. Church historians — United States. I. T.
BR138.B68     270/.09     *LC* 72-156134     *ISBN* 0807811769

**Bettenson, Henry Scowcroft. ed.**     • **1.2272**
Documents of the Christian Church; selected and edited by Henry Bettenson. — 2nd ed. — London; New York [etc.]: Oxford U.P., 1967. xvii, 343 p.; 21 cm. — (Oxford paperbacks, no. 125) 1. Church history — Sources I. T.
BR141.B4 1967     270     *LC* 68-109402

**González, Justo L.**     **1.2273**
The early church to the dawn of the Reformation / Justo L. González. — 1st ed. — San Francisco: Harper & Row, c1984. xviii, 429 p.: ill.; 24 cm. — (The Story of Christianity; v. 1) 1. Church history — Primitive and early church, ca. 30-600 2. Church history — Middle Ages, 600-1500 I. T.
BR142.G66 1984 vol.1     270 s 270 19     *LC* 83-48430     *ISBN* 0060633158

**González, Justo L.**     **1.2274**
The Reformation to the present day / Justo L. González. — 1st ed. — San Francisco: Harper & Row, c1984. xii, 414 p.: ill.; 24 cm. (The Story of Christianity; v. 2) Includes index. 1. Church history — Modern period, 1500- I. T.
BR142.G66 1984 vol. 2 BR290     270 s 270s 19     *LC* 83-49187     *ISBN* 0060633166

**Hughes, Philip, 1895-.**     • **1.2275**
A history of the church. New York, Sheed & Ward, 1947-. v. 1. Church history I. T.
BR145.H812     *LC* 49-48690

**Latourette, Kenneth Scott.**     • **1.2276**
A history of Christianity / Kenneth Scott Latourette. — New York: Harper, 1953. xxvii, 1516 p.: maps (some fold.). 1. Church history I. T.
BR145L28     270     *LC* 53-5004

**Latourette, Kenneth Scott, 1884-1968.**    • **1.2277**
A history of the expansion of Christianity. — Grand Rapids: Zondervan Pub. House, [1970] 7 v.: illus., maps.; 22 cm. — (Contemporary evangelical perspectives) 1. Church history I. T.
BR145.L33     209     *LC* 73-120050

**Schaff, Philip, 1819-1893.**    • **1.2278**
History of the Christian church / by Philip Schaff. — Grand Rapids, Mich.: W.B. Eerdmans, 1949-1966. 8 v.: maps; 23 cm. Vols. 5-6 by David Schley Schaff. 1. Church history 2. Reformation I. Schaff, David Schley, 1852- II. T.
BR145 S3

**Walker, Williston, 1860-1922.**    • **1.2279**
A history of the Christian church / by Williston Walker and Richard A. Norris, David W. Lotz, Robert T. Handy. — 4th ed. — New York: Scribner, c1985. xii, 756 p.: ill.; 25 cm. Includes index. 1. Church history I. T.
BR145.W34 1985    270 19    *LC* 84-23614    *ISBN* 0684184176

**Aland, Kurt.**    **1.2280**
[Geschichte der Christenheit. English] A history of Christianity / Kurt Aland; translated by James L. Schaaf. — Philadelphia: Fortress Press, c1985-. v. < 1 >; 24 cm. Translation of: Geschichte der Christenheit. Includes index. 1. Church history I. T.
BR145.2.A413 1985    270 19    *LC* 84-47913    *ISBN* 0800607252

**Jedin, Hubert, 1900- ed.**    **1.2281**
History of the church / edited by Hubert Jedin and John Dolan. — New York: Seabury Press, 1980-. v.; 24 cm. Translation of Handbuch der Kirchengenschichte. 'A Crossroad book.' 1. Church history — Collected works. I. Dolan, John Patrick. II. T.
BR145.2.J413 1980    270    *LC* 79-29649    *ISBN* 0816404496

**Wilken, Robert Louis, 1936-.**    • **1.2282**
The myth of Christian beginnings; history's impact on belief [by] Robert L. Wilken. — [1st ed.]. — Garden City, N.Y.: Doubleday, 1971. x, 218 p.; 22 cm. 1. Church history 2. Christianity — Essence, genius, nature I. T.
BR145.2.W5    270/.09 19    *LC* 71-123712

**Latourette, Kenneth Scott.**    • **1.2283**
Christianity through the ages. Harper and Row, 1965. 321 p., bibl. (Harper chapel books, CB1.) 1. Church history I. T.
BR146.L3    270    *LC* 65-11348

**Marty, Martin E., 1928-.**    • **1.2284**
A short history of Christianity. — New York: Meridian Books, [1959] 384 p.; 19 cm. — (Living age books [LA24]) 1. Church history I. T.
BR146.M28    270    *LC* 59-7187

**World Christian encyclopedia: a comparative study of churches**    **1.2285**
**and religions in the modern world, AD 1900–2000 / edited by David B. Barrett.**
Nairobi; New York: Oxford University Press, 1982. xii, 1010 p.: ill. (some col.); 33 cm. Includes indexes. 1. Christian sects — Dictionaries. 2. Christianity — 20th century — Dictionaries. 3. Religions — Dictionaries. I. Barrett, David B.
BR157.W67 1982    203/.21 19    *LC* 82-199409    *ISBN* 0195724356

# BR160–240 To 600

**Stevenson, James, 1901- ed.**    • **1.2286**
Creeds, councils, and controversies; documents illustrative of the history of the church A.D. 337–461. Edited by J. Stevenson. New York, Seabury Press [1966] xix, 390 p. map (on lining papers) 23 cm. 'Based upon the collection edited by the late B. J. Kidd.' 'Intended to be a successor to vol. II of the late B. J. Kidd's Documents, published in 1923.' 1. Church history — Primitive and early church, ca. 30-600 — Sources 2. Christian literature, Early I. Kidd, B. J. (Beresford James), 1863-1948. ed. Documents illustrative of the history of the church. II. T.
BR160.A2 S7 1966a    270.2 19    *LC* 66-16652

**Grant, Robert McQueen, 1917-.**    **1.2287**
Eusebius as church historian / Robert M. Grant. — Oxford: Clarendon Press, 1980. 184 p.; 23 cm. Includes indexes. 1. Eusebius, of Caesarea, Bishop of Caesarea, ca. 260-ca. 340. 2. Church history — Primitive and early church, ca. 30-600 — Historiography. I. T.
BR160.E55 G73 1980    270.1/092/4 19    *LC* 80-40342    *ISBN* 0198264410

**Bainton, Roland Herbert, 1894-.**    • **1.2288**
Early and medieval Christianity. Boston, Beacon Press [1962] iv, 261 p. 21 cm. (His collected papers in church history, ser. 1) 1. Church history — Primitive and early church, ca. 30-600 — Addresses, essays, lectures. 2. Church history — Middle Ages, 600-1500 — Addresses, essays, lectures. I. T.
BR162.B25    270.082    *LC* 62-7894

**Cannon, William Ragsdale, 1916-.**    • **1.2289**
History of Christianity in the Middle Ages: from the fall of Rome to the fall of Constantinople. — New York, Abingdon Press (1960) 352 p. 24 cm. 1. Church history — Middle Ages. I. T.
BR162.2.C3    270.2    *LC* 60-6928

**Daniélou, Jean.**    • **1.2290**
The first six hundred years, by Jean Daniélou and Henri Marrou. Translated by Vincent Cronin, with illus. selected and annotated by Peter Ludlow. — New York: McGraw-Hill, [1964] xxx, 522 p.: illus., maps (1 fold.) ports.; 23 cm. — (The Christian centuries, v. 1) Issued also in French under title: Des origines à saint Grégoire le Grand, and in German under title: Von der Gründung der Kirche bis zu Gregor dem Grossen. 1. Church history — Primitive and early church, ca. 30-600 I. Marrou, Henri Irénée. II. T.
BR162.2.D3x    270.1    *LC* 63-22123

**Frend, W. H. C.**    **1.2291**
The rise of Christianity / W.H.C. Frend. — Philadelphia: Fortress Press, 1984 (1985 printing) xvii, 1022 p.: ill., maps; 25 cm. 1. Church history — Primitive and early church, ca. 30-600 I. T.
BR162.2.F733 1984    270.1 19    *LC* 84-3994    *ISBN* 0800607139

**Wallace-Hadrill, J. M. (John Michael)**    **1.2292**
The Frankish Church / J.M. Wallace-Hadrill. — Oxford [Oxfordshire]: Clarendon Press; New York: Oxford University Press, c1983. x, 463 p: map; 24 cm. — (Oxford history of the Christian Church.) Includes index. 1. Church history — Primitive and early church, ca. 30-600 2. Church history — Middle Ages, 600-1500 I. T. II. Series.
BR162.2.W27 1983    274.4/02 19    *LC* 83-13051    *ISBN* 0198269064

**Chadwick, Henry, 1920-.**    • **1.2293**
The early church. Grand Rapids, Mich., Eerdmans [1968, c1967] 304 p. 22 cm. (The Pelican history of the church, v.1) 1. Church history — Primitive and early church, ca. 30-600 I. T.
BR165.C48 1968b    270.1    *LC* 68-92647

**Conzelmann, Hans.**    **1.2294**
[Geschichte des Urchristentums. English] History of primitive Christianity. Translated by John E. Steely. Nashville, Abingdon Press [1973] 190 p. 24 cm. Translation of Geschichte des Urchristentums. 1. Church history — Primitive and early church, ca. 30-600 I. T.
BR165.C6613    270.1    *LC* 72-8818    *ISBN* 0687172519 *ISBN* 0687172527

**Grant, Robert McQueen, 1917-.**    **1.2295**
Augustus to Constantine; the thrust of the Christian movement into the Roman world [by] Robert M. Grant. — [1st ed.]. — New York, Harper & Row [1970] xiv, 334 p. ports. 25 cm. Includes bibliographical references. 1. Church history — Primitive and early church. I. T.
BR165.G66 1970    281/.1    *LC* 73-109065

**Harnack, Adolf von, 1851-1930.**    • **1.2296**
The mission and expansion of Christianity in the first three centuries. Translated and edited by James Moffatt. — New York, Harper [1962] 527 p. illus. 21 cm. — (Harper torchbooks. The cloister library, TB92) First ed. in English published in 1904 under title: The expansion of Christianity in the first three centuries. Torchbook ed. consists of v. 1 of the 2d English ed. Includes bibliography. 1. Church history — Primitive and early church. I. Moffatt, James, 1870-1944. tr. II. T.
BR165.H4 1962    270.1    *LC* 62-4721

**Kidd, B. J. (Beresford James), 1863-1948.**    • **1.2297**
A history of the church to A.D. 461 / by B. J. Kidd. — Oxford: Clarendon Press, 1922. 3 v. 1. Church history — Primitive and early church, ca. 30-600 I. T.
BR165.K46    *LC* 22-18691

**Leitzmann, Hans, 1875-1942.**    • **1.2298**
A history of the early church / Hans Leizmann; translated by Bertram Lee Woolf. — Cleveland: World Pub. Co., 1961. 4 v. in 2; 20 cm. — (Meridian books; MG26A-B) 1. Church history — Primitive and early church. I. T.
BR165.L47 1961

**Loisy, Alfred Firmin, 1857-1940.**    • **1.2299**
[Naissance du christianisme. English] The birth of the Christian religion (La naissance du christianisme) and The origins of the New Testament (Les origines du Nouveau Testament) Authorized translation from the French by L. P. Jacks. New Hyde Park, N.Y., University Books [1962] xix, 413, 332 p. 24 cm. 1. Bible. N.T. — Criticism, interpretation, etc. 2. Church history — Primitive and early church. I. Loisy, Alfred Firmin, 1857-1940. Les origines du Nouveau Testament. English 1962. II. T. III. Title: Origins of the New Testament.
BR165.L834 1962    270.1    *LC* 62-18073

**Tyson, Joseph B.**    **1.2300**
A study of early Christianity [by] Joseph B. Tyson. New York, Macmillan [1973] xv, 447 p. illus. 24 cm. 1. Jesus Christ — History of doctrines — Early

church, ca. 30-600 2. Bible. N.T. — Criticism, interpretation, etc. 3. Church history — Primitive and early church, ca. 30-600 4. Christian literature, Early — History and criticism. I. T.
BR165.T9 1973     270.1 19     *LC* 74-190674

**Gager, John G.**             **1.2301**
Kingdom and community: the social world of early Christianity / John G. Gager. — Englewood Cliffs, N.J.: Prentice-Hall, [1975] xiii, 158 p.; 24 cm. — (Prentice-Hall studies in religion series) 1. Sociology, Christian — History — Early church, ca. 30-600 I. T.
BR166.G33     270.1     *LC* 74-28199     *ISBN* 0135162114. *ISBN* 0135162033 pbk

**Meeks, Wayne A.**             **1.2302**
The first urban Christians: the social world of the Apostle Paul / Wayne A. Meeks. — New Haven: Yale University Press, c1983. x, 299 p.: map; 24 cm. Includes indexes. 1. Paul, the Apostle, Saint. 2. Sociology, Christian — History — Early church, ca. 30-600 I. T.
BR166.M44 1983     270.1 19     *LC* 82-8447     *ISBN* 0300028768

**Cochrane, Charles Norris, 1889-1945.**      • **1.2303**
Christianity and classical culture; a study of thought and action from Augustus to Augustine. — London; New York, Oxford University Press, 1957. 523 p. 21 cm. 1. Civilization, Christian 2. Civilization, Greco-Roman 3. Church history — Primitive and early church. I. T.
BR170.C6 1957     270.1     *LC* 57-13990

**Goodenough, Erwin Ramsdell, 1893-1965.**      • **1.2304**
The church in the Roman Empire. — New York: Cooper Square Publishers, 1970 [c1931] xii, 132 p.; 23 cm. — (The Berkshire studies in European history) 1. Church history — Primitive and early church, 30-600. I. T. II. Series.
BR170.G63 1970     270.1     *LC* 77-122754     *ISBN* 0815403372

**Cureton, William, 1808-1864.**      • **1.2305**
Ancient Syriac documents relative to the earliest establishment of Christianity in Edessa and the neighbouring countries, from the year after our Lord's ascension to the beginning of the fourth century / discovered, edited, translated, and annotated by W. Cureton; with a preface by W. Wright. — Amsterdam: Oriental Press, 1967. xiv, 196, 112 p. Includes texts in English, Latin, French, or Syriac. 1. Church history — Primitive and early church, ca. 30-600 — Sources I. T. II. Title: Ancient Syriac documents relative to the earliest establishment of Christianity in Edessa.
BR185.C9 1967     270.1/08     *LC* 67-108685

## BR250–280 Medieval. Renaissance. Reformation

**Deanesly, Margaret.**      • **1.2306**
A history of the medieval Church, 590–1500. — 9th ed. — London: Methuen, 1969. 283 p.: map.; 22 cm. 1. Church history — Middle Ages, 600-1500 I. T.
BR252.D4 1969     270     *LC* 74-471166     *ISBN* 0416168302

**Knowles, David, 1896-.**      **1.2307**
The Middle Ages / by David Knowles with Dimitri Obolensky. — [1st ed.]. — London: Darton, Longman and Todd, [1969] xxxii, 519 p.: maps, 72 plates.; 23 cm. — (The Christian centuries, v. 2) Issued also in French under title: Le moyen age, and in German under title: Früh- und Hochmittelalten. 1. Church history — Middle Ages, 600-1500 2. Middle Ages — History I. Obolensky, Dimitri, 1918- joint author. II. T.
BR252.K6x     270     *LC* 70-6783

**Oakley, Francis.**      **1.2308**
The Western church in the later Middle Ages / Francis Oakley. — Ithaca, N.Y.: Cornell University Press, 1979. 345 p.; 23 cm. Includes index. 1. Europe — Church history — Middle Ages, 600-1500 I. T.
BR252.O15     282/.09/023     *LC* 79-7621     *ISBN* 0801412080

**Southern, R. W. (Richard William), 1912-.**      **1.2309**
Western society and the Church in the Middle Ages [by] R. W. Southern. — [Harmondsworth, Eng.]: Penguin Books, [1970] 376 p.: maps.; 18 cm. — (The Pelican history of the Church, 2) (Pelican books) 1. Church history — Middle Ages, 600-1500 2. Civilization, Medieval I. T.
BR252.S6     270     *LC* 75-21956     *ISBN* 0140205039

**Sumption, Jonathan.**      **1.2310**
Pilgrimage: an image of mediaeval religion / Jonathan Sumption. — Totawa, N.J.: Rowman and Littlefield, c1975. 391 p., [2] leaves of plates: ill.; 23 cm. Includes index. 1. Christianity — Middle Ages, 600-1500 2. Christian pilgrims and pilgrimages I. T.
BR252.S9 1975     209/.02     *ISBN* 0874716772

**Runciman, Steven, Sir.**      • **1.2311**
The medieval Manichee: a study of the Christian dualist heresy / Steven Runciman. — Cambridge: Cambridge University Press, 1947. 212 p. 1. Manicheism. 2. Heresies and heretics — Middle Ages, 600- 1500. I. T.
BR253.R8     *LC* 47-30740     283

**Turberville, Arthur Stanley, 1888-1945.**      **1.2312**
Mediaeval heresy & the Inquisition / by A. S. Turberville. — London; Hamden, Conn.: Archon Books, 1964. vi, 264 p.; 22 cm. 'First published 1920'. 1. Inquisition. 2. Sects, Medieval 3. Heresy I. T.
BR253.T7 1964     270.5     *LC* 64-11061

**Vlasto, A. P.**      • **1.2313**
The entry of the Slavs into Christendom; an introduction to the medieval history of the Slavs [by] A. P. Vlasto. — Cambridge [Eng.]: University Press, 1970. xii, 435 p.: fold. map.; 24 cm. 1. Slavs — Church history. I. T.
BR253.V57     301.29/174/91804     *LC* 70-98699     *ISBN* 0521074592

**Cohn, Norman Rufus Colin.**      • **1.2314**
The pursuit of the millennium; revolutionary millenarians and mystical anarchists of the Middle Ages [by] Norman Cohn. — Rev. and expanded ed. — New York: Oxford University Press, 1970. 412 p.: illus., port.; 24 cm. 1. Church history — Middle Ages, 600-1500 2. Sects, Medieval 3. Millennium — History of doctrines I. T.
BR270.C6 1970b     270.5     *LC* 79-12811

**Ozment, Steven E.**      **1.2315**
The age of reform (1250–1550): an intellectual and religious history of late medieval and Reformation Europe / Steven Ozment. — New Haven: Yale University Press, 1980. xii, 458 p.: ill.; 26 cm. 1. Church history — Middle Ages, 600-1500 2. Reformation 3. Theology, Doctrinal — History — Middle Ages, 600-1500 4. Theology, Doctrinal — History — 16th century 5. Civilization, Medieval I. T.
BR270.O9     274     *LC* 79-24162     *ISBN* 0300024770

## BR290–481 Modern

## BR300–430 Reformation. Counter-Reformation

**Christianity and revolution: radical Christian testimonies,**      **1.2316**
**1520–1650 / edited by Lowell H. Zuck.**
Philadelphia: Temple University Press, 1975. xiv, 310 p.; 23 cm. (Documents in free church history) Includes indexes. 1. Reformation — Sources. 2. Anabaptists — History — Sources. I. Zuck, Lowell H. II. Series.
BR301.C45     270.6     *LC* 74-25355     *ISBN* 0877220409

**Karlstadt's battle with Luther: documents in a liberal–radical**      **1.2317**
**debate / edited by Ronald J. Sider.**
Philadelphia: Fortress Press, c1978. xi, 161 p.; 22 cm. Includes index. 1. Karlstadt, Andreas Rudolff-Bodenstein von, ca. 1480-1541. 2. Luther, Martin, 1483-1546. 3. Theology — Collected works — 16th century. 4. Reformation — Sources. I. Karlstadt, Andreas Rudolff-Bodenstein von, ca. 1480-1541. II. Luther, Martin, 1483-1546. Selections. 1977 III. Sider, Ronald J.
BR301.K3     230/.08     *LC* 77-78642     *ISBN* 0800613120

**Kidd, B. J. (Beresford James), 1863-1948.**      • **1.2318**
Documents illustrative of the Continental Reformation; edited by B. J. Kidd. 1st ed. reprinted. Oxford, Clarendon P., 1967. xix, 743 p. 20 cm. Contributions in English, Latin and French. 1. Reformation — Sources. I. T.
BR301.K4 1967     270.6/08     *LC* 68-75422

**Spinka, Matthew, 1890-1972. ed.**      • **1.2319**
Advocates of reform, from Wyclif to Erasmus. Philadelphia, Westminster Press [1953] 399 p. 24 cm. (The Library of Christian classics; v. 14) 1. Reformation — Sources. 2. Reformation — Early movements I. T. II. Series.
BR301.S65     270.5     *LC* 53-13092

**Spiritual and Anabaptist writers. Documents illustrative of the**      • **1.2320**
**Radical Reformation, edited by George Huntston Williams, and**
**Evangelical Catholicism as represented by Juan de Valdés,**
**edited by Angel M. Mergal.**
Philadelphia: Westminster Press, [1957] 421 p.; 24 cm. — (The Library of Christian classics, v. 25) 1. Reformation — Sources. 2. Anabaptists I. Williams, George Huntston, 1914- ed. II. Valdés, Juan de, d. 1541.
BR301.S67     270.6     *LC* 57-5003

**Chadwick, Owen.**　　　　　　　　　　　　　**1.2321**
The Reformation. — [1st ed.], reprinted with revisions. — Harmondsworth: Penguin, 1972. 463 p.; 18 cm. — (The Pelican history of the church, v. 3) (Pelican books) 1. Reformation I. T.
BR305.2.C5 1972　　　270.6　　　*LC* 73-331082　　　*ISBN* 0140205047

**Dickens, A. G. (Arthur Geoffrey), 1910-.**　　　　• **1.2322**
Reformation and society in sixteenth–century Europe [by] A. G. Dickens. [1st American ed. New York] Harcourt, Brace & World [1966] 216 p. illus. (part col.) facsims., maps (1 fold.) ports. (part col.) 21 cm. (History of European civilization library) 1. Reformation I. T.
BR305.2.D5 1966a　　　270.6　　　*LC* 66-19863

**Grimm, Harold John, 1901-.**　　　　　　　　• **1.2323**
The Reformation era, 1500–1650 [by] Harold J. Grimm. — 2d ed. — New York: Macmillan, [1973] xiii, 594 p.: illus.; 24 cm. 1. Reformation I. T.
BR305.2.G74 1973　　　270.6　　　*LC* 72-91167

**Hillerbrand, Hans Joachim. ed.**　　　　　　　• **1.2324**
The Reformation; a narrative history related by contemporary observers and participants [edited by] Hans J. Hillerbrand. — [1st ed.]. — New York: Harper & Row, [1964] 495 p.: illus., facsims., ports.; 25 cm. London ed. (Student Christian Movement Press) has title: The Reformation in its own words. 1. Reformation I. T.
BR305.2.H5 1964　　　270.6082　　　*LC* 64-15480

**Hillerbrand, Hans Joachim.**　　　　　　　　**1.2325**
The world of the Reformation [by] Hans J. Hillerbrand. — New York: Scribner, [1973] x, 229 p.: map.; 24 cm. 1. Reformation I. T.
BR305.2.H53 1973　　　270.6　　　*LC* 73-5175　　　*ISBN* 0684135345

**Pietas et societas: new trends in Reformation social history:**　　**1.2326**
**essays in memory of Harold J. Grimm / edited by Kyle C.**
**Sessions and Phillip N. Bebb.**
Kirksville, Mo.: Sixteenth Century Journal Publishers, c1985. xix, 224 p.: ill.; 24 cm. (Volume 4 of Sixteenth century essays & studies) 1. Grimm, Harold John, 1901- — Addresses, essays, lectures. 2. Reformation — Addresses, essays, lectures. 3. Europe — Social life and customs — Addresses, essays, lectures. I. Grimm, Harold John, 1901- II. Sessions, Kyle C. III. Bebb, Phillip N., 1941-
BR305.2.P54 1985　　　270.6 19　　　*LC* 85-14395　　　*ISBN* 0940474042

**Reformation Europe: a guide to research / edited by Steven**　　**1.2327**
**Ozment.**
St. Louis: Center for Reformation Research, c1982. 390 p.; 22 cm. 1. Reformation — Addresses, essays, lectures. 2. Counter-Reformation — Addresses, essays, lectures. 3. Reformation — Research — Addresses, essays, lectures. 4. Counter-Reformation — Research — Addresses, essays, lectures. 5. Reformation — Bibliography. 6. Counter-Reformation — Bibliography. I. Ozment, Steven E.
BR305.2.R39 1982　　　270.6 19　　　*LC* 82-19776　　　*ISBN* 0910345015

**Spitz, Lewis William, 1922-.**　　　　　　　　**1.2328**
The Protestant Reformation, 1517–1559 / by Lewis W. Spitz. — 1st ed. — New York: Harper & Row, c1985. xiii, 444 p.: ill.; 22 cm. (Rise of modern Europe.) Includes index. 1. Reformation I. T. II. Series.
BR305.2.S66 1985　　　270.6 19　　　*LC* 83-48805　　　*ISBN* 0060139587

**Friesen, Abraham.**　　　　　　　　　　　　**1.2329**
Reformation and utopia; the Marxist interpretation of the Reformation and its antecedents. Wiesbaden, F. Steiner, 1974. xv, 271 p. 25 cm. (Veröffentlichungen des Instituts für Europäische Geschichte Mainz. Abteilung abendländische Religionsgeschichte, Bd. 71) Originally presented as the author's thesis, Institut für Europäische Geschichte at Mainz. 1. Zimmermann, Wilhelm, 1807-1878. 2. Reformation — Historiography. 3. Peasants' War, 1524-1525 4. Communism and Christianity I. T.
BR307.F74 1974　　　270.6　　　*LC* 74-183374　　　*ISBN* 3515018182

**Moeller, Bernd, 1931-.**　　　　　　　　　　**1.2330**
[Reichsstadt und Reformation. English] Imperial cities and the Reformation; three essays. Edited and translated by H. C. Erik Midelfort and Mark U. Edwards, Jr. Philadelphia, Fortress Press [1972] xi, 115 p. illus. 22 cm. 'Translated from the expanded French version of 1966 [of Reichsstadt und Reformation]' Includes Problems of Reformation research (translation of Probleme der Reformationsgeschichtsforschung) and The German humanists and the beginnings of the Reformation (translation of Die deutschen Humanisten und die Anfänge der Reformation). 1. Reformation — Germany 2. Imperial cities (Holy Roman Empire) 3. Germany — Church history — 16th century I. Moeller, Bernd, 1931- Probleme der Reformationsgeschichtsforschung. English. 1972. II. Moeller, Bernd, 1931- Die deutschen Humanisten und die Anfänge der Reformation. English. 1972. III. T.
BR307.M613　　　274.3　　　*LC* 72-75660　　　*ISBN* 0800601211

**Williams, George Huntston, 1914-.**　　　　　　**1.2331**
The Radical Reformation. — Philadelphia: Westminster Press, [1962] xxxi, 924 p.: map (on lining paper); 24 cm. 1. Reformation 2. Anabaptists I. T.
BR307.W5　　　270.5　　　*LC* 62-7066

**Kingdon, Robert McCune, 1927-.**　　　　　　**1.2332**
Transition and revolution; problems and issues of European Renaissance and Reformation history, edited by Robert M. Kingdon. — Minneapolis: Burgess Pub. Co., [1974] viii, 274 p.; 23 cm. 1. Reformation 2. State, The — History. 3. Humanism 4. Witchcraft — History. 5. Printing — History I. T.
BR309.K5　　　914/.03/23　　　*LC* 74-75575　　　*ISBN* 0808711180

**Ozment, Steven E. comp.**　　　　　　　　　• **1.2333**
The Reformation in medieval perspective. Edited with an introd. by Steven E. Ozment. — Chicago: Quadrangle Books, 1971. xiv, 267 p.; 22 cm. — (Modern scholarship on European history) 1. Reformation — Addresses, essays, lectures. I. T.
BR309.O93　　　270.6　　　*LC* 72-152100　　　*ISBN* 0812901940

## BR315–350 BIOGRAPHY

**Gerrish, B. A. (Brian Albert), 1931-.**　　　　　**1.2334**
Reformers in profile. — Philadelphia: Fortress Press, 1967. vii, 264 p.; 23 cm. 1. Reformation — Biography I. T.
BR 315 G37 1967

**Rupp, E. Gordon (Ernest Gordon), 1910-.**　　　**1.2335**
Patterns of reformation, by Gordon Rupp. Philadelphia, Fortress Press [1969] xxiii, 427 p. illus. 26 cm. 1. Oecolampadius, Joannes, 1482-1531. 2. Karlstadt, Andreas Rudolff-Bodenstein von, ca. 1480-1541. 3. Münzer, Thomas, 1490 (ca.)-1525. 4. Vadianus, Joachim, 1484-1551. 5. Kessler, Johannes, 1502?-1574. I. T.
BR315.R86　　　270.6/0922　　　*LC* 69-14626

**Bainton, Roland Herbert, 1894-.**　　　　　　**1.2336**
Women of the Reformation in France and England [by] Roland H. Bainton. — Minneapolis: Augsburg Pub. House, [1973] 287 p.: illus.; 23 cm. 1. Reformation — Biography. 2. Women — Biography I. T.
BR317.B29　　　270.6/092/2 B　　　*LC* 73-78269　　　*ISBN* 0806613335

**Bainton, Roland Herbert, 1894-.**　　　　　　**1.2337**
Women of the Reformation in Germany and Italy / by Roland H. Bainton. — Minneapolis: Augsburg Pub. House, [1971] 279 p.: ill., facsims., geneal. table, maps, ports.; 23 cm. 1. Reformation — Biography. 2. Women — Biography I. T.
BR317.B3 1971　　　270.6/0922 B　　　*LC* 70-135235

**Bainton, Roland Herbert, 1894-.**　　　　　　• **1.2338**
Here I stand; a life of Martin Luther. — New York: Abingdon-Cokesbury Press, [1950] 422 p.: illus., ports., music.; 24 cm. 1. Luther, Martin, 1483-1546. I. T.
BR325.B26　　　922.443　　　*LC* 50-9795

**Brecht, Martin.**　　　　　　　　　　　　　**1.2339**
[Martin Luther. English] Martin Luther: his road to Reformation, 1483–1521 / Martin Brecht; translated by James L. Schaaf. — Philadelphia: Fortress Press, c1985. xv, 557 p., [16] p. of plates: ill.; 24 cm. Translation of: Martin Luther: Sein Weg zur Reformation, 1483-1521. Includes index. 1. Luther, Martin, 1483-1546. 2. Reformation — Biography. I. T.
BR325.B69313 1985　　　284.1/092/4 B 19　　　*LC* 84-47911　　　*ISBN* 0800607384

**Edwards, Mark U.**　　　　　　　　　　　　**1.2340**
Luther and the false brethren / Mark U. Edwards, Jr. — Stanford, Calif.: Stanford University Press, 1975. viii, 242 p.; 23 cm. 1. Luther, Martin, 1483-1546. I. T.
BR325.E34　　　270.6/092/4　　　*LC* 75-181　　　*ISBN* 0804708835

**Erikson, Erik H. (Erik Homburger), 1902-.**　　　• **1.2341**
Young man Luther; a study in psychoanalysis and history. [1st ed.] New York, Norton [1958] 288 p. 22 cm. (Austen Riggs monograph no. 4) 1. Luther, Martin, 1483-1546. I. T.
BR325.E7　　　922.443　　　*LC* 58-11113

**Haile, Harry Gerald, 1931-.**　　　　　　　　**1.2342**
Luther, an experiment in biography / H. G. Haile. — 1st ed. — Garden City, N.Y.: Doubleday, 1980. x, 422 p.: map (on lining papers); 22 cm. 1. Luther, Martin, 1483-1546. 2. Reformation — Biography. I. T.
BR325.H23　　　284.1/092/4　　　*LC* 79-6282　　　*ISBN* 0385159609

**Manns, Peter.**　　　　　　　　　　　　　　**1.2343**
[Martin Luther. English] Martin Luther: an illustrated biography / text by Peter Manns; photographs by Helmuth Nils Loose; introduction by Jaroslav Pelikan; [translated by Michael Shaw]. — New York: Crossroad, 1982. 223 p.:

ill. (some col.); 31 cm. 1. Luther, Martin, 1483-1546. 2. Reformation — Germany — Biography. I. T.
BR325.M28513 1982      284.1/092/4 B 19      *LC* 82-14972      *ISBN* 0824505107

**Bornkamm, Heinrich, 1901-.**            **1.2344**
[Martin Luther in der Mitte seines Lebens. English] Luther in mid–career, 1521–1530 / Heinrich Bornkamm; edited, and with a foreward by Karin Bornkamm; translated by E. Theodore Bachmann. — Philadelphia: Fortress Press, c1983. xx, 709 p.; 24 cm. Translation of: Martin Luther in der Mitte seines Lebens. Includes indexes. 1. Luther, Martin, 1483-1546. 2. Reformation — Biography. I. Bornkamm, Karin, 1928- II. T.
BR326.6.B6713 1983      284.1/092/4 B 19      *LC* 82-48591      *ISBN* 0800606922

**Edwards, Mark U.**            **1.2345**
Luther's last battles: politics and polemics, 1531–46 / Mark U. Edwards, Jr. — Ithaca, N.Y.: Cornell University Press, 1983. xii, 254 p.: ill.; 24 cm. 1. Luther, Martin, 1483-1546. I. T.
BR326.8.E38 1983      284.1/092/4 19      *LC* 82-72363      *ISBN* 0801415640

**Luther, Martin, 1483-1546.**         • **1.2346**
Early theological works. Edited and translated by James Atkinson. — Philadelphia, Westminster Press [1962] 380 p. 24 cm. — (The Library of Christian classics, v. 16) 1. Theology — Collected works I. Atkinson, James, 1914- ed. and tr. II. T. III. Series.
BR330.E4 1962      230.41      *LC* 62-12358

**Luther, Martin, 1483-1546.**         • **1.2347**
Works. Edited by Jaroslav Pelikan. Saint Louis, Concordia Pub. House 1955-1986. 55 v. General editor: Helmut T. Lehmann. Vols. 31-55 have imprint: Philadelphia, Fortress Press (formerly Muhlenberg Press). 1. Lutheran Church — Collected works. 2. Bible — Criticism, interpretation, etc. — History 3. Theology — Collected works — 16th century. I. T. II. Title: Luther the expositor.
BR330.E5 1955      *LC* 55-9893

**Luther, Martin, 1483-1546.**         • **1.2348**
Three treatises / Martin Luther; [translated by Charles M. Jacobs, A.T.W. Steinhäuser, W.A. Lambert]. — Philadelphia: Muhlenberg Press, 1947. 290 p. 1. Lutheran Church — Collected works. 2. Theology — Collected works — 16th century. I. T.
BR331.E5 J323 1947

**Gritsch, Eric W.**            **1.2349**
Martin— God's court jester: Luther in retrospect / Eric W. Gritsch. — Philadelphia: Fortress Press, c1983. xiv, 289 p.; 23 cm. Includes indexes. 1. Luther, Martin, 1483-1546. 2. Reformation — Biography. I. T.
BR332.5.G74 1983      284.1/092/4 B 19      *LC* 83-48004      *ISBN* 0800617533

**Ebeling, Gerhard, 1912-.**            **1.2350**
[Luther. English] Luther; an introduction to his thought. Translated by R. A. Wilson. Philadelphia, Fortress Press [1970] 287 p. 22 cm. 1. Luther, Martin, 1483-1546 — Theology. I. T.
BR333.2.E313 1970      230.4/1/0924      *LC* 77-99612

**Holl, Karl, 1866-1926.**            **1.2351**
[Gesammelte Aufsätze zur Kirchengeschichte. Was verstand Luther unter Religion? English] What did Luther understand by religion? / Karl Holl; edited by James Luther Adams and Walter F. Bense; translated by Fred W. Meuser and Walter R. Wietzke. — Philadelphia: Fortress Press, c1977. iv, 123 p.; 22 cm. 'Translation of the essay 'Was verstand Luther unter Religion?' found in ... Gesammelte Aufsätze zur Kirchengeschichte, volume 1, pp. 1-110.' 1. Luther, Martin, 1483-1546 — Theology. 2. Luther, Martin, 1483-1546 — Religion. I. T.
BR333.2.H6413      230/.4/10924      *LC* 76-62611      *ISBN* 0800612604

**Pauck, Wilhelm, 1901- comp.**         • **1.2352**
Melanchthon and Bucer. Philadelphia, Westminster Press [1969] xx, 406 p. 24 cm. (The Library of Christian classics, v. 19) 1. Theology — 16th century I. Melanchthon, Philipp, 1497-1560. Loci communes rerum theologicarum. English. 1969. II. Bucer, Martin, 1491-1551. De regno Christi. English. 1969. III. T. IV. Series.
BR336.L62 1969      230.4/1      *LC* 69-12309      *ISBN* 0664220193

**Potter, George Richard, 1900-.**            **1.2353**
Zwingli / G. R. Potter. Cambridge; New York: Cambridge University Press, 1976. xvii, 432 p.: maps; 24 cm. 1. Zwingli, Ulrich, 1484-1531. I. T.
BR345.P68      270.6/092/4 B      *LC* 75-46136      *ISBN* 0521209390

**Zwingli, Ulrich, 1484-1531.**         • **1.2354**
Zwingli and Bullinger; selected translations with introductions and notes by G. W. Bromiley. — Philadelphia, Westminster Press [1953] 364 p. 24 cm. — (The Library of Christian classics, v. 24) Bibliography: p. 353-357. 1. Reformed

Church — Collected works. 2. Theology — Collected works — 16th cent. I. Bullinger, Heinrich, 1504-1575. II. Bromiley, G. W., ed. and tr. III. T. IV. Series.
BR346.A24      270.6      *LC* 53-1533

## BR358–420 REFORMATION IN SPECIAL COUNTRIES

**Dickens, A. G. (Arthur Geoffrey), 1910-.**            **1.2355**
The English Reformation [by] A. G. Dickens. New York, Schocken Books [1964] x, 374 p. 24 cm. 1. Reformation — England I. T.
BR375.D5      274.2      *LC* 64-22987

**Dickens, A. G. (Arthur Geoffrey), 1910-.**         • **1.2356**
The Reformation in England, to the accession of Elizabeth I / edited by A. G. Dickens and Dorothy Carr. — New York: St. Martin's Press, 1968, c1967. vii, 167, [1] p.; 20 cm. — (Documents of modern history) 1. Reformation — England — Sources. I. Carr, Dorothy. II. T.
BR375.D52 1968      270.6/0942      *LC* 67-29568

**Parker, T. H. L. (Thomas Henry Louis), ed.**         • **1.2357**
English reformers, edited by T. H. L. Parker. Philadelphia, Westminster Press [1966] xxiv, 360 p. 24 cm. (The Library of Christian classics, v. 26) 1. Reformation — England — Collections. I. T.
BR375.P26 1966      274.2      *LC* 66-10354

**Thomas, Keith Vivian.**            **1.2358**
Religion and the decline of magic [by] Keith Thomas. — New York: Scribner, [1971] xviii, 716 p.; 25 cm. 1. Occultism — England. 2. Great Britain — Religion I. T.
BR377.T48 1971b      133      *LC* 74-141707      *ISBN* 0684106027

**Cowan, Ian Borthwick.**            **1.2359**
The Scottish Reformation: church and society in sixteenth century Scotland / Ian B. Cowan. — New York: St. Martin's Press, 1982. x, 244 p.: map; 23 cm. Includes index. 1. Reformation — Scotland. 2. Scotland — Church history — 16th century I. T.
BR385.C76 1982      274.11/06 19      *LC* 82-5834      *ISBN* 0312705190

**Donaldson, Gordon.**         • **1.2360**
The Scottish Reformation. — Cambridge [Eng.] University Press, 1960. 242 p. illus. 23 cm. 'Based on the Birkbeck lectures delivered in the University of Cambridge in 1957-8.' Includes bibliography. 1. Reformation — Scotland. 2. Scotland — Church history — 16th cent. 3. Church of Scotland — Hist. 4. Scotland — Soc. life & cust. I. T.
BR385.D6 1970      274.1      *LC* 60-16183

**Knox, John, 1505-1572.**         • **1.2361**
History of the Reformation in Scotland. Edited by William Croft Dickinson. — London, New York, Nelson [1949] 2 v. 25 cm. Bibliography: v. 2, p. 343-350. 1. Reformation — Scotland. I. T.
BR385.K6 1949      274.1      *LC* 50-12368

## BR430 COUNTER–REFORMATION

**Kidd, B. J. (Beresford James), 1863-1948.**         • **1.2362**
The Counter–Reformation, 1550–1600 / by B. J. Kidd. — London: Society for Promoting Christian Knowledge, 1933. 270 p.; 23 cm. 1. Counter-Reformation I. T.
BR430.K5      270.6

**Wright, A. D. (Anthony David)**            **1.2363**
The counter–reformation: Catholic Europe and the non–Christian world / A.D. Wright. — New York: St. Martin's Press, 1982. 344 p.; 24 cm. Includes index. 1. Catholic Church — Missions — History. 2. Counter-Reformation I. T.
BR430.W7 1982      270.6 19      *LC* 82-3210      *ISBN* 0312170211

## BR450–481 1648–

**Cragg, Gerald R. (Gerald Robertson)**         • **1.2364**
The church and the age of reason, 1648–1789 / Gerald R. Cragg. — New York: Atheneum, 1961. 299 p. — (The Pelican history of the church; v. 4) 1. Church history — 17th century 2. Church history — 18th century 3. Enlightenment I. T. II. Series.
BR455 C7 1961      *LC* 61-3977

**Latourette, Kenneth Scott, 1884-1968.**         • **1.2365**
Christianity in a revolutionary age; a history of Christianity in the nineteenth and twentieth centuries. — Westport, Conn.: Greenwood Press, [1973,

c1958-62] 5 v.; 23 cm. 1. Church history — 19th century 2. Church history —
20th century I. T.
BR475.L33      270.8      *LC* 77-138141      *ISBN* 0837157005

**Vidler, Alexander Roper, 1899-.**                          • **1.2366**
The Church in an age of revolution: 1789 to the present day [by] Alec R. Vidler.
— Baltimore: Penguin Books, c1965. 287 p.; 19cm. (Pelican history of the
church; v. 5) (Pelican books, A506) 1. Church history — Modern period, 1500-
I. T. II. Series.
BR475.V5 1965      270.8

**Tillich, Paul, 1886-1965.**                          • **1.2367**
The religious situation. Translated by H. Richard Niebuhr. — New York,
Meridian Books, 1956 [c1932] 219 p. 19 cm. — (Living age books, LA 6)
Translation of Die religiöse Lage der Gegenwart. 1. Religious thought — 20th
cent. I. T.
BR479.Tx      270.8      *LC* 56-9242

## BR513–569 UNITED STATES

**Yearbook of American and Canadian churches.**                          **1.2368**
41st- 1973-. Nashville, Abingdon Press. v. 23 cm. Annual. 1. Christian sects —
United States — Directories. 2. Christian sects — Canada — Directories.
I. National Council of the Churches of Christ in the United States of America.
Office of Research, Evaluation and Planning.
BR513.Y4      277/.05      *LC* 75-640866

**Smith, H. Shelton (Hilrie Shelton), 1893-.**                          **1.2369**
American Christianity: an historical interpretation with representative
documents / by H. Shelton Smith, Robert T. Handy and Lefferts A. Loetscher.
— New York: Scribner, 1960-1963. 2 v.: ill.; 24 cm. 1. United States — Church
history — Sources. 2. United States — Church history I. T.
BR514.S55      *LC* 60-8117

**Ahlstrom, Sydney E.**                          • **1.2370**
A religious history of the American people [by] Sydney E. Ahlstrom. — New
Haven: Yale University Press, 1972. xvi, 1158 p.; 26 cm. 1. United States —
Religion I. T.
BR515.A4 1972      200/.973      *LC* 72-151564      *ISBN* 0300014759

**Baird, Robert, 1798-1863.**                          • **1.2371**
[Religion in the United States of America] Religion in America. A critical
abridgment with introd. by Henry Warner Bowden. New York, Harper &
Row [1970] xxxvii, 314 p. 21 cm. (Harper torchbooks, TB 1509) First published
in 1844 under title: Religion in the United States of America. 1. United States
— Church history I. Bowden, Henry Warner. ed. II. T.
BR515.B322B3      209/.73      *LC* 75-114093

**Clebsch, William A.**                          **1.2372**
American religious thought: a history / William A. Clebsch. — Chicago:
University of Chicago Press, 1973. xxi, 212 p.; 22 cm. (Chicago history of
American religion) Includes index. 1. Religious thought — United States. I. T.
BR515.C53      209/.73      *LC* 73-82911      *ISBN* 0226109607

**Greeley, Andrew M., 1928-.**                          • **1.2373**
The denominational society; a sociological approach to religion in America [by]
Andrew M. Greeley. Academic advisor in sociology: Peter H. Rossi. —
Glenview, Ill.: Scott, Foresman, [1972] 266 p.; 23 cm. 1. Religion and sociology
— United States. 2. United States — Religion I. T.
BR515.G74      200/.973      *LC* 70-173239

**Greven, Philip J.**                          **1.2374**
The protestant temperament: patterns of child–rearing, religious experience,
and the self in early America / Philip Greven. — 1st ed. — New York: Knopf,
1977. xiv, 431 p.; 25 cm. Includes index. 1. Protestantism 2. Child
development 3. Temperament 4. Experience (Religion) 5. Religious thought
— United States. I. T.
BR515.G75 1977      301.5/8      *LC* 77-74989      *ISBN* 0394404238

**Handy, Robert T.**                          • **1.2375**
A Christian America; Protestant hopes and historical realities [by] Robert T.
Handy. — New York: Oxford University Press, 1971. x, 282 p.; 22 cm.
1. Protestant churches — U.S. 2. Christianity and culture 3. U.S. — Church
history. I. T.
BR515.H354      280/.4/0973      *LC* 78-161888      *ISBN* 0195014537

**Hudson, Winthrop Still, 1911-.**                          • **1.2376**
American Protestantism. — [Chicago]: University of Chicago Press, [1961]
198 p.; 21 cm. — (The Chicago history of American civilization) 1. Protestant
churches — United States. 2. United States — Church history I. T.
BR515.H78      277.3      *LC* 61-15936

**Hudson, Winthrop Still, 1911-.**                          • **1.2377**
Religion in America: an historical account of the development of American
religious life / Winthrop S. Hudson. — 3rd ed. — New York: Scribner, c1981.

p. cm. Includes index. 1. Christianity — United States 2. United States —
Religion I. T.
BR515.H79 1981      291/.0973 19      *LC* 81-2152      *ISBN* 0684170108

**Marty, Martin E., 1928-.**                          **1.2378**
A nation of behavers / Martin E. Marty. — Chicago: University of Chicago
Press, c1976. xi, 239 p.; 21 cm. 1. Sociology, Christian — United States.
2. United States — Religion — 1945-1960 3. United States — Religion —
1960- I. T.
BR515.M32      200/.973      *LC* 76-7997      *ISBN* 0226508919

**Marty, Martin E., 1928-.**                          **1.2379**
Pilgrims in their own land: 500 years of religion in America / Martin E. Marty.
— 1st ed. — Boston: Little, Brown, c1984. xii, 500 p.: ill.; 25 cm. Includes
index. 1. United States — Church history 2. United States — Religion I. T.
BR515.M324 1984      291/.0973 19      *LC* 84-821      *ISBN* 0316548677

**Marty, Martin E., 1928-.**                          **1.2380**
Protestantism in the United States: righteous empire / Martin E. Marty. — 2nd
ed. — New York: Scribner's; London: Collier Macmillan, c1986. xi, 290 p.; 24
cm. Rev. ed. of: Righteous empire. 1970. Includes index. 1. Protestant
churches — United States. 2. United States — Church history I. Marty,
Martin E., 1928- Righteous empire. II. T.
BR515.M328 1986      280/.4/0973 19      *LC* 85-10475      *ISBN*
0023765003

**Mead, Sidney Earl, 1904-.**                          • **1.2381**
The lively experiment: the shaping of Christianity in America. — [1st ed.]. —
New York, Harper & Row [1963] 220 p. 22 cm. 1. U.S. — Church history.
I. T.
BR515.M43      277.3      *LC* 63-10750

**Mead, Sidney Earl, 1904-.**                          **1.2382**
The old religion in the brave new world: reflections on the relation between
Christendom and the Republic / Sidney E. Mead. — Berkeley: University of
California Press, c1977. xii, 189 p.; 21 cm. — (The Jefferson memorial lectures)
1. Christianity — United States — Addresses, essays, lectures. I. T. II. Series.
BR515.M453      209/.73      *LC* 76-24588      *ISBN* 0520033221

**Schaff, Philip, 1819-1893.**                          • **1.2383**
America, a sketch of its political, social, and religious character / by Philip
Schaff; translated from the German; edited by Perry Miller. — Cambridge:
Belknap Press of Harvard University Press, 1961. 241 p. — (John Harvard
library.) 1. United States — Religion 2. United States — Church history
3. United States — Civilization I. T. II. Series.
BR515.S3 1961      *LC* 61-8871/L

**Smith, James Ward, 1917-.**                          • **1.2384**
Religion in American life. / Editors: James Ward Smith and A. Leland
Jamison. Princeton, N.J.: Princeton U.P., 1961-. v. in : ill., plans. (Princeton
studies in American civilization, no.5.) Vol. 4 by Nelson R. Burr in
collaboration with the editors. 1. United States — Religion 2. United States —
Civilization I. Burr, Nelson Rollin, 1904- II. Jamison, A. Leland (Albert
Leland), 1911- III. T. IV. Title: The shaping of American religion. V. Title:
Religious perspectives in American culture. VI. Title: A critical bibliography
of religion in America. VII. Series.
BR515.S6      277.3      *LC* 61-5383

**Sperry, Willard Learoyd, 1882-1954.**                          **1.2385**
Religion in America. Cambridge [Eng.] The University press; New York, The
Macmillan company, 1946. x, [1], 317, [1] p. 21 cm. 1. United States — Church
history 2. United States — Religion I. Lazzaro, Ralph. II. T.
BR515.S67 1946      *LC* 46-7760

**Strout, Cushing.**                          **1.2386**
The new heavens and new earth; political religion in America. — [1st ed.]. —
New York: Harper & Row, [1973, c1974] xv, 400 p.; 24 cm. 1. United States —
Religion I. T.
BR515.S77 1973      200/.973      *LC* 73-4128      *ISBN* 0060141719

**Women and religion in America / [edited by] Rosemary**                          **1.2387**
**Radford Ruether, Rosemary Skinner Keller.**
1st ed. — San Francisco: Harper & Row, c1981-. xiv, 353 p.: ill. 1. Women in
Christianity — United States — History — 19th century — Addresses, essays,
lectures. 2. Women in Judaism — United States — History — 19th century —
Addresses, essays, lectures. 3. United States — Religion — Addresses, essays,
lectures. I. Ruether, Rosemary Radford. II. Keller, Rosemary Skinner.
BR515.W648 1981      280/.088042 19      *LC* 80-8346      *ISBN*
0060668296

**Women in American religion / Paul Boyer ... [et al.]; edited by**                          **1.2388**
**Janet Wilson James.**
Philadelphia: University of Pennsylvania Press, 1980, c1978. 274 p.: ill.; 24 cm.
1. Women in Christianity — United States — Addresses, essays, lectures.
2. Women in church work — United States — Addresses, essays, lectures.
3. Women in Judaism — United States — Addresses, essays, lectures.

4. Women — United States — Addresses, essays, lectures. 5. United States — Religion — Addresses, essays, lectures. I. Boyer, Paul S. II. James, Janet Wilson, 1918-
BR515.W65 1980     261.8/344     *LC* 79-5261     *ISBN* 0812277805

**Braden, Charles Samuel, 1887-.**        • **1.2389**
These also believe: a study of modern American cults & minority religious movements / Charles Samuel Braden. — New York: Macmillan, 1949. xv, 491 p. 1. Sects — United States. I. T.
BR516.B697     280.973     *LC* 49-8917

**Judah, J. Stillson.**        **1.2390**
The history and philosophy of the metaphysical movements in America, by J. Stillson Judah. — Philadelphia: Westminster Press, [1967] 317 p.; 24 cm. 1. Sects — United States. I. T.
BR516.J8     280/.0973     *LC* 67-11672

**Lowell, C. Stanley.**        **1.2391**
The great church–state fraud [by] C. Stanley Lowell. — Washington: R. B. Luce, [1973] 224 p.; 23 cm. 1. Church and state — United States I. T.
BR516.L783     261.7/0973     *LC* 72-94949

**Smith, Elwyn A. (Elwyn Allen), 1919-.**        • **1.2392**
Religious liberty in the United States; the development of church–state thought since the Revolutionary era [by] Elwyn A. Smith. — Philadelphia: Fortress Press, [1972] xiv, 386 p.; 24 cm. 1. Freedom of religion — United States. 2. Church and state — United States I. T.
BR516.S57     261.7/2     *LC* 70-178093     *ISBN* 0800600711

**Stokes, Anson Phelps, 1874-1958.**        • **1.2393**
Church and state in the United States ... Introd. by Ralph Henry Gabriel. New York, Harper [1950] 3 v. illus. 1. Church and state — United States I. T.
BR516.S85     261.7     *LC* 50-7978

**Gaustad, Edwin Scott.**        **1.2394**
Dissent in American religion / Edwin Scott Gaustad. — Chicago: University of Chicago Press, 1973. xii, 184 p.; 22 cm. (Chicago history of American religion) Includes index. 1. Dissenters, Religious — United States. 2. United States — Religion I. T.
BR516.5.G35     200/.973     *LC* 73-77131     *ISBN* 0226284360

**Mead, Frank Spencer, 1898-.**        • **1.2395**
Handbook of denominations in the United States / Frank S. Mead. — New 8th ed. / revised by Samuel S. Hill. — Nashville: Abingdon Press, c1985. 320 p.; 23 cm. Includes index. 1. Christian sects — United States 2. Sects — United States. I. Hill, Samuel S. II. T.
BR516.5.M38 1985     291/.0973 19     *LC* 84-24342     *ISBN* 0687165717

**Zaretsky, Irving I.**        **1.2396**
Religious movements in contemporary America, edited by Irving I. Zaretsky and Mark P. Leone. — Princeton, N.J.: Princeton University Press, [c1974] xxxvi, 837 p.: illus.; 25 cm. 1. United States — Religious life and customs 2. United States — Religion — 1945- I. Leone, Mark P., joint author. II. T.
BR516.5.Z37     200/.973     *LC* 73-39054     *ISBN* 0691071861

**Vidich, Arthur J.**        **1.2397**
American sociology: worldly rejections of religion and their directions / Arthur J. Vidich and Stanford M. Lyman. — New Haven: Yale University Press, c1985. xiii, 380 p.; 25 cm. Includes index. 1. Sociology, Christian — United States. I. Lyman, Stanford M. II. T.
BR517.V47 1985     301/.0973 19     *LC* 84-2268     *ISBN* 0300030371

## BR520–526 Special Periods

**Davidson, James West.**        **1.2398**
The logic of millennial thought: eighteenth–century New England / James West Davidson. — New Haven: Yale University Press, 1977. xii, 308 p.; 22 cm. (Yale historical publications. Miscellany. 112) Includes index. 1. Bible. N.T. Revelation — Criticism, interpretation, etc. — History — 18th century. 2. Millennium — History of doctrines 3. Religious thought — New England. I. T. II. Series.
BR520.D29     261     *LC* 75-43315     *ISBN* 0300019475

**Gaustad, Edwin Scott.**        • **1.2399**
The Great Awakening in New England. — Gloucester, Mass., P. Smith, 1965 [c1957] 173 p. illus., maps. 21 cm. Bibliographical references included in 'Notes' (p. 141-159) Bibliography: p. 160-168. 1. Great Awakening I. T.
BR520.G2 1965     277.4     *LC* 65-4750

**Goen, C. C.**        • **1.2400**
Revivalism and separatism in New England, 1740–1800; Strict Congregationalists and Separate Baptists in the Great Awakening, by C. C. Goen. With a new preface by the author. [Hamden, Conn.] Archon Books, 1969

[c1962] xii, 370 p. 23 cm. 1. Dissenters, Religious — New England. 2. New England — Church history. I. T.
BR520.G6 1969     277.4     *LC* 69-19225     *ISBN* 0208008020

**Hall, David D.**        • **1.2401**
The faithful shepherd; a history of the New England ministry in the seventeenth century, by David D. Hall. Chapel Hill, Published for the Institute of Early American History and Culture, Williamsburg, Va., by the University of North Carolina Press [1972] xvi, 301 p. 24 cm. 1. Pastoral theology — New England — History — 17th century. 2. Clergy — New England. 3. New England — Church history. I. T.
BR520.H3     253     *LC* 72-81326     *ISBN* 0807811939

**Heimert, Alan.**        • **1.2402**
Religion and the American mind, from the Great Awakening to the Revolution [by] Alan Heimert. Cambridge, Harvard University Press, 1966. x, 668 p. 25 cm. 'Biographical glossary': p. 555-563. 1. Religious thought — United States. 2. United States — Church history I. T.
BR520.H4     261.70973     *LC* 66-14444

**Lovejoy, David S. (David Sherman), 1919-.**        **1.2403**
Religious enthusiasm in the New World: heresy to revolution / David S. Lovejoy. — Cambridge, Mass.: Harvard University Press, 1985. viii, 291 p.; cm. Includes index. 1. Dissenters, Religious — United States. 2. Enthusiasm — Religious aspects — Christianity 3. United States — Church history — Colonial period, ca. 1600-1775 4. United States — History — Colonial period, ca. 1600-1775 I. T.
BR520.L633 1985     280/.4 19     *LC* 84-22377     *ISBN* 0674758641

**Marini, Stephen A., 1946-.**        **1.2404**
Radical sects of revolutionary New England / Stephen A. Marini. — Cambridge, Mass.: Harvard University Press, 1982. 213 p.; 24 cm. Includes index. 1. Christian sects — New England. 2. New England — Church history. I. T.
BR520.M36 1982     289 19     *LC* 81-6913     *ISBN* 0674746252

**Carter, Paul Allen, 1926-.**        • **1.2405**
The spiritual crisis of the gilded age [by] Paul A. Carter. — DeKalb: Northern Illinois University Press, 1971. xiii, 295 p.: illus.; 25 cm. 1. United States — Religion — 19th century I. T.
BR525.C37     209/.73     *LC* 72-156938     *ISBN* 0875800262

**Moorhead, James H.**        **1.2406**
American apocalypse: Yankee Protestants and the Civil War, 1860–1869 / James H. Moorhead. — New Haven: Yale University Press, 1978. xiv, 278 p.; 22 cm. Originally presented as the author's thesis, Yale, 1975. Includes index. 1. Millennialism — History. 2. Messianism, Political — United States 3. Protestant churches — United States — History. 4. United States — History — Civil War, 1861-1865 — Religious aspects I. T.
BR525.M56 1978     280/.4/0973     *LC* 77-14360     *ISBN* 0300021526

**The Rise of Adventism; religion and society in mid–nineteenth–century America.** Edwin S. Gaustad, editor.        **1.2407**
[1st ed.]. — New York: Harper & Row, [1974] xx, 329 p.; 24 cm. Lectures delivered during 1972-73 at the University Church, Loma Linda University, Loma Linda, Calif. 1. Adventists 2. United States — Religion — 19th century I. Gaustad, Edwin Scott. ed.
BR525.R57 1974     286/.773     *LC* 74-4637     *ISBN* 0060630949

**Schneider, Herbert Wallace, 1892-.**        • **1.2408**
Religion in 20th century America. — Cambridge: Harvard University Press, 1952. x, 244 p.: illus.; 22 cm. — (The Library of Congress series in American civilization) 1. United States — Religion — 1901-1945 2. United States — Church history — 20th century I. T. II. Series.
BR525.S34     277.3     *LC* 52-8219

**McLoughlin, William Gerald.**        • **1.2409**
Religion in America, edited by William G. McLoughlin and Robert N. Bellah. Boston, Houghton Mifflin, 1968. xxiv, 433 p. illus. 24 cm. (The Daedalus library [v. 12]) Papers, by contributors chosen by the editors, based on preparatory conferences held at the American Academy of Arts and Sciences, Boston. 1. United States — Religion — 1945-1960 2. United States — Religion — 1960- I. Bellah, Robert Neelly, 1927- joint author. II. American Academy of Arts and Sciences. III. T. IV. Series.
BR526.M32     209.73     *LC* 68-17174

## BR530–560 Special Regions

**Holifield, E. Brooks.**        **1.2410**
The gentlemen theologians: American theology in Southern culture, 1795–1860 / E. Brooks Holifield. — Durham: Duke University Press, 1978. x, 262 p.; 25 cm. 1. Theology, Doctrinal — Southern States — History. 2. Religious thought — Southern States. I. T.
BR535.H57     277/.5     *LC* 78-59580     *ISBN* 0822304147

**Mathews, Donald G.**                                                      **1.2411**
Religion in the old South / Donald G. Mathews. — Chicago: University of Chicago Press, 1977. xx, 274 p.; 21 cm. — (Chicago history of American religion) Includes index. 1. Christianity — Southern States. 2. Evangelicalism — Southern States. I. T.
BR535.M37        277.5      *LC* 77-587        *ISBN* 0226510018

**Miyakawa, Tetsuo Scott.**                                              • **1.2412**
Protestants and pioneers; individualism and conformity on the American frontier [by] T. Scott Miyakawa. Chicago, University of Chicago Press [1964] 306 p. 23 cm. 1. Protestants — West (U.S.) 2. West (U.S.) — Religion. I. T.
BR545.M5      *LC* 64-22247

**Cross, Whitney R.**                                                    • **1.2413**
The Burned–over District; the social and intellectual history of enthusiastic religion in western New York, 1800–1850. Ithaca: Cornell University Press, 1982. — xiii, 383 p. maps. 24 cm. 1. Enthusiasm 2. New York (State) — Church history. I. T.
BR555.N7 C7 1982      277.47      *LC* 50-12161      *ISBN* 0801492327

**Buckley, Thomas E., 1939-.**                                           **1.2414**
Church and state in Revolutionary Virginia, 1776–1787 / Thomas E. Buckley. — Charlottesville: University Press of Virginia, 1977. 217 p.: maps; 24 cm. Includes index. 1. Church and state — Virginia — History. 2. Freedom of religion — Virginia — History. I. T.
BR555.V8 B8      261.7/09755      *LC* 77-4283      *ISBN* 081390692X

**Gewehr, Wesley Marsh, 1888-.**                                         • **1.2415**
The great awakening in Virginia, 1740–1790, by Wesley M. Gewehr. Gloucester, Mass., P. Smith, 1965 [c1930] viii, 292 p. maps, ports. 21 cm. (Duke University publications) 1. Revivals — Virginia. 2. Great Awakening 3. Virginia — Church history. I. T.
BR555.V8G4 1965      *LC* 66-1635

**Caplow, Theodore.**                                                    **1.2416**
All faithful people: change and continuity in Middletown's religion / Theodore Caplow, Howard M. Bahr, Bruce A. Chadwick, and Dwight W. Hoover ... [et al.]. — Minneapolis: University of Minnesota Press, c1983. x, 378 p.; 24 cm. Includes indexes. 1. Christianity — Indiana — Muncie. 2. Muncie (Ind.) — Religious life and customs. I. Bahr, Howard M. II. Chadwick, Bruce A. III. T.
BR560.M86 C36 1983      306/.6/0977265 19      *LC* 82-24759      *ISBN* 0816612307

## BR563 By Race or Ethnic Group

**Afro–American religious history: a documentary witness** / edited      **1.2417**
by Milton C. Sernett.
Durham [N.C.]: Duke University Press, 1985. xii, 504 p.; 24 cm. 1. Afro-Americans — Religion — Addresses, essays, lectures. I. Sernett, Milton C., 1942-
BR563.N4 A37 1985      200/.8996073 19      *LC* 84-24686      *ISBN* 0822305917

**Clarke, Erskine, 1941-.**                                              **1.2418**
Wrestlin' Jacob: a portrait of religion in the Old South / Erskine Clarke. — Atlanta: John Knox Press, c1979. xv, 207 p. [8 leaves of plates]: ill. 1. Jones, Charles Colcock, 1840-1863. 2. Afro-Americans — Georgia — Liberty Co. — Religion. 3. Afro-Americans — South Carolina — Charleston — Religion. 4. Slavery in the United States — Georgia — Condition of slaves. 5. Liberty County (Ga.) — Church history. 6. Charleston (S.C.) — Church history. 7. Slavery in the United States — South Carolina — Condition of slaves. I. T.
BR563.N4 C57      277.58/733      *LC* 78-52453      *ISBN* 0804210888

**Frazier, Edward Franklin, 1894-1962.**                                 • **1.2419**
The Negro church in America. New York, Schocken Books [1964, c1963] xii, 92 p. 23 cm. (Studies in sociology) 1. Afro-American churches I. T.
BR563.N4 F7      277.3      *LC* 62-19390

**Raboteau, Albert J.**                                                  **1.2420**
Slave religion: the 'invisible institution' in the Antebellum South / Albert J. Raboteau. — New York: Oxford University Press, 1978. xp. cm. Includes index. 1. Afro-Americans — Southern States — Religion. 2. Slaves — Southern States — Religion. 3. Southern States — Church history. I. T.
BR563.N4 R25      299/.6/0975      *LC* 78-7275      *ISBN* 0195024389

**Sernett, Milton C., 1942-.**                                           **1.2421**
Black religion and American evangelicalism: white Protestants, plantation missions, and the flowering of Negro Christianity, 1787–1865 / by Milton C. Sernett; with a foreword by Martin E. Marty. — Metuchen, N.J.: Scarecrow Press, 1975. 320 p.: ill.; 23 cm. — (ATLA monograph series; no. 7) A revision of the author's thesis, University of Delaware. Includes index. 1. Afro-Americans — Religion 2. Evangelicalism — Southern States. I. T.
BR563.N4 S47 1975      280/.4/0975      *LC* 75-4754      *ISBN* 081080803X

**Sobel, Mechal.**                                                       **1.2422**
Trabelin' on: the slave journey to an Afro–Baptist faith / Mechal Sobel. — Westport, Conn.: Greenwood Press, c1979. xxv, 454 p.: ill.; 25 cm. — (Contributions in Afro-American and African studies. no. 36 0069-9624) Includes indexes. 1. Afro-Americans — Religion 2. Afro-American Baptists — History. 3. Slavery in the United States. 4. Africa, West — Religion. I. T. II. Series.
BR563.N4 S64      286/.173      *LC* 77-84775      *ISBN* 0837198879

**Washington, Joseph R.**                                                • **1.2423**
Black religion; the Negro and Christianity in the United States [by] Joseph R. Washington, Jr. Boston, Beacon Press [1964] ix, 308 p. 22 cm. 1. Afro-Americans — Religion I. T. II. Title: Negro and Christianity in the United States.
BR563.N4 W3      277.3      *LC* 64-13529

**Williams, Melvin D., 1933-.**                                          **1.2424**
Community in a Black Pentecostal church; an anthropological study [by] Melvin D. Williams. [Pittsburgh] University of Pittsburgh Press [1974] xii, 202 p. 24 cm. 1. Afro-Americans — Religion 2. Pentecostal churches — Pennsylvania — Pittsburgh. 3. Afro-Americans — Pennsylvania — Pittsburgh I. T.
BR563.N4 W523      301.5/8      *LC* 74-5108      *ISBN* 0822932903

**Wilmore, Gayraud S.**                                                  **1.2425**
Black religion and Black radicalism, by Gayraud S. Wilmore. [1st ed.] Garden City, N.Y., Doubleday, 1972. xiii, 344 p. 22 cm. (The C. Eric Lincoln series on Black religion) 1. Afro-Americans — Religion I. T. II. Series.
BR563.N4 W53      291/.08996073 19      *LC* 75-180116

## BR600–730 Latin America

**Churches and politics in Latin America** / edited by Daniel H.         **1.2426**
Levine; pref. by John P. Harrison.
Beverly Hills: Sage Publications, c1980. 288 p.; 23 cm. (Sage focus editions. 14) 1. Catholic Church — Latin America — History — Addresses, essays, lectures. 2. Church and state — Latin America — Addresses, essays, lectures. 3. Christianity and politics — Addresses, essays, lectures. 4. Latin America — Politics and government — 1948- — Addresses, essays, lectures. 5. Latin America — Church history — Addresses, essays, lectures. I. Levine, Daniel H. II. Series.
BR600.C46      322/.1/098      *LC* 79-23827      *ISBN* 0803912986

## BR735–1050 Europe

**Monter, E. William.**                                                  **1.2427**
Ritual, myth, and magic in early modern Europe / William Monter. — Athens, Ohio: Ohio University Press, 1984, c1983. 184 p.; 23 cm. 1. Superstition — History. 2. Religious tolerance — Europe — History. 3. Europe — Church history I. T.
BR735.M66 1984      274/.06 19      *LC* 83-43136      *ISBN* 0821407627

## BR740–799 Great Britain. Ireland

**An Ecclesiastical history of England.**                                **1.2428**
New York: Oxford University PRess, 1961-1970. 7 v. in 8: facsim.; 25 cm. 1. Great Britain — Church history
BR743.2.E3      274.2      *LC* 61-65215

**Moorman, John R.H. (John Richard Humpidge), Bishop of**                • **1.2429**
**Ripon, 1905-.**
A history of the Church in England / by John R. H. Moorman. — [1st American ed.] New York: Morehouse-Gorham, 1954. 460 p.; 24 cm. 1. Great Britain — Church history I. T.
BR743.2.M6 1973      274.2      *LC* 73-181161      *ISBN* 0713613467

**Norman, Edward R.**                                                    **1.2430**
Church and society in England 1770–1970: a historical study / by E. R. Norman. Oxford: Clarendon Press, 1976. 507 p.; 24 cm. Includes index. 1. Sociology, Christian — England — History. I. T.
BR744.N67      261      *LC* 76-377182      *ISBN* 0198264356

**Bede, the Venerable, Saint, 673-735.**                                 **1.2431**
[Historia ecclesiastica gentis Anglorum English and Latin] Bede's ecclesiastical history of the English people; edited by Bertram Colgrave and R. A. B. Mynors. Oxford, Clarendon P., 1969. lxxvi, 618 p. 23 cm. (Oxford medieval texts.) Parallel Latin text and English translation with English notes. 1. England — Church history — Anglo Saxon period, 449-1066 I. Colgrave, Bertram. ed. II. Mynors, R. A. B. (Roger Aubrey Baskerville), Sir, 1903- ed. III. T. IV. Series.
BR746.B5 1969      274.2      *LC* 71-465643      *ISBN* 0198222025

**Edwards, David Lawrence.**                                **1.2432**
Christian England / David L. Edwards. — New York: Oxford University Press, 1980- < 1984 > . v. < 1, 3 > : ill.; 24 cm. 1. England — Church history I. T.
BR746.E38     274.2 19     *LC* 81-102729     *ISBN* 0195202295

**McNeill, John Thomas, 1885-.**                                **1.2433**
The Celtic churches; a history A.D. 200 to 1200 [by] John T. McNeill. — Chicago: University of Chicago Press, [1974] xiii, 289 p.; 24 cm. 1. Celtic Church — History. I. T.
BR748.M33     274     *LC* 73-84193     *ISBN* 0226560953

**Mayr-Harting, Henry.**                                • **1.2434**
The coming of Christianity to England. — New York: Schocken Books, [1972] 334 p.: illus.; 23 cm. 1. Church history — To 449. 2. Great Britain — Church history — Anglo Saxon period, 449-1066 I. T.
BR748.M38 1972     274.2     *LC* 74-169818

**Barlow, Frank.**                                **1.2435**
The English church, 1000–1066: a history of the later Anglo–Saxon church / Frank Barlow. — 2d ed. — London; New York: Longman, 1979. xii, 354 p.: maps; 24 cm. 1. England — Church history — Anglo Saxon period, 449-1066 I. T.
BR749.B3 1979     274.2     *LC* 78-40984     *ISBN* 0582490499

**Deanesly, Margaret, 1885-.**                                • **1.2436**
The pre–conquest church in England. New York Oxford University Press 1961. 374p. (An Ecclesiastical history of England, 1) 1. Celtic Church 2. Great Britain — Church history — Early period 3. Great Britain — Church history — Anglo-Saxon period I. T. II. Series.
BR749 D43

**Barlow, Frank.**                                **1.2437**
The English church, 1066–1154: a history of the Anglo–Norman church / Frank Barlow. — London; New York: Longman, 1979. xii, 340 p.: ill.; 24 cm. 1. England — Church history — Medieval period, 1066-1485 I. T.
BR750.B37     274.2     *LC* 78-40458     *ISBN* 0582502365

**Brooke, Zachary Nugent, 1883-.**                                • **1.2438**
The English church & the papacy, from the conquest to the reign of John, by Z. N. Brooke. Cambridge [Eng.] The University press, 1931. xii, 260 p. 23 cm. ([Birkbeck lectures, 1929-1931]) 1. Catholic Church in England. 2. Church and state in England. 3. Ecclesiastical law — Great Britain. 4. Great Britain — Church history — Medieval period, 1066-1485 I. T.
BR750.B76     274.2     *LC* 32-8453

**Cheney, C. R. (Christopher Robert), 1906-.**                                **1.2439**
English bishops' chanceries, 1100–1250. [Manchester] Manchester University Press 1950. 176p. (Publications of the Faculty of Arts of the University of Manchester, no. 3) 1. Chanceries, Diocesan — England 2. Diplomatics I. T.
BR750 C43

**Moorman, John Richard Humpidge.**                                • **1.2440**
Church life in England in the thirteenth century / by John R.H. Moorman. — Cambridge [Eng.]: The University Press, 1945. xxviii, 444 p., [6] leaves of plates: ill., facsims. 1. Great Britain — Church history — Medieval period, 1066-1485 I. T.
BR750 M6     BR750 M6.     274.2     *LC* 45-7788

**Knowles, David, 1896-.**                                • **1.2441**
Saints and scholars: twenty–five medieval portraits / by David Knowles. — London: Cambridge University Press, 1962. x, 207 p.: ill. 1. Saints — Great Britain. 2. Scholars — Great Britain. I. T.
BR754.A1 K57     *LC* 62-4142

**Cheney, C. R. (Christopher Robert), 1906-.**                                **1.2442**
Hubert Walter / by C.R. Cheney. — London: Nelson, 1967. x, 198 p.: facsims. (Leaders of religion) 1. Hubert Walter, Abp. of Canterbury, d.1205. I. T. II. Series.
BR754.H8 C45     *LC* 67-108884

**Gilbert, Alan D.**                                **1.2443**
Religion and society in industrial England: church, chapel, and social change, 1740–1914 / Alan D. Gilbert. — London; New York: Longman, 1976. ix, 251 p.; 22 cm. (Themes in British social history) (A Longman paper-back) Includes index. 1. Sociology, Christian — England. 2. England — Religion I. T.
BR755.G54     301.5/8/0942     *LC* 76-360904     *ISBN* 0582483220

**Walzer, Michael.**                                • **1.2444**
The revolution of the saints; a study in the origins of radical politics. — Cambridge: Harvard University Press, 1965. x, 334 p.; 24 cm. 1. Puritans 2. Calvinism 3. Christianity and politics — History. 4. Great Britain — Church history — Modern period, 1485- I. T.
BR756.W34     274.2     *LC* 65-22048

**Inglis, Kenneth Stanley.**                                • **1.2445**
Churches and the working classes in Victorian England. — London, Routledge and K. Paul [1963] vii, 350 p. 23 cm. — (Studies in social history) Bibliographical footnotes. 1. Gt. Brit. — Church history — 19th cent. 2. Church and social problems — Gt. Brit. 3. Sects — Gt. Brit. I. T.
BR759.I48     *LC* 63-23763

**Machin, G. I. T.**                                **1.2446**
Politics and the churches in Great Britain, 1832–1868 / G. I. T. Machin. — Oxford [Eng.]; New York: Clarendon Press, 1977. viii, 438 p.; 25 cm. Includes index. 1. Church and state — Great Britain — History. 2. Great Britain — Church history — 19th century I. T.
BR759.M26     322/.1/0941     *LC* 77-30296     *ISBN* 0198264364

**Ward, W. Reginald (William Reginald)**                                **1.2447**
Religion and society in England, 1790–1850 / W. R. Ward. — New York: Schocken Books, 1973,c1972. ix, 339 p.; 23 cm. 1. Sociology, Christian — England. 2. Dissenters, Religious — England 3. Great Britain — Church history — 19th century I. T.
BR759.W29 1973     274/.2     *LC* 72-85591     *ISBN* 0805234756

**McLeod, Hugh.**                                **1.2448**
Class and religion in the late Victorian city. — Hamden, Conn.: Archon Books, [1974] xii, 360 p.: illus.; 23 cm. 1. Sociology, Christian — England — London region. 2. London region, Eng. — Religious life and customs. I. T.
BR764.M23 1974b     301.5/8/09421     *LC* 74-13765     *ISBN* 0208014748

**Burleigh, John H. S.**                                • **1.2449**
A church history of Scotland. London, New York, Oxford University Press, 1960. 456 p. illus. 22 cm. 1. Scotland — Church history I. T.
BR782.B8     274.1     *LC* 60-50629

**Whyte, John Henry, 1928-.**                                **1.2450**
Church and state in modern Ireland, 1923–1979 / J.H. Whyte. — 2d ed. — Dublin: Gill and Macmillan; Totowa, N.J.: Barnes & Noble Books, 1980. xiv, 491 p.; 23 cm. Includes index. 1. Church and state in Ireland — History — 20th century. I. T.
BR793.W49 1980     322/.1/09417 19     *LC* 79-55700     *ISBN* 0064976386

**Watt, John A.**                                **1.2451**
The church in medieval Ireland [by] John Watt. — [Dublin]: Gill and Macmillan, [c1972] 232 p.: maps.; 19 cm. — (The Gill history of Ireland, 5) 1. Ireland — Church history — Medieval period, 600-1500 I. T. II. Series.
BR794.W353     282/.415     *LC* 74-173096     *ISBN* 0717105628

## BR840–1050 OTHER EUROPEAN COUNTRIES

**Garrett, Clarke, 1935-.**                                **1.2452**
Respectable folly: millenarians and the French Revolution in France and England / Clarke Garrett. — Baltimore: Johns Hopkins University Press, [1975] x, 237 p.; 23 cm. 1. Millennialism — France. 2. Millennialism — England. 3. France — History — Revolution. I. T.
BR845.G36     209/.44     *LC* 74-24378     *ISBN* 0801816181

**Barth, Karl, 1886-1968.**                                • **1.2453**
The German church conflict. [Translated by P. T. A. Parker]. — Richmond, John Knox Press [1965] 77 p. 22 cm. — (Ecumenical studies in history, no. 1) Translation of Karl Barth zum Kirchenkampf. Bibliographical footnotes. 1. Germany — Church history — 1933-1945 I. T. II. Series.
BR856.B2513     274.3     *LC* 65-15427

**Helmreich, Ernst Christian.**                                **1.2454**
The German churches under Hitler: background, struggle, and epilogue / Ernst Christian Helmreich. — Detroit: Wayne State University Press, 1979. 616 p.; 26 cm. Includes index. 1. Church and state — Germany — History — 20th century 2. Germany — Church history — 20th century I. T.
BR856.H443     261.7/0943     *LC* 78-17737     *ISBN* 0814316034

**International Scholars' Conference. 1st, Wayne State University,**     **1.2455**
**1970.**
The German church struggle and the Holocaust. Edited by Franklin H. Littell [and] Hubert G. Locke. — Detroit: Wayne State University Press, 1974. 328 p.; 24 cm. Sponsored by the Walker and Gertrude Cisler Library of the Grosberg Religious Center. 1. Church and state in Germany — 1933-1945 — Congresses. 2. Holocaust, Jewish (1939-1945) — Congresses. I. Littell, Franklin Hamlin. ed. II. Locke, Hubert G. ed. III. Walker and Gertrude Cisler Library. IV. T.
BR856.I57 1970     261.7/0943     *LC* 72-9352     *ISBN* 0814314929

**Ginzburg, Carlo.**                                **1.2456**
[Formaggio e i vermi. English] The cheese and the worms: the cosmos of a sixteenth–century miller / Carlo Ginzburg; translated by John and Anne Tedeschi. — Baltimore: Johns Hopkins University Press, 1980. xxvii, 177 p.:

ill.; 24 cm. Translation of Il formaggio e i vermi. 1. Scandella, Domenico, 1532-1601. 2. Heretics, Christian — Italy — Udine (Province) 3. Heresies, Christian — History — Modern period, 1500- 4. Peasantry — Italy — Udine (Province) 5. Udine (Italy: Province) — Religious life and customs. 6. Udine (Italy: Province) — Civilization. 7. Udine (Italy: Province) — Church history. I. T.
BR877.F74 G5613          273/.6 19          LC 79-3654          ISBN 0801823366

**Tschiżewskij, Dmitrij, 1894-.**                                                   **1.2457**
[Russische Geistesgeschichte. English] Russian intellectual history / Dmitrij Tschizewskij; translated by John C. Osborne; edited by Martin P. Rice. — Ann Arbor: Ardis, c1978. 283 p., [13] leaves of plates: ill.; 24 cm. Translation of th 1959-1961 ed. of Russische Geistesgeschichte. Includes index. 1. Russia — Religion. 2. Russia — Church history. 3. Russia — Intellectual life. I. Rice, Martin P. II. T.
BR932.C4513      001.2/0947      LC 78-110675      ISBN 0882332198

**Lane, Christel.**                                                                 **1.2458**
Christian religion in the Soviet Union: a sociological study / by Christel Lane. — Albany: State University of New York Press, 1978. 256 p.: map (on lining papers); 24 cm. Includes index. 1. Sociology, Christian — Russia. 2. Sects — Russia. I. T.
BR933.L36        301.5/8        LC 77-801        ISBN 0873953274

**Simon, Gerhard.**                                                                 **1.2459**
[Kirchen in Russland. English] Church, state, and opposition in the U.S.S.R. Translated by Kathleen Matchett in collaboration with the Centre for the Study of Religion and Communism. Berkeley, University of California Press [1974] x, 248 p. 23 cm. Translation of Die Kirchen in Russland. 1. Church and state in Russia. I. T.
BR933.S5413      322/.1/0947      LC 73-87754      ISBN 0520026128

**Alexander, Stella.**                                                              **1.2460**
Church and state in Yugoslavia since 1945 / Stella Alexander. — Cambridge; New York: Cambridge University Press, 1979. xxi, 351 p.: maps; 23 cm. (Soviet and East European studies.) Includes index. 1. Church and state — Yugoslavia 2. Communism and Christianity — Yugoslavia. 3. Yugoslavia — Church history. I. T. II. Series.
BR966.3.A4       261.7/09497       LC 77-88668       ISBN 0521219426

## BR1060–1355 ASIA

**Betts, Robert Brenton.**                                                          **1.2461**
Christians in the Arab East: a political study / by Robert Brenton Betts. — Rev. ed. — Atlanta: John Knox Press, c1978. xvii, 318 p.; 21 cm. Includes index. 1. Christians — Arab countries 2. Arab countries — Politics and government I. T.
BR1067.A7 B47 1978      209/.17/4927      LC 78-8674      ISBN 0804207968

**Haddad, Robert M., 1930-.**                                                    • **1.2462**
Syrian Christians in Muslim society; an interpretation, by Robert M. Haddad. — Princeton, N.J.: Princeton University Press, 1970. viii, 118 p.; 23 cm. — (Princeton studies on the Near East.) 1. Christianity — Syria. 2. Christianity and other religions — Islam 3. Islam — Relations — Christianity I. T. II. Series.
BR1110.H33      301.45/28/095691      LC 75-113002      ISBN 0691030863

**Anderson, Gerald H.**                                                          • **1.2463**
Studies in Philippine church history. Edited by Gerald H. Anderson. Ithaca [N.Y.] Cornell University Press [1969] xiv, 421 p. 24 cm. 1. Philippines — Church history — Addresses, essays, lectures. I. T.
BR1260.A5        279.14        LC 69-18208        ISBN 0801404851

**Boxer, C. R. (Charles Ralph), 1904-.**                                         • **1.2464**
The Christian century in Japan, 1549–1650 / by C. R. Boxer. — Berkeley: University of California Press, 1974. xx, $35 p., 8 leaves of plates: ill., facsims., maps (1 fold. inserted), ports. — (California library reprint series.) Reprint of the 1967 ed. 1. Catholic Church — Japan. 2. Japan — Church history 3. Japan — History — To 1868 I. T. II. Series.
BR1305.B6 1974        275.2        ISBN 0520027027

**Picken, Stuart D. B.**                                                            **1.2465**
Christianity and Japan: meeting, conflict, hope / Stuart D.B. Picken; introduction by Edwin O. Reischauer. — Tokyo; New York: Kodansha International; New York, N.Y.: Distributed in the U.S. by Kodansha International/USA through Harper & Row, c1983. 80 p.: ill. (some col.), col. maps; 31 cm. Maps on lining papers. 1. Christianity — Japan. I. T.
BR1305.P52 1983      275.2 19      LC 82-48787      ISBN 0870115898

## BR1360–1470 AFRICA

**African Christianity: patterns of religious continuity / edited by**            **1.2466**
**George Bond, Walton Johnson, Sheila S. Walker.**
New York: Academic Press, c1979. xvi, 175 p.; 24 cm. — (Studies in anthropology) 1. Christianity — Africa — Addresses, essays, lectures. 2. Christian sects — Africa — Addresses, essays, lectures. 3. Africa — Church history — Addresses, essays, lectures. I. Bond, George C. II. Johnson, Walton R. III. Walker, Sheila S.
BR1360.A526        289.9        LC 79-51668        ISBN 0121134504

**Christianity in independent Africa / edited by Edward Fasholé–**                **1.2467**
**Luke ... [et al.].**
London: R. Collings; Bloomington, IN: Indiana University Press, c1978. 630 p.; 24 cm. 1. Christianity — Africa — Congresses. 2. Christianity — 20th century — Congresses. I. Fasholé-Luke, Edward W.
BR1360.C48        209/.6        LC 77-26351        ISBN 0253375061

**Groves, Charles Pelham.**                                                      • **1.2468**
The planting of Christianity in Africa / by C. P. Groves. — London: Lutterworth Press [1964] 4 v.: maps; 23 cm. First published 1948-[58] reprinted 1964. 1. Missions — Africa. 2. Africa — Church history. I. T.
BR1360.G884        LC 65-7593 cd

**Hastings, Adrian.**                                                               **1.2469**
African Christianity / Adrian Hastings. — New York: Seabury Press, [1977] c1976. vi, 105 p.; 22 cm. 'A Crossroad book.' Includes index. 1. Christianity — Africa. I. T.
BR1360.H3 1977        209/.6        LC 77-1890        ISBN 0816403368

**Sundkler, Bengt Gustaf Malcolm, 1909-.**                                       • **1.2470**
Bantu prophets in South Africa. — 2d ed. — London, New York, Published for the International African Institute by the Oxford University Press, 1961. 381 p. illus. 23 cm. Includes bibliography. 1. Zulus — Church history. 2. Sects — Africa, South. I. T.
BR1367.Z8S8 1961        276.8        LC 61-65161

**Taddesse Tamrat.**                                                                **1.2471**
Church and state in Ethiopia, 1270–1527 / by Taddesse Tamrat. — Oxford, 1972. xv, 327 p., [6] leaves: ill., maps, plan; 23 cm. — (Oxford studies in African affairs.) Based on research done for the author's thesis, University of London. Includes index. 1. Church and state — Ethiopia 2. Ethiopia — Church history. 3. Ethiopia — History — To 1490 4. Ethiopia — History — 1490-1889 I. T. II. Series.
BR1370.T35        276.3        LC 76-381840        ISBN 0198216718

**Welbourn, Frederick Burkewood.**                                                  **1.2472**
A place to feel at home: a study of two independent churches in Western Kenya [by] F. B. Welbourn [and] B. A. Ogot. London, Nairobi [etc.] Oxford U.P., 1966. xv, 157 p. front. (map) 4 plates (incl. ports). diagrs. 22 1/2 cm. 1. African Israel Church Nineveh. 2. Church of Christ in Africa. 3. Kenya — Church history. I. Ogot, Bethwell A. joint author. II. T.
BR1443.K4 W4        276.762        LC 66-77111

**Lātūkefu, Sione.**                                                                **1.2473**
Church and state in Tonga: the Wesleyan Methodist missionaries and political development, 1822–1875. — Honolulu: University Press of Hawaii, [1974] xvii, 302 p.: maps.; 23 cm. A revision of the author's thesis, Australian National University. 1. Methodist Church — Missions 2. Church and state — Tonga 3. Missions — Tonga. 4. Tonga — Constitutional law. I. T.
BR1495.T66 L37 1974      322/.1/099612      LC 73-91461      ISBN 0824803221

# BR1600–1617 Persecution. Toleration. Liberalism

**Frend, W. H. C.**                                                              • **1.2474**
Martyrdom and persecution in the early church; a study of a conflict from the Maccabees to Donatus, by W. H. C. Frend. Garden City, N.Y., Anchor Books, 1967 [c1965] xviii, 577 p. 18 cm. 1. Persecution — History — Early church, ca. 30-600 I. T.
BR1604.2.F7 1967        272/.1        LC 66-24325

**Foxe, John, 1516-1587.**                                                       • **1.2475**
Christian martyrs of the world: from the celebrated work by John Foxe, and other eminent authorities. — Newly revised and illustrated. — Chicago: Moody Press, [1963?] vi,590 p.: ill.; 23 cm. — 1. Martyrs 2. Persecution 3. Chruch history. I. T.
BR1607.Fx        LC 63-22993

**Lecler, Joseph.**      • **1.2476**
Toleration and the Reformation. Translated by T. L. Westow. — New York, Association Press [1960] 2 v. ; 25 cm. Translation of Histoire de la tolérance au siécle de la Réforme. Bibliography: v. 2, p. 507-535. I. T.
BR1610.L433     *LC* 60-12723 rev

# BR1640–1653 Evangelicalism. Pietism

**Essig, James D.**      **1.2477**
The bonds of wickedness: American evangelicals against slavery, 1770–1808 / James D. Essig. — Philadelphia: Temple University Press, 1982. xiv, 208 p. ; 22 cm. 1. Evangelicalism — United States. 2. Slavery — United States I. T.
BR1642.U5 E85 1982    241/.675 19    *LC* 82-10670    *ISBN* 0877222827

**The New Christian right: mobilization and legitimation / edited**    **1.2478**
**by Robert C. Liebman, Robert Wuthnow; with contributions by James L. Guth ... [et al.].**
Hawthorne, N.Y.: Aldine Pub. Co., c1983. viii, 256 p. ; 24 cm. Includes index. 1. Moral Majority, Inc — Addresses, essays, lectures. 2. Evangelicalism — United States — Addresses, essays, lectures. 3. Christianity and politics — Addresses, essays, lectures. I. Liebman, Robert C. II. Wuthnow, Robert. III. Guth, James L.
BR1642.U5 N48 1983    322/.1/0973 19    *LC* 83-13443    *ISBN* 0202303071

**Varieties of southern evangelicalism / edited by David Edwin**    **1.2479**
**Harrell, Jr.; foreword by Martin E. Marty.**
Macon, Ga.: Mercer University Press, c1981. xii, 114 p. ; 24 cm. 'Essays ... written by the participants in the Fourth Annual Hugo Black Symposium held at the University of Alabama in Birmingham in 1979'—Pref. 1. Evangelicalism — Southern States — Congresses. 2. Southern States — Religion — Congresses. I. Harrell, David Edwin. II. Hugo Black Symposium in American History. (4th: 1979: University of Alabama in Birmingham)
BR1642.U5 V37    280/.4/0975 19    *LC* 81-11312    *ISBN* 0865540152

**Presence, power, praise: documents on the charismatic renewal /**    **1.2480**
**edited by Kilian McDonnell.**
Collegeville, Minn.: Liturgical Press, 1980. 3 v.; 24 cm. 1. Pentecostalism — Addresses, essays, lectures. I. McDonnell, Kilian.
BR1644.P73    269    *LC* 79-26080    *ISBN* 0814611265

# BR1690–1725 Biography

**Vitae Patrum.**      • **1.2481**
The desert fathers; translations from the Latin with an introduction by Helen Waddell. New York, H. Holt [c1936] xi, 297 p. 21 cm. Translated from Rosweyde's second revised edition of the Vitae patrum, published in 1628. cf. Pref. 1. Saints 2. Hermits I. Waddell, Helen, 1889-1965. tr. II. T.
BR1705.A2V525 1936a    *LC* 36-23900

**Campenhausen, Hans, Freiherr von, 1903-.**      • **1.2482**
The fathers of the Greek Church / Hans von Campenhausen; translated by Stanley Godman. — New York: Pantheon, 1959. 170 p. Original title: Griechische Kirchenväter. 1. Fathers of the church, Greek. I. T.
BR1705.C273    *LC* 59-8588

**Campenhausen, Hans, Freiherr von, 1903-.**      • **1.2483**
[Lateinische Kirchenväter. English] The fathers of the Latin Church. Translated by Manfred Hoffman. Stanford, Calif., Stanford University Press [1969, c1964] vii, 328 p. 23 cm. Translation of Lateinische Kirchenväter. 1. Fathers of the Church, Latin. I. T.
BR1706.C313 1969    281/.3/0922 B    *LC* 76-75260

**Battenhouse, Roy Wesley, 1912- ed.**      • **1.2484**
A companion to the study of St. Augustine. — New York, Oxford University Press, 1955. 425 p. 22 cm. 1. Augustinus, Aurelius, Saint, Bp. of Hippo. I. T.
BR1720.A9B33    281.4    *LC* 55-6253

**Brown, Peter Robert Lamont.**      • **1.2485**
Augustine of Hippo; a biography, by Peter Brown. — Berkeley: University of California Press, 1967. 463 p.; 23 cm. 1. Augustine, Saint, Bishop of Hippo. I. T.
BR1720.A9 B7 1967b    270.2/0924 B    *LC* 67-13137

**O'Donnell, James Joseph, 1950-.**      **1.2486**
Cassiodorus / James J. O'Donnell. — Berkeley: University of California Press, c1979. xvi, 303 p.; 23 cm. Includes index. 1. Cassiodorus, Senator, ca. 487-ca. 580. 2. Christian biography — Italy. I. T.
BR1720.C4 O36    271/.0092/4 B    *LC* 77-93470    *ISBN* 0520036468

**Clemens, Titus Ilavius, Alexandrinus.**      • **1.2487**
The exhortation to the Greeks, the rich man's salvation, and the fragment of an address entitled To the newly baptized / Clement of Alexandria; with an English translation by G.W. Butterworth. — London: William Heinemann, 1919. xx, 409 p.: ill.; 17 cm. (Loeb classical library.) Includes index and bibliographical footnotes. 1. Clement, of Alexandria, Saint, ca. 150-ca. 215. I. Butterworth, George William, 1879- II. T. III. Title: The Rich man's salvation. IV. Title: To the newly baptized. V. Title: Clement of Alexandria. VI. Series.
BR1720.C6 E9    *LC* 19-16236

**A new Eusebius: documents illustrative of the history of the**    **1.2488**
**church to A.D. 337 / edited by J. Stevenson; based upon the collection edited by the late B. J. Kidd.**
London: S.P.C.K., 1957. xix, 427 p.: maps; 22 cm. (S.P.C.K. large paperbacks; 1) '319 extracts in translation.' 1. Church history — Primitive and early church, ca. 30-600 — Sources 2. Christian literature, Early I. Eusebius, of Caesarea, Bishop of Caesarea, ca. 260-ca. 340. II. Stevenson, James, 1901-
BR1720.E8 Sx    *ISBN* 0281008027

**Kelly, J. N. D. (John Norman Davidson)**      **1.2489**
Jerome: his life, writings, and controversies / J. N. D. Kelly. — 1st U.S. ed. — New York: Harper & Row, c1975. xi, 353 p.: map (on lining papers); 24 cm. 1. Jerome, Saint, d. 419 or 20. I. T.
BR1720.J5 K44 1975b    270.2/092/4 B    *LC* 75-36732    *ISBN* 0060643331

**Warfield, Benjamin Breckinridge, 1851-1921.**      • **1.2490**
Studies in Tertullian and Augustine. Westport, Conn., Greenwood Press [1970] v, 412 p. 23 cm. Reprint of the 1930 ed. 1. Tertullian, ca. 160-ca. 230. 2. Augustine, Saint, Bishop of Hippo — Addresses, essays, lectures. 3. Trinity — History of doctrines — Early church, ca. 30-600. 4. Knowledge, Theory of (Religion) 5. Pelagianism I. T.
BR1720.T3 W3 1970    230.1/3/0922    *LC* 73-109980    *ISBN* 0837144906

# BS BIBLE

# BS1–400 Texts and Versions

**Bible. English. Layman's parallel. 1973.**      **1.2491**
The layman's parallel Bible: King James version, Modern Language Bible, Living Bible, Revised Standard version. — Grand Rapids, Mich.: Zondervan Bible Publishers, [c1973] xiii, 3037 p.; 25 cm. I. Bible. English. Authorized. 1973 II. Bible. English. Modern language. 1973. III. Bible. English. Living Bible. 1973. IV. Bible. English. Revised standard. 1973. V. T.
BS125 1973    220.52    *LC* 73-15435

**Mozley, James Frederic, 1887-.**      • **1.2492**
Coverdale and his Bibles / by J.F. Mozley. — London: Lutterworth Press, c1953. x, 359 p.: facsim. 'Coverdale's works': p. 324-335. 1. Coverdale, Miles, 1488-1568. 2. Bible English — Versions — Coverdale. 3. Bible. English — History I. T.
BS146.M6    *LC* 53-4419

**Bible. English. Authorized. 1963.**      • **1.2493**
The Holy Bible. The Authorized or King James version of 1611 now reprinted with the Apocrypha. With reproductions of 105 of the sixteenth–century woodcuts of Bernard Salomon. London, Nonesuch Press; New York, Random House, 1963. 3 v. illus. 25 cm. I. Salomon, Bernard, 16th cent., illus. II. T.
BS185 1963.L6    220.52    *LC* 63-24703

**Bridges, Ronald.**      • **1.2494**
The Bible word book: concerning obsolete or archaic words in the King James version of the Bible / by Ronald Bridges and Luther A. Weigle. — New York: Nelson, 1960. vii, 422 p.; 22 cm. 1. Bible. English — Versions — Authorized 2. Bible English — Versions — Revised standard. 3. Bible. English — Glossaries, vocabularies, etc. 4. English language — Words — History. I. Weigle, Luther A. (Luther Allan), 1880- II. T.
BS186.B7    *LC* 60-6749

**Opfell, Olga S.**  1.2495
The King James Bible translators / Olga S. Opfell. — Jefferson, N.C.: McFarland, 1982. v, 173 p.; 24 cm. Includes index. 1. Bible. English — Versions — Authorized I. T.
BS186.O63 1982     220.5/2038 19     *LC* 81-20885     *ISBN* 0899500412

**Bible. English. American Revised. 1901.**  • 1.2496
The Holy Bible: containing the Old and New Testaments, translated out of the original tongues, being the version set forth A.D. 1611; compared with the most ancient authorities and revised A.D. 1881–1885 / newly edited by the American Revision Committee 1901. — Standard ed. — New York: T. Nelson, [c1901]. 2 v. in 1: 12 maps.; 21 cm. New Testament, v.2, has title: 'The New Covenant, commonly called the New Testament of Our Lord and Saviour Jesus Christ; translated out of the Greek; being the version set forth A.D. 1611 compared with the most ancient authorities and revised A.D. 1881. Newly edited by the New Testament members of the American Revision Committee A.D. 1900.' Special t.p. only. I. T.
BS190.A1 1901.N4     *LC* 01-20361

**Bible. English. Revised standard. 1973.**  1.2497
The new Oxford annotated Bible with the Apocrypha. Rev. standard version, containing the 2d ed. of the New Testament. Edited by Herbert G. May [and] Bruce M. Metzger. New York, Oxford University Press, 1973. xxviii, 1564, xxii, 298 p. illus. 23 cm. At head of title: An ecumenical study Bible. I. May, Herbert Gordon, 1904- ed. II. Metzger, Bruce Manning. ed. III. T.
BS191.A1 1973.N43     220.5/204     *LC* 72-96564

**Bible. English. New English. 1970.**  • 1.2498
The New English Bible with the Apocrypha. — London: Oxford U.P., 1970. xxi, 336 p.; 21 cm. Includes the 2nd ed. of the New English Bible New Testament. 'A completely new translation [by] the Joint Committee on the New Translation of the Bible.' I. Joint Committee on the New Translation of the Bible. II. T.
BS192.A1 1970.L6     220.52     *LC* 75-498997     *ISBN* 019180004X

**Bible. English. 1966. Jerusalem Bible.**  • 1.2499
The Jerusalem Bible. General editor: Alexander Jones. Garden City, N.Y., Doubleday, 1966. xvi, 1547, 498 p. maps (part col.) 25 cm. 'The principal collaborators in translation and literary revision were: Joseph Leo Alston [and others]' I. Jones, Alexander, 1906- ed. II. T.
BS195.J4 1966     220.5204     *LC* 66-24278

**Bible. English. Smith-Goodspeed. 1939.**  • 1.2500
The complete Bible: an American translation. The Old Testament translated by J. M. Powis Smith and a group of scholars. The Apocrypha and the New Testament translated by Edgar J. Goodspeed. Chicago, University of Chicago Press [1939] 883, 202, 246 p. 20 cm. The Old Testament: an American translation by A. R. Gordon, T. J. Meek, J. M. P. Smith, Leroy Waterman; edited by J. M. P. Smith; revised by T. J. Meek. I. Smith, J. M. Powis (John Merlin Powis), 1866-1932. ed. II. Goodspeed, Edgar Johnson, 1871-1962. tr. III. Meek, Theophile James, 1881-1966, ed. IV. T.
BS 195 S6     *LC* 39-28964

**Bible. English. Today's English. 1979.**  1.2501
Good news Bible: with Deuterocanonicals/Apocrypha: The Bible in Today's English version. — New York: American Bible Society, 1979. 1041, 217, 59, 413 p.: ill., maps. Maps on lining papers. I. American Bible Society. II. Bible. O.T. Apocrypha. English. 1979. III. T.
BS195 T63 1979

# BS410–680 Works About the Bible

## BS410–440 Reference

**Ellison, John W. (John William), 1920-.**  • 1.2502
Nelson's complete concordance of the Revised standard version of the Bible. Compiled under the supervision of John W. Ellison. New York, Nelsoo [c1957] 2157 p. 28 cm. 1. Bible — Concordances, English — Revised Standard I. Thomas Nelson & Sons. II. T.
BS425.E4 1957     220.2     *LC* 57-7122

**Strong, James, 1822-1894.**  • 1.2503
The exhaustive concordance of the Bible: showing every word of the text of the common English version of the canonical books, and every occurrence of each word in regular order; together with a comparative concordance of the Authorized and Revised versions, including the American variations; also brief dictionaries of the Hebrew and Greek words of the original, with references to

the English words. New York: Abingdon-Cokesbury Press, [1947] 1340, 262, 126, 79 p.; 30 cm. Published in 1976 under title: Strong's exhaustive concordance. 1. Bible — Concordances, English 2. Hebrew language — Dictionaries — English. 3. Greek language, Biblical — Dictionaries — English. I. T.
BS425.S8 1947     220.2     *LC* 47-7147

**Young, Robert, 1822-1888.**  • 1.2504  [Rf.] BS 425 Y75
Analytical concordance to the Bible on an entirely new plan containing about 311,000 references, subdivided under the Hebrew and Greek originals, with the literal meaning and pronunciation of each; designed for the simplest reader of the English Bible. Also index lexicons to the Old and New Testaments, being a guide to parallel passages and a complete list of Scripture proper names showing their modern pronunciation. — 22d American ed., rev. by Wm. B. Stevenson. To which is added a supplement entitled Recent discoveries in Bible lands, by William F. Albright. — New York: Funk & Wagnalls, [1955] ix, 1090, 93, 23, 51 p.; 29 cm. 'Recent discoveries in Bible lands' has special t.p. On cover: Authorized edition. 1. Bible — Concordances, English 2. Bible — Antiquities 3. Hebrew language — Dictionaries — English. 4. Greek language, Biblical — Dictionaries — English. 5. Palestine — Antiquities I. Albright, William Foxwell, 1891-1971. II. T. III. Title: Recent discoveries in Bible lands.
BS425.Y7 1955     220.2     *LC* 55-5338

**Gehman, Henry Snyder, 1888-.**  • 1.2505
The new Westminster dictionary of the Bible. Edited by Henry Snyder Gehman. — Philadelphia: Westminster Press, [1970] xi, 1027, 4 p.: illus., maps (incl. 6 col.); 25 cm. — (Westminster aids to the study of the Scriptures) Based on A dictionary of the Bible, by J. D. Davis. 1. Bible — Dictionaries I. Davis, John D., 1854-1926. A dictionary of the Bible. II. T. III. Series.
BS440.G4     220/.3     *LC* 69-10000     *ISBN* 0664212778

**Harper's Bible dictionary / general editor, Paul J. Achtemeier;**  1.2506
**associate editors, Roger S. Boraas ... [et al.] with the Society of Biblical Literature.**
1st ed. — San Francisco: Harper & Row, c1985. xxii, 1178, [16] p., [8] p. of plates: ill. (some col.), col. maps; 24 cm. Includes index. 1. Bible — Dictionaries I. Achtemeier, Paul J. II. Harper & Row. III. Society of Biblical Literature. IV. Title: Bible dictionary.
BS440.H237 1985     220.3 19     *LC* 85-42767     *ISBN* 0060698632

**Hastings, James, 1852-1922.**  • 1.2507
Dictionary of the Bible / edited by James Hastings. — Rev. ed. / by Frederick C. Grant and H.H.Rowley. — New York: Scribner, 1963. xxi, 1059 p. ill., col. maps. 1. Bible — Dictionaries I. Grant, Frederick C. (Frederick Clifton), 1891-1974. II. Rowley, Harold Henry, 1890- III. T.
BS440.H5 1963     220.3     *LC* 62-21697

**The Interpreter's dictionary of the Bible; an illustrated**  • 1.2508
**encyclopedia identifying and explaining all proper names and significant terms and subjects in the Holy Scriptures, including the Aprocrypha, with attention to archaeological discoveries and researches into the life and faith of ancient times. [Editorial board: George Arthur Buttrick, dictionary editor, and others].**
New York: Abingdon Press, [1962] 4 v.: illus (part col.) maps (part col.); 27 cm. 1. Bible — Dictionaries I. Buttrick, George Arthur, 1892- ed.
BS440.I63     220.3     *LC* 62-9387

## BS445–481 Introductions

**The Cambridge history of the Bible.**  • 1.2509
Cambridge, University Press, 1963-70. [v. 1, 1970; v. 3, 1963] 3 v. illus., facsims. 24 cm. 1. Bible — History 2. Bible — Versions I. Ackroyd, Peter R. ed. II. Evans, Christopher Francis. ed. III. Lampe, G. W. H. (Geoffrey William Hugo), 1912-1980. ed. IV. Greenslade, S. L. (Stanley Lawrence), 1905- ed.
BS445.C26     220/.09     *LC* 63-24435

**Kenyon, Frederic G. (Frederic George), Sir, 1863-1952.**  • 1.2510  — O —
Our Bible and the ancient manuscripts. Rev. by A. W. Adams. Introd. by G. R. Driver. New York, Harper [1958] 352 p. ill., facsims. 23 cm. 1. Bible — History 2. Bible — Versions 3. Bible — Manuscripts I. T.
BS445.K46 1958a     *LC* 58-7098

**Robinson, H. Wheeler (Henry Wheeler), 1872-1945. ed.**  • 1.2511
The Bible in its ancient and English versions. Edited by H. Wheeler Robinson. Westport, Conn., Greenwood Press [1970] vii, 337 p. 23 cm. Reprint of the 1940 ed. 1. Bible — History 2. Bible — Versions 3. Bible. English — Versions I. T.
BS445.R66 1970     220.4     *LC* 76-109832     *ISBN* 0837143233

**Bruce, F. F. (Frederick Fyvie), 1910-.**  • 1.2512
The English Bible; a history of translations from the earliest English versions to the New English Bible, by F. F. Bruce. [New and rev. ed.] New York, Oxford University Press, 1970. xiv, 262 p. illus., facsims., ports. 23 cm. Third ed. (1978)

published under title: The history of the Bible in English. 1. Bible. English — Versions I. T.
BS455.B74 1970    220.5/2/009    *LC* 74-15923

**MacGregor, Geddes.**    • **1.2513**
A literary history of the Bible; from the Middle Ages to the present day. Nashville, Abingdon Press [1968] 400 p. 25 cm. 1. Bible. English — History I. T.
BS455.M32    220.5/09    *LC* 68-11477

**Campenhausen, Hans, Freiherr von, 1903-.**    **1.2514**
[Entstehung der christlichen Bibel. English] The formation of the Christian Bible, by Hans von Campenhausen. Translated by J. A. Baker. Philadelphia, Fortress Press [1972] xiv, 342 p. 23 cm. Translation of Die Entstehung der christlichen Bibel. 1. Bible — Canon I. T.
BS465.C313 1972    220.1/2    *LC* 73-171495    *ISBN* 0800602234

**Goodspeed, Edgar Johnson, 1871-1962.**    • **1.2515**
The story of the Bible, by Edgar J. Goodspeed. — Chicago, Ill.: The University of Chicago press, [c1936] xvi, 187, iii, 150 p.; 20 cm. 'The New Testament' has special half-title and separate paging. Previously published as the author's 'The story of the Old Testament' (Chicago, 1934) and his 'The story of the New Testament' (Chicago, 1916) 1. Bible — Introductions I. T.
BS475.G65    220.6    *LC* 36-21666

**Soggin, J. Alberto.**    **1.2516**
[Introduzione all'Antico Testamento. English] Introduction to the Old Testament, from its origins to the closing of the Alexandrian canon / J. Alberto Soggin; [translated by John Bowden from the Italian]. — Philadelphia: Westminster Press, c1976. xxxii, 510 p.; 23 cm. — (Old Testament library.) Translation of the 2d rev. and updated ed. of Introduzione all'Antico Testamento. 1. Bible. O.T — Introductions. I. T. II. Series.
BS475.2.S613    221/.6/6    *LC* 76-20650    *ISBN* 0664213391

**Krentz, Edgar.**    **1.2517**
The historical–critical method / by Edgar Krentz. — Philadelphia: Fortress Press, c1975. vi, 88 p.; 22 cm. (Guides to Biblical scholarship) 1. Bible — Hermeneutics I. T.
BS476.K73    220.6/3    *LC* 74-26345    *ISBN* 0800604601

**Ricoeur, Paul.**    **1.2518**
Essays on Biblical interpretation / Paul Ricoeur; edited with an introd. by Lewis S. Mudge. — Philadelphia: Fortress Press, 1980. ix, 182 p.; 22 cm. Essays translated from French and published in English between 1974 and 1979. 1. Bible — Hermeneutics — Addresses, essays, lectures. I. Mudge, Lewis Seymour. II. T.
BS476.R52    220.6/01    *LC* 80-8052    *ISBN* 0800614070

**Robinson, James McConkey, 1924- ed.**    • **1.2519**
The new hermeneutic, edited by James M. Robinson [and] John B. Cobb, Jr. — [1st ed.]. — New York, Harper & Row [1964] xii, 243 p. 22 cm. — (Newfrontiers in theology; discussions among continental and American theologians, v. 2) 1. Bible — Hermeneutics 2. Theology 3. Theology, Doctrinal — Hist. — 20th cent. I. Cobb, John B. joint ed. II. T.
BS476.R6    220.601    *LC* 64-14380

**Thiselton, Anthony C.**    **1.2520**
The two horizons: New Testament hermeneutics and philosophical description with special reference to Heidegger, Bultmann, Gadamer, and Wittgenstein / by Anthony C. Thiselton; with a foreword by J. B. Torrance. — 1st American ed. — Grand Rapids: W. B. Eerdmans Pub. Co., 1980. xx, 484 p.; 24 cm. Includes indexes. 1. Heidegger, Martin, 1889-1976. 2. Bultmann, Rudolf Karl, 1884-1976. 3. Gadamer, Hans Georg, 1900- 4. Wittgenstein, Ludwig, 1889-1951. 5. Bible. N.T — Hermeneutics. 6. Hermeneutics I. T.
BS476.T46 1980    225.6/01    *LC* 79-14387    *ISBN* 0802835201

**Daniélou, Jean.**    • **1.2521**
From shadows to reality: studies in the Biblical typology of the Fathers / by Jean Danielou; [translation by Wulstan Hibberd]. — Westminster, Md.: Newman Press, [c1960] 296 p.; 23 cm. Translation of Sacramentum futuri. 1. Bible. O.T. Hexateuch — Hermeneutics 2. Bible — Criticism, interpretation, etc. — History 3. Typology (Theology) I. T.
BS478.D3 1960    221.6    *LC* 60-14811

**Burtchaell, James Tunstead.**    • **1.2522**
Catholic theories of Biblical inspiration since 1810: a review and critique. London, Cambridge U.P., 1969. viii, 342 p. 23 cm. 1. Bible — Inspiration — History of doctrines I. T.
BS480.B79    220.1/3/09    *LC* 77-77284    *ISBN* 0521074851

## BS482–498 COMMENTARIES

**Calvin, Jean, 1509-1564.**    • **1.2523**
Calvin: commentaries. Newly translated and edited by Joseph Haroutunian, in collaboration with Louise Pettibone Smith. — Philadelphia, Westminster Press [1958] 414 p. 24 cm. — (The Library of Christian classics. v. 23) Cover title: Calvin: commentaries and letters. 1. Bible — Commentaries I. Haroutunian, Joseph, 1904- ed. and tr. II. T. III. Series.
BS485.C333 1958    220.7    *LC* 58-5060

**Black, Matthew. ed.**    • **1.2524**
Peake's commentary on the Bible. General editor and New Testament editor: Matthew Black. Old Testament editor: H. H. Rowley. — London; New York: T. Nelson, 1962. xv, 1126, 4 p.: 16 col. maps.; 27 cm. 'An entirely new work.' 'Based on the text of the Revised standard-version.' 1. Bible — Commentaries I. Rowley, Harold Henry, 1890- ed. II. Peake, Arthur Samuel, 1865-1929, ed. A commentary on the Bible. III. T.
BS491.B57    220.7    *LC* 62-6297

**Brown, Raymond Edward. comp.**    • **1.2525**
The Jerome Biblical commentary, edited by Raymond E. Brown, Joseph A. Fitzmyer [and] Roland E. Murphy. With a foreword by Augustin Cardinal Bea. — Englewood Cliffs, N.J.: Prentice-Hall, [1968] 2 v. in 1.: illus., geneal. table, maps (1 fold.); 28 cm. 1. Bible — Commentaries I. Fitzmyer, Joseph A. joint comp. II. Murphy, Roland Edmund, 1917- joint comp. III. T.
BS491.2.B7    220.7    *LC* 68-9140

**The Interpreter's Bible: the Holy Scriptures in the King James**    • **1.2526**
**and Revised standard versions with general articles and introduction, exegesis, exposition for each book of the Bible. [Editorial board: George Arthur Buttrick, commentary editor, and others]**
New York, Abingdon-Cokesbury Press [1951-57, v. 1, 1952] 12 v. col. plates, maps. 27 cm. 'How to use the Interpreter's Bible [by] George Arthur Buttrick.' (16 p.) inserted in v. 8. 1. Bible — Commentaries I. Buttrick, George Arthur, 1892- ed. II. Bible. English. 1951. Authorized. III. Bible. English. 1951. Revised standard.
BS491.2.I55    220.7    *LC* 51-12276

**The Interpreter's one volume commentary on the Bible: introd.**    • **1.2527**
**and commentary for each book of the Bible including the Apocrypha, with general articles. Edited by Charles M. Laymon.**
Nashville, Abingdon Press [1971] xiv, 1386 p. illus., maps (16 col.) 27 cm. Rev. ed. published as: Interpreter's concise commentary. c1983- 1. Bible — Commentaries I. Laymon, Charles M. ed.
BS491.2.I57    220.7    *LC* 71-144392    *ISBN* 0687192994

## BS500–534 CRITICISM AND INTERPRETATION

**Reventlow, Henning, Graf.**    **1.2528**
[Bibelautorität und Geist der Moderne. English] The authority of the Bible and the rise of the modern world / Henning Graf Reventlow. — 1st Fortress Press ed. — Philadelphia: Fortress Press, 1985. xx, 668 p.; 24 cm. Translation of: Bibelautorität und Geist der Moderne. 1. Bible — Criticism, interpretation, etc. — England — History. 2. England — Intellectual life I. T.
BS500.R4713 1985    220.6/0942 19    *LC* 83-48921    *ISBN* 0800602889

**Rogers, Jack Bartlett.**    **1.2529**
The authority and interpretation of the Bible: an historical approach / by Jack B. Rogers & Donald K. McKim. — 1st ed. — San Francisco: Harper & Row, c1979. xxiv, 484 p.; 24 cm. 1. Bible — Criticism, interpretation, etc. — History 2. Bible — Evidences, authority, etc. — History. 3. Theology, Reformed Church — Doctrines — History. I. McKim, Donald K. joint author. II. T.
BS500.R63 1979    220.6/09    *LC* 78-20584    *ISBN* 006066696X

**Smalley, Beryl.**    **1.2530**
The study of the Bible in the Middle Ages. [2d ed.] Oxford Blackwell 1952. 406p. 1. Bible — Criticism, interpretation, etc. — History I. T.
BS500 S5 1952

**Arnold, Matthew, 1822-1888.**    • **1.2531**
Literature and dogma. Edited, abridged, and with an introd. by James C. Livingston. — New York: Ungar, [1970] xxix, 162 p.; 20 cm. — (Milestones of thought in the history of ideas) 1. Bible — Criticism, interpretation, etc. I. Livingston, James C., 1930- ed. II. T. III. Series.
BS511.A7 1970    201    *LC* 79-107032    *ISBN* 0804460116

**Koch, Klaus, 1926-.**    • **1.2532**
[Was ist Formgeschichte? English] The growth of the Biblical tradition; the form–critical method. Translated from the 2d German ed. by S. M. Cupitt. New

York, Scribner [1969] xv, 233 p. 23 cm. (Scribner studies in biblical interpretation) Translation of Was ist Formgeschichte? 1. Bible — Criticism, Form I. T.
BS511.2.K613        220.6/7        LC 68-17350

**Miranda, José Porfirio.**                                       **1.2533**
[Marx y la Biblia. English] Marx and the Bible: a critique of the philosophy of oppression. Translated by John Eagleson. Maryknoll, N.Y., Orbis Books [1974] xxi, 338 p. 23 cm. 1. Bible — Criticism, interpretation, etc. 2. Communism and religion I. T.
BS511.2.M5713        220.6/6        LC 73-89053        *ISBN* 0883443066 *ISBN* 0883443074

# BS535–580 THE BIBLE AS LITERATURE. BIBLE BIOGRAPHY

**Berlin, Adele.**                                       **1.2534**
Poetics and interpretation of biblical narrative / Adele Berlin. — Sheffield: Almond Press, 1983. 180 p.: ill.; 23 cm. (Bible and literature series. 0260-4493; 9) Includes indexes. 1. Bible as literature I. T. II. Series.
BS535.B39 1983        220.6/6 19        LC 83-221266        *ISBN* 0907459234

**Ryken, Leland.**                                       **1.2535**
How to read the Bible as literature / Leland Ryken. — Grand Rapids, Mich.: Academie books, c1984. 208 p.; 21 cm. 1. Bible — Criticism, interpretation, etc. 2. Bible as literature I. T.
BS535.R89 1984        220.6/6 19        LC 84-19667        *ISBN* 0310390214

**Caird, G. B. (George Bradford), 1917-.**                                       **1.2536**
The language and imagery of the Bible / G. B. Caird. — Philadelphia: Westminster Press, c1980. viii, 280 p.; 23 cm. 1. Bible — Language, style I. T.
BS537.C33        220.6 19        LC 79-27586        *ISBN* 0664213782

**Fowler, David C., 1921-.**                                       **1.2537**
The Bible in early English literature / by David C. Fowler. — Seattle: University of Washington Press, c1976. x, 263 p.; 24 cm. Includes index. 1. Higden, Ranulf, d. 1364. Polychronicon. 2. Bible — Criticism, interpretation, etc. — History — Middle Ages, 600-1500 3. Bible. English — Versions 4. Cursor mundi. 5. Bible — Influence — History. 6. Bible in literature I. T.
BS538.7.F68        820/.9/001 19        LC 76-7786        *ISBN* 0295954388

**Barr, James.**                                       **1.2538**
The scope and authority of the Bible / by James Barr. — Philadelphia: Westminster Press, c1980. xi, 150 p.; 21 cm. Includes index. 1. Bible — Criticism, interpretation, etc. — Addresses, essays, lectures. I. T.
BS540.B323        220.6 19        LC 80-21394        *ISBN* 0664243614

**Mollenkott, Virginia R.**                                       **1.2539**
The divine feminine: the biblical imagery of God as female / Virginia Ramey Mollenkott. — New York, NY: Crossroad Pub. Co., 1983. 119 p.; 22 cm. 1. Femininity of God — Biblical teaching. I. T.
BS544.M64 1983        220.6/4 19        LC 82-23542        *ISBN* 0824505654

**Digges, Mary Laurentia, 1910-.**                                       **1.2540**
Adam's haunted sons / Laurentia Digges; with a foreword by Barnabas Ahern. — New York: Macmillan, 1966. xvi, 302 p. 1. Bible. O.T. — Biography I. T.
BS571 D5        LC 66-21162

**Samuel, Maurice, 1895-1972.**                                       **1.2541**
Certain people of the Book. [1st ed.] New York, Knopf, 1955. 363 p. 22 cm. 1. Bible. O.T. — Biography I. T.
BS572.S3        LC 55-8887

**Freud, Sigmund, 1856-1939.**                                       **● 1.2542**
Moses and monotheism / translated from the German by Katherine Jones. — New York: Vintage Books, 1955 [c1939] viii, 178, iv p.; 19 cm. (A Vintage book, K-14) Translation of Der Mann Moses und die monotheistische Religion. Bibliographical footnotes. 1. Moses (Biblical leader) 2. Monotheism 3. Judaism — Relations — Egyptian. 4. Psychology, Religious I. T.
BS580.M6Fx        221.92        LC 55-152

# BS620–680 OTHER TOPICS

**Cornfeld, Gaalyahu, 1902-.**                                       **1.2543**
Archaeology of the Bible: book by book / Gaalyah Cornfeld; David Noel Freedman, consulting editor. — 1st U.S. ed. — New York: Harper & Row,

c1976. 334, [9] p.: ill., maps, plans. 1. Bible — Antiquities 2. Bible — History of Biblical events I. T.
BS621.C6415 1976        BS621 C672 1976.        220.93        LC 76-9979
    *ISBN* 0060615842

**Freedman, David Noel, 1922- comp.**                                       **● 1.2544**
The Biblical archaeologist reader. Edited by David Noel Freedman and G. Ernest Wright. [1st ed.] Garden City, N.Y., Anchor Books, 1961-70. 3 v. illus., maps, plans. 19 cm. Vols. 2-3 edited by E.F. Campbell, Jr., and D.N. Freedman. 1. Bible — Antiquities — Addresses, essays, lectures. I. Wright, George Ernest, 1909-1974. joint comp. II. Campbell, Edward Fay. joint comp. III. Biblical archaeologist. IV. T.
BS621.F73        220.93        LC 61-7649

**Kenyon, Kathleen Mary, Dame.**                                       **1.2545**
The Bible and recent archaeology / Kathleen M. Kenyon. — Atlanta: John Knox Press, c1978. 105 p.: ill.; 24 cm. Includes index. 1. Bible — Antiquities — Addresses, essays, lectures. I. T.
BS621.K4 1978        220.9/5        LC 78-4089        *ISBN* 0804200106

**Paul, Shalom M.**                                       **1.2546**
Biblical archaeology / edited by Shalom M. Paul and William G. Dever. — New York: Quadrangle/New York Times Book Co., [1975] c1974. xiii, 290 p.: ill.; 25 cm. — (The New York times library of Jewish knowledge) Includes index. 1. Bible — Antiquities I. Dever, William G. joint author. II. T.
BS621.P38 1975        221.9/3        LC 73-77034        *ISBN* 081290351X

**Wright, George Ernest, 1909-1974.**                                       **● 1.2547**
Biblical archaeology. — [New and rev. ed.]. — Philadelphia: Westminster Press, [1962] 291 p.: illus.; 29 cm. 1. Bible — Antiquities I. T.
BS621.W72 1962        220.93        LC 63-906

**Gaster, Theodor Herze, 1906-.**                                       **● 1.2548**
Myth, legend, and custom in the Old Testament; a comparative study with chapters from Sir James G. Frazer's Folklore in the Old Testament. — [1st ed.]. — New York: Harper & Row, [1969] lv, 899 p.; 24 cm. 1. Bible. O.T — Criticism, interpretation, etc. 2. Jews — Folklore 3. Mythology I. Frazer, James George, Sir, 1854-1941. Folk-lore in the Old Testament. II. T.
BS625.G3        221.6        LC 69-17018

**Aharoni, Yohanan, 1919-1976.**                                       **● 1.2549**
[Erets-Yiśra'el bi-tekufat ha-Mikra. English] The land of the Bible: a historical geography / by Yohanan Aharoni; translated from the Hebrew by A. F. Rainey. — Philadelphia: Westminster Press [1967] xiv, 409 p.: maps; 25 cm. Translation of Erets-Yiśra'el bi-tekufat ha-Mikra. 1. Bible. O.T — Geography. 2. Jews — History — To 70 A.D. I. T.
BS630.A4213 1967        221.9/1 19        LC 67-11273

**Baly, Denis.**                                       **1.2550**
The geography of the Bible. New and rev. ed. New York, Harper & Row [1974] xv, 288 p. illus. 24 cm. 1. Bible — Geography I. T.
BS630.B34 1974        220.9/1        LC 73-6340        *ISBN* 0060603712

**Oxford Bible atlas** / edited by Herbert G. May; with the    **1.2551**
**assistance of G.N.S. Hunt; in consultation with R.W. Hamilton.**
3rd ed. / rev. for the 3rd ed. by John Day. — New York: Oxford University Press, 1984. 144 p.: ill., col. maps; 26 cm. 1. Bible — Geography 2. Bible — Geography — Maps I. May, Herbert Gordon, 1904- II. Hunt, G. N. S. III. Hamilton, R. W. IV. Day, John, 1948-
BS630.O96 1984        220.9/1 19        LC 84-10052        *ISBN* 0191434523

**Wright, George Ernest, 1909-1974.**                                       **● 1.2552**
The Westminster historical atlas to the Bible, edited by George Ernest Wright and Floyd Vivian Filson. With an introductory article by William Foxwell Albright. — Rev. ed. — Philadelphia: Westminster Press, [1956] 130 p.: illus., maps.; 37 cm. — (Westminster aids to the study of the Scriptures) 1. Bible — Geography 2. Bible — Geography — Maps I. Filson, Floyd Vivian, 1896- joint author. II. T. III. Series.
BS630.W7 1956        220.91        LC 56-9123

**Finegan, Jack, 1908-.**                                       **● 1.2553**
Handbook of Biblical chronology; principles of time reckoning in the ancient world and problems of chronology in the Bible. — Princeton, N. J., Princeton University Press, 1964. xxvi, 338 p. 24 cm. Includes bibliographical references. 1. Bible — Chronology I. T.
BS637.2.F5        220.9        LC 63-18642

**Collins, John Joseph, 1946-.**                                       **1.2554**
The apocalyptic imagination: an introduction to the Jewish matrix of Christianity / John J. Collins. — New York: Crossroad, 1984. viii, 280 p.; 24 cm. Includes index. 1. Apocalyptic literature — History and criticism. I. T.
BS646.C65 1984        229/.913 19        LC 84-17581        *ISBN* 0824506235

**Rowland, Christopher, 1947-.**                                       **1.2555**
The open heaven: a study of apocalyptic in Judaism and early Christianity / Christopher Rowland. — New York: Crossroad, 1982. xiii, 562 p.; 24 cm.

Includes indexes. 1. Apocalyptic literature 2. Rabbinical literature — History and criticism. I. T.
BS646.R58 1982     220 19     *LC* 82-7409     *ISBN* 0824504550

**Buber, Martin, 1878-1965.**     **1.2556**
[Ben 'am le-artso. English] On Zion; the history of an idea. With a new foreword by Nahum N. Glatzer. [Translated from the German by Stanley Godman] New York, Schocken Books [1973] xxii, 165 p. 23 cm. Translation of Ben 'am le-artso. 1. Jews — Restoration — History of doctrines 2. Zionism — History. I. T.
BS649.J5 B7713 1973     956.94/001     *LC* 72-88533

**Zohary, Michael, 1898-.**     **1.2557**
Plants of the Bible: a complete handbook to all the plants with 200 full–color plates taken in the natural habitat / Michael Zohary. — London; New York: Cambridge University Press, 1982. 223 p.: ill. (some col.); 25 cm. Includes index. 1. Plants in the Bible I. T.
BS665.Z64 1982     220.8/582 19     *LC* 82-4535     *ISBN* 0521249260

**Ellul, Jacques.**     • **1.2558**
[Sans feu ni lieu. English] The meaning of the city. Introd. by John Wilkinson. Translated by Dennis Pardee. Grand Rapids, Eerdmans [1970] xix, 209 p. 23 cm. Translation of Sans feu ni lieu. 1. Cities and towns — Biblical teaching I. T.
BS680.C5 E413     301.3/64     *LC* 70-103446

**Walzer, Michael.**     **1.2559**
Exodus and revolution / Michael Walzer. — New York: Basic Books, c1985. xii, 177 p.; 22 cm. Includes index. 1. Exodus, The — Typology 2. Revolutions — Religious aspects — Christianity I. T.
BS680.E9 W35 1985     222/.12064 19     *LC* 84-45306     *ISBN* 0465021646

**Feminist interpretation of the Bible / Letty M. Russell, editor.**     **1.2560**
1st ed. — Philadelphia: Westminster Press, c1985. 166 p.; 23 cm. 1. Bible and feminism — Addresses, essays, lectures. I. Russell, Letty M.
BS680.W7 F46 1985     220.6/088042 19     *LC* 84-17342     *ISBN* 0664246397

**Swidler, Leonard J.**     **1.2561**
Biblical affirmations of woman / by Leonard Swidler. — 1st ed. — Philadelphia: Westminster Press, c1979. 382 p.; 21 cm. Includes indexes. 1. Woman (Theology) — Biblical teaching. 2. Women in the Bible 3. Woman (Theology) — History of doctrines. I. T.
BS680.W7 S97     261.8/34/12     *LC* 79-18886     *ISBN* 0664213774

# BS701–1830 Old Testament

## BS701–1055 Texts and Versions

**Bible. O.T. English. Jewish Publication Society. 1985.**     **1.2562**
[Tanakh] = Tanakh: a new translation of the Holy Scriptures according to the traditional Hebrew text. — 1st ed. — Philadelphia: Jewish Publication Society, 1985. xxvi, 1624 p.; 24 cm. I. Jewish Publication Society. II. T.
BS896.A1 P45 1985     221.5/2 19     *LC* 85-10006     *ISBN* 0827602529

## BS1110–1199 Works About the Old Testament

**Society for Old Testament Study.**     • **1.2563**
The Old Testament and modern study; a generation of discovery and research. Essays by members of the Society, edited by H.H. Rowley. Oxford Clarendon Press 1951. 405p. 1. Bible. O.T. — Criticism, interpretation, etc. 2. Bible. O.T — Addresses, essays, lectures I. Rowley, Harold Henry, 1890- ed. II. T.
BS1110 S6

**Eissfeldt, Otto, 1887-.**     • **1.2564**
The Old Testament; an introduction, including the Apocrypha and Pseudepigrapha, and also the works of similar type from Qumran; the history of the formation of the Old Testament. / Translated by Peter R.Ackroyd. New York: Harper and Row, [1965] xxiv,861p.bibl. Translation from the 3d German ed.of a work first published in Tübingen in 1934 under title:Einleitungin dasAlte Testament. 1. Bible. O.T. — Introductions. 2. Bible. O.T — Apocrypha and Apocryphal books — Introductions. I. T.
BS1140.E583 1965     *LC* 65-15399

**Childs, Brevard S.**     **1.2565**
Introduction to the Old Testament as Scripture / Brevard S. Childs. — 1st American ed. — Philadelphia: Fortress Press, 1979. 688 p.; 24 cm. 1. Bible. O.T — Introductions. I. T.
BS1140.2.C48 1979     221.6     *LC* 78-14665     *ISBN* 0800605322

**Kuntz, John Kenneth.**     **1.2566**
The people of ancient Israel; an introduction to Old Testament literature, history, and thought [by] J. Kenneth Kuntz. — New York: Harper & Row, [1974] xv, 559 p.: illus.; 24 cm. 1. Bible. O.T — Introductions. 2. Bible. O.T — History of Biblical events. I. T.
BS1140.2.K86     221.9/5     *LC* 74-8042     *ISBN* 0060438223

**The Hebrew Bible and its modern interpreters / edited by**     **1.2567**
**Douglas A. Knight and Gene M. Tucker.**
Philadelphia, Pa.: Fortress Press; Chico, Calif.: Scholars Press, c1985. xxvii, 516 p.: maps. — (Society of Biblical Literature. Centennial publications.) (The Bible and its modern interpreters; 1) 1. Bible. O.T — Criticism, interpretation, etc. — History — 20th century — Addresses, essays, lectures. I. Knight, Douglas A. II. Tucker, Gene M. III. Series.
BS1160.H43 1985     221.6/09/04 19     *LC* 84-25936     *ISBN* 080060721X

**Alter, Robert.**     **1.2568**
The art of Biblical narrative / Robert Alter. — New York: Basic Books, c1981. xii, 195 p.; 24 cm. 1. Bible. O.T — Language, Style. 2. Narration in the Bible I. T.
BS1171.2.A45     221.4/4 19     *LC* 80-68958     *ISBN* 0465004245

**Fishbane, Michael A.**     **1.2569**
Text and texture: close readings of selected Biblical texts / Michael Fishbane. — New York: Schocken Books, 1979. xiv, 154 p.; 21 cm. 1. Bible. O.T — Criticism, interpretation, etc. I. T.
BS1171.2.F57     221.6     *LC* 79-14083     *ISBN* 0805237240

**Fromm, Erich, 1900-.**     **1.2570**
You shall be as gods: a radical interpretation of the Old Testament and its tradition. — [1st ed.] New York: Holt, Rinehart and Winston [1966] 240 p.; 22 cm. 1. Bible. O.T. — Criticism, interpretation, etc. I. T.
BS1171.2.F7 1966     221.6     *LC* 66-22066

**Trible, Phyllis.**     **1.2571**
God and the rhetoric of sexuality / Phyllis Trible. — Philadelphia: Fortress Press, c1978. xvii, 206 p.; 22 cm. (Overtures to biblical theology.) 1. Bible. O.T. — Criticism, interpretation, etc. 2. Bible. O.T — Hermeneutics. 3. God — Biblical teaching 4. Image of God — Biblical teaching. 5. Sex — Religious aspects — Christianity — Biblical teaching. I. T. II. Series.
BS1171.2.T74     221.6     *LC* 77-78647     *ISBN* 0800604644

**Ancient Near Eastern texts relating to the Old Testament /**     • **1.2572**
**edited by James B. Pritchard; translators and annotators, W.F.**
**Albright ... [et al.].**
3d ed. with supplement. Princeton, N.J.: Princeton University Press, 1969. xxiii, 710 p.; 29 cm. Includes indexes. 1. Bible. O.T — History of contemporary events, etc. 2. Oriental literature — Translations into English. I. Pritchard, James Bennett, 1909-
BS1180.P822     *LC* 78-76499     *ISBN* 0691035032

**Pritchard, James Bennett, 1909-.**     • **1.2573**
The ancient Near East; supplementary texts and pictures relating to the Old Testament, edited by James B. Pritchard. Princeton, N.J., Princeton University Press, 1969. viii, 274 p. illus., plans. 29 cm. Contains supplementary materials for the author's The ancient Near East in pictures and Ancient Near Eastern texts. 1. Bible. O.T — Antiquities. 2. Bible. O.T — History of contemporary events. 3. Middle Eastern literature — Translations into English. 4. English literature — Translations from Near Eastern languages. 5. Middle East — Antiquities. I. T.
BS1180.P826     221.95     *LC* 78-76500

**Pritchard, James Bennett, 1909-.**     • **1.2574**
The ancient Near East in pictures, relating to the Old Testament. 2nd ed. with supplement. Princeton, N.J. Princeton University Press 1969. 396p. 1. Bible. O.T — Antiquities 2. Near East — Antiquities I. T.
BS1180.P8x

**Jacobs, Louis. comp.**     **1.2575**
Jewish biblical exegesis. Front. by Eleanor Schick. New York, Behrman House [1973] xii, 196 p. front. 24 cm. (The Chain of tradition series, v. 4) 1. Bible. O.T — Criticism, interpretation, etc., Jewish 2. Bible. O.T — Commentaries. I. T.
BS1186.J3     221.6/6     *LC* 73-1487     *ISBN* 0874412250

**Tradition and interpretation / essays by members of the Society**     **1.2576**
**for Old Testament Study; edited by G. W. Anderson.**
Oxford: Clarendon Press; New York: Oxford University Press, 1979. xxi, 462 p.; 23 cm. Successor to the Society's The Old Testament and modern study

published in 1951. 1. Bible. O.T — Criticism, interpretation, etc. — Addresses, essays, lectures. I. Anderson, George Wishart. II. Society for Old Testament Study.
BS1192.T68      221      *LC* 78-40252      *ISBN* 0198263155

**Eichrodt, Walther, 1890-.** • **1.2577**
Theology of the Old Testament. Translated by J. A. Baker. — Philadelphia, Westminster Press [1961-1967] 2 v. 23 cm. — (Old Testament library.) 1. Bible. O.T — Theology. I. T. II. Series.
BS1192.5.E353      221.6      *LC* 61-11867

**Hasel, Gerhard F.** • **1.2578**
Old Testament theology: basic issues in the current debate, by Gerhard F. Hasel. — Grand Rapids, Mich.: Eerdmans, [1972] 103 p.; 21 cm. 1. Bible. O.T — Theology. I. T.
BS1192.5.H37      221.6/6      *LC* 72-77181      *ISBN* 0802814786

**Rad, Gerhard von, 1901-1971.** • **1.2579**
[Theologie des Alten Testaments. English] Old Testament theology. Translated by D. M. G. Stalker. New York, Harper, 1962-[65] 2 v. 24 cm. Vol. 2 published by Harper & Row. 1. Bible. O.T — Theology. I. T.
BS1192.5.R3132      221.6      *LC* 62-7306

**Anderson, Bernhard W.** • **1.2580**
Understanding the Old Testament [by] Bernhard W. Anderson. 2d ed. Englewood Cliffs, N.J., Prentice-Hall [1966] xxi, 586 p. illus., maps (part col.) col. plates. 24 cm. 1. Jews — History — To 70 A.D. 2. Bible. O.T — History of Biblical events. I. T.
BS1197.A63 1966      221.95      *LC* 66-11713

**Herrmann, Siegfried, 1926-.** **1.2581**
[Geschichte Israels in alttestamentlicher Zeit. English] A history of Israel in Old Testament times / Siegfried Herrmann; translated by John Bowden from the German. — 1st American ed. — Philadelphia: Fortress Press, 1975. xiii, 364 p.: maps; 23 cm. Translation of Geschichte Israels in alttestamentlicher Zeit. Includes index. 1. Bible. O.T — History of Biblical events. 2. Jews — History — To 70 A.D. I. T.
BS1197.H3913 1975      221.9/5      *LC* 74-24918      *ISBN* 0800604059

**Blenkinsopp, Joseph, 1927-.** **1.2582**
A history of prophecy in Israel / Joseph Blenkinsopp. — 1st ed. — Philadelphia: Westminster Press, c1983. 287 p.; 23 cm. 1. Bible. O.T — Prophecies — History. 2. Prophets I. T.
BS1198.B53 1983      224/.06 19      *LC* 83-10178      *ISBN* 0664244793

**Brueggemann, Walter.** **1.2583**
The prophetic imagination / Walter Brueggemann. — Philadelphia: Fortress Press, 1980. 127 p.; 22 cm. 1. Prophets 2. Pastoral theology I. T.
BS1198.B84      221.1/5      *LC* 78-54546      *ISBN* 0800613376

**Koch, Klaus, 1926-.** **1.2584**
[Profeten. English] The prophets / Klaus Koch. — 1st Fortress Press ed. — Philadelphia: Fortress Press, 1983-1984, c1982. 2 v.: ill.; 22 cm. Translation of: Die Profeten. 1. Prophets I. T.
BS1198.K6313 1983      224/.06 19      *LC* 79-8894      *ISBN* 0800616480

**Wilson, Robert R., 1942-.** **1.2585**
Prophecy and society in ancient Israel / Robert R. Wilson. — Philadelphia: Fortress Press, c1980. xii, 322 p.; 24 cm. Includes indexes. 1. Bible. O.T. Prophets — Criticism, interpretation, etc. 2. Prophets 3. Sociology, Biblical I. T.
BS1198.W55      224/.06      *LC* 78-14677      *ISBN* 0800605373

**Wolff, Hans Walter.** **1.2586**
Anthropology of the Old Testament / Hans Walter Wolff; [translated by Margaret Kohl from the German]. — Philadelphia: Fortress Press, c1974. x, 293 p.; 23 cm. Rev. translation of Anthropologie des Alten Testaments. Includes indexes. 1. Bible. O.T. — Criticism, interpretation, etc. 2. Man (Theology) — Biblical teaching. I. T.
BS1199.M2 W6413 1974      233      *LC* 74-21591      *ISBN* 0800602986

**Gottwald, Norman K. (Norman Karol), 1926-.** **1.2587**
The tribes of Yahweh: a sociology of the religion of liberated Israel, 1250–1050 B.C.E. / Norman K. Gottwald. — Maryknoll, N.Y.: Orbis Books, c1979. xxv, 916 p.; 26 cm. 1. Jews — History — 1200-953 B.C. 2. Bible. O.T — Theology. 3. Sociology, Biblical 4. Twelve tribes of Israel I. T.
BS1199.S6 G67      301.5/8      *LC* 78-24333      *ISBN* 0883444984

# BS1200–1830 SPECIAL BOOKS

## BS1201–1375 Historical Books

**Bible. O.T. Pentateuch. English. 1963. Jewish Publication Society.** • **1.2588**
The Torah, [Torah (romanized form)] the five books of Moses. — [1st ed., 2d impression]. — Philadelphia: Jewish Publication Society of America, [1963, c1962] 393 p.; 22 cm. 'A new translation of the Holy Scriptures according to the Masoretic text. First section.' I. Jewish Publication Society of America. II. T.
BS1223 1963      222/.1/052      *LC* 62-12948

**Noth, Martin, 1902-1968.** **1.2589**
[Überlieferungsgeschichte des Pentateuch. English] A history of Pentateuchal traditions. Translated with an introd. by Bernhard W. Anderson. Englewood Cliffs, N.J., Prentice-Hall [1972] xxxv, 296 p. port. 24 cm. Translation of the 1st ed. of Überlieferungsgeschichte des Pentateuch. 1. Bible. O.T. Pentateuch — Criticism, interpretation, etc. I. T.
BS1225.2.N613      222/.106 19      *LC* 73-132171      *ISBN* 0133912353

**Westermann, Claus.** **1.2590**
[Genesis 37-50. English] Genesis 37–50: a commentary / Claus Westermann; translated by John J. Scullion. — Minneapolis: Augsburg Pub. House, 1986. p. cm. Includes indexes. 1. Bible. O.T. Genesis XXXVII-L — Commentaries. I. T.
BS1235.3.W3713 1986      222/.11077 19      *LC* 85-26802      *ISBN* 0806621974

**Westermann, Claus.** **1.2591**
[Genesis 1-11. English] Genesis 1–11: a commentary / Claus Westermann; translated by John J. Scullion. — Minneapolis: Augsburg Pub. House, 1984. xii, 636 p.; 24 cm. 1. Bible. O.T. Genesis I-XI — Commentaries. I. T. II. Title: Genesis one to eleven.
BS1235.3.W4413 1984      222/.1107 19      *LC* 82-72655      *ISBN* 0806619627

**Westermann, Claus.** **1.2592**
[Genesis 12-36. English] Genesis 12–36: a commentary / Claus Westermann; translated by John J. Scullion. — Minneapolis: Augsburg Pub. House, 1985. 604 p.; 25 cm. 1. Bible. O.T. Genesis XII-XXXVI — Commentaries. I. T.
BS1235.3.W44313 1985      222/.11077 19      *LC* 85-7449      *ISBN* 0806621729

**Childs, Brevard S.** **1.2593**
The book of Exodus; a critical, theological commentary [by] Brevard S. Childs. Philadelphia, Westminster Press [1974] xxv, 659 p. 23 cm. (Old Testament library.) 1. Bible. O.T. Exodus — Commentaries. I. Bible. O.T. Exodus. English. Childs. 1974. II. T. III. Series.
BS1245.3.C45      222/.12/077      *LC* 73-23120      *ISBN* 0664209858

**Bible. O.T. Leviticus. English. Revised standard. 1965.** • **1.2594**
Leviticus; a commentary /[by] Martin Noth. Philadelphia, Westminster Press [1965] 208 p. 23 cm. (Old Testament library.) 'Translated by J. S. Anderson from ... Das dritte Buch Mose, Leviticus.' 1. Bible. O.T. Leviticus — Commentaries. 2. Bible. O.T. Leviticus. English. Revised standard. 1965. I. Noth, Martin, 1902-1968. II. T. III. Series.
BS1255.3.N613      222.13077      *LC* 65-11498 rev

**Noth, Martin, 1902-1968.** • **1.2595**
[Vierte Buch Mose, Numeri. English] Numbers: a commentary. [Translated by James D. Martin from the German.] Philadelphia, Westminster Press [1968] x, 258 p. 24 cm. (Old Testament library.) Translation of Das vierte Buch Mose, Numeri. 1. Bible. O.T. Numbers — Commentaries. I. Bible. O.T. Numbers. English. Revised standard. 1968. II. T. III. Series.
BS1265.3.N613 1968      222/.14/077      *LC* 69-12129      *ISBN* 066420841X

**Rad, Gerhard von, 1901-1971.** • **1.2596**
[Bible. O.T. Deuteronomy. English. 1966. Revised standard] Deuteronomy; a commentary. [Translated by Dorothea Barton] Philadelphia, Westminster Press [1966] 211 p. 23 cm. (Old Testament library.) Translation of Das fünfte Buch Mose: Deuteronomium, which was first published in 1964 as v. 8 of Das Alte Testament deutsch, edited by V. Herntrich and A. Weiser. 1. Bible. O.T. Deuteronomy — Commentaries. I. Bible. O.T. Deuteronomy. English. 1966. Revised standard. II. T. III. Series.
BS1275.3.R3 1966      222.1507      *LC* 66-23088

**Soggin, J. Alberto.** **1.2597**
[Livre de Josué. English] Joshua: a commentary [by] J. Alberto Soggin. Philadelphia, Westminster Press [1972] xvii, 245 p. 23 cm. (Old Testament library.) Translation of Le livre de Josué. 1. Bible. O.T. Joshua — Commentaries. I. Bible. O.T. Joshua. English. 1972. II. T. III. Series.
BS1295.3.S613      222/.2/077      *LC* 72-76954      *ISBN* 0664209386

**Soggin, J. Alberto.**     **1.2598**
Judges, a commentary / J. Alberto Soggin; [translated by John Bowden from the Italian original]. — Philadelphia: Westminster Press, c1981. xx, 305 p.; 23 cm. — (Old Testament library.) 1. Bible. O.T. Judges — Commentaries. I. T. II. Series.
BS1305.3.S6313     222/.32077 19     *LC* 81-7600     *ISBN* 0664213685

**Bible. O.T. Hagiographa. English. Jewish Publication Society.**     **1.2599**
**1982.**
The Writings = [Ketuvim] = Kethubim: a new translation of the Holy Scriptures according to the Masoretic text: third section. — Philadelphia: Jewish Publication Society of America, c1982. vii, 624 p.; 22 cm. I. Jewish Publication Society of America. II. T. III. Title: Ketuvim. IV. Title: Kethubim.
BS1308.A3 J48 1982     223/.052 19     *LC* 81-85106     *ISBN* 0827602022

BS
1325.3
HS7

**Hertzberg, Hans Wilhelm, 1895-.**     • **1.2600**
[Samuelbücher. English] I & II Samuel, a commentary. [Translated by J. S. Bowden] Philadelphia, Westminster Press [c1964] 416 p. 23 cm. (Old Testament library.) 1. Bible. O.T. Samuel — Commentaries. I. Bible. O.T. Samuel. English. 1964. II. T. III. Series.
BS1325.3.H413     222.407     *LC* 65-10074

**Gray, John, 1913-.**     • **1.2601**
I & II Kings; a commentary. 2d, fully rev. ed. Philadelphia, Westminster Press [1970] xviii, 802 p. maps. 23 cm. (Old Testament library.) 1. Bible. O.T. Kings — Commentaries. I. Bible. O.T. Kings. English. 1970. II. T. III. Series.
BS1335.3.G7 1970b     222/.5/077     *LC* 73-134271     *ISBN* 0664208983

**Bible. O.T. Chronicles. English. New English. 1976.**     **1.2602**
The first and second books of the Chronicles: commentary / by R. J. Coggins. — Cambridge, Eng.; New York: Cambridge University Press, 1976. x, 314 p.; 20 cm. — (The Cambridge Bible commentary on the New English Bible) Includes index. 1. Bible. O.T. Chronicles — Commentaries. I. Coggins, R. J., 1929- II. T.
BS1345.3.C63     222/.6/077     *LC* 75-17117     *ISBN* 0521086477.
*ISBN* 0521097584 pbk

**Bible. O.T. Ezra. English. New English. 1976.**     **1.2603**
The books of Ezra and Nehemiah. Commentary by R. J. Coggins. Cambridge [Eng.] Cambridge University Press, 1976. 150 p. 20 cm. (The Cambridge Bible commentary, New English Bible) 1. Bible. O.T. Ezra — Commentaries. 2. Bible. O.T. Nehemiah — Commentaries. I. Coggins, R. J., 1929- II. Bible. O.T. Nehemiah. English. New English. 1976. III. T. IV. Series.
BS 1353 C617 1976     *LC* 75-26278     *ISBN* 0521086485

# BS1401–1490 Poetical Books. Psalms. Proverbs

**Robinson, Theodore Henry, 1881-.**     • **1.2604**
The poetry of the Old Testament. London, Duckworth [1947] 231 p. 19 cm. (Studies in theology) 1. Bible. O.T. Poetical books — Introductions. 2. Hebrew poetry — History and criticism. I. T. II. Series.
BS1405.R55     223     *LC* 48-10111

**Alter, Robert.**     **1.2605**
The art of Biblical poetry / Robert Alter. — New York: Basic Books, c1985. xii, 228 p.; 24 cm. Includes indexes. 1. Bible. O.T — Language, style. 2. Hebrew poetry, Biblical — History and criticism. I. T.
BS1405.2.A48 1985     809/.93522144 19     *LC* 85-47550     *ISBN* 046500430X

**Habel, Norman C.**     **1.2606**
The Book of Job: a commentary / Norman C. Habel. — Philadelphia: Westminster Press, c1985. 586 p.; 23 cm. (Old Testament library.) 1. Bible. O.T. Job — Commentaries. I. Bible. O.T. Job. English. 1985. II. T. III. Series.
BS1415.3.H29 1985     223/.107 19     *LC* 84-21580     *ISBN* 0664218318

**Bible. O.T. Psalms. English. New English. 1977.**     **1.2607**
Psalms / commentary by J. W. Rogerson and J. W. McKay. — Cambridge; New York: Cambridge University Press, 1977. 3 v.; 21 cm. (The Cambridge Bible commentary, New English Bible) 1. Bible. O.T. Psalms — Commentaries. I. Rogerson, J. W. (John William), 1935- II. McKay, John William, 1941- III. T. IV. Series.
BS1430.3.R63     223/.2/077     *LC* 76-27911     *ISBN* 0521214637

**Rad, Gerhard von, 1901-1971.**     **1.2608**
[Weisheit in Israel. English] Wisdom in Israel. Nashville, Abingdon Press [1972] x, 330 p. 23 cm. Translation of Weisheit in Israel. 1. Wisdom literature — Criticism, interpretation, etc. I. T.
BS1455.R2313 1972b     222/.1/066     *LC* 73-152746     *ISBN* 0687457564

**McKane, William.**     • **1.2609**
Proverbs, a new approach. Philadelphia, Westminster Press [1970] xxii, 670 p. 23 cm. (Old Testament library.) 1. Bible. O.T. Proverbs — Commentaries. I. T. II. Series.
BS1465.3.M25 1970b     223/.7/077     *LC* 75-108185     *ISBN* 0664208878

# BS1501–1675 Prophets

**Heschel, Abraham Joshua, 1907-1972.**     • **1.2610**
The Prophets. [1st ed.] New York, Harper & Row [1962] 518 p. 25 cm. 1. Bible. O.T. Prophets — Criticism, interpretation, etc. 2. Prophets I. T.
BS1505.2.H4     224.06     *LC* 62-7290

**Westermann, Claus.**     • **1.2611**
[Grundformen prophetischer Rede] Basic forms of prophetic speech. Translated by Hugh Clayton White. Philadelphia, Westminster Press [1967] 222 p. 21 cm. 1. Bible. O.T. Prophets — Criticism, Form. I. T.
BS1505.2.W413     224/.06/6     *LC* 67-10512

**Bible. O.T. Isaiah I-XXXIX. English. New English. 1973.**     **1.2612**
The book of the prophet Isaiah, chapters 1–39. Commentary by A. S. Herbert. Cambridge [Eng.] University Press, 1973. x, 218 p. maps. 21 cm. (The Cambridge Bible commentary: New English Bible) 1. Bible. O.T. Isaiah I-XXXIX — Commentaries. I. Herbert, Arthur Sumner. II. T. III. Series.
BS1515.3.H47     224/.1/077     *LC* 73-79495     *ISBN* 0521086248 *ISBN* 0521097665

**Westermann, Claus.**     • **1.2613**
[Buch Jesaia, 40-66. English] Isaiah 40–66; a commentary. [Translated by David M. G. Stalker from the German] Philadelphia, Westminster Press [1969] xv, 429 p. 23 cm. (Old Testament library.) Translation of Das Buch Jesaia, 40-66. 1. Bible. O.T. Isaiah XL-LXVI — Commentaries. I. T. II. Series.
BS1520.W413 1969b     224/.1     *LC* 69-18647     *ISBN* 0664208517

**Bible. O.T. Jeremiah. English. Bright. 1964.**     **1.2614**
Jeremiah. Introd., translation, and notes by John Bright. — [1st ed.]. — Garden City, N. Y., Doubleday, 1965. cxliv, 372 p. 24 cm. — (Bible. Anchor Bible. 1964. 21) Bibliography: p. [cxliii]-cxliv. 1. Bible O.T. Jeremiah — Commentaries. I. Bright, John, 1908- ed. and tr. II. T. III. Series.
BS1523.B7x     224.2     *LC* 65-13603

**Zimmerli, Walther, 1907-.**     **1.2615**
Ezekiel 1: a commentary on the book of the prophet Ezekiel, chapters 1–24 / by Walther Zimmerli; translated by Ronald E. Clements; ed. by Frank Moore Cross and Klaus Baltzer, with the assistance of Leonard Jay Greenspoon. — Philadelphia: Fortress Press, c1979-1983. 2 v.; 25 cm. — (Hermeneia, a critical and historical commentary on the Bible) 'Translated from the German Ezechiel 1, I. Teilband ... Biblischer Kommentar Altes Testament, Band XIII/1.' Vol.2 translated by James D. Martin; edited by Paul D. Hanson with Leonard Jay Greenspoon. 1. Bible. O.T. Ezekiel — Commentaries. I. Cross, Frank Moore. II. Baltzer, Klaus, 1928- III. Greenspoon, Leonard Jay. IV. Bible. O.T. Ezekiel. English. Zimmerli. 1979. V. T.
BS1545.3.Z5613     *LC* 75-21540     *ISBN* 0800660080

**Lacocque, André.**     **1.2616**
[Livre de Daniel. English] The book of Daniel / by André Lacocque; translated by David Pellauer; English ed. rev. by the author; foreword by Paul Ricoeur. — Atlanta: John Knox Press, c1979. xxvi, 302 p.; 24 cm. Translation of Le livre de Daniel. Includes indexes. 1. Bible. O.T. Daniel — Commentaries. I. T.
BS1555.3.L313 1979     224/.5/077     *LC* 78-2036     *ISBN* 0804200904

**Wolff, Hans Walter.**     **1.2617**
[Dodekapropheton. 1. Hosea. English] Hosea: a commentary on the book of the Prophet Hosea / by Hans Walter Wolff; translated by Gary Stansell; edited by Paul D. Hanson. — Philadelphia: Fortress Press, [1974] xxxii, 259 p.: facsim.; 25 cm. — (Hermeneia) Translation of Dodekapropheton 1: Hosea (2. Aufl.) 1. Bible. O.T. Hosea — Commentaries. I. Bible. O.T. Hosea. English. Wolff. 1974. II. T. III. Series.
BS1565.3.W64213     224/.6/077     *LC* 70-179634     *ISBN* 0800660048

**Wolff, Hans Walter.**     **1.2618**
[Dodekapropheton. 2. Joel and Amos. English] Joel and Amos: a commentary on the books of the Prophets Joel and Amos / by Hans Walter Wolff; translated by Waldemar Janzen, S. Dean McBride, Jr., and Charles A. Muenchow; edited by S. Dean McBride, Jr. — Philadelphia: Fortress Press, c1977. xxiv, 392 p., [1] leaf of plates: ill.; 25 cm. — (Hermeneia) Translation of Dodekapropheton 2:

Joel and Amos (2. Aufl.) Includes index. 1. Bible. O.T. Joel — Commentaries. 2. Bible. O.T. Amos — Commentaries. I. McBride, S. Dean (Samuel Dean), 1937- II. Bible. O.T. Joel. English. Wolff. 1977. III. Bible. O.T. Amos. English. Wolff. 1977. IV. T. V. Series.
BS1575.3.W64213       224/.7/077       LC 75-76932       ISBN 0800660072

**Mays, James Luther.**                                                        **1.2619**
Micah: a commentary / James Luther Mays. Philadelphia: Westminster Press, c1976. xii, 169 p.; 23 cm. (Old Testament library.) 1. Bible. O.T. Micah — Commentaries. I. Bible. O.T. Micah. English. 1976. II. T. III. Series.
BS1615.3.M39 1976     224/.93/07     LC 76-2599     ISBN 0664208177

# BS1691–1830 Apocrypha

**Bible. O.T. Apocrypha. English. New English. Selections. 1972.**  • **1.2620**
The shorter books of the Apocrypha: Tobit, Judith, Rest of Esther, Baruch, Letter of Jeremiah, additions to Daniel and Prayer of Manasseh. Commentary by J. C. Dancy, with contributions by W. J. Fuerst and R. J. Hammer. Cambridge [Eng.] University Press, 1972. ix, 252 p. 21 cm. (The Cambridge Bible commentary: New English Bible) I. Dancy, John Christopher. II. Fuerst, Wesley J., 1930- III. Hammer, R. J. (Raymond J.) IV. T. V. Series.
BS1695.D3 1972     BS1695D3 1972.     229/.22/05206     LC 72-76358
    ISBN 0521086040 ISBN 0521097290

**Metzger, Bruce Manning.**                                                    • **1.2621**
An introduction to the Apocrypha / Bruce M. Metzger. — New York: Oxford University Press, 1977, c1957. ix, 274 p.; 21 cm. — (Oxford University Press paperback) 1. Bible. O.T. Apocrypha — Introductions. I. T.
BS1700.M4 1977     ISBN 0195023404

**Bible. O.T. Apocrypha. Esdras, 1st. English. New English. 1979.**     **1.2622**
The first and second books of Esdras / commentary on 1 Esdras by R. J. Coggins and commentary on 2 Esdras by M. A. Knibb. — Cambridge; New York: Cambridge University Press, 1979. xii, 314 p.; 21 cm. (The Cambridge Bible commentary, New English Bible) 1. Bible. O.T. Apocrypha. Esdras, 1st — Commentaries. 2. Bible. O.T. Apocrypha. Esdras, 2nd — Commentaries. I. Coggins, R. J., 1929- II. Knibb, Michael A. (Michael Anthony), 1938- III. Bible. O.T. Apocrypha. Esdras, 2nd English. New English. 1979. IV. T. V. Series.
BS1713 1979     229/.1/077     LC 78-16420     ISBN 0521086566

**Clarke, Ernest G. (Ernest George)**                                          **1.2623**
The Wisdom of Solomon; commentary by Ernest G. Clarke. Cambridge [Eng.] University Press, 1973. xii, 136 p. 21 cm. (The Cambridge Bible commentary: New English Bible) 1. Bible. O.T. Apocrypha. Wisdom of Solomon — Commentaries. I. Bible. O.T. Apocrypha. Wisdom of Solomon II. T. III. Series.
BS1755.3.C55     229/.3/077     LC 74-155266     ISBN 0521086353
ISBN 0521097568

**Snaith, John G.**                                                            **1.2624**
Ecclesiasticus, or the wisdom of Jesus son of Sirach, commentary by John G. Snaith. [London, New York] Cambridge University Press, [1974] x, 271 p. 21 cm. (The Cambridge Bible commentary: New English Bible) 1. Bible. O.T. Apocrypha. Ecclesiasticus — Commentaries. I. Bible. O.T. Apocrypha. Ecclesiasticus. New English Bible. 1974. II. T. III. Series.
BS1765.3.S6     229/.4/077     LC 73-82459     ISBN 0521086574 ISBN 0521097754

**Bible. O.T. Apocrypha. 1-2 Maccabees. English. New English.**     **1.2625**
**1973.**
The First and Second Books of the Maccabees. Commentary by John R. Bartlett. Cambridge [Eng.] University Press, 1973. xiv, 357 p. 21 cm. (The Cambridge Bible commentary: New English Bible) 1. Bible. O.T. Apocrypha. 1-2 Maccabees — Commentaries. I. Bartlett, John R. (John Raymond) II. T. III. Series.
BS1825.3.B37     229/.73/07     LC 72-87436     ISBN 0521086582 ISBN 0521097495

# BS1901–2970 New Testament

## BS2280–2545 WORKS ABOUT THE NEW TESTAMENT

**Robinson, John A. T. (John Arthur Thomas), 1919-.**               **1.2626**
Redating the New Testament / John A.T. Robinson. — Philadelphia: Westminster Press, c1976. xiii, 369 p.; 24 cm. 1. Bible — Authorship — Date of authorship I. T.
BS2315.5.R67 1976     225.1/4     LC 76-17554     ISBN 0664213367

**Dibelius, Martin, 1883-1947.**                                         • **1.2627**
A fresh approach to the New Testament and early Christian literature / by Martin Dibelius. — London: Nicholson and Watson, 1936. 280 p.; 23 cm. — (The international library of Christian knowledge) 1. Bible. N.T — Introductions. 2. Christian literature, Early — History and criticism. I. T. II. Series.
BS2330.D5     225.6     LC 37-8570

**Kümmel, Werner Georg, 1905-.**                                         • **1.2628**
[Einleitung in das Neue Testament] Introduction to the New Testament / by Werner Georg Kümmel; translated by Howard Clark Kee. — Rev. ed. — Nashville, Tenn.: Abingdon Press, [1975] 629 p.; 23 cm. Revised and updated translation of Einleitung in das Neue Testament by P. Feine and J. Behm. 1. Bible. N.T — Introductions. I. Feine, Paul, 1859-1933. Einleitung in das Neue Testament. II. T.
BS2330.F413 1975     225.6     LC 74-26804     ISBN 0687195756

**McNeile, Alan Hugh, 1871-1933.**                                       • **1.2629**
An introduction to the study of the New Testament. — 2d ed. rev. by C. S. C. Williams. — Oxford, Clarendon Press, 1953. viii, 486 p. 23 cm. Includes bibliographies. 1. Bible N. T. — Introductions. I. T.
BS2330.M33 1953     225     LC 53-3555

**Fuller, Reginald Horace.**                                               **1.2630**
A critical introduction to the New Testament / by Reginald H. Fuller. — London: G. Duckworth, 1966. 221 p.: diagr. — (Studies in theology; [no. 55]) I. T. II. Series.
BS2330.2 F8     225.61     LC 66-68195     ISBN 0715605828

**Martin, Ralph P.**                                                       **1.2631**
New Testament foundations: a guide for Christian students, by Ralph P. Martin. Grand Rapids, Eerdmans [1975-78] 2 v. 25 cm. 1. Bible. N.T — Introductions. I. T.
BS2330.2.M28 1975     225.6     LC 74-19163     ISBN 0802834442

**Perrin, Norman.**                                                        **1.2632**
The New Testament, an introduction: proclamation and parenesis, myth and history / Norman Perrin, Dennis C. Duling. — 2nd ed. / under the general editorship of Robert Ferm. — New York: Harcourt Brace Jovanovich, c1982. xx, 516 p.: ill.; 24 cm. Includes index. 1. Bible. N.T — Introductions. I. Duling, Dennis C. II. Ferm, Robert L. III. T.
BS2330.2.P46 1982     225.6/1 19     LC 82-80524     ISBN 0155657267

**Collins, Raymond F., 1935-.**                                            **1.2633**
Introduction to the New Testament / Raymond F. Collins. — 1st ed. — Garden City, N.Y.: Doubleday, 1983. xxix, 449 p.; 24 cm. 1. Bible. N.T — Hermeneutics. I. T.
BS2331.C64 1983     225.6/01 19     LC 82-45070     ISBN 0385181264

**McKnight, Edgar V.**                                                     **1.2634**
Meaning in texts: the historical shaping of a narrative hermeneutics / by Edgar V. McKnight. — Philadelphia: Fortress Press, c1978. xi, 332 p.; 24 cm. 1. Bible. N.T — Hermeneutics. 2. Hermeneutics 3. Structuralism (Literary analysis) I. T.
BS2331.M3     225.6/3     LC 77-15238     ISBN 0800605187

## BS2350–2397 Criticism. Interpretation. Theology

**Henry, Patrick, 1939-.**                                                 **1.2635**
New directions in New Testament study / by Patrick Henry. — 1st ed. — Philadelphia: Westminster Press, c1979. 300 p.; 23 cm. Includes index.

1. Bible. N.T — Criticism, interpretation, etc. — History — 20th century.
I. T.
BS2350.H43        225.6/09/04        *LC* 79-16267        *ISBN* 0664213766

**Kümmel, Werner Georg, 1905-.**                                    **1.2636**
[Neue Testament. English] The New Testament: the history of the investigation
of its problems. Translated by S. McLean Gilmour and Howard C. Kee.
Nashville, Abingdon Press [1972] 510 p. 24 cm. Translation of Das Neue
Testament: Geschichte der Erforschung seiner Probleme. 1. Bible. N.T. —
Criticism, interpretation, etc. — History I. T.
BS2350.K813        225.6/09        *LC* 74-185554        *ISBN* 0687279267

**Grant, Frederick C. (Frederick Clifton), 1891-1974.**        • **1.2637**
An introduction to New Testament thought / by Frederick C. Grant. — New
York: Abington-Cokesbury Press, [1950] 339 p.; 21 cm. Includes indexes.
1. Bible. N.T — Theology. I. T.
BS2361 G65        *LC* 50-8047

**Sandmel, Samuel.**                                    **1.2638**
A Jewish understanding of the New Testament. Cincinnati, Hebrew Union
College Press, 1956. 321 p. 25 cm. 1. Bible. N.T. — Criticism, interpretation,
etc. 2. Judaism — Relations — Christianity 3. Christianity and other religions
— Judaism I. T.
BS2361.S24        225.7        *LC* 56-8371

**Daube, David.**                                    • **1.2639**
The New Testament and Rabinic Judaism. [London], University of London,
Athlone Press, 1956. xviii, 460 p., 23 cm. (Jordan lectures in comparative
religion, 2) 1. Bible. N.T. — Criticism, interpretation, etc. 2. Christianity and
other religions — Judaism 3. Judaism — Relations — Christianity I. T.
BS2361.2.D3        221.7        *LC* 56-2915

**Malina, Bruce J.**                                    **1.2640**
The New Testament world: insights from cultural anthropology / Bruce J.
Malina. — Atlanta, Ga.: John Knox Press, c1981. ix, 169 p.: ill.; 23 cm.
1. Bible. N.T. — Criticism, interpretation, etc. 2. Jews — Palestine — Social
life and customs. I. T.
BS2361.2.M15        225.9/5 19        *LC* 80-84650        *ISBN* 0804204233

**Patte, Daniel.**                                    **1.2641**
What is structural exegesis? / By Daniel Patte. — Philadelphia: Fortress Press,
c1976. vi, 90 p.: diagrs.; 22 cm. — (Guides to Biblical scholarship: New
Testament series) Includes index. 1. Bible. N.T. — Criticism, interpretation,
etc. 2. Bible. N.T — Hermeneutics. I. T.
BS2361.2.P36        225.6        *LC* 75-36454        *ISBN* 0800604628

**Petersen, Norman R., 1933-.**                                    **1.2642**
Literary criticism for New Testament critics / by Norman R. Petersen. —
Philadelphia: Fortress Press, c1978. 92 p.; 22 cm. — (Guides to Biblical
scholarship: New Testament series) 1. Bible. N.T. — Criticism, interpretation,
etc. I. T.
BS2361.2.P47        225.6/1        *LC* 77-15241        *ISBN* 0800604652

**Brown, Raymond Edward.**                                    **1.2643**
Antioch and Rome: New Testament cradles of Catholic Christianity /
Raymond E. Brown, John P. Meier. — New York: Paulist Press, c1983. xii,
242 p.; 21 cm. Includes indexes. 1. Bible. N.T. — Criticism, interpretation, etc.
2. Church history — Primitive and early church, ca. 30-600 3. Jewish
Christians — History — Early church, ca. 30-600 4. Gentiles in the New
Testament 5. Christianity — Origin 6. Antioch (Turkey) — Church history.
7. Rome (Italy) — Church history. I. Meier, John P. II. T.
BS2370.B76 1983        274.5/63201 19        *LC* 82-63171        *ISBN*
0809103397

**Wilder, Amos Niven, 1895-.**                                    • **1.2644**
The language of the Gospel: early Christian rhetoric / Amos N. Wilder. — New
York: Harper & Row, c1964. 143 p. Also published under title: Early Christian
rhetoric. 'The present volume ... represents the text of the Haskell lectures for
1961-1962 ...' 1. Bible. N.T. — Language, style I. T. II. Title: Early Christian
rhetoric.
BS2370 W5 1964        *LC* 64-15479

**Finegan, Jack, 1908-.**                                    • **1.2645**
The archeology of the New Testament; the life of Jesus and the beginning of the
early church. — Princeton, N.J.: Princeton University Press, 1969. xxiv, 273 p.:
illus., maps.; 29 cm. 1. Bible. N.T — Antiquities. I. T.
BS2375.F5        225.93        *LC* 69-18057        *ISBN* 0691035342

**Finegan, Jack, 1908-.**                                    **1.2646**
The archeology of the New Testament: the Mediterranean world of the early
Christian Apostles / Jack Finegan. — Boulder, Colo.: Westview Press; London,
England: Croom Helm, c1981. xxxii, 250 p.: ill., maps, ports.; 27 cm.
Companion vol. to: The archeology of the New Testament, the life of Jesus and
the beginning of the early church. 1. Bible. N.T — Antiquities.

2. Mediterranean Region — Description and travel 3. Mediterranean Region
— Antiquities. I. T.
BS2375.F52        225.9/3 19        *LC* 81-177982        *ISBN* 0865310645

**Kennedy, George Alexander, 1928-.**                                    **1.2647**
New Testament interpretation through rhetorical criticism / George A.
Kennedy. — Chapel Hill: University of North Carolina Press, c1984. x, 171 p.;
21 cm. — (Studies in religion) Includes index. 1. Bible. N.T. — Language, style
I. T.
BS2385.K39 1984        225.6/6 19        *LC* 83-23577        *ISBN* 0807816019

**Shires, Henry M.**                                    **1.2648**
Finding the Old Testament in the New, by Henry M. Shires. Philadelphia,
Westminster Press [1974] 251 p. 21 cm. 1. Bible. N.T — Relation to O.T. I. T.
BS2387.S54        220.6/6        *LC* 73-19600        *ISBN* 0664209939

**Fitzmyer, Joseph A.**                                    • **1.2649**
Essays on the Semitic background of the New Testament [by] Joseph A.
Fitzmyer. London, G. Chapman, 1971. xix, 524 p. 23 cm. 1. Bible. N.T —
Criticism, interpretation, etc. — Addresses, essays, lectures. 2. Dead Sea
scrolls — Addresses, essays, lectures. I. T.
BS2393.F58        225.6/6        *LC* 70-859191        *ISBN* 0225488841

**New Testament interpretation: essays on principles and methods**        **1.2650**
/ edited by I. Howard Marshall.
1st American ed. — Grand Rapids: Eerdmans, 1977. 406 p.; 24 cm. Includes
indexes. 1. Bible. N.T — Criticism, interpretation, etc. — Addresses, essays,
lectures. I. Marshall, I. Howard.
BS2393.N49 1977        225/.07        *LC* 77-9619        *ISBN* 0802835031

**Bultmann, Rudolf Karl, 1884-1976.**                                    **1.2651**
The New Testament and mythology and other basic writings / Rudolf
Bultmann; selected, edited, and translated by Schubert M. Ogden. —
Philadelphia: Fortress Press, c1984. x, 168 p.; 23 cm. 1. Bible. N.T —
Criticism, interpretation, etc. — Addresses, essays, lectures.
2. Demythologization — Addresses, essays, lectures. I. Ogden, Schubert
Miles, 1928- II. T.
BS2395.B83 1984        225.6/8 19        *LC* 84-47912        *ISBN* 0800607279

**Käsemann, Ernst.**                                    • **1.2652**
Essays on New Testament themes / [translated by W. J. Montague]. —
Naperville, Ill.: A.R. Allenson, [1964] 200 p.; 22 cm. — (Studies in Biblical
theology; no. 41) 'Translated ... from selections from ... [the author's] ...
Exegetische Versuche und Besinnungen, erster Band (2nd edition,
Vandenhoeck und Ruprecht, 1960)' 1. Bible. N.T — Addresses, essays,
lectures. I. T. II. Series.
BS2395.K313        *LC* 65-106

**Taylor, Vincent, 1887-1968.**                                    **1.2653**
New Testament essays. London, Epworth P., 1970. vii, 146 p., plate. port. 23
cm. 1. Bible. N.T — Addresses, essays, lectures. I. T.
BS2395.T3 1970        225/.08        *LC* 79-492391        *ISBN* 0716200465

**Bultmann, Rudolf Karl, 1884-1976.**                                    **1.2654**
Theology of the New Testament; translated by Kendrick Grobel. — New York,
Scribner, 1951-55. 2 v. 22 cm. Includes bibliographies. 1. Bible. N.T —
Theology. I. T.
BS2397.B813        230        *LC* 51-14678 rev

**Conzelmann, Hans.**                                    • **1.2655**
[Grundriss der Theologie des Neuen Testaments. English] An outline of the
theology of the New Testament. [1st U.S. ed.] New York, Harper & Row [1969]
xviii, 373 p. 22 cm. Translation of Grundriss der Theologie des Neuen
Testaments. 1. Bible. N.T — Theology. I. T.
BS2397.C6513 1969        225        *LC* 69-17019

**Ladd, George Eldon, 1911-.**                                    **1.2656**
A theology of the New Testament. — Grand Rapids, Mich.: Eerdmans, [1974]
661 p.; 25 cm. 1. Bible. N.T — Theology. I. T.
BS2397.L33        225.6/6        *LC* 74-766        *ISBN* 0802834434

## BS2407–2520 History. Biography

**Bruce, F. F. (Frederick Fyvie), 1910-.**                                    • **1.2657**
New Testament history [by] F. F. Bruce. [1st U.S. ed.] Garden City, N.Y.,
Doubleday, 1971 [c1969] xiv, 462 p. 22 cm. 1. Bible. N.T — History of Biblical
events. 2. Bible. N.T — History of contemporary events. I. T.
BS2407.B69 1971        225/.95        *LC* 78-144253

**Kee, Howard Clark.**                                    **1.2658**
Understanding the New Testament / Howard Clark Kee. — 4th ed. —
Englewood Cliffs, N.J.: Prentice-Hall, c1983. viii, 408 p.: ill.; 24 cm. 1. Bible.
N.T — History of Biblical events. 2. Bible. N.T — Introductions. I. T.
BS2407.K37 1983        225.6/1 19        *LC* 82-16482        *ISBN* 0139365915

**Koester, Helmut, 1926-.**    **1.2659**
[Einführung in das Neue Testament. English] Introduction to the New Testament / Helmut Koester. — Philadelphia: Fortress Press; Berlin [Germany]; New York: De Gruyter, c1982. 2 v.: ill.; 25 cm. (Hermeneia—foundations and facets.) Translation of: Einführung in das Neue Testament. 1. Bible. N.T — History of contemporary events. I. T. II. Series.
BS2410.K613 1982   225.9/5   *LC* 82-71828   *ISBN* 080062100X

**Lohse, Eduard, 1924-.**    **1.2660**
[Umwelt des Neuen Testaments. English] The New Testament environment / Eduard Lohse; translated by John E. Steely. — Nashville: Abingdon, c1976. 296 p.: ill.; 22 cm. Translation of Umwelt des Neuen Testaments. Includes indexes. 1. Bible. N.T — History of contemporary events. I. T.
BS2410.L6413   225.9/5   *LC* 75-43618   *ISBN* 0687279453. *ISBN* 0687279445 pbk

**Weiss, Johannes, 1863-1914.**    • **1.2661**
[Urchristentum. English] Earliest Christianity; a history of the period A.D. 30–150. English translation edited with a new introd. and bibliography by Frederick C. Grant. New York, Harper [1959] 2 v. 21 cm. (Harper torchbooks, TB53-54) 1. Bible. N.T — History of Biblical events. 2. Bible. N.T — Theology. 3. Theology, Doctrinal — History — Early church, ca. 30-600 4. Church history — Primitive and early church, ca. 30-600 I. T.
BS2410.W2822   225.95   *LC* 59-6651

**Perrin, Norman.**    **1.2662**
Rediscovering the teaching of Jesus. — [1st ed.]. — New York, Harper & Row [1967] 272 p. 22 cm. 1. Jesus Christ — Teachings I. Bible. N.T. English. Selections. 1967. Revised standard. II. T.
BS2415.P4   232.95/4   *LC* 67-11510

**Wilder, Amos Niven, 1895-.**    • **1.2663**
Eschatology and ethics in the teaching of Jesus / Amos N. Wilder. — Rev. ed. — New York: Harper, 1950. 223 p.; 22 cm. 1. Jesus Christ — Teachings 2. Jesus Christ — Ethics 3. Eschatology — Biblical teaching 4. Kingdom of God — Biblical teaching I. T.
BS2417.E7 W5 1950   236   *LC* 50-6434

**Deissmann, Gustav Adolf, 1866-1937.**    • **1.2664**
[Paulus] Paul; a study in social and religious history. Translated by William E. Wilson. [1st Harper torchbook ed.] New York, Harper [1957] 323 p. illus. 21 cm. (Harper torchbooks, TB15) 1. Paul, the Apostle, Saint. I. T.
BS2505.D42 1957   225.92 922.1   *LC* 57-7533

**Munck, Johannes, 1904-1965.**    **1.2665**
Paul and the salvation of mankind / [translated by Frank Clarke from the German]. — 1st English ed. — Atlanta: John Knox Press, 1977, c1959. 351 p.; 24 cm. 1. Paul, the Apostle, Saint. I. T.
BS2505.M933 1959   225.92   *LC* 60-5412   *ISBN* 0804203733

**Bornkamm, Günther.**    • **1.2666**
[Paulus. English] Paul, Paulus. Translated by D. M. G. Stalker. [1st U.S. ed.] New York, Harper & Row [1971] xxviii, 259 p. 22 cm. 1. Paul, the Apostle, Saint. 2. Bible. N.T. Epistles of Paul — Theology. I. T.
BS2506.B6213   225.9/24 B   *LC* 75-22728

**Longenecker, Richard N.**    • **1.2667**
Paul, apostle of liberty, by Richard N. Longenecker. [1st ed.] New York, Harper & Row [1964] x, 310p. 22cm. 1. Paul, the Apostle, Saint. I. T.
BS2506.L6   *LC* 64-19500

**Lüdemann, Gerd.**    • **1.2668**
[Paulus, der Heidenapostel. 1. Studien zur Chronologie. English] Paul, apostle to the Gentiles: studies in chronology / Gerd Luedemann; foreword by John Knox; translated by F. Stanley Jones. — Philadelphia: Fortress Press, c1984. xxii, 311 p.; 24 cm. Translation of: Paulus, der Heidenapostel. Bd. 1, Studien zur Chronologie. Includes indexes. 1. Paul, the Apostle, Saint — Chronology. 2. Bible. N.T. Epistles of Paul — Chronology. 3. Bible. N.T. Acts — Chronology. 4. Christian saints — Turkey — Tarsus — Biography. 5. Tarsus (Turkey) — Biography. I. T.
BS2506.L8313 1984   225.9/24 B 19   *LC* 83-48919   *ISBN* 0800607147

**Cullmann, Oscar.**    • **1.2669**
Peter; disciple, apostle, martyr: a historical and theological study. Translated from the German by Floyd V. Filson. — 2d rev. and expanded ed. — Philadelphia, Westminster Press [1962] 252 p. 22 cm. — (The Library of history and doctrine) Includes bibliography. 1. Peter, Saint, apostle. I. T.
BS2515.C813 1962   225.92   *LC* 62-10169

**Peter in the New Testament; a collaborative assessment by Protestant and Roman Catholic scholars. Edited by Raymond E. Brown, Karl P. Donfried, and John Reumann, from discussions by Paul J. Achtemeier [and others]**    **1.2670**
Minneapolis, Augsburg Pub. House, 1973. ix, 181 p. 21 cm. 1. Peter, the Apostle, Saint. 2. Bible. N.T. — Criticism, interpretation, etc. I. Brown, Raymond Edward. ed. II. Donfried, Karl P. ed. III. Reumann, John Henry Paul. ed.
BS2515.P475   225.9/24 B   *LC* 73-83787   *ISBN* 0806614013

## BS2545 Other Topics

**Furnish, Victor Paul.**    **1.2671**
The love command in the New Testament. Nashville, Abingdon Press [c1972] 240 p. 24 cm. 1. Love — Biblical teaching. I. T.
BS2545.L6 F87   225.8/231/6   *LC* 75-172814   *ISBN* 0687228093

**Davies, William David, 1911-.**    **1.2672**
The Gospel and the land; early Christianity and Jewish territorial doctrine, by W. D. Davies. — Berkeley: University of California Press, [1974] xiv, 521 p.: illus.; 24 cm. 1. Palestine in the Bible 2. Palestine in Judaism I. T.
BS2545.P43 D38   236   *LC* 72-82228   *ISBN* 0520022785

*[handwritten margin note: BS 2545 P43 D38]*

**Perkins, Pheme.**    **1.2673**
Resurrection: New Testament witness and contemporary reflection / Pheme Perkins. — 1st ed. — Garden City, N.Y.: Doubleday, 1984. 504 p.; 25 cm. Includes index. 1. Jesus Christ — Resurrection 2. Bible. N.T. — Criticism, interpretation, etc. 3. Resurrection — Biblical teaching. I. T.
BS2545.R47 P47 1984   232/.5 19   *LC* 83-25473   *ISBN* 0385172567

## BS2549–2970 SPECIAL BOOKS

## BS2549–2617 Gospels

**Bultmann, Rudolf Karl, 1884-1976.**    • **1.2674**
The history of the synoptic tradition / Rudolf Bultmann. Translated by John Marsh. — Rev. ed. — New York: Harper & Row, 1976. viii, 462 p.; 24 cm. Translation of Die Geschichte der synoptischen Tradition. 1. Bible. N.T. Gospels — Criticism, Form. I. T.
BS2555.B7233 1976   226   *LC* 62-7282   *ISBN* 0060611723

**Dibelius, Martin, 1883-1947.**    • **1.2675**
From tradition to Gospel / by Martin Dibelius. Translated from the revised second edition of Die formgeschichte des evangeliums, in collaboration with the author, by Bertram Lee Woolf. New York: Scribner, 1965? 311 p. 1. Bible. N.T. Gospels — Criticism, interpretation, etc. 2. Bible — Criticism, interpretation, etc. N. T. Gospels. I. Woolf, Bertram Lee, 1884- II. T.
BS2555.D52 1965   226

**Streeter, Burnett Hillman, 1874-1937.**    • **1.2676**
The four Gospels; a study of origins, treating of the manuscript tradition, sources, authorship, & dates, by Burnett Hillman Streeter. 4th impression, revised. London, Macmillan and co., limited, 1930. xxiv, 624 p. illus. (map.) diagrs. 22 cm. 1. Bible. N.T. Gospels — Criticism, interpretation, etc. 2. Bible. N.T. Gospels — Criticism, Textual. I. T.
BS2555.S915 1930 BS2555.S   226   *LC* a 32-2865

**Edwards, Richard Alan.**    **1.2677**
A theology of Q: eschatology, prophecy, and wisdom / Richard A. Edwards. — Philadelphia: Fortress Press, c1976. xiii, 173 p.; 24 cm. Includes indexes. 1. Q document (Biblical criticism) I. T.
BS2555.2.E34   226/.06   *LC* 75-13042   *ISBN* 0800604326

**Talbert, Charles H.**    **1.2678**
What is a Gospel?: The genre of the canonical Gospels / Charles H. Talbert. — Philadelphia: Fortress Press, c1977. xi, 147 p.; 23 cm. 1. Bible. N.T. Gospels — Criticism, interpretation, etc. 2. Religious biography — History and criticism 3. Bible as literature I. T.
BS2555.2.T34   226/.06   *LC* 77-78645   *ISBN* 0800605128

**Documents for the study of the Gospels / David R. Cartlidge, David L. Dungan.**    **1.2679**
Cleveland: Collins, 1980. 298 p.; 23 cm. Label on title page: Fortress Press, Philadelphia. 1. Bible. N.T. Gospels — Extra-canonical parallels. 2. Rome — Religion. I. Cartlidge, David R. II. Dungan, David L.
BS2555.5.D62 1980   226/.06   *LC* 79-21341   *ISBN* 0529056836

**Grant, Frederick C. (Frederick Clifton), 1891-1974.**    • **1.2680**
The Gospels, their origin and their growth / by Frederick C. Grant. — New York: Harper & Row, c1957. vii, 216 p.; 21 cm. Includes indexes. 1. Bible. N.T. Gospels — Criticism, interpretation, etc. I. T.
BS2555.5 G73 1957   226.07   *LC* 57-7352

**Wilder, Amos Niven, 1895-.**                                                    **1.2681**
Jesus' parables and the war of myths: essays on imagination in the Scripture /
Amos N. Wilder; edited, with a preface, by James Breech. — Philadelphia:
Fortress Press, [1982] 168 p.; 24 cm. 1. Jesus Christ — Parables — Addresses,
essays, lectures. 2. Bible. N.T. Gospels — Hermeneutics — Addresses, essays,
lectures. 3. Bible. N.T. Gospels — Criticism, interpretation, etc. — Addresses,
essays, lectures. I. Breech, James. II. T.
BS2555.5.W53 1982        226/.806 19       *LC* 81-43083       *ISBN*
080060668X

**Bible. N.T. Gospels. English. Harmonies. American revised.**    • **1.2682**
**1945.**
A harmony of the synoptic gospels: for historical and critical study / by Ernest
DeWitt Burton and Edgar Johnson Goodspeed. — New York: Scribner, c1917.
xv, 275 p., [1] leaf of plates: col. map. I. Burton, Ernest De Witt, 1856-1925.
II. Goodspeed, Edgar Johnson, 1871-1962. III. T.
BS2560 B8        *LC* 17-25996

**Bible. N.T. Gospels. English. 1964. Revised standard.**         • **1.2683**
Gospel parallels; a synopsis of the first three Gospels, with alternative readings
from the manuscripts and noncanonical parallels. Text used is the Revised
standard version, 1952; the arrangement follows the Huck–Lietzmann synopsis,
9th ed., 1936. Edited by Burton H. Throckmorton, Jr. [2d ed., rev.] New York
Nelson [1964] 191p. 1. Bible. N.T. Gospels — Harmonies, English
I. Throckmorton, Burton Hamilton, 1921- ed. II. International Council of
Religious Education. American Standard Bible Committee III. T.
BS2560 I5 1964

**Kingsbury, Jack Dean.**                                                         **1.2684**
Matthew: structure, Christology, kingdom / by Jack Dean Kingsbury.
Philadelphia: Fortress Press, c1975. xiv, 178 p.; 24 cm. 1. Jesus Christ —
History of doctrines — Early church, ca. 30-600 2. Bible. N.T. Matthew —
Criticism, interpretation, etc. I. T.
BS2575.2.K49        226/.2/06       *LC* 75-13043       *ISBN* 0800604342

**Gundry, Robert Horton.**                                                        **1.2685**
Matthew, a commentary on his literary and theological art / by Robert H.
Gundry. — Grand Rapids, Mich.: W.B. Eerdmans Pub. Co., c1982. xviii,
652 p.; 24 cm. Includes indexes. 1. Bible. N.T. Matthew — Commentaries.
I. Bible. N.T. Matthew. II. T.
BS2575.3.G85        226/.206 19       *LC* 81-12448       *ISBN* 080283549X

**Kee, Howard Clark.**                                                            **1.2686**
Community of the new age: studies in Mark's Gospel / by Howard Clark Kee.
Philadelphia: Westminster Press, c1977. xi, 225 p.; 24 cm. 1. Bible. N.T. Mark
— Criticism, interpretation, etc. I. T.
BS2585.2.K43        226/.3/06       *LC* 76-49484       *ISBN* 0664207707

**Kelber, Werner H.**                                                             **1.2687**
The kingdom in Mark; a new place and a new time [by] Werner H. Kelber. —
Philadelphia: Fortress Press, [1974] xii, 173 p.; 24 cm. Based on the author's
thesis, University of Chicago, 1970. 1. Bible. N.T. Mark I-XIII — Criticism,
interpretation, etc. 2. Kingdom of God — Biblical teaching I. T.
BS2585.2.K44        236       *LC* 73-88353       *ISBN* 0800602684

**The Passion in Mark: studies on Mark 14–16 / edited by**        **1.2688**
**Werner H. Kelber; with contributions by John R. Donahue ...**
**[et al.].**
Philadelphia: Fortress Press, c1976. xvii, 203 p.; 24 cm. Includes indexes.
1. Bible. N.T. Mark XIV-XVI — Criticism, interpretation, etc. — Addresses,
essays, lectures. I. Kelber, Werner H. II. Donahue, John R.
BS2585.2.P3        226/.3/06       *LC* 75-36453       *ISBN* 0800604393

**Bible. N.T. Mark. English. 1974.**                                             **1.2689**
The Gospel according to Mark; the English text with introduction, exposition,
and notes, by William L. Lane. Grand Rapids, Eerdmans [1974] xvi, 652 p. 23
cm. 1. Bible. N.T. Mark — Commentaries. I. Lane, William L., 1931- II. T.
BS2585.3.L36        226/.3/066       *LC* 73-76529       *ISBN* 0802823408

**Schweizer, Eduard, 1913-.**                                                     **1.2690**
[Evangelium nach Markus. English] The good news according to Mark.
Translated by Donald H. Madvig. Richmond, John Knox Press [1970] 395 p.
21 cm. Translation of Das Evangelium nach Markus. 'The English language
edition is based on the text of Today's English version (Good news for modern
man)' 1. Bible. N.T. Mark — Commentaries. I. Bible. N.T. Mark. English.
Today's English. 1970. II. T.
BS2585.3.S3613        226/.3/077       *LC* 77-93828       *ISBN* 0804202508

**Tiede, David Lenz.**                                                            **1.2691**
Prophecy and history in Luke–Acts / David L. Tiede. — Philadelphia: Fortress
Press, c1980. ix, 166 p.; 23 cm. Includes indexes. 1. Bible. N.T. Luke and Acts
— Criticism, interpretation, etc. I. T.
BS2589.T53        226/.406       *LC* 79-8897       *ISBN* 0800606329

**Bible. N.T. Luke IX. English. Fitzmyer. 1981.**                                **1.2692**
The gospel according to Luke (I–IX) / Introduction, translation, and notes by
Joseph A. Fitzmyer. — Garden City, N.Y.: Doubleday, 1981. xxvi, 837 p. —
(The Anchor Bible; no. 28) 1. Bible. N.T. Luke — Commentaries. I. Fitzmyer,
Joseph A. II. T.
BS192.2.A1 1964.G3 vol. 28 BS2593        BS2593 1981.        220.7/7 s
226/.4077 19        *LC* 80-702        *ISBN* 0385005156

**Cullmann, Oscar.**                                                              **1.2693**
[Johanneische Kreis. English] The Johannine circle / Oscar Cullmann;
translated by John Bowden. — Philadelphia: Westminster Press, c1976. xi,
124 p.; 24 cm. Translation of Der johanneische Kreis. Includes indexes.
1. Bible. N.T. John — Criticism, interpretation, etc. 2. Johannine school I. T.
BS2615.2.C8413 1976        226/.5/01        *LC* 75-42249       *ISBN* 0664207448

**Culpepper, R. Alan.**                                                           **1.2694**
Anatomy of the fourth gospel: a study in literary design / R. Alan Culpepper;
foreword by Frank Kermode. — Philadelphia: Fortress Press, c1983. — xii,
266 p.; 24 cm. — (Foundations and facets. New Testament.) Includes indexes.
1. Bible. N.T. John — Criticism, interpretation, etc. I. T. II. Series.
BS2615.2.C85 1983        226/.506 19        *LC* 82-16302       *ISBN* 0800621026

**Martyn, J. Louis (James Louis), 1925-.**                        • **1.2695**
History and theology in the Fourth Gospel [by] J. Louis Martyn. [1st ed.] New
York, Harper & Row [1968] xxi, 168 p. 21 cm. 1. Bible. N.T. John —
Criticism, interpretation, etc. 2. Bible. N.T. John — Theology. I. T.
BS2615.2.M34        226/.5/06        *LC* 68-17588

**Sanders, Joseph Newbould.**                                     • **1.2696**
A commentary on the Gospel according to St. John [by] J. N. Sanders. Edited
and completed by B. A. Mastin. — [1st United States ed.]. — New York:
Harper & Row, [1968] x, 480 p.; 22 cm. — (Harper's New Testament
commentaries) 1. Bible. N.T. John — Commentaries. I. Mastin, B. A., ed.
II. T.
BS2615.3.S19 1968b        226/.5/077        *LC* 69-10469

**Schnackenburg, Rudolf, 1914-.**                                                **1.2697**
[Johannesevangelium.] The Gospel according to St. John / Rudolf
Schnackenburg. — New York: Seabury Press, 1980-1982. 3 v.; 24 cm. (Herder's
theological commentary on the New Testament) 'A Crossroad book.'
Translation of Das Johannesevangelium. Includes indexes. Imprint varies.
1. Bible. N.T. John — Commentaries. I. T. II. Title: Johannesevangelium.
BS2615.3.S313 1980        226/.5/07        *LC* 79-67156       *ISBN* 0816412103

**Dodd, Charles Harold, 1884-1973.**                              • **1.2698**
Historical tradition in the Fourth Gospel. — Cambridge [Eng.] University
Press, 1963. xii, 453 p. 25 cm. 1. Bible. N.T. John — Criticism, interpretation,
etc. I. T.
BS2615.52.D6        *LC* 63-23896

# BS2620–2627 Acts of the Apostles

**Haenchen, Ernst, 1894-.**                                                       **1.2699**
The Acts of the Apostles; a commentary. [Translated by Bernard Noble and
Gerald Shinn, under the supervision of Hugh Anderson, and with the
translation rev. and brought up to date by R. McL. Wilson]. — Philadelphia:
Westminster Press, [1971] xxiii, 737 p.: col. map; 24 cm. Translation of 14th ed.
of Die Apostelgeschichte. 1. Bible. N.T. Acts — Commentaries. I. Bible. N.T.
Acts. English. II. T.
BS2625.3.H313        226/.6/077        *LC* 78-161218       *ISBN* 066420919X

# BS2630–2815 Epistles

**Pagels, Elaine H., 1943-.**                                                     **1.2700**
The gnostic Paul: gnostic exegesis of the Pauline letters / Elaine Hiesey Pagels.
— Philadelphia: Fortress Press, c1975. xii, 180 p.; 24 cm. Includes indexes.
1. Bible. N.T. Epistles of Paul — Criticism, interpretation, etc. 2. Gnosticism
I. T.
BS2650.2.P33        227/.07/7        *LC* 74-26350       *ISBN* 0800604032

**Schmithals, Walter.**                                                           **1.2701**
Paul & the Gnostics. Translated by John E. Steely. — Nashville: Abingdon
Press, [c1972] 279 p.; 25 cm. Rev. translation of Paulus und die Gnostiker.
Continues the author's Gnosticism in Korinth; continued by Paul and James.
1. Bible. N.T. Epistles of Paul — Criticism, interpretation, etc. I. T.
BS2650.2.S34        227        *LC* 70-175130       *ISBN* 068730492X

**Caird, G. B. (George Bradford), 1917-.**                                       **1.2702**
Paul's letters from prison: Ephesians, Philippians, Colossians, Philemon, in the
Revised standard version / introd. and commentary by G. B. Caird. — Oxford:
Oxford University Press, 1976. 223 p.; 19 cm. — (The New Clarendon Bible)
'The actual text of the letters is not included.' Includes index. 1. Bible. N.T.

Ephesians — Commentaries. 2. Bible. N.T. Philippians — Commentaries. 3. Bible. N.T. Colossians — Commentaries. 4. Bible. N.T. Philemon — Commentaries. I. T. II. Series.
BS2650.3.C28     227     *LC* 76-368451     *ISBN* 0198369190

**Beker, Johan Christiaan, 1924-.**         **1.2703**
Paul the apostle: the triumph of God in life and thought / J. Christiaan Beker. — Philadelphia: Fortress Press, c1980. xi, 452 p.; 24 cm. Includes indexes. 1. Bible. N.T. Epistles of Paul — Theology. 2. Bible. N.T. Epistles of Paul — Hermeneutics. I. T.
BS2651.B44     230/.092/4     *LC* 79-8904     *ISBN* 0800606337

**Keck, Leander E.**         **1.2704**
Paul and his letters / Leander E. Keck. — Philadelphia: Fortress Press, c1979. viii, 135 p.; 22 cm. (Proclamation commentaries: The New Testament witnesses for preaching) Includes index. 1. Paul, the Apostle, Saint. 2. Bible. N.T. Epistles of Paul — Theology. I. T.
BS2651.K42     227/.06     *LC* 78-54554     *ISBN* 080060587X

**Schütz, John Howard.**         **1.2705**
Paul and the anatomy of apostolic authority / John Howard Schütz. — London; New York: Cambridge University Press, 1975. x, 307 p.; 23 cm. (Monograph series - Society for New Testament studies; 26) Includes indexes. 1. Bible. N.T. Epistles of Paul — Theology. 2. Authority (Religion) — Biblical teaching. I. T.
BS2655.A8 S38     262/.8     *LC* 74-76573     *ISBN* 052120464X

**Furnish, Victor Paul.**         **1.2706**
The moral teaching of Paul / Victor Paul Furnish. — Nashville: Abingdon, c1979. 143 p.; 20 cm. 1. Bible. N.T. Epistles of Paul — Criticism, interpretation, etc. 2. Ethics in the Bible I. T.
BS2655.E8 F79     227/.06     *LC* 78-10633     *ISBN* 0687271800

**Sanders, E. P.**         **1.2707**
Paul, the law, and the Jewish people / E.P. Sanders. — Philadelphia: Fortress Press, c1983. xi, 227 p.; 24 cm. Includes indexes. 1. Paul, the Apostle, Saint — Views on Judaism 2. Bible. N.T. Epistles of Paul — Criticism, interpretation, etc. 3. Law (Theology) — Biblical teaching 4. Judaism — History — Postexilic period, 586 B.C.-210 A.D. I. T.
BS2655.L35 S26 1983     241/.2 19     *LC* 82-17487     *ISBN* 0800606981

## BS2660–2815.5 Individual Epistles

**Barth, Karl, 1886-1968.**         • **1.2708**
[Römerbrief. English] The Epistle to the Romans, by Karl Barth; translated from the 6th edition by Edwyn C. Hoskyns, bart., with a new preface by the author. London, Oxford university press, H. Milford, 1933. xxi, 547, [1] p. 23 cm. German original first published 1918. 'Biographical note': p. [xvii] 'Modern German commentaries on the Epistle to the Romans': p. [xviii] 1. Bible. N.T. Romans — Commentaries. I. Hoskyns, Edwyn Clement, Sir, 1884-1937. tr. II. T.
BS2665.B34 1933     227.1     *LC* 33-33633

**Luther, Martin, 1483-1546.**         • **1.2709**
Lectures on Romans. Newly translated and edited by Wilhelm Pauck. Philadelphia, Westminster Press [1961] lxvi, 444 p. 24 cm. (The Library of Christian classics; v. 15) 'Translation is based on the critical edition of Luther's Römerbriefvorlesung by Johannes Ficker, published as vol. 56 of the so-called Weimar edition.' Translation includes Luther's scholia and parts of his gloss. 1. Bible. N.T. Romans — Commentaries. I. Pauck, Wilhelm, 1901- ed. and tr. II. T. III. Series.
BS2665.L7613     227.107     *LC* 61-13626

**Cranfield, C. E. B.**         **1.2710**
A critical and exegetical commentary on the Epistle to the Romans / by C. E. B. Cranfield. — 6th ed. (entirely rewritten). — Edinburgh: Clark, 1975-1979. 2 v. (xxvii, 927 p.); 22 cm. — (The International critical commentary; [32]) Vol. 2 has no edition statement. First-5th ed. by W. Sanday. Includes the text of the Epistle. 1. Bible. N.T. Romans — Commentaries. I. Sanday, W. (William), 1843-1920. A critical and exegetical commentary on the Epistle to the Romans. II. Bible. N.T. Romans. English. 1975. III. T. IV. Series.
BS2665.3.C73     220.7 s 227/.107     *LC* 75-332732     *ISBN* 0567050408

**Käsemann, Ernst.**         **1.2711**
[An die Römer. English] Commentary on Romans / by Ernst Käsemann; translated and edited by Geoffrey W. Bromiley. — Grand Rapids, Mich.: Eerdmans, c1980. xxix, 428 p.; 24 cm. Commentary with text of Paul's epistle to the Romans. Translation of An die Römer. 1. Bible. N.T. Romans — Commentaries. I. Bromiley, Geoffrey William. II. Bible. N.T. Romans. English. 1980. III. T.
BS2665.3.K3313     227/.1077     *LC* 79-27866     *ISBN* 080283499X

**Barrett, C. K. (Charles Kingsley), 1917-.**         • **1.2712**
A commentary on the First Epistle to the Corinthians [by] C. K. Barrett. [1st ed.] New York, Harper & Row [1968] xi, 410 p. 22 cm. (Harper's New

Testament commentaries) 1. Bible. N.T. Corinthians, 1st — Commentaries. I. T.
BS2675.3.B3     227/.2/077     *LC* 68-17594

**Conzelmann, Hans.**         **1.2713**
[Erste Brief an die Korinther. English] 1 Corinthians: a commentary on the First Epistle to the Corinthians / by Hans Conzelmann; translated by James W. Leitch; bibliography and references by James W. Dunkly; edited by George W. MacRae. — Philadelphia: Fortress Press, [1975] xxii, 323 p.; 25 cm. — (Hermeneia) Translation of Der erste Brief an die Korinther. Includes the text of 1 Corinthians in a translation produced for this edition. Includes indexes. 1. Bible. N.T. Corinthians, 1st — Commentaries. I. Bible. N.T. Corinthians, 1st. English. Leitch-MacRae. 1975. II. T. III. Series.
BS2675.3.C6613     227/.2/077     *LC* 73-88360     *ISBN* 0800660056

**Bible. N.T. Corinthians, 2nd. English. Furnish. 1984.**         **1.2714**
II Corinthians / translated with introduction, notes, and commentary by Victor Paul Furnish. — 1st ed. — Garden City, N.Y.: Doubleday, 1984. xxii, 619 p., [8] p. of plates: ill.; 24 cm. (The Anchor Bible; v. 32A) Includes indexes. 1. Bible. N.T. Corinthians, 2nd — Commentaries. I. Furnish, Victor Paul. II. T. III. Title: Second Corinthians.
BSBS2675.3.F8x     220.7/7 s 227/.3077 19     *LC* 83-2056     *ISBN* 0385111991

**Howard, George, 1935-.**         **1.2715**
Paul: crisis in Galatia: a study in early Christian theology / George Howard. — Cambridge; New York: Cambridge University Press, 1979. xii, 114 p.; 23 cm. (Society for New Testament studies monograph series; 35) Includes indexes. 1. Bible. N.T. Galatians — Criticism, interpretation, etc. I. T.
BS2685.2.H68     227/.4/06     *LC* 77-84002     *ISBN* 0521217091

**Betz, Hans Dieter.**         **1.2716**
Galatians: a commentary on Paul's letter to the churches in Galatia / by Hans Dieter Betz. — Philadelphia: Fortress Press, c1979. xxx, 352 p.; 25 cm. — (Hermeneia) Includes indexes. 1. Bible. N.T. Galatians — Commentaries. I. Bible. N.T. Galatians. English. Betz. 1979. II. T. III. Series.
BS2685.3.B47     227/.4077     *LC* 77-78625     *ISBN* 0800660099

**Bible. N.T. Ephesians. English. Barth. 1974,**         **1.2717**
Ephesians. Introd., translation, and commentary by Markus Barth. [1st ed.] Garden City, N.Y., Doubleday, 1974. 2 v. (xxxiv, 849 p.) 25 cm. (Bible. Anchor Bible. 1964. v. 34-34A) 1. Bible. N.T. Ephesians — Commentaries. I. Barth, Markus. ed. II. T. III. Series.
BS2693.B3x     220.6/6 s 227/.5/077     *LC* 72-79373     *ISBN* 0385044127

**Lohse, Eduard, 1924-.**         • **1.2718**
[Briefe an die Kolosser und an Philemon. English] Colossians and Philemon; a commentary on the Epistles to the Colossians and to Philemon. Translated by William R. Poehlmann and Robert J. Karris. Edited by Helmut Koester. Philadelphia, Fortress Press [1971] xviii, 233 p. 25 cm. (Hermeneia) Translation of Die Briefe an die Kolosser und an Philemon. 1. Bible. N.T. Colossians — Commentaries. 2. Bible. N.T. Philemon — Commentaries. I. Bible. N.T. Colossians. English. Poehlmann & Karris. 1971. II. Bible. N.T. Philemon. English. Poehlmann & Karris. 1971. III. T. IV. Series.
BS2715.3.L6413     227.7/07     *LC* 76-157550

**Best, Ernest.**         • **1.2719**
[Bible. N.T. Thessalonians. English. Best. 1972] A commentary on the First and Second Epistles to the Thessalonians. [1st U.S. ed.] New York, Harper & Row [c1972] xvi, 376 p. 23 cm. (Harper's New Testament commentaries) Includes the texts, translated by the author. 1. Bible. N.T. Thessalonians — Commentaries. I. Bible. N.T. Thessalonians. Best. 1972. II. T.
BS2725.3.B47 1972     227/.81/077     *LC* 72-82235     *ISBN* 0713613068 *ISBN* 0713613076

**Dibelius, Martin, 1883-1947.**         • **1.2720**
[Pastoralbriefe. English] The Pastoral epistles; a commentary on the Pastoral epistles, by Martin Dibelius and Hans Conzelmann. Translated by Philip Buttolph and Adela Yarbro. Edited by Helmut Koester. Philadelphia, Fortress Press [1972] xx, 175 p. illus. 25 cm. (Hermeneia) Translation of Die Pastoralbriefe, 4th rev. ed. by H. Conzelmann. 1. Bible. N.T. Pastoral Epistles — Commentaries. I. Conzelmann, Hans. II. Bible. N.T. Pastoral Epistles. English. Koester. 1972. III. T. IV. Series.
BS2735.D513 1972     227/.8     *LC* 71-157549     *ISBN* 0800660021

**Houlden, J. L. (James Leslie)**         **1.2721**
The pastoral Epistles: I and II Timothy, Titus / [by] J. L. Houlden. — Harmondsworth: Penguin, 1976. 168 p.; 19 cm. — (The Pelican New Testament commentaries) (A Pelican book) Includes indexes. Includes an introductory essay by the editor and the Revised Standard Version text of the Epistles. 1. Bible. N.T. Pastoral Epistles — Commentaries. I. Bible. N.T. Pastoral Epistles. English. Revised standard. 1976. II. T.
BS2735.3.H68     227/.83/077     *LC* 76-383585     *ISBN* 0140218149

**Jewett, Robert.**                                                    **1.2722**
Letter to Pilgrims: a commentary on the Epistle to the Hebrews / Robert
Jewett. — New York: Pilgrim Press, 1981. 248 p.; 21 cm. 1. Bible. N.T.
Hebrews — Commentaries. I. T.
BS2775.3.J48        227/.87077 19        LC 80-28102        ISBN 0829804250

**Dibelius, Martin, 1883-1947.**                                       **1.2723**
[Brief des Jakobus. English] James: a commentary on the Epistle of James / by
Martin Dibelius; rev. by Heinrich Greeven; translated by Michael A. Williams;
edited by Helmut Koester. — Philadelphia: Fortress Press, c1976. xxii, 285 p.;
25 cm. — (Hermeneia) Translated from Der Brief des Jakobus, 11th rev. ed.
prepared by H. Greeven. 1. Bible. N.T. James — Commentaries. I. Greeven,
Heinrich, 1906- II. Bible. N.T. James. English. 1976. III. T. IV. Series.
BS2785.D513        227/.91/077        LC 74-80428        ISBN 0800660064

**Laws, Sophie.**                                                      **1.2724**
A commentary on the Epistle of James / Sophie Laws. — San Francisco:
Harper & Row, c1980. x, 273 p.; 22 cm. — (Harper's New Testament
commentaries) Includes indexes. 1. Bible. N.T. James — Commentaries.
I. Bible. N.T. James. English. Laws. 1980. II. T.
BS2785.3.L38 1980        227/.91077 19        LC 80-8349        ISBN
0060649186

**Elliott, John Hall.**                                                **1.2725**
A home for the homeless: a sociological exegesis of 1 Peter, its situation and
strategy / John H. Elliott. — Philadelphia: Fortress Press, c1981. xiv, 306 p.:
map; 24 cm. 1. Bible. N.T. Peter, 1st — Criticism, interpretation, etc.
2. Sociology, Biblical I. T.
BS2795.2.E42        227/.9206 19        LC 80-2394        ISBN 0800606590

**Bible. N.T. Epistles of John. English. Brown. 1982.**              **1.2726**
The Epistles of John / translated, with introduction, notes, and commentary, by
Raymond E. Brown. — 1st ed. — Garden City, N.Y.: Doubleday, 1982. xxviii,
812 p.; 25 cm. — (The Anchor Bible; v. 30) Includes indexes. 1. Bible. N.T.
Epistles of John — Commentaries. I. Brown, Raymond Edward. II. T.
BS2803.B72x        227/.94077 19        LC 81-43380        ISBN 0385056869

**Bible. N.T. John. English. 1966. Brown.**                           **1.2727**
The Gospel according to John. Introd., translation, and notes by Raymond E.
Brown. [1st ed.] Garden City, N.Y., Doubleday, 1966-70. 2 v. (cxlvi, 1208 p.) 25
cm. (Bible. Anchor Bible. 1964. no. 29-29A) 1. Bible. N.T. John —
Commentaries. I. Brown, Raymond Edward. ed. II. T. III. Series.
BS2803.B7x        226/.5/077        LC 66-12209

**Bultmann, Rudolf Karl, 1884-1976.**                                  **1.2728**
[Drei Johannesbriefe. English] The Johannine epistles; a commentary on the
Johannine epistles, by Rudolf Bultmann. Translated by R. Philip O'Hara with
Lane C. McGaughy and Robert Funk. Edited by Robert W. Funk.
Philadelphia, Fortress Press [1973] xiv, 143 p. illus. 25 cm. (Hermeneia)
Translation of Die drei Johannesbriefe. 1. Bible. N.T. Epistles of John —
Commentaries. I. Bible. N.T. Epistles of John. 1973. II. T. III. Series.
BS2805.3.B8413        227/.94077 19        LC 75-171510        ISBN
080066003X

## BS2820–2970 Revelation. Apocrypha

**Lawrence, D. H. (David Herbert), 1885-1930.**                        **1.2729**
Apocalypse and the writings on Revelation / D. H. Lawrence; edited by Mara
Kalnins. — Cambridge [Eng.]; New York: Cambridge University Press, 1980.
xiii, 249 p.; 23 cm. (The Cambridge edition of the letters and works of D. H.
Lawrence) 1. Bible. N.T. Revelation — Criticism, interpretation, etc. —
Collected works. I. Kalnins, Mara. II. T.
BS2825.L36 1980        228/.06        LC 79-41417        ISBN 0521224071

**Collins, Adela Yarbro.**                                             **1.2730**
Crisis and catharsis: the power of the Apocalypse / Adela Yarbro Collins. —
1st ed. — Philadelphia: Westminster Press, c1984. 179 p.; 23 cm. 1. Bible. N.T.
Revelation — Criticism, interpretation, etc. I. T.
BS2825.2.C583 1984        228/.06 19        LC 83-26084        ISBN 0664245218

**Ellul, Jacques.**                                                    **1.2731**
[Apocalypse, architecture en mouvement. English] Apocalypse: the book of
Revelation / Jacques Ellul; translated by George W. Schreiner. — New York:
Seabury Press, 1977. 283 p.; 22 cm. Translation of L'Apocalypse, architecture
en mouvement. 'A Crossroad book.' 1. Bible. N.T. Revelation — Criticism,
interpretation, etc. I. T.
BS2825.2.E4413        228/.06        LC 76-54322        ISBN 0816403309

**Caird, G. B. (George Bradford), 1917-.**                            **1.2732**
A commentary on the Revelation of St. John the Divine / G.B. Caird. — 2nd
ed. — London: A. & C. Black, 1984. xvi, 318 p. — (Black's New Testament
commentaries) 1. Bible. N.T. Revelation — Commentaries I. Bible. N.T.
Revelation. English. Caird. 1984 II. T.
BS2825.3C3 1984        ISBN 0713626216

**Mounce, Robert H.**                                                  **1.2733**
The Book of Revelation / by Robert H. Mounce. — Grand Rapids: Eerdmans,
c1977. 426 p.; 23 cm. — (The New international commentary on the New
Testament; 17) Includes indexes. 1. Bible. N.T. Revelation — Commentaries.
I. Bible. N.T. Revelation. English. American revised. 1977. II. T.
BS2825.3.M69        228/.06        LC 77-7664        ISBN 0802823483

**Sweet, John Philip McMurdo.**                                        **1.2734**
Revelation / J. P. M. Sweet. — Philadelphia: Westminster Press, c1979. xv,
361 p.: map; 23 cm. (Westminster Pelican commentaries) Includes indexes.
1. Bible. N.T. Revelation — Commentaries. I. Bible. N.T. Revelation.
English. Revised standard. 1979. II. T. III. Series.
BS2825.3.S93        228/.07/7        LC 78-26383        ISBN 0664213758

**Bible. N.T. Apocryphal books. English. 1963.**                    • **1.2735**
New Testament Apocrypha, edited by Wilhelm Schneemelcher. English
translation [by A. J. B. Higgins and others] edited by R. McL. Wilson.
Philadelphia, Westminster Press [1963-66, c1963-65] 2 v. 24 cm. Original
German ed., edited by Edgar Hennecke. I. Hennecke, Edgar, 1865-1951, ed.
II. Schneemelcher, Wilhelm, 1914- ed. III. Wilson, R. McL. (Robert
McLachlan) ed. IV. T.
BS2832.S3        229        LC 63-7492

**Crossan, John Dominic.**                                             **1.2736**
Four other gospels: shadows on the contours of canon / by John Dominic
Crossan. — Minneapolis: Winston Press, c1985. 208 p.; 23 cm. 'A Seabury
book.' Includes indexes. 1. Bible. N.T. Gospels — Criticism, interpretation,
etc. 2. Apocryphal books (New Testament) — Criticism, interpretation, etc.
I. T.
BS2851.C76 1985        229/.806 19        LC 84-52137        ISBN 0866839593

**Smith, Morton, 1915-.**                                              **1.2737**
The Secret Gospel; the discovery and interpretation of the Secret Gospel
according to Mark. — [1st ed.]. — New York: Harper & Row, [1973] ix, 148 p.:
illus.; 22 cm. 1. Secret Gospel according to Mark. I. T.
BS2860.S42 S55 1973        229/.8        LC 72-11363        ISBN 0060674113

## BT DOCTRINAL THEOLOGY

(see also: BX1746-1759)

**Abelard, Peter, 1079-1142.**                                         **1.2738**
Christian theology [selected and translated] by J. Ramsay McCallum. Oxford,
Blackwell, 1948. vii, 117 p. I. McCallum, James Ramsay, ed. and tr. II. T.
BT7.M23        LC A50-4879

**Oberman, Heiko Augustinus.**                                         **1.2739**
Forerunners of the Reformation: the shape of late medieval thought / Heiko
Augustinus Oberman; illustrated by key documents; [translations by Paul L.
Nyhus]. — 1st Fortress Press ed. — Philadelphia: Fortress Press, 1981. xiii,
333 p.; 22 cm. Originally published: New York: Holt, Rinehart, and Winston,
1966. Includes index. 1. Theology — Collected works — Middle Ages,
600-1500 2. Theology, Doctrinal — History — Middle Ages, 600-1500 I. T.
BT10.O23 1981        230/.09/02 19        LC 81-66518        ISBN 0800616170

**Bultmann, Rudolf Karl, 1884-1976.**                                  **1.2740**
Existence and faith; shorter writings of Rudolf Bultmann. Selected, translated,
and introduced by Schubert M. Ogden. — New York: Meridian Books, [1960]
320 p.; 19 cm. — (Living age books) 1. Theology — Addresses, essays, lectures.
I. T.
BT15.B78        230.4        LC 60-6774

**Bultmann, Rudolf Karl, 1884-1976.**                                • **1.2741**
[Glauben und verstehen. English] Faith and understanding, [by] Rudolf
Bultmann. Edited with an introd. by Robert W. Funk. Translated by Louise
Pettibone Smith. [1st U.S. ed.] New York, Harper & Row [1969- v. 22 cm.
Essays. Translation of Glauben und verstehen. 1. Bible — Theology
2. Theology — Addresses, essays, lectures. I. T.
BT15.B8213        230/.08        LC 69-10471

**Ebeling, Gerhard, 1912-.**                                         • **1.2742**
Word and faith. — [1st English ed. Translated by James W. Leitch]. —
Philadelphia, Fortress Press [1963] 442 p. 23 cm. Bibliography: p. [16]
Bibliographical footnotes. 1. Theology, Doctrinal — Addresses, essays,
lectures. I. T.
BT15.E213        230.082        LC 63-13878

# BT19–33 Doctrine and Dogma

**Harnack, Adolf von, 1851-1930.**      • **1.2743**
History of dogma. Translated from the 3d German ed., by Neil Buchanan. — New York: Dover Publications, [1961] 7 v. in 4.; 21 cm. Translation of Lehrbuch der Dogmengeschichte. 'An unabridged republication of the English translation of the third German edition that appeared circa 1900.' 1. Theology, Doctrinal — History I. T.
BT21.H33 1961     230.09     *LC* 61-4455

**Burkill, T. Alec.**      • **1.2744**
The evolution of Christian thought, by T. A. Burkill. — Ithaca [N.Y.]: Cornell University Press, [1971] x, 504 p.; 24 cm. 1. Theology, Doctrinal — History I. T.
BT21.2.B86     201/.1/09     *LC* 76-127601     *ISBN* 0801405815

**A History of Christian doctrine: in succession to the earlier**     **1.2745**
**work of G. P. Fisher, published in the International**
**technological library series / edited by Hubert Cunliffe–Jones,**
**assisted by Benjamin Drewery.**
1st Fortress Press ed. — Philadelphia: Fortress Press, 1980, c1978. x, [iii], 601 p.; 22 cm. Includes indexes. 1. Theology, Doctrinal — History — Addresses, essays, lectures. I. Cunliffe-Jones, Hubert. II. Drewery, Benjamin. III. Fisher, George Park, 1827-1909. History of Christian doctrine.
BT21.2.H57 1980     230/.09     *LC* 79-21689     *ISBN* 0800606264

**Lohse, Bernhard, 1928-.**      **1.2746**
[Epochen der Dogmengeschichte. English] A short history of Christian doctrine. Translated by F. Ernest Stoeffler. Philadelphia, Fortress Press [1966] xiv, 304 p. 23 cm. Translation of Epochen der Dogmengeschichte. 1. Theology, Doctrinal — History I. T.
BT21.2.L613     230/.09     *LC* 66-21732

**Placher, William C. (William Carl), 1948-.**      **1.2747**
A history of Christian theology: an introduction / by William C. Placher. — 1st ed. — Philadelphia: Westminster Press, c1983. 324 p.; 23 cm. Includes index. 1. Theology, Doctrinal — History I. T.
BT21.2.P57 1983     230/.09 19     *LC* 83-16778     *ISBN* 0664244963

**Kelly, J. N. D. (John Norman Davidson)**      • **1.2748**
Early Christian doctrines. — New York: Harper, [1959, c1958] 500 p.; 22 cm. 1. Theology, Doctrinal — History — Early church, ca. 30-600 I. T.
BT25.K4 1959     230.11     *LC* 58-12933

**Pelikan, Jaroslav Jan, 1923-.**      • **1.2749**
The Christian tradition: a history of the development of doctrine / [by] Jaroslav Pelikan. — Chicago: University of Chicago Press, [1971- . –. v.   ; 24 cm. — 1. Theology, Doctrinal — History — Early church, ca. 30-600 I. T.
BT25.P43     230.2     *LC* 79-142042     *ISBN* 0226653706

**Wolfson, Harry Austryn, 1887-1974.**      • **1.2750**
The philosophy of the Church fathers. 3d ed., rev. Cambridge, Harvard University Press [1970-. v. 23 cm. (His Structure and growth of philosophic systems from Plato to Spinoza, 3) 1. Theology, Doctrinal — History — Early church, ca. 30-600 2. Incarnation — History of doctrines 3. Trinity — History of doctrines — Early church, ca. 30-600. 4. Heresies, Christian — History — Early church, ca. 30-600 I. T.
BT25.W63     230     *LC* 70-119077     *ISBN* 0674665511

**Chenu, Marie-Dominique, 1895-.**      **1.2751**
[Théologie au douzième siècle. English] Nature, man, and society in the twelfth century; essays on new theological perspectives in the Latin West, by M. D. Chenu, with a pref. by Etienne Gilson. Selected, edited, and translated by Jerome Taylor and Lester K. Little. Chicago, University of Chicago Press [1968] xxi, 361 p. 25 cm. Translation of nine essays selected from La théologie au douzième siècle. 1. Theology, Doctrinal — History — Middle Ages, 600-1500 2. Philosophy, Medieval — History. 3. Scholasticism — History. I. T.
BT26.C5132 1968     230     *LC* 68-15574

**Oberman, Heiko Augustinus.**      • **1.2752**
The harvest of medieval theology; Gabriel Biel and late medieval nominalism. — [Rev. ed.]. — Grand Rapids: W. B. Eerdmans Pub. Co., [1967] xv, 495 p.; 22 cm. (Robert Troup Paine prize-treatise. 1962) 1. Biel, Gabriel, d. 1495. 2. Theology, Doctrinal — History — Middle Ages, 600-1500 3. Nominalism I. T. II. Series.
BT26.O2 1967     230/.09/02     *LC* 67-19313

**Barth, Karl, 1886-1968.**      **1.2753**
The humanity of God. — Richmond, John Knox Press [1960] 96 p. 21 cm. 1. Theology, Doctrinal — Hist. — 19th cent. 2. Theology, Doctrinal — Hist. — 20th cent. 3. Freedom (Theology) I. T.
BT28.B273     230.0903     *LC* 60-5479

**Berger, Peter L.**      **1.2754**
The heretical imperative: contemporary possibilities of religious affirmation / Peter L. Berger. — 1st ed. — Garden City, N.Y.: Anchor Press, 1979. xv, 220 p.; 22 cm. 1. Theology — 20th century 2. Religion and sociology 3. Experience (Religion) 4. Religions I. T.
BT28.B43 1979     200/.1     *LC* 78-20106     *ISBN* 0385142862

**Cooper, John Charles.**      • **1.2755**
Radical Christianity and its sources. Philadelphia, Westminster Press [1968] 171 p. 21 cm. 1. Theology, Doctrinal — History — 20th century 2. Christianity — 20th century 3. Death of God theology 4. United States — Religion — 1946-1960. 5. United States — Religion — 1960- I. T.
BT28.C58     230/.09/04     *LC* 68-21411

**A Handbook of Christian theologians / edited by Dean G.**     **1.2756**
**Peerman and Martin E. Marty.**
Enl. ed. — Nashville: Abingdon Press, c1984. 735 p.; 21 cm. 1. Theology, Doctrinal — History — 19th century — Handbooks, manuals, etc. 2. Theology, Doctrinal — History — 20th century — Handbooks, manuals, etc. 3. Theologians — Handbooks, manuals, etc. I. Peerman, Dean G. II. Marty, Martin E., 1928-
BT28.H33 1984     230/.092/2 19     *LC* 84-16879     *ISBN* 0687165636

**Mackintosh, H. R. (Hugh Ross), 1870-1936.**      • **1.2757**
Types of modern theology: Schleiermacher to Barth / by Hugh Ross Mackintosh. — London: Nisbet, 1937. vii, 333 p. 1. Theology, Doctrinal — History — 19th century 2. Theology, Doctrinal — History — 20th century I. T.
BT28.M25     *LC* 37-37828

**Tillich, Paul, 1886-1965.**      • **1.2758**
Perspectives on 19th and 20th century Protestant theology. Edited and with an introd. by Carl E. Braaten. [1st ed.] New York, Harper & Row [1967] xxiv, 252 p. 22 cm. 'Lectures ... delivered at the Divinity School of the University of Chicago ... spring ... 1963.' 1. Protestant churches — Doctrines — History. 2. Theology, Doctrinal — History — 19th century 3. Theology, Doctrinal — History — 20th century I. Braaten, Carl E., 1929- ed. II. T.
BT28.T5     230/.4     *LC* 67-11507

**Tracy, David.**      **1.2759**
Blessed rage for order, the new pluralism in theology / David Tracy. — New York: Seabury Press, [1975] xiv, 271 p.; 24 cm. 'A Crossroad book.' Includes bibliographical references and indexes. 1. Theology — 20th century 2. Languages — Religious aspects — Christianity I. T.
BT28.T65     230     *LC* 75-8803     *ISBN* 0816402779

**Welch, Claude.**      • **1.2760**
Protestant thought in the nineteenth century. New Haven, Yale University Press, 1972-. v. 24 cm. 1. Theology, Doctrinal — History — 19th century 2. Protestant churches — Doctrines — History — 19th century. I. T.
BT28.W394     209/.034     *LC* 72-75211     *ISBN* 0300015356

**Wingren, Gustaf, 1910-.**      • **1.2761**
Theology in conflict: Nygren, Barth, Bultmann / by Gustaf Wingren; translated by Eric H. Wahlstrom. — Philadelphia: Muhlenberg Press, c1958. xxii, 170 p. Translation of Teologiens metodfråga. 1. Nygren, Anders, 1890- 2. Barth, Karl, 1886-1968. 3. Bultmann, Rudolf Karl, 1884-1976. 4. Theology, Doctrinal — History — 20th century 5. Law and gospel I. T.
BT28 W513

**Asian voices in Christian theology / edited and with an introd.**     **1.2762**
**by Gerald H. Anderson.**
Maryknoll, N.Y.: Orbis Books, c1976. 321 p.; 22 cm. 1. Theology, Doctrinal — Asia — History — Addresses, essays, lectures. I. Anderson, Gerald H.
BT30.A8 A78     230/.095     *LC* 75-13795     *ISBN* 0883440172

**Barth, Karl, 1886-1968.**      **1.2763**
[Protestantische Theologie im 19. Jahrhundert. English] Protestant theology in the nineteenth century; its background & history. Valley Forge [Pa.] Judson Press [1973, c1972] 669 p. 23 cm. 'The first complete translation of Die protestantische Theologie im 19. Jahrhundert.' 1. Theology, Doctrinal — Germany — History. 2. Theology, Doctrinal — History — 18th century 3. Theology, Doctrinal — History — 19th century 4. Protestant churches — Germany — Doctrines — History. I. T.
BT30.G3 B313 1973     230/.09/034     *LC* 72-1956     *ISBN* 0817005722

**Haroutunian, Joseph, 1904-.**      • **1.2764**
Piety versus moralism: the passing of the New England theology / by Joseph Haroutunian. — Hamden, Conn.: Archon Books, 1964. xxv, 329, 4 p.; 20 cm.

— 1. New England theology I. T. II. Title: The Passing of the New England Theology.
BT30.U5 H3       *LC* 64-24715

**Ahlstrom, Sydney E. comp.**                                    • **1.2765**
Theology in America; the major Protestant voices from puritanism to neo-orthodoxy. Indianapolis, Bobbs-Merrill, 1967. 630 p. (American heritage series, 73.) 1. Theology, Doctrinal — United States — History 2. Theology — Collections — Protestant authors. I. T.
BT30.U55 A6       230.0973       *LC* 67-21401

**Fackre, Gabriel J.**                                    **1.2766**
The Religious Right and Christian faith / by Gabriel Fackre. — Grand Rapids, Mich.: Eerdmans, c1982. xiii, 126 p.: ill.; 22 cm. 1. Falwell, Jerry. 2. Moral Majority, Inc. 3. Theology, Doctrinal — United States — History — 20th century. 4. Fundamentalism — History — 20th century. 5. Christianity and politics — History — 20th century. I. T.
BT30.U6 F33 1982       230/.044 19       *LC* 82-2488       *ISBN* 080283566X

**Ferm, Deane William, 1927-.**                                    **1.2767**
Contemporary American theologies: a critical survey / Deane William Ferm. — New York: Seabury Press, 1981. x, 182 p.; 21 cm. Includes index. 1. Theology, Doctrinal — United States — History — 20th century. I. T.
BT30.U6 F4       230/.0973 19       *LC* 81-5678       *ISBN* 0816423415

# BT40–55 Philosophical Theology

**Farrer, Austin Marsden.**                                    **1.2768**
Reflective faith; essays in philosophical theology. Edited by Charles C. Conti. — Grand Rapids: Eerdmans, [1974, c1972] xv, 234 p.; 21 cm. 1. Philosophical theology I. T.
BT40.F36 1974       230/.3       *LC* 73-14737       *ISBN* 0802815197

**Flew, Antony, 1923-.**                                    • **1.2769**
New essays in philosophical theology / edited by Antony Flew [and] Alasdair MacIntyre. — New York: Macmillan, 1964. x, 274 p.; 22 cm. — (Macmillan paperback edition) 1. Philosophical theology I. MacIntyre, Alasdair C. II. T.
BT40.F54 1964       230.01

**Tillich, Paul, 1886-1965.**                                    • **1.2770**
Theology of culture, edited by Robert C. Kimball. — New York: Oxford University Press, 1959. ix, 213 p.; 20 cm. 1. Christianity — Philosophy 2. Culture I. T.
BT40.T5       201       *LC* 59-9814

**Robinson, John A. T. (John Arthur Thomas), 1919-.**                                    • **1.2771**
Honest to God. Philadelphia, Westminster Press [1963] 143 p. 19 cm. 1. Christianity — Essence, genius, nature 2. Apologetics — 20th century I. T.
BT55.R6       230       *LC* 63-13819

# BT65–83 Doctrinal, Dogmatic, Systematic Theology

**Aulén, Gustaf, 1879-.**                                    • **1.2772**
The faith of the Christian church. Translated from the 5th Swedish ed by Eric H. Wahlstrom. — Philadephia, Muhlenberg Press [c1960] 403 p. 22 cm. Translation of Den allmänneliga kristna tron. Includes bibliography. 1. Theology, Doctrinal I. T.
BT75.A763 1960       230       *LC* 61-5302

**Barth, Karl, 1886-1968.**                                    • **1.2773**
[Kirchliche Dogmatik. English] Church dogmatics / by Karl Barth; editors, G. W. Bromiley, T. F. Torrance; [translator, G. W. Bromiley]. — 2d ed. — Edinburgh: T. & T. Clark, 1975-. v.; 24 cm. Translation of Die kirchliche Dogmatik. Each pt. also has special t.p. Includes indexes. 1. Theology, Doctrinal I. Bromiley, Geoffrey William. II. Torrance, Thomas Forsyth, 1913- III. T.
BT75.B283 1975       230       *LC* 78-315267       *ISBN* 0567090132

**Heim, Karl, 1874-1958.**                                    • **1.2774**
Christian faith and natural science. [1st Harper torchbook ed.] New York, Harper [1957] 256 p. 21 cm. (Harper torchbooks, TB16) Translation by N. Horton Smith of Der christliche Gottenglaube und die Naturwissenschaft, I. Grundiegung. 1. Religion and science — 1946- I. T.
BT75.H536 1957       *LC* 57-7536

**Schleiermacher, Friedrich, 1768-1834.**                                    **1.2775**
[Christliche Glaube. English] The Christian faith / by Friedrich Schleiermacher; edited by H. R. Mackintosh and J. S. Stewart. — Philadelphia: Fortress Press, 1976. xii, 760 p.; 23 cm. Translation of the 2d ed. of Der christliche Glaube. 1. Theology, Doctrinal I. T.
BT75.S58513 1976       230       *LC* 76-53313       *ISBN* 0800604873

**Cox, Harvey Gallagher.**                                    **1.2776**
Religion in The secular city: toward a postmodern theology / by Harvey Cox. — New York: Simon and Schuster, c1984. 304 p.; 22 cm. Includes index. 1. Theology — 20th century I. T.
BT75.2.C69 1984       230 19       *LC* 83-19619       *ISBN* 0671453440

**Fiorenza, Francis Schüssler.**                                    **1.2777**
Foundational theology: Jesus and the church / Francis Schüssler Fiorenza. — New York: Crossroad, 1984. xviii, 326 p.; 24 cm. 1. Jesus Christ — Resurrection 2. Hermeneutics 3. Theology, Doctrinal 4. Church 5. Mission of the church I. T.
BT75.2.F56 1984       230/.2 19       *LC* 84-7764       *ISBN* 0824504941

**Kaufman, Gordon D.**                                    **1.2778**
Systematic theology: a historicist perspective / by Gordon D. Kaufman. — New York: Scribner, c1978. xxiv, 543 p.; 21 cm. 1. Theology, Doctrinal I. T.
BT75.2.K38 1978       230       *LC* 78-50761       *ISBN* 0684157969

**Macquarrie, John.**                                    **1.2779**
Principles of Christian theology / John Macquarrie. 2d ed. — New York: Scribner, c1977. xiii, 544 p.; 24 cm. 1. Theology, Doctrinal I. T.
BT75.2.M3 1977       230       *LC* 76-23182       *ISBN* 0684147769

**Rahner, Karl, 1904-.**                                    **1.2780**
[Grundkurs des Glaubens English] Foundations of Christian faith: an introduction to the idea of Christianity / Karl Rahner; translated by William V. Dych. — New York: Seabury Press, 1978. xv, 470 p.; 24 cm. 'A Crossroad book.' Translation of Grundkurs des Glaubens. 1. Catholic Church — Doctrinal and controversial works — Catholic authors. 2. Theology, Doctrinal I. T.
BT75.2.R3313       230/.2       *LC* 77-13336       *ISBN* 0816403546

**Roberts, J. Deotis (James Deotis), 1927-.**                                    **1.2781**
A Black political theology, by J. Deotis Roberts. Philadelphia, Westminster Press [1974] 238 p. 19 cm. 1. Theology, Doctrinal 2. Afro-Americans — Religion I. T.
BT75.2.R6       230       *LC* 74-4384       *ISBN* 0664249884

**Thielicke, Helmut, 1908-.**                                    **1.2782**
The evangelical faith. Translated and edited by Geoffrey W. Bromiley. — Grand Rapids: Eerdmans, [1974-. 3v.   ; 25 cm. Translation of Der evangelische Glaube. 1. Theology, Doctrinal I. T.
BT75.2.T4513       230       *LC* 74-7010       *ISBN* 0802823424

**Tillich, Paul, 1886-1965.**                                    • **1.2783**
Systematic theology. — [Chicago]: University of Chicago Press, [1967, c1951-63] 3 v. in 1; 24 cm. 1. Theology, Doctrinal I. T.
BT75.2.T5 1967       230/.0924       *LC* 66-20786

**Tracy, David.**                                    **1.2784**
The analogical imagination: Christian theology and the culture of pluralism / David Tracy. — New York: Crossroad, 1981. xiv, 467 p. 1. Theology, Doctrinal I. T.
BT75.2.T645       BT75.2 T645.       230 19       *LC* 81-629       *ISBN* 0824501225

**Wainwright, Geoffrey, 1939-.**                                    **1.2785**
Doxology: the praise of God in worship, doctrine, and life: a systematic theology / by Geoffrey Wainwright. — New York: Oxford University Press, 1980. vii, 609 p.; 24 cm. Includes indexes. 1. Theology, Doctrinal 2. Liturgics I. T.
BT75.2.W34 1980       230       *LC* 80-11886       *ISBN* 0195201922

**Cone, James H.**                                    • **1.2786**
A Black theology of liberation [by] James H. Cone. — [1st ed.] — Philadelphia: Lippincott, [1970] 254 p.; 21 cm. — (C. Eric Lincoln series in Black religion) 1. Black theology I. T. II. Series.
BT78.C59 1970       200       *LC* 74-120333

**Cullmann, Oscar.**                                    • **1.2787**
Christ and time: the primitive Christian conception of time and history / Oscar Cullmann; translated from the German by Floyd V. Filson. — Rev. ed. — Philadelphia: Westminster Press, 1964. xvi, 253 p. 1. Theology, Doctrinal 2. Church history — Philosophy 3. Salvation I. T.
BT78.C83 1964       *LC* 64-2336

**Van Buren, Paul Matthews, 1924-.**                                    **1.2788**
Discerning the way: a theology of the Jewish Christian reality / Paul M. Van Buren. — New York: Seabury Press, 1980. vii, 207 p. 'A Crossroad book.'

1. Theology, Doctrinal 2. Christianity and other religions — Judaism 3. Judaism — Relations — Christianity I. T.
BT78.V28      BT78 V28.      230      *LC* 79-27373      *ISBN* 0816401241

**Christian theology: an introduction to its traditions and tasks /**      **1.2789**
**edited by Peter C. Hodgson and Robert H. King.**
2nd ed., rev. and enl. — Philadelphia: Fortress Press, 1985. xiii, 400 p.; 23 cm. 1. Theology, Doctrinal — Addresses, essays, lectures. I. Hodgson, Peter Crafts, 1934- II. King, Robert Harlen, 1935-
BT80.C49 1985      230 19      *LC* 84-48720      *ISBN* 0800618483

**Ogden, Schubert Miles, 1928-.**      **1.2790**
The reality of God, and other essays / by Schubert M. Ogden. — [1st ed.]. — New York: Harper & Row, 1966. xii, 237 p.; 22 cm. 1. Theology, Doctrinal — Addresses, essays, lectures. I. T.
BT80.O4      230      *LC* 66-20783

**Pannenberg, Wolfhart, 1928-.**      **1.2791**
[Grundfragen systematischer Theologie English] Basic questions in theology: collected essays / Wolfhart Pannenberg; translated by George H. Kehm. — Philadelphia: Westminster Press, 1983, c1970-c1971. 2 v.; 22 cm. Translation of Grundfragen systematischer Theologie. Reprint. Originally published: Philadelphia: Fortress Press, [1970-1971] 1. Theology, Doctrinal — Addresses, essays, lectures. I. T.
BT80.P3413 1983      230/.044 19      *LC* 82-15984      *ISBN* 0664244661

**Hutchison, William R.**      **1.2792**
The modernist impulse in American Protestantism / William R. Hutchison. — Cambridge, Mass.: Harvard University Press, 1976. x, 347 p.: ports.; 25 cm. Includes index. 1. Modernism I. T.
BT82.H87      273/.9      *LC* 75-20190      *ISBN* 0674580583

**Barr, James.**      **1.2793**
Fundamentalism / by James Barr. — Philadelphia: Westminster Press, c1978. vii, 379 p.; 22 cm. Includes indexes. 1. Fundamentalism — Controversial literature. I. T.
BT82.2.B37      230      *LC* 77-14512      *ISBN* 0664241913

**Marsden, George M., 1939-.**      **1.2794**
Fundamentalism and American culture: the shaping of twentieth century evangelicalism, 1870–1925 / George M. Marsden. — New York: Oxford University Press, 1980. xiv, 306 p.: ill.; 24 cm. 1. Fundamentalism — History. 2. Christianity — United States I. T.
BT82.2.M37      280/.4      *LC* 80-11209      *ISBN* 0195027582

**Sandeen, Ernest Robert, 1931-.**      • **1.2795**
The roots of fundamentalism; British and American millenarianism, 1800–1930 [by] Ernest R. Sandeen. — Chicago: University of Chicago Press, [1970] xix, 328 p.; 23 cm. 1. Fundamentalism 2. Millennialism I. T.
BT82.2.S18      280/.4      *LC* 79-112739      *ISBN* 0226734676

**Black theology: a documentary history, 1966–1979 / edited by**      **1.2796**
**Gayraud S. Wilmore and James H. Cone.**
Maryknoll, N.Y.: Orbis Books, c1979. ix, 657 p.; 24 cm. Includes index. 1. Black theology — Addresses, essays, lectures. 2. Afro-Americans — Religion — Addresses, essays, lectures. 3. Black power — Addresses, essays, lectures. I. Wilmore, Gayraud S. II. Cone, James H.
BT82.7.B56      230      *LC* 79-12747      *ISBN* 0883440415

**Cone, James H.**      **1.2797**
A Black theology of liberation / James H. Cone; [foreword by Paulo Freire]. — 2nd ed. — Maryknoll, N.Y.: Orbis Books, c1986. xxii, 154 p.; 21 cm. Includes index. 1. Black theology I. T.
BT82.7.C666 1986      230/.08996 19      *LC* 85-18749      *ISBN* 0883442450

**Cone, James H.**      **1.2798**
For my people: Black theology and the Black church / James H. Cone. — Maryknoll, N.Y.: Orbis Books, c1984. xiii, 271 p.; 21 cm. (Bishop Henry McNeal Turner studies in North American Black religion. vol. 1) 1. Black theology 2. Afro-American churches I. T. II. Series.
BT82.7.C67 1984      230/.08996073 19      *LC* 84-5195      *ISBN* 0883441063

**Bonhoeffer, Dietrich, 1906-1945.**      • **1.2799**
[Akt und Sein. English] Act and being. Translated by Bernard Noble. Introd. by Ernst Wolf. [1st American ed.] New York, Harper [1962, c1961] 192 p. 22 cm. 1. Dialectical theology 2. Act (Philosophy) I. T.
BT83.B613 1962a      230      *LC* 62-7951

**Robinson, James McConkey, 1924-.**      • **1.2800**
The beginnings of dialectic theology. Edited by James M. Robinson. — Richmond: John Knox Press, [1968-. v.     ; 24 cm. Vol. 1 contains a translation of p. 37-49, 77-218, and 322-347 of Teil 1 and p. 11-218 of Teil 2, of Anfänge der dialektischen Theologie, München, 1962-63, comp. by J. Moltmann. Vol. 1, pt. 1 translated by Keith R. Crim; pt. 2 translated by Louis

De Grazia and Keith R. Crim. 1. Dialectical theology — Collections. 2. Theology — Collections — 20th century. I. Moltmann, Jürgen, ed. Anfänge der dialektischen Theologie. English. 1968. II. T.
BT83.R63      230      *LC* 67-12941

# BT83.5–83.7 Death of God. Theology. Liberation Theology. Process Theology. Secularization

**Altizer, Thomas J. J.**      **1.2801**
Radical theology and the death of God [by] Thomas J. J. Altizer and William Hamilton. — Indianapolis: Bobbs-Merrill, [1966] xiii, 202 p.; 20 cm. 1. Death of God theology I. Hamilton, William, 1924- II. T. III. Title: The death of God.
BT83.5.A46      230      *LC* 66-20111

**Toward a new Christianity: readings in the death of God**      • **1.2802**
**theology / edited by Thomas J.J. Altizer.**
New York: Harcourt, Brace and World, 1967. viii, 374 p. 1. Death of God theology — Collected works. I. Altizer, Thomas J. J.
BT83.5.A47      BT83.5.T68.      *LC* 67-15337

**Boff, Leonardo.**      **1.2803**
[Da libertação. English] Salvation and liberation / Leonardo and Clodovis Boff; translated from the Portuguese by Robert R. Barr. — Maryknoll, N.Y.: Orbis Books, c1984. viii, 119 p.; 21 cm. Translation of: Da libertação. 1. Liberation theology I. Boff, Clodovis. II. T.
BT83.57.B613 1984      261.8/098 19      *LC* 84-7220      *ISBN* 0883444518

**Comblin, Joseph, 1923-.**      **1.2804**
The church and the national security state / José Comblin. — Maryknoll, N.Y.: Orbis Books, c1979. xiii, 236 p.; 24 cm. 1. Catholic Church — Latin America 2. Liberation theology 3. Church and state — Latin America I. T.
BT83.57.C65      261.7/098      *LC* 79-10881      *ISBN* 0883440822

**Míguez Bonino, José.**      **1.2805**
Doing theology in a revolutionary situation / José Míguez Bonino. — Philadelphia: Fortress Press, [1975] xxviii, 179 p.; 20 cm. (Confrontation books) 1. Liberation theology I. T.
BT83.57.M53      261.8      *LC* 74-80424      *ISBN* 0800614518

**Frontiers of theology in Latin America / edited by Rosino**      **1.2806**
**Gibellini; translated by John Drury; Gustavo Gutiérrez ... [et**
**al.].**
Maryknoll, N.Y.: Orbis Books, c1979. xii, 321 p.: ill.; 24 cm. Translation of La Nuova frontiera della teologia in America Latina. 1. Liberation theology — Addresses, essays, lectures. 2. Theology, Doctrinal — Addresses, essays, lectures. I. Gibellini, Rosino.
BT83.57.N8613      261.8/098      *LC* 78-9147      *ISBN* 0883441446 pbk

**Segundo, Juan Luis.**      **1.2807**
[Liberación de la teología. English] Liberation of theology / Juan Luis Segundo; translated by John Drury. — Maryknoll, N.Y.: Orbis Books, c1976. vi, 240 p.; 24 cm. Translation of Liberación de la teología. 1. Liberation theology 2. Sociology, Christian 3. Theology — 20th century I. T.
BT83.57.S4413      230 19      *LC* 76-7049      *ISBN* 088344285X

**Witvliet, Theo.**      **1.2808**
[Plaats onder de zon. English] A place in the sun: liberation theology in the Third World / Theo Witvliet; [translated by John Bowden from the Dutch]. — Maryknoll, N.Y.: Orbis Books, 1985. ix, 182 p.; 22 cm. Translation of: Een plaats onder de zon. Includes index. 1. Liberation theology 2. Black theology 3. Ras Tafari movement 4. Theology, Doctrinal — Developing countries. I. T.
BT83.57.W5713 1985      230 19      *LC* 84-27229      *ISBN* 0883444046

**Cobb, John B.**      **1.2809**
Process theology: an introductory exposition / John B. Cobb, Jr., and David Ray Griffin. — Philadelphia: Westminster Press, c1976. 192 p.; 21 cm. Includes index. 1. Process theology I. Griffin, David, 1939- joint author. II. T.
BT83.6.C6      230      *LC* 76-10352      *ISBN* 0664247431

**Ford, Lewis S.**      **1.2810**
The lure of God: a Biblical background for process theism / Lewis S. Ford. — Philadelphia: Fortress Press, c1978. xiii, 144 p.; 24 cm. 1. Bible — Theology 2. Process theology I. T.
BT83.6.F67      230      *LC* 77-15230      *ISBN* 0800605160

**Schillebeeckx, Edward, 1914-.**       • **1.2811**
God, the future of man, by E. Schillebeeckx. Translated by N. D. Smith. New York, Sheed and Ward [1968] xi, 207 p. 22 cm. Essays. 1. Church and the world 2. Secularization (Theology) I. T.
BT83.7.S3      260      *LC* 68-26036

# BT88–94 Authority. Kingdom of God

**Tavard, Georges Henri, 1922-.**       • **1.2812**
Holy Writ or Holy Church: the crisis of the Protestant Reformation / George H. Tavard. — New York: Harper, 1959. x, 250 p.; 23 cm. 1. Catholic Church — Relations — Protestant churches 2. Authority (Religion) — History of doctrines 3. Protestant churches — Relations — Catholic Church I. T.
BT88.T35      230      *LC* 60-5299

**Campenhausen, Hans, Freiherr von, 1903-.**       • **1.2813**
[Kirchliches Amt und geistliche Vollmacht. English] Ecclesiastical authority and spiritual power in the church of the first three centuries [by] Hans von Campenhausen. Translated by J. A. Baker. Stanford, Calif., Stanford University Press, 1969. vii, 308 p. 23 cm. Translation of Kirchliches Amt und geistliche Vollmacht in den ersten drei Jahrhunderten. 1. Church — Authority 2. Church — History of doctrines — Early church. I. T.
BT91.C313      262/.8      *LC* 68-54827

**Buber, Martin, 1878-1965.**       • **1.2814**
Kingship of God. Translated by Richard Scheimann. — [1st American ed.]. — New York, Harper & Row [1967] 228 p. 22 cm. Translation of the 3d, newly enl. ed. of Königtum Gottes. Bibliographical references included in 'Notes' (p. [163]-222) 1. Bible O.T. — Theology. 2. Kingdom of God I. T.
BT94.B813      231/.7      *LC* 67-14929

**Niebuhr, H. Richard (Helmut Richard), 1894-1962.**       • **1.2815**
The kingdom of God in America. Hamden, Conn.: Shoe String Press, 1956 [c1935] 215 p. 21 cm. 1. Kingdom of God 2. United States — Church history I. T.
BT94.N5 1956      231.7      *LC* 56-6352

**Pannenberg, Wolfhart, 1928-.**       **1.2816**
Theology and the kingdom of God / by Wolfhart Pannenberg. — Philadelphia: Westminster Press, [1969] 143 p.; 21 cm. 1. Pannenberg, Wolfhart, 1928- 2. Kingdom of God I. Newhaus, Richard John. II. T.
BT94.P33      231/.7      *LC* 69-12668      *ISBN* 066424842X

**Perrin, Norman.**       **1.2817**
The kingdom of God in the teaching of Jesus. Philadelphia, Westminster Press [1963] 215 p. 23 cm. (The New Testament library) Revision of thesis— Göttingen. 1. Jesus Christ — Teachings 2. Kingdom of God 3. Theology, Doctrinal — History — 20th century I. T.
BT94.P39      *LC* 63-14641

**Schnackenburg, Rudolf, 1914-.**       **1.2818**
[Gottes Herrschaft und Reich. English] God's rule and kingdon; translated [from the German] by John Murray. 2nd enlarged ed. London, Burns & Oates; New York, Herder and Herder, 1968. 400 p. 22 cm. Translation of Gottes Herrschaft und Reich. 1. Kingdom of God I. T.
BT94.S343 1968      231/.7      *LC* 68-133720

**Schweitzer, Albert, 1875-1965.**       • **1.2819**
[Reich Gottes und Christentum. English] The kingdom of God and primitive Christianity. Edited, with an introd. by Ulrich Neuenschwander. Translated by L. A. Garrard. New York, Seabury Press [1968] xiv, 193 p. 22 cm. Translation of Reich Gottes und Christentum. 1. Kingdom of God — Biblical teaching I. Neuenschwander, Ulrich. ed. II. T.
BT94.S3523 1968      231/.7      *LC* 68-24007

# BT98–180 God

**Grant, Robert McQueen, 1917-.**       • **1.2820**
The early Christian doctrine of God [by] Robert M. Grant. — Charlottesville, University Press of Virginia [1966] vi, 141 p. illus. 23 cm. — (Richard lectures, 1965-66) Bibliography: p. [127]-132. 1. God — History of doctrines 2. Trinity — History of doctrines I. T.
BT98.G68      231      *LC* 66-22845

**Evans, G. R. (Gillian Rosemary)**       **1.2821**
Anselm and talking about God / by G. R. Evans. — Oxford: Clarendon Press; New York: Oxford University Press, 1978. [12], 211 p.; 23 cm. Includes index. 1. Anselm, Saint, Archbishop of Canterbury, 1033-1109. 2. God — History of doctrines — Middle Ages, 600-1500 I. T.
BT100.A57 E9      230/.2/0924      *LC* 78-40314      *ISBN* 0198266472

**Burrell, David B.**       **1.2822**
Aquinas: God and action / David B. Burrell. — Notre Dame, Ind.: University of Notre Dame Press, 1979. xiii, 194 p.; 24 cm. 1. Thomas, Aquinas, Saint, 1225?-1274 — Contributions in theology 2. God — Proof — History of doctrines I. T.
BT100.T4 B87 1979      231/.042      *LC* 78-51519      *ISBN* 0268005885

**Kenny, Anthony John Patrick.**       **1.2823**
The five ways: St. Thomas Aquinas' proofs of God's existence / Anthony Kenny. — Notre Dame, Ind.: University of Notre Dame Press, 1980, c1969. 131 p.; 21 cm. Reprint of the ed. published by Schocken Books, New York, in series: Studies in ethics and the philosophy of religion. Includes index. 1. Thomas, Aquinas, Saint, 1225?-1274 — Contributions in theology 2. God — Proof I. T.
BT100.T4 K46 1980      231/.042      *LC* 80-10416      *ISBN* 026800952X

**Thomas, Aquinas, Saint, 1225?-1274.**       • **1.2824**
Concerning being and essence: De ente et essentia / translated from the Latin with the addition of a preface by George G. Leckie. New York: Appleton-Century-Crofts, c1937. 47 p. 'Appleton-Century philosophy sourcebooks' 1. Ontology 2. Substance (Philosophy) I. Leckie, George Gaines. II. T.
BT100.T4 06 1937      *LC* 37-2104

**Gilson, Etienne, 1884-1978.**       • **1.2825**
God and philosophy, by Étienne Gilson ... — New Haven, Yale University Press; [1961] 147 p. 21 cm. — (Half-title: Powell lectures on philosophy at Indiana University) Bibliographical foot-notes. 1. God — Knowableness 2. God — Proof I. T.
BT101.G53      231      *LC* 41-8742

**Royce, Josiah, 1855-1916.**       • **1.2826**
The conception of God; a philosophical discussion concerning the nature of the divine idea as a demonstrable reality, by Josiah Royce [and others] New York, Macmillan Co., 1898. — St. Clair Shores, Mich.: Scholarly Press, 1971 [c1897] xxxviii, 354 p.; 22 cm. 1. God I. T.
BT101.R8 1971      211      *LC* 79-107189      *ISBN* 0403003091

**Critiques of God / edited by Peter Angeles.**       **1.2827**
Buffalo, N.Y.: Prometheus Books, 1976. xvii, 371 p.; 23 cm. 1. God — Addresses, essays, lectures. 2. Atheism — Addresses, essays, lectures. 3. Religion — Philosophy — Addresses, essays, lectures. I. Angeles, Peter Adam, 1931-
BT102.C74      211      *LC* 76-43520

**Hartshorne, Charles, 1897-.**       • **1.2828**
Anselm's discovery: a re-examination of the ontological proof for God's existence. — La Salle, Ill., Open Court [1965] xvi, 333 p. 21 cm. — (The Open Court library of philosophy) Bibliography: p. [305]-310. 1. Anselm, Saint, Archbishop of Canterbury, 1033-1109. 2. God — Proof, Ontological I. T.
BT102.H36      211      *LC* 65-20278

**Kaufman, Gordon D.**       **1.2829**
God the problem [by] Gordon D. Kaufman. — Cambridge, Mass.: Harvard University Press, 1972. xx, 276 p.; 22 cm. 1. God — Addresses, essays, lectures. I. T.
BT102.K34      211      *LC* 70-174543      *ISBN* 0674355253

**Küng, Hans, 1928-.**       **1.2830**
[Existiert Gott? English] Does God exist?: An answer for today / Hans Küng; translated by Edward Quinn. — Garden City, N.Y.: Doubleday, 1980. xxiv, 839 p.; 24 cm. Translation of Existiert Gott? 1. God 2. God — History of doctrines I. T.
BT102.K8213 1980      231      *LC* 79-6576      *ISBN* 0385135920

**Plantinga, Alvin.**       • **1.2831**
God and other minds; a study of the rational justification of belief in God. — Ithaca, N.Y.: Cornell University Press, [1967] xi, 277 p.; 23 cm. — (Contemporary philosophy) 1. God — Proof 2. Theism I. T.
BT102.P55      211/.3      *LC* 67-20519

**Swinburne, Richard.**       **1.2832**
The existence of God / by Richard Swinburne. — Oxford: Clarendon Press; New York: Oxford University Press, 1979. 296 p.; 23 cm. Includes index. 1. God — Proof — Addresses, essays, lectures. 2. Theism — Addresses, essays, lectures. I. T.
BT102.S95      212      *LC* 79-40606      *ISBN* 0198246110

**Fortman, Edmund J., 1901-.**     **1.2833**
The Triune God; a historical study of the doctrine of the Trinity [by] Edmund J. Fortman. — Philadelphia: Westminster, [1972] xxvi, 382 p.; 24 cm. — (Theological resources) 1. Trinity — History of doctrines I. T.
BT109.F67 1972     231     *LC* 73-137395     *ISBN* 0664209173

**Lonergan, Bernard J. F.**     **1.2834**
[De Deo Trino. 1. Pars dogmatica, p. 17-112. English] The way to Nicea: the dialectical development of trinitarian theology / Bernard Lonergan; a translation by Conn O'Donovan of the first part of De Deo Trino. — Philadelphia: Westminster Press, c1976. xxxi, 142 p.; 23 cm. 'A translation of pages 17-112, Pars dogmatica, of De Deo Trino, Rome, Gregorian University Press, 1964.' 1. Trinity — History of doctrines 2. Dogma, Development of 3. Sects I. T.
BT109.L6613     231     *LC* 76-20792     *ISBN* 0664213405

**The Trinitarian controversy / translated and edited by William**     **1.2835**
**G. Rusch.**
Philadelphia: Fortress Press, c1980. viii, 182 p.; 22 cm. — (Sources of early Christian thought.) 1. Trinity — History of doctines — Early church, ca. 30-600. 2. Trinity — Early works to 1800. I. Rusch, William G. II. Series.
BT109.T74     231/.044     *LC* 79-8889     *ISBN* 0800614100

**Hodgson, Leonard, 1889-.**     ● **1.2836**
The doctrine of the trinity: Croall lectures, 1942–1943 / by Leonard Hodgson. — New York: Scribners, 1944. 237 p.; 18 cm. (Croall lectures; 1942-1943) 1. Trinity I. T. II. Series.
BT111.H6 1943     *LC* 44-5605

**Jenson, Robert W.**     **1.2837**
The triune identity: God according to the gospel / by Robert W. Jenson. — Philadelphia: Fortress Press, c1982. xv, 191 p.; 24 cm. 1. Trinity I. T.
BT111.2.J46 1982     231/.044 19     *LC* 81-43091     *ISBN* 0800606728

**Moltmann, Jürgen.**     **1.2838**
[Trinität und Reich Gottes. English] The Trinity and the kingdom: the doctrine of God / Jürgen Moltmann; [translated by Margaret Kohl]. — 1st U.S. ed. — San Francisco: Harper & Row, c1981. xvi, 256 p.; 24 cm. Translation of Trinität und Reich Gottes. 1. Trinity 2. Kingdom of God I. T.
BT111.2.M613 1981     231/.044 19     *LC* 80-8352     *ISBN* 0060659068

**Baillie, John, 1886-1960.**     ● **1.2839**
The idea of revelation in recent thought. — New York: Columbia University Press, 1956. 151 p.; 21 cm. — (Bampton lectures in America, no. 7) 1. Revelation I. T.
BT127.B234     231.74     *LC* 56-8158

**Niebuhr, H. Richard (Helmut Richard), 1894-1962.**     ● **1.2840**
The meaning of revelation, by H. Richard Niebuhr .... — New York: The Macmillan Company, 1941. x p., 2 l., 196 p.; 20 cm. 'First printing.' 'Contains, with some additions and revisions, the Nathanael W. Taylor lectures given at the Divinity School of Yale university in April, 1940.'—Pref. 1. Revelation I. T.
BT127.N5 1941     *LC* 41-5080

**Schillebeeckx, Edward, 1914-.**     ● **1.2841**
[Openbaring en Theologie. English] Revelation and theology, by E. Schillebeeckx. Translated by N. D. Smith. New York, Sheed and Ward [1967-. v. 22 cm. (His Theological soundings) 'Originally published as parts 1 and 2 of Openbaring en Theologie ... 1964. This translation is based on the second revised edition of 1966.' 1. Revelation 2. Theology, Doctrinal I. T.
BT127.2.S3313     231/.74     *LC* 67-21907

**Swinburne, Richard.**     **1.2842**
The coherence of theism / Richard Swinburne. — Oxford [Eng.]: Clarendon Press, 1977. 302 p.; 23 cm. (Clarendon library of logic and philosophy) 1. God — Attributes 2. Languages — Religious aspects I. T.
BT130.S94     211/.3     *LC* 77-5802     *ISBN* 019824410X

**Griffin, David, 1939-.**     **1.2843**
God, power, and evil: a process theodicy / by David Ray Griffin. Philadelphia: Westminster Press, c1976. 336 p.; 24 cm. 1. Theodicy — History of doctrines 2. Theodicy 3. Process theology I. T.
BT160.G74     231/.8     *LC* 76-21631     *ISBN* 0664207537

**Hick, John Harwood, 1922-.**     **1.2844**
Evil and the god of love / John Hick. — Rev. ed. — New York: Harper & Row, c1978. x, 389 p.; 21 cm. 1. Theodicy I. T.
BT160.H5 1978     *LC* 80-925812     *ISBN* 0060639024 pa

**Maritain, Jacques, 1882-1973.**     ● **1.2845**
God and the permission of evil / translated by Joseph W. Evans. — Milwaukee: Bruce Pub. Co., 1966. ix, 121 p. : ill.; 21 cm. — (Christian culture and philosophy series) 1. Theodicy I. T.
BT160.M313     231.8     *LC* 66-17003

# BT198–590 Jesus Christ

## BT198–199 CHRISTOLOGY

**Cullmann, Oscar.**     **1.2846**
The Christology of the New Testament / translated by Shirley C. Guthrie and Charles A. M. Hall. — Revised edition. — Philadelphia: Westminster Press, c1963. 342 p.; 24 cm. 1. Jesus Christ — History of doctrines — Early church, ca. 30-600 2. Jesus Christ — Person and offices 3. Bible. N.T — Theology. I. T.
BT198.C813 1959     232     *BT 683 C96 1963*

**Fuller, Reginald Horace.**     **1.2847**
The foundations of New Testament Christology, by Reginald H. Fuller. New York, Scribner [1965] 268 p. 22 cm. 1. Jesus Christ — History of doctrines — Early church, ca. 30-600 I. T.
BT198.F9     232     *LC* 65-27240

**Grillmeier, Alois, 1910-.**     **1.2848**
Christ in Christian tradition / Aloys Grillmeier; translated by John Bowden. — 2d rev. ed. — Atlanta: John Knox Press, [1975-. v. ; 24 cm. Includes indexes. 1. Jesus Christ — History of doctrines — Early church, ca. 30-600 I. T.
BT198.G743 1975     232     *LC* 75-13456     *ISBN* 0804204926

**Hengel, Martin.**     **1.2849**
The Son of God: the origin of Christology and the history of Jewish–Hellenistic religion / Martin Hengel; [translated by John Bowden from the German]. — 1st American ed. — Philadelphia: Fortress Press, 1976. xii, 100 p.; 22 cm. Translation of Der Sohn Gottes. 1. Son of God — History of doctrines. 2. Jesus Christ — History of doctrines — Early church, ca. 30-600 I. T.
BT198.H4613 1976     232     *LC* 75-37151     *ISBN* 0800612272

**Meyendorff, John, 1926-.**     **1.2850**
[Christ dans la théologie byzantine. English] Christ in Eastern Christian thought / John Meyendorff. — [Crestwood, N.Y.]: St. Vladimir's Seminary Press, 1975. 248 p.; 22 cm. Translation of Le Christ dans la théologie byzantine. 1. Jesus Christ — History of doctrines 2. Orthodox Eastern Church — Doctrines — History. I. T.
BT198.M4313 1975     232     *LC* 75-31979     *ISBN* 0913836273

**Moule, C. F. D. (Charles Francis Digby), 1908-.**     **1.2851**
The origin of Christology / C. F. D. Moule. — Cambridge; New York: Cambridge University Press, 1977. x, 187 p.; 22 cm. 1. Jesus Christ — History of doctrines — Early church, ca. 30-600 — Addresses, essays, lectures. I. T.
BT198.M68     232/.09/015     *LC* 76-11087     *ISBN* 0521212901

**Pelikan, Jaroslav Jan, 1923-.**     **1.2852**
Jesus through the centuries: his place in the history of culture / Jaroslav Pelikan. — New Haven [Conn.]: Yale University Press, c1985. xvi, 270 p., [12] p. of plates: ill. (some col.); 24 cm. Includes indexes. 1. Jesus Christ — History of doctrines 2. Jesus Christ — Influence I. T.
BT198.P44 1985     232.9/04 19     *LC* 85-2428     *ISBN* 0300034962

**Perrin, Norman.**     **1.2853**
A modern pilgrimage in New Testament christology. — Philadelphia: Fortress Press, [1974] x, 148 p.; 23 cm. 1. Jesus Christ — History of doctrines — Early church, ca. 30-600 I. T.
BT198.P47     232/.09     *LC* 73-88352     *ISBN* 0800602676

**Stanton, G. N.**     **1.2854**
Jesus of Nazareth in New Testament preaching / G. N. Stanton. — London; New York: Cambridge University Press, 1974. xi, 207 p.; 23 cm. (Monograph series - Society for New Testament Studies; 27) Originally presented as the author's thesis, Cambridge, 1969. 1. Jesus Christ — History of doctrines — Early church, ca. 30-600 2. Bible. N.T. — Criticism, interpretation, etc. I. T.
BT198.S69 1974     232     *LC* 73-92782     *ISBN* 0521204658

**Hardy, Edward Rochie, 1908- ed.**     ● **1.2855**
Christology of the later Fathers, edited by Edward Rochie Hardy, in collaboration with Cyril C. Richardson. — Philadelphia, Westminster Press [1954] 400 p. 24 cm. (The Library of Christian classics, v. 3) Includes bibliographies. 1. Jesus Christ — History of doctrines 2. Christian literature, Early (Selections: Extracts, etc.) 3. Fathers of the church I. T.
BT199.H4     232.082     *LC* 54-9949

## BT202 GENERAL WORKS

**Boff, Leonardo.**                                                    **1.2856**
[Jesus Cristo libertador. English] Jesus Christ liberator: a critical Christology for our times / Leonardo Boff; translated by Patrick Hughes. — Maryknoll, N.Y.: Orbis Books, c1978. xii, 323 p.; 21 cm. Translation of Jesus Cristo libertador. 1. Jesus Christ — Person and offices I. T.
BT202.B5313        232        LC 78-969        ISBN 0883442361 pbk

**Christ, faith and history: Cambridge studies in Christology;**        **1.2857**
**edited by S. W. Sykes and J. P. Clayton.**
London: Cambridge University Press, 1972. x, 303 p.; 23 cm. Papers presented to a graduate Christology seminar, Cambridge. 1. Jesus Christ — Person and offices I. Sykes, Stephen. ed. II. Clayton, John Powell. ed.
BT202.C5        232/.08        LC 70-176257        ISBN 0521084512

**Cobb, John B.**                                                     **1.2858**
Christ in a pluralistic age / by John B. Cobb, Jr. — Philadelphia: Westminster Press, [1975] 287 p.; 25 cm. 1. Jesus Christ — Person and offices I. T.
BT202.C62        232        LC 74-820        ISBN 0664208614

**Conzelmann, Hans.**                                                 **1.2859**
Jesus; the classic article from RGG expanded and updated. Translated by J. Raymond Lord. Edited with an introd. by John Reumann. — Philadelphia, Fortress Press [1973] xii, 116 p. 18 cm. 'A translation of Jesus Christus, published in [the 3d ed. of] Die Religion in Geschichte und Gegenwart: Handwörterbuch für Theologie und Religionswissenschaft ... vol. 3 (1959)' 1. Jesus Christ — Person and offices I. T.
BT202.C6713        232        LC 73-79011        ISBN 0800610008

**Jeremias, Joachim, 1900-.**                                       • **1.2860**
[Neutestamentliche Theologie. English] New Testament theology. New York, Scribner [1971-. v. 24 cm. Translation of Neutestamentliche Theologie. 1. Jesus Christ — Person and offices I. T.
BT202.J3913        232        LC 70-143936        ISBN 0684123630

**Jesús, ni vencido ni monarca celestial. English.**                 **1.2861**
Faces of Jesus: Latin American christologies / edited by José Míguez Bonino; translated from the Spanish by Robert R. Barr. — Maryknoll, N.Y.: Orbis Books, c1984. vi, 186 p.; 24 cm. Translation of: Jesús, ni vencido ni monarca celestial. 1. Jesus Christ — Person and offices — Addresses, essays, lectures. 2. Theology, Doctrinal — Latin America — History — 20th century — Addresses, essays, lectures. I. Míguez Bonino, José. II. T.
BT202.J43613 1984        232/.098 19        LC 83-19375        ISBN 0883441292

**Kappen, Sebastian.**                                                **1.2862**
Jesus and freedom / Sebastian Kappen. Maryknoll, N.Y.: Orbis Books, 1980. viii, 178 p.; 22 cm. 1. Jesus Christ — Person and offices 2. Freedom (Theology) 3. Liberation theology I. T.
BT202.K27        232        LC 76-25927        ISBN 0883442329

**Kasper, Walter.**                                                   **1.2863**
[Jesus der Christus. English] Jesus the Christ / Walter Kasper; [translation by V. Green]. — London: Burns & Oates; New York: Paulist Press, 1976. 289 p.; 23 cm. Translation of Jesus der Christus. 1. Jesus Christ — Person and offices I. T.
BT202.K313 1976        232        LC 76-20021        ISBN 0809102110

**Machovec, Milan.**                                                  **1.2864**
[Jesus für Atheisten. English] A Marxist looks at Jesus / Milan Machovec; with an introd. by Peter Hebblethwaite. — 1st American ed. — Philadelphia: Fortress Press, 1976. 231 p.; 22 cm. Translation of Jesus für Atheisten. Includes indexes. 1. Jesus Christ — Person and offices I. T.
BT202.M2913 1976        335.43/8/232        LC 76-10053        ISBN 0800612442

**Moltmann, Jürgen.**                                                 **1.2865**
The crucified God: the cross of Christ as the foundation and criticism of Christian theology / Jürgen Moltmann; [translated by R. A. Wilson and John Bowden from the German]. — 1st U.S. ed. — New York: Harper & Row, c1974. 346 p.; 22 cm. Translation of Der gekreuzigte Gott. 1. Jesus Christ — Person and offices 2. Jesus Christ — Crucifixion I. T.
BT202.M5513 1974b        232        LC 73-18703        ISBN 0060659017

**Ogden, Schubert Miles, 1928-.**                                     **1.2866**
The point of Christology / Schubert M. Ogden. — 1st ed. — San Francisco: Harper & Row, c1982. xii, 191 p.; 22 cm. Lectures given during 1980-81 at University of Oxford as Sarum Lectures. Includes index. 1. Jesus Christ — Person and offices — Addresses, essays, lectures. I. T.
BT202.O32 1982        232 19        LC 81-47842        ISBN 0060663529

**Pannenberg, Wolfhart, 1928-.**                                      **1.2867**
[Grundzüge der Christologie. English] Jesus, God and man / Wolfhart Pannenberg; translated by Lewis L. Wilkins and Duane A. Priebe. — 2d ed. —

Philadelphia: Westminster Press, c1977. 427 p.; 24 cm. Translation of Grundzüge der Christologie. 1. Jesus Christ — Person and offices I. T.
BT202.P313 1977        232        LC 76-26478        ISBN 0664212891

**Schillebeeckx, Edward, 1914-.**                                     **1.2868**
[Gerechtigheid en liefde. English.] Christ, the experience of Jesus as Lord / Edward Schillebeeckx; translated by John Bowden. — New York: Seabury Press, 1980. 925 p.; 23 cm. Translation of Gerechtigheid en liefde. Continues the author's Jesus. 'A Crossroad book.' 1. Jesus Christ — Person and offices 2. Bible. N.T — Theology. 3. Grace (Theology) — Biblical theology. 4. Salvation — Biblical teaching 5. Experience (Religion) I. T.
BT202.S33313        234        LC 80-50120        ISBN 0816401365

**Schillebeeckx, Edward, 1914-.**                                     **1.2869**
[Jezus. English] Jesus: an experiment in Christology / Edward Schillebeeckx; translated by Hubert Hoskins. — New York: Seabury Press, 1979. 767 p.; 24 cm. 'A Crossroad book.' Translation of Jezus. 1. Jesus Christ — Person and offices 2. Jesus Christ — History of doctrines — Early church, ca. 30-600 I. T.
BT202.S33513 1979        232/.09        LC 78-10225        ISBN 0816403457

**Schillebeeckx, Edward, 1914-.**                                     **1.2870**
Interim report on the books Jesus & Christ / Edward Schillebeeckx. — New York: Crossroad, 1981. 151 p.; 24 cm. Translation with revisions of Tussentijds verhaal over twee Jezus boeken. 1. Schillebeeckx, Edward, 1914- Jezus. 2. Schillebeeckx, Edward, 1914- Gerechtigheid en liefde. 3. Jesus Christ — Person and offices I. T.
BT202.S335313        232 19        LC 80-26708

**Sobrino, Jon.**                                                     **1.2871**
[Cristología desde América Latina. English] Christology at the crossroads: a Latin American approach / Jon Sobrino; translated by John Drury. — Maryknoll, N.Y.: Orbis Books, c1978. xxvi, 432 p.; 21 cm. Translation of Cristología desde América Latina. 1. Jesus Christ — Person and offices 2. Liberation theology I. T.
BT202.S6213        232        LC 77-25025        ISBN 0883440768 pbk

**Vermès, Géza, 1924-.**                                              **1.2872**
Jesus the Jew: a historian's reading of the Gospels. [1st American Edition] New York, Macmillan [1974] 286 p. 22 cm. Includes index. 1. Jesus Christ — Person and offices 2. Jesus Christ — Name I. T.
BT202.V45        232        LC 73-18516        ISBN 0002153734

## BT205–295 SPECIAL TOPICS

**Pawlikowski, John.**                                                **1.2873**
Christ in the light of the Christian–Jewish dialogue / John Pawlikowski. — New York: Paulist Press, c1982. 168 p.; 22 cm. — (Studies in Judaism and Christianity.) (A Stimulus book) 1. Jesus Christ — Person and offices 2. Christianity and other religions — Judaism 3. Judaism — Relations — Christianity I. T. II. Series.
BT205.P28 1982        233 19        LC 81-83186        ISBN 0809124165

**Aulén, Gustaf, 1879-.**                                           • **1.2874**
Christus victor; an historical study of the three main types of the idea of atonement, by Gustaf Aulen. Authorized translation by A. G. Hebert. American ed. New York, Macmillan, 1951. xvi, 163 p. 19 cm. 1. Atonement — History. I. Hebert, Arthur Gabriel, 1886- tr. II. T.
BT265.Ax        LC a 52-9812

## BT296–500 LIFE OF CHRIST

**Renan, Ernest, 1823-1892.**                                       • **1.2875**
The life of Jesus, by Ernest Renan; introduction by John Haynes Holmes. — New York, Modern library [1955] 4 p. 1. vii-ix, 15-393 p. 19 cm. — (Half-title: Modern library of the world's best books) 1. Jesus Christ — Biog. I. T.
BT301.R4 1955        LC 28-713

**Schleiermacher, Friedrich, 1768-1834.**                             **1.2876**
[Leben Jesu. English] The life of Jesus / by Friedrich Schleiermacher; edited and with an introd. by Jack C. Verheyden; translated by S. Maclean Gilmour. — Philadelphia: Fortress Press, c1975. lxii, 481 p.; 22 cm. (Lives of Jesus series) Translation of Das Leben Jesu. 1. Jesus Christ — Biography I. T.
BT301.S3613 1975        232.9/01 B        LC 72-87056        ISBN 0800612728

**Strauss, David Friedrich, 1808-1874.**                              **1.2877**
[Christus des Glaubens und der Jesus der Geschichte. English] The Christ of faith and the Jesus of history: a critique of Schleiermacher's Life of Jesus / by David Friedrich Strauss; translated, edited, and with an introduction by Leander E. Keck. — Philadelphia: Fortress Press, c1977. cxii, 169 p.; 19 cm. (Lives of Jesus series) Translation of Der Christus des Glaubens und der Jesus

der Geschichte. 1. Schleiermacher, Friedrich, 1768-1834. Das Leben Jesu. 2. Jesus Christ — Biography I. T.
BT301.S363 S813    232.9/01    *LC* 75-37152    *ISBN* 0800612736

**Strauss, David Friedrich, 1808-1874.**    • **1.2878**
[Leben Jesu. English] The life of Jesus, critically examined. Edited and with an introd. by Peter C. Hodgson. Translated from the 4th German ed. by George Eliot. Philadelphia, Fortress Press [1973, c1972] lviii, 39-812 p. 22 cm. (Lives of Jesus series) 1. Jesus Christ — Biography I. T.
BT301.S72 1973    232.9/01    *LC* 72-75655    *ISBN* 080061271X

**Bornkamm, Günther.**    • **1.2879**
[Jesus von Nazareth. English] Jesus of Nazareth. Translated by Irene and Fraser McLuskey with James M. Robinson. New York, Harper [1960] 239 p. 22 cm. 1. Jesus Christ — Person and offices I. T.
BT301.2.B583 1960a    232    *LC* 61-5256

**Schweitzer, Albert, 1875-1965.**    • **1.2880**
[Von Reimarus zu Wrede. English] The quest of the historical Jesus; a critical study of its progress from Reimarus to Wrede. [With a new] introd. by James M. Robinson. [Translated by W. Montgomery] New York, Macmillan [1968] xxxiii, 413 p. 21 cm. (Macmillan paperbacks) Reprint of the 1910 ed. Translation of Von Reimarus zu Wrede. 1. Jesus Christ — Biography — History and criticism 2. Jesus Christ — Historicity I. Montgomery, W. (William), 1871-1930. tr. II. Robinson, James McConkey, 1924- III. T.
BT303.S42 1968    232.9/08    *LC* 68-29509

**Anderson, Hugh, 1920-.**    • **1.2881**
Jesus and Christian origins; a commentary on modern viewpoints. — New York, Oxford University Press, 1964. xii, 368 p. 22 cm. Bibliography: p. 355-360. 1. Jesus Christ — Historicity 2. Kerygma 3. Theology, Doctrinal — Hist. — 20th cent. I. T.
BT303.2.A6    232.8    *LC* 64-10235

**Harvey, A. E. (Anthony Ernest)**    **1.2882**
Jesus and the constraints of history / A.E. Harvey. — Philadelphia: Westminster Press, c1982. 184 p.; 24 cm. 1. Jesus Christ — Historicity I. T.
BT303.2.H37 1982    232.9/08 19    *LC* 81-16095    *ISBN* 0664218253

**Kähler, Martin, 1835-1912.**    **1.2883**
The so-called historical Jesus and the historic biblical Christ / by Martin Kähler; translated, edited, and with an introduction by Carl E. Braaten; foreword by Paul Tillich. — Philadelphia: Fortress, c1964. xi, 153 p.; 21 cm. (Seminar editions.) 'This book is a translation of the first and second essays in the 1896 edition of Der sogenannte historische Jesus und der geschichtliche, biblische Christus...' 1. Jesus Christ — Historicity 2. Bible. N.T — Historiography. I. Braaten, Carl E., 1929- II. T.
BT303.2.K313    *LC* 64-12994

**Augstein, Rudolf, 1923-.**    **1.2884**
[Jesus Menschensohn. English] Jesus, Son of Man / by Rudolf Augstein; translated by Hugh Young; pref. by Gore Vidal; afterword by David Noel Freedman. — 1st American ed. — New York: Urizen Books, c1977. 408 p.; 24 cm. Translation of Jesus Menschensohn. Includes index. 1. Jesus Christ — Rationalistic interpretations 2. Christianity — Controversial literature I. T.
BT304.95.A8313 1977    232    *LC* 76-57698    *ISBN* 0916354636

**Crossan, John Dominic.**    **1.2885**
In fragments: the aphorisms of Jesus / John Dominic Crossan. — 1st ed. — San Francisco: Harper & Row, c1983. x, 389 p.; 21 cm. Includes indexes. 1. Jesus Christ — Words 2. Aphorisms and apothegms I. T.
BT306.C76 1983    232.9/54 19    *LC* 83-47719    *ISBN* 0060616083

**Dungan, David L.**    **1.2886**
The sayings of Jesus in the churches of Paul; the use of the Synoptic tradition in the regulation of early church life, by David L. Dungan. — Philadelphia: Fortress Press, [1971] xxxiii, 180 p.; 22 cm. 1. Jesus Christ — Words 2. Bible. N.T. Epistles of Paul — Criticism, interpretation, etc. I. T.
BT306.D85    227/.06    *LC* 70-155785    *ISBN* 0800600568

**Dodd, Charles Harold, 1884-1973.**    • **1.2887**
The parables of the kingdom. [Rev. ed.] New York, Scribner [1961] 176 p. 21 cm. 1. Jesus Christ — Parables 2. Kingdom of God — Biblical teaching I. T.
BT375.D55 1961    226.806    *LC* 61-3521

**Jeremias, Joachim, 1900-.**    • **1.2888**
The parables of Jesus. — Rev. ed. — New York, Scribner [c1963] 248 p. 24 cm. Bibliographical footnotes. Translated by S. H. Hooke from the German Die Gleichnisse Jesu, 6 th ed., 1962. 1. Jesus Christ — Parables I. T.
BT375.J413 1963    226.806    *LC* 63-22114

**Breech, James.**    **1.2889**
The silence of Jesus: the authentic voice of the historical man / James Breech. — 1st Fortress Press ed. — Philadelphia: Fortress Press, 1983. x, 245 p.; 24 cm.

1. Jesus Christ — Parables 2. Jesus Christ — Words 3. Jesus Christ — Character 4. Bible. N.T. Gospels — Criticism, interpretation, etc. I. T.
BT375.2.B73 1983    226/.806 19    *LC* 82-71825    *ISBN* 0800606914

**Kissinger, Warren S., 1922-.**    **1.2890**
The parables of Jesus: a history of interpretation and bibliography / by Warren S. Kissinger. — Metuchen, N.J.: Scarecrow Press, 1979. xxiv, 439 p.; 23 cm. — (ATLA bibliography series; no. 4) Includes indexes. 1. Jesus Christ — Parables 2. Jesus Christ — Parables — Bibliography. I. T.
BT375.2.K56    226/.8/06    *LC* 78-23271    *ISBN* 0810811863

**Via, Dan Otto, 1928-.**    **1.2891**
The parables; their literary and existential dimension. — Philadelphia: Fortress Press, [1967] xii, 217 p.; 22 cm. 1. Jesus Christ — Parables I. T.
BT375.2.V5    226/.8/063    *LC* 67-11910

**Bonhoeffer, Dietrich, 1906-1945.**    • **1.2892**
[Nachfolge. English] The cost of discipleship. [Translated from the German by R. H. Fuller, with some revision by Irmgard Booth] Rev. [i.e. 2d] & unabridged ed. containing material not previously translated. New York, Macmillan [1959] 285 p. 23 cm. Translation of Nachfolge. 1. Sermon on the mount. I. T.
BT380.B66 1959    226.2    *LC* 60-677

**Davies, William David, 1911-.**    **1.2893**
The setting of the Sermon on the Mount. — Cambridge [Eng.] University Press, 1964. xiii, 546 p. 24 cm. Bibliography: p. 481-504. 1. Sermon on the mount I. T.
BT380.D37    *LC* 64-630

**Taylor, Vincent, 1887-1968.**    **1.2894**
The passion narrative of St. Luke; a critical and historical investigation. Edited by Owen E. Evans. Cambridge [Eng.] University Press [1971] 1972. xii, 141 p. 22 cm. (Society for New Testament Studies monograph series, 19) 1. Jesus Christ — Passion 2. Bible. N.T. Luke — Criticism, interpretation, etc. I. T.
BT431.T34 1972    226/.4    *LC* 79-163057    *ISBN* 0521082951

**Rivkin, Ellis, 1918-.**    **1.2895**
What crucified Jesus? / Ellis Rivkin. — Nashville: Abingdon Press, c1984. 124 p.; 21 cm. 1. Jesus Christ — Passion — Role of Romans 2. Jesus Christ — Jewish interpretations 3. Jews — History — 168 B.C.-135 A.D. 4. Rome — Politics and government — 30 B.C.-68 A.D. I. T.
BT431.6.R58 1984    232.9/6 19    *LC* 83-15570    *ISBN* 0687446376

**Brandon, S. G. F. (Samuel George Frederick), 1907-1971.**    **1.2896**
The trial of Jesus of Nazareth [by] S. G. F. Brandon. New York, Stein and Day [1968] 223 p. illus. 23 cm. (Historic trials series) 1. Jesus Christ — Trial I. T.
BT440.B7 1968    232.96/2    *LC* 68-9206

**Sloyan, Gerard Stephen, 1919-.**    **1.2897**
Jesus on trial; the development of the Passion narratives and their historical and ecumenical implications. Edited, with an introd., by John Reumann. Philadelphia, Fortress Press [1973] xix, 156 p. 18 cm. 1. Jesus Christ — Trial 2. Jesus Christ — Passion — Role of Jews 3. Passion narratives (Gospels) — Criticism, interpretation, etc. I. T.
BT440.S56    232.9/62    *LC* 73-79040    *ISBN* 0800610334

## BT587–590 OTHER TOPICS

**Wilson, Ian, 1941-.**    **1.2898**
The Shroud of Turin: the burial cloth of Jesus Christ? / by Ian Wilson. — 1st ed. — Garden City, N.Y.: Doubleday, 1978. xii, 272 p., [20] leaves of plates: ill.; 22 cm. 1. Holy Shroud I. T.
BT587.S4 W53    232.9/66    *LC* 77-81551    *ISBN* 0385127367

**Sanders, E. P.**    **1.2899**
Jesus and Judaism / by E.P. Sanders. — 1st Fortress Press ed. — Philadelphia: Fortress Press, 1985. xiv, 444 p.; 24 cm. Includes indexes. 1. Jesus Christ — Views on Judaism I. T.
BT590.J8 S26 1985    232.9 19    *LC* 84-48806    *ISBN* 0800607430

## BT595–690 Mary. Mariology

**Warner, Marina, 1946-.**    **1.2900**
Alone of all her sex: the myth and the cult of the Virgin Mary / Marina Warner. — 1st American ed. — New York: Knopf: distributed by Random House, 1976. xxv, 400, xix p., [20] leaves of plates: ill.; 25 cm. Includes index. 1. Mary, Blessed Virgin, Saint. I. T.
BT602.W37 1976    232.91    *LC* 76-13682    *ISBN* 0394499131

Mary in the New Testament: a collaborative assessment by **1.2901**
Protestant and Roman Catholic scholars / edited by Raymond
E. Brown ... [et al.]; from discussions by Paul J. Achtemeier ...
[et al.]; sponsored by the United States Lutheran–Roman
Catholic Dialogue.
Philadelphia: Fortress Press, 1978. xii, 323 p.; 21 cm. Includes indexes.
1. Mary, Blessed Virgin, Saint — Biblical teaching. 2. Bible. N.T. — Criticism,
interpretation, etc. I. Brown, Raymond Edward. II. Achtemeier, Paul J.
III. United States Lutheran-Roman Catholic Dialogue (Group)
BT611.M37        232.91        *LC* 78-8797        *ISBN* 0800613457

**Rahner, Karl, 1904-.**                                          **1.2902**
Mary, Mother of the Lord / [by] Karl Rahner; [translated from the German by
W. J. O'Hara]. — Wheathampstead: A. Clarke, 1974. 107 p.: 19 cm.
Translation of Maria, Mutter des Herrn. 1. Mary, Blessed Virgin, Saint —
Theology I. T.
BT613.R353 1974        232.91        *LC* 75-301920        *ISBN* 0856500364

**Ashe, Geoffrey.**                                               **1.2903**
The virgin / Geoffrey Ashe. — London: Routledge & Paul, 1976. vi, 261 p.; 23
cm. Includes index. 1. Mary, Blessed Virgin, Saint — Cult 2. Women and
religion I. T.
BT645.A85        232.91        *LC* 76-364472        *ISBN* 0710083424

# BT695–748 Creation. Man.
# Doctrinal Anthropology

**Gilkey, Langdon Brown, 1919-.**                                 **1.2904**
Maker of heaven and earth: a study of the Christian doctrine of creation /
Langdon Gilkey. — Lanham, MD: University Press of America, 1985, c1959.
p. cm. Reprint. Originally published: Garden City, N.Y.: Doubleday, 1959.
Includes index. 1. Creation I. T.
BT695.G5 1985        231.7/65 19        *LC* 85-22607        *ISBN* 0819149764

**Innocent III, Pope, 1160 or 61-1216.**                          **1.2905**
De miseria condicionis humane / Lotario dei Segni (Pope Innocent III); edited
by Robert E. Lewis. — Athens, GA: University of Georgia Press, c1978.
xiv,303p.: facsim. Also entitled: De contemptu mundi. Latin and English.
1. Man (Theology) I. Lewis, Robert E. II. Innocent III, Pope, 1160 or
61-1216. De contemptu mundi III. T.
BX890.I57 C6        BT700 I6 1978.        *LC* 75-26119        *ISBN* 082030395X

**Brunner, Emil, 1889-1966.**                                    • **1.2906**
Man in revolt, a Christian anthropology [by] Emil Brunner ... translated by
Olive Wyon. — Philadelphia, The Westminster press [1947] 2 p. l., 564 p. 23.5
cm. 'An unabridged translation of the book ... first published in German in 1937
... under the title: Der mensch im widerspruch.'—Translator's note. 1. Man
(Theology) 2. Dialectic (Theology) I. Wyon, Olive, tr. II. T.
BT701.B72 1947        233        *LC* 47-2442

**Niebuhr, Reinhold, 1892-1971.**                                • **1.2907**
The nature and destiny of man: a Christian interpretation / by Reinhold
Niebuhr. — New York: C. Scribner's Sons, 1949. 2 v. in 1. — (Gifford lectures.
1939) 1. Man (Theology) I. T. II. Series.
BT701.N5214        *LC* 49-3134

**Niebuhr, Reinhold, 1892-1971.**                                • **1.2908**
The self and the dramas of history. — New York, Scribner, 1955. ix, 246 p. 21
cm. Bibliographical footnotes. 1. Man (Theology) 2. Self 3. Christianity and
politics 4. Sociology, Christian I. T.
BT701.N53        233        *LC* 55-7197

**Clark, Elizabeth A. (Elizabeth Ann), 1938-.**                  **1.2909**
Women and religion: a feminist sourcebook of Christian thought / Elizabeth
Clark and Herbert Richardson. — 1st ed. — New York: Harper & Row, c1977.
viii, 296 p.; 21 cm. — (Harper forum books; RD 178) 1. Woman (Theology) —
Addresses, essays, lectures. 2. Women and religion — Addresses, essays,
lectures. I. Richardson, Herbert Warren. joint author. II. T.
BT704.C53 1977        261.8/34/12        *LC* 76-9975        *ISBN* 006061398X

**Hammett, Jenny Yates.**                                        **1.2910**
Woman's transformations: a psychological theology / Jenny Yates Hammett.
— New York: E. Mellen Press, c1982. 120 p.: ill.; 21 cm. — (Symposium series;
v. 8) 1. Woman (Christian theology) 2. Women — Psychology I. T.
BT704.H35 1982        230/.088042 19        *LC* 82-14287        *ISBN*
0889469180

**Plaskow, Judith.**                                             **1.2911**
Sex, sin, and grace: women's experience and the theologies of Reinhold Niebuhr
and Paul Tillich / by Judith Plaskow. — Washington: University Press of

America, c1980. viii, 216 p.; 22 cm. Based on the author's thesis, Yale, 1975.
1. Niebuhr, Reinhold, 1892-1971. 2. Tillich, Paul, 1886-1965. 3. Woman
(Christian theology) — History of doctrines. 4. Sin — History of doctrines
5. Grace (Theology) — History of doctrines I. T.
BT704.P56        231        *LC* 79-5434        *ISBN* 0819108820

**Ruether, Rosemary Radford.**                                   **1.2912**
Sexism and God–talk: toward a feminist theology / Rosemary Radford
Ruether. — Boston: Beacon Press, c1983. xi, 289 p.; 24 cm. 1. Woman
(Christian theology) I. T.
BT704.R83 1983        230/.088042 19        *LC* 82-72502        *ISBN*
0807011045

**Ricoeur, Paul.**                                               • **1.2913**
[Symbolique de mal. English] The symbolism of evil. Translated from the
French by Emerson Buchanan. [1st ed.] New York, Harper & Row [1967] xv,
357 p. 22 cm. (Religious perspectives. v. 17) Translation of La symbolique du
mal, the 2d pt. of Finitude et culpabilité, which was published as v. 2 of the
author's Philosophie de la volonté. 1. Sin 2. Good and evil I. T. II. Series.
BT715.R48        233/.2        *LC* 67-11506

**Kierkegaard, Søren, 1813-1855.**                               **1.2914**
[Begrebet Angest.] The concept of anxiety: a simple psychologically orienting
deliberation on the dogmatic issue of hereditary sin / by Søren Kierkegaard;
edited and translated with introd. and notes by Reidar Thomte, in collaboration
with Albert B. Anderson. — Princeton, N.J.: Princeton University Press,
c1980. xviii, 273 p.; 23 cm. (Kierkegaard's writings; 8) Translation of Begrebet
Angest. Includes index. 1. Sin, Original 2. Psychology, Religious 3. Anxiety
— Religious aspects — Christianity. I. Thomte, Reidar. II. Anderson, Albert,
1928- III. T.
BT720.K52 1980        233/.14        *LC* 79-3217        *ISBN* 0691072442

**Jones, William Ronald.**                                       **1.2915**
Is God a white racist? A preamble to Black theology, by William R. Jones. [1st
ed.] Garden City, N.Y., Anchor Press, 1973. xxii, 239 p. 22 cm. (C. Eric
Lincoln series on Black religion) 1. Race — Religious aspects — Christianity
2. Afro-Americans — Religion I. T. II. Series.
BT734.J66        231        *LC* 72-96245        *ISBN* 0385009097 *ISBN*
038500995X

**Cone, James H.**                                               • **1.2916**
Black theology and black power [by] James H. Cone. New York, Seabury Press
[1969] x, 165 p. 21 cm. (An Original Seabury paperback, SP 59) 1. Race
relations — Religious aspects 2. Black theology I. T. II. Title: Black power.
BT734.2.C6        261.8/3        *LC* 70-76462

**Merton, Thomas, 1915-1968.**                                   • **1.2917**
Seeds of destruction. New York, Farrar, Straus and Giroux [1965, c1964] xvi,
328 p. 21 cm. 1. Catholic Church — Clergy — Correspondence 2. Race
relations — Religious aspects — Catholic Church 3. Christianity — 20th
century — Addresses, essays, lectures. 4. United States — Race relations I. T.
BT734.2.M4        261        *LC* 64-19515

**Smith, H. Shelton (Hilrie Shelton), 1893-.**                   **1.2918**
In his image, but ... Racism in Southern religion, 1780–1910 [by] H. Shelton
Smith. Durham, N.C., Duke University Press, 1972. x, 318 p. 25 cm. 1. Race
relations — Religious aspects 2. Southern States — Race relations. I. T.
BT734.2.S56        261.8/34/5196073075        *LC* 72-81338        *ISBN*
082230273X

**Ellul, Jacques.**                                              • **1.2919**
Violence; reflections from a Christian perspective. Translated by Cecelia Gaul
Kings. New York, Seabury Press [1969] 179 p. 22 cm. 1. Violence — Religious
aspects — Christianity I. T.
BT736.15.E413        261.8/3        *LC* 69-13540

**Hengel, Martin.**                                              **1.2920**
[Gewalt und Gewaltlosigkeit. English] Victory over violence, Jesus and the
revolutionists. Translated by David E. Green. With an introd. by Robin
Scroggs. Philadelphia, Fortress Press [1973] xxvi, 67 p. 19 cm. Translation of
Gewalt und Gewaltlosigkeit. 1. Violence — Religious aspects — Christianity
I. T.
BT736.15.H4513        261.8        *LC* 73-79035        *ISBN* 080060167X

**Merton, Thomas, 1915-1968.**                                   **1.2921**
Faith and violence; Christian teaching and Christian practice. [Notre Dame,
Ind.] University of Notre Dame Press, 1968. x, 291 p. 21 cm. 1. Violence —
Religious aspects — Christianity I. T.
BT736.15.M4        261.8        *LC* 68-20438

**Bainton, Roland Herbert, 1894-.**                              • **1.2922**
Christian attitudes toward war and peace; a historical survey and critical re-
evaluation. New York, Abingdon Press [1960] 299 p. illus. 24 cm. 1. War —
Religious aspects — Christianity — History of doctrines 2. Church history
I. T.
BT736.2.B3        261.63        *LC* 60-12064

**Russell, Frederick H.**                                        **1.2923**
The just war in the middle ages / Frederick H. Russell. — Cambridge; New
York: Cambridge University Press, 1975. xi, 332 p.; 23 cm. (Cambridge studies
in life and thought; 3d ser., v. 8) Includes index. 1. Just war doctrine — History
of doctrines. I. T. II. Series.
BT736.2.R85      230      *LC* 74-25655      *ISBN* 0521206901

**Gutiérrez, Gustavo, 1928-.**                                   **1.2924**
[Teologia de la liberación. English] A theology of liberation: history, politics,
and salvation. Translated and edited by Sister Caridad Inda and John Eagleson.
Maryknoll, N.Y., Orbis Books, 1973. xi, 323 p. 22 cm. 1. Liberation theology
I. T.
BT738.G8613      201/.1      *LC* 72-85790

**Handy, Robert T. ed.**                                        • **1.2925**
The Social Gospel in America, 1870–1920, edited by Robert T. Handy. — New
York: Oxford University Press, 1966. xii, 399 p.; 24 cm. — (A Library of
Protestant thought) 1. Social gospel 2. Sociology, Christian — History I. T.
II. Series.
BT738.H29      261      *LC* 66-14977

**Rauschenbusch, Walter, 1861-1918.**                            **1.2926**
Christianity and the social crisis. Edited by Robert D. Cross. — New York,
Harper & Row [1964] xxv, 429 p. 21 cm. — (American perspectives) Harper
torchbooks. The University library, TB3059. Bibliographical footnotes.
1. Sociology, Christian I. T.
BT738.R34 1964      261      *LC* 64-57260

**Stackhouse, Max L.**                                           **1.2927**
Ethics and the urban ethos; an essay in social theory and theological
reconstruction [by] Max L. Stackhouse. — Boston, Beacon Press [1972] 220 p.
21 cm. 1. Sociology, Christian 2. Sociology, Urban I. T.
BT738.S695 1972      261.1      *LC* 77-179155      *ISBN* 0807011363

**White, Donald Cedric, 1939-.**                                 **1.2928**
The social gospel: religion and reform in changing America / Ronald C. White,
Jr. and C. Howard Hopkins; with an essay by John C. Bennett. — Philadelphia:
Temple University Press, 1976. xix, 306 p.: ill.; 22 cm. 1. Social gospel
2. Sociology, Christian — United States. I. Hopkins, Charles Howard, 1905-
joint author. II. T.
BT738.W45      261/.0973      *LC* 75-34745      *ISBN* 0877220832

**Ruether, Rosemary Radford.**                                   • **1.2929**
The radical kingdom; the Western experience of Messianic hope. — [1st ed.]. —
New York: Harper & Row, [1970] viii, 304 p.; 22 cm. 1. Revolutions —
Religious aspects — Christianity 2. Messianism 3. Sociology, Christian I. T.
BT738.3.R8 1970      261.8      *LC* 70-109080

**Miles, Margaret Ruth.**                                        **1.2930**
Fullness of life: historical foundations for a new asceticism / by Margaret R.
Miles. — 1st ed. — Philadelphia: Westminster Press, c1981. 186 p. 1. Body,
Human — Religious aspects — Christianity 2. Asceticism I. T.
BT741.2.M54      BT741.2 M54.      233/.5 19      *LC* 81-11535      *ISBN*
0664243894

## BT750–810 Salvation

**Weingart, Richard E.**                                         • **1.2931**
The logic of divine love: a critical analysis of the soteriology of Peter Abailard
[by] Richard E. Weingart. London, Clarendon, 1970. xiv, 220 p. 23 cm.
1. Abelard, Peter, 1079-1142. 2. Salvation — History of doctrines — Middle
Ages, 600-1500 I. T.
BT751.2.W4      230.2/0924      *LC* 78-521215      *ISBN* 0198266235

**Küng, Hans, 1928-.**                                           • **1.2932**
Justification; the doctrine of Karl Barth and a Catholic reflection. With a letter
by Karl Barth. Translated from the German by Thomas Collins, Edmund E.
Tolk, and David Granskou. — New York, Nelson [1964] xxvi, 332 p. 22 cm.
Bibliography: p. 308-321. 1. Barth, Karl, 1886-1968. 2. Justification —
History of doctrines I. T.
BT764.2.K813      234.7      *LC* 64-25285

**Wesley, John, 1703-1791.**                                     • **1.2933**
A plain account of Christian perfection. — London, Epworth Press [1952]
116 p. 19 cm. Label mounted on t.p.: Chicago, A. R. Allenson. 1. Perfection
I. T.
BT766.W52 1952      234      *LC* 53-30884

**Tillich, Paul, 1886-1965.**                                    • **1.2934**
Dynamics of faith. — New York: Harper, [1958, c1957] 134 p.; 20 cm. —
(Harper torchbooks, TB42) 1. Faith I. T.
BT771.T54 1958      234.2      *LC* 58-10150

**Gogarten, Friedrich, 1887-1967.**                              • **1.2935**
The reality of faith; the problem of subjectivism in theology. Translated by Carl
Michalson, and others. — Philadelphia, Westminster Press [1959] 192 p. 21 cm.
1. Faith I. T. II. Title: Subjectivism in theology.
BT771.2.G613      234.2      *LC* 59-5048

**Kahlefeld, Heinrich.**                                         • **1.2936**
Parables and instructions in the Gospels / translated by Arlene Swidler. —
[New York]: Herder and Herder, [1966-]. v.; 21 cm. 1. Jesus Christ — Parables
I. T.
BT375.2.K313      *LC* 66-13073

**Erasmus, Desiderius, d. 1536.**                                • **1.2937**
Discourse on free will [by] Erasmus [and] Luther. Translated and edited by
Ernst F. Winter. — New York: Ungar, [1961] xiii, 138 p.; 20 cm. — (Milestones
of thought in the history of ideas, M114) 1. Free will and determinism
I. Erasmus, Desiderius, d. 1536. The free will. II. Luther, Martin, 1483-1546.
The bondage of the will. III. T. IV. Series.
BT810.E63      234.9      *LC* 60-53363

**Ruether, Rosemary Radford.**                                   • **1.2938**
Liberation theology: human hope confronts Christian history and American
power. New York: Paulist Press, [1972] vi, 194 p.; 21 cm. 1. Liberation
theology — Addresses, essays, lectures. 2. Sociology, Christian — Addresses,
essays, lectures. I. T.
BT810.2.R8      230      *LC* 72-92263      *ISBN* 0809117444

**Russell, Letty M.**                                            **1.2939**
Human liberation in a feminist perspective—a theology, by Letty M. Russell. —
Philadelphia: Westminster Press, [1974] 213 p.; 21 cm. 1. Freedom (Theology)
2. Salvation 3. Woman (Christian theology) I. T.
BT810.2.R87      261.8/34/12      *LC* 74-10613      *ISBN* 0664249914

## BT819–950 Eschatology. Immortality

**Pelikan, Jaroslav Jan, 1923-.**                                • **1.2940**
The shape of death; life, death, and immortality in the early fathers. New York,
Abingdon Press, [1961] 128 p. 20 cm. 1. Eschatology — History of doctrines —
Early church, ca. 30-600 2. Death 3. Immortality — History of doctrines —
Early church, ca. 30-600. 4. Fathers of the church I. T.
BT819.5.P44 1961      236      *LC* 61-5197

**Brunner, Emil, 1889-1966.**                                    • **1.2941**
Eternal hope; translated by Harold Knight. — Philadelphia, Westminster Press
[1954] 232 p. 23 cm. Translation of Das Ewige als Zukunft und Gegenwart.
Bibliographical references included in 'Notes' (p. 221-232) 1. Eschatology
I. T.
BT821.B733 1954      236      *LC* 54-3507

**Moltmann, Jürgen.**                                            • **1.2942**
[Theologie der Hoffnung. English] Theology of hope; on the ground and the
implications of a Christian eschatology. [1st U.S. ed.] New York, Harper &
Row [1967] 342 p. 22 cm. Translation of Theologie der Hoffnung. 1. Hope —
Religious aspects — Christianity 2. Eschatology I. T.
BT821.2.M6313 1967b      236      *LC* 67-21550

**Rahner, Karl, 1904-.**                                         **1.2943**
On the theology of death. [Translated by Charles H. Henkey. — New York]
Herder and Herder [1961] 127 p. 22 cm. — (Quaestiones disputatae, 2)
1. Death 2. Martyrdom I. T.
BT825.R313      *LC* 61-11443

**Stannard, David E.**                                           **1.2944**
The Puritan way of death: a study in religion, culture, and social change /
David E. Stannard. — New York: Oxford University Press, 1977. xii, 236 p.:
ill.; 22 cm. 1. Death 2. Puritans — New England. I. T.
BT825.S76      230/.5/9      *LC* 76-42647      *ISBN* 0195022262

**Walker, D. P. (Daniel Pickering)**                             • **1.2945**
The decline of hell: seventeenth–century discussions of eternal torment / by D.
P. Walker. — Chicago: University of Chicago Press, 1964. vii, 272 p. 1. Hell —
History of doctrines. I. T.
BT836.2.W3      *LC* 64-19849

**Le Goff, Jacques, 1924-.**     **1.2946**
[Naissance du purgatoire. English] The birth of purgatory / Jacques Le Goff; translated by Arthur Goldhammer. — Chicago: University of Chicago Press, c1984. ix, 430 p.; 24 cm. Translation of: La naissance du purgatoire. 1. Purgatory — History of doctrines I. T.
BT842.L413 1984  236/.5/09 19  *LC* 83-1108  *ISBN* 0226470822

**Visions of the end: apocalyptic traditions in the Middle Ages /** **1.2947**
**Bernard McGinn.**
New York: Columbia University Press, 1979. xvii, 377 p.; 24 cm. (Records of civilization, sources and studies. no. 96) Includes indexes. 1. End of the world — History of doctrines. 2. Millennium — History of doctrines 3. Apocalyptic literature 4. Church history — Middle Ages, 600-1500 I. McGinn, Bernard, 1937- II. Series.
BT876.V58  236  *LC* 79-4303  *ISBN* 0231045948

**Apocalyptic spirituality: treatises and letters of Lactantius, Adso** **1.2948**
**of Montier–en–Der, Joachim of Fiore, the Franciscan spirituals,**
**Savonarola / translation and introd. by Bernard McGinn; pref.**
**by Marjorie Reeves.**
New York: Paulist Press, c1979. xviii, 334 p.; 23 cm. — (The Classics of Western spirituality) Includes indexes. 1. Second Advent — Early works to 1800 — Addresses, essays, lectures. 2. Antichrist — Early works to 1800 — Addresses, essays, lectures. 3. Apocalyptic literature — Early works to 1800 — Addresses, essays, lectures. I. McGinn, Bernard, 1937-
BT885.A65  236  *LC* 79-90834  *ISBN* 0809103052

**Barkun, Michael.**     **1.2949**
Disaster and the millennium / Michael Barkun. — New Haven: Yale University Press, 1974. x, 246 p.; 23 cm. Includes index. 1. Millennialism 2. Disasters I. T.
BT891.B37  301.5/8  *LC* 73-86884  *ISBN* 0300017251

**Thrupp, Sylvia Lettice, 1903- ed.**   **1.2950**
Millennial dreams in action; studies in revolutionary religious movements, edited by Sylvia L. Thrupp. — New York: Schocken Books, [1970] 229 p.; 21 cm. 'This volume is the outcome of a conference held at the University of Chicago on April 8th and 9th, 1960 ... Some of the papers were made available in draft form beforehand but since have been revised; others were not written until after the conference.' 1. Millennium I. T.
BT891.T5 1970  236/.3  *LC* 70-107614

**Lamont, Corliss, 1902-.**    • **1.2951**
The illusion of immortality. Introd. by John Dewey. — 4th ed. — New York, F. Ungar Pub. Co. [1965] xiii, 303 p. 21 cm. Bibliographical references included in 'Notes' (p. [279]-295) 1. Immortality I. T.
BT921.L167 1965  129.6  *LC* 65-25140

# BT960–985 Invisible World. Devil

**Russell, Jeffrey Burton.**    **1.2952**
Lucifer, the Devil in the Middle Ages / Jeffrey Burton Russell. — Ithaca, N.Y.: Cornell University Press, 1984. 356 p.: ill.; 24 cm. Includes index. 1. Devil — History of doctrines — Middle Ages, 600-1500. I. T.
BT981.R86 1984  235/.47 19  *LC* 84-45153  *ISBN* 0801415039

**Russell, Jeffrey Burton.**    **1.2953**
Satan: the early Christian tradition / Jeffrey Burton Russell. — Ithaca: Cornell University Press, 1981. 258 p.: ill.; 24 cm. Includes index. 1. Devil — History of doctrines — Early church, ca. 30-600. I. T.
BT981.R87  235/.47/09015 19  *LC* 81-66649  *ISBN* 0801412676

# BT990–1255 Creeds. Apologetics

**Creeds of the churches: a reader in Christian doctrine, from the** **1.2954**
**Bible to the present / edited by John H. Leith.**
3rd ed. — Atlanta: John Knox Press, 1982. x, 736 p.; 19 cm. 1. Creeds — Collected works. 2. Theology — Collected works I. Leith, John H.
BT990.C655 1982  238 19  *LC* 82-48029  *ISBN* 0804205264

**The Creeds of Christendom: with a history and critical notes /** **1.2955**
**ed. by Philip Schaff; rev. by David S. Schaff.**
6th edition. Grand Rapids, Mich.: Baker Book House, 1983. 3v. 1. Creeds — History and criticism. I. Schaff, David Schley, 1852-1941 II. Schaff, Philip, 1819-1893.
BT990.C7x  238  *ISBN* 0801082323

**Kelly, J. N. D. (John Norman Davidson)**  **1.2956**
Early Christian creeds [by] J. N. D. Kelly. 3d ed. New York, D. McKay Co. [1972] xi, 446 p. 23 cm. 1. Creeds I. T.
BT990.K4 1972b  238/.1  *LC* 72-172064

**Pannenberg, Wolfhart, 1928-.**   **1.2957**
[Glaubensbekenntnis. English] The Apostles' Creed in the light of today's questions. [Translated from the German by Margaret Kohl] Philadelphia, Westminster Press [1972] viii, 178 p. 22 cm. Translation of Das Glaubensbekenntnis, ausgelegt und verantwortet vor den Fragen der Gegenwart. 1. Apostles' Creed. I. T.
BT993.2.P3513  238/.11  *LC* 72-5767  *ISBN* 0664209475

**Butler, Joseph, 1692-1752.**   • **1.2958**
The analogy of religion / Joseph Butler; Introd. by Ernest C. Mossner. — New York: F. Ungar, 1961. xii, 259 p. (Milestones of thought in the history of ideas) 1. Analogy (Religion) 2. Natural theology 3. Apologetics — 18th cent. 4. Revelation — Early works to 1800. 5. Eschatology — Early works to 1800. I. T. II. Series.
BT1100.B9 1961  *LC* 60-53362

**Küng, Hans, 1928-.**     **1.2959**
[Christ sein. English] On being a Christian / Hans Küng; translated by Edward Quinn. — Garden City, N.Y.: Doubleday, c1976. 720 p.; 24 cm. Translation of Christ sein. 1. Apologetics — 20th century 2. Theology I. T.
BT1102.K8313  230  *LC* 75-36597  *ISBN* 0385027125

**Walker, D. P. (Daniel Pickering)**  • **1.2960**
The ancient theology; studies in Christian Platonism from the fifteenth to the eighteenth century [by] D. P. Walker. Ithaca, N.Y., Cornell University Press [1972] 276 p. 23 cm. 1. Apologetics — History 2. Christianity — Philosophy 3. Platonists I. T.
BT1106.W3 1972  239/.3/09  *LC* 72-3841  *ISBN* 0801407494

# BT1313–1480 Heresies.
# Gnosticism

**Bauer, Walter, 1877-1960.**   • **1.2961**
[Rechtgläubigkeit und Ketzerei im ältesten Christentum. English] Orthodoxy and heresy in earliest Christianity. Translated by a team from the Philadelphia Seminar on Christian Origins, and edited by Robert A. Kraft and Gerhard Krodel. Philadelphia, Fortress Press [1971] xxv, 326 p. 24 cm. Translation of Rechtgläubigkeit und Ketzerei im ältesten Christentum. 1. Heresies, Christian — History — Early church, ca. 30-600 2. Church history — Primitive and early church, ca. 30-600 3. Apologetics — Early church, ca. 30-600. I. Kraft, Robert A. ed. II. Krodel, Gerhard, 1926- ed. III. T.
BT1315.B313 1971  273/.1  *LC* 71-141252  *ISBN* 080060055X

**Leff, Gordon.**      • **1.2962**
Heresy in the later Middle Ages: the relation of heterodoxy to dissent, c. 1250–c. 1450. Manchester, Manchester U.P.; New York, Barnes & Noble [1967] 2 v. 25 cm. 1. Christian sects, Medieval 2. Theology, Doctrinal — History — Middle Ages, 600-1500 3. Heresies, Christian — History — Middle Ages, 600-1500 I. T.
BT1315.2.L4 1967  273/.09/02  *LC* 67-113563

**Lambert, Malcolm (Malcolm D.)**  **1.2963**
Medieval heresy: popular movements from Bogomil to Hus / Malcolm Lambert. — New York: Holmes & Meier Publishers, 1977, c1976. xvi, 430 p.: ill.; 24 cm. Includes index. 1. Heresies, Christian — History — Middle Ages, 600-1500 I. T.
BT1319.L35 1977  273/.6  *LC* 76-49949  *ISBN* 0841902984

**Frend, W. H. C.**      **1.2964**
The Donatist Church: a movement of protest in Roman North Africa, by W. H. C. Frend. — Oxford: Clarendon Press, 1971. xviii, 361 p., 3 fold. plates;: 3 maps.; 23 cm. 1. Donatists I. T.
BT1370.F7 1971  273/.4  *LC* 75-595861  *ISBN* 0198264089

**Dart, John, 1936-.**     **1.2965**
The laughing Savior: the discovery and significance of the Nag Hammadi gnostic library / John Dart. — 1st ed. — New York: Harper & Row, c1976. xxi, 154 p.: ill.; 22 cm. Includes index. 1. Nag Hammadi codices. 2. Gnosticism I. T.
BT1390.D35 1976  273/.1  *LC* 75-36749  *ISBN* 006061692X

**Foerster, Werner, 1897- comp.**      • **1.2966**
[Gnosis. English] Gnosis; a selection of Gnostic texts. English translation edited by R. McL. Wilson. Oxford, Clarendon Press, 1972-. v. 22 cm. Translation of Die Gnosis. 1. Gnosticism I. Wilson, Robert MacLachlan, ed. II. T.
BT1390.F613     273/.1     LC 73-156488     ISBN 019826433X

**Grant, Robert McQueen, 1917-.**      • **1.2967**
Gnosticism and early Christianity, by R. M. Grant. — 2d ed. — New York: Columbia University Press, 1966. viii, 241 p.; 21 cm. 1. Gnosticism I. T.
BT1390.G72 1966a     273.1     LC 66-31334

**The Nag Hammadi Library in English / translated by members**      **1.2968**
**of the Coptic Gnostic Library Project of the Institute for**
**Antiquity and Christianity.**
San Francisco: Harper & Row, [1981] c1977. xv, 493 p.; 24 cm. Includes index. 1. Gnosticism — Collected works. 2. Gnostic literature I. Coptic Gnostic Library Project. II. Nag Hammadi codices.
BT1390.N34 1981     299/.932 19     LC 77-7853     ISBN 0060669292

**Pagels, Elaine H., 1943-.**      **1.2969**
The gnostic Gospels / by Elaine Pagels. — 1st ed. — New York: Random House, c1979. xxxvi, 182 p.; 24 cm. 1. Gnosticism 2. Chenoboskion manuscripts. I. T.
BT1390.P3     273/.1     LC 79-4764     ISBN 0394502787

**Perkins, Pheme.**      **1.2970**
The gnostic dialogue: the early church and the crisis of gnosticism / Pheme Perkins. — New York: Paulist Press, c1980. xi, 239 p.; 21 cm. — (Theological inquiries.) Includes indexes. 1. Gnosticism 2. Theology, Doctrinal — History — Early church, ca. 30-600 I. T. II. Series.
BT1390.P4     230/.99 19     LC 80-81441     ISBN 0809123207

**Rudolph, Kurt.**      **1.2971**
[Gnosis. English] Gnosis: the nature and history of gnosticism / Kurt Rudolph; translation edited by Robert McLachlan Wilson. — San Francisco: Harper & Row, 1983. xii, 411 p., [1] folded leaf of plates: ill. (some col.); 22 cm. Translation of: Die Gnosis. Includes index. 1. Gnosticism I. Wilson, R. McL. (Robert McLachlan) II. T.
BT1390.R7713 1983     299/.932 19     LC 81-47437     ISBN 0060670177

**Frend, W. H. C.**      **1.2972**
The rise of the monophysite movement; chapters in the history of the church in the fifth and sixth centuries [by] W. H. C. Frend. — Cambridge, [Eng.]: University Press, 1972. xvii, 405 p.; 24 cm. Revised ed. of the Birkbeck lectures for 1968 on the Rise of the monophysite empire. 1. Monophysites 2. Church history — Primitive and early church, ca. 30-600 I. T.
BT1425.F73     281/.6     LC 72-75302     ISBN 0521081300

**Evans, Robert F.**      • **1.2973**
Pelagius; inquiries and reappraisals [by] Robert F. Evans. — New York: Seabury Press, [1968] xvi, 171 p.; 22 cm. 1. Pelagius. I. T.
BT1450.E9 1968     273/.5     LC 67-20939

**The Polish brethren: documentation of the history and thought**      **1.2974**
**of Unitarianism in the Polish–Lithuanian Commonwealth and in**
**the Diaspora 1601–1685 / edited, translated, and interpreted by**
**George Hunston Williams.**
Missoula, Mont.: Scholars Press, c1980. 2 v. (xxxii, 773 p.): ill.; 23 cm. — (Harvard theological studies. no. 30) Includes indexes; index references to p. 363 cf seq. must have 4 subtracted, e.g., a term indexed as occurring on p. 363 will be found on p. 359. 1. Socinianism — History — Sources. 2. Unitarianism — Poland — History — Sources. 3. Unitarianism — Netherlands — History — Sources. I. Williams, George Hunston, 1914- II. Series.
BT1480.A18     288/.438 19     LC 77-21277     ISBN 089130343X

**Kot, Stanislaw, 1885-.**      **1.2975**
Socinianism in Poland; the social and political ideas of the Polish Antitrinitarians in the sixteenth and seventeenth centuries / Stanislas Kot. — Boston, Starr King Press, [c1957] xxvii, 226 p.; 22 cm. 1. Socinianism — Poland. I. T.
BT1480.K58 1957     LC 57-12746

# BV PRACTICAL THEOLOGY

## BV5–525 Worship. Symbolism. Liturgies

**Cullmann, Oscar.**      **1.2976**
[Urchristentum und Gottesdienst. English] Early Christian worship / Oscar Cullmann; [translation by A. Stewart Todd and James B. Torrance.]. — Philadelphia: Westminster Press, [1978] c1953. 126 p.; 22 cm. 'A translation of the second edition of Urchristentum und Gottesdienst ... and contains also an extra chapter on 'Jesus and the day of rest' from the French translation of Part 2, which appeared under the title Les Sacrements dans l'évangile Johannique.' 1. Bible. N.T. John — Criticism, interpretation, etc. 2. Worship — History — Early church, ca. 30-600 3. Sabbath 4. Sacraments — Biblical teaching. I. Cullmann, Oscar. Les sacrements dans l'Évangile johannique. English. 1978. II. T.
BV6.C8413 1978     264/.009     LC 78-6636     ISBN 0664242200

**Hahn, Ferdinand, 1926-.**      **1.2977**
The worship of the early church. Translated by David E. Green. Edited, with an introd., by John Reumann. — Philadelphia: Fortress Press, [1973] xxvi, 118 p.; 18 cm. Translation of Der urchristliche Gottesdienst. 1. Worship — History — Early church, ca. 30-600 I. T.
BV6.H2713     264/.01/1     LC 72-87063     ISBN 0800601270

**Martin, Ralph P.**      **1.2978**
Worship in the early church / by Ralph P. Martin. — [Rev. ed.]. — Grand Rapids: Eerdmans, 1974, 1975 printing, c1964. 144 p.; 22 cm. 1. Worship — History — Early church, ca. 30-600 I. T.
BV6.M37 1975     264/.01/1     LC 75-14079     ISBN 0802816134

**Underhill, Evelyn, 1875-1941.**      • **1.2979**
Worship / by Evelyn Underhill. — Westport, Conn.: Hyperion Press, 1979, c1937. xxi, 350 p.; 22 cm. Reprint of the ed. published by Harper, New York, in series: The library of constructive theology. 1. Worship I. T.
BV10.U5 1979     264     LC 78-20499     ISBN 0883558742

**Allmen, Jean-Jacques von, 1917-.**      • **1.2980**
Worship; its theology and practice / by J.J.von Allmen. — New York: Oxford University Press, 1965. 317 p.; 23 cm. 1. Worship I. T.
BV10.2.A44     264     LC 65-23571

**Smart, Ninian, 1927-.**      • **1.2981**
The concept of worship. — [London]: Macmillan; [New York]: St. Martin's Press, [1972] 77 p.; 22 cm. — (New studies in the philosophy of religion) 1. Worship 2. Religion — Philosophy I. T.
BV10.2.S59     291.3     LC 72-77773     ISBN 0333102738

**Solberg, Winton U.**      **1.2982**
Redeem the time: the Puritan Sabbath in early America / Winton U. Solberg. Cambridge: Harvard University Press, 1977. xii, 406 p.; 24 cm. (A Publication of the Center for the Study of the History of Liberty in America, Harvard University) Includes index. 1. Sabbath — History. 2. Sunday — History. 3. Puritans I. T.
BV111.S64     263/.0973     LC 76-26672     ISBN 0674751302

**Webber, Frederick Roth, 1887-1963.**      **1.2983**
Church symbolism; an explanation of the more important symbols of the Old and New Testament, the primitive, the mediaeval, and the modern church. Introd. by Ralph Adams Cram. — 2d ed., rev. — Detroit: Gale Research Co., 1971. ix, 413 p.: illus.; 22 cm. 'Facsimile reprint of the 1938 edition.' 1. Christian art and symbolism I. T.
BV150.W4 1938a     704.948/2     LC 79-107627

**Daniélou, Jean.**      • **1.2984**
Primitive Christian symbols. Translated by Donald Attwater. — Baltimore, Helicon Press [1964] xvi, 151 p. illus. 22 cm. Bibliographical footnotes. 1. Christian art and symbolism I. T.
BV155.D313     246.2     LC 64-12383

**The Study of liturgy / edited by Cheslyn Jones, Geoffrey**      **1.2985**
**Wainwright, Edward Yarnold.**
New York: Oxford University Press, 1978. xxvii, 547 p., [8] leaves of plates: ill.; 24 cm. 1. Liturgics — Addresses, essays, lectures. I. Jones, Cheslyn. II. Wainwright, Geoffrey, 1939- III. Yarnold, Edward.
BV176.S76 1978     264     LC 78-18464     ISBN 0195200756

**Dix, Gregory.**     **1.2986**
The shape of the liturgy / by Gregory Dix; additional notes by Paul V. Marshall. — New York: Seabury Press, 1982, c1945. xxi, 777 p., [1] folded leaf of plates; 22 cm. Reprint. Originally published: 2nd ed. 1945. 1. Lord's Supper (Liturgy) 2. Lord's Supper — History I. T.
BV178.D5 1982    264/.36/09 19    *LC* 82-222965    *ISBN* 0816424187

**Emswiler, Sharon Neufer, 1944-.**     **1.2987**
Women and worship: a guide to nonsexist hymns, prayers, and liturgies / Sharon Neufer Emswiler, Thomas Neufer Emswiler. — Rev. and expanded ed. — San Francisco: Harper & Row, c1984. xiv, 142 p.; 20 cm. Cover title: Women & worship. 1. Sexism in liturgical language 2. Liturgies I. Emswiler, Thomas Neufer, 1941- II. T. III. Title: Women & worship.
BV178.E48 1984    264 19    *LC* 83-48459    *ISBN* 0060661011

**Thompson, Bard, 1925- ed.**     **1.2988**
Liturgies of the Western church. — Cleveland: Meridian Books, [c1961] xiv, 434 p.; 19 cm. — (Living age books, LA35) 1. Liturgies I. T.
BV186.5.T5    264    *LC* 61-15750

**Heiler, Friedrich, 1892-1967.**     • **1.2989**
Prayer: a study in the history and psychology of religion / by Friedrich Heiler; translated and edited by Samuel McComb; with the assistance of J. Edgar Park. — London: Oxford University Press, 1932. xxviii, 376 p. 1. Prayer I. McComb, Samuel, 1864- II. Park, John Edgar, 1879- III. T.
BV210.H38    *LC* 32-12970

**Anselm, Saint, Archbishop of Canterbury, 1033-1109.**     **1.2990**
The prayers and meditations of St. Anselm; translated [from the Latin] and with an introduction by Sister Benedicta Ward; with a foreword by R. W. Southern. Harmondsworth, Penguin, 1973. 287 p. 18 cm. (Penguin classics) 1. Prayers 2. Meditations. I. Ward, Benedicta, 1933- tr. II. T.
BV245.A5    242/.802    *LC* 73-178518    *ISBN* 0140442782

**Frankiel, Sandra Sizer, 1946-.**     **1.2991**
Gospel hymns and social religion: the rhetoric of nineteenth–century revivalism / Sandra S. Sizer. — Philadelphia: Temple University Press, c1978. xi, 222 p.; 22 cm. (American civilization.) Based on the author's thesis, University of Chicago. 1. Revivals — Hymns — History and criticism. 2. Revivals — United States. 3. Sociology, Christian — United States. I. T. II. Series.
BV460.F7 1978    264/.2    *LC* 78-10165    *ISBN* 0877221421

# BV590–1650 Ecclesiastical Theology

**Welch, Claude, 1922-.**     • **1.2992**
The reality of the church / by Claude Welch. — New York: Scribners, [c1958]. 254 p.; 21 cm. 1. Church I. T.
BV593.W45 1958    *LC* 58-11639

**Moltmann, Jürgen, 1926-.**     **1.2993**
The Church in the power of the Spirit: a contribution to messianic ecclesiology / Jürgen Moltmann. — New York: Harper & Row, 1977. xvii, 407 p.; 24 cm. Traduction de Kirche in der Kraft des Geistes. 1. Church I. T.
BV600.2.M64    BV600.2.M6413 1977b.

**Küng, Hans, 1928-.**     • **1.2994**
[Unfehlbar? eine Anfrage. English] Infallible? An inquiry. Translated by Edward Quinn. Garden City, N.Y., Doubleday, 1971. 262 p. 22 cm. Translation of Unfehlbar? Eine Anfrage. 1. Catholic Church — Infallibility 2. Popes — Infallibility I. T.
BV601.6.I5 K813    262/.131    *LC* 77-139784

**Childress, James F.**     • **1.2995**
Civil disobedience and political obligation; a study in Christian social ethics [by] James F. Childress. New Haven, Yale University Press, 1971. xv, 250 p. 21 cm. (Yale publications in religion, 16) 1. Government, Resistance to — Religious aspects — Christianity 2. Political ethics I. T. II. Series.
BV630.2.C55 1971    172/.1    *LC* 75-158137    *ISBN* 0300014937

**Tierney, Brian.**     **1.2996**
The crisis of church & state, 1050–1300. With selected documents. — Englewood Cliffs, N.J.: Prentice-Hall, [1964] xi, 211 p.; 21 cm. — (A Spectrum book) 1. Church and state — History. I. T.
BV630.2.T5    270.4    *LC* 64-23072

**Abell, Aaron Ignatius.**     • **1.2997**
The urban impact on American Protestantism 1865–1900 / by Aaron Ignatius Abell. — Hamden [Conn.]: Archon, 1962, c1943. x, 275 p. Includes index. 1. City churches 2. Church and social problems — United States.

3. Protestant churches — United States. 4. Church work 5. Theology, Doctrinal — History — United States. 6. Missions — United States I. T.
BV637.A3 1962    277.3    *LC* a 62-5420//r

**Cross, Robert D., ed.**     **1.2998**
The church and the city, 1865–1910. Edited by Robert D. Cross. — Indianapolis, Bobbs-Merrill Co. [1967] xlv, 359 p. 21 cm. — (American heritage series;) 1. City churches — Collections. 2. United States — Religion — Collections. I. T. II. Series.
BV637.C7    254.2/208    *LC* 66-17273

**Ruether, Rosemary Radford.**     **1.2999**
Religion and sexism; images of woman in the Jewish and Christian traditions. Edited by Rosemary Radford Ruether. — New York: Simon and Schuster, [1974] 356 p.; 22 cm. 1. Women in Christianity 2. Women in the Bible 3. Women in rabbinical literature I. T.
BV639.W7 R8    261.8/34/12    *LC* 74-2791    *ISBN* 0671216929

**Women of spirit: female leadership in the Jewish and Christian**     **1.3000**
**traditions / edited by Rosemary Ruether and Eleanor McLaughlin.**
New York: Simon and Schuster, c1979. 400 p.; 22 cm. 1. Women in Christianity — Addresses, essays, lectures. 2. Women in Judaism — Addresses, essays, lectures. 3. Woman (Theology) — Addresses, essays, lectures. I. Ruether, Rosemary Radford. II. McLaughlin, Eleanor.
BV639.W7 W62    261.8/34/12    *LC* 78-11995    *ISBN* 0671228439

**Horsfield, Peter G.**     **1.3001**
Religious television: the American experience / Peter G. Horsfield. — New York: Longman, c1984. xv, 197 p.; 24 cm. — (Communication and human values.) Includes index. 1. Television in religion — United States. I. T. II. Series.
BV656.3.H67 1984    269/.2 19    *LC* 83-11313    *ISBN* 0582284325

**Ministry in America: a report and analysis, based on an in-**     **1.3002**
**depth survey of 47 denominations in the United States and Canada, with interpretation by 18 experts / David S. Schuller, Merton P. Strommen, and Milo L. Brekke, editors.**
1st ed. — San Francisco: Harper & Row, c1980. xxv, 582 p.: graphs; 24 cm. 'A project of the Association of Theological Schools in the United States and Canada and of Search Institute.' 1. Clergy — Office — Evaluation — Addresses, essays, lectures. 2. Clergy — United States — Addresses, essays, lectures. 3. Clergy — Canada — Addresses, essays, lectures. 4. Christian sects — United States — Addresses, essays, lectures. 5. Christian sects — Canada — Addresses, essays, lectures. I. Schuller, David S. II. Strommen, Merton P. III. Brekke, Milo. IV. Association of Theological Schools in the United States and Canada. V. Search Institute.
BV660.2.M53 1980    253    *LC* 79-2990    *ISBN* 006067721X

**The Ministry in historical perspectives / edited by H. Richard**     **1.3003**
**Niebuhr and Daniel D. Williams.**
2nd ed. — San Francisco: Harper & Row, c1983. xi, 253 p.; 21 cm. 1. Clergy — History — Addresses, essays, lectures. I. Niebuhr, H. Richard (Helmut Richard), 1894-1962. II. Williams, Daniel Day, 1910-1973.
BV660.2.M535 1983    262/.1/09 19    *LC* 80-8899    *ISBN* 0060662328

**Rahner, Karl, 1904-.**     • **1.3004**
The episcopate and the primacy [by] Karl Rahner [and] Joseph Ratzinger. [Translated by Kenneth Barker and others]. — Freiburg, Herder [1962] 134 p. 22 cm. — (Quaestiones disputatae, 4) 1. Episcopacy I. Ratzinger, Joseph. II. T.
BV670.R313 1962a    *LC* 62-19565

## BV676 WOMEN. ORDINATION

**Hewitt, Emily C.**     **1.3005**
Women priests: yes or no? [By] Emily C. Hewitt [and] Suzanne R. Hiatt. New York, Seabury Press [1973] 128 p. 21 cm. 1. Ordination of women — Episcopal Church. I. Hiatt, Suzanne R., joint author. II. T.
BV676.H48    253/.2    *LC* 72-81027    *ISBN* 0816420769

**Jewett, Paul King.**     **1.3006**
The ordination of women: an essay on the office of Christian ministry / by Paul K. Jewett. — Grand Rapids, Mich.: Eerdmans, c1980. xi, 148 p.; 21 cm. 1. Ordination of women I. T.
BV676.J48    262/.14    *LC* 80-15644    *ISBN* 0802818501

## BV740–741 FREEDOM AND AUTHORITY

**Rahner, Karl, 1904-.**      • **1.3007**
Free speech in the church. — New York, Sheed & Ward [1960, c1959] 112 p. 20 cm. 1. Freedom of speech in the church 2. Public opinion 3. Christianity — 20th cent. I. T.
BV740.R313 1960     282     *LC* 60-7313 rev

**Bainton, Roland Herbert, 1894-.**      • **1.3008**
The travail of religious liberty; nine biographical studies, by Roland H. Bainton. — [Hamden, Conn.]: Archon Books, 1971 [c1951] 272 p.: illus.; 23 cm. 1. Freedom of religion 2. Christian biography I. T.
BV741.B26 1971     261.7/2/0922     *LC* 76-122412     *ISBN* 0208010858

**Bates, M. Searle (Miner Searle), 1897-1978.**      **1.3009**
Religious liberty: an inquiry, by M. Searle Bates. New York, Da Capo Press, 1972 [c1945] xviii, [2], 604 p. 23 cm. (Civil liberties in American history) 1. Freedom of religion I. T. II. Series.
BV741.B3 1972     323.44/2     *LC* 77-166096     *ISBN* 0306702355

**Carrillo de Albornoz, Angel Francisco, 1905-.**      • **1.3010**
The basis of religious liberty. — New York, Association Press [1963] 182 p. 23 cm. Includes bibliography. 1. Freedom of religion I. T.
BV741.C34     261.72     *LC* 63-16047

**Murray, John Courtney. ed.**      • **1.3011**
Freedom and man. [Contributors] Hans Küng [and others]. — New York: P. J. Kenedy, [1965] 217 p.; 22 cm. — (A Wisdom and discovery book) 1. Liberty of conscience I. Küng, Hans, 1928- II. T.
BV741.M87     233     *LC* 65-23957

## BV800–890 SACRAMENTS

**Berkouwer, G. C. (Gerrit Cornelis), 1903-.**      **1.3012**
[Sacramenten. English] The sacraments, by G. C. Berkouwer. [Translated by Hugo Bekker] Grand Rapids, Eerdmans [1969] 304 p. 23 cm. (His Studies in dogmatics) Translation of De Sacramenten. 1. Sacraments I. T.
BV800.B4713     265     *LC* 66-27410

**Holifield, E. Brooks.**      **1.3013**
The covenant sealed: the development of Puritan sacramental theology in old and New England, 1570–1720 / E. Brooks Holifield. — New Haven: Yale University Press, 1974. xi, 248 p.; 25 cm. Includes index. 1. Sacraments — History of doctrines 2. Puritans I. T.
BV800.H64     234/.16     *LC* 73-92695     *ISBN* 0300017332

**Jenson, Robert W.**      **1.3014**
Visible words: the interpretation and practice of Christian sacraments / Robert W. Jenson. — Philadelphia: Fortress Press, c1978. xi, 212 p.; 24 cm. 1. Sacraments I. T.
BV800.J45     234/.16     *LC* 77-78631     *ISBN* 0800605071

**Beasley-Murray, George Raymond, 1916-.**      **1.3015**
Baptism in the New Testament / by G. R. Beasley–Murray. — 1st American paperback ed. — Grand Rapids, Mich.: W. B. Eerdmans, 1973. ix, 422 p. 1. Baptism I. T.
BV806.B4 1973     *ISBN* 080281493X

**Cullmann, Oscar.**      **1.3016**
[Tauflehre des Neuen Testaments. English] Baptism in the New Testament / Oscar Cullmann. — Philadelphia: Westminster Press, [1978] c1950. 84 p.; 22 cm. Translation of Die Tauflehre des Neuen Testaments. This ed. first published by SCM Press, London, which was issued as no. 1 of Studies in Biblical theology. 1. Baptism — Biblical teaching. I. T.
BV806.C84 1978     234/.161     *LC* 78-6937     *ISBN* 0664242197

**Barth, Karl, 1886-1968.**      • **1.3017**
The teaching of the church regarding baptism. Translated by Ernest A. Payne. — London, SCM Press [1948] 64 p. 19 cm. 1. Baptism I. T.
BV811.B393     265.1     *LC* 51-1026

**Jeremias, Joachim, 1900-.**      • **1.3018**
Infant baptism in the first four centuries. Translated by David Cairns. Philadelphia, Westminster Press [1960] 111 p. illus. 23 cm. (The Library of history and doctrine) 1. Infant baptism — History I. T.
BV813.2.J413     265.1     *LC* 61-5625

**Tentler, Thomas N., 1932-.**      **1.3019**
Sin and confession on the eve of the Reformation / Thomas N. Tentler. Princeton, N.J.: Princeton University Press, c1977. xxiv, 395 p.; 25 cm. Includes index. 1. Penance — History I. T.
BV840.T43     234/.166     *LC* 76-3022     *ISBN* 0691072191

# BV2000–3705 Missions

**Sundkler, Bengt Gustaf Malcolm, 1909-.**      **1.3020**
The world of mission, by Bengt Sundkler. [English translation by Eric J. Sharpe]. — Grand Rapids, Mich.: Wm. B. Eerdmans Pub., 1966. 318 p. 20 cm. 1. Missions I. T.
BV2061.S831     266     *LC* 66-3153

**Classics of Christian missions / Francis M. DuBose, editor.**      **1.3021**
Nashville: Broadman Press, c1979. 462 p.; 21 cm. Includes indexes. 1. Missions — Addresses, essays, lectures. I. DuBose, Francis M.
BV2070.C55     266     *LC* 78-53147     *ISBN* 0805463135

**Neill, Stephen, 1900-.**      **1.3022**
Colonialism and Christian missions / by Stephen Neill. New York: McGraw-Hill, [1966] 445 p.; 22 cm. 1. Missions I. T.
BV2080.N4     266     *LC* 66-21153

**Glover, Robert Hall, 1871-1947.**      **1.3023**
The progress of world–wide missions. Rev. and enl. by J. Herbert Kane. — New York: Harper, [1960] x, 502 p.: maps.; 22 cm. 1. Missions — History I. Kane, J. Herbert. ed. II. T.
BV2100.G5 1960     266.09     *LC* 60-11775

**Neill, Stephen, 1900-.**      **1.3024**
A history of Christian missions / Stephen Neill. — Harmondsworth: Penguin Books, 1964. 622 p. (Pelican history of the church; 6.) 1. Missions — History I. T. II. Series.
BV2100 N43     266.009     *LC* 64-3926     *ISBN* 0140206280

**Hill, Patricia Ruth.**      **1.3025**
The world their household: the American woman's foreign mission movement and cultural transformation, 1870–1920 / Patricia R. Hill. — Ann Arbor: University of Michigan Press, c1985. 231 p.; 24 cm. (Women and culture series.) Includes index. 1. Women in missionary work 2. Women missionaries — United States. 3. Missions, American 4. Protestant churches — Missions 5. United States — Church history — 19th century 6. United States — Church history — 20th century I. T. II. Series.
BV2610.H55 1985     266/.023/73 19     *LC* 84-13206     *ISBN* 0472100556

**Anderson, Courtney.**      **1.3026**
To the Golden Shore; the life of Adoniram Judson. Boston, Little, Brown [c1956] 530 p. ill. 22 cm. 1. Judson, Adoniram, 1788-1850. 2. Missions, American — India. 3. Missionaries — India — Biography. 4. Missionaries — United States — Biography. I. T.
BV 3271 J81 A54 1956     *LC* 56-6766

**Latourette, Kenneth Scott, 1884-1968.**      • **1.3027**
A history of Christian missions in China. — New York, Russell & Russell [1967] xii, 930 p. fold. map. 22 cm. 'First published in 1929.' 1. Missions — China I. T.
BV3415.L35 1967     266/.023/0951     *LC* 66-24721

**Fairbank, John King, 1907-.**      **1.3028**
The missionary enterprise in China and America / edited and with an introd. by John K. Fairbank. — Cambridge: Harvard University Press, 1974. 442 p.; 25 cm. — (Harvard studies in American-East Asian relations. 6) 1. Missions — China 2. Protestant churches — Missions 3. Missions, American — China. I. T. II. Series.
BV3415.2.F34     266/.023/0951     *LC* 74-82191     *ISBN* 0674576551

**Covell, Ralph R.**      **1.3029**
W. A. P. Martin, pioneer of progress in China / by Ralph Covell. — Washington: Christian University Press, c1978. viii, 303 p.; 21 cm. Includes index. 1. Martin, W. A. P. (William Alexander Parsons), 1827-1916. 2. Missionaries — China — Biography. 3. Missionaries — United States — Biography. 4. Missions — China I. T.
BV3427.M295 C68     266/.023/0924 B     *LC* 77-13321     *ISBN* 0802817157

**Spence, Jonathan D.**      **1.3030**
The memory palace of Matteo Ricci / Jonathan D. Spence. — New York, N.Y.: Viking Penguin, 1984. xii, 350 p., [1] leaf of plates: 10 ill.; 24 cm. 'Elisabeth Sifton books.' Includes index. 1. Ricci, Matteo, 1552-1610. 2. Jesuits — Missions — China. 3. Missionaries — China — Biography. 4. Missionaries — Italy — Biography. 5. China — History — Ming dynasty, 1368-1644 I. T.
BV3427.R46 S66 1984     266/.2/0924 B 19     *LC* 83-40653     *ISBN* 0670468304

**Williams, Walter L., 1948-.**        **1.3031**
Black Americans and the evangelization of Africa, 1877–1900 / Walter L. Williams. — Madison, Wis.: University of Wisconsin Press, 1982. xviii, 259 p.: ill.; 24 cm. Includes index. 1. Missions — Africa, Sub-Saharan. 2. Afro-American missionaries — Africa, Sub-Saharan. 3. Afro-Americans — Religion I. T.
BV3520.W49 1982     266/.023/73067 19     *LC* 81-69830     *ISBN* 0299089207

---

# BV3750–3799 Revivals

**Finney, Charles Grandison, 1792-1875.**      • **1.3032**
Lectures on revivals of religion / by Charles Grandison Finney; edited by William G. McLoughlin. — Cambridge, Mass.: Belknap Press of Harvard University Press, 1960. lix, 470 p.; 24 cm. (John Harvard library.) 1. Revivals I. T. II. Series.
BV3770.F55 1960     *LC* 60-11558

**Boles, John B.**      • **1.3033**
The Great Revival, 1787–1805: the origins of the Southern evangelical mind [by] John B. Boles. — [Lexington]: University Press of Kentucky, [1972] xiii, 236 p.: illus.; 24 cm. 1. Revivals — Southern States. I. T.
BV3773.B65     269/.2/0975     *LC* 77-183349     *ISBN* 0813112605

**Carwardine, Richard.**      **1.3034**
Transatlantic revivalism: popular evangelicalism in Britain and America, 1790–1865 / Richard Carwardine. — Westport, Conn.: Greenwood Press, 1978. xviii, 249 p.: ill.; 25 cm. — (Contributions in American history; no. 75 0084-9219) Includes index. 1. Revivals — United States — History. 2. Revivals — Great Britain — History. 3. Evangelicalism — Great Britain — History. 4. Evangelicalism — United States — History. 5. United States — Church history 6. Great Britain — Church history I. T.
BV3773.C35     269/.2/0973     *LC* 77-94740     *ISBN* 0313203083

**Harrell, David Edwin.**      **1.3035**
All things are possible: the healing & charismatic revivals in modern America / David Edwin Harrell, Jr. — Bloomington: Indiana University Press, [1975] xi, 304 p.: ill.; 24 cm. Includes index. 1. Revivals — United States. 2. Spiritual healing — History. 3. Pentecostalism — United States — History. I. T.
BV3773.H37 1975     269/.2/0973     *LC* 75-1937     *ISBN* 0253100909

**McLoughlin, William Gerald.**      • **1.3036**
Modern revivalism: Charles Grandison Finney to Billy Graham / William G. McLoughlin. — New York: Ronald Press, c1959. vii, 551 p. 1. Revivals — United States I. T.
BV3773.M3     *LC* 58-12959

**McLoughlin, William Gerald.**      **1.3037**
Revivals, awakenings, and reform: an essay on religion and social change in America, 1607–1977 / William G. McLoughlin. — Chicago: University of Chicago Press, 1978. xv, 239 p.; 21 cm. — (Chicago history of American religion) Includes index. 1. Revivals — United States. 2. United States — Church history 3. United States — Civilization I. T.
BV3773.M32     269/.2/0973     *LC* 77-27830     *ISBN* 0226560910

**Smith, Timothy Lawrence, 1924-.**      **1.3038**
[Revivalism and social reform in mid-nineteenth-century America] Revivalism and social reform: American Protestantism on the eve of the Civil War / Timothy L. Smith; with a new afterword by the author. — Baltimore: Johns Hopkins University Press, 1980. 269 p.; 20 cm. Originally published in 1957 by Abingdon Press, New York, under title: Revivalism and social reform in mid-nineteenth-century America. Includes index. 1. Protestant churches — United States. 2. Revivals — United States — History. 3. Church and social problems — United States. 4. United States — Church history — 19th century I. T.
BV3773.S6 1980     269/.24/0973 19     *LC* 80-8114     *ISBN* 080182477X

**Weisberger, Bernard A., 1922-.**      • **1.3039**
They gathered at the river; the story of the great revivalists and their impact upon religion in America. — [1st ed.]. — Boston: Little, Brown, [1958] 345 p.: illus.; 22 cm. 1. Revivals — United States. 2. Evangelists I. T.
BV3773.W4     *LC* 58-7848

**Johnson, Paul E., 1942-.**      **1.3040**
A shopkeeper's millennium: society and revivals in Rochester, New York, 1815–1837 / Paul E. Johnson. — 1st ed. — New York: Hill and Wang, 1978. ix, 210 p.: maps; 22 cm. (American century series) 1. Revivals — New York (State) — Rochester. 2. Rochester (N.Y.) — History. 3. Rochester (N.Y.) — Church history. I. T.
BV3775.R62 J63 1978     269/.24/0974789 19     *LC* 78-10533     *ISBN* 0809086549

**Frady, Marshall.**      **1.3041**
Billy Graham, a parable of American righteousness / Marshall Frady. — 1st ed. — Boston: Little, Brown, c1979. xi, 546 p.; 24 cm. 1. Graham, Billy, 1918- 2. Evangelists — United States — Biography. I. T.
BV3785.G69 F7     269/.2/0924 B     *LC* 79-9947     *ISBN* 0316291307

**Pollock, John Charles.**      **1.3042**
Billy Graham, evangelist to the world: an authorized biography of the decisive years / John Pollock. — 1st ed. — San Francisco: Harper & Row, c1979. x, 324 p., [8] leaves of plates: ill.; 24 cm. Includes index. 1. Graham, Billy, 1918- 2. Evangelists — United States — Biography. I. T.
BV3785.G69 P597 1979     269/.2/0924 B 19     *LC* 76-62949     *ISBN* 0060666919

**Haliburton, Gordon MacKay.**      **1.3043**
The prophet Harris; a study of an African prophet and his mass–movement in the Ivory Coast and the Gold Coast, 1913–1915. — New York: Oxford University Press, 1973. xv, 155 p.: illus.; 21 cm. 1. Harris, William Wade. I. T.
BV3785.H348 H3 1973     266/.3/0924 B     *LC* 72-83851     *ISBN* 0195016262

**Findlay, James F., 1930-.**      • **1.3044**
Dwight L. Moody, American evangelist, 1837–1899 [by] James F. Findlay, Jr. With a foreword by Martin E. Marty. — Chicago: University of Chicago Press, [1969] ix, 440 p.; 23 cm. 1. Moody, Dwight Lyman, 1837-1899. I. T.
BV3785.M7 F47     269/.2/0924     *LC* 69-13200

---

# BV4000–4470 Pastoral Theology

**Mather, Cotton, 1663-1728.**      • **1.3045**
Manuductio ad ministerium: directions for a candidate of the ministry / by Cotton Mather; with a bibliographical note by Thomas J. Holmes and Kenneth B. Murdock. — 1st AMS ed. — New York: AMS Press, 1978. xix, 151 p.; 19 cm. Reprint of the 1938 ed. published by Columbia University Press, New York, which was issued as Publication no. 42 of the Facsimile Text Society, and which was reproduced from the original edition, Boston, 1726. 1. Clergy — Training of I. T. II. Title: Directions for a candidate of the ministry.
BV4020.M35 1978     207/.1     *LC* 75-41190     *ISBN* 0404146856

**Mitchell, Henry H.**      **1.3046**
Black preaching [by] Henry H. Mitchell. [1st ed.] Philadelphia, Lippincott [1970] 248 p. 21 cm. (C. Eric Lincoln series on Black religion) 1. Preaching — United States — History. 2. Afro-Americans — Religion 3. Afro-American preaching I. T.
BV4208.U6 M57 1970     251/.00973     *LC* 72-124546

**Sermons in American history; selected issues in the American pulpit, 1630–1967. Prepared under the auspices of the Speech Communication Association. DeWitte Holland, editor. Hubert Vance Taylor and Jess Yoder, assistant editors.**      **1.3047**
[Nashville: Abingdon Press, 1971] 542 p.; 25 cm. 1. Sermons, American I. Holland, DeWitte Talmadge, 1923- ed. II. Speech Communication Association.
BV4241.S4186     261     *LC* 76-148072     *ISBN* 0687377943

**Schweitzer, Albert, 1875-1965.**      • **1.3048**
[Strassburger Predigten. English] Reverence for life. Translated by Reginald H. Fuller. [1st ed.] New York, Harper & Row [1969] 153 p. 22 cm. Translation of Strassburger Predigten. 1. Sermons, English — Translations from German. 2. Sermons, German — Translations into English. I. T.
BV4244.S3613     252/.04     *LC* 71-85052

**Barth, Karl, 1886-1968.**      • **1.3049**
[Den Gefangenen Befreiung. English] Deliverance to the captives. [Sermons; translated by Marguerite Wieser. 1st ed.] New York, Harper [1961] 160 p. 22 cm. 1. Prisons — Sermons. I. T.
BV4316.P7 B33     252     *LC* 61-7333

**Lea, Henry Charles, 1825-1909.**      • **1.3050**
The history of sacerdotal celibacy in the Christian church. New York, Russell & Russell, 1957. xvii, 611 p. 22 cm. First published in 1867 under title: An historical sketch of sacerdotal celibacy in the Christian church. 1. Catholic Church — Clergy 2. Celibacy I. T.
BV4390.L4 1957     *LC* 57-8673

**Richardson, James T., 1941-.**      **1.3051**
Organized miracles: a study of a contemporary, youth, communal, fundamentalist organization / James T. Richardson, Mary White Stewart, Robert B. Simmonds. — New Brunswick, N.J.: Transaction Books, c1979. xxviii, 368 p.: ill.; 24 cm. Includes index. 1. Christ Communal Organization.

I. Stewart, Mary White, 1945- joint author. II. Simmonds, Robert B., 1945-
joint author. III. T.
BV4407.3.R52　　301.5/8　　*LC* 78-55937　　*ISBN* 0878552847

research; v. 44) Includes index. 1. College students — United States —
Religious life. 2. Apostasy I. Sherrow, Fred, joint author. II. T.
BV4531.2.C33　　301.5/8　　*LC* 77-1043　　*ISBN* 0803907141. *ISBN*
080390715X pbk

# BV4485–5099 Practical Religion. Christian Life

**Bynum, Caroline Walker.**　　　　　　　　　　**1.3052**
Jesus as mother: studies in the spirituality of the High Middle Ages / Caroline
Walker Bynum. — Berkeley: University of California Press, c1984. xiv, 279 p.;
25 cm. (Publications of the Center for Medieval and Renaissance Studies,
UCLA; 16) 1. Spiritual life — Middle Ages, 600-1500 — Addresses, essays,
lectures. 2. Monastic and religious life — History — Middle Ages, 600-1500 —
Addresses, essays, lectures. 3. God — Motherhood — History of doctrines —
Middle Ages, 600-1500 — Addresses, essays, lectures. I. T.
BV4490.B96 1982　　255 19　　*LC* 81-13137　　*ISBN* 0520041941

**Christian spirituality: origins to the twelfth century / edited by**　　**1.3053**
**Bernard McGinn and John Meyendorff in collaboration with**
**Jean Leclercq.**
New York: Crossroad, 1985. xxv, 502 p.: ill.; 25 cm. (Vol. 16 of World
spirituality) 1. Spiritual life — History of doctrines — Addresses, essays,
lectures. I. McGinn, Bernard, 1937- II. Meyendorff, John, 1926-
III. Leclercq, Jean, 1911-
BV4490.C464 1985　　248/.09 19　　*LC* 85-7692　　*ISBN* 0824506812

**Hambrick-Stowe, Charles E.**　　　　　　　　　**1.3054**
The practice of piety: Puritan devotional disciplines in seventeenth–century
New England / Charles E. Hambrick–Stowe. — Chapel Hill: Published for the
Institute of Early American History and Culture, Williamsburg, Virginia by the
University of North Carolina Press, c1982. xvi, 298 p.: ill.; 24 cm. 1. Spiritual
life — History of doctrines — 17th century. 2. Puritans — New England.
3. New England — Religious life and customs. I. Institute of Early American
History and Culture (Williamsburg, Va.) II. T.
BV4490.H3 1982　　248.4/0974 19　　*LC* 81-19806　　*ISBN* 0807815187

**Law, William, 1686-1761.**　　　　　　　　　　**1.3055**
A serious call to a devout and holy life; The spirit of love / William Law; edited
from the first editions by Paul G. Stanwood; introd. by Austin Warren and Paul
G. Stanwood; pref. by John Booty. — New York: Paulist Press, c1978. x,
526 p.; 23 cm. — (Classics of Western spirituality.) Errata slip inserted.
Includes indexes. 1. Christian life I. Stanwood, P. G. II. Law, William,
1686-1761. The spirit of love. 1978. III. T. IV. Series.
BV4500.L3 1978　　248/.4　　*LC* 78-61418　　*ISBN* 080910265X

**Arndt, Johann, 1555-1621.**　　　　　　　　　　**1.3056**
[Wahres Christenthum. English. Selections] True Christianity / Johann Arndt;
translation and introd. by Peter Erb; pref. by Heiko A. Oberman. — New York:
Paulist Press, c1979. xvii, 301 p.; 23 cm. — (Classics of Western spirituality.)
Translation of book 1 and parts of books 2-6 of Wahres Christenthum.
1. Christian life — Lutheran authors. 2. Mysticism I. T. II. Series.
BV4503.A76213 1979　　248/.48/41　　*LC* 78-72046　　*ISBN*
0809102811

**Kierkegaard, Søren, 1813-1855.**　　　　　　　　● **1.3057**
Edifying discourses by Søren Kierkegaard ... translated from the Danish by
David F. Swenson and Lillian Marvin Swenson. — Minneapolis, Minn.,
Augsburg publishing house [1943-1946] 4 v. 22 cm. 1. Spiritual life
I. Swenson, David F. (David Ferdinand), 1876-1940. tr. II. Swenson, Lillian
B. (Marvin), joint tr. III. T.
BV4505.K44　　248　　*LC* 43-15536

**Erasmus, Desiderius, d. 1536.**　　　　　　　　● **1.3058**
The enchiridion. Translated and edited by Raymond Himelick. —
Bloomington, Indiana University Press [1963] 222 p. 20 cm. — (Midland
books, MB-52) Translation of Enchiridion militis Christiani. Bibliographical
references included in 'Notes' (p. 201-222) 1. Christian life — Middle Ages.
I. Himelick, Raymond, ed. and tr. II. T.
BV4509.L2E833　　248.4　　*LC* 63-16615

**Ochs, Carol.**　　　　　　　　　　　　　　**1.3059**
Women and spirituality / Carol Ochs. — Totowa, N.J.: Rowman & Allanheld,
1983. 156 p.; 22 cm. (New feminist perspectives series.) Includes index.
1. Women — Religious life 2. Spirituality — Christianity. I. T. II. Series.
BV4527.O25 1983　　248.8/43 19　　*LC* 83-3397　　*ISBN* 0847672328

**Caplovitz, David.**　　　　　　　　　　　　**1.3060**
The religious drop–outs: apostasy among college graduates / David Caplovitz,
Fred Sherrow, with the assistance of Stanley Raffel and Steven Cohen. —
Beverly Hills: Sage Publications, c1977. 199 p.; 22 cm. (Sage library of social

# BV4610–4780 Moral Theology. Love

**Geach, P. T. (Peter Thomas), 1916-.**　　　　　　**1.3061**
The virtues / Peter Geach. — Cambridge: Cambridge University Press, 1977.
xxxv, 173 p.; 21 cm. — (The Stanton lectures; 1973-4) Includes index.
1. Virtues — Addresses, essays, lectures. I. T. II. Series.
BV4630.G4　　241/.4　　*LC* 76-19628　　*ISBN* 0521213509

**Conference on Hope and the Future of Man, New York, 1971.**　● **1.3062**
Hope and the future of man. Ewert H. Cousins, editor. Philadelphia, Fortress
Press [1972] xii, 148 p. 21 cm. Sponsored by the American Teilhard de Chardin
Association, and others. 1. Hope — Religious aspects — Christianity —
Addresses, essays, lectures. I. Cousins, Ewert H. ed. II. American Teilhard de
Chardin Association. III. T.
BV4638.C58 1971　　236　　*LC* 72-75647　　*ISBN* 0800605403

**Lewis, C. S. (Clive Staples), 1898-1963.**　　　　● **1.3063**
The four loves. New York, Harcourt, Brace [1960] 192 p. 21 cm. 1. Love
2. Love — Religious aspects — Christianity I. T.
BV4639.L45 1960a　　241　　*LC* 60-10920

**Nygren, Anders, 1890-.**　　　　　　　　　　● **1.3064**
[Kristna kärlekstanken. English] Agape and Eros. Translated by Philip S.
Watson. New York, Harper & Row [1969] 764 p. 21 cm. (Harper torchbooks.
The Library of religion and culture, TB1430) Reprint of the 1953 ed.
Translation of Den kristna kärlekstanken genom tiderna. 1. Love — Religious
aspects — Christianity 2. Agape I. T.
BV4639.N813 1969　　231/.6　　*LC* 77-3058

**Outka, Gene H.**　　　　　　　　　　　　● **1.3065**
Agape; an ethical analysis, by Gene Outka. — New Haven: Yale University
Press, 1972. viii, 321 p.; 23 cm. — (Yale publications in religion, 17) A revision
of the author's thesis, Yale University. 1. Agape 2. Ethics I. T. II. Series.
BV4639.O95 1972　　231/.6　　*LC* 72-88070　　*ISBN* 0300013841

**Williams, Daniel Day, 1910-1973.**　　　　　　● **1.3066**
The spirit and the forms of love. [1st U.S. ed.] New York, Harper & Row [1968]
ix, 306 p. 22 cm. Based on lectures at the General Council of the Congregational
Christian Churches in Claremont, California, in 1952 and the Nathaniel W.
Taylor lectures at the Yale Divinity School in 1953. 1. Love — Religious
aspects — Christianity I. T.
BV4639.W484 1968　　241.4　　*LC* 68-29561

**Bernard, de Clairvaux, saint, 1090-91-1153.**　　● **1.3067**
The steps of humility / by Bernard, abbot of Clairvaux; translated, with
introduction and notes, as a study of epistemology by George Bosworth Bruch.
— Cambridge, Mass.: Harward University Press, 1940. xi, 287 p. Texte latin en
regard de la traduction anglaise de: Tractatus de gradibus humilitatis et
superbiae. I. Burch, George Bosworth, 1902- II. T.
BV4647.H8 B45　　BR75.B522 T759 1940 A.　　189.4　　*LC* 40-32426

**Little, Lester K.**　　　　　　　　　　　　**1.3068**
Religious poverty and the profit economy in medieval Europe / Lester K. Little.
— Ithaca, NY: Cornell University Press, 1978. xi, 267 p.; 25 cm. 1. Poverty —
Religious aspects — Christianity — History of doctrines 2. Monastic and
religious life — History of doctrines 3. Civilization, Medieval 4. Economic
history — Medieval, 500-1500 I. T.
BV4647.P6 L57 1978　　241/.4　　*LC* 78-58630　　*ISBN* 0801412137

# BV4800–4911 Works of Meditation and Devotion. Consolation and Cheer

**Weil, Simone, 1909-1943.**　　　　　　　　　**1.3069**
Waiting for God; translated by Emma Gruafurd. With an introd. by Leslie A.
Fiedler. New York, Putnam [1951] 227 p. 22 cm. 1. God — Worship and love.
I. T.
BV4817.W413　　248　　*LC* 51-7174

**Imitatio Christi. English.**　　　　　　　　　● **1.3070**
The imitation of Christ, from the first edition of an English translation made c.
1530 by Richard Whitford, edited with an introduction by Edward J. Klein.

New York and London, Harper & brothers [1943] xxv, 261, [1] p. 16 cm. I. Klein, Edward J. II. Whitford, Richard, fl. 1495-1555? III. T. BV4821.A1 1943    *LC* 43-10542

**Donne, John, 1573-1631.**      • **1.3071**
Devotions upon emergent occasions; together with Death's duel. — [Ann Arbor] University of Michigan Press [1959] li, 188 p. 21 cm. — (Ann Arbor paperbacks, AA30) Includes 'The life of Dr. John Donne, taken from the life by Izaak Walton.' 1. Meditations. I. T. II. Title: Death's duel. BV4831.D6 1959    242    *LC* 59-16355

**Julian, of Norwich, b. 1343.**      **1.3072**
[Revelations of divine love] Showings / Julian of Norwich; translated from the critical text, with an introd., by Edmund Colledge and James Walsh; pref. by Jean Leclercq. — New York: Paulist Press, c1978. 369 p.; 23 cm. — (Classics of Western spirituality.) Commonly known as the Revelations of divine love. Includes both the long and short texts. Includes indexes. 1. Devotional literature I. Colledge, Edmund. II. Walsh, James, 1920- III. T. IV. Series. BV4831.J8 1978    242    *LC* 77-90953    *ISBN* 080910234X. *ISBN* 0809120917 pbk

**The Seventeenth–century resolve: a historical anthology of a**    **1.3073**
**literary form / edited by John L. Lievsay.**
Lexington, Ky.: University Press of Kentucky, c1980. 211 p.; 23 cm. Includes index. 1. Meditations. 2. English prose literature — Early modern, 1500-1700 I. Lievsay, John Leon. BV4831.S36    242    *LC* 79-4004    *ISBN* 0813113938

**Traherne, Thomas, d. 1674.**      • **1.3074**
Centuries, poems, and thanksgivings. Edited by H. M. Margoliouth. — Oxford, Clarendon Press, 1958. 2 v. facsims. 23 cm. 1. Devotional literature I. Margoliouth, Herschel Maurice, 1887- ed. II. T. BV4831.T72 1958    242    *LC* 58-4245

**Lewis, C. S. (Clive Staples), 1898-1963.**      • **1.3075**
Surprised by joy; the shape of my early life. [1st American ed.] New York, Harcourt, Brace [1956, c1955] 238 p. 22 cm. 1. Lewis, C. S. (Clive Staples), 1898-1963. 2. Converts, Anglican I. T. BV4935.L43 A3 1956    248    *LC* 56-5329

# BV5015–5095 ASCETICISM. MYSTICISM

**Chadwick, Owen. ed.**      • **1.3076**
Western asceticism; selected translations, with introductions and notes. — Philadelphia, Westminster Press [1958] 368 p. 24 cm. — (The Library of Christian classics, v. 12) Bibliography: p. 361-362. 1. Asceticism I. T. II. Series. BV5017.C5 1958    248    *LC* 58-8713

**Symeon, the New Theologian, Saint, 949-1022.**      **1.3077**
[Catecheses English] Symeon the New Theologian: the discourses / translation by C. J. de Catanzaro; introd. by George Maloney; pref. by Basile Krivocheine. — New York: Paulist Press, c1980. xvii, 396 p.; 23 cm. (The Classics of Western spirituality) Translation of Catéchèses. 1. Asceticism — History — Middle Ages, 600-1500 2. Spiritual life — Middle Ages, 600-1500 I. T. BV5039.G7 S913    248.4/8140942 19    *LC* 80-82414    *ISBN* 0809102927

**Leech, Kenneth.**      **1.3078**
Soul friend: a study of spirituality / Kenneth Leech. — London: Harper & Row, 1977. 250 p.; 22 cm. Includes index. 1. Spiritual direction I. T. BV5053.L43 1977    248.4 19    *LC* 77-363211    *ISBN* 0859691136

**Petry, Ray C, 1903- ed.**      • **1.3079**
Late medieval mysticism. Philadelphia, Westminster Press [1957] 424 p. 24 cm. (The Library of Christian classics, v. 13) 1. Mysticism — History — Middle Ages, 600-1500 I. T. II. Series. BV5072.P4    *LC* 57-5092

**Butler, Edward Cuthbert, 1858-1934.**      • **1.3080**
Western mysticism; the teaching of Augustine, Gregory, and Bernard on contemplation and the contemplative life. 3d ed. with Afterthoughts, and a new foreword by David Knowles. New York, Barnes & Noble [1968, c1967] lxxii, 242 p. 22 cm. 1. Augustine, Saint, Bishop of Hippo. 2. Bernard, of Clairvaux, Saint, 1090 or 91-1153. 3. Gregory I, Pope, ca. 540-604. 4. Contemplation 5. Mysticism I. T. BV5075.B8 1968    248.2/2    *LC* 68-6959

**Knowles, David, 1896-.**      • **1.3081**
The English mystical tradition. — [1st ed.] — New York, Harper [1961] 197 p. 22 cm. Includes bibliography. 1. Mysticism — Gt. Brit. I. T. BV5077.G7K58    248.220942    *LC* 61-7343

**Peers, E. Allison (Edgar Allison), 1891-1952.**      • **1.3082**
Studies of the Spanish mystics. — 2d ed., rev. — London, S. P. C. K.; New York, Macmillan, 1951-1960. 3 v. 22 cm. Includes bibliography. 1. Mysticism — Spain. 2. Spanish literature — Hist. & crit. I. T. II. Title: Spanish mystics. BV5077.S7P52    149.3    *LC* 57-22935

**Böhme, Jakob, 1575-1624.**      • **1.3083**
Confessions. Compiled and edited by W. Scott Palmer [pseud.] With an introduction by Evelyn Underhill. [2d ed.] New York: Gordon Press, 1976. xxxv, 153 p. 1. Mysticism I. Palmer, William Scott, pseud., ed. II. T. BV5080.B65E5 1976    *LC* 75-44330

**Böhme, Jakob, 1575-1624.**      **1.3084**
[Weg zu Christo. English] The way to Christ / Jacob Boehme; translation and introd. by Peter Erb; pref. by Winfried Zeller. — New York: Paulist Press, c1978; xviii, 307 p.; 23 cm. — (Classics of Western spirituality.) Translation of Der weg zu Christo. 1. Mysticism — History I. Erb, Peter C., 1943- II. T. III. Series. BV5080.B7 W413 1978    248/.22    *LC* 77-95117    *ISBN* 0809102374. *ISBN* 0809121026 pbk

**Cloud of unknowing.**      **1.3085**
The cloud of unknowing / edited, with an introduction, by James Walsh; preface by Simon Tugwell. — New York: Paulist Press, c1981. xxvi, 293 p.; 23 cm. — (Classics of Western spirituality.) Includes indexes. 1. Mysticism — Early works to 1800. I. Walsh, James, 1920- II. T. III. Series. BV5080.C5 1981    248.2/2 19    *LC* 81-82201    *ISBN* 0809123320

**Eckhart, Meister, d. 1327.**      **1.3086**
Breakthrough, Meister Eckhart's creation spirituality, in new translation / introd. and commentaries by Matthew Fox. — Garden City, N.Y.: Doubleday, 1980. xx, 579 p.; 22 cm. 1. Mysticism — History — Middle Ages, 600-1500 — Collected works. 2. Mysticism — Germany — Collected works. I. Fox, Matthew, 1940- II. T. BV5080.E3213 1980    230/.2 19    *LC* 80-909    *ISBN* 0385170459

**Eckhart, Meister, d. 1327.**      • **1.3087**
[Selections. English. 1981. Paulist Press] Meister Eckhart, the essential sermons, commentaries, treatises, and defense / translation and introduction by Edmund Colledge, and Bernard McGinn; preface by Huston Smith. — New York: Paulist Press, c1981. xviii, 366 p.; 24 cm. (Classics of Western spirituality.) Includes indexes. 1. Catholic Church — Sermons 2. Mysticism — Early works to 1800 — Addresses, essays, lectures. 3. Sermons, Latin — Translations into English. 4. Sermons, English — Translations from Latin. I. Colledge, Edmund. II. McGinn, Bernard, 1937- III. T. IV. Series. BV5080.E3213 1981a    248.2/2 19    *LC* 81-82206    *ISBN* 0809103222

**Eckhart, Meister, d.1327**      **1.3088**
Meister Eckhart, an introduction to the study of his works, with an anthology of his sermons. Selected, annotated, and translated by James M. Clark. London, Nelson [1957] xii, 267 p. illus. I. Clark, James Midgley, 1888-1961. ed. and tr. II. T. BV5080E45 E43    *LC* a58-1986

**Gregory, of Nyssa, Saint, ca. 335-ca. 394.**      **1.3089**
From glory to glory; texts from Gregory of Nyssa's mystical writings, selected and with an introd. by Jean Daniélou. Translated and editied by Herbert Musurillo. — New York, Scribner [1961] xiv, 298 p. illus. 22 cm. Includes bibliographical references. 1. Mysticism — Early church. I. Daniélou, Jean. ed. II. Musruliio, Herbert Anthony, ed. and tr. III. T. BV5080.G73    248.22    *LC* 61-13370

**Richard, of St. Victor, d. 1173.**      **1.3090**
[Benjamin minor. English.] The twelve patriarchs; The mystical ark; Book three of The Trinity / Richard of St. Victor; translation and introd. by Grover A. Zinn; pref. by Jean Châtillon. — New York: Paulist Press, c1979. xviii, 425 p.; 23 cm. (Classics of Western spirituality.) 1. Mysticism — History — Middle Ages, 600-1500 I. Richard, of St. Victor, d. 1173. Benjamin major. English. 1979. II. Richard, of St. Victor, d. 1173. De Trinitate. Book 3. English. 1979. III. T. IV. Series. BV5080.R5513    248/.22    *LC* 79-83834    *ISBN* 0809102412

**Underhill, Evelyn, 1875-1941.**      • **1.3091**
Mysticism; a study in the nature and development of man's spiritual consciousness. Rev. ed. New York, E. P. Dutton and company, inc. [1930] xviii p., 1 l.515, [1] p. 23 cm. 1. Mysticism I. T. BV5081.U55 1930    *LC* 31-26805

**Inge, William Ralph.**      • **1.3092**
Christian mysticism. 7th ed. New York: Meridian, 1956. xx, 332 p. (Living age books, 3.) 1. Mysticism I. T. II. Series. BV5082.I6 1956    149.3    *LC* 56-9239

**Dupré, Louis K., 1925-.**                                                   **1.3093**
The deeper life: an introduction to Christian mysticism / by Louis Dupré. —
New York: Crossroad, 1981. 92 p.; 21 cm. 1. Mysticism — Addresses, essays,
lectures. I. T.
BV5082.2.D86 1981      248.2/2 19      *LC* 81-3275      *ISBN* 0824500075

**Yungblut, John R.**                                                         **1.3094**
Discovering God within / John R. Yungblut. — 1st ed. — Philadelphia:
Westminster Press, c1979. 197 p.; 21 cm. 1. Mysticism I. T.
BV5082.2.Y86      248/.22      *LC* 78-21713      *ISBN* 0664242316

**An Introduction to the medieval mystics of Europe: fourteen**              **1.3095**
**original essays / edited by Paul E. Szarmach.**
Albany: State University of New York Press, c1984. vi, 376 p.; 24 cm. Includes
index. 1. Mystics — Europe — Biography — Addresses, essays, lectures.
2. Mysticism — History — Middle Ages, 600-1500 — Addresses, essays,
lectures. 3. Mysticism — Europe — History — Addresses, essays, lectures.
I. Szarmach, Paul E.
BV5095.A1 I57 1984      248.2/2/0922 B 19      *LC* 84-225213      *ISBN*
0873958349

# BX Denominations

## BX1–9 Church Unity. Ecumenical Movement

**Jordan, Philip D., 1940-.**                                                 **1.3096**
The Evangelical Alliance for the United States of America, 1847–1900:
ecumenism, identity, and the religion of the Republic / Philip D. Jordan. —
New York: E. Mellen Press, c1982. ix, 277 p.; 24 cm. — (Studies in American
religion. v. 7) Includes index. 1. Evangelical Alliance for the United States of
America. 2. Christian Union — United States — History — 19th century.
3. Evangelicalism — United States — History — 19th century. 4. United
States — Religion — 19th century I. T. II. Series.
BX4.J67 1982      277.3/081 19      *LC* 82-24953      *ISBN* 0889466505

**Gaines, David P.**                                                        • **1.3097**
The World Council of Churches, a study of its background and history, by
David P. Gaines. — [1st ed.]. — Peterborough, N.H.: R. R. Smith, [1966] xviii,
1302 p.; 25 cm. 1. World Council of Churches. I. T.
BX6.W78 G3      262.001      *LC* 63-17177

**Brown, Robert McAfee, 1920-.**                                             **1.3098**
The ecumenical revolution: an inuerpretation of the Catholic–Protestant
dialogue. — [1st ed.] Garden City, N.Y.: Doubleday, 1967. xix, 388 p.; 22 cm.
Based on the William Belden Noble lectures for 1964-65. 1. Catholic Church
— Relations — Protestant churches 2. Ecumenical movement — History.
3. Protestant churches — Relations — Catholic Church I. T. II. Title:
William Belden Noble lectures.
BX6.5.B75      262/.001      *LC* 67-12862

**Rouse, Ruth, ed.**                                                        • **1.3099**
A history of the ecumenical movement, edited by Ruth Rouse and Stephen
Charles Neill. 2d ed. with rev. bibliography. Philadelphia, Westminster Press,
1967-[70] 2 v. 23 cm. Vol. 2, without edition statement, edited by Harold E. Fey
and published on behalf of the Committee on Ecumenical History, Geneva.
1. Ecumenical movement 2. Church history — Modern period. I. Neill,
Stephen, 1900- joint ed. II. Fey, Harold Edward, 1898- ed. III. T.
BX6.5.R62      270      *LC* 67-14834

**Fries, Heinrich.**                                                          **1.3100**
[Einigung der Kirchen—reale Möglichkeit. English] Unity of the churches—an
actual possibility / Heinrich Fries and Karl Rahner; translated by Ruth C.L.
Gritsch and Eric W. Gritsch. — Philadelphia: Fortress Press; New York:
Paulist Press, c1985. xi, 146 p.; 22 cm. Translation of: Einigung der Kirchen—
reale Möglichkeit. 1. Christian Union. I. Rahner, Karl, 1904- II. T.
BX8.2.F6813 1985      262/.0011 19      *LC* 84-48481      *ISBN* 0800618203

# BX100–750 Eastern Churches

**Florovsky, Georges, 1893-1979.**                                            **1.3101**
Bible, church, tradition: an Eastern Orthodox view. Belmont, Mass., Nordland
Pub. Co. [c1972] 127 p. 23 cm. (Collected works of Georges Florovsky, v. 1)
1. Bible — Criticism, interpretation, etc. 2. Tradition (Theology) 3. Church
I. T.
BX260.F55 vol. 1 BT90      230/.1/908 s 230/.1/9      *LC* 72-89502
      *ISBN* 0913124028

**Meyendorff, John, 1926-.**                                                • **1.3102**
The Orthodox Church: its past and its role in the world today / by John
Mayendorff; translated from the French by John Chapin. — New York:
Pantheon Books, 1962. xii, 290 p.; 21 cm. Translation of L'Église orthodoxe:
hier et aujourd'hui. 1. Orthodox Eastern Church — History I. T.
BX290 M413      BX290.M4.      281.9      *LC* 62-14260

**Schmemann, Alexander, 1921-.**                                            • **1.3103**
The historical road of Eastern Orthodoxy. Translated by Lydia W. Kesich. —
[1st ed.]. — New York, Holt, Rinehart and Winston [1963] viii, 343 p. 22 cm.
Bibliography: p. 342-343. 1. Orthodox Eastern Church — Hist. I. T.
BX290.S373      281.9      *LC* 63-11873

**Runciman, Steven, Sir, 1903-.**                                             **1.3104**
The Byzantine theocracy / Steven Runciman. Cambridge; New York:
Cambridge University Press, 1977. viii, 197 p.; 20 cm. (The Weil lectures; 1973)
1. Church and state — Byzantine Empire — History — Addresses, essays,
lectures. I. T. II. Series.
BX300.R86      274.95      *LC* 76-47405      *ISBN* 0521214017

**Congar, Yves Marie Joseph, 1904-.**                                       • **1.3105**
After nine hundred years; the background of the schism between the Eastern
and Western churches [by] Yves Congar. — New York, Fordham University
Press [1959] 150 p. 23 cm. 'A translation of Neuf cents ans après, originally
published as part of 1054-1954, l'Église et les Églises.' Includes bibliography.
1. Schism — Eastern and Western Church I. T.
BX303.C613      270.3      *LC* 59-15643

**Bulgakov, Sergeĭ Nikolaevich, 1871-1944.**                                • **1.3106**
The Orthodox Church [by] Sergius Bulgakov. [Translated by Elizabeth S.
Cram; edited by Donald A. Lowrie] London Centenary Press [1935] 224p.
1. Orthodox Eastern Church — Doctrinal and controversial works I. Cram,
Elizabeth S. II. Lowrie, Donald Alexander III. T.
BX320 B813

**Benz, Ernst, 1907-.**                                                     • **1.3107**
[Geist und Leben der Ostkirche. English] The Eastern Orthodox Church, its
thought and life. Translated from the German by Richard and Clara Winston.
[1st ed.] Garden City, N.Y., Anchor Books, 1963. 230 p. 18 cm. (Anchor,
A332) Translation of Geist und Leben der Ostkirche. 1. Orthodox Eastern
Church. I. T.
BX320.2.B413      281.9      *LC* 63-7690

**Constantelos, Demetrios J.**                                                **1.3108**
Understanding the Greek Orthodox church: its faith, history, and practice /
Demetrios J. Constantelos. — New York, N.Y.: Seabury Press, 1982. xiii,
178 p.; 22 cm. Includes irdexes. 1. Orthodox Eastern Church. 2. Orthodoxos
Ekklēsia tēs Hellados. I. T.
BX320.2.C66 1982      281.9/3 19      *LC* 81-21313      *ISBN* 0816405158

**Maloney, George A., 1924-.**                                                **1.3109**
A history of Orthodox theology since 1453 / by George A. Maloney. —
Belmont, Mass.: Nordland Pub. Co., 1976. 388 p.; 23 cm. 1. Orthodox Eastern
Church — Doctrines — History. I. T.
BX320.2.M34      230/.1/909      *LC* 75-27491      *ISBN* 0913124125

**Meyendorff, John, 1926-.**                                                  **1.3110**
Byzantine theology: historical trends and doctrinal themes / John Meyendorff.
— 1st ed. — New York: Fordham University Press, 1974. 243 p.; 22 cm.
Includes index. 1. Orthodox Eastern Church — Doctrines — History. I. T.
BX320.2.M47      230/.1/9      *LC* 72-94167      *ISBN* 0823209652

**Zernov, Nicolas.**                                                        • **1.3111**
Eastern Christendom, a study of the origin and development of the Eastern
Orthodox Church. — [1st American ed.]. — New York, Putnam [1961] 326 p.
illus. 24 cm. — (The Putnam history of religion) Includes bibliography.
1. Orthodox Eastern Church. I. T.
BX320.2.Z45 1961      281.9      *LC* 61-5715

**Runciman, Steven, Sir, 1903-.**                                           • **1.3112**
The Orthodox churches and the secular state. — Oxford: [s.n.], 1973. 110 p.; 23
cm. Based on four lectures delivered at the University of Auckland, September,

1970. 1. Orthodox Eastern Church — History 2. Church and state — History.
I. T.
BX323.R85    261.7    *LC* 72-193983

**The Way of a pilgrim and The pilgrim continues his way: a new**    **1.3113**
**translation / by Helen Bacovcin.**
Garden City, N.Y.: Image Books, 1978. 196 p.; 18 cm. Translation of
Otkrovennye rasskazy strannika dukhovnomu svoemu ottsu. 1. Spiritual life —
Orthodox Eastern authors. 2. Jesus prayer I. Bacovcin, Helen, 1934-
BX382.O8513    248/.48/19    *LC* 76-52000    *ISBN* 0385124007

**Fedotov, G. P. (Georgiĭ Petrovich), 1886-1951.**    • **1.3114**
The Russian religious mind. — Cambridge, Harvard University Press, 1946-66.
2 v. 24 cm. 'Selected literature': v. 1, p. [413]-424. 'Bibliography of the writings
of George P. Fedotov (1886-1951) compiled and edited by Thomas E. Bird': v.
2, p. [397]-413. Bibliographical footnotes. 1. Religious thought — Russia.
2. Russia — Church history. 3. Orthodox Eastern church, Russian — Hist.
4. Spirituality I. T.
BX485.F4    281.947    *LC* A 47-1236 rev

**Curtiss, John Shelton, 1899-.**    **1.3115**
Church and state in Russia; the last years of the empire, 1900–1917. New York
Columbia University Press 1940. 442 p.; 24 cm. Issued also as thesis (Ph.D.)
Columbia University. 1. Church and state — Soviet Union 2. Soviet Union —
Church history I. T.
BX491 C8    *LC* 40-14852

**Pospielovsky, Dimitry, 1935-.**    **1.3116**
The Russian church under the Soviet regime, 1917–1982 / Dimitry
Pospielovsky. Crestwood, N.Y.: St. Vladimir's Seminary Press, 1984. 2 v.
(535 p.); 22 cm. Pre-publication title: The Russian church and the Soviet
regime, 1917-1982. Includes index. 1. Russkaia pravoslavnaia tserkov' —
History — 20th century. 2. Orthodox Eastern Church — Soviet Union —
History — 20th century. 3. Soviet Union — Church history — 1917- I. T.
II. Title: The Russian church and the Soviet regime, 1917-1982.
BX492.P67 1984    281.9/3    *LC* 84-5336    *ISBN* 0881410152

# BX801–4795 Roman Catholic Church

**Piehl, Mel.**    **1.3117**
Breaking bread: the Catholic worker and the origin of Catholic radicalism in
America / Mel Piehl. — Philadelphia: Temple University Press, 1982. xv,
296 p.: ill.; 24 cm. Includes index. 1. Day, Dorothy, 1897-1980. 2. Maurin,
Peter. 3. Catholic Church — United States — History — 20th century.
4. Catholic Worker Movement — History. 5. Radicalism — United States —
History — 20th century. I. T.
BX810.C393 P53 1982    267/.182 19    *LC* 82-10327    *ISBN*
0877222576

## BX820–837 Councils

**Jedin, Hubert, 1900-.**    **1.3118**
Ecumenical councils of the Catholic Church; an historical outline. [Translation
by Ernest Graf. — New York] Herder and Herder [c1960] 253 p. 19 cm.
Translation of Kleine Konziliengeschichte. Includes bibliography. 1. Councils
and synods, Ecumenical I. T.
BX825.J4 1960a    282    *LC* 59-15483

**Loomis, Louise Ropes, 1874-1958.**    • **1.3119**
The Council of Constance: the unification of the church / edited and annotated
by John Hine Mundy and Kennerly M. Woody. New York: Columbia
University Press, 1961. xiii, 562 p. (Records of civilization, sources and studies.
63) Includes Richental's Chronicle of the Council of Constance, Fillastre's
Diary of the Council of Constance, and Cerretano's Journal. 1. Council of
Constance (1414-1418) I. Mundy, John Hine, 1917- II. Woody, Kennerly M.
III. T. IV. Series.
BX830 1414.L6    *LC* 61-9659

**Jedin, Hubert, 1900-.**    • **1.3120**
A history of the Council of Trent. Translated from the German by Ernest Graf.
— St. Louis, B. Herder Book Co. [1957- v. illus. 25 cm. Includes bibliographies.
1. Council of Trent (1545-1563) I. T.
BX830 1545.J3513    *LC* A 58-1432

**Butler, Edward Cuthbert, 1858-1934.**    • **1.3121**
The Vatican Council, 1869–1870, based on Bishop Ullathorne's letters. Edited
by Christopher Butler. — Westminster, Md., Newman Press, 1962. 510 p. 20

cm. 1. Vatican Council (1st: 1869-1870) I. Ullathorne, William Bernard, Abp.,
1806-1889. II. T.
BX830 1869.B822    262.5    *LC* 61-16567

**Hennesey, James J.**    • **1.3122**
The First Council of the Vatican: the American experience. — [New York]
Herder and Herder [1963] 341 p. 22 cm. Bibliographical footnotes. 1. Vatican
Council (1st: 1869-1870) I. T.
BX830 1869.H4    262.5    *LC* 63-18150

**Vatican Council (2nd: 1962-1965).**    • **1.3123**
The documents of Vatican II. Introductions and commentaries by Catholic
bishops and experts. Responses by Protestant and Orthodox scholars. Walter
M. Abbott, general editor. Joseph Gallagher, translation editor. New York,
Guild Press [1966] xxi, 794 p. 19 cm. (An Angelus book, 31185) I. Abbott,
Walter M., ed. II. T.
BX830 1962 .A3 G3    262.5    *LC* 66-20201

**Vatican Council (2nd: 1962-1965).**    • **1.3124**
The Declaration on the relation of the Church to non–Christian religions,
promulgated by Pope Paul VI, October 28, 1965. Commentary by René
Laurentin and Joseph Neuner. [Study-club ed.] Glen Rock, N.J., Paulist Press,
1966. 104 p. (Vatican II documents) 1. Catholic Church — Relations
2. Vatican Council. 2d. Declaratio de Ecclesiae habitudine ad religiones non-
Christianas. I. Laurentin, René. II. Neuner, Josef. III. T.
BX830 1962.A45D353    261

**Lindbeck, George A.**    • **1.3125**
The future of Roman Catholic theology; Vatican II – catalyst for change [by]
George A. Lindbeck. — Philadelphia, Fortress Press [1970] xvi, 125 p. 22 cm.
1. Catholic Church — Relations — Protestant churches 2. Vatican Council
(2nd: 1962-1965). 3. Theology, Catholic. 4. Protestant churches — Relations
— Catholic Church I. T.
BX830 1962.L513    230.2    *LC* 75-83678

**Rynne, Xavier, pseud.**    **1.3126**
The fourth session: the debates and decrees of Vatican Council II, September 14
to December 8, 1965 / Xavier Rynne. — New York: Farrar, Straus and Giroux,
1966. xi, 368 p.: ill., facsims, tables. 1. Vatican Council (2nd: 1962-1965). I. T.
II. Title: The debates and decrees of Vatican Council II, September 14 to
December 8, 1965.
BX830 1962 R88    262.5    *LC* 66-15322

**Rynne, Xavier, pseud.**    **1.3127**
Letters from Vatican City; Vatican Council II, first session: background and
debates. — New York, Farrar, Straus [1963] 289 p. illus. 22 cm. 1. Vatican
Council, 2d. I. T.
BX830 1962.R9    262.5    *LC* 63-13197

**Rynne, Xavier, pseud.**    • **1.3128**
The second session: the debates and decrees of Vatican Council II, September
29 to December 4, 1963 / Xavier Rynne. — New York: Farrar, Straus, [1964]
xxiii, 390 p.: facsims.; 22 cm. Facsimiles in Latin. 1. Vatican Council (2nd:
1962-1965). I. T. II. Title: The debates and decrees of Vatican Council II.
BX830 1962.R92    262.5    *LC* 64-17815

**Rynne, Xavier, pseud.**    • **1.3129**
The third session; the debates and decrees of Vatican Council II, September 14
to November 21, 1964. — New York, Farrar, Straus & Giroux [1965] xiii,
399 p. facsims. 22 cm. 1. Vatican Council, 2d. I. T. II. Title: The debates and
decrees of Vatican Council II.
BX830 1962.R93    262.5    *LC* 65-20915

**Council of Trent (1545-1563)**    • **1.3130**
Canons and decrees of the Council of Trent / original text with English
translation by H. J. Schroeder. — St. Louis, Mo.: B. Herder Book Co., [1955,
c1941]. xxxiii, 608 p.; 23 cm. 'The Latin text of the Canons and decrees given in
the second part of this book (p. 279-578) and upon which the accompanying
translation is based, is that of the Neapolitan edition of 1859, which was made
from the Roman edition of 1834 issued by the Collegium Urbanus de
Propaganda Fide.' I. Schroeder, Henry Joseph, 1875-, tr. II. T.
BX830 1545.A3 S35

## BX841–875 Dictionaries. Encyclopedias. Documents

**New Catholic encyclopedia. Prepared by an editorial staff at the**    • **1.3131**
**Catholic University of America.**
New York: McGraw-Hill, 1967. 15 v.: illus. (part col.), facsims., maps, ports.
(part col.); 29 cm. 1. Catholic Church — Dictionaries I. Catholic University of
America. II. Title: Catholic Encyclopedia.
BX841.N44 1967    282/.03    *LC* 66-22292

**Catholic Church. Pope.** • **1.3132**
The papal encyclicals in their historical context, by Anne Fremantle. With an introd. by Gustave Weigel. — [New York]: New American Library, [1956] 317 p.; 18 cm. — (A Mentor book, MD177) (A Mentor religious classic.) 1. Encyclicals, Papal I. Fremantle, Anne Jackson, 1909- ed. II. T.
BX860.A36 1956    262.8    *LC* 56-11328

## BX880–891 COLLECTIONS

**Pegis, Anton Charles, 1905- ed.** • **1.3133**
The wisdom of Catholicism. — New York, Random House [1949] xxix, 988 p. 24 cm. — (The Random House lifetime library) Bibliography: p. 985-988. 1. Theology — Collections — Catholic authors. 2. Catholic literature I. T.
BX880.P36    208.2    *LC* 49-9822

**Bonaventure, Saint, Cardinal, ca. 1217-1274.** **1.3134**
[Selected works. English. 1978] Bonaventure / translation and introd. by Ewert Cousins; pref. by Ignatius Brady. — New York: Paulist Press, c1978. xx, 353 p.; 23 cm. — (Classics of Western spirituality.) Translated from the Latin. Includes indexes. 1. Catholic Church — Collected works 2. Theology — Collected works — Middle Ages, 600-1500 I. Cousins, Ewert H. II. T. III. Series.
BX890.B6731313 1978    230/.2    *LC* 78-60723    *ISBN* 0809102404.
*ISBN* 0809121212 pbk

**Francis, of Assisi, Saint, 1182-1226.** **1.3135**
[Works. English. 1982] Francis and Clare: the complete works / translation and introduction by Regis J. Armstrong and Ignatius C. Brady; preface by John Vaughn. — New York: Paulist Press, c1982. xvi, 256 p.; 23 cm. (Classics of Western spirituality.) Includes indexes. 1. Catholic Church — Collected works 2. Theology — Collected works — Middle Ages, 600-1500 3. Spiritual life — Catholic authors — Collected works. I. Armstrong, Regis J. II. Brady, Ignatius C. III. Clare, of Assisi, Saint, 1194-1253. Works. English. 1982 IV. T. V. Series.
BX890.F665 1982    271/.3/022 19    *LC* 82-62693    *ISBN* 0809124467

**John of the Cross, Saint, 1542-1591.** **1.3136**
The Collected works of St. John of the Cross / translated by Kieran Kavanaugh and Otilio Rodriguez; with introductions by Kieran Kavanaugh. — 2d paperback ed. — Washington: Institute of Carmelite Studies, 1979. 773 p.; 22 cm. — (ICS publications) Translation of Obras de San Juan de la Cruz. Includes index. 1. Mysticism — Collected works 2. Theology — Collected works I. T.
BX890.J623 1979    *LC* 78-65789    *ISBN* 0960087656

**Newman, John Henry, 1801-1890.** • **1.3137**
The essential Newman / edited by Vincent Ferrer Blehl. — New York: New American Library, [1963] 350 p.; 18 cm. — (A Mentor-Omega book; MT 488) 1. Catholic Church — Collected works 2. Theology — Collected works — 19th century. I. Blehl, Vincent Ferrer. II. T.
BX890.N417    *LC* 63-25953

**Teresa, of Avila, Saint, 1515-1582.** **1.3138**
[Works. English. 1976] The collected works of St. Teresa of Avila / translated by Kieran Kavanaugh and Otilio Rodriguez. — Washington: Institute of Carmelite Studies, 1976-<1980>. v. <1-2>; 22 cm. 1. Catholic Church — Collected works 2. Theology — Collected works — 16th century. I. T.
BX890.T353 1976    248    *LC* 75-31305    *ISBN* 0960087621

**Thomas, Aquinas, Saint, 1225?-1274.** • **1.3139**
[English. 1948] Introduction to Saint Thomas Aquinas, ed., with an introd. by Anton C. Pegis. New York, Modern Library [1948] xxx, 690 p. 19 cm. (The Modern library of the world's best books [259]) 'Selections ... from Basic writings of St. Thomas Aquinas ... published in 1945.' 1. Theology — Collected works — Middle Ages, 600-1500 I. Pegis, Anton Charles, 1905- ed. II. T.
BX890.T62 E6 1948    208.1    *LC* 48-2954

**Rahner, Karl, 1904-.** **1.3140**
[Selections. English. 1975] A Rahner reader. Edited by Gerald A. McCool. New York, Seabury Press [1975] xxviii, 381 p. 24 cm. 'A Crossroad book.' 1. Catholic Church — Collected works 2. Theology — Collected works — 20th century. I. McCool, Gerald A. ed. II. T.
BX891.R253 1975    230/.2    *LC* 74-16138    *ISBN* 0816411735 *ISBN* 0816421072

**Rahner, Karl, 1904-.** • **1.3141**
Inquiries. New York: Herder and Herder. 1964. 462 p.; 22 cm. "Studies which appeared separately in the series Questiones disputatae as nos.1,10,9,4,11." 1. Theology — Collected works — 20th century. 2. Catholic Church — Collected works I. T.
BX891 R3    208.1    *LC* 64-20435

## BX938–1745 HISTORY

**Holmes, J. Derek.** **1.3142**
A short history of the Catholic Church / J. Derek Holmes and Bernard W. Bickers. — New York: Paulist Press, 1984. 315 p.; 22 cm. Includes index. 1. Catholic Church — History I. Bickers, Bernard W. II. T.
BX945.2.H63 1984    282/.09 19    *LC* 83-63193    *ISBN* 0809126230

**Bernard, of Clairvaux, Saint, 1090 or 91-1153.** **1.3143**
[De consideratione. English] Five books on consideration: advice to a Pope / translated by John D. Anderson & Elizabeth T. Kennan. — Kalamazoo, Mich.: Cistercian Publications, 1976. 222 p.; 22 cm. — (His The works of Bernard of Clairvaux; v. 13) (Cistercian Fathers series; no. 37) Translation of De consideratione. Includes index. 1. Papacy I. T.
BX953.B3x    230/.2 s 262/.13    *LC* 75-27953    *ISBN* 0879071370.
*ISBN* 0879077379 pbk

**Giles, Edward.** • **1.3144**
Documents illustrating papal authority, A.D. 96–454. London, S.P.C.K., 1952. xxi, 344 p. 19 cm. Bibliographical footnotes. 1. Papacy — History — Sources. 2. Church history — Primitive and early church — Sources. 3. Christian literature, Early (Selections: Extracts, etc.) I. T. II. Title: Papal authority.
BX953.G5    262.13    *LC* 53-8048

**Ranke, Leopold von, 1795-1886.** • **1.3145**
History of the popes, their church and state, and especially of their conflicts with Protestantism in the sixteenth and seventeenth centuries, by Leopold von Ranke; translated by E. Foster. London, G. Bell and sons, 1896. 3 v. illus. 19 cm. (Bohn's standard library) 1. Popes — Hist. I. Foster, E., tr. II. T.
BX955.Rx    *LC* 04-16241

**Barraclough, Geoffrey, 1908-.** • **1.3146**
The medieval papacy. — [1st American ed. — New York]: Harcourt, Brace & World, [1968] 216 p.: illus., facsims., maps, ports.; 22 cm. — ([History of European civilization library]) Part of illustrative matter colored. 1. Papacy — History — To 1309 I. T.
BX955.2.B3 1968b    262/.13/09    *LC* 68-29667

**Ullmann, Walter, 1910-.** • **1.3147**
The growth of Papal government in the Middle Ages; a study in the ideological relation of clerical to lay power. — [3d ed.]. — London: Methuen, [1970] xxiv, 496 p.: front.; 22 cm. 'Distributed in the USA by Barnes & Noble.' 1. Papacy — History — To 1309 2. Popes — Temporal power 3. Church and state — History. I. T.
BX955.2.U5 1970    262/.13/09021    *LC* 72-476873    *ISBN* 0416158900

**Ullmann, Walter, 1910-.** **1.3148**
A short history of the Papacy in the Middle Ages / Walter Ullmann. [1st ed.] reprinted with corrections. London: Methuen, 1974. [6], 393 p.; 22 cm. (University paperbacks) Distributed in the U.S. by Harper & Row, New York. 1. Papacy — History I. T.
BX955.2.U53 1974    262/.13/0902    *LC* 75-310360    *ISBN* 0416086500. *ISBN* 0416749704 pbk

**Richards, Jeffrey.** **1.3149**
The popes and the papacy in the early Middle Ages, 476–752 / Jeffrey Richards. — London; Boston: Routledge & Kegan Paul, 1979. viii, 422 p.; 22 cm. Includes index. 1. Papacy — History — To 1309 2. Europe — Church history I. T.
BX970.R48    262/.13/09021    *LC* 78-41023    *ISBN* 0710000987

**Catholic Church. Pope (1073-1085: Gregory VII)** • **1.3150**
[Registrum. English. Selections] The correspondence of Pope Gregory VII; selected letters from the Registrum. Translated with an introd. by Ephraim Emerton. New York, Norton [1969, c1932] xxxi, 212 p. 21 cm. (Records of civilization, sources and studies. [14]) I. Emerton, Ephraim, 1851-1935, ed. & tr. II. T. III. Series.
BX1187.A4 1969    262/.13/0924    *LC* 70-8470

**Robinson, I. S. (Ian Stuart), 1947 Feb. 11-.** **1.3151**
Authority and resistance in the Investiture Contest: the polemical literature of the late eleventh century / I. S. Robinson. — Manchester: Manchester University Press; New York: Holmes & Meier Publishers, 1978. x, 195 p.; 23 cm. 1. Investiture I. T.
BX1198.R62 1978    262.7    *LC* 78-9110    *ISBN* 0841904073

**Chodorow, Stanley.** **1.3152**
Christian political theory and church politics in the mid–twelfth century; the ecclesiology of Gratian's Decretum. Berkeley, University of California Press, 1972. xi, 300 p. 24 cm. (Publications of the Center for Medieval and Renaissance Studies, U.C.L.A., 5) 1. Gratian, 12th cent. Decretum. 2. Canon law — History 3. Church history — 12th century I. T.
BX1210.C5x    262.9/23    *LC* 71-138512    *ISBN* 0520018508

**Pennington, Kenneth.**     **1.3153**
Pope and bishops: the papal monarchy in the twelfth and thirteenth centuries / Kenneth Pennington. — [Philadelphia]: University of Pennsylvania Press, c1984. xiii, 225 p.; 24 cm. — (Middle Ages.) Includes indexes. 1. Catholic Church — Bishops — History. 2. Papacy — History — To 1309 3. Church and state — Catholic Church — History. I. T. II. Series.
BX1210.P46 1984    262/.13/09022 19    *LC* 83-21799    *ISBN* 0812279182

**Renouard, Yves.**     ● **1.3154**
The Avignon papacy, 1305–1403. Translated by Denis Bethell. — [Hamden, Conn.]: Archon Books, 1970. 157 p.: maps, port.; 23 cm. Translation of La papauté à Avignon. 1. Papacy — History — 1309-1378 I. T.
BX1270.R413    262/.13/09023    *LC* 70-21164    *ISBN* 0208011560

**Ullmann, Walter, 1910-.**     ● **1.3155**
The origins of the great schism; a study in fourteenth–century ecclesiastical history. With a 1972 pref. by the author. — [Hamden, Conn.]: Archon Books, 1972. xxvii, 244 p.: illus.; 22 cm. Reprint of the 1948 ed. published by Burns, Oates, & Washbourne, London. 1. Schism, The Great Western, 1378-1417 I. T.
BX1301.U55 1972    282/.09/023    *LC* 79-39365    *ISBN* 020801277X

**Chadwick, Owen.**     **1.3156**
The Popes and European revolution / Owen Chadwick. — Oxford: Clarendon Press; New York: Oxford University Press, 1981. ix, 646 p.; 25 cm. — (Oxford history of the Christian Church.) Includes index. 1. Catholic Church in Europe — History. 2. Papacy — History — 1566-1799 3. Papacy — History — 19th century. 4. Europe — Politics and government — 18th century 5. Europe — Politics and government — 1789-1900 I. T. II. Series.
BX1361.C45    262/.13/09033 19    *LC* 80-40673    *ISBN* 0198269196

**Hales, Edward Elton Young, 1908-.**     ● **1.3157**
Revolution and Papacy, 1769-1846. Garden City, N.Y.: Hanover House, 1960. 320 p. 1. Catholic Church — History — 18th century 2. Catholic Church — History — 19th century I. T.
BX1361.H3    *LC* 60-13527

BX 1105 A88

**Aubert, Roger.**     **1.3158**
The church in a secularised society / by Roger Aubert ... [et al.]; the French texts of Roger Aubert, J. Bruhls [i.e. Bruls] and J. Hajjar were translated by Janet Sondheimer; the ill. were selected and annotated by Peter Ludlow. — 1st ed. — New York: Paulist Press, 1978. xxxi, 719 p., [32] leaves of plates: ill.; 23 cm. — (The Christian centuries; v. 5) Issued also in French under title: L'Église dans le monde moderne, and in German under title: Vom Kirchenstaat zur Weltkirche.Includes indexes. 1. Catholic Church — History — Modern period, 1500- I. T. II. Series.
BX1365.A8x    282 s 282/.09/03    *LC* 78-53496    *ISBN* 0809102447

**Moody, Joseph Nestor, 1904- ed.**     ● **1.3159**
Church and society; Catholic social and political thought and movements, 1789-1950. Edited by Joseph N. Moody in collaboration with: Edgar Alexander [and others]. — New York, Arts, inc. [c1953] 914 p. 24 cm. Includes bibliographical references. 1. Catholic Church — Hist. 2. Church and social problems — Catholic Church 3. Church and state — Catholic Church I. T.
BX1365.M6    282.09    *LC* 53-10712

**John XXIII, Pope, 1881-1963.**     ● **1.3160**
[Giornale dell' anima. English] Journal of a soul [by] Pope John XXIII. Translated by Dorothy White. New York, McGraw-Hill [1965] lvii, 453 p. illus., coat of arms, facsims., ports. 25 cm. I. T.
BX1378.2.A383    922.21    *LC* 64-8610

**Hebblethwaite, Peter.**     **1.3161**
[John XXIII, pope of the council] Pope John XXIII, shepherd of the modern world / Peter Hebblethwaite. — Garden City, N.Y.: Doubleday, 1985. 550 p., [16] p. of plates: ill.; 24 cm. Originally published in England under title: John XXIII, pope of the council. Includes index. 1. John XXIII, Pope, 1881-1963. 2. Popes — Biography. I. T. II. Title: Pope John 23rd, shepherd of the modern world.
BX1378.2.H34 1985    282/.092/4 B 19    *LC* 82-45483    *ISBN* 0385172982

**Williams, George Huntston, 1914-.**     **1.3162**
The mind of John Paul II: origins of his thought and action / George Huntston Williams. — New York: Seabury Press, 1981. xvi, 415 p.: map; 24 cm. 1. John Paul II, Pope, 1920- I. T.
BX1378.5.W55    282/.092/4 19    *LC* 80-19947    *ISBN* 0816404631

**Hales, Edward Elton Young, 1908-.**     ● **1.3163**
The Catholic Church in the modern world; a survey from the French Revolution to the present. [1st ed.] Garden City, N.Y., Hanover House, 1958. 312 p. 22 cm. Includes bibliography. 1. Catholic Church — History — Modern period, 1500- 2. Church history — 19th century 3. Church history — 20th century I. T.
BX1386.H3    282.0903    *LC* 58-5943

**Holmes, J. Derek.**     **1.3164**
The Papacy in the modern world, 1914–1978 / J. Derek Holmes; foreword by John Tracy Ellis. — New York: Crossroad, 1981. viii, 275 p.; ill.; 22 cm. Includes index. 1. Catholic Church — History — 20th century 2. Papacy — History — 20th century I. T.
BX1389.H64 1981b    282/.09/04 19    *LC* 81-65110    *ISBN* 0824500474

**Murphy, Francis Xavier, 1914-.**     **1.3165**
The papacy today / Francis X. Murphy. — New York: Macmillan, c1981. viii, 269 p.; 22 cm. 1. Papacy — History — 20th century I. T.
BX1389.M8    262/.13/0904 19    *LC* 81-869    0025888900

**Loome, Thomas Michael, 1935-.**     **1.3166**
Liberal catholicism, reform catholicism, modernism: a contribution to a new orientation in modernist research / Thomas Michael Loome. — Mainz: Matthias-Grünewald-Verlag, 1979. vii, 452 p.; 23 cm. — (Tübinger theologische Studien. Bd. 14) 1. Modernism — Catholic Church I. T. II. Series.
BX1396.L66    282/.09/04    *LC* 79-312816    *ISBN* 3786706603

**Ratté, John, 1936-.**     ● **1.3167**
Three modernists: Alfred Loisy, George Tyrrell, William L. Sullivan. — New York, Sheed and Ward [1967] viii, 370 p. 22 cm. Includes bibliographical references. 1. Loisy, Alfred Firmin, 1857-1940. 2. Sullivan, William Laurence, 1872-1935. 3. Tyrell, George, 1861-1909. 4. Modernism — Catholic Church I. T.
BX1396.R3    282/.0922    *LC* 67-13763

# BX1401–1695 By Country

**Whyte, John Henry, 1928-.**     **1.3168**
Catholics in western democracies: a study in political behaviour / John H. Whyte. — New York: St. Martin's Press, 1981. 193 p.; 23 cm. Includes index. 1. Catholics — Political activity. I. T.
BX1401.A1 W48 1981    322/.1/091713 19    *LC* 81-9375    *ISBN* 0312124465

## BX1404–1418 United States

**Toward Vatican III: The work that needs to be done / edited by David Tracy with Hans Küng and Johann B. Metz.**     **1.3169**
Nijmegen, Holland: Concilium; New York: Seabury Press, 1978. xi, 333 p.; 23 cm. Papers originally presented at a colloquium at the University of Notre Dame, May 29-June 1, 1977. 1. Catholic Church in the United States — Congresses. 2. Church renewal — Catholic Church — Congresses. I. Tracy, David. II. Küng, Hans, 1928- III. Metz, Johannes Baptist, 1928- IV. Title: Vatican III.
BX1404.T68    262/.5/2    *LC* 77-28606    *ISBN* 0816403791

**Ellis, John Tracy, 1905- comp.**     **1.3170**
Documents of American Catholic history. [Rev. ed.] Chicago, H. Regnery Co. [1967] 2 v. (xii, 702 p.) 17 cm. (Logos) 1. Catholic Church — United States — History — Sources. 2. United States — Church history — Sources. I. T.
BX1405.E42    282/.73    *LC* 67-5312

**Billington, Ray Allen, 1903-.**     ● **1.3171**
The Protestant Crusade, 1800–1860: a study of the origins of American nativism. — New York: Rinehart, [1952, c1938]. viii, 514 p.: ill., maps; 21 cm. 1. Catholics in the United States. 2. American Party. 3. Protestants in the United States. 4. Persecution 5. Nativism 6. United States — History — 1783-1865 7. United States — Politics & government — 1815-1861. I. T.
BX1406.B5 1952    *LC* 52-14020

**Colaianni, James F., 1922-.**     ● **1.3172**
The Catholic left: the crisis of radicalism within the church. Introd. by Donald J. Thorman. — [1st ed.]. — Philadelphia: Chilton, [1968] xx, 232 p.; 21 cm. 1. Catholic Church in the United States. 2. Church renewal — Catholic Church. I. T.
BX1406.2.C6    282.73    *LC* 68-29313

**Dolan, Jay P., 1936-.**     **1.3173**
The American Catholic experience: a history from colonial times to the present / Jay P. Dolan. — 1st ed. — Garden City, N.Y.: Doubleday, 1985. 504 p.; 24 cm. Includes index. 1. Catholic Church — United States — History 2. United States — Church history I. T.
BX1406.2.D637 1985    282/.73 19    *LC* 84-26026    *ISBN* 038515206X

**Ellis, John Tracy, 1905-.**    • **1.3174**
American Catholicism. — 2d ed., rev. — Chicago: University of Chicago Press, [1969] xviii, 322 p.; 21 cm. — (The Chicago history of American civilization) 1. Catholic Church in the United States — History. I. T. II. Series.
BX1406.2.E37 1969    282.73    *LC* 69-19274

**Ellis, John Tracy, 1905-.**    • **1.3175**
Catholics in Colonial America. — Baltimore, Helicon [1965] 486 p. 24 cm. — (Benedictine studies, v. 8) Bibliographical footnotes. 1. Catholic church in the U.S. — Hist. — Colonial period. I. T. II. Series.
BX1406.2.E39    282.73    *LC* 64-10920

**Gleason, Philip. comp.**    • **1.3176**
Catholicism in America. — New York: Harper & Row Pub., [1970] 159 p.; 21 cm. — (Interpretations of American history) 1. Catholics — United States — Addresses, essays, lectures. I. T.
BX1406.2.G57    282.73    *LC* 74-121629

**Hennesey, James J.**    **1.3177**
American Catholics: a history of the Roman Catholic community in the United States / James Hennesey; with a foreword by John Tracy Ellis. — New York: Oxford University Press, 1981. xvi, 397 p.; 24 cm. 1. Catholic Church — United States — History 2. Catholics — United States — History. I. T.
BX1406.2.H37    282/.73 19    *LC* 81-1074    *ISBN* 0195029461

**Hitchcock, James.**    • **1.3178**
The decline and fall of radical Catholicism. — [New York]: Herder and Herder, [1971] 228 p.; 21 cm. 1. Catholic Church — History — 1965- 2. Catholic Church in the United States. I. T.
BX1406.2.H5    282.73    *LC* 73-146297

**Hoge, Dean R., 1937-.**    **1.3179**
Converts, dropouts, returnees, a study of religious change among Catholics / by Dean R. Hoge, with Kenneth McGuire, Bernard F. Stratman [and] concluding chapter by Alvin Illig. — Washington, DC: United States Catholic Conference; New York: Pilgrim Press, c1981. xii, 226 p.: ill.; 24 cm. A study sponsored by the National Conference of Catholic Bishops' Committee on Evangelization. 1. Catholics — United States 2. Converts, Catholic — United States. 3. Ex-church members — Catholic Church 4. Evangelistic work I. McGuire, Kenneth. II. Stratman, Bernard F. III. Catholic Church. National Conference of Catholic Bishops. Committee on Evangelization. IV. T.
BX1406.2.H59    282/.73 19    *LC* 81-15351    *ISBN* 0829804838

**Cross, Robert D.**    **1.3180**
The emergence of liberal Catholicism in America. — Cambridge, Mass., Harvard University Press, 1958. 328 p. 22 cm. Includes bibliography. 1. Americanism. I. T.
BX1407.A5C7    282.73    *LC* 58-5593

**McAvoy, Thomas Timothy, 1903-1969.**    • **1.3181**
The great crisis in American Catholic history, 1895–1900 / by Thomas T. McAvoy. — Chicago: H. Regnery, 1957. 402 p.; 22 cm. 1. Americanism (Catholic controversy) I. T.
BX1407.A5 M18    *LC* 57-11728

**Dolan, Jay P., 1936-.**    **1.3182**
The immigrant church: New York's Irish and German Catholics, 1815–1865 / Jay P. Dolan; foreword by Martin E. Marty. — Baltimore: Johns Hopkins University Press, [1975] xiv, 221 p.: ill.; 21 cm. 1. Catholics — New York (N.Y.) 2. Irish Americans — New York (N.Y.) — History — 19th century. 3. German Americans — New York (N.Y.) — History — 19th century. I. T.
BX1418.N5 D64    282/.747/1    *LC* 75-12552    *ISBN* 0801817080

## BX1419–1695 Other Countries

**Cleary, Edward L.**    **1.3183**
Crisis and change: the Church in Latin America today / Edward L. Cleary. — Maryknoll, N.Y.: Orbis Books, c1985. vi, 202 p.; 21 cm. Includes index. 1. Catholic Church — Latin America. 2. Latin America — Church history. I. T.
BX1426.2.C54 1985    282.8 19    *LC* 84-16478    *ISBN* 0883441497

**Greenleaf, Richard E. comp.**    • **1.3184**
The Roman Catholic Church in colonial Latin America, edited with an introduction by Richard E. Greenleaf. — [1st ed.]. — New York: Knopf, [1971] xi, 272 p.; 19 cm. — (Borzoi books on Latin America) 1. Catholic Church in Latin America — History — Addresses, essays, lectures. 2. Latin America — Church history — Addresses, essays, lectures. I. T.
BX1426.2.G73 1971    282.8    *LC* 71-130774    *ISBN* 0394302907

**Ricard, Robert.**    • **1.3185**
The spiritual conquest of Mexico: an essay on the apostolate and the evangelizing methods of the mendicant orders in New Spain, 1523–1572 / by Robert Ricard; translated by Lesley Byrd Simpson. — Berkeley: University of California Press, 1966. xii, 423 p., [4] leaves of plates: ill.; 24 cm. Translation of

La conquête spirituelle du Mexique. Includes index. 1. Catholic Church — Mexico. 2. Indians of Mexico — Missions 3. Indians of Mexico — Languages — Bibliography. 4. Mexico — Church history 5. Mexico — History — Conquest, 1519-1540 I. T.
BX1428.R51    282/.72    *LC* 66-16286

**Costeloe, Michael P.**    • **1.3186**
Church wealth in Mexico: a study of the 'Juzgado de Capellanias' in the archbishopric of Mexico 1800–1856, by Michael P. Costeloe. — London: Cambridge U.P., 1967. ix, 139 p.; 22 1/2 cm. — (Cambridge Latin American studies, no. 2) 1. Catholic Church in Mexico — Finance. 2. Church and state in Mexico. I. T. II. Title: Juzgado de Capellanias.
BX1428.2.C6    254.8    *LC* 67-18310    *ISBN* 0521047293

**Bruneau, Thomas C.**    **1.3187**
The church in Brazil: the politics of religion / by Thomas C. Bruneau. — 1st ed. — Austin: University of Texas Press, 1982. xvi, 237 p.: map; 24 cm. — (Latin American monographs / Institute of Latin American Studies, the University of Texas at Austin; no. 56) 'This book is in many respects a logical continuation of The political transformation of the Brazilian Catholic Church, published in 1974'.—Pref. Includes index. 1. Catholic Church — Brazil 2. Brazil — Church history I. T.
BX1466.2.B77 1982    282/.81 19    *LC* 81-16391    *ISBN* 0292710712

**Levine, Daniel H.**    **1.3188**   ← *BX 4734 L48 1981*
Religion and politics in Latin America: the Catholic Church in Venezuela and Colombia / Daniel H. Levine. — Princeton, N.J.: Princeton University Press, c1981. xii, 342 p.; 25 cm. Includes index. 1. Catholic Church — Venezuela 2. Catholic Church — Colombia 3. Christianity and politics 4. Venezuela — Politics and government — 1830- 5. Colombia — Politics and government — 1946-1974 6. Venezuela — Church history. 7. Colombia — Church history — 20th century I. T.
BX1488.2.L48    282/.861 19    *LC* 80-20110    *ISBN* 0691076243

**Bossy, John.**    **1.3189**
The English Catholic community, 1570–1850 / John Bossy. — New York: Oxford University Press, c1976. xii, 446 p.: ill., maps; 22 cm. Includes index. 1. Catholic Church — England — History. 2. Catholics — England — History. 3. England — Church history I. T.
BX1492.B67x 1976    *LC* 84-672164    *ISBN* 0195198476

**Bieler, Ludwig.**    **1.3190**
St. Patrick and the coming of Christianity. — Dublin: Gill, [1967] [8], 100 p.; 22 cm. — (A History of Irish Catholicism, v. 1, 1) 1. Patrick, Saint, 373?-463? I. T. II. Series.
BX1503.H55 vol. 1, no. 1    282.415 s    *LC* 74-17605

**Lewy, Guenter, 1923-.**    • **1.3191**
The Catholic Church and Nazi Germany. — [1st ed.]. — New York: McGraw-Hill, [1964] xv, 416 p.: map; 22 cm. 1. Catholic Church in Germany — History — 1933-1945. I. T.
BX1536.L4    282.43    *LC* 64-21072

**Halperin, Samuel William.**    • **1.3192**
The separation of church and state in Italian thought from Cavour to Mussolini, by S. William Halperin. — New York: Octagon Books, 1971 [c1937] ix, 115 p.; 23 cm. 1. Church and state — Italy 2. Roman question I. T.
BX1545.H3 1971    322/.1/0945    *LC* 71-120623

**Payne, Stanley G.**    **1.3193**
Spanish catholicism: an historical overview / Stanley G. Payne. — Madison, Wis.: University of Wisconsin Press, 1984. xiii, 263 p.; 24 cm. Includes index. 1. Catholic Church — Spain — History. 2. Spain — Religious life and customs. 3. Spain — Church history I. T.
BX1583.P29 1984    282/.46 19    *LC* 83-25946    *ISBN* 0299098001

**Callahan, William James, 1937-.**    **1.3194**
Church, politics, and society in Spain, 1750–1874 / William J. Callahan. — Cambridge, Mass.: Harvard University Press, 1984. 325 p.: ill.; 24 cm. — (Harvard historical monographs. v. 73) Includes index. 1. Catholic Church — Spain — History. 2. Spain — Church history I. T. II. Series.
BX1585.C214 1984    282/.46 19    *LC* 83-26503    *ISBN* 0674131258

**Schumacher, John N.**    **1.3195**
Readings in Philippine church history / John N. Schumacher. — Quezon City: Loyola School of Theology, Ateneo de Manila University, 1979. xi, 428 p., [3] p. of plates: ill.; 27 cm. 1. Catholic Church — Philippines — History — Sources. 2. Philippines — Church history — Sources. I. T.
BX1656.S38    282/.599 19    *LC* 81-185342

## BX1746–1759 THEOLOGY. DOCTRINE. SERMONS

**Küng, Hans, 1928-.** • **1.3196**
[Kirche. English] The church. [Translation by Ray and Rosaleen Ockenden] New York, Sheed and Ward [1968, c1967] xiv, 515 p. 22 cm. 1. Church I. T.
BX1746.K813x    262.7    *LC* 68-13844

**Thomas, Aquinas, Saint, 1225?-1274.** • **1.3197**
[Summa theologica English & Latin] Summa theologiae. Latin text and English translation, introductions, notes, appendices, and glossaries. [Cambridge? Eng.] Blackfriars; New York, McGraw-Hill 1964-1981. 61 v.; 23 cm. 1. Theology, Doctrinal I. T.
BX1749.T48 1964    230.2    *LC* 63-11128

**Adam, Karl, 1876-.** • **1.3198**
The spirit of Catholicism. Translated by Justin McCann. — Rev. ed. — Garden City, N. Y., Image Books [1954] 260 p. 18 cm. — (Image books, P 502) 1. Catholic Church — Doctrinal and controversial works — Catholic authors. I. T.
BX1751.A4 1954    230.2    *LC* 54-12995 rev

**Lubac, Henri de, 1896-.** • **1.3199**
Catholicism; a study of dogma in relation to the corporate destiny of mankind. — New York: Sheed and Ward, 1958. xiv, 283 p. 23 cm. Translated from the 4th French ed. by Lancelot C. Sheppard. 1. Theology, Doctrinal 2. Sociology, Christian — Catholic authors. I. T.
BX1751.L913 1958    282    *LC* 58-14969

BT
344
S41

→ **Segundo, Juan Luis.** **1.3200**
[Esa comunidad llamada iglesia. English] The community called church, by Juan Luis Segundo in collaboration with the staff of the Peter Faber Center in Montevideo, Uruguay. Translated by John Drury. Maryknoll, N.Y. [Orbis Books, 1973] xi, 172 p. 24 cm. (His A theology for artisans of a new humanity, v. 1) Translation of Esa comunidad llamada iglesia. 1. Church 2. Christian life — Catholic authors. 3. Church and the world I. Centro Pedro Fabro de Montevideo. II. T.
BX1751.2.A1 S413 vol. 1 BX1746    230/.2 s 282    *LC* 72-85795
    *ISBN* 088344481X

**McBrien, Richard P.** **1.3201**
Catholicism / by Richard P. McBrien. — Minneapolis, MN: Winston Press, c1980. 2 v. (xcii, 1186 p.); 24 cm. 1. Catholic Church — Doctrinal and controversial works — Catholic authors. I. T.
BX1751.2.M24    230/.2 19    *LC* 79-55963    *ISBN* 0030569079

**Rahner, Karl, 1904-.** • **1.3202**
[Schriften zur Theologie. English] Theological investigations / by Karl Rahner;translated with an introduction by Cornelius Ernst. — Baltimore: Helicon Press, [1961]- < 1979 >. v. < 1-8, 11, 13-14, 16 >; 22 cm. Translation of: Schriften zur Theologie. Translators vary. Imprint varies: v. 7-8: London: Darton, Longman & Todd; New York: Herder and Herder; v. 11: London: Darton, Longman & Todd; New York: Seabury Press; v. 13: New York: Seabury Press; v. 16: London: Darton, Longman & Todd. 1. Catholic Church — Doctrinal and controversial works — Catholic authors. 2. Theology, Catholic. I. T.
BX1751.2.R313    *LC* 61-8189    *ISBN* 0232356165

**Curran, Charles E.** **1.3203**
American Catholic social ethics: twentieth–century approaches / Charles E. Curran. — Notre Dame: University of Notre Dame Press, c1982. x, 353 p.; 24 cm. 1. Catholic Church — United States — History — 20th century. 2. Christian ethics — History of doctrines — 20th century. 3. Social ethics — History — 20th century. 4. Sociology, Christian (Catholic) — History of doctrines — 20th century. I. T.
BX1753.C86 1982    261.8/0973 19    *LC* 82-4829    *ISBN* 0268006032

**Newman, John Henry, 1801-1890.** • **1.3204**
Sermons and discourses. — New ed., edited with a pref. and introd. by Charles Frederick Harrold. — New York, Longmans, Green, 1949. 2 v. p. 21 cm. 1. Catholic Church — Sermons 2. Sermons, English I. Harrold, Charles Frederick, 1897-1948, ed. II. T.
BX1756.A3N4 1949    252.02    *LC* 49-7580 *

**Häring, Bernhard, 1912-.** • **1.3205**
Toward a Christian moral theology [by] Bernard Häring. — [Notre Dame, Ind.]: University of Notre Dame Press, 1966. viii, 230 p.; 22 cm. — (The Cardinal O'Hara series. Studies and research in Christian theology at Notre Dame, v. 2) 1. Christian ethics — Catholic authors I. T. II. Title: A Christian moral theology.
BX1758.2.H32    248.482    *LC* 66-15502

## BX1760–1955 CATHOLIC CHURCH – RELATIONS. CHURCH AND STATE. CHURCH GOVERNMENT. LAITY

**Pelikan, Jaroslav Jan, 1923-.** • **1.3206**
The riddle of Roman Catholicism. — New York, Abingdon Press [1959] 272 p. 24 cm. Includes bibliography. 1. Catholic Church — Doctrinal and controversial works — Protestant authors. 2. Catholic Church — Relations — Protestant churches 3. Protestant churches — Relations — Catholic Church I. T.
BX1765.2.P4    282    *LC* 59-10367

**Minus, Paul M.** **1.3207**
The Catholic rediscovery of Protestantism: a history of Roman Catholic ecumenical pioneering / by Paul M. Minus, Jr. — New York: Paulist Press, c1976. vi, 261 p.; 21 cm. (An Exploration book) 1. Catholic Church — Relations — Protestant churches 2. Christian Union — Catholic Church — History. 3. Protestant churches — Relations — Catholic Church I. T.
BX1784.M56    262/.001    *LC* 75-44804    *ISBN* 0089119447

**Sturzo, Luigi, 1871-1959.** **1.3208**
Church and state. With an introd. by A. Robert Caponigri. [Translated by Barbara Barclay Carter. — Notre Dame, Ind.] University of Notre Dame Press, 1962. 2 v. (584 p.) 21 cm. — (Notre Dame paperbooks, NDP13a-b) Bibliography: p. 565-569. 1. Church and state — Catholic Church 2. Church and social problems — Catholic Church I. T.
BX1790.S78 1962    261.7    *LC* 62-12467    *ISBN* 0268000476

**Tellenbach, Gerd, 1903-.** • **1.3209**
[Libertas; Kirch und Weltordnung im Zeitalter des Investiturstreites] Church, state, and Christian society at the time of the investiture contest. Translated by R. F. Bennett. New York, Harper & Row [1970, c1959] xxiii, 196 p. 21 cm. (Harper torchbooks) Translation of Libertas; Kirche und Weltordnung im Zeitalter des Investiturstreites. 1. Church and state — History. 2. Investiture 3. Liberty. I. T.
BX1790.T43 1970    261.7/09/021    *LC* 75-19373

**McKenzie, John L.** **1.3210**
Authority in the Church [by] John L. McKenzie. — New York: Sheed and Ward, [1966] vi, 184 p.; 22 cm. 1. Catholic Church — Discipline 2. Church — Authority I. T.
BX1802.M23    262.8    *LC* 66-12270

**Tierney, Brian.** **1.3211**
Origins of papal infallibility, 1150–1350; a study on the concepts of infallibility, sovereignty and tradition in the Middle Ages. — Leiden: E. J. Brill, 1972. viii, 298 p.; 25 cm. — (Studies in the history of Christian thought. v. 6) 1. Popes — Infallibility — History. I. T. II. Series.
BX1806.T54    262/.131/0902    *LC* 72-188202

**Congar, Marie Joseph, 1904-.** • **1.3212**
Lay people in the church: a study for a theology of laity / Yves M.J. Congar; translated by Donald Attwater. — Rev. ed. — Westminster, Md.: Newman Press, 1967. xxi, 498 p.: ill.; 22 cm. Translation of: Jalons pour une théologie du laïcat. 1. Laity 2. Catholic Church. 3. Priesthood, Universal 4. Catholic action I. T.
BX1920.C612 1963    BX1920.C66 1967.    262.2    *LC* 56-10002

**Barraclough, Geoffrey, 1908-.** • **1.3213**
Papal provisions; aspects of church history, constitutional, legal and administrative in the later Middle Ages. — Westport, Conn.: Greenwood Press, [1971] xvi, 187 p.; 23 cm. Reprint of the 1935 ed. 1. Catholic Church — Government 2. Benefices, Ecclesiastical 3. Papacy 4. Church history — Middle Ages, 600-1500 I. T.
BX1955.B3 1971    262/.22    *LC* 74-109707    *ISBN* 0837141982

## BX1958–2315 CREEDS. LITURGY. MEDITATIONS. SACRAMENTS

**Nijmegen, Netherlands. Hoger Katechetisch Instituut.** • **1.3214**
[Nieuwe katechismus. English] A New catechism: Catholic faith for adults. [Translation by Kevin Smyth. New York] Herder and Herder [1967] xviii, 510 p. 21 cm. Translation of De nieuwe katechismus. 1. Catholic Church — Catechisms and creeds — Dutch. I. T.
BX1966.D8 N6213 1967b    238    *LC* 68-3626

**Bouyer, Louis, 1913-.** **1.3215**
Rite and man: natural sacredness and Christian liturgy / translated by M. Joseph Costelloe. — Notre Dame, Ind.: University of Notre Dame Press, 1963.

220 p. 24 cm. — (University of Notre Dame. Liturgical studies; v.7) 1. Catholic Church — Liturgy and ritual. I. T. II. Series.
BX1970.B66      264.02      *LC* 62-20224

**Hardison, O. B.**                                                                            • **1.3216**
Christian rite and Christian drama in the Middle Ages; essays in the origin and early history of modern drama, by O. B. Hardison, Jr. — Baltimore: Johns Hopkins Press, [1965] xiii, 328 p.: illus.; 24 cm. 1. Catholic Church Liturgy and ritual — History. 2. Drama — History and criticism 3. Liturgical drama I. T.
BX1970.H28      809.251      *LC* 65-25479

**Francis, de Sales, Saint, 1567-1622.**                                                        • **1.3217**
Treatise on the love of God, translated into English by the Rev. Henry Benedict Mackey, O. S. B., with an introduction by the translator. — Westminster, Md., The Newman book shop, 1942. xliv, 555 p. 19 cm. At head of title: St. Francis de Sales. 1. Love — Religious aspects — Christianity 2. God — Worship and love 3. Spiritual life — Catholic authors I. Mackey, Benedict, 1846-1906, tr. II. T.
BX2179.F8T74 1942      242      *LC* 43-2793

**Francis, de Sales, Saint, 1567-1622.**                                                        • **1.3218**
Introduction to the devout life. London, J.M. Dent; New York, Dutton [1961] 261 p. (Everyman's library, 324) 1. Meditations. I. Day, Michael. tr. II. T.
BX2179.F81x      *LC* 61-65003

**Ignatius, of Loyola, Saint, 1491-1556.**                                                       **1.3219**
[Exercitia spiritualia English] The spiritual exercises of St. Ignatius: a literal translation and a contemporary reading / David L. Fleming. — St. Louis: Institute of Jesuit Sources, 1978. xxiv, 244 p.; 24 cm. (Series IV—Study aids on Jesuit topics. no. 7) Translation of Exercitia spiritualia. Edition for 1976 by D. L. Fleming published under title: A contemporary reading of The spiritual exercises. Includes index. 1. Spiritual exercises I. Fleming, David L., 1934- II. Fleming, David L., 1934- A contemporary reading of The spiritual excercises. III. T. IV. Series.
BX2179.L7 E5 1978      248.3 19      *LC* 77-93429      *ISBN* 0912422327

**Rolle, Richard, of Hampole, 1290?-1349.**                                                      **1.3220**
[Incendium amoris. English] The fire of love; translated [from the Latin] into modern English with an introduction by Clifton Wolters. Harmondsworth, Penguin, 1972. 192 p. 19 cm. (The Penguin classics) Translation of Incendium amoris. 1. Devotional literature I. Wolters, Clifton. tr. II. T.
BX2180.R613 1972      242/.1      *LC* 72-190574      *ISBN* 0140442561

**Hugh, of Saint-Victor, 1096?-1141.**                                                          • **1.3221**
Hugh of Saint Victor on the sacraments of the Christian faith (De sacramentis) / English version by Roy J. Deferrari. — Cambridge, Mass.: Mediaeval Academy of America, 1951. xx, 486 p. — (Mediaeval Academy of America. Publications; no. 58) 1. Sacraments — Early works to 1800. I. T. II. Title: On the sacraments of the Christian faith. III. Series.
BX2200.H843      *LC* 51-7939

**Martos, Joseph, 1943-.**                                                                      **1.3222**
Doors to the sacred: a historical introduction to sacraments in the Catholic Church / Joseph Martos. — 1st ed. — Garden City, N.Y.: Doubleday, 1981. xiii, 531 p.; 22 cm. 1. Catholic Church — Doctrinal and controversial works — Catholic authors. 2. Sacraments — Catholic Church — History. I. T.
BX2200.M355      234/.16 19      *LC* 80-626      *ISBN* 038515738X

**Rahner, Karl, 1904-.**                                                                        • **1.3223**
The church and the sacraments. [Translated by W. J. O'hara]. — Freiburg, Herder [1963] 116 p. 22 cm. — (Questiones disputate, 9) 1. Sacraments — Catholic Church 2. Church I. T.
BX2200.R313      265      *LC* 63-10582

**Schillebeeckx, Edward, 1914-.**                                                               • **1.3224**
[Christusontmoeting als Sacrament Van de Godsontmoeting. English] Christ, the sacrament of the encounter with God, by E. Schillebeeckx. [Translation by Paul Barrett. English text rev. by Mark Schoof and Laurence Bright] New York, Sheed and Ward [1963] xvii, 222 p. 22 cm. 1. Sacraments — Catholic Church I. T.
BX2200.S4143      265      *LC* 63-17144

**Balasuriya, Tissa.**                                                                          **1.3225**
The Eucharist and human liberation / Tissa Balasuriya. — Maryknoll, N.Y.: Orbis Books, 1979, c1977. 1 v. 1. Lord's Supper — Catholic Church I. T.
BX2215.2.B33      234/.163      *LC* 78-9160      *ISBN* 0883441187

## BX2325–2333 SAINTS. HAGIOLOGY
(see also: BX4654, BX4700)

**Brown, Peter Robert Lamont.**                                                                 **1.3226**
The cult of the saints: its rise and function in Latin Christianity / Peter Brown. — Chicago: University of Chicago Press, c1981. xv, 187 p.; 23 cm. (Haskell

lectures on history of religions; new ser., no. 2) 1. Christian saints — Cult — History — Addresses, essays, lectures. I. T. II. Series.
BX2333.B74      270.2      *LC* 80-11210      *ISBN* 0226076210

## BX2347–4556 CHRISTIAN LIFE. MONASTIC AND RELIGIOUS LIFE

**International Ecumenical Congress of Theology. (4th: 1980: São**      **1.3227**
**Paulo, Brazil)**
The challenge of basic Christian communities: papers from the International Ecumenical Congress of Theology, February 20–March 2, 1980, São Paulo, Brazil / edited by Sergio Torres and John Eagleson; translated by John Drury. — Maryknoll, N.Y.: Orbis Books, c1981. xx, 283 p.; 24 cm. 1. Christian communities — Catholic Church — Congresses. 2. Christian communities — Latin America — Congresses. 3. Christian communities — Congresses. I. Torres, Sergio. II. Eagleson, John. III. T.
BX2347.72.L37 I57 1980      261.8 19      *LC* 81-38361      *ISBN* 0883445034

**Merton, Thomas, 1915-1968.**                                                                  • **1.3228**
No man is an island. — [1st ed.]. — New York: Harcourt, Brace, [1955] 264 p.; 22 cm. 1. Spiritual life — Catholic authors I. T.
BX2350.M535      248      *LC* 55-7420

**Merton, Thomas, 1915-1968.**                                                                  • **1.3229**
Seeds of contemplation. Norfolk, Conn. : New Directions, 1949. 201 p. 1. Spiritual life — Catholic authors I. T.
BX2350.M54      *LC* 49-1562

**Paris, Matthew, 1200-1259.**                                                                  **1.3230**
[Selections. 1984] Chronicles of Matthew Paris: monastic life in the thirteenth century / edited, translated, and with an introduction by Richard Vaughan. — Gloucester [Gloucestershire]: A. Sutton; New York: St. Martin's Press, 1985 (c1984). 286 p.; 23 cm. Translated from Latin. Includes index. 1. Monastic and religious life — Addresses, essays, lectures. I. Vaughan, Richard, 1927- II. T.
BX2435.P2542      940.1/84 19      *LC* 83-40602      *ISBN* 0312134525

**Leclercq, Jean, 1911-.**                                                                      **1.3231**
[Amour des lettres et le désir de Dieu. English] The love of learning and the desire for God: a study of monastic culture / Jean Leclercq; translated by Catharine Misrahi. — 3rd ed. — New York: Fordham University Press, 1982. viii, 282 p.; 23 cm. Translation of: L'amour des lettres et le désir de Dieu. 1. Monasticism and religious orders — History — Middle Ages, 600-1500 2. Christian literature, Early — History and criticism. 3. Theology — History — Middle Ages, 600-1500 I. T.
BX2470.L413 1982      255 19      *LC* 82-242178      *ISBN* 0823204073

**Knowles, David, 1896-.**                                                                      **1.3232**
The heads of religious houses, England and Wales, 940–1216; edited by David Knowles, C. N. L. Brooke [and] Vera C. M. London. — Cambridge [Eng.]: University Press, 1972. xlviii, 277 p.; 24 cm. 1. Monasticism and religious orders — Great Britain — Registers. 2. Superiors, Religious — Great Britain. I. Brooke, Christopher Nugent Lawrence. joint author. II. London, Vera C. M. joint author. III. T.
BX2592.K55      271/.00942      *LC* 79-171676      *ISBN* 0521083672

**Knowles, David, 1896-.**                                                                      **1.3233**
Medieval religious houses, England and Wales, by David Knowles and R. Neville Hadcock. New York, St. Martin's Press [1972, c1971] xv, 565 p. fold. maps. 24 cm. 1. Monasticism and religious orders — England. 2. Monasticism and religious orders — Wales. I. Hadcock, R. Neville (Richard Neville) joint author. II. T.
BX2592.K56 1972      271/.00942      *LC* 76-167756

**Knowles, David, 1896-.**                                                                      • **1.3234**
The religious orders in England. — Cambridge [Eng.] University Press, 1948-59. 3 v. fronts. 26 cm. Includes bibliographies. 1. Monasticism and religious orders — England. I. T.
BX2592.K583      271.0942      *LC* 48-10465 rev 3*

**Woodward, George William Otway.**                                                             • **1.3235**
The dissolution of the monasteries / G.W.O. Woodward. — New York: Walker, c1966. ix, 186 p.: ill. (Blanford history series.) Includes index. 1. Monasticism and religious orders — England. 2. Secularization — Great Britain. I. T.
BX2592.W67 1966a      *LC* 67-13243

**Evans, Joan, 1893-.**                                                                         • **1.3236**
Monastic life at Cluny, 910–1157. [Hamden, Conn.] Archon Books, 1968. xix, 137 p. illus., facsims. maps. 22 cm. Includes music. 1. Cluny (Benedictine abbey) I. T.
BX2615.C63 E8 1968      271/.1      *LC* 68-20376

**Horn, Walter William, 1908-.** 1.3237
The Plan of St. Gall: a study of the architecture & economy of & life in a paradigmatic Carolingian monastery / by Walter Horn and Ernest Born; with a foreword by Wolfgang Braunfels; a translation into English by Charles W. Jones of the Directives of Adalhard, 753–826, the Ninth Abbot of Corbie; and with a note by A. Hunter Dupree on the Significance of the Plan of St. Gall to the history of measurement. — Berkeley: University of California Press, 1980 [c1979] 3 v.: ill.; 37 cm. (California studies in the history of art. 19) The Plan is in the library of the former monastery of St. Gall (Stiftsbibliothek, Ms. 1092) Errata slip for v. 3 inserted. Includes index. 1. Kloster St. Gallen. I. Born, Ernest, 1898- joint author. II. Adalard, Saint, d. 826. Consuetudines corbeienses. English. 1979. III. Stiftsbibliothek Sankt Gallen. Manuscript. 1092. IV. T. V. Series.
BX2659.S32 H67          271/.1/04947 19          *LC* 71-118844          *ISBN* 0520017242

**Butler, Edward Cuthbert, 1858-1934.** • 1.3238
Benedictine monachism; studies in Benedictine life and rule. With a new foreword by David Knowles. Cambridge [Eng.] Speculum Historiale; New York, Barnes & Noble [1962] [12], 424 p. 22 cm. 'Second edition: Longmans: 1924, photographically reprinted: 1961 for Speculum Historiale.' 1. Benedict, Saint, Abbot of Monte Cassino. 2. Benedictines. I. T.
BX3002.B8 1962          271.1          *LC* 62-4053

**Benedict, Saint, Abbot of Monte Cassino.** • 1.3239
The rule of Saint Benedict; in Latin and English / edited & translated by Justin McCann. Westminster, Md., Newman Press [1963, 1952] 214 p. (The Orchard books) 1. Benedictines. I. T.
BX3004.E6 1952          *LC* 53-863

**Hinnebusch, William A.** 1.3240
The history of the Dominican Order [by] William A. Hinnebusch. — Staten Island, N.Y.: Alba House, [1966-. v.      ; 24 cm. 1. Dominicans. I. T.
BX3506.2.H5          271.2          *LC* 65-17977          *ISBN* 0818902663

**Weigle, Marta.** 1.3241
Brothers of light, brothers of blood: the Penitentes of the Southwest / Marta Weigle. — 1st ed. — Albuquerque: University of New Mexico Press, c1976. xix, 300 p., [7] leaves of plates: ill.; 25 cm. Includes index. 1. Hermanos Penitentes. I. T.
BX3653.U6 W39          271/.093/0789          *LC* 75-21188

**Guibert, Joseph de.** • 1.3242
The Jesuits: their spiritual doctrine and practice; a historical study. William J. Young, translator. George E. Ganss, editor. Chicago, Institute of Jesuit Sources, 1964. xxv, 692 p.; 24 cm. Translation of La spiritualité de la Compagnie de Jésus; esquisse historique. 1. Ignatius, of Loyola, Saint, 1491-1556. 2. Ignatius, of Loyola, Saint, 1491-1556. Exercitia spiritualia. 3. Jesuits. I. T.
BX3703.G813          271.5          *LC* 64-21430

**Mitchell, David J.** 1.3243
The Jesuits, a history / by David Mitchell. — New York: F. Watts, 1981, c1980. 320 p., [8] leaves of plates: ill.; 24 cm. Includes index. 1. Jesuits — History I. T.
BX3706.2.M57 1981          271/.53 19          *LC* 80-25316          *ISBN* 0531099474

**Ricci, Matteo, 1552-1610.** • 1.3244
China in the sixteenth century: the journals of Matthew Ricci, 1583–1610; translated from the Latin by Louis J. Gallagher. With a foreword by Richard J. Cushing, Archbishop of Boston. — New York, Random House [1953] xxii, 616 p. ports. 24 cm. 'Translation of Trigault's 1615 Latin version of the Ricci commentaries [entitled De Christiana expeditione apud Sinas suscepta ab Societate Jesu]' 1. Jesuits — China 2. Missions — China 3. Jesuits — Missions I. Trigault, Nicolas, 1577-1628. II. T.
BX3746.C5R473          271.5          *LC* 53-9708

**Merton, Thomas, 1915-1968.** • 1.3245
The waters of Siloe. — [1st ed.]. — New York, Harcourt, Brace [1949] xxxvii, 377 p. illus. 22 cm. Bibliography: p. 353-358. 1. Trappists. I. T.
BX4102.M4          271.125          *LC* 49-10495 *

## BX4650–4705 BIOGRAPHY

**Butler, Alban, 1711-1773.** • 1.3246
Lives of the saints; edited, rev., and supplemented by Herbert Thurston and Donald Attwater. Complete ed. New York, Kenedy [1956] 4 v. 24 cm. 1. Catholic Church — Prayer-books and devotions — English 2. Christian saints — Biography 3. Devotional calendars — Catholic Church. I. Thurston, Herbert, 1856-1939. II. Attwater, Donald, 1892-1977. III. T.
BX4654.B8 1956          922.22          *LC* 56-5383

**Jacobus, de Voragine, ca. 1229-1298.** 1.3247
The golden legend: or, Lives of the saints / as Englished by William Caxton. London, J. M. Dent, 1900–39. [v. 1, 1931-. New York: AMS Press, 1974. 7 v. in 4.; 19 cm. Original ed. issued in series: The Temple classics. 1. Saints I. Caxton, William, ca. 1422-1491. tr. II. T. III. Title: Lives of the saints.
BX4654.J33 1973          282/.092/2 B          *LC* 76-170839          *ISBN* 0404067700

**The saints: a concise biographical dictionary / edited by John** • 1.3248
**Coulson; with an introduction by C.C. Martindale, S.J.**
New York: Hawthorn Books, 1958. 496 p.: ill. (some col.); 25 cm. 1. Saints I. Coulson, John, 1919-
BX4655.S28          235/.2          *LC* 58-5626

**Cunningham, Lawrence.** 1.3249
The meaning of saints / Lawrence S. Cunningham. — 1st ed. — San Francisco, CA: Harper & Row, c1980. 186 p.; 22 cm. Includes index. 1. Christian saints I. T.
BX4662.C86 1980          235/.2          *LC* 80-7754          *ISBN* 0060616490

**Delehaye, Hippolyte, 1859-1941.** • 1.3250
The legends of the saints; an introduction to hagiography, from the French of H. Delehaye. With an introd. by Richard J. Schoeck. Translated by V.M. Crawford. [Notre Dame, Ind.] University of Notre Dame Press, 1961. 241 p. (Notre Dame publications; NDP7) 1. Hagiography I. T.
BX4662.D343 1961          235.2

**Bouyer, Louis, 1913-.** • 1.3251
The spirit and forms of Protestantism. Translated by A. V. Littledale. — Westminster, Md., Newman Press, 1961. xi, 234 p. 22 cm. 1. Converts, Catholic 2. Protestantism I. T.
BX4668.B67 1961          284          *LC* 56-10001

## BX4700 Individual Saints

**Eadmer, d. 1124?** • 1.3252
The life of St. Anselm, Archbishop of Canterbury. Edited with introd., notes, and translation by R. W. Southern. London, New York, T. Nelson [c1962] xxxvi, 171, 171, 172-179p. (Medieval classics (London)) Added t.p. in Latin: Vita Sancti Anselmi, archiepiscopi Cantuariensis. Latin and English on opposite pages, numbered in duplicate. 1. Anselm, Saint, 1033-1109. I. T.
BX4700.A58E2 1962          *LC* a 63-603

**Hopkins, Jasper.** • 1.3253
A companion to the study of St. Anselm. Minneapolis, University of Minnesota Press [1972] ix, 291 p. 24 cm. Cover title: Study of St. Anselm. Appendixes (p. [213]-253): 1. Anselm's Philosophical fragments.—2. Anselm's Methods of arguing. 1. Anselm, Saint, Archbishop of Canterbury, 1033-1109. I. T. II. Title: Study of St. Anselm.
BX4700.A58 H66 1972          230/.2          *LC* 72-79097          *ISBN* 0816606579

**Southern, R. W. (Richard William), 1912-.** 1.3254
Saint Anselm and his biographer; a study of monastic life and thought, 1059–c. 1130. — Cambridge [Eng.] University Press, 1963. xvi, 389 p. facsim. 23 cm. — (The Birkbeck lectures, 1959) Bibliography: p. xiv-xvi. Bibliographical footnotes. 1. Anselm, Saint, Archbishop of Canterbury, 1033-1109. 2. Eadmer, d. 1124? I. T. II. Series.
BX4700.A58S6          922.242          *LC* 63-4322

**Chapman, John, Father, 1865-1933.** • 1.3255
Saint Benedict and the sixth century. Westport, Conn., Greenwood Press [1971] vi, 239 p. 23 cm. Reprint of the 1929 ed. 1. Benedict, Saint, Abbot of Monte Cassino. 2. Benedict, Saint, Abbot of Monte Cassino. Regula 3. Monasticism and religious orders I. T.
BX4700.B3 C5 1971          271/.1/024 B          *LC* 79-109719          *ISBN* 0837142091

**Gregory I, Pope, ca. 540-604.** • 1.3256
[Dialogi de vita. Bk. 2. English] Life and miracles of St. Benedict: book two of the Dialogues / by Gregory the Great; translated by Odo J. Zimmermann and Benedict R. Avery. — Collegeville, Min.: St. John's Abbey Press, 1949. xv, 87 p.; 23 cm. Translation of Book 2 of Dialogi de vita. 1. Benedict, Saint, Abbot of Monte Cassino. 2. Christian saints — Italy — Biography. I. Zimmermann, Odo John, 1906- II. Avery, Benedict Raymund, 1919- III. T.
BX4700.B3 G7213 1949          281/.4/0924 B 19          *LC* 50-5458

**Bernard, of Clairvaux, Saint, 1090 or 91-1153.** • 1.3257
The letters of St. Bernard of Clairvaux / newly translated by Bruno Scott James. — New York: H. Regnery, c1953. xx, 530 p. I. James, Bruno Scott. tr. II. T.
BX4700.B5 A413 1953          *LC* 53-30189

**Habig, Marion Alphonse, 1901- comp.** 1.3258
St. Francis of Assisi: writings and early biographies: English omnibus of the sources for the life of St. Francis / edited by Marion A. Habig; translations by

Raphael Brown ... [et al.]. — 3d rev. ed., including A new Fioretti / by John R. H. Moorman. — Chicago: Franciscan Herald Press, [1977] c1973. xx, 1904 p.; 21 cm. Includes indexes. 1. Francis, of Assisi, Saint, 1182-1226. 2. Christian saints — Italy — Assisi — Biography. 3. Assisi (Italy) — Biography. I. Moorman, John R. H. (John Richard Humpidge), 1905- A new Fioretti. 1977. II. T.
BX4700.F6 H27 1977     271/.3/024 B     *LC* 76-58903     *ISBN* 0819906581

**Fioretti di San Francesco.**              • **1.3259**
The little flowers of St. Francis. The mirror of perfection. St. Bonaventure's Life of St. Francis. Introd. by Hugh McKay. London,: Dent; New York,: Dutton, 1963, 1910. xi, 397 p. 19 cm. (Everyman's library; no.485.) Early printings have title: 'The little flowers' & the Life of St. Francis with the 'Mirror of perfection'. I. Okey, Thomas, 1852-1935, ed. and tr. II. Leo, Brother, d. 1271. III. Bonaventure, Saint, Cardinal, ca. 1217-1274. IV. Mirror of perfection. V. T. VI. Title: The mirror of perfection.
BX4700.F63 E5 1963     *LC* 36-37424

**Brenan, Gerald.**                     **1.3260**
St John of the Cross; his life and poetry. With a translation of his poetry by Lynda Nicholson. Cambridge [Eng.] University Press, 1973. xii, 232 p. illus. 23 cm. Includes the poems of Juan de la Cruz in the original Spanish with parallel English translations. 1. John of the Cross, Saint, 1542-1591. I. John of the Cross, Saint, 1542-1591. Poems. English & Spanish. 1973. II. Nicholson, Lynda, tr. III. T.
BX4700.J7 B64     271/.73/024 B     *LC* 72-83577     *ISBN* 0521200067

**Thérèse, de Lisieux, Saint, 1873-1897.**     • **1.3261**
Autobiography; the complete and authorized text of L'histoire d'une âme. Newly translated by Ronald Knox. With a foreword by Vernon Johnson. — New York, Kenedy [1958] 320 p. illus., ports. 22 cm. I. T.
BX4700.T5A5 1958     922.244     *LC* 58-7325

## BX4705 Others

**Gilson, Etienne, 1884-1978.**         • **1.3262**
Heloise and Abelard. [Authorized translation by L. K. Shook. Ann Arbor] University of Michigan Press [1960] 194 p. 21 cm. 1. Abelard, Peter, 1079-1142. 2. Héloïse, 1101-1164. I. T.
BX4705.A2Gx     *LC* a 62-8647

**Berrigan, Daniel.**                 • **1.3263**
The geography of faith; conversations between Daniel Berrigan, when underground, and Robert Coles. — Boston: Beacon Press, [1971] 179 p.: ports.; 22 cm. 1. Berrigan, Daniel. I. Coles, Robert. II. T.
BX4705.B3845 A294 1971     201.1     *LC* 70-159844     *ISBN* 080700538X

**Brown, Judith C.**                 **1.3264**
Immodest acts: the life of a lesbian nun in Renaissance Italy / Judith C. Brown. — New York: Oxford University Press, 1986. viii, 214 p.; 22 cm. (Studies in the history of sexuality.) Includes index. 1. Carlini, Benedetta. 2. Lesbian nuns — Italy — Biography. 3. Lesbianism — History 4. Lesbians — Attitudes. 5. Women — Sexual behavior — History. I. T. II. Series.
BX4705.C3134 B76 1986     306.7/663/0924 B 19     *LC* 85-5031     *ISBN* 0195036751

**Carroll, John, Abp., 1735-1815.**         **1.3265**
[Works. 1976] The John Carroll papers / Thomas O'Brien Hanley, editor; under the auspices of the American Catholic Historical Association; endorsed by the National Historical Publications and Records Commission. — Notre Dame: University of Notre Dame Press, c1976. 3 v.: ill.; 25 cm. Includes some papers in original French, Italian, or Latin, with English translations. 1. Carroll, John, Abp., 1735-1815. 2. Catholic Church in the United States — Collected works. 3. United States — Politics and government — Revolution, 1775-1783 — Collected works. I. Hanley, Thomas O'Brien. II. American Catholic Historical Association. III. T.
BX4705.C33 A2 1976     282/.092/4 B     *LC* 75-19879     *ISBN* 0268011869

**Kotre, John N.**                 **1.3266**
The best of times, the worst of times: Andrew Greeley and American Catholicism, 1950-1975 / John N. Kotre. — Chicago: Nelson-Hall Co., c1978. xvii, 274 p.; 23 cm. 'Books by Andrew M. Greeley': p. 263-265. 1. Greeley, Andrew M., 1928- 2. Catholic Church — Clergy — Biography 3. Catholic Church — United States — History 4. Clergy — United States — Biography. I. T.
BX4705.G6185 K67     282/.092/4 B     *LC* 78-14224     *ISBN* 088229380X. *ISBN* 0882295977 pbk

**Electio Hugonis. English.**          **1.3267**
The chronicle of the election of Hugh, Abbot of Bury St. Edmunds and later Bishop of Ely / edited and translated by R. M. Thomson. — Oxford: Clarendon

Press, 1974. li, 208 p.: 1 ill., port.; 23 cm. — (Oxford medieval texts.) Parallel Latin text and English translation; English introd. and notes. Sometimes attributed to Master Nicholas of Dunstable. Written at Bury St. Edmunds Abbey in the 1220's. A revision of the author's thesis (M.A.), University of Melbourne. Includes indexes. 1. Hugh of Northwold, Bishop of Ely. 2. Church and state in England — History. I. Thomson, Rodney M. II. Nicholas of Dunstable. III. T. IV. Series.
BX4705.H785 E413 1974     262/.12/0924     *LC* 76-378746     *ISBN* 0198222270

**Fitzgerald, Penelope.**              **1.3268**
The Knox brothers: Edmund (Evoe), 1881-1971, Dillwyn, 1883-1943, Wilfred, 1886-1950, Ronald, 1888-1957 / Penelope Fitzgerald. — 1st American ed. — New York: Coward, McCann & Geoghegan, 1978 (c1977). 293 p., [4] leaves of plates: ill.; 23 cm. Includes index. 1. Knox, Ronald Arbuthnott, 1888-1957. 2. Knox, E. V. (Edmund Valpy), 1881-1971. 3. Knox, Wilfred Lawrence, 1886-1950. 4. Knox, Dillwyn, 1883-1943. 5. England — Biography. I. T.
BX4705.K6 F57     920/.042     *LC* 77-22621     *ISBN* 0698108604

**Stearns, Peter N.**               • **1.3269**
Priest and revolutionary; Lamennais and the dilemma of French Catholicism [by] Peter N. Stearns. [1st ed.] New York, Harper & Row [1967] x, 209 p. 22 cm. (Character in crisis) 1. Lamennais, Félicité Robert de, 1782-1854. 2. Catholic Church in France. I. T.
BX4705.L26 S7     282/.0924     *LC* 66-20760

**Merton, Thomas, 1915-1968.**         **1.3270**
The seven storey mountain / Thomas Merton. — 1st Harvest/HBJ ed. — New York: Harcourt-Brace Jovanovich, 1978, c1948. 429 p.; 21 cm. (A Harvest/HBJ book) Autobiography. Includes index. 1. Merton, Thomas, 1915-1968. 2. Trappists — United States — Biography. I. T.
BX4705.M542 A3 1978     271/.125/024 B     *LC* 78-7109     *ISBN* 0156806797

**Mott, Michael.**               **1.3271**
The seven mountains of Thomas Merton / Michael Mott. — Boston: Houghton Mifflin, 1984. xxvi, 690 p., [16] p. of plates: ill., ports.; 24 cm. Includes index. 1. Merton, Thomas, 1915-1968. 2. Trappists — United States — Biography. I. T.
BX4705.M542 M67 1984     271/.125/024 B 19     *LC* 84-10944     *ISBN* 0395313244

**Pelotte, Donald E.**             **1.3272**
John Courtney Murray: theologian in conflict / by Donald E. Pelotte. New York: Paulist Press, c1976. xi, 210 p.; 24 cm. Includes index. 1. Murray, John Courtney. 2. Catholics — Biography 3. Theologians — United States — Biography. I. T.
BX4705.M977 P44     261.7/092/4     *LC* 76-18046     *ISBN* 0809102129

**Newman, John Henry, 1801-1890.**     • **1.3273**
Apologia pro vita sua. An authoritative text, basic texts of the Newman-Kingsley controversy, origin and reception of the Apologia [and] essays in criticism. Edited by David J. DeLaura. [1st ed.] New York, Norton, [1968] xviii, 506 p. 21 cm. (Norton critical editions) 1. Newman, John Henry, 1801-1890. 2. Catholics — England — Biography. 3. Catholic Church — Doctrines I. DeLaura, David J., ed. II. T.
BX4705.N5 A3 1968     230.2 19     *LC* 67-16618

**Bouyer, Louis, 1913-.**             • **1.3274**
Newman: his life and spirituality / by Louis Bouyer; with a preface by H. Francis Davis; [translated by J. Lewis May]. — New York: P.J. Kenedy, 1958. xiii, 391 p.: portr. Traduction de: Newman, sa vie, sa spiritualité. I. T.
BX4705.N5 B653     922.242     *LC* 58-5667

**Chadwick, Owen.**               **1.3275**
Newman / Owen Chadwick. — Oxford; New York: Oxford University Press, 1983. 83 p.; 22 cm. (Past masters.) Includes index. 1. Newman, John Henry, 1801-1890. 2. Catholic Church — Doctrines — History — 19th century. I. T. II. Series.
BX4705.N5 C38 1983     230/.2/0924 19     *LC* 83-170464     *ISBN* 019287568X

**Walgrave, J. H.**                • **1.3276**
Newman the theologian; the nature of belief and doctrine as exemplified in his life and works. Translated by A. V. Littledale. — New York, Sheed & Ward [1960] 378 p. 22 cm. Translation, revised and expanded, of the author's thesis, Louvain, published in 1944 under title: Kardinaal Newman's theorie over de ontwikkeling van het dogma. Includes bibliography. 1. Newman, John Henry, 1801-1890. 2. Dogma, Development of I. T.
BX4705.N5W233     230.2     *LC* 60-16895

**Sigmund, Paul E.**              • **1.3277**
Nicholas of Cusa and medieval political thought. — Cambridge, Mass., Harvard University Press, 1963. viii, 335 p. port. 22 cm. — (Harvard political

studies) Bibliography: p. 317-330. 1. Nicholas, of Cusa, Cardinal, 1401-1464. 2. Conciliar theory 3. Church and state — Catholic Church I. T. II. Series.
BX4705.N58S5     262     LC 63-20772

**Kress, Robert.**                                                               **1.3278**
A Rahner handbook / Robert Kress. — Atlanta, Ga.: John Knox Press, c1982. vii, 118 p.; 21 cm. Includes index. 1. Rahner, Karl, 1904- 2. Theology, Doctrinal — History — 20th century 3. Theology, Catholic — History — 20th century. I. T.
BX4705.R287 K74 1982     230/.2/0924 19     LC 81-85333     ISBN 080420652X

**A World of grace: an introduction to the themes and**                          **1.3279**
**foundations of Karl Rahner's theology** / edited by Leo J.
**O'Donovan.**
New York: Seabury Press, 1980. xiii, 198 p.; 23 cm. 'A Crossroad book.' 1. Rahner, Karl, 1904- — Addresses, essays, lectures. I. O'Donovan, Leo J. II. T.
BX4705.R287 W67     230/.2/0924     LC 79-25588     ISBN 0816402124

# BX4800–9999 Protestantism

**Dillenberger, John.**                                                          • **1.3280**
Protestant Christianity interpreted through its development [by] John Dillenberger [and] Claude Welch. — New York: Scribner, 1954. 340 p.; 22 cm. 1. Protestantism — History I. Welch, Claude. joint author. II. T.
BX4807.D5     284     LC 54-10367

**Pauck, Wilhelm, 1901-.**                                                       • **1.3281**
The heritage of the Reformation. — Rev. and enl. ed. — London; New York [etc.]: Oxford University Press, [1968] x, 399 p.; 21 cm. — (A Galaxy book, GB251) 1. Protestantism I. T.
BX4810.P3 1968     280/.4     LC 68-115753

**Tillich, Paul, 1886-1965.**                                                    • **1.3282**
The Protestant era; tr., and with a concluding essay, by James Luther Adams. Chicago, Univ. of Chicago Press [1948] xxxi, 323 p. Essays and addresses. 1. Protestantism 2. Theology, Doctrinal — Addresses, essays, lectures. 3. Christianity — Philosophy I. T.
BX4817.T53     LC 48-6650

# BX4827 Biography

**Berkouwer, G. C. (Gerrit Cornelis), 1903-.**                                   • **1.3283**
The triumph of grace in the theology of Karl Barth / G.C. Berkouwer; [translated by Harry R. Boer]. — Grand Rapids, Mich.: W.B. Eerdmans, 1956. 414 p. 1. Barth, Karl, 1886-1968. 2. Grace (Theology) 3. Dialectical theology I. T.
BX4827B3 B433

**Busch, Eberhard, 1937-.**                                                      **1.3284**
[Karl Barths Lebenslauf. English] Karl Barth: his life from letters and autobiographical texts / Eberhard Busch; translated by John Bowden. — Philadelphia: Fortress Press, c1976. xvii, 569 p.: ill.; 23 cm. Translation of Karl Barths Lebenslauf. 1. Barth, Karl, 1886-1968. 2. Theologians — Switzerland — Basel — Biography. 3. Basel (Switzerland) — Biography. I. T.
BX4827.B3 B86313     230/.092/4 B     LC 76-15881     ISBN 0800604857

**Casalis, Georges.**                                                            • **1.3285**
Portrait of Karl Barth / Georges Casalis; translated with an introd. by Robert McAfee. — Garden City, N. Y.: Doubleday, 1963. viii, 135 p. 1. Barth, Karl, 1886-1968. II. Barth, Karl. III. T.
BX4827.B3C33 1963     230     LC 63-7483

**Hodgson, Peter Crafts, 1934-.**                                                • **1.3286**
The formation of historical theology; a study of Ferdinand Christian Baur [by] Peter C. Hodgson. — [1st ed.]. — New York: Harper & Row, [1966] xv, 299 p.: port.; 22 cm. — (Makers of modern theology) 1. Baur, Ferdinand Christian, 1792-1860. 2. History (Theology) I. T.
BX4827.B33 H6     230.0924     LC 66-15039

**Bonhoeffer, Dietrich, 1906-1945.**                                             **1.3287**
[Widerstand und Ergebung. English] Letters and papers from prison. Edited by Eberhard Bethge. [1st American] enl. ed. New York, Macmillan [1972, c1971] x, 437 p. maps. 22 cm. Translation of Widerstand und Ergebung. 1. Bonhoeffer, Dietrich, 1906-1945. I. T.
BX4827.B57 A43 1972     230/.092/4 B     LC 78-184531

**Kierkegaard, Søren, 1813-1855.**                                               • **1.3288**
The point of view for my work as an author: a report to history and related writings / Søren Kierkegaard; translated with introd. and notes by Walter Lowrie. — Newly edited with a pref. / by Benjamin Nelson. — New York: Harper & Row, 1962. xxiv, 170 p.: port.; 21 cm. — (Harper torchbooks: the cloister library; TB 88) I. Lowrie, Walter, 1868-1959. II. Nelson, Benjamin. III. T.
BX4827.K5 A5 1962     LC 62-852     ISBN 0061300888

**Diem, Hermann, 1900-.**                                                        • **1.3289**
Kierkegaard: an introduction / by Hermann Diem; translated by David Green. — Richmond, Va.: John Knox Press, c1966. 124 p. 1. Kierkegaard, Søren, 1813-1855. I. T.
BX4827.K5 D523     LC 66-17278

**Eller, Vernard.**                                                              • **1.3290**
Kierkegaard and radical discipleship, a new perspective. Princeton, N.J., Princeton University Press, 1968. xii, 445 p. 23 cm. 1. Kierkegaard, Søren, 1813-1855. 2. Church of the Brethren. I. T.
BX4827.K5 E4     230/.0924     LC 67-21021

**Sponheim, Paul R.**                                                            • **1.3291**
Kierkegaard on Christ and Christian coherence [by] Paul Sponheim. [1st ed.] New York, Harper & Row [1968] xix, 332 p. port. 22 cm. (Makers of modern theology) 1. Kierkegaard, Søren, 1813-1855. I. T.
BX4827.K5 S6 1968b     230/.0924     LC 68-17590

**Niebuhr, Reinhold, 1892-1971.**                                                • **1.3292**
Leaves from the notebook of a tamed cynic / by Reinhold Niebuhr. — Hamden, Ct: Shoestring Press, 1956. xii, 198 p. 1. Clergy — Correspondence, reminiscences, etc. I. T.
BX4827N5 A25 1960

**Fackre, Gabriel J.**                                                           • **1.3293**
The promise of Reinhold Niebuhr, by Gabriel Fackre. — [1st ed.]. — Philadelphia: Lippincott, [1970] 101 p.; 21 cm. — (The Promise of theology) 1. Niebuhr, Reinhold, 1892-1971. I. T.
BX4827.N5 F3     230/.0924     LC 79-120329

**Kegley, Charles W. ed.**                                                       • **1.3294**
Reinhold Niebuhr: his religious, social, and political thought, edited by Charles W. Kegley and Robert W. Bretall. — New York, Macmillan, 1956. xiv, 486 p. port. 22 cm. — (The Library of living theology, v. 2) 1. Niebuhr, Reinhold, 1892-1971. I. Bretall, Robert Walter, 1913- joint ed. II. T.
BX4827.N5K4     922.473     LC 56-13522

**Niebuhr, Richard R.**                                                          • **1.3295**
Schleiermacher on Christ and religion: a new introduction. New York: Scribner, 1964. 267p.,bibl. 1. Schleiermacher, Friedrich Ernst Daniel. I. T.
BX4827S3 N5     230.4     LC 64-22393

**Tillich, Paul, 1886-1965.**                                                    • **1.3296**
On the boundary; an autobiographical sketch. — New York, Scribner [1966] 104 p. 22 cm. 'A revision, newly translated, of Part I of [the author's] The interpretation of history.' Bibliography: p. 102-104. 1. Theology — Addresses, essays, lectures. 2. Protestantism — Addresses, essays, lectures. I. T.
BX4827.T53A33     230.0924     LC 66-18546

**Kegley, Charles William, 1912-.**                                              • **1.3297**
The theology of Paul Tillich, edited by Charles W. Kegley & Robert W. Bretall. New York, Macmillan, 1952. 370 p. ill. (The Library of living theology; v. 1) 1. Tillich, Paul, 1886-1965. I. Bretall, Robert Walter, 1913- II. T. III. Series.
BX4827.T53K4     230     LC 52-13200

**Pauck, Wilhelm, 1901-.**                                                       **1.3298**
Paul Tillich, his life & thought / Wilhelm & Marion Pauck. 1st ed. — New York: Harper & Row, c1976. 340 p.: ill.; 22 cm. 1. Tillich, Paul, 1886-1965. 2. Theologians — United States — Biography. 3. Theologians — Germany — Biography. I. Pauck, Marion. joint author. II. T.
BX4827.T53 P28 1976     230/.092/4 B     LC 74-25709     ISBN 0060664746

# BX4837–4946 European Sects

**Petr z Mladenovic, d.1451.**                                                   • **1.3299**
John Hus at the Council of Constance / [Peter of Mladoňovice]; translated from the Latin and the Czech with notes and introd. by Matthew Spinka. — New York: Columbia University Press, c1965 [i.e. 1966]. xii, 327 p.; 24 cm. — (Records of civilization, sources and studies. no.73) Translation of Relatio de Magistri Joannis Hus causa. 1. Hus, Jan, 1369?-1415. 2. Council of Constance (1414-1418) I. Spinka, Matthew, 1890-1972. II. T. III. Series.
BX4917.P413     LC 65-11019

**Spinka, Matthew, 1890-1972.**      • **1.3300**
John Hus; a biography. — Princeton, N.J.: Princeton University Press, 1968. v, 344 p.: illus., maps.; 23 cm. 1. Hus, Jan, 1369?-1415. I. T.
BX4917.S69     284.3     *LC* 68-20880

**Spinka, Matthew, 1890-1972.**      • **1.3301**
John Hus and the Czech reform. — Hamden, Conn., Archon Books, 1966 [c1941] vii, 81 p. 22 cm. Bibliographical footnotes. 1. Hus, Jan, 1369?-1415. I. T.
BX4917.S7 1966     284.3     *LC* 66-18645

**Littell, Franklin Hamlin.**      • **1.3302**
The Anabaptist view of the church: a study in the origins of sectarian Protestantism / by Franklin Hamlin Littell. — 2d ed., rev. and enl. — Boston: Starr King Press, 1958. xviii, 229 p.; 21 cm. 1. Anabaptists 2. Church I. T.
BX4931.L5 1958     *LC* 58-6338

**Clasen, Claus Peter.**      **1.3303**
Anabaptism; a social history, 1525–1618: Switzerland, Austria, Moravia, South and Central Germany. — Ithaca: Cornell University Press, [1972] xviii, 523 p.: maps.; 24 cm. 1. Anabaptists — History. I. T.
BX4931.2.C57     284/.3     *LC* 78-37751     *ISBN* 080140696X

**Bender, Harold Stauffer, 1897-1962.**      **1.3304**
Conrad Grebel: c. 1498–1526, the founder of the Swiss Brethren sometimes called Anabaptists / by Harold S. Bender. — Scottdale, Pa.: Herald Press [1971, c1950] xvi, 326 p.: ill.; 23 cm. (Studies in Anabaptist and Mennonite history. 6) Originally published in 1950 as v. 1 of The life and letters of Conrad Grebel. 1. Grebel, Konrad, 1498?-1526. I. T. II. Series.
BX4946.G7 B42 1950

**Gritsch, Eric W.**      **1.3305**
Reformer without a church; the life and thought of Thomas Muentzer, 1488?–1525, by Eric W. Gritsch. — Philadelphia: Fortress Press, [1967] xiv, 214 p.: map, port.; 24 cm. 1. Münzer, Thomas, 1490 (ca.)-1525. I. T.
BX4946.M8 G7     284/.3 B     *LC* 67-20144

# BX5003–6093 ANGLICAN COMMUNION

**Soloway, R. A.**      **1.3306**
Prelates and people; ecclesiastical social thought in England, 1783–1852, by R. A. Soloway. — London: R. Routledge & K. Paul; Toronto: University of Toronto P., 1969. [7] 464 p.; 22 cm. — (Studies in social history) 1. Church of England — History 2. Church and social problems — Gt. Brit. 3. Gt. Brit. — Church history — 19th century. I. T.
BX5093.S6     261.8     *LC* 77-414213     *ISBN* 0710063318

**Chadwick, Owen. ed.**      • **1.3307**
The mind of the Oxford movement. — Stanford, Calif., Stanford University Press [c1960] 239 p. 23 cm. — (A Library of modern religious thought) 1. Oxford movement I. T.
BX5099.C45     283.42     *LC* 60-15256

**The English sermon: an anthology.**      **1.3308**
Cheadle: Carcanet Press, 1976. 3 v.; 22 cm. 1. Church of England — Sermons. 2. Sermons, English I. Seymour-Smith, Martin, 1928- II. Sisson, C. H. (Charles Hubert), 1914- III. Nye, Robert.
BX5133.A1 E53     BX5133A1 E53.     252/.03     *LC* 76-375017
*ISBN* 0856350931

**Donne, John, 1572-1631.**      • **1.3309**
Sermons / edited, with introductions and critical apparatus by George R. Potter and Evelyn M. Simpson. — Berkeley: University of California Press, 1962. 10 v.: facsims. 1. Church of England — Sermons. 2. Sermons, English I. Potter, George Reuben, 1895-1954. II. Simpson, Evelyn Mary Spearing, 1885-1963. III. T.
BX5133.D61 P68 1962     BX5133.D6 S42 1962.     252.03

**Brooks, Nicholas.**      **1.3310**
The early history of the Church of Canterbury: Christ Church from 597 to 1066 / Nicholas Brooks. — [Leicester, Leicestershire]: Leicester University Press; Atlantic Highlands, N.J.: Humanities Press, [North American distributors], 1984. xiv, 402 p.: ill.; 24 cm. (Studies in the early history of Britain.) 1. Canterbury Cathedral — History. 2. Canterbury (England) — History. 3. Canterbury (England) — Church history. 4. England — Church history — Anglo Saxon period, 449-1066 I. T. II. Series.
BX5195.C3 B76 1984     274.22/3402 19     *LC* 84-235058     *ISBN* 0718511824

**Hill, W. Speed, ed.**      **1.3311**
Studies in Richard Hooker; essays preliminary to an edition of his works. Edited by W. Speed Hill. Cleveland, Press of Case Western Reserve University,
1972. xiv, 363 p. 24 cm. 1. Hooker, Richard, 1553 or 4-1600. I. Hill, W. Speed (William Speed), 1935- ed. II. T.
BX5199.H813 S85     230/.3     *LC* 74-170151     *ISBN* 0829502203

**Josselin, Ralph, 1617-1683.**      **1.3312**
The diary of the Rev. Ralph Josselin 1616–1683 / edited by Alan Macfarlane. — London: Oxford University Press for the British Academy, 1976. xxvi, 727 p., [1] leaf of plates: ill.; 26 cm. — (Records of social and economic history. new ser., 3) 1. Josselin, Ralph, 1617-1683. 2. Church of England — Clergy — Biography. 3. Clergy — England — Essex — Biography. I. Macfarlane, Alan. II. T. III. Series.
HC251.B7 n.s., no. 3 BX5199.J66     309.1/41 s 283/.092/4 B     *LC* 76-379883     *ISBN* 0197259553

**Watts, Michael R.**      **1.3313**
The dissenters / by Michael R. Watts. — Oxford [Eng.]: Clarendon Press, 1978-. v.: ill.; 23 cm. Includes index. 1. Dissenters, Religious — England — History. 2. England — Church history I. T.
BX5203.2.W37     274.1     *LC* 77-30144     *ISBN* 0198224605

**Addison, James Thayer, 1887-.**      • **1.3314**
The Episcopal Church in the United States, 1789–1931. [Hamden, Conn.] Archon Books, 1969 [c1951] xii, 400 p. 23 cm. 1. Episcopal Church — History. I. T.
BX5880.A33 1969     283/.73     *LC* 69-15786     *ISBN* 0208007415

**Bridenbaugh, Carl.**      • **1.3315**
Mitre and sceptre; transatlantic faiths, ideas, personalities, and politics, 1689–1775. — New York: Oxford University Press, 1962. xiv, 354 p.: illus.; 24 cm. 1. Church of England — United States 2. Episcopacy I. T.
BX5881.B77     283.73     *LC* 62-16574

**Woolverton, John Frederick, 1926-.**      **1.3316**
Colonial Anglicanism in North America / by John Frederick Woolverton. — Detroit: Wayne State University Press, 1984. 331 p.; 24 cm. Includes indexes. 1. Church of England — United States — History — 17th century. 2. Church of England — United States — History — 18th century. 3. United States — Church history — Colonial period, ca. 1600-1775 I. T.
BX5881.W65 1984     283/.73 19     *LC* 83-27400     *ISBN* 0814317553

**Chorley, Edward Clowes, 1865-1949.**      • **1.3317**
Men and movements in the American Episcopal Church. Hamden, Conn., Archon Books, 1961 [c1946] ix, 501 p. 21 cm. (The Hale lectures) 1. Episcopal Church — Parties and movements 2. Episcopal Church — History. I. T.
BX5925.C5 1961     283.73     *LC* 61-4971

**Dean, David M.**      **1.3318**
Defender of the race: James Theodore Holly, Black nationalist and bishop / David M. Dean. — Boston, Ma.: Lambeth Press, c1979. 150 p.; 24 cm. Includes indexes. 1. Holly, James Theodore, 1829-1911. 2. Église Orthodox Apostolique Haitienne — Bishops — Biography. 3. Bishops — Haiti — Biography. I. T.
BX5999.5.Z8 H643     283/.092/4 B     *LC* 78-26913     *ISBN* 0931186021

# BX6196–6197 ARMINIANS

**Bangs, Carl, 1922-.**      **1.3319**
Arminius: a study in the Dutch Reformation / Carl Bangs. — 2nd ed. — Grand Rapids, Mich.: F. Asbury Press, c1985. 388 p.: ill.; 22 cm. Includes indexes. 1. Arminius, Jacobus, 1560-1609. 2. Reformed Church — Netherlands — Clergy — Biography. 3. Theologians — Netherlands — Biography. I. T.
BX6196.B28 1985     284/.9/0924 B 19     *LC* 85-6050     *ISBN* 0310294819

# BX6201–6495 BAPTISTS

**Harrison, Paul Mansfield.**      • **1.3320**
Authority and power in the free church tradition; a social case study of the American Baptist Convention. Princeton, N. J., Princeton University Press, 1959. 248 p. 23 cm. 'A major portion of this book was a dissertation presented for the degree of doctor of philosophy in Yale University.' Includes bibliography. 1. American Baptist Convention — Government. 2. Church polity I. T.
BX6207.A36H3     262.4     *LC* 59-11077

**McLoughlin, William Gerald.**      • **1.3321**
New England dissent, 1630–1833; the Baptists and the separation of church and state [by] William G. McLoughlin. — Cambridge, Mass.: Harvard University

Press, 1971. 2 v.; 25 cm. 1. Baptists — New England — History. 2. Dissenters, Religious — New England. 3. Church and state — New England I. T.
BX6239.M25     322/.1     *LC* 70-131464     *ISBN* 0674611756

**King, Martin Luther, Jr., 1929-1968.**     • **1.3322**
Strength to love. [1st ed.] New York, Harper & Row [1963] 146 p. 22 cm. 1. Baptists — Sermons. 2. Sermons, American I. T.
BX6452.K5     252.06     *LC* 63-12051

**Brumberg, Joan Jacobs.**     **1.3323**
Mission for life: the story of the family of Adoniram Judson, the dramatic events of the first American foreign mission, and the course of evangelical religion in the nineteenth century / Joan Jacobs Brumberg. — New York: Free Press, c1980. xvi, 302 p., [8] leaves of plates: ill.; 25 cm. Includes index. 1. Judson family 2. Baptists — United States — Biography. 3. Missions, American — History. 4. Evangelicalism — United States — History. I. T.
BX6493.B73     286/.1/0922     *LC* 79-54667     *ISBN* 0029051002

**McLoughlin, William Gerald.**     • **1.3324**
Isaac Backus and the American pietistic tradition [by] William G. McLoughlin. Edited by Oscar Handlin. — Boston: Little, Brown, [1967] xii, 252 p.; 20 cm. — (Library of American biography.) 1. Backus, Isaac, 1724-1806. I. T. II. Series.
BX6495.B32 M28     286/.0924 B     *LC* 67-19143

**Miller, Robert Moats.**     **1.3325**
Harry Emerson Fosdick: preacher, pastor, prophet / Robert Moats Miller. — New York: Oxford University Press, 1985. xvi, 608 p.; 24 cm. Includes index. 1. Fosdick, Harry Emerson, 1878-1969. 2. Baptists — United States — Clergy — Biography. I. T.
BX6495.F68 M54 1985     286/.1/0924 B 19     *LC* 84-7168     *ISBN* 0195035127

**Gilpin, W. Clark.**     **1.3326**
The millenarian piety of Roger Williams / W. Clark Gilpin. — Chicago: University of Chicago Press, 1979. viii, 214 p.; 23 cm. Includes index. 1. Williams, Roger, 1604?-1683. 2. Millennium — History of doctrines I. T.
BX6495.W55 G54     286/.1/0924     *LC* 78-20786

## BX6600 CATHOLIC APOSTOLIC CHURCH

**Omoyajowo, J. Akinyele.**     **1.3327**
Cherubim and Seraphim: the history of an African independent church / by J. Akinyele Omoyajowo. — New York: NOK Publishers International, c1982. xvi, 256 p.: ill.; 24 cm. Revision of thesis (Ph.D.)—Univerity of Ibadan, 1971. Includes index. 1. Cherubim and Seraphim (Society) 2. Nigeria — Church history. I. T.
BX6600.C373 O46 1982     289.9 19     *LC* 78-64624     *ISBN* 0883570688

## BX6901–6996 CHRISTIAN SCIENCE

**Eddy, Mary Baker, 1821-1910.**     • **1.3328**
Prose works other than science and health, with key to the scriptures / by Mary Baker Eddy. — Boston: Trustees under the will of Mary Baker G. Eddy, 1925. 13 v. in 1.; 17 cm. Each part has special t.p. and separate paging. 1. Boston. First Church of Christ, Scientist. 2. Christian Science I. T.
BX6941.A4 1925     289.5     *LC* 25-18131

**Eddy, Mary Baker, 1821-1910.**     • **1.3329**
Science and health with key to the Scriptures, by Mary Baker Eddy. Boston: Published by the Trustees under the will of Mary Baker G. Eddy, 1941. 5 p.;., vii-xii, 724 p., 1 l.; 36 1/2 cm. Half-title:...Subscription edition. 'Limited to one thousand copies for sale and twenty-six copies to be presented to the leading libraries of the world.' 1. Christian Science I. T.
BX6941.S4 1941     *LC* 42-51081

**Gottschalk, Stephen.**     **1.3330**
The emergence of Christian Science in American religious life. — Berkeley: University of California Press, [1973] xxix, 305 p.; 25 cm. 1. Christian Science — United States. I. T.
BX6943.G66     289.5/73     *LC* 72-85530     *ISBN* 0520023080

**Silberger, Julius.**     **1.3331**
Mary Baker Eddy, an interpretive biography of the founder of Christian Science / Julius Silberger, Jr. — 1st ed. — Boston: Little, Brown, c1980. x, 274 p.: ill.; 22 cm. Includes index. 1. Eddy, Mary Baker, 1821-1910. 2. Christian Scientists — United States — Biography. I. T.
BX6995.S513     289.5/092/4 B     *LC* 80-11098     *ISBN* 0316790907

## BX7101–7260 CONGREGATIONALISM

**Edwards, Jonathan, 1703-1758.**     • **1.3332**
[Works. 1957] The works of Jonathan Edwards / Perry Miller, general editor. — [New Haven: Yale University Press, 1957-< 1985 >. v. < 1-7 >: ill.; 24 cm. Each vol. has also special t.p. General editor, v. 3-< 6: > John E. Smith, v. 7— edited by Norman Pettit. 1. Congregational churches — Collected works. 2. Theology — Collected works — 18th century. I. Miller, Perry, 1905-1963. II. Smith, John Edwin. III. Pettit, Norman. IV. T.
BX7117.E3 1957     230/.58/0924 19     *LC* 57-2336     *ISBN* 0300022824

**Mather, Cotton, 1663-1728.**     • **1.3333**
Selections. Edited, with an introd. and notes, by Kenneth B. Murdock. — New York: Hafner Pub. Co., [1960, c1926] 377 p.; 21 cm. — (The Hafner library of classics, no. 20) American authors series. 1. Congregational churches — Collected works. 2. Theology — Collected works — 18th century. I. T.
BX7117.M25 1960     285.8081     *LC* 60-11056

**Sweet, William Warren, 1881-1959. ed.**     • **1.3334**
The Congregationalists, a collection of source materials, by William Warren Sweet. Chicago, Ill., The University of Chicago press [1939] xi, 435 p. front., ill. (maps) 22 cm. (His Religion on the American frontier, 1783-1850, v.3) 1. Congregational churches in the U. S. — History — Sources. 2. Congregational churches in the U. S. — History. 3. Frontier and pioneer life — United States. I. T.
BX7131.S9     *LC* 39-33291

**Beecher, Henry Ward, 1813-1887.**     • **1.3335**
Lectures and orations. Edited by Newell Dwight Hillis. — New York: AMS Press, [1970] 330 p.; 19 cm. Reprint of the 1913 ed. I. Hillis, Newell Dwight, 1858-1929. II. T.
BX7260.B3 A54 1970     081     *LC* 72-126662     *ISBN* 040400699X

**McLoughlin, William Gerald.**     • **1.3336**
The meaning of Henry Ward Beecher; an essay on the shifting values of mid–Victorian America, 1840–1870 [by] William G. McLoughlin. — [1st ed.]. — New York: Knopf, 1970. xiii, 275 p.; 22 cm. 1. Beecher, Henry Ward, 1813-1887. 2. U.S. — Religion — 19th century. 3. U.S. — Civilization — 19th century. I. T.
BX7260.B3 M33 1970     200     *LC* 77-111239     *ISBN* 039443563X

**Griffin, Edward M., 1937-.**     **1.3337**
Old Brick, Charles Chauncy of Boston, 1705–1787 / by Edward M. Griffin. — Minneapolis: University of Minnesota Press, c1980. x, 248 p.: port.; 24 cm. — (Minnesota monographs in the humanities; v. 11) 'The works of Charles Chauncy': p. 219-229. 1. Chauncy, Charles, 1705-1787. 2. Congregational churches — Clergy — Biography. 3. Clergy — Massachusetts — Biography. 4. Boston (Mass.) — Biography. I. T. II. Series.
BX7260.C527 G74     285.8/32/0924 B     *LC* 79-27203     *ISBN* 0816609071

**Aldridge, Alfred Owen, 1915-.**     • **1.3338**
Jonathan Edwards. — New York: Washington Square Press, [1964] 181 p.; 18 cm. — (The Great American thinkers series, W881) 1. Edwards, Jonathan, 1703-1758. I. T.
BX7260.E3 A59     922.573     *LC* 65-935

**Critical essays on Jonathan Edwards / [edited by] William J. Scheick.**     **1.3339**
Boston: G. K. Hall, c1980. xxv, 310 p.; 24 cm. — (Critical essays on American literature.) Includes bibliographical references and index. 1. Edwards, Jonathan, 1703-1758 — Addresses, essays, lectures. I. Scheick, William J. II. Series.
BX7260.E3 C67     285/.8/0924     *LC* 79-17053     *ISBN* 081618304X

**Miller, Perry, 1905-1963.**     • **1.3340**
Jonathan Edwards / Perry Miller. — New York: W. Sloane Associates, 1949. xv, 348 p.: port.; 22 cm. (The American men of letters series) 1. Edwards, Jonathan, 1703-1758. I. T.
BX7260.E3 M5 1949     285/.8/0924     *LC* 49-50164

**Winslow, Ola Elizabeth.**     • **1.3341**
Jonathan Edwards, 1703–1758; a biography. — New York: Octagon Books, 1973 [c1940] xii, 406 p.: illus.; 24 cm. Reprint of the ed. published by Macmillan. 1. Edwards, Jonathan, 1703-1758. I. T.
BX7260.E3 W5 1973     285/.8/0924 B     *LC* 73-9771

**Burg, B. R. (Barry Richard), 1938-.**     **1.3342**
Richard Mather of Dorchester / B. R. Burg. — [Lexington, Ky.]: University Press of Kentucky, c1976. xiii, 207 p.; 23 cm. Includes index. 1. Mather, Richard, 1596-1669. 2. Congregational churches — Clergy — Biography. 3. Clergy — Massachusetts — Biography. I. T.
BX7260.M368 B87     285/.8/0924 B     *LC* 75-41987     *ISBN* 0813113431

**Shepard, Thomas, 1605-1649.**     1.3343
God's plot; the paradoxes of Puritan piety; being The autobiography & journal of Thomas Shepard. Edited with an introd. by Michael McGiffert. — [Amherst]: University of Massachusetts Press, 1972. vii, 252 p.; 24 cm. — (The Commonwealth series [v. 1]) 1. Shepard, Thomas, 1605-1649. I. Shepard, Thomas, 1605-1649. The autobiography. 1972. II. Shepard, Thomas, 1605-1649. The journal. 1972. III. T.
BX7260.S53 A32     285/.9/0924 B     *LC* 71-181364

# BX7350 Father Divine

**Weisbrot, Robert.**     1.3344
Father Divine and the struggle for racial equality / Robert Weisbrot. — Urbana: University of Illinois Press, c1983. 241 p., [8] leaves of plates: ill.; 24 cm. (Blacks in the New World) Includes index. 1. Father Divine. 2. Afro-Americans — Civil rights 3. Race relations — Religious aspects — Catholic Church 4. United States — Race relations I. T.
BX7350.A4 W44 1983     299/.93 19     *LC* 82-2644     *ISBN* 0252009738

**Harris, Sara.**     1.3345
Father Divine, by Sara Harris, with the assistance of Harriet Crittendon [i.e.] Crittenden. — Newly rev. and expanded, and with an introd. by John Henrik Clarke. — New York: Collier Books, [1971] xxxiv, 377 p.; 19 cm. 1. Father Divine. I. Crittenden, Harriet, joint author. II. T.
BX7350.H37 1971     289.9 B     *LC* 78-146617

# BX7601–7795 Society of Friends

**Barbour, Hugh. comp.**     1.3346
Early Quaker writings, 1650–1700. Edited by Hugh Barbour and Arthur O. Roberts. Grand Rapids, Eerdmans [1973] 622 p. 24 cm. 1. Society of Friends — Collected works. I. Roberts, Arthur O. joint comp. II. T.
BX7615.B34     289.6/08     *LC* 72-93617     *ISBN* 080283423X

**Penn, William, 1644-1718.**     • 1.3347
The witness of William Penn. Edited with an introd. [by] Frederick B. Tolles and E. Gordon Alderfer. New York, Macmillan, 1957. xxx, 205 p. 22 cm. Selected passages from the author's works. 1. Society of Friends — Collected works. 2. Theology — Collected works — 18th century. I. Tolles, Frederick Barnes, 1915- ed. II. Alderfer, E. Gordon (Everett Gordon), 1915- ed. III. T.
BX7617.P5 A1 1957     *LC* 57-10894

**Tolles, Frederick Barnes, 1915-.**     • 1.3348
Quakers and the Atlantic culture. New York, Macmillan, 1960. 160 p. 22 cm. 1. Society of Friends — History. 2. Society of Friends — Influence. 3. United States — Civilization I. T.
BX7631.2.T6     *LC* 60-7085

**Frost, J. William (Jerry William)**     1.3349
The Quaker family in colonial America; a portrait of the Society of Friends [by] J. William Frost. New York, St. Martin's Press [1973] vi, 248 p. 25 cm. 1. Society of Friends. 2. Friends in the United States. 3. United States — Church history — Colonial period, ca. 1600-1775 I. T.
BX7636.F76     289.6/73     *LC* 72-95835

**Marietta, Jack D.**     1.3350
The reformation of American Quakerism, 1748–1783 / Jack D. Marietta. — Philadelphia: University of Pennsylvania Press, c1984. xvii, 356 p.: ill.; 24 cm. Includes index. 1. Society of Friends — United States — History — 18th century. 2. Society of Friends — Doctrines 3. United States — Church history — Colonial period, ca. 1600-1775 I. T.
BX7636.M37 1984     289.6/73 19     *LC* 83-23502     *ISBN* 0812279220

**Doherty, Robert W.**     • 1.3351
The Hicksite separation; a sociological analysis of religious schism in early nineteenth century America, by Robert W. Doherty. New Brunswick, N.J., Rutgers University Press [1967] vii, 157 p. map. 22 cm. 1. Society of Friends — History. I. T.
BX7637.D6     289.6/09     *LC* 67-13077

**Tolles, Frederick Barnes, 1915-.**     • 1.3352
Meeting house and counting house; the Quaker merchants of colonial Philadelphia, 1682–1763. Chapel Hill, Pub. for the Institute of Early American History and Culture at Williamsburg, Va., by the Univ. of North Carolina Press, 1948. xiv,292 p. ill.,ports. 25 cm. 1. Friends, Society of Philadelphia 2. Philadelphia (Pa.) — Industries — History I. T.
BX7649.P5T64     *LC* 49-49

**Quaker spirituality: selected writings / edited and introduced by**     1.3353
**Douglas V. Steere; preface by Elizabeth Gray Vining.**
New York: Paulist Press, c1984. xii, 334 p.; 24 cm. — (Classics of Western spirituality. 41) 1. Spirituality — Society of Friends — Addresses, essays, lectures. 2. Society of Friends — Doctrines — Addresses, essays, lectures. I. Steere, Douglas Van, 1901- II. Series.
BX7738.Q34 1984     248.4/896 19     *LC* 83-63537     *ISBN* 0809125102

**Jorns, Auguste.**     • 1.3354
[Studien über die Sozialpolitik der Quäker. English] The Quakers as pioneers in social work. Translated by Thomas Kite Brown, Jr. Montclair, N.J., Patterson Smith, 1969. 269 p. 22 cm. (Patterson Smith reprint series in criminology, law enforcement, and social problems. Publication no. 27) Translation of Studien über die Sozialpolitik der Quäker. Reprint of the 1931 edition. 1. Society of Friends. I. T.
BX7747.J65 1969b     289.6     *LC* 69-14934     *ISBN* 0875850278

**Fox, George, 1624-1691.**     • 1.3355
The journal of George Fox. Edited from the MSS. by Norman Penney, with an introd. by T. Edmund Harvey. Cambridge University Press 1911. 2 v.: ports., facsims.; 24 cm. — I. Penney, Norman, 1858-, ed. II. T.
BX7795 F7 A25 1911     *LC* 12-4945

**Woolman, John, 1720-1772.**     • 1.3356
The journal and major essays of John Woolman. Edited by Phillips P. Moulton. — New York: Oxford University Press, 1971. xviii, 336 p.; 24 cm. — (A Library of Protestant thought) 1. Woolman, John, 1720-1772. 2. Slavery in the United States — Controversial literature. 3. Poor I. T. II. Series.
BX7795.W7 A3 1971b     289.6/0924 B     *LC* 71-171970

# BX7990–8080 German Reformed Church. Lutheran Churches

**Dieter, Melvin Easterday.**     1.3357
The holiness revival of the nineteenth century / by Melvin Easterday Dieter. — Metuchen, N.J.: Scarecrow Press, 1980. x, 356 p.; 22 cm. — (Studies in evangelicalism; no. 1) Includes index. 1. Holiness churches — United States — History — 19th century. 2. Holiness churches — Europe — History — 19th century. 3. Revivals — United States — History — 19th century. 4. Revivals — Europe — History — 19th century. 5. United States — Church history — 19th century 6. Europe — Church history — 19th century I. T.
BX7990.H6 D53     269/.24/0973     *LC* 80-17259     *ISBN* 0810813289

**Jones, Charles Edwin, 1932-.**     1.3358
Perfectionist persuasion: the holiness movement and American Methodism, 1867–1936. Metuchen, N.J., Scarecrow Press, 1974. xx, 242 p. illus. 22 cm. (ATLA monograph series, no. 5) 1. Holiness churches — United States. I. T.
BX7990.H6 J66     287/.6     *LC* 74-13766     *ISBN* 0810807475

**The Lutherans in North America / edited by E. Clifford Nelson,**     1.3359
**in collaboration with Theodore G. Tappert ... [et al.].**
Philadelphia: Fortress Press, c1975. xi, 541 p.: ill.; 26 cm. 1. Lutheran Church — North America. 2. Lutherans — North America I. Nelson, E. Clifford, 1911-
BX8041.L87     284/.173     *LC* 74-26337     *ISBN* 0800604091

**Tappert, Theodore Gerhardt, 1904- comp.**     1.3360
Lutheran confessional theology in America, 1840–1880. Edited by Theodore G. Tappert. New York, Oxford University Press, 1972. viii, 364 p. 24 cm. (A Library of Protestant thought) 1. Lutheran Church — Collected works. 2. Theology — Collected works — 19th century. I. T. II. Series.
BX8065.T33     230/.4/173     *LC* 72-81463

**Gritsch, Eric W.**     1.3361
Lutheranism: the theological movement and its confessional writings / Eric W. Gritsch and Robert W. Jenson. — Philadelphia: Fortress Press, c1976. x, 214 p.; 24 cm. Includes index. 1. Lutheran Church — Doctrines — History. I. Jenson, Robert W. joint author. II. T.
BX8065.2.G74     230/.4/1     *LC* 76-7869     *ISBN* 080060458X

**Lindberg, Carter, 1937-.**     1.3362
The third reformation: charismatic movements and the Lutheran tradition / by Carter Lindberg. — Macon, Ga.: Mercer University Press, c1983. ix, 345 p.; 24 cm. Includes index. 1. Lutheran Church — Doctrines 2. Pentecostalism — Lutheran Church. I. T.
BX8065.5.L56 1983     284.1/09 19     *LC* 83-11371     *ISBN* 0865540756

**Konkordienbuch.**     • 1.3363
The Book of Concord: the confessions of the Evangelical Lutheran Church / translated and edited by Theodore G. Tappert in collaboration with Jaroslav Pelikan, Robert H. Fisher, Arthur C. Piepkorn. — Philadelphia: Mühlenberg

Press, [1959] vii, 717 p.; 23 cm. Includes index. 1. Lutheran Church —
Catechisms and creeds I. Tappert, Theodore Gerhardt, 1904- II. T.
BX8068.A3 1959a     *LC* 59-11369     *ISBN* 0800608259

**Confessing one faith: a joint commentary on the Augsburg**     **1.3364**
**Confession by Lutheran and Catholic theologians / edited by**
**George Wolfgang Forell and James F. McCue, in cooperation**
**with Wenzel Lohff ... [et al.].**
Minneapolis: Augsburg Pub. House, c1982. 344 p.; 22 cm. 1. Confessio
Augustana — Addresses, essays, lectures. I. Forell, George Wolfgang.
II. McCue, James F.
BX8069.C64 1982     238/.41 19     *LC* 80-65557     *ISBN* 0806618027

**The Place of Bonhoeffer: problems and possibilities in his**     • **1.3365**
**thought / edited and introduced by Martin E. Marty, with Peter**
**Berger ... [et al.].**
New York: Association Press, 1962. 224 p.; 21 cm. 1. Bonhoeffer, Dietrich,
1906-1945. I. Marty, Martin E., 1928-
BX8080.B645.M3     193     *LC* 62-16875

# BX8101–8143 MENNONITES

**Sawatzky, Harry Leonard, 1931-.**     **1.3366**
They sought a country; Mennonite colonization in Mexico. With an appendix
on Mennonite colonization in British Honduras. — Berkeley: University of
California, 1971. xi, 387 p.: illus., maps.; 24 cm. 1. Mennonites — Mexico
2. Mennonites — Belize I. T.
BX8128.C6 S29     301.45/28/87072     *LC* 78-92673     *ISBN*
0520017048

**Hostetler, John Andrew, 1918-.**     • **1.3367**
Amish society. Baltimore, Johns Hopkins Press [1963] 347 p. 1. Mennonites —
Social life and customs. 2. Mennonites — United States I. T.
BX8129.A6H6     *LC* 63-19553

**Zablocki, Benjamin David, 1941-.**     **1.3368**
The joyful community: an account of the Bruderhof, a communal movement
now in its third generation / Benjamin David Zablocki. — Phoenix ed. —
Chicago: University of Chicago Press, 1980. 362 p.; 18 cm. (A Phoenix book.)
Includes index. 1. Hutterian Society of Brothers (Rifton, N.Y.) I. T.
BX8129.B64 Z3 1980     301.45/28/87     *LC* 79-24992     *ISBN*
0226977498

**Hostetler, John Andrew, 1918-.**     **1.3369**
Hutterite society [by] John A. Hostetler. — Baltimore: Johns Hopkins
University Press, [1974] xvi, 403 p.: illus.; 24 cm. 1. Hutterite Brethren.
2. Collective settlements I. T.
BX8129.H8 H63     289.7/73     *LC* 74-6827     *ISBN* 0801815843

# BX8201–8495 METHODISTS

**Norwood, Frederick Abbott.**     **1.3370**
The story of American Methodism; a history of the United Methodists and their
relations [by] Frederick A. Norwood. — Nashville: Abingdon Press, [1974]
448 p.; 23 cm. 1. Methodist Church in the United States. I. T.
BX8235.N65     287/.673     *LC* 74-10621     *ISBN* 0687396409

**Baker, Frank, 1910-.**     **1.3371**
From Wesley to Asbury: studies in early American Methodism / by Frank
Baker. — Durham, N.C.: Duke University Press, 1976. xiv, 223 p.; 25 cm.
Includes index. 1. Wesley, John, 1703-1791. 2. Asbury, Francis, 1745-1816.
3. Methodist Church in the United States. I. T.
BX8236.B34     287/.0973     *LC* 75-39454     *ISBN* 0822303590

**Richardson, Harry Van Buren.**     **1.3372**
Dark salvation: the story of Methodism as it developed among Blacks in
America / Harry V. Richardson. — 1st ed. — Garden City, N.Y.: Anchor
Press, 1976. viii, 324 p.; 22 cm. — (C. Eric Lincoln series on Black religion)
1. Afro-American Methodists 2. Methodist Church in the United States. I. T.
II. Series.
BX8435.R5     287/.8/09     *LC* 76-3009     *ISBN* 0385002459

**Walker, Clarence Earl.**     **1.3373**
A rock in a weary land: the African Methodist Episcopal Church during the
Civil War and Reconstruction / Clarence E. Walker. — Baton Rouge:
Louisiana State University Press, c1982. 157 p.; 24 cm. Revision of thesis (Ph.
D.)—University of California, Berkeley, 1976. Includes index. 1. African
Methodist Episcopal Church — History. I. T.
BX8443.W27 1982     287/.83 19     *LC* 81-11731     *ISBN* 0807108839

**Johnson, Charles Albert, 1916-.**     • **1.3374**
The frontier camp meeting: religion's harvest time / Charles A. Johnson; with a
new introduction by Ferenc M. Szasc. — Dallas: Southern Methodist
University Pr., 1985. xxi, 325 p.: ill., ports. 1. Methodism — History 2. Camp-
meetings I. T.
BX8475.J64 1985     *LC* 55-8783     *ISBN* 0870742019

**Garrettson, Freeborn, 1752-1827.**     **1.3375**
American Methodist pioneer: the life and journals of the Rev. Freeborn
Garrettson, 1752–1827: social and religious life in the U.S. during the
revolutionary and federal periods / introductory biographical essay and notes
by Robert Drew Simpson, editor. — Rutland, Vt.: Published under the
sponsorship of Drew University Library, Madison, N.J. by Academy Books,
c1984. ix, 433 p.: ill.; 24 cm. Includes index. 1. Garrettson, Freeborn,
1752-1827. 2. Methodist Church (U.S.) — Clergy — Biography. I. Simpson,
Robert Drew. II. Drew University. Library. III. T.
BX8495.G3 A34 1984     287/.632/0924 B 19     *LC* 83-72532     *ISBN*
0914960490

**Schmidt, Martin, 1909-.**     • **1.3376**
John Wesley: a theological biography. Translated by Norman P. Goldhawk. —
New York, Abingdon Press [1963, c1962-. v. 23 cm. Includes bibliography.
1. Wesley, John, 1703-1791. I. T.
BX8495.W5S283     922.742     *LC* 63-3396

# BX8525–8530 MILLENIAL DAWNISTS.
## JEHOVAH'S WITNESSES

**Penton, M. James, 1932-.**     **1.3377**
Apocalypse delayed: the story of Jehovah's Witnesses / M. James Penton. —
Toronto; Buffalo: University of Toronto Press, c1985. xvii, 400 p., [10] p. of
plates: ill.; 24 cm. Includes index. 1. Jehovah's Witnesses I. T.
BX8526.P46 1985     289.9/2 19     *LC* 85-244517     *ISBN* 0802025404

# BX8601–8695 MORMONS

**Shipps, Jan, 1929-.**     **1.3378**
Mormonism: the story of a new religious tradition / Jan Shipps. — Urbana:
University of Illinois Press, c1985. xviii, 211 p.; 24 cm. Includes index.
1. Mormon Church — History — Addresses, essays, lectures. 2. Church of
Jesus Christ of Latter-Day Saints — History — Addresses, essays, lectures.
I. T.
BX8611.S49 1985     289.3 19     *LC* 84-2672     *ISBN* 0252011597

**Book of Mormon.**     • **1.3379**
The Book of Mormon; an account written by the hand of Mormon upon plates
taken from the plates of Nephi. Translated by Joseph Smith, Jr. — Salt Lake
City: Church of Jesus Christ of Latter-Day Saints, 1964 [c1963] 558 p.; 18 cm.
I. Smith, Joseph, 1805-1844. II. Church of Jesus Christ of Latter-Day Saints.
III. T.
BX8623 1964     289.3/22     *LC* 72-8846

**Doctrine and covenants.**     • **1.3380**
The doctrine and covenants, of the Church of Jesus Christ of Latter-Day
Saints, containing the revelations given to Joseph Smith, Jun., the prophet, for
the building up of the Kingdom of God in the last days. Divided into verses,
with references, by Orson Pratt, Sen. Westport, Conn., Greenwood Press [1971]
503 p. 23 cm. Reprint of the 1880 ed. 1. Mormon Church — Doctrinal and
controversial works. I. Smith, Joseph, 1805-1844. II. Pratt, Orson, 1811-1881.
III. Church of Jesus Christ of Latter-Day Saints. IV. T.
BX8628.A3 1971b     289.3/2     *LC* 69-14082     *ISBN* 083714101X

**Smith, Joseph, 1805-1844.**     • **1.3381**
The pearl of great price: a selection from the revelations, translations, and
narrations of Joseph Smith, first prophet, seer, and revelator to the Church of
Jesus Christ of Latter–day saints. — Salt Lake City, Utah: The Church of Jesus
Christ of Latter-day Saints, 1939, c1921. iv, 63 p.: ill. 1. Mormons and
Mormonism — Doctrinal and controversial works I. T.
BX8629.P52 1939

**Hansen, Klaus J.**     **1.3382**
Mormonism and the American experience / Klaus J. Hansen. — Chicago:
University of Chicago Press, c1981. xviii, 257 p.; 21 cm. — (Chicago history of
American religion) Includes index. 1. Mormons and Mormonism.
2. Mormons and Mormonism in the United States. I. T.
BX8635.2.H36     289.3/73 19     *LC* 80-19312     *ISBN* 0226315525

**Bushman, Richard L.**     **1.3383**
Joseph Smith and the beginnings of Mormonism / Richard L. Bushman. —
Urbana: University of Illinois Press, c1984. 262 p.; 24 cm. Includes index.

1. Smith, Joseph, 1805-1844. 2. Mormon Church — History — 19th century. I. T.
BX8695.S6 B87 1984      289.3/09/034 19      *LC* 84-2451      *ISBN* 0252011430

**Arrington, Leonard J.**            **1.3384**
Brigham Young: American Moses / Leonard J. Arrington. — 1st ed. — New York: Knopf: Distributed by Random House, 1985. xvii, 522, [16] p. of plates: ill.; 25 cm. Errata slip inserted. Includes index. 1. Young, Brigham, 1801-1877. 2. Mormon Church — Presidents — Biography. 3. Church of Jesus Christ of Latter-Day Saints — Presidents — Biography. I. T.
BX8695.Y7 A85 1985      289.3/32/0924 B 19      *LC* 84-48650      *ISBN* 0394510224

## BX8701–8749 New Jerusalem Church. Swedenborgianism

**Swedenborg, Emanuel, 1688-1772.**            **1.3385**
[Arcana coelestia. English. Selections] The universal human and Soul–body interaction / Emanuel Swedenborg; edited and translated by George F. Dole; introduction by Stephen Larsen; preface by Robert H. Kirven. — New York: Paulist Press, c1984. xvi, 267 p.; 23 cm. (Classics of Western spirituality.) The material presented under the title The universal human has been translated and extracted from Swedenborg's Arcana coelestia; Soul-body interaction is the complete translation of his De commercio animae et corporis. Includes indexes. 1. New Jerusalem Church — Doctrines 2. Body, Human — Religious aspects I. Dole, George F. II. Swedenborg, Emanuel, 1688-1772. De commercio animae et corporis. English. III. T. IV. Series.
BX8712.A8 Z73 1984      230/.94 19      *LC* 84-60734      *ISBN* 0809125544

## BX8762–8795 Pentecostal Churches

**Hollenweger, Walter J., 1927-.**            **1.3386**
[Enthusiastisches Christentum. English] The Pentecostals; the charismatic movement in the churches [by] W. J. Hollenweger. [Translated by R. A. Wilson with revisions by the author. 1st U.S. ed.] Minneapolis, Augsburg Pub. House [1972] xx, 572 p. illus. 25 cm. Translation of Enthusiastisches Christentum. 1. Pentecostalism I. T.
BX8763.H613      289.9      *LC* 70-176103      *ISBN* 080661210X

**Nichol, John Thomas.**            • **1.3387**
Pentecostalism. — [1st ed.]. — New York: Harper & Row, [1966] xv, 264 p.; 22 cm. 'Much of this material was originally submitted to satisfy the doctoral requirements at the Boston University Graduate School.' 1. Pentecostal churches 2. Pentecostalism I. T.
BX8763.N5      289.9      *LC* 66-20782

**Paris, Arthur E., 1945-.**            **1.3388**
Black Pentecostalism: Southern religion in an urban world / Arthur E. Paris. — Amherst: University of Massachusetts Press, 1982. vii, 183 p.; 23 cm. Includes index. 1. Mt. Calvary Holy Church of America (Boston, Mass.) 2. Afro-Americans — Massachusetts — Boston — Religion. 3. Boston (Mass.) — Church history. I. T.
BX8770.A4 P37 1982      289.9 19      *LC* 81-16169      *ISBN* 087023353X

**Bloch-Hoell, Nils.**            **1.3389**
The Pentecostal movement; its origin, development, and distinctive character. — [Oslo] Universitetforlaget [c1964] 255 p. 24 cm. — (Scandinavian university books) Label on t.p.: Humanities Press, New York. Bibliography: p. 239-[249] 1. Pentecostal churches — Norway. I. T.
BX8795.P25B553      289.9      *LC* 65-3204

## BX8901–9225 Presbyterians

**Trinterud, Leonard J., 1904-.**            • **1.3390**
The forming of an American tradition: a re–examination of colonial Presbyterianism / Leonard J. Trinterud. — Philadelphia: Westminster Press, c1949. 352 p. 1. Presbyterian Church in the United States (General) — History I. T.
BX8936.T7      *LC* 49-4887

**Thompson, Ernest Trice, 1894-.**            **1.3391**
Presbyterians in the South. Richmond, John Knox Press [1963-73] 3 v. map (on lining papers) 24 cm. (v. 2-3: Presbyterian Historical Society. Publication series,

13) 1. Presbyterian Church in the Southern States. 2. Presbyterian Church in the U.S — History. I. T.
BX8941.T5      *LC* 63-19121      *ISBN* 0804209979

**Makey, Walter.**            **1.3392**
The Church of the Covenant, 1637–1651: revolution and social change in Scotland / Walter Makey. — Edinburgh: John Donald Publishers, 1979. vii, 216 p.; 24 cm. Includes index. 1. Church of Scotland — History. 2. Church and state — Scotland — History. 3. Scotland — Church history — 17th century. I. T.
BX9071.M28      285/.2/411      *LC* 79-314845      *ISBN* 0859760359

**Ridley, Jasper Godwin.**            • **1.3393**
John Knox [by] Jasper Ridley. — New York: Oxford University Press, [1968] vi, 596 p.: ports.; 22 cm. 1. Knox, John, 1505-1572. I. T.
BX9223.R5      285/.2/0924 B      *LC* 68-55648

**Pilcher, George William.**            • **1.3394**
Samuel Davies; apostle of dissent in colonial Virginia. — [1st ed.] — Knoxville: University of Tennessee Press, [1971] xi, 229 p.: map, port.; 24 cm. 1. Davies, Samuel, 1723-1761. I. T.
BX9225.D33 P55      285/.1/0924 B      *LC* 77-134737      *ISBN* 0870491210

**Dallimore, Arnold A.**            • **1.3395**
George Whitefield; the life and times of the great evangelist of the eighteenth–century revival [by] Arnold A. Dallimore. — [London]: Banner of Truth Trust, [1970-. v. : illus., ports.; 23 cm. 1. Whitefield, George, 1714-1770. 2. Presbyterian Church — Clergy — Biography. 3. Clergy — Great Britain — Biography. I. T.
BX9225.W4 D34      285/.2/0924 B      *LC* 70-515723

## BX9301–9359 Puritans

**Schneider, Herbert Wallace, 1892-.**            • **1.3396**
The Puritan mind. — [Ann Arbor]: University of Michigan Press, [1958] 267 p.; 21 cm. — (Ann Arbor paperbacks, AA21) 1. Puritans 2. New England — Church history. I. T.
BX9321.S4 1958      285.9      *LC* 58-14941

**Simpson, Alan.**            • **1.3397**
Puritanism in old and New England. — [Chicago] University of Chicago Press [1955] 125 p. 22 cm. — (Charles R. Walgreen Foundation lectures) 1. Puritans I. T.
BX9321.S55      285.9      *LC* 55-13637

**Morgan, Edmund Sears.**            • **1.3398**
Visible saints; the history of a Puritan idea. — [New York] New York University Press, 1963. 159 p. 22 cm. 1. Puritans 2. Church — History of doctrines I. T.
BX9322.M6      285.9      *LC* 63-9999

**Pope, Robert G.**            • **1.3399**
The half-way covenant; church membership in Puritan New England, by Robert G. Pope. — Princeton, N.J.: Princeton University Press, 1969. xi, 321 p.; 21 cm. 1. Church membership 2. Covenants (Church polity) 3. Puritans — New England. I. T.
BX9353.P6      254/.5/0974      *LC* 69-18067      *ISBN* 069107156X

## BX9401–9595 Reformed Church. Calvinism

**Graham, W. Fred, 1930-.**            • **1.3400**
The constructive revolutionary; John Calvin & his socio–economic impact, by W. Fred Graham. Richmond, John Knox Press [1971] 251 p. port. 21 cm. 1. Calvin, Jean, 1509-1564 — Contributions in sociology. I. T.
BX9418.G7      261.8      *LC* 72-107321      *ISBN* 0804208808

**Niesel, Wilhelm.**            • **1.3401**
The theology of Calvin. Translated by Harold Knight. — Philadelphia, Westminster Press [1956] 254 p. 23 cm. 1. Calvin, Jean, 1509-1564 — Theology. I. T.
BX9418.N53      230.42      *LC* 56-8047

**Parker, T. H. L. (Thomas Henry Louis)**            **1.3402**
John Calvin: a biography / by T. H. L. Parker. — Philadelphia: Westminster Press, c1975. xviii, 190 p., [5] leaves of plates: ill.; 24 cm. Includes indexes. 1. Calvin, Jean, 1509-1564. I. T.
BX9418.P344      230/.4/20924 B      *LC* 75-33302      *ISBN* 066420810X

**Wendel, François.**       **1.3403**
[Calvin] Calvin: the origins and development of his religious thought. — London: Collins, 1963. 383 p.: ill.; 22 cm. 1. Calvin, Jean, 1509-1564. I. T. BX9418.W3833 1963a    *LC* 63-5919

**Calvin, Jean, 1509-1564.**      ● **1.3404**
[Institutio Christianae religionis English] Institutes of the Christian religion. Edited by John T. McNeill. Translated by Ford Lewis Battles, in collaboration with the editor and a committee of advisers. Philadelphia, Westminster Press [c1960] 2 v. (lxxi, 1734 p.) 24 cm. (The Library of Christian classics, v. 20-21) 1. Reformed Church — Doctrines 2. Theology, Doctrinal I. T. II. Series. BX9420.I65 1960    230.42    *LC* 60-5379

**Calvin, Jean, 1509-1564.**      ● **1.3405**
Theological treatises. Translated with introductions and notes by J. K. S. Reid. Philadelphia, Westminster Press [1954] 355 p. 24 cm. (The Library of Christian classics, v. 22) 1. Reformed Church — Collected works. 2. Theology — Collected works — 16th century. I. T. BX9420.T68    284.2    *LC* 54-9956

**McNeill, John Thomas, 1885-.**      ● **1.3406**
The history and character of Calvinism. New York, Oxford University Press, 1954. x, 466 p. 22 cm. 1. Calvinism I. T. BX9422.M32    284.2    *LC* 54-6911

**Gerrish, B. A. (Brian Albert), 1931-.**      **1.3407**
Tradition and the modern world: reformed theology in the nineteenth century / B. A. Gerrish. — Chicago: University of Chicago Press, c1978. xii, 263 p.; 24 cm. — (The Andrew C. Zenos memorial lectures; 1977) Includes index. 1. Reformed Church — Doctrines — History — 18th century — Addresses, essays, lectures. 2. Theology, Doctrinal — History — 19th century — Addresses, essays, lectures. I. T. II. Series. BX9422.2.G47    230    *LC* 78-4982    *ISBN* 0226288668

**Kingdon, Robert McCune, 1927-.**      ● **1.3408**
Geneva and the consolidation of the French Protestant movement, 1564–1572; a contribution to the history of Congregationalism, Presbyterianism, and Calvinist resistance theory [by] Robert M. Kingdon. Madison, University of Wisconsin Press, 1967. 241 p. facsims. 25 cm. 1. Bèze, Théodore de, 1519-1605. 2. Huguenots — France 3. France — Church history — 16th century I. T. BX9454.2.K5    284/.5    *LC* 67-24373

## BX9701–9743 SALVATION ARMY

**McKinley, Edward H.**      **1.3409**
Marching to glory: the history of the Salvation Army in the United States of America, 1880–1980 / Edward H. McKinley. — 1st ed. — San Francisco: Harper & Row, c1980. xviii, 286 p., [4] leaves of plates: ill.; 21 cm. 1. Salvation Army — United States — History. I. T. BX9716.M32 1980    267/.15/0973    *LC* 79-2997    *ISBN* 0060655380

## BX9750 SEGYE KIDOKKYO T'ONGIL SILLYONG HYOPHOE (SUN MYUNG MOON). UNIFICATION CHURCH

**Bromley, David G.**      **1.3410**
Moonies in America: cult, church, and crusade / David G. Bromley and Anson D. Shupe, Jr.; foreword by John Lofland. — Beverly Hills: Sage Publications, c1979. 269 p.; 23 cm. (Sage library of social research; v. 92) Includes index. 1. Moon, Sun Myung. 2. Unification Church. I. Shupe, Anson D. joint author. II. T. BX9750.S4 B76    301.5/8    *LC* 79-16456    *ISBN* 0803910606

## BX9751–9793 SHAKERS

**Morse, Flo.**      **1.3411**
The Shakers and the world's people / by Flo Morse. — New York: Dodd, Mead, c1980. xxii, 378 p.; 24 cm. Includes index. 1. Shakers — Collected works. I. T. BX9759.M67    289/.8/0973    *LC* 79-27271    *ISBN* 0396078095

**Andrews, Edward Deming.**      ● **1.3412**
The people called Shakers: a search for the perfect society / by Edward Deming Andrews. — New enl. ed. — New York: Dover Publications, 1963. xvi, 351 p.: ill., facsims.; 22 cm. Includes index. 1. Shakers — History. I. T. BX9765.A6 1963    *LC* 63-17896    *ISBN* 0486210812

## BX9801–9869 UNITARIANISM. UNIVERSALISM

**Channing, William Ellery, 1780-1842.**      **1.3413**
The works of William E. Channing. New York, B. Franklin [1970] iv, 931 p. 24 cm. (Burt Franklin research & source works series 626. American classics in history and social science 163) Reprint of the 1882 ed. 1. Unitarian Universalist churches — Collected works. 2. Theology — Collected works — 19th century. I. T. BX9815.C4 1970    201/.1    *LC* 70-114815    *ISBN* 083370530X

**Parker, Theodore, 1810-1860.**      ● **1.3414**
An anthology. Edited, with an introd. and notes, by Henry Steele Commager. Boston, Beacon Press [1960] 391 p. 22 cm. 1. Unitarian Universalist churches — Collected works. 2. Theology — Collected works — 19th century. I. Commager, Henry Steele, ed. II. T. BX9815.P32 1960    *LC* 60-14677

**Robinson, David, 1947-.**      **1.3415**
The Unitarians and the universalists / David Robinson. — Westport, Conn.: Greenwood Press, 1985. xiii, 368 p.; 24 cm. (Denominations in America. 0193-6883; no. 1) 1. Unitarianism — United States — History. 2. Universalists — United States — History. 3. Liberalism (Religion) — United States — History. I. T. II. Series. BX9833.R63 1985    288/.73 19    *LC* 84-9031    *ISBN* 0313209464

**Wright, Conrad.**      ● **1.3416**
The beginnings of Unitarianism in America. Boston, Starr King Press; distributed by Beacon Press [1955] 305 p. maps. 22 cm. 'Biographical appendix': p. [281]-291. 'Bibliographical note': p. [292]-294. 1. Unitarianism — United States I. T. BX9833.W7    288.73    *LC* 55-8138

**Mendelsohn, Jack, 1918-.**      ● **1.3417**
Channing, the reluctant radical; a biography. — [1st ed.]. — Boston: Little, Brown, [1971] 308 p.: illus.; 22 cm. 1. Channing, William Ellery, 1780-1842. 2. Unitarians — Clergy — Biography. 3. Clergy — United States — Biography. I. Channing, William Ellery, 1780-1842. II. T. BX9869.C4 M45 1971    288/.0924 B    *LC* 75-161863

**Albrecht, Robert C.**      ● **1.3418**
Theodore Parker by Robert C. Albrecht. — New York: Twayne Publishers, [1971] 160 p.; 21 cm. — (Twayne's United States authors series, 179) 1. Parker, Theodore, 1810-1860. I. T. BX9869.P3 A43    288/.0924 B    *LC* 76-120521

**Dirks, John Edward, 1919-.**      ● **1.3419**
The critical theology of Theodore Parker. — Westport, Conn.: Greenwood Press, [1970, c1948] viii, 173 p.: port.; 23 cm. — (Columbia studies in American culture, no. 19) 1. Parker, Theodore, 1810-1860. I. T. II. Series. BX9869.P3 D5 1970    230.8    *LC* 70-100156    *ISBN* 0837136822

**Bainton, Roland Herbert, 1894-.**      ● **1.3420**
Hunted heretic; the life and death of Michael Servetus, 1511-1553. With a new foreword by the author. Boston, Beacon Press [1960] 270 p. illus. 21 cm. (Beacon series in liberal religion, LR2) Includes bibliography. 1. Servet, Miguel, 1511-1553. I. T. BX9869.S4B3 1960    922.8146    *LC* 60-16079

**Miller, Russell E.**      **1.3421**
The larger hope: the first century of the Universalist Church in America, 1770–1870 / Russell E. Miller. — Boston: Unitarian Universalist Association, c1979. xxviii, 1009 p.: ill.; 24 cm. Includes index. 1. Universalist Church of America — History. 2. Universalism — History. I. T. BX9933.M54    289.1/73    *LC* 79-13789    093340004

# M  Music

**The Norton scores: an anthology for listening / edited by Roger**                    **1.3422**
**Kamien.**
4th ed. expanded. — New York: W.W. Norton, 1984. Score (2 v.); 22 cm.
1. Music — Analysis, appreciation 2. Music appreciation — Music collections
I. Kamien, Roger.
M1.N7x     780/.8     *LC* 83-19428     *ISBN* 0393953041

**Norton anthology of western music: in two volumes / edited by**                    **1.3423**
**Claude V. Palisca.**
1st ed. — New York: Norton, c1980. 2 v. Includes indexes. 1. Vocal music
2. Instrumental music I. Palisca, Claude Victor
M1 N825     M1 N73.     *LC* 80-11916     *ISBN* 039395143X

**Scores: an anthology of new music / selection and commentary**                    **1.3424**
**by Roger Johnson.**
New York: Schirmer Books, c1981. — xvi, 351 p. of music; 23 x 28 cm. Includes
index. 'Recent musical compositions selected for their interest, artistic quality,
and accessibility to performance ... all readily performable by a wide range of
people - musicians and nonmusicians both.' 'Selected bibliography': p. 347-348.
1. Chance compositions 2. Vocal music — Scores. 3. Instrumental music —
Scores. 4. Electronic music I. Johnson, Roger Orville II. Title: An anthology
of new music.
M1.S36     *LC* 80-53302/M     *ISBN* 0028711904

**Davison, Archibald T. (Archibald Thompson), 1883-1961. ed.**     • **1.3425**
Historical anthology of music, by Archibald T. Davison and Willi Apel. — Rev.
ed. — Cambridge: Harvard University Press, 1949-. v.     ; 32 cm.
1. Instrumental music I. Apel, Willi, 1893- joint ed. II. T.
M2.D25 H6     *LC* 49-4539

**Marrocco, W. Thomas (William Thomas), 1909- ed.**                    **1.3426**
Music in America: an anthology from the landing of the Pilgrims to the close of
the Civil War, 1620–1865 Compiled and edited with historical and analytical
notes, by W. Thomas Marrocco and Harold Gleason. — New York: Norton,
[1964] 371 p.: facsims.; 28 cm. 'Biographical notes': p. 355-361.
1. Instrumental music 2. Instrumental music — To 1800. 3. Vocal music
4. Vocal music — To 1800. 5. Music, American — Hist. & crit. I. Gleason,
Harold, 1892- joint editor. II. T.
M2.M267M9     780.973     *LC* 62-8635

**Parrish, Carl, ed.**                    **1.3427**
Masterpieces of music before 1750; an anthology of musical examples from
Gregorian chant to J. S. Bach, compiled and edited with historical and
analytical notes by Carl Parrish and John F. Ohl. [1st ed.] New York, Norton
[1951] x, 235 p. 25 cm. 1. Instrumental music 2. Vocal music 3. Music —
History and criticism I. Ohl, John F., joint ed. II. T.
M2.P25 M3     780.82     *LC* 51-11051

**A treasury of early music: an anthology of masterworks of the**                    **1.3428**
**Middle Ages, the Renaissance, and the Baroque era / compiled**
**and edited with notes by Carl Parrish.**
New York: W.W. Norton, 1958. x, 331 p.: music. 1. Music — History and
criticism I. Parrish, Carl.
M2.P25 T7     *LC* M 53-638     *ISBN* 0393094448

**Stevens, Denis, 1922-.**     • **1.3429**
The Penguin book of English madrigals: for 4 voices / edited by Denis Stevens.
— [Harmondsworth, Middlesex; Baltimore]: Penguin Books, [1967]. –.
miniature score (158 p.); 20 cm. — Critical notes by the editor and the words,
printed as text, precede each madrigal. - 1. Part-songs, English — To 1800.
I. T.
M1579.4 .S84 P4     *LC* 67-8709     *ISBN* 0140708332

**MacClintock, Carol, 1910-.**                    **1.3430**
The solo song, 1580–1730. Edited by Carol MacClintock. [1st ed.] New York,
W. W. Norton [1973] xxvi, [i] 345 p. music. 28 cm. (A Norton music anthology)
Words in Italian, French, German, and/or English; figured bass realized for
keyboard instrument. 1. Songs 2. Songs — History and criticism I. T.
M 1619 M12 1973     *LC* 70-146039     *ISBN* 0393099822

**Shaw, Martin Fallas, 1875-1958.**                    **1.3431**
National anthems of the world. Edited by Martin Shaw, Henry Coleman and
T.M. Cartledge. [4th ed. rev. and enl.] New York, Arco Pub., 1976. 477 p.
music. 25 cm. Principally for voice and piano; words in English or in original
language with English translation. 1. National songs I. Coleman, Henry,
1888-1965. II. Cartledge, T. M. III. T.
M 1627 S53 N2 1976     *LC* 75-13887     *ISBN* 0668038497

**Lomax, Alan, 1915-.**     • **1.3432**
The folk songs of North America, in the English language. Melodies and guitar
chords transcribed by Peggy Seeger, with one hundred piano arrangements by
Matyas Seiber and Don Banks. Illustrated by Michael Leonard. Editorial
assistant, Shirley Collins. Garden City, N.Y., Doubleday [1960] 623 p. illus. 27
cm. 1. Folk-songs, American. 2. Folk-songs, American — Discography. I. T.
M1629.L83 F6 1960a     *LC* m 60-1043

**Lomax, Alan, 1915- comp.**     • **1.3433**
Hard hitting songs for hard–hit people; American folk songs of the Depression
and the labor movement of the 1930's. Notes on the songs by Woody
Guthrie.Music transcribed and edited by Pete Seeger. New York: Oak Pub.,
1967. 368 p.: ill. Unacc. melodies, with chord symbols. 1. Folk-songs,
American. 2. Ballads, American. 3. Depressions — 1929 — United States —
Songs and music. 4. Labor and laboring classes — Songs and music I. Guthrie,
Woody, 1912-1967. II. Seeger, Pete, 1919- arr. III. T.
M1629.L83 H4     *LC* 66-19058

**Lomax, Alan, 1915- comp.**     • **1.3434**
The Penguin book of American folk songs. Compiled and edited with notes by
Alan Lomax; piano arrangements by Elizabeth Poston. [Harmondsworth, Eng.;
Baltimore] Penguin Books [1966, c1964] 159 p. 28 cm. "American folk guitar
style": p. 145-151. 1. Folk-songs, American — Discography. 2. Folk-songs,
American. I. T.
M1629.L83 P5     *LC* 68-40518

**Traditional American folk songs from the Anne & Frank**                    **1.3435**
**Warner collection / [edited by] Anne Warner; Jeff Warner,**
**associate editor; Jerome S. Epstein, music editor; foreword by**
**Alan Lomax.**
1st ed. — [Syracuse, N.Y.]: Syracuse University Press, 1984. xxiii p., 501 p.: ill.,
music; 24 cm. Includes indexes. 1. Folk-songs, English — Atlantic States.
2. Folk music — Atlantic States. I. Warner, Anne. II. Warner, Frank.
III. Warner, Jeff. IV. Epstein, Jerome S. V. Title: Anne & Frank Warner
collection.
M1629.6.A7 T7 1984     784.4974     *LC* 84-95     *ISBN* 0815601859

**Ozark folksongs / Vance Randolph; edited and abridged by**                    **1.3436**
**Norm Cohen.**
Urbana: University of Illinois Press, c1982. xxvi, 590 p.: music. — (Music in
American life.) Includes indexes. 1. Folk-songs, American — Ozark
Mountains. I. Randolph, Vance, 1892- II. Cohen, Norm. III. Series.
M1629.6.O9 V36 1982     *LC* 81-4403     *ISBN* 0252008154

**Hispanic folk music of New Mexico and the Southwest: a self–**                    **1.3437**
**portrait of a people / [compiled] by John Donald Robb.**
Norman: University of Oklahoma Press, c1980. xviii, 891 p.: ill., music, ports.;
27 cm. Principally unacc. melodies; the songs have Spanish words with English
translations. Includes indexes. 1. Hispanic American folk music — New
Mexico. 2. Hispanic American folk music — Southwest, New. I. Robb, John
Donald, 1892-
M1668.4.H52     784.75     *LC* 78-21392     *ISBN* 0806114924

**Allen, William Francis, 1830-1889, comp.**     • **1.3438**
Slave songs of the United States. New York, P. Smith, 1929. 1 p. l., xliv p., 2 l.,
115 p. 23 cm. 'Copyright 1867. Reprinted 1929.' 1. Negro songs. I. Ware,
Charles Pickard, 1840-1921, joint comp. II. Garrison, Lucy McKim, joint
comp. III. T.
M1670.A42 1929     *LC* 30-26184

**The Books of American Negro spirituals: including The book of**                    **1.3439**
**American Negro spirituals and The second book of Negro**
**spirituals / [compiled by] James Welden Johnson and J.**
**Rosamond Johnson.**
New York: Viking Press, 1940. 1 score (187, 189 p.); 26 cm. For voice and
piano. A reissue of the volumes first published separately in 1925 and 1926.
Each volume has special t.p. Musical arrangements by J. Rosamond Johnson,
additional numbers by Lawrence Brown. 1. Spirituals (Songs) 2. Afro-
Americans — Music 3. Folk music — United States 4. Folk-songs, English —
United States. I. Johnson, James Weldon, 1871-1938. II. Johnson, J.

Rosamond (John Rosamond), 1873-1954. III. Brown, Lawrence. IV. Title: Book of American Negro spirituals. V. Title: Second book of Negro spirituals.
M1670.J67 B65      *LC* 41-546

**Parrish, Lydia (Austin), Mrs., d1953, comp.**      • **1.3440**
Slave songs of the Georgia Sea islands. New York, Creative age press, inc., 1942. xxxi, [1], 256 p. incl. map. front., plates, ports. 29 x 22 cm. Includes words and music (melodies unaccompanied) of 60 songs. 1. Negro songs. 2. Music — Negroes. 3. Negroes — Sea islands, Ga. I. Churchill, Creighton. II. MacGimsey, Robert. III. T.
M1670.P236 S6      784.756      *LC* 42-10485

**Everyman's book of British ballads / edited by Roy Palmer.**      **1.3441**
London; Toronto: J.M. Dent, 1980. 256 p.: ill., music; 25 cm. Includes index. 1. Ballads, British. I. Palmer, Roy.
M1678.E94      784/306      *ISBN* 0460044524

**Greenberg, Noah. ed.**      • **1.3442**
An Elizabethan song book; lute songs, madrigals, and rounds. Music edited by Noah Greenberg. Text edited by W. H. Auden and Chester Kallman. London, Faber and Faber [1957] xv, 240 p. illus. 29 cm. Principally for voice and piano. 1. Song-books 2. Songs with lute — To 1800. I. Auden, W. H. (Wystan Hugh), 1907-1973. ed. II. Kallman, Chester, 1921- ed. III. T.
M1740.G83E4 1957      784.306      *LC* 65-661

**Foner, Philip Sheldon, 1910- comp.**      **1.3443**
American labor songs of the nineteenth century / [selected by] Philip S. Foner. — Urbana: University of Illinois Press, [1975] c1974. xvii, 356 p.: facsims.; 29 cm. +1 sound recording (1 sound disc: 33 1/3 rpm., stereo.; 7 in.). — (Music in American life) Without the music. Includes indexes. 1. Labor and laboring classes — Songs and music 2. American ballads and songs. I. T.
M1977.L3 F74      784.6/8/3310973      *LC* 74-20968      *ISBN* 0252001877

**White, Benjamine Franklin, 1800-1879.**      • **1.3444**
The sacred harp / by B.F. White and E.J. King. — Nashville: Broadman Press, [1968] xxxii, 432 p.; 16 x 24 cm. For 3-4 voices; shape-note notation. 1. Tune-books 2. Hymns, English 3. Choruses, Sacred (Mixed voices) I. King, E. J. (Earl Judson), 1901-1962. II. Jackson, George Pullen, 1874-1953. Story of the The sacred harp. III. T.
M2117.W45      783.952      *LC* 68-18032

# ML LITERATURE OF MUSIC

**International Repertory of Music Literature (Organization)**      • **1.3445**
RILM abstracts. 1- Jan./Apr. 1967-. [New York, RILM] v. 28 cm. Quarterly. Official journal of Repértoire International de Littérature Musicale. 1. Music — Abstracts — Periodicals. I. International Musicological Society. II. International Association of Music Libraries. III. American Council of Learned Societies. IV. T.
ML1.I83      780/.5      *LC* 70-200921

**Musical America: annual directory issue.**      **1.3446**
1968/69-. Great Barrington, Mass., Billboard Publications. v. ill., ports. 29 cm. Annual. 1. Music — United States — Directories.
ML12.M88      780.25/73      *LC* 70-5637

**Who's new wave in music: an illustrated encyclopedia, 1976–1982 (the first wave) / compiled and edited by David Bianco.**      **1.3447**
Ann Arbor, MI: Pierian Press, 1985. xvii, 430 p.: ill.; 29 cm. (Rock & roll reference series; 14) 1. New wave music — Directories. 2. Rock groups — Directories. 3. New wave music — Discography. I. Bianco, David.
ML12.W5 1985      784.5/4/0025 19      *LC* 84-61228      *ISBN* 0876501730

**Music industry directory.**      **1.3449**
7th (1983). — Chicago, Ill.: Marquis Professional Pub. 1 v.; 29 cm. 1. Music — United States — Directories. 2. Music trade — United States — Directories.
ML13.M505      338.7/6178/02573 19      *LC* 83-645913

**Harris, Ernest E.**      **1.3450**
Music education: a guide to information sources / Ernest E. Harris. — Detroit: Gale Research Co., c1978. xvii, 566 p.; 23 cm. (Gale information guide library. Education information guide series. v. 1) Includes indexes. 1. Music — Instruction and study — Directories. 2. School music — Instruction and study — Directories. 3. Music — Bibliography I. T. II. Series.
ML19.H37      780/.7      *LC* 74-11560      *ISBN* 081031309X

**Lynch, Richard Chigley, 1932-.**      **1.3451**
Musicals!: a directory of musical properties available for production / by Richard Chigley Lynch. — Chicago: American Library Association, 1984. xi, 197 p.; 24 cm. Includes index. 1. Musical revue, comedy, etc — Directories. I. T.
ML19.L9 1984      782.81/029/473 19      *LC* 84-468      *ISBN* 0838904041

**Sandberg, Larry.**      **1.3452**
The folk music source book / Larry Sandberg and Dick Weissman. — 1st ed. — New York: Knopf: distributed by Random House, 1976. x, 260, xiv p.: ill.; 31 cm. Includes index. 1. Folk music — North America — Directories. 2. Folk music — North America — Bibliography. 3. Folk music — North America — Discography. I. Weissman, Dick. joint author. II. T.
ML19.S26      016.7817/0973      *LC* 75-34472      *ISBN* 0394496841

**Great rock musicals / edited, with an introd. and notes on the plays, authors, and composers by Stanley Richards.**      **1.3453**
New York: Stein and Day, c1979. x,, 562 p., [8] leaves of plates: ill.; 25 cm. Librettos. 1. Musical revues, comedies, etc — Librettos. I. Richards, Stanley, 1918-
ML48.G7      782.8/1/2      *LC* 78-7005      *ISBN* 0812825098

**Richards, Stanley, 1918- comp.**      **1.3454**
Great musicals of the American theatre / edited, with an introd. and notes on the plays, authors, and composers, by Stanley Richards. — Radnor, Pa.: Chilton Book Co., c1973-. v.: ill.; 24 cm. Vol. 1 originally published under title: Ten great musicals of the American theatre. 1. Musical revues, comedies, etc — Librettos. I. T.
ML48.R5 1973b      782.8/1/2      *LC* 78-113020      *ISBN* 0801957311

**Britten, Benjamin, 1913-1976.**      **1.3455**
[Operas. Librettos. English] The operas of Benjamin Britten: the complete librettos: illustrated with designs of the first productions / edited by David Herbert; pref. by Peter Pears; contributions by Janet Baker ... [et al.]. — New York: Columbia University Press, 1979. xxxi, 382 p.: ill.; 29 cm. Includes index. 1. Britten, Benjamin, 1913-1976 — Operas. 2. Operas — Librettos I. Herbert, David. II. T.
ML49.B74 H5 1979b      782.1/2 19      *LC* 79-2052      *ISBN* 0231048688

**Coffin, Berton.**      **1.3456**
Word–by–word translations of song and arias / by Berton Coffin, Werner Singer and Pierre Delattre. — Metuchen, N.J.: Scarecrow P., 1966-1972. 2 v.; 22 cm. "Companion to The singer's repertoire." 1. Songs — Texts I. Singer,Werner. II. Delattre,Pierre. III. T.
ML54.6.C7W7      781.96      *LC* 66-13746

**Downhome blues lyrics: an anthology from the post–World War II era / selected and transcribed by Jeff Todd Titon.**      **1.3457**
[Boston, MA.]: Twayne Publishers, 1981. xv, 214 p.; 21 cm. 1. Blues (Music) — United States — Texts. 2. Blues (Music) — United States — History and criticism. I. Titon, Jeff.
ML54.6.D69      784.5/305 19      *LC* 81-1174      *ISBN* 0805794514

**Mercer, Johnny, 1909-.**      **1.3458**
Our huckleberry friend: the life, times, and lyrics of Johnny Mercer / collected and edited by Bob Bach and Ginger Mercer; designed by Christopher Simon. — 1st ed. — Secaucus, N.J.: Lyle Stuart, 1982. 252 p.: ill., ports.; 29 cm. 1. Mercer, Johnny, 1909- 2. Popular music — United States — Texts. 3. Librettists — United States — Biography. I. Bach, Bob. II. Mercer, Ginger. III. T.
ML54.6.M45 O9 1982      784.5/05 19      *LC* 82-10503      *ISBN* 0818403314

**Miller, Philip Lieson, 1906- comp. and tr.**      **1.3459**
The ring of words; an anthology of song texts. The original texts selected and translated, with an introd. by Philip L. Miller. — New York: W. W. Norton, [1973] xxviii, 518 p.; 20 cm. — (The Norton library) German, French, Italian, Spanish, Russian, Norwegian, and Swedish, with English translations. Reprint of the 1966 ed. 1. Songs — Texts I. T.
ML54.6.M5 R5 1973      781.9/6      *LC* 72-10270      *ISBN* 0393006778

**Prawer, Siegbert Salomon, 1925- ed. and tr.**      • **1.3460**
The Penguin book of Lieder. Edited and translated by S. S. Prawer. Baltimore, Penguin Books [1964] 208 p. 20 cm. (Penguin reference book, R25) Without the music; German and English words. 'Notes on the poets': p. [179]-189. 1. Songs — Texts 2. Poets 3. Songs, German — Discography. I. T.
ML54.6.P75 P5      784.3      *LC* 64-6693

# ML55–60 Essays: Collections

**Boretz, Benjamin. comp.**    • **1.3461**
Perspectives on Schoenberg and Stravinsky. Edited by Benjamin Boretz and Edward T. Cone. Princeton, N.J., Princeton University Press, 1968. x, 284 p. music. 21 cm. Essays derived principally from the periodical Perspectives of New Music. 1. Schoenberg, Arnold, 1874-1951. 2. Stravinsky, Igor, 1882-1971. 3. Music — Addresses, essays, lectures. I. Cone, Edward T. joint comp. II. T.
ML55.B663P5    780/.922    *LC* 68-28031

**LaRue, Jan. ed.**    • **1.3462**
Aspects of medieval and Renaissance music; a birthday offering to Gustave Reese. Associate editors: Martin Bernstein, Hans Lenneberg [and] Victor Yellin. [1st ed.] New York, W.W. Norton [1966] xvii, 891 p. ill., facsims., music, ports. 1. Musicology — Addresses, essays, lectures 2. Music — History and criticism — Medieval 3. Music — 16th century — History and criticism I. Reese, Gustave, 1899-1977. II. T.
ML55 R3 L4    *LC* 64-22450MN

**Reese, Gustave, 1899-1977. ed.**    • **1.3463**
The commonwealth of music, edited by Gustave Reese and Rose Brandel in honor of Curt Sachs. New York, Free Press [1965] 374 p. music, plates (incl. facsims.) Includes vocal music (1-4 pts.) 1. Sachs, Curt, 1881-1959. 2. Music — Addresses, essays, lectures I. Brandel, Rose, 1928 II. T.
ML55 S13 R4    *LC* 64-23082MN

## ML60 Individual Authors, A–Z

**Abraham, Gerald, 1904-.**    • **1.3464**
Slavonic and Romantic music; essays and studies, by Gerald Abraham. New York, St. Martin's Press [1968] 360 p. music. 26 cm. 1. Music — 19th century — History and criticism — Addresses, essays, lectures. I. T.
ML60.A215 S6    780    *LC* 68-13029

**Abraham, Gerald, 1904-.**    **1.3465**
The tradition of Western music [by] Gerald Abraham. Berkeley, University of California Press [1974] 130 p. music. 23 cm. Based on the author's Ernest Bloch lectures, Apr.-May 1969. 1. Music — Addresses, essays, lectures. I. T.
ML60.A215 T7    780    *LC* 72-97738    *ISBN* 0520024141

**Blume, Friedrich, 1893-.**    • **1.3466**
Classic and romantic music; a comprehensive survey. Translated by M. D. Herter Norton. [1st ed.] New York, W. W. Norton [1970] viii, 213 p. 22 cm. Translation of two essays first published in Die Musik in Geschichte und Gegenwart. 1. Music — Addresses, essays, lectures. 2. Music — 18th century — History and criticism 3. Music — 19th century — History and criticism I. T.
ML60.B688    780.9033    *LC* 78-77390    *ISBN* 0393021378

**Cage, John.**    • **1.3467**
Silence; lectures and writings. — [1st ed.]. — Middletown, Conn.: Wesleyan University Press, [1961] 276 p.; 24 cm. 1. Music — Addresses, essays, lectures. I. T.
ML60.C13 S5    780.8    *LC* 61-14238

**Carter, Elliott, 1908-.**    **1.3468**
The writings of Elliott Carter: an American composer looks at modern music / compiled, edited, and annotated by Else Stone and Kurt Stone. — Bloomington: Indiana University Press, c1977. xvii, 390 p.: ill.; 24 cm. Includes index. 1. Music — 20th century — History and criticism — Addresses, essays, lectures. I. Stone, Else, 1912- II. Stone, Kurt. III. T.
ML60.C22    780/.904    *LC* 76-48539    *ISBN* 0253367204

**Cone, Edward T.**    **1.3469**
The composer's voice [by] Edward T. Cone. — Berkeley: University of California Press, [1974] ix, 184 p.: illus.; 23 cm. — (Ernest Bloch lectures.) 1. Music — Addresses, essays, lectures. 2. Music — Philosophy and aesthetics I. T. II. Series.
ML60.C773 C6    780/.1    *LC* 73-80830    *ISBN* 0520025083

**Einstein, Alfred, 1880-1952.**    • **1.3470**
Essays on music / Alfred Einstein. — New York: Norton, 1956. 265 p.: ill. — (Norton library.) 1. Music — Addresses, essays, lectures. I. T.
ML60.E38    *LC* 56-10095

**Gould, Glenn.**    **1.3471**
The Glenn Gould reader / edited and with an introduction by Tim Page. — 1st ed. — New York: Knopf, 1984. xvi, 473 p.: music. 1. Music — Addresses, essays, lectures. I. Page, Tim. II. T.
ML60.G68 1984    780 19    *LC* 84-47819    *ISBN* 0394540670

**Hanslick, Eduard, 1825-1904.**    • **1.3472**
Music criticisms, 1846–99 / Eduard Hanslick; translated and edited by Henry Pleasants. — Baltimore: Penguin Books, 1963, c1950. 312 p. — (Peregrine books; Y32) 1. Music — 19th century — History and criticism I. Pleasants, Henry. II. T.
ML60.H2043    *LC* 64-143

**Schoenberg, Arnold, 1874-1951.**    • **1.3473**
Style and idea. — New York, Philosophical Library [1950] vii, 224 p. music. 23 cm. 'Several of the essays ... were originally written in German [and translated by Dika Newlin]' 1. Music — Addresses, essays, lectures. I. T.
ML60.S374    780.4    *LC* 50-8187

**Schoenberg, Arnold, 1874-1951.**    **1.3474**
Style and idea: selected writings of Arnold Schoenberg / edited by Leonard Stein; with translations by Leo Black. — New York: St. Martins Press, 1975. 559 p.: music; 26 cm. Includes index. 1. Music — Addresses, essays, lectures. I. Stein, Leonard. II. T.
ML60.S374 1975    780/.8    *LC* 72-85510

**Seeger, Pete, 1919-.**    **1.3475**
The incompleat folksinger, by Pete Seeger. Edited by Jo Metcalf Schwartz. New York, Simon and Schuster [1972] viii, 596 p. illus. 25 cm. 1. Folk music — Addresses, essays, lectures. 2. Folk music — United States 3. Folk-songs I. Schwartz, Jo Metcalf, ed. II. T.
ML60.S444 I5    784.4    *LC* 73-156161    *ISBN* 067120954X

**Sessions, Roger, 1896-.**    • **1.3476**
The musical experience of composer, performer, listener. — Princeton: Princeton University Press, 1950. 127 p.: music.; 23 cm. 'Six lectures delivered in the summer of 1949, at the Julliard [sic] School of Music, New York City.' 1. Music — Addresses, essays, lectures. I. T.
ML60.S5    780.4    *LC* 50-10912

**Sessions, Roger, 1896-.**    • **1.3477**
Questions about music. — Cambridge, Mass.: Harvard University Press, 1970. 166 p.; 22 cm. — (The Charles Eliot Norton lectures, 1968-1969) 1. Music — Addresses, essays, lectures. I. T. II. Series.
ML60.S513    780    *LC* 72-102672    *ISBN* 0674743504

**Sessions, Roger, 1896-.**    **1.3478**
Roger Sessions on music: collected essays / edited by Edward T. Cone. — Princeton, N.J.: Princeton University Press, c1979. xi, 388 p.: ill.; 23 cm. 1. Music — Addresses, essays, lectures. I. Cone, Edward T. II. T.
ML60.S514    780/.8    *LC* 78-51190    *ISBN* 0691091269

**Thomson, Virgil, 1896-.**    **1.3479**
[Selections. 1981] A Virgil Thomson reader / by Virgil Thomson; with an introduction by John Rockwell. — Boston: Houghton Mifflin, 1981. x, 582 p.; 24 cm. Includes index. 1. Music — Addresses, essays, lectures. I. T.
ML60.T515    780 19    *LC* 81-6375    *ISBN* 0395313309

**Tovey, Donald Francis, Sir, 1875-1940.**    • **1.3480**
Musical articles from the Encyclopaedia britannica, by Donald Francis Tovey ... with an editorial preface by Hubert J. Foss. — London: Oxford university press, H. Milford, 1944. vii, 251, [1] p.: illus. (incl. music); 22 cm. 1. Music I. Encyclopaedia britannica. II. T.
ML60.T668    780.4    *LC* 45-3169

**Tovey, Donald Francis, Sir, 1875-1940.**    • **1.3481**
A musician talks ... London, New York [etc.] Oxford university press, 1941. 2 v. 19 cm. 1. Music — Addresses, essays, lectures. I. Foss, Hubert James, 1899- ed. II. Cramb lectures, 1936. III. Alsop lectures, 1938. IV. T.
ML60.T67 M8    780.4    *LC* 41-14700

**Vaughan Williams, Ralph, 1872-1958.**    • **1.3482**
Some thoughts on Beethoven's Choral symphony, with writings on other musical subjects. London, New York, Oxford University Press, 1953. 172 p. music. 21 cm. 1. Beethoven, Ludwig van, 1770-1827. Symphonies, no. 9, op. 125, D minor 2. Music — Addresses, essays, lectures. I. T.
ML60.V29    780.4    *LC* 53-4467

# ML62–89 Special Topics

**Copland, Aaron, 1900-.**    • **1.3483**
Copland on music. — [1st ed.]. — Garden City, N.Y.: Doubleday, 1960. 280 p.; 22 cm. 1. Music I. T.
ML63.C48    780.8    *LC* 60-15171

**Hurst, Jack.**     **1.3484**
Grand Ole Opry / text by Jack Hurst; introd. by Roy Acuff. — New York: H. N. Abrams, [1975] 404 p.: ill., music; 36 cm. Includes index. 1. Grand ole opry (Radio program) I. T.
ML68.H87     ML68 H87.     791.44/7     *LC* 75-14486     *ISBN* 0810902680

**D'Urfey, Thomas, 1653-1723.**     • **1.3485**
The songs of Thomas D'Urfey, selected and edited by Cyrus Lawrence Day. Cambridge, Mass., Harvard university press, 1933. x, 168 p. incl. facsims. (music) front. (port.) 21 cm. (Harvard studies in English. vol. IX) I. Day, Cyrus Lawrence, 1900-1968. II. T. III. Series.
ML80.D95 D33     *LC* 34-49

**Bowen, Zack R.**     **1.3486**
Musical allusions in the works of James Joyce: early poetry through Ulysses [by] Zack Bowen. — [1st ed.]. — Albany: State University of New York Press, 1974. 372 p.: music.; 24 cm. 1. Joyce, James, 1882-1941 — Knowledge — Music. 2. Joyce, James, 1882-1941. Ulysses. I. T.
ML80.J75 B7     823/.9/12     *LC* 74-13314     *ISBN* 0873952480

**Seng, Peter J.**     • **1.3487**
The vocal songs in the plays of Shakespeare; a critical history. — Cambridge, Mass.: Harvard University Press, 1967. xiv, 314 p.; 25 cm. 1. Shakespeare, William, 1564-1616 — Songs and music — History and criticism. I. T.
ML80.S5 S35     822/.3/3     *LC* 66-18256

**Sternfeld, Frederick William, 1914-.**     • **1.3488**
Music in Shakespearean tragedy. — London: Routledge & K. Paul; New York: Dover Publications, 1963. xxvi, 334 p.: ill., ports., facsims., music; 22 cm. — (Studies in the history of music) Includes settings of melodies with and without realizations of figured bass in appendices of chapters. 1. Shakespeare, William, 1564-1616 — Musical settings 2. Shakespeare, William, 1564-1616 — Stage history — To 1625 3. Music — 16th century — History and criticism I. T. II. Series.
ML80.S5 S8     782.83     *LC* 64-2673

**Ammer, Christine.**     **1.3489**
Unsung: a history of women in American music / Christine Ammer. — Westport, Conn.: Greenwood Press, c1980. x, 317 p.; 24 cm. — (Contributions in women's studies. no. 14 0147-104X) Includes index. 1. Women musicians 2. Women composers 3. Musicians — United States. I. T. II. Series.
ML82.A45     780/.92/2 B     *LC* 79-52324     *ISBN* 0313220077

**Dahl, Linda, 1949-.**     **1.3490**
Stormy weather: the music and lives of a century of jazzwomen / by Linda Dahl. — 1st ed. — New York: Pantheon Books, c1984. xii, 371 p.: ill.; 25 cm. Includes index. 1. Women jazz musicians — United States. I. T.
ML82.D3 1984     785.42/088042 19     *LC* 83-19456     *ISBN* 0039453553

**Women in music: an anthology of source readings from the**     **1.3491**
**Middle Ages to the present / edited by Carol Neuls–Bates.**
1st ed. — New York: Harper & Row, c1982. xvi, 351 p.: ill., ports.; 21 cm. Includes index. 1. Women musicians 2. Women composers I. Neuls-Bates, Carol.
ML82.W65 1982     780/.88042 19     *LC* 81-48045     *ISBN* 0060149922

**Winternitz, Emanuel.**     **1.3492**
Musical instruments and their symbolism in Western art: studies in musical iconology / Emanuel Winternitz. — New Haven: Yale University Press, 1979. 253 p., 96 [i.e. 48] leaves of plates: ill.; 26 cm. 1. Musical instruments in art I. T.
ML85.W58 1979     704.94/9/78191     *LC* 78-65482     *ISBN* 0300023243

**Kinsky, Georg, 1882-1951. ed.**     • **1.3493**
A history of music in pictures, edited by George Kinsky, with the co–operation of Robert Haas, Hans Schnoor and other experts. With an introd. by Eric Blom. New York, Dover Publications [c1951] xiv, 363 p. ill., ports., music. 1. Music — History and criticism I. T.
ML89 K62 1951     *LC* A53-9805

**Lang, Paul Henry.**     • **1.3494**
A pictorial history of music / Paul Henry Lang and Otto Bettmann. — New York: Norton, 1960. vii, 242 p.: ill., facsims., ports.; 29 cm. 'Text based on Music in Western civilization, by Paul Henry Lang, copyright 1941.' 1. Music — History and criticism 2. Music in art 3. Musicians — Portraits 4. Musical instruments in art I. Bettmann, Otto. joint author. II. T.
ML89.L15     780.9     *LC* 60-6822     *ISBN* 0393021076

## ML90–98 Musicians as Authors. Music Manuscripts

**Chase, Gilbert, 1906- ed.**     • **1.3495**
The American composer speaks; a historical anthology, 1770–1965. — [Baton Rouge]: Louisiana State Universtiy Press, [c1966] ix, 318 p.; 24 cm. 1. Musicians as authors 2. Composers, American. I. T.
ML90.C55     780.07110973     *LC* 66-11661

**Morgenstern, Sam. comp.**     • **1.3496**
Composers on music; an anthology of composers' writings from Palestrina to Copland. Edited by Sam Morgenstern. — New York, Greenwood Press [1969, c1956] xxiii, 584 p. music. 24 cm. 1. Musicians as authors 2. Music — History and criticism I. T.
ML90.M6 1969     780/.8     *LC* 69-14005     *ISBN* 837111471

**Three classics in the aesthetic of music: Monsieur Croche the**     • **1.3497**
**dilettante hater, by Claude Debussy. Sketch of a new esthetic of**
**music, by Ferruccio Busoni. Essays before a sonata, by Charles**
**E. Ives.**
New York, Dover Publications [1962] iv, 188 p. 1. Musicians as authors 2. Music — Philosophy and aesthetics I. Debussy, Claude, 1862-1918. II. Busoni, Ferruccio, 1866-1924. III. Ives, Charles, 1874-1954.
ML90 T47     *LC* 62-52796

**Weiss, Piero. comp.**     • **1.3498**
Letters of composers through six centuries. Compiled and edited by Piero Weiss. Foreword by Richard Ellmann. — [1st ed.]. — Philadelphia: Chilton Book Co., [1967] xxix, 619 p.: music.; 24 cm. 1. Musicians — Correspondence, reminiscences, etc. I. T.
ML90.W44     780/.922     *LC* 67-28895

**Winternitz, Emanuel.**     • **1.3499**
Musical autographs from Monteverdi to Hindemith / by Emanuel Winternitz. — New York: Dover Publications, 1965. 2 v.: ill., facsims., music, port. 1. Music — Manuscripts 2. Musical notation 3. Paleography, Musical 4. Composers — Autographs I. T.
ML96.4.W5 1965     *LC* 65-12261 MN

## ML100–110 Dictionaries. Encyclopedias

**The International cyclopedia of music and musicians / editor in**     **1.3500**
**chief, Oscar Thompson; editor, fifth–eighth editions, Nicolas**
**Slonimsky; editor, ninth edition, Robert Sabin; editor, tenth and**
**eleventh editions, Bruce Bohle.**
11th ed. — New York: Dodd, Mead, 1985. viii, 2609 p.: ill.; 29 cm. 1. Music — Dictionaries 2. Music — Bio-bibliography I. Thompson, Oscar, 1887-1945. II. Bohle, Bruce.
ML100.I57 1985     780/.3/21 19     *LC* 84-13736     *ISBN* 0396084125

**Kennedy, Michael, 1926-.**     **1.3501**
The Oxford dictionary of music / Michael Kennedy. — Oxford; New York: Oxford University Press, 1985. xiv, 810 p.: ill. Rev. and enl. ed. of: The concise Oxford dictionary of music. 3rd ed. 1980. 1. Music — Dictionaries 2. Music — Bio-bibliography I. Kennedy, Michael, 1926- Concise Oxford dictionary of music. II. T.
ML100.K35 1985     780/.3/21 19     *LC* 84-22803     *ISBN* 0193113333

**Die Musik in Geschichte und Gegenwart; allgemeine**     • **1.3502**
**Enzyklopädie der Musik. Unter Mitarbeit zahlreicher**
**Musikforscher des In– und Auslandes, hrsg. von Friedrich**
**Blume.**
Kassel: Bärenreiter-Verlag, 1949-79. 16 v.: illus., ports., facsims, music.; 28 cm. 1. Music — Dictionaries — German. 2. Music — Bio-bibliography I. Blume, Friedrich, 1893- ed.
ML100.M92     780/.3     *LC* a 50-3662

**The New Grove dictionary of music and musicians / edited by**     **1.3503**
**Stanley Sadie.**
London: Macmillan Publishers; Washington, D.C.: Grove's Dictionaries of Music, 1980. 20 v.: ill.; 26 cm. 1. Music — Dictionaries 2. Music — Bio-bibliography I. Grove, George, Sir, 1820-1900, ed. Grove's dictionary of music and musicians. II. Sadie, Stanley.
ML100.N48     780/.3     *LC* 79-26207     *ISBN* 0333231112

**The New Harvard dictionary of music** / edited by Don Michael    **1.3504**
**Randel.**
Cambridge, Mass.: Belknap Press of Harvard University Press, 1986. xxi,
942 p.: ill., music; 26 cm. Rev. ed. of: Harvard dictionary of music / Willi Apel.
2nd ed. 1969. 1. Music — Dictionaries I. Randel, Don Michael. II. Apel,
Willi, 1893- Harvard dictionary of music.
ML100.N485 1986     780/.3/21 19     *LC* 86-4780     *ISBN* 0674615255

**The New Oxford companion to music** / general editor, Denis    **1.3505**
**Arnold.**
Oxford; New York: Oxford University Press, 1983. 2 v.: (xii, 2017 p.): ill.; 26 cm.
Based on: The Oxford companion to music / by Percy A. Scholes. 1. Music —
Dictionaries 2. Music — Bio-bibliography I. Arnold, Denis. II. Scholes,
Percy Alfred, 1877-1958. Oxford companion to music.
ML100.N5 1983     780/.3/21 19     *LC* 83-233314     *ISBN* 0193113163

**Randel, Don Michael.**    **1.3506**
Harvard concise dictionary of music / compiled by Don Michael Randel. —
Cambridge, Mass.: Belknap Press, 1978. 577 p.: ill.; 22 cm. 1. Music —
Dictionaries 2. Music — Bio-bibliography I. T.
ML100.R28     780/.3 19     *LC* 78-5948     *ISBN* 0674374711

**Roche, Jerome.**    **1.3507**
A dictionary of early music: from the troubadours to Monteverdi / by Jerome &
Elizabeth Roche; [line drawings by Alec Roth]. — New York: Oxford
University Press, 1981. 208 p.: ill.; 19 cm. 1. Music — Dictionaries I. Roche,
Elizabeth. II. T.
ML100.R695     780/.902 19     *LC* 81-82688     *ISBN* 0195202554

**Vinton, John.**    **1.3508**
Dictionary of contemporary music. John Vinton, editor. [1st ed.] New York, E.
P. Dutton [1974] xiv, 834 p. 25 cm. 1. Music — 20th century — Dictionaries.
2. Music — 20th century — Bio-bibliography. I. T.
ML100.V55     780/.904     *LC* 73-78096     *ISBN* 0525091254

**Westrup, J. A. (Jack Allan), 1904-1975.**    **1.3509**
[Collins encyclopedia of music] The new college encyclopedia of music / J. A.
Westrup and F. Ll. Harrison. — Rev. ed. / rev. by Conrad Wilson. — New
York: W. W. Norton, 1976. 608 p.: ill.; 27 cm. 'Published in Great Britain ...
under the title of Collins encyclopedia of music.' 1. Music — Dictionaries
2. Music — Bio-bibliography I. Harrison, Frank Llewellyn, 1905- joint
author. II. Wilson, Conrad, music critic. III. T.
ML100.W48 1976     780/.3/21 19     *LC* 76-22891     *ISBN* 0393021912

**The New Grove dictionary of American music** / edited by H.    **1.3510**
**Wiley Hitchcock and Stanley Sadie.**
New York, N.Y.: Grove's Dictionaries of Music, 1986. 4 v.: ill.; 29 cm.
1. Music — United States — Dictionaries. 2. Music — United States — Bio-
bibliography. I. Hitchcock, H. Wiley (Hugh Wiley), 1923- II. Sadie, Stanley.
ML101.U6 N48 1986     781.773/03/21 19     *LC* 86-404     *ISBN*
0943818362

**Harris, Sheldon.**    **1.3511**
Blues who's who: a biographical dictionary of Blues singers / Sheldon Harris.
— New Rochelle, N.Y.: Arlington House, c1979. 775 p.: ports; 29 cm. Includes
indexes. 1. Blues (Music) — United States — Bio-bibliography. I. T.
ML102.B6 H3     784/.092/2 B     *LC* 78-27073     *ISBN* 0870004255

**Studwell, William E. (William Emmett), 1936-.**    **1.3512**
Christmas carols: a reference guide / William E. Studwell; indexes by David A.
Hamilton. — New York: Garland Pub., 1985. xxxiii, 278 p.; 23 cm. Includes
indexes. 1. Carols — Dictionaries. 2. Carols — Indexes. 3. Carols —
Bibliography. I. T.
ML102.C3 S9 1985     783.6/5 19     *LC* 84-48240     *ISBN* 0824088999

**Stambler, Irwin.**    **1.3513**
Encyclopedia of folk, country, & western music / Irwin Stambler and Grelun
Landon. — 2nd ed. — New York, N.Y.: St. Martin's Press, c1983. 902 p.,
[56] p. of plates: ill., ports.; 24 cm. 1. Folk music — United States —
Dictionaries. 2. Country music — United States — Dictionaries. 3. Musicians
— United States — Biography. 4. Country musicians — United States —
Biography. I. Landon, Grelun. II. T.
ML102.F66 S7 1983     781.773/03/21 19     *LC* 82-5702     *ISBN*
0312248180

**Buchner, Alexandr.**    **1.3514**
Colour encyclopedia of musical instruments / by Alexander Buchner;
translated by Simon Pellar. — London; Toronto: Hamlyn, c1980. 351 p.: ill.
(some col.) 1. Musical instruments 2. Musical instruments — Pictorial works.
I. T.
ML102I5 B813     *ISBN* 0600364216

**Marcuse, Sibyl.**    **1.3515**
Musical instruments: a comprehensive dictionary / by Sibyl Marcuse. — Corr.
ed. — New York: Norton, 1975. xii, 608 p. 20 cm. (The Norton library; N758)
1. Musical instruments — Dictionaries I. T.
ML102.I5 M37 1975     781.9/1/03     *LC* 74-30050     *ISBN*
0393007588

**The New Grove dictionary of musical instruments** / edited by    **1.3516**
**Stanley Sadie.**
London: Macmillan Press; New York, NY: Grove's Dictionaries of Music,
c1984. 3 v.: ill.; 26 cm. 1. Musical instruments — Dictionaries I. Sadie,
Stanley.
ML102.I5 N48 1984     781.91/03/21 19     *LC* 84-9062     *ISBN*
0943818052

**Feather, Leonard G.**    **1.3517**
The encyclopedia of jazz / [by Leonard Feather; appreciations by Duke
Ellington, Benny Goodman, and John Hammond]. — New York: Horizon
Press, c1960. 527 p.: ill.; 26 cm. Includes index. 1. Jazz music — Bio-
bibliography. 2. Jazz musicians — Bibliography. 3. Jazz music —
Discography. I. T.
ML102.J3 F4 1960     785.42/092/2 B 19     *LC* 84-166016     *ISBN*
081801203X

**Loewenberg, Alfred.**    **1.3518**
Annals of opera, 1597–1940 / compiled from the original sources by Alfred
Loewenberg; with an introd. by Edward J. Dent. — 3d ed. rev. and corrected.
— Totowa, N.J.: Rowman and Littlefield, 1978. xxv p., 1756 columns; 26 cm.
1. Opera — Dictionaries I. T.
ML102.O6 L6 1978     782.1/09     *LC* 79-105243     *ISBN* 0874718511

**Moore, Frank Ledlie.**    • **1.3519**
Crowell's handbook of world opera. Introd. by Darius Milhaud. — New York:
Crowell, [1961] 683 p.: maps, music.; 24 cm. — (A Crowell reference book)
'Recordings of complete operas': p. 654-662. 1. Opera — Dictionaries
2. Operas — Stories, plots, etc. 3. Operas — Discography I. T.
ML102.O6 M6     782.03     *LC* 61-6139

**The Simon and Schuster book of the opera: a complete**    **1.3520**
**chronological reference to opera from 1597 to the present** /
[translated from the Italian by Catherine Atthill ... et al.;
editore–in–chief, Riccardo Mezzanotte].
1st Fireside ed. — New York: Simon and Schuster, 1985, c1978. 512 p.: ill.
(some col.); 26 cm. Translation of L'Opera: repértorio della lirica dal 1597.
Cover title: The Simon & Schuster book of the opera. 'A Fireside Book.'
Includes indexes. 1. Opera — Dictionaries 2. Opera — Chronology. 3. Operas
— Stories, plots, etc. I. Mezzanotte, Riccardo. II. Title: Simon & Schuster
book of the opera.
ML102.O6 O63 1985     782.1/03     *LC* 79-1317     *ISBN* 0671248863

**Rosenthal, Harold D.**    **1.3521**
The concise Oxford dictionary of opera / by Harold Rosenthal and John
Warrack. — 2d ed. — London; New York: Oxford University Press, 1979. [14],
561 p.; 21 cm. 1. Opera — Dictionaries I. Warrack, John Hamilton, 1928-
joint author. II. T.
ML102.O6 R67 1979     782.1/03     *LC* 79-318553     *ISBN*
019311318X

**Who's who in opera: an international biographical directory of**    **1.3522**
**singers, conductors, directors, designers, and administrators, also**
**including profiles of 101 opera companies** / Maria F. Rich,
**editor.**
1st ed. — New York: Arno Press, 1976. xxi, 684 p.; 25 cm. 1. Opera —
Biography — Dictionaries. 2. Opera — Directories. I. Rich, Maria F.
ML102.O6 W5     782.1/092/2 B     *LC* 75-7963     *ISBN* 040506652X

**Booth, Mark W., 1943-.**    **1.3523**
American popular music: a reference guide / Mark W. Booth. — Westport,
Conn.: Greenwood Press, 1983. xvi, 212 p.; 25 cm. — (American popular
culture. 0193-6859) 1. Popular music — United States — Dictionaries.
2. Popular music — United States — Bio-bibliography. 3. Popular music —
United States — History and criticism. I. T. II. Series.
ML102.P66 B65 1983     016.78/042/0973 19     *LC* 82-21062     *ISBN*
0313213054

**Kinkle, Roger D., 1916-.**    **1.3524**
The complete encyclopedia of popular music and jazz, 1900–1950 [by] Roger D.
Kinkle. — New Rochelle, N.Y.: Arlington House, [1974] 4 v. (xl, 2644 p.):
illus.; 24 cm. 1. Popular music — Dictionaries. 2. Jazz music — Dictionaries.
3. Musicians — United States — Biography. 4. Jazz musicians — Biography.
I. T.
ML102.P66 K55     780/.42/0973     *LC* 74-7109     *ISBN* 0870002295

**Roxon, Lillian.**    **1.3525**
Lillian Roxon's Rock encyclopedia / compiled by Ed Naha. — Rev. ed. — New
York: Grosset & Grosset & Dunlap, 1978. x, 565 p., [8] leaves of plates.

1. Rock music — Dictionaries. 2. Rock music — Bio-bibliography. I. Naha, Ed. II. Rock encyclopedia. III. T.
ML102.P66 R7 1978     784     *LC* 78-112332     *ISBN* 0448145715

**Shaw, Arnold.**                               **1.3526**
Dictionary of American pop/rock / written and compiled by Arnold Shaw. — New York, N.Y.: Schirmer Books; London: Collier Macmillan, 1983, c1982. vii, 440 p.; 24 cm. 1. Popular music — Dictionaries. 2. Popular music — Bio-bibliography. I. T.
ML102.P66 S5 1982     780/.42/0321 19     *LC* 82-50382     *ISBN* 0028723600

**Stambler, Irwin.**                             **1.3527**
Encyclopedia of pop, rock and soul / by Irwin Stambler. — New York: St. Martin's Press, [1975] c1974. 609 p.: ports.; 25 cm. 1. Popular music — Dictionaries. 2. Popular music — Bio-bibliography. 3. Rock music — Dictionaries. 4. Rock music — Bio-bibliography. 5. Blues (Music) — Dictionaries. 6. Blues (Music) — Bio-bibliography. I. T.
ML102.P66 S8     784/.092/2 B     *LC* 73-87393

**Jasper, Tony.**                                **1.3528**
The international encyclopedia of hard rock & heavy metal / Tony Jasper and Derek Oliver, Steve Hammond, Dave Reynolds. — New York, N.Y.: Facts on File, [1985], c1983. vii, 400 p.; 24 cm. 1. Rock music — Bio-bibliography. 2. Rock groups 3. Rock music — Discography. I. Oliver, Derek. II. T. III. Title: Hard rock & heavy metal. IV. Title: Hard rock and heavy metal.
ML102.R6 J37 1985     784.5/4 19     *LC* 84-10236     *ISBN* 0816011001

*[Ref]*
*ML*
*105*
*B16*
*1984*

**Baker, Theodore, 1851-1934.**               **1.3529**
[Biographical dictionary of musicians] Baker's Biographical dictionary of musicians. — 7th ed. / revised by Nicolas Slonimsky. — New York: Schirmer Books; London: Collier Macmillan, c1984. xlii, 2577 p.; 25 cm. 1. Music — Bio-bibliography I. Slonimsky, Nicolas, 1894- II. T. III. Title: Biographical dictionary of musicians.
ML105.B16 1984     780/.92/2 B 19     *LC* 84-5595     *ISBN* 0028702700

**Claghorn, Charles Eugene, 1911-.**        **1.3530**
Biographical dictionary of jazz / Charles Eugene Claghorn. — Englewood Cliffs, N.J.: Prentice-Hall, c1982. 377 p.; 26 cm. 1. Jazz musicians — Biography. I. T.
ML105.C59 1982     785.42/092/2 B 19     *LC* 82-10409     *ISBN* 0130779660

**Cohen, Aaron I.**                             **1.3531**
International encyclopedia of women composers / Aaron I. Cohen. — New York: Bowker, 1981. xviii, 597 p.: ports.; 29 cm. 1. Women composers — Biography. 2. Music — Bio-bibliography I. T.
ML105.C7     780/.92/2 B 19     *LC* 81-12233     *ISBN* 0835212882

**Ewen, David, 1907-.**                         **1.3532**
Musicians since 1900: performers in concert and opera / compiled and edited by David Ewen. — New York: H. W. Wilson Co., 1978. 974 p.: ports.; 26 cm. 1. Music — Bio-bibliography. 2. Opera — Bio-bibliography. I. T.
ML105.E97     780/.92/2 B     *LC* 78-12727     *ISBN* 0824205650

*[Ref]*
*ML*
*105*
*F28*

**Feather, Leonard G.**                      • **1.3533**
The encyclopedia of jazz in the sixties, by Leonard Feather. Foreword by John Lewis. New York, Horizon Press [1966] 1 v. (unpaged) ports. 1. Jazz musicians 2. Jazz music — Discography I. T.
ML105.F32     *LC* 66-26705

**Feather, Leonard G.**                         **1.3534**
The encyclopedia of jazz in the seventies / by Leonard Feather and Ira Gitler; introduction by Quincy Jones. — New York: Horizon Press, c1976. 393 p.: ill.; 27 cm. 1. Jazz music — Bio-bibliography. 2. Jazz musicians — Biography. 3. Jazz music — Discography. I. Gitler, Ira. joint author. II. T.
ML105.F36     785.4/2/0922     *LC* 76-21196     *ISBN* 0818012153

**Laurence, Anya.**                           **1.3535**
Women of notes: 1,000 women composers born before 1900 / by Anya Laurence. — 1st ed. — New York: R. Rosen Press, 1978. xix, 101 p.: ports; 29 cm. (The Theatre student) 1. Women composers — Biography. I. T.
ML105.L28     780/.92/2 B     *LC* 78-7862     *ISBN* 0823902636

**Nite, Norm N.**                              **1.3536**
Rock on; the illustrated encyclopedia of rock n'roll, by Norm N. Nite. Special introd. by Dick Clark. — New York: T. Y. Crowell Co., c1974-1978. 2 v.: ports.; 24 cm. 1. Rock music — Bio-bibliography. I. T.
ML105.N49     784/.092/2 B     *LC* 74-12247     *ISBN* 0690005830

**Southern, Eileen.**                           **1.3537**
Biographical dictionary of Afro–American and African musicians / Eileen Southern. — Westport, Conn.: Greenwood Press, 1982. xviii, 478 p.; 29 cm. — (Greenwood encyclopedia of Black music. 0272-0264) Includes index. 1. Afro-

American musicians — Bio-bibliography. 2. Musicians — Africa — Bio-bibliography. I. T. II. Series.
ML105.S67 1982     780/.92/2 B 19     *LC* 81-2586     *ISBN* 0313213399

**Encyclopedia of music in Canada / edited by Helmut Kallmann,**     **1.3538**
**Gilles Potvin, Kenneth Winters.**
Toronto; Buffalo: University of Toronto Press, c1981. xxix, 1076 p.: ill.; 31 cm. 1. Music — Canada — Dictionaries. 2. Music — Canada — Bio-bibliography. I. Kallmann, Helmut. II. Potvin, Gilles, 1923- III. Winters, Kenneth, 1929-
ML106.C3 E5     780/.971 19     *LC* 82-116808     *ISBN* 0802055095

**International who's who in music and musicians' directory.**     **1.3539**
7th- ed.; 1975-. Cambridge, Eng. [Melrose Press] 26 cm. 1. Music — Bio-bibliography
ML106.G7 W4     780/.92/2 [B]     *LC* 76-641873

**American Society of Composers, Authors and Publishers.**     **1.3540**
ASCAP biographical dictionary / compiled for the American Society of Composers, Authors, and Publishers by Jaques Cattell Press. — 4th ed. — New York: R.R. Bowker Co., 1980. xii, 589 p.; 29 cm. Includes index. Previously published as: The ASCAP biographical dictionary of composers, authors and publishers. 3rd ed. 1966. 1. American Society of Composers, Authors and Publishers — Biography. 2. Music — United States — Bio-bibliography. I. Jaques Cattell Press. II. T. III. Title: A.S.C.A.P. biographical dictionary.
ML106.U3 A5 1980     780/.92/2 B 19     *LC* 80-65351     *ISBN* 0835212831

**Chilton, John, 1931 or 2-.**                    • **1.3541**   *[R*
Who's who of jazz! Storyville to Swing Street. Foreword by Johnny Simmen. —  *ML*
[1st American ed.]. — Philadelphia: Chilton Book Co., [1972] 419 p.: illus.; 24  *1C*
cm. 1. Jazz musicians — United States — Biography. 2. Jazz musicians  *U3*
— United States — Biography. I. T.
ML106.U3 C5 1972     785.4/2/0922 B     *LC* 72-188159     *ISBN*  *C5*
0801957052                                                     *19*

**District of Columbia Historical Records Survey.**     **1.3542**
Bio–bibliographical index of musicians in the United States of America since colonial times. Washington, Music Section, Pan American Union, 1956. 2d ed. [New York, AMS Press, 1972] xxiii, 439 p. 27 cm. Prepared under the supervision of Leonard Ellinwood and Keyes Porter. Reprint of the 1956 ed. 1. Music — Bio-bibliography 2. Music — United States — Bio-bibliography. I. Ellinwood, Leonard Webster, 1905- ed. II. Porter, Keyes, 1887- ed. III. T.
ML106.U3 H6 1972     780/.922 B     *LC* 76-39375     *ISBN* 0404080758

**Who's who in American music. Classical.**     **1.3543**
1st ed. (1983)-    . — New York: R.R. Bowker Co., c1983-    . — v.; 29 cm. Biennial. 1. Musicians — United States — Bio-bibliography. 2. Musicians — United States — Directories.
ML106.U3 W35     780/.92/2 B     *LC* 84-642464

---

# ML111–158 Bibliography

**Dichter, Harry, 1899-.**                         **1.3544**
[Early American sheet music] Handbook of early American sheet music, 1768–1889 / by Harry Dichter and Elliott Shapiro. — New York: Dover Publications, 1977. xxvii, 287 p.: ill.; 24 cm. Reprint, with corrections, of the 1941 ed. published by Bowker Co., New York, under title: Early American sheet music. Includes index. 1. Music — United States — Bibliography. 2. Publishers and publishing — United States. 3. Music printing I. Shapiro, Elliott, 1895- II. T.
ML112.D53 1977     016.7817/73     *LC* 77-70454     *ISBN* 0486233642

**Wolfe, Richard J.**                            **1.3545**
Early American music engraving and printing: a history of music publishing in America from 1787 to 1825 with commentary on earlier and later practices / Richard J. Wolfe. — Urbana: Published in cooperation with the Bibliographical Society of America by the University of Illinois Press, c1980. xix, 321 p., [19] leaves of plates: ill.; 24 cm. — (Music in American life) Includes index. 1. Music printing 2. Publishers and publishing — United States. 3. Music — United States — History and criticism. I. T.
ML112.W64     686.2/84/0973     *LC* 79-12955     *ISBN* 0252007263

**A Basic music library: essential scores and books / compiled by**     **1.3546**
**the Music Library Association Committee on Basic Music**
**Collection under the direction of Pauline S. Bayne; edited by**
**Robert Michael Fling.**
2nd ed. — Chicago: American Library Association, 1983. xii, 357 p.; 23 cm. Includes index. 1. Music — Bibliography I. Bayne, Pauline Shaw. II. Fling, Robert Michael, 1941- III. Music Library Association. Committee on Basic Music Collection.
ML113.B3 1983     016.78 19     *LC* 83-2768     *ISBN* 0838903754

**Brook, Barry S.**                                                    **1.3547**
Thematic catalogues in music, an annotated bibliography; including printed, manuscript, and in–preparation catalogues; related literature and reviews; an essay on the definitions, history, functions, historiography, and future of the thematic catalogue, by Barry S. Brook. Hillsdale, N.Y., Pendragon Press [1972] xxxvi, 347 p. facsims. 27 cm. (RILM retrospectives, no. 1) 'Published under the sponsorship of the Music Library Association and RILM abstracts of music literature.' 1. Music — Thematic catalogs — Bibliography. I. T.
ML113.B86      016.78      LC 72-7517

**Cooper, David Edwin, 1944-.**                                        **1.3548**
International bibliography of discographies: classical music and jazz & blues, 1962–1972: a reference book for record collectors, dealers, and libraries / by David Edwin Cooper; with a pref. by Guy A. Marco. — Littleton, Colo.: Libraries Unlimited, 1975. 272 p.; 24 cm. (Keys to music bibliography; no. 2) Includes index. 1. Music — Discography — Bibliography. 2. Jazz music — Discography — Bibliography. 3. Blues (Music) — Discography — Bibliography. I. T. II. Series.
ML113.C655 I6      016.78      LC 75-4516      ISBN 0872871088

**Diamond, Harold J., 1934-.**                                         **1.3549**
Music criticism: an annotated guide to the literature / by Harold J. Diamond. — Metuchen, N.J.: Scarecrow Press, 1979. x, 316 p.; 23 cm. Includes indexes. 1. Music — History and criticism — Bibliography. 2. Musical criticism — Bibliography. I. T.
ML113.D5      016.78/09      LC 79-22279      ISBN 0810812681

**Fuld, James J., 1916-.**                                             **1.3550**
The book of world–famous music: classical, popular, and folk / James J. Fuld. — 3rd ed., rev. and enl. — New York: Dover, 1985. xiii, 714 p., [8] p. of plates: ill., music; 22 cm. 1. Music — Thematic catalogs 2. Popular music — Thematic catalogs. 3. Bibliography — First editions I. T.
ML113.F8 1985      016.78 19      LC 84-21232      ISBN 0486248577

**Heyer, Anna Harriet, 1909-.**                                        **1.3551**
Historical sets, collected editions, and monuments of music: a guide to their contents / compiled by Anna Harriet Heyer. — 3d ed. — Chicago: American Library Association, 1980. 2 v. (xvii, 1105 p.); 26 cm. Includes index. 1. Music — Bibliography I. T.
ML113.H52 1980      016.78 19      LC 80-22893      ISBN 083890288X

**Marco, Guy A.**                                                      **1.3552**
Information on music: a handbook of reference sources in European languages / by Guy A. Marco, with the assistance of Sharon Paugh Ferris; foreword by James Coover. — Littleton, Colo.: Libraries Unlimited, 1975-<1984 >. v. <1-3 >; 24 cm. Vol. 3- 'with the assistance of Sharon Paugh Ferris, Ann G. Olszewski.' Includes indexes. 1. Music — Bibliography 2. Music — Discography — Bibliography. 3. Bibliography — Bibliography — Music. I. Ferris, Sharon Paugh. II. Olszewski, Ann G. III. T.
ML113.M33      016.78      LC 74-32132      ISBN 0872870960

**The Pro/Am guide to U.S. books about music: annotated**              **1.3553**
**subject guide to current and backlist titles / prepared by**
**Thomas P. Lewis.**
1986 ed. — White Plains, NY: Pro/Am Music Resources, Inc., c1987. viii, 203 p.; 28 cm. 1. Music — Bibliography I. Lewis, Thomas P. II. Title: Guide to U.S. books about music.
ML113.P7x 1987      ISBN 0912483032

**Sendrey, Alfred, 1884-.**                                          • **1.3554**
Bibliography of Jewish music. New York, Columbia University Press, 1951. xli, 404 p. 26 cm. Covers the literature of music and music itself, with a brief list of recordings. 1. Jews — Music — Bibliography. 2. Jews — Music — Discography. 3. Music — Bibliography 4. Music — Discography I. T.
ML113.S5      781.971      LC 50-11111

**Hilton, Ruth B.**                                                    **1.3555**
An index to early music in selected anthologies / by Ruth B. Hilton. — Clifton, N.J.: European American Music Corporation, c1978. xii, 127 p.; 29 cm. — (Music Indexes and Bibliographies; no. 13) 1. Music — Bibliography I. T. II. Series.
ML116.H54      016.78      LC 78-109998      ISBN 0913574139

**The Music index.**                                                 • **1.3556**
v. 1- 1949-. Detroit: Information Coordinators [etc.] v.; 26 cm. Monthly. Vol. 1, no. 12, Dec. 1949, is the first annual cumulation. 1. Music — Indexes. 2. Subject headings — Music
ML118.M84      016.78      LC 50-13627

**Wenk, Arthur B.**                                                    **1.3557**
Analyses of nineteenth–century music: 1940–1980 / compiled by Arthur Wenk. — 2nd ed. — Boston: Music Library Association, c1984. 83 p.; 26 cm. (MLA index and bibliography series, 0094-6478; no. 15) 'A companion to Analyses of twentieth–century music'—P. 1. Includes index. 1. Music — 19th century —

History and criticism — Bibliography. I. Wenk, Arthur B. Analyses of twentieth–century music, 1940-1970. II. T.
ML118.W43 1984      016.78/0903/4 19      LC 84-2017      ISBN 0914954296

**Wenk, Arthur B.**                                                    **1.3558**
Analyses of twentieth–century music, 1940–1970 / compiled by Arthur Wenk. — Ann Arbor, Mich.: Music Library Association, 1975. 94 p.; 26 cm. — (MLA index and bibliography series; no. 13) 'The checklist covers some hundred fifty composers represented in thirty-nine periodicals ... in addition an attempt has been made to glean as many analyses as possible from biographies, book-length surveys, doctoral dissertation[s], and Festschriften.' Includes index. 1. Music — 20th century — History and criticism — Bibliography. 2. Musical analysis — Bibliography. I. T.
ML118.W46      016.78/0904      LC 76-375324      ISBN 0914954040

## ML120 SPECIAL COUNTRIES

**Eagon, Angelo.**                                                   • **1.3559**
Catalog of published concert music by American composers. 2d ed. Metuchen, N.J., Scarecrow Press, 1969. viii, 348 p. 22 cm. 1. Music — United States — Bibliography. I. T.
ML120.U5 E23 1969      016.78/0973      LC 68-9327      ISBN 0810801752

**Horn, David, 1942-.**                                                **1.3560**
The literature of American music in books and folk music collections: a fully annotated bibliography / by David Horn. — Metuchen, N.J.: Scarecrow Press, 1977. xiv, 556 p.; 23 cm. Includes index. 1. Music — United States — History and criticism — Bibliography. 2. Music — United States — Bibliography. I. T.
ML120.U5 H7      016.7817/73      LC 76-13160      ISBN 0810809966

**Jackson, Richard, 1936-.**                                           **1.3561**
United States music; sources of bibliography and collective biography [by] Richard Jackson. [Brooklyn] Institute for Studies in American Music, Dept. of Music, Brooklyn College of the City University of New York [c1973] vii, 80 p. 22 cm. (I.S.A.M. monographs, no. 1) 1. Music — United States — Bibliography. 2. Music — United States — Bio-bibliography. I. T.
ML120.U5 J2      016.78/0973      LC 73-80637

**Resources of American music history: a directory of source**        **1.3562**
**materials from Colonial times to World War II / D. W.**
**Krummel ... [et al.].**
Urbana: University of Illinois Press, c1981. 463 p.; 29 cm. — (Music in American life) Includes index. 1. Music — United States — Bibliography — Union lists. 2. Music — United States — Directories. I. Krummel, Donald William, 1929-
ML120.U5 R47      016.78/0973      LC 80-14873      ISBN 0252008286

**Sonneck, Oscar George Theodore, 1873-1928.**                       • **1.3563**
A bibliography of early secular American music, 18th century. — Rev. and enl. by William Treat Upton. With a pref. to the Da Capo ed. by Irving Lowens. — New York: Da Capo Press, 1964. x, xvi, 616 p.: music.; 24 cm. 'A Da Capo reprint edition.' 1. Music — United States — Bibliography. 2. Composers, American. I. Upton, William Treat, 1870-1961, ed. II. T.
ML120.U5 S6 1964      781.97      LC 64-18992

**Wolfe, Richard J.**                                                • **1.3564**
Secular music in America, 1801–1825; a bibliography. Introd. by Carleton Sprague Smith. — [1st ed.]. — New York: The New York Public Library, 1964. 3 v.; 26 cm. 1. Music — United States — Bibliography. 2. Composers, American. I. T.
ML120.U5 W57      781.97      LC 64-25006

## ML128 SPECIAL TOPICS, A–Z

**De Lerma, Dominique-René.**                                          **1.3565**
Bibliography of Black music / Dominique–René de Lerma; foreword by Jessie Carney Smith. — Westport, Conn.: Greenwood Press, 1981-1984. 4 v.; 29 cm. — (Greenwood encyclopedia of Black music. 0272-0264) Vol. 2: Foreword by Georgia Ryder; v. 3: Foreword by Samuel A. Floyd, Jr.; v. 4: Foreword by Geneva H. Southall. 1. Blacks — Music — Bibliography. 2. Afro-Americans — Music — Bibliography. 3. Music — Bibliography I. T. II. Series.
ML128.B45 D44      016.7817/296073 19      LC 80-24681      ISBN 0313213402

**Floyd, Samuel A.**                                                   **1.3566**
Black music in the United States: an annotated bibliography of selected reference and research materials / Samuel A. Floyd, Marsha J. Reisser. — Millwood, N.Y.: Kraus International Publications, 1983. xv, 234 p.; 24 cm.

Includes indexes. 1. Afro-Americans — Music — Bibliography. 2. Music — United States — Bibliography. I. Reisser, Marsha J. II. T.
ML128.B45 F6 1983    781.7/296073 19    *LC* 82-49044    *ISBN* 0527301647

**Hinson, Maurice.**      **1.3567**
The piano in chamber ensemble: an annotated guide / Maurice Hinson. — Bloomington: Indiana University Press, c1978. xxxiii, 570 p.; 24 cm. Includes indexes. 1. Piano with instrumental ensemble — Bibliography. 2. Chamber music — Bibliography. I. T.
ML128.C4 H5    016.7857    *LC* 77-9862    *ISBN* 025334493X

**Tjepkema, Sandra L., 1953-.**      **1.3568**
A bibliography of computer music: a reference for composers / Sandra L. Tjepkema. — Iowa City: University of Iowa Press, c1981. xvii, 276 p.; 24 cm. Includes index. 1. Computer music — Bibliography. I. T.
ML128.E4 T55    016.789/7 19    *LC* 81-2967    *ISBN* 0877451109

**Barlow, Harold.**      **1.3569**
A dictionary of musical themes / by Harold Barlow and Sam Morgenstern; introd. by John Erskine. Rev. ed. — New York: Crown Publishers, c1975. 642 p.: music; 23 cm. Includes indexes. 1. Instrumental music — Thematic catalogs. I. Morgenstern, Sam. joint author. II. T.
ML128.I65 B3 1975    016.78    *LC* 75-15687    *ISBN* 0517524465

**Brown, Howard Mayer.**      • **1.3570**
Instrumental music printed before 1600; a bibliography. Cambridge, Mass., Harvard University Press, 1965. 559 p. facsims. 1. Instrumental music — To 1800 — Bibliography I. T.
ML128 I65 B77    *LC* 65-12783MN

**Parsons, Denys.**      **1.3571**
The directory of tunes and musical themes / Denys Parsons; introd. by Bernard Levin. — Cambridge, Eng.: S. Brown, 1975. 288 p.: music; 24 cm. 1. Instrumental music — Thematic catalogs. 2. Vocal music — Thematic catalogs I. T.
ML128.I65 P33    016.78    *LC* 75-314448    *ISBN* 090474700X

**Kennington, Donald.**      **1.3572**
The literature of jazz: a critical guide / by Donald Kennington and Danny L. Read. — 2d ed., rev. — Chicago: American Library Association, 1980. xi, 236 p.; 22 cm. Includes indexes. 1. Jazz music — Bibliography. I. Read, Danny L., 1946- joint author. II. T.
ML128.J3 K45 1980    016.781/57 19    *LC* 80-19837    *ISBN* 0838903134

**Merriam, Alan P., 1923-.**      **1.3573**
A bibliography of jazz, by Alan P. Merriam. With the assistance of Robert J. Benford. — New York: Da Capo Press, 1970. xiii, 145 p.; 24 cm. — (Da Capo Press music reprint series) Reprint of the 1954 ed. 1. Jazz music — Bibliography. I. T.
ML128.J3 M4 1970    016.7854/2    *LC* 75-127282    *ISBN* 0306700360

**Bloom, Ken.**      **1.3574**
American song: the complete musical theatre companion / Ken Bloom. — New York, N.Y.: Facts on File, c1985. 2 v.; 29 cm. Spine title: American song: musical theater companion, 1900-1984. Vol. 2: Index. 1. Musical revues, comedies, etc — Bibliography. 2. Songs, English — United States — Indexes. I. T.
ML128.M78 B6 1985    782.81/0973 19    *LC* 84-24728    *ISBN* 0871969610

**Gerboth, Walter.**      • **1.3575**
An index to musical festschriften and similar publications. — [1st ed.]. — New York: W. W. Norton, [1969] ix, 188 p.; 24 cm. 1. Musicology — Bibliography. 2. Festschriften — Bibliography. I. T.
ML128.M8 G4    016.780/8    *LC* 68-12182    *ISBN* 0393021343

**Drone, Jeanette Marie, 1940-.**      **1.3576**
Index to opera, operetta, and musical comedy synopses in collections and periodicals / by Jeanette Marie Drone. — Metuchen, N.J.: Scarecrow Press, 1978. v, 171 p.; 23 cm. 1. Operas — Stories, plots, etc. — Indexes. 2. Musical revues, comedies, etc — Stories, plots, etc. — Indexes. I. T.
ML128.O4 D76    016.7821/3    *LC* 77-25822    *ISBN* 0810811006

**Marco, Guy A.**      **1.3577**
Opera: a research and information guide / Guy A. Marco. — New York: Garland Pub., 1984. xvii, 373 p.; 23 cm. (Garland reference library of the humanities. v. 468) Includes indexes. 1. Opera — Bibliography. I. T. II. Series.
ML128.O4 M28 1984    016.7821 19    *LC* 83-49312    *ISBN* 0824089995

**Daniels, David, 1933-.**      **1.3578**
Orchestral music: a handbook / by David Daniels. — 2nd ed. — Metuchen, N.J.: Scarecrow Press, 1982. xii, 413 p.; 22 cm. 1. Orchestral music — Bibliography. I. T.
ML128.O5 D3 1982    016.785 19    *LC* 81-16678    *ISBN* 0810814846

**Farish, Margaret K.**      **1.3579**
Orchestral music in print / edited by Margaret K. Farish. — 1st ed. — Philadelphia: Musicdata, 1979. xii, 1029 p. (p. 1017-1029 advertisement; 29 cm. — (Music-in-print series. v. 5 0146-1883.) 1. Orchestral music — Bibliography. I. T. II. Series.
ML128.O5 F33    016.785    *LC* 79-24460    *ISBN* 0884780104

**Frankel, Walter A., 1938-.**      **1.3580**
Organ music in print / edited by Walter A. Frankel and Nancy K. Nardone. — 2nd ed. — Philadelphia: Musicdata, 1984. xiii, 354 p.: ill.; 29 cm. — (Music-in-print series, 0146-7883; vol. 3) 1. Organ music — Bibliography. I. Nardone, Nancy K. II. T.
ML128.O6 F7 1984    016.7868 19    *LC* 83-26956    *ISBN* 0884780155

**Nardone, Thomas R.**      **1.3581**
Organ music in print / edited by Thomas R. Nardone. — 1st ed. — Philadelphia: Musicdata, 1975. x, 262 p.; 29 cm. (Music-in-print series. v. 3) 1. Organ music — Bibliography I. T. II. Series.
ML128.O6 N37    016.7868    *LC* 75-16504    *ISBN* 0884780066

**Hinson, Maurice.**      **1.3582**
Guide to the pianist's repertoire. Edited by Irwin Freundlich. — Bloomington: Indiana University Press, [1973] xlv, 831 p.; 25 cm. 'An effort has been made to grade representative works of each composer.' 'Specifically related bibliographic entries of books and periodical articles have been incorporated into the main body of the text.' 1. Piano music — Bibliography 2. Piano music — Bibliography — Graded lists I. Freundlich, Irwin, ed. II. T.
ML128.P3 H5    016.7864/05    *LC* 72-75983    *ISBN* 0253327008

**Hinson, Maurice.**      **1.3583**
Music for more than one piano: an annotated guide / Maurice Hinson. — Bloomington: Indiana University Press, c1983. xxvii, 218 p.; 25 cm. Includes indexes. 1. Piano music (Pianos (2)) — Bibliography. 2. Chamber music — Bibliography.
ML128.P3 H52 1983    016.7864/95 19    *LC* 82-49245    *ISBN* 0253339529

**Hinson, Maurice.**      **1.3584**
Music for piano and orchestra: an annotated guide / Maurice Hinson. — Bloomington: Indiana University Press, c1981. xxiii, 327 p.; 24 cm. Includes indexes. 1. Piano with orchestra — Bibliography. 2. Concertos (Piano) — Bibliography.
ML128.P3 H53    016.7856/61 19    *LC* 80-8380    *ISBN* 0253124352

**Hinson, Maurice.**      **1.3585**
The piano teacher's source book: an annotated bibliography of books related to the piano and piano music / Maurice Hinson. — 2d ed. — Melville, N.Y.: Belwin Mills Pub. Corp., c1980. 187 p.; 23 cm. Includes indexes. 1. Piano — Bibliography. 2. Piano music — Bibliography I. T.
ML128.P3 H55 1980    016.7861 19    *LC* 79-57320

**Taylor, Paul.**      **1.3586**
Popular music since 1955: a critical guide to the literature / Paul Taylor. — Boston, Mass.: G.K. Hall, 1985. xvi, 533 p.; 25 cm. Includes indexes. 1. Popular music — Bibliography. I. T.
ML128.P63 T39 1985b    016.78/042/0904 19    *LC* 85-8732    *ISBN* 0816187843

**Hoffmann, Frank W., 1949-.**      **1.3587**
The literature of rock, 1954-1978 / by Frank Hoffmann. — Metuchen, N.J.: Scarecrow Press, 1981. xi, 337 p.: ill.; 23 cm. Includes index. 1. Rock music — Bibliography. I. T.
ML128.R6 H6    016.7845/4 19    *LC* 80-23459    *ISBN* 0810813718

**De Charms, Desiree.**      • **1.3588**
Songs in collections; an index [by] Desiree de Charms & Paul F. Breed. — [Detroit]: Information Service, [c1966] xxxix, 588 p.; 26 cm. 1. Songs — Indexes. I. Breed, Paul Francis, 1916- II. T.
ML128.S3 D37    783.6016    *LC* 65-27601

**Espina, Noni.**      **1.3589**
Repertoire for the solo voice: a fully annotated guide to works for the solo voice published in modern editions and covering material from the 13th century to the present / by Noni Espina; with a foreword by Berton Coffin. — Metuchen, N.J.: Scarecrow Press, 1977. 2 v. Includes indexes. 1. Songs — Bibliography. I. T.
ML128.S3 E8    ML128S3 E8.    016.784/3061    *LC* 76-30441    *ISBN* 0810809435

**Havlice, Patricia Pate.**      **1.3590**
Popular song index / by Patricia Pate Havlice. — Metuchen, N.J.: Scarecrow Press, 1975. 933 p.; 22 cm. 1. Songs — Indexes. I. T.
ML128.S3 H4     016.784     *LC* 75-9896     *ISBN* 081080820X

**Lax, Roger.**      **1.3591**
The great song thesaurus / Roger Lax, Frederick Smith. — New York: Oxford University Press, 1984. 665 p.; 25 cm. 1. Popular music — Indexes. I. Smith, Frederick. II. T.
ML128.S3 L4 1984     784.5/0016 19     *LC* 83-24927     *ISBN* 0195032225

**Lewine, Richard.**      **1.3592**
Songs of the theater / Richard Lewine and Alfred Simon. — New York: H.W. Wilson Co., 1984. 897 p.; 26 cm. Includes indexes. 1. Musical revues, comedies, etc — Excerpts — Bibliography. 2. Popular music — United States — Bibliography. I. Simon, Alfred, 1907- II. T.
ML128.S3 L55 1984     016.78281 19     *LC* 84-13068

**Sears, Minnie Earl, 1873-1933.**      • **1.3593**
Song index; an index to more than 12,000 songs in 177 song collections comprising 262 volumes and supplement, 1934. Assisted by Phyllis Crawford. — [n.p.]: Shoe String Press, 1966. 2 v. in 1.; 26 cm. The suppl. consists of an index to more than 7,000 songs in 104 song collections comprising 124 vols. 'This vol. is a facsim. reproduction of both the Song index and Song index suppl.' 'Classified list of collections indexed': v. 2, p. xxi-xxxvii. 1. Songs — Indexes. I. Crawford, Phyllis, 1899- II. T.
ML128.S3 S31 1966     016.784     *LC* 66-25185

**Farish, Margaret K.**      • **1.3594**
String music in print, by Margaret K. Farish. New York, R. R. Bowker Co., 1965. xiii, 420 p. 26 cm. 1. Violin music — Bibliography 2. Viola music — Bibliography. 3. Violoncello music — Bibliography. 4. Double-bass music — Bibliography. 5. Chamber music — Bibliography. I. T.
ML128.S7 F4     016.7857 19     *LC* 65-14969

**Farish, Margaret K.**      **1.3595**
String music in print / edited by Margaret K. Farish. — 2d ed. — Philadelphia: Musicdata, 1980. xv, 464 p.; 26 cm. — (Music-in-print series. v. 6 0146-4729) Reprint of the 1973 ed. published by R. R. Bowker, New York. Includes index. 1. Violin music — Bibliography 2. Viola music — Bibliography. 3. Violoncello music — Bibliography. 4. Double-bass music — Bibliography. I. T. II. Series.
ML128.S7 F4 1980     016.787/015 19     *LC* 80-18425     *ISBN* 0884780112

**Barlow, Harold.**      **1.3596**
A dictionary of opera and song themes: including cantatas, oratorios, lieder, and art songs = originally published as A dictionary of vocal themes / compiled by Harold Barlow and Sam Morgenstern. — Rev. ed. — New York: Crown Publishers, c1976. 547 p.: music; 25 cm. Includes indexes. 1. Vocal music — Thematic catalogs I. Morgenstern, Sam. joint author. II. T.
ML128.V7 B3 1976     016.784     *LC* 75-30751     *ISBN* 0517525038

**Coffin, Berton.**      • **1.3597**
Singer's repertoire. — 2d ed. — New York: Scarecrow Press, 1960-62. 5 v.; 23 cm. (v. 5: 21 cm.) Joint author for v. 5: Werner Singer. 1. Vocal music — Bibliography 2. Vocal music — Analysis, appreciation. I. Singer, Werner, joint author. II. T.
ML128.V7 C67 1960     781.97     *LC* 60-7265

**Eslinger, Gary S., 1953-.**      **1.3598**
Sacred choral music in print / edited by Gary S. Eslinger and F. Mark Daugherty. — 2nd ed. — Philadelphia: Musicdata, 1985. 2 v. (xiii, 1322); 29 cm. (Music-in-print series, 0146-7883; v. 1) 'In addition to revising information in the original volume (1974), this edition contains listings from the Supplement to Choral music in print (1976), the Supplement to Sacred choral music in print (1981), and the Music-in-print annual supplements, 1982-1984'—P. v. 1. Choral music — Bibliography. I. Daugherty, F. Mark, 1951- II. T. III. Series.
ML128.V7 E78 1985     016.783/02/6 19     *LC* 85-15368     *ISBN* 0884780171

**Hovland, Michael A.**      **1.3599**
Musical settings of American poetry: a bibliography / compiled by Michael Hovland. — Westport, Conn.: Greenwood Press, 1986. xli, 531 p.; 25 cm. (Music reference collection. 0736-7740; no. 8) Includes indexes. 1. Vocal music — Bibliography 2. American poetry — Musical settings — Bibliography. I. T. II. Series.
ML128.V7 H67 1986     016.7843 19     *LC* 86-402     *ISBN* 0313229384

**Kagen, Sergius.**      • **1.3600**
Music for the voice; a descriptive list of concert and teaching material. — Rev. ed. — Bloomington: Indiana University Press, [c1968] xx, 780 p.; 24 cm. I. T.
ML128.V7 K3 1968     781/.97     *LC* 68-27348

**Mattfeld, Julius, 1893-1968.**      **1.3601**
Variety music cavalcade, 1620–1969; a chronology of vocal and instrumental music popular in the United States. With an introd. by Abel Green. — 3d ed. — Englewood Cliffs, N.J.: Prentice-Hall, [1971] xx, 766 p.; 24 cm. 1. Popular music — United States — Bibliography. 2. Music — United States — Chronology. I. T.
ML128.V7 M4 1971     *LC* 70-129240     *ISBN* 0139407189

**Nardone, Nancy K.**      **1.3602**
Secular choral music in print. 1982 supplement / edited by Nancy K. Nardone. — Philadelphia: Musicdata, 1982. xiii, 210 p.; 29 cm. — (Music-in-print series) 'Companion volume to Choral music in print, vol. 2 (1974) and the 1976 supplement to Choral music in print'—Preface. Includes index. 1. Choral music — Bibliography. I. Nardone, Thomas R. Choral music in print. II. T. III. Series.
ML128.V7 N325 1982     016.7841 19     *LC* 82-8131     *ISBN* 0884780139

**Voxman, Himie.**      **1.3603**
Woodwind music guide / compiled by Himie Voxman & Lyle Merriman. — [Rev. ed.]. — Evanston, Ill.: Instrumentalist Co., 1982-1984. 2 v.; 24cm. (Music guide series; no.2,3) 1. Woodwind instruments — Bibliography. 2. Woodwind ensembles — Bibliography. I. Merriman, Lyle. II. T.
ML128.W5V6x

**Block, Adrienne Fried.**      **1.3604**
Women in American music: a bibliography of music and literature / compiled and edited by Adrienne Fried Block and Carol Neuls–Bates. — Westport, Conn.: Greenwood Press, 1979. xxvii, 302 p., [4] leaves of plates: ill.; 29 cm. Includes indexes. 1. Women musicians — United States — Bibliography. 2. Music — United States — Bibliography. I. Neuls-Bates, Carol. II. T.
ML128.W7 B6     780/.92/2 B     *LC* 79-7722     *ISBN* 0313214107

# ML134 THEMATIC CATALOGUES

**Schmieder, Wolfgang.**      • **1.3605**
Thematisch–systematisches Verzeichnis der musikalischen Werke von Johann Sebastian Bach; Bach–Werke–Verzeichnis (BWV). — [3., unveränderte Aufl.]. — Leipzig: Breitkopf & Härtel Musikverlag, 1961 [c1950] xxii, 747 p.; 27 cm. 1. Bach, Johann Sebastian — Thematic catalogs. I. T.
ML134.B1 S3 1961     *LC* 63-47794

**Kinsky, Georg, 1882-1951.**      • **1.3606**
Das Werk Beethovens; thematisch–bibliographisches Verzeichnis seiner sämtlichen vollendeten Kompositionen. Nach dem Tode des Verfassers abgeschlossen und hrsg. von Hans Halm. München, G. Henle Verlag [c1955] xxii, 808 p. music. 27 cm. 1. Beethoven, Ludwig van, 1770-1827 — Thematic catalogs. 2. Beethoven, Ludwig van, 1770-1827 — Bibliography. I. Halm, Hans, 1887- ed. II. T.
ML134.B4 K5     780/.92/4 19     *LC* a 56-1737

**McCorkle, Margit L.**      **1.3607**
Johannes Brahms: thematisch–bibliographisches Werkverzeichnis / von Margit L. McCorkle; herausgegeben nach gemeinsamen Vorarbeiten mit Donald M. McCorkle. — München: G. Henle, c1984. lxxvii, 841 p.: ill.; 27 cm. Includes indexes. 1. Brahms, Johannes, 1833-1897 — Thematic catalogs. I. McCorkle, Donald. II. T.
ML134.B8 A3 1984     780/.92/4 19     *LC* 85-110072     *ISBN* 3873280418

**Kobylańska, Krystyna.**      **1.3608**
[Rekopisy utworów Chopina. German] Frédéric Chopin: thematisch–bibliographisches Werkverzeichnis von / Krystyna Kobylańska. — München: G. Henle, c1979. xxii, 362 p.; 26 cm. Translation of Rekopisy utworów Chopina. Includes indexes. 1. Chopin, Frédéric, 1810-1849 — Thematic catalogs 2. Chopin, Frédéric, 1810-1849 — Bibliography I. T.
ML134.C54 A315     ML134C54 K5915.     786.1/092/4 19     *LC* 80-492707     *ISBN* 3873280299

**Brown, Maurice John Edwin.**      • **1.3609**
Chopin: an index of his works in chronological order. London, Macmillan, 1960. xiii, 199 p. music. 1. Chopin, Frédéric, 1810-1849 — Thematic catalogs I. T.
ML134 C54 B84     *LC* 60-50966

**Hoboken, Anthony van, 1887-.**      • **1.3610**
Joseph Haydn; thematisch–bibliographisches Werkverzeichnis. — Mainz: B. Schott's Söhne, [1957-1978] 3 v.: facsims., music.; 27 cm. 'Beilage zu Band I': in pocket of v. 1. 'Beilage zu Band I and II': in pocket of v. 2. 1. Haydn, Joseph, 1732-1809 — Thematic catalogs. I. T.
ML134.H272 H6     *LC* 57-43073

**Köchel, Ludwig von, Ritter, 1800-1877.**     • **1.3611**
Chronologisch–thematisches Verzeichnis sämtlicher Tonwerke Wolfgang Amadé Mozarts; nebst Angabe der verlorengegangenen, angefangenen, von fremder Hand bearbeiteten, zweifelhaften und unterschobenen Kompositionen. — 6. Aufl., bearb. von Franz Giegling, Alexander Weinmann [und] Gerd Sievers. — Wiesbaden: Breitkopf & Härtel; sole agents in U.S.A.: C. F. Peters Corp., New York, 1964. cxliii, 1024 p.: port., facsim., music.; 28 cm. 1. Mozart, Johann Chrysostom Wolfgang Amadeus — Thematic catalogs. I. Giegling, Franz, 1921- ed. II. Weinmann, Alexander, 1901- ed. III. Sievers, Gerd, ed. IV. T.
ML134.M9 K55 1964      *LC* 64-4363

**Zimmerman, Franklin B.**     • **1.3612**
Henry Purcell, 1659-1695; an analytical catalogue of his music. London, Macmillan; New York, St. Martin's Press, 1963. xxiv, 575 p. music. 24 cm. 1. Purcell, Henry, 1659-1695 — Thematic catalogs. I. T.
ML134.P95 A4      *LC* 63-24476

**Rufer, Josef, 1893-.**     • **1.3613**
The works of Arnold Schoenberg; a catalogue of his compositions, writings and paintings. Translated by Dika Newlin. [New York] Free Press of Glencoe [1963, c1962] 214 p. illus., ports., facsims. (music) 26 cm. 1. Schoenberg, Arnold, 1874-1951 — Bibliography. I. T.
ML134.S33 R83 1963      016.78

**Deutsch, Otto Erich, 1883-1967.**     • **1.3614**
Schubert; thematic catalogue of all his works in chronological order, by Otto Erich Deutsch in collaboration with Donald R. Wakeling. New York, W. W. Norton [1951] xxiv, 566 p. music. 22 cm. 1. Schubert, Franz, 1797-1828 — Thematic catalogs. I. T.
ML134.S38 D44 1951a      780.81      *LC* 52-1005

## M155–157 PHONORECORDS

**Coover, James, 1925-.**     **1.3615**
Musical instrument collections: catalogues and cognate literature / James Coover. — Detroit: Information Coordinators, 1981. 464 p.; 24 cm. — (Detroit studies in music bibliography; no. 47) Includes indexes. 1. Musical instruments — Catalogs and collections — Bibliography. I. T.
ML155.C63      016.78191/074 19      *LC* 81-19901      *ISBN* 0899900135

**Bibliography of discographies.**     **1.3616**
New York: Bowker, 1977- < 1983 >. v. < 1-3 >; 26 cm. Includes indexes. 1. Music — Discography — Bibliography. I. Gray, Michael H., 1946- II. Gibson, Gerald D., 1938- III. Allen, Daniel.
ML156.2.B49      016.0167899/12 19      *LC* 77-22661      *ISBN* 0835210235

**Croucher, Trevor.**     **1.3617**
Early music discography: from plainsong to the sons of Bach / compiled by Trevor Croucher. — 1981 ed. — Phoenix, AZ: Oryx Press, c1981. 2 v.; 21 cm. 1. Music — Discography I. T.
ML156.2.C76      016.7899/12 19      *LC* 81-16794      *ISBN* 0897740181

**Fox, Charles, 1921-.**     **1.3618**
Jazz on record: a critical guide / Charles Fox, Peter Gammond, Alun Morgan; with additional material by Alexis Korner. — Westport, Conn.: Greenwood Press, 1978, c1960. 352 p.; 22 cm. Reprint of the ed. published by Hutchinson, London. Includes index. 1. Jazz music — Discography. I. Gammond, Peter. joint author. II. Morgan, Alun, 1928- joint author. III. T.
ML156.4.J3 F7 1978      789.9/136/542      *LC* 78-8189      *ISBN* 0313205132

**Raymond, Jack, 1923-.**     **1.3619**
Show music on record: from the 1890s to the 1980s / Jack Raymond. — New York: F. Ungar, c1982. v, 253 p., [32] p. of plates: ill.; 29 cm. Includes index. 1. Musical revues, comedies, etc — Discography. I. T.
ML156.4.O46 R4 1982      016.7899/12281 19      *LC* 81-40471      *ISBN* 0804457743

**The New Trouser Press record guide / Ira A. Robbins, editor.**     **1.3620**
2nd ed. — New York: C. Scribner's Sons, c1985. 463 p.; 24 cm. Rev. ed. of: The Trouser Press guide to new wave records. 1983. 1. Popular music — Discography. 2. Sound recordings — Reviews. I. Robbins, Ira A. II. Trouser Press guide to new wave records.
ML156.4.P6 N48 1985      789.9/13645 19      *LC* 85-11820      *ISBN* 0684183773

**Tudor, Dean.**     **1.3621**
Popular music, an annotated guide to recordings / by Dean Tudor. — Littleton, Colo.: Libraries Unlimited, 1983. xxii, 647 p.; 25 cm. Includes index. 1. Popular music — United States — Discography. I. T.
ML156.4.P6 T85 1983      016.7899/13 19      *LC* 83-18749      *ISBN* 0872873951

**Hounsome, Terry.**     **1.3622**
Rock record / Terry Hounsome and Tim Chambre. — New York, N.Y.: Facts on File, 1981. x, 526 p.; 23 cm. 'Original limited edition (Rockmaster, 1978) and revised, expanded edition (Rock record, 1979) published and produced in the United Kingdom by Terry Hounsome. This edition published in the United Kingdom in 1981 by Blandford Books Ltd., as New rock record.'—p. [iv] Includes index. 1. Rock music — Discography. I. Chambre, Tim. II. T.
ML156.4.R6 H68      016.7899/12454 19      *LC* 81-12489      *ISBN* 087196547X

**Creighton, James Lesley, 1934-.**     **1.3623**
Discopaedia of the violin, 1889-1971 [by] James Creighton. — [Toronto; Buffalo]: University of Toronto Press, [1974] xvi, 987 p.; 28 cm. 1. Violin music — Discography. I. T.
ML156.4.V5 C7      016.7899/12      *LC* 79-185708      *ISBN* 0802018106

**Stahl, Dorothy.**     **1.3624**
A selected discography of solo song: a cumulation through 1971. — Detroit: Information Coordinators, 1972. 137 p.; 23 cm. — (Detroit studies in music bibliography. 24) 1. Songs — Discography. I. T. II. Series.
ML156.4.V7 S8 1972      016.7899/12      *LC* 72-90432      *ISBN* 0911772359

**Cohen, Aaron I.**     **1.3625**
International discography of women composers / compiled by Aaron I. Cohen. — Westport, Conn.: Greenwood Press, 1984. xx, 254 p.; 25 cm. — (Discographies. 0192-334X; no. 10) Includes indexes. 1. Women composers — Discography. I. T. II. Series.
ML156.4.W6 C6 1984      016.7899/12/088042 19      *LC* 83-26445      *ISBN* 0313242720

**Castleman, Harry.**     **1.3626**
All together now: the first complete Beatles discography, 1961–1975 / by Harry Castleman & Walter J. Podrazik. — Ann Arbor, Mich.: Pierian Press, 1975. xv, 379 p.: ill.; 24 cm. 1. Beatles — Discography. I. Podrazik, Walter J. II. T.
ML156.7.B4 C36      016.7899/12454 19      *LC* 75-29523      *ISBN* 0876500750

**Christgau, Robert.**     **1.3627**
[Record guide] Christgau's Record guide: rock albums of the seventies / Robert Christgau. — New Haven: Ticknor & Fields, 1981. 471 p.; 24 cm. 1. Sound recordings — Reviews. 2. Rock music — Discography. I. T. II. Title: Record guide.
ML156.9.C53      789.9/136454 19      *LC* 81-1977      *ISBN* 0899190251

**Myers, Kurtz.**     **1.3628**
Index to record reviews: based on material originally published in Notes, the quarterly journal of the Music Library Association between 1949 and 1977 / compiled and edited by Kurtz Myers. — Boston: G. K. Hall, 1978-1980. 5 v.; 29 cm. Includes indexes to the index. 1. Music — Discography 2. Sound recordings — Reviews — Indexes. I. Music Library Association. Notes. II. T.
ML156.9.M89      789.9/131/016 19      *LC* 79-101459      *ISBN* 081610087X

**Myers, Kurtz.**     **1.3629**
Index to record reviews, 1978–1983: based on material originally published in Notes, the quarterly journal of the Music Library Association, between 1978 and 1983 / compiled and edited by Kurtz Myers. — Boston, Mass.: G.K. Hall, 1985. xxv, 873 p.; 28 cm. Includes indexes to the index. 1. Music — Discography 2. Sound recordings — Reviews — Indexes. I. Notes (Music Library Association) II. T.
ML156.9.M89 1985      789.9/131 19      *LC* 86-135431      *ISBN* 0816104352

## ML159–3797 History and Criticism

**Hawkins, John, Sir, 1719-1789.**     **1.3630**
A general history of the science and practice of music. With a new introd. by Charles Cudworth. — New York: Dover Publications, [1963] 2 v. (963 p.): illus., plates, ports., diagrs., facsims., music.; 28 cm. — (American Musicological Society Music Library Association. Reprint series) Reprint of

the 1853 ed. 1. Music — History and criticism 2. Musicians — Portraits I. T. II. Series.
ML159.H39 1963     780.9     *LC* 63-4484

**Abraham, Gerald, 1904-.**        **1.3631**
The concise Oxford history of music / Gerald Abraham. — London; New York: Oxford University Press, 1979. 968 p.: ill., music; 26 cm. Includes index. 1. Music — History and criticism I. T.
ML160.A27     780/.9     *LC* 79-40540     *ISBN* 0193113198

**Blume, Friedrich, 1893-.**        • **1.3632**
Renaissance and Baroque music; a comprehensive survey. Translated by M. D. Herter Norton. [1st ed.] New York, W. W. Norton [1967] ix, 180 p. 22 cm. 1. Music — 16th century — History and criticism 2. Music — 17th century — History and criticism 3. Music — 18th century — History and criticism I. T.
ML160.B655 R5     780.9031     *LC* 65-13323

**Borroff, Edith, 1925-.**        • **1.3633**
Music in Europe and the United States; a history. — Englewood Cliffs, N.J.: Prentice-Hall, [1971] xvi, 752 p.: illus. (part col.), facsims., music.; 25 cm. 1. Music — Europe — History and criticism. 2. Music — U.S. — History and criticism. I. T.
ML160.B784 M9     780/.94     *LC* 73-140092     *ISBN* 0136080839

**Grout, Donald Jay.**        **1.3634**
A history of western music / Donald Jay Grout. — 3d ed. / with Claude V. Palisca. — New York: Norton, c1980. xii, 849 p.: ill.; 24 cm. Includes index. 1. Music — History and criticism I. Palisca, Claude V. joint author. II. T.
ML160.G87 1980     780/.9     *LC* 80-12224     *ISBN* 0393951367

**Láng, Paul Henry, 1900-.**        **1.3635**
Music in western civilization, by Paul Henry Láng ... — New York, W. W. Norton & company, inc. [c1941] xvi, 1107 p. front, plates, 3 double maps. 24 cm. Bibliography: p. 1045-1065. 1. Music — Hist. & crit. I. T.
ML160.L25M8     780.9     *LC* 41-9128

**New Oxford history of music.**        • **1.3636**
[London; New York: Oxford University Press, 1954- < 1973 > . v. < 1-5, 7 >: ill.; 26 cm. 1. Music — History and criticism I. Title: Oxford history of music.
ML160.N44     780/.9 19     *LC* 54-12578

**Strunk, W. Oliver (William Oliver), 1901- comp.**        • **1.3637**
Source readings in music history. Selected and annotated by Oliver Strunk. New York, W.W. Norton, 1965. 5 v. music. 21 cm. 1. Music — History and criticism — Sources. I. T.
ML 160 S92 1965     *LC* 66-489     *ISBN* 0393096807

**Wörner, Karl Heinrich, 1910-1969.**        **1.3638**
[Geschichte der Musik. English] History of music; a book for study and reference. Translated and supplemented by Willis Wager. 5th ed. New York, Free Press [1973] xx, 712 p. 26 cm. Translation of Geschichte der Musik. 1. Music — History and criticism — Outlines, syllabi, etc. I. T.
ML161.W613     780/.9     *LC* 72-90547

## ML162–197 BY PERIOD

## ML162–169 Ancient

**Goldron, Romain.**        • **1.3639**
Ancient and Oriental music [by] Romain Goldron. [n.p.] H. S. Stuttman Co.; distributed by Doubleday [1968] 121, [4] p. illus. (part col.), facsims. 22 cm. (History of music, v. 1) 1. Music — To 500 — History and criticism 2. Music — Asia — History and criticism. I. T. II. Series.
ML162.B87     780/.901     *LC* 68-1787

**Sachs, Curt, 1881-1959.**        • **1.3640**
The rise of music in the ancient world, East and West. New York, W. W. Norton & company, inc. [1943] 324 p. illus. (incl. music) plates, diagrs. 24 cm. 'First edition.' 1. Music — To 500 — History and criticism 2. Music — Asia — History and criticism. 3. Music, Greek and Roman I. T.
ML162.S14     781.8     *LC* 43-16820

**Galpin, Francis William, 1858-1945.**        • **1.3641**
The music of the Sumerians and their immediate successors, the Babylonians & Assyrians. Described and illustrated from original sources. New York, Da Capo Press, 1970. ix, 110 p. illus., music, 12 plates. 29 cm. (Da Capo Press music reprint series) Reprint of the 1937 ed. 1. Music — Sumeria — History and criticism. 2. Music — Assyria — History and criticism. 3. Music — Babylonia — History and criticism. I. T.
ML164.G17M9 1970b     781.7/35     *LC* 78-87458     *ISBN* 0306714620

**Rothmüller, Aron Marko.**        • **1.3642**
[Musik der Juden. English] The music of the Jews; an historical appreciation. [Translated from the German by H. S. Stevens] New and rev. ed. South Brunswick, T. Yoseloff [1967] 320 p. music, 26 plates (incl. facsims., ports.) 22 cm. Translation of Die Musik der Juden. 1. Jews — Music — History and criticism. 2. Music — History and criticism I. T.
ML166.R6512 1967     781.7/2/924     *LC* 65-14229

**Werner, Eric.**        • **1.3643**
[Sacred bridge. Volume 1. 1. Historic-liturgical] The sacred bridge; liturgical parallels in synagogue and early church. New York, Schocken Books [1970] xviii, 364 p. 21 cm. 'This volume comprises Part 1 of The sacred bridge, originally published ... in 1959.' 1. Catholic Church — Liturgy — History 2. Judaism — Rituals — History. I. T.
ML166.W43 1970     783.2     *LC* 75-127818     *ISBN* 0805202781

**Greek musical writings / edited by Andrew Barker.**        **1.3644**
Cambridge; New York: Cambridge University Press, 1984-. v. < 1 >: ill.; 24 cm. — (Cambridge readings in the literature of music.) Includes index. 1. Music, Greek and Roman — Sources. 2. Music — To 500 — Sources. I. Barker, Andrew, 1943- II. Series.
ML167.G73 1984     781.738 19     *LC* 83-20924     *ISBN* 0521235936

**Scott, William C. (William Clyde), 1937-.**        **1.3645**
Musical design in Aeschylean theater / William C. Scott. — Hanover: Published for Dartmouth College by University Press of New England, 1984. xxi, 228 p.; 23 cm. Includes index. 1. Aeschylus — Dramatic production. 2. Aeschylus — Stage history. 3. Music, Greek and Roman — History and criticism. 4. Greek drama — Incidental music — History and criticism. 5. Drama — Chorus (Greek drama) I. T.
ML169.S37 1984     782.8/3/0938 19     *LC* 83-40560     *ISBN* 0874512913

## ML170–190 Medieval

**Medieval music / ed. by W. Thomas Marrocco and Nicholas Sandon.**        **1.3646**
[s.l.]: Oxford U P, 1977. 239 p music. (The Oxford anthology of music) 1. Music — 500-1400 — Addresses, essays, lectures. I. Series.
ML170.M45 1985     *LC* 85-16034

**Brown, Howard Mayer.**        **1.3647**
Music in the Renaissance / Howard Mayer Brown. — Englewood Cliffs, N.J.: Prentice-Hall, c1976. xiv, 384 p.: music; 24 cm. — (Prentice-Hall history of music series) 1. Music — 15th century — History and criticism 2. Music — 16th century — History and criticism I. T.
ML172.B86     780/.9031     *LC* 75-28352     *ISBN* 0136085059

**Caldwell, John, 1938-.**        **1.3648**
Medieval music / John Caldwell. — Bloomington: Indiana University Press, c1978. 304 p.: music; 24 cm. Includes indexes. 1. Music — 400-1500 — History and criticism. I. T.
ML172.C28     780/.902     *LC* 77-94060     *ISBN* 0253337313

**Hoppin, Richard H.**        **1.3649**
Medieval music / Richard H. Hoppin. — 1st ed. — New York: W. W. Norton, c1978. xxiii, 566 p.: ill.; 24 cm. — (The Norton introduction to music history) Includes index. 1. Music — 500-1400 — History and criticism I. T.
ML172.H8     780/.902     *LC* 78-7010     *ISBN* 0393090906

**Reese, Gustave, 1899-1977.**        • **1.3650**
Music in the Renaissance. Rev. ed. New York, Norton [1959] xvii, 1022 p. illus., facsims., music. 24 cm. 1. Music — 15th century — History and criticism 2. Music — 16th century — History and criticism I. T.
ML172.R42 1959     780.94     *LC* 59-12879

**Reese, Gustave, 1899-1977.**        • **1.3651**
Music in the middle ages, with an introduction on the music of ancient times, by Gustave Reese. New York, W. W. Norton & company [c1940] xvii, 502 p. illus. (music) viii pl. (incl. facsims. (music)) 24 cm. 'First edition.' 1. Music — 500-1400 — History and criticism 2. Music — To 500 — History and criticism I. T.
ML172.R74 M8     780.902     *LC* 41-557

**Seay, Albert.**        • **1.3652**
Music in the medieval world. Englewood Cliffs, N.J., Prentice-Hall [1965] 182 p. facsims., music. 22 cm. (Prentice-Hall history of music series) 1. Music — 500-1400 — History and criticism I. T.
ML172.S4 M9     780.902     *LC* 65-17795

**Waite, William G.**        • **1.3653**
The rhythm of twelfth-century polyphony, its theory and practice. New Haven, Yale University Press, 1954. x, 141 p. music (254 p.) (Yale studies in the history

of music [v. 2]) 1. Organum I. Leoninus Magister, fl. 1160-1170. Magnus liber organi de gradali et antiphonario II. T. III. Series.
ML174 W14        *LC* 54-5093

**Collins, Fletcher.**                                                    **1.3654**
The production of medieval church music–drama. — Charlottesville: University Press of Virginia, [1972] xiii, 356 p.: ill.; 26 cm. 1. Liturgical drama I. T.
ML178.C64        782.8        *LC* 78-168610        *ISBN* 0813903734

# ML193–197 Modern

**Bukofzer, Manfred F., 1910-1955.**                                   • **1.3655**
Music in the baroque era, from Monteverdi to Bach. [1st ed.] New York, W. W. Norton [1947] xv, 489 p. illus., ports., facsims., music. 24 cm. 1. Music — 17th century — History and criticism 2. Music — 18th century — History and criticism I. T.
ML193.B8        780.903        *LC* 47-12355

**Palisca, Claude V.**                                                  • **1.3656**
Baroque music [by] Claude V. Palisca. Englewood Cliffs, N.J., Prentice-Hall [1968] 230 p. music. 22 cm. (Prentice-Hall history of music series) 1. Music — 17th century — History and criticism 2. Music — 18th century — History and criticism I. T.
ML193.P34        780/.94        *LC* 68-12336

## ML194–196 18TH–19TH CENTURIES

**Burney, Charles, 1726-1814.**                                        • **1.3657**
[The present state of music in Germany, The Netherlands, and United Provinces. English] An eighteenth–century musical tour in Central Europe and the Netherlands. London, New York, Oxford University Press, 1959. xii, 268 p. port., maps (on lining papers) facsim., music. 26 cm. (Burney, Charles, Musical tours in Europe, v.2.) 1. Music — Europe. 2. Musicians — Correspondence, reminiscences, etc. 3. Europe — Description and travel I. Scholes, Percy Alfred, 1877-1958. ed. II. The present state of music in Germany, The Netherlands, and United Provinces. English III. T. IV. Series.
ML195.B862 1959        *LC* 59-3383

**Burney, Charles, 1726-1814.**                                        • **1.3658**
An eighteenth–century musical tour in France and Italy; being Dr. Charles Burney's account of his musical experiences as it appears in his published volume with which are incorporated his travel experiences according to his original intention. Edited by Percy A. Scholes. London, Oxford University Press, 1959. xxxv, 328 p. port., maps (on lining papers) facsim., music. (His Musical tours in Europe, v. 1) 1. Music — France 2. Music — Italy 3. Musicians — Correspondence, reminiscences, etc. 4. Europe — Description and travel I. Scholes, Percy Alfred, 1877-1958. II. T. III. Series.
ML195 B963 1959        *LC* 59-3382

**Pauly, Reinhard G.**                                                  • **1.3659**
Music in the classic period [by] Reinhard G. Pauly. Englewood Cliffs, N.J., Prentice-Hall [1965] 214 p. illus., facsims., map, music. 22 cm. (Prentice-Hall history of music series) 1. Music — 18th century — History and criticism I. T.
ML195.P38        780.9033        *LC* 65-17797

**Ratner, Leonard G.**                                                    **1.3660**
Classic music: expression, form, and style / Leonard G. Ratner. — New York: Schirmer Books; London: Collier Macmillan Publishers, c1980. xvii, 475 p.; 25 cm. Includes indexes. 1. Music — 18th century — History and criticism 2. Classicism in music I. T.
ML195.R38 1980        780/.903/3 19        *LC* 76-57808        *ISBN* 0028720202

**Rosen, Charles, 1927-.**                                                **1.3661**
The classical style: Haydn, Mozart, Beethoven. New York, W. W. Norton [1972] 467 p. illus. 20 cm. (The Norton library, N653) 1. Haydn, Joseph, 1732-1809 — Criticism and interpretation. 2. Mozart, Wolfgang Amadeus, 1756-1791 — Criticism and interpretation. 3. Beethoven, Ludwig van, 1770-1827 — Criticism and interpretation. 4. Classicism in music 5. Music — 18th century — History and criticism I. T.
ML195.R68 1972        780/.9033        *LC* 72-8920        *ISBN* 0393006530

**Abraham, Gerald, 1904-.**                                            • **1.3662**
A hundred years of music. [3d ed.] Chicago, Aldine Pub. Co. [1964] 325 p. 22 cm. 1. Music — 19th century — History and criticism 2. Music — 20th century — History and criticism I. T.
ML196.A3 1964        780.9034        *LC* 63-22210

**Einstein, Alfred, 1880-1952.**                                       • **1.3663**
[Romantik in der Musik. English] Music in the romantic era. New York, W. W. Norton & company, inc. [1947] xii, 371 p., 1 l. ports. 24 cm. 'First edition.'

1. Music — 19th century — History & criticism. 2. Romanticism in music I. T.
ML196.E35        780.903        *LC* 47-3745

**Longyear, Rey M. (Rey Morgan), 1930-.**                              **1.3664**
Nineteenth–century romanticism in music [by] Rey M. Longyear. 2d ed. Englewood Cliffs, N.J., Prentice-Hall [1973] xiv, 289 p. music. 23 cm. (Prentice-Hall history of music series) 1. Music — 19th century — History and criticism 2. Romanticism in music I. T.
ML196.L65 1973        780/.9034        *LC* 72-3962        *ISBN* 0136226701
*ISBN* 0136226477

**Plantinga, Leon.**                                                      **1.3665**
Romantic music: a history of musical style in nineteenth–century Europe / Leon Plantinga. — 1st ed. — New York: W.W. Norton, c1984. xiii, 523 p.: ill.; music; 24 cm. (Norton introduction to music history.) Includes index. 1. Music — 19th century — History and criticism I. T. II. Series.
ML196.P6 1984        780/.903/4 19        *LC* 84-4012        *ISBN* 0393951960

## ML197 20TH CENTURY

**Austin, William W.**                                                  • **1.3666**
Music in the 20th century, from Debussy through Stravinsky [by] William W. Austin. [1st ed.] New York, W. W. Norton [1966] xx, 708 p. illus., music, ports. 24 cm. 1. Music — 20th century — History and criticism I. T.
ML197.A9        780.904        *LC* 65-18776

**Boulez, Pierre, 1925-.**                                             • **1.3667**
[Penser la musique aujourd'hui. English] Boulez on music today. Translated by Susan Bradshaw and Richard Rodney Bennett. Cambridge, Mass., Harvard University Press, 1971. 144 p. music. 23 cm. Translation of Penser la musique aujourd'hui. 1. Music — 20th century — History and criticism I. T.
ML197.B7213        781        *LC* 74-142073        *ISBN* 0674080068

**Copland, Aaron, 1900-.**                                             • **1.3668**
[Our new music] The new music, 1900–1960. Rev. and enl. ed. New York, W. W. Norton [1968] 194 p. music. 21 cm. Previously published in 1941 under title: Our new music. 1. Music — 20th century — History and criticism I. T.
ML197.C76 1968        780/.904        *LC* 68-10878

**Forte, Allen.**                                                      • **1.3669**
Contemporary tone–structures. New York, Teachers College, Columbia University, 1955. 194 p. 22 cm. (Teachers College studies in education) 'Scores and analytic sketches' (music) p. [145]-194. Additional copy printed separately, and laid in. Photocopy. Ann Arbor, Mich., Xerox University Microfilms, 1975. 1. Music — 20th century — History and criticism I. T. II. Series.
ML 197 F73 1955        *LC* 55-12410

**Hansen, Peter S.**                                                      **1.3670**
An introduction to twentieth century music / Peter S. Hansen. — 4th ed. — Boston: Allyn and Bacon, c1978. xiv, 457 p.: ill.; 24 cm. 1. Music — 20th century — History and criticism 2. Music appreciation I. T.
ML197.H25 1978        780/.904        *LC* 77-9296        *ISBN* 020505921X

**European music in the twentieth century / edited by Howard Hartog.**  • **1.3671**
New York: Praeger, 1957. viii, 341 p.; 23 cm. — (Praeger paperbacks; 12) 1. Music — 20th century — History and criticism 2. Music — Europe — History and criticism. 3. Composers I. Hartog, Howard, 1913-
ML197.H27 1957b        780/.94        *LC* 57-12772

**Hodeir, André, 1921-.**                                                **1.3672**
Since Debussy: a view of contemporary music / by André Hodeir; translated by Noel Burch. — London: Secker & Warburg, [1961] 256 p., [4] leaves of plates: ill.; 22 cm. — 1. Music — 20th century — History and criticism 2. Composers 3. Music — Discography I. T.
ML197.H63        780/.904

**Krenek, Ernst, 1900-.**                                              • **1.3673**
Music here and now. Translated by Barthold Fles. — New York, Russell & Russell [1967, c1966] 306 p. 22 cm. Discography: p. 295-297. 1. Music — 20th century — History and criticism I. Fles, Barthold, 1902- II. T.
ML197.K92M9 1967        780.904        *LC* 66-24718

**Lang, Paul Henry, 1901- ed.**                                       • **1.3674**
Problems of modern music; the Princeton seminar in advanced musical studies. New York, W. W. Norton [1962, c1960] 121 p. diagrs., music. 20 cm. (The Norton library, N115) 1. Music — 20th century — History and criticism — Addresses, essays, lectures. I. T.
ML197.L27        780.904        *LC* 62-3417

**Machlis, Joseph, 1906-.**   • **1.3675**
Introduction to contemporary music. New York, W. W. Norton [1961] 714 p. illus. 24 cm. 1. Music — 20th century — History and criticism 2. Composers 3. Music appreciation 4. Music — Discography I. T.
ML197.M11 I5    780.904    *LC* 61-7480

**Peyser, Joan.**   • **1.3676**
The new music; the sense behind the sound. With an introd. by Jacques Barzun. New York, Delacorte Press [1971] xvii, 204 p. illus., ports. 24 cm. 1. Schoenberg, Arnold, 1874-1951. 2. Stravinsky, Igor, 1882-1971. 3. Varèse, Edgard, 1883-1965. 4. Music — 20th century — History and criticism I. T.
ML197.P42    780/.904    *LC* 71-125575

**Reynolds, Roger, 1934-.**   **1.3677**
Mind models: new forms of musical experience. New York, Praeger [1975] xiii, 238 p. illus. 22 cm. 1. Music — 20th century — History and criticism 2. Music and society I. T.
ML197.R5    780/.07    *LC* 75-189923    *ISBN* 0275536203

**Salzman, Eric.**   **1.3678**
Twentieth–century music: an introduction. 2d ed. Englewood Cliffs, N.J., Prentice-Hall [1974] xiii, 242 p. illus. 24 cm. (Prentice-Hall history of music series) 1. Music — 20th century — History and criticism I. T.
ML197.S17 1974    780/.904    *LC* 73-17211    *ISBN* 0139350152
*ISBN* 0139350071

**Schwartz, Elliott, 1936- comp.**   • **1.3679**
Contemporary composers on contemporary music. Edited by Elliott Schwartz and Barney Childs. [1st ed.] New York, Holt, Rinehart and Winston [1967] xxi, 375 p. illus., music. 24 cm. 1. Music — 20th century — History and criticism — Addresses, essays, lectures. I. Childs, Barney. joint comp. II. T.
ML197.S33    780/.904    *LC* 66-25594

**Slonimsky, Nicolas, 1894-.**   • **1.3680**
Music since 1900. 4th ed. New York, C. Scribner's Sons [1971] xvii, 1595 p. 25 cm. 1. Music — 20th century — History and criticism 2. Music — 20th century — Chronology. I. T.
ML197.S634 1971    780/.904    *LC* 70-114929    *ISBN* 0684105500

**Sternfeld, Frederick William, 1914-.**   **1.3681**
Music in the modern age. Edited by F. W. Sternfeld. New York, Praeger [1973] 515 p. music. 25 cm. (A History of Western music, 5) 1. Music — 20th century — History and criticism I. T. II. Series.
ML197.S7655 M9    780/.904    *LC* 78-190596

**Stuckenschmidt, Hans Heinz, 1901-.**   • **1.3682**
Twentieth century music. Translated from the German by Richard Deveson. New York, McGraw-Hill Book Co. [1969] 249 p. illus., facsims., music, ports. 19 cm. (World university library) 1. Music — 20th century — History and criticism I. T.
ML197.S7752    780/.9/04    *LC* 68-21853

## ML198–370 BY COUNTRY

## ML200–203 United States

**Chase, Gilbert, 1906-.**   • **1.3683**
America's music, from the pilgrims to the present. — Rev. 2d ed. — New York: McGraw-Hill Book Co., [1966] xxi, 759 p.: music.; 23 cm. 1. Music — United States — History and criticism. I. T.
ML200.C5 1966    780.973    *LC* 66-23622

**Ellinwood, Leonard Webster, 1905-.**   **1.3684**
The history of American church music, by Leonard Ellinwood. — Rev. ed. — New York: Da Capo Press, 1970. xiv, 274 p.: illus., ports.; 24 cm. — (Da Capo Press music reprint series) 1. Church music — U.S. I. T.
ML200.E4 1970    783/.026/0973    *LC* 69-12683    *ISBN* 0306712334

**Gentry, Linnell.**   • **1.3685**
A history and encyclopedia of country, western, and gospel music. — 2d ed., completely rev. — [Nashville, Tenn.: Clairmont Corp., 1969] xiv, 598 p.; 23 cm. 1. Country music — United States — History and criticism. 2. Musicians — United States. I. T. II. Title: Country, western, and gospel music.
ML200.G4 1969    784.4/9/73    *LC* 70-7208

**Hamm, Charles.**   **1.3686**
Music in the New World / Charles Hamm. — 1st ed. — New York: Norton, c1983. xiv, 722 p.: ill., music; 24 cm. Includes index. 1. Music — United States — History and criticism. I. T.
ML200.H17 1983    781.773 19    *LC* 82-6481    *ISBN* 0393951936

**Hitchcock, H. Wiley (Hugh Wiley), 1923-.**   **1.3687**
Music in the United States; a historical introduction [by] H. Wiley Hitchcock. 2d ed. Englewood Cliffs, N.J., Prentice-Hall, [1974] xvii, 286 p. illus. 24 cm. (Prentice-Hall history of music series) 1. Music — United States — History and criticism. I. T.
ML200.H58 1974    781.7/73    *LC* 73-19751    *ISBN* 0136083986
*ISBN* 0136083803

**Howard, John Tasker, 1890-1964.**   • **1.3688**
Our American music; a comprehensive history from 1620 to the present. 4th ed. New York, T. Y. Crowell Co. [1965] xxii, 944 p. facsims. (incl. music), ports. 22 cm. 1. Music — United States — History and criticism. I. T.
ML200.H8 1965    780.973    *LC* 65-18697

**Lowens, Irving, 1916-.**   • **1.3689** [Ref.] ML 200 L91
Music and musicians in early America. — [1st ed.]. — New York: W. W. Norton, [1964] 328 p.: facsims. (incl. music); 22 cm. 'A check-list of writings about music in the periodicals of American transcendentalism (1835-50)': p. 311-321. 1. Music — United States — History and criticism. 2. Composers, American — Biography. I. T.
ML200.L7    780.973    *LC* 64-17518

**Mellers, Wilfrid Howard, 1914-.**   • **1.3690**
Music in a new found land; themes and developments in the history of American music [by] Wilfrid Mellers. [1st American ed.] New York, A.A. Knopf, 1965 [c1964] xv, 543 p. music. 22 cm. 1. Music — United States — History and criticism. 2. Music, American — Discography. I. T.
ML200.M44 1965    780.973    *LC* 64-17706

**Mueller, John Henry, 1895-.**   • **1.3691**
The American symphony orchestra; a social history of musical taste. Bloomington, Indiana University Press, 1951. xii, 437 p. ill., ports. 1. Music — United States — History and criticism 2. Symphony orchestras — United States 3. Composers 4. Orchestra I. T.
ML200 M8    *LC* 51-13728

**Music in American society, 1776–1976: from Puritan hymn to synthesizer / edited by George McCue.**   **1.3692**
New Brunswick, N.J.: Transaction Books, c1977. 201 p.; 24 cm. 1. Music — United States — Addresses, essays, lectures. I. McCue, George.
ML200.1.M9    781.7/73    *LC* 76-24527    *ISBN* 087855209X

**Sonneck, Oscar George Theodore, 1873-1928.**   • **1.3693**
Early concert–life in America. (1731–1800) O. G. Sonneck. — Wiesbaden: M. Sändig, [1969] 338 p.; 22 cm. Reprint of original edition published in Leipzig 1907. 1. Music — U.S. — History and criticism. I. T.
ML200.3.S6 1969    780/.973    *LC* 74-387578

**Mussulman, Joseph A.**   **1.3694**
Music in the cultured generation; a social history of music in America, 1870–1900 [by] Joseph A. Mussulman. Evanston, Ill., Northwestern University Press, 1971. xiii, 298 p. illus. 24 cm. (Pi Kappa Lambda studies in American music) 1. Music — United States — 19th century — History and criticism. 2. Music and society I. T.
ML200.4.M9    780.07/0973    *LC* 77-149920    *ISBN* 0810103508

**Mead, Rita H.**   **1.3695**
Henry Cowell's New Music, 1925–1936: the Society, the music editions, and the recordings / by Rita Mead. — Ann Arbor, Mich.: UMI Research Press, c1981. xx, 616 p.: ill.; 24 cm. — (Studies in musicology. No. 40) Includes index. 1. Music — United States — 20th century — History and criticism. I. Cowell, Henry, 1897-1965. II. New Music Society of California. III. T. IV. Series.
ML200.5.M35 1981    781.773/06/0794 19    *LC* 81-1510    *ISBN* 0835711706

**Rockwell, John.**   **1.3696**
All American music: composition in the late twentieth century / John Rockwell. — 1st ed. — New York: Knopf: Distributed by Random House, c1983. x, 286 p.; 22 cm. Includes index. 1. Music — United States — 20th century — History and criticism. I. T.
ML200.5.R6 1983    781.773/09/04 19    *LC* 82-48738    *ISBN* 0394511638

**Tischler, Barbara L., 1949-.**   **1.3697**
An American music: the search for an American musical identity / Barbara L. Tischler. — New York: Oxford University Press, 1986. viii, 225 p., [10] p. of plates: ill., ports.; 24 cm. Includes index. 1. Music — United States — 20th century — History and criticism. 2. Music and society I. T.
ML200.5.T55 1986    781.773/09/042 19    *LC* 85-29882    *ISBN* 0195040236

**Woodworth, George Wallace.**   **1.3698**
The world of music. Cambridge, Mass., Belknap Press of Harvard University Press, 1964. 207 p. 22 cm. 1. Music — United States — History and criticism. 2. Music — 20th century — History and criticism I. T.
ML200.5.W65    *LC* 64-13432

**Johnson, Harold Earle.**                                                    **1.3699**
Musical interludes in Boston, 1795–1830, by H. Earle Johnson. New York, Columbia university press, 1943. xv p., 2 l., [3]-366 p. front., ports., map. 25 cm. (Columbia university studies in musicology, no. 5) 'The Sonneck memorial fund in the Library of Congress, through an award in 1942, and the American council of learned societies have ... contributed funds to assist in the publication of this volume.' 'Von Hagen publications': p. [299]-303. 'Catalogue of Graupner publications': p. [305]-337. 'Lesser publishers in Boston': p. [338]-342. 'Complete list of musical works for which copyright was granted by the clerk of the District court, Boston, between January 1, 1791, and September 1, 1827': p. [343]-349. 1. Music — Massachusetts — Boston. 2. Music — United States — History and criticism. I. T. II. Series.
ML200.8.B7 J6      780.9744      *LC* 43-11010

## ML205 Canada

**Aspects of music in Canada, edited by Arnold Walter.**          • **1.3700**
Toronto: University of Toronto Press, 1969. x, 336 p.; 24 cm. Sponsored by the Canadian Music Council. 1. Music — Canada — History and criticism. I. Walter, Arnold M., ed. II. Canadian Music Council.
ML205.A86      780.9/71      *LC* 74-418249      *ISBN* 0802015360

**MacMillan, Ernest, 1893- ed.**                                    • **1.3701**
Music in Canada. — [Toronto] University of Toronto Press, 1955. 232 p. illus. 24 cm. 1. Music — Canada. I. T.
ML205.M3      780.971      *LC* 55-4629

## ML240–325 Europe

**The Musical quarterly.**                                          • **1.3702**
Contemporary music in Europe; a comprehensive survey, edited by Paul Henry Lang and Nathan Broder. New York, G. Schirmer; W. W. Norton/distributor to the book trade [1966, c1965] viii, 308 p. illus., facsim., music, ports. 26 cm. 'These essays were written for the fiftieth anniversary issue of the Musical quarterly, January, 1965.' 1. Music — Europe — 20th century — History and criticism. I. Lang, Paul Henry, 1901- ed. II. Broder, Nathan. ed. III. T.
ML240.5.M83 1966      780.94      *LC* 65-18020

### ML245–249 Austria. Hungary

**Szabolcsi, Bence, 1899-1973.**                                    • **1.3703**
[A magyar zenetörténet Kézikönyve. English.] A concise history of Hungarian music. London, Barrie and Rockliff [1964] 239 p. facsims. (incl. music) ports. 23 cm. 'Musical illustrations': p. 97-200. 1. Music — Hungary — History and criticism. I. A magyar zenetortenet Kezikonyve. English. II. T.
ML248.S963 1964a      *LC* 66-1403

### ML270–284 France. Germany

**Anthony, James R.**                                                    **1.3704**
French Baroque music; from Beaujoyeulx to Rameau [by] James R. Anthony. [1st American ed.] New York, W. W. Norton [1974] xi, 429 p. illus. 23 cm. 1. Music — France — 17th century — History and criticism. 2. Music — France — 18th century — History and criticism. 3. Music — France — 16th century — History and criticism. I. T.
ML270.2.A6 1974      781.7/44      *LC* 73-179328      *ISBN* 0393021734

**Brown, Howard Mayer.**                                            • **1.3705**
Music in the French secular theater, 1400–1550. Cambridge, Harvard University Press, 1963. x, 338 p. ill., music. 'A catalogue of theatrical chansons': p. [181]-282. 'Note' inserted. 1. Music — France — History and criticism 2. Music — History and criticism — Medieval 3. Music — 16th century — History and criticism 4. Music, Incidental — History and criticism 5. Theater — France — History I. T.
ML270.2 B8 M9      *LC* 62-19214MN

**Cooper, Martin, 1910-.**                                          • **1.3706**
French music, from the death of Berlioz to the death of Fauré. London, Oxford University Press, 1951. viii, 239 p. ill., ports., music. 1. Music, French — History and criticism I. T.
ML270.4 C7      *LC* 51-13449

**Myers, Rollo H.**                                                  • **1.3707**
Modern French music, from Fauré to Boulez [by] Rollo Myers. New York, Praeger Publications [c1971] 210 p. illus. 24 cm. 1. Music — France — 20th century — History and criticism. I. T.
ML270.5.M9M6      781.7/44      *LC* 77-154606      *ISBN* 0631130209

**Harding, James.**                                                      **1.3708**
The Ox on the Roof; scenes from the musical life in Paris in the twenties. New York, St. Martin's Press [1972] 261 p. illus. 23 cm. 1. Bo euf sur le toit (Restaurant) 2. Music — France — Paris — 20th century — History and criticism. I. T.
ML270.8.P2 H4 1972b      780/.944/361 19      *LC* 72-76750

**Helm, Ernest Eugene.**                                            • **1.3709**
Music at the court of Frederick the Great. [1st ed.] Norman, University of Oklahoma Press [1960] 268 p. ill. 1. Frederick II, King of Prussia, 1712-1786. 2. Music — Prussia I. T.
ML279 H4      *LC* 60-14105

### ML285–289 Great Britain

**The Athlone history of music in Britain.**                            **1.3710**
London: Athlone Press; New Jersey: Humanities Press distributor, < 1981- >. v. < 5 >: music; 25 cm. At head of title: Music in Britain. Includes index. 1. Music — Great Britain — History and criticism. I. Title: Music in Britain.
ML285.A83      780/.941 19      *LC* 82-120824      *ISBN* 048513005X

**Ehrlich, Cyril.**                                                      **1.3711**
The music profession in Britain since the eighteenth century: a social history / Cyril Ehrlich. — Oxford: Clarendon Press; New York: Oxford University Press, 1985. 269 p., [8] p. of plates: ill., ports.; 24 cm. Includes index. 1. Music — Great Britain — 19th century — History and criticism. 2. Music — Great Britain — 20th century — History and criticism. 3. Music and society 4. Music — Economic aspects I. T.
ML285.E35 1985      780/.941 19      *LC* 85-15570      *ISBN* 0198226659

**Scholes, Percy Alfred, 1877-1958.**                              • **1.3712**
The mirror of music, 1844–1944; a century of musical life in Britain as reflected in the pages of the Musical times. Freeport, N.Y., Books for Libraries Press [1970, c1947] 2 v. (xix, 964 p.) illus., music, ports. 24 cm. 1. Musical times. London. 2. Music — Great Britain — History and criticism. I. T.
ML285.S35 1970      780/.942      *LC* 71-124255      *ISBN* 0836954432

**Walker, Ernest, 1870-1949.**                                      • **1.3713**
A history of music in England. — 3d ed., rev. and enl. by J. A. Westrup. — Oxford, Clarendon Press, 1952. xi, 468 p. music. 23 cm. Bibliography: p. 403-414. 1. Music — England — Hist. & crit. I. T.
ML285.W18 1952      780.942      *LC* 52-12668

**Young, Percy M. (Percy Marshall), 1912-.**                        • **1.3714**
A history of British music [by] Percy M. Young. — New York: W. W. Norton, [1967] x, 641 p.: music.; 24 cm. 1. Music — Great Britain — History and criticism. I. T.
ML285.Y68 1967b      780/.942      *LC* 67-9236

**Harrison, Frank Llewellyn, 1905-.**                              • **1.3715**
Music in medieval Britain / by Frank Ll. Harrison. — New York: Praeger, 1959. xix, 491 p., [8] leaves of plates: ill., map, music; 23 cm. — (Studies in the history of music) Includes indexes. 1. Music — Great Britain — History and criticism. 2. Music — History and criticism — Medieval, 400-1500 I. T.
ML285.2.H3 1958a      780.942

**Howes, Frank Stewart, 1891-.**                                    • **1.3716**
The English musical renaissance / Frank Howes. — New York: Stein and Day, 1966. 381 p.: ill., music; 22 cm. 1. Music — England — History and criticism. I. T.
ML286.H69 1966a      780.942      *LC* 66-13763

**Mackerness, Eric David.**                                          • **1.3717**
A social history of English music, by E. D. Mackerness. — London, Routledge and K. Paul [1964] x, 307 p. 7 plates (incl. facsims.) 22 cm. — (Studies in social history) 'Bibliographical note': p. 290-294. 1. Music — England — Hist. & crit. 2. Music and society I. T.
ML286.M25      780.942      *LC* 65-1052

**Pattison, Bruce.**                                                  • **1.3718**
Music and poetry of the English Renaissance. London, Methuen [1948] ix, 220 p. music. 1. Music — England — History and criticism 2. Music — 16th century — History and criticism 3. English poetry — Early modern (to 1700) — History and criticism 4. Music and literature 5. Music — 17th century — History and criticism I. T.
ML286.2 P3      *LC* A48-9889

**Price, David C.**                                                      **1.3719**
Patrons and musicians of the English Renaissance / David C. Price. — Cambridge [Eng.]; New York: Cambridge University Press, 1981. xix, 250 p.: ill.; 24 cm. — (Cambridge studies in music.) Includes index. 1. Music — England — 16th century — History and criticism. 2. Music — England — 17th century — History and criticism. I. T. II. Series.
ML286.2.P7      338.4/778/0942      *LC* 80-40054      *ISBN* 0521228069

**Stevens, John E., 1921-.**        • **1.3720**
Music & poetry in the Early Tudor Court. London, Methuen [1961] xi, 483 p. music. 25 cm. 1. Music — England — 15th century — History and criticism. 2. Music — England — 16th century — History and criticism. 3. English poetry — Early modern, 1500-1700 — History and criticism. 4. Music and literature I. T.
ML286.2.S8 1961b     780/.942     LC 78-3531

**Shaw, Bernard, 1856-1950.**        • **1.3721**
How to become a musical critic. Edited with an introd. by Dan H. Laurence. New York, Hill and Wang [1961] 358 p. 21 cm. 1. Music — England — London. 2. Musical criticism 3. Music appreciation I. T.
ML286.8.L5 S36 1961     780.942     LC 61-8460

**Shaw, Bernard, 1856-1950.**        • **1.3722**
London music in 1888–89 as heard by Corno di Bassetto (later known as Bernard Shaw) with some further autobiographical particulars. New York, Dodd, Mead & company, 1937. 3 p.l., 3-439 p. 1 illus. (music) 21 cm. Critisims contributed weekly to the Star. of.Pref. 1. Music — England — London. I. T.
ML286.8.L5 S38 1937a     780.9421     LC 37-25998

**Shaw, Bernard, 1856-1950.**        • **1.3723**
Music in London, 1890–1894, by Bernard Shaw ... London, Constable and company limited [1932] 3 v. 21 cm. 'Revised and reprinted for this standard edition 1932.' 'These criticisms were contributed week by week to the World.' 1. Music — England — London. I. T.
ML286.8.L5 S4     780.9421     LC 32-19127

**Shaw, Bernard, 1856-1950.**        • **1.3724**
[Prose works. 1955] Shaw on music; a selection from the music criticism of Bernard Shaw, made by Eric Bentley. Garden City, N.Y., Doubleday, 1955. 307 p. 19 cm. (A Doubleday anchor book, A53) 1. Music — England — London — Addresses, essays, lectures. I. T.
ML286.8.L5 S44     780.4     LC 55-5501

## ML290 ITALY

**Palisca, Claude V.**        **1.3725**
Humanism in Italian Renaissance musical thought / Claude V. Palisca. — New Haven: Yale University Press, c1985. xiii, 471 p.: ill., music; 25 cm. Includes index. 1. Music — Italy — 15th century — History and criticism. 2. Music — Italy — 16th century — History and criticism. 3. Renaissance — Italy. 4. Humanism — Italy. I. T.
ML290.2.P34 1985     781.745 19     LC 85-8190     ISBN 0300033028

## ML300–309 RUSSIA

**Abraham, Gerald, 1904-.**        • **1.3726**
Studies in Russian music; critical essays on the most important of Rimsky–Korsakov's operas, Borodin's Prince Igor, Dargomizhky's Stone guest, etc., with chapters on Glinka, Mussorgsky, Balakirev and Tchaikovsky, by Gerald Abraham. Freeport, N.Y., Books for Libraries Press [1968] vi, 355 p. music, ports. 22 cm. (Essay index reprint series) 1. Rimsky-Korsakov, Nikolay, 1844-1908. 2. Music — Soviet Union — 19th century — History and criticism. 3. Opera — Soviet Union — 19th century. I. T.
ML300.A16S8 1968     780/.9/47     LC 68-20285

**Abraham, Gerald, 1904-.**        • **1.3727**
On Russian music; critical and historical studies of Glinka's operas, Balakirev's works, etc., with chapters dealing with compositions by Borodin, Rimsky-Korsakov, Tchaikovsky, Mussorgsky, Glazunov, and various other aspects of Russian music, by Gerald E. H. Abraham. Freeport, N.Y., Books for Libraries Press [1970] 279 p. music, port. 23 cm. (Essay index reprint series) Reprint of the 1939 ed. Complementary volume to the author's Studies in Russian music. Cf. Pref. 1. Music — Soviet Union — History and criticism. 2. Operas, Russian — History and criticism. I. T.
ML300.A16S82 1970     780/.947     LC 73-134046     ISBN 0836919009

**Asaf'ev, B. V. (Boris Vladimirovich), 1884-1949.**        • **1.3728**
Russian music from the beginning of the nineteenth century; translated from the Russian by Alfred J. Swan. Ann Arbor, Published for American Council of Learned Societies by J.W. Edwards [1953] viii, 329 p. (Russian Translation Project series of the American Council of Learned Societies, 22) 1. Music — Russia — History and criticism I. T.
ML300 A833

**Leonard, Richard Anthony.**        • **1.3729**
A history of Russian music / Richard Anthony Leonard. New York: Macmillan, 1957. 395 p.: ports. 1. Music — Russia — History and criticism. I. T.
ML300.L45 1968     781.7/47     780.947     LC 57-7295

**Seaman, Gerald R.**        • **1.3730**
History of Russian music, by Gerald R. Seaman. — New York: F. A. Praeger, [1967-. v.: illus., facsims., music, ports.; 22 cm. 1. Music — Russia — History and criticism. I. T.
ML300.S33     781.7/47     LC 67-21754

**Schwarz, Boris, 1906-.**        **1.3731**
Music and musical life in Soviet Russia / Boris Schwarz. — Enl. ed., 1917-1981. — Bloomington: Indiana University Press, c1983. xiii, 722 p.; 22 cm. Includes index. 1. Music — Soviet Union — 20th century — History and criticism. I. T.
ML300.5.S37 1983     780/.947 19     LC 82-48267     ISBN 0253339561

## ML315 SPAIN

**Chase, Gilbert, 1906-.**        • **1.3732**
The music of Spain. — 2d rev. ed. — New York: Dover Publications, [1959] 383 p.: illus.; 21 cm. 1. Music — Spain. 2. Music — Latin America 3. Music — Portugal. I. T.
ML315.C4 1959     780.946     LC 59-16808

**Stevenson, Robert Murrell.**        • **1.3733**
Spanish music in the age of Columbus. The Hague, M. Nijhoff, 1960. xiv, 335 p. music. 1. Music — Spain — History and criticism 2. Music — History and criticism — Medieval 3. Music — 16th century — History and criticism I. T.
ML315.2 S74     LC 61-45749

## ML330–370 Asia. Africa

**Malm, William P.**        **1.3734**
Music cultures of the Pacific, the Near East, and Asia / William P. Malm. — 2d ed. — Englewood Cliffs, N.J.: Prentice-Hall, c1977. xv, 236 p.: ill.; 24 cm. — (Prentice-Hall history of music series) 1. Music — Asia — History and criticism. 2. Music — Oceanica — History and criticism. I. T.
ML330.M3 1977     780/.95     LC 76-44027     ISBN 0136080006. ISBN 0136079946 pbk

**Deva, Bigamudre Chaitanya, 1922-.**        **1.3735**
An introduction to Indian music [by] B. Chaitanya Deva. Thompson, Conn.: InterCulture Associates, 1975 [c1973]. 130 p. illus. 25 cm. 1. Music — India — History and criticism. I. T.
ML338.D495 I6     781.7/54     ISBN 0882539205

**Neuman, Daniel M., 1944-.**        **1.3736**
The life of music in north India: the organization of an artistic tradition / by Daniel M. Neuman. — Detroit: Wayne State University Press, 1980. 296 p.: ill.; 24 cm. Includes index. 1. Music, Hindustani — History and criticism. 2. Music — India — History and criticism. 3. Musicians — India. 4. Music and society I. T.
ML338.N44     781.7/54     LC 79-16889     ISBN 0814316328

**Nijenhuis, Emmie te.**        **1.3737**
Musicological literature / Emmie te Nijenhuis. — Wiesbaden: Harrassowitz, 1977. 51 p.; 25 cm. — (A History of Indian literature; v. 6: Scientific and technical literature; Fasc. 1) Includes index. 1. Music — India — History and criticism — Sources. I. T.
ML338.N55     LC 78-339902     ISBN 3447018313

**Shankar, Ravi.**        • **1.3738**
My music, my life. With an introd. by Yehudi Menuhin. — New York: Simon and Schuster, [1968] 160 p.: illus., map, music.; 28 cm. 1. Music, Indic — History and criticism. I. T.
ML338.S475M9     781.7/54     LC 68-28918 MN

**Wade, Bonnie C.**        **1.3739**
Music in India: the classical traditions / Bonnie C. Wade. — Englewood Cliffs, N.J.: Prentice-Hall, c1979. xix, 252 p.: ill.; 23 cm. — (Prentice-Hall history of music series) Includes index. 1. Music — India — History and criticism. I. T.
ML338.W32     781.7/54     LC 77-28488     ISBN 0136070361

**White, Emmons E.**        • **1.3740**
Appreciating India's music; an introduction, with an emphasis on the music of South India, by Emmons E. White. Boston, Crescendo Pub. Co. [1971] ii, 96 p. illus., music. 23 cm. 1. Music — India — History and criticism. 2. Music, Karnatic — History and criticism. I. T.
ML338.W53     781.7/54     LC 70-131051     ISBN 0875970591

**Kishibe, Shigeo.**        **1.3741**
The traditional music of Japan / by Kishibe Shigeo. — 2nd ed. — Tokyo: Japan Foundation, 1982. x, 92 p., [57] p. of plates: ill.; 25 cm. Includes index. 1. Music — Japan — History and criticism. I. T.
ML340.K59 1982     781.752 19     LC 82-244291

**Malm, William P.**    • **1.3742**
Japanese music and musical instruments. [1st ed.] Tokyo, Rutland, Vt., C. E. Tuttle Co. [1959] 299 p. illus. (part col.) ports., music. 27 cm. 1. Music — Japan — History and criticism. 2. Musical instruments — Japan I. T.
ML340.M3    780.951    *LC* 59-10411

**Malm, William P.**    • **1.3743**
Nagauta: the heart of kabuki music. Rutland, Vt., C.E. Tuttle Co. [1963] xvi, 344 p. ill., 6 plates, music, 54 tables. 1. Music, Japanese — History & criticism 2. Kabuki I. T.
ML340 M33    *LC* 62-9362MN

**Sakata, Hiromi Lorraine.**    **1.3744**
Music in the mind: the concepts of music and musician in Afghanistan / Hiromi Lorraine Sakata. — Kent, Ohio: Kent State University Press, c1983. xii, 243 p.: ill., music; 24 cm. Includes index. 1. Music — Afghanistan — History and criticism. I. T.
ML345.A35 S24 1983    781.758/1 19    *LC* 82-23296    *ISBN* 087338265X

**McPhee, Colin, 1901-1964.**    • **1.3745**
Music in Bali; a study in form and instrumental organization in Balinese orchestral music. With photos. by the author. New Haven, Yale University Press, 1966. xviii, 430 p. map, music, 120 plates. 29 cm. 1. Music — Indonesia — Bali Island. 2. Gamelan 3. Musical instruments — Indonesia — Bali Island. I. T.
ML345.B3 M25    781.7923    *LC* 62-8252

**Morton, David, 1920-.**    **1.3746**
The traditional music of Thailand / David Morton. — Berkeley: University of California Press, 1976. xv, 258: ill.; 29 cm. Includes index. 1. Music — Thailand — History and criticism. I. T.
ML345.T5 M66    781.7/593    *LC* 70-142048    *ISBN* 0520018761

**Bebey, Francis.**    **1.3747**
[Musique de l'Afrique. English] African music: a people's art / Francis Bebey; translated by Josephine Bennett. — 1st U.S. ed. — New York: L. Hill, 1975. vii, 184 p.: ill.; 23 cm. Translation of Musique de l'Afrique. 1. Music — Africa — History and criticism. I. T.
ML350.B4213    780/.96    *LC* 74-9348    *ISBN* 0882080512

**Nketia, J. H. Kwabena.**    **1.3748**
The music of Africa [by] J. H. Kwabena Nketia. [1st ed.] New York, W. W. Norton [1974] x, 278 p. illus. 21 cm. 1. Music — Africa — History and criticism. I. T.
ML350.N595 M9    780/.96    *LC* 74-4178    *ISBN* 0393021777 *ISBN* 0393092496

# ML385–429 BIOGRAPHY

## ML385–390 COMPOSERS (COLLECTED)

**Dance, Stanley.**    **1.3749**
The world of Count Basie / Stanley Dance. — New York: C. Scribner's Sons, c1980. xxi, 399 p., [12] leaves of plates: ill.; 24 cm. Includes index. 1. Basie, Count, 1904- 2. Jazz musicians — United States — Biography. 3. Jazz music 4. Big bands I. T.
ML385.D26    785.42/092/4 B    *LC* 80-15641    *ISBN* 0684166046

**Martin, George Whitney.**    **1.3750**
The Damrosch dynasty: America's first family of music / George Martin. — Boston: Houghton Mifflin, 1983. xiii, 526 p., [16] p. of plates: ill., ports.; 24 cm. Includes index. 1. Damrosch family 2. Musicians — United States — Biography. I. T.
ML385.M275 1983    780/.92/2 B 19    *LC* 83-315    *ISBN* 0395344085

**Trotter, James M.**    • **1.3751**
Music and some highly musical people: containing brief chapters on I. A description of music. II. The music of nature. III. A glance at the history of music. IV. The power, beauty, and uses of music. Following which are given sketches of the lives of remarkable musicians of the colored race. With portraits, and an appendix containing copies of music composed by colored men, by James M. Trotter. — Chicago: Afro-Am Press, 1969. 353, 152 p. of music.: ports.; 22 cm. 'The original edition was published in 1880.' 1. Negro musicians — Biography. I. T.
ML385.T76 1969    780/.922    *LC* 71-99415    *ISBN* 0841100888

**Abraham, Gerald, 1904-.**    • **1.3752**
Eight Soviet composers [by] Gerald Abraham. Westport, Conn., Greenwood Press [1970] 102 p. music. 23 cm. Reprint of the 1943 ed. 1. Composers —

Soviet Union — Biography. 2. Music — Soviet Union — 20th century — History and criticism. I. T.
ML390.A13 1970    780/.922 B    *LC* 71-106679    *ISBN* 0837133505

**Anderson, E. Ruth, 1928-.**    **1.3753**
Contemporary American composers: a biographical dictionary / compiled by E. Ruth Anderson. — 2nd ed. — Boston, Mass.: G.K. Hall, 1982. 578 p.; 29 cm. 1. Composers — United States — Biography. I. T.
ML390.A54 1982    780/.92/2 B 19    *LC* 81-7047    *ISBN* 081618223X

**The Black composer speaks** / edited by David N. Baker, Lida    **1.3754**
M. Belt, and Herman C. Hudson; a project of the Afro–American Arts Institute, Indiana University.
Metuchen, N.J.: Scarecrow Press, 1978. v, 506 p.; 23 cm. 1. Composers — United States — Interviews. 2. Afro-American composers — Interviews. I. Baker, David, 1931- II. Belt, Lida M. III. Hudson, Herman. IV. Indiana. University. Afro-American Arts Institute.
ML390.B64    780/.92/2 B    *LC* 77-24146    *ISBN* 081081045X

**Leibowitz, René, 1913-1972.**    • **1.3755**
[Schoenberg et son école. English] Schoenberg and his school; the contemporary stage of the language of music. Translated from the French by Dika Newlin. New York, Da Capo Press, 1970 [c1949]. xxvi, 305 p. music. 24 cm. (Da Capo Press music reprint series) 1. Schoenberg, Arnold, 1874-1951. 2. Berg, Alban, 1885-1935. 3. Webern, Anton, 1883-1945. 4. Music — 20th century — History and criticism I. T.
ML390.L462 1970    780/.904    *LC* 75-115338    *ISBN* 030671681X

**Seroff, Victor Ilyitch, 1902-.**    • **1.3756**
The Mighty Five; the cradle of Russian national music. New York, Allen, Towne & Heath [1948] 280 p. ports. 1. Balakirev, Miliĭ Alekseevich, 1837-1910. 2. Mussorgsky, Modest Petrovich, 1839-1881. 3. Borodin, Aleksandr Porfir'evich, 1833-1887. 4. Cui, César, 1835-1918. 5. Rimsky-Korsakov, Nikolay, 1844-1908. I. T.
ML390 S47    *LC* 48-6401

## ML394–402 PERFORMERS. CONDUCTORS (COLLECTED)

**Goldberg, Joe.**    • **1.3757**
Jazz masters of the fifties. — New York: Macmillan Co., [1965] 246 p.; 22 cm. — (The Macmillan jazz masters series) 1. Jazz musicians — Biography. I. T.
ML394.G63    927.8    *LC* 65-13117

**Hadlock, Richard.**    • **1.3758**
Jazz masters of the twenties. — New York: Macmillan, [1965] 255 p.; 22 cm. — (The Macmillan jazz masters series) 1. Jazz musicians — Biography. 2. Jazz music 3. Jazz music — Discography. I. T.
ML394.H33    780.922    *LC* 65-18469

**Spellman, A. B., 1935-.**    • **1.3759**
[Four lives in the bebop business] Black music, four lives, by A. B. Spellman. New York, Schocken Books [1970, c1966] xiv, 241 p. 21 cm. First ed., 1966, has title: Four lives in the bebop business. 1. Jazz musicians — Biography. 2. Afro-American musicians — Biography. I. T.
ML394.S74 1970    780.92/2 B    *LC* 76-123365    *ISBN* 0805202811

**Gitler, Ira.**    • **1.3760**
Jazz masters of the forties. — New York: Macmillan Co., [1966] 290 p.: ports.; 22 cm. — (The Macmillan jazz masters series) 1. Jazz musicians — Biography. I. T.
ML395.G58    781.570922    *LC* 66-17874

**Schonberg, Harold C.**    • **1.3761**
The great pianists. — New York: Simon and Schuster, 1963. 448 p.: ports., music.; 24 cm. 1. Pianists — Biography. I. T.
ML397.S3    927.8    *LC* 63-15367

**Heriot, Angus, 1927-.**    • **1.3762**
The castrati in opera. — London: Secker & Warburg, 1956. 243 p.: ill.; 23 cm. — 1. Singers — Biography. 2. Castrati — Biography. 3. Opera I. T.
ML400.H47 1974    782.1/09/033    *LC* 57-82

**Kutsch, K. J.**    • **1.3763**
[Unvergängliche Stimmen: Kleines Sängerlexikon. English] A concise biographical dictionary of singers; from the beginning of recorded sound to the present, by K. J. Kutsch and Leo Riemens. Translated from German, expanded and annotated by Harry Earl Jones. [1st American ed.] Philadelphia, Chilton Book Co. [1969] xxiv, 487 p. 21 cm. Translation of Unvergängliche Stimmen: Kleines Sängerlexikon. 1. Singers — Biography. I. Riemens, Leo. joint author. II. T.
ML400.K9813 1969    784/.0922 B    *LC* 79-94106

**Mellers, Wilfrid Howard, 1914-.**                                                **1.3764**
Angels of the night: popular female singers of our time / Wilfrid Mellers. — New York: B. Blackwell, 1986. x, 227 p., [24] p. of plates: ill.; 24 cm. Includes index. 1. Women singers — United States — Biography. 2. Popular music — United States — History and criticism. I. T.
ML400.M44 1986        784.5/0088042 19        *LC* 85-18659        *ISBN* 0631146962

**Pleasants, Henry.**                                                              • **1.3765**
The great singers; from the dawn of opera to our own time. — New York: Simon and Schuster, [1966] 382 p.: illus., music, ports.; 24 cm. 1. Singers — Biography. I. T.
ML400.P65        782.0922        *LC* 66-20250

**Steane, J. B.**                                                                  **1.3766**
The grand tradition; seventy years of singing on record [by] J. B. Steane. — New York: C. Scribner's Sons, [1974] xii, 628 p.: illus.; 25 cm. 1. Singers 2. Sound recordings I. T.
ML400.S82 1974b        789.9/136/210922        *LC* 73-10839        *ISBN* 0684136341

**Hart, Philip, 1914-.**                                                           **1.3767**
Conductors: a new generation / Philip Hart. — New York: C. Scribner's Sons, 1979. xviii, 302 p.: ports.; 24 cm. Includes index. 1. Conductors (Music) — Biography. I. T.
ML402.H37        785/.092/2 B        *LC* 79-18083        *ISBN* 0684163896

**Matheopoulos, Helena.**                                                          **1.3768**
Maestro: encounters with conductors of today / Helena Matheopoulos. — 1st U.S. ed. — New York: Harper & Row, c1982. xxi, 536 p., [32] p. of plates: ill.; 25 cm. Includes index. 1. Conductors (Music) — Interviews. I. T.
ML402.M37 1982        785/.092/2 B 19        *LC* 82-48125        *ISBN* 006015103X

**Schonberg, Harold C.**                                                           • **1.3769**
The great conductors [by] Harold C. Schonberg. — New York: Simon and Schuster, [1967] 384 p.: illus., facsims., music, ports.; 24 cm. 1. Conductors (Music) — Biography. I. T.
ML402.S387 G7        780.922        *LC* 67-19821

**Langwill, Lyndesay Graham, 1897-.**                                              **1.3770**
An index of musical wind–instrument makers / by Lyndesay G. Langwill. — 6th ed., rev., enl., and illustrated. — Edinburgh, Scotland: L.G. Langwill, 1980. xix, 331 p., [2] leaves of plates: ill.; 26 cm. Spine title: Index of wind-instrument makers. 1. Wind instrument makers I. T. II. Title: Index of wind-instrument makers.
ML404.L3 1980        338.4/7681818 19        *LC* 81-101213

## ML410 Composers, A–Z

## ML410 Ba

**Arnold, Denis.**                                                                 **1.3771**
Bach / Denis Arnold. — Oxford; New York: Oxford University Press, 1984. vii, 103 p.; 18 cm. — (Past masters.) Includes index. 1. Bach, Johann Sebastian, 1685-1750. 2. Composers — Germany — Biography. I. T. II. Series.
ML410.B1 A96 1984        780/.92/4 B 19        *LC* 83-15141        *ISBN* 019287554X

**Boyd, Malcolm.**                                                                 **1.3772**
Bach / Malcolm Boyd. — London: J.M. Dent, 1983. xiv, 290 p., [12] p. of plates: ill., music, ports.; 23 cm. — (The Master musicians) Includes index. 1. Bach, Johann Sebastian, 1685-1750. 2. Composers — Germany — Biography. I. T.
ML410.B1 B73 1983        780/.92/4 19        *LC* 83-226639        *ISBN* 0460044664

**Carrell, Norman.**                                                               • **1.3773**
Bach the borrower; preface by Basil Lam. — London: Allen & Unwin, 1967. 3-396 p.: illus. (music), tables. 1. Bach, Johann Sebastian, 1685-1750. I. T.
ML410.B1 C277        780/.924        *LC* 67-91819

**David, Hans Theodore, 1902- ed.**                                                • **1.3774**
The Bach reader; a life of Johann Sebastian Bach in letters and documents, edited by Hans T. David and Arthur Mendel. — Rev., with a supplement. — New York: W. W. Norton, [1966] 474 p.: illus., facsims., music, ports.; 22 cm. 1. Bach, Johann Sebastian, 1685-1750. I. Mendel, Arthur, 1905- joint ed. II. T.
ML410.B1 D24 1966        780.924        *LC* 66-10768

**Forkel, Johann Nikolaus, 1749-1818.**                                            • **1.3775**
[Ueber Johann Sebastian Bachs Leben. English] Johann Sebastian Bach; his life, art, and work. Notes and appendices by Charles Sanford Terry. New York, Da Capo Press, 1970. xxxii, 321 p. illus., geneal. tables, ports. 24 cm. (Da Capo

Press music reprint series) Translation of Ueber Johann Sebastian Bachs Leben, Kunst und Kunstwerke. 1. Bach, Johann Sebastian, 1685-1750. I. T.
ML410.B1 F83 1970        780/.924 B        *LC* 75-125044        *ISBN* 0306700107

**Geiringer, Karl, 1899-.**                                                        • **1.3776**
The Bach family; seven generations of creative genius [by] Karl Geiringer in collaboration with Irene Geiringer. — New York: Oxford University Press, 1954. xiv, 514 p.: illus., 26 plates (incl. ports., facsims.) map, music.; 25 cm. 1. Bach family 2. Bach, Johann Sebastian, 1685-1750. I. T.
ML410.B1 G397        927.8        *LC* 54-13129

**Geiringer, Karl, 1899-.**                                                        • **1.3777**
Johann Sebastian Bach; the culmination of an era [by] Karl Geiringer, in collaboration with Irene Geiringer. — New York: Oxford University Press, 1966. xi, 382 p.: geneal. table, music, 8 plates (inc. facsims., ports.); 24 cm. 1. Bach, Johann Sebastian, 1685-1750. I. Geiringer, Irene. II. T.
ML410.B1 G43        780.924        *LC* 66-22262

**Herz, Gerhard, 1911-.**                                                          **1.3778**
Essays on J.S. Bach / by Gerhard Herz. — Ann Arbor, Mich.: UMI Research Press, c1985. xxxi, 276 p.: ill.; 24 cm. (Studies in musicology. no. 73) In part a translation, with new introd., of the author's dissertation, Johann Sebastian Bach im Zeitalter des Rationalismus und der Frühromantik (University of Zurich, 1934) 1. Bach, Johann Sebastian, 1685-1750. I. Herz, Gerhard, 1911- Johann Sebastian Bach im Zeitalter des Rationalismus und der Frühromantik. English. 1985. II. T. III. Series.
ML410.B1 H348 1985        780/.92/4 19        *LC* 84-22222        *ISBN* 0835714756

**Johann Sebastian Bach (Kassel, Germany). English.**                              **1.3779**
Johann Sebastian Bach: life, times, influence / edited by Barbara Schwendowius and Wolfgang Dömling. — New Haven: Yale University Press, c1984. 179 p.: ill. (some col.); 32 cm. Translated from the German. Includes index. 1. Bach, Johann Sebastian, 1685-1750 — Addresses, essays, lectures. 2. Composers — Germany — Biography. I. Schwendowius, Barbara. II. Dömling, Wolfgang, 1938- III. T.
ML410.B1 J6713 1984        780/.92/4 19        *LC* 84-50475        *ISBN* 0300032684

**Marshall, Robert Lewis.**                                                        **1.3780**
The compositional process of J. S. Bach; a study of the autograph scores of the vocal works. [Princeton, N.J.] Princeton University Press, 1972. 2 v. illus. 29 cm. (Princeton studies in music, no. 4) 1. Bach, Johann Sebastian, 1685-1750. Vocal music. 2. Bach, Johann Sebastian, 1685-1750 — Manuscripts. 3. Composition (Music) — History. 4. Vocal music — Analysis, appreciation. I. T. II. Series.
ML410.B1 M285        783/.092/4        *LC* 76-113005        *ISBN* 0691091137

**Schweitzer, Albert, 1875-1965.**                                                 • **1.3781**
J. S. Bach / by Albert Schweitzer; translated by Ernest Newman. — New York: Macmillan, 1952, c1911. 2 v.: music, port.; 22 cm. 'English translation from the German ed., with alterations and additions by the author, published in 1911 by Breitkopf and Hartel, London.' 1. Bach, Johann Sebastian, 1685-1750. I. T.
ML410.B1 S34 1966        780/.924 B

**Spitta, Philipp, 1841-1894.**                                                    • **1.3782**
Johann Sebastian Bach, his work and influence on the music of Germany, 1685–1750. Translated from the German by Clara Bell and J. A. Fuller–Maitland. — London: Novello; New York: Dover Publications, [1951] 3 v. in 2.: port.; 21 cm. 'Not merely ... a translation, but ... a revised and improved edition.' 'Musical supplement': v. 3, p. 363-405. 1. Bach, Johann Sebastian, 1685-1750. I. T.
ML410.B1 S7 1951        927.8        *LC* 52-6022

**Terry, Charles Sanford, 1864-1936.**                                             • **1.3783**
Bach's orchestra / by Charles Sanford Terry. — London: Oxford University Press: H. Milford, 1932. xv, 250 p., [9] leaves of plates: ill., music, port.; 23 cm. 1. Bach, Johann Sebastian, 1685-1750. 2. Orchestra 3. Musical instruments 4. Musical instruments — History — 17th century. 5. Musical instruments — History — 18th century. I. T.
ML410.B13 T4        *LC* 33-6682

**Terry, Charles Sanford, 1864-1936.**                                             • **1.3784**
John Christian Bach. — 2nd ed. with a foreword by H. C. Robbins Landon. — London; New York: Oxford U.P., 1967. lv, 373 p.: illus. (music), 22 plates.; 22 1/2 cm. 1. Bach, Johann Christian, 1735-1782. 2. Bach, Johann Christian, 1735-1782 — Thematic catalogs. I. T.
ML410.B15 T3 1967        780/.924 B        *LC* 67-77649

**Bach, Carl Philipp Emanuel, 1714-1788.**                                         • **1.3785**
Carl Philip Emanuel Bach's autobiography / Facsimile of the original edition of 1773 with critical annotations by William S. Newman. — Hilversum: Frits A. M. Knuf, 1967. 20 p.: port. — (Facsimiles of early biographies; v. 4) First published in the Hamburg section of J. J. P. Bodes German translation of Charles Burneys The present state of music in Germany, the Netherlands and

the United Provinces. 1. Musicians — Biography I. Newman, William S. II. T. III. Series.
ML410.B16 A3 1773a     *LC* 67-21063/MN

**Broder, Nathan.**      • **1.3786**
Samuel Barber. New York, G. Schirmer [1954] 111 p. ill. 19 cm. Photocopy. Ann Arbor.: Mich.: University Microfilms, 1979. 1. Barber, Samuel, 1910-2. Barber, Samuel, 1910- — Discography. I. T.
ML 410 B23 B86 1954     *LC* 54-13121

**Bartók, Béla, 1881-1945.**      • **1.3787**
[Levelek. English] Béla Bartók letters. Collected, selected, edited, and annotated by János Demény. Prefaced by Sir Michael Tippett. Translated into English by Péter Balabán and István Farkas. Translation rev. by Elisabeth West and Colin Mason. New York, St. Martin's Press [1971] 466 p. illus. 25 cm. 1. Bartók, Béla, 1881-1945. 2. Musicians — Correspondence, reminiscences, etc. I. Demény, János. ed. II. T.
ML410.B26 A42 1971b     780/.924 B     *LC* 70-124146

**Griffiths, Paul.**      **1.3788**
Bartók / Paul Griffiths. — London: J.M. Dent, 1984. ix, 224 p., [8] p. of plates: ill., music; 23 cm. — (Master musicians series.) Includes index. 1. Bartók, Béla, 1881-1945. 2. Composers — Hungary — Biography. I. T. II. Series.
ML410.B26 G7 1984     780/.92/4 B 19     *LC* 84-141807     *ISBN* 0460031821

**Lesznai, Lajos.**      **1.3789**
[Béla Bartók. English] Bartok. Translated from the German by Percy M. Young. New York, Octagon Books [1973] xii, 219 p. illus. 20 cm. (Master musicians series.) Imprint on mounted label. Translation of Béla Bartók; sein Leben, seine Werke. 1. Bartók, Béla, 1881-1945. I. T. II. Series.
ML410.B26 L53 1973b     780/.92/4 B     *LC* 73-7004     *ISBN* 0460031368

**Milne, Hamish.**      **1.3790**
Bartók: his life and times / Hamish Milne. — Tunbridge Wells: Midas, 1982. 112 p.: ill., facsims., map, music, ports.; 26 cm. — (Composers, their lives and times.) 1. Bartók, Béla, 1881-1945. 2. Composers — Hungary — Biography. I. T. II. Series.
ML410.B26 M5x     ML410B26 M54.     780/.92/4 19     *ISBN* 0859362736

**Stevens, Halsey, 1908-.**      • **1.3791**
The life and music of Béla Bartók. — Rev. ed. — New York: Oxford University Press, 1964. xvi, 364 p.: illus., facsim., music, ports.; 22 cm. 1. Bartók, Béla, 1881-1945. I. T.
ML410.B26 S8 1964     780.92     *LC* 64-24867

**Szabolcsi, Bence, 1899-1973.**      • **1.3792**
Béla Bartók, his life in pictures. Introductory study by Bence Szabolcsi. Photos, collected and edited by Ferenc Bónis. [Translated by Sára Karig and Lili Halápy] London Boosey & Hawkes [1964] 68p. 1. Bartók, Béla, 1881-1945. 2. Bartók, Béla, 1881-1945 — Iconography I. Bónis, Ferenc. II. T.
ML410 B26 S896 1964

**Ujfalussy, József.**      • **1.3793**
[Bartók Béla. English] Béla Bartók. [Translated by Ruth Pataki. 1st U.S. ed.] Boston, Crescendo Pub. Co. [1972, c1971] 459 p. port. 21 cm. 1. Bartók, Béla, 1881-1945. I. T.
ML410.B26 U383     780/.924 B     *LC* 72-200879     *ISBN* 087597077X

## ML410 Be

**Beethoven, Ludwig van, 1770-1827.**      • **1.3794**
The letters of Beethoven / collected, translated and edited with an introd., appendixes, notes and indexes by Emily Anderson. — New York: St. Martin's Press, 1961. 3 v. (liii, 1489, [7] p., [41] l. of plates): facsims., music, ports. I. Anderson, Emily. II. T.
ML410.B4 A43     *LC* 61-65707

**Beethoven, Ludwig van, 1779-1827.**      • **1.3795**
New Beethoven letters. 1st ed. Norman, University of Oklahoma Press [1957] xxxix, 577 p. facsims. 25 cm. I. Briefe. English. II. T.
ML410.B4 A4376     *LC* 57-7331

**Arnold, Denis.**      • **1.3796**
[Beethoven companion] The Beethoven reader. Edited by Denis Arnold and Nigel Fortune. New York, W. W. Norton [1971] 542 p. illus., facsims., music, port. 25 cm. London ed. (Faber) has title: The Beethoven companion. 1. Beethoven, Ludwig van, 1770-1827. I. Fortune, Nigel. joint author. II. T.
ML410.B4 A75 1971b     780/.924     *LC* 77-139374     *ISBN* 0303021491

**Beethoven: impressions by his contemporaries. Edited by O. G.**      • **1.3797**
**Sonneck.**
New York: Dover Publications, [1967, c1964] vi, 231 p.: music, ports.; 22 cm. 'This Dover edition is an unabridged and unaltered republication of the work originally published in 1926 under the title Beethoven: impressions of contemporaries.' 1. Beethoven, Ludwig van, 1770-1827. I. Sonneck, Oscar George Theodore, 1873-1928. comp.
ML410.B4 B28 1967     780.924     *LC* 66-30379

**Cooper, Martin, 1910-.**      • **1.3798**
Beethoven; the last decade 1817–1827, with a medical appendix by Edward Larkin. — London; New York: Oxford University Press, 1970. x, 483, p.: facsim., music, port.; 23 cm. 1. Beethoven, Ludwig van, 1770-1827. I. T.
ML410.B4 C75     780/.924     *LC* 76-116137     *ISBN* 0193153106

**Johnson, Douglas Porter.**      **1.3799**
The Beethoven sketchbooks: history, reconstruction, inventory / Douglas Johnson, Alan Tyson & Robert Winter; edited by Douglas Johnson. — Berkeley: University of California Press, c1985. xx, 611 p.: ill.; 27 cm. — (California studies in 19th century music. 4) 1. Beethoven, Ludwig van, 1770-1827. Selections (Sketches) I. Tyson, Alan. II. Winter, Robert, 1945- III. T. IV. Series.
ML410.B4 J58 1985     780/.92/4 19     *LC* 82-25920     *ISBN* 0520048350

**Landon, Howard Chandler Robbins, 1926- comp.**      • **1.3800**
[Beethoven. English] Beethoven; a documentary study. Compiled and edited by H. C. Robbins Landon. [1st American ed. New York] Macmillan [1970] 400 p. illus. (part col.), facsims., ports. 33 cm. Translation of Beethoven; sein Leben und seine Welt in zeitgenössischen Bildern und Texten. 1. Beethoven, Ludwig van, 1770-1827. 2. Beethoven, Ludwig van, 1770-1827 — Iconography. I. T.
ML410.B4 L287     780/.924     *LC* 77-101293

**Marek, George Richard, 1902-.**      • **1.3801**
Beethoven: biography of a genius, by George R. Marek. — London: Kimber, 1970. xix, 696 p., plate.: illus., facsims., ports. (1 col.).; 26 cm. 1. Beethoven, Ludwig van, 1770-1827. I. T.
ML410.B4 M227 1970     780/.924 B     *LC* 77-513910     *ISBN* 071830411X

**Mies, Paul, 1889-.**      • **1.3802**
Beethoven's sketches; an analysis of his style based on a study of his sketch-books, by Paul Mies. Translated by Doris L. Mackinnon. — London, Oxford university press, H. Milford, 1929. 4 p. l., 198 p., 1 l. illus. (music) 22 cm. Bibliography: p. 189-190. Translation of Die bedeutung der skizzen Beethovens zur erkenntnis seines stiles. 1. Beethoven, Ludwig van, 1770-1827. I. Mackinnon, Doris Livingston. tr. II. T.
ML410.B4M62     *LC* 29-17403

**Scherman, Thomas, comp.**      • **1.3803**
The Beethoven companion. Edited by Thomas K. Scherman and Louis Biancolli. — [1st ed.]. — Garden City, N.Y.: Doubleday, 1972. xl, 1230 p.; 25 cm. 1. Beethoven, Ludwig van, 1770-1827. I. Biancolli, Louis Leopold. joint comp. II. T.
ML410.B4 S27     780/.924 B     *LC* 74-125530

**Schindler, Anton Felix, 1795-1864.**      • **1.3804**
Beethoven as I knew him; a biography by Anton Felix Schindler. Edited by Donald W. MacArdle and translated by Constance S. Jolly. — Chapel Hill, University of North Carolina Press [1966] 547 p. facsims., music, plates. 26 cm. Translation of Biographie von Ludwig van Beethoven (Münster, Aschendorff, 1860) 1. Beethoven, Ludwig van, 1770-1827. I. MacArdle, Donald W. ed. II. T.
ML410.B4S3333 1966a     780.924 (B)     *LC* 66-7988

**Solomon, Maynard.**      **1.3805**
Beethoven / Maynard Solomon. — New York: Schirmer Books, c1977. xvi, 400 p.: ill.; 24 cm. Includes indexes. 1. Beethoven, Ludwig van, 1770-1827. 2. Composers — Biography. I. T.
ML410.B4 S64     780/.92/4 B     *LC* 77-5242     *ISBN* 0028724607

**Thayer, Alexander Wheelock, 1817-1897.**      • **1.3806**
[Ludwig van Beethoven's Leben. English] Life of Beethoven. Rev. and edited by Elliot Forbes. Princeton, N.J., Princeton University Press, 1964. 2 v. (1136 p.) ports., music. 25 cm. Although some portions of Thayer's original text have been deleted because recent Beethoven research has proved them inaccurate, 'the majority of the text used consists of the coordinated treatment of Thayer's notes and manuscript by these three editors [H. Deiters, H. Riemann, and H. Krehbiel]' with additions and corrections by the present editor. 'First publication of works after Beethoven's death': v. 2, p. 1077-1084. 1. Beethoven, Ludwig van, 1770-1827. I. Forbes, Elliot. ed. II. Deiters, Hermann, 1833-1907. ed. III. Riemann, Hugo, 1849-1919. ed. IV. Krehbiel, Henry Edward, 1854-1923. ed. V. T.
ML410.B4 T33 1964     927.8     *LC* 63-16239

**Tovey, Donald Francis, Sir, 1875-1940.**    • **1.3807**
Beethoven [by] Donald Francis Tovey ... with an editorial preface by Hubert J. Foss. London, New York [etc.] Oxford University Press, 1946,c1945. vii, 138 p. illus. (music) diagrs. 22 cm. A discussion of Beethoven's music. 1. Beethoven, Ludwig van, 1770-1827. I. Foss, Hubert James, 1899- II. T.
ML410.B4 T68 1946    780.81    *LC* 45-10300

**Berlioz, Hector, 1803-1869.**    • **1.3808**
A critical study of Beethoven's nine symphonies: with 'A few words on his trios and sonatas,' a criticism of 'Fidelio' and an introductory essay on music / by Hector Berlioz; translated from the French by Edwin Evans. — London: W. Reeves, c1958. 165 p.: port. Translation of Étude critique des symphonies de Beethoven. 1. Beethoven, Ludwig van, 1770-1827. Symphonies. 2. Beethoven, Ludwig van, 1770-1827. Fidelio (1814) 3. Music — Addresses, essays, lectures. I. T.
ML410.B42 B413    *LC* 63-6584

**Beethoven studies.**    **1.3809**
[1]-. New York, N.Y.: Norton, c1973-. v.: ill.; 24 cm. Imprint varies. I. Tyson, Alan.
ML410.B42 T9    *LC* 83-642519

**Schmidt-Görg, Joseph, 1897-.**    • **1.3810**
[Ludwig van Beethoven. English] Ludwig van Beethoven; edited by Joseph Schmidt-Görg & Hans Schmidt [translated from the German] London, Pall Mall P., 1970. 275 p. illus. (some col.), facsims. (some col.), music, ports. (some col.) 32 cm. 1. Beethoven, Ludwig van, 1770-1827. I. Schmidt, Hans, Dr., joint author. II. T.
ML410.B43 S253 1970b    780/.924 B    *LC* 78-523662    *ISBN* 0269026193

**Weinstock, Herbert, 1905-.**    • **1.3811**
Vincenzo Bellini; his life and his operas. — [1st ed.]. — New York: A. A. Knopf, 1971. xx, 554, xxxvii p.: illus.; 25 cm. 1. Bellini, Vincenzo, 1801-1835. I. T.
ML410.B44 W4    782.1/0924 B    *LC* 70-111256    *ISBN* 0394416562

**Jarman, Douglas.**    **1.3812**
The Music of Alban Berg / Douglas Jarman. — Berkeley: University of California Press, c1979. xii, 266 p.: music; 27 cm. Includes index. 1. Berg, Alban, 1885-1935 — Criticism and interpretation. I. T.
ML410.B47 J33    780/.92/4    *LC* 77-76687    *ISBN* 0520034856

**Perle, George, 1915-.**    **1.3813**
The operas of Alban Berg / George Perle. — Berkeley: University of California Press, c1980-c1985. 2 v.: ill.; 26 cm. Includes indexes. 1. Berg, Alban, 1885-1935. 2. Berg, Alban, 1885-1935. Wozzeck. 3. Berg, Alban, 1885-1935. Lulu. I. T.
ML410.B47 P48    782.1/092/4    *LC* 76-52033    *ISBN* 0520034406

**Redlich, Hans Ferdinand, 1903-1968.**    • **1.3814**
Alban Berg: the man and his music / Hans F. Redlich. — New York: Abelard-Schuman [1957]. 316 p.: ill., ports., facsims., music; 22 cm. 1. Berg, Alban, 1885-1935. I. T.
ML410.B47 R3    *LC* 57-513

**Berlioz, Hector, 1803-1869.**    • **1.3815**
[Soirées de l'orchestre. English] Evenings with the orchestra. Translated and edited with an introd. and notes by Jacques Barzun at the request of the Berlioz Society. [1st ed.] New York, Knopf, 1956. xviii, 376 p. illus., ports. 24 cm. 1. Music — France — Paris. 2. Music — Addresses, essays, lectures. I. T.
ML410.B5 A245 1956    780.883    *LC* 56-5294

**Berlioz, Hector, 1803-1869.**    **1.3816**
[Mémoires. English] The memoirs of Hector Berlioz, member of the French Institute: including his travels in Italy, Germany, Russia, and England, 1803–1865 / translated and edited by David Cairns. — Corr. ed. — New York: Norton, 1975. 636 p., [12] leaves of plates: ill.; 20 cm. — (The Norton library; N698) Includes index. 1. Berlioz, Hector, 1803-1869. 2. Composers — France — Biography. I. Cairns, David. ed. II. T.
ML410.B5 A42 1975    780/.92/4 B    *LC* 74-32133    *ISBN* 0393006980

**Barzun, Jacques, 1907-.**    • **1.3817**
Berlioz and the romantic century. — 3d ed. — New York: Columbia University Press, 1969. 2 v.: illus., ports.; 24 cm. 'Errors in the 'complete' edition of the scores': v. 2, p. [358]-381. 1. Berlioz, Hector, 1803-1869. I. T.
ML410.B5 B2 1969    780/.924 B    *LC* 77-97504    *ISBN* 0231031351

**Holoman, D. Kern, 1947-.**    **1.3818**
The creative process in the autograph musical documents of Hector Berlioz, c. 1818–1840 / D. Kern Holoman. — Ann Arbor, Mich.: UMI Research Press, [1980] xxii, 379 p.: ill.; 24 cm. — (Studies in musicology. no. 7) Includes index. 1. Berlioz, Hector, 1803-1869 — Manuscripts — History and criticism.

2. Creation (Literary, artistic, etc.) 3. Musical sketches — History and criticism. I. T. II. Series.
ML410.B5 H6    780/.92/4    *LC* 79-11879    *ISBN* 0835709884

## ML410 Bi–By

**McKay, David Phares.**    **1.3819**
William Billings of Boston: eighteenth–century composer, by David P. McKay and Richard Crawford. — [Princeton, N.J.]: Princeton University Press, [1975] xii, 303 p.: illus.; 24 cm. 1. Billings, William, 1746-1800. I. Crawford, Richard, 1935- joint author. II. T.
ML410.B588 M3    783/.092/4 B    *LC* 74-19035    *ISBN* 0691091188

**Dean, Winton.**    • **1.3820**
Georges Bizet, his life and work. London, J.M. Dent [1965] xiv, 304 p. ill., facsims., music, ports. 1. Bizet, Georges, 1838-1875. I. T.
ML410 B62 D355    *LC* 65-6938

**Geiringer, Karl, 1899-.**    • **1.3821**
[Johannes Brahms; Leben und Schaffen] Brahms, his life and work [tr. by H. B. Weiner and Bernard Miall] 2d ed., rev. and enl., with a new appendix of Brahms's letters. New York, Oxford University Press, 1947. xv, 383 p. illus., ports., music. 22 cm. 1. Brahms, Johannes, 1883-1897. I. Weiner, H. B., tr. II. T.
ML410.B8 G42 1947    927.8    *LC* 47-11223

**James, Burnett.**    • **1.3822**
Brahms; a critical study. — New York: Praeger, [1972] xiii, 202 p.: illus.; 23 cm. 1. Brahms, Johannes, 1833-1897. I. T.
ML410.B8 J3    780/.92/4    *LC* 78-165844

**Evans, Peter Angus, 1929-.**    **1.3823**
The music of Benjamin Britten / Peter Evans; illustrated with over 300 music examples and diagrams. — Minneapolis: University of Minnesota Press, 1979. vii, 564 p.: ill.; 25 cm. Includes index. 1. Britten, Benjamin, 1913-1976 — Criticism and interpretation. I. T.
ML410.B853 E9 1979    780/.92/4    *LC* 78-31606

**Mitchell, Donald, 1925- ed.**    • **1.3824**
Benjamin Britten; a commentary on his works from a group of specialists. Edited by Donald Mitchell and Hans Keller. Westport, Conn., Greenwood Press [1972, c1952] xvi, 410 p. illus. 23 cm. 1. Britten, Benjamin, 1913-1976 — Criticism and interpretation. I. Keller, Hans, 1919- ed. II. T.
ML410.B853 M5 1972    780/.924    *LC* 70-138166    *ISBN* 0837156238

**Doernberg, Erwin.**    • **1.3825**
The life and symphonies of Anton Bruckner. With a foreword by Robert Simpson. — New York: Dover Publications, [1968, c1960] xii, 235 p.: illus., facsims., music, ports.; 22 cm. 'This Dover edition is an unabridged and unaltered republication of the work originally published in 1960.' 1. Bruckner, Anton, 1824-1896. 2. Bruckner, Anton, 1824-1896. Symphonies. I. T.
ML410.B88 D6 1968    780/.924 B    *LC* 68-19176

**Redlich, Hans Ferdinand, 1903-1968.**    • **1.3826**
Bruckner and Mahler / by H.F. Redlich. — London: Dent, 1955. xi, 300 p.: ill., facsims., music, ports.; 20 cm. — (The Master musicians) 1. Bruckner, Anton, 1824-1896. 2. Mahler, Gustav, 1860-1911. I. T.
ML410.B88 R4    780/.92/2 B

**Schönzeler, Hans Hubert.**    • **1.3827**
Bruckner. — New York: Grossman Publishers, 1970. 190 p.: illus.; 22 cm. — ([Library of composers, 3]) 1. Bruckner, Anton, 1824-1896. I. T. II. Series.
ML410.B88 S24 1970b    780/.92/4 B    *LC* 78-114931

**Simpson, Robert Wilfred Levick, 1921-.**    • **1.3828**
The essence of Bruckner; an essay toward the understanding of his music, by Robert Simpson. — [1st American ed.]. — Philadelphia: Chilton Book Co., [1968] 206 p.: music, port.; 23 cm. 1. Bruckner, Anton, 1824-1896. I. T.
ML410.B88 S46 1968    780/.924    *LC* 68-28040

**Cunningham, Walker.**    **1.3829**
The keyboard music of John Bull / by Walker Cunningham. — Ann Arbor, Mich.: UMI Research Press, c1984. xviii, 274 p.: music; 24 cm. (Studies in musicology. no. 71) Revision of thesis (Ph.D.)—University of California-Berkeley, 1981. Includes indexes. 1. Bull, John, d. 1628. Keyboard music I. T. II. Series.
ML410.B93 C8 1984    786.1/092/4 19    *LC* 84-59    *ISBN* 0835714667

**Fellowes, Edmund Horace, 1870-1951.**    • **1.3830**
William Byrd. 2d ed. London; New York: Oxford University Press, 1948. 271 p. 'Byrd's motets': p. 252-263. 1. Byrd, William, 1542 or 3-1623. I. T.
ML410.B996 F34 1948    *LC* 48-10154

## ML410 C

**Kostelanetz, Richard. comp.**    • **1.3831**
John Cage. Edited by Richard Kostelanetz. — New York: Praeger, [1970] xvi, 237 p.: illus., facsims., ports.; 23 cm. — ([Documentary monographs in modern art]) 'Told mostly in his [Cage's] own words and writings.' 1. Cage, John. I. Cage, John. II. T.
ML410.C24 K7     780/.924     *LC* 77-121714

**Edwards, Allen, 1944-.**    • **1.3832**
Flawed words and stubborn sounds; a conversation with Elliott Carter. [1st ed.] New York, W. W. Norton [1972, c1971] 128 p. 22 cm. 1. Carter, Elliott, 1908- 2. Music — 20th century — History and criticism I. Carter, Elliott, 1908- II. T.
ML410.C3293 E3    780/.924 B    *LC* 77-152660    *ISBN* 0393021599

**Myers, Rollo H.**    • **1.3833**
Emmanuel Chabrier and his circle [by] Rollo Myers. — [1st American ed.]. — Rutherford [N.J.]: Fairleigh Dickinson University Press, [1970, c1969] xii, 178 p.: illus., facsims., music, ports.; 22 cm. 1. Chabrier, Emmanuel, 1841-1894. I. T.
ML410.C393 M9 1970    780/.924 B    *LC* 70-141868    *ISBN* 0838678335

**Brown, David, 1929-.**    **1.3834**
Tchaikovsky / by David Brown. — New York: W. W. Norton, 1978-. 3v.: ill,. music, ports.; 24 cm. 1. Tchaikovsky, Peter Ilyitch, 1840-1893. I. T.
ML410.C4. B76    *LC* 78-61150    *ISBN* 0393075352

**Wiley, Roland John.**    **1.3835**
Tchaikovsky's ballets: Swan lake, Sleeping beauty, Nutcracker / Roland John Wiley. — Oxford [Oxfordshire]: Clarendon Press; New York: Oxford University Press, 1985. xv, 429 p.: ill., music; 25 cm. Includes index. 1. Tchaikovsky, Peter Ilich, 1840-1893. Ballets 2. Ballet I. T.
ML410.C4 W53 1985    782.9/5/0924 19    *LC* 83-23843    *ISBN* 0193153149

**Abraham, Gerald, 1904-.**    • **1.3836**
Chopin's musical style, by Gerald Abraham. London, Oxford university press [1960] xli, 116 p. ill. (music) 1. Chopin, Frédéric, 1810-1849. I. T.
ML410 C54 A4 1960    *LC* 40-9515

**Liszt, Franz, 1811-1886.**    • **1.3837**
Frederic Chopin. Translated, with an introd. by Edward N. Waters. London, Free Press of Glencoe, Collier-Macmillan [1963] vii, 184 p. 1. Chopin, Frédéric, 1810-1849. I. T.
ML410 C54 L513    *LC* 63-10651

**Walker, Alan, writer on music, ed.**    • **1.3838**
Frederic Chopin; profiles of the man and the musician [by] Paul Badura-Skoda [et al.] Edited by Alan Walker. — [1st Amer. ed.]. — New York, Taplinger Pub. Co. [1966] 334 p. facsims., music, port. 24 cm. Bibliography: p. [323]-324; discography: p. [301]-321. 1. Chopin, Frédéric, 1810-1849. I. T.
ML410.C54W16 1967    786.1/0924    *LC* 67-16594

**Weinstock, Herbert, 1905-.**    • **1.3839**
Chopin, the man and his music. [1st ed.] New York, A.A. Knopf, 1949. x, 336, xxii p. illus., ports., music. 25 cm. 1. Chopin, Frédéric, 1810-1849. I. T.
ML410.C54 W26    927.8    *LC* 49-7744

**Plantinga, Leon.**    **1.3840**
Clementi: his life and music / Leon Plantinga. London; New York: Oxford University Press, 1977. xiii, 346 p., [4] leaves of plates: ill.; 24 cm. Includes index. 1. Clementi, Muzio, 1752-1832. I. T.
ML410.C64 P5    786.1/092/4 B    *LC* 77-359247    *ISBN* 0193152274

**Copland, Aaron, 1900-.**    **1.3841**
Copland: 1900 through 1942 / by Aaron Copland and Vivian Perlis. — 1st ed. — New York: St. Martin's /Marek, c1984. xii, 402 p.: ill.; 25 cm. Includes index. 1. Copland, Aaron, 1900- 2. Composers — United States — Biography. I. Perlis, Vivian. II. T.
ML410.C756 A3 1984    780/.92/4 B 19    *LC* 84-11703    *ISBN* 0312169620

**Berger, Arthur, 1912-.**    • **1.3842**
Aaron Copland [by] Arthur Berger. Westport, Conn., Greenwood Press [1971, c1953] vii, 120 p. illus. 23 cm. 1. Copland, Aaron, 1900- I. T.
ML410.C756 B4 1971    780/.92/4 B 19    *LC* 79-136055    *ISBN* 0837152054

**Pincherle, Marc, 1888-1974.**    • **1.3843**
Corelli: his life, his work. Translated from the French by Hubert E. M. Russell. — [1st ed.]. — New York, Norton [1956] 236 p. illus., ports., facsims., music. 22 cm. Translation of Corelli et son temps. Bibliographical references included

in 'Notes' (p. 188-205) 'Musical bibliography': p. 206-225. Bibliography: p. 226-230. 1. Corelli, Arcangelo, 1653-1713. I. T.
ML410.C78P52    927.8    *LC* 56-10096

**Mellers, Wilfrid Howard, 1914-.**    • **1.3844**
François Couperin and the French classical tradition. — New York: Dover Publications, [1968] 408 p.: illus.; 22 cm. 'This Dover edition is an unabridged republication of the work originally published in 1950.' 1. Couperin, François, 1668-1733. I. T.
ML410.C855 M4 1968    780/.924    *LC* 68-19894

## ML410 D

**Vlad, Roman, 1919-.**    **1.3845**
Luigi Dallapiccola / Roman Vlad; [English translation by Cynthia Jolly]. — St. Clair Shores, Mich.: Scholarly Press, 1977. 62 p., [1] leaf of plates: ill.; 22 cm. Reprint of the 1957 ed. published by Edizioni Suvini Zerboni, Milano. 1. Dallapiccola, Luigi, 1904-1975 — Criticism and interpretation. I. T.
ML410.D138 V6 1977    780/.92/4    *LC* 76-51492    *ISBN* 0403072158

**Debussy, Claude, 1862-1918.**    **1.3846**
[Monsieur Croche et autres écrits. English] Debussy on music: the critical writings of the great French composer Claude Debussy / collected and introduced by François Lesure; translated and edited by Richard Langham Smith. — 1st American ed. — New York: A. A. Knopf, 1977. xxv, 353 p.; 22 cm. Translation of Monsieur Croche et autres écrits. Includes index. 1. Music — Addresses, essays, lectures. I. T.
ML410.D28 A333    780/.8    *LC* 76-13717    *ISBN* 0394481208

**Lockspeiser, Edward, 1905-1973.**    **1.3847**
Debussy / by Edward Lockspeiser. — 5th ed. — London: Dent, 1980. xvi, 301 p., [4] leaves of plates: ill., music; 20 cm. — (The Master musicians series) Revisions by R. L. Smith. Includes index. 1. Debussy, Claude, 1862-1918. 2. Composers — France — Biography. I. T.
ML410.D28 L8 1980    780/.92/4 B 19    *LC* 80-491637    *ISBN* 0460031732

**Lockspeiser, Edward, 1905-1973.**    **1.3848**
Debussy: his life and mind. — London, Cassell [1962-65] 2 v.: ill.; 23 cm. 1. Debussy, Claude, 1862-1918. I. T.
ML410.D28 L85    *LC* 62-51320

**Vallas, Léon, 1879-1956.**    • **1.3849**
[Claude Debussy et son temps. English] Claude Debussy, his life and works / translated from the French by Marie and Grace O'Brien. London: Oxford University Press, 1933. 275, lxxxiii, xv p. illus. 22 cm. Translation of Claude Debussy et son temps. 1. Debussy, Claude, 1862-1918. 2. Composers — France — Biography I. O'Brien, Marie, tr. II. O'Brien, Grace, joint tr. III. T.
ML410.D28 V1673 1973    780/.92/4 B    *LC* 33-25069

**A Delius companion / edited, with a pref. by Christopher**    **1.3850**
**Redwood.**
New York: Da Capo Press, 1977. 270 p., [10] leaves of plates: ill.; 23 cm. (Da Capo Press music reprint series) 1. Delius, Frederick, 1862-1934. 2. Composers — England — Biography. I. Redwood, Christopher, 1939-
ML410.D35 D44 1977    780/.92/4 B    *LC* 76-57756    *ISBN* 0306708809

**Fenby, Eric, 1906-.**    **1.3851**
Delius as I knew him / Eric Fenby. — New and rev. ed. — Cambridge [Cambridgeshire]; New York: Cambridge University Press, 1981. xxii, 262 p., [8] p. of plates: ill.; 21 cm. Includes index. 1. Delius, Frederick, 1862-1934. 2. Fenby, Eric, 1906- 3. Composers — England — Biography. 4. Composers — France — Biography. I. T.
ML410.D35 F4 1981    780/.92/4 B 19    *LC* 81-83295    *ISBN* 0521245346

**Warlock, Peter, 1894-1930.**    • **1.3852**
Frederick Delius, by Peter Warlock (Philip Heseltine) Reprinted with additions, annotations, and comments by Hubert Foss. Westport, Conn., Greenwood Press [1974] 224 p. port. 23 cm. Reprint of the 1952 ed. published by Oxford University Press, New York. 1. Delius, Frederick, 1862-1934. I. T.
ML410.D35 H36 1974    780/.92/4 B    *LC* 73-19570    *ISBN* 0837172926

**International Josquin Festival-Conference, New York, 1971.**    **1.3853**
Josquin des Prez: proceedings of the International Josquin Festival–Conference held at the Julliard School at Lincoln Center in New York City, 21–25 June 1971 / sponsored by the American Musicological Society, in cooperation with the International Musicological Society, and the Renaissance Society of America; edited by Edward E. Lowinsky, in collaboration with Bonnie J. Blackburn. — London; New York: Oxford University Press, 1976. xviii, 787 p., [24] leaves of plates (1 fold.): ill. (some col.); 27 cm. & phonodiscs (6 s.: 7 in.: 33 1/3 rpm.) Includes index. 1. Josquin, des Prez, d. 1521. 2. Music —

Congresses. 3. Music — Addresses, essays, lectures. I. Lowinsky, Edward E. (Edward Elias), 1908-1985. II. Blackburn, Bonnie J. III. American Musicological Society. IV. International Musicological Society. V. Renaissance Society of America. VI. T.
ML410.D367 I6 1971     780/.92/4     *LC* 77-361746     *ISBN* 0193152290

**Ashbrook, William, 1922-.**                                          **1.3854**
Donizetti and his operas / William Ashbrook. — Cambridge, [Eng.]: Cambridge University Press, 1982. viii, 744 p.: music; 24 cm. Includes index. 1. Donizetti, Gaetano, 1797-1848. Operas. I. T.
ML410.D7 A83 1982     782.1/092/4 19     *LC* 81-12235     *ISBN* 052123526X

**Weinstock, Herbert, 1905-.**                                          • **1.3855**
Donizetti and the world of opera in Italy, Paris and Vienna in the first half of the nineteenth century. — New York: Pantheon Books, [1963] xxii, 453 p.: 20 plates (incl. illus., ports., facsims., music); 25 cm. 1. Donizetti, Gaetano, 1797-1848. 2. Opera — Italy. 3. Opera — Paris. 4. Opera — Vienna. I. T.
ML410.D7 W4     927.8     *LC* 63-13703

**Poulton, Diana.**                                          • **1.3856**
John Dowland; his life and works. Berkeley, University of California Press, 1972. 520 p. illus. 26 cm. 1. Dowland, John, 1563?-1626. I. T.
ML410.D808 P7 1972b     780/.92/4 B     *LC* 76-169229     *ISBN* 0520021096

**Fallows, David.**                                          **1.3857**
Dufay / David Fallows. — London: J.M. Dent, 1982. viii, 321 p., [12] p. of plates: ill., music; 23 cm. — (Master musicians series.) Includes index. 1. Dufay, Guillaume, d. 1474. 2. Composers — Biography. I. T. II. Series.
ML410.D83 F3 1982     780/.92/4 B 19     *LC* 82-200447     *ISBN* 0460031805

**Clapham, John.**                                          **1.3858**
Dvořák / John Clapham. — 1st American ed. — New York: Norton, 1979. 238 p.: ill.; 25 cm. Includes indexes. 1. Dvořák, Antonín, 1841-1904. 2. Composers — Czechoslovakia — Biography. I. T.
ML410.D99 C63 1979b     780/.92/4 B     *LC* 78-70265     *ISBN* 0393012042

**Robertson, Alec.**                                          • **1.3859**
Dvořák / by Alec Robertson. — London: Dent, 1945. viii, 234 p., [8] p. of plates: ill., music. — (The master musicians. New series.) 1. Dvořák, Antonín, 1841-1904. I. T. II. Series.
ML410.D99 R6x

## ML410 E–F

**Kennedy, Michael, 1926-.**                                          • **1.3860**
Portrait of Elgar. London, New York, [etc.] Oxford U.P., 1968. xi, 324 p. 15 plates, illus., facsims., music, ports. 23 cm. 1. Elgar, Edward, 1857-1934. I. T.
ML410.E41 K5     780/.924 B     *LC* 68-101411

**Parrott, Ian.**                                          **1.3861**
Elgar. London, Dent; New York, Farrar, Straus and Giroux, 1971. xi, 143 p., 8 plates; illus., facsims., music, ports. 20 cm. (Master musicians series.) 1. Elgar, Edward, 1857-1934. I. T. II. Series.
ML410.E41 P37     780/.924 B     *LC* 76-851212     *ISBN* 0460031090

**Young, Percy M. (Percy Marshall), 1912-.**                                          • **1.3862**
Elgar, O. M.: a study of a musician / by Percy M. Young. — London: Collins, 1955. — 447 p., [8] leaves of plates: ill., facsims., music, ports.; 21 cm. Includes index. 1. Elgar, Edward, 1857-1934. I. T.
ML410.E41 Y7 1955     780/.92/4 B     *LC* 56-100

**Ellington, Duke, 1899-1974.**                                          **1.3863**
Music is my mistress, by Edward Kennedy Ellington. [1st ed.]. — Garden City, N.Y.: Doubleday, 1973. xv, 522 p.: illus.; 27 cm. 1. Ellington, Duke, 1899-1974. 2. Composers — United States — Biography. I. T.
ML410.E44 A3     785.4/2/0924 B     *LC* 73-83189     *ISBN* 0385022352

**Jewell, Derek.**                                          **1.3864**
Duke: a portrait of Duke Ellington / Derek Jewell. New York: Norton, c1977. 264 p.: ill.; 24 cm. Includes index. 1. Ellington, Duke, 1899-1974. 2. Jazz musicians — United States — Biography. I. T.
ML410.E44 J5     785.4/2/0924 B     *LC* 77-2271     *ISBN* 0393075125

**Demarquez, Suzanne.**                                          • **1.3865**
Manuel de Falla. Translated from the French by Salvator Attanasio. — [1st ed.]. — Philadelphia: Chilton Book Co., [1968] viii, 253 p.; 21 cm. 1. Falla, Manuel de, 1876-1946. I. T.
ML410.F215 D43     780/.924 B     *LC* 68-25858

**Koechlin, Charles, 1867-1950.**                                          • **1.3866**
Gabriel Fauré, 1845–1924 / Charles Koechlin. London: D. Dobson, [1945] viii, 98 p.: port.; 23 cm. 1. Fauré, Gabriel, 1845-1924. I. T.
ML410.F27 K72 1976     780/.92/4 B     *LC* 46-3523

**Suckling, Norman.**                                          • **1.3867**
Fauré. New York, Pellegrini & Cydahy, 1951. vii, 229 p. illus., ports., facsim. 19 cm. (The Master musician) 1. Fauré, Gabriel, 1845-1924. I. T. II. Series.
ML410.F27 S9     928.4     *LC* 52-483

**Austin, William W.**                                          **1.3868**
'Susanna,' 'Jeanie,' and 'the old folks at home': the songs of Stephen C. Foster from his time to ours / William W. Austin. — New York: Macmillan, 1975. xxiv, 420 p.; 24 cm. 1. Foster, Stephen Collins, 1826-1864. Songs. I. T.
ML410.F78 A9     784/.092/4     *LC* 75-17635     *ISBN* 0025045008

**Howard, John Tasker, 1890-.**                                          **1.3869**
Stephen Foster, America's troubadour. New York, Thomas Y. Crowell company [1935] xviii, 445 p. col. front., plates, ports., map, facsims. (incl. music) 23 cm. 1. Foster, Stephen Collins, 1826-1864. I. Hodges, Fletcher, Jr. II. T.
ML410.F78 H6 1935     *LC* 35-25367

**Davies, Laurence.**                                          **1.3870**
César Franck and his circle. — [1st American ed.]. — Boston: Houghton Mifflin Co., 1970. 380 p.: illus., facsims., music, ports.; 23 cm. 1. Franck, César, 1822-1890. I. T.
ML410.F82 D29     780/.0924 B     *LC* 73-108305

**Indy, Vincent d', 1851-1931.**                                          • **1.3871**
César Franck; a translation from the French. With an introd. by Rosa Newmarch. New York, Dover Publications [1965] 286 p. illus., music, ports. 21 cm. (Dover books on music) 'An unabridged and unaltered republication of the work first published by John Lane, The Bodley Head, London, in 1910.' 1. Franck, César, 1822-1890. I. T.
ML410.F82 I63 1965     780.92     *LC* 65-14031

**Vallas, Léon, 1879-1956.**                                          • **1.3872**
[Véritable histoire de César Franck. English] César Franck. Translated by Hubert Foss. Westport, Conn., Greenwood Press [1973] 283 p. illus. 22 cm. Translation of La véritable histoire de César Franck. Reprint of the 1951 ed. published by Harrap, London. 1. Franck, César, 1822-1890. I. T.
ML410.F82 V33 1973     780/.92/4 B     *LC* 73-5210     *ISBN* 0837168732

## ML410 G

**Arnold, Denis.**                                          **1.3873**
Giovanni Gabrieli / Denis Arnold. — London; New York: Oxford University Press, 1974. 70 p.; 22 cm. (Oxford studies of composers. 12) 1. Gabrieli, Giovanni, 1557-1612. I. T. II. Series.
ML410.G11 A7     780/.92/4 B     *LC* 75-304565     *ISBN* 0193152312

**Schwartz, Charles.**                                          **1.3874**
Gershwin, his life and music. — Indianapolis: Bobbs-Merrill Co., [c1973] 428 p.: illus.; 26 cm. 'Compositions by George Gershwin': p. 335-352. 1. Gershwin, George, 1898-1937. I. T.
ML410.G288 S33     780/.92/4 B     *LC* 73-1715     *ISBN* 0672516624

**Fellowes, Edmund Horace, 1870-1951.**                                          • **1.3875**
[Orlando Gibbons; a short account of his life and work] Orlando Gibbons and his family; the last of the Tudor school of musicians [by] Edmund H. Fellowes. 2d ed. [Hamden, Conn.] Archon Books, 1970. 109 p. facsims., ports. 22 cm. First published in 1925 under title: Orlando Gibbons; a short account of his life and work. 1. Gibbons, Orlando, 1583-1625. 2. Gibbons family I. T.
ML410.G295 F4 1970     780/.924 B     *LC* 79-95024     *ISBN* 0208008489

**Einstein, Alfred, 1880-1952.**                                          • **1.3876**
[Gluck, sein Leben, seine Werke. English] Gluck. Translated by Eric Blom. New York, McGraw-Hill Book Co. [1972, c1964] ix, 238 p. music, port. 21 cm. (McGraw-Hill paperbacks) Translation of Gluck, sein Leben, seine Werke. 1. Gluck, Christoph Willibald, Ritter von, 1714-1787. I. T.
ML410.G5 E5 1972     782.1/092/4 B     *LC* 72-189735     *ISBN* 0070195307

**Newman, Ernest, 1868-1959.**                                          • **1.3877**
Gluck and the opera; a study in musical history. — London: Gollancz, 1967. ix, 300 p.; 21 cm. 1. Gluck, Christoph Willibald, Ritter von, 1714-1787. 2. Opera I. T.
ML410.G5 N3 1967     782/.0924     *LC* 74-355466

**Gottschalk, Louis Moreau, 1829-1869.**                                          • **1.3878**
Notes of a pianist / Louis Moreau Gottschalk; edited, with a prelude, a postlude, and explanatory notes, by Jeanne Behrend. — New York: Alfred A.

Knopf, 1964. xxxviii, 420 p.: ill. — (A Borzoi book) 1. Musicians — Correspondence, reminiscences, etc. 2. United States — Description and travel — 1848-1865 3. South America — Description and travel I. Behrend, Jeanne, 1911- ed. II. T.
ML410.G68 G6 1964      927.8      *LC* 64-12302

**Bird, John.**               **1.3879**
Percy Grainger / John Bird. — London: P. Elek, 1976. xv, 317 p., [8] leaves of plates: ill.; 24 cm. Includes index. 1. Grainger, Percy, 1882-1961. 2. Composers — Biography. I. T.
ML410.G75 B6     786.1/092/4 B     *LC* 77-355788     *ISBN* 0236400045

**Abraham, Gerald, 1904- ed.**        • **1.3880**
Grieg; a symposium. Edited by Gerald Abraham. Westport, Conn., Greenwood Press [1971] 144 p., 40 p. of music. 23 cm. Reprint of the 1950 ed. 1. Grieg, Edvard, 1843-1907. I. T.
ML410.G9 A47 1971     780/.924     *LC* 71-138196     *ISBN* 0837155495

**Levarie, Siegmund, 1914-.**         • **1.3881**
Guillaume de Machaut. Edited by John J. Becker. New York, Da Capo Press, 1969 [c1954] 114 p. illus. 24 cm. (Da Capo Press music reprint series) 'This Da Capo Press edition is an unabridged republication of the first edition published in 1954.' 1. Guillaume, de Machaut, ca. 1300-1377. I. T.
ML410.G966 1969     783/.0924 B     *LC* 70-98309

## ML410 H

**Handel, George Frideric, 1685-1759.**      • **1.3882**
The letters and writing of George Frideric Handel. Edited by Erich H. Müller. Freeport, N.Y., Books for Libraries Press [1970] viii,98 p. 23 cm. In English, French or German; 'translations of those letters appearing in the text in French and German': p. 78-92. Reprint of the 1935 ed. 1. Handel, George Frideric, 1685-1759. I. T.
ML410.H13 A3 1970     780/.924     *LC* 70-114882     *ISBN* 0836952863

**Abraham, Gerald, 1904- ed.**        • **1.3883**
Handel, a symposium. London, New York, Oxford University Press, 1954. vi, 328 p. music. 23 cm. 1. Handel, George Frideric, 1685-1759. I. T.
ML410.H13 A66     780.81     *LC* 54-8770

**Cudworth, Charles.**          • **1.3884**
Handel; a biography, with a survey of books, editions, and recordings. [Hamden, Conn.] Linnet Books [1972] 112 p. 23 cm. (The Concertgoer's companions) 1. Handel, George Frideric, 1685-1759. I. T.
ML410.H13 C88     780/.92/4 B     *LC* 72-176705     *ISBN* 0208010688

**Dean, Winton.**          • **1.3885**
Handel's dramatic oratorios and masques. London, Oxford University Press, 1959. xii, 694 p. ill., ports., music. 1. Handel, George Frideric, 1685-1759. I. T.
ML410 H13 D35     *LC* 59-2150

**Dean, Winton.**          **1.3886**
Handel's operas, 1704–1726 / Winton Dean and John Merrill Knapp. — Oxford [Oxfordshire]; New York: Clarendon Press, 1987. xx, 751 p., [17] p. of plates: ill., music, ports.; 25 cm. Includes indexes. 1. Handel, George Frideric, 1685-1759. Operas. 2. Opera I. Knapp, John Merrill. II. T.
ML410.H13 D37 1987     782.1/092/4 19     *LC* 85-11580     *ISBN* 0193152193

**Deutsch, Otto Erich, 1883-1967.**      • **1.3887**
Handel, a documentary biography. New York, Da Capo Press, 1974. xiv, 942 p. illus. 23 cm. (Da Capo Press music reprint series) Reprint of the 1955 ed. published by W. W. Norton, New York. 1. Handel, George Frideric, 1685-1759. I. T.
ML410.H13 D47 1974     780/.92/4 B     *LC* 74-3118     *ISBN* 0306706245

**Hogwood, Christopher.**         **1.3888**
Handel / Christopher Hogwood; chronological table by Anthony Hicks. — London: Thames and Hudson, 1984. 312 p.: ill. (some col.), music, map, ports; 25 cm. Chronological table of Handel's life and contemporary performances of his works: p. 277-294. Includes select bibliography and indexes. 1. Handel, George Frideric, 1685-1759. 2. Composers — Germany — Biography. 3. Composers — England — Biography I. Hicks, Anthony. II. T.
ML410.H13 H64     780.924     *LC* 84-72765     *ISBN* 0500013551

**Keates, Jonathan, 1946-.**         **1.3889**
Handel, the man and his music / by Jonathan Keates. — New York: St. Martin's Press, 1985. 346 p.: col. port.; 24 cm. Includes index. 1. Handel, George Frideric, 1685-1759. 2. Composers — Biography. I. T.
ML410.H13 K33 1985     780/.92/4 B 19     *LC* 85-40017     *ISBN* 0312358466

**Lang, Paul Henry, 1901-.**         • **1.3890**
George Frideric Handel. [1st ed.] New York, W. W. Norton [1966] xviii, 731 p. music, 16 plates (incl. facsims., ports.) 24 cm. 1. Handel, George Frideric, 1685-1759. I. T.
ML410.H13 L16     780.924 B     *LC* 66-11793

**Larsen, Jens Peter, 1902-.**         • **1.3891**
Handel's Messiah; origins, composition, sources. 2d ed. New York, W. W. Norton [1972] 337 p. illus., facsims., music. 20 cm. (The Norton library, N657) 1. Handel, George Frideric, 1685-1759. Messiah 2. Handel, George Frideric, 1685-1759 — Bibliography — Manuscripts. I. T.
ML410.H13 L2 1972     783.3/092/4     *LC* 72-5025     *ISBN* 0393006573

**Handy, W. C. (William Christopher), 1873-1958.**    • **1.3892**
Father of the blues, an autobiography. Edited by Arna Bontemps, with a foreword by Abbe Niles. — [New York]: Macmillan, 1955. [xix], 317 p.: illus.; 18 cm. 1. Handy, W. C. (William Christopher), 1873-1958. 2. Jazz music I. Bontemps, Arna Wendell, 1902-1973. ed. II. T.
ML410.H18 B6 1970     784/.092/4 B

**Haydn, Joseph, 1732-1809.**         • **1.3893**
The collected correspondence and London notebooks. [By] H.C. Robbins Landon. Fair Lawn, N.J., Essential Books, 1959. xxix, 367 p. illus. 23 cm. I. Landon, Howard Chandler Robbins, 1926- II. T. III. Title: London notebooks.
ML410.H4A4     *LC* 59-3697

**Landon, Howard Chandler Robbins, 1926-.**      **1.3894**
Haydn, a documentary study / H.C. Robbins Landon. — New York: Rizzoli, c1981. 224 p.: ill. (some col.), facsims.; 31 cm. Includes index. 1. Haydn, Joseph, 1732-1809. 2. Composers — Austria — Biography. I. T.
ML410.H4 L257     780/.92/4 B 19     *LC* 81-50279     *ISBN* 0847803880

**Landon, Howard Chandler Robbins, 1926-.**      **1.3895**
Haydn: chronicle and works / H. C. Robbins Landon. — 1st American ed. — Bloomington: Indiana University Press, 1976-1980. 5 v.: ill.; 26 cm. 1. Haydn, Joseph, 1732-1809. 2. Composers — Biography. I. T.
ML410.H4 L26     780/.92/4 B 19     *LC* 76-14630     0253370035

**Landon, Howard Chandler Robbins, 1926-.**      • **1.3896**
The symphonies of Joseph Haydn. London, Universal Edition [c1955] xvii, 862 p. ports., facsims., music. 1. Haydn, Joseph, 1732-1809. Symphonies 2. Haydn, Joseph, 1732-1809 — Thematic catalogs 3. Symphonies — To 1800 — Scores I. T.
ML410 H4 L28     *LC* 56-716

**Holst, Imogen, 1907-.**         • **1.3897**
The music of Gustav Holst. 2nd ed. London, Oxford U.P., 1968. xii, 169 p. 4 plates, facsims., music. 23 cm. 1. Holst, Gustav, 1874-1934 — Criticism and interpretation. I. T.
ML410.H748 H63 1968     780/.924     *LC* 74-353260     *ISBN* 0193154161

**Honegger, Arthur, 1892-1955.**         • **1.3898**
I am a composer. Translated from the French by Wilson O. Clough in collaboration with Allan Arthur Willman. New York, St. Martin's Press [1966] 141 p. port. I. T.
ML410 H79 A313 1966     *LC* 66-11638

## ML410 I–L

**Ives, Charles, 1874-1954.**         • **1.3899**
Memos. Edited by John Kirkpatrick. [1st ed.] New York, W. W. Norton [1972] 355 p. illus. 25 cm. 'Memos' (Ives' own title): p. [25]-142; 'Appendices': p. [143]-324. 1. Musicians — Correspondence, reminiscences, etc. I. Kirkpatrick, John, 1905- ed. II. T.
ML410.I94 A3     780/.92/4 B     *LC* 76-77407     *ISBN* 039302153X

**Burkholder, J. Peter (James Peter)**      **1.3900**
Charles Ives, the ideas behind the music / J. Peter Burkholder. — New Haven: Yale University Press, c1985. xiv, 166 p.: ports.; 25 cm. Includes index. 1. Ives, Charles, 1874-1954. 2. Composers — United States — Biography. 3. Music — Philosophy and aesthetics I. T.
ML410.I94 B48 1985     780/.92/4 B 19     *LC* 85-2469     *ISBN* 0300032617

**Charles Ives Centennial Festival-Conference, New York and**    **1.3901**
**New Haven, 1974.**
An Ives celebration: papers and panels of the Charles Ives Centennial Festival–Conference / edited by H. Wiley Hitchcock, Vivian Perlis. — Urbana: University of Illinois Press, c1977. xi, 282 p.: ill.; 27 cm. — (Music in American life) 'The Ives Festival-Conference was sponsored by the Institute for Studies in American Music at Brooklyn College of the City University of New York and

the School of Music of Yale University.' 1. Ives, Charles, 1874-1954 — Anniversaries, etc. 2. Ives, Charles, 1874-1954 — Congresses. I. Hitchcock, H. Wiley (Hugh Wiley), 1923- II. Perlis, Vivian. III. Brooklyn College. Institute for Studies in American Music. IV. Yale University. School of Music. V. T.
ML410.I94 C4 1974b        780/.92/4        *LC* 77-7987        *ISBN* 0252006194

**Cowell, Henry, 1897-1965.**                              • **1.3902**
Charles Ives and his music, by Henry Cowell and Sidney Cowell. New York, Oxford University Press, 1955. x, 245 p. ports., facsim., music. 21 cm. Includes: Soliloquy; or, A study in 7ths and other things (p. 158) and Paracelsus (p. 183-185) for voice and piano. 'A list of the compositions of Charles Edward Ives': p. 207-233. 1. Ives, Charles, 1874-1954. I. Cowell, Sidney Robertson, Mrs., joint author. II. T.
ML410.I94 C6        927.8        *LC* 54-10000

**Hitchcock, H. Wiley (Hugh Wiley), 1923-.**                              **1.3903**
Ives / H. Wiley Hitchcock. — London; New York: Oxford University Press, 1977. 95 p.; 22 cm. (Oxford studies of composers. 14) 1. Ives, Charles, 1874-1954 — Criticism and interpretation. I. T. II. Series.
ML410.I94 H6        780/.92/4        *LC* 77-367800        *ISBN* 0193154390

**Perlis, Vivian.**                              **1.3904**
Charles Ives remembered: an oral history / by Vivian Perlis. — New Haven: Yale University Press, 1974. xviii, 237 p.: ill.; 27 cm. 1. Ives, Charles, 1874-1954. I. T.
ML410.I94 P5        780/.92/4 B        *LC* 74-75288        *ISBN* 0300017588

**Rossiter, Frank R.**                              **1.3905**
Charles Ives and his America / Frank R. Rossiter. — 1st ed. — New York: Liveright, [1975] xv, 420 p., [4] leaves of plates: ill.; 24 cm. Includes index. 1. Ives, Charles, 1874-1954. I. T.
ML410.I94 R68        780/.92/4 B        *LC* 75-12663        *ISBN* 0871406101

**Tyrrell, John.**                              **1.3906**
Leoš Janáček, Káta Kabanová / compiled by John Tyrrell. — Cambridge [Cambridgeshire]; New York: Cambridge University Press, 1982. xv, 234 p.: ill.; 23 cm. — (Cambridge opera handbooks.) Includes index. 1. Janáček, Leoš, 1854-1928. Káta Kabanová I. T. II. Series.
ML410.J18 L49 1982        782.1/092/4 19        *LC* 81-38505        *ISBN* 0521231809

**Bordman, Gerald Martin.**                              **1.3907**
Jerome Kern: his life and music / Gerald Bordman. — New York: Oxford University Press, 1980. viii, 438 p., [8] leaves of plates: ill.; 24 cm. Includes indexes. 1. Kern, Jerome, 1885-1945. 2. Composers — United States — Biography. I. T.
ML410.K385 B7        782.8/1/0924 B        *LC* 79-13826        *ISBN* 0195026497

**Young, Percy M. (Percy Marshall), 1912-.**                              • **1.3908**
Zoltán Kodály, a Hungarian musician [by] Percy M. Young. London, E. Benn [1964] xvi, 231 p. music, plates (incl. facsims.) 1. Kodály, Zoltán, 1882-1967. I. T.
ML410 K6 Y7        *LC* 64-54500

**Eősze, László.**                              • **1.3909**
Zoltán Kodály: his life and work / László Eösze; translated by Istvan Farkas and Gyula Gulyás. — London: Collet's c1962. 183 p.: ill., ports. Translation of Kodály Zoltán élete és müvészete. 1. Kodály, Zoltán, 1882-1967. I. T.
ML410.K732 E582        *LC* 67-59649 MN

**Sitwell, Sacheverell, 1897-.**                              • **1.3910**
Liszt. New York, Dover Publications [1967] xxxvi, 400 p. illus., ports. 22 cm. 'This Dover edition is an unabridged republication, with minor corrections, of the revised edition published in 1955.' 1. Liszt, Franz, 1811-1886. I. T.
ML410.L7 S62 1967        780.924 B        *LC* 66-26822

**Walker, Alan, 1930-.**                              **1.3911**
Franz Liszt / by Alan Walker. — 1st American ed. — New York: Knopf: Distributed by Random House, 1983-. v. <1 >: ill. (some col.); 25 cm. Includes index. 1. Liszt, Franz, 1811-1886. 2. Composers — Biography. I. T.
ML410.L7 W27 1983        780/.92/4 B 19        *LC* 82-47821        *ISBN* 039452540X

**Walker, Alan, 1930-.**                              • **1.3912**
Franz Liszt; the man and his music. Edited by Alan Walker. — New York: Taplinger Pub. Co., [1970] xiv, 471 p.: illus., facsims., music, ports.; 24 cm. 1. Liszt, Franz, 1811-1886. I. T.
ML410.L7 W28        780/.924        *LC* 72-108274        *ISBN* 0800829905

**Luening, Otto, 1900-.**                              **1.3913**
The Odyssey of an American composer: the autobiography of Otto Luening. — New York: Scribner, c1980. x, 605 p., [4] leaves of plates: ill.; 24 cm. Includes

index. 1. Luening, Otto, 1900- 2. Composers — United States — Biography. I. T.
ML410.L947 A3        780/.92/4 B        *LC* 80-11624        *ISBN* 0684164965

**Stucky, Steven.**                              **1.3914**
Lutosławski and his music / Steven Stucky. — Cambridge: Cambridge University Press, 1981. ix, 252 p.: music, 3 ports.; 24 cm. I. T.
ML410.L965        780/.92/4 18        780/.92/4 19        *LC* 80-40982        *ISBN* 0521227992


## ML410 M

**Gilman, Lawrence, 1878-1939.**                              • **1.3915**
Edward MacDowell; a study. New introd. by Margaret L. Morgan. New York, Da Capo Press, 1969. xv, xii, 190 p. illus., facsims., music, ports. 20 cm. (Da Capo Press music reprint series) 'Unabridged republication of the first edition published in New York and London in 1908.' 1. MacDowell, Edward, 1861-1908. I. T.
ML410.M12 G5 1969        780/.924        *LC* 67-27455

**Blaukopf, Kurt.**                              **1.3916**
Gustav Mahler. Translated by Inge Goodwin. — New York: Praeger, [1973] 279 p.: illus.; 23 cm. 1. Mahler, Gustav, 1860-1911. I. T.
ML410.M23 B63        780/.92/4 B        *LC* 73-109467

**Walter, Bruno, 1876-1962.**                              • **1.3917**
[Gustav Mahler. English] Gustav Mahler. Translation from the German supervised by Lotte Walter Lindt. New York, Knopf, 1958 [c1957] 175 p. illus. 20 cm. 1. Mahler, Gustav, 1860-1911. I. T.
ML410.M23 W25 1958        927.8        *LC* 57-7551

**Mitchell, Donald, 1925-.**                              **1.3918**
Gustav Mahler: songs and symphonies of life and death: interpretations and annotations / Donald Mitchell. — Berkeley: University of California Press, [1986], c1985. 659 p.: ill.; 26 cm. On spine: Gustav Mahler, volume III: Songs and symphonies of life and death. Includes indexes. 1. Mahler, Gustav, 1860-1911. 2. Mahler, Gustav, 1860-1911. Songs. 3. Mahler, Gustav, 1860-1911. Symphonies. 4. Composers — Austria — Biography. I. T. II. Title: Songs and symphonies of life and death.
ML410.M23 M48 1986        780/.92/4 19        *LC* 85-40494        *ISBN* 0520055780

**Mitchell, Donald, 1925-.**                              **1.3919**
Gustav Mahler: the early years / Donald Mitchell; rev. and edited by Paul Banks and David Matthews. — Rev. ed. — Berkeley: University of California Press, c1980. xxii, 338 p., [6] leaves of plates: ill.; 26 cm. Includes indexes. 1. Mahler, Gustav, 1860-1911. 2. Composers — Austria — Biography. I. Banks, Paul, 1957- II. Matthews, David, 1943- III. T.
ML410.M23 M5 1980        780/.92/4 B        *LC* 79-9694        *ISBN* 0520041410

**Mitchell, Donald, 1925-.**                              **1.3920**
Gustav Mahler: the Wunderhorn years: chronicles and commentaries / by Donald Mitchell. — 1st Calif. pbk. ed. — Berkeley: University of California Press, 1980, c1975. 461 p.: ill.; 24 cm. Includes index. 1. Mahler, Gustav, 1860-1911. 2. Composers — Austria — Biography. I. T.
ML410.M23 M53 1980        780/.92/4        *LC* 75-23204        *ISBN* 0520042204

**Mahler, Alma, 1879-1964.**                              • **1.3921**
Gustav Mahler; memories and letters, by Alma Mahler. — Enl. ed., rev. and edited with an introd. by Donald Mitchell. Translated by Basil Creighton. — New York: Viking Press, [1969] xl, 369 p.: facsims. (incl. music), ports.; 25 cm. 1. Mahler, Gustav, 1860-1911. I. T.
ML410.M23 W532 1969        780/.924        *LC* 69-18800        *ISBN* 0670358096

**Šafránek, Miloš, 1894-.**                              • **1.3922**
Bohuslav Martinů: his life and works / by Miloš Šafránek; translated by Roberta Finlayson–Samsourová. — London: A. Wingate, c1962. 367 p., [11] leaves of plates: ill., music, ports. Translation of Bohuslav Martinů; život a dílo. 1. Martinů, Bohuslav, 1890-1959. I. T.
ML410M382 S43        ML410M382 S343 1962.        *LC* 64-55362/MN

**Mason, Daniel Gregory, 1873-1953.**                              • **1.3923**
Music in my time, and other reminiscences. — Westport, Conn.: Greenwood Press, [1970] 409 p.: illus., facsims, music, ports.; 23 cm. Reprint of the 1938 ed. 1. Mason, Daniel Gregory, 1873-1953. 2. Musicians — Correspondence, reminiscences, etc. I. T.
ML410.M397 A2 1970b        780/.924        *LC* 71-109784        *ISBN* 0837142741

**Massenet, Jules, 1842-1912.**                              • **1.3924**
My recollections, by Jules Massenet. The authorized translation done at the master's express desire by his friend H. Villiers Barnett. Westport, Conn.,

Greenwood Press [1970] 304 p. illus., ports. 23 cm. 'Originally published in 1919.' 1. Massenet, Jules, 1842-1912. 2. Musicians — Correspondence, reminiscences, etc. I. T.
ML410.M41 A33 1970b     780/.92/2 B     *LC* 79-109786     *ISBN* 0837142768

**Mendelssohn-Bartholdy, Felix, 1809-1847.**       • **1.3925**
Letters, edited by G. Selden–Goth; with 33 illustrations. [New York] Pantheon [1945] 372, [1] p. front., illus. (incl. music, facsims.) plates, ports. 24 cm. At head of title: Felix Mendelssohn. 1. Musicians — Correspondence, reminiscences, etc. I. Selden-Goth, Gisella, 1884- ed. II. T.
ML410.M5A28     *LC* 45-5930

**Blunt, Wilfrid, 1901-.**       **1.3926**
On wings of song; a biography of Felix Mendelssohn. — New York: Scribner, [1974] 288 p.: illus.; 26 cm. 1. Mendelssohn-Bartholdy, Felix, 1809-1847. I. T.
ML410.M5 B62     780/.92/4 B     *LC* 73-10840     *ISBN* 0684136333

**Radcliffe, Philip, 1905-.**       • **1.3927**
Mendelssohn. — Revised ed. — London: Dent; New York: Farrar, Straus and Giroux, 1967. xi, 210 p.: 16 plates, illus., facsims., ports.; 20 cm. — (Master musicians series.) 1. Mendelssohn-Bartholdy, Felix, 1809-1847. 2. Composers — Biography. I. T. II. Series.
ML410.M5 R25 1967     780/.92/4 B 19     *LC* 68-74768

**Griffiths, Paul.**       **1.3928**
Olivier Messiaen and the music of time / Paul Griffiths. — Ithaca, N.Y.: Cornell University Press, 1985. 274 p.: ill.; 24 cm. Includes indexes. 1. Messiaen, Olivier, 1908- — Criticism and interpretation. I. T.
ML410.M595 G7 1985     780/.92/4 19     *LC* 84-45797     *ISBN* 0801418135

**Johnson, Robert Sherlaw.**       **1.3929**
Messiaen / Robert Sherlaw Johnson. — Berkeley: University of California Press, 1975. 221 p.: ill.; 26 cm. Includes indexes. 1. Messiaen, Olivier, 1908- — Criticism and interpretation. I. T.
ML410.M595 J6     780/.92/4     *LC* 74-81434     *ISBN* 0520028120

**Milhaud, Darius, 1892-1974.**       • **1.3930**
[Notes sans musique. English] Notes without music; an autobiography. [Translated from the French by Donald Evans] New York, Da Capo Press, 1970 [c1953] x, 355, xxii p. illus., ports. 24 cm. (Da Capo Press music reprint series) 1. Milhaud, Darius, 1892-1974. 2. Musicians — Correspondence, reminiscences, etc. I. T.
ML410.M674 A32 1970     780/.924     *LC* 72-87419     *ISBN* 0306715651

**Arnold, Denis.**       • **1.3931**
Monteverdi. — London: J. M. Dent; New York: Farrar, Straus and Cudahy, [1963] 212 p.: illus.; 20 cm. — (The Master musicians series) 1. Monteverdi, Claudio, 1567-1643. I. T.
ML410.M77 A8     927.8     *LC* 63-2544

**Schrade, Leo, 1903-1964.**       • **1.3932**
Monteverdi, creator of modern music. — [1st ed.]. — New York: Norton, [1950] 384 p.: illus., ports., music; 24 cm. 1. Monteverdi, Claudio, 1567-1643. I. T.
ML410.M77 S35     780.81     *LC* 50-10675

**Lomax, Alan, 1915-.**       • **1.3933**
Mister Jelly Roll; the fortunes of Jelly Roll Morton, New Orleans Creole and inventor of jazz. Drawings by David Stone Martin. 2d ed. Berkeley, University of California Press [1973] xvii, 318 p. illus. 21 cm. 1. Morton, Jelly Roll, d. 1941. 2. Morton, Jelly Roll, d. 1941 — Discography. 3. Jazz music — Discography. I. T.
ML410.M82 L6 1973     785.4/2/0924 B     *LC* 74-189222     *ISBN* 0520024028 *ISBN* 0520022378

**Mozart, Wolfgang Amadeus, 1756-1791.**       **1.3934**
The letters of Mozart and his family / chronologically arranged, translated and edited with an introduction, notes and indexes by Emily Anderson. — 3rd ed. — New York: Norton, 1985. li, 1038 p.: ill., ports.; 23 cm. Includes indexes. 1. Mozart, Wolfgang Amadeus, 1756-1791. 2. Composers — Austria — Correspondence. I. Anderson, Emily Ann. II. T.
ML410M9 A402 1985     ML410.M9 A187 1985x.     780/.92/4 19
    *ISBN* 039302248X

**Badura-Skoda, Eva.**       **1.3935**
[Mozart-Interpretation. English] Interpretating Mozart on the keyboard / Eva and Paul Badura–Skoda; translated by Leo Black; new preface by Eva Badura–Skoda. — New York: Da Capo Press, 1985. ix, 319 p., [2] leaves of plates: ill.; 24 cm. — (Da Capo Press music reprint series.) Translation of: Mozart-Interpretation. Reprint. Originally published: New York: St. Martin's, 1962. Includes index. 1. Mozart, Wolfgang Amadeus, 1756-1791. Instrumental

music. 2. Piano music — Interpretation (Phrasing, dynamics, etc.) I. Badura-Skoda, Paul. II. T. III. Series.
ML410.M9 B1413 1986     786.1/092/4 19     *LC* 85-24566     *ISBN* 030676265X

**Dent, Edward Joseph, 1876-1957.**       • **1.3936**
Mozart's operas: a critical study / Edward J. Dent. — 2nd ed. — London: Oxford University Press, 1947. — xi, 276 p. [9] leaves of plates: ill., facsims., music, ports.; 23 cm. Includes index. 1. Mozart, Wolfgang Amadeus, 1756-1791. Operas I. T.
ML410.M9 D32     782.10924     *LC* 47-31287

**Deutsch, Otto Erich, 1883-1967.**       • **1.3937**
[Mozart; Dokumente seines Lebens. English] Mozart, a documentary biography. Translated by Eric Blom, Peter Branscombe, and Jeremy Noble. Stanford, Stanford University Press [1965] ix, 680 p. 24 cm. 1. Mozart, Wolfgang Amadeus, 1756-1791. I. T.
ML410.M9 D4782     927.8     *LC* 64-12077

**Einstein, Alfred, 1880-1952.**       • **1.3938**
[Mozart, sein Charakter, sein Werk. English] Mozart, his character, his work [by] Alfred Einstein; translated by Arthur Mendel and Nathan Broder. New York, London [etc.] Oxford university press, 1945. x p., 2 l., 3-492 p. front. (facsim.) illus. (music) ports. 24 cm. 'First edition.' 1. Mozart, Wolfgang Amadeus, 1756-1791. I. Mendel, Arthur, 1905- tr. II. Broder, Nathan. joint tr. III. T.
ML410.M9 E4     927.8     *LC* 45-1487

**Jahn, Otto, 1813-1869.**       • **1.3939**
[W. A. Mozart. English] Life of Mozart. Translated from the German by Pauline Townsend, with a pref. by George Grove. New York, Cooper Square Publishers, 1970. 3 v. facsims., music, ports. 22 cm. Translation of W. A. Mozart. Reprint of the 1891 ed. 1. Mozart, Wolfgang Amadeus, 1756-1791. I. T.
ML410.M9 J413 1970     780/.924 B     *LC* 78-125917

**Landon, Howard Chandler Robbins, 1926- ed.**       • **1.3940**
The Mozart companion. New York, Oxford University Press, 1956. xv, 397 p. illus., ports., facsims., music. 22 cm. 1. Mozart, Wolfgang Amadeus, 1756-1791. I. Abraham, Gerald, 1904- II. Mitchell, Donald, 1925- joint ed. III. T.
ML410.M9 L24 1956     *LC* 56-13858

**Calvocoressi, Michel D., 1877-1944.**       **1.3941**
Modest Mussorgsky, his life and works. Fair Law, N.J., Essential Books, 1956. xix, 322 p. illus., ports., facsim. 23 cm. 1. Musorgskiĭ, Modest Petrovich, 1839-1881. I. Abraham, Gerald Ernest Heal, 1904- ed. II. T.
ML410.M97 C33     *LC* 56-14349

## ML410 N–P

**Simpson, Robert Wilfred Levick, 1921-.**       **1.3942**
Carl Nielsen, symphonist / Robert Simpson; biographical appendix by Torben Meyer. — [Rev. and expanded ed]. — New York: Taplinger Pub. Co., 1979. 260 p.: ill.; 23 cm. 'A Crescendo book.' Includes index. 1. Nielsen, Carl, 1865-1931. Works. I. T.
ML410.N625 S48     785.1/1/0924     *LC* 79-63622     *ISBN* 0800812603

**Liess, Andreas, 1903-.**       • **1.3943**
Carl Orff. Translated by Adelheid and Herbert Parkin. — London, Calder & Boyars, 1966. 184 p. illus., facsim., music, ports. 21 cm. Bibliography: p. [171]-174. 1. Orff, Carl, 1895- I. T.
ML410.O65L57 1966a     782.0924     *LC* 64-16423

**Coates, Henry, 1880-.**       • **1.3944**
Palestrina. London, J. M. Dent and sons, ltd.; New York, E. P. Dutton and co., inc. [1938] ix, 243, [1] p. front., illus., (music) plates, ports., facsims., (music) 19 cm. (The matter musicians. New series) 'First published 1938.' 1. Palestrina, Giovanni Pierluigi da, 1525?-1594. I. T. II. Series.
ML410.P15 C7     927.8     *LC* 38-15063

**Schwartz, Charles.**       **1.3945**
Cole Porter: a biography / by Charles Schwartz. — New York: Dial Press, 1977. xvi, 365 p., [8] leaves of plates: ill.; 24 cm. Includes index. 1. Porter, Cole, 1891-1964. 2. Composers — United States — Biography. I. T.
ML410.P7844 S4     782.8/1/0924 B     *LC* 77-6907     *ISBN* 0803714645

**Bernac, Pierre.**       **1.3946**
[Francis Poulenc et ses mélodies. English] Francis Poulenc, the man and his songs / by Pierre Bernac; translated by Winifred Radford; with a foreword by Sir Lennox Berkeley. — New York: Norton, c1977. 233 p., [3] leaves of plates:

ill.; 23 cm. Includes index. Translation of Francis Poulenc et ses mélodies. 1. Poulenc, Francis, 1899-1963. Songs I. T.
ML410.P787 B53 1977b    784/.3/00924    *LC* 77-156191    *ISBN* 0393021963

**Hell, Henri.**       **1.3947**
Francis Poulenc. Translated from the French and introduced by Edward Lockspeiser. New York, Grove Press [c1959] 118 p. illus., music. 23 cm. 1. Poulenc, Francis, 1899-1963. I. T.
ML410.P787 H42    *LC* 59-11658

**Nest'ev, I. V. (Izrail' Vladimirovich), 1911-.**    • **1.3948**
Prokofiev. Translated from the Russian by Florence Jonas; with a foreword by Nicolas Slonimsky. Stanford, Calif., Stanford University Press, 1960. 528 p. ill., ports., facsim., music. 1. Prokofiev, Sergey, 1891-1953. I. Jonas, Florence. II. T.
ML410 P865 N463    *LC* 60-11631

**Puccini, Giacomo, 1858-1924.**    • **1.3949**
[Correspondence English. 1971] Letters of Giacomo Puccini, mainly connected with the composition and production of his operas. Edited by Giuseppe Adami. Translated from the Italian and edited for the English ed. by Ena Makin. New York, AMS Press [1971] 335 p. facsims., port. 23 cm. Reprint of Lippincott ed., 1931. 1. Composers — Italy — Correspondence. I. Adami, Giuseppe, 1878-1946. ed. II. T.
ML410.P89 A23 1971    782.1/0924 B    *LC* 71-140038    *ISBN* 0404051499

**Carner, Mosco.**       **1.3950**
Puccini: a critical biography / by Mosco Carner. 2d ed. — New York: Holmes & Meier Publishers, 1977, c1974. xvi, 520 p., [11] leaves of plates: ill.; 26 cm. Includes indexes. 1. Puccini, Giacomo, 1858-1924. 2. Composers — Italy — Biography. I. T.
ML410.P89 C3 1977    782.1/092/4 B    *LC* 76-30456    *ISBN* 0841903026

**Price, Curtis Alexander, 1945-.**       **1.3951**
Henry Purcell and the London stage / Curtis Alexander Price. — Cambridge [Cambridgeshire]; New York: Cambridge University Press, 1984. xiv, 380 p., [6] p. of plates: ill., music; 24 cm. Includes index. 1. Purcell, Henry, 1659-1695 — Criticism and interpretation. 2. English drama — Restoration, 1660-1700 — History and criticism. 3. Music in theaters I. T.
ML410.P93 P7 1984    782.8/3/0924 19    *LC* 83-15170    *ISBN* 0521238315

**Westrup, J. A. (Jack Allan), 1904-1975.**    • **1.3952**
Purcell. — London: T. M. Dent, 1965. 323 p. (Great composers series; BS114X) 'Catalogue of works': p. 297-311. 1. Purcell, Henry, 1659-1695. I. T. II. Series.
ML410.P93 W52 1962    *LC* 66-884

## ML410 R

**Bertensson, Sergei, 1885-1962.**    • **1.3953**
Sergei Rachmaninoff, a lifetime in music, by Sergei Bertensson and Jay Leyda, with the assistance of Sophia Satin. — New York: New York University Press, 1956. viii, 464 p.: illus., ports., facsims., music.; 24 cm. 1. Rachmaninoff, Sergei, 1873-1943. 2. Rachmaninoff, Sergei, 1873-1943 — Discography. I. Leyda, Jay, 1910- joint author. II. Satina, Sophie, 1879- III. T.
ML410.R12 B47    927.8    *LC* 55-10065

**Culshaw, John.**       **1.3954**
Sergei Rachmaninov. London, D. Dobson, 1949. 174 p. ports., music. (Contemporary composers.) 1. Rachmaninoff, Sergei, 1873-1943. I. T. II. Series.
ML410 R12 C8    *LC* 49-6844

**Girdlestone, Cuthbert Morton, 1895-.**    • **1.3955**
Jean–Philippe Rameau: his life and work, by Cuthbert Girdlestone. — [Rev. and enl. ed.]. — New York: Dover Publications, [1969] x, 631 p.: illus., music, ports.; 22 cm. 1. Rameau, Jean Philippe, 1683-1764. I. T.
ML410.R2 G5 1969    780/.924 B    *LC* 74-78058    *ISBN* 0486214168

**Demuth, Norman, 1898-.**    • **1.3956**
Ravel. London: J.M. Dent, c1947, 1956 printing. ix, 214 p. (The Master musicians. New series) 'Catalogue of Ravel's works': p. 192-197. 1. Ravel, Maurice, 1875-1937. I. T. II. Series.
ML410.R23 D4    *LC* 48-7354

**Myers, Rollo H.**    • **1.3957**
Ravel: life & works / Rollo H. Myers. — New York: Yoseloff, 1960. 239 p.: ill. 1. Composers, French — Biography. I. T.
ML410.R23M9 1960a    927.8

**Orenstein, Arbie.**       **1.3958**
Ravel: man and musician / by Arbie Orenstein. — New York: Columbia University Press, 1975. xvi, 290 p., [16] leaves of plates: ill.; 24 cm. 1. Ravel, Maurice, 1875-1937. I. T.
ML410.R23 O73    780/.92/4 B    *LC* 74-34022    *ISBN* 0231039026

**Abraham, Gerald, 1904-.**       **1.3959**
Rimsky–Korsakov: a short biography / by Gerald Abraham. — New York: AMS Press, 1976. 142 p.; 18 cm. Reprint of the 1945 ed. published by Duckworth, London. 1. Rimsky-Korsakov, Nikolay, 1844-1908. 2. Composers — Russia — Biography. I. T.
ML410.R52 A62 1976    780/.92/4 B    *LC* 75-41002    *ISBN* 0404145000

**Rodgers, Richard, 1902-.**       **1.3960**
Musical stages: an autobiography / Richard Rodgers. 1st ed. — New York: Random House, [1975] 341 p.: ill.; 24 cm. Includes index. 1. Rodgers, Richard, 1902- 2. Composers — United States — Biography. I. T.
ML410.R6315 A3    782.8/1/0924 B    *LC* 75-10259    *ISBN* 0394479568

**Toye, Francis, 1883-.**    • **1.3961**
Rossini: a study in tragi–comedy. — [New ed.] — London: A. Barker, [1954]. 269 p.: ill.; 23 cm. I. T.
ML410.R8 T73 1954    *LC* 55-3363

**Weinstock, Herbert, 1905-.**    • **1.3962**
Rossini, a biography. [1st ed.] New York, A. A. Knopf, 1968. xviii, 560 p. illus., facsims., music, ports. 25 cm. 1. Rossini, Gioacchino, 1792-1868. I. T.
ML410.R8 W35    780/.924 B    *LC* 67-18622

**Rubinstein, Anton, 1829-1894.**    • **1.3963**
[Avtobiograficheskīia vospominanīia. English] Autobiography. Translated from the Russian by Aline Delano. St. Clair Shores, Mich., Scholarly Press, 1970. xii, 171 p. 21 cm. Translation of Avtobiograficheskīia vospominanīia. 'Reprint of the 1890 ed. 'Supplement: Rubinstein as a composer (p. [141]-163); Rubinstein as a pianist (p. 163-171)' 1. Rubinstein, Anton, 1829-1894. 2. Rubinstein, Anton, 1829-1894. 3. Composers — Soviet Union — Biography. I. T.
ML410.R89 A32 1970    780/.924 B    *LC* 70-131820    *ISBN* 0403007070

## ML410 S–Sc

**Harding, James.**       **1.3964**
Erik Satie / James Harding. New York: Praeger, 1975. xiii, 269 p., [4] leaves of plates; 23 cm. Includes index. 1. Satie, Erik, 1866-1925. 2. Composers — France — Biography. I. T.
ML410.S196 H3 1975    786.1/092/4 B    *LC* 75-5829    *ISBN* 027553720X

**Dent, Edward Joseph, 1876-1957.**    • **1.3965**
Alessandro Scarlatti: his life and works. New impression, with pref. and additional notes by Frank Walker. London, E. Arnold [1960] xii, 252 p. port., music. 1. Scarlatti, Alessandro, 1660-1725. I. T.
ML410 S22 D2 1960    *LC* 60-4215

**Kirkpatrick, Ralph.**    • **1.3966**
Domenico Scarlatti. — Princeton: Princeton University Press, 1953. xix, 473 p.: illus., fold. geneal. table, music.; 24 cm. 'Keyboard works': p. 399-412. 'Vocal music': p. 413-424. 'Miscellaneous, doubtful and spurious works': p. 425-428. 'Catalogue of Scarlatti sonatas and table of principle sources in approximately chronological order': p. 442-456. 'Table of sonatas in the order of Longo's edition': p. 457-459. 1. Scarlatti, Domenico, 1685-1757. I. T.
ML410.S221 K5    927.8    *LC* 53-6387

**Schoenberg, Arnold, 1874-1951.**    • **1.3967**
Letters. Selected and edited by Erwin Stein. Translated from the original German by Eithne Wilkins and Ernst Kaiser. — New York, St Martin's Press [1965, c1964] 309 p. music, port. 24 cm. First pub. in 1958 under title Arnold Schönberg: Ausgewählte Briefe. 1. Musicians — Correspondence, reminiscences, etc. I. Stein, Erwin, 1885-1958. ed. II. T.
ML410.S283A42    927.8    *LC* 65-12618 rev/MN

**Reich, Willi, 1898-.**    • **1.3968**
[Arnold Schönberg, oder Der konservative Revolutionär. English] Schoenberg: a critical biography. Translated by Leo Black. New York, Praeger [1971] xi, 268 p. illus., facsims., ports. 23 cm. Translation of Arnold Schönberg, oder Der konservative Revolutionär. 1. Schoenberg, Arnold, 1874-1951. I. T.
ML410.S283 R43 1971b    780/.924 B    *LC* 73-134527

**Rosen, Charles, 1927-.**      • **1.3969**
Arnold Schoenberg / Charles Rosen. — New York: Viking Press, 1975. xiv, 113 p.: music; 20 cm. (Modern masters) Includes index. 1. Schoenberg, Arnold, 1874-1951. I. T.
ML410.S283 R65    780/.92/4    *LC* 72-78996    *ISBN* 0670133167.
*ISBN* 0670019860 pbk

**Stuckenschmidt, Hans Heinz, 1901-.**      • **1.3970**
Arnold Schoenberg. Translated by Edith Temple Roberts and Humphrey Searle. — London, J. Calder [1959] 168 p. illus. 22 cm. 1. Schoenberg, Arnold, 1874-1951. I. T.
ML410.S283S92 1959b    927.8    *LC* 59-11750

**Stuckenschmidt, Hans Heinz, 1901-.**      **1.3971**
Schoenberg: his life, world and work / H. H. Stuckenschmidt; translated from the German by Humphrey Searle. — 1st American ed. — New York: Schirmer Books, 1978, c1977. 581 p.: ill., facsims, ports.; 23 cm. Translation of 'Schoenberg, leben, umwelt, werk.' 1. Schoenberg, Arnold, 1874-1951. 2. Composers — Austria — Biography. I. T.
ML410.S283 S 93    780/.92/4    *LC* 77-81649    *ISBN* 0028724801

**Wörner, Karl Heinrich, 1910-1969.**      • **1.3972**
Schoenberg's 'Moses and Aaron;' with the complete libretto in German and English. Translated by Paul Hamburger. New York: St. Martin's Press, [c1963] 208 p. ill., music. Libretto by the composer. Cf. Grove 5th ed. 1. Schoenberg, Arnold, 1874-1951. Moses und Aron I. Schoenberg, Arnold, 1874-1951. Moses und Aron. Libretto. English & German. II. T.
ML410 S283 W643    *LC* 64-14229

**Schubert, Franz, 1797-1828.**      • **1.3973**
Franz Schubert's letters and other writings. Edited by Otto Erich Deutsch and translated by Venetia Savile. With a foreword by Ernest Newman. Westport, Conn., Greenwood Press [1970] xx, 143 p. 23 cm. Reprint of the 1928 ed. 1. Schubert, Franz, 1797-1828. I. Deutsch, Otto Erich, 1883-1967. ed. II. T.
ML410.S3 A413 1970b    780/.924 B    *LC* 76-109840    *ISBN* 0837143319

**Abraham, Gerald, 1904-.**      • **1.3974**
The music of Schubert, edited by Gerald Abraham. Port Washington, N.Y., Kennikat Press [1969] 342 p. 23 cm. (Essay and general literature index reprint series) 1. Schubert, Franz, 1797-1828. I. T.
ML410.S3 A56 1969    780/.924    *LC* 68-8226

**Brown, Maurice John Edwin.**      • **1.3975**
Essays on Schubert / by Maurice J.E. Brown. London, Macmillan, 1966. xii, 315 p. front., ill. (music) 14 plates (incl. ports.) facsims. 1. Schubert, Franz, 1797-1828. I. T.
ML410 S3 B67    *LC* 65-22791

**Brown, Maurice John Edwin.**      • **1.3976**
Schubert: a critical biography. London: Macmillan; New York: St. Martin's Press, 1958. 414 p.: facsims., music, ports.; 23 cm. Works by Schubert not included in the 'Gesamtausgabe': p.362-367. 'The works in chronological order': p.368-397. 1. Schubert, Franz, 1797-1828. I. T.
ML410.S3 B7    927.8    *LC* 58-2878

**Einstein, Alfred, 1880-1952.**      • **1.3977**
Schubert; a musical portrait. New York, Oxford University Press, 1951. ix, 343 p. music. 22 cm. 1. Schubert, Franz, 1797-1828. I. T.
ML410.S3 E5    927.8    *LC* 51-578

**Deutsch, Otto Erich, 1883-1967. ed.**      • **1.3978**
The Schubert reader: A life of Franz Schubert in letters and documents / tr. by Eric Blom; being an English version of Franz Schubert: die Dokumente seines Lebens; Rev. and augm., with a commentary by the author. — 1st American ed. — New York: W. W. Norton, 1947. xxxii, 1039 p.: ill., ports, map, facsims.; 25 cm. London ed., J. M. Dent, has title: Schubert, a documentary biography. 1. Schubert, Franz, 1797-1828. I. Blom, Eric, 1888- , tr. II. T.
ML410.S3 D52 1947a    *LC* 47-12315

**Reed, John, 1909-.**      **1.3979**
The Schubert song companion / by John Reed; with prose translations by Norma Deane and Celia Larner. — New York, N.Y.: Universe Books, c1985. p. cm. 1. Schubert, Franz, 1797-1828. Songs I. T.
ML410.S3 R265 1985    784.3/0092/4 19    *LC* 84-9665    *ISBN* 0876634773

**Moser, Hans Joachim, 1889-1967.**      • **1.3980**
[Heinrich Schütz] Heinrich Schütz; his life and work. Translated from the 2d rev. ed. by Carl F. Pfatteicher. Saint Louis, Concordia Pub. House [c1959] xxvi, 740 p. illus. (music) plates (incl. ports) fold. table. 25 cm. 'Works of Schütz known to have existed, now lost': p. 720-722. 'The works of Schütz discussed': p. 737. 1. Schütz, Heinrich, 1585-1672. I. T.
ML410.S35 M62    *LC* a 60-2810

**Schumann, Robert, 1810-1856.**      • **1.3981**
On music and musicians / Robert Schumann; [edited by Konrad Wolff; translated by Paul Rosenfeld]. — New York: Pantheon, 1946. 274 p., [18]p. of plates: ill., facsims., music, pots; 24 cm. Translation of Gesammelte Schriften über musik und musiker, with rearrangement of material and some omissions. 1. Music — History and criticism — Modern. 2. Musicians I. Wolff, Konrad. II. T. III. Title: Music and musicians.
ML410.S4 A134    780.15    *LC* 47-831

**Abraham, Gerald, 1904- ed.**      • **1.3982**
Schumann; a symposium. London, New York, Oxford University Press, 1952. vi, 319 p. music. 22 cm. 1. Schumann, Robert, 1810-1856. I. T.
ML410.S4A6317    *LC* 52-7806

**Moore, Gerald.**      **1.3983**
Poet's love: the songs and cycles of Schumann / Gerald Moore. — New York: Taplinger Pub. Co., 1981. xii, 247 p.: music; 25 cm. 'A Crescendo book.' Includes indexes. 1. Schumann, Robert, 1810-1856. Songs. I. T.
ML410.S4 M65    784.3/007 19    *LC* 81-50607    *ISBN* 0800863909

**Plantinga, Leon.**      • **1.3984**
Schumann as critic / by Leon B. Plantinga. — New Haven: Yale University Press, 1967. xiii, 354 p.: facsims., music. 25 cm. — (Yale studies in the history of music; 4) Bibliography: p. [335]-342. 1. Schumann, Robert, 1810-1856. 2. Musical criticism I. T. II. Series.
ML410.S4P6    780.15/0924    *LC* 67-13446 rev/MN

**Taylor, Ronald, 1924-.**      **1.3985**
Robert Schumann, his life and work / Ronald Taylor. — New York: Universe Books, 1982. 354 p., [8] p. of plates: ill.; 24 cm. Includes indexes. 1. Schumann, Robert, 1810-1856. 2. Composers — Germany — Biography. I. T.
ML410.S4 T2 1982    780/.92/4 B 19    *LC* 82-8526    *ISBN* 0876634064

**Young, Percy M. (Percy Marshall), 1912-.**      **1.3986**
Tragic muse: the life and works of Robert Schumann. — [Enl. ed.] London, D. Dobson [1961] 256 p. illus. 22 cm. 1. Schumann, Robert, 1810-1856. I. T.
ML410.S4 Y7 1961    *LC* 61-19293

## ML410 Sh–Sz

**Shostakovich, Dmitriĭ Dmitrievich, 1906-1975.**      **1.3987**
Testimony: the memoirs of Dmitri Shostakovich / as related to and edited by Solomon Volkov; translated from the Russian by Antonina W. Bouis. — New York: Harper & Row, c1979. xli, 289 p., [48] leaves of plates: ill.; 25 cm. 'Major compositions, titles, and awards': p. 277-281. Includes index. 1. Shostakovich, Dmitriĭ Dmitrievich, 1906-1975. 2. Composers — Russia — Biography. I. Volkov, Solomon. II. T.
ML410.S53 A3    785/.092/4 B    *LC* 79-2236    *ISBN* 0060144769

**Kay, Norman Forber.**      • **1.3988**
Shostakovich; [by] Norman Kay. London, New York, Oxford University Press, 1971. 80 p. music. 22 cm. (Oxford studies of composers. 8) 1. Shostakovich, Dmitriĭ Dmitrievich, 1906-1975 — Criticism and interpretation. I. T. II. Series.
ML410.S53 K4    785/.0924    *LC* 76-31858    *ISBN* 0193154226

**Johnson, Harold Edgar, 1915-.**      • **1.3989**
Jean Sibelius. [1st ed.] New York, Knopf, 1959. xviii, 287, xi p. ill., ports. 1. Sibelius, Jean, 1865-1957. I. T.
ML410 S54 J6    *LC* 59-8580

**Layton, Robert.**      **1.3990**
Sibelius / by Robert Layton. — [2d ed.]. — London: J. M. Dent, 1978. xi, 210 p., [4] leaves of plates: ill.; 20 cm. — (Master musicians series.) Includes music and index. 1. Sibelius, Jean, 1865-1957. 2. Composers — Finland — Biography. I. T. Series.
ML410.S54 L35 1978    780/.92/4 B    *LC* 79-309169    *ISBN* 0460031694

**Swan, Alfred Julius, 1890-.**      • **1.3991**
Scriabin, by Alfred J. Swan. New York, Da Capo Press, 1969. 119 p. 21 cm. (Da Capo Press music reprint series) 1. Scriabin, Aleksandr Nikolayevich, 1872-1915. I. T.
ML410.S5988 S9 1969    786.1/0924 B    *LC* 75-76423

**Large, Brian.**      • **1.3992**
Smetana. — New York, Praeger [1970] xvii, 473 p. illus., facsims., geneal. table, music, 27 plates (incl. ports.) 26 cm. 1. Smetana, Bedřich, 1824-1884. I. T.
ML410.S63 L4 1970b    780/.924 B    *LC* 78-100938

**Bierley, Paul E.**                                                        **1.3993**
John Philip Sousa; American phenomenon [by] Paul E. Bierley. — New York: Appleton-Century-Crofts, [1973] xxiii, 261 p.: illus.; 25 cm. 1. Sousa, John Philip, 1854-1932. I. T.
ML410.S688 B5      785/.092/4 B      LC 73-1712

**Arvey, Verna, 1910-.**                                                    **1.3994**
In one lifetime / Verna Arvey; with an introduction and notes by B.A. Nugent. — Fayetteville: University of Arkansas Press, 1984. xii, 262 p.: ports.; 25 cm. 1. Still, William Grant, 1895- 2. Composers — United States — Biography. I. T.
ML410.S855 A78 1984      780/.92/4 B 19      LC 83-24226      ISBN 0938626310

**Maconie, Robin.**                                                         **1.3995**
The works of Karlheinz Stockhausen / Robin Maconie; with a foreword by Karlheinz Stockhausen. — London; New York: Oxford University Press, 1976. ix, 341 p.: ill.; 26 cm. Includes indexes. 1. Stockhausen, Karlheinz, 1928- — Criticism and interpretation. I. T.
ML410.S858 M3      780/.92/4      LC 76-371987      ISBN 0193154293

**Wörner, Karl Heinrich, 1910-1969.**                                       **1.3996**
Stockhausen; life and work. Introduced, translated, and edited by Bill Hopkins. — [Rev. ed.]. — Berkeley: University of California Press, 1973. 270 p.: illus.; 23 cm. German ed. published in 1963 under title: Karlheinz Stockhausen. 1. Stockhausen, Karlheinz, 1928- I. Hopkins, Bill. ed. II. T.
ML410.S858 W62      785/.092/4      LC 76-174460      ISBN 0520021436

**Strauss, Richard, 1864-1949.**                                           **• 1.3997**
[Betrachtungen und Erinnerungen. English] Recollections and reflections. Edited by Willi Schuh. English translation by L. J. Lawrence. London: Boosey & Hawkes, [1953] 173 p. illus. 19 cm. Translation of Betrachtungen und Erinnerungen. 1. Strauss, Richard, 1864-1949. 2. Composers — Biography. I. T.
ML410.S93 A372 1953      780/.8      LC 53-4368      ISBN 0837173663

**Strauss, Richard, 1864-1949.**                                           **• 1.3998**
Working friendship: the correspondence between Richard Strauss and Hugo von Hofmannsthal. New York: Random House, 1961. xx, 558 p.: ill., ports., facsims. 1. Hofmannsthal, Hugo von, 1874-1929. I. T.
ML410.S93 A453      927.8      LC 61-13839

**Del Mar, Norman, 1919-.**                                                **• 1.3999**
Richard Strauss; a critical commentary on his life and works, by Norman Del Mar. Philadelphia, Chilton Book Co. [1969, v. 1, c1962] 2 v. illus., music, ports. 23 cm. Includes lists of compositions. 1. Strauss, Richard, 1864-1949. I. T.
ML410.S93 D4 1969      780/.924 B      LC 69-11425

**Petersen, Barbara A., 1945-.**                                            **1.4000**
Ton und Wort: the Lieder of Richard Strauss / by Barbara A. Petersen. — Ann Arbor, Mich.: UMI Research Press, c1980. xvii, 254 p.: music; 24 cm. — (Studies in musicology. no. 15) Includes index. 1. Strauss, Richard, 1864-1949. Songs I. T. II. Series.
ML410.S93 P35 1980      784/.3/00924      LC 79-24415      ISBN 0835710726

**Stravinsky, Igor, 1882-1971.**                                           **• 1.4001**
[Poétique musicale sous forme de six leçons. English & French] Poetics of music in the form of six lessons [by] Igor Stravinsky. English translation by Arthur Knodell and Ingolf Dahl. Pref. by George Seferis. Bilingual ed. Cambridge, Mass., Harvard University Press, 1970. ix, 187 p. port. 22 cm. (Charles Eliot Norton lectures. 1939-40) In French and English. 1. Music — Addresses, essays, lectures. I. T. II. Series.
ML410.S932 A13 1970      780      LC 79-99520      ISBN 0674678559

**Stravinsky, Igor, 1882-1971.**                                           **• 1.4002**
Igor Stravinsky, an autobiography. — New York: Norton, 1962, c1936. 176 p.; 20 cm. — (The Norton Library; N161) Translation of Chroniques de ma vie. I. T.
ML410.S932 A22      LC 63-197

**Stravinsky, Igor, 1882-1971.**                                           **• 1.4003**
Conversations with Igor Stravinsky / Igor Stravinsky and Robert Craft. — [1st ed]. — Garden City, N.Y.: Doubleday, 1959. — 162 p., [16] p. of plates: ill., facsims, ports.; 22cm. Includes index. 1. Composers — Interviews. I. Craft, Robert. II. T.
ML410.S932 A33      780.924      LC 59-6375

**Stravinsky, Igor, 1882-1971.**                                           **1.4004**
Dialogues and a diary [by] Igor Stravinsky and Robert Craft. — London, Faber, 1968. 3-328 p. 9 plates, illus., facsims., music, ports. 23 cm. 1. Stravinsky, Igor, 1882-1971. 2. Music I. Craft, Robert. II. T.
ML410.S932 A335 1968      780/.924      LC 68-143871

**Stravinsky, Igor' Fedorovich.**                                          **• 1.4005**
Expositions and developments by Igor Stravinsky and Robert Craft. Doubleday 1962. 191p.illus. 1. Musicians — Correspondence,reminiscences etc. I. Craft, Robert. II. T.
ML410.S932 A34      927.8      LC 61-12588

**Stravinsky, Igor, 1882-1971.**                                           **• 1.4006**
Memories [by] Igor Stravinsky and Robert Craft. and commentaries. [1st ed.] Garden City, N.Y., Doubleday, 1960 [c1959] 167 p. ill. 1. Music I. Craft, Robert. II. T.
ML410 S932 A35      LC 60-10684

**Stravinsky, Igor, 1882-1971.**                                           **• 1.4007**
Themes and episodes [by] Igor Stravinsky and Robert Craft. [1st ed.] New York, A. A. Knopf, 1966. x, 352, xvi p. music. (Borzoi books) 1. Music I. Craft, Robert. jt. author II. T.
ML410 S932 A38      LC 66-19373

**Craft, Robert.**                                                         **• 1.4008**
Stravinsky; chronicle of a friendship, 1948–1971. — [1st ed.]. — New York: A. A. Knopf, 1972. xvi, 424, xvi p.: illus.; 25 cm. 1. Stravinsky, Igor, 1882-1971. I. T.
ML410.S932 C8      780/.924 B      LC 79-173776      ISBN 0394476123

**Goldner, Nancy.**                                                        **1.4009**
The Stravinsky festival of the New York City Ballet. Written and edited by Nancy Goldner. With photos. by Martha Swope and others. New York, Eakins Press [1974, c1973] 302 p. illus., music. 15 x 19 cm. 1. Stravinsky, Igor, 1882-1971 — Anniversaries, etc., 1972. 2. Stravinsky, Igor, 1882-1971. Ballets 3. Ballets — Analysis, appreciation. I. New York City Ballet. II. T.
ML410.S932 G64      792.8/4      LC 73-84996      ISBN 0871300370

**Stravinsky, Vera.**                                                      **1.4010**
Stravinsky in pictures and documents / by Vera Stravinsky and Robert Craft. — New York: Simon and Schuster, c1978. 688 p., [16] leaves of plates: ill.; 28 cm. 1. Stravinsky, Igor, 1882-1971. 2. Composers — Biography. I. Craft, Robert. joint author. II. T.
ML410.S932 S787      780/.92/4 B      LC 78-15375      ISBN 0671243829

**Van den Toorn, Pieter C., 1938-.**                                       **1.4011**
The music of Igor Stravinsky / Pieter C. van den Toorn. — New Haven: Yale University Press, c1983. xxi, 512 p.: music; 25 cm. (Composers of the twentieth century.) Includes index. 1. Stravinsky, Igor, 1882-1971 — Criticism and interpretation. I. T. II. Series.
ML410.S932 V36 1983      780.924 19      LC 82-2560      ISBN 0300026935

**Vlad, Roman, 1919-.**                                                    **• 1.4012**
Stravinsky; translated from the Italian by Frederick and Ann Fuller. 2nd ed. London, New York [etc.] Oxford U.P., 1967. [vii], 264 p. plate, music. 23 cm. 1. Stravinsky, Igor, 1882-1971. I. T.
ML410.S932 V52 1967      780/.924      LC 68-71387

**White, Eric Walter, 1905-.**                                             **1.4013**
Stravinsky, the composer and his works / Eric Walter White. — 2d ed. — Berkeley: University of California Press, 1979. 656 p.: ill.; 26 cm. Register of works: p. 162-551. 1. Stravinsky, Igor, 1882-1971. 2. Composers — Biography. I. T.
ML410.S932 W47 1979      780/.92/4 B      LC 80-110579      ISBN 0520039831

**Jacobs, Arthur.**                                                        **1.4014**
Arthur Sullivan, a Victorian musician / Arthur Jacobs. — Oxford; New York: Oxford University Press, 1984. xvi, 470 p., [16] p. of plates: ill.; 25 cm. Includes index. 1. Sullivan, Arthur, Sir, 1842-1900. 2. Composers — England — Biography. I. T.
ML410.S95 J28 1984      782.81/092/4 B 19      LC 83-8207      ISBN 0193154439

**Jefferson, Alan.**                                                       **1.4015**
The complete Gilbert & Sullivan opera guide / Alan Jefferson. — New York: Facts on File, c1984. 352 p.: ill. (some col.); 27 cm. Includes librettos. Includes index. 1. Sullivan, Arthur, Sir, 1842-1900. Operas. 2. Operas — 19th century — History and criticism. I. Sullivan, Arthur, Sir, 1842-1900. Operas. Librettos. Selections. 1984. II. Gilbert, W. S. (William Schwenck), 1836-1911. III. T. IV. Title: Complete Gilbert and Sullivan opera guide. V. Title: Gilbert & Sullivan opera guide. VI. Title: Gilbert and Sullivan opera guide.
ML410.S95 J43 1984      782.81/092/4 19      LC 83-20654      ISBN 0871968576

**Sullivan, Herbert.**                                                     **• 1.4016**
Sir Arthur Sullivan, his life, letters & diaries / by Herbert Sullivan and Newman Flower. — 2nd ed. — London: Cassell, 1950. ix, 306 p., [6] leaves of plates: ill., facsims., ports. 'List of works, compiled by William C. Smith': p. 350-357.

1. Sullivan, Arthur, Sir, 1842-1900. 2. Musicians — England — Correspondence I. Flower, Newman, Sir, 1879- II. T.
ML410.S95 S95 1950    927/8    *LC* 54-27545

## ML410 T–V

### (Tchaikovskii: see Chaikovskii)

**Petzoldt, Richard, 1907-.**    **1.4017**
[Georg Philipp Telemann. English] Georg Philipp Telemann. Translated by Horace Fitzpatrick. New York, Oxford University Press, 1974. xv, 255 p. illus. 22 cm. 1. Telemann, Georg Philipp, 1681-1767. I. T.
ML410.T26 P53    780/.92/4 B    *LC* 73-82633    *ISBN* 0195197224

**Ouellette, Fernand.**    • **1.4018**
Edgard Varèse. Translated from the French by Derek Coltman. — New York: Orion Press, [1968] ix, 270 p.: illus., facsims., ports.; 24 cm. Translation of Edgard Varèse published in 1966. 1. Varèse, Edgard, 1883-1965. I. T.
ML410.V27 O83    780/.924 B    *LC* 68-15461

**Vaughan Williams, Ralph, 1872-1958.**    • **1.4019**
Heirs and rebels; letters written to each other and occasional writings on music, by Ralph Vaughan Williams and Gustav Holst. Edited by Ursula Vaughan Williams and Imogen Holst. London, Oxford University Press, 1959. 111 p. ill. I. Holst, Gustav, 1874-1934. II. Vaughan Williams, Ursula. III. Holst, Imogen, 1907- IV. T.
ML410 V3 A4    *LC* 60-238

**Kennedy, Michael, 1926-.**    • **1.4020**
The works of Ralph Vaughan Williams. London, Oxford University Press, 1964. xvi, 776 p. front. (port.), music, 8 plates (incl. facsims., ports.) 1. Vaughan Williams, Ralph, 1872-1958. Works I. T.
ML410 V3 K4    *LC* 64-56920

**Verdi, Giuseppe, 1813-1901.**    • **1.4021**
[Correspondence. English] Verdi, the man in his letters. As edited and selected by Franz Werfel and Paul Stefan. Translated by Edward Downes. Freeport, N.Y., Books for Libraries Press [1970] 469 p. illus., ports. 23 cm. Reprint of the 1942 ed. 1. Verdi, Giuseppe, 1813-1901. 2. Verdi, Giuseppe, 1813-1901. 3. Composers — Italy — Correspondence. I. Werfel, Franz, 1890-1945. ed. II. Stefan, Paul, 1879-1943. ed. III. T.
ML410.V4 A385 1970    782.1/092/4 B 19    *LC* 71-130565    *ISBN* 0836955382

**Budden, Julian.**    **1.4022**
The operas of Verdi / Julian Budden. — New York: Oxford University Press, 1978-1981. 3 v.: music; 24 cm. Includes index. 1. Verdi, Giuseppe, 1813-1901. Operas. I. T.
ML410.V4 B88 1978    782.1/0924    *LC* 70-187275    *ISBN* 0195200306

**Encounters with Verdi / edited, introduced, and annotated by**    **1.4023**
**Marcello Conati; translated by Richard Stokes; with a foreword by Julian Budden.**
Ithaca, N.Y.: Cornell University Press, 1984. xxvii, 417 p., [24] p. of plates: ill.; 24 cm. Includes index. 1. Verdi, Giuseppe, 1813-1901. 2. Composers — Italy — Addresses, essays, lectures. I. Conati, Marcello.
ML410.V4 E48 1984    782.1/092/4 B 19    *LC* 83-73736    *ISBN* 0801417171

**Godefroy, Vincent.**    **1.4024**
The dramatic genius of Verdi: studies of selected operas / by Vincent Godefroy; with an introd. by Charles Osborne. — New York: St. Martin's Press, 1976-78, c1975-77. 2 v.: music; 23 cm. 1. Verdi, Giuseppe, 1813-1901. Operas. 2. Libretto I. T.
ML410.V4 G6 1976    782.1/092/4    *LC* 75-13981    *ISBN* 0312219466

**Martin, George Whitney.**    • **1.4025**
Verdi; his music, life and times. Illustrated with drawings by Everett Raymond Kinstler, photos., maps, and Delfico cartoons. — New York: Dodd, Mead, 1963. xxi, 633 p.: illus.; 24 cm. 1. Verdi, Giuseppe, 1813-1901. I. T.
ML410.V4 M266    927.8    *LC* 63-15475

**Toye, Francis, 1883-.**    • **1.4026**
Giuseppe Verdi, his life and works. Introd. by Herbert Weinstock. — New York: Knopf, [c1946] xxi, 414, xiv p.: ill.; 24 cm. 1. Verdi, Giuseppe, 1813-1901. I. T.
ML410.V4 T7 1972    782.1/092/4 B    *LC* 72-81577    *ISBN* 0844300675

**Verdi: a documentary study / compiled, edited, and translated**    **1.4027**
**by William Weaver.**
[London]: Thames & Hudson, [1977?] 256 p.: ill. (some col.); 31 cm. Includes index. 1. Verdi, Giuseppe, 1813-1901. 2. Composers — Italy — Biography. I. Weaver, William, 1923-
ML410.V4 V29    782.1/092/4 B    *LC* 77-376231    *ISBN* 0500011842

**The Verdi companion / edited by William Weaver and Martin**    **1.4028**
**Chusid.**
1st ed. — New York: W. W. Norton, c1979. xvi, 366 p.: ill.; 22 cm. Includes indexes. 1. Verdi, Giuseppe, 1813-1901. I. Weaver, William, 1923- II. Chusid, Martin.
ML410.V4 V295    782.1/092/4    *LC* 79-14793    *ISBN* 0393012158

**Verdi's Aida: the history of an opera in letters and documents /**    **1.4029**
**collected and translated by Hans Busch.**
Minneapolis: University of Minnesota Press, c1978. lv, 688 p.: ill.; 24 cm. Includes index. 1. Verdi, Giuseppe, 1813-1901. Aïda 2. Composers — Italy — Correspondence. I. Verdi, Giuseppe, 1813-1901. Correspondence. English. Selections. 1978. II. Busch, Hans, 1914-
ML410.V4 V33    782.1/092/4    *LC* 76-11495    *ISBN* 0816607982

**Walker, Frank, 1907-1962.**    • **1.4030**
The man Verdi. New York, Knopf, 1962. xiii, 526 p. plates. 25 cm. 1. Verdi, Giuseppe, 1813-1901. I. T.
ML410.V4 W3    *LC* 62-8686

**Kolneder, Walter.**    • **1.4031**
[Antonio Vivaldi. English] Antonio Vivaldi; his life and work. Translated by Bill Hopkins. Berkeley, University of California Press, 1970. x, 288 p. illus., facsims., music, ports. (part col.) 25 cm. 1. Vivaldi, Antonio, 1678-1741. I. T.
ML410.V82 K553    780/.924 B    *LC* 71-101341    *ISBN* 0520016297

**Pincherle, Marc, 1888-1974.**    • **1.4032**
[Vivaldi. English] Vivaldi, genius of the baroque. Translated from the French by Christopher Hatch. [1st ed.] New York, W.W. Norton [1957] 278 p. illus. 22 cm. 1. Vivaldi, Antonio, 1678-1741. I. T.
ML410.V82 P532    927.8    *LC* 57-11245

**Talbot, Michael.**    **1.4033**
Vivaldi / Michael Talbot. — London: Dent, 1978. 275 p., [4] leaves of plates: ill.; 20 cm. — (Master musicians series.) Includes music and indexes. 1. Vivaldi, Antonio, 1678-1741. 2. Composers — Italy — Biography. I. T. II. Series.
ML410.V82 T34    780/.92/4 B    *LC* 79-302925    *ISBN* 0460031643

## ML410 Wagner

**James, Burnett, 1919-.**    **1.4034**
Wagner and the romantic disaster / Burnett James. — New York: Hippocrene; Tunbridge Wells: Midas, 1983. 202 p.; 25 cm. 1. Composers — Germany — Biography. I. T.
ML410.W1    782.1/092/4 19    *ISBN* 0859361063

**Wagner, Richard, 1813-1883.**    • **1.4035**
[Correspondence: Liszt. English] Correspondence of Wagner and Liszt. Translated into English, with a pref., by Francis Hueffer. New ed. rev., and furnished with an index, by W. Ashton Ellis. New York, Greenwood Press [1969] 2 v. port., music. 23 cm. Reprinted from the 1897 ed. 1. Wagner, Richard, 1813-1883. I. Liszt, Franz, 1811-1886. II. T.
ML410.W1 A365 1969b    782.1/0924    *LC* 68-31009    *ISBN* 0837127432

**Barth, Herbert, 1910-.**    **1.4036**
[Wagner. English] Wagner: a documentary study / compiled and edited by Herbert Barth, Dietrich Mack, Egon Voss; pref. by Pierre Boulez. — New York: Oxford University Press, 1975. 256 p.: ill., facsims., music (some col.); 31 cm. Translation of: Wagner: sein Leben und seine Welt in zeitgenöss. Bildern u. Texten. Includes index. 1. Wagner, Richard, 1813-1883. 2. Composers — Germany — Biography. I. Mack, Dietrich. joint author. II. Voss, Egon. joint author. III. T.
ML410.W1 B1853 1975b    782.1/092/4 B    *LC* 75-4097    *ISBN* 0195198182

**Gutman, Robert W.**    • **1.4037**
Richard Wagner; the man, his mind, and his music, by Robert W. Gutman — [1st ed.]. — New York: Harcourt, Brace & World, [1968] xx, 490 p.; 24 cm. 1. Wagner, Richard, 1813-1883. I. T.
ML410.W1 G83    782/.1/0924 B    *LC* 67-20310

**Wagner, Richard, 1813-1883.**    **1.4038**
[Mein Leben. English] My life / Richard Wagner; translated by Andrew Gray; edited by Mary Whittall. — Cambridge [Cambridgeshire]; New York: Cambridge University Press, 1983. ix, 786 p.; 24 cm. Translation of: Mein

Leben. 1. Wagner, Richard, 1813-1883. 2. Composers — Germany — Biography. I. Gray, Andrew. II. Whittall, Mary. III. T.
ML410.W1 M146 1983    782.1/092/4 B 19    *LC* 82-23568    *ISBN* 0521229294

**Millington, Barry.**                     **1.4039**
Wagner / Barry Millington. — London: J.M. Dent, 1984. x, 342 p., [12] p. of plates: ill.; 23 cm. (The Master musicians) Includes index. 1. Wagner, Richard, 1813-1883. 2. Composers — Germany — Biography. I. T.
ML410.W1 M58 1984    782.1/092/4 B 19    *LC* 84-186075    *ISBN* 0460031813

**Newman, Ernest, 1868-1959.**             • **1.4040**
The life of Richard Wagner ... — New York: A. A. Knopf, 1933-46. 4 v.: front. (v. 1, 3-4) illus. (music) plates, ports., map, facsims. (incl. music); 24 1/2 cm. 'First American edition.' 'The works of Ernest Newman': v. 1, p. 511-512. 'Sources': v. 1. p. xix-xxvii. 'Additional sources and references': v. 2, p. xv-xx; v. 3, p. xiii-xvi; v. 4, p. xv-xvii. 1. Wagner, Richard, 1813-1883. I. T.
ML410.W1 N53    927.8    *LC* 33-4967

**Newman, Ernest, 1868-1959.**             • **1.4041**
Wagner as a man & artist. [2d American ed.] New York, A.A. Knopf, 1924. 399 p.: ill.; music. 1. Wagner, Richard, 1813-1883. I. T.
ML410.W1 N55 1924    780.924 B    *LC* 24-30743

**Stein, Jack Madison.**                 • **1.4042**
Richard Wagner & the synthesis of the arts. Detroit, Wayne University, 1960. 229 p. illus. 24 cm. 1. Wagner, Richard, 1813-1883. 2. Music and literature I. T.
ML410.W1S83    *LC* 59-7831

**Taylor, Ronald, 1924-.**                 **1.4043**
Richard Wagner: his life, art and thought / Ronald Taylor. — New York: Taplinger Pub. Co., 1979. 285 p., [8] leaves of plates: ill.; 25 cm. 'A Crescendo book.' 1. Wagner, Richard, 1813-1883. 2. Composers — Germany — Biography. I. T.
ML410.W1 T4    782.1/092/4 B    *LC* 78-63053    *ISBN* 080084792X

**Watson, Derek.**                   **1.4044**
Richard Wagner: a biography / Derek Watson. — 1st American ed. — New York: Schirmer Books, 1981, c1979. 352 p., [32] p. of plates: ill.; 25 cm. Includes index. 1. Wagner, Richard, 1813-1883. 2. Composers — Germany — Biography. I. T.
ML410.W1 W38 1981    780/.92/4 B 19    *LC* 81-1161    *ISBN* 0028727002

**Westernhagen, Curt von.**             **1.4045**
[Wagner. English] Wagner: a biography / Curt von Westernhagen; translated by Mary Whittall. — Cambridge; New York: Cambridge University Press, 1978. 2 v. (xxiii, 654 p.), [16] leaves of plates: ill.; 24 cm. Includes index. 1. Wagner, Richard, 1813-1883. 2. Composers — Germany — Biography. I. T.
ML410.W1 W543    782.1/092/4 B    *LC* 78-2397    *ISBN* 0521219302

**Wagner, Richard, 1813-1883.**           **1.4046**
[Braune Buch. English] The diary of Richard Wagner 1865–1882: the brown book / presented and annotated by Joachim Bergfeld; translated by George Bird. — London; New York: Cambridge University Press, 1980. 218 p.: music; 24 cm. Translation of Das braune Buch. Includes index. 1. Wagner, Richard, 1813-1883. 2. Composers — Germany — Biography. I. Bergfeld, Joachim, 1906- II. T.
ML410.W11 W122    782.1/092/4 B 19    *LC* 79-56128    *ISBN* 0521233119

**Dahlhaus, Carl, 1928-.**               **1.4047**
[Richard Wagners Musikdramen. English] Richard Wagner's music dramas / Carl Dahlhaus; translated by Mary Whittall. — Cambridge; New York: Cambridge University Press, 1979. 161 p.: music; 24 cm. Translation of Richard Wagners Musikdramen. 1. Wagner, Richard, 1813-1883. Operas I. T.
ML410.W13 D153    782.1/092/4    *LC* 78-68359    *ISBN* 0521223970

**Mander, Raymond.**                **1.4048**
The Wagner companion / Raymond Mander & Joe Mitchenson; with a musical appreciation and an essay on the Bayreuth Festival Centenary Celebrations by Barry Millington. — New York: Hawthorn Books, 1978 [c1977]. x, 265 p., [16] leaves of plates: ill.; 25 cm. Includes index. 1. Wagner, Richard, 1813-1883. Operas 2. Wagner, Richard, 1813-1883 — Stories of operas I. Mitchenson, Joe. joint author. II. Millington, Barry. III. T.
ML410.W13 M14 1978    782.1/092/4    *LC* 78-52877    *ISBN* 080158356X

**Deathridge, John.**                 **1.4049**
Wagner's Rienzi: a reappraisal based on a study of the sketches and drafts / John Deathridge. — Oxford; New York: Clarendon Press, 1977. xvi, 199 p., [3]

leaves of plates: ill.; 28 cm. — (Oxford monographs on music) Includes index. 1. Wagner, Richard, 1813-1883. Rienzi. I. T.
ML410.W132 D4    782.1/092/4    *LC* 78-303657    *ISBN* 019816131X

**Donington, Robert.**               **1.4050**
Wagner's 'Ring' and its symbols; the music and the myth. — New York: St. Martin's Press, [1974] 342 p.; 22 cm. 'Appendix of music examples': p. 275-306. 1. Wagner, Richard, 1813-1883. Der Ring des Nibelungen. I. T.
ML410.W15 D6 1974b    782.1/092/4    *LC* 74-75421

**Ewans, Michael, 1946-.**              **1.4051**
Wagner and Aeschylus: the Ring and the Oresteia / Michael Ewans. — Cambridge [Cambridgeshire]; New York: Cambridge University Press, 1983, c1982. 271 p.: music; 23 cm. Includes index. 1. Wagner, Richard, 1813-1883. Ring des Nibelungen 2. Aeschylus. Oresteia. I. T.
ML410.W15 E9 1983    782.1/092/4 19    *LC* 82-12762    *ISBN* 0521250730

**Penetrating Wagner's Ring: an anthology / edited by John**    **1.4052**
**Louis DiGaetani.**
Rutherford [N.J.]: Fairleigh Dickinson University Press, c1978. 453 p.: ill.; 24 cm. 1. Wagner, Richard, 1813-1883. Der Ring des Nibelungen. I. DiGaetani, John Louis, 1943-
ML410.W15 P46    782.1/092/4    *LC* 76-14285    *ISBN* 0838617956

**Fischer-Dieskau, Dietrich, 1925-.**         **1.4053**
[Wagner und Nietzsche. English] Wagner and Nietzsche / Dietrich Fischer–Dieskau; translated from the German by Joachim Neugroschel. — New York: Seabury Press, c1976. 232 p.; 24 cm. — (A Continuum book) 1. Wagner, Richard, 1813-1883. 2. Nietzsche, Friedrich Wilhelm, 1844-1900. I. T.
ML410.W19 F563    782.1/092/4    *LC* 75-45489    *ISBN* 0816492808

**Bayreuth, the early years: an account of the early decades of**    **1.4054**
**the Wagner festival as seen by the celebrated visitors &**
**participants / compiled, edited, and introduced by Robert**
**Hartford.**
London; New York: Cambridge University Press, 1981 [c1980]. 284 p., [16] p. of plates: ill.; 24 cm. Includes indexes. 1. Wagner, Richard, 1813-1883. 2. Bayreuther Festspiele. I. Hartford, Robert.
ML410.W2 B265 1980    782.1/07/94331 19    *LC* 80-67459    *ISBN* 0521238226

**Skelton, Geoffrey.**                 • **1.4055**
Wagner at Bayreuth: experiment and tradition. Foreword by Wieland Wagner. — [1st American ed.]. — New York: G. Braziller, [c1965] 239 p.: illus. (part col.), ports.; 22 cm. 1. Wagner family 2. Bayreuther Festspiele. I. T.
ML410.W2 S55 1966a    780.924    *LC* 66-20191

# ML410 W–Z

**Warrack, John Hamilton, 1928-.**        **1.4056**
Carl Maria von Weber / John Warrack. — 2d ed. — Cambridge, Eng.: New York: Cambridge University Press, c1976. 411 p.: ill.; 24 cm. Includes index. 1. Weber, Carl Maria von, 1786-1826. 2. Composers — Germany — Biography. I. T.
ML410.W3 W26 1976    780/.92/4 B    *LC* 76-26655    *ISBN* 0521213541

**Kolneder, Walter.**               • **1.4057**
[Anton Webern, Einführung in Werk und Stil. English] Anton Webern; an introduction to his works. Translated by Humphrey Searle. Berkeley, University of California Press, 1968. 232 p. music, port. 23 cm. Originally published in 1961 under title: Anton Webern; Einführung in Werk und Stil. 1. Webern, Anton, 1883-1945. I. T.
ML410.W33 K63    780/.924    *LC* 68-10663

**Moldenhauer, Hans.**              **1.4058**
Anton von Webern, a chronicle of his life and work / Hans Moldenhauer and Rosaleen Moldenhauer. — New York: Knopf: distributed by Random House, 1979, c1978. 803 p., [8] leaves of plates: ill.; 25 cm. Includes index. 1. Webern, Anton, 1883-1945. 2. Composers — Austria — Biography. I. Moldenhauer, Rosaleen. II. T.
ML410.W33 M55 1979    780/.92/4 B    *LC* 77-20370    *ISBN* 0394472373

**Moldenhauer, Hans. comp.**           • **1.4059**
Anton Von Webern perspectives. Edited by Demar Irvine. Introductory interview with Igor Stravinsky. Seattle, University of Washington Press [1966] xxvii, 191 p. facsims., music, ports. 1. Webern, Anton, 1883-1945. I. T.
ML410 W33 M58    *LC* 66-13539 MN

**Jarman, Douglas.**    1.4060
Kurt Weill, an illustrated biography / Douglas Jarman. — Bloomington: Indiana University Press, c1982. 160 p., [24] p. of plates: ill.; 24 cm. Includes index. 1. Weill, Kurt, 1900-1950. 2. Composers — Biography. I. T.
ML410.W395 J37 1982    782.81/092/4 B 19    LC 82-47949    ISBN 025314650X

**Kowalke, Kim H., 1948-.**    1.4061
Kurt Weill in Europe / by Kim H. Kowalke. — Ann Arbor, Mich.: UMI Research Press, 1979. vii, 589 p.: ill.; facsims. — (Studies in musicology. no. 14) 'Catalogue of Weill's compositions, 1900-1935': p. 369-452. Includes index. 1. Weill, Kurt, 1900-1950. Works. I. T. II. Series.
ML410.W395 K7    780/.92/4    LC 79-23221    ISBN 0835710769

**Sanders, Ronald.**    1.4062
The days grow short: the life and music of Kurt Weill / Ronald Sanders. — 1st ed. — New York: Holt, Rinehart and Winston, c1980. viii, 469 p.: ill.; 24 cm. 'Kurt Weill's principal compositions': p. 434-441. Includes index. 1. Weill, Kurt, 1900-1950. 2. Composers — Biography. I. T.
ML410.W395 S2    782.8/1/0924 B    LC 79-17331    ISBN 0030194113

**Townsend, Charles R.**    1.4063
San Antonio Rose: the life and music of Bob Wills / Charles R. Townsend; with a discography and filmusicography by Bob Pinson. — Urbana: University of Illinois Press, c1976. xv, 395 p. [44] leaves of plates: ill.; 26 cm. (Music in American life) Includes index. 1. Wills, Bob, 1905-1975. I. T.
ML410.W7138 T7    785/.092/4 B    LC 75-45431    ISBN 0252004701

**Newman, Ernest, 1868-1959.**    • 1.4064
Hugo Wolf. With a new introd. by Walter Legge. — New York: Dover Publications, [1966] xxv, 279 p.: illus., facsims., music, ports.; 22 cm. 'This Dover edition is an unabridged and corrected republication of the work first published in 1907.' 1. Wolf, Hugo, 1860-1903. I. T.
ML410.W8 N5 1966    784/.0924 B    LC 66-23973

**Walker, Frank, 1907-1962.**    • 1.4065
Hugo Wolf; a biography. — 2d enl. ed. — New York: A. A. Knopf, 1968. x, 522 p.: facsim., music, ports.; 26 cm. 1. Wolf, Hugo, 1860-1903. I. T.
ML410.W8 W25 1968b    784/.0924 B    LC 68-10870

## ML416–419 PERFORMERS

**Plaskin, Glenn.**    1.4066
Horowitz: a biography of Vladimir Horowitz / by Glenn Plaskin. — 1st ed. — New York: W. Morrow, 1983. 607 p., [32] p. of plates: ill.; 25 cm. 1. Horowitz, Vladimir, 1904- 2. Pianists — Biography. I. T.
ML417.H8 P6 1983    786.1/092/4 B 19    LC 82-14275    ISBN 0688016162

**Landowska, Wanda.**    1.4067
Landowska on music / collected, edited and translated by Denise Restout; assisted by Robert Hawkins. — New York: Stein and Day, c1964. 434 p., [8] leaves of plates: ill. 1. Landowska, Wanda — Discography. 2. Landowska, Wanda. 3. Music — Addresses, essays, lectures. I. Restout, Denise. II. T.
ML417.L26 A33 1969    ML60.L226.    LC 64-22698

**Wallace, Robert K., 1944-.**    1.4068
A century of music–making: the lives of Josef & Rosina Lhevinne / Robert K. Wallace. — Bloomington: Indiana University Press, c1976. xi, 350 p., [9] leaves of plates: ill.; 24 cm. Includes index. 1. Lhévinne, Josef, 1874-1944. 2. Lhevinne, Rosina, 1880-1976. 3. Pianists — Biography. I. T.
ML417.L65 W3    786.1/092/2 B    LC 75-28908    ISBN 0253313309

**Rubinstein, Artur, 1887-.**    1.4069
My many years / Arthur Rubinstein. — 1st ed. — New York: Knopf: distributed by Random House, 1980. 626 p., [12] leaves of plates: ill.; 25 cm. Includes index. 1. Rubinstein, Artur, 1887- 2. Pianists — Biography. I. T.
ML417.R79 A28    786.1/092/4 B    LC 79-2231    ISBN 0394422538

**Rubinstein, Artur, 1887-.**    1.4070
My young years [by] Arthur Rubinstein. [1st ed.] New York, Knopf; [distributed by Random House] 1973. xi, 478, xiii p. illus. 25 cm. 1. Rubinstein, Artur, 1887- 2. Musicians — Correspondence, reminiscences, etc. I. T.
ML417.R79 A3    786.1/092/4 B    LC 70-171147    ISBN 0394468902

**Schnabel, Artur, 1882-1951.**    • 1.4071
My life and music; &, Reflections on music. With a foreword by Sir Robert Mayer and an introd. by Edward Crankshaw. — New York: St. Martin's Press, [1972, c1961] xv, 248 p.; 22 cm. — (St. Martin's music paperbacks) 1. Schnabel, Artur, 1882-1951. 2. Musicians — Correspondence, reminiscences, etc. I. Schnabel, Artur, 1882-1951. Reflections on music. 1972. II. T.
ML417.S36 A3 1972    786.1/092/4 B    LC 70-166527

**Schnabel, Artur, 1882-1951.**    • 1.4072
Music and the line of most resistance. New York: Da Capo Press, 1969 [c1942] 90 p.; 21 cm. — (Da Capo Press music reprint series) 'This Da Capo Press edition is an unabridged republication of the first edition published in 1942.' 1. Music — Philosophy and aesthetics 2. Music — Performance 3. Musical criticism I. T.
ML417.S36 M8 1969    780.15    LC 69-12690

**Wolff, Konrad.**    1.4073
The teaching of Artur Schnabel: a guide to interpretation. — New York: Praeger, [1972] 189 p.: music, port.; 23 cm. 1. Schnabel, Artur, 1882-1951. 2. Piano music — Interpretation (Phrasing, dynamics, etc.) I. T.
ML417.S36 W64 1972b    786.4/04/1    LC 77-165841

**Chissell, Joan.**    1.4074
Clara Schumann, a dedicated spirit: a study of her life and work / by Joan Chissell. — New York: Taplinger Pub. Co., 1983. xvi, 232 p., [8] p. of plates: ill.; 24 cm. 'A Crescendo book.' Includes index. 1. Schumann, Clara, 1819-1896. 2. Pianists — Germany — Biography. I. T.
ML417.S4 C5 1983b    786.1/092/4 B 19    LC 83-50182    ISBN 0800816242

**Reich, Nancy B.**    1.4075
Clara Schumann, the artist and the woman / Nancy B. Reich. — Ithaca, N.Y.: Cornell University Press, 1985. 346 p.: ill.; 25 cm. Includes index. 1. Schumann, Clara, 1819-1896. 2. Pianists — Germany — Biography. I. T.
ML417.S4 R4 1985    786.1/042/4 B 19    LC 84-45798    ISBN 0801417481

**Casals, Pablo, 1876-1973.**    • 1.4076
Joys and sorrows; reflections, by Pablo Casals as told to Albert E. Kahn. — New York: Simon and Schuster, [1970] 314 p.: illus., ports.; 24 cm. 1. Casals, Pablo, 1876-1973. 2. Musicians — Correspondence, reminiscences, etc. I. Kahn, Albert Eugene, 1912-1979. II. T.
ML418.C4 A35    787/.3/0924 B    LC 73-101879    ISBN 0671204858

**Blum, David, 1935-.**    1.4077
Casals and the art of interpretation / David Blum. New York: Holmes & Meier Publishers, 1977. xvi, 223 p., [2] leaves of plates: ill.; 23 cm. Includes indexes. 1. Casals, Pablo, 1876-1973. 2. Music — Performance I. T.
ML418.C4 B6    780/.92/4    LC 77-1444    ISBN 0841903077

**Armstrong, Louis, 1900-1971.**    • 1.4078
Satchmo; my life in New Orleans. New York, Prentice-Hall [1954] 240 p. ill. 21 cm. 1. Armstrong, Louis, 1900-1971. 2. Musicians — Biography 3. Jazz music I. T.
ML 419 A75 A4 1954    LC 54-9628

**Jones, Max.**    • 1.4079
Louis; the Louis Armstrong story, 1900–1971 [by] Max Jones & John Chilton. — [1st American ed.]. — Boston: Little, Brown, [1971] 256 p.: illus.; 26 cm. 1. Armstrong, Louis, 1900-1971. I. Chilton, John, joint author. II. T.
ML419.A75 J625    788/.1/0924 B    LC 76-175031

**Bechet, Sidney, 1897-1959.**    1.4080
Treat it gentle. Among those who helped record and edit the tapes on which this book is based are: Joan Reid, Desmond Flower, and John Ciardi. New York, Hill and Wang [1960] 245 p. illus. 22 cm. 1. Musicians — Correspondence, reminiscences, etc. I. T.
ML419.B23 A3    LC 60-15935

**Sudhalter, Richard M.**    1.4081
Bix: man & legend, by Richard M. Sudhalter & Philip R. Evans, with William Dean–Myatt. — New Rochelle, N.Y.: Arlington House, [1974] 512 p.: illus.; 24 cm. 1. Beiderbecke, Bix, 1903-1931. 2. Beiderbecke, Bix, 1903-1931 — Discography. 3. Jazz music I. Evans, Philip R., 1935- joint author. II. T.
ML419.B25 S8    788/.1/0924 B    LC 74-6326    ISBN 0870002686

**Cole, Bill, 1937-.**    1.4082
John Coltrane / by Bill Cole. — New York: Schirmer Books, c1976. vi, 264 p.: ill.; 24 cm. Includes indexes. 1. Coltrane, John, 1926-1967. 2. Jazz musicians — United States — Biography. I. T.
ML419.C645 C6    788/.66/0924 B    LC 76-14289    ISBN 0028706609

**Carr, Ian.**    1.4083
Miles Davis: a biography / Ian Carr; foreword by Len Lyons. — 1st U.S. ed. — New York: Morrow, 1982. 310 p., [16] p. of plates: ill.; 25 cm. British ed. has subtitle: A critical biography. Includes indexes. 1. Davis, Miles. 2. Jazz musicians — United States — Biography. I. T.
ML419.D39 C35 1982    788/.1/0924 B 19    LC 82-6469    ISBN 068801321X

**Gillespie, Dizzy, 1917-.**    1.4084
To be, or not ... to BOP: memoirs / Dizzy Gillespie, with Al Fraser. — 1st ed. — Garden City, N.Y.: Doubleday, 1979. xix, 552 p., [28] leaves of plates: ill.; 24

cm. 1. Gillespie, Dizzy, 1917- 2. Jazz musicians — United States — Biography. I. T.
ML419.G54 A3        785.420924 B      *LC* 77-76237      *ISBN* 0385120524

**Reisner, Robert George.**                                              **1.4085**
Bird: the legend of Charlie Parker / by Robert George Reisner. — New York: Da Capo Press, 1975, c1962. 256 p.: ill.; 26 cm. (The Roots of jazz) Reprint of the ed. published by Citadel Press, New York. 1. Parker, Charlie, 1920-1955. I. T.
ML419.P4 R4 1975       788/.66/0924 B       *LC* 74-30084      *ISBN*
0306706776

## ML420 SINGERS

**Anderson, Marian, 1902-.**                                         • **1.4086**
My Lord, what a morning; an autobiography. — New York: Viking Press, 1956. 312 p.: illus.; 22 cm. 'A condensed version ... appeared in serial form in the Woman's home companion.' 1. Anderson, Marian, 1902- 2. Singers — United States — Biography. I. T.
ML420.A6 A3        927.8       *LC* 56-10402

**Berry, Chuck.**                                                        **1.4087**
Chuck Berry: the autobiography. — 1st ed. — New York: Harmony Books, 1987. xxii, 346 p.: ill.; 25 cm. Includes index. 1. Berry, Chuck. 2. Rock musicians — United States — Biography. I. T.
ML420.B365 A3 1987       784.5/4/00924 B 19       *LC* 87-11825      *ISBN*
0517566664

**DeWitt, Howard A.**                                                    **1.4088**
Chuck Berry, rock 'n' roll music / by Howard A. DeWitt; with research assistance and a discography by Morten Reff. — 2nd ed. — Ann Arbor, MI: Pierian Press, 1985. xvi, 291 p.: ill.; 24 cm. — (Rock & roll reference series; 12) 1. Berry, Chuck. 2. Rock musicians — United States — Biography. I. Reff, Morten. II. T. III. Series.
ML420.B365 D5 1985       784.5/4/00924 B 19       *LC* 84-61230      *ISBN*
0876501714

**Mellers, Wilfrid Howard, 1914-.**                                      **1.4089**
A darker shade of pale: a backdrop to Bob Dylan / Wilfrid Mellers. — New York: Oxford University Press, 1985, c1984. 255 p., [16] p. of plates: ill., ports.; 21 cm. Includes index. 1. Dylan, Bob, 1941- 2. Popular music — United States — History and criticism. I. T.
ML420.D98 M4 1985       784.4/924 19       *LC* 85-272      *ISBN*
0195036220

**Flagstad, Kirsten, 1895-1962.**                                    • **1.4090**
The Flagstad manuscript [by] Louis Biancolli. New York, Putnam [1952] 293 p. ports. An autobiography narrated to Louis Biancolli. I. Biancolli, Louis Leopold. II. T.
ML420 F55 A3        *LC* 52-9828

**Goreau, Laurraine.**                                                   **1.4091**
Just Mahalia, baby / Laurraine Goreau. — Waco, Tex.: Word Books, [1975] x, 611 p.: ill.; 25 cm. 1. Jackson, Mahalia, 1911-1972. 2. Gospel musicians — United States — Biography. I. T.
ML420.J17 G67       784/.092/4 B       *LC* 74-82654

**Jones, Bessie, 1902-.**                                                **1.4092**
For the ancestors: autobiographical memories / Bessie Jones; collected and edited by John Stewart. — Urbana: University of Illinois Press, c1983. xxv, 203 p.: ill., ports.; 24 cm. 1. Jones, Bessie, 1902- 2. Singers — United States — Biography. I. Stewart, John, 1933- II. T.
ML420.J75 A3 1983       783.6/7/0924 B 19       *LC* 82-8593      *ISBN*
0252009592

**Wiener, Jon.**                                                         **1.4093**
Come together: John Lennon in his time / Jon Wiener. — 1st ed. — New York: Random House, c1984. xix, 379 p., [8] p. of plates: ill.; 24 cm. Includes index. 1. Lennon, John, 1940- 2. Rock musicians — Biography. I. T.
ML420.L38 W5 1984       784.5/4/00924 19       *LC* 83-43194      *ISBN*
0394535707

**Bushnell, Howard.**                                                    **1.4094**
Maria Malibran: a biography of the singer / Howard Bushnell; foreword by Elaine Brody. — University Park: Pennsylvania State University Press, c1979. xix, 264 p.: ill.; 24 cm. Includes index. 1. Malibran, Maria, 1808-1836. 2. Singers — Biography. I. T.
ML420.M2 B87        782.1/092/4 B       *LC* 79-14880      *ISBN* 0271002220

**Merman, Ethel.**                                                       **1.4095**
Merman / by Ethel Merman with George Eells. — New York: Simon and Schuster, c1978. 320 p., [8] leaves of plates: ill.; 25 cm. Includes index. 1. Merman, Ethel. 2. Singers — United States — Biography. I. Eells, George. joint author. II. T.
ML420.M39 A32       782.8/1/0924 B       *LC* 78-92      *ISBN* 0671227122

**Goldman, Albert Harry, 1927-.**                                        **1.4096**
Elvis / by Albert Goldman. — New York: McGraw-Hill, c1981. x, 598 p., [16] p. of plates: ill.; 25 cm. 'A Kevin Eggers book.' Includes index. 1. Presley, Elvis, 1935-1977. 2. Singers — United States — Biography. I. T.
ML420.P96 G66       784.5/4/00924 B 19       *LC* 81-8130      *ISBN*
0070236577

**Lieb, Sandra R.**                                                      **1.4097**
Mother of the blues: a study of Ma Rainey / Sandra R. Lieb. — [Amherst]: University of Massachusetts Press, 1981. xvii, 226 p.: ill.; 25 cm. Includes indexes. 1. Rainey, Ma, 1886-1939. 2. Afro-American singers — Biography. I. T.
ML420.R274 L5       784.5/3/00924 B 19       *LC* 81-1168      *ISBN*
0870233343

**Dunaway, David King.**                                                 **1.4098**
How can I keep from singing: Pete Seeger / by David King Dunaway. — New York: McGraw-Hill Book Co., c1981. 386 p. [10] leaves of plates: ill., ports. Includes index. 1. Seeger, Pete, 1919- 2. Folk singers — United States — Biography. I. T.
ML420.S445 D8       ML420S4315 D8.       784.7/92/4 B 19       *LC*
80-29374       *ISBN* 0070181500

**Mellers, Wilfrid Howard, 1914-.**                                      **1.4099**
Twilight of the gods; the music of the Beatles [by] Wilfrid Mellers. — New York: Viking Press, [1974, c1973] 215 p.: illus.; 22 cm. 1. The Beatles. I. T.
ML421.B4 M44 1974       784/.092/2 B       *LC* 73-3508      *ISBN*
0670735981

**Schaffner, Nicholas, 1953-.**                                          **1.4100**
The Beatles forever / Nicholas Schaffner. — Harrisburg, Pa.: Cameron House., c1977. 222 p., [2] leaves of plates: ill.; 29 cm. Includes index. 1. The Beatles. I. T.
ML421.B4 S28       784/.092/2       *LC* 77-76774      *ISBN* 0811702251

## ML422–429 CONDUCTORS. OTHERS

**Heyworth, Peter, 1921-.**                                              **1.4101**
Conversations with Klemperer; compiled and edited by Peter Heyworth. London, Gollancz, 1973. 128, [12] p. illus., ports. 27 cm. 1. Klemperer, Otto, 1885-1973. 2. Conductors (Music) — Germany — Interviews. I. Klemperer, Otto, 1885-1973. II. T.
ML422.K67 H5       785/.092/4       *LC* 73-169562      *ISBN* 0575016523

**Leinsdorf, Erich, 1912-.**                                             **1.4102**
Cadenza: a musical career / Erich Leinsdorf. — Boston: Houghton Mifflin, 1976. x, 321 p., [8] leaves of plates: ill.; 24 cm. Includes index. 1. Leinsdorf, Erich, 1912- 2. Conductors (Music) — Correspondence, reminiscences, etc.
ML422.L38 A3       785/.092/4 B       *LC* 76-3553      *ISBN* 0395244013

**Rodzinski, Halina.**                                                   **1.4103**
Our two lives / Halina Rodzinski. — New York: Scribner, c1976. ix, 403 p., [16] leaves of plates: ill.; 24 cm. Includes index. 1. Rodzinski, Halina. 2. Rodzinski, Artur, 1892-1958. 3. Musicians — Correspondence, reminiscences, etc. I. T.
ML422.R7 R6       785/.092/4 B       *LC* 75-37519      *ISBN* 0684145111

**Horowitz, Joseph, 1948-.**                                             **1.4104**
Understanding Toscanini: how he became an American culture–god and helped create a new audience for old music / Joseph Horowitz. — 1st ed. — New York: A.A. Knopf, 1987. x, 492 p., [24] p. of plates: ill., ports.; 25 cm. Includes index. 1. Toscanini, Arturo, 1867-1957. 2. Conductors (Music) — Biography. 3. Music — United States — History and criticism. I. T.
ML422.T67 H65 1987       785/.092/4 B 19       *LC* 86-45373      *ISBN*
0394529189

**Matthews, Denis.**                                                     **1.4105**
Arturo Toscanini / Denis Matthews; with selected discography by Ray Burford. — Tunbridge Wells, Kent: Midas Books; New York: Hippocrene Books, 1982. 176 p.: ill.; 24 cm. 'Great performers series'—Jacket. Includes index. 1. Toscanini, Arturo, 1867-1957. 2. Conductors (Music) — Biography. I. Burford, Ray. II. T. III. Title: Great performers series.
ML422.T67 M34 1982       785/.092/4 B 19       *LC* 83-101763      *ISBN*
0882546570

**Walter, Bruno, 1876-1962.**                                        • **1.4106**
Of music and music–making. Translated by Paul Hamburger. — [1st American ed.]. — New York: W. W. Norton, [1961] 222 p.: illus.; 22 cm. 1. Musicians — Correspondence, reminiscences, etc. 2. Music — Addresses, essays, lectures. I. T.
ML422.W27 A312       927.8       *LC* 61-5616

**Kendall, Alan.** 1.4107
The tender tyrant: Nadia Boulanger; a life devoted to music, a biography / by Alan Kendall; introduction by Yehudi Menuhin. — Wilton, Conn.: Lyceum Books, 1977. xvi, 144 p., [8] p. of plates: ill. 1. Boulanger, Nadia. 2. Music teachers — France — Biography. I. T.
ML423.B52 K4x    LC 76-27098    ISBN 0915336170

**Young, Percy M. (Percy Marshall), 1912-.** 1.4108
George Grove, 1820–1900: a biography / by Percy M. Young. — Washington, D.C.: Grove's Dictionaries of Music, 1980. 344 p., [6] leaves of plates: ill.; 22 cm. Includes index. 1. Grove, George, Sir, 1820-1900. 2. Musicians — Great Britain — Biography. I. T.
ML423.G8 Y7    780/.92/4 B    LC 79-29705    ISBN 0333196023

**Fordin, Hugh, 1935-.** 1.4109
Getting to know him: a biography of Oscar Hammerstein II / Hugh Fordin. — 1st ed. — New York: Random House, c1977. xiv, 383 p., [8] leaves of plates: ill.; 25 cm. Includes index. 1. Hammerstein, Oscar, 1895-1960. 2. Librettists — United States — Biography. I. T.
ML423.H24 F7    782.8/1/0924 B    LC 77-6021    ISBN 0394494415

**The Music theater of Walter Felsenstein: collected articles,** 1.4110
**speeches, and interviews / by Felsenstein and others; translated, edited, and annotated by Peter Paul Fuchs.**
1st ed. — New York: Norton, [1975] xx, 188 p., [8] leaves of plates: ill.; 21 cm. 1. Felsenstein, Walter. 2. Opera — Addresses, essays, lectures. 3. Opera — Dramaturgy I. Felsenstein, Walter. II. Stamm, H. Peter Paul.
ML429.F43 M9    782.1/071    LC 75-6648    ISBN 0393021866

**Klein, Joe, 1946-.** 1.4111
Woody Guthrie: a life / Joe Klein. — 1st ed. — New York: A. A. Knopf: distributed by Random House, 1980. xv, 475 p., [16] leaves of plates: ill.; 25 cm. Includes index. 1. Guthrie, Woody, 1912-1967. 2. Musicians — United States — Biography. I. T.
ML429.G95 K6    784.4/924 B    LC 80-7634    ISBN 0394501527

**Rumiantsev, Pavel Ivanovich.** 1.4112
[Stanislavskiĭ i opera. English] Stanislavski on opera / by Constantin Stanislavski and Pavel Rumyantsev; translated and edited by Elizabeth Reynolds Hapgood. — New York: Theatre Arts Books, c1975. x, 374 p.: ill.; 25 cm. Based on the teachings of Stanislavskiĭ. 1. Stanislavsky, Konstantin, 1863-1938. 2. Acting in opera 3. Opera — Soviet Union. I. T.
ML429.S8 R813    782/.13    LC 72-87119    ISBN 0878301321

## ML430–455 COMPOSITION

**Mickelsen, William C.** 1.4113
Hugo Riemann's Theory of harmony: a study / by William C. Mickelsen and History of music theory, book III / by Hugo Riemann; translated and edited by William C. Mickelsen. — Lincoln: University of Nebraska Press, c1977. xv, 263 p.: ill.; 24 cm. Includes indexes. 1. Riemann, Hugo, 1849-1919. Geschichte der Musiktheorie im IX.-XIX. Jahrhundert. 2. Composition (Music) — History. 3. Harmony I. Riemann, Hugo, 1849-1919. Geschichte der Musiktheorie im IX.-XIX. Jahrhundert. Book 3. English. 1977. II. T.
ML430.M5    781.3    LC 76-15366    ISBN 080320891X

**Crocker, Richard L.** • 1.4114
A history of musical style [by] Richard L. Crocker. New York, McGraw-Hill Book Co. [1966] vii, 573 p. music. (McGraw-Hill series in music) 1. Style, Musical 2. Music — Performance — History I. T.
ML430.5 C76    LC 65-28233/MN

**Dart, Thurston, 1921-1971.** • 1.4115
The interpretation of music. — 4th ed. — London, Hutchinson, 1967. 190 p. illus. (music), tables. 22 cm. — (Hutchinson university library; music) Bibliography: p. [179]-184. 1. Music — Interpretation (Phrasing, dynamics, etc.) 2. Music — Performance I. T.
ML430.5.D3 1967    781.6/3    LC 67-101007

**Dorian, Frederick, 1902-.** • 1.4116
The history of music in performance: the art of musical interpretation from the Renaissance to our day / by Frederick Dorian. — 1st ed. — New York: W.W. Norton, c1942. 387 p., [6] feuillets de planches: fac-sim., musique; 22 cm. 1. Music — Performance — History 2. Music — Interpretation (Phrasing, dynamics, etc.) — History I. T. II. Title: The art of musical interpretation...
ML430.5.D66    ML430.5 D66.    781.63    LC 43-2216

**Apel, Willi, 1893-.** • 1.4117
The notation of polyphenic music, 900–1600. 5th ed. rev. and commentary. Cambridge, Mass., Mediaeval Academy of America, 1953 [i.e. 1961] xxv, 464, [30] p. facsims., music. (The Mediaeval Academy of America. Publication no. 38) 1. Musical notation I. T. II. Series.
ML431 A6 1961    LC 61-12067

**Parrish, Carl.** • 1.4118
The notation of medieval music / Carl Parrish. 1st ed. — New York: W.W. Norton, c1957. xvii, 228 p., [31] feuillets de planches: musique; 25 cm. I. T.
ML 431. P37    781.24    LC 57-11708

**Rastall, Richard.** 1.4119
The notation of Western music: an introduction / Richard Rastall. — 1st U.S. ed. — New York, N.Y.: St. Martin's Press, c1982. xiv, 306 p.: ill.; 25 cm. Includes index. 1. Musical notation I. T.
ML431.R27 1982    781/.24 19    LC 82-62938    ISBN 0312579632

**Sachs, Curt, 1881-1959.** • 1.4120
Rhythm and tempo; a study in music history. — [1st ed. — New York, Norton [c1953] 391 p. music. 25 cm. Bibliographical footnotes. 1. Musical meter and rhythm 2. Tempo (Music) I. T.
ML437.S3    781.62    LC 52-4911

**Oldroyd, George.** • 1.4121
The Technique and spirit of fugue: an historical study / George Oldroyd; with a foreword by Sir Stanley Marchant. — London; Toronto: Oxford University Press, 1948. viii, 220 p.: music. 1. Fugue I. T.
ML448.O4    LC 48-8826    ISBN 0193173115

**Carse, Adam von Ahn, 1878-1958.** • 1.4122
The history of orchestration. — New York, Dover Publications [1964] xiii, 348 p. illus., music. 22 cm. 'An unabridged and corrected republication of the work first published by Kegan Paul, Trench, Trubner and Company, Limited, in 1925.' 1. Instrumentation and orchestration — Hist. I. T.
ML455.C32 1964    781.632    LC 64-17314

## ML457 INTERPRETATION

**Donington, Robert.** 1.4123
The interpretation of early music. — New version. — New York: St. Martin's Press, [1974] 766 p.: music.; 26 cm. 1. Music — Performance 2. Style, Musical 3. Music — History and criticism — Sources. 4. Musical instruments I. T.
ML457.D64 1974    781.6/3    LC 73-81205

**Readings in the history of music in performance / selected,** 1.4124
**translated, and edited by Carol MacClintock.**
Bloomington: Indiana University Press, c1979. xii, 432 p.: music; 25 cm. 1. Music — Performance 2. Music — History and criticism — Sources. I. MacClintock, Carol, 1910-
ML457.R4    780/.9    LC 78-9511    ISBN 0253144957

## ML460–1092 MUSICAL INSTRUMENTS

**Baines, Anthony.** • 1.4125
European and American musical instruments. — New York: Viking Press, [1966] x, 174 p.: music, 112 plates.; 31 cm. — (A Studio book) 1. Musical instruments I. T.
ML460.B13 1966    781.91    LC 66-25611

**Baines, Anthony. ed.** 1.4126
Musical instruments through the ages / edited by Anthony Baines for the Galpin Society. — New ed. — New York: Walker, 1976, c1961. 344 p., [16] leaves of plates: ill.; 24 cm. Includes index. 1. Musical instruments — History. I. Galpin Society. II. T.
ML460.B14 1976    781.9/1/09    LC 74-83196    ISBN 0802704697

**Donington, Robert.** • 1.4127
The instruments of music. — [3d ed., rev. and enl.]. — London: Methuen, [1970] xxvi, 262 p.: illus., music.; 22 cm. 'Distributed in the U.S.A. by Barnes and Noble.' 1. Musical instruments I. T.
ML460.D6 1970    781.91    LC 77-17993    ISBN 0416172105

**Donington, Robert.** 1.4128
Music and its instruments / Robert Donington. — London; New York: Methuen, 1982. xii, 232 p., [16] p. of plates: ill.; 23 cm. Includes index. 1. Musical instruments I. T.
ML460.D63 1982    781.91 19    LC 82-8012    ISBN 0416722709

**Galpin, Francis William, 1858-1945.** • 1.4129
A textbook of European musical instruments: their origin, history, and character / by Francis W. Galpin. — New York: J. De Graff, [1956, c1937]. 256 p., [10] leaves of plates: ill.; 23 cm. Includes index. 1. Musical instruments — History. I. T.
ML460.G14 T35    781.9/1    LC 56-58142

**Geiringer, Karl, 1899-.**     **1.4130**
Instruments in the history of Western music / Karl Geiringer. — 3d ed. — New York: Oxford University Press, 1978. 318 p., [35] leaves of plates: ill.; 24 cm. 1943 and 1945 editions published under title: Musical instruments. Includes indexes. 1. Musical instruments — History. I. T.
ML460.G4 1978     781.9/1/09     LC 78-14802     ISBN 0195200577

**Montagu, Jeremy.**     **1.4131**
The world of Medieval & Renaissance musical instruments / Jeremy Montagu. — Woodstock [N. Y.]: Overlook Press, 1976. 136 p.: ill. (part col.); 26 cm. 1. Musical instruments — History I. T.
ML460.M65     781.91     LC 76-5987     ISBN 0879510455

**Munrow, David.**     **1.4132**
Instruments of the Middle Ages and Renaissance / David Munrow; foreword by André Previn. London: Oxford University Press, Music Dept., c1976. 95 p.: ill.; 29 cm. 1. Musical instruments I. T.
ML460.M94     781.9/1/0902     LC 76-366364     ISBN 0193213214

**Rock hardware: the instruments, equipment, and technology of**     **1.4133**
**rock** / edited by Tony Bacon.
1st ed. — New York: Harmony Books, c1981. 224 p.: ill. (some col.); 31 cm. Includes index. 1. Musical instruments — Handbooks, manuals, etc. 2. Rock music — Handbooks, manuals, etc. I. Bacon, Tony.
ML460.R62 1981     784.5/4 19     LC 81-1473     ISBN 0517545217

**Sachs, Curt, 1881-1959.**     • **1.4134**
The history of musical instruments [by] Curt Sachs. — New York: W. W. Norton & company, inc., [c1940] 505 p., 1 l.: illus., xxiv pl.; 25 cm. 'First edition.' 1. Musical instruments — History. I. T.
ML460.S24 H5     781.9109     LC 41-559

**Montagu, Jeremy.**     **1.4135**
The world of baroque & classical musical instruments / Jeremy Montagu. — Woodstock, N.Y.: Overlook Press, 1979. 136 p.: ill. (some col.) Continues The world of medieval and Renaissance musical instruments. Includes index. 1. Musical instruments I. T.
ML465.M65     781.9/1/0903     LC 78-25814     ISBN 0879510897

**Dolmetsch, Arnold, 1858-1940.**     • **1.4136**
The interpretation of the music of the XVII and XVIII centuries revealed by contemporary evidence / by Arnold Dolmetsch. — London: Novello, 1946. — x, 493 p.: music; 19 cm. — (Handbooks for musicians) Includes index. 1. Music — Interpretation (Phrasing, dynamics, etc.) 2. Music — Performance I. T. II. Series.
ML467.D65 1946     LC 49-5608

**Carse, Adam von Ahn, 1878-1958.**     • **1.4137**
The orchestra from Beethoven to Berlioz; a history of the orchestra in the first half of the 19th century, and of the development of orchestral baton-conduction. — Cambridge [Eng.]: W. Heffer, [1948] xiii, 514 p.: illus. (part col.) ports., music; 28 cm. 1. Orchestra 2. Conducting 3. Conductors (Music) I. T.
ML469.C3     785.09     LC 49-2416

**Galpin, Francis William, 1858-1945.**     • **1.4138**
Old English instruments of music; their history and character, [by] Francis W. Galpin. 4th ed., rev. with supplementary notes by Thurston Dart. New York, Barnes and Noble [1965] xxviii, 254 p. ill., facsims., music. '[List of] some illustrations of musical instruments in manuscripts, carvings and paintings from the eighth to the eighteenth century (British examples only):' p. 222-231. 1. Musical instruments — England I. T.
ML501 G2 1965     LC 65-6937

**Kirby, Percival Robson.**     **1.4139**
The musical instruments of the native races of South Africa, by Percival R. Kirby. 2d ed. Johannesburg, Witwatersrand University Press, 1965. xxiii, 293 p. 73 plates, map, music. 1. Musical instruments — Africa, South 2. Musical instruments, Primitive I. T.
ML544 K5 1965     LC 66-8755

## ML549–1092 Special Instruments

**Ferguson, Howard, 1908-.**     **1.4140**
Keyboard interpretation from the 14th to the 19th century: an introduction / Howard Ferguson. — New York: Oxford University Press, 1975. ix, 211 p.: music; 22 cm. 1. Organ music — Interpretation (Phrasing, dynamics, etc.) 2. Harpsichord music — Interpretation (Phrasing, dynamics, etc.) 3. Piano music — Interpretation (Phrasing, dynamics, etc.) 4. Music — Performance — History I. T.
ML549.F47     786.1/07     LC 75-4207     ISBN 0193184192

## ML550–649 Organ

**Andersen, Poul Gerhard.**     • **1.4141**
[Orgelbogen; klangteknik, arkitektur og historie. English] Organ building and design. Translated by Joanne Curnutt. New York, Oxford University Press, 1969. 359 p. illus. 24 cm. Translation of Orgelbogen; klangteknik, arkitektur og historie. 1. Organ 2. Organ — Construction I. T.
ML550.A513 1969b     786.6/3     LC 74-5578

**Sumner, William Leslie, 1904-1973.**     **1.4142**
The organ; its evolution, principles of construction and use. — [4th ed., rev. and enl.]. — New York: St. Martin's, [1973, c1962] 603 p.: illus.; 23 cm. 'A selection of organ specifications': p. 385-567. 1. Organ — History I. T.
ML550.S9 1973     786.6     LC 73-78871

**Williams, Peter F.**     **1.4143**
A new history of the organ from the Greeks to the present day / Peter Williams. — Bloomington: Indiana University Press, c1980. 233 p., [24] leaves of plates: ill.; 24 cm. 1. Organ — History I. T.
ML550.W38     786.6/2     LC 79-2176     ISBN 0253157048

**Ochse, Orpha Caroline, 1925-.**     • **1.4144**
The history of the organ in the United States [by] Orpha Ochse. — Bloomington: Indiana University Press, [1975] xv, 494 p.: illus.; 24 cm. 1. Organs — United States. 2. Organ — History 3. Organ-builders — United States. I. T.
ML561.O3     786.6/273     LC 73-22644     ISBN 0253328306

**Douglass, Fenner.**     • **1.4145**
The language of the classical French organ, a musical tradition before 1800. — New Haven: Yale University Press, 1969. xi, 235 p.: illus., charts, facsims., map, music.; 25 cm. — (Yale studies in the history of music, 5) 1. Organ — History 2. Organs — France I. T. II. Series.
ML574.D69     786.6/2/44     LC 72-81415

**Arnold, Corliss Richard.**     • **1.4146**
Organ literature: a comprehensive survey / by Corliss Richard Arnold. — 2nd ed. — Metuchen, N.J.: Scarecrow Press, 1984. 2 v.: ill.; 23 cm. 1. Organ music — History and criticism 2. Organ music — Bibliography I. T.
ML600.A76 1984     786.8/09 19     LC 83-20075     ISBN 0810816628

## ML650–747 Piano. Harpsichord

**The Book of the piano** / edited by Dominic Gill.     **1.4147**
Ithaca, N.Y.: Cornell University Press, 1981. 288 p.: ill., ports. (some col.); 29 cm. 'A Phaidon book'—T.p. Includes index. 1. Piano 2. Piano music — History and criticism I. Gill, Dominic.
ML650.B64     786.1 19     LC 80-69990     ISBN 0801413990

**Loesser, Arthur, 1894-1969.**     • **1.4148**
Men, women and pianos; a social history. — New York: Simon and Schuster, 1954. xvi, 654 p.; 24 cm. 1. Piano — History I. T.
ML650.L64     786.2     LC 54-9801

**Matthews, Denis. comp.**     **1.4149**
Keyboard music. — New York: Praeger, [1972] 386 p.: music.; 23 cm. 1. Piano music — History and criticism 2. Harpsichord music — History and criticism. I. T.
ML650.M25     786.4/04     LC 77-185335

**Hubbard, Frank.**     • **1.4150**
Three centuries of harpsichord making. Cambridge, Mass., Harvard University Press, 1965. xviii, 369 p. 41 plates. 1. Harpsichord — Construction I. T.
ML651 H83     LC 65-12784

**Zuckermann, Wolfgang, 1922-.**     • **1.4151**
The modern harpsichord; twentieth century instruments and their makers. [New York] October House [1969] 255 p. illus., ports. 29 cm. 1. Harpsichord 2. Harpsichord makers I. T.
ML651.Z83     786.2/21     LC 70-99498     ISBN 0807901652

**Dolge, Alfred, 1848-.**     **1.4152**
Pianos and their makers; a comprehensive history of the development of the piano from the monochord to the concert grand player piano / by Alfred Dolge. — New York Dover Publications London Constable 1972. 2-478p ill, ports 22cm Pbk. I. T.
ML652.D6x 1972     786.2 1 09     LC 72-188952     ISBN 0486228568

**Ehrlich, Cyril.**     **1.4153**
The piano: a history / [by] Cyril Ehrlich. London: Dent, 1976. 254 p., [8] p. of plates: ill., facsims.; 26 cm. Includes index. 1. Piano — History I. T.
ML652.E4     786.2/1/09     LC 76-376624     ISBN 0460042467

**Good, Edwin M. (Edwin Marshall), 1928-.**     **1.4154**
Giraffes, black dragons, and other pianos: a technological history from Cristofori to the modern concert grand / Edwin M. Good. — Stanford, Calif.: Stanford University Press, 1982. xvii, 305 p.: ill.; 24 cm. Includes index. 1. Piano — History 2. Piano — Construction I. T.
ML652.G6 1982    786.2/1/09 19    *LC* 81-50787    *ISBN* 0804711208

**Apel, Willi.**     • **1.4155**
Masters of the keyboard: a brief survey of pianoforte music / by Willi Apel. — Cambridge, Mass.: Harvard University Press, 1947. 323 p.:ill., music. 1. Piano music — History and criticism 2. Organ music — History and criticism I. T.
ML700.A6    786.409    *LC* 47-12245    *ISBN* 0674553004

**Gerig, Reginald, 1919-.**     **1.4156**
Famous pianists & their technique [by] Reginald R. Gerig. — Washington: R. B. Luce, [1974] xvi, 560 p.: illus.; 24 cm. 1. Pianists 2. Piano music — Interpretation (Phrasing, dynamics, etc.) I. T.
ML700.G44    786.1/092/2 B    *LC* 73-18804    *ISBN* 088331066X

**Taylor, Billy, 1921-.**     **1.4157**
Jazz piano: history and development / Billy Taylor. — Dubuque, Iowa: W.C. Brown, c1982. viii, 264 p.: ill.; 23 cm. 1. Piano music (Jazz) — History and criticism. I. T.
ML700.T4 1982    786.4/041 19    *LC* 82-70521    *ISBN* 0697034941

**Wolff, Konrad, 1907-.**     **1.4158**
Masters of the keyboard: individual style elements in the piano music of Bach, Haydn, Mozart, Beethoven, and Schubert / Konrad Wolff. — Bloomington: Indiana University Press, c1983. xi, 248 p.: ill.; 25 cm. Includes index. 1. Piano music — 18th century — History and criticism. 2. Piano music — 19th century — History and criticism. I. T.
ML705.W64 1983    786.1/09/033 19    *LC* 83-47677    *ISBN* 0253336902

**Caldwell, John, 1938-.**     **1.4159**
English keyboard music before the nineteenth century. New York, Praeger [1973] xxi, 328 p. music 24 cm. 1. Harpsichord music — History and criticism. 2. Organ music — History and criticism 3. Music — England — History and criticism. I. T.
ML728.C3    786.4/04/210942    *LC* 79-158091

## ML750–846 String Instruments

**Woodfield, Ian.**     **1.4160**
The early history of the viol / Ian Woodfield. — Cambridge [Cambridgeshire]; New York: Cambridge University Press, 1984. xiii, 266 p.: ill.; 26 cm. — (Cambridge musical texts and monographs.) Includes index. 1. Viol — History. I. T. II. Series.
ML760.V55 W66 1984    787/.42/09031 19    *LC* 83-18876    *ISBN* 0521242924

**Bachmann, Alberto Abraham, 1875- .**     • **1.4161**
An encyclopedia of the violin / Alberto Bachmann; original introd. by Eugène Ysaÿe; pref. to the Da Capo ed. by Stuart Canin; [translated by Frederick H. Martens]. — New York: Da Capo Press, 1966. vi, xiv, 470 p.: ill., facsims., music, ports.; 24 cm. — (Da Capo Press music titles) Includes index. 1. Violin 2. Violinists, violoncellists, etc. 3. Violin makers I. T.
ML800.B13 1966    787.1    *LC* 65-23406

**Straeten, Edmund Sebastian Joseph van der, 1855-1934.**     • **1.4162**
The history of the violin; its ancestors and collateral instruments from earliest times, by E. van der Straeten. New York, Da Capo Press, 1968. 2 v. illus., music, 48 plates, ports. 22 cm. (Da Capo Press music reprint series) 'This Da Capo Press edition is an unabridged republication of the first edition published in London in 1933.' 1. Violin — History. 2. Violinists I. T.
ML800.S89 H5 1968    787/.1/09    *LC* 68-21090

## ML930–990 Wind Instruments

**Baines, Anthony.**     • **1.4163**
Woodwind instruments and their history / by Anthony Baines; with a foreword by Sir Adrian Boult. — Rev. ed. — New York: Norton, 1963, c1962. 384 p., music. [16] leaves of plates: ill. map; 23 cm. 1. Wind instruments I. T.
ML930.B3 1967    788/.05    *LC* 63-1528    *ISBN* 0393097234

**Carse, Adam von Ahn, 1878-1958.**     • **1.4164**
Musical wind instruments, by Adam Carse. With an introd. to the Da Capo ed. by Himie Voxman. New York, Da Capo Press, 1965. xi, xv, 381 p. incl. 30 plates on 15 l. ill., music. 1. Wind instruments I. T.
ML930 C38 M9 1965    *LC* 65-18502

**Baines, Anthony.**     **1.4165**
Brass instruments: their history and development / Anthony Baines. — New York: Scribner, [1978] c1976. 298 p., [8] leaves of plates: ill.; 23 cm. Includes index. 1. Brass instruments I. T.
ML933.B33 1978    788/.01    *LC* 77-74716    *ISBN* 0684152290

**Bate, Philip.**     • **1.4166**
The flute: a study of its history, development and construction. — London: Benn; New York: W. W. Norton, 1969. xvi, 268 p.: 23 plates, illus., facsim., music, ports.; 23 cm. — (Instruments of the orchestra) 1. Flute — History. 2. Flute — Construction I. T.
ML935.B25    788/.51    *LC* 74-382066    *ISBN* 0510363512

**Hunt, Edgar, 1909-.**     • **1.4167**
The recorder and its music. London, H. Jenkins [1962] 176 p. illus. 22 cm. 1. Recorder (Musical instrument) — History. 2. Recorder (Musical instrument) — Instruction and study. I. T.
ML935.H85    *LC* 62-6190

**Toff, Nancy.**     **1.4168**
The flute book: a complete guide for students and performers / Nancy Toff. — New York: C. Scribner's Sons, c1985. xix, 472 p.: ill.; 24 cm. (Scribner music library.) Series statement from jacket. Includes index. 1. Flute I. T. II. Series.
ML935.T65 1985    788/.51 19    *LC* 84-27729    *ISBN* 0684182416

**Bate, Philip.**     **1.4169**
The oboe: an outline of its history, development, and construction / Philip Bate. — 3d ed. — London: E. Benn; New York: W. W. Norton, 1975. xv, 236 p., viii leaves of plates: ill.; 23 cm. (Instruments of the orchestra) Includes indexes. 1. Oboe — History. I. T.
ML940.B37 1975    788/.7    *LC* 75-317958    *ISBN* 0393021161

**Brymer, Jack.**     **1.4170**
Clarinet / Jack Brymer. 1st American ed. — New York: Schirmer Books, 1977, c1976. xii, 267 p., [12] leaves of plates: ill.; 21 cm. (Yehudi Menuhin music guides) Includes index. 1. Clarinet I. T.
ML945.B8 1977    788/.62    *LC* 77-275    *ISBN* 002871430X

**Kroll, Oskar.**     • **1.4171**
[Klarinette; ihre Geschichte, ihre Literatur, ihre grossen Meister. English] The clarinet. Revised, and with a repertory by Diethard Riehm. Translated by Hilda Morris. Translation edited by Anthony Baines. New York, Taplinger Pub. Co. [1968] 183 p. illus., music, 39 plates (incl. ports.) 23 cm. Translation of Die Klarinette; ihre Geschichte, ihre Literatur, ihre grossen Meister. 1. Clarinet — History. 2. Clarinet music — Bibliography. I. Riehm, Diethard. II. T.
ML945.K7613    788/.62/09    *LC* 68-22701

**Langwill, Lyndesay Graham, 1897-.**     • **1.4172**
The bassoon and contrabassoon [by] Lyndesay G. Langwill. London, E. Benn; New York, W. W. Norton [1965] xiv, 269 p. illus., facsims., music. 23 cm. (Instruments of the orchestra) 1. Bassoon — History. 2. Bassoonists 3. Bassoon music — Bibliography. 4. Bassoon music — Discography. 5. Contrabassoon — History. I. T.
ML950.L29    788.8    *LC* 65-29708

**Gregory, Robin.**     • **1.4173**
The horn; a comprehensive guide to the modern instrument & its music. — [Rev. and enl. ed.] — New York: F. A. Praeger, [1969] 410 p.: illus., music.; 23 cm. 'A list of music for the horn': p. 181-393. I. T.
ML955.G7 1969b    781/.97    *LC* 69-20022

**Bate, Philip.**     **1.4174**
The trumpet and trombone: an outline of their history, development, and construction / [by] Philip Bate. — 2nd ed. — London: E. Benn; New York: W. W. Norton, 1978. xix, 300 p., [23] p. of plates: ill., music, port.; 23 cm. — (Instruments of the orchestra) (A Benn study: Music) Includes indexes. 1. Trumpet — History. 2. Trumpet — Construction. 3. Trombone — History. 4. Trombone — Construction. I. T.
ML960.B38 1978    788/.1    *LC* 78-313868    *ISBN* 0393021297

**Smithers, Don L., 1933-.**     **1.4175**
The music and history of the baroque trumpet before 1721 [by] Don L. Smithers. — [1st ed. — Syracuse, N.Y.]: Syracuse University Press, 1973. 323 p.: illus.; 24 cm. 1. Trumpet 2. Trumpet music — History and criticism. I. T.
ML960.S63    788/.1/09    *LC* 73-8765    *ISBN* 0815621574

**Gregory, Robin.**     **1.4176**
The trombone; the instrument and its music. — New York: Praeger, [1973] 328 p.: illus.; 23 cm. 1. Trombone 2. Trombone music — Bibliography. I. T.
ML965.G74    788/.2    *LC* 70-141651

**Bevan, Clifford.**     **1.4177**
The tuba family / by Clifford Bevan. — New York: Scribner, c1978. 303 p., [8] leaves of plates: ill.; 25 cm. Includes index. 1. Tuba — History. I. T.
ML970.B48 1978    788/.48    *LC* 77-82241    *ISBN* 0684154773

## ML1000–1092 Other Instruments

**Turnbull, Harvey.**                                                   **1.4178**
The guitar, from the Renaissance to the present day. — New York: C. Scribner's Sons, [1974] vii, 168 p.: illus.; 23 cm. 1. Guitar — History. I. T.
ML1015.G9 T9 1974b      787/.61/09      *LC* 72-9038      *ISBN* 068413215X

**Tyler, James.**                                                      **1.4179**
The early guitar: a history and handbook / by James Tyler. — London: Music Dept., Oxford University Press, 1980. xiii, 176 p.: ill.; 25 cm. (Early music series; 4) 1. Guitar I. T.
ML1015.G9 T95      787.6/1 19      *LC* 80-504118      *ISBN* 0193231824

**Blades, James.**                                                    **• 1.4180**
Percussion instruments and their history. — New York: F. A. Praeger, [1970] 509 p.: illus., music, plates.; 26 cm. 1. Percussion instruments I. T.
ML1030.B6      789/.01      *LC* 79-90411

**Holland, James, 1933–.**                                             **1.4181**
Percussion / James Holland; foreword by Pierre Boulez. — 1st American ed. — New York: Schirmer Books, 1981, c1978. xii, 283 p.: ill.; 21 cm. — (Yehudi Menuhin music guides.) 1. Percussion instruments I. T. II. Series.
ML1030.H64 1981      789/.01 19      *LC* 81-1171      *ISBN* 0028716000

**Peters, Gordon B.**                                                  **1.4182**
The drummer, man: a treatise on percussion / by Gordon B. Peters. — Rev. ed. — Wilmette, Ill.: Kemper-Peters Publications, c1975. xii, 356 p.: ill.; 23 cm. Previous ed. published under title: Treatise on percussion. Includes index. 1. Percussion instruments I. T.
ML1030.P48 1975      789/.01      *LC* 74-79909

**Richards, Martin. Emil.**                                            **1.4183**
World of percussion; a catalog of 300 standard, ethnic, and special musical instruments and effects. — Sherman Oaks, Calif.: Gwyn Pub. Co., c1972. 94 p.: illus.; 29 cm. 1. Percussion instruments I. T.
ML1030.R52      789/.01/2      *LC* 74-164408

**Chávez, Carlos, 1899–.**                                            **• 1.4184**
Toward a new music: music and electricity / by Carlos Chavez; translated from the Spanish by Herbert Weinstock. — New York: Nortom, 1937. 180 p.: ill.; 22 cm. — 1. Musical instruments, Electronic 2. Music — 20th century — History and criticism 3. Music — Acoustics and physics 4. Musical films I. Weinstock, Herbert, 1905- tr. II. T.
ML1092.C4T6      789.9

## ML1100–1354 INSTRUMENTAL MUSIC

## ML1100–1165 Chamber Music

**Cobbett, Walter Willson, 1847-1937, ed.**                           **• 1.4185**
Cyclopedic survey of chamber music. Compiled and edited by Walter Willson Cobbett. With supplementary material edited by Colin Mason. — 2d ed. — London; New York: Oxford University Press, 1963. 3 v.: music.; 24 cm. 1. Chamber music — Dictionaries 2. Music — Bio-bibliography I. Mason, C. M. (Colin M.) ed. II. T.
ML1100.C7 1963      785.7003      *LC* 64-1302

**Tovey, Donald Francis, Sir, 1875-1940.**                            **• 1.4186**
Essays in musical analysis: chamber music. With an editor's note by Hubert J. Foss. London: Oxford U.P., 1944. 217 p.: ill., music. Contains the greater part of the author's chamber music analysis. Not part of author's 6 v. set under same title. 1. Chamber music 2. Music — Analytical guides. I. Foss, Hubert James, 1899- II. T. III. Title: Musical analysis.
ML1100.T7      785.7      *LC* 44-5779

**Ulrich, Homer, 1906–.**                                             **• 1.4187**
Chamber music. — 2d ed. — New York: Columbia University Press, 1966. xvi, 401 p.: charts, music.; 23 cm. 1. Chamber music — History and criticism I. T.
ML1100.U4 1966      785.7009      *LC* 66-17909

**Newman, William S.**                                                **• 1.4188**
The sonata in the Baroque era, by William S. Newman. — Rev. ed. — Chapel Hill, University of North Carolina Press [1966] xvi, 463 p. facsim, map, music. 24 cm. Bibliography: p. [407]-449. 1. Sonata 2. Music, Baroque. 3. Music — 17th century — History and criticism 4. Composers I. T.
ML1156.N4S6 1966      781.52      *LC* 66-19475

**Newman, William S.**                                                **• 1.4189**
The sonata in the classic era. — Chapel Hill: University of North Carolina Press, [1963] xxii, 897 p.: map, charts, facsims., music, tables.; 24 cm. 1. Sonata

2. Classicism in music 3. Music — 18th century — History and criticism 4. Composers I. T.
ML1156.N4 S62      781.52      *LC* 63-22802

**Newman, William S.**                                                **• 1.4190**
The sonata since Beethoven; the third and final volume of a history of the sonata idea, by William S. Newman. — Chapel Hill: University of North Carolina Press, [1969] xxvi, 854 p.: facsims., music., 24 cm. 1. Sonata I. T.
ML1156.N4S63      785.3/1      *LC* 76-80924

**Rosen, Charles, 1927–.**                                            **1.4191**
Sonata forms / by Charles Rosen. — 1st ed. — New York: W. W. Norton, c1980. 344 p.: ill.; 24 cm. 1. Sonata I. T.
ML1156.R67      781/.52      *LC* 79-27538      *ISBN* 0393012034

**Griffiths, Paul.**                                                   **1.4192**
The string quartet / Paul Griffiths. — New York, N.Y.: Thames and Hudson, 1983. 240 p.: music; 24 cm. Includes index. 1. String quartet I. T.
ML1160.G74 1983      785.7/0471 19      *LC* 83-70402      *ISBN* 050001311X

## ML1200–1270 Orchestral Music

**Del Mar, Norman, 1919–.**                                           **1.4193**
Anatomy of the orchestra / Norman Del Mar. — Berkeley: University of California Press, c1981. 528 p.: ill.; 25 cm. 1. Orchestra 2. Music — Performance I. T.
ML1200.D45      785/.06/61 19      *LC* 81-11559      *ISBN* 0520045009

**Ulrich, Homer, 1906–.**                                             **• 1.4194**
Symphonic music, its evolution since the Renaissance. New York, Columbia University Press, 1952. 352 p. illus. 25 cm. 1. Orchestral music — History and criticism. I. T.
ML1200.U4      785.11      *LC* 52-12033

**McCarthy, Albert J.**                                                **1.4195**
Big band jazz / Albert McCarthy. — New York: Berkley Pub. Corp., 1977, c1974. 360 p.: ill.; 28 cm. Includes index. 1. Big bands I. T.
ML1206.M2 1977      785/.06/6709      *LC* 73-78636      *ISBN* 0425035352

**Hart, Philip, 1914–.**                                              **1.4196**
Orpheus in the New World; the symphony orchestra as an American cultural institution. — [1st ed.]. — New York: W. W. Norton, [1973] xix, 562 p.: illus.; 25 cm. 1. Symphony orchestras — United States. I. T.
ML1211.H3      785/.06/610973      *LC* 73-3151      *ISBN* 0393021696

**Lindsay, Jennifer.**                                                 **1.4197**
Javanese Gamelan / Jennifer Lindsay. — Kuala Lumpur; New York: Oxford University Press, 1979. x, 58 p., [8] leaves of plates: ill.; 22 cm. 1. Music — Indonesia — Java — History and criticism. 2. Gamelan I. T.
ML1251.J4 L56      781.7598/2      *LC* 80-112919      *ISBN* 0195804139

**Carse, Adam von Ahn, 1878-1958.**                                   **• 1.4198**
18th century symphonies: a short history of the symphony in the 18th century with special reference to the works in the two series: Early classical symphonies and 18th century overtures. — London: Augener 1951. –. 75 p.: facsim., music, 22 cm. — 1. Symphony 2. Symphonies — To 1800 — Analysis, appreciation. I. T.
ML1255.C3      785.110903      *LC* 51-24298

**Hutchings, Arthur, 1906–.**                                         **• 1.4199**
The Baroque concerto. — New York, W. W. Norton [1961] 363 p. illus., ports., maps, facims., music. 22 cm. Bibliography: p. 351-356. 1. Concerto I. T.
ML1263.H85 1961a      785.6      *LC* 61-65772

**Veinus, Abraham.**                                                  **• 1.4200**
The concerto. — New York: Dover Publications, [1964] 317 p.; 22 cm. — (Dover books on music) 'Revised republication of the work first published by Doubleday, Doran and Company in 1945, and by Cassell and Company Limited in 1948.' 1. Concerto I. T.
ML1263.V4 1964      785.6      *LC* 63-19503

## ML1300–1354 Bands. Military Music

**Farmer, Henry George, 1882–.**                                      **• 1.4201**
The rise & development of military music. With an introd. by Albert Williams. — Freeport, N.Y.: Books for Libraries Press, [1970] xxi, 156 p.: illus., facsims., music.; 23 cm. 'First published 1912.' At head of title: Military music and its story. 1. Military music — History and criticism I. T. II. Title: Military music and its story.
ML1300.F33 1970      785.06/71      *LC* 79-107801      *ISBN* 0836952049

**Goldman, Richard Franko, 1910-.**    • **1.4202**
The wind band, its literature and technique. Boston, Allyn and Bacon [c1962] xvi, 286 p. ill., ports., facsims. (incl. music) 1. Bands (Music) I. T.
ML1300 G65    *LC* 62-8835

**Camus, Raoul F.**    **1.4203**
Military music of the American Revolution / by Raoul F. Camus. — Chapel Hill: University of North Carolina Press, c1976. xii, 218 p.; 24 cm. Includes index. 1. Military music — United States — History and criticism. 2. Bands (Music) — United States. 3. United States — History — Revolution, 1775-1783 — Songs and music — History and criticism. I. T.
ML1311.C35    785/.06/71    *LC* 75-38947    *ISBN* 0807812633

# ML1400–3275 VOCAL MUSIC

**Partch, Harry, 1901-.**    **1.4204**
Genesis of a music; an account of a creative work, its roots and its fulfillments. — 2d ed., enl. — New York: Da Capo Press, 1974. xxv, 517 p.: illus.; 26 cm. 1. Vocal music — History and criticism 2. Musical intervals and scales 3. Musical instruments 4. Musical temperament I. T.
ML1400.P3 1974    780/.92/4    *LC* 76-87373    *ISBN* 030671597X

**Anhalt, István.**    **1.4205**
Alternative voices: essays on contemporary vocal and choral composition / Istvan Anhalt. — Toronto; Buffalo: University of Toronto Press, c1984. x, 336 p.: ill.; 24 cm. Includes indexes. 1. Vocal music — 20th century — History and criticism. I. T.
ML1406.A53 1984    784/.09/04 19    *LC* 84-148317    *ISBN* 0802055311

**Hines, Jerome, 1921-.**    **1.4206**
Great singers on great singing / Jerome Hines. — 1st ed. — Garden City, N.Y.: Doubleday, 1983. 356 p.: ill.; 22 cm. 1. Singing 2. Singers — Interviews. I. T.
ML1460.H46 1982    784.9/3 19    *LC* 81-43280    *ISBN* 0385146388

# ML1700–2100 Opera. Musical Theatre

**Dent, Edward Joseph, 1876-1957.**    **1.4207**
Opera / Edward J. Dent; illustrated by Kay Ambrose. — Rev. ed. — Westport, Conn.: Greenwood Press, 1978, c1949. 206 p., [8] leaves of plates: ill.; 22 cm. Reprint of the ed. published by Penguin Books, Baltimore. Includes index. 1. Opera I. T.
ML1700.D46 O7 1978    782.1    *LC* 78-14482    *ISBN* 0313205639

**Donington, Robert.**    **1.4208**
The opera / Robert Donington. — New York: Harcourt Brace Jovanovich, 1978. x, 238 p.: ill.; 24 cm. — (The Harbrace history of musical forms) Includes index. 1. Opera I. T.
ML1700.D66    782.1    *LC* 77-93589    *ISBN* 0155675362

**Donington, Robert.**    **1.4209**
The rise of opera / Robert Donington. — New York: C. Scribner's Sons, c1981. 399 p., [16] p. of plates: ill.; 26 cm. Includes index. 1. Opera I. T.
ML1700.D67    782.1/09/032 19    *LC* 81-50730    *ISBN* 0684171651

**Grout, Donald Jay.**    • **1.4210**
A short history of opera. — 2d ed. — New York: Columbia University Press, 1965. xviii, 852 p.: music; 24 cm. 1. Opera I. T.
ML1700.G83 1965    782.09    *LC* 64-11043

**Mordden, Ethan, 1947-.**    **1.4211**
The splendid art of opera: a concise history / by Ethan Mordden. — 1st ed. — New York: Methuen, c1980. 413 p.: ill.; 24 cm. Includes index. 1. Opera I. T.
ML1700.M73    782.1/09    *LC* 80-15647    *ISBN* 0416007317

**Orrey, Leslie.**    **1.4212**
A concise history of opera. — New York: C. Scribner's Sons, [c1972] 252 p.: illus. (part color.); 22 cm. 1. Opera I. T.
ML1700.O77 1972b    782.1/09    *LC* 73-5192    *ISBN* 0684135698

**Dent, Edward Joseph, 1876-1957.**    **1.4213**
The rise of romantic opera / Edward J. Dent; edited by Winton Dean. Cambridge; New York: Cambridge University Press, 1976. x, 198 p.; 23 cm. Lectures originally delivered at Cornell University, 1937-8. Includes index. 1. Opera — Addresses, essays, lectures. I. T.
ML1704.D46    782.1/094    *LC* 76-14029    *ISBN* 0521213371

**Mordden, Ethan, 1947-.**    **1.4214**
Opera in the twentieth century: sacred, profane, Godot / Ethan Mordden. — New York: Oxford University Press, 1978. ix, 357 p.; 22 cm. Cover title: Sacred, profane, Godot. Includes index. 1. Opera — 20th century — History and criticism. I. T. II. Title: Sacred, profane, Godot.
ML1705.M67    782.1/09    *LC* 77-23745    *ISBN* 0195022882

**Bordman, Gerald Martin.**    **1.4215**
American musical revue: from The passing show to Sugar babies / Gerald Bordman. — New York: Oxford University Press, 1985. vi, 184 p., [16] p. of plates: ill.; 22 cm. Includes index. 1. Musical revue, comedy, etc — United States. I. T.
ML1711.B665 1985    782.81/0973 19    *LC* 85-4816    *ISBN* 0195036301

**Bordman, Gerald Martin.**    **1.4216**
American musical theatre: a chronicle / Gerald Bordman. — New York: Oxford University Press, 1978. viii, 749 p.; 24 cm. Includes indexes. 1. Musical revue, comedy, etc — United States. I. T.
ML1711.B67    782.8/1/0973    *LC* 77-18748    *ISBN* 0195023560

**Engel, Lehman, 1910-.**    **1.4217**
The American musical theater / by Lehman Engel. — Rev. ed. — New York: Macmillan, 1975. xx, 266 p.; 21 cm. Includes index. 1. Musical revue, comedy, etc — United States. I. T.
ML1711.E5 1975    782.8/1/0973    *LC* 74-31255    *ISBN* 0025360809

**Ewen, David, 1907-.**    • **1.4218**
[Complete book of American musical theater] New complete book of the American musical theater. [1st ed.] New York, Holt, Rinehart, and Winston [1970] xxv, 800 p. illus., ports. 25 cm. Previous editions have title: Complete book of the American musical theater. 1. Musical revue, comedy, etc — United States. 2. Musical revues, comedies, etc. — Stories, plots, etc. I. T. II. Title: American musical theater.
ML1711.E9 1970    782.8/1/0973    *LC* 70-117257    *ISBN* 0030850606

**Mates, Julian, 1927-.**    **1.4219**
America's musical stage: two hundred years of musical theatre / Julian Mates. — Westport, Conn.: Greenwood Press, 1985. xii, 252 p., 20 p. of plates: ill., ports.; 22 cm. (Contributions in drama and theatre studies. 0163-3821; no. 18) Includes index. 1. Musical revue, comedy, etc — United States. I. T. II. Series.
ML1711.M42 1985    782.81/0973 19    *LC* 85-935    *ISBN* 0313239487

**Smith, Cecil Michener, 1906-.**    **1.4220**
Musical comedy in America. — 2nd ed. — New York: Theatre Arts Books, c1981. xv, 367 p., [16] p. of plates: ill.; 24 cm. Includes index. 1. Musical revue, comedy, etc — United States. I. Litton, Glenn. II. T.
ML1711.S6 1981    782.81/0973 19    *LC* 80-51638    *ISBN* 0878305645

**Sonneck, Oscar George Theodore, 1873-1928.**    • **1.4221**
Early opera in America. — New York: B. Blom, [1963, c1943] viii, 230 p.: illus. (part fold.), ports., facsims.; 24 cm. — (Roots and sources of the American theatre) 1. Opera — United States — History and criticism. I. T.
ML1711.S73 1963    782.10973    *LC* 63-23189

**Toll, Robert C.**    **1.4222**
Blacking up: the minstrel show in nineteenth century America / Robert C. Toll. — New York: Oxford University Press, 1974. x, 310 p.: ill.; 24 cm. Includes index. 1. Musical revue, comedy, etc — United States. 2. Minstrel shows I. T.
ML1711.T64    791.1/2/0973    *LC* 74-83992

**Baral, Robert.**    **1.4223**
Revue: a nostalgic reprise of the great Broadway period / by Robert Baral; introduction by Abel Green. — New York: Fleet Pub. Corp., c1962. 288 p.: illus., facsims., ports.; 26 cm. 1. Musical revue, comedy, etc — New York (N.Y.) 2. Musicians — United States. I. T.
ML1711.8.N3 B3    782.8/1/097471    *LC* 62-7579

**Kolodin, Irving, 1908-.**    • **1.4224**
The Metropolitan Opera, 1883–1966; a candid history. — [4th ed.]. — New York: A. A. Knopf, 1966. xxi, 762, xlvii p.: illus., ports.; 25 cm. — (A Borzoi book) 'The Metropolitan repertory, 1883-1966': p. 753-762. 1. New York. Metropolitan Opera. 2. Opera — New York (City) I. T.
ML1711.8.N3 M44 1966    782.107    *LC* 66-19384

**Seltsam, William H., comp.**    • **1.4225**
Metropolitan Opera annals; a chronicle of artists and performances, with an introd. by Edward Johnson. New York, H. W. Wilson, in association with the Metropolitan Opera Guild, 1947. 751 p. ill. 26 cm. 1. Metropolitan Opera (New York, N.Y.) 2. Concerts — Programs I. T.
ML 1711.8 N3 M59 S5 1947    *LC* 47-11435 rev 2

**Robinson, Paul A., 1940-.**    **1.4226**
Opera & ideas: from Mozart to Strauss / by Paul A. Robinson. — 1st ed. — New York: Harper & Row, c1985. 279 p.; 24 cm. Includes index. 1. Opera —

Europe. 2. Opera 3. Song cycles — History and criticism. 4. Europe — Intellectual life I. T. II. Title: Opera and ideas.
ML1720.R6 1985     782.1/09 19     *LC* 84-48822     *ISBN* 0060154500

**White, Eric Walter, 1905-.**           **1.4227**
A history of English opera / Eric Walter White. — London: Faber and Faber, 1983. 472 p., 32 p. of plates: ill.; 26 cm. 1. Opera — England — History and criticism. I. T.
ML1731.W58 1983     782.1/0942 19     *LC* 83-1599     *ISBN* 0571107885

**Dent, Edward Joseph, 1876-1957.**        • **1.4228**
Foundations of English opera; a study of musical drama in England during the seventeenth century, by Edward J. Dent. — With an introd. to the Da Capo ed. by Michael M. Winesanker. — New York, Da Capo Press, 1965. xv, ix, 241 p. music. 23 cm. 'A Da Capo reprint edition.' Bibliographical footnotes. 1. Opera, English — Hist. & crit. I. T.
ML1731.2.D4 1965     782.10942     *LC* 65-18501

**Fiske, Roger.**               **1.4229**
English theatre music in the eighteenth century. — London; New York: Oxford University Press, 1973. xv, 684, 16 p., leaf.: illus., music, ports.; 24 cm. 1. Music, Incidental — History and criticism. 2. Opera — England — History and criticism. 3. English drama — 18th century — History and criticism. I. T.
ML1731.3.F58     782.1/09421     *LC* 73-163752     *ISBN* 0193164027

**Rosselli, John.**             **1.4230**
The opera industry in Italy from Cimarosa to Verdi: the role of the impresario / John Rosselli. — Cambridge [Cambridgeshire]; New York: Cambridge University Press, 1984. viii, 214 p., [1] leaf of plates: ill.; 24 cm. Includes index. 1. Opera — Italy — 18th century. 2. Opera — Italy — 19th century. 3. Impresarios — Italy. I. T.
ML1733.R78 1984     782.1/0945 19     *LC* 83-7688     *ISBN* 0521257328

**Traubner, Richard.**            **1.4231**
Operetta: a theatrical history / Richard Traubner. — 1st ed. — Garden City, N.Y.: Doubleday, 1983. xvii, 461 p.: ill.; 24 cm. Includes index. 1. Operetta — History and criticism. I. T.
ML1900.T7 1983     782.81/09 19     *LC* 77-27684     *ISBN* 0385132328

**Bazelon, Irwin.**             **1.4232**
Knowing the score: notes on film music / Irwin Bazelon. — New York: Van Nostrand Reinhold Co., 1975. 352 p.: ill.; 25 cm. Includes index. 1. Motion picture music — History and criticism. I. T.
ML2075.B36     782.8/5     *LC* 73-16701     *ISBN* 0442205945

## ML2500–2881 Songs

**Fellowes, Edmund Horace, 1870-1951.**     • **1.4233**
The English madrigal composers. — 2d ed. — London, New York, Oxford University Press, 1948. 364 p. music. 22 cm. 'Contains a complete index of the first lines of the whole series of English madrigals, and also separate lists of works of this class at the conclusion of the biographical and critical notice of each composer.' 1. Madrigal 2. Composers, English. I. T.
ML2631.F46 1948     784.1     *LC* 49-9603

**Kerman, Joseph, 1924-.**          • **1.4234**
The Elizabethan madrigal; a comparative study. [New York?] American Musicological Society; distributor: Galaxy Music Corp., New York [1962] xxii, 318 p. music, 15 tables. (American Musicological Society. Studies and documents, no. 4) 1. Madrigal 2. Composers, English 3. Music — 16th century — History and criticism 4. Music — England — History and criticism I. T. II. Series.
ML2631 K47     *LC* 62-52131

**Einstein, Alfred, 1880-1952.**        • **1.4235**
The Italian madrigal; tr. by Alexander H. Krappe, Roger H. Sessions and Oliver Strunk. — Princeton, Princeton Univ. Press, 1949. 3 v. illus., ports., facsims., music. 28 cm. Vol. 3 contains texts and scores of 97 madrigals. 1. Madrigal 2. Music — Italy — Hist. & crit. 3. Composers, Italian. 4. Part-songs — To 1800. I. Krappe, Alexander Haggerty, 1894-1947. tr. II. Sessions, Roger, 1896- tr. III. Strunk, W. Oliver (William Oliver), 1901- tr. IV. T.
ML2633.E32     784.1     *LC* 49-7773 *

**Stevens, Denis, 1922- ed.**        • **1.4236**
A history of song. [1st American ed.] New York, W. W. Norton [1961, c1960] 491 p. illus. 24 cm. 1. Songs — History and criticism I. T.
ML2800.S8 1961     784.09     *LC* 61-5622

**Spaeth, Sigmund Gottfried, 1885-1965.**     • **1.4237**
A history of popular music in America. New York, Random House [1948] xv, 729 p. 22 cm. 1. Popular music — United States — History and criticism.

2. Popular music — United States — History and criticism. 3. Jazz music — United States — History and criticism. I. T.
ML2811.S7     784     *LC* 48-8954

**Brody, Elaine.**              • **1.4238**
The German lied and its poetry [by] Elaine Brody and Robert A. Fowkes. — New York: New York University Press, 1971. viii, 316 p.: music.; 27 cm. 1. Songs, German — History and criticism. 2. German poetry — 19th century — History and criticism. I. Fowkes, Robert Allen, 1913- joint author. II. T.
ML2829.B76     784/.3/00943     *LC* 76-124520     *ISBN* 0814709583

**Routley, Erik.**             • **1.4239**
The English carol. New York, Oxford University Press, 1959 [c1958] 272 p. illus. 23 cm. 1. Carols — History and criticism. 2. Hymns, English — History and criticism. I. T.
ML2881.E5R7 1959     783.60942     *LC* 59-3696

## ML2900–3275 Church Music

**Stevens, Denis, 1922-.**          • **1.4240**
Tudor church music, by Denis Stevens. [2d ed.] New York, W. W. Norton [1966] 97 p. music. 26 cm. and phonodisc (2 s. 7 in. 45 rpm.) in pocket. Phonodisc contains works by Fayrfax, Stone, Blithemann, and Byrd performed by the Ambrosian Singers. 1. Church music — England — History and criticism. I. T.
ML2931.S8 1966a     783.0942     *LC* 65-13528

**Fellerer, Karl Gustav, 1902-.**       • **1.4241**
The history of Catholic Church music. Translated by Francis A. Brunner. Baltimore, Helicon Press, 1961. 235 p. music. 1. Church music — Catholic Church I. T.
ML3002 F443 1961     *LC* 60-15631

**Stevenson, Robert Murrell.**       • **1.4242**
Spanish cathedral music in the Golden Age. Berkeley, University of California Press, 1961. 523 p. music. 1. Church music — Spain — History and criticism 2. Church music — Catholic Church 3. Music — 16th century — History and criticism I. T.
ML3047 S83     *LC* 61-7518

**Wellesz, Egon, 1885-1974.**       • **1.4243**
Studies in Eastern chant / general editors, Egon Wellesz and Miloš Velimirović. London: Oxford U.P., 1966-. 1 v.: ill., music. Vol.1&3 edited by Miloš Velimirović. 1. Chants (Byzantine) — History and criticism 2. Church music — Orthodox Eastern Church — History and criticism I. Velimirović, Miloš M. II. T.
ML3060 W35     783.5     *LC* 66-75827     *ISBN* 019316320

**Apel, Willi, 1893-.**           • **1.4244**
Gregorian chant. — Bloomington: Indiana University Press, [1958] xiv, 529 p.: 8 facsims., music.; 24 cm. Includes chapters on the Ambrosian chant, by R. Jesson and the Old Roman chant, by R. J. Snow. 1. Chants (Plain, Gregorian, etc.) — History & criticism. I. T.
ML3082.A64     783.5     *LC* 57-10729

**Blume, Friedrich, 1893-.**        **1.4245**
[Evangelische Kirchenmusik. English] Protestant church music; a history. By Friedrich Blume, in collaboration with Ludwig Finscher [and others] Foreword by Paul Henry Lang. [1st ed.] New York, W. W. Norton 1975 [c1974]. 831 p. illus. 24 cm. Translation of Geschichte der evangelischen Kirchenmusik, 2. Aufl., published by Bärenreiter Verlag, Kassel, New York, 1965; with 3 additional chapters written for the English ed. 1. Church music — Protestant churches I. T.
ML3100.B5913     783/.026     *LC* 74-8392     *ISBN* 0393021769

**Cobb, Buell E.**             **1.4246**
The sacred harp: a tradition and its music / Buell E. Cobb, Jr. — Athens: University of Georgia Press, c1978. ix, 245 p., [2] leaves of plates: ill.; 24 cm. Includes index. 1. White, Benjamin Franklin, comp. The sacred harp. 2. Hymns, English — History and criticism. 3. Church music — Southern States. I. T.
ML3111.C6     783.6/7     *LC* 77-6323     *ISBN* 0820304263

**Fellowes, Edmund Horace, 1870-1951.**     • **1.4247**
English cathedral music [by] Edmund H. Fellowes. — 5th ed.; revised by J. A. Westrup. — London: Methuen, 1969. xi, 283 p.: music.; 23 cm. 'Distributed in the U.S.A. by Barnes & Noble.' First ed. published in 1941 under title: English cathedral music from Edward VI to Edward VII. 1. Church music — Church of England 2. Church music — England I. Westrup, J. A. (Jack Allan), 1904-1975. II. T.
ML3131.F3 1969     783/.0942     *LC* 70-456990     *ISBN* 0416148506

**Long, Kenneth R.**                                    • **1.4248**
The music of the English church, by Kenneth R. Long. — New York: St. Martin's, [1972, c1971] 479 p.: music.; 26 cm. 1. Church music — Church of England — History and criticism. 2. Church music — England — History and criticism. I. T.
ML3131.L6 1972b          783/.026/342          *LC* 74-175525

**Routley, Erik.**                                    • **1.4249**
Twentieth century church music / by Erik Routley. — New York: Oxford University Press, 1964. 244 p.: music; 23 cm. — (Studies in church music) 1. Church music — England — History and criticism. 2. Church music — Protestant churches 3. Music — 20th century — History and criticism 4. Church music — Discography. I. T. II. Series.
ML3131.R68          *LC* 64-5901

**Temperley, Nicholas.**                                    **1.4250**
The music of the English parish church / Nicholas Temperley. — Cambridge; New York: Cambridge University Press, 1979. 2 v.: ill.; 26 cm. (Cambridge studies in music.) Vol. 2 is an anthology of music. Vol. 1 includes index. 1. Church music — England 2. Church music — Church of England 3. Sacred vocal music — England. I. T. II. Series.
ML3131.T44          783/.026/342          *LC* 77-84811          *ISBN* 0521220459

**Patterson, Daniel W. (Daniel Watkins)**                                    **1.4251**
The Shaker spiritual / by Daniel W. Patterson. — Princeton, N.J.: Princeton University Press, c1979. xix, 562 p.: ill.; 29 cm. 'Checklist of additional manuscripts cited': [529]-537. 1. Shakers — Hymns — History and criticism. 2. Shakers — Hymns 3. Folk-songs, English — United States — History and criticism. 4. Folk dancing — United States. 5. Folk music — United States — History and criticism. I. T.
ML3178.S5 P4          783/.026/98          *LC* 77-85557          *ISBN* 0691091242

**Smither, Howard E.**                                    **1.4252**
A history of the oratorio / by Howard E. Smither. Chapel Hill: University of North Carolina Press, 1977. 2 v.: ill., music; 24 cm. 1. Oratorio — History and criticism. I. T.
ML3201.S6          782.8/2/09          *LC* 76-43980          *ISBN* 0807812749

# ML3475–3547 POPULAR MUSIC. NATIONAL MUSIC. FOLK MUSIC

**Roberts, John S.**                                    **1.4253**
The Latin tinge: the impact of Latin American music on the United States / John Storm Roberts. — New York: Oxford University Press, 1979. ix, 246 p.: ill.; 22 cm. Includes index. 1. Popular music — United States — History and criticism. 2. Popular music — Latin America — History and criticism. I. T.
ML3475.R6          780/.42          *LC* 78-26534          *ISBN* 0195025644

**Dennison, Sam.**                                    **1.4254**
Scandalize my name: Black imagery in American popular music / Sam Dennison. — New York: Garland Publishing, 1982. xxiii, 594 p.: ill.; 23 cm. — (Critical studies on Black life and culture; v. 13) Includes indexes. 1. Afro-Americans — Songs and music — History and criticism. 2. Popular music — United States — History and criticism. 3. Racism — United States. 4. United States — Popular culture 5. United States — Race relations I. T.
ML3477.D46 1982          784.6/8305896073 19          *LC* 80-9027          *ISBN* 0824093097

**Hamm, Charles.**                                    **1.4255**
Yesterdays: popular song in America / Charles Hamm. — 1st ed. — New York: Norton, c1979. xxii, 533 p.: ill.; 24 cm. Includes index. 1. Popular music — United States — History and criticism. I. T.
ML3477.H35          784          *LC* 79-12953          *ISBN* 0393012573

**Malone, Bill C.**                                    **1.4256**
Southern music, American music / Bill C. Malone. — Lexington: University Press of Kentucky, c1979. x, 203 p., [4] leaves of plates: ill.; 22 cm. — (New perspectives on the South.) Includes index. 1. Popular music — Southern States — History and criticism. I. T. II. Series.
ML3477.M34          781.775 19          *LC* 79-4005          *ISBN* 0813103002

**Litweiler, John.**                                    **1.4257**
The freedom principle: jazz after 1958 / John Litweiler. — 1st ed. — New York: W. Morrow, 1984. 324 p.; 22 cm. Includes index. 1. Jazz music — History and criticism. I. T.
ML3506.L57 1984          781/.57/09 19          *LC* 83-63296          *ISBN* 0688022464

**Stewart, Rex William, 1907-1967.**                                    **1.4258**
Jazz masters of the thirties / by Rex Stewart. — New York: Da Capo Press, 1980, c1972. 223 p., [4] leaves of plates: ill.; 23 cm. — (The Roots of jazz) Reprint of the ed. published by Macmillan Co., New York, in series: The

Macmillan jazz masters series. 1. Jazz music 2. Jazz musicians — Biography. I. T.
ML3506.S84 1980          785.42/092/2 B          *LC* 79-27879          *ISBN* 0306760304

**Ullman, Michael, 1945-.**                                    **1.4259**
Jazz lives: portraits in words and pictures / by Michael Ullman. — Washington, D.C.: New Republic Books, 1980. 244 p.: ports.; 22 cm. 1. Jazz music 2. Jazz musicians I. T.
ML3506.U44          785.42/092/2 B          *LC* 80-399          *ISBN* 0915220512

**Williams, Martin T.**                                    **1.4260**
Jazz masters in transition, 1957–69 / by Martin Williams. — New York: Da Capo Press, 1980, c1970. 288 p., [4] leaves of plates: ill.; 23 cm. — (The Roots of jazz) Reprint of the ed. published by Macmillan Co., New York, in series: The Macmillan jazz masters series. 1. Jazz music 2. Jazz musicians — Biography. I. T.
ML3506.W54 1980          785.42/092/2 B          *LC* 79-27874          *ISBN* 0306796120

**Williams, Martin T.**                                    **1.4261**
Where's the melody?: a listener's introduction to jazz / by Martin Williams. — New York: Da Capo Press, [1983], c1966. xvi, 205 p.; 21 cm. — (A Da Capo paperback) Reprint. Originally published: 1st ed. New York: Pantheon Books, c1966. 1. Jazz music — History and criticism. 2. Jazz music — Discography. I. T.
ML3506.W547 1983          781/.57 19          *LC* 82-23644          *ISBN* 0306801833

**Balliett, Whitney.**                                    **1.4262**
Jelly Roll, Jabbo, and Fats: 19 portraits in jazz / Whitney Balliett. — New York: Oxford University Press, 1983. x, 197 p.; 22 cm. 1. Jazz musicians — Addresses, essays, lectures. 2. Jazz music — Addresses, essays, lectures. I. T.
ML3507.B35 1983          785.42/092/2 19          *LC* 82-22557          *ISBN* 0195032756

**Giddins, Gary.**                                    **1.4263**
Rhythm–a–ning: jazz tradition and innovation in the '80s / Gary Giddins. — New York: Oxford University Press, 1985. xviii, 291 p.; 22 cm. Includes index. 1. Jazz music — Addresses, essays, lectures. I. T.
ML3507.G5 1985          785.42 19          *LC* 84-20658          *ISBN* 0195035585

**Giddins, Gary.**                                    **1.4264**
Riding on a blue note: jazz and American pop / Gary Giddins. — New York: Oxford University, 1981. xv, 313 p.; 22 cm. Includes index. 1. Jazz music — Addresses, essays, lectures. I. T.
ML3507.G52          785.42 19          *LC* 80-21238          *ISBN* 019502835X

**Jazz panorama: from the pages of the Jazz review / edited by**                                    **1.4265**
**Martin T. Williams.**
New York: Da Capo Press, 1979, c1962. 318 p., [4] leaves of plates: ill.; 22 cm. (The Roots of jazz) Reprint of the ed. published by Crowell-Collier Press, New York. 1. Jazz music — Addresses, essays, lectures. I. Williams, Martin T. II. Jazz review.
ML3507.J4 1979          785.4/2          *LC* 79-16173          *ISBN* 0306795744

**Williams, Martin T.**                                    **1.4266**
Jazz heritage / Martin Williams. — New York: Oxford University Press, 1985. xiiv, 253 p.; 22 cm. Includes index. 1. Jazz music — Addresses, essays, lectures. 2. Jazz musicians I. T.
ML3507.W53 1985          785.42 19          *LC* 85-4815          *ISBN* 0195036115

**Young, Al, 1939-.**                                    **1.4267**
Bodies & soul: musical memoirs / by Al Young. — Berkeley: Creative Arts Book Co., 1981. 129 p.; 23 cm. 1. Jazz music — Addresses, essays, lectures. 2. Jazz music — United States — History and criticism. 3. Jazz musicians — United States. I. T.
ML3507.Y68          785.42/092/2 B 19          *LC* 81-215880          *ISBN* 0916870391

**Balliett, Whitney.**                                    **1.4268**
Night creature: a journal of jazz, 1975–1980 / Whitney Balliett. — New York: Oxford University Press, 1981. 285 p.: ill.; 22 cm. Includes index. 1. Jazz music — New York (City) I. T.
ML3508.B34          785.42/09747/1 19          *LC* 80-24678          *ISBN* 0195029089

**Lyttelton, Humphrey, 1921-.**                                    **1.4269**
Basin Street to Harlem: jazz masters and masterpieces, 1917–1930 / Humphrey Lyttelton. — New York: Taplinger, 1979. 214 p., [4] leaves of plates: ill.; 22 cm. — (The Best of jazz / Humphrey Lyttelton; [1]) 'A Crescendo book.' Includes index. 1. Jazz music — United States. 2. Jazz music — United States. I. T.
ML3508.L95 1979 vol. 1          785.42/092/2 s 785.42/092/2 19          *LC* 79-13159          *ISBN* 0800807278

**Placksin, Sally.** 1.4270
American women in jazz: 1900 to the present: their words, lives, and music / Sally Placksin. — 1st ed. — New York: Seaview Books, c1982. xvii, 332 p., [16] p. of plates: ill.; 24 cm. Includes index. 1. Women jazz musicians — United States. 2. Jazz music — United States — History and criticism. I. T. ML3508.P58 1982　　785.42/092/2 B 19　　*LC* 81-50324　　*ISBN* 0872237567

**Simon, George Thomas.** 1.4271
The big bands / George T. Simon; with a foreword by Frank Sinatra. — 4th ed. — New York: Schirmer Books; London: Collier Macmillan, c1981. xvii, 614 p.: ill.; 25 cm. Includes index. 1. Big bands — United States. 2. Jazz musicians — United States — Biography. I. T. ML3518.S55 1981　　785/.06/66 19　　*LC* 81-51633　　*ISBN* 0028724208

**Cantwell, Robert, 1945-.** 1.4272
Bluegrass breakdown: the making of the old southern sound / Robert Cantwell. — Urbana: University of Illinois Press, c1984. xiii, 309 p.; 24 cm. (Music in American life.) Includes index. 1. Bluegrass music — United States — History and criticism. I. T. II. Series. ML3520.C36 1984　　784.5/2/00973 19　　*LC* 83-4861　　*ISBN* 025201054X

**Broven, John.** 1.4273
[Walking to New Orleans] Rhythm and blues in New Orleans / John Broven. — Gretna, La.: Pelican Pub. Co., 1978, c1974. xxiii, 250 p., [26] leaves of plates; 23 cm. British ed. published under title: Walking to New Orleans. Includes index. 1. Rhythm and blues music — Louisiana — New Orleans — History and criticism. 2. Rock music — Louisiana — New Orleans — History and criticism. I. T. ML3521.B63 B76 1978　　784　　*LC* 77-13351　　*ISBN* 0882891251

**Evans, David, fl. 1971-.** 1.4274
Big road blues: tradition and creativity in folk blues / David Evans. — Berkeley: University of California Press, c1982. p. cm. Includes index. 1. Blues (Music) — United States — History and criticism. I. T. ML3521.E9　　784.5/3　　*LC* 77-76177　　*ISBN* 0520034848

**Palmer, Robert.** 1.4275
Deep blues / Robert Palmer. — New York: Viking Press, 1981. viii, 310 p.; 24 cm. Includes index. 1. Blues (Music) — History and criticism. 2. Blues musicians — United States — Biography. 3. Afro-American musicians — Biography. I. T. ML3521.P34　　784.5/3/009 19　　*LC* 80-52000　　*ISBN* 0670495115

**Malone, Bill C.** 1.4276
Country music, U.S.A. / by Bill C. Malone. — Rev. ed. — Austin: University of Texas Press, c1985. xii, 562 p.: ill.; 25 cm. 1. Country music — United States — History and criticism. I. T. II. Title: Country music, USA. ML3524.M34 1985　　784.5/2/00973 19　　*LC* 84-21896　　*ISBN* 029271095X

**Berlin, Edward A.** 1.4277
Ragtime: a musical and cultural history / Edward A. Berlin. — Berkeley: University of California Press, c1980. xix, 248 p.: ill.; 24 cm. 'Location index for piano rags in selected anthologies': p. [199-213] Includes index. 1. Ragtime music — History and criticism. I. T. ML3530.B47　　781/.572/09 19　　*LC* 78-51759　　*ISBN* 0520036719

**Ragtime: its history, composers, and music / edited by John Edward Hasse.** 1.4278
New York: Schirmer Books, c1985. x, 400 p.: ill. Includes index. 1. Ragtime music — Addresses, essays, lectures. I. Hasse, John Edward, 1948- ML3530.R33 1985　　781/.572 19　　*LC* 84-13952　　*ISBN* 0028716507

**Macken, Bob.** 1.4279
The rock music source book / Bob Macken, Peter Fornatale, and Bill Ayres. — 1st ed., Anchor Books ed. — Garden City, N.Y.: Anchor Books, 1980. 644 p.; 21 cm. 1. Rock music — Miscellanea. 2. Rock music — Themes, motives, Literary. I. Fornatale, Peter. joint author. II. Ayres, Bill. joint author. III. T. ML3534.M3　　784.5/4　　*LC* 78-1196　　*ISBN* 0385141394

**Ochs, Michael, 1943-.** 1.4280
Rock archives / Michael Ochs. — Garden City, N.Y.: Doubleday, 1984. xiii, 401 p.: ill.; 31 cm. 'A Dolphin book.' Includes index. 1. Rock music — United States — Pictorial works. 2. Rock musicians — Portraits. I. T. ML3534.025 1984　　784.5/4/00973 19　　*LC* 84-4063　　*ISBN* 0385194331

**Pollock, Bruce.** 1.4281
When the music mattered: rock in the 1960's / Bruce Pollock. — 1st ed. — New York: Holt, Rinehart and Winston, 1984, c1983. x, 243 p.: ill., ports.; 24 cm. Includes index. 1. Rock music — United States — History and criticism. I. T. ML3534.P65 1984　　784.5/4/00973 19　　*LC* 83-10853

**The Rolling Stone illustrated history of rock & roll / edited by Jim Miller.** 1.4282
Rev. and updated. — New York: Rolling Stone, c1980. 474 p.: ill.; 28 cm. Edition statement also appears as: First edition. 'A Random House/ Rolling Stone Press book.' 1. Rock music — History and criticism. I. Miller, Jim, 1947- II. Rolling stone. ML3534.R64 1980　　784.5/4/00973　　*LC* 80-5265　　*ISBN* 0394513223

*[handwritten: [Ref] ML 3534 R64 1980]*

**Belz, Carl.** 1.4283
The story of rock. — 2d ed. — New York: Oxford University Press, 1972. xv, 286 p.: ports.; 22 cm. 1. Popular music — History and criticism. I. T. ML3545.B4 1972　　784　　*LC* 77-183870

**Lomax, Alan, 1915-.** • 1.4284
Folk song style and culture. With contributions by the cantometrics staff and with the editorial assistance of Edwin E. Erickson. Washington, American Association for the Advancement of Science [1968] xix, 363 p. illus. 27 cm. (American Association for the Advancement of Science. Publication no. 88) 1. Folk-songs — History and criticism. I. Erickson, Edwin E., ed. II. American Association for the Advancement of Science. III. T. ML3545.L63　　784.4/9　　*LC* 68-21545

**Nettl, Bruno, 1930-.** 1.4285
Folk and traditional music of the western continents [by] Bruno Nettl, with chapters on Latin America by Gérard Béhague. — 2d ed. — Englewood Cliffs, N.J.: Prentice-Hall, [1973] xiii, 258 p.: illus.; 23 cm. — (Prentice-Hall history of music series) 1. Folk music — History and criticism. 2. Music, Primitive. I. Béhague, Gerard. II. T. ML3545.N285 1973　　781.7/09182/1　　*LC* 72-10010　　*ISBN* 0133229416

**Buchner, Alexandr.** 1.4286
[Hudební nástroje národů. English] Folk music instruments [by] Alexander Buchner. [Translated by Alžběta Nováková. New York] Crown [1972] 292 p. illus. (part col.) 34 cm. Title on spine: Folk music instruments of the world. Translation of Hudební nástroje národů. 1. Musical instruments, Primitive. I. T. ML3547.B913　　781.9/1　　*LC* 76-173297

*[handwritten: ML 3547 B913]*

**Nettl, Bruno, 1930-.** • 1.4287
Music in primitive culture. — Cambridge: Harvard University Press, 1956. xviii, 182 p., music (16 p.); 24 cm. 1. Music, Primitive. 2. Musicology I. T. ML3547.N4　　781.71　　*LC* 56-8551

## ML3549–3780 MUSIC, BY COUNTRY

## ML3549–3562 United States

**Lawless, Ray McKinley, 1896-.** • 1.4288
Folksingers and folksongs in America; a handbook of biography, bibliography, and discography, by Ray M. Lawless. Illustrated from paintings by Thomas Hart Benton and others, and from designs in Steuben glass. New York, Duell, Sloan and Pearce [1965] xviii, 750 p. illus., facsim., ports. 22 cm. 1. Folk singers — United States — Biography. 2. Folk-songs, English — United States — Bibliography. 3. Folk-songs, English — United States — Discography. 4. Folk music — United States — Bibliography. 5. Folk music — United States — Discography. I. T. ML3550.L4 1965　　784.4973　　*LC* 65-21677

**Cohen, Norm.** 1.4289
Long steel rail: the railroad in American folksong / Norm Cohen; music edited by David Cohen. — Urbana: University of Illinois Press, c1981. xx, 710 p.: ill.; 27 cm. (Music in American life) Includes melodies with chord symbols and index. 1. Folk-songs, English — United States — History and criticism. 2. Railroads — Songs and music — History and criticism. 3. Railroads — Songs and music 4. Folk music — United States — History and criticism. I. T. ML3551.C57　　784.6/8385/0973　　*LC* 80-14874　　*ISBN* 0252003438

**Jackson, George Pullen, 1874-1953.** • 1.4290
White spirituals in the southern uplands; the story of the fasola folk, their songs, singings, and 'buckwheat notes.' New York, Dover Publications [1965] xvi, 444 p. illus., facsims., music, ports. 22 cm. (Dover books, T1425) Includes unacc. melodies. 'An unabridged and unaltered republication of the work first published in 1933.' 1. Solmization 2. Folk-songs, English — Appalachian Mountains, Southern — History and criticism. 3. Folk music — Appalachian Mountains, Southern — History and criticism. 4. Ballads, English — Appalachian Mountains, Southern — History and criticism. 5. Musical notation 6. Choral societies — Southern States. 7. Mountain whites (Southern States) I. T. II. Title: Spirituals in the southern uplands. ML3551.J2 1965　　784.4　　*LC* 65-24348

**Lawrence, Vera Brodsky.**     **1.4291**
Music for patriots, politicians, and presidents: harmonies and discords of the first hundred years / Vera Brodsky Lawrence. — New York: Macmillan, 1975. 480 p.: ill.; 31 cm. 1. Music — United States — History and criticism. 2. Patriotic music — United States — History and criticism. 3. Political ballads and songs — United States — History and criticism. I. T.
ML3551.L29    784.7/1973    LC 75-28041    ISBN 0025693905

**Nettl, Bruno, 1930-.**     **1.4292**
Folk music in the United States: an introduction / by Bruno Nettl. — 3d ed. / rev. and expanded by Helen Myers. — Detroit: Wayne State University Press, 1976. 187 p.: music; 21 cm. (Wayne books; WB41; Humanities) Previous editions published under title: An introduction to folk music in the United States. Includes index. 1. Folk music — United States I. Myers, Helen, 1946- II. T.
ML3551.N47 1976    781.7/73    LC 76-84    ISBN 0814315569

**Wilder, Alec.**     **1.4293**
American popular song; the great innovators, 1900–1950. Edited and with an introd. by James T. Maher. — New York: Oxford University Press, 1972. xxxix, 536 p.: music.; 24 cm. 1. Popular music — United States — History and criticism. I. T.
ML3551.W54    784/.0973    LC 70-159643    ISBN 0195014456

**Wilgus, D. K.**     **1.4294**
Anglo–American folksong scholarship since 1898. — New Brunswick, N. J., Rutgers University Press, 1959. xx, 466 p. 22 cm. 'Grown out of a doctoral dissertation completed at the Ohio State University.' 'A selected discography of folk music performances on long-playing records': p. [365]-382. Bibliographical references included in 'Notes' (p. [383]-407) Bibliography: p. [409]-427. 1. Folk-songs, American — Hist. & crit. 2. Folk-songs, British — Hist. & crit. 3. Folk-songs — Discography. I. T.
ML3553.W48    782.812    LC 59-7517

## ML3556 AFRO–AMERICAN MUSIC

**Blues / Robert Neff & Anthony Connor.**     **1.4295**
Boston: D. R. Godine, 1975. 141 p.: ill.; 27 cm. Interviews. Includes biographical notes and index. 1. Blues musicians — United States — Interviews. 2. Afro-American musicians — Interviews. 3. Blues (Music) — United States — History and criticism. I. Neff, Robert, 1930- II. Connor, Anthony, 1946-
ML3556.B65    784/.092/2 B    LC 75-11468    ISBN 0879231521

**Brooks, Tilford.**     **1.4296**
America's Black musical heritage / Tilford Brooks. — Englewood Cliffs, N.J.: Prentice-Hall, c1984. xvi, 336 p.: ill., music; 24 cm. Includes index. 1. Afro-Americans — Music — History and criticism. I. T.
ML3556.B76 1984    781.7/296073 19    LC 83-11184    ISBN 0130243159

**Courlander, Harold, 1908-.**     • **1.4297**
Negro folk music, U.S.A. New York, Columbia University Press, 1963. x, 324 p. illus., music. 24 cm. 'The music' (melodies with words): p. [221]-287. 1. Afro-American music — History and criticism. 2. Afro-American songs — History and criticism. 3. Afro-American songs — Discography. 4. Afro-American songs. I. T.
ML3556.C7    784.756    LC 63-18019

**Epstein, Dena J.**     **1.4298**
Sinful tunes and spirituals: Black folk music to the Civil War / Dena J. Epstein. — Urbana: University of Illinois Press, c1977. xix, 433 p.: ill.; 24 cm. — (Music in American life) Includes index. 1. Afro-Americans — Music — History and criticism. 2. Spirituals (Songs) — History and criticism. I. T.
ML3556.E8    784.7/56/009    LC 77-6315    ISBN 0252005201

**Haralambos, Michael.**     **1.4299**
Right on: From blues to soul in Black America / Michael Haralambos. — New York: Drake Publishers, [1975] 187 p.: ill.; 22 cm. Includes index. 1. Afro-Americans — Music — History and criticism. 2. Blues (Music) — United States — History and criticism. 3. Soul music — United States — History and criticism. I. T.
ML3556.H295 R5 1975    784    LC 74-22598    ISBN 0877498121

**Hare, Maud (Cuney), Mrs., 1874-1936.**     • **1.4300**
Negro musicians and their music. Washington, D.C., The Associated publishers, inc. [c1936] xii, 439 p. plates, ports., facsim. 21 cm. 1. Negro musicians. 2. Negro songs — History and criticism. 3. Music — United States — History and criticism. 4. Folk-songs, African. 5. Music — Africa. I. T.
ML3556.H3 N4    780.96    LC 36-11223

**Jones, LeRoi.**     • **1.4301**
Blues people; Negro music in white America. New York, W. Morrow, 1963. xii, 244 p. 22 cm. 1. Blues (Music) — United States — History and criticism.

2. Afro-American music — History and criticism. 3. Jazz music 4. Afro-Americans I. T.
ML3556.J73    781.773    LC 63-17688

**Keil, Charles.**     • **1.4302**
Urban blues. Chicago, University of Chicago Press [1966] ix, 231 p. 22 cm. 1. Blues (Music) — United States — History and criticism. 2. Afro-American music — History and criticism. 3. Jazz music 4. Afro-American musicians 5. Afro-Americans I. T.
ML3556.K43    781.57    LC 66-13876

**Locke, Alain LeRoy, 1886-1954.**     • **1.4303**
The Negro and his music: Negro art: past and present / [by] Alain Locke. — New York: Arno Press, 1969. — 142, 122 p.; 23 cm. (The American Negro, his history and literature. Afro-American culture series.) 1. Negro musicians. 2. Negro songs — History and criticism. 3. Music — United States — History and criticism. 4. Jazz music 5. Music — Discography 6. Negro art — United States. I. T. II. Series.
ML3556.L6 N4 1969    LC 69-18592

**Rowe, Mike.**     **1.4304**
Chicago breakdown / Mike Rowe. — New York: Drake Publishers, 1975. 226 p.: ill.; 22 cm. Includes index. 1. Afro-American music — History and criticism. 2. Blues (Music) — United States — History and criticism. I. T.
ML3556.R7 1975    784    LC 74-22597    ISBN 087749813X

**Southern, Eileen.**     **1.4305**
The music of Black Americans: a history / Eileen Southern. — 2nd ed. — New York: Norton, c1983. xx, 602 p.: ill.; 24 cm. Includes index. 1. Afro-Americans — Music — History and criticism. I. T.
ML3556.S74 1983    781.7/296073 19    LC 82-25960    ISBN 0393952797

## ML3557 NATIVE AMERICAN MUSIC

**Densmore, Frances, 1867-1957.**     **1.4306**
Chippewa music. New York, Da Capo Press, 1972. 2 v. illus. 22 cm. (Da Capo Press music reprint series) Reprint of the 1910-13 ed., which was issued as no. 45 and 53 of the Smithsonian Institution, Bureau of American Ethnology bulletins. 1. Indians of North America — Music 2. Chippewa Indians — Music. I. T.
ML3557.D355 1972    781.7/1/701    LC 77-164513    ISBN 0306704595

**Densmore, Frances, 1867-1957.**     **1.4307**
Teton Sioux music. New York, Da Capo Press, 1972. xxviii, 561 p. illus. 23 cm. (Da Capo Press music reprint series) Reprint of the 1918 ed., which was issued as Bulletin 61 of Smithsonian Institution. Bureau of American Ethnology. 1. Indians of North America — Great Plains — Music. 2. Teton Indians — Music. I. T.
ML3557.D376 1972    784.7/51    LC 72-1889    ISBN 0306705168

**Frisbie, Charlotte Johnson.**     **1.4308**
Music and dance research of Southwestern United States Indians: past trends, present activities, and suggestions for future research / by Charlotte J. Frisbie. — Detroit: Information Coordinators, 1977. 109 p.: ill.; 24 cm. — (Detroit studies in music bibliography; no. 36) 1. Indians of North America — Southwest, New — Music. 2. Indians of North America — Southwest, New — Dances 3. Indians of North America — Southwest, New — History — Sources. I. T.
ML3557.F8    781.7/297 19    LC 77-74663    ISBN 0911772863

**McAllester, David Park, 1916-.**     **1.4309**
Enemy way music: a study of social and esthetic values as seen in Navaho music / by David P. McAllester. — Milwood, N.Y.: Kraus Reprint Co., 1973. ix, 96 p., [52] p. of music; 28 cm. Reprint of the 1954 ed. published by the Peabody Museum of American Archaeology and Ethnology, Harvard University, Cambridge, which was issued as v. 41, no. 3 of its Papers and no. 3 of Reports of the Rimrock project; values series. 1. Indians of North America — Southwest, New — Music. 2. Navajo Indians — Music I. T.
ML3557.M25 1973    781.7/79    LC 78-316098

**Underhill, Ruth Murray, 1884-.**     **1.4310**
Singing for power: the song magic of the Papago Indians of southern Arizona / Ruth Murray Underhill. Berkeley: University of California Press, 1976, c1938. vii, 158 p.: ill.; 21 cm. (California library reprint series.) 1. Papago Indians — Music 2. Indians of North America — Arizona — Music I. T. II. Series.
ML3557.U53 1976    299/.7    LC 77-354970    ISBN 0520033108

## ML3561.B6 BLUEGRASS. BLUES

**Price, Steven D.**                                                          **1.4311**
Old as the hills: the story of bluegrass music / Steven D. Price. — New York:
Viking Press, 1975. x, 110 p.: ill.; 22 cm. 1. Bluegrass music — United States —
History and criticism. I. T.
ML3561.B62 P7        780/.42        LC 74-20637        ISBN 067052204X

**Charters, Samuel Barclay.**                                             • **1.4312**
The bluesmen; the story and the music of the men who made the blues, by
Samuel Charters. — New York: Oak Publications, [1967-77] 2 v.: illus., music,
ports.; 27 cm. 1. Blues (Music) — United States — History and criticism.
2. Afro-American musicians — Biography. I. T.
ML3561.B63 C5        784/.092/2 s B        LC 67-24017

**Murray, Albert.**                                                          **1.4314**
Stomping the blues / Albert Murray; produced and art directed by Harris
Lewine. New York: McGraw-Hill, c1976. 264 p.: ill.; 26 cm. Erratum slip
inserted. Includes index. 1. Blues (Music) — United States — History and
criticism. I. T.
ML3561.B63 M9        784        LC 76-14949        ISBN 0070440743

**Titon, Jeff.**                                                             **1.4315**
Early downhome blues: a musical and cultural analysis / Jeff Todd Titon. —
Urbana: University of Illinois Press, c1977. xvii, 296 p.: ill.; 26 cm. & disc. (33
1/3 rpm. mono. 7 in.) in pocket. (Music in American life) Includes index.
1. Blues (Music) — History and criticism. I. T.
ML3561.B63 T58        784        LC 77-8053        ISBN 0252001877

## ML3561.J3 JAZZ

**Berendt, Joachim Ernst.**                                                  **1.4316**
[Jazzbuch. English] The jazz book; from New Orleans to rock and free jazz, by
Joachim Berendt. Translated by Dan Morgenstern and Helmut and Barbara
Bredigkeit. New York, L. Hill; [distributed by Independent Publishers Group,
1975] xvi, 459 p. 21 cm. 1. Jazz music I. T.
ML3561.J3 B4122        785.4/2/09        LC 73-81750        ISBN 088208027X
ISBN 0882080288

**Blesh, Rudi, 1899-.**                                                    • **1.4317**
Shining trumpets: a history of jazz / by Rudi Blesh. — 2d ed., rev. and enl. —
New York: Knopf, c1958. 408 p.: music. Includes indexes. 1. Jazz music I. T.
ML3561.J3 B47 1958        785.4/2/0973        LC 58-9674

**Blesh, Rudi, 1899-.**                                                    • **1.4318**
They all played ragtime, the true story of an American music [by] Rudi Blesh &
Harriet Janis. [1st ed.] New York, Knopf, 1950. xviii, 338, xviii p. illus., ports.,
facsims., music. 22 cm. 'Musical compositions': p. 283-324. 'A selected list of
phonograph records': p. 325-332. 'A selected list of cylinder phonograph
records': p. 333-334. 'A list of player-piano rolls': p. 335-638. 1. Jazz music
2. Jazz music — Bibliography. 3. Jazz music — Discography. I. Janis, Harriet
Grossman. joint author. II. T.
ML3561.J3B49 1950        780.973        LC 50-12082

**Charters, Samuel Barclay.**                                             • **1.4319**
Jazz, New Orleans, 1885–1963: an index to the Negro musicians of New
Orleans. — Rev. ed. — New York: Oak Publications, 1963. 173 p., [8] leaves of
plates: ill. 'Discographical appendix: The New Orleans recordings': p. 130-154.
1. Jazz musicians 2. Jazz music 3. Jazz music — Bibliography. 4. Music —
Louisiana — New Orleans. I. T.
ML3561.J3.C43 1963        LC 63-23662

**Collier, James Lincoln, 1928-.**                                          **1.4320**
The making of jazz: a comprehensive history / James Lincoln Collier. —
Boston: Houghton Mifflin Co., 1978. xi, 543 p.: ill.; 24 cm. Includes index.
1. Jazz music I. T.
ML3561.J3 C5725        781.5/7/09        LC 77-25030        ISBN 0395262860

**Dance, Stanley.**                                                         **1.4321**
The world of swing. — New York: C. Scribner's Sons, [1974-. v.        : illus.; 24
cm. 1. Jazz music 2. Jazz musicians I. T.
ML3561.J3 D322        785.4/2/0922 B        LC 73-1112        ISBN
068413778X

**Feather, Leonard G.**                                                     **1.4322**
The book of jazz, from then till now; a guide to the entire field, by Leonard
Feather. — [Rev. and up-to-date ed.]. — New York: Horizon Press, [1965] viii,
280 p.: music.; 22 cm. 1. Jazz music — History and criticism. I. T.
ML3561.J3 F387 1965        781.5709        LC 65-15364

**Feather, Leonard G.**                                                     **1.4323**
Inside jazz / by Leonard Feather. — New York: Da Capo Press, 1977, c1949.
103 p., [11] leaves of plates: ill.; 24 cm. — (The Roots of jazz) Reprint of the ed.

published by J. J. Robbins, New York, under title: Inside be-bop. 1. Jazz music
2. Jazz musicians 3. Jazz music — Discography. I. T. II. Title: Inside be-bop.
ML3561.J3 F4 1977        785.4/2        LC 77-23411        ISBN 0306774372

**Gleason, Ralph J.**                                                       **1.4324**
Celebrating the Duke, and Louis, Bessie, Billie, Bird, Carmen, Miles, Dizzy,
and other heroes / Ralph J. Gleason; pref. by Studs Terkel. Boston: Little,
Brown, c1975. xx, 280 p.: ports.; 22 cm. 'An Atlantic Monthly Press book.'
Includes index. 1. Jazz music 2. Jazz musicians I. T.
ML3561.J3 G5595        784        LC 75-15685        ISBN 0316315850

**Gridley, Mark C., 1947-.**                                                **1.4325**
Jazz styles / Mark C. Gridley. — Englewood Cliffs, N.J.: Prentice-Hall, c1978.
x, 410 p.: ill.; 25 cm. Includes index. 1. Jazz music 2. Style, Musical 3. Jazz
musicians I. T.
ML3561.J3 G67        785.4/2        LC 77-8580        ISBN 0135098858

**Harrison, Max.**                                        -                 **1.4326**
A jazz retrospect / Max Harrison. Newton Abbot [Eng.]: David & Charles;
Boston: Crescendo Pub. Co., 1976. 223 p.; 22 cm. 1. Jazz music — Addresses,
essays, lectures. I. T.
ML3561.J3 H35        785.4/2        LC 77-351080        ISBN 0875971016

**Hentoff, Nat. comp.**                                                     **1.4327**
Jazz; new perspectives on the history of jazz by twelve of the world's foremost
jazz critics and scholars. Edited by Nat Hentoff and Albert J. McCarthy. —
New York: Da Capo Press, 1974 [c1959] 387 p.: illus.; 22 cm. — (The Roots of
jazz) Reprint of the 1st ed. published by Rinehart, New York. 1. Jazz music
I. McCarthy, Albert J. joint comp. II. T.
ML3561.J3 H44 1974        785.4/2/0973        LC 70-171383        ISBN
0306705923

**Hobson, Wilder, 1906-1964.**                                              **1.4328**
American jazz music / Wilder Hobson. — New York: Da Capo Press, 1976,
c1939. 230 p., [4] leaves of plates: ill.; 23 cm. — (The Roots of jazz) Reprint of
the ed. published by Norton, New York. Includes index. 1. Jazz music I. T.
ML3561.J3 H62 1976        785.4/2/0973        LC 76-22565        ISBN
0306708167

**Hodeir, André, 1921-.**                                                   **1.4329**
[Hommes et problèmes du jazz. English] Jazz, its evolution and essence / by
André Hodeir; translated by David Noakes. — New York: Da Capo Press,
1975, c1956. ix, 295 p.: music.; 22 cm. — (The Roots of jazz) Translation of
Hommes et problèmes du jazz. Reprint of the 1st ed. published by Grove Press,
New York. Includes index. 1. Jazz music 2. Jazz music — Discography. I. T.
ML3561.J3 H6383 1975        785.4/2        LC 74-23387        ISBN
0306706822

**Keepnews, Orrin.**                                                       • **1.4330**
A pictorial history of jazz; people and places from New Orleans to modern jazz.
Compiled by Orrin Keepnews and Bill Grauer, Jr. Text and captions by Orrin
Keepnews. New ed. rev. by Orrin Keepnews. New York, Crown Publishers
[1966] 297 p. illus., facsims., ports. 29 cm. 1. Jazz music — Pictorial works.
2. Jazz musicians — Portraits. I. Grauer, Bill, 1922-1963. joint author. II. T.
ML3561.J3 K4 1966        781.570973 19        LC 66-4300

**Panassié, Hugues.**                                                       **1.4331**
[Jazz hot. English] Hot jazz; the guide to swing music. Translated by Lyle &
Eleanor Dowling from 'Le jazz hot.' Especially rev. by the author for the
English ed. Westport, Conn., Negro Universities Press [1970] xvi, 363 p. 23 cm.
Reprint of the 1936 ed. 1. Jazz music I. T.
ML3561.J3 P352 1970        781.5/74        LC 74-135606        ISBN
0837151813

**Ramsey, Frederic, 1915- ed.**                                             **1.4332**
Jazzmen / edited by Frederic Ramsey, Jr. and Charles Edward Smith. — New
York: Harcourt Brace Jovanovich, 1977, c1967. xv, 360 p., [16] leaves of plates:
ill.; 20 cm. — (A Harvest/HBJ book) Reprint of the 1959 ed. published by
Harcourt, Brace, New York. 1. Jazz music 2. Jazz musicians — Biography.
I. Smith, Charles Edward. joint ed. II. T.
ML3561.J3 R3 1977        785.4/2/0922 B        LC 77-4215        ISBN
0156462052

**Russell, Ross.**                                                          **1.4333**
Jazz style in Kansas City and the Southwest / by Ross Russell. — 1st pbk. ed.
— Berkeley: University of California Press, 1973, c1971. xviii, 292 p.: ill.; 25
cm. Includes index. 1. Jazz music I. T.
ML3561.J3 R848        785.4/2/09778411        LC 72-138507        ISBN
0520047850

**Sargeant, Winthrop, 1903-.**                                              **1.4334**
Jazz, hot and hybrid / Winthrop Sargeant. — 3d ed., enl. — New York: Da
Capo Press, 1975. 302 p.: ill.; 22 cm. Includes index. 1. Jazz music I. T.
ML3561.J3 S3 1975        785.4/2        LC 74-20823        ISBN 0306706563

**Schuller, Gunther.**    • **1.4335**
The history of jazz. — New York: Oxford University Press, 1968-. v. <1- >: map, music.; 24 cm. 'A selected discography': v. 1, p. 385-389. 1. Jazz music — History and criticism. 2. Jazz music — Discography. I. T.
ML3561.J3 S3295     781.5/7     LC 68-17610

**Stearns, Marshall Winslow.**    • **1.4336**
The story of jazz. — New York: Oxford University Press, 1956. 367 p.: illus.; 21 cm. 1. Jazz music — History and criticism. I. T.
ML3561.J3 S8     780.973 785.42*     LC 56-8012

**Tirro, Frank.**    **1.4337**
Jazz: a history / by Frank Tirro. — 1st ed. — New York: Norton, c1977. xix, 457 p.: ill.; 25 cm. Includes index. 1. Jazz music I. T.
ML3561.J3 T5     781.5/7/09     LC 77-22623     ISBN 0393021947

**Ulanov, Barry.**    • **1.4338**
A history of jazz in America. — New York: Da Capo Press, 1972 [c1952] x, 382 p.; 22 cm. — (Da Capo Press music reprint series) 1. Jazz music 2. Music — U.S. — History and criticism. I. T.
ML3561.J3 U5 1972     785.4/2/0973     LC 74-37324     ISBN 0306704277

**Williams, Martin T. ed.**    **1.4339**
The art of jazz: essays on the nature and development of jazz / edited by Martin T. Williams. — New York: Da Capo Press, 1979, c1959. 248 p.: ill.; 23 cm. — (The Roots of jazz) Includes index. 1. Jazz music 2. Jazz musicians I. T.
ML3561.J3 W53 1979     785.4/2     LC 79-10083     ISBN 0306795566

**Williams, Martin T.**    • **1.4340**
The jazz tradition [by] Martin Williams. — New York: Oxford University Press, 1970. viii, 232 p.; 22 cm. 1. Jazz music 2. Jazz musicians I. T.
ML3561.J3 W5317     785.4/2     LC 71-83058

**Wilson, John Steuart, 1913-.**    **1.4341**
Jazz: the transition years, 1940–1960 [by] John S. Wilson. New York, Appleton-Century- Crofts [1966] x, 185 p. ports. 1. Jazz music 2. Jazz music — Discography I. T.
ML3561 J3 W543     LC 66-24251

## ML3572–3776 Other Countries

**Kodály, Zoltán, 1882-1967.**    • **1.4342**
Folk music of Hungary. Enl. ed. rev. by Lajos Vargyas. Translated by Ronald Tempest and Cynthia Jolly. Translation rev. by Laurence Picken. New York, Praeger [1971, i.e. 1972] 195 p. illus. 25 cm. Translation of A magyar népzene. 1. Folk music — Hungary — History and criticism. 2. Folk-songs, Hungarian — Hungary. I. T.
ML3593.K4952 1972     781.7/439     LC 75-125391

**Vargyas, Lajos.**    **1.4343**
[Magyar népballada és Európa. English] Hungarian ballads and the European ballad tradition / by Lajos Vargyas; [translated by Imre Gombos]. — Budapest: Akadémiai Kiadó, 1983. 2 v.: ill., music; 25 cm. Translation of: A magyar népballada és Európa. Includes unacc. melodies. 1. Folk music — Hungary — History and criticism. 2. Ballads, Hungarian — History and criticism. 3. Ballads — Europe — History and criticism. I. T.
ML3593.V37313 1983     784.4/9439 19     LC 83-235297     ISBN 9630529904

**Bronson, Bertrand Harris, 1902- ed.**    • **1.4344**
The traditional tunes of the Child ballads; with their texts, according to the extant records of Great Britain and America. Princeton, N.J., Princeton University Press, 1959-72. 4 v. music. 1. English ballads and songs 2. Scottish ballads and songs 3. Ballads, English 4. Ballads, Scottish I. Child, Francis James, 1825-1896. English and Scottish popular ballads II. T.
ML3650 B82     LC 57-5468

**Wells, Evelyn Kendrick.**    • **1.4345**
The ballad tree, a study of British and American ballads, their folklore, verse and music, together with sixty traditional ballads and their tunes. — New York, Ronald Press Co. [1950] ix, 370 p. illus., ports. 24 cm. Bibliography: p. 353-360. 1. English ballads and songs. 2. Ballads, English 3. American ballads and songs. 4. Ballads, American. I. T.
ML3650.W4     784.3     LC 50-7548

**Brandel, Rose.**    • **1.4346**
The music of Central Africa; an ethnomusicological study: former French Equatorial Africa, the former Belgian Congo, Ruanda–Urundi, Uganda, Tanganyika. — The Hague, M. Nijhoff [1973, c1961] xii, 272 p. illus., music. 27 cm. Transcriptions: p. 111-245. Bibliography: p. [261]-266. 1. Music — Africa, Central — Hist. & crit. 2. Ethnomusicology 3. Music, African. I. T.
ML3740.B7     LC 62-6547

**Slobin, Mark.**    **1.4347**
Music in the culture of northern Afghanistan / Mark Slobin. — Tucson: Published for the Wenner-Gren Foundation for Anthropological Research [by] University of Arizona Press, c1976. xiv, 297 p.: ill.; 23 cm. (Viking Fund publications in anthropology. no. 54) Includes index. 1. Music — Afghanistan — History and criticism. 2. Folk music — Afghanistan — History and criticism. I. T. II. Series.
ML3758.A3 S6     781.7/581     LC 76-358067     ISBN 0816504989

**Chernoff, John Miller.**    **1.4348**
African rhythm and African sensibility: aesthetics and social action in African musical idioms / John Miller Chernoff. — Chicago: University of Chicago Press, 1979. xv, 261 p., [11] leaves of plates: ill.; 24 cm. Includes index. 1. Music — Africa — History and criticism. 2. Aesthetics, African I. T.
ML3760.C48     780/.96     LC 79-189     ISBN 0226103447

**Jones, A.M.**    • **1.4349**
Studies in African music. London, Oxford University Press, 1959. 2 v. xviii plates (photos.), charts (part fold., part col.) music. 1. Music, African — History and criticism 2. Music, Primitive 3. Music, African I. T.
ML3760 J63     LC 59-1858

**Mitcalfe, Barry.**    **1.4350**
Maori poetry: the singing word / Barry Mitcalfe. — Wellington: Price Milburn for Victoria University Press, 1974. 208 p., [8] leaves of plates: ill.; 25 cm. Music. 1. Songs, Maori — New Zealand — History and criticism. 2. Maoris — New Zealand — History and criticism. 3. Maoris — Music — History and criticism. I. T.
ML3770.M6     784.7/6/994     LC 74-183400     ISBN 0705503690

**Idelsohn, Abraham Zebi, 1882-1938.**    • **1.4351**
Jewish music in its historical development, by A. Z. Idelsohn. New York, Schocken Books [1967, c1956] xi, 535 p. facsims., music. 21 cm. 1. Jews — Music — History and criticism. 2. Synagogue music — History and criticism 3. Folk-songs — History and criticism. 4. Musicians, Jewish I. T.
ML3776.I3 1967     781.7/2924 19     LC 67-25236

**Rubin, Ruth.**    **1.4352**
Voices of a people: the story of Yiddish folksong. 2d ed. New York, McGraw-Hill [1973] 558 p. illus. 24 cm. 1. Jews — Music — History and criticism. 2. Folk music — History and criticism. 3. Folk-songs, Yiddish — History and criticism. I. T.
ML3776.R77 1973     784.7/6924     LC 73-6983     ISBN 0070541949

**Green, Archie.**    **1.4353**
Only a miner; studies in recorded coal–mining songs. Urbana, University of Illinois Press [1972] xiv, 504 p. illus. 27 cm. (Music in American life) 1. Miners — Songs and music — History and criticism. 2. Folk-songs, English — United States — History and criticism. 3. Folk music — United States — History and criticism. I. T.
ML3780.G74     784.6/8/6220973     LC 78-155499     ISBN 0252001818

## ML3785–3795 Music Industry. Music and Society

**Chapple, Steve.**    **1.4354**
Rock 'n' roll is here to pay: the history and politics of the music industry / Steve Chapple & Reebee Garofalo. — Chicago: Nelson-Hall, c1977. xv, 354 p.; 24 cm. Includes index. 1. Music trade — United States. 2. Rock music — United States — History and criticism. I. Garofalo, Reebee, joint author. II. T.
ML3790.C44     338.4/7/784     LC 77-10488     ISBN 0882293958

**Shemel, Sidney.**    **1.4355**
This business of music / by Sidney Shemel and M. William Krasilovsky; original edition edited by Paul Ackerman. — Rev. & enl. 5th ed. — New York: Billboard Publications, c1985. xxvi, 646 p.: charts, forms; 25 cm. Includes index. 1. Music trade — United States. 2. Music — Economic aspects 3. Copyright — Music 4. Popular music — Writing and publishing I. Krasilovsky, M. William. II. T.
ML3790.S5 1985     338.4/778/0973 19     LC 85-1293     ISBN 0823077543

**Denisoff, R. Serge.**    • **1.4356**
Great day coming; folk music and the American left [by] R. Serge Denisoff. — Urbana: University of Illinois Press, [1971] 219 p.: ports.; 26 cm. — (Music in American life) 1. Music and society 2. Radicalism — Songs and music — History and criticism. 3. Radicalism — U.S. I. T.
ML3795.D34     784.6     LC 74-155498     ISBN 0252001796

**Mellers, Wilfrid Howard, 1914-.**                             • **1.4357**
Music and society: England and the European tradition / by Wilfrid Mellers. — 2nd ed. — London: Dobson, 1950. 230 p.: ill. 1. Music and society 2. Music — England — History and criticism. 3. Music — History and criticism I. T. ML3795.M4 1950     *LC* 51-1247

**Raynor, Henry.**                                             • **1.4358**
A social history of music, from the Middle Ages to Beethoven. — New York: Schocken Books, [1972] viii, 373 p.; 25 cm. 1. Music and society 2. Music — History and criticism 3. Music — Economic aspects I. T. ML3795.R4     780/.9     *LC* 79-183616     *ISBN* 0805234462

## ML3797–3798 MUSICOLOGY.
### ETHNOMUSICOLOGY

**Dahlhaus, Carl, 1928-.**                                         **1.4359**
[Grundlagen der Musikgeschichte. English] Foundations of music history / Carl Dahlhaus; translated by J.B. Robinson. — Cambridge, [Cambridgeshire]; New York: Cambridge University Press, 1983. x, 177 p.; 23 cm. Translation of: Grundlagen der Musikgeschichte. Includes index. 1. Music — Historiography I. T. ML3797.D2313 1983     780/.01 19     *LC* 82-9591     *ISBN* 0521232813

**Kerman, Joseph, 1924-.**                                         **1.4360**
Contemplating music: challenges to musicology / Joseph Kerman. — Cambridge, Mass.: Harvard University Press, 1985. 255 p.; 24 cm. Includes index. 1. Musicology I. T. ML3797.K47 1985     780/.01 19     *LC* 84-25217     *ISBN* 0674166779

**Kunst, Jaap, 1891-.**                                         • **1.4361**
Ethnomusicology; a study of its nature, its problems, methods and representative personalities to which is added a bibliography. 3d much enl. ed. of Musicologica. The Hague, M. Nijhoff, 1959. 303 p. ill., ports., music. 1. Ethnomusicology 2. Ethnomusicology — Bibliography I. T. ML3797 K8 1959     *LC* 59-16807

**Adorno, Theodor W., 1903-1969.**                                 **1.4362**
[Einleitung in die Musiksoziologie. English] Introduction to the sociology of music / Theodor W. Adorno; translated from the German by E. B. Ashton. — New York: Seabury Press, c1976. xii, 233 p.; 22 cm. — (A Continuum book) Translation of Einleitung in die Musiksoziologie. 1. Music and society I. T. ML3797.1.A3413     780/.07     *LC* 75-33883     *ISBN* 0816492662

**Musics of many cultures: an introduction / Elizabeth May,**         **1.4363**
**editor; foreword by Mantle Hood.**
Berkeley: University of California Press, c1980. xix, 431 p.: ill.; 26 cm. & 3 discs (33 1/3 rpm. mono. 7 in.). 1. Ethnomusicology 2. Music — History and criticism 3. Music and society I. May, Elizabeth, writer on music. ML3798.M87     781.7     *LC* 76-50251     *ISBN* 0520033930

**Nettl, Bruno, 1930-.**                                         **1.4364**
The study of ethnomusicology: twenty–nine issues and concepts / Bruno Nettl. — Urbana: University of Illinois Press, c1983. xii, 410 p.; 24 cm. Includes index. 1. Ethnomusicology I. T. ML3798.N47 1983     781.7 19     *LC* 82-7065     *ISBN* 025200986X

**Worlds of music: an introduction to the music of the world's**     **1.4365**
**peoples / Jeff Todd Titon, general editor.**
New York: Schirmer Books; London: Collier Macmillan, 1984. 386 p.: ill., music; 24 cm. + 2 cassettes. 1. Ethnomusicology 2. Music — History and criticism 3. Music and society I. Titon, Jeff. ML3798.W67 1984     781.7 19     *LC* 83-13380     *ISBN* 0028726006

## ML3800–3923 Philosophy and Physics of Music

**Allen, Warren Dwight, 1885-.**                                 • **1.4366**
Philosophies of music history: a study of general histories of music, 1600–1960 / by Warren Dwight Allen. — New York: Dover Publications, c1962. xxxiv, 382 p. ill. — (Dover books on music) 'Unabridged and corrected republication of the work originally published by the American Book Company in 1939.' 1. Music — Historiography 2. Music — Bibliography I. T. ML3800.A43 P5 1962     *LC* 63-1070/MN     *ISBN* 0486202828

**Hindemith, Paul, 1895-1963.**                                 • **1.4367**
A composer's world, horizons and limitations. — Gloucester, Mass.: P. Smith, 1969 [c1952] xi, 257 p.; 21 cm. — (The Charles Eliot Norton lectures, 1949-1950) 1. Music — Philosophy and aesthetics I. T. II. Series. ML3800.H55 1969     780.1     *LC* 70-11458

**Meyer, Leonard B.**                                         • **1.4368**
Emotion and meaning in music. — [Chicago]: University of Chicago Press, [1956] 307 p.: illus.; 24 cm. 1. Music — Philosophy and aesthetics 2. Music — Psychology I. T. ML3800.M63     780.1     *LC* 56-9130

**Meyer, Leonard B.**                                         • **1.4369**
Music, the arts, and ideas; patterns and predictions in twentieth–century culture, by Leonard B. Meyer. Chicago, University of Chicago Press [1967] xi, 342 p. Essays. 1. Music — Philosophy and aesthetics 2. Music — 20th century — History and criticism I. T. ML3800.M633     780.15     *LC* 67-25515

**Weber, Max, 1864-1920.**                                     • **1.4370**
The rational and social foundations of music. Translated and edited by Don Martindale, Johannes Riedel [and] Gertrude Neuwirth. [Carbondale] Southern Illinois University Press, 1958. 148 p. 1. Music — Theory 2. Music — Philosophy and aesthetics I. T. ML3800 W3712     *LC* 56-12134

**Zuckerkandl, Victor.**                                         • **1.4371**
Sound and symbol. Translated from the German by Willard R. Trask [and] Norbert Guterman. [New York]: Pantheon Books, [1956-73] 2 v.: illus., music.; 24 cm. — (Bollingen series. 44) 1. Music — Philosophy and aesthetics I. T. II. Series. ML3800.Z813     780.1     *LC* 55-11489     *ISBN* 0691099251

## ML3805–3817 ACOUSTICS AND PHYSICS

**Backus, John.**                                             • **1.4372**
The acoustical foundations of music. [1st ed.] New York, W. W. Norton [1969] xiv, 312 p. illus. 25 cm. 1. Music — Acoustics and physics I. T. ML3805.B245A3     781.1     *LC* 68-54957     *ISBN* 0393098346

**Benade, Arthur H.**                                             **1.4373**
Fundamentals of musical acoustics / Arthur H. Benade. — New York: Oxford University Press, 1976. xii, 596 p.: ill.; 25 cm. 1. Music — Acoustics and physics I. T. ML3805.B328     781/.1     *LC* 75-25460

**Jeans, James Hopwood, Sir, 1877-1946.**                         • **1.4374**
Science & music, by Sir James Jeans. — New York: Dover Publications, [1968] x, 258 p.: illus.; 22 cm. 'This Dover edition is an unabridged republication of the work originally published in 1937.' 1. Music — Acoustics and physics 2. Sound I. T. ML3805.J43S3 1968     781.1     *LC* 68-24652

**Musical acoustics: piano and wind instruments / edited by Earle**     **1.4375**
**L. Kent.**
Stroudsburg, Pa.: Dowden, Hutchinson & Ross, c1977. xiii, 367 p.: ill.; 26 cm. (Benchmark papers in acoustics; 9) Includes indexes. 1. Music — Acoustics and physics — Addresses, essays, lectures. 2. Piano — Construction — Addresses, essays, lectures. 3. Wind instruments — Construction — Addresses, essays, lectures. I. Kent, Earle Lewis, 1910- ML3805.M885     786.2/1     *LC* 76-20464     *ISBN* 087933245X

**Schafer, R. Murray.**                                         **1.4376**
The tuning of the world / R. Murray Schafer. 1st ed. — New York: Knopf, 1977. xii, 301 p.: ill.; 25 cm. 1. Music — Acoustics and physics 2. Sound 3. Music — Philosophy and aesthetics I. T. ML3805.S3     781/.1     *LC* 76-49508     *ISBN* 0394409663

**Winckel, Fritz.**                                             • **1.4377**
[Phänomene des musikalisches Hörens. English] Music, sound and sensation, a modern exposition. Translated from the German by Thomas Binkley. New York, Dover Publications [1967] ix, 189 p. illus., music. 22 cm. 'This Dover edition is a new English translation of Phänomene musikalischen Hörens. The author has revised the text and written a new Preface for this English edition.' 1. Music — Acoustics and physics I. T. ML3805.W5533     781.2/2     *LC* 66-28273

**Miller, Dayton Clarence, 1866-1941.**                         • **1.4378**
The science of musical sounds / by Dayton Clarence Miller.— 2d ed.— New York: Macmillan, 1926. xi, 286 p.: ill., musique; 23 cm. I. T. ML3807.M56 1926     *LC* 62-55167

**Barbour, James Murray, 1897-.** • **1.4379**
Tuning and temperament, a historical survey. East Lansing, Michigan State
College Press, 1951. 228 p.    24 cm. 1. Tuning 2. Musical temperament
I. T.
ML3809.B234    *LC* 51-14140

**Forte, Allen.** **1.4380**
The structure of atonal music. New Haven, Yale University Press, 1973. ix,
224 p. music. 27 cm. 1. Tonality 2. Musical pitch 3. Music — 20th century —
History and criticism I. T.
ML3811.F66    781/.22    *LC* 72-91295    *ISBN* 0300016107

**Yasser, Joseph.** **1.4381**
A theory of evolving tonality / by Joseph Yasser. — New York: Da Capo Press,
1975, c1932. x, 381 p.: ill.; 23 cm. (Da Capo Press music reprint series) Reprint
of the ed. published by American Library of Musicology, New York, which was
issued as v. 1 of Contemporary series. 1. Tonality 2. Musical intervals and
scales I. T.
ML3811.Y2 T4 1975    781/.22    *LC* 74-34376    *ISBN* 0306707292

## ML3820–3838 PHYSIOLOGY.
## PSYCHOLOGY

**Helmholtz, Hermann Ludwig Ferdinand von, 1821-1894.** • **1.4382**
On the sensations of tone as a physiological basis for the theory of music. 2d
English ed., translated, thoroughly rev. and corrected, rendered conformal to
the 4th (and last) German ed. of 1877, with numerous additional notes and a
new additional appendix bringing down information to 1885, and especially
adapted to the use of music students, by Alexander J. Ellis. With a new introd.
(1954) by Henry Margenau. New York, Dover Publications [1954] xix, 576 p.
ill., diagrs., music, tables. 1. Sound 2. Music — Physiological aspects 3. Music
— Acoustics and physics I. Ellis, Alexander John, 1814-1890. II. T.
ML3820 H42 1954    *LC* 54-3730

**Davies, John Booth.** **1.4383**
The psychology of music / John Booth Davies. — Stanford, Calif.: Stanford
University Press, 1978. 240 p.: ill.; 24 cm. Includes index. 1. Music —
Psychology I. T.
ML3830.D28 1978b    781/.15    *LC* 77-92339    *ISBN* 0804709807

**Farnsworth, Paul Randolph, 1899-.** • **1.4384**
The social psychology of music [by] Paul R. Farnsworth. — 2d ed. — [Ames,
Iowa]: Iowa State University Press, [1969] xvi, 298 p.; 24 cm. 1. Music —
Psychology I. T.
ML3830.F215 1969    781.1/5    *LC* 74-84944    *ISBN* 0813815479

**Lundin, Robert W. (Robert William), 1920-.** • **1.4385**
An objective psychology of music. 2d ed. New York, Ronald Press Co. [c1967]
vii, 345 p. illus. 24 cm. 1. Music — Psychology I. T.
ML3830.L9 1967    *LC* 67-14486

**Mursell, James Lockhart, 1893-.** • **1.4386**
The psychology of music. [1st ed.] New York, W.W. Norton [c1937] 389 p. ill.
(music) diagrs. 1. Music — Psychology I. T.
ML3830 M96 P96 1937A    *LC* 37-28429

**The Psychology of music / edited by Diana Deutsch.** **1.4387**
New York: Academic Press, c1982. xvii, 542 p.: ill., music; 24 cm. —
(Academic Press series in cognition and perception.) 1. Music — Psychology
I. Deutsch, Diana. II. Series.
ML3830.P9 1982    781/.15 19    *LC* 82-1646    *ISBN* 0122135601

**Seashore, Carl Emil, 1866-1949.** • **1.4388**
Psychology of music, by Carl E. Seashore. — New York: Dover Publications,
[1967] xix, 408 p.: illus., music.; 22 cm. 'This Dover edition is an unabridged
and unaltered republication of the work originally published in 1938.' 1. Music
— Psychology I. T.
ML3830.S32 P8 1967    781.1/5    *LC* 67-27877

**Blacking, John.** **1.4389**
How musical is man?. — Seattle: University of Washington Press, [1973] xii,
116 p.: illus.; 23 cm. — (The John Danz lectures) 1. Musical ability
2. Ethnomusicology I. T. II. Series.
ML3838.B6    780/.1    *LC* 72-6710    *ISBN* 0295952180

**Shuter-Dyson, Rosamund.** • **1.4390**
The psychology of musical ability. London, Methuen, 1968. 347 p. 23 cm.
(Methuen's manuals of modern psychology) 1. Music — Psychology
2. Musical ability I. T.
ML3838.S525 P9    781.1/5    *LC* 68-122648

## ML3845–3925 AESTHETICS. CRITICISM.
## MUSIC THERAPY

**Dahlhaus, Carl, 1928-.** **1.4391**
[Musikästhetik. English] Esthetics of music / Carl Dahlhaus; translated by
William W. Austin. — Cambridge; New York: Cambridge University Press,
1982. xii, 115 p.; 23 cm. Translation of: Musikästhetik. Includes index.
1. Music — Philosophy and aesthetics I. T.
ML3845.D2913 1982    780/.1 19    *LC* 81-10080    *ISBN* 0521235081

**Gurney, Edmund, 1847-1888.** • **1.4392**
The power of sound. With an introductory essay by Edward T. Cone. — New
York: Basic Books, [1966] xxiii, 559 p.: music.; 26 cm. 'First published in 1880.'
1. Music — Philosophy and aesthetics 2. Music — Psychology I. T.
ML3845.G98 1966    780.1    *LC* 66-28360

**Kivy, Peter.** **1.4393**
Sound and semblance: reflections on musical representation / by Peter Kivy. —
Princeton, N.J.: Princeton University Press, c1984. 235 p.: ill., music; 25 cm.
(Princeton essays on the arts.) Includes index. 1. Music — Philosophy and
aesthetics 2. Music — Theory I. T. II. Series.
ML3845.K59 1984    780/.1 19    *LC* 83-43081    *ISBN* 0691072825

**Music and aesthetics in the eighteenth and early–nineteenth** **1.4394**
**centuries / edited by Peter le Huray and James Day.**
Cambridge [Eng.]; New York: Cambridge University Press, 1981. xvi, 597 p.:
ill.; 24 cm. — (Cambridge readings in the literature of music.) Includes indexes.
1. Music — Philosophy and aesthetics — Addresses, essays, lectures. I. Le
Huray, Peter. II. Day, James. III. Series.
ML3845.M97    781 19    *LC* 80-49805    *ISBN* 0521234263

**Seashore, Carl Emil, 1866-.** • **1.4395**
In search of beauty in music, a scientific approach to musical esthetics, by Carl
E. Seashore ... — New York, The Ronald press company [1947] xvi, 389 p.:
illus., diagrs. 22 cm. 1. Music — Philosophy and esthetics. 2. Music —
Psychology I. T.
ML3845.S398    780.1    *LC* 47-3744

**Einstein, Alfred, 1880-1952.** • **1.4396**
Greatness in music. Translated by César Saerchinger. New York, Oxford
University Press, 1941. vii, 288 p. 1. Music — Philosophy and aesthetics
2. Genius I. T.
ML3847 E563

**Hanslick, Eduard, 1825-1904.** • **1.4397**
The beautiful in music. Translated by Gustav Cohen. Edited, with an introd., by
Morris Weitz. — New York, Liberal Arts Press [1957] 127 p. 21 cm. — (The
Library of liberal arts, no. 45) Translation of Vom Musikalisch-Schönen.
1. Music — Philosophy and aesthetics I. T.
ML3847.H3 1957    780.1    *LC* 57-14627

**Forsyth, Michael.** **1.4398**
Buildings for music: the architect, the musician, and the listener from the
seventeenth century to the present day / by Michael Forsyth. — Cambridge,
Mass.: MIT Press, 1985. 370 p., [16] p. of plates: ill. (some col.); 27 cm. Includes
index. 1. Music and architecture 2. Music — Acoustics and physics I. T.
ML3849.F74 1985    725/.81 19    *LC* 83-18770    *ISBN* 0262060892

**Hollander, John.** • **1.4399**
The untuning of the sky; ideas of music in English poetry, 1500–1700.
Princeton, N.J., Princeton University Press, 1961. xii, 467 p. ill., facsims.
1. Music and literature 2. English poetry — Early modern (to 1700) —
History and criticism I. T.
ML3849 H54    *LC* 60-12231

**Jorgens, Elise Bickford.** **1.4400**
The well-tun'd word: musical interpretations of English poetry, 1597–1651 /
Elise Bickford Jorgens. — Minneapolis: University of Minnesota Press, c1982.
xx, 298 p.: music; 24 cm. Includes index. 1. Music and literature 2. Songs,
English — England — 17th century — History and criticism. 3. English poetry
— Early modern, 1500-1700 — Musical settings — History and criticism. I. T.
ML3849.J67    784.3/001/5 19    *LC* 81-13090    *ISBN* 0816610290

**Kramer, Lawrence, 1946-.** **1.4401**
Music and poetry, the nineteenth century and after / Lawrence Kramer. —
Berkeley: University of California Press, c1984. xiii, 251 p.: ill.; 27 cm.
(California studies in 19th century music; 3) Includes index. 1. Music and
literature 2. Music — 19th century — Philosophy and aesthetics. 3. Music —
20th century — Philosophy and aesthetics. I. T.
ML3849.K7 1984    780/.08 19    *LC* 83-1173    *ISBN* 0520048733

**Winn, James Anderson, 1947-.**  1.4402
Unsuspected eloquence: a history of the relations between poetry and music / James Anderson Winn. — New Haven, CT: Yale University Press, c1981. xiv, 381 p.: music; 24 cm. Includes index. 1. Music and literature I. T.
ML3849.W58    780/.3.08 19    LC 80-27055    ISBN 0300026153

**Copland, Aaron, 1900-.**  • 1.4403
Music and imagination. Cambridge, Harvard University Press, 1952. 116 p. 22 cm. (The Charles Elliot Norton lectures, 1951-52) 1. Creation (Literary, artistic, etc.) 2. Music — 20th century — History & criticism. 3. Imagination I. T.
ML3853.C7    780.1    LC 52-9385

**Kerman, Joseph, 1924-.**  • 1.4404
Opera as drama. — [1st ed.]. — New York: Knopf, 1956. 269 p.; 21 cm. 1. Opera — Dramaturgy I. T.
ML3858.K4    782    LC 56-5790

**Schmidgall, Gary, 1945-.**  1.4405
Literature as opera / Gary Schmidgall. — New York: Oxford University Press, 1977. xi, 431 p.; 24 cm. 1. Opera 2. Music and literature I. T.
ML3858.S37    782.1/3    LC 76-57264    ISBN 0195022130

**Clifton, Thomas, 1935-1978.**  1.4406
Music as heard: a study in applied phenomenology / Thomas Clifton. — New Haven: Yale University Press, c1983. xi, 316 p.: music, ill.; 25 cm. Includes index. 1. Music — Philosophy and aesthetics 2. Phenomenology I. T.
ML3877.C6 1983    780/.1 19    LC 82-10944    ISBN 0300020910

**Cowart, Georgia.**  1.4407
The origins of modern musical criticism: French and Italian music, 1600–1750 / by Georgia Cowart. — Ann Arbor, Mich.: UMI Research Press, c1981. xi, 215 p.: music; 24 cm. — (Studies in musicology. [no. 38]) Revision of thesis (Ph.D)—Rutgers University, 1980. Includes index. 1. Musical criticism — History and criticism. 2. Music — France — 17th century — History and criticism. 3. Music — France — 18th century — History and criticism. 4. Music — Italy — 17th century — History and criticism. 5. Music — Italy — 18th century — History and criticism. I. T. II. Series.
ML3916.C7 1981    780/.944 19    LC 81-641    ISBN 0835711668

**Alvin, Juliette.**  1.4408
Music therapy / Juliette Alvin. — New York: Basic Books, 1975, c1966. 180 p., [4] leaves of plates: ill.; 22 cm. 1. Music therapy I. T.
ML3920.A66 1975    615/.837    LC 74-25290    ISBN 0465047432

# MT Musical Instruction and Study

**Bessom, Malcolm E.**  1.4409
Teaching music in today's secondary schools: a creative approach to contemporary music education / Malcolm E. Bessom, Alphonse M. Tatarunis, Samuel L. Forcucci. — 2d ed. — New York: Holt, Rinehart, and Winston, 1980. xiv, 386 p.: ill.; 24 cm. 1. School music — Instruction and study. I. Tatarunis, Alphonse M., joint author. II. Forcucci, Samuel L. joint author. III. T.
MT1.B555 1980    780/.72973    LC 79-23828    ISBN 0030215560

**Choksy, Lois.**  1.4410
The Kodály context: creating an environment for musical learning / Lois Choksy. — Englewood Cliffs, N.J.: Prentice-Hall, c1981. xxi, 281 p.: music; 24 cm. 1. Kodály, Zoltán, 1882-1967. 2. School music — Instruction and study. I. Kodály, Zoltán, 1882-1967. II. T.
MT1.C536    780/.7 19    LC 80-22149    ISBN 0135166748

**Gordon, Edwin, 1927-.**  1.4411
Learning sequences in music: skill, content, and patterns / by Edwin E. Gordon. — Chicago: G.I.A. Publications, c1984. x, 301 p.: ill.; 23 cm. Includes index. 1. Music — Instruction and study I. T.
MT1.G646    MT1.G646 1984x.    780/.7

**Leonhard, Charles, 1915-.**  1.4412
Foundations and principles of music education [by] Charles Leonhard [and] Robert W. House. — 2d ed. — New York: McGraw-Hill Book, [c1972] viii, 432 p.; 21 cm. 1. School music — Instruction and study. I. House, Robert William, 1920- joint author. II. T.
MT1.L575F7 1972    780.7/2    LC 72-160711    ISBN 0070371997

**Madsen, Clifford K. comp.**  1.4413
Research in music behavior: modifying music behavior in the classroom. Edited by Clifford K. Madsen, R. Douglas Greer, and Charles H. Madsen, Jr. — New York: Teachers College Press, [1975] vii, 277 p.: illus.; 24 cm. 1. Music — Instruction and study — Addresses, essays, lectures. 2. School music — Addresses, essays, lectures. I. Greer, R. Douglas, 1942- joint comp. II. Madsen, Charles H., 1933- joint comp. III. T.
MT1.M135    372.8/7/019    LC 74-16362    ISBN 080772436X

**Schafer, R. Murray.**  1.4414
Creative music education: a handbook for the modern music teacher / R. Murray Schafer. — New York: Schirmer Books, c1976. x, 275 p.: ill.; 24 cm. 1. Music — Instruction and study 2. School music — Instruction and study. I. T.
MT1.S29    780/.72    LC 75-30286    ISBN 0028723309

**Swanwick, Keith.**  1.4415
Discovering music: developing the music curriculum in secondary schools / Keith Swanwick, Dorothy Taylor. — London: Batsford, c1982. 141 p.: ill., music. 'A Batsford educational book'. 1. School music — Instruction and study I. Taylor, Dorothy. II. T.
MT1S945 D5    ISBN 0713440651

**Teaching music in the twentieth century / Lois Choksy ... [et al.].**  1.4416
Englewood Cliffs, N.J.: Prentice-Hall, c1986. xx, 343 p.: ill., music; 24 cm. 1. School music — Instruction and study. I. Choksy, Lois. II. Title: Teaching music in the 20th century.
MT1.T38 1986    780/.7/2 19    LC 85-6340    ISBN 013892662X

**Wieck, Friedrich, 1785-1873.**  1.4417
[Clavier und Gesang. English] Piano and song: how to teach, how to learn, and how to form a judgment of musical performances / translated from the German of Friedrich Wieck; new preface by Nancy Reich. — New York: Da Capo Press, 1982. ix, x, 189 p.; 19 cm. — (Da Capo Press music reprint series) Translation of: Clavier und Gesang. Reprint. Originally published: Boston: Lockwood, Brooks, 1875. Translated by Mary P. Nichols. 1. Piano — Instruction and study 2. Singing I. Nichols, Mary Pickering. II. T.
MT1.W6313 1982    786.3/041 19    LC 81-12536    ISBN 030676122X

**Keene, James A., 1932-.**  1.4418
A history of music education in the United States / James A. Keene. — Hanover, [N.H.]: University Press of New England, 1982. ix, 396 p., [4] p. of plates: ill., music; 24 cm. 1. Music — Instruction and study — United States — History. I. T.
MT3.U5 K3 1982    780/.7/2973 19    LC 81-51610    ISBN 0874512123

**Klotman, Robert H.**  1.4419
The school music administrator and supervisor; catalysts for change in music education [by] Robert H. Klotman. — Englewood Cliffs, N.J.: Prentice-Hall, [1973] vii, 248 p.: illus.; 24 cm. 1. School music supervision 2. School music — Instruction and study — United States. I. T.
MT3.U5 K5    375/.78    LC 72-6635    ISBN 0137937113

**Lasker, Henry.**  1.4420
Teaching creative music in secondary schools. — Boston: Allyn and Bacon, [1971] xii, 385 p.: illus., music.; 24 cm. 1. School music — Instruction and study — U.S. I. T.
MT3.U5 L38    780.7/29/73    LC 79-124939

**Regelski, Thomas A., 1941-.**  1.4421
Teaching general music: action learning for middle and secondary schools / Thomas A. Regelski. — New York: Schirmer Books; London: Collier Macmillan, c1981. 421 p.: ill.; 24 cm. Includes index. 1. School music — Instruction and study — United States. I. T.
MT3.U5 R43    780/.7/2973 19    LC 80-5561    ISBN 0028720709

**Juilliard School of Music.**  • 1.4422
The Juilliard report on teaching the literature and materials of music. Westport, Conn., Greenwood Press [1970, c1953] 223 p. 23 cm. 1. Music — Instruction and study I. T.
MT4.N5J86 1970    780.7/2/097471    LC 79-97384    ISBN 0837130085

**Zarlino, Gioseffo, 1517-1590.**  1.4422a
[Istitutioni harmoniche. 4a pt. English] On the modes: part four of Le istitutioni harmoniche, 1558 / Gioseffo Zarlino; translated by Vered Cohen; edited with an introduction by Claude V. Palisca. — New Haven: Yale University Press, c1983. xxiii, 120 p.: ill.; 27 cm. — (Music theory translation series.) Includes indexes. 1. Music — Theory — 16th century 2. Musical intervals and scales — Early works to 1800. I. Cohen, Vered. II. Palisca, Claude V. III. T. IV. Title: Istitutioni harmoniche. V. Series.
MT5.5.Z3813 1983    781/.22 19    LC 83-2477    ISBN 0300029373

# MT6 Music Theory

**Aspects of Schenkerian theory / edited by David Beach.**    **1.4423**
New Haven: Yale University Press, c1983. xi, 222 p.: music; 24 cm.
1. Schenkerian analysis I. Beach, David, 1938-
MT6.A766 1983    781 19    *LC* 82-13498    *ISBN* 0300028008

**Boatwright, Howard.**    • **1.4424**
Introduction to the theory of music. — New York: W. W. Norton, [1956]
289 p.: illus.; 25 cm. 1. Music — Theory I. T.
MT6.B648    781    *LC* 56-11456

**Cogan, Robert, 1930-.**    **1.4425**
Sonic design: the nature of sound and music / Robert Cogan, Pozzi Escot. —
Englewood Cliffs, N.J.: Prentice-Hall, c1976. xvi, 496 p.: ill.; 25 cm. 1. Music
— Theory I. Escot, Pozzi. joint author. II. T.
MT6.C63 S6    781    *LC* 75-25735    *ISBN* 0138227268

**Copland, Aaron, 1900-.**    • **1.4426**
What to listen for in music. [Rev. ed.] New York, McGraw-Hill [1957] 307 p.
illus. 21 cm. 780.15* 1. Music appreciation I. T.
MT6.C78 1957    *LC* 57-7228

**Forte, Allen.**    **1.4427**
Introduction to Schenkerian analysis / Allen Forte, Steven E. Gilbert. — New
York: Norton, c1982. vii, 397 p.: music; 25 cm. 1. Schenkerian analysis
I. Gilbert, Steven E. II. T.
MT6.F642 I6 1982    781 19    *LC* 81-22502    *ISBN* 0393951928

**LaRue, Jan.**    **1.4428**
Guidelines for style analysis. [1st ed.] New York, W. W. Norton [1970] xii,
244 p. illus. 22 cm. 1. Musical analysis 2. Style, Musical I. T.
MT6.L146G8    781.2    *LC* 73-77409    *ISBN* 0393099466

**Lerdahl, Fred, 1943-.**    **1.4429**
A generative theory of tonal music / Fred Lerdahl, Ray Jackendoff. —
Cambridge, Mass.: MIT Press, c1983. xiv, 368 p.: ill.; 26 cm. — (MIT Press
series on cognitive theory and mental representation.) Includes index. 1. Music
— Theory 2. Music — Psychology 3. Music and language I. Jackendoff, Ray
S. II. T. III. Series.
MT6.L36 G4 1983    781 19    *LC* 82-17104    *ISBN* 0262120941

**Machlis, Joseph, 1906-.**    • **1.4430**
The enjoyment of music; an introduction to perceptive listening. 3d ed. New
York, W. W. Norton [1970] xx, 682 p. illus. (part col.), facsims., music, ports.
25 cm. 1. Music appreciation I. T.
MT6.M134 1970    780.15    *LC* 77-90980    *ISBN* 0393099296

**Marquis, G. Welton.**    • **1.4431**
Twentieth–century music idioms. Englewood Cliffs, N.J., Prentice-Hall [1964]
xv, 269 p. music. 1. Music — Theory 2. Twelve-tone system I. T.
MT6 M34    *LC* 64-10844

**Messiaen, Olivier, 1908-.**    • **1.4432**
The technique of my musical language. Translated by John Satterfield. — Paris,
A. Leduc [1956-. v. 30 cm. — (Bibliothèque-Leduc, 831) 'Olivier Messiaen:
catalogue of works': v. 1, p. [71]-74. 1. Music — Theory I. T.
MT6.M4482    781    *LC* 59-28742

**Morley, Thomas, 1557-1603?**    • **1.4433**
A plain and easy introduction to practical music. Edited by R. Alec Harman;
with a foreword by Thurston Dart. New York, Norton [1953] xxix, 326 p.
diagrs., facsims., music. 26 cm. 'The various sections of the book have been
arranged in a more convenient form ... All the pieces which Morley includes
between the Peroratio and the Annotations have been omitted.' Retained are 2
motets by the author, Domine fac mecum and Agnus Dei, each in facsim. (part-
books) and in modern transcription(score: SATB). 1. Music — Theory —
16th-17th century. I. Morley, Thomas, 1557-1603? Domine fac mecum.
II. Morley, Thomas, 1557-1603? Plaine and easie introduction to practicall
musicke. Agnus Dei III. T.
MT6.M86 1953    *LC* 52-12671

**Ratner, Leonard G.**    • **1.4434**
Music, the listener's art [by] Leonard G. Ratner. 2d ed. New York, McGraw-
Hill [1966] vi, 463 p. ill., facsims., music. (McGraw-Hill series in music)
1. Music — Analysis, appreciation I. T.
MT6 R24 1966    *LC* 65-27679

**Regelski, Thomas A., 1941-.**    **1.4435**
Principles and problems of music education [by] Thomas A. Regelski. —
Englewood Cliffs, N.J.: Prentice-Hall, [1975] xix, 330 p.; 24 cm. 1. Music —
Instruction and study — Programmed instruction. I. T.
MT6.R278 P7    372.8/7/044    *LC* 74-14967    *ISBN* 0137098405

**Schwartz, Elliott, 1936-.**    **1.4436**
Music, ways of listening / Elliott Schwartz. — New York: Holt, Rinehart, and
Winston, c1982. xvi, 534 p.: ill.; 24 cm. Includes index. 1. Music — Analysis,
appreciation. I. T.
MT6.S354 M9    780/.1/5 19    *LC* 81-20327    *ISBN* 0030446767

**The Suzuki concept: an introduction to a successful method for**    **1.4437**
**early music education, by Shinichi Suzuki [and others] Edited**
**by Elizabeth Mills and Therese Cecile Murphy with an**
**introduction by Masaaki Honda.**
[Berkeley]: Diablo Press, [c1973] vi, 216 p.: illus.; 22 cm. 1. Suzuki, Shin'ichi,
1898- 2. Music — Instruction and study — Juvenile I. Suzuki, Shin'ichi, 1898-
II. Mills, Elizabeth. ed. III. Murphy, Therese Cecile, ed.
MT6.S927    787/.1/0712    *LC* 72-97891    *ISBN* 0872970027

**Wennerstrom, Mary H. comp.**    **1.4438**
Anthology of twentieth–century music [by] Mary H. Wennerstrom. New York,
Appleton-Century-Crofts [1969] x p., score (246 p.) 31 cm. 'For use in theory
and literature courses or for private study.' Includes biographical notes and a
brief history of each work. Contains works by Bartók, Berg, Elliott Carter,
Copland, Gaburo, Hindemith, Ives, Persichetti, Mel Powell, Schoenberg,
Schuller, Stravinsky, and Webern. 1. Musical analysis — Music collections
2. Music — 20th century I. T.
MT6.W334A6    780/.82    *LC* 79-80886    *ISBN* 0390930504

**White, John David, 1931-.**    **1.4439**
The analysis of music / John D. White. — 2nd ed. — Metuchen, N.J.:
Scarecrow Press, 1984. xii, 216 p.: ill., music; 23 cm. 1. Musical analysis I. T.
MT6.W4147 A6 1984    780/.1/5 19    *LC* 84-5437    *ISBN*
0810817012

**Burkhart, Charles (Charles L.)**    **1.4440**
Anthology for musical analysis / Charles Burkhart. — 4th ed. — New York:
Holt, Rinehart and Winston, 1986. xv, 602 p.: music; 28 cm. Includes indexes.
1. Musical analysis — Music collections I. T.
MT6.5.B87 1986    781 19    *LC* 85-8513    *ISBN* 0030012899

**Jaques-Dalcroze, Emile, 1865-1950.**    • **1.4441**
Eurhythmics, art, and education. Translated from the French by Frederick
Rothwell. Edited and prepared for the press by Cynthia Cox. New York, B.
Blom, 1972. ix, 265 p. illus. 21 cm. Reprint of the 1930 ed. 1. Music —
Instruction and study 2. Musical meter and rhythm 3. Gymnastics
4. Dancing I. T.
MT22.A74 1972    780/.77    *LC* 78-180027

# MT35–38 Notation

**Donato, Anthony.**    • **1.4442**
Preparing music manuscript. Englewood Cliffs, N.J., Prentice-Hall [1963]
181 p. ill. 1. Musical notation I. T.
MT35 D65    *LC* 63-16352

**Hindemith, Paul, 1895-1963.**    • **1.4443**
Elementary training for musicians / by Paul Hindemith. — New York:
Associated Music, 1946. — xiii, 237 p.: ill., music; 25 cm. 1. Sight-reading
(Music) 2. Ear training 3. Musical dictation 4. Music — Instruction and
study I. T.
MT35.H6 1946

**Karkoschka, Erhard.**    **1.4444**
[Schriftbild der Neuen Musik. English] Notation in new music; a critical guide
to interpretation and realisation. Translated from the German by Ruth Koenig.
New York, Praeger [1972] xii, 183 p. 32 cm. Translation of Das Schriftbild der
Neuen Musik. 1. Musical notation I. T.
MT35.K185 S33 1972    781/.24/0904    *LC* 75-134522

**Read, Gardner, 1913-.**    **1.4445**
Modern rhythmic notation / Gardner Read. — Bloomington: Indiana
University Press, c1978. ix, 202 p.: music; 24 cm. Includes index. 1. Musical
notation 2. Musical meter and rhythm I. T.
MT35.R253 M6    781.6/2    *LC* 77-9860    *ISBN* 0253338670

**Read, Gardner, 1913-.**     ● **1.4446**
Music notation: a manual of modern practice / Gardner Read. — 2d ed. — Boston: Crescendo Publishers, c1969. x, 482 p.: music.; 24 cm. 1. Musical notation I. T.
MT35.R253 M9 1972     781/.24     *LC* 68-54213     *ISBN* 087597080X

**Stone, Kurt.**     **1.4447**
Music notation in the twentieth century: a practical guidebook / by Kurt Stone. — 1st ed. — New York: W. W. Norton, c1980. xxii, 357 p.: ill.; 24 cm. Includes index. 1. Musical notation I. T.
MT35.S87     781/.24/0904     *LC* 79-23093     *ISBN* 0393950530

# MT40–68 Composition. Improvisation

**Fux, Johann Joseph, 1660-1741.**     ● **1.4448**
The study of counterpoint / from Johann Joseph Fux's Gradus ad Parnassum; translated and edited by Alfred Mann; with the collaboration of John Edmunds. — Rev. ed. — New York: W.W. Norton, 1965. xvi, 156 p.: music. — (The Norton library; N277) Original title: Gradus ad Parnassum. 1. Counterpoint 2. Composition (Music) I. Mann, Alfred, 1917- II. Edmunds, John, 1913- III. Fux, Johann Joseph, 1660-1741. Gradus ad Parnassum. IV. T. V. Title: Steps to Parnassus.
MT40F83 1965     781.42     *LC* 65-4836     *ISBN* 0393002772

**Garcia, Russell.**     **1.4449**
The professional arranger composer / Russell Garcia. — New York: Criterion Music Corp. by arrangement with Barrington House, c1954, 197-? printing. 172 p.: ill., music.; 28 cm. 1. Composition (Music) 2. Arrangement (Music) 3. Instrumentation and orchestration I. T.
MT40.G37 1970z

**Hindemith, Paul, 1895-1963.**     ● **1.4450**
The craft of musical composition, by Paul Hindemith ... New York, Associated Music Publishers, inc.; London, Schott, [c1941-45] 2 v. ill. (music) 21 cm. Translation of Unterweisung im Tonsatz. 'Revised edition ... 1945.' 1. Composition (Music) 2. Harmony I. T. II. Title: Unterweisung im Tonsatz.
MT 40 H66     *LC* 45-18358

**Perle, George, 1915-.**     **1.4451**
Serial composition and atonality: an introduction to the music of Schoenberg, Berg, and Webern / by George Perle. — 5th ed., rev. — Berkeley: University of California Press, 1981, c1980. xiv, 164 p.: ill.; 27 cm. 1. Twelve-tone system 2. Composition (Music) I. T.
MT40.P45 1981     781.3 19     *LC* 80-53772     *ISBN* 0520043650

**Perle, George, 1915-.**     **1.4452**
Twelve–tone tonality / George Perle. — Berkeley: University of California Press, c1977. xi, 174 p.: music; 24 cm. 1. Twelve-tone system I. T.
MT40.P46     781.3     *LC* 76-50258     *ISBN* 0520033876

**Reti, Rudolph Richard, 1885-1957.**     ● **1.4453**
The thematic process in music. New York, Macmillan, 1951. x, 362 p. music. 1. Composition (Music) 2. Music — Theory 3. Music — Analysis, appreciation I. T.
MT40 R46     *LC* 51-10953

**Russo, William.**     ● **1.4454**
Jazz composition and orchestration. — Chicago: University of Chicago Press, [1968] xvii, 825 p.: music.; 25 cm. 1. Composition (Music) 2. Instrumentation and orchestration (Dance orchestra) I. T.
MT40.R89     781.6/1     *LC* 67-20580

**Salzer, Felix.**     ● **1.4455**
Structural hearing; tonal coherence in music. With a foreword by Leopold Mannes. [Unabridged and corr.]. — New York, Dover Publications [1962] 2 v. 22 cm. — ([Dover books on music]) 'Based on Heinrich Schenker's conceptions of tonality and musical coherence.' 1. Schenker, Heinrich, 1868-1935. 2. Music — Theory 3. Harmony I. T.
MT40.S2 1962     781.22     *LC* 63-5537

**Schenker, Heinrich, 1868-1935.**     **1.4456**
[Neue musikalische Theorien und Phantasien. v. 1. Harmonielehre. English] Harmony. Edited and annotated by Oswald Jonas. Translated by Elisabeth Mann Borgese. [Chicago] University of Chicago Press [1954] xxxii, 359 p. 24 cm. Translation of Neue musikalische Theorien und Phantasien, 1. Bd., Harmonielehre. 1. Schenkerian analysis I. T.
MT40.S2912     781     *LC* 54-11213     *ISBN* 0226737330

**Bateman, Wayne, 1951-.**     **1.4457**
Introduction to computer music / Wayne Bateman. — New York: J. Wiley, c1980. vii, 314 p.: ill.; 24 cm. 'A Wiley-Interscience publication.' 1. Computer music — Instruction and study. 2. Computer composition I. T.
MT41.B37     781.6/1/02854     *LC* 79-26361     *ISBN* 0471052663

**Chamberlin, Hal.**     **1.4458**
Musical applications of microprocessors / Hal Chamberlin. — 2nd ed. — Hasbrouck Heights, N.J.: Hayden Book Co., 1985. 802 p.: ill.; 24 cm. Includes index. 1. Computer music — Instruction and study. 2. Computer composition 3. Microprocessors I. T.
MT41.C5 1985     789.9/9 19     *LC* 85-24842     *ISBN* 0810457687

**Howe, Hubert S.**     **1.4459**
Electronic music synthesis; concepts, facilities, techniques [by] Hubert S. Howe, Jr. [1st ed.] New York, W. W. Norton [1975] xv, 272 p. illus. 25 cm. 1. Electronic music — Instruction and study. 2. Music — Acoustics and physics 3. Musical instruments, Electronic 4. Computer composition I. T.
MT41.H735 E4     789.9     *LC* 74-10722     *ISBN* 0393092573

**Keane, David.**     **1.4460**
Tape music composition / David Keane. — London; New York: Oxford University Press, 1980. x, 148 p.: ill.; 22 cm. Includes index. 1. Composition (Music) — Mechanical aids 2. Electronic music — Instruction and study. 3. Magnetic recorders and recording I. T.
MT41.K4     789.9/9     *LC* 80-40292     *ISBN* 0193119196

**Cooper, Grosvenor.**     ● **1.4461**
The rhythmic structure of music [by] Grosvenor W. Cooper and Leonard B. Meyer. — [Chicago]: University of Chicago, [1960] ix, 212 p.: illus., music.; 25 cm. 1. Musical meter and rhythm I. Meyer, Leonard B. joint author. II. T.
MT42.C642     781.62     *LC* 60-14068

**Keller, Hermann, 1885-1967.**     ● **1.4462**
Thoroughbass method; with excerpts from the theoretical works of Praetorius [and others] and numerous examples from the literature of the 17th and 18th centuries. Translated and edited by Carl Parrish. — [1st ed.]. — New York, W. W. Norton [1965] xiv, 97 p. music. 28 cm. First published in 1931 under title: Schule des Generalbass-Spiels. Bibliography: p. xi-xiii. 1. Thorough bass I. T.
MT49.K2952     781.3     *LC* 64-23882

## MT50 HARMONY

**Bobbitt, Richard, 1924-.**     **1.4463**
Harmonic technique in the rock idiom: the theory & practice of rock harmony / Richard Bobbitt. Belmont, Calif.: Wadsworth Pub. Co., c1976. 246 p.: music; 26 cm. Includes index. 1. Harmony 2. Rock music — Instruction and study. I. T.
MT50.B65     784     *LC* 76-12492     *ISBN* 0534004741

**Forte, Allen.**     **1.4464**
Tonal harmony in concept and practice / Allen Forte. — 3d ed. — New York: Holt, Rinehart and Winston, c1979. 564 p.; 24 cm. Includes indexes. 1. Harmony I. T.
MT50.F713 T7 1979     781.3     *LC* 78-12229     *ISBN* 0030207568

**Hindemith, Paul, 1895-1963.**     ● **1.4465**
A concentrated course in traditional harmony with emphasis on exercises and a minimum of rules, by Paul Hindemith. Rev. ed. New York, Associated music publishers, inc. [1944] v, 125 p. music. 1. Harmony I. T.
MT50 H658 1944     *LC* 45-239

**Persichetti, Vincent, 1915-.**     ● **1.4466**
Twentieth–century harmony; creative aspects and practice. — [1st ed.]. — New York: W. W. Norton, [1961] 287 p.: illus.; 24 cm. 1. Harmony I. T.
MT50.P455 T9     781.3     *LC* 61-5615

**Piston, Walter, 1894-1976.**     **1.4467**
Harmony / Walter Piston. — 5th ed. / revised and expanded by Mark DeVoto. — New York: Norton, c1987. xvi, 575 p.: music; 24 cm. Includes indexes. 1. Harmony. I. DeVoto, Mark. II. T.
MT50.P665 1987     781.3 19     *LC* 86-23901     *ISBN* 0393954803

**Schoenberg, Arnold, 1874-1951.**     **1.4468**
[Harmonielehre. English] Theory of harmony / Arnold Schoenberg; translated by Roy E. Carter. — Berkeley: University of California Press, 1978. xxi, 440 p.: music; 26 cm. Translation of Harmonielehre. 1. Harmony I. T.
MT50.S37413 1978b     781.3     *LC* 77-73502     *ISBN* 0520034643

**Schoenberg, Arnold, 1874-1951.**      • **1.4469**
Structural functions of harmony. Rev. ed. with corrections. Edited by Leonard Stein. New York, W. W. Norton [1969] xvi, 203 p. music. 20 cm. (The Norton library, N478) 1. Harmony I. Stein, Leonard. ed. II. T.
MT50.S37417 1969     781.3     *LC* 74-81181

**Sessions, Roger, 1896-.**      • **1.4470**
Harmonic practice / by Roger Sessions. — New York: Harcourt, Brace, c1951. xxiv, 441 p.: music; 25 cm. 1. Harmony I. T.
MT50.S487     MT50 S487.     781/3     *LC* 51-8476

## MT55 COUNTERPOINT

**Jeppesen, Knud, 1892-.**      • **1.4471**
[Kontrapunkt (vokalpolyfoni) English] Counterpoint, the polyphonic vocal style of the sixteenth century, by Knud Jeppesen. Translated, with an introduction, by Glen Haydon. New York, Prentice-Hall, inc., 1939. xviii, 302 p. illus. (music) 25 cm. ([The Prentice-Hall music series: Douglas Moore, editor]) 1. Counterpoint I. Haydon, Glen, 1896-1966. tr. II. T.
MT55.J45 K63     781.4     *LC* 39-15933

**Kennan, Kent Wheeler, 1913-.**      **1.4472**
Counterpoint; based on eighteenth–century practice. — 2d ed. — Englewood Cliffs, N.J.: Prentice-Hall, [1972] xiii, 289 p.: music.; 24 cm. 1. Counterpoint I. T.
MT55.K53 1972     781.4/2     *LC* 73-168625     *ISBN* 0131842919

**Piston, Walter, 1894-1976.**      • **1.4473**
Counterpoint, by Walter Piston. — New York: W. W. Norton & company, inc., [1947] 235 p.; 24 cm. 'Musical illustrations drawn by Mario Carmosino.' 'First edition.' 1. Counterpoint I. T.
MT55.P67     781.4     *LC* 47-1928

## MT58–67 MUSICAL FORMS

**Berry, Wallace.**      **1.4475**
Form in music: an examination of traditional techniques of musical form and their applications in historical and contemporary styles / Wallace Berry. — 2nd ed. — Englewood Cliffs, N.J.: Prentice-Hall, c1986. xx, 439 p.: music; 24 cm. 1. Musical form I. T.
MT58.B34 1986     781/.5 19     *LC* 85-3374     *ISBN* 0133292851

**Cone, Edward T.**      **1.4476**
Musical form and musical performance [by] Edward T. Cone. — [1st ed.]. — New York: W. W. Norton, [1968] 103 p.: music.; 21 cm. 1. Musical form 2. Music — Interpretation (Phrasing, dynamics, etc.) 3. Style, Musical 4. Music — Philosophy and aesthetics I. T.
MT58.C65     781.5     *LC* 68-11157

**Epstein, David.**      **1.4477**
Beyond Orpheus: studies in musical structure / David Epstein. — Cambridge, Mass.: MIT Press, c1979. xiv, 244 p.: ill.; 26 cm. Includes index. 1. Music — Theory 2. Musical form 3. Music — Philosophy and aesthetics I. T.
MT58.E67     781.3     *LC* 78-232     *ISBN* 0262050161

**Leichtentritt, Hugo, 1874-1951.**      • **1.4478**
Musical form. — [1st English ed.]. — Cambridge, Harvard University Press, 1951. xii, 467 p. music. 25 cm. Translated and enlarged from the 3d German edition, Musikalische Formenlehre, 1927. 1. Musical form I. T.
MT58.L452     781.508     *LC* 51-11139

**Tovey, Donald Francis, Sir, 1875-1940.**      • **1.4479**
A companion to 'The art of fugue' (Die Kunst der Fuge) J.S. Bach / by Donald Francis Tovey. — London: Oxford University Press: H. Milford, 1931, 1982 printing. 79 p. : music; 19 cm. 'Bach's Die Kunst der Fuge, edited and completed by Professor Tovey, is published in a complete edition in open score for the use of students by the Oxford University Press.'—Note. 1. Bach, Johann Sebastian, 1685-1750. Kunst der Fuge 2. Canon (Music) 3. Fugue I. T.
MT59.B21 T71     781.42     *LC* 32-16723     *ISBN* 0193231514

**Gedalge, André, 1856-1926.**      • **1.4480**
Treatise on the fugue. Translated and edited by Ferdinand Davis, with a foreword by Darius Milhaud. — [1st ed.]. — Norman, University of Oklahoma Press [c1965] xi, 435 p. music. 27 cm. 'Fugal subjects': 296-312; 'Fugues with several subjects': p. 313-335; 'Representative scholastic fugues': p. 336-423. 1. Fugue I. T.
MT59.G4T75     781.42     *LC* 65-11241

**Verrall, John, 1908-.**      • **1.4481**
Fugue and invention in theory and practice, by John W. Verrall. — Palo Alto, Calif.: Pacific Books, [1966] x, 149 p.: music.; 26 cm. 1. Fugue I. T.
MT59.V47     781.42     *LC* 66-23124

**Engel, Lehman, 1910-.**      **1.4482**
The making of a musical / Lehman Engel. — New York: Macmillan Pub. Co., c1977. xvii, 157 p.: music; 22 cm. Includes index. 1. Musical revue, comedy, etc. — Writing and publishing 2. Musical revue, comedy, etc. — Production and direction I. T.
MT67.E6 M3     782.8/1     *LC* 77-23595     *ISBN* 0025360701

## MT68–74 Improvisation. Accompaniment

**Adler, Kurt Herbert, 1905-.**      • **1.4483**
The art of accompanying and coaching [by] Kurt Adler. Minneapolis, University of Minnesota Press [1965] 260 p. ill., music. 1. Musical accompaniment 2. Singing — Diction 3. Style, Musical I. T.
MT68 A3     *LC* 64-25906

**Baker, David, 1931-.**      **1.4484**
Jazz improvisation: a comprehensive method of study for all players / by David Baker. — Chicago: Maher Publications, c1969. 179 p.: ill.; 28 cm. 1. Improvisation (Music) I. T.
MT68.B25     *LC* 72-206818

**Coker, Jerry.**      **1.4485**
Improvising jazz. Englewood Cliffs, N.J., Prentice-Hall [1964] xii, 115 p. illus. music. 21 cm. (A Spectrum book S-89) 1. Improvisation (Music) 2. Jazz music I. T.
MT68.C64     781.65     *LC* 64-14024

**Kynaston, Trent P.**      **1.4486**
Jazz improvisation / Trent P. Kynaston, Robert J. Ricci. — Englewood Cliffs, N.J.: Prentice-Hall, c1978. 218 p.: music; 28 cm. — (A Spectrum book) Includes index. 1. Improvisation (Music) 2. Jazz music I. Ricci, Robert, joint author. II. T.
MT68.K95     781.6/5     *LC* 77-28290     *ISBN* 0135093155

## MT70–86 Orchestra. Orchestration

**Adler, Samuel, 1928-.**      **1.4487**
The study of orchestration / Samuel Adler; [photographs by Louis Ouzer; drawings by Ralph Bentley]. — 1st ed. — New York: Norton, c1982. xiii, 560 p.: ill., music; 24 cm. Includes index. 1. Instrumentation and orchestration I. T.
MT70.A3 1982     785/.028/4 19     *LC* 81-14209     *ISBN* 039395188X

**Berlioz, Hector, 1803-1869.**      • **1.4488**
Treatise on instrumentation, enl. and rev. by Richard Strauss, including Berlioz' essay On conducting. Tr. by Theodore Front. New York, E.F. Kalmus, c1948. iii, 424 p. music. 1. Instrumentation and orchestration 2. Conducting I. Strauss, Richard, 1864-1949. II. T.
MT70 B482 1948     *LC* 48-21781

**Kennan, Kent Wheeler, 1913-.**      • **1.4489**
The technique of orchestration. — 2d ed. — Englewood Cliffs, N.J.: Prentice-Hall, [1970] xiii, 364 p.: illus., music.; 24 cm. 1. Instrumentation and orchestration I. T.
MT70.K37 1970     785/.0284     *LC* 77-79830     *ISBN* 0139003169

**Piston, Walter, 1894-1976.**      • **1.4490**
Orchestration. — [1st ed.]. — New York: Norton, [1955] 477 p.: illus.; 24 cm. 1. Instrumentation and orchestration I. T.
MT70.P56     781.632     *LC* 55-14230

**Read, Gardner, 1913-.**      • **1.4491**
Thesaurus of orchestral devices. — New York: Greenwood Press, [1969] xxi, 631 p.: music; 29 cm. First published in 1953. 1. Instrumentation and orchestration 2. Musical instruments I. T.
MT70.R37 1969     785/.0284     *LC* 69-14045     *ISBN* 0837118840

**Rimsky-Korsakov, Nikolay, 1844-1908.**                         • **1.4492**
[Osnovy orkestrovki. English] Principles of orchestration, with musical examples drawn from his own works [by] Nikolay Rimsky–Korsakov. Edited by Maximilian Steinberg. English translation by Edward Agate. New York, Dover Publications [1964] 2 v. in 1 music. 24 cm. (Dover books on music) 'This Dover edition is an unabridged and corrected republication of the work first published by Edition russe de musique in 1922.' 1. Instrumentation and orchestration I. Shteĭnberg, Maksimilian Oseevich, 1883-1946. II. Agate, Edward. tr. III. T.
MT70.R62 1964       781.632       LC 64-24418

**Sebesky, Don.**                                                **1.4493**
The contemporary arranger / by Donald Sebesky. — New York: Alfred Pub. Co., 1979. xv, 233 p.: music; 31 cm. & 3 discs (33 1/3 rpm. mono. 7 in.) in pocket. 1. Instrumentation and orchestration 2. Arrangement (Music) I. T.
MT70.S4       781.6/4       LC 75-23493       ISBN 0882840320

**Wagner, Joseph Frederick, 1900-1974.**                         **1.4494**
Band scoring. New York, McGraw-Hill, 1960. xiv, 448 p. music. (McGraw-Hill series in music) 1. Instrumentation and orchestration (Band) I. T.
MT73 W27       LC 60-8044

## MT75 INTERPRETATION

**Barra, Donald.**                                               **1.4495**
The dynamic performance: a performer's guide to musical expression and interpretation / Donald Barra; with a foreword by Yehudi Menuhin. — Englewood Cliffs, N.J.: Prentice-Hall, c1983. viii, 181 p.: music; 24 cm. Includes index. 1. Music — Interpretation (Phrasing, dynamics, etc.) I. T.
MT75.B29 1983       781.6/3 19       LC 82-5366       ISBN 013221556X

**Keller, Hermann, 1885-1967.**                                  **1.4496**
[Phrasierung und Artikulation. English] Phrasing and articulation; a contribution to a rhetoric of music, with 152 musical examples. Translated by Leigh Gerdine. New York, W. W. Norton [1973] v, 117 p. 20 cm. (The Norton library) Translation of Phrasierung und Artikulation. 1. Music — Interpretation (Phrasing, dynamics, etc.) I. T.
MT75.K443 1973       781.6/3       LC 72-13069       ISBN 0393006816

**Leinsdorf, Erich, 1912-.**                                     **1.4497**
The composer's advocate: a radical orthodoxy for musicians / Erich Leinsdorf. — New Haven: Yale University Press, c1981. viii, 216 p.: music; 24 cm. Includes index. 1. Music — Interpretation (Phrasing, dynamics, etc.) 2. Conducting 3. Music — Performance I. T.
MT75.L44       781.6/3       LC 80-17614       ISBN 0300024274

## MT85–86 CONDUCTING

**Berlioz, Hector, 1803-1869.**                                  • **1.4498**
[Chef d'orchestre. English] The conductor; the theory of his art. Extrait du Grand d'instrumentation et d'orchestration modernes. Translated by John Broadhouse. London, W. Reeves [19—] St. Clair Shores, Mich., Scholarly Press, 1970. 63 p. illus., music. 22 cm. Translation of Le chef d'orchestre. 1. Conducting I. T.
MT85.B52C74 1970       781.6/35       LC 71-107160       ISBN 0403002478

**Davison, Archibald T. (Archibald Thompson), 1883-1961.**       • **1.4499**
Choral conducting / by Archibald T. Davison. — Cambridge, Mass.: Harvard University Press, c1940. xii, 73 p.: ill., music, diagrs. 1. Conducting, Choral I. T.
MT85.D28 C4       LC 40-27315

**Decker, Harold A., comp.**                                     **1.4500**
Choral conducting; a symposium. Edited by Harold A. Decker and Julius Herford. — New York: Appleton-Century-Crofts, [1973] x, 251 p.: music.; 25 cm. 1. Conducting, Choral I. Herford, Julius, joint comp. II. T.
MT85.D313 C5       784.9/63       LC 72-94347

**Green, Elizabeth A. H.**                                       **1.4501**
The modern conductor: a college text on conducting based on the technical principles of Nicolai Malko as set forth in his The conductor and his baton / Elizabeth A.H. Green. — 4th ed. — Englewood Cliffs, N.J.: Prentice-Hall, 1987. ix, 273 p.: ill.; 24 cm. Includes indexes. 1. Conducting I. Malko, Nicolai, 1883-1961. Conductor and his baton II. T.
MT85.G785 1987       781.6/35 19       LC 86-15054       ISBN 0135901839

**Rudolf, Max.**                                                 • **1.4502**
The grammar of conducting; a practical study of modern baton technique. With a foreword by George Szell. — New York: G. Schirmer, 1950. xvi, 350 p.: diagrs., music.; 26 cm. 1. Conducting I. T.
MT85.R8       781.63       LC 50-1281

**Scherchen, Hermann, 1891-1966.**                               • **1.4503**
Handbook of conducting / by Hermann Scherchen; translated from the German by M. D. Calvocoressi. — London: Oxford University Press, 1933. xiii, 243 p.; 22 cm. Translation of Lehrbuch des Dirigierens. 1. Conducting 2. Orchestral music I. T.
MT85.S33 L42       781.6       LC 33-33439

**Henry, Robert E.**                                             **1.4504**
The jazz ensemble: a guide to technique / Robert E. Henry. — Englewood Cliffs, N.J.: Prentice-Hall, c1981. x, 117 p.: music; 29 cm. — (A Spectrum book) Includes index. 1. Jazz music — Instruction and study. 2. Jazz ensembles — Instruction and study. 3. Big band music — Instruction and study. I. T.
MT86.H47       785.42 19       LC 80-23360       ISBN 0135099927

## MT90–150 Analytical Guides

**Tovey, Donald Francis, Sir, 1875-1940.**                       • **1.4505**
Essays in musical analysis, by Donald Francis Tovey ... London, Oxford university press, H. Milford, 1935-39. 6 v. illus. (music) 23 cm. 1. Musical analysis I. T.
MT90.T6 E8       780.072       LC 35-11193

**Cooke, Deryck.**                                               **1.4506**
Gustav Mahler: an introduction to his music / Deryck Cooke. — Cambridge [Eng.]; New York: Cambridge University Press, 1980. 127 p.; 22 cm. Includes index. 1. Mahler, Gustav, 1860-1911. Works. I. T.
MT92.M14 C66       780/.92/4 19       LC 79-8588       ISBN 0521231752

**Howes, Frank Stewart, 1891-.**                                 **1.4507**
The music of William Walton [by] Frank Howes. 2d ed. London, New York, Oxford University Press, 1974 [i.e. 1973] xvi, 248 [8] p. illus., music, ports. 23 cm. 1. Walton, William, 1902- Works. I. T.
MT92.W16 H6 1974       780/.92/4       LC 74-156945       ISBN 0193154315

## MT95–110 OPERA. BALLET

**Balanchine, George.**                                          **1.4508**
[Complete stories of the great ballets] Balanchine's Complete stories of the great ballets / by George Balanchine; and Francis Mason. — Rev. and enl. ed. — Garden City, N.Y.: Doubleday, 1977. xxvi, 838 p., [32] leaves of plates: ill.; 24 cm. Edition for 1968 published under title: Balanchine's New complete stories of the great ballets. Includes index. 1. Ballets — Stories, plots, etc. I. Mason, Francis, joint author. II. T. III. Title: Complete stories of the great ballets.
MT95.B3 1977       792.8/4       LC 76-55684       ISBN 0385113811

**Kobbé, Gustave.**                                              **1.4509**
Kobbé's complete opera book. — 10th ed. / edited and revised by the Earl of Harewood. — London: Putnam, 1987. [1408] p.: ill.; 24 cm. 1. Opera I. Harewood, George Lascelles, Earl of, 1923- II. T.
ML1700 ML1700       MT95.K52 1987x.       782.1/09 19       ISBN 0370310179

**Martin, George Whitney.**                                      **1.4510**
[Companion to twentieth-century opera] The opera companion to twentieth–century opera / by George Martin. — New York: Dodd, Mead, 1979. xvi, 653 p.; 24 cm. Also published as: The companion to twentieth-century opera. Includes index. 1. Operas — 20th century — Stories, plots, etc. I. T. II. Title: Opera companion to 20th-century opera.
MT95.M253       782.1/3       LC 78-22048       ISBN 0396075940

**The Metropolitan Opera stories of the great operas / by John**   **1.4511**
**W. Freeman.**
1st ed. — New York: Metropolitan Opera Guild: W.W. Norton, c1984. xxxii, 547 p.: ports.; 24 cm. 1. Operas — Stories, plots, etc. I. Freeman, John. II. Metropolitan Opera (New York, N.Y.) III. Title: Stories of the great operas.
MT95.M49 1984       782.1/3 19       LC 84-8030       ISBN 0393018881

**The Victor book of the opera. Rev. by Henry W. Simon.**        • **1.4512**
**Picture editor: Gerald Fitzgerald.**
13th ed. — New York: Simon and Schuster, [1968] 475 p.: illus., ports.; 29 cm. First published in 1912. 1. Operas — Stories, plots, etc. 2. Operas — Discography I. Simon, Henry William, 1901- ed.
MT95.V5x       782.13       LC 68-11017

**Reich, Willi, 1898-.**      • **1.4513**
Alban Berg's Wozzeck: a guide to the text and Music of the opera / by Willi Reich. — New York: G. Schirmer, c1952. 22 p.: ill. 1. Berg, Alban, 1885-1935. Wozzeck. I. T. II. Title: Wozzeck.
MT100.B4R4 1952     782.13     LC 52-66231

**Mann, William, 1924-.**      **1.4514**
The operas of Mozart / William Mann. — New York: Oxford University Press, 1977. 656 p.: music; 26 cm. Includes index. 1. Mozart, Wolfgang Amadeus, 1756-1791. Operas. I. T.
MT100.M76 M3     782.1/092/4     LC 76-9279     ISBN 0195198913

**Ashbrook, William, 1922-.**      • **1.4515**
The operas of Puccini. — New York: Oxford University Press, 1968. xv, 269 p.: music, port.; 25 cm. 1. Puccini, Giacomo, 1858-1924. Operas. I. T.
MT100.P95 A8     782.13     LC 68-8407

**Mann, William, 1924-.**      **1.4516**
Richard Strauss: a critical study of the operas / William S. Mann. New York: Oxford University Press, 1964. 402 p.: ill., music. I. Strauss, Richard, 1864-1949. Operas. II. T.
MT100.S84 M3     782.10924     LC 66-2148

**Newman, Ernest, 1868-1959.**      • **1.4517**
The Wagner operas. 1st ed. New York, Knopf, 1949. xii, 723, v p. port., music. 25 cm. 'Published in England under the title Wagner nights.' Analyses of the operas, omitting Die Feen, Das Liebesverbot and Rienzi. 1. Wagner, Richard. Operas. Selections. I. T.
MT100.W2 N53 1949     782.2     LC 49-11607

**Osborne, Charles, 1927-.**      **1.4518**
The world theatre of Wagner: a celebration of 150 years of Wagner productions / Charles Osborne; preface by Sir Colin Davis. — 1st American ed. — New York: Macmillan, 1982. 224 p.: ill. (some col.); 32 cm. 1. Wagner, Richard, 1813-1883. Operas 2. Opera — Production and direction 3. Operas — Stories, plots, etc. I. Davis, Colin, 1927- II. T.
MT100.W2 O8 1982     782.1/092/4 19     LC 82-130     ISBN 0025940503

**Shaw, Bernard, 1856-1950.**      • **1.4519**
The perfect Wagnerite; a commentary on the Niblung's ring. New York, Dover Publications [1967] xx, 136 p. 22 cm. (Dover books on music, T1707) 'This Dover edition is an unabridged and unaltered republication of the fourth edition (1923)' 1. Wagner, Richard, 1813-1883. Der Ring des Nibelungen. I. T.
MT100.W25 S5 1967     782.1/0924     LC 66-29055

## MT115 CANTATAS. SONGS

**Whittaker, W. G. (William Gillies), 1876-1944.**      • **1.4520**
The cantatas of Johann Sebastian Bach, sacred and secular. London, Oxford University Press, 1959. 2 v. music. 1. Bach, Johann Sebastian, 1685-1750. Cantatas I. T.
MT115 B2 W5     LC 59-65215

**Brown, Maurice John Edwin.**      • **1.4521**
Schubert songs / by Maurice J. E. Brown. — London: British Broadcasting Corporation, 1967. — 64 p.: ill.; 20 cm. (BBC music guides.) 1. Schubert, Franz, 1797-1828. Songs I. T. II. Series.
MT 115 S37 B87 1967     LC 67-109894     ISBN 0563073020

**Sams, Eric.**      • **1.4522**
The songs of Hugo Wolf. Foreword by Gerald Moore. New York: Oxford University Press, 1962, [c1961] 268 p.: ill.; 22 cm. 1. Wolf, Hugo, 1860-1903. Songs. I. T.
MT115.W6 S3 1961     LC 62-2823

## MT125–130 ORCHESTRAL MUSIC

**Downes, Edward, 1911-.**      **1.4523**
Guide to the symphony / by Edward Downes. — New York: Walker, c1981. — xxix, 1058 p.: ill., music; 24 cm. Previously published under title: The New York Philharmonic guide to the symphony. Includes index. 1. Orchestral music — Analysis, appreciation I. T.
MT125.D68 1981     785/.01/5 19     LC 81-7442     ISBN 0802771777

**Grove, George, Sir, 1820-1900.**      • **1.4524**
Beethoven and his nine symphonies. 3d ed. New York, Dover Publications [1962] 407 p. illus. 21 cm. (Dover books, T334) 1. Beethoven, Ludwig van, 1770-1827. Symphonies. I. T.
MT130.B43 G8 1962     785.11     LC 63-234

**Hutchings, Arthur, 1906-.**      • **1.4525**
A companion to Mozart's piano concertos / by Arthur Hutchings. — 2d ed. — London; Toronto: Oxford University Press, 1950. xiv, 211 p.: musique. 'Thematic guide to Mozart's concertos': pp. [xi]-xiv. 1. Mozart, Wolfgang Amadeus, 1756-1791 — Thematic catalogs. 2. Mozart, Wolfgang Amadeus, 1756-1791. Concertos, piano, orchestra I. T.
MT130.M8 H8 1950     LC 50-14482

## MT140–145 CHAMBER MUSIC. SOLO INSTRUMENTAL MUSIC

**Hutcheson, Ernest, 1871-1951.**      • **1.4526**
The literature of the piano; a guide for amateur and student. — 3d ed., rev. and brought up to date by Rudolph Ganz. — New York: A. A. Knopf, 1964. xvi, 436, xxxiv p.: music.; 25 cm. — (A Borzoi book) 1. Piano music — Analysis, appreciation 2. Piano music — Interpretation (Phrasing, dynamics, etc.) I. Ganz, Rudolph, 1877- ed. II. T.
MT140.H95 1964     786.4     LC 63-9130

**Barford, Philip.**      • **1.4527**
The keyboard music of C. P. E. Bach, considered in relation to his musical aesthetic and the rise of the sonata principle. — New York: October House, [1966, c1965] xv, 186 p.: facsim., music.; 26 cm. 1. Bach, Carl Philipp Emanuel, 1714-1788. Works, keyboard. 2. Music — Philosophy and aesthetics 3. Sonata I. T.
MT145.B12 B4 1966     786.0924     LC 66-23121

**Bodky, Erwin, 1896-1958.**      • **1.4528**
The interpretation of Bach's keyboard works. — Cambridge, Harvard University Press, 1960. ix, 421 p. illus., facsims., music. 26 cm. Bibliography: p. 401-407. 1. Bach, Johann Sebastian, 1685-1750. Works, Keyboard. I. T.
MT145.B14B6     786.4081     LC 58-10396

**Kirkpatrick, Ralph.**      **1.4529**
Interpreting Bach's Well–tempered clavier: a performer's discourse of method / Ralph Kirkpatrick. — New Haven: Yale University Press, c1984. xvii, 132 p.; 22 cm. Includes index. 1. Bach, Johann Sebastian, 1685-1750. Wohltemperierte Klavier. I. T. II. Title: Well-tempered clavier.
MT145.B14 K57 1984     786.1/092/4 19     LC 84-5811     ISBN 0300030584

**Williams, Peter F.**      **1.4530**
The organ music of J.S. Bach / by Peter Williams. — Cambridge [Eng.]; New York: Cambridge University Press, 1980-1984. 3 v.: music; 26 cm. (Cambridge studies in music) 1. Bach, Johann Sebastian, 1685-1750. Organ music. 2. Organ music — Analysis, appreciation. I. T. II. Series.
MT145.B14 W53 1980     786.6/22/4     LC 77-71431     ISBN 0521217237

**Blom, Eric, 1888-1959.**      • **1.4531**
Beethoven's pianoforte sonatas discussed. New York, Da Capo Press, 1968. viii, 251 p. music. 24 cm. (A Da Capo Press reprint edition) 'This Da Capo Press edition is an unabridged republication of the first edition published in 1938.' 'A republication of a series of annotations and essays contributed by degrees to the albums of records published by the Beethoven Sonata Society under the auspices of 'His master's voice.''—Foreword. 1. Beethoven, Ludwig van, 1770-1827. Sonatas, piano 2. Sonatas (Piano) — Analysis, appreciation. I. T.
MT145.B42 B59 1968     786.4/1/0924 19     LC 68-21092

**Tovey, Donald Francis, Sir, 1875-1940.**      • **1.4532**
A companion to Beethoven's pianoforte sonatas: complete analyses / by Donald Francis Tovey. — New York: AMS Press, 1976. xiv, 301 p.: music; 23 cm. Reprint of the 1931 ed. published by the Associated Board of the R.A.M and the R.C.M., London. 1. Beethoven, Ludwig van, 1770-1827. Sonatas, piano 2. Sonatas (Piano) — Analysis, appreciation. I. T.
MT145.B42 T6 1976     786.4/1/0924 19     LC 74-24243     ISBN 0404131174

**Kerman, Joseph, 1924-.**      **1.4533**
The Beethoven quartets / Joseph Kerman. — 1st ed. — Westport, Conn.: Greenwood Press, 1982, c1966. 386, viii p.: ill., port.; 24 cm. Reprint. Originally published: New York: Knopf, 1967. Includes indexes. 1. Beethoven, Ludwig van, 1770-1827. Quartets, strings. 2. String quartets — Analysis, appreciation. I. T.
MT145.B425 K47 1982     785.7/0092/4 19     LC 81-20275     ISBN 0313233721

**Schmitz, E. Robert (Elie Robert), 1889-1949.**      • **1.4534**
The piano works of Claude Debussy, by E. Robert Schmitz. Foreword by Virgil Thomson. New York, Dover Publications [1966, c1950] x, 234 p. illus., facsims., music, ports. 22 cm. 'An unabridged and corrected republication of

the work originally published in 1950.' 1. Debussy, Claude, 1862-1918. Works, piano. I. T.
MT145.D4 S3 1966     786.10924     *LC* 66-20423

## MT165–728 Instruments: Tuning. Techniques

**Meffen, John.**                                      **1.4535**
A guide to tuning musical instruments / John Meffen. — Newton Abbot, Devon; North Pomfret, Vt.: David & Charles, c1982. 160 p.: ill.; 23 cm. Includes index. 1. Tuning 2. Musical temperament I. T.
MT165.M44 1982     781.91 19     *LC* 84-121683     *ISBN* 0715381695

**Read, Gardner, 1913-.**                              **1.4536**
Contemporary instrumental techniques / by Gardner Read. — New York: Schirmer Books, c1976. xii, 259 p.: ill.; 26 cm. Includes indexes. 1. Instrumental music — Instruction and study I. T.
MT170.R39     785/.07     *LC* 75-27455     *ISBN* 0028721004

**Newman, William S.**                                 **1.4537**
The pianist's problems; a modern approach to efficient practice and musicianly performance [by] William S. Newman. With a pref. by Arthur Loesser. Illustrated by John V. Allcott. — 3d expanded ed. — New York: Harper & Row, [1974] xiv, 208 p.: illus.; 21 cm. 1. Piano — Practicing I. T.
MT220.N5 1974     786.3/04/1     *LC* 73-14275     *ISBN* 0060131810

**Clementi, Muzio, 1752-1832.**                        **1.4538**
Introduction to the art of playing on the piano forte; containing the elements of music, preliminary notions on fingering, and fifty fingered lessons. New introd. by Sandra P. Rosenblum. — New York: Da Capo Press, 1974. xxxix, 63 p.: music.; 31 cm. — (Da Capo Press music reprint series) Reprint of the 1st ed., 2d issue, 1801, published by Clementi, Banger, Hyde, Collard & Davis, London. 1. Piano — Methods I. T.
MT222.C617 1974     786.3/04/1     *LC* 70-125067     *ISBN* 0306700042

**Leimer, Karl, 1858-1944.**                           **1.4539**
[Modernes Klavierspiel nach Leimer-Gieseking. English] Piano technique consisting of the two complete books The shortest way to pianistic perfection and Rhythmics, dynamics, pedal and other problems of piano playing [by] Walter Gieseking [and] Karl Leimer. New York, Dover Publications [1972] 140 p. ports. 22 cm. 1. Piano — Methods I. Gieseking, Walter, 1895-1956. II. T. III. Title: Rhythmics, dynamics, pedal and other problems of piano playing.
MT222.L4983 1972     786.3/04/1     *LC* 72-82075     *ISBN* 0486228673

**Türk, Daniel Gottlob, 1750-1813.**                   **1.4540**
[Klavierschule. English] School of clavier playing, or, Instructions in playing the clavier for teachers & students / by Daniel Gottlob Türk; translation, introduction & notes by Raymond H. Haggh; [music autography by Helen M. Jenner]. — Lincoln: University of Nebraska Press, c1982. xxxvi, 563 p.: music; 24 cm. Translation of: Klavierschule. Based on the 1789 ed. 1. Keyboard instruments — Methods — Early works to 1800. I. Haggh, Raymond H., 1920- II. T.
MT222.T8513 1982     786.3/041 19     *LC* 81-14626     *ISBN* 0803223161

**Bach, Carl Philipp Emanuel, 1714-1788.**             • **1.4541**
Essay on the true art of playing keyboard instruments, translated and edited by William J. Mitchell. — [1st ed.]. — New York: W. W. Norton, [1949] xiii, 449 p.: port., music.; 24 cm. 1. Piano — Instruction and study — To 1800. 2. Musical accompaniment 3. Harpsichord — Instruction and study — To 1800. I. Mitchell, William John, 1906- ed. and tr. II. T.
MT224.B132     786.3     *LC* 48-9749

**Banowetz, Joseph.**                                  **1.4542**
The pianist's guide to pedaling / Joseph Banowetz; contributors, Dean Elder ... [et al.]. — Bloomington: Indiana University Press, c1985. x, 309 p.: music; 24 cm. Includes index. 1. Piano — Instruction and study — Pedaling I. Elder, Dean. II. T.
MT227.B2 1985     786.3/5 19     *LC* 84-47534     *ISBN* 0253344948

**Neĭgauz, Genrikh Gustavovich, 1888-1964.**           **1.4543**
The art of piano playing [by] Heinrich Neuhaus. Translated by K. A. Leibovitch. — New York: Praeger Publishers, [1973] xiii, 240 p.: illus.; 23 cm. Translation of Ob iskusstve fortep'iannoĭ igry. 1. Piano music — Interpretation (Phrasing, dynamics, etc.) 2. Piano — Instruction and study I. T.
MT235.N413     786.3/04/1     *LC* 72-93432

**Nurmi, Ruth.**                                       **1.4544**
A plain & easy introduction to the harpsichord / Ruth Nurmi. — 1st ed. — Albuquerque: University of New Mexico Press, [1974] xiv, 248 p.: ill., music; 26 cm. Includes index. 1. Harpsichord — Instruction and study. I. T.
MT252.N87     786.2/21     *LC* 73-92998     *ISBN* 0826303242

## MT260–338 String Instruments

**Szigeti, Joseph, 1892-1973.**                        • **1.4545**
Szigeti on the violin. New York, F. A. Praeger [1970, c1969] x, 234 p. music, port. 24 cm. 1. Violin — Instruction and study I. T.
MT260.S99 1970     787.1/07/12 19     *LC* 71-95361

**Mozart, Leopold, 1719-1787.**                        • **1.4546**
A treatise on the fundamental principles of violin playing / by Leopold Mozart; translated by Editha Knocker; with a pref. by Alfred Einstein. — 2d ed. — London: Oxford University Press, 1951. — xxxv, 234 p.: ill., facsims., music; 22 cm. Includes index. 1. Violin — Instruction and study — To 1800 I. T.
MT262.M913 1951     *LC* 51-7192     *ISBN* 0193185024

## MT339–538 Wind Instruments

**Farkas, Philip.**                                    **1.4547**
The art of brass playing: a treatise on the formation and use of the brass player's embouchure / by Philip Farkas. — Bloomington: Ind., Brass Publications, c1962. 65 p.: ill. 1. Wind instruments — Instruction and study. I. T.
MT339.F27     *LC* 62-20149

**Porter, Maurice M.**                                 **1.4548**
The embouchure, by Maurice M. Porter. — London: Boosey & Hawkes, 1967. xiii, 144 p.: table, diagrs.; 22 cm. 1. Brass instruments — Instruction and study. I. T.
MT339.P67     788/.07     *LC* 67-20054

**Bartolozzi, Bruno.**                                 **1.4549**
New sounds for woodwind / Bruno Bartolozzi; translated and edited by Reginald Smith Brindle. — 2d ed. — London; New York: Oxford University Press, 1982. 113 p., [1] folded leaves of plates: ill., music; 23 cm. + 1 sound disc (45 rpm., mono.; 6 in.) Sound disc in pocket. 1. Woodwind instruments — Instruction and study. I. T.
MT339.5.B37 1982     788/.05/0712 19     *LC* 80-40519     *ISBN* 0193186071

**Saucier, Gene Allen.**                               **1.4550**
Woodwinds: fundamental performance techniques / Gene A. Saucier. — New York: Schirmer Books; London: Collier Macmillan, c1981. xi, 241 p.: ill.; 28 cm. 1. Woodwind instruments — Instruction and study. I. T.
MT339.5.S3     788/.05/0712 19     *LC* 80-5223     *ISBN* 0028723007

**Rowland-Jones, Anthony.**                            **1.4551**
Recorder technique. — London; New York: Oxford University Press, [1969] 159 p.: ill; 19cm. 'Fifth impression, corrected 1969.' 'Based upon a series of articles printed in The recorder news.' 'The recorder repertoire': p.[16]-28. 'Summary of makes of recorders':p.[136]-140. 'Supplement':p.[141]-147. I. T.
MT340.R6x

**Quantz, Johann Joachim, 1697-1773.**                 • **1.4552**
On playing the flute / Johann Joachim Quantz; a complete translation [from the German] with an introduction and notes by Edward R. Reilly. — London: Faber, [c1966]. xxxix, 365 p., [3] f. de planches: musique; 26 cm. Translation of Versuch einer Anweisung die Flüte traversiere zu spielen. 1752. 1. Flute — Instruction and study. 2. Flute music — Interpretation (Phrasing, dynamics, etc.) 3. Musical accompaniment I. Reilly, Edward R. II. T.
MT342 Q313     788.51     *LC* 65-22285     *ISBN* 0571066984

**Goossens, Leon, 1897-.**                             **1.4553**
Oboe / Leon Goossens and Edwin Roxburgh. — 1st American ed. — New York: Schirmer Books, 1977. xv, 238 p., [8] leaves of plates: ill.; 22 cm. — (Yehudi Menuhin music guides) Includes index. 1. Oboe — Instruction and study. I. Roxburgh, Edwin. joint author. II. T.
MT360.G66     788/.7/07     *LC* 77-15886     *ISBN* 0028714504

**Sprenkle, Robert.**                                  **1.4554**
The art of oboe playing, by Robert Sprenkle [and] David Ledet. Evanston, Ill., Summy-Birchard Pub. Co. [1961] 96 p. ill. 1. Oboe — Instruction and study I. Ledet, David. II. T.
MT360 S77     *LC* 61-39356

**Stein, Keith.**      **1.4555**
The art of clarinet playing / by Keith Stein. — Princeton, N.J.: Summy-Birchard Music, 1958. 80 p.: ill., music; 28 cm. — 'Suggested literature for the clarinet': p. 62-70. 1. Clarinet — Instruction and study. I. T.
MT380.S84 1958x

**Thurston, Frederick.**      **1.4556**
Clarinet technique. — 4th ed. — London; New York: Oxford University Press, 1985. viii, 107 p.: ill music; 19cm. I. T.
MT380.T5

**Camden, Archie, 1888-1979.**      • **1.4557**
Bassoon technique. London, Oxford University Press, 1962. 74 p. ill. 1. Bassoon — Instruction and study 2. Bassoon music — Bibliography I. T.
MT400 C3      *LC* 63-1150

**Spencer, William G.**      **1.4558**
The art of bassoon playing / by William Spencer. Revised by Frederick A. Mueller. — Evanston, Ill.: Summy-Birchard, 1969. 72 p.: ill; 28cm. 'Selected literature and discography': p. 67-72. 1. Bassoon — Instrument and study. 2. Bassoon music — Discography. I. Mueller, Frederick A. II. T.
MT400.S74 1969

**Schuller, Gunther.**      • **1.4559**
Horn technique. London, Oxford University Press, 1962. 118 p. ill. 1. Horn (Musical instrument) — Instruction and study 2. Horn music — Bibliography I. T.
MT420 S35      *LC* 62-2101

**Dale, Delbert A.**      • **1.4560**
Trumpet technique / by Delbert A. Dale. — London; New York; Toronto: Oxford University Press, 1965. viii, 93 p.: ill., music; 19 cm. 1. Trumpet — Instruction and study. 2. Trumpet music — Bibliography. I. T.
MT440.D34      788.10712      *LC* 66-4613

## MT655–720 PERCUSSION INSTRUMENTS

**Blades, James.**      • **1.4561**
Orchestral percussion technique. London, Oxford University Press, 1961. 85 p. ill. 1. Percussion instruments — Instruction and study I. T.
MT655 B6      *LC* 62-2634

## MT820–892 Singing

**Burgin, John Carroll.**      **1.4562**
Teaching singing. — Metuchen, N.J.: Scarecrow Press, 1973. 290 p.; 22 cm. 1. Singing — Instruction and study I. T.
MT820.B94      784.9/32      *LC* 72-10594      *ISBN* 0810805650

**Rose. Arnold.**      • **1.4563**
The singer and the voice; vocal physiology and technique for singers. Foreword by Harold Rosenthal. — [2d ed.]. — New York: St. Martin's Press, [1971] 267 p.: illus.; 23 cm. 1. Singing — Instruction and study I. T.
MT820.R797S6 1971      784.9/32      *LC* 72-155764

**Schiøtz, Aksel, 1906-.**      • **1.4564**
The singer and his art. — [1st ed.]. — New York: Harper & Row, [1969, c1970] xvi, 214 p.: music; 22 cm. 1. Singing I. T.
MT820.S353S5      784/.023      *LC* 69-15259

**Miller, Richard, 1926-.**      **1.4565**
English, French, German and Italian techniques of singing: a study in national tonal preferences and how they relate to functional efficiency / by Richard Miller. Metuchen, N.J.: Scarecrow Press, 1977. xviii, 257 p.: ill.; 23 cm. Includes index. 1. Singing — Instruction and study — History and criticism. I. T.
MT823.M55      784.9/32      *LC* 76-58554      *ISBN* 0810810204

**Christy, Van Ambrose, 1900-.**      • **1.4566**
Expressive singing; a textbook for school or studio class or private teaching [by] Van A. Christy. — Rev. ed. — Dubuque, Iowa: W. C. Brown Co., [1967-. v.: illus., music.; 28 cm. — (Brown music series) 1. Singing — Methods I. T.
MT825.C5 1967      784/.9/3      *LC* 67-22708

**Vennard, William.**      • **1.4567**
Singing, the mechanism and the technic / by William Vennard; illus. by the author. — Rev. ed., greatly enl. — New York: C. Fischer, 1967. v, 275 p.: ill., music; 28 cm. 1. Singing — Methods I. T.
MT825.V4 1967      *LC* 67-49163

**Garcia, Manuel, 1805-1906.**      **1.4568**
A complete treatise on the art of singing / by Manuel Garcia II. 2d part, complete and unabridged; the editions of 1847 and 1872 collated, edited, and translated by Donald V. Paschke. — New York: Da Capo Press, 1975, c1972. xvi, 261 p.: ill.; 25 cm. (Da Capo Press music reprint series) Translation of v. 2 of École de Garcia: traité complet de l'art du chant. Reprint of the ed. published by D. V. Paschke. 1. Singing — Methods I. Paschke, Donald V. tr. II. T.
MT835.G313 1975      784.9/3      *LC* 74-23382      *ISBN* 0306706601

**Ottman, Robert W.**      **1.4569**
Music for sight singing / Robert W. Ottman. — 3rd ed. — Englewood Cliffs, N.J.: Prentice-Hall, c1986. xviii p., 339 p. of music; 23 cm. Some selections contain words. 1. Sight-singing I. T.
MT870.O86 1986      *LC* 85-25616      *ISBN* 0136075320

**Bernac, Pierre.**      • **1.4570**
The interpretation of French song. Translations of song texts, by Winifred Radford. New York, Praeger [1970] xiv, 326 p. music. 23 cm. 1. Songs — France — Interpretation (Phrasing, dynamics, etc.) I. T.
MT892.B4      784.9/34      *LC* 76-79069

**Lehmann, Lotte.**      **1.4571**
Eighteen song cycles; studies in their interpretation. With a foreword by Neville Cardus. New York, Praeger Publishers [1972] xiii, 185 p. 21 cm. 1. Singing — Interpretation (Phrasing, dynamics, etc.) 2. Song cycles — Interpretation (Phrasing, dynamics, etc.) I. T.
MT892.L46 E4 1972      784.3/007      *LC* 73-171026

## MT955 Opera Production

**Eaton, Quaintance.**      • **1.4572**
Opera production, a handbook. Minneapolis, University of Minnesota Press [1961-74] 2 v. 24 cm. Vol. 2 includes Production problems of Handel's operas, by Randolph Mickelson. 1. Handel, George Frideric, 1685-1759. Operas. 2. Operas — Stories, plots, etc. 3. Opera — Production and direction I. Mickelson, Randolph. Production problems in Handel's operas. II. T. III. Title: Production problems in Handel's operas.
MT955.E25      782.07      *LC* 61-16843      *ISBN* 0816606897

**Van Witsen, Leo, 1912-.**      **1.4573**
Costuming for opera: who wears what and why / Leo Van Witsen. — Bloomington: Indiana University Press, c1981. xxiii, 232 p.: ill. 1. Operas — Stage guides 2. Costume 3. Opera — Production and direction I. T.
MT955.V36      MT955 V36      782.1/07/3 19      *LC* 79-3250      *ISBN* 0253132258

# N    Fine Arts

## N Visual Arts (General)

### N25–55 Reference Works

**The Encyclopedia of visual art / general editor, Sir Lawrence** **1.4574**
**Gowing.**
American ed. — Englewood Cliffs, N.J.: Prentice-Hall, 1983. 2 v. 'An Equinox book.' 1. Art — Collected works. I. Gowing, Lawrence.
N25.E53 1983    709 19    *LC* 83-3428    *ISBN* 0132765438

**Encyclopedia of world art.** • **1.4575**
New York, McGraw-Hill [1959-c1983] 16 v. illus., maps, plans., plates (part col.) 31 cm. Added t.p., in Italian. Added t.p., v. 16: Supplement: World art in our time. Vol. 15: Index. Vol. 16 edited by Bernard S. Myers. 'All articles have been translated into English from the original language ... and correlated with the final editorial work of the Italian edition.' 1. Art — Dictionaries. I. Myers, Bernard Samuel, 1908- II. Title: Enciclopedia universale dell' arte.
N31.E4833    703 19    *LC* 59-13433

**Murray, Peter, 1920-.** • **1.4576**
The Penguin dictionary of art and artists / Peter and Linda Murray. — 5th ed. — Harmondsworth, Middlesex, England; New York, N.Y., U.S.A.: Penguin, 1983. xiv, 457 p.; 20 cm. Rev. ed. of: A dictionary of art and artists. 4th ed. 1976. 1. Art — Dictionaries. 2. Artists — Biography. I. Murray, Linda. II. Murray, Peter, 1920- A dictionary of art and artists. III. T.
N31.M8 1983    703/.21 19    *LC* 84-113289    *ISBN* 0140511334

**The Thames and Hudson dictionary of art and artists /** **1.4577**
**consulting editor, Herbert Read.**
Rev. ed. / Nikos Stangos. — London: Thames and Hudson, 1985, c1984. 352 p.: ill., ports.; 22 cm. 1. Art — Dictionaries 2. Artists — Dictionaries. I. Stangos, Nikos. II. Read, Herbert Edward, Sir, 1893-1968. III. Title: Dictionary of art and artists IV. Title: Art and artists V. Title: The Thames and Hudson encyclopaedia of the arts
N31.R4 1985    *LC* 84-50342    *ISBN* 0500234027

**McGraw–Hill dictionary of art. Edited by Bernard S. Myers.** • **1.4578**
**Assistant editor: Shirley D. Myers.**
New York: McGraw-Hill, [1969] 5 v.: illus. (part col.); 29 cm. 1. Art — Dictionaries. I. Myers, Bernard Samuel, 1908- ed. II. Myers, Shirley D. ed.
N33.M23    703    *LC* 68-26314

**The Oxford companion to art; edited by Harold Osborne.** • **1.4579**
Oxford: Clarendon P., 1970. xii, 1277 p., 2 plates.: illus. (incl. 8 col.), plans.; 25 cm. 1. Art — Dictionaries. 2. Artists — Dictionaries. I. Osborne, Harold, 1905- ed.
N33.O9    703    *LC* 71-526168    *ISBN* 019866107X

**Walker, John Albert, 1938-.** **1.4580**
Glossary of art, architecture, and design since 1945: terms and labels describing movements styles and groups derived from the vocabulary of artists and critics / John A Walker. — 2d rev. ed. — London: Bingley; Hamden, Ct.: Linnet Books, 1977. 352 p.; 23 cm. 1. Art — Terminology. I. T.
N34.W34 1977    709/.04    *LC* 77-3201    *ISBN* 0208015434

**Bénézit, Emmanuel, 1854-1920.** **1.4581**
Dictionnaire critique et documentaire des peintres, scu!pteurs, dessinateurs et graveurs de tous les temps et de tous les pays / par un groupe d'écrivains spécialistes français et étrangers. Nouv. éd. entièrement refondue, revue et corr. sous la direction des héritiers de E. Bénézit. — Paris: Gründ, c1976. 10 v.; 25 cm. At head of title: E. Bénézit. On cover: Dictionnaire des peintres, sculpteurs, dessinateurs et graveurs. 1. Artists — Biography. 2. Artists' marks 3. Monograms I. T. II. Title: Dictionnaire critique et documentaire des peintres, sculpteurs, dessinateurs et graveurs ... III. Title: Dictionnaire des peintres, sculpteurs, dessinateurs et graveurs.
N40.B47 1976    709/.2/2 B    *LC* 76-479549    *ISBN* 2700001494

**Havlice, Patricia Pate.** **1.4582**
Index to artistic biography. — Metuchen, N.J.: Scarecrow Press, 1973. 2 v. (viii, 1362 p.); 22 cm. 1. Artists — Biography — Indexes. I. T.
N40.H38    709/.2/2    *LC* 72-6412    *ISBN* 0810805405

**Petersen, Karen, 1943-.** **1.4583**
Women artists: recognition and reappraisal from the early Middle Ages to the twentieth century / Karen Petersen & J. J. Wilson. — New York: New York University Press, 1976. 212 p.: ill.; 25 cm. Includes index. 1. Women artists — Biography. I. Wilson, J. J., 1936- joint author. II. T.
N40.P45 1976b    709/.2/2 B    *LC* 76-23505    *ISBN* 081476567X

**Thieme, Ulrich, 1865-1922. ed.** • **1.4584**
Allgemeines Lexikon der bildenden Künstler von der Antike bis zur Gegenwart. Unter Mitwirkung von 300 Fachgelehrten des In– und Auslandes hrsg. von Ulrich Thieme und Felix Becker. Leipzig, W. Engelmann, 1907-50. 37 v. Statement of contributors varies. 1. Artists — Dictionaries I. Becker, Felix, 1864-1928. II. Willis, Frederick Charles, 1883- III. Vollmer, Hans, 1878- IV. T.
N40 T4

**Vollmer, Hans, 1878-.** **1.4585**
Allgemeines Lexikon der bildenden Künstler des XX. Jahrhunderts. Unter Mitwirkung von Fachgelehrten des In–und Auslandes. Leipzig, E. A. Seemann, 1953-62. 6 v. 27 cm. A continuation of Ulrich Thieme's 'Allgemeines Lexikon der bildenden Künstler von der Antike bis zur Gegenwart.' 1. Artists — Dictionaries — German. I. Thieme, Ulrich, 1865-1922. Allgemeines Lexikon der bildenden Künstler von der Antike bis zur Gegenwart. II. T.
N40.V6    *LC* 54-19064

**Women as interpreters of the visual arts, 1820–1979 / edited by** **1.4586**
**Claire Richter Sherman with Adele M. Holcomb.**
Westport, Conn.: Greenwood Press, c1981. 483 p.: ill. — (Contributions in women's studies. no. 18 0147-104X) Includes index. 1. Women artists — Biography. 2. Art, Modern — 19th century 3. Art, Modern — 20th century I. Sherman, Claire Richter. II. Holcomb, Adele M. III. Series.
N40.W7    709/.2/2 B    *LC* 80-785    *ISBN* 0313220565

**Fine, Elsa Honig.** **1.4587**
Women & art: a history of women painters and sculptors from the renaissance to the 20th century. — Montclair, N.J.: Allanheld & Schram/Prior, c1978. xiii, 240 p., [1] leaf of plates: ill.; 26 cm. Includes index. 1. Women artists — Biography. 2. Art, Renaissance 3. Art, Modern I. T.
N43.F56 1978    709/.2/2 B    *LC* 77-15897    *ISBN* 0839001878

**Petteys, Chris.** **1.4588**
Dictionary of women artists: an international dictionary of women artists born before 1900 / Chris Petteys, with the assistance of Hazel Gustow, Ferris Olin, Verna Ritchie. — Boston, Mass.: G.K. Hall, c1985. xviii, 851 p.: port.; 29 cm. Includes index. 1. Women artists — Biography — Dictionaries. I. T.
N43.P47 1985    709/.2/2 B 19    *LC* 84-22511    *ISBN* 0816184569

**Slatkin, Wendy.** **1.4589**
Women artists in history: from antiquity to the 20th century / Wendy Slatkin. — Englewood Cliffs, N.J.: Prentice-Hall, c1985. xv, 191 p.: ill.; 23 cm. Includes index. 1. Women artists — Biography. I. T.
N43.S57 1985    709/.2/2 B 19    *LC* 84-11481    *ISBN* 013961821X

**American art directory. v. [1]– 1898–.** • **1.4590**
New York, R. R. Bowker. v. illus. (part col.) ports. 23-27 cm. Vols. 36-37 (1941/45-1945/48) called pt. 1, Organizations. Frequency varies. At head of title, v. 38-    ; American Federation of Arts. Title varies: 1898-1945/48 (v. 1-37) American art annual. Founded and for many years edited by F. N. Levy. Vols. 1-37 published in Washington [etc.] by the American Federation of Arts [etc.] The biographical material formerly included in the directory is issued separately as Who's who in American art, 1933/37- 1. Art — U.S. — Directories. 2. Art — Canada — Directories. 3. Art — Spanish America — Directories. I. Levy, Florence Nightingale, 1870-1947, ed. II. American Federation of Arts.
N50.A54    705.8    *LC* 99-1016

**Fine arts market place. 1973/74 / ed. by Paul Cummings.** **1.4591**
New York: R. R. Bowker, 1973. 258 p. 1. Art — United States — Directories. I. R.R. Bowker Company.
N51.F55    380.1/45/7002573    *LC* 73-2497    *ISBN* 0835206262

# N61–79 Theory. Philosophy. Aesthetics

**Hegel, Georg Wilhelm Friedrich, 1770-1831.**      **1.4592**
[Ästhetik. English] Aesthetics: lectures on fine art / by G. W. F. Hegel; translated by T. M. Knox. — Oxford: Clarendon Press, 1975. 2 v. (xxi, 1289 p, [1] leaf of plates): ill.; 23 cm. Translation of Ästhetik. 1. Aesthetics I. T.
N64.H413    700/.1    *LC* 75-318549    *ISBN* 0198243715

**Lessing, Gotthold Ephraim, 1729-1781.**      • **1.4593**
Laocoön, Nathan the Wise, Minna von Barnhelm [by] Lessing. London, J.M. Dent; New York, E. P. Dutton; 1930. xiv p., 1 l., 296 p. 1 illus. (Everyman's library. Poetry and the drama; 843) 'Translated with an introduction by William A. Steel.' 1. Aesthetics — Early works to 1800. I. Steel, William A. II. T. III. Title: Nathan the Wise. IV. Title: Minna von Barnhelm.
N64.L413    *LC* 37-5588

**Panofsky, Erwin, 1892-1968.**      • **1.4594**
The Codex Huygens and Leonardo da Vinci's art theory; the Pierpont Morgan Library, Codex M.A. 1139. Westport, Conn., Greenwood Press [1971] 138, [90] p. 117 illus. 24 cm. Reprint of the 1940 ed. 1. Leonardo, da Vinci, 1452-1519. 2. Huygens, Constantijn, heer van Zuilichem, 1628-1697. 3. Anatomy, Artistic 4. Proportion (Art) 5. Perspective I. Pierpont Morgan Library. Mss. (M.A. 1139) II. T.
N65.L4 P3 1971    701    *LC* 79-109814    *ISBN* 0837143063

**Bernheimer, Richard.**      • **1.4595**
The nature of representation; a phenomenological inquiry. Edited by H. W. Janson. New York, New York University Press [c1961] 249 p. 22 cm. 1. Art — Philosophy I. T.
N66.B46    701.17    *LC* 61-8057

**Dewey, John, 1859-1952.**      • **1.4596**
Art as experience. — New York: Capricorn Books, [1959, c1934] vii, 355 p.; 19 cm. — (A Putnam Capricorn book, Cap 1) 1. Aesthetics 2. Experience I. T.
N66.D4 1959    701    *LC* 58-59756

**Kubler, George, 1912-.**      • **1.4597**
The shape of time; remarks on the history of things. New Haven, Yale University Press, 1962. 136 p. 1. Art — Philosophy 2. Aesthetics I. T.
N66 K8    *LC* 62-8250

**Neutra, Richard Joseph, 1892-1970.**      • **1.4598**
Survival through design. — London; New York: Oxford University Press, [1969] xvi, 384 p.: illus., ports.; 21 cm. — (A Galaxy book, GB285) 1. Art — Philosophy I. T.
N66.N38 1969    720/.1    *LC* 76-94526

**Read, Herbert Edward, Sir, 1893-1968.**      • **1.4599**
Icon and idea: the function of art in the development of human consciousness / Herbert Read. — New York: Schocken Books, 1965. 161 p., 44 leaves of plates: ill.; 21 cm. — (Schocken paperbacks; SB105) 1. Art — Philosophy 2. Aesthetics I. T.
N66.R4 1965    701    *LC* 65-25410

**Santayana, George, 1863-1952.**      • **1.4600**
The sense of beauty, being the outlines of aesthetic theory. With a foreword by Philip Blair Rice. — New York: Modern Library, [1955] xii, 268 p.; 19 cm. — (The Modern library of the world's best books, 292) 1. Aesthetics I. T.
N66.S23 1955a    701.17 101*    *LC* 55-10656

**Kandinsky, Wassily, 1866-1944.**      • **1.4601**
Concerning the spiritual in art, and painting in particular. 1912 / a version of the Sadleir translation, with considerable re–translation by Francis Golffing, Michael Harrison and Ferdinand Ostertag. New York: Wittenborn, Schultz, 1947. 95 p.: illus., port.; 26 cm. (The Documents of modern art) 'Prose poems (1912-1937)': p. 79-91. 1. Aesthetics 2. Painting I. Sadleir, Michael, 1888-1957. II. Golffing, Francis. III. T. IV. Series.
N68.K3 1947    *LC* 47-12026

**Worringer, Wilhelm, 1881-1965.**      • **1.4602**
Abstraction and empathy; a contribution to the psychology of style. Translated by Michael Bullock. New York, International Universities Press, 1953. 144 p. 1. Aesthetics 2. Art — Philosophy I. T.
N68 W613    *LC* 53-12034

**Croce, Benedetto, 1866-1952.**      • **1.4603**
Guide to aesthetics = (Breviario di estetica) / translated, with an introd., by Patrick Romanell. — Indianapolis: Bobbs-Merrill, 1965. — xxxii, 88 p.; 21 cm.

— (Library of liberal arts.) 1. Aesthetics — Addresses, essays, lectures I. T. II. Series.
N69.C813    *LC* 65-26527

## N70 SPECIAL ASPECTS

**Arnheim, Rudolf.**      • **1.4604**
Toward a psychology of art; collected essays. — Berkeley: University of California Press, 1966. viii, 369 p.: illus. (part col.); 27 cm. 1. Art — Psychology 2. Perception I. T.
N70.A69    701.15    *LC* 66-10692

**Arnheim, Rudolf.**      • **1.4605**
Visual thinking. — Berkeley: University of California Press, [1969] xi, 345 p.: illus. (part col.); 26 cm. 1. Visual perception 2. Art — Philosophy I. T.
N70.A693    701    *LC* 71-76335

**Berenson, Bernard, 1865-1959.**      **1.4606**
Aesthetics and history, [by] Bernard Berenson. London, Constable, [1955] 242 p. 1. Aesthetics 2. Art — History and criticism I. T.
N70.B465x    *LC* 52-1732

**Burnham, Jack, 1931-.**      **1.4607**
Great western salt works; essays on the meaning of post–formalist art. — New York: G. Braziller, [1974] 165 p.: illus.; 23 cm. 1. Art — Philosophy 2. Symbolism of numbers 3. Signs and symbols I. T.
N70.B835    701    *LC* 73-92677    *ISBN* 0807607401

**Collingwood, R. G. (Robin George), 1889-1943.**      • **1.4608**
The Principles of art / by R.G. Collingwood. — Oxford: Clarendon Press, 1938. xi, 317, [1] p.; 23 cm. 1. Aesthetics 2. Art — Philosophy I. T.
N70.C63    *LC* 38-22978

**Gombrich, E. H. (Ernst Hans), 1909-.**      • **1.4609**
Art and illusion; a study in the psychology of pictorial representation [by] E. H. Gombrich. [2d ed., 3d print. Princeton, N.J.] Princeton University Press [1969] xxxi, 466 p. illus. (part col.) 26 cm. (Bollingen series, 35. The A. W. Mellon lectures in the fine arts, 5) 1. Art — Psychology I. T.
N70.G615 1969    701.15    *LC* 71-12016

**Hogarth, William, 1697-1764.**      • **1.4610**
The analysis of beauty. With the rejected passages from the manuscript drafts and autobiographical notes. Edited with an introd. by Joseph Burke. Oxford, Clarendon Press, 1955. lxii, 244 p. plates, facsims. With facsimile reproduction of original title page. 1. Aesthetics — Early works to 1800 I. T.
N70 H7 1955    *LC* 55-13860

**Kris, Ernst, 1900-1957.**      • **1.4611**
Psychoanalytic explorations in art / Ernst Kris. — New York: International Universities Press, c1952, (1979 printing). 358 p., 18 leaves of plates: ill. 1. Art — Psychology 2. Psychoanalysis I. T.
N70.K84    *LC* 52-10509    *ISBN* 0823644405

**Langer, Susanne Katherina Knauth, 1895-.**      • **1.4612**
Problems of art; ten philosophical lectures. — New York: Scribner, [1957] 184 p.; 21 cm. 1. Art — Philosophy 2. Aesthetics — Addresses, essays, lectures. I. T.
N70.L28    701    *LC* 57-6068

**Léger, Fernand, 1881-1955.**      **1.4613**
[Fonctions de la peinture. English] Functions of painting, by Fernand Léger. Translated by Alexandra Anderson. Edited and introduced by Edward F. Fry. With a pref. by George L. K. Morris. New York, Viking Press [1973] xxxiv, 221 p. illus. 22 cm. (The Documents of 20th-century art) Translation of Fonctions de la peinture. 1. Art — Philosophy 2. Aesthetics 3. Art and society I. T. II. Series.
N70.L45213 1973    701    *LC* 71-184540    *ISBN* 0670332216 *ISBN* 0670019453

**Malraux, André, 1901-1976.**      • **1.4614**
The psychology of art; translated by Stuart Gilbert. [New York] Pantheon Books [1949-50] 3 v. illus. (part mounted col.) 29 cm. (Bollingen series. 24) Translation of Psychologie de l'art. 1. Art — Psychology 2. Art — Philosophy I. T. II. Title: Psychologie de l'art. III. Series.
N70.M33    701.15    *LC* 49-48802 rev 2*

**Margolis, Joseph Zalman, 1924-.**      **1.4615**
Art and philosophy / by Joseph Margolis. — Atlantic Highlands, N.J.: Humanities Press, 1980. vi, 350 p.; 24 cm. — (Eclipse books) Includes indexes. 1. Art — Philosophy I. T.
N70.M34 1980    701    *LC* 76-19063    *ISBN* 0391006452

**Taine, Hippolyte, 1828-1893.**    • **1.4616**
Lectures on art, by H. Taine .. tr. by John Durand ... New York: Holt, 1889. 2 v. 20 cm. 1. Art — Addresses, essays, lectures. I. Durand, John, 1822-1908. II. T.
N70.T18     *LC* 36-16839

**Tolstoy, Leo, graf, 1828-1910.**    • **1.4617**
What is art? and essays on art, by Tolstóy, translated by Aylmer Maude. [London, New York,] Oxford university press, H. Milford [1932?] xix, [1], 339 p. 16 cm. (The World's classics. 331) "What is art?' first appeared in 1898; the other essays in the years given in the contents. In 'The World's classics' the Maude translation was first published in 1930.' —On art (c. 1895-7).—Tolstóy's preface to 'What is art?' (1898).—What is art? (1898).—Appendices to What is art?—Preface to von Polenz's novel Der Büttnerbauer (1902).—An afterword, by Tolstóy, to Chékhov's story, Darling (1905) 1. Arts I. Maude, Aylmer, 1858-1938. tr. II. T.
N70.T72 1932    701     *LC* 33-5715

# N71 PSYCHOLOGY OF ART

**Arnheim, Rudolf.**    **1.4618**
Art and visual perception: a psychology of the creative eye / Rudolf Arnheim. — New version, expanded and rev. ed. — Berkeley: University of California Press, [1974] x, 508 p., [2] leaves of plates: ill.; 23 cm. Includes index. 1. Art — Psychology 2. Visual perception I. T.
N71.A67 1974    701/.15    *LC* 73-87587     *ISBN* 0520023277

**Berger, John.**    **1.4619**
About looking / John Berger. — 1st American ed. — New York: Pantheon Books, c1980. 198 p.: ill.; 22 cm. 1. Art — Psychology 2. Visual perception 3. Meaning (Psychology) I. T.
N71.B398 1980    701/.1/5    *LC* 79-3615     *ISBN* 0394511247

**Burnham, Jack, 1931-.**    **1.4620**
The structure of art / by Jack Burnham; assisted by Charles Harper and Judith Benjamin Burnham. — Revised edition. New York: G. Braziller, c1973. xii, 195 p.: ill., facsims.; 25 cm. Includes index. 1. Art — Psychology 2. Form (Aesthetics) I. Harper, Charles. joint author. II. Burnham, Judith Benjamin, joint author. III. T.
N71.B86 1973    701.15    *LC* 75-143195     *ISBN* 0807605956

**Ehrenzweig, Anton, 1908-1966.**    • **1.4621**
The hidden order of art; a study in the psychology of artistic imagination. — Berkeley: University of California Press, 1967. xiv, 306 p.: illus.; 23 cm. 1. Art — Psychology 2. Imagination I. T.
N71.E5 1967    701.15    *LC* 67-20443

**Feldman, Edmund Burke.**    **1.4622**
Varieties of visual experience / Edmund Burke Feldman. — 3rd ed. — Englewood Cliffs, N.J.: Prentice-Hall; New York: H.N. Abrams, 1987. 528 p.: ill. (some col.); 30 cm. Includes index. 1. Art — Psychology 2. Composition (Art) 3. Visual perception I. T.
N71.F4 1987    701 19    *LC* 86-9333     *ISBN* 0139406026

**Feldman, Edmund Burke.**    **1.4623**
The artist / Edmund Burke Feldman. — Englewood Cliffs, N.J.: Prentice-Hall, c1982. viii, 231 p.: ill.; 24 cm. Includes index. 1. Artists — Psychology 2. Art and society I. T.
N71.F43 1982    701/.1/5 19    *LC* 81-21040     *ISBN* 0130490318

**Gombrich, E. H. (Ernst Hans), 1909-.**    **1.4624**
Art, perception and reality [by] E. H. Gombrich, Julian Hochberg [and] Max Black. Baltimore, Johns Hopkins University Press [1972] x, 132 p. illus. 24 cm. (Alvin and Fanny Blaustein Thalheimer lectures. 1970) 1. Art — Psychology 2. Visual perception I. Hochberg, Julian E. II. Black, Max, 1909- III. T. IV. Series.
N71.G64    701/.17    *LC* 76-186514     *ISBN* 0801813549

**Wittkower, Rudolf.**    **1.4625**
Born under Saturn; the character and conduct of artists: a documented history from antiquity to the French Revolution [by] Rudolf and Margot Wittkower. New York, Random House [1963] 344 p. illus. 25 cm. Includes bibliography. 1. Artists — Psychology 2. Artists I. Wittkower, Margot. joint author. II. T.
N71.W54    706.972    *LC* 63-7128

**Cardinal, Roger.**    **1.4626**
Outsider art. — New York: Praeger Publishers, [1972, i.e. 1973] 192 p.: illus. (part col.); 26 cm. 1. Art and mental illness I. T.
N71.5.C37 1973    709/.2/2    *LC* 72-81584

# N72 ART IN RELATION TO OTHER SUBJECTS, A–Z

**Nishida, Kitarō, 1870-1945.**    **1.4627**
Art and morality. Translated by David A. Dilworth [and] Valdo H. Viglielmo. — Honolulu: University Press of Hawaii, [1973] xi, 216 p.; 24 cm. 'An East-West Center book.' Translation of Geijutsu to dōtoku. 1. Art and morals I. T.
N72.E8 N5713 1973    111.8    *LC* 72-92067     *ISBN* 082480256X

**Feminism and art history: questioning the litany / edited by**    **1.4628**
**Norma Broude and Mary D. Garrard.**
1st ed. — New York: Harper & Row, c1982. ix, 358 p.: ill.; 24 cm. — (Icon editions) 1. Feminism and art — Addresses, essays, lectures. 2. Feminism in art — Addresses, essays, lectures. I. Broude, Norma. II. Garrard, Mary D.
N72.F45 F44 1982    701/.03 19    *LC* 81-48062     *ISBN* 0064305252

**Gerbrands, A. A. (Adrianus Alexander), 1917-.**    • **1.4629**
Art as an element of culture, especially in Negro–Africa. Leiden E.J. Brill 1957. 158p. (Mededelingen van het Rijksmuseum voor Volkenkunde, Leiden, no. 12) 1. Art and society 2. Art, Primitive 3. Art, African 4. Negro art I. T.
N72 G413    *LC* 59-25978

**Hauser, Arnold, 1892-1978.**    • **1.4630**
The social history of art / Arnold Hauser; translated in collaboration with the author by Stanley Godman. — New York: Knopf, 1952. 2 v. (1022 p.): ill. 1. Art and society 2. Art — History I. T.
N72.S6 H353 1951a    N72.H353 1951a.    *LC* 51-13993

**Herbert, Eugenia W.**    • **1.4631**
The artist and social reform: France and Belgium, 1885–1898. New Haven, Yale University Press, 1961. xvi, 236 p. ill. (Yale historical publications. Miscellany 74) 1. Art and society 2. Art — France 3. Art — Belgium 4. France — Social conditions 5. Belgium — Social conditions I. T.
N72 H46    *LC* 61-6313

**Leeuw, G. van der (Gerardus), 1890-1950.**    • **1.4632**
[Vom Heiligen in der Kunst. English] Sacred and profane beauty; the holy in art. Pref. by Mircea Eliade. Translated by David E. Green. London, Weidenfeld and Nicolson [1963] xx, 357 p. 25 cm. Translation of Vom Heiligen in der Kunst. 1. Art and religion 2. Religion and literature I. T.
N72.L4x    701    *LC* 79-6528

**Malraux, André, 1901-1976.**    • **1.4633**
The metamorphosis of the gods. Translated by Stuart Gilbert. — [1st ed. in English]. — Garden City, N.Y.: Doubleday, 1960-. v.    : illus. (part col.); 24 cm. 1. Art — Philosophy 2. Art and religion I. T.
N72.M2643    701.1    *LC* 60-10395

**Coke, Van Deren, 1921-.**    **1.4634**
The painter and the photograph; from Delacroix to Warhol. [Rev. and enl. ed.]. — Albuquerque: University of New Mexico Press, [1972] 324 p.: illus.; 29 cm. Rev. and enl. from the 1964 exhibition catalog issued under the same title. 1. Painting from photographs 2. Painting — Exhibitions. 3. Photography — Exhibitions I. T.
N72.P5 C6 1972    759/.06    *LC* 75-129804

**Scharf, Aaron, 1922-.**    • **1.4635**
Art and photography. — London: Allen Lane, 1968. xv, 314 p.: illus., facsims.; 29 cm. 1. Painting from photographs I. T.
N72.P5 S3    770.1/1    *LC* 78-367336

**Kuhns, Richard Francis, 1924-.**    **1.4636**
Psychoanalytic theory of art: a philosophy of art on developmental principles / Richard Kuhns. — New York: Columbia University Press, 1983. xi, 169 p.; 24 cm. Includes index. 1. Psychoanalysis and art 2. Art — Philosophy I. T.
N72.P74 K8 1983    701 19    *LC* 82-23499     *ISBN* 0231056206

**Brandon, S. G. F. (Samuel George Frederick), 1907-1971.**    **1.4637**
Man and God in art and ritual; a study of iconography, architecture and ritual action as primary evidence of religious belief and practice [by] S. G. F. Brandon. New York, Scribner [c1975] xiv, 514 p. illus. 29 cm. 1. Art and religion 2. Ritual I. T.
N72.R4 B72    246    *LC* 73-1358     *ISBN* 0684136570

**Layton, Robert.**    **1.4638**
The anthropology of art / Robert Layton. — New York: Columbia University Press, 1981. x, 227 p.: ill.; 25 cm. 1. Art and anthropology I. T.
N72.S6 L39 1981    709/.01/1 19    *LC* 80-39919     *ISBN* 0231052820

**Read, Herbert Edward, Sir, 1893-1968.**    • **1.4639**
Art and society [by] Herbert Read. — New York: Schocken Books, [1966] xvii, 152 p.: illus., ports.; 21 cm. 1. Art and society 2. Art and religion I. T.
N72.S6 R4 1966    701.1    *LC* 66-26728

## N75 TASTE

**Alison, Archibald, 1757-1839.**      **1.4640**
Essays on the nature and principles of taste. (1790.). — (Reprografischer Nachdruck der Ausg. London 1790.). — Hildescheim: G. Olms, 1968. xiii, 415 p.; 18 cm. — (Anglistica & Americana. 26) 1. Aesthetics — Early works to 1800. I. T. II. Series.
N75.A5 1968     111.8/5     *LC* 73-390264

**Gerard, Alexander, 1728-1795.**      • **1.4641**
An essay on taste (1759), together with observations concerning the imitative nature of poetry. A facsimile reproduction of the 3d ed. (1780) with an introd. by Walter J. Hipple, Jr. Gainesville, Fla., Scholars' Facsimiles & Reprints, 1963. xxviii p., facsim.: xi, 284 p. 1. Aesthetics — Early works to 1800 I. T.
N75 G3 1780A     *LC* 63-7081

**Kepes, Gyorgy, 1906- ed.**      • **1.4642**
Module, proportion, symmetry, rhythm. New York, G. Braziller [1966] 233 p. illus., music. 29 cm. (Vision+value series) 'Duality and synthesis in the music of Béla Bartók [by] Ernö Lendvai': p. 174-193. 1. Bartók, Béla, 1881-1945. 2. Symmetry (Art) I. T.
N76.K4     701.17     *LC* 66-13044

**Goldwater, Robert John, 1907-1973. ed. and tr.**      • **1.4643**
Artists on art, from the XIV to the XX century. 100 illustrations. Compiled and edited by Robert Goldwater and Marco Treves. — [New York]: Pantheon books, [1945] 1 p.l., v-xv, 497, [1] p.: illus. (incl. ports.); 24 cm. 'We have translated into English for the first time nearly one-half of the artists' writing quoted, and have reworked other selections for this book.'—Foreword. 1. Art 2. Artists I. Treves, Marco, joint ed. and tr. II. T.
N79.G57     704.92     *LC* 45-11131

**Langer, Susanne Katherina Knauth, 1895- ed.**      • **1.4644**
Reflections on art; a source book of writings by artists, critics, and philosophers. Baltimore, Johns Hopkins Press [1959, c1958] 364 p. ill. 1. Art — Philosophy 2. Aesthetics — Addresses, essays, lectures 3. Music — Philosophy and aesthetics I. T.
N79 L2     *LC* 58-59767

# N81–390 Study and Teaching. Schools

**Jones, Lois Swan.**      **1.4645**
Art research methods and resources: a guide to finding art information / Lois Swan Jones. — Dubuque, Iowa: Kendall/Hunt Pub. Co., c1978. xii, 243 p.: facsims.; 28 cm. 1. Art — Research. I. T.
N85.J64     707/.2     *LC* 77-93281     *ISBN* 0840318464

**McFee, June King.**      **1.4646**
Art, culture, and environment: a catalyst for teaching / June King McFee, Rogena M. Degge. Belmont, Calif.: Wadsworth Pub. Co., c1977. xviii, 398 p.: ill.; 25 cm. Includes indexes. 1. Art — Study and teaching I. Degge, Rogena M. joint author. II. T.
N85.M24     707     *LC* 76-42286     *ISBN* 0534004725

**Pevsner, Nikolaus, Sir, 1902-.**      • **1.4647**
Academies of art, past and present / by Nikolaus Pevsner. — Cambridge: University press, 1940. xiv, 323, 17 leaves of plates: ill., port. 1. Art schools 2. Art — Study and teaching I. T.
N325.P4     *LC* 41-6058

**Design in America: the Cranbrook vision, 1925–1950 / text by Robert Judson Clark ... [et al.]; [catalog coordinator, Andrea P.A. Belloli].**      **1.4648**
New York: Abrams, in association with the Detroit Institute of Arts and the Metropolitan Museum of Art, c1983. 352 p.: ill. (some col.); 29 cm. Published in conjunction with an exhibition held at the Detroit Institute of Arts, Dec. 14, 1983-Feb. 19, 1984, and elsewhere. 1. Cranbrook Academy of Art — Exhibitions. 2. Art, Modern — 20th century — Michigan — Bloomfield — Exhibitions. 3. Design — Michigan — Bloomfield — History — 20th century — Exhibitions. I. Clark, Robert Judson. II. Belloli, Andrea P. A. III. Detroit Institute of Arts. IV. Metropolitan Museum of Art (New York, N.Y.)
N330.B55 C74 1983     709/.774/38 19     *LC* 83-6343     *ISBN* 0810908018

**Itten, Johannes, 1888-1967.**      • **1.4649**
[Mein Vorkurs am Bauhaus; Gestaltungs und Formenlehre. English] Design and form; the basic course at the Bauhaus. Translated by John Maass. New York, Reinhold Pub. Corp. [1964] 190 p. illus. 29 cm. Translation of Mein Vorkurs am Bauhaus; Gestaltungs- und Formenlehre. 1. Art — Study and teaching — Germany, West. 2. Art — Technique I. Bauhaus. II. T.
N332.B38 I83     707     *LC* 63-19225

**Boime, Albert.**      **1.4650**
The Academy and French painting in the Nineteenth century. London, Phaidon, 1971. xi, 330 p. illus. 28 cm. Distributors in the United States: Praeger Publishers, New York. 1. Académie des beaux-arts (France) 2. Painting, French — History. 3. Painting, Modern — 19th century — France I. T.
N332.F83 P33     759.4     *LC* 78-112622     *ISBN* 0714814016

**Whitford, Frank.**      **1.4651**
Bauhaus / Frank Whitford. — London: Thames and Hudson, c1984. 216 p.: ill. (some col.); 21 cm. (World of art.) Includes index. 1. Bauhaus. I. T. II. Series.
N332.G33 B487 1984     707/.114322 19     *LC* 83-50527     *ISBN* 0500201935

**Lowenfeld, Viktor.**      **1.4652**
Creative and mental growth / Viktor Lowenfeld, W. Lambert Brittain. — 8th ed. — New York: Macmillan; London: Collier Macmillan, c1987. xvi, 510 p., [24] p. of plates: ill. (some col.); 24 cm. Includes index. 1. Art — Study and teaching 2. Creation (Literary, artistic, etc.) 3. Children as artists 4. Artists — Psychology I. Brittain, W. Lambert. II. T.
N350.L62 1987     707 19     *LC* 86-8529     *ISBN* 0023721103

**Mattil, Edward L.**      **1.4653**
Meaning in children's art: projects for teachers / Edward L. Mattil, Betty Marzan. — Englewood Cliffs, N.J.: Prentice-Hall, c1981. x, 324 p.: ill.; 28 cm. 1. Art — Study and teaching (Elementary) 2. Children as artists 3. Project method in teaching I. Marzan, Betty. joint author. II. T.
N350.M34     372.5/044 19     *LC* 80-23915     *ISBN* 0135671078

**Smith, Nancy R.**      **1.4654**
Experience and art: teaching children to paint / Nancy R. Smith. — New York: Teachers College, Columbia University, 1983. p. cm. Includes index. 1. Painting — Study and teaching (Elementary) 2. Children as artists 3. Children's art I. T.
N350.S67 1983     372.5/2 19     *LC* 82-10287

**Podro, Michael.**      **1.4655**
The critical historians of art / Michael Podro. — New Haven: Yale University Press, 1982. xxvi, 257 p.: ill.; 24 cm. Includes index. 1. Art — Historiography 2. Art criticism I. T.
N380.P53 1982     701/.1/80943 19     *LC* 82-4934     *ISBN* 0300028628

**Roskill, Mark W., 1933-.**      **1.4656**
What is art history? / Mark Roskill. — 1st U. S. ed. — New York: Harper & Row, 1976. 192 p.: ill. — (Icon editions) 1. Art — Historiography 2. Art criticism I. T.
N380.R67 1976     701.18 707.2     *LC* 75-34872     *ISBN* 0064384756

# N400–3990 Art Museums. Galleries

**Museums in crisis. Edited, with an introd. by Brian O'Doherty. Foreword by Nancy Hanks.**      **1.4657**
New York: G. Braziller, [1972] ix, 178 p.: illus.; 22 cm. 'Articles ... first appeared in the special museum issue of Art in America, v. 59, no. 4.' 1. Art museums — Addresses, essays, lectures. I. O'Doherty, Brian. ed. II. Art in America.
N430.M8 1972     069     *LC* 79-183186     *ISBN* 0807606294

**Museum of Fine Arts, Boston.**      **1.4658**
Museum of Fine Arts, Boston: Western art / Adolph S. Cavallo [et al.]. — Greenwich, Conn.: Distributed by New York Graphic Society, 1972 [c1971] 211 p.: ill.; 37 cm. — 1. Museum of Fine Arts, Boston. 2. Art — Boston — Catalogs. I. Cavallo, Adolph S. II. T. III. Title: Western art.
N520.C3     708.14461     *LC* 74-10138     *ISBN* 0878460543

**Cleveland Museum of Art.**      **1.4659**
European paintings before 1500 / Cleveland Museum of Art. Cleveland: The Museum, 1974. xvi, 183 p., [14] leaves of plates: ill. (some col.); 29 cm. (Its Catalogue of paintings; pt. 1) Includes index. 1. Panel painting, Gothic — Catalogs. 2. Panel painting — Cleveland — Catalogs. I. T.
N552.A556 pt. 1 ND144     750/.74/017132 s 759.94/074/017132     *LC* 72-83626     *ISBN* 0910386196

**Yale University. Art Gallery.**      **1.4660**
Selected paintings and sculpture from the Yale University Art Gallery. Introd.: Andrew Carnduff Ritchie. Commentaries: Katharine B. Neilson. — New

Haven: Published for the Yale University Art Gallery by Yale University Press, 1972. 154 p. 1. Art — New Haven — Catalogs. I. Neilson, Katharine Bishop. II. T.
N590.A65     750/.74/01468     *LC* 76-179475     *ISBN* 0300015623

**Frick Collection.**             **1.4661**
The Frick Collection; an illustrated catalogue. New York; Distrubuted by Princeton University Press [Princeton, N.J.] 1968-. v. illus. (part col.), ports. (part col.) 27 cm. I. T.
N620.F6 A6     708/.147/1     *LC* 68-57985     *ISBN* 0691038112

**Museum of Modern Art (New York, N.Y.)**     **1.4662**
The Museum of Modern Art, New York: the history and the collection / introduction by Sam Hunter. — New York, N.Y.: H.N. Abrams in association with the Museum of Modern Art, New York, 1984. 599 p., [6] p. of plates: ill. (some col.). Includes index. 1. Museum of Modern Art (New York, N.Y.) I. Hunter, Sam, 1923- II. T.
N620.M9 A85 1984     709/.04/007401471 19     *LC* 83-15769     *ISBN* 0810913089

**Rudenstine, Angelica Zander.**         **1.4663**
The Guggenheim Museum collection: paintings 1880–1945 / by Angelica Zander Rudenstine. New York: Solomon R. Guggenheim Museum, 1976. 2 v. I. T.
N620.S63 R83     *LC* 75-37356     *ISBN* 0892070021

**Walker, John, 1906 Dec. 24-.**        **1.4664**
National Gallery of Art, Washington / by John Walker; foreword by J. Carter Brown. — Rev. ed. — New York: H.N. Abrams, [1984] 696 p.: ill. Includes index. 1. National Gallery of Art (U.S.) I. T.
N856.W33 1984     708.153 19     *LC* 83-27545     *ISBN* 0810913704

**National Portrait Gallery (Great Britain).**     **1.4665**
National Portrait Gallery: complete illustrated catalogue, 1856–1979 / compiled by K.K. Yung; edited by Mary Pettman. — New York: St Martin's Press, c1981. — x, 749 p.: ill.; 26 cm. Includes index. 1. National Portrait Gallery (Great Britain). 2. Portraits — England — London — Catalogs. 3. Great Britain — Biography — Portraits — Catalogs. I. Yung, Kai Kin. II. Pettman, Mary. III. T.
N1090.A52     757.9094212     *ISBN* 0312157770

**Art treasures of the Vatican: architecture, painting, sculpture /**     **1.4666**
**edited by D. Redig de Campos; contributors, Maria Donati**
**Barcellona ... [et al.; translated by J. Gerber].**
1st American ed. — Englewood Cliffs, N.J.: Prentice-Hall, 1975, c1974. 398 p.: ill. (some col.); 31 cm. 1. Vatican Palace (Vatican City) 2. Art — Vatican City. I. Redig de Campos, D. (Deoclecio) II. Donati Barcellona, Maria.
N2940.A77 1975     708/.5/634     *LC* 74-18699     *ISBN* 0130490644

**The Shogun age exhibition / from the Tokugawa Art Museum,**     **1.4667**
**Japan.**
Tokyo: Shogun Age Exhibition Executive Committee, 1984, [c1983]. 279 p.: ill. (some col.); 29 cm. Includes index. 1. Tokugawa family — Art collections. 2. Tokugawa Bijutsukan — Catalogs. 3. Art, Japanese — Edo period, 1600-1868 — Exhibitions. 4. Shōguns 5. Decorative arts — Japan — History — Edo period, 1600-1868 — Exhibitions. 6. Japan — History — Tokugawa period, 1600-1868 I. Tokugawa Bijutsukan.
N3750.N3 A58

**Weng, Wango H. C.**            **1.4668**
The Palace Museum, Peking: treasures of the Forbidden City / Wan-go Weng, Yang Boda. — New York: Abrams, 1982. 319 p.: ill. (some col.); 35 cm. 'A Wan-go Weng book.' Includes index. 1. Ku kung po wu yüan (China) I. Yang, Boda. II. Ku kung po wu yüan (China) III. T.
N3750.P3 W4 1982     709/.51/0740951156 19     *LC* 82-1703     *ISBN* 0810914778

# N4390–5299 Exhibitions. Private Collections. Art Patronage

**Brown, Milton Wolf, 1911-.**           • **1.4669**
The story of the Armory show / by Milton W. Brown. — [s.l.]: Joseph H. Hirshhorn Foundation; distributed by New York Graphic Society [Greenwich, Conn.], 1963. 320 p., [32] leaves of plates: ill. Includes an account of the International exhibition of modern art (1913) sponsored by the Association of American Painters and Sculptors, and a catalogue raisonné. 1. Art — Exhibitions I. Association of American Painters and Sculptors, New York. II. T. III. Title: The Armory show. IV. Title: International exhibition of modern art.
N5015.A8 B7     *LC* 63-13496

**Baudelaire, Charles, 1821-1867.**        **1.4670**
Art in Paris, 1845–1862: salons and other exhibitions / reviewed by Charles Baudelaire; translated and edited by Jonathan Mayne. — Ithaca, N.Y.: Cornell University Press, 1981, c1965. xiv, 241 p., [70] p. of plates: ill.; 21 cm. — (Landmarks in art history.) (Cornell paperbacks) Reprint. Originally published: 1st ed. London; New York: Phaidon, 1965. 'Cornell/Phaidon books.' 1. Salon (Exhibition) 2. Art, French — Exhibitions. 3. Art, Modern — 19th century — France — Exhibitions. 4. Art — France — Paris — Exhibitions. I. Mayne, Jonathan. II. T. III. Series.
N5064.B313 1981     709/.44/07404361 19     *LC* 81-66146     *ISBN* 0801492270

**Haskell, Francis, 1928-.**           **1.4671**
Rediscoveries in art: some aspects of taste, fashion, and collecting in England and France / Francis Haskell. — Ithaca, N.Y.: Cornell University Press, 1976. x, 246 p.: ill.; 28 cm. (The Wrightsman lectures; 7th) Includes index. 1. Art patronage — Great Britain. 2. Aesthetics, British 3. Art patronage — France. 4. Aesthetics, French I. T. II. Series.
N5208.G7 H37     704/.7     *LC* 75-21656     *ISBN* 0801409950

**Kean, Beverly Whitney.**           **1.4672**
All the empty palaces: the merchant patrons of modern art in pre-Revolutionary Russia / Beverly Whitney Kean. — New York: Universe Books, 1983. xviii, 342 p., [4] p. of plates: ill. (some col.); 25 cm. Includes index. 1. Shchukin, Sergeĭ Ivanovich, 1854-1936 — Art collections. 2. Morozov, Ivan Abramovich — Art collections. 3. Art patronage — Soviet Union — History — 20th century. 4. Impressionism (Art) — France. 5. Post-impressionism — France. 6. Painting, French — Soviet Union. 7. Painting, French — Influence. I. T.
N5276.2.S5 K4 1983     759.4/074/07 19     *LC* 82-8536     *ISBN* 0876634129

# N5300–6494 History, by Period

**Gardner, Helen.**            • **1.4673**
[Art through the ages] Gardner's Art through the ages / revised by Horst de la Croix and Richard G. Tansey. — 7th ed. — New York: Harcourt Brace Jovanovich, c1980. xiii, 922 p.: ill. (some col.); 29 cm. Includes index. 1. Art — History I. De la Croix, Horst. II. Tansey, Richard G. III. T. IV. Title: Art through the ages.
N5300.G25 1980     709     *LC* 79-65963     *ISBN* 0155037587

**Gombrich, E. H. (Ernst Hans), 1909-.**     • **1.4674**
The story of art / E.H. Gombrich. — 14th ed., enl. and reset. — Oxford [Oxfordshire]: Phaidon, 1984. 520 p.: ill.; 25 cm. 'A note on art books': p. 510-515. Includes index. 1. Art — History I. T.
N5300.G643 1984     709 19     *LC* 85-201275     *ISBN* 0714822779

**Honour, Hugh.**             **1.4675**
The visual arts: a history / Hugh Honour, John Fleming. — 1st ed. — Englewood Cliffs, N.J.: Prentice-Hall, c1982. 639 p.: ill. (some col.); 24 cm. Published in Great Britain under the title: A world history of art. Includes index. 1. Art — History I. Fleming, John, 1919- II. T.
N5300.H68 1982     709 19     *LC* 82-5351     *ISBN* 0139423591

**Janson, H. W. (Horst Woldemar), 1913-.**     • **1.4676**
History of art / by H.W. Janson. — 3rd ed. / rev. and expanded by Anthony F. Janson. — New York: H.N. Abrams; Englewood Cliffs, N.J.: Prentice-Hall, 1986. 824 p.: ill. (some col.); 30 cm. Includes index. 1. Art — History I. Janson, Anthony F. II. T.
N5300.J3 1986b     709 19     *LC* 85-12406     *ISBN* 013389388X

**Readings in art history / edited by Harold Spencer.**     • **1.4677**
3rd ed. — New York: Scribner, c1982-c1983. 2 v.: ill.; 23 cm. 1. Art — History — Addresses, essays, lectures. I. Spencer, Harold, 1920-
N5300.R38 1982     709 19     *LC* 82-5521     *ISBN* 068417619X

**Wölfflin, Heinrich, 1864-1945.**        • **1.4678**
[Kunstgeschichtliche Grundbegriffe. English] Principles of art history; the problem of the development of style in later art. Translated by M. D. Hottinger. — [New York]: Dover Publications, [1950] xvi, 237 p.: illus.; 24 cm. Translation of: Kunstgeschichtliche Grundbegriffe. Reprint. Originally published London: G. Bell, 1932. 1. Art — History I. T. II. Title: Kunstgeschichtliche Grundbegriffe. English
N5300.W82     709     *LC* 50-4154     *ISBN* 486202763

**Janson, H. W. (Horst Woldemar), 1913- ed.**     • **1.4679**
Key monuments of the history of art; a visual survey, edited by H. W. Janson, with Dora Jane Janson. Text ed. Englewood Cliffs, N. J., Prentice-Hall [1959] 1068 p. plates. 26 cm. 1. Art — History I. T.
N5301.J3     709     *LC* 59-6934

**Elsen, Albert Edward, 1927-.**      **1.4680**
Purposes of art: an introduction to the history and appreciation of art / Albert E. Elsen. — 4th ed. — New York: Holt, Rinehart, and Winston, 1981. p. cm. Includes index. 1. Art — History 2. Art — Themes, motives 3. Art appreciation I. T.
N5303.E45 1981     709 19     *LC* 80-26290     *ISBN* 0030497663

**Holt, Elizabeth Basye Gilmore. ed.**      • **1.4681**
A documentary history of art. [2d ed.] Garden City, N.Y., Doubleday, 1957-. v. illus. 19 cm. (Doubleday anchor books, A114a, 114b) Expansion and revision of the editor's Literary sources of art history, published in 1947. 1. Art — History — Sources. I. T.
N5303.H762     709     *LC* 57-10457

**Rowland, Benjamin, 1904-1972.**      • **1.4682**
The classical tradition in Western art. Cambridge, Harvard University Press, 1963. xx, 379 p. plates. 1. Classicism in art 2. Art — History I. T.
N5303 R68     *LC* 63-17211

## N5310 PREHISTORIC ART

**Boas, Franz, 1858-1942.**      • **1.4683**
Primitive art. — [New ed.]. — New York: Dover Publications, [1955] 372 p.: illus.; 21 cm. 1. Art, Primitive 2. Folk literature — History and criticism I. T.
N5310.B6 1955     709.01     *LC* 55-12840

**Fraser, Douglas. comp.**      **1.4684**
The many faces of primitive art; a critical anthology. — Englewood Cliffs, N.J.: Prentice-Hall, [1966] xi, 300 p.: illus.; 23 cm. 1. Art, Primitive — Addresses, essays, lectures. I. T.
N5310.F68     709.011     *LC* 66-15402

**Laming-Emperaire, Annette, 1917-1977.**      • **1.4685**
Lascaux: paintings and engravings. Translated by Eleanore Frances Armstrong. [Harmondsworth, Middlesex, Baltimore, Md.] Penguin Books [1959] 208 p. illus. 18 cm. (Pelican books, A419) 1. Cave-drawings 2. Petroglyphs — France. 3. Lascaux Cave (France) I. T.
N5310.L373 1959     571.709447     *LC* 59-1209

**Mead, Margaret, 1901-1978.**      • **1.4686**
Technique & personality [by] Margaret Mead, Junius B. Bird [and] Hans Himmelheber. New York, Museum of Primitive Art; distributed by the New York Graphic Society, 1963. 110 p. ill. (part. col.) ([New York] Museum of Primitive Art. Lecture series, no. 3) 1. Art, Primitive — Addresses, essays, lectures I. T. II. Series.
N5310 M36     *LC* 63-19321

**Sandars, N. K. (Nancy K.)**      **1.4687**
Prehistoric art in Europe [by] N. K. Sandars. Harmondsworth, Penguin, 1968. xlix, 350 p. 189 plates, illus. (incl. 1 col.), maps. 27 cm. (Pelican history of art. Z30) In slip case. 1. Art, Prehistoric — Europe. 2. Europe — Antiquities I. T. II. Series.
N5310.S32     709/.01/10936 19     *LC* 79-352957

**Sieveking, Ann.**      **1.4688**
The cave artists / Ann Sieveking. — London: Thames and Hudson, c1979. 221 p.: ill. (some col.); 25 cm. — (Ancient peoples and places; 93) Includes index. 1. Art, Prehistoric 2. Cave-drawings I. T.
N5310.S47     709/.01/120944     *LC* 80-473767     *ISBN* 0500020922

**Wingert, Paul S. (Paul Stover), 1900-1974.**      • **1.4689**
Primitive art: its traditions and styles. New York, Oxford University Press, 1962. 421 p. ill. 1. Art, Primitive I. T.
N5310 W766     *LC* 62-20161

**Phelps, Steven.**      **1.4690**
Art and artefacts of the Pacific, Africa and the Americas: the James Hooper Collection / [by] Steven Phelps. London: Hutchinson [for Christie, Manson & Woods], 1976. 487 p., leaf of plate, [8] p. of plates: ill. (some col.); 31 cm. Includes a catalog of the collections. Includes index. 1. Hooper, James T. — Art collections. 2. Art, Primitive I. T.
N5310.8.G7 H666     709/.01/1     *LC* 76-380837     *ISBN* 0091250005

**Ethnic and tourist arts: cultural expressions from the fourth world / Nelson H. H. Graburn, editor.**      **1.4691**
Berkeley: University of California Press, 1977 (c1976). xv, 412 p., [4] leaves of plates: ill. (some col.); 23 cm. Some of the papers were presented at the Symposium on the Arts of Acculturation at the annual meeting of the American Anthropological Association in San Diego, Calif., Nov. 1970. Includes index. 1. Art, Primitive — Addresses, essays, lectures. I. Graburn, Nelson H. H.
N5311.E73     709/.01/1     *LC* 74-30521     *ISBN* 0520029496

**Giedion, S. (Sigfried), 1888-1968.**      **1.4692**
The eternal present. A contribution on constancy and change. [New York, Bollingen Foundation; distributed by] Pantheon Books [1962-64] 2 v. illus., col. plates, col. maps (part fold.), plans. 27 cm. (Bollingen series, 35.6.1- The A.W. Mellon lectures in the fine arts, 1957) 1. Art, Primitive 2. Architecture, Ancient 3. Art — Psychology I. T.
N5311.G48 1962     709/.01 19     *LC* 62-7942

**Jopling, Carol F., comp.**      **1.4693**
Art and aesthetics in primitive societies; a critical anthology. Edited by Carol F. Jopling. — [1. ed.]. — New York: E. P. Dutton, 1971. xx, 426 p.: illus.; 21 cm. 1. Art, Primitive — Addresses, essays, lectures. 2. Aesthetics — Addresses, essays, lectures. I. T.
N5311.J66 1971     709.01/1     *LC* 73-87202     *ISBN* 0525057838

## N5315–5390 ANCIENT ART. ANCIENT MIDDLE EAST

**Age of spirituality: a symposium / edited by Kurt Weitzmann; contributors to this vol., Hans–Georg Beck ... [et al.].**      **1.4694**
New York: Metropolitan Museum of Art; Princeton, N.J.: distributed by Princeton University Press, c1980. viii, 174 p.: ill.; 29 cm. Held in conjunction with the exhibition, Age of spirituality: late antique and early Christian art. third to seventh century, held at the Metropolitan Museum of Art, Nov. 19, 1977-Feb. 12, 1978. 1. Art, Ancient — Addresses, essays, lectures. 2. Art, Early Christian — Addresses, essays, lectures. 3. Christian art and symbolism — Medieval, 500-1500 — Addresses, essays, lectures. 4. Jewish art and symbolism — Addresses, essays, lectures. I. Weitzmann, Kurt, 1904- II. Beck, Hans Georg, 1910- III. Metropolitan Museum of Art (New York, N.Y.)
N5340.A34     709/.01/5     *LC* 80-11497

**Age of spirituality: late antique and early Christian art, third to seventh century: catalogue of the exhibition at the Metropolitan Museum of Art, November 19, 1977, through February 12, 1978 / edited by Kurt Weitzmann.**      **1.4695**
New York: The Museum, c1979. xxxi, 735 p., [8] leaves of plates: ill. (some col.); 29 cm. Published in association with Princeton University Press. Includes index. 1. Art, Ancient — Exhibitions. 2. Art, Early Christian — Exhibitions. 3. Christian art and symbolism — Medieval, 500-1500 — Exhibitions. 4. Jewish art and symbolism — Exhibitions. I. Weitzmann, Kurt, 1904- II. Metropolitan Museum of Art (New York, N.Y.)
N5340.A35     709/.01/507401471     *LC* 78-23512     *ISBN* 0870991795

**Amiet, Pierre.**      **1.4696**
[Art antique du Proche-Orient. English] Art of the ancient Near East / Pierre Amiet; translated from the French by John Shepley and Claude Choquet; [editor, Naomi Noble Richard]. — New York: H. N. Abrams, 1980, c1977. 618 p.: ill. (some col.); 32 cm. Translation of L'art antique du Proche-Orient. Includes index. 1. Art, Ancient — Near East. 2. Art — Middle East 3. Middle East — Antiquities. I. Richard, Naomi Noble. II. T.
N5345.A7413 1980     709/.39     *LC* 79-4411     *ISBN* 0810906384

**Frankfort, Henri, 1897-1954.**      **1.4697**
The art and architecture of the ancient Orient. [4th rev. impression] [Harmondsworth, Eng.] Penguin Books [1970] 456 p. illus., map. 21 cm. (Pelican history of art. PZ7) 1. Art — Middle East 2. Architecture — Middle East I. T. II. Series.
N5345.F7 1970     709.3     *LC* 70-128007     *ISBN* 0140561072

**Frankfort, Henriette Antonia (Groenewegen) 1896-.**      **1.4698**
Arrest and movement; an essay on space and time in the representational art of the ancient Near East, by H. A. Groenewegen–Frankfort. — New York: Hacker Art Books, 1972. xxiv, 222 p.: illus.; 25 cm. Reprint of the 1951 ed. 1. Composition (Art) 2. Perspective 3. Art, Ancient — Near East. I. T.
N5345.F72 1972     701/.8     *LC* 70-143349     *ISBN* 0878170693

**Michałowski, Kazimierz.**      **1.4699**
[Art de l'ancienne Égypte. English] Art of ancient Egypt. [Translated and adapted from the Polish and French by Norbert Guterman] New York, H. N. Abrams [1969] 600 p. illus., maps, plans, plates (part col.) 32 cm. Translation of the author's L'art de l'ancienne Égypte which was based on his Nie tylko piramidy. 1. Art, Egyptian — History. 2. Egypt — Civilization I. Guterman, Norbert, 1900- tr. II. Michałowski, Kazimierz. Nie tylko piramidy. III. T.
N5350.M61423     709/.32     *LC* 68-26865

**Schäfer, Heinrich, 1868-1957.**      **1.4700**
Principles of Egyptian art / Heinrich Schäfer; edited, with an epilogue by Emma Brunner–Traut; translated and edited, with an introd. by John Baines. — Oxford [Eng.]: Clarendon Press, 1974. xxviii, 470 p., [72] leaves of plates: ill.; 24 cm. Includes index. 1. Art, Egyptian I. Brunner-Traut, Emma. ed. II. T.
N5350.S313     N5350 S313.     709/.32     *LC* 75-300260     *ISBN* 0198171986

**Smith, William Stevenson.**    • **1.4701**
The art and architecture of ancient Egypt. — [Harmondsworth, Middlesex]: Penguin Books, [1958] xxvii, 301 p.: illus., 192 plates, maps, plans.; 27 cm. — (Pelican history of art. z14) 1. Art, Egyptian 2. Architecture — Egypt 3. Egypt — Antiquities I. T. II. Series.
N5350.S5     709.32     *LC* 58-3043

**Yoyotte, Jean.**    **1.4702**
[Trésors des pharaons. English] Treasures of the pharaohs. The early period, the New Kingdom, the late period. Introd. by Christiane Desroches Noblecourt. Text by Jean Yoyotte. (Translated from the French by Robert Allen. Geneva,) Skira (1968) xii, 259 p. illus. 34 cm. (Treasures of the world, v. 7) 'Distributed in the United States by the World Publishing Company, Cleveland, Ohio.' Translation of Les trésors des pharaons. 1. Art, Egyptian I. T.
N5350.Y613     709/.32     *LC* 68-56859

**Lange, Kurt.**    • **1.4703**
[Aegypten. Architektur, Plastik, in drei Jahrtausenden. English] Egypt: architecture, sculpture, painting in three thousand years [by] Kurt Lange and Max Hirmer; with contributions by Eberhard Otto and Christiane Desroches–Noblecourt; translated by R. H. Boothroyd from the original German. 4th ed. revised and enlarged; with additional material in the fourth German ed. translated by Judith Filson and Barbara Taylor. London, New York, Phaidon, 1968. viii, 559 p. 60 plates, illus. (incl. 60 col.), plans. 31 cm. Translation of Aegypten, Architektur, Plastik, Malerei in drei Jahrtausenden. 1. Art — Egypt — History. I. Hirmer, Max, joint author. II. T.
N5351.L313 1968     709/.32     *LC* 68-12257     *ISBN* 0714813494

**Moortgat, Anton, 1897-.**    • **1.4704**
[Kunst des alten Mesopotamien. English] The art of ancient Mesopotamia; the classical art of the Near East. [Translated by Judith Filson] London, New York, Phaidon [1969] x, 356 p. illus., map, plans. 26 cm. Translation of Die Kunst des alten Mesopotamien. 1. Art, Assyro-Babylonian 2. Art, Ancient — Iraq. 3. Iraq — Antiquities I. T.
N5370.M6613     709/.35     *LC* 69-12789     *ISBN* 0714813710

**Parrot, André, 1901-.**    • **1.4705**
The arts of Assyria. Translated by Stuart Gilbert and James Emmons. — New York: Golden Press, [1961] xviii, 383 p.: illus. (part col.) maps.; 29 cm. — (The Arts of mankind) 1. Art, Assyro-Babylonian 2. Art — Iraq. I. T.
N5370.P333     709.35     *LC* 61-11170

**Parrot, André, 1901-.**    • **1.4706**
Sumer: the dawn of art. Translated by Stuart Gilbert and James Emmons. New York, Golden Press [1961] L, 397 p. illus. (part col.) ports., maps (part col.) 29 cm. (Arts of mankind) Bibliography: p. 361-370. 1. Art, Sumerian — History. I. T. II. Series.
N5370.P343     709.35     *LC* 61-6746

**Strommenger, Eva.**    • **1.4707**
[Fünf Jahrtausende Mesopotamien. English] 5000 years of the art of Mesopotamia. Photos. by Max Hirmer. [Translated by Christina Haglund] New York, H. N. Abrams [1964] 480 p. illus., maps ( 1 fold.) 44 col. plates. 32 cm. Translation of Fünf Jahrtausende Mesopotamien. 1. Art — Iraq — History. I. Hirmer, Max. II. T. III. Title: Art of Mesopotamia.
N5370.S713     709.35     *LC* 64-15231

**Akurgal, Ekrem.**    • **1.4708**
The art of the Hittites. Photos. by Max Hirmer. [Translated by Constance McNab] New York, H. N. Abrams [1962] 315 p. illus., plates (part col.) map, plans. 32 cm. Bibliography: p. 306-312. 1. Art, Hittite — History. I. T.
N5385.A413     709.39     *LC* 62-11624

**Ghirshman, Roman.**    • **1.4709**
[Iran: Parthes et Sassanides. English] Persian art, Parthian and Sassanian dynasties, 249 B.C.–A.D. 651. Translated by Stuart Gilbert and James Emmons. New York, Golden Press [1962] 401 p. illus. (part col.) maps (1 fold.) 28 cm. (The Arts of mankind) Translation of Iran; Parthes et Sassanides. 1. Art, Iranian — History. I. T. II. Series.
N5390.G513     709.55     *LC* 62-19125

**Porada, Edith, 1912-.**    • **1.4710**
[Alt-Iran. English] The art of ancient Iran; pre–Islamic cultures [by] Edith Porada with the collaboration of R. H. Dyson and contributions by C. K. Wilkinson. New York Crown Publishers [1965] 279 p. illus. (part mounted col.) map, plans. 24 cm. (Art of the world, non-European cultures; the historical, sociological, and religious backgrounds) Translation of Alt-Iran. 1. Art, Iranian — History. I. T.
N5390.P613     *LC* 65-15839

# N5605–5896 Classic Art

**Pliny, the Elder.**    • **1.4711**
[Naturalis historia English and Latin] The Elder Pliny's chapters on the history of art. Translated by K. Jex–Blake. With commentary and historical introd. by E. Sellers, and additional notes contributed by Heinrich Ludwig Urlichs. [1st American ed.] Chicago, Argonaut, 1968. [A]-Y, c, 252 p. facsim., geneal. tables. 20 cm. The text is a reprint of the 1896 ed. Translation of selected portions of Naturalis historia; Latin and English on facing pages. 1. Art — History 2. Art, Greco-Roman — History. I. Strong, Eugénie Sellers. ed. II. T.
N5610.P6 1968     709/.38     *LC* 66-19183

## N5630–5720 GREECE. CRETE

**Brilliant, Richard.**    **1.4712**
Arts of the ancient Greeks. — New York: McGraw-Hill, [1973] xxiii, 406 p.: illus. (part col.); 30 cm. 1. Art, Greek I. T.
N5630.B74     709/.38     *LC* 72-14098     *ISBN* 0070078505

**Carpenter, Rhys, 1889-.**    • **1.4713**
Greek art; a study of the formal evolution of style. Philadelphia, University of Pennsylvania Press [c1962] 256 p. ill. 1. Art, Greek — History I. T.
N5630 C33     *LC* 61-6619

**Charbonneaux, Jean, 1895-1969.**    **1.4714**
[Grèce archaïque. English] Archaic Greek art (620–480 B.C.) [by] Jean Charbonneaux, Roland Martin [and] François Villard. [Translated from the French by James Emmons [and] Robert Allen. New York, G. Braziller [1971] xi, 437 p. illus. (part. fold. col.), fold. col. maps. 29 cm. (The Arts of mankind, v. 14) Translation of Grèce archaïque. 1. Art, Greek — History. I. Martin, Roland, 1912- joint author. II. Villard, François. joint author. III. T. IV. Series.
N5630.C45713     709/.38     *LC* 78-136166     *ISBN* 0807605875

**Charbonneaux, Jean, 1895-1969.**    **1.4715**
[Grèce classique (480-330 avant J.-C.). English] Classical Greek art (480–330 B.C.) [by] Jean Charbonneaux, Roland Martin [and] François Villard. Translated from the French by James Emmons] New York, G. Braziller [1972] xi, 422 p. illus. (part col.) 29 cm. (The Arts of mankind, v. 16) Translation of Grèce classique (480-330 avant J.-C.) 1. Art, Greek I. Martin, Roland, 1912- joint author. II. Villard, François. joint author. III. T. IV. Series.
N5630.C4613 1972b     709/.38     *LC* 72-80015     *ISBN* 0807606278

**Charbonneaux, Jean, 1895-1969.**    **1.4716**
[Grèce hellénistique. English] Hellenistic art (330–50 B.C.) [by] Jean Charbonneaux, Roland Martin [and] François Villard. [Translated from the French by Peter Green] New York, G. Braziller [1973] ix, 421 p. illus. (part col.) 28 cm. (The Arts of mankind, v. 18) Translation of Grèce hellénistique. 1. Art, Hellenistic I. Martin, Roland, 1912- II. Villard, François. III. T. IV. Series.
N5630.C46513 1973b     709/.38     *LC* 72-89850     *ISBN* 0807606669

**Greek art and architecture [by] John Boardman [and others]**    **1.4717**
**Photos. by Max Hirmer.**
New York, H. N. Abrams [1967] 600p. illus.(part col.) map,plans 30cm. Translation of Die Griechische Kunst. 1. Art, Greek 2. Architecture, Greek I. Boardman, John, 1927- II. Hirmer, Max.
N5630.G713     *LC* 67-22850

**Matz, Friedrich, 1890-1974.**    • **1.4718**
[Kreta und frühes Griechenland. English] The art of Crete and early Greece; the prelude to Greek art. [Translated by Ann E. Keep] New York, Crown Publishers [1962] 260 p. illus. (part mounted col.) maps, plans. 24 cm. (Art of the world, European cultures; the historical, sociological, and religious backgrounds.) Translation of Kreta und frühes Griechenland. 1. Art, Minoan 2. Art, Cretan — History. 3. Art, Mycenaean — History. I. T.
N5630.M313     709.3     *LC* 62-20056

**Pollitt, J. J. (Jerome Jordan), 1934-.**    **1.4719**
Art and experience in classical Greece [by] J. J. Pollitt. Cambridge [Eng.] Cambridge University Press, 1972. xiv, 205 p. illus. 25 cm. 1. Art, Greek 2. Art — Psychology I. T.
N5630.P54 1972     709/.38     *LC* 74-160094     *ISBN* 0521080657 *ISBN* 0521096626

**Richter, Gisela Marie Augusta, 1882-1972.**    **1.4720**
A handbook of Greek art [by] Gisela M. A. Richter. — [6th ed., redesigned]. — London; New York: Phaidon, [1969] 431 p.: illus., maps.; 26 cm. — (Phaidon paperback) 1. Art, Greek I. T.
N5630.R49 1969     709/.38     *LC* 75-443770     *ISBN* 0714813516

**Robertson, Martin.**    **1.4721**
A history of Greek art / Martin Robertson. — London: Cambridge University Press, 1975. 2 v. ([23], 835 p., [202] p. of plates): ill., maps, plans; 29 cm.

Abridged ed. published in 1981 under title: A shorter history of Greek art. Includes indexes. 1. Art, Greek — History. I. T.
N5630.R63     709/.38     LC 73-79317     ISBN 0521202779

**Schweitzer, Bernhard, 1892-1966.**     • **1.4722**
Greek geometric art. [Edited by Ulrich Hausmann in co–operation with Jochen Briegleb. Translated by Peter and Cornelia Usborne. — New York]: Phaidon, [1971] 352 p.: illus., map (on lining paper), plans, ports.; 26 cm. Translation of Die geometrische Kunst Griechenlands. 1. Art, Greek I. T.
N5630.S3913 1971     709/.38     LC 71-111066     ISBN 0714814113

**Marinatos, Spyridon, 1901-.**     • **1.4723**
Crete and Mycenae. Photos. by Max Hirmer. — New York: H. N. Abrams, [1960] 177, [13] p.: illus. (part mounted col.) 236 plates, map, plans.; 32 cm. 1. Art, Minoan 2. Art, Mycenaean I. Hirmer, Max, 1893- illus. II. T.
N5660.M35     709.391     LC 60-8399

## N5740–5849 ROMAN ART

**Matt, Leonard von.**     • **1.4724**
Magna Graecia / Leonard von Matt; explanatory text by Umberto Zanotti–Bianco; translated from the Italian by Herbert Hoffmann. — [1st American ed.] New York: Universe Books, 1962. — 231 p.: ill. (part col.) map., 29 cm. 1. Art — Magna Grecia. 2. Art, Greek I. Zanotti-Bianco, Umberto. II. T.
N5740.M433 1962     709.377     LC 61-14580

**Brendel, Otto, 1901-1973.**     **1.4725**
Etruscan art / Otto J. Brendel. — Harmondsworth, Eng.: New York: Penguin Books, 1978. 507 p.: ill.; 21 cm. — (Pelican history of art.) Includes index. 1. Art, Etruscan I. T. II. Series.
N5750.B67 1978     709/.37/5     LC 77-22662     ISBN 0140561439 pbk

**Andreae, Bernard.**     **1.4726**
[Römische Kunst. English] The art of Rome / Bernard Andreae; translated from the German by Robert Erich Wolf. — New York: H. N. Abrams, 1978, [c1977]. 655 p.: ill. (some col.); 32 cm. Translation of Römische Kunst. Includes index. 1. Art, Roman I. T.
N5760.A4813 1977     709/.37     LC 75-8855     ISBN 0810906260

**Bianchi Bandinelli, Ranuccio, 1900-1975.**     • **1.4727**
[Rome, le centre du pouvoir. English] Rome, the center of power, 500 B.C. to A.D. 200. Translated by Peter Green. New York, G. Braziller [1970] xii, 437 p. illus. (part col.), col. plans. 29 cm. (The Arts of mankind, v. 15) Translation of Rome, le centre du pouvoir. 1. Art, Roman 2. Rome — Antiquities I. T. II. Series.
N5760.B513     709/.37     LC 70-116985     ISBN 080760559X

**L'Orange, Hans Peter, 1903-.**     **1.4728**
Art forms and civic life in the late Roman Empire, by H. P. L'Orange. [Translated from the Norwegian by Dr. and Mrs. Knut Berg]. — Princeton, N. J., Princeton University Press, 1965. 131 p. illus. 23 cm. Translation of Fra principat til dominat. Bibliographical footnotes. 1. Discletianus, Emperor of Rome, 245-313. 2. Art, Roman — Hist. I. T.
N5760.L613     709.37     LC 65-10831

**Strong, Donald Emrys.**     **1.4729**
Roman art / Donald Strong; prepared for press by J. M. C. Toynbee. Harmondsworth; Baltimore [etc.]: Penguin, 1976. xxvii, 197 p., [81] leaves of plates: ill. (some col.); 27 cm. (Pelican history of art.) Includes index. 1. Art, Roman — History. I. Toynbee, J. M. C. (Jocelyn M. C.), d. 1985. II. T. III. Series.
N5760.S68     709/.37     LC 76-380183     ISBN 0140560394

**Toynbee, J. M. C. (Jocelyn M. C.), d. 1985.**     **1.4730**
The Art of the Romans. — New York: Praeger, c1965. 271 p. : illus.; 21 cm. — (Ancient peoples and places; v. 43) 1. Art, Roman — History. I. T. II. Series.
N5760.T58     LC 65-20080

**Bianchi Bandinelli, Ranuccio, 1900-1975.**     **1.4731**
[Rome, la fin de l'art antique. English] Rome, the late Empire; Roman art, A.D. 200–400. Translated by Peter Green. New York, G. Braziller [1971] x, 463 p. illus. (part col.), col. maps (part fold.) 29 cm. (Arts of mankind series, v. 17) Translation of Rome, la fin de l'art antique. 1. Art, Roman 2. Art, Early Christian I. T. II. Series.
N5763.B513 1971     709/.37     LC 71-136167     ISBN 080760593X

**Hanfmann, George Maxim Anossov, 1911-.**     **1.4732**
From Croesus to Constantine: the cities of western Asia Minor and their arts in Greek and Roman times / George M. A. Hanfmann. — Ann Arbor: University of Michigan Press, [1975] xiii, 127 p.: [31] leaves of plates: ill.; 29 cm. (Jerome lectures. 10th ser.) Includes index. 1. Art, Classical — Ionia, Asia Minor. 2. Art — Ionia, Asia Minor. 3. Ionia, Asia Minor — Antiquities. I. T. II. Series.
N5865.A3 I564 1975     709/.392     LC 73-80574     ISBN 0472084208

**Rosenfield, John M.**     **1.4733**
The dynastic arts of the Kushans [by] John M. Rosenfield. — Berkeley: University of California Press, 1967. xliii, 377, [131] p.: illus., maps, plans, plates.; 29 cm. — (California studies in the history of art. 6) 1. Art, Kushan 2. Kushans I. T. II. Series.
N5899.K8 R6     709/.34     LC 65-14981

**Hachmann, Rolf.**     **1.4734**
[Germanen. English] The Germanic peoples / Rolf Hachmann; translated from the German by James Hogarth. — Geneva; Paris; Munich: Nagel, 1971. 208 p.: ill.; 24 cm. — (Archaeologia mundi) Translation of Die Germanen. Includes index. 1. Art, Germanic I. T.
N5930.H313 1971b     936.3     LC 75-519222

## N5940–6494 MEDIEVAL ART. MODERN ART (GENERAL)

## N5950–6320 Medieval Art

**Calkins, Robert G.**     **1.4735**
Monuments of medieval art / Robert G. Calkins. — 1st ed. — New York: Dutton, c1979. xx, 299 p., [12] leaves of plates: ill. (some col.); 24 cm. Includes index. 1. Art, Medieval I. T.
N5970.C34 1979     709/.02     LC 78-75288     ISBN 0525159320

**Duby, Georges.**     **1.4736**
[Temps des cathédrales. English] The age of the cathedrals: art and society, 980–1420 / Georges Duby; translated by Eleanor Levieux and Barbara Thompson. — Chicago: University of Chicago Press, c1981. v, 312 p., [16] leaves of plates: ill.; 24 cm. Translation of Le temps des cathédrales. Includes index. 1. Art, Medieval 2. Art and society 3. Civilization, Medieval I. T.
N5970.D8313     701/.03 19     LC 80-22769     ISBN 0226167690

**Kitzinger, Ernst, 1912-.**     **1.4737**
[Early medieval art in the British Museum] Early medieval art, with illustrations from the British Museum and British Library collections / Ernst Kitzinger. — Rev. ed. — Bloomington: Indiana University Press, 1983. 127 p., [16] p. of plates: ill. (some col.); 25 cm. (Midland book; MB-65) Previously published as: Early medieval art in the British Museum. 'Second Midland Book edition'—T.p. verso. 1. British Museum. 2. Art, Medieval I. British Museum. II. British Library. III. T.
N5970.K55 1983     709/.02 19     LC 83-47900     ISBN 0253200652

**Zarnecki, George.**     **1.4738**
Art of the medieval world: architecture, sculpture, painting, the sacred arts / George Zarnecki. Englewood Cliffs, N.J.: Prentice-Hall, 1975. 476 p.: ill. (some col.); 31 cm. (Library of art history) Includes index. 1. Art, Medieval — History. I. T.
N5970.Z37 1975b     709/.02     LC 75-25576     ISBN 081090361X

**Davis-Weyer, Caecilia, comp.**     **1.4739**
Early medieval art, 300–1150; sources and documents [compiled by] Caecilia Davis–Weyer. — Englewood Cliffs, N.J.: Prentice-Hall, [1971] x, 182 p.: front.; 23 cm. — (Sources and documents in the history of art series.) 1. Art, Medieval — History — Sources. I. T. II. Series.
N5975.D3     709.02     LC 70-135404     ISBN 0132223643

**Henderson, George, 1931-.**     **1.4740**
Early medieval. Harmondsworth, Penguin, 1972. 272 p. illus., facsims., plan, ports. 20 cm. (Style and civilization) 1. Art, Medieval I. T.
N5975.H35     709/.4     LC 72-171390     ISBN 0140214208

**Hubert, Jean.**     • **1.4741**
[Empire carolingien. English] The Carolingian renaissance [by] J. Hubert, J. Porcher [and] W. F. Volbach. New York, G. Braziller [1970] xi, 380 p. illus. (part col.), col. maps (part fold.), plans (part col.) 25 cm. (The Arts of mankind) Translation of L'Empire carolingien. 'Translated by James Emmons: parts one and four, Stuart Gilbert: part two, and Robert Allen: part three.' 1. Art, Carolingian 2. Architecture, Carlovingian I. Porcher, Jean. joint author. II. Volbach, Wolfgang Friedrich, 1892- joint author. III. T. IV. Series.
N6245.H813     709/.4     LC 72-99513

**Lasko, Peter.**     **1.4742**
Ars sacra, 800–1200 / Peter Lasko. — Harmondsworth, Middlesex: Penguin Books, c1972. xxix, 338 p., [19] p. of plates: ill. (Pelican history of art.) 1. Art, Carolingian 2. Art, Ottonian 3. Art, Romanesque I. T. II. Series.
N6245.L37     730/.094     LC 73-162318     ISBN 014056036X

**Beckwith, John, 1918-.**     **1.4743**
The art of Constantinople: an introduction to Byzantine art 330–1453. — 2nd ed. — London; New York: Phaidon, 1968. viii, 184 p.: 203 illus.; 26 cm. —

(Phaidon paperback) Distributors in the United States: Frederick A. Praeger, New York. 1. Art, Byzantine — Istanbul. 2. Art — Istanbul — History. I. T.
N6250.B4 1968      709/.561      *LC* 68-18908      *ISBN* 071481332X

**Kitzinger, Ernst, 1912-.**      **1.4744**
The art of Byzantium and the medieval West: selected studies / by Ernst Kitzinger; edited by W. Eugene Kleinbauer. Bloomington: Indiana University Press, c1976. xvii, 419 p.: ill.; 29 cm. 1. Art, Byzantine — Addresses, essays, lectures. 2. Art, Medieval — Byzantine influences — Addresses, essays, lectures. I. T.
N6250.K57 1976      709/.39/5      *LC* 75-34728      *ISBN* 0253310555

**Kitzinger, Ernst.**      **1.4745**
Byzantine art in the making: main lines of stylistic development in Mediterranean art, 3rd–7th century / Ernst Kitzinger. — Cambridge, Mass.: Harvard University Press, 1977. xii, 175 p., [68] leaves of plates: ill. (some col.); 26 cm. 1. Art, Byzantine I. T.
N6250.K58      709/.02      *LC* 77-73578      *ISBN* 0674089553

**Mango, Cyril A. comp.**      **1.4746**
The art of the Byzantine Empire, 312–1453; sources and documents [by] Cyril Mango. — Englewood Cliffs, N.J.: Prentice-Hall, [1972] xvi, 272 p.: front.; 23 cm. — (Sources and documents in the history of art series.) 1. Art, Byzantine — History — Sources. I. T. II. Series.
N6250.M25      709/.02      *LC* 72-380      *ISBN* 0130470279

**Burckhardt, Titus.**      **1.4747**
Art of Islam: language and meaning / by Titus Burckhardt; with photographs by Roland Michaud; translated by J. Peter Hobson; foreword by Seyyed Hossein Nasr. — [London]: World of Islam Festival Pub. Co., 1976. xvi, 204 p.: ill. (some col.); 31 cm. Includes index. 1. Art, Islamic 2. Islamic art and symbolism I. T.
N6260.B87 1976      709/.17/671 19      *LC* 82-136134      *ISBN* 0905035003

**Grabar, Oleg.**      **1.4748**
The formation of Islamic art. — New Haven: Yale University Press, 1973. xix, 233, [80] p.: 131 illus.; 27 cm. 1. Art, Islamic — History. I. T.
N6260.G69      709/.1/7671      *LC* 72-75193      *ISBN* 0300015054

**Papadopoulo, Alexandre.**      **1.4749**
[Islam et l'art musulman. English] Islam and Muslim art / Alexandre Papadopoulo; translated from the French by Robert Erich Wolf. — New York: H. N. Abrams, 1979, c1976. 631 p.: ill. (some col.); 32 cm. Includes index. 1. Art, Islamic I. T.
N6260.P3613 1979      709/.1/7671      *LC* 78-31690      *ISBN* 0810906414

**Focillon, Henri, 1881-1943.**      **1.4750**
[Art d'Occident, le moyen âge, roman et gothique. English] The art of the West in the Middle Ages; edited and introduced by Jean Bony; [translated from the French by Donald King]. 2d ed. London, New York, Phaidon, 1969. 2 v. illus. 26 cm. (Phaidon paperback, PH 58, 59) Translation of Art d'Occident, le moyen âge, roman et gothique. 1. Art, Romanesque 2. Art, Gothic I. T.
N6280.F613 1969      709/.4      *LC* 71-444367      *ISBN* 0714813524

**Swarzenski, Hanns, 1903-.**      • **1.4751**
Monuments of Romanesque art: the art of church treasures in north–western Europe / by Hanns Swarzenski. — 2nd ed. — Chicago: University of Chicago Press, 1967 (1974, printing). 102 p., 238 p. of plates: ill., facsims. 1. Art, Romanesque 2. Christian art and symbolism 3. Art objects, Romanesque I. T.
N6280 S9 1967a      *ISBN* 0226786064

**The Year 1200.**      **1.4752**
[New York] Metropolitan Museum of Art; distributed by New York Graphic Society [1970] 2 v. illus. (part col.), facsims., plans. 26 cm. (The Cloisters studies in medieval art, 1-2) 1. Art, Romanesque — Exhibitions. 2. Art, Gothic — Exhibitions. I. Hoffmann, Konrad, 1938- II. Deuchler, Florens, 1931- ed. III. Metropolitan Museum of Art (New York, N.Y.) IV. Series.
N6280.Y4      709.02/1      *LC* 73-109964      *ISBN* 0870990004

## N6310–6320 GOTHIC ART
### (12th-16th Centuries)

**Frisch, Teresa Grace.**      • **1.4753**
Gothic art 1140–c. 1450; sources and documents [by] Teresa G. Frisch. — Englewood Cliffs, N.J.: Prentice-Hall, [1971] x, 181 p.: front.; 23 cm. — (Sources and documents in the history of art series) 1. Art, Gothic — History — Sources. I. T.
N6310.F7      709.02/2      *LC* 77-135403      *ISBN* 0133605450

**Henderson, George, 1931-.**      **1.4754**
Gothic. Harmondsworth Penguin 1967. 223p. (Style and civilization) 1. Art, Gothic I. T.
N6310 H4

**Worringer, Wilhelm, 1881-1965.**      **1.4755**
Form in Gothic. Authorized translation edited with an introd. by Sir Herbert Read. [Rev. ed.] Containing the original illus. New York, Schocken Books [1964] xv, 180 p. illus. 21 cm. (Schocken paperbacks) 'SB70.' Translation of Formprobleme der Gotik. 1. Art, Gothic 2. Architecture, Gothic 3. Aesthetics I. Read, Herbert Edward, Sir, 1893-1968. ed. and tr. II. T.
N6310.W6 1964      709.02      *LC* 63-22688

**Swaan, Wim.**      **1.4756**
The late Middle Ages: art and architecture from 1350 to the advent of the Renaissance / Wim Swaan; with photos. by the author. — Ithaca, N.Y.: Cornell University Press, 1977. 232 p.: ill. (some col.); 32 cm. Includes index. 1. Art, Gothic — Late Gothic I. T.
N6320.S92 1977b      709/.02/3      *LC* 77-77552      *ISBN* 0801411416

## N6350–6494 Modern Art

**Harris, Ann Sutherland.**      **1.4757**
Women artists, 1550–1950 / Ann Sutherland Harris, Linda Nochlin. — 1st ed. — Los Angeles: Los Angeles County Museum of Art/Knopf, 1977, [c1976] 367 p.: ill. (some col.); 27 cm. Exhibition catalog. Includes index. 1. Art, Modern — Exhibitions. 2. Women artists I. Nochlin, Linda, joint author. II. Los Angeles County Museum of Art. III. T.
N6350.H35 1976      709/.03/074019494      *LC* 76-39955      *ISBN* 0875870732

**Pevsner, Nikolaus, Sir, 1902-.**      • **1.4758**
Studies in art, architecture, and design. New York, Walker [1968] 2 v. illus., plans. 30 cm. 1. Art, Modern I. T.
N6350.P4 1968b      709.03      *LC* 68-27371

**Rodman, Selden, 1909-.**      • **1.4759**
The eye of man; form and content in Western painting. New York, Devin-Adair, 1955. 181 p. illus. 26 cm. 1. Art, Modern 2. Painting I. T.
N6350.R6      750.903      *LC* 55-10833

### N6370–6375 RENAISSANCE ART
### (15th-16th Centuries)

**Benesch, Otto, 1896-1964.**      • **1.4760**
The art of the Renaissance in northern Europe: its relation to the contemporary spiritual and intellectual movements / Otto Benesch. — Rev. ed. — London: Phaidon, 1965. ix, 195 p.: 90 ill., port. 1. Art, Renaissance 2. Art, European 3. Renaissance I. T.
N6370.B37 1965      709.4      *LC* 66-177

**Gilbert, Creighton.**      **1.4761**
History of Renaissance art: painting, sculpture, architecture throughout Europe. — New York: H. N. Abrams, [1973] 460 p.: illus. (part col.); 30 cm. — (The Library of art history) 1. Art, Renaissance — History. I. T.
N6370.G45 1973      709/.02/4      *LC* 72-4791      *ISBN* 0810901692

**Gombrich, E. H. (Ernst Hans), 1909-.**      **1.4762**
Symbolic images, by E. H. Gombrich. [London] Phaidon [distributed by Praeger, New York, 1972] viii, 247 p. illus. 25 cm. (His Studies in the art of the Renaissance 2) 1. Symbolism in art 2. Art, Renaissance I. T. II. Series.
N6370.G58 1972      704.94/6      *LC* 74-158098      *ISBN* 0714814954

**Hauser, Arnold, 1892-1978.**      **1.4763**
Mannerism: the crisis of the Renaissance & the origin of modern art / Arnold Hauser; translated in collaboration with the author by Eric Mosbacher. — New York: Knopf, 1965. 2 v.: ill.; 27 cm. Translation of Der Manierismus: die Krise der Renaissance und der Ursprung der modernen Kunst. 1. Mannerism (Art) 2. Literature — History and criticism I. T.
N6370.H313      709.03      *LC* 65-11130

**Hocke, Gustav René, 1908-.**      **1.4764**
Die Welt als Labyrinth: Manier und Manie in der europäischen Kunst von 1520 bis 1650 und der Gegenwart / Gustav René Hocke. — Hamburg: Rowohlt, 1957. 252 p., [48] leaves of plates: ill. — (Rowohlts deutsche Enzyklopädie. Sachgebiet: Kunstgeschichte; 50/51) 1. Mannerism (Art) 2. Art, Renaissance 3. Art, Modern — 20th century I. T.
N6370.H57      *LC* 59-25248

**Panofsky, Erwin, 1892-1968.**      • **1.4765**
Renaissance and renascences in Western art. — New York: Harper & Row, [1969, c1960] xx, 242 p., [119] p. of illus.; 21 cm. — (Harper torchbooks, TB1447) 1. Art, Renaissance I. T.
N6370.P28 1969      709/.4      *LC* 75-5834

**Panofsky, Erwin, 1892-1968.**      • **1.4766**
Studies in iconology: humanistic themes in the art of the Renaissance / by Erwin Panofsky. — New York: Harper & Row, 1962. xliii, 262 p.: ill., 93 plates;

21 cm. — (Harper torchbooks; TB1077) (The Academy library) 1. Art, Renaissance 2. Humanism I. T. II. Title: Iconology
N6370.P3 1962    *LC* 62-6203

**Shearman, John K. G.**       **1.4767**
Mannerism [by] John Shearman. Harmondsworth, Penguin, 1967. 216 p. 102 illus., plan. 20 cm. (Style and civilization) (Pelican book, A808.) 1. Mannerism (Art) I. T.
N6370.S48 1967    709.03/1    *LC* 67-98470

**Snyder, James.**       **1.4768**
Northern Renaissance art: painting, sculpture, the graphic arts from 1350 to 1575 / James Snyder. — Englewood Cliffs, N.J.: Prentice-Hall; New York: Abrams, 1985. 559 p.: ill. (some col.); 30 cm. Includes index. 1. Art, Renaissance — Europe, Northern. 2. Art — Europe, Northern. I. T.
N6370.S6 1985    709/.02/4 19    *LC* 84-11435    *ISBN* 0136235964

**Stechow, Wolfgang, 1896-1974. ed.**       **1.4769**
Northern Renaissance art, 1400–1600; sources and documents. — Englewood Cliffs, N.J.: Prentice-Hall, [1966] x, 187 p.: port.; 23 cm. — (Sources and documents in the history of art series.) 1. Art, Renaissance — History — Sources. I. T. II. Series.
N6370.S66    709.024    *LC* 66-16399

**Sypher, Wylie.**       • **1.4770**
Four stages of Renaissance style; transformations in art and literature, 1400–1700. [1st ed.] Garden City, N.Y., Doubleday, 1955. 312 p. illus. 18 cm. (A Doubleday anchor original A45) 1. Arts, Renaissance I. T.
N6370.S95    709.03    *LC* 55-6749

**Wölfflin, Heinrich, 1864-1945.**       • **1.4771**
The sense of form in art: a comparative psychological study / by H. Wölfflin; translated from the German by Alice Muehsam and Norma H. Shatan. — New York: Chelsea Pub. Co, c1958. 230 p.: ill. Translation of: Die Kunst der Renaissance: Italien und das deutsche Formgefühl. 1. Art, Renaissance 2. Art, German 3. Art, Italian 4. Art — Psychology I. T.
N6370.W553    *LC* 57-12877

## N6410–6425 17TH–18TH CENTURIES

**Gloag, John, 1896-.**       • **1.4772**
Georgian grace; a social history of design from 1660–1830. London, A. and C. Black [1956] xix, 426 p. illus., ports., facsims. 26 cm. Bibliography: p. 349-359. 'Books on furniture published between 1660 and 1830': p. 384. 1. Art, Modern — 17th-18th centuries — History 2. Design I. T.
N6410.G55    709.03    *LC* 57-412

**Praz, Mario, 1896-.**       **1.4773**
[Gusto Neoclassico. English] On Neoclassicism; translated from the Italian by Angus Davidson. London, Thames & Hudson, 1969. 400 p. 71 illus. 26 cm. Translation of Gusto Neoclassico. 1. Neoclassicism (Art) 2. Art, Modern — 17th-18th centuries I. T.
N6410.P713    709.03    *LC* 70-386455    *ISBN* 050023101X

**Rosenblum, Robert.**       **1.4774**
Transformations in late eighteenth century art. — Princeton, N.J.: Princeton University Press, 1967. xxvi, 203 p.: illus.; 25 cm. 1. Art — History — 17th-18th century. 2. Classicism in art I. T.
N6410.R66    709.033    *LC* 66-21841

**Held, Julius Samuel, 1905-.**       **1.4775**
17th and 18th century art; baroque painting, sculpture, architecture [by] Julius S. Held [and] Donald Posner. — New York: H. N. Abrams, [1971] 439 p.: illus. (part col.); 30 cm. — (Library of art history) 1. Art, Baroque I. Posner, Donald. II. T.
N6415.B3 H4    709/.03/2    *LC* 79-127417    *ISBN* 0810900327

**Martin, John Rupert.**       **1.4776**
Baroque / John Rupert Martin. — 1st U. S. ed. — New York: Harper & Row, c1977. 367 p.: ill.; 24 cm. Icon editions. 1. Art, Baroque I. T.
N6415.B3 M37 1977    N6415.B3 M37 1977b.    709/.03/2    *LC* 77-156098

**Eitner, Lorenz. comp.**       • **1.4777**
Neoclassicism and romanticism, 1750–1850; sources and documents [compiled by] Lorenz Eitner. Englewood Cliffs, N.J., Prentice-Hall [1970] 2 v. illus. 23 cm. (Sources and documents in the history of art series.) 1. Neoclassicism (Art) 2. Romanticism in art I. T. II. Series.
N6425.N4 E35    709/.033    *LC* 74-94425    *ISBN* 0136109071

**Honour, Hugh.**       **1.4778**
Neo–classicism. — Harmondsworth: Penguin, 1968. 221 p.: illus.; 20 cm. — (Style and civilization) (Pelican book A978.) 1. Neoclassicism (Art) I. T.
N6425.N4 H6    709/.033    *LC* 71-384062

**Rosenblum, Robert.**       **1.4779**
19th century art / painting by Robert Rosenblum, sculpture by H.W. Janson. — New York: Abrams, 1984. 527 p.: ill. (some col.); 30 cm. 'Published in Great Britain under the title: Art of the nineteenth century'—T.p. verso. 1. Neoclassicism (Art) 2. Art, Modern — 19th century I. Janson, H. W. (Horst Woldemar), 1913- II. T. III. Title: Nineteenth century art.
N6425.N4 R65 1984    709/.03/4 19    *LC* 83-3882    *ISBN* 0810913623

## N6447 19TH AND 20TH CENTURIES

**Canaday, John, 1907-.**       • **1.4780**
Mainstreams of modern art / John Canaday. — 2d ed. — New York: Holt, Rinehart and Winston, c1981. xii, 484 p.: ill.; 26 cm. Includes index. 1. Art, Modern — 19th century 2. Art, Modern — 20th century I. T.
N6447.C36 1981    709/.03/4 19    *LC* 80-25696    *ISBN* 0030576385

**Dunlop, Ian, 1940-.**       **1.4781**
The shock of the new; seven historic exhibitions of modern art. — New York: American Heritage Press, [1972] 272 p.: illus. (part col.); 26 cm. 1. Art, Modern — 19th century — Exhibitions — History. 2. Art, Modern — 20th century — Exhibitions — History. 3. Art and society I. T.
N6447.D86    709/.04/074    *LC* 77-39481    *ISBN* 0070182671

**Hughes, Robert, 1936-.**       **1.4782**
The shock of the new / Robert Hughes. — 1st American ed. — New York: Knopf: distributed by Random House, 1981, c1980. 423 p.: ill. (some col.); 28 cm. Includes index. 1. Art, Modern — 19th century 2. Art, Modern — 20th century I. T.
N6447.H83 1981    709/.04    *LC* 80-7631    *ISBN* 0394513789

**Kramer, Hilton.**       **1.4783**
The age of the avant–garde; an art chronicle of 1956–1972. — New York: Farrar, Straus and Giroux, [1973] xviii, 565 p.: illus.; 24 cm. 1. Art, Modern — 19th century 2. Art, Modern — 20th century 3. Art — Philosophy I. T.
N6447.K72 1973    709/.04    *LC* 72-89885    *ISBN* 0374102384

**Modern art and modernism: a critical anthology / edited by**       **1.4784**
**Francis Frascina and Charles Harrison; with the assistance of**
**Deirdre Paul.**
New York: Harper & Row, [1982] 312 p., [8] leaves of plates: ill.; 24 cm. (Icon editions) 1. Art, Modern — 19th century — Addresses, essays, lectures. 2. Art, Modern — 20th century — Addresses, essays, lectures. 3. Modernism (Art) — Addresses, essays, lectures. I. Frascina, Francis. II. Harrison, Charles, 1942- III. Paul, Deirdre.
N6447.M6 1982    709/.04 19    *LC* 82-48153    *ISBN* 0064332152

**Russell, John, 1919-.**       **1.4785**
The meanings of modern art / John Russell. — [Rev. and updated ed.]. — New York: Museum of Modern Art: Harper & Row, c1981. 429 p.: ill. (some col.); 27 cm. Includes index. 1. Art, Modern — 19th century 2. Art, Modern — 20th century I. T.
N6447.R87 1981    709/.04 19    *LC* 80-8217    *ISBN* 0060137010

**Schapiro, Meyer, 1904-.**       **1.4786**
Modern art, 19th & 20th centuries / Meyer Schapiro. — New York: G. Braziller, 1978, 1979 printing. xi, 277 p., [39] leaves of plates: ill. (some col.); 25 cm. — (His Selected papers; v. 2) 1. Art, Modern — 19th century 2. Art, Modern — 20th century I. T.
N6447.S33    709/.04    *LC* 78-6831    *ISBN* 0807608998

## N6450–6465 19TH CENTURY

**The Art of all nations, 1850–73: the emerging role of exhibitions**       **1.4787**
**and critics / selected and edited by Elizabeth Gilmore Holt.**
Princeton, N.J.: Princeton University Press, 1982, c1981. xxx, 606 p., [48] p. of plates: ill.; 23 cm. Originally published: Garden City, N.Y.: Anchor Books, 1981. Includes index. 1. Art, Modern — 19th century — Themes, motives — Exhibitions. 2. Art and society 3. Salon (Exhibition) 4. Art criticism I. Holt, Elizabeth Basye Gilmore.
N6450.A79 1982    701/.03 19    *LC* 81-47989    *ISBN* 0691039968

**Chipp, Hershel Browning, comp.**       **1.4788**
Theories of modern art; a source book by artists and critics / Herschel B. Chipp; contributions by Peter Selz and Joshua C. Taylor. Berkeley: University of California Press, 1968. xv, 664 p.: ill., ports. — (California studies in the history of art. 11) 1. Art, Modern — 19th century — History — Addresses, essays, lectures. 2. Art, Modern — 20th century — History — Addresses, essays, lectures I. T. II. Series.
N6450.C62    *LC* 68-12038    *ISBN* 0520014502

**Galassi, Peter.**       **1.4789**
Before photography: painting and the invention of photography / Peter Galassi. — New York: Museum of Modern Art; Boston: Distributed by New York

Graphic Society, c1981. 151 p.: ill. (some col.); 22 x 26 cm. Catalog of an exhibition held at the Museum of Modern Art, New York, May 9–July 5, 1981, and other institutions. Includes index. 1. Art, Modern — 19th century — Exhibitions. 2. Art and photography — Exhibitions. 3. Photography, Artistic — Exhibitions. I. Museum of Modern Art (New York, N.Y.) II. T.
N6450.G23      760/.09/034074013 19      *LC* 81-80568      *ISBN* 0870702548

**Nochlin, Linda.**                                           **1.4790**
Realism and tradition in art, 1848–1900; sources and documents. — Englewood Cliffs, N.J.: Prentice-Hall, [1966] x, 189 p.; 23 cm. — (Sources and documents in the history of art series.) 1. Realism in art 2. Naturalism in art 3. Art, Modern — 19th century — Sources. I. T. II. Series.
N6450.N57      709.034      *LC* 66-23609

**Pevsner, Nikolaus, Sir, 1902-.**                          ● **1.4791**
[Pioneers of the modern movement] Pioneers of modern design, from William Morris to Walter Gropius. [Rev. ed. Harmondsworth, Middlesex] Penguin Books [1964, c1960] 253 p. illus. 20 cm. (Pelican books, A497) First published in 1936 under title: Pioneers of the modern movement, from William Morris to Walter Gropius. 1. Art, Modern — 19th century 2. Art, Modern — 20th century I. T.
N6450.P4 1964      709.035      *LC* 64-4000

**Schultze, Jürgen.**                                         **1.4792**
Art of nineteenth-century Europe / text by Jürgen Schultze, [translated from the German by Barbara Forryan].— New York: Abrams, 1970. 264 p.: ill.; 24 cm.— (Panorama of world art) Traduction de Neunzehntes Jahrhundert. 1. Art, Modern — 19th century — Europe. I. T. II. Series.
N6450.S34      *LC* 79-92913      *ISBN* 0810980177

**Holt, Elizabeth Basye Gilmore.**                           **1.4793**
The Triumph of art for the public: the emerging role of exhibitions and critics / selected and edited by Elizabeth Gilmore Holt. — Princeton, N.J.: Princeton University Press, 1983. xxviii, 530 p., [16] leaves of plates: ill.; 18 cm. Includes index. 1. Art, Modern — 19th century 2. Art — Exhibitions 3. Art exhibition audiences 4. Art criticism I. T.
N6450.T7 1983      709/.03/4 19      *LC* 83-60461      *ISBN* 0691003491

**Schmutzler, Robert.**                                       **1.4794**
[Art nouveau. English] Art nouveau / Robert Schmutzler. — New York: Abrams, 1978. 224 p.: ill. (some col.); 30 cm. Includes index. 1. Art nouveau 2. Art, Modern — 19th century I. T.
N6465.A7 S3513 1978      709/.04      *LC* 78-8781      *ISBN* 0810906767.      *ISBN* 0810921774 pbk

**Selz, Peter Howard, 1919- ed.**                            **1.4795**
Art nouveau: art and design at the turn of the century / edited by Peter Selz and Mildred Constantine; with articles by Greta Daniel ... [et al.]. New rev. ed. — New York: Museum of Modern Art; Boston: distributed by New York Graphic Society, 1975. 192 p., [4] leaves of plates: ill. (some col.); 24 cm. Includes index. 1. Art nouveau 2. Art, Modern — 19th century I. Constantine, Mildred. II. T.
N6465.A7 S4 1975      709/.04      *LC* 75-15064      *ISBN* 087070222X

**Rewald, John, 1912-.**                                     ● **1.4796**
The history of impressionism / John Rewald. — 4th, rev. ed. — New York: Museum of Modern Art; Greenwich, Conn.: distributed by New York Graphic Society, 1973. 672 p., [1] leaf of plates: ill. (some col.); 26 cm. Includes index. 1. Impressionism (Art) — History. 2. Art, Modern — 19th century — History I. T.
N6465.I4 R48 1973      759.05      *LC* 68-17468      *ISBN* 0870703606

**Nochlin, Linda.**                                           **1.4797**
Realism. — Harmondsworth: Penguin, 1971. 283 p.: illus.; 20 cm. — (Style and civilization) 1. Realism in art 2. Art, Modern — 19th century I. T.
N6465.R4 N6      709/.03/4      *LC* 71-149557      *ISBN* 0140213058

**Vaughan, William.**                                         **1.4798**
Romantic art / William Vaughan. — London: Thames and Hudson, c1978. 288 p.: ill. (some col.); 22 cm. — 1. Romanticism in art 2. Art, Modern — 19th century I. T.
N6465.R6 V39 1978      N6465R6 V39 1978.      *LC* 77-76818      *ISBN* 0500181608

**Delevoy, Robert L.**                                        **1.4799**
Symbolists and symbolism / by Robert L. Delevoy; [translated from the French by Barbara Bray, Elizabeth Wrightson, and Bernard C. Swift]. — New York: Rizzoli, 191978. 247 p.: ill. Translation of Journal du symbolisme. Includes index. 1. Symbolism (Art movement) 2. Art, Modern — 19th century I. T.
N6465.S9 D4413      700/.9/034      *LC* 77-79717

**Goldwater, Robert John, 1907-1973.**                       **1.4800**
Symbolism / Robert Goldwater. — 1st U.S. ed. — New York: Harper & Row, c1979. 286 p.: ill.; 24 cm. 1. Symbolism (Art movement) 2. Art, Modern — 19th century I. T.
N6465.S9 G64      N6465S9 G64.      *LC* 77-82780      *ISBN* 0064332659

## N6485–6494 20TH CENTURY

**Zeitgeist: international art exhibition, Berlin, 1982: Martin–**    **1.4801**
**Gropius–Bau: [catalogue / edited by Christos M. Joachimides,**
**Norman Rosenthal].**
New York: G. Brazilier, c1983. 296 p.: ill.; 29 cm. '... arranged through the Neuer Berliner Kunstverein e.V., Berlin.' 1. Art, Modern — 20th century — Exhibitions. I. Joachimides, Christos M. II. Rosenthal, Norman. III. Neuer Berliner Kunstverein. IV. Martin-Gropius-Bau (Berlin, Germany) V. Title: Zeit-Geist. VI. Title: International art exhibition, Berlin, 1982.
N6488.G3 B38993      *ISBN* 0807680331

**American Abstract Artists.**                               ● **1.4802**
The World of abstract art. — New York: G. Wittenborn, 1957? viii, 167 p.: ill. (part col.). 'Artists from different parts of the world ... write on aspects of the movement in their respective countries.' 1. Art, Abstract 2. Art, Modern — 20th century I. T.
N6490.A64      *LC* 57-8548

**Arnason, H. Harvard.**                                      **1.4803**
History of modern art: painting, sculpture, architecture / H.H. Arnason. — 3rd ed. / rev. and updated by Daniel Wheeler. — Englewood Cliffs, N.J.: Prentice-Hall; New York: H.N. Abrams, 1986. p. cm. Includes index. 1. Art, Modern — 20th century I. Wheeler, Daniel. II. T.
N6490.A713 1986b      709/.04 19      *LC* 86-3411      *ISBN* 0133903605

**Art actuel. Actual art.**                                  **1.4804**
no. 1- 1975-. [Genève, Suisse, Éditions d'art Albert Skira, etc.] no. ill. 33 cm. Annual. 'Skira annuel.' 1. Art, Modern — 20th century — Yearbooks.
N6490.A7165      709/.04      *LC* 80-642930

**Battcock, Gregory, 1937- ed.**                             **1.4805**
The new art; a critical anthology. — [1st ed.]. — New York: Dutton, 1966. 254 p.: illus.; 19 cm. 1. Art, Modern — 20th century — Addresses, essays, lectures. 2. Art criticism I. T.
N6490.B35      709.04      *LC* 66-3422

**Benthall, Jonathan.**                                       **1.4806**
Science and technology in art today. — New York: Praeger, [1972] 180 p.: illus.; 22 cm. — (Praeger world of art series) 1. Art, Modern — 20th century 2. Art and science 3. Art and technology I. T.
N6490.B375 1972b      701      *LC* 78-183061

**Contemporary artists / Muriel Emanuel ... [et al.], editors.**    **1.4807**
2nd ed. — New York: St. Martin's Press, 1983. vii, 1041 p.: ill.; 29 cm. — (Contemporary arts series) 1. Art, Modern — 20th century — Bio-bibliography. I. Emanuel, Muriel.
N6490.C6567 1983      709/.2/2 B 19      *LC* 82-25048      *ISBN* 0312166435

**Herbert, Robert L., 1929- ed.**                            ● **1.4808**
Modern artists on art; ten unabridged essays, edited by Robert L. Herbert. — Englewood Cliffs, N.J.: Prentice-Hall, [1965, c1964] ix, 149 p.; 21 cm. — (A Spectrum book) 1. Art, Modern — 20th century — Addresses, essays, lectures. I. T.
N6490.H45      709.04      *LC* 64-7568

**An international survey of recent painting and sculpture / the**    **1.4809**
**Museum of Modern Art, New York; Kynaston McShine.**
New York: The museum, 1984. 364 p.: ill. (some col.); 29 x 26 cm. 1. Art, Modern — 20th century — Exhibitions. I. McShine, Kynaston. II. Museum of Modern Art (New York, N.Y.)
N 6490 I625 1984      *LC* 84-60766      *ISBN* 0870703919

**Janis, Harriet Grossman.**                                 ● **1.4810**
Collage: personalities, concepts [and] techniques [by] Harriet Janis and Rudi Blesh. — [Rev. ed.]. — Philadelphia: Chilton Book Co., [1967] 342 p.: 497 illus.; 28 cm. 1. Collage I. Blesh, Rudi, 1899- joint author. II. T.
N6490.J3 1967      751.4/9      *LC* 67-5494

**Kandinsky, Wassily, 1866-1944. ed.**                       ● **1.4811**
[Blaue Reiter. English] The Blaue Reiter almanac. Edited by Wassily Kandinsky and Franz Marc. New documentary ed. Edited and with an introd. by Klaus Lankheit. New York, Viking Press [1974] 296 p. illus. 22 cm. (The Documents of 20th-century art) Translation of Der Blaue Reiter. 1. Blaue Reiter (Group of artists) 2. Art, Modern — 20th century — Addresses, essays,

N
6487
N4
M85
1984

lectures. I. Marc, Franz, 1880-1916. joint ed. II. Lankheit, Klaus. joint ed. III. T.
N6490.K2913 1974     759.3 19     *LC* 75-170678     *ISBN* 067017355X
*ISBN* 0670019313

**Kepes, Gyorgy, 1906- ed.**     • **1.4812**
The visual arts today. — Middletown, Conn.: Wesleyan University Press, [1960] 272 p.: illus.; 27 cm. 1. Art, Modern — 20th century — Addresses, essays, lectures. 2. Art — Philosophy I. T.
N6490.K4     709.04     *LC* 60-13159

**Klee, Paul, 1879-1940.**     • **1.4813**
[Über die moderne Kunst. English] On modern art; translated [from the German] by Paul Findlay with an introd. by Herbert Read. London, Faber, 1966. 55 p. illus. 19 cm. (Faber paper covered editions) 1. Modernism (Art) I. Findlay, Paul, tr. II. T.
N6490.K553 1966     709.04     *LC* 71-356501

**Krauss, Rosalind E.**     **1.4814**
The originality of the avant–garde and other modernist myths / Rosalind E. Krauss. — Cambridge, Mass.: MIT Press, c1985. 307 p.: ill.; 24 cm. 1. Avant-garde (Aesthetics) — History — 20th century. 2. Modernism (Art) — Themes, motives. 3. Creation (Literary, artistic, etc.) — Psychological aspects. I. T.
N6490.K727 1985     709/.04 19     *LC* 84-11315     *ISBN* 0262110938

**Lewis, Wyndham, 1886-1957.**     • **1.4815**
Demon of progress in the arts. Chicago, H. Regnery Co., 1955. 97 p. illus. 1. Art, Modern — 20th century 2. Art — England I. T.
N6490 L4     709.04     *LC* 55-4030

**Lynton, Norbert.**     **1.4816**
The story of modern art / Norbert Lynton. — Ithaca, N.Y.: Cornell University Press, 1980. 382 p.: ill. (some col.); 25 cm. — (Cornell paperbacks.) 'A Phaidon book.' Includes index. 1. Art, Modern — 20th century — History I. T.
N6490.L93 1980b     709/.04 19     *LC* 80-67606     *ISBN* 0801413516

**Mondrian, Piet, 1872-1944.**     • **1.4817**
Plastic art and pure plastic art, 1937, and other essays, 1941–1943 / Piet Mondrian. — 1st ed. — New York: Wittenborn, 1945. 64 p.: ill. (some col.); 26 cm. — (The Documents of modern art) 1. Art, Modern — 20th century 2. Art, Abstract I. T. II. Series.
N6490 M6     *LC* 45-35141

**Museum of Modern Art (New York, N.Y.)**     • **1.4818**
Fantastic art, dada, surrealism. Edited by Alfred H. Barr, Jr. Essays by Georges Hugnet. New York, Museum of Modern Art. Reprint ed. [New York] Published for the Museum of Modern Art by Arno Press, 1968 [c1947] 271 p. illus. 26 cm. 'This volume is a revision of that originally published to record and explain the exhibition ... held at the Museum of Modern Art, December 1936-January 1937.' 1. Dadaism 2. Surrealism 3. Fantasy in art I. Barr, Alfred Hamilton, 1902- ed. II. Hugnet, Georges, 1906-1974. III. T.
N6490.N374 1968     709.04     *LC* 68-8367

**Museum of Modern Art (New York, N.Y.)**     • **1.4819**
Masters of modern art; edited by Alfred H. Barr, Jr. New York, Distributed by Simon and Schuster [1954] 239 p. illus. (part mounted col.) 29 cm. 'Prepared by the Museum of Modern Art on the occasion of the twenty-fifth anniversary.' 1. Art, Modern — 20th century I. Barr, Alfred Hamilton, 1902- ed. II. T.
N6490.N38     709.04     *LC* 54-13277

**The Oxford companion to twentieth–century art / edited by**     **1.4820**
**Harold Osborne.**
Oxford; New York: Oxford University Press, 1982, [c1981]. x, 656 p., [128] p. of plates: ill. (some col.); 24 cm. 1. Art, Modern — 20th century — Dictionaries. 2. Artists — Biography. I. Osborne, Harold, 1905-
N6490.O94     709/.04/00321 19     *LC* 82-126560     *ISBN* 0198661193

**Parry, Pamela Jeffcott.**     **1.4821**
Contemporary art and artists: an index to reproductions / compiled by Pamela Jeffcott Parry. — Westport, Conn.: Greenwood Press, 1978. xlix, 327 p.; 24 cm. 1. Art, Modern — 20th century — Indexes. 2. Artists — Indexes. I. T.
N6490.P3234     709/.04     *LC* 78-57763     *ISBN* 0313205442

**Phaidon dictionary of twentieth–century art.**     **1.4822**
London; New York: Phaidon Press, 1973. [6], 420, [48] p.: illus.; 26 cm. Distributed by Praeger Publishers, New York. 1. Art, Modern — 20th century — Dictionaries. 2. Artists — Biography — Dictionaries. I. Title: Dictionary of twentieth-century art.
N6490.P46     709/.04     *LC* 72-86572     *ISBN* 0714815578

**Public Education Association of the City of New York.**     • **1.4823**
Seven decades, 1895-1965; crosscurrents in modern art; [exhibition] April 26–May 21, 1966. Text by Peter Selz. [New York, s.n., 1966] 192 p. ill. (some col.) 28 cm. 1. Art, Modern — 20th century — Exhibitions. I. Selz, Peter Howard, 1919- II. T. III. Title: Crosscurrents in modern art.
N 6490 P97 1966     *LC* 66-57731

**Read, Herbert Edward, Sir, 1893-1968.**     • **1.4824**
Art now; an introduction to the theory of modern painting and sculpture. — [Rev. ed.]. — New York: Pitman, [1960] 131 p.: 196 plates (part col.); 23 cm. 1. Art, Modern — 20th century 2. Aesthetics, Modern — 20th century I. T.
N6490.R4 1960     709.04     *LC* 61-19203

**Read, Herbert Edward, Sir, 1893-1968.**     • **1.4825**
The philosophy of modern art; collected essays. — Freeport, N.Y.: Books for Libraries Press, [1971, c1953] 278 p.: illus.; 23 cm. — (Essay index reprint series) 1. Art — Philosophy 2. Art, Modern — 20th century I. T.
N6490.R43 1971     709.04     *LC* 70-128294     *ISBN* 0836920236

**Richardson, Tony, 1941-1969.**     **1.4826**
Concepts of modern art. Edited by Tony Richardson and Nikos Stangos. — [1st U.S. ed.]. — New York: Harper & Row, [1974] xii, 281 p.: illus.; 23 cm. — (Icon editions) 1. Art, Modern — 20th century I. Stangos, Nikos. joint author. II. T.
N6490.R53458 1974     709/.04     *LC* 73-9334     *ISBN* 0064384454

**Rickey, George.**     • **1.4827**
Constructivism; origins and evolution. — New York: G. Braziller, [1967] xi, 305 p.: illus.; 25 cm. 1. Constructivism. I. T.
N6490.R54     701.8     *LC* 67-24210

**Rischbieter, Henning. comp.**     • **1.4828**
[Bühne und bildende Kunst im XX. Jahrhundert. English] Art and the stage in the 20th century; painters and sculptors work for the theater. Documented by Wolfgang Storch. [Translated from the German by Michael Bullock. French and Italian texts translated by Michael Bullock. Catalog translated by Andreas Schroeder] Greenwich, Conn., New York Graphic Society [c1968] 306 p. illus. (part col.) 31 cm. Translation of Bühne und bildende Kunst im XX. Jahrhundert. 1. Art, Modern — 20th century 2. Theaters — Stage-setting and scenery I. Storch, Wolfgang. II. T.
N6490.R5473     709/.04     *LC* 72-86261     *ISBN* 0821203525

**Rosenberg, Harold.**     • **1.4829**
The anxious object; art today and its audience. — New York: Horizon Press, [1964] 270 p.: illus.; 24 cm. 1. Art, Modern — 20th century I. T. II. Title: Art today and its audience.
N6490.R59     709.04     *LC* 64-24539

**Rosenberg, Harold.**     • **1.4830**
Artworks and packages. — New York: Horizon Press, [1969] 232 p.: 171 illus. (incl. 8 col. plates); 32 cm. 1. Art, Modern — 20th century 2. Art — Technique I. T.
N6490.R592     709/.04     *LC* 68-54185

**Rubin, William Stanley.**     • **1.4831**
Dada, Surrealism, and their heritage, by William S. Rubin. New York, Museum of Modern Art; distributed by New York Graphic Society, Greenwich, Conn. [1968] 251 p. illus. (part col.), ports. 24 cm. Exhibition shown Mar. 27-June 9, 1968, at the Museum of Modern Art; July 16-Sept. 8, 1968, at the Los Angeles County Museum of Art; and Oct. 19-Dec. 8, 1968, at the Art Institute of Chicago. 1. Dadaism 2. Surrealism (Art) 3. Art, Modern — 20th century — Exhibitions. I. New York, Museum of Modern Art. II. Los Angeles County Museum. III. Art Institute of Chicago. IV. T.
N6490.R77     709.04     *LC* 68-17466

**Schmutzler, Robert.**     • **1.4832**
[Art nouveau. English] Art nouveau. [English translation by Edouard Roditi] New York, H. N. Abrams [c1962] 322 p. illus. (part mounted col.) 31 cm. 1. Art nouveau I. T.
N6490.S2953     709.04     *LC* 64-10765

**Seitz, William Chapin.**     • **1.4833**
The art of assemblage. — New York: Museum of Modern Art; distributed by Doubleday, Garden City, N.Y., [1961] 176 p.: illus. (part col.); 25 cm. 1. Assemblage (Art) 2. Art — Exhibitions I. T.
N6490.S35     709.04     *LC* 61-17803

**Selz, Peter Howard, 1919-.**     • **1.4834**
Art nouveau; art and design at the turn of the century, edited by Peter Selz and Mildred Constantine, with articles by Greta Daniel [and others] New York, Museum of Modern Art; distributed by Doubleday, Garden City [1960, c1959] 192 p. illus. 25 cm. 'Issued in conjunction with the art nouveau exhibition at the Museum of Modern Art [and others]' 1. Art nouveau I. Constantine, Mildred. II. T.
N6490.S37     709.04     *LC* 60-11987

**Smagula, Howard J., 1942-.**     **1.4835**
Currents, contemporary directions in the visual arts / Howard J. Smagula. — Englewood Cliffs, N.J.: Prentice-Hall, c1983. ix, 336 p., [8] p. of plates: ill. (some col.); 24 cm. 1. Art, Modern — 20th century — Themes, motives 2. Art — Philosophy I. T.
N6490.S565 1983     709/.04 19     *LC* 82-15075     *ISBN* 0131957430

**Steinberg, Leo, 1920-.**        **1.4836**
Other criteria: confrontations with twentieth–century art. — New York: Oxford University Press, 1972. viii, 436 p.: illus.; 27 cm. 1. Art, Modern — 20th century I. T.
N6490.S74     709/.04     *LC* 72-77502     *ISBN* 0195015770

**Zero.**        **1.4837**
1-3; 1958-1961. [Cambridge, Mass.: MIT Press, 1973.] 3 v. in 1 (xxv, 331 p.): ill.; 21 cm. 1. Art, Modern — 20th century — Periodicals. I. Piene, Otto. II. Mack, Heinz.
N6490.Z38     709/.04     *LC* 78-130276

**Battersby, Martin.**        **1.4838**
The decorative Twenties. New York, Walker [1969] 211 p. illus. (part col.) 30 cm. 1. Art, Modern — 20th century 2. Decorative arts — History — 20th century. I. T.
N6493 1920.B372     745.2     *LC* 71-84213

## N6494 Special Movements, A–Z

**Arwas, Victor.**        **1.4839**
Art deco / Victor Arwas; [editor, Frank Russell]. — New York: Abrams, 1980. 315 p.: ill. (some col.); 32 cm. Includes index. 1. Art deco 2. Art, Modern — 20th century I. Russell, Frank D., 1923- II. T.
N6494.A7 A65     709/.04/012     *LC* 80-12363     *ISBN* 0810906910

**Bann, Stephen. comp.**        **1.4840**
The tradition of constructivism. Edited and with an introd. by Stephen Bann. New York, Viking Press [1974] xlix, 334 p. illus. 22 cm. (The Documents of 20th-century art) 1. Constructivism (Art) — Addresses, essays, lectures. 2. Art, Modern — 20th century — Addresses, essays, lectures. I. T. II. Series.
N6494.C64 B36 1974     709/.04     *LC* 72-75748     *ISBN* 0670723010 *ISBN* 0670019569

**New York. Museum of Modern Art.**        • **1.4841**
Cubism and abstract art, by Alfred H. Barr, Jr. — Reprint ed. — New York: Published for the Museum of Modern Art by Arno Press, 1966 [c1936] 249 p.: illus.; 27 cm. Includes catalog of an exhibition. 1. Cubism 2. Art, Abstract I. Barr, Alfred Hamilton, 1902- II. T.
N6494.C8     709.04     *LC* 66-26123

**Cooper, Douglas, 1911-.**        • **1.4842**
The Cubist epoch. [New York] Phaidon [1971] 320 p. illus. (part col.) 26 cm. Based on an exhibition of 321 paintings, sculpture, drawings, and prints shown at the Los Angeles County Museum of Art, 1970 and at the Metropolitan Museum of Art, 1971. 1. Cubism — Exhibitions. 2. Art, Modern — 20th century I. Los Angeles County Museum of Art. II. Metropolitan Museum of Art (New York, N.Y.) III. T.
N6494.C8 C6     759.06     *LC* 74-112621     *ISBN* 0714814482

**Kozloff, Max.**        **1.4843**
Cubism/futurism. — New York: Charterhouse, [1973] xix, 234 p.: illus.; 23 cm. 1. Cubism 2. Futurism (Art) I. T.
N6494.C8 K69     759.06     *LC* 72-84221

**Rosenblum, Robert.**        • **1.4844**
Cubism and twentieth–century art / Robert Rosenblum. — New York: H. N. Abrams, [1976?] 346 p.: ill. (some col.); 25 cm. Includes index. 1. Cubism 2. Art, Modern — 20th century I. T.
N6494.C8 R67 1976b     709/.04/032 19     *LC* 80-488131     *ISBN* 0810907674

**Beardsley, John.**        **1.4845**
Earthworks and beyond: contemporary art in the landscape / John Beardsley. — 1st ed. — New York: Abbeville Press, c1984. 144 p.: ill. (some col.); 29 cm. Includes index. 1. Earthworks (Art) 2. Avant-garde (Aesthetics) — 20th century. I. T.
N6494.E27 B4 1984     709/.04/076 19     *LC* 83-21424     *ISBN* 089659422X

**Elderfield, John.**        **1.4846**
The 'wild beasts': Fauvism and its affinities / John Elderfield. — New York: Museum of Modern Art: distributed by Oxford University Press, c1976. 167 p.: ill. (some col.); 24 cm. Published on the occasion of an exhibition of Fauvist art held at the Museum of Modern Art, March 26-June 1, 1976, at the San Francisco Museum of Modern Art, June 29-Aug. 15, 1976, and at the Kimbell Art Museum, Fort Worth, Sept. 11-Oct. 31, 1976. 1. Fauvism — Exhibitions. 2. Art, Modern — 20th century — Exhibitions. I. Museum of Modern Art (New York, N.Y.) II. San Francisco Museum of Modern Art. III. Kimbell Art Museum. IV. T. V. Title: Fauvism.
N6494.F3 E42     759.4     *LC* 76-1491     *ISBN* 087070639X

**Tisdall, Caroline.**        **1.4847**
Futurism / Caroline Tisdall, Angelo Bozzolla [i.e. A. Bozzola]. — New York; Toronto: Oxford University Press, 1978, c1977. 216 p.: ill.; 21 cm. — (World of art.) 1. Futurism (Art) I. Bozzola, Angelo, joint author. II. T. III. Series.
N6494.F8 T57     *LC* 77-76819     *ISBN* 0195199804 Pbk

**Tovey, John.**        **1.4848**
The technique of kinetic art. — London: Batsford; New York: Van Nostrand Reinhold, 1971, [c1972]. 144 p., 4 plates.: illus. (some col.); 26 cm. 1. Kinetic art I. T.
N6494.K5 T6 1971     700     *LC* 72-161979

**Battcock, Gregory, 1937- comp.**        **1.4849**
Minimal art; a critical anthology. — [1st ed.]. — New York: E. P. Dutton, 1968. 448 p.: illus.; 21 cm. 1. Minimal art — Addresses, essays, lectures. I. T.
N6494.M5 B3 1968     709.04     *LC* 68-5528

**Kultermann, Udo.**        **1.4850**
[Radikaler Realismus. English] New realism. Greenwich, Conn., New York Graphic Society [1972] 1 v. (various pagings) illus. (part col.) 25 cm. Translation of Radikaler Realismus. 1. Pop art 2. Art, Modern — 20th century I. T.
N6494.P6 K813     759.13     *LC* 76-181341     *ISBN* 0821204327

**'Primitivism' in 20th century art: affinity of the tribal and the**        **1.4851**
**modern / edited by William Rubin.**
New York: Museum of Modern Art; Boston: Distributed by New York Graphic Society Books, c1984. 2 v. (xv, 689 p.): ill. (some col.); 32 cm. 'Published in conjunction with an exhibition of the same title shown at the following museums: The Museum of Modern Art, New York, Detroit Institute of Arts, Dallas Museum of Art'—T.p. verso. 1. Primitivism in art — Addresses, essays, lectures. 2. Art, Modern — 20th century — Addresses, essays, lectures. I. Rubin, William Stanley. II. Museum of Modern Art (New York, N.Y.) III. Detroit Institute of Arts. IV. Dallas Museum of Art. V. Title: 'Primitivism' in twentieth century art.
N6494.P7 P75 1984     709/.04 19     *LC* 84-60915     *ISBN* 0870705180

**Carrà, Massimo, 1922- comp.**        **1.4852**
[Metafisica. English] Metaphysical art [compiled by] Massimo Carrà, with Patrick Waldberg and Ewald Rathke. Translation and historical foreword by Caroline Tisdall. New York, Praeger Publishers [1971] 216 p. illus. 22 cm. Translation of Metafisica. 1. Surrealism — Addresses, essays, lectures. I. Waldberg, Patrick. II. Rathke, Ewald. III. T.
N6494.S8 C313     750/.1     *LC* 79-116640

**Rubin, William Stanley.**        • **1.4853**
Dada and surrealist art [by] William S. Rubin. — New York: H. N. Abrams, [1968] 525 p.: illus. (part col.), ports.; 31 cm. 1. Dadaism 2. Surrealism I. T.
N6494.S8 R8     709/.04     *LC* 68-13064

# N6501–7418 MEDIEVAL ART. MODERN ART (BY COUNTRY)

## N6502 Latin America: General

**Cali, François.**        **1.4854**
The art of the Conquistadors / by François Cali; photographs by Claude Arthaud and François Hébert-Stevens; [translated by Bryan Rhys]. — London: Thames and Hudson, c1961. 300 p.: ill. (some col.), map. Translation of L'art des conquistadors. 1. Art, Latin American — History I. Arthaud, Claude, 1927- II. Hébert-Stevens, François, 1922- III. T.
N6502 C253

**Catlin, Stanton Loomis.**        **1.4855**
Art of Latin America since independence, by Stanton Loomis Catlin. [Rev. ed. New Haven, Conn., Yale University, 1966] xiv, 246 p. 118 plates (part col.) 22 x 23 cm. Exhibition sponsored by Yale University and the University of Texas and various departments within the two universities. Held at the Yale University Art Gallery, Jan. 27-Mar. 13, 1966; the University of Texas Art Museum, Apr. 17-May 15, 1966, and other museums of art. 1. Art, Latin American — Exhibitions. 2. Artists, Latin American. I. Grieder, Terence. joint author. II. Yale University. III. University of Texas. Art Museum. IV. T.
N6502.C33     709.8     *LC* 66-18340

**Chase, Gilbert, 1906-.**        • **1.4856**
Contemporary art in Latin America: painting, graphic art, sculpture, architecture. — New York: Free Press, [1970] viii, 292 p.: illus.; 22 cm. 1. Art, Latin American 2. Art, Modern — 20th century — Latin America. I. T.
N6502.C42     709/.8     *LC* 70-78890

**Keleman, Pál.**      • **1.4857**
Baroque and rococo in Latin America / by Pál Kelemen. — 2d ed. — New York: Dover Publications, 1967. 2 v.: ill., map. 1. Art, Latin American 2. Art, Baroque — Latin America. I. T.
N6502.K42      709.8

# N6505–6538 United States

**The Britannica encyclopedia of American art: a special**    **1.4858**
**educational supplement to the Encyclopaedia Britannica.**
Chicago: Encyclopaedia Britannica Educational Corp.; New York: distribution by Simon and Schuster, [1976?] 669 p.: ill. (some col.); 29 cm. 'A Chanticleer Press edition.' 1. Art, American — Dictionaries. 2. Artists — United States — Biography.
N6505.B73 1976     709/.73     LC 73-80529     ISBN 0878271600

**Dunlap, William, 1766-1839.**      • **1.4859**
History of the rise and progress of the arts of design in the United States. Introd. by William P. Campbell. Newly edited by Alexander Wyckoff, incorporating the notes and additions compiled by Frank W. Bayley and Charles Goodspeed. [New ed., rev. and enl. New York] B. Blom [1965] 3 v. Running title: History of the arts of design. 1. Artists, American 2. Art, American — History I. Wyckoff, Alexander II. T. III. Title: History of the arts of design IV. Title: The arts of design
N6505 D9 1965     LC 65-16236

**Larkin, Oliver W.**      • **1.4860**
Art and life in America / Oliver W. Larkin. — Rev. and enl. ed. — New York: Holt, Rinehart and Winston, 1960. xvii, 559 p.: ill. (part col.). 1. Art — United States — History. I. T.
N6505.L37 1960     709.73     LC 60-6491     ISBN 0030089107

**Rubinstein, Charlotte Streifer.**      **1.4861**
American women artists: from early Indian times to the present / Charlotte Streifer Rubinstein. — New York, N.Y.: Avon; Boston, Mass.: G.K. Hall, c1982. x, 560 p., [32] p. of plates: ill. (some col.); 24 cm. Includes index. 1. Women artists — United States 2. Indians of North America — Art 3. Indians of North America — Women I. T.
N6505.R8 1982     704/.042/0973 19     LC 81-20135     ISBN 0816185352

**Von Blum, Paul.**      **1.4862**
The critical vision: a history of social and political art in the U.S. / Paul Von Blum; with editorial assistance and contributions by Mark Resnick. — Boston, MA: South End Press, c1982. xviii, 169 p.: ill.; 26 cm. Includes index. 1. Art, American 2. Politics in art — United States. 3. Art and society — United States. I. T.
N6505.V66 1982     709/.73 19     LC 82-61156     ISBN 0896081710

**Wilmerding, John.**      **1.4863**
American art / John Wilmerding. Harmondsworth, Eng.; New York: Penguin Books, 1976. xxiii, 322 p., [97] leaves of plates: ill. (1 col.); 27 cm. (Pelican history of art.) Includes index. 1. Art, American — History. I. T. II. Series.
N6505.W54     709/.73     LC 75-18755     ISBN 0140560408

**The Arts in America: the colonial period [by] Louis B. Wright**    **1.4864**
**[and others].**
New York, Scribner [1966] xvi, 368 p. illus. (part col.) 28 cm. 1. Art, American I. Wright, Louis B. (Louis Booker), 1899-
N6507.A7     709.73     LC 66-12921

**Little, Nina Fletcher, 1903-.**      **1.4865**
Country arts in early American homes / Nina Fletcher Little; foreword by Wendell Garrett. — 1st ed. — New York: Dutton, 1975. xv, 221 p., [8] leaves of plates: ill. (some col.); 22 cm. 1. Art, American 2. Art, Modern — 17th-18th centuries — United States. 3. Art, Modern — 19th century — United States. I. T.
N6507.L57 1975     745/.0973     LC 74-33139     ISBN 0525086803

**Brooklyn Museum.**      **1.4866**
The American renaissance, 1876–1917. — Brooklyn, N.Y.: Brooklyn Museum; New York: distributed by Pantheon Books, c1979. 232 p.: ill. (some col.); 31 cm. 'Published for the exhibition the American renaissance, 1876-1917.' Includes indexes. 1. Art, American — Exhibitions. 2. Art, American — 19th century — United States — Exhibitions. 3. Art, Modern — 20th century — United States — Exhibitions. I. T.
N6510.B75 1979     709/.73/074014723     LC 79-13325     ISBN 0394508076

## N6512 20TH CENTURY

**Alloway, Lawrence, 1926-.**      **1.4867**
Topics in American art since 1945 / Lawrence Alloway. — 1st ed. — New York: Norton, [1975] 283 p.: ill.; 24 cm. 1. Art, American 2. Art, Modern — 20th century — United States I. T.
N6512.A5663 1975     709/.73     LC 74-34361     ISBN 0393044017

**American artists on art from 1940 to 1980 / edited by Ellen H.**    **1.4868**
**Johnson.**
1st ed. — New York: Harper & Row, c1982. xii, 274 p.: ill.; 23 cm. — (Icon editions) 1. Art, American 2. Art, Modern — 20th century — United States 3. Happening (Art) — United States. 4. Artists as authors — United States. I. Johnson, Ellen H.
N6512.A586 1982     700/.973 19     LC 80-8702     ISBN 0064334260

**Baur, John I. H. (John Ireland Howe), 1909-1987.**      **1.4869**
Revolution and tradition in modern American art [by] John I. H. Baur. New York, F. A. Praeger [1967] xxii, 170 p. illus. 24 cm. (Praeger paperbacks, p-228) 1. Art — United States. 2. Art, Modern — 20th century — United States I. T.
N6512.B3 1967     709/.73     LC 67-27417

**Hunter, Sam, 1923-.**      **1.4870**
American art of the 20th century. — New York: H. N. Abrams, [1972] 487 p.: illus. (part col.); 28 cm. 1. Art, Modern — 20th century — United States 2. Art, American I. T.
N6512.H78     709/.73     LC 72-3634     ISBN 0810900300

**Miller, Lynn F.**      **1.4871**
Lives and works, talks with women artists / Lynn F. Miller, Sally S. Swenson. — Metuchen, N.J.: Scarecrow Press, 1981. vii, 244 p.: ill.; 22 cm. 1. Women artists — United States — Interviews. 2. Feminism and art — United States. 3. Art, Modern — 20th century — United States I. Swenson, Sally S. II. T.
N6512.M518     709/.2/2 B 19     LC 81-9043     ISBN 0810814587

**Müller, Grégoire.**      **1.4872**
The new avant–garde; issues for the art of the seventies. Text by Grégoire Müller. Photos. by Gianfranco Gorgoni. — New York: Praeger, [1972] 177 p.: illus.; 24 cm. 1. Artists, American. 2. Art, Modern — 20th century — United States 3. Art — Philosophy I. Gorgoni, Gianfranco. illus. II. T.
N6512.M75     709/.04     LC 72-166514

**Munro, Eleanor C.**      **1.4873**
Originals: American women artists / Eleanor Munro. — New York: Simon and Schuster, c1979. 528 p., [16] leaves of plates: ill. (some col.); 24 cm. 'An outgrowth of the television series 'The originals/women in art' produced by WNET/Thirteen.' Includes index. 1. Art, American 2. Art, Modern — 20th century — United States 3. Women artists — United States — Biography. I. T.
N6512.M78     709/.2/2 B     LC 78-31814     ISBN 067123109X

**Museum of Modern Art (New York, N.Y.)**      • **1.4874**
American realists and magic realists. Edited by Dorothy C. Miller and Alfred H. Barr, Jr., with statements by the artists and an introd. by Lincoln Kirstein. [New York] Published for the Museum of Modern Art by Arno Press, 1969 [c1943] 67 p. illus. 27 cm. 1. Art, American — Exhibitions. 2. Realism in art — United States. I. Miller, Dorothy Canning, 1904- ed. II. Barr, Alfred Hamilton, 1902- joint ed. III. T.
N6512.N4 1969     760/.0973     LC 77-86431

**Museum of Modern Art (New York, N.Y.)**      • **1.4875**
15 Americans / The Museum of Modern Art, New York; edited by Dorothy C. Miller; with statements by the artists and others. — New York: The Museum, 1952. 47 p.: ill.; 26 cm. 'One of a series of exhibitions initiated by the Museum of Modern Art in 1929.' 1. Art, American — Exhibitions 2. Artists — United States I. Miller, Dorothy Canning, 1904- II. T.
N6512 N42     LC 52-2347

**Museum of Modern Art (New York, N.Y.)**      • **1.4876**
12 Americans / edited by Dorothy C. Miller; with statements by the artists and others. — New York: The Museum: distributed by Simon and Schuster, 1956. 95 p.: ill. (some col.), ports.; 24 cm. 'Catalog of the exhibition, May 29 through September 9, 1956': p. 92-[96] 1. Art, American — Exhibitions. I. Miller, Dorothy Canning, 1904- II. T.
N6512.N45     LC 56-3810

**Museum of Modern Art (New York, N.Y.)**      • **1.4877**
Americans, 1942; 18 artists from 9 states. Edited by Dorothy C. Miller, with statements by the artists. New York, Museum of Modern Art [1942] 128 p. ill. 26 cm. 1. Art, American — Exhibitions. 2. Artists — United States I. Miller, Dorothy Canning, 1904- II. T.
N 6512 N5557 1942     LC 42-36115 rev.2

**Painters painting: a candid history of the modern art scene,**   **1.4878**
**1940–1970 / in the words of Josef Albers ... [et. al.]; [compiled**
**by] Emile de Antonio and Mitch Tuchman.**
1st ed. — New York: Abbeville Press, c1984. 192 p.: ill.; 24 cm. Based on
transcripts from the film Painters painting, made by Emile de Antonio in 1972.
Includes index. 1. Artists — United States — Interviews. 2. Modernism (Art)
— United States. I. Albers, Josef. II. De Antonio, Emile. III. Tuchman,
Mitch. IV. Painters painting (Motion picture)
N6512.P27 1984     709/.73 19     *LC* 83-21526     *ISBN* 0896594181

**Pollock and after: the critical debate / edited by Francis**   **1.4879**
**Frascina.**
New York: Harper & Row, 1985. 266 p.: ill.; 24 cm. 'Icon editions' 1. Art,
American 2. Art, Modern — 20th century — United States I. Frascina,
Francis.
N6512.P64     709/.73 19     *LC* 84-48596     *ISBN* 0064331261

**Rose, Barbara.**     • **1.4880**
American art since 1900. — Rev. and expanded ed. — New York: Praeger,
[1975] 320 p.: illus.; 21 cm. — (Praeger world of art series) 1. Art, American —
History. 2. Art, Modern — 20th century — United States I. T.
N6512.R63 1975     709/.73     *LC* 72-83563     *ISBN* 0275439003

**Rose, Barbara. comp.**     • **1.4881**
Readings in American art since 1900; a documentary survey. — New York: F.
A. Praeger, [1968] xiv, 224 p.: illus., ports.; 22 cm. — (Praeger world of art
series) 1. Art, American — History — Addresses, essays, lectures. 2. Art,
Modern — 20th century — United States — Addresses, essays, lectures. I. T.
II. Title: American art since 1900.
N6512.R64     709.73     *LC* 68-16421

**Whitney Museum of American Art.**     • **1.4882**
American art of our century [by] Lloyd Goodrich, director [and] John I. H.
Baur, associate director. — New York: Praeger, [1961] 309 p.: illus. (part col.);
29 cm. — (Books that matter) The illustrations are of works in the museum's
collection. 'Catalogue of the collection': p. 267-297. 1. Art, American 2. Art
— New York (City) — Catalogs. 3. Art, Modern — 20th century — United
States I. Goodrich, Lloyd, 1897- II. Baur, John I. H. (John Ireland Howe),
1909-1987. III. T.
N6512.W46     708.1471     *LC* 61-15642

**Abstract painting and sculpture in America, 1927–1944 / edited**   **1.4883**
**by John R. Lane and Susan C. Larsen.**
Pittsburgh: Museum of Art, Carnegie Institute; New York: In Assocation with
H.M. Abrams, 1984, c1983. 256 p.: ill. (some col.); 29 cm. Accompanies the
exhibition: Abstract painting and sculpture in America, 1927-1944. Includes
index. 1. Art, Abstract — United States — Exhibitions. 2. Art, American —
Exhibitions. 3. Art, Modern — 20th century — United States — Exhibitions.
I. Lane, John R., 1944- II. Larsen, Susan C. III. Carnegie Institute. Museum
of Art.
N6512.5.A2 A27 1984     759.13/074/013 19     *LC* 83-3850     *ISBN*
0810918056

**Goodyear, Frank Henry, 1944-.**     **1.4884**
Contemporary American realism since 1960 / Frank H. Goodyear, Jr. — 1st
ed. — Boston: New York Graphic Society in association with the Pennsylvania
Academy of the Fine Arts, c1981. 255 p.: ill. (some col.); 29 cm. 'Published in
connection with the exhibition opening at the Pennsylvania Academy of the
Fine Arts, Philadelphia, September 18, 1981'—T.p. verso. Includes index. 1.
Photo-realism — United States. 2. Realism in art — United States 3. Art,
Modern — 20th century — United States I. Pennsylvania Academy of the Fine
Arts. II. T.
N6512.5.P45 G6     709/.73 19     *LC* 81-11012     *ISBN* 0821211269

**Bowie, Theodore Robert.**     • **1.4885**
East–West in art; patterns of cultural & aesthetic relationships, by Theodore
Bowie in collaboration with J. Leroy Davidson [and others] With an introd. by
Rudolf Wittkower. Bloomington, Indiana University Press [1966] 191 p. ill.,
facsims., maps. (Indiana University international studies) 1. Art — History
2. East and West 3. Intercultural communication I. T.
N6525 B6     *LC* 66-12723

**O'Hara, Frank.**     **1.4886**
Art chronicles, 1954–1966 / Frank O'Hara. — New York: G. Braziller, [1975]
165 p.: ill.; 26 cm. 'A Venture book.' 1. Art, American 2. Art, Modern — 20th
century — New York (City) I. T.
N6535.N5 O37 1975     709/.73     *LC* 74-77526     *ISBN* 080760755X

**Simpson, Charles R.**     **1.4887**
SoHo: the artist in the city / Charles R. Simpson; [maps by Jonathan Williams;
photos. by Woody Goldberg]. — Chicago: University of Chicago Press, c1981.
ix, 276 p., [4] leaves of plates: ill.; 24 cm. 1. Avant-garde (Aesthetics) — New
York (N.Y.) 2. Artists — New York (N.Y.) — Socio-economic status.
3. SoHo (New York, N.Y.) — Description. I. T.
N6535.N5 S53     306/.4 19     *LC* 80-27083     *ISBN* 0226759377

## N6536–6538 BIOGRAPHY

**Cummings, Paul.**     • **1.4888**
Dictionary of contemporary American artists / Paul Cummings. — 4th ed., 1st
ed. — New York: St. Martin's Press, c1982. x, 653 p.: ill.; 24 cm. Includes
index. 1. Artists — United States — Biography. 2. Art, Modern — 20th
century — United States I. T. II. Title: Contemporary American artists.
N6536.C8 1982     709/.2/2 B 19     *LC* 82-7337     *ISBN* 0312200978

**Who's who in American art.**     • **1.4889**
v. 1- 1936/37-. New York [etc.] R. R. Bowker. v. 23-26 cm. Irregular. Vols. for
1936/37-1940/47 called v. 1-4. 1. Artists — United States — Biography —
Yearbooks. I. American Federation of Arts.
N6536.W5     709/.22     *LC* 36-27014

**Bearden, Romare, 1914-.**     **1.4890**
The art of Romare Bearden; the prevalence of ritual. Text by M. Bunch
Washington, with an introd. by John A. Williams. — New York: Abrams,
[1973] 230 p.: illus. (part col.); 35 cm. 1. Bearden, Romare, 1914-
I. Washington, M. Bunch. II. T.
N6537.B4 W37     759.13     *LC* 72-4399     *ISBN* 0810900335

**Baur, John I. H. (John Ireland Howe), 1909-1987.**     **1.4891**
The inlander: life and work of Charles Burchfield, 1893–1967 / John I.H. Baur.
— Newark: University of Delaware Press; New York: Cornwall Books, c1982.
280 p., [18] leaves of plates: ill. (some col.); 31 cm. 'An American art journal
book.' Includes index. 1. Burchfield, Charles Ephraim, 1893-1967. 2. Artists
— United States — Biography. I. T.
N6537.B86 B38 1982     759.13 B 19     *LC* 80-51780     *ISBN*
0874131863

**Calder, Alexander, 1898-1976.**     **1.4892**
Calder's universe / Jean Lipman; Ruth Wolfe, editorial director. — New York:
Viking Press in cooperation with the Whitney Museum of American Art, 1976.
351 p.: ill. (some col.); 28 cm. (A Studio book) An exhibition based on this book
is scheduled to be held at the Whitney Museum of American Art, Oct. 14, 1976
to May 1, 1977, and at other museums at later dates. Includes index. 1. Calder,
Alexander, 1898-1976. 2. Artists — United States — Biography. I. Lipman,
Jean, 1909- II. Whitney Museum of American Art. III. T.
N6537.C33 L56 1976     709/.2/4 B     *LC* 76-28232     *ISBN*
0670199664

**Chicago, Judy, 1939-.**     **1.4893**
The birth project / by Judy Chicago. — Garden City, N.Y.: Doubleday, 1985.
231 p.: ill.; 28 cm. Includes index. 1. Chicago, Judy, 1939- 2. Needlework —
United States. 3. Group work in art — United States. I. T.
N6537.C48 A4 1985     746/.092/4 19     *LC* 84-18783     *ISBN*
0385187106

*[handwritten margin note: N 6537 C48 A4 1985]*

**Ashton, Dore.**     **1.4894**
A Joseph Cornell album. With special contributions by John Ashbery [and
others] and assorted ephemera, readings, decorations, and reproductions of
works by Joseph Cornell. — New York: Viking Press, [1974] xiv, 240 p.: illus.;
23 x 25 cm. 1. Cornell, Joseph. I. T.
N6537.C66 A93 1974     709/.2/4     *LC* 74-10815     *ISBN* 0670408840

**Joseph Cornell / edited by Kynaston McShine; essays by Dawn**   **1.4895**
**Ades ... [et al.].**
New York: Museum of Modern Art, c1980. 295 p.: ill. (some col.); 29 cm.
Published on the occasion of the exhibition 'Joseph Cornell,' Nov. 17, 1980-Jan.
20, 1981, at the Museum of Modern Art. 1. Cornell, Joseph — Addresses,
essays, lectures. I. McShine, Kynaston. II. Ades, Dawn. III. Museum of
Modern Art (New York, N.Y.)
N6537.C66 J67     709/.2/4 19     *LC* 80-84102     *ISBN* 0870702718

**Goodrich, Lloyd, 1897-.**     **1.4896**
Thomas Eakins / Lloyd Goodrich. — Cambridge, Mass.: Published for the
National Gallery of Art [by] Harvard University Press, 1982. 2 v.: ill. (some
col.); 29 cm. — (Ailsa Mellon Bruce studies in American art. v. 2) 1. Eakins,
Thomas, 1844-1916. 2. Artists — United States — Biography. I. Eakins,
Thomas, 1844-1916. II. National Gallery of Art (U.S.) III. T. IV. Series.
N6537.E3 G6 1982     709/.2/4 B 19     *LC* 82-12170     *ISBN*
0674884906

**Kass, Ray.**     **1.4897**
Morris Graves, vision of the inner eye / Ray Kass; introduction by Theodore F.
Wolff. — 1st ed. — New York: Braziller, in association with the Phillips
Collection, Washington, D.C., c1983. 174 p., [1] leaf of plates: ill. (some col.);
29 cm. Published in conjunction with the exhibition held in Washington, D.C.,
Apr. 9-May 29, 1983, etc. 1. Graves, Morris, 1910- — Exhibitions. 2. Graves,
Morris, 1910- 3. Artists — United States — Biography. I. Graves, Morris,
1910- II. Phillips Collection. III. T.
N6537.G688 A4 1983     759.13 19     *LC* 83-2606     *ISBN* 0807610682

**Crichton, Michael, 1942-.**                                    **1.4898**
Jasper Johns / by Michael Crichton. — New York: Abrams, in association with the Whitney Museum of American Art, c1977. 243 p. (some fold.): ill. (some col.); 29 cm. 'The Jasper Johns exhibition was organized for the Whitney Museum of American Art by David Whitney.' 1. Johns, Jasper, 1930- 2. Artists — United States — Biography. I. Whitney Museum of American Art. II. T.
N6537.J6 C74      709/.2/4      LC 77-78150      ISBN 0810911612

**Driscoll, John Paul.**                                    **1.4899**
John Frederick Kensett, an American master / John Paul Driscoll, John K. Howat, with contributions by Dianne Dwyer, Oswaldo Rodriguez Roque; edited by Susan E. Strickler. — 1st ed. — New York: Worcester Art Museum in association with Norton, c1985. 208 p.: ill. (some col.); 29 cm. Catalogue of an exhibition held at the Worcester Art Museum, Los Angeles County Museum of Art, and the Metropolitan Museum of Art. Includes index. 1. Kensett, John Frederick, 1816-1872 — Exhibitions. 2. Landscape in art — Exhibitions. I. Howat, John K. II. Strickler, Susan E. III. Worcester Art Museum. IV. Los Angeles County Museum of Art. V. Metropolitan Museum of Art (New York, N.Y.) VI. T.
N6537.K43 A4 1985      759.13 19      LC 84-29440      ISBN 0393019349

**Lewitt, Sol, 1928-.**                                    **1.4900**
Sol Lewitt: the Museum of Modern Art, New York: [exhibition] / edited and introduced by Alicia Legg; designed by Sol Lewitt; essays by Lucy R. Lippard, Bernice Rose, Robert Rosenblum. — New York: The Museum, c1978. 181 p.: ill. (some col.); 28 cm. 'Illustrations, works by Sol Lewitt, 1962-1977, with his commentaries': p. 50-165. Catalog: p. 43-48. 1. Lewitt, Sol, 1928- — Exhibitions. I. Legg, Alicia. II. Lippard, Lucy R. III. Rose, Bernice. IV. Rosenblum, Robert. V. Museum of Modern Art (New York, N.Y.) VI. T.
N6537.L46 A4 1978      709/.2/4      LC 77-15309      ISBN 0870704273.
ISBN 0870704281 pbk

**Newman, Barnett, 1905-1970.**                                    **1.4901**
Barnett Newman / Harold Rosenberg. — New York: Abrams, 1978. 260 p.: ill. (some col.); 28 x 30 cm. Includes index. 1. Newman, Barnett, 1905-1970. 2. Artists — United States — Biography. I. Rosenberg, Harold. II. T.
N6537.N48 A4 1978      709/.2/4      LC 77-25433      ISBN 0810913607

**Pollock, Jackson, 1912-1956.**                                    **1.4902**
Jackson Pollock: a catalogue raisonné of paintings, drawings, and other works / edited by Francis Valentine O'Connor and Eugene Victor Thaw. — New Haven: Yale University Press, 1978. 4 v.: ill.; 29 cm. 1. Pollock, Jackson, 1912-1956. I. O'Connor, Francis V. II. Thaw, Eugene V. III. T.
N6537.P57 A4 1978      709/.2/4      LC 77-16390      ISBN 0300021097

**Pollock, Jackson, 1912-1956.**                                    **1.4903**
Jackson Pollock, drawing into painting / Bernice Rose. — New York: Museum of Modern Art, c1980. 96 p.: ill. (some col.); 25 x 28 cm. Exhibition held at the Museum of Modern Art, Feb. 4-Mar. 16, 1980. 'Text is a revision of an original text written for 'Jackson Pollock: works on paper', published by the Museum of Modern Art and the Drawings Society in 1969.' 1. Pollock, Jackson, 1912-1956 — Exhibitions. I. Rose, Bernice. II. Pollock, Jackson, 1912-1956. Jackson Pollock. III. Museum of Modern Art (New York, N.Y.) IV. T.
N6537.P57 A4 1980      759.13 19      LC 79-92490      ISBN 0870705164

**Hassrick, Peter H.**                                    **1.4904**
Frederic Remington: paintings, drawings, and sculpture in the Amon Carter Museum and the Sid W. Richardson Foundation collections, by Peter H. Hassrick. Foreword by Ruth Carter Johnson. [New York] Abrams [1973] 218 p. illus. (part col.) 32 x 35 cm. 1. Remington, Frederic, 1861-1909. 2. West (U.S.) in art. I. Remington, Frederic, 1861-1909. II. Amon Carter Museum of Western Art. III. Sid W. Richardson Foundation. IV. T.
N6537.R4 H38      709/.2/4      LC 72-8852      ISBN 0810904446

**Fry, Edward F.**                                    **1.4905**
David Smith, painter, sculptor, draftsman / Edward F. Fry and Miranda McClintic. — New York: G. Braziller; Washington, D.C.: Hirshhorn Museum and Sculpture Garden, Smithsonian Institution, c1982. 144 p.: ill. (some col.); 28 cm. Catalog of an exhibition to be held at the Hirshhorn Museum and Sculpture Garden, Nov. 4, 1982-Jan. 2, 1983 and at the San Antonio Museum of Art, Mar. 27-June 4, 1983. 1. Smith, David, 1906-1965 — Exhibitions. I. Smith, David, 1906-1965. II. McClintic, Miranda. III. Hirshhorn Museum and Sculpture Garden. IV. San Antonio Museum of Art. V. T.
N6537.S616 A4 1982      709/.2/4 19      LC 82-15446      ISBN 0807610569

**Vedder, Elihu, 1836-1923.**                                    **1.4906**
Perceptions and evocations: the art of Elihu Vedder / with an introd. by Regina Soria and essays by Joshua C. Taylor, Jane Dillenberger, Richard Murray. — Washington: Published for the National Collection of Fine Arts by the Smithsonian Institution Press, 1979. ix, 246 p.: ill.; 27 cm. 'Published on the occasion of an exhibition at the National Collection of Fine Arts, Smithsonian Institution, Washington, D.C., October 13, 1978-February 4, 1979 and the Brooklyn Museum, New York, April 28-July 9, 1979. Includes index. 1. Vedder, Elihu, 1836-1923 — Exhibitions. I. Taylor, Joshua Charles, 1917-

II. Dillenberger, Jane. III. Murray, Richard, 1942- IV. National Collection of Fine Arts (U.S.) V. Brooklyn Museum. VI. T.
N6537.V43 A4 1979      709/.2/4      LC 78-9915      ISBN 0874749026

**Curry, David Park.**                                    **1.4907**
James McNeill Whistler at the Freer Gallery of Art / David Park Curry. — [Washington]: Freer Gallery of Art, Smithsonian Institution; New York: W.W. Norton, 1984. 319 p.: ill. (some col.); 31 cm. 'Published on the occasion of the exhibition 'James McNeill Whistler' ... exhibition dates: Freer Gallery of Art, Washington, D.C., May 11, 1984-November 5, 1984'—T.p. verso. Includes index. 1. Whistler, James McNeill, 1834-1903 — Exhibitions. 2. Freer Gallery of Art — Exhibitions. I. Whistler, James McNeill, 1834-1903. II. T.
N6537.W4 A4 1984      759.13 19      LC 83-25525      ISBN 0393018474

# N6538 Afro–American Artists

**Doty, Robert M.**                                    **1.4908**
Contemporary Black artists in America, by Robert Doty. New York, Whitney Museum of American Art [1971] 64 p. illus. (part col.) 25 cm. Catalogue of an exhibition held at Whitney Museum of American Art, April 6-May 16, 1971. 1. Afro-American art — Exhibitions. I. Whitney Museum of American Art. II. T.
N6538.N5 D58      709.73/074/01471      LC 74-154608

**Dover, Cedric.**                                    **• 1.4909**
American Negro art. [Greenwich, Conn.] New York Graphic Society [1960] 186 p. illus., col. plates, ports. 25 cm. 1. Afro-American art — United States. 2. Art, American I. T.
N6538.N5 D6 1960      709.73      LC 60-51364

**Driskell, David C.**                                    **1.4910**
Two centuries of Black American art: [exhibition], Los Angeles County Museum of Art, the High Museum of Art, Atlanta, Museum of Fine Arts, Dallas, the Brooklyn Museum / David C. Driskell; with catalog notes by Leonard Simon. — 1st ed. — New York: Knopf, 1976. 221 p.: ill. (some col.); 28 cm. Includes index. 1. Afro-American art — Exhibitions. I. Simon, Leonard, 1936- II. Los Angeles County Museum of Art. III. T.
N6538.N5 D74      709/.73      LC 76-13691

**Fax, Elton C.**                                    **1.4911**
Black artists of the new generation / Elton C. Fax; foreword by Romare Bearden. — New York: Dodd, Mead, c1977. xiv, 370 p., [8] leaves of plates: ill.; 22 cm. Includes index. 1. Afro-American artists — Biography. 2. Afro-American art 3. Art, Modern — 20th century — United States I. T.
N6538.N5 F29      709/.2/2 B      LC 77-7053      ISBN 0396074340

**Fax, Elton C.**                                    **1.4912**
Seventeen black artists [by] Elton C. Fax. New York, Dodd, Mead [1971] xiv, 306 p. illus., ports. 22 cm. 1. Afro-American artists I. T.
N6538.N5 F3      709/.22      LC 72-165671      ISBN 0396063918

**Fine, Elsa Honig.**                                    **1.4913**
The Afro–American artist; a search for identity. New York, Holt, Rinehart and Winston [1973] x, 310 p. illus. 26 cm. 1. Afro-American art 2. Afro-American artists I. T.
N6538.N5 F56      709/.73      LC 73-1235

**Lewis, Samella S.**                                    **1.4914**
Art: African American / Samella Lewis. — New York: Harcourt Brace Jovanovich, c1978. x, 246 p.: ill. (some col.); 25 cm. Includes index. 1. Afro-American art I. T.
N6538.N5 L39      709/.73      LC 77-78732      ISBN 0155034103

**Lewis, Samella S.**                                    **1.4915**
Black artists on art, [edited by] Samella S. Lewis and Ruth G. Waddy. [Los Angeles, Contemporary Crafts Publishers, 1969-. v. illus. (part col.), ports. (part col.) 27 cm. 1. Afro-American art 2. Afro-American artists I. Waddy, Ruth G., 1909- joint author. II. T.
N6538.N5 L4      709/.22      LC 76-97788

**Livingston, Jane.**                                    **1.4916**
Black folk art in America, 1930–1980 / by Jane Livingston and John Beardsley with a contribution by Regenia Perry. — Jackson: Published for the Corcoran Gallery of Art by the University Press of Mississippi; [s.l.]: Center for the Study of Southern Culture, c1982. 186 p.: ill. (some col.); 28 cm. Catalog of an exhibition held at the Corcoran Gallery of Art and other institutions. 1. Afro-American art — Exhibitions. 2. Primitivism in art — United States — Exhibitions. 3. Ethnic art — United States — Exhibitions. I. Beardsley, John. II. Perry, Regenia. III. Corcoran Gallery of Art. IV. T.
N6538.N5 L58 1982      704/.0396073/074013 19      LC 81-24072      ISBN 0878051589

**Vlach, John Michael, 1948-.**                                    **1.4917**
The Afro–American tradition in decorative arts / John Michael Vlach. — Cleveland: Cleveland Museum of Art, c1978. xii, 175 p.: ill. (some col.); 28 cm.

Catalog of an exhibition held Feb 1-Apr. 2, 1978 at the Cleveland Museum of Art and at other museums later. 1. Afro-American art — Exhibitions. 2. Afro-American art — African influences — Exhibitions. 3. Afro-American art — European influences — Exhibitions. I. Cleveland Museum of Art. II. T.
N6538.N5 V57     745/.0973/074017132     *LC* 77-19326     *ISBN* 0910386390

# N6540–6739 Canada. Latin America, by Country

**Burnett, David G.**            **1.4918**
Contemporary Canadian art / David Burnett & Marilyn Schiff. — Edmonton, Alta.: Hurtig in co-operation with the Art Gallery of Ontario, c1983. 300 p.: ill. (some col.); 23 cm. Includes index. 1. Art, Canadian 2. Art, Modern — 20th century — Canada. I. Schiff, Marilyn, 1939- II. T.
N6545.B87 1983     709/.71 19     *LC* 84-123925     *ISBN* 0888302428

**Harper, J. Russell.**            • **1.4919**
Early painters and engravers in Canada [by] J. Russell Harper. — [Toronto]: University of Toronto Press, [c1970] xv, 376 p.; 26 cm. 1. Artists — Canada — Dictionaries. I. T.
N6548.H37     759.11 B     *LC* 70-151373     *ISBN* 0802016308

**Toussaint, Manuel, 1895-1955.**            • **1.4920**
[Arte colonial en México. English] Colonial art in Mexico. Translated and edited by Elizabeth Wilder Weismann. Austin, University of Texas Press [1967] xxvi, 493 p. illus. (part col.), facsims., ports. 29 cm. (The Texas pan-American series) 1. Art, Mexican — History. 2. Art, Colonial — Mexico — History. I. T.
N6553.T6813     709/.72     *LC* 66-15696

**Weismann, Elizabeth Wilder, 1908-.**            **1.4921**
Art and time in Mexico: from the Conquest to the Republic / text by Elizabeth Wilder Weismann; photographs by Judith Hancock Sandoval. — 1st ed. — New York: Harper & Row, c1985. xviii, 284 p., 16 p. of plates: ill. (some col.). — (Icon editions) Includes index. 1. Art, Mexican 2. Art, Colonial — Mexico. I. Sandoval, Judith Hancock de. II. T.
N6553.W44 1985     709/.72 19     *LC* 84-48202     *ISBN* 006438506X

**Schmeckebier, Laurence Eli, 1906-.**            • **1.4922**
Modern Mexican art [by] Laurence E. Schmeckebier. — Westport, Conn.: Greenwood Press, [1971, c1939] xvii, 190 p.: 216 plates.; 27 cm. 1. Art, Mexican 2. Art, Modern — 20th century — Mexico. I. T.
N6555.S3 1971     709/.72     *LC* 70-141418     *ISBN* 0837146925

**Lemos, Carlos Alberto Cerqueira.**            **1.4923**
The art of Brazil / by Carlos Lemos, José Roberto Teixeira Leite, and Pedro Manuel Gismonti; with an introduction by Pietro Maria Bardi, and an essay by Oscar Niemeyer; [translated by Jennifer Clay]. — 1st U.S. ed. — New York: Harper & Row, c1983. 318 p.: ill. (some col.); 32 cm. — (Icon editions) Based on: Arte no Brasil. Includes index. 1. Art, Brazilian 2. Art — Brazil. I. Leite, José Roberto Teixeira. II. Gismonti, Pedro Manuel. III. Arte no Brasil. IV. T.
N6650.L4 1983     709/.81 19     *LC* 83-47557     *ISBN* 0064352897

**Dark, Philip John Crosskey.**            • **1.4924**
Bush negro art: an African art in the Americas, by Philip J. C. Dark. London, Tiranti, 1970. viii, 54 p., 48 plates. illus., map. 26 cm. 1. Art — Surinam. 2. Art, Primitive — Surinam. 3. Art, Black — Surinam. 4. Blacks — Surinam I. T.
N6696.D3 1970     732/.2     *LC* 78-851356     *ISBN* 0854582304

**Wethey, Harold E. (Harold Edwin), 1902-1984.**            • **1.4925**
Colonial architecture and sculpture in Peru [by] Harold E. Wethey. — Westport, Conn.: Greenwood Press, [1971, c1949] xvii, 330 p.: 367 illus., map.; 26 cm. 1. Architecture — Peru — History. 2. Sculpture — Peru — History. I. T.
N6713.W48 1971     720/.985     *LC* 73-97337     *ISBN* 0837140803

# N6750–7255 Europe

**Novotny, Fritz, 1902-.**            • **1.4926**
Painting and sculpture in Europe, 1780 to 1880. — Baltimore: Penguin Books, [1960] xxii, 288 p.: illus., 192 plates.; 27 cm. — (Pelican history of art. Z20) 1. Art — Europe — History. I. T. II. Series.
N6750.N6     759.94     *LC* 60-51441

**Hempel, Eberhard, 1886-.**            **1.4927**
Baroque art and architecture in central Europe: Germany, Austria, Switzerland, Hungary, Czechoslovakia, Poland. Painting and sculpture: seventeenth and eighteenth centuries; architecture: sixteenth to eighteenth centuries. [Translated from the German by Elisabeth Hempel and Marguerite Kay]. — Baltimore: Penguin Books, [1965] xxiii, 370 p.: illus., maps, plans, 200 plates.; 27 cm. — (Pelican history of art. Z22) 1. Art, Baroque — Europe — History. 2. Architecture, Baroque — History. 3. Art, European — History. I. T. II. Series.
N6756.H413     709.43     *LC* 65-28970

**Hamilton, George Heard.**            **1.4928**
Painting and sculpture in Europe, 1880–1940 / George Heard Hamilton. — 2nd ed. — Harmondsworth, Middlesex, England; New York: Penguin Books, 1981. 616 p.: ill.; 21 cm. — (Pelican history of art.) Includes index. 1. Art, European 2. Art, Modern — 19th century — Europe. 3. Art, Modern — 20th century — Europe. I. T. II. Series.
N6757.H3 1981     759.94 19     *LC* 81-189238     *ISBN* 0140561293

**Tschudi-Madsen, Stephan, 1923-.**            • **1.4929**
Sources of art nouveau. [English translation by Ragnar Christophersen] New York, G. Wittenborn [1956] 488 p. 264 ill. 1. Art — Europe 2. Art — Great Britain I. T.
N6757 M313     *LC* 56-12801

# N6761–6797 Britain. Ireland

**The Oxford history of English art; edited by T.S.R. Boase.**            • **1.4930**
[Oxford, Clarendon Press, 1949-. ill., plates, maps, plans. Half title; each vol. has also special t.p., with title: English art ... 1. Art — England — History I. Boase, T. S. R. (Thomas Sherrer Ross), 1898-1974. II. Title: English art
N6761 O9     *LC* 53-4155

**Pevsner, Nikolaus, Sir, 1902-.**            • **1.4931**
The Englishness of English art: an expanded and annotated version of the Reith lectures broadcast in October and November 1955 / Sir Nikolaus Pevsner. — New York: Praeger, 1956. 208 p.: ill. — (Books that matter) 1. Art, English 2. England in art. I. T.
N6761.P48     709/.42     *LC* 56-8431

**Saxl, Fritz, 1890-1948.**            • **1.4932**
British art and the Mediterranean, by F. Saxl and R. Wittkower. London, Oxford University Press, 1948. 86 p., [86] p. of ill. 1. Art, British 2. Art — Mediterranean Region I. Wittkower, Rudolf. joint author II. T.
N6761 S38     *LC* 48-10062

**Dodwell, C. R. (Charles Reginald)**            **1.4933**
Anglo–Saxon art: a new perspective / C.R. Dodwell. — Ithaca, N.Y.: Cornell University Press, 1982. x, 353 p., [8] p. of plates: ill. (some col.); 26 cm. Includes index. 1. Art, Anglo-Saxon I. T.
N6763.D62 1982     709/.42 19     *LC* 82-71592     *ISBN* 0801415160

**English romanesque art, 1066–1200: Hayward Gallery, London, 5 April–8 July 1984 / [edited by George Zarnecki, Janet Holt and Tristram Holland].**            **1.4934**
London: Weidenfeld and Nicolson in association with the Arts Council of Great Britain, c1984. 416 p.: ill.; 27 cm. 1. Art, English — Exhibitions. 2. Art, Romanesque — England — Exhibitions. I. Zarnecki, George. II. Holt, Janet. III. Holland, Tristram. IV. Hayward Gallery. V. Arts Council of Great Britain.
N6763.E53 1984     709/.42/07402165 19     *LC* 84-175635     *ISBN* 0297784129

**The Golden age of Anglo–Saxon art, 966–1066 / edited by Janet Backhouse, D.H. Turner, Leslie Webster; with contributions by Marion Archibald ... [et al.].**            **1.4935**
Bloomington: Indiana University Press, c1984. 216 p.: ill. (some col.); 29 cm. An exhibition held at the British Museum and the British Library. 1. Art, Anglo-Saxon — Exhibitions. I. Backhouse, Janet. II. Turner, D. H. III. Webster, Leslie. IV. Archibald, Marion. V. British Museum. VI. British Library.
N6763.G65 1984     709/.41/0740214 19     *LC* 84-48492     *ISBN* 0253133262

**Kendrick, T. D. (Thomas Downing)**            • **1.4936**
Late Saxon and Viking art. London, Methuen [1949] xv, 152, xcvi p. ill. 1. Art — Great Britain — History 2. Art, Anglo-Saxon 3. Art, Viking I. T.
N6763 K46     *LC* 49-48888

**Wilson, David McKenzie.**            **1.4937**
Anglo–Saxon art: from the seventh century to the Norman conquest / David M. Wilson. — Woodstock, N.Y.: Overlook Press, c1984. 224 p.: ill. (some col.); 28 cm. Includes index. 1. Art, Anglo-Saxon I. T.
N6763.W55 1984     709/.42 19     *LC* 84-4447     *ISBN* 0879519762

**Irwin, David G.**                                                      **1.4938**
English neoclassical art; studies in inspiration and taste. Greenwich, Conn.,
New York Graphic Society [1966] 230 p. 158 illus. (1. col.) 26 cm. 1. Art,
English — History. 2. Classicism in art I. T.
N6766.I7    *LC* 66-18856

**Paulson, Ronald.**                                                     **1.4939**
Emblem and expression: meaning in English art of the eighteenth century /
Ronald Paulson. — Cambridge, Mass.: Harvard University Press, 1975. 256 p.:
ill.; 26 cm. 1. Art, English 2. Art, Modern — 17th-18th centuries — England.
3. Allegories 4. Emblems — England. I. T.
N6766.P38 1975b    700/.942    *LC* 74-31988    *ISBN* 0674247787

**Watkinson, Raymond.**                                               • **1.4940**
Pre–Raphaelite art and design. — Greenwich, Conn.: New York Graphic
Society, [1970] 208 p.: illus. (part col.); 26 cm. 1. Preraphaelitism I. T.
N6767.5.P7 W3 1970b    709/.42    *LC* 79-120101    *ISBN* 0821203983

**Harrison, Charles.**                                                   **1.4941**
English art in the modern period, 1900–1939 / Charles Harrison. —
Bloomington: Indiana University Press, 1981, c1980. 416 p;: ill. Includes index.
1. Art, English 2. Modernism (Art) — England. I. T.
N6768.H37 1981    709/.42 19    *LC* 80-8611    *ISBN* 0253137225

**Rothenstein, John, Sir, 1901-.**                                     • **1.4942**
British art since 1900, an anthology. With 155 illus. London, Phaidon Press
[1962] 181 p. plates (part col.) 1. Art, British — History I. T.
N6768 R6    *LC* 62-52392

**Treasures of early Irish art, 1500 B.C. to 1500 A.D.: from the         1.4943
collections of the National Museum of Ireland, Royal Irish
Academy, Trinity College, Dublin / exhibited at the
Metropolitan Museum of Art ... [et al.]; photography by Lee
Boltin.**
[New York: Metropolitan Museum of Art, 1977] 221 p.: col. ill.; 28 cm. 1. Art,
Irish — Exhibitions. 2. Art, Prehistoric — Ireland — Exhibitions. 3. Art,
Ancient — Ireland — Exhibitions. 4. Art, Medieval — Ireland — Exhibitions.
I. Boltin, Lee. II. National Museum of Ireland. III. Royal Irish Academy.
IV. Trinity College (Dublin, Dublin) V. Metropolitan Museum of Art (New
York, N.Y.)
N6782.T73    709/.415/074013    *LC* 77-8692    *ISBN* 0870991647

**Treasures of Ireland: Irish art 3000 B.C.–1500 A.D.**                  **1.4944**
Dublin: Royal Irish Academy, [c1983] 203 p.: ill. (some col.); 24 cm. 1. Art,
Irish I. Royal Irish Academy.
N6783.T73 1983    709/.415 19    *LC* 83-210162    *ISBN* 0901714283

**Henry, Françoise.**                                                  • **1.4945**
Irish art in the early Christian period, to 800 A. D. Ithaca, N. Y., Cornell
University Press [1965] xvi, 256, [120] p. illus., maps (part fold.) plates (part
col.) 23 cm. Bibliography: p. 225-232. Bibliographical footnotes. 1. Art, Irish
— History. I. T.
N6784.H42    709.415    *LC* 65-22854

## N6797 Individual Artists, A–Z

**Bain, Iain.**                                                          **1.4946**
Thomas Bewick: an illustrated record of his life and work / by Iain Bain. —
Newcastle-upon-Tyne: The Laing Gallery, Tyne and Wear County Council
Museums, 1980, [c1979]. 112 p.: ill., facsims., ports.; 25 cm. 1. Bewick,
Thomas, 1753-1828. 2. Artists — England — Biography. I. T.
N6797.B48 B34    769.92/4 B 19    *LC* 80-147439    *ISBN* 0905974026

**Butlin, Martin.**                                                      **1.4947**
The paintings and drawings of William Blake / Martin Butlin. — New Haven:
Published for the Paul Mellon Centre for Studies in British Art by Yale
University Press, 1981. 2 v.: ill. (some col.); 30 cm. — (Studies in British art.)
Includes indexes. 1. Blake, William, 1757-1827. I. Blake, William, 1757-1827.
II. Paul Mellon Centre for Studies in British Art. III. T. IV. Series.
N6797.B57 B87    760/.092/4 19    *LC* 80-6221    *ISBN* 0300025505

**Keynes, Geoffrey, Sir, 1887-.**                                        **1.4948**
Blake studies: essays on his life and work, by Geoffrey Keynes, Kt. 2nd ed.
Oxford, Clarendon Press, 1971. xii, 263 p., 64 plates; illus., facsims. 26 cm.
1. Blake, William, 1757-1827. I. T.
N6797.B57 K4 1971    760/.0924 B    *LC* 72-870938    *ISBN*
0198120036

**The Visionary hand: essays for the study of William Blake's art        1.4949
and aesthetics / edited and with an introd. by Robert N. Essick.**
Los Angeles: Hennessey & Ingalls, 1973. xviii, 558 p.: ill.; 24 cm. 1. Blake,
William, 1757-1827 — Addresses, essays, lectures. I. Essick, Robert N.
N6797.B57 V57    760/.092/4    *LC* 72-96392    *ISBN* 0912158220

**Crook, J. Mordaunt (Joseph Mordaunt), 1937-.**                         **1.4950**
William Burges and the High Victorian dream / J. Mordaunt Crook. —
Chicago: University of Chicago Press, 1981. 454 p., [77] p. of plates: ill. (some
col.); 25 cm. 1. Burges, William, 1827-1881. 2. Artists — Great Britain —
Biography. 3. Art, Victorian — Great Britain. 4. Middle Ages — Influence.
I. T.
N6797.B85 C76 1981    720/.92/4 B 19    *LC* 81-1592    *ISBN*
0226121178

**Reynolds, Graham.**                                                    **1.4951**
The later paintings and drawings of John Constable / Graham Reynolds. —
New Haven: Published for the Paul Mellon Centre for Studies in British Art by
Yale University Press, 1984. 2 v.: ill (some col.); 31 cm. (Studies in British art.)
Includes indexes. 1. Constable, John, 1776-1837 — Catalogs. I. Paul Mellon
Centre for Studies in British Art. II. T. III. Series.
N6797.C63 A4 1984    759.2 19    *LC* 84-40186    *ISBN* 0300031513

**Robertson, David Allan.**                                              **1.4952**
Sir Charles Eastlake and the Victorian art world / by David Robertson. —
Princeton, N.J.: Princeton University Press, 1978, [c1976]. xvii, 468 p., [2]
leaves of plates: ill. (some col.); 28 cm. 1. Eastlake, Charles Lock, Sir,
1793-1865. 2. Art, Victorian — England. I. T.
N6797.E15 R62    709/.2/4 B    *LC* 75-43797    *ISBN* 069103902X

**John Flaxman / edited by David Bindman.**                             **1.4953**
London: Thames and Hudson, c1979. 188 p.: ill.; 25 cm. 'Published
simultaneously in paperback as a catalogue for the exhibition, John Flaxman,
R. A., at the Royal Academy of Arts, London, 26 October-9 December, 1979.'
1. Flaxman, John, 1755-1826 — Exhibitions. I. Flaxman, John, 1755-1826.
II. Bindman, David. III. Royal Academy of Arts (Great Britain)
N6797.F54 A4 1979a    709/.2/4 19    *LC* 80-491569    *ISBN*
0500091390

**Bindman, David.**                                                      **1.4954**
Hogarth / David Bindman. — New York: Oxford University Press, 1981.
216 p.: ill.; 21 cm. — (The World of art) Includes index. 1. Hogarth, William,
1697-1764. 2. Artists — England — Biography. I. T.
N6797.H6 B56    760/.092/4 B 19    *LC* 80-39785    *ISBN* 0195202392

**Surtees, Virginia.**                                                   **1.4955**
The paintings and drawings of Dante Gabriel Rossetti (1828–1882): a catalogue
raisonné. — Oxford: Clarendon Press, 1971. 2 v. (xvi, 267) p., 225 plates, illus.;
30 cm. 1. Rossetti, Dante Gabriel, 1828-1882. I. T.
N6797.R58 S9    760/.0924    *LC* 70-25419    *ISBN* 0198171749

**Stubbs, George, 1724-1806.**                                          **1.4956**
George Stubbs, 1724-1806. — London: Tate Gallery; Salem, N.H.: Salem
House, 1984 (1985 printing) 248 p.: ill. (some col.); 33 cm. 'The exhibition and
catalogue sponsored by United Technologies Corporation.' Exhibition held at
the Tate Gallery and Yale Center for British Art. 1. Stubbs, George, 1724-1806
— Exhibitions. I. United Technologies Corporation. II. Tate Gallery.
III. Yale Center for British Art. IV. T.
N6797.S84 A4 1984    759.2 19    *LC* 85-234990    *ISBN* 0881620386

## N6801–6838 Austria. Hungary.
### Czechoslovakia

**Rasmo, Nicolò.**                                                       **1.4957**
[Michele Pacher. English] Michael Pacher; translated (from the Italian) by
Philip Waley. London, Phaidon, 1971. 264 p. illus. (some col.), geneal. table. 29
cm. Distributed in the U.S. by Praeger Publishers, New York. 1. Pacher,
Michael, 15th cent. I. T.
N6811.5.P3 R313    759.3    *LC* 70-111063    *ISBN* 0714814172

## N6841–6853 France

**Stoddard, Whitney S.**                                               • **1.4958**
Monastery and cathedral in France; medieval architecture, sculpture, stained
glass, manuscripts, the art of the church treasuries, by Whitney S. Stoddard. —
[1st ed.]. — Middletown, Conn.: Wesleyan University Press, [1966] xxi, 412 p.:
illus., map, plans.; 29 cm. 1. Church architecture — France. 2. Art, French
3. Art, Medieval I. T.
N6843.S7    726.0944    *LC* 66-23923

**Blunt, Anthony, 1907-1983.**                                          **1.4959**
Art and architecture in France, 1500 to 1700 / Anthony Blunt. — 4th ed. —
Harmondsworth, Middlesex; New York: Penguin Books, 1980, c1981. 476 p.:
ill.; 21 cm. — (Pelican history of art.) Includes index. 1. Art, French
2. Mannerism (Art) — France. 3. Art, Baroque — France. 4. Classicism in art
— France. I. T. II. Series.
N6845.B59 1981    709/.44 19    *LC* 81-189237    *ISBN* 0140561048

**Kalnein, Wend von, 1914-.**                                      **1.4960**
Art and architecture of the eighteenth century in France [by] Wend Graf
Kalnein and Michael Levey. Translation of pt. 2 by J. R. Foster.
[Harmondsworth, Eng.] Penguin Books 1973, [c1972] xxv, 443 p. illus. 27 cm.
(Pelican history of art.) 1. Art, French 2. Art, Modern — 17th-18th centuries
— France. I. Levey, Michael. joint author. II. T. III. Series.
N6846.K2613        709/.44        LC 73-167862        ISBN 0140560378

**Eriksen, Svend.**                                               **1.4961**
Early Neo–Classicism in France: the creation of the Louis Seize style in
architectural decoration, furniture and ormolu, gold and silver, and sevres
porcelain in the mid–eighteenth century / by Svend Eriksen; translated from
the Danish [MS.] and edited by Peter Thornton. — London: Faber, 1974.
3-432 p., [8] leaves of plates, [285] p. of plates: ill. (some col.) geneal. table; 29
cm. (Faber monographs on furniture) Includes chapters in French with English
translations. Ill. on lining papers. 1. Neoclassicism (Art) — France.
2. Decoration and ornament — Louis XVI style I. T.
N6846.5.N4 E7413        745.4/49/44        LC 74-186862        ISBN
0571087175

**Kimball, Fiske, 1888-1955.**                                    **1.4962**
[Creation of the rococo.] The creation of the rococo decorative style / by Fiske
Kimball. — New York: Dover Publications, 1980. xvii, 242 p., [52] leaves of
plates: ill.; 28 cm. Reprint of the 1943 ed. published by Philadelphia Museum of
Art under title: The creation of the rococo. 1. Art, Rococo — France.
2. Decoration and ornament, Rococo — France. I. T.
N6846.5.R6 K55 1980        729/.3/0944 19        LC 79-55748        ISBN
0486239896

**Baudelaire, Charles, 1821-1867.**                             • **1.4963**
The mirror of art; critical studies, by Charles Baudelaire. Translated and edited
with notes and illus. by Jonathan Mayne. Garden City, N.Y. Doubleday, 1956.
xxi, 370 p. illus., plates, ports. 18cm. (Doubelday anchor books, A84) 1. Art —
France 2. Art criticism I. Mayne, Jonathan. ed. II. T.
N6847.B3x        LC 57-2188

**Clark, T. J. (Timothy J.)**                                     **1.4964**
The absolute bourgeois: artists and politics in France, 1848–1851 [by] T. J.
Clark. Greenwich, Conn., New York Graphic Society [c1973] 224 p. illus. 25
cm. 1. Politics in art — France. 2. France — History — Second Republic,
1848-1852 — Art I. T.
N6847.C53 1973        700/.944        LC 72-93942        ISBN 082120517X

**Japonisme: Japanese influence on French art, 1854–1910:**       **1.4965**
[exhibition catalog] / Gabriel P. Weisberg ... [et al.].
Cleveland: Cleveland Museum of Art, [1975] xii, 220 p.: ill. (some col.); 27 cm.
Catalog of an exhibition shown at the Cleveland Museum of Art, July 9-Aug.
31, 1975; the Rutgers University Art Gallery, Oct. 4-Nov. 16, 1975; and the
Walters Art Gallery, Dec. 10, 1975-Jan. 26, 1976. 1. Art, French —
Exhibitions. 2. Art, Japanese — Exhibitions. 3. Art, Modern — 19th century
— France — Exhibitions. 4. Art, French — Japanese influences I. Weisberg,
Gabriel P. II. Cleveland Museum of Art. III. Rutgers University. Art Gallery.
IV. Walters Art Gallery.
N6847.J34        709/.44/074013        LC 75-16127        ISBN 0910386226

**Yeldham, Charlotte, 1951-.**                                    **1.4966**
Women artists in nineteenth–century France and England: their art education,
exhibition opportunities and membership of exhibiting societies and academies,
with an assessment of the subject matter of their work and summary
biographies / Charlotte Yeldham. — New York: Garland, 1984. 2 v.: ill.; 24 cm.
— (Outstanding theses from the Courtauld Institute of Art.) Originally
presented as the author's thesis (doctoral—Courtauld Institute of Art)
1. Women artists — France — Biography. 2. Art, Modern — 19th century —
France 3. Women artists — England — Biography. 4. Art, Modern — 19th
century — England I. T. II. Series.
N6847.Y4 1984        704/.042/0942 B 19        LC 83-48689        ISBN
0824059891

**Levitine, George.**                                             **1.4967**
The dawn of Bohemianism: the Barbu rebellion and primitivism in neoclassical
France / George Levitine. — University Park: Pennsylvania State University
Press, c1978. xi, 163 p., [24] leaves of plates: ill.; 26 cm. Includes index.
1. Painting, French 2. Primitivism in art — France 3. Painting, Modern —
19th century — France 4. Avant-garde (Aesthetics) — France. I. T.
N6847.5.P68 L48        759.4        LC 77-13892        ISBN 0271005270

**Weisberg, Gabriel P.**                                          **1.4968**
The realist tradition: French painting and drawing, 1830–1900 / Gabriel P.
Weisberg. — Cleveland: Cleveland Museum of Art; Bloomington, Ind.:
distributed by Indiana University Press, c1980. xiii, 346 p., [20] leaves of plates:
ill. (some col.); 29 cm. Catalog of a Special exhibition at the Cleveland Museum
of Art, Nov. 12, 1980-Jan. 18, 1981; the Brooklyn Museum, Mar. 7-May 10,
1981; the St. Louis Art Museum, Jul. 23-Sept. 20, 1981; and the Glasgow Art
Gallery and Museum, Kelvingrove, Nov. 5, 1981-Jan. 4, 1982. Includes index.
1. Realism in art — France — Exhibitions. 2. Art, French — Exhibitions.

3. Art, Modern — 19th century — France — Exhibitions. I. Cleveland
Museum of Art. II. T.
N6847.5.R4 W44        759.4/074/017132        LC 80-16579        ISBN
0910386609

## N6853 Individual Artists, A–Z

**Schnapper, Antoine.**                                           **1.4969**
[David. English] David / Antoine Schnapper; [English translation by Helga
Harrison]. — New York: Alpine Fine Arts Collection, 1982, c1980. 311 p.: ill.
(some col.); 29 cm. Includes index. 1. David, Jacques Louis, 1748-1825.
2. Artists — France — Biography. I. T.
N6853.D315 S313 1982        759.4 B 19        LC 84-244240        ISBN
0933516592

**Dubuffet, Jean, 1901-.**                                        **1.4970**
Jean Dubuffet: a retrospective. [New York, Solomon R. Guggenheim
Foundation, 1973] 304 p. 296 illus. (part col.) 28 cm. Errata slip inserted.
'Exhibition 73/3.' Catalogue of a loan exhibition organized by the Solomon R.
Guggenheim Museum and the Centre national d'art contemporain; presented at
the Solomon R. Guggenheim Museum, New York and the Grand Palais, Paris.
1. Dubuffet, Jean, 1901- I. Solomon R. Guggenheim Museum. II. Centre
national d'art contemporain. III. Galeries nationales du Grand Palais (France)
IV. T.
N6853.D78 S64        709/.2/4        LC 73-77081

**Duchamp, Marcel, 1887-1968.**                                   **1.4971**
[Marchand du sel. English] Salt seller; the writings of Marcel Duchamp.
Marchand du sel. Edited by Michel Sanouillet and Elmer Peterson. New York,
Oxford University Press, 1973. xii, 196 p. illus. 24 cm. 1. Duchamp, Marcel,
1887-1968. 2. Art — Philosophy I. T.
N6853.D8 A57        759.4        LC 73-87343        ISBN 0195197496

**D'Harnoncourt, Anne, 1943-.**                                   **1.4972**
Marcel Duchamp. Edited by Anne d'Harnoncourt and Kynaston McShine.
[New York] Museum of Modern Art; distributed by New York Graphic
Society, Greenwich, Conn. [c1973] 345 p. illus. 29 cm. 'Published on the
occasion of an exhibition organized by the Philadelphia Museum of Art and the
Museum of Modern Art.' 1. Duchamp, Marcel, 1887-1968. I. McShine,
Kynaston. joint author. II. Philadelphia Museum of Art. III. Museum of
Modern Art (New York, N.Y.) IV. T.
N6853.D8 D52 1973        700/.924        LC 72-95075        ISBN 0870702963
ISBN 0870702955

**Dufy, Raoul, 1877-1953.**                                       **1.4973**
Raoul Dufy: paintings, drawings, illustrated books, mural decorations,
Aubusson tapestries, fabric designs and fabrics for Bianchini–Férier, Paul
Poiret dresses, ceramics, posters, theatre designs: Arts Council of Great Britain,
Hayward Gallery, London, 9 November 1983–5 February 1984: an exhibition /
sponsored by Cognac Courvoisier. — London: Arts Council of Great Britain,
c1983. 185 p.: ill. (some col.); 22 x 24 cm. 'Texts translated by Roberta Bailey
and Sarah Wilson'—T.p. verso. 1. Dufy, Raoul, 1877-1953 — Exhibitions.
I. Hayward Gallery. II. Cognac Courvoisier (Firm) III. T.
N6853.D83 A4 1983        709/.2/4 19        LC 84-134653        ISBN
0728703815

**Russell, H. Diane (Helen Diane)**                               **1.4974**
Claude Lorrain, 1600–1682 / H. Diane Russell. — Washington, D.C.: National
Gallery of Art, c1982. 480 p.: ill. (some col.); 28 cm. Exhibition held at the
National Gallery of Art, Oct. 17 1982-Jan 2, 1983. 1. Lorrain, Claude,
1600-1682. I. Lorrain, Claude, 1600-1682. II. National Gallery of Art (U.S.)
III. T.
N6853.L64 R87 1982        760/.092/4 19        LC 82-14250        ISBN
0894680579

**Manet, Edouard, 1832-1883.**                                    **1.4975**
Manet, 1832–1883: Galeries nationales du Grand Palais, Paris, April
22–August 8, 1983, the Metropolitan Museum of Art, New York, September
10–November 27, 1983 / curators of the exhibition, Françoise Cachin, Charles
S. Moffett, in collaboration with Michel Melot. — New York: Metropolitan
Museum of Art: Abrams, c1983. 548 p.: ill. (some col.); 29 cm. Includes
catalogue by Françoise Cachin, Charles S. Moffett, Juliet Wilson Bareau.
Includes indexes. 1. Manet, Edouard, 1832-1883 — Exhibitions. I. Cachin,
Françoise. II. Melot, Michel. III. Moffett, Charles S. IV. Bareau, Juliet
Wilson. V. Galeries nationales du Grand Palais (France) VI. Metropolitan
Museum of Art (New York, N.Y.) VII. T.
N6853.M233 A4 1983        760/.092/4 19        LC 83-8278        ISBN
0870993593

**Elderfield, John.**                                             **1.4976**
Matisse in the collection of the Museum of Modern Art, including remainder-
interest and promised gifts / John Elderfield, with additional texts by William S.
Lieberman and Riva Castleman. — New York: Museum of Modern Art, c1978.
232 p.: ill. (some col.); 25 cm. Issued in connection with an exhibition held at
the Museum of Modern Art, New York. 1. Matisse, Henri, 1869-1954.
2. Museum of Modern Art (New York, N.Y.) I. Matisse, Henri, 1869-1954.

II. Lieberman, William Slattery, 1924- joint author. III. Castleman, Riva. joint author. IV. Museum of Modern Art (New York, N.Y.) V. T.
N6853.M33 E38  709/.2/4  LC 78-56155  ISBN 0870704702

**Schneider, Pierre.**             **1.4977**
[Matisse. English] Matisse / Pierre Schneider; translated by Michael Taylor and Bridget Strevens Romer. — New York: Rizzoli, 1984. 752 p.: ill. (some col.); 35 cm. Includes index. 1. Matisse, Henri, 1869-1954. 2. Artists — France — Biography. I. T.
N6853.M33 S3513 1984  759.4 19  LC 84-42644  ISBN 0847805468

**Herbert, Robert L., 1929-.**         **1.4978**
Jean–François Millet: [exhibition], Hayward Gallery, 22 January–7 March 1976 / Arts Council of Great Britain. — [London]: [The Council], 1976. 235 p.: ill.; 25 cm. Catalog by Robert Herbert in consultation with Michel Laclotte and Roseline Bacou. 'An exhibition organized by the Réunion des musées nationaux and first held in the Galeries nationales d'exposition du Grand Palais, Paris from 17 October 1975 to 5 January 1976.' 1. Millet, Jean François, 1814-1875. I. Laclotte, Michel. joint author. II. Bacou, Roseline. joint author. III. Millet, Jean François, 1814-1875. IV. Arts Council of Great Britain. V. Hayward Gallery. VI. Réunion des musées nationaux (France) VII. T.
N6853.M52 H46  759.4  LC 76-365275  ISBN 0728700794

**Picasso, Pablo, 1881-1973.**        **1.4979**
Pablo Picasso, a retrospective / edited by William Rubin; chronology by Jane Fluegel. — New York: Museum of Modern Art; Boston: distributed by New York Graphic Society, c1980. 463 p.: chiefly ill. (some col.); 29 cm. 'Published on the occasion of the exhibition 'Pablo Picasso: a retrospective,' May 22-September 16, 1980, organized by the Museum of Modern Art, New York, with the collaboration of the Réunion des musées nationaux de France.' Errata slip inserted. 1. Picasso, Pablo, 1881-1973 — Catalogs. I. Rubin, William Stanley. II. Fluegel, Jane. III. Museum of Modern Art (New York, N.Y.) IV. Réunion des musées nationaux (France) V. T.
N6853.P5 A4 1980a  709/.2/4 19  LC 80-80107  ISBN 0870705288

**Viollet–le–Duc: [exposition], Galeries nationales du Grand** **1.4980**
**Palais, 19 février–5 mai 1980.**
Paris: Editions de la Réunion des musées nationaux, Ministère de la culture et de la communication, c1980. 415 p.: ill. (some col.); 25 cm. 1. Viollet-le-Duc, Eugène-Emmanuel, 1814-1879 — Exhibitions. I. Viollet-le-Duc, Eugène-Emmanuel, 1814-1879. II. Galeries nationales du Grand Palais (France)
N6853.V52 A4 1980  720/.92/4 19  LC 80-115247  ISBN 2711801373

**Grasselli, Margaret Morgan, 1951-.**     **1.4981**
Watteau, 1684–1721 / Margaret Morgan Grasselli and Pierre Rosenberg, with the assistance of Nicole Parmantier. — Washington: National Gallery of Art, c1984. 580 p.: ill. (some col.); 28 cm. 'Exhibition dates: National Gallery of Art, June 17-September 23, 1984; Galeries nationales du Grand Palais, Paris, October 23, 1984-January 28, 1985; Schloss Charlottenburg, Berlin, February 22-May 26, 1985'–T.p. verso. Includes index. 1. Watteau, Antoine, 1684-1721 — Exhibitions. I. Rosenberg, Pierre. II. Parmantier, Nicole. III. Watteau, Antoine, 1684-1721. IV. National Gallery of Art (U.S.) V. Galeries nationales du Grand Palais (France) VI. Schloss Charlottenburg. VII. T.
N6853.W38 A4 1984  760/.092/4 19  LC 84-4918  ISBN 0894680749

## N6861–6888 Germany

**German masters of the nineteenth century: paintings and** **1.4982**
**drawings from the Federal Republic of Germany.**
New York: Metropolitan Museum of Art: Distributed by H.N. Abrams, [1981] 280 p.: ill. (some col.); 30 cm. 'Published in connection with an exhibition at the Metropolitan Museum of Art, New York, from May 2-July 5, 1981, and at the Art Gallery of Ontario, Canada, from August 1-October 11, 1981.'–Verso t.p. 1. Art, German — Catalogs. 2. Art, Modern — 19th century — Germany — Catalogs. 3. Art — Germany (West) — Catalogs. I. Metropolitan Museum of Art (New York, N.Y.) II. Art Gallery of Ontario.
N6867.G47  759.3/074/01471 19  LC 81-179477  ISBN 0870992635

**Paret, Peter.**            **1.4983**
The Berlin Secession: modernism and its enemies in imperial Germany / Peter Paret. — Cambridge, Mass.: Belknap Press of Harvard University Press, 1980. 269 p., [2] leaves of plates: ill. (some col.); 24 cm. Includes index. 1. Berliner Secession. 2. Modernism (Art) — Germany. 3. Politics in art — Germany. 4. Politics and culture — Germany. 5. Germany — History — William II, 1888-1918 I. T.
N6868.5.B3 P37  709/.431/55  LC 80-15117  ISBN 0674067738

**Dube, Wolf Dieter.**          **1.4984**
[Expressionists] Expressionism. Translated by Mary Whittall. New York, Praeger Publishers [1973, c1972] 215 p. illus. (part col.) 22 cm. London ed.

published under title: The expressionists. 1. Expressionism (Art) — Germany. 2. Art, Modern — 20th century — Germany. I. T.
N6868.5.E9 D8213 1973  760/.09/04  LC 72-79505

**Smith, Jeffrey Chipps, 1951-.**       **1.4985**
Nuremberg, a Renaissance city, 1500–1618 / by Jeffrey Chipps Smith. — 1st ed. — Austin: Published for the Archer M. Huntington Art Gallery, the University of Texas at Austin [by the] University of Texas Press, 1983. xiv, 322 p.: ill.; 31 cm. Catalog of an exhibition held at the Archer M. Huntington Art Gallery at the University of Texas at Austin. Includes index. 1. Art, German — Germany (West) — Nuremberg — Exhibitions. 2. Art, Renaissance — Germany (West) — Nuremberg — Exhibitions. 3. Reformation in art — Germany (West) — Nuremberg — Exhibitions. 4. Nuremberg (Germany) — Civilization — Exhibitions. I. Archer M. Huntington Art Gallery. II. T.
N6886.N9 S64 1983  709/.43/32 19  LC 83-10559  ISBN 0292755279

## N6888 Individual Artists, A–Z

**Hans Baldung Grien, prints & drawings: National Gallery of** **1.4986**
**Art, Washington, from January 25 through April 5 [and] Yale**
**University Art Gallery, New Haven, April 23 through June 14,**
**1981: exhibition / organized and catalogue edited by James H.**
**Marrow & Alan Shestack; with three essays on Baldung and his**
**art by Alan Shestack, Charles W. Talbot, and Linda C. Hults.**
New Haven: Yale University Art Gallery; [Chicago]: Distributed by the Universtiy of Chicago Press, c1981. xiv, 281 p.: ill.; 28 cm. 1. Baldung, Hans, d. 1545 — Exhibitions. I. Baldung, Hans, d. 1545. II. Marrow, James H. III. Shestack, Alan. IV. National Gallery of Art (U.S.) V. Yale University. Art Gallery. VI. Title: Hans Baldung Grien, prints and drawings.
N6888.B293 A4 1981  760/.092/4 19  LC 80-52733  ISBN 0894670131

**Windsor, Alan.**           **1.4987**
Peter Behrens, architect and designer / Alan Windsor. — New York, N.Y.: Whitney Library of Design, c1981. 186 p.: ill.; 24 cm. Includes index. 1. Behrens, Peter, 1868-1940. 2. Behrens, Peter, 1868-1940 — Influence. 3. Artists — Germany — Biography. I. T.
N6888.B433 W56 1981  709/.2/4 B 19  LC 81-12976  ISBN 0823074218

**Tisdall, Caroline.**          **1.4988**
Joseph Beuys / Caroline Tisdall. — New York: Thames and Hudson, c1979. 288 p.: ill.; 31 cm. Includes index. 1. Beuys, Joseph. I. Beuys, Joseph. II. Solomon R. Guggenheim Museum. III. T.
N6888.B463 T57  700/.92/4  LC 79-63886

**Strieder, Peter.**          **1.4989**
Albrecht Dürer, paintings, prints, drawings / by Peter Strieder; translated by Nancy M. Gordon and Walter L. Strauss. — English translation, 1st ed. — New York: Abaris Books, 1982. 400 p.: ill. (some col.); 34 cm. Translation of: Albrecht Dürer. Includes index. 1. Dürer, Albrecht, 1471-1528. 2. Artists — Germany — Biography. I. Dürer, Albrecht, 1471-1528. II. T. III. Title: Albrecht Dürer.
N6888.D8 S713 1982  760/.092/4 B 19  LC 79-50679  ISBN 0898350425

**Wölfflin, Heinrich, 1864-1945.**      **1.4990**
[Kunst Albrecht Dürers. English] The art of Albrecht Dürer. Translated by Alastair & Heide Grieve. [New York] Phaidon [distributed in the U.S. by Praeger, 1971] 311 p. illus., 8 col. plates. 26 cm. Translation of Die Kunst Albrecht Dürers. 1. Dürer, Albrecht, 1471-1528. I. T.
N6888.D8 W613  760/.0924  LC 70-139837  ISBN 0714814679

**Andrews, Keith.**          **1.4991**
Adam Elsheimer: paintings, drawings, prints / Keith Andrews. — New York: Rizzoli, 1977. 178 p.: ill. (some col.); 29 cm. Includes indexes. 1. Elsheimer, Adam, 1578-1610. 2. Artists — Italy — Rome (City) — Biography. 3. Artists — Germany — Biography. I. Elsheimer, Adam, 1578-1610. II. T.
N6888.E63 A5  760/.092/4  LC 77-73365  ISBN 084780089X

**Max Ernst / [compiled and edited by] Edward Quinn;** **1.4992**
**contributors: Max Ernst ... [et al.].**
Boston: New York Graphic Society, 1977. 444 p., [1] fold. leaf of col. plates: ill. (some col.); 32 cm. 1. Ernst, Max, 1891-1976 — Addresses, essays, lectures. I. Quinn, Edward. II. Ernst, Max, 1891-1976.
N6888.E7 M382  709.2/4  LC 77-77340  ISBN 0821207113

**Russell, John, 1919-.**         **1.4993**
[Max Ernst: Leben und Werk. English] Max Ernst: life and work. New York, H. N. Abrams [1967] 359 p. illus. (part col.), facsims., ports. 31 cm. 1. Ernst, Max, 1891-1976. I. T.
N6888.E7 R83 1967b  709/.44  LC 67-22852

**George Grosz. English.**     **1.4994**
George Grosz: his life and work / [edited] by Uwe M. Schneede; with contributions by Georg Bussmann and Marina Schneede–Sczesny; translated by Susanne Flatauer. — New York: Universe Books, 1979. 182 p.: ill. (some col.); 23 cm. Translation of: George Grosz. Includes index. 1. Grosz, George, 1893-1959. 2. Artists — Germany — Biography. I. Grosz, George, 1893-1959. II. Schneede, Uwe M. III. Bussmann, Georg. IV. Schneede-Sczesny, Marina. V. T.
N6888.G742 G4613 1979b    741/.092/4 B 19    *LC* 78-64969    *ISBN* 0876633335

**Jordan, Jim M.**     **1.4995**
Paul Klee and cubism / by Jim M. Jordan. — Princeton, N.J.: Princeton University Press, c1984. xxiii, 233 p.: ill.; 29 cm. Includes index. 1. Klee, Paul, 1879-1940. 2. Cubism I. Klee, Paul, 1879-1940. II. T.
N6888.K55 J67 1984    760/.092/4 19    *LC* 83-13898    *ISBN* 0691040257

**'s Levens felheid. English.**     **1.4996**
The Master of the Amsterdam Cabinet, or, The Housebook Master, ca. 1470–1500 / compiled by J.P. Filedt Kok; introductions and appendixes by K.G. Boon ... [et al.]; translations from the Dutch and German by Arno Pomerans, Gary Schwartz and Patricia Wardle]. — Amsterdam: Rijksmuseum in association with the Rijksprentenkabinet; Princeton, N.J.: Princeton University Press, 1985. 309 p.: ill. (some col.); 31 cm. Translation of: 's Levens felheid. Catalogue of an exhibition held in the Rijksprentenkabinet, Rijksmuseum, Amsterdam, Mar. 19-June 9, 1985. 1. Master of the Housebook, 15th cent — Exhibitions. I. Filedt Kok, J. P. II. Rijksmuseum (Netherlands). Rijksprentenkabinet. III. T.
N6888.M3455 A4 1985    709/.2/4 19    *LC* 85-6359    *ISBN* 0691040354

**Perry, Gillian.**     **1.4997**
Paula Modersohn–Becker, her life and work / Gillian Perry. — 1st U.S. ed. — New York: Harper & Row, c1979. ix, 149 p.: ill. (some col.), ports. An Icon edition. 1. Modersohn-Becker, Paula, 1876-1907. 2. Artists, German — Biography. I. T.
N6888.M5 P4 1979    *LC* 79-1913    *ISBN* 0064384217

**Pois, Robert A.**     **1.4998**
Emil Nolde / Robert Pois. — Washington, D.C.: University Press of America, c1982. xxx, 263 p., [15] p. of plates: ill., port.; 22 cm. Includes index. 1. Nolde, Emil, 1867-1956. 2. Artists — Germany — Biography. I. T.
N6888.N6 P64 1982    760/.092/4 B 19    *LC* 81-43498    *ISBN* 0819123676

**Elderfield, John.**     **1.4999**
Kurt Schwitters / John Elderfield. — London: Thames and Hudson, c1985. 424 p.: ill. (some col.) 'Published on the occasion of an exhibition ... at the Museum of Modern Art, New York, in 1985.' 1. Schwitters, Kurt, 1887-1948. I. Schwitters, Kurt, 1887-1948. II. Museum of Modern Art (New York, N.Y.) III. T.
N6888.S42 E42    *ISBN* 0500234264

## N6911–6923 ITALY

**Blunt, Anthony Sir, 1907-.**     • **1.5000**
Artistic theory in Italy, 1450–1600 / by Anthony Blunt. — Oxford: Clarendon Press, 1940. vi, 168 p., 12 leaves of plates: ill.; 21 cm. 1. Aesthetics 2. Art, Italian 3. Art, Renaissance 4. Painting, Italian I. T.
N6915.B55 1956    *LC* a 41-144

**Hartt, Frederick.**     **1.5001**
History of Italian Renaissance art: painting, sculpture, architecture. — New York: H. N. Abrams, [1969] 636 p.: illus., 80 col. plates.; 30 cm. 1. Art, Italian 2. Art, Renaissance — Italy I. T.
N6915.H37    709/.45    *LC* 74-95193    *ISBN* 0810901838

**Italian art, 1400–1500: sources and documents / [selected and translated by] Creighton E. Gilbert.**     **1.5002**
Englewood Cliffs, N.J.: Prentice-Hall, c1980. xxviii, 226 p.; 23 cm. — (Sources and documents in the history of art series.) Principal contents made up of writings translated from the original French, Italian, or Latin. 1. Art, Italian — Addresses, essays, lectures. 2. Art, Renaissance — Early Renaissance — Italy — Addresses, essays, lectures. I. Gilbert, Creighton. II. Series.
N6915.I78    709/.45    *LC* 79-11069    *ISBN* 0135079470

**White, John.**     • **1.5003**
Art and architecture in Italy, 1250 to 1400 / John White. Baltimore: Penguin, 1966. xxvi, 449 p.: ill., map, plans. — (Pelican history of art. Z28.) 1. Art, Italian — History. 2. Architecture, Italian — History. I. T. II. Series.
N6915.W45    *LC* 67-5664

**Wölfflin, Heinrich.**     **1.5004**
Classic art: an introduction to the Italian Renaissance / Heinrich Wölfflin. — Ithaca, N.Y.: Cornell University Press, 1980. xviii, 294 p.: ill. — (Landmarks in art history.) Translation [from the eighth German ed.] of: Die Klassische Kunst. 'A Phaidon book.' First published: New York: Phaidon Press, 1952. 1. Art — Italy — History. 2. Art, Renaissance — Italy I. T. II. Series.
N6915.W6x 1980    *LC* 80-7483    *ISBN* 0801491932

**Haskell, Francis, 1928-.**     **1.5005**
Patrons and painters: a study in the relations between Italian art and society in the age of the Baroque / Francis Haskell. — Rev. and enl. ed. — New Haven: Yale University Press, 1980. xviii, 474 p., [34] leaves of plates: ill.; 26 cm. Includes index. 1. Art, Italian 2. Art, Baroque — Italy. 3. Art patrons 4. Art and society — Italy. I. T.
N6916.H37 1980    709/.45    *LC* 80-5213    *ISBN* 0300025378

**Wittkower, Rudolf.**     **1.5006**
Art and architecture in Italy, 1600 to 1750 / Rudolf Wittkower. — 3rd rev. ed., reprinted with corrections and augmented bibliography. — Harmondsworth, Middlesex; New York, N.Y.: Penguin Books, 1980. 664 p.: ill.; 21 cm. — (Pelican history of art.) Includes index. 1. Art, Italian 2. Art, Modern — 17th-18th centuries — Italy. I. T. II. Series.
N6916.W5 1980    709/.45 19    *LC* 80-151645    *ISBN* 0140561161

**Antal, Frederick.**     • **1.5007**
Florentine painting and its social background; the bourgeois republic before Cosimo de' Medici's advent to power: 14 and early 15 centuries. London, K. Paul [1948] xxiii, 388 p. plates. 1. Art — Florence 2. Florence (Italy) — Social life and customs 3. Florence (Italy) — History I. T.
N6921 F7 A54    *LC* 48-10125

**Wackernagel, Martin, 1881-.**     **1.5008**
[Lebensraum des Künstlers in der florentinischen Renaissance. English] The world of the Florentine Renaissance artist: projects and patrons, workshop and art market / Martin Wackernagel; translated by Alison Luchs. — Princeton, N.J.: Princeton University Press, c1981. xxx, 447 p.; 24 cm. Translation of Der Lebensraum des Künstlers in der florentinischen Renaissance. 1. Art, Italian — Italy — Florence. 2. Art, Renaissance — Italy — Florence. 3. Artists — Italy — Florence. 4. Art patronage — Italy — Florence. I. T.
N6921.F7 W313    709/.45/51 19    *LC* 80-39683    *ISBN* 0691039666

**Vasari, Giorgio, 1511-1574.**     • **1.5009**
[Vite de' più eccellenti architetti, pittori et scultori italiani English] The lives of the painters, sculptors, and architects. Edited with an introd. by William Gaunt. London, Dent; New York, Dutton [1963] 4 v. ports. 19 cm. (Everyman's library, no. 784-787) 1. Artists, Italian. 2. Art — Italy — History. I. T.
N6922.V48    927    *LC* 63-5456

## N6923 Individual Artists, A–Z

**Bernini, Gian Lorenzo, 1598-1680.**     • **1.5010**
[Zeichnungen des Gianlorenzo Bernini. English] Bernini's drawings, by Heinrich Brauer and Rudolf Wittkower. [New York] Collectors Editions [1970] 2 v. illus. 33 cm. (Römische Forschungen der Bibliotheca Hertziana, v. 9-10) Reprint of the German 1931 ed., with a new pref. in German and English. Original title on spine: Die Zeichnungen des Gianlorenzo Bernini. I. Brauer, Heinrich, ed. II. Wittkower, Rudolf. ed. III. T.
N6923.B5 A3 1970    741.945    *LC* 75-101393

**Baldinucci, Filippo, 1625-1696.**     • **1.5011**
The life of Bernini. Translated from the Italian by Catherine Enggass. Foreword by Robert Enggass. University Park, Pennsylvania State University Press, 1966. xviii, 177 p. ill., port. 1. Bernini, Gian Lorenzo, 1598-1680. I. T.
N6923 B5 B33    *LC* 65-26094

**Lavin, Irving, 1927-.**     **1.5012**
Bernini and the unity of the visual arts / by Irving Lavin. — New York: [Published for] Pierpont Morgan Library [by] Oxford University Press, c1980. 2 v.: ill.; 29 cm. (Franklin Jasper Walls lectures. 1975) 1. Bernini, Gian Lorenzo, 1598-1680. I. Pierpont Morgan Library. II. T. III. Series.
N6923.B5 L38    709/.2/40 19    *LC* 80-80573    *ISBN* 0195201841

**Condivi, Ascanio, b. ca. 1520.**     **1.5013**
[Vita di Michelagnolo Buonarroti. English] The life of Michelangelo / by Ascanio Condivi; translated by Alice Sedgwick Wohl; edited by Hellmut Wohl. — Baton Rouge: Louisiana State University Press, c1976. xxii, 156 p.: ill.; 26 cm. Translation of Vita di Michelagnolo Buonarroti. Includes index. 1. Michelangelo Buonarroti, 1475-1564. I. T.
N6923.B9 C613 1976    700/.92/4 B    *LC* 74-27197

**De Tolnay, Charles, 1899-.**      • **1.5014**
Michelangelo. [Princeton, Princeton University Press, 1943-. v. plates. 31 cm. Half title: each vol. has also special t.p. 1. Michelangelo Buonarroti, 1475-1564. I. T.
N6923.B9 D395     *LC* 62-4630

**Spear, Richard E., 1940-.**      **1.5015**
Domenichino / Richard E. Spear. — New Haven: Yale University Press, 1983 (c1982). 2 v.: col. ill.; 29 cm. Errata slip inserted in vol. 1. Includes indexes. 1. Domenichino, 1581-1641 — Catalogs. I. T.
N6923.D63 S6     759.5 19     *LC* 82-2844     *ISBN* 0300023596

**Knox, George.**      **1.5016**
Piazzetta: a tercentenary exhibition of drawings, prints, and books / George Knox. — Washington: National Gallery of Art; Cambridge: Cambridge University Press, c1983. — 258 p.: ill.; 29 cm. 'Exhibition dates ... 20 November 1983-26 February 1984'—T.p. verso. Includes indexes. 1. Piazzetta, Giovanni Battista — Exhibitions. I. Piazzetta, Giovanni Battista. II. National Gallery of Art (U.S.) III. T.
N6923.P457 A4 1983     760/.092/4 19     *LC* 83-17484     *ISBN* 0521264316

**Wilton-Ely, John.**      **1.5017**
The mind and art of Giovanni Battista Piranesi / John Wilton-Ely. — London: Thames and Hudson, c1978. 304 p.: ill.; 32 cm. Includes index. 1. Piranesi, Giambattista, 1720-1778. 2. Neoclassicism (Art) — Italy. I. T.
N6923.P495 W54     769/.92/4     *LC* 77-92272     *ISBN* 0500091226

**Jones, Roger, 1947-.**      **1.5018**
Raphael / Roger Jones and Nicholas Penny. — New Haven: Yale University Press, 1983. 256 p.: ill. (some col.); 30 cm. Includes index. 1. Raphael, 1483-1520. I. Penny, Nicholas, 1949- II. T.
N6923.R3 J6 1983     759.5 19     *LC* 83-1390     *ISBN* 0300030614

## N6925–6973 Netherlands. Belgium

**Osten, Gert von der.**      **1.5019**
Painting and sculpture in Germany and the Netherlands, 1500 to 1600 [by] Gert von der Osten & Horst Vey; [translated from the German MS. by Mary Hottinger]. — Harmondsworth, Penguin, 1969. xxii, 403 p., 193 plates. illus. (incl. 1 col.), 2 maps. 27 cm. — (Pelican history of art. Z 31) 1. Art, German — History. 2. Art, Flemish — History. 3. Art, Dutch — History. I. Vey, Horst. II. T. III. Series.
N6925.O813 1969     759.3     *LC* 79-514834     *ISBN* 140560319

**De Stijl, 1917–1931: visions of Utopia / introduction by Hans**      **1.5020**
**L.C. Jaffé; essays by Manfred Bock ... [et al.]; Mildred**
**Friedman, editor.**
Minneapolis: Walker Art Center; New York: Abbeville Press, c1982. 255 p.: ill. (some col.); 28 cm. Catalog of an exhibition organized by the Walker Art Center. Includes index. 1. De Stijl — Exhibitions. I. Bock, Manfred. II. Friedman, Mildred S. III. Walker Art Center.
N6948.5.S8 S8     709/.04 19     *LC* 81-19063     *ISBN* 089659257X

**Troy, Nancy J.**      **1.5021**
The De Stijl environment / Nancy J. Troy. — Cambridge, Mass.: MIT Press, c1983. ix, 254 p.: ill. (some col.); 23 x 28 cm. Includes index. 1. Stijl. 2. Neoplasticism 3. Art, Modern — 20th century — Netherlands I. T.
N6948.5.S8 T7 1983     709/.492 19     *LC* 82-12517     *ISBN* 0262200465

**Ernst, Bruno.**      **1.5022**
The magic mirror of M. C. Escher / Bruno Ernst; [translated from the Dutch by John E. Brigham]. — 1st American ed. — New York: Random House, c1976. 112 p.: ill. (some col.); 32 cm. Includes index. 1. Escher, M. C. (Maurits Cornelis), 1898-1972. I. T.
N6953.E82 E76 1976     769/.92/4     *LC* 75-664     *ISBN* 039449217X

**Veldman, Ilja M.**      **1.5023**
Maarten van Heemskerck and Dutch humanism in the sixteenth century / Ilja M. Veldman; translated from the Dutch by Michael Hoyle. — Maarssen: G. Schwartz, 1977. 176 p.: ill.; 31 cm. 1. Heemskerck, Martin van, 1498-1574. 2. Artists — Netherlands — Biography. 3. Humanism in art I. Heemskerck, Martin van, 1498-1574. II. T.
N6953.H33 V34     *LC* 78-372316     *ISBN* 0839002009

**Slive, Seymour, 1920-.**      **1.5024**
Jacob van Ruisdael / Seymour Slive, H.R. Hoetink; [editor, Mark Greenberg]. — New York: Abbeville Press, 1982 (c1981). 271 p.: ill. (some col.); 29 cm. Catalogue of an exhibition held at the Mauritshuis, the Royal Cabinet of Paintings, the Hague, 1 Oct. 1981-3 Jan. 1982 and at the Fogg Art Museum, Harvard University, Cambridge, Mass., 18 Jan. 1982-11 April 1982. 1. Ruisdael, Jacob van, 1628 or 9-1682 — Exhibitions. I. Hoetink, Hendrik

Richard. II. Ruisdael, Jacob van, 1628 or 9-1682. III. Greenberg, Mark. IV. Mauritshuis (Hague, Netherlands) V. Fogg Art Museum. VI. T.
N6953.R8 A4     760/.092/4 19     *LC* 81-65933     *ISBN* 089659226X

**Gerson, H. (Horst)**      • **1.5025**
Art and architecture in Belgium, 1600 to 1800 [by] H. Gerson [and] E.H. ter Kuile. [Translated from the Dutch by Olive Renier. Harmondsworth, Middlesex] Penguin Books [1960] xix, 236 p. 160 plates (incl. ports.) (Pelican history of art. Z18) 1. Art — Belgium — History 2. Architecture — Belgium — History I. Kuile, Engelbert Hendrik ter, joint author II. T. III. Series.
N6966 G43     *LC* 60-3193

**Flemish art from Ensor to Permeke / [general supervision],**      **1.5026**
**Albert Smeets; [translations, Arthur Birt, Guido Eeckels, Henri**
**Schoup].**
[s.l.]: Abner Schram, 1972. 303 p.: ill. (some col.), ports. Includes indexes. 1. Art, Flemish 2. Art, Modern — 19th century — Flanders. 3. Art, Modern — 20th century — Flanders. I. Smeets, Albert.
N6969.F5 S613     709/.493/1     *ISBN* 9020903861

**Collon-Gevaert, Suzanne.**      **1.5027**
A treasury of Romanesque art; metalwork, illuminations and sculpture from the valley of the Meuse [by] Suzanne Collon–Gevaert, Jean Lejeune [and] Jacques Stiennon. Foreword and introd. by Germaine Faider–Feytmans. Translated by Susan Waterston. [New York] Phaidon; [distributed by Praeger, 1972] 327 p. illus. (part col.) 31 cm. Translation of Art roman dans la vallée de la Meuse aux XIe, XIIe et XIIIe siècles. 1. Art — Meuse River Valley. 2. Art, Romanesque — Meuse River Valley. I. Lejeune, Jean, joint author. II. Stiennon, Jacques. joint author. III. T.
N6969.M4 C59513     709/.02/1     *LC* 76-161220     *ISBN* 0714814210

**Held, Julius Samuel, 1905-.**      **1.5028**
Rubens and his circle: studies / by Julius S. Held; edited by Anne W. Lowenthal, David Rosand, John Walsh, Jr. — Princeton, N.J.: Princeton University Press, c1982. xxiv, 207 p., [36] leaves of plates: ill. (some col.); 29 cm. 1. Rubens, Peter Paul, Sir, 1577-1640 — Addresses, essays, lectures. 2. Rubens, Peter Paul, Sir, 1577-1640 — Influence — Addresses, essays, lectures. I. Lowenthal, Anne W. II. Rosand, David. III. Walsh, John, 1937- IV. T.
N6973.R9 H44 1982     759.9493 19     *LC* 80-27441     *ISBN* 0691039682

## N6976–6999 Russia

**Hamilton, George Heard.**      **1.5029**
The art and architecture of Russia / George Heard Hamilton. 2d ed. — Harmondsworth [Eng.]; Baltimore: Penguin Books, 1975. xxiv, 342 p., [91] leaves of plates: ill.; 27 cm. (Pelican history of art.) Includes index. 1. Art, Russian — History. 2. Architecture — Russia — History. I. T. II. Series.
N6981.H34 1975     709/.47     *LC* 77-352526     *ISBN* 0140560068

**Introduction to Russian art and architecture / edited by Robert**      **1.5030**
**Auty and Dimitri Obolensky, with the editorial assistance of**
**Anthony Kingsford; with chapters by Robin Milner–Gulland &**
**John Bowlt.**
Cambridge; New York: Cambridge University Press, 1980. xiii, 194 p.: ill.; 24 cm. — (Companion to Russian studies; v. 3) 1. Art, Russian 2. Architecture — Russia. I. Auty, Robert. II. Obolensky, Dimitri, 1918- III. Kingsford, Anthony. IV. Series.
N6981.I57     709/.47     *LC* 75-10691     *ISBN* 0521208955

**Williams, Robert Chadwell, 1938-.**      **1.5031**
Russian art and American money, 1900–1940 / Robert C. Williams. — Cambridge, Mass.: Harvard University Press, 1980. vi, 309 p.: ill.; 24 cm. Includes index. 1. Art, Russian — United States. 2. Art — United States — Marketing. 3. Art — Russia — Marketing. 4. United States — Commerce — Russia. 5. Russia — Commerce — United States. I. T.
N6981.W54     382/.45/70947     *LC* 79-16925

**Art of the October Revolution / compiled and introduced by**      **1.5032**
**Mikhail Guerman; translation from the Russian, W. Freeman,**
**D. Saunders, and C. Binns].**
New York: Abrams, 1979. 34 p., [100] leaves of plates: ill. (some col.); 32 cm. Includes index. 1. Art, Russian 2. Art, Modern — 20th century — Russia. 3. Socialist realism in art — Russia. 4. Performing arts — Russia. 5. Russia — History — Revolution, 1917-1921 — Art and the Revolution. I. German, Mikhail IUr'evich.
N6988.A762     704.94/9/94708410947     *LC* 77-20741     *ISBN* 0810906759

**Gray, Camilla.**      • **1.5033**
[Great experiment: Russian art, 1863-1922] The Russian experiment in art, 1863–1922. New York, H. N. Abrams [1971, c1962] 296 p. illus. (part col.) 22

cm. First published under title: The great experiment: Russian art, 1863-1922.
1. Art, Russian — History. I. T.
N6988.G7 1971b     709.47     LC 79-106516     ISBN 0810904659

**New art from the Soviet Union: the known and the unknown /**     **1.5034**
**[prepared by] Norton Dodge & Alison Hilton.**
Washington: Acropolis Books, c1977. 127 p.: ill. (some col.); 29 cm. 1. Art,
Russian 2. Dissident art — Russia 3. Art, Modern — 20th century — Russia.
I. Dodge, Norton T. II. Hilton, Alison.
N6988.N47 1977     709/.47     LC 77-13442     ISBN 0874912091

**Russian art of the avant–garde: theory and criticism, 1902–1934**     **1.5035**
**/ edited and translated by John E. Bowlt.**
New York: Viking Press, [1976] xl, 360 p.: ill.; 22 cm. (The Documents of 20th-
century art) Includes index. 1. Art, Russian — History — Collected works.
2. Art, Modern — 20th century — Soviet Union — Collected works. I. Bowlt,
John E. II. Series.
N6988.R84 1976     709/.47     LC 73-17687     ISBN 067061257X

**Russian avant–garde art: the George Costakis Collection /**     **1.5036**
**general editor, Angelica Zander Rudenstine; introduction by S.**
**Frederick Starr; Collecting art of the avant–garde, by George**
**Costakis.**
New York: Abrams, 1981. 527 p.: ill. (some col.); 30 cm. 1. Costakis, Georgi —
Art collections. 2. Art, Russian 3. Art, Modern — 20th century — Soviet
Union. 4. Avant-garde (Aesthetics) — Soviet Union. 5. Art — Private
collections — Soviet Union. 6. Artists — Soviet Union — Biography.
I. Costakis, Georgi. II. Rudenstine, Angelica Zander. III. Starr, S. Frederick.
N6988.R85     709/.47/074 19     LC 81-1406     ISBN 0810915561

**Lodder, Christina, 1948-.**     **1.5037**
Russian constructivism / Christina Lodder. — New Haven: Yale University
Press, 1983. viii, 328 p.: ill. (some col.); 27 cm. Includes index.
1. Constructivism (Art) — Soviet Union. 2. Art, Russian 3. Art, Modern —
20th century — Soviet Union. I. T.
N6988.5.C64 L63 1983     709/.47 19     LC 83-40002     ISBN
0300027273

**Compton, Susan P.**     **1.5038**
Chagall / Susan Compton. — New York: H.N. Abrams, [1985] 280 p.: ill.
(some col.); 29 cm. Catalog of an exhibition to be held in April 1985 at the
Philadelphia Museum of Art, originating at the Royal Academy of Arts.
1. Chagall, Marc, 1887- — Exhibitions. I. Philadelphia Museum of Art.
II. Royal Academy of Arts (Great Britain) III. T.
N6999.C46 A4 1985     709/.2/4 19     LC 84-24273     ISBN
0810907976

## N7000–7193 OTHER EUROPEAN COUNTRIES

**Stang, Ragna Thiis.**     **1.5039**
[Edvard Munch. English] Edvard Munch: the man and his art / by Ragna
Stang; translation from the Norwegian by Geoffrey Culverwell. — New York:
Abbeville Press, c1979. 319 p.: ill. (some col.); 30 cm. Translation of Edvard-
Munch. Includes indexes. 1. Munch, Edvard, 1863-1944. 2. Artists — Norway
— Biography. I. T.
N7073.M8 S7313     709/.2/4 B 19     LC 78-31813     ISBN 0896590259

**Kubler, George, 1912-.**     • **1.5040**
Art and architecture in Spain and Portugal and their American dominions,
1500 to 1800 / by George Kubler and Martin Soria. — [Harmondsworth,
Middlesex]: Penguin Books, 1959. xxviii, 445 p. illus., 192 plates, maps, plans.
27 cm. (Pelican history of art. Z17) 1. Art — Spain — History. 2. Architecture
— Spain — History. 3. Art — Portugal — History. 4. Architecture —
Portugal — History. 5. Art — Latin America — History. 6. Architecture —
Latin America — History. I. Soria, Martin Sebastian. II. T. III. Series.
N7104.K8 1959a     LC 60-666

**Christo, 1935-.**     **1.5041**
[Running fence English] The running fence project / Christo; text by Werner
Spies; photos. by Wolfgang Volz; [translated from the German by Kathleen
Cheesmond]. — New York: H. N. Abrams, 1977. [23] p., [46] leaves of plates (2
fold.): ill. (some col.); 20 x 23 cm. Translation of The running fence. 1. Christo,
1935- Running fence I. Spies, Werner, 1937- II. Volz, Wolfgang. III. T.
N7193.C5 A4 1977     709/.2/4     LC 77-77150     ISBN 0810920808

**Hovdenakk, Per.**     **1.5042**
Christo, complete editions, 1964-1982: catalogue raisonné and introduction /
by Per Hovdenakk; [editor, German translation, Jörg Schellmann]. — New
York, N.Y.: New York University Press, 1983, c1982. ca 150 p.: ill. (some col.);
25 cm. English and German. 1. Christo, 1935- — Catalogs. I. Schellmann,
Jörg. II. T.
N7193.C5 A4 1982     709/.2/4 19     LC 82-6468     ISBN 0814734170

## N7260–7369 Asia

**Binyon, Laurence, 1869-1943.**     • **1.5043**
The spirit of man in Asian art, being the Charles Eliot Norton lectures delivered
in Harvard university, 1933–34, by Laurence Binyon ... Cambridge, Mass.,
Harvard university press, 1935. xv, 217 p. 70 pl. 22.5 cm. 1. Arts — Asia. I. T.
II. Title: Asian art.
N7260.B53     709.5     LC 35-3032

**Coomaraswamy, Ananda Kentish, 1877-1947.**     • **1.5044**
History of Indian and Indonesian art, by Ananda K. Coomaraswamy. New
York, Dover Publications [1965] 295, cxxviii p. illus., maps. 24 cm. 'First
published in ... 1927.' 1. Art, Indic 2. Art, Indonesian 3. Art — Asia,
Southeastern. I. T.
N7260.C65 1965     709.54     LC 65-24018

## N7280–7289 IRAN. PERSIA

**Pope, Arthur Upham, 1881-1969. ed.**     **1.5045**
A survey of Persian art from prehistoric times to the present. Arthur Upham
Pope, editor; Phillis Ackerman, assistant editor. [2d ed.] London Oxford
University Press 1964-. v. ill. (part col.) maps, plans. (An Asia Institute book)
'Published under the auspices of the Asia Institute'. 'Index volume, compiled by
Theodore Besterman': 63 supplementary pages at end of v. 6. Proposed v. 13 not
published; incorporated into v. 15. Imprint varies. Vols. 1-13, a reissue, with
corrigenda and addenda, of 6-vol. ed. published 1938-39. 1. Art — Iran —
History I. Ackerman, Phyllis, 1893- jt. ed. II. Besterman, Theodore,
1904-1976. III. T.
N7280 P63 1964

## N7300–7310 SOUTH ASIA. INDIA

**Chandra, Pramod.**     **1.5046**
On the study of Indian art / Pramod Chandra. — Cambridge, Mass.: Published
for the Asia Society, by Harvard University Press, 1983. 134 p., [12] p. of plates:
ill.; 22 cm. — (Polsky lectures in Indian and Southeast Asian art and
archaeology.) Includes index. 1. Art, Indic I. T. II. Series.
N7301.C474 1983     709/.54 19     LC 83-8393     ISBN 0674637623

**Huntington, Susan L.**     **1.5047**
The art of ancient India: Buddhist, Hindu, Jain / by Susan L. Huntington with
contributions by John C. Huntington. — 1st ed. — New York: Weatherhill,
1985. xxix, 786 p., [12] p. of plates: ill. (some col.); 27 cm. Ill. on lining papers.
Includes indexes. 1. Art, Indic 2. Architecture — India I. Huntington, John
C. II. T.
N7301.H86 1985     709/.54 19     LC 83-5742     ISBN 0834801833

**Rowland, Benjamin, 1904-1972.**     • **1.5048**
The art and architecture of India: Buddhist, Hindu, Jain / Benjamin Rowland.
— 1st integrated ed., reprinted with revisions and updated bibliography / by J.
C. Harle. — Harmondsworth, Eng.: Penguin Books, 1977. 512 p.: ill.; 21 cm. —
(Pelican history of art. PZ2) 1. Art, Indic 2. Architecture, Indic. I. Harle,
James C. II. T. III. Series.
N7301.R68 1977     704.948/9/40954     ISBN 0140561021

**Zimmer, Heinrich Robert, 1890-1943.**     • **1.5049**
The art of Indian Asia, its mythology and transformations. Completed and
edited by Joseph Campbell; with photos by Eliot Elisofon and others. [New
York] Pantheon Books [1955] 2 v. ill., plates, maps. (Bollingen series. 39)
1. Art — India — History 2. Art, Indic 3. Mythology, Hindu I. T. II. Series.
N7301 Z5     LC 54-11742

**Griswold, Alexander B.**     • **1.5050**
[Burma, Korea, Tibet. English] The art of Burma, Korea, Tibet, by Alexander
B. Griswold, Chewon Kim [and] Peter H. Pott. New York, Crown Publishers
[1964] 277 p. illus. (part mounted col.), maps. 24 cm. (Art of the world, non-
European cultures; the historical, sociological and religious backgrounds)
Translation of Burma, Korea, Tibet. 1. Art, Burmese — History. 2. Art,
Korean — History. 3. Art, Tibetan — History. I. T.
N7306.G7     709.51     LC 63-20855

**Lyons, Islay, 1922-.**     • **1.5051**
Gandhāran art in Pakistan; with 577 illustrations photographed by Islay Lyons,
and 77 pictures from other sources. Introd. and descriptive catalogue by Harald
Ingholt. [New York] Pantheon Books [c1957] 203 p. illus., maps. 31 cm.
Bibliographical references included in 'Notes' (p. 41-45) 1. Art — Peshawar,
India (District) 2. Art, Buddhist I. Ingholt, Harald, 1896- II. T.
N7307.P3L9     709.54     LC 57-10237

**Macdonald, Alexander W.**     **1.5052**
Newar art: Nepalese art during the Malla period / A.W. Macdonald & Anne
Vergati Stahl. — Warminster, Eng.: Aris & Phillips, 1979. xiv, 154 p.: ill. (some

col.); 31 cm. Seven col. ill. tipped in. Errata slip inserted. Includes index. 1. Art, Newari 2. Nepal — Civilization. I. Stahl, Anne Vergati. joint author. II. T. N7310.8.N4 M32 1979b   709/.549/6   LC 80-474657   ISBN 0856680567

**Pal, Pratapaditya.**      **1.5053**
The arts of Nepal / by Pratapaditya Pal. — Leiden: E. J. Brill, 1974-. v.    : ill.; 25 cm. (Handbuch der Orientalistik: 7. Abt., Kunst und Archäologie; 3. Bd.; Innerasien, 3. Abschnitt; Tibet, Nepal, Mongolei, 2. Lfg.) Based on the author's thesis, Cambridge, originally presented under title: Sculpture and painting of Nepal. Includes index. 1. Art, Nepali I. T. N7310.8.N4 P34   709/.549/6   LC 75-500108   ISBN 9004037764

## N7311–7332 SOUTHEAST ASIA

**Groslier, Bernard Philippe.**    • **1.5054**
The art of Indochina, including Thailand, Vietnam, Laos and Cambodia. [Translated by George Lawrence] New York, Crown Publishers [1962] 261 p. ill. (part mounted col.) maps (part fold.) plans, tables. (Art of the world, non-European cultures: the historical sociological and religious backgrounds) 1. Art, Indochinese I. T. N7311 G713 1962   LC 62-11805

**Le May, Reginald Stuart, 1885-.**    • **1.5055**
A concise history of Buddhist art in Siam / by Reginald Le May. — 2d ed. — Rutland, Vt.: C. E. Tuttle Co., 1963, c1962. xxiii, 169 p., [40] leaves of plates: ill., [2] fold. maps; 28 cm. Includes index. 1. Art, Thai — History. 2. Art, Buddhist — History. I. T. II. Title: Buddhist art in Siam. N7321.L4 1963   709.593   LC 62-18359   ISBN 0804801207

**Bernet Kempers, August Johan, 1906-.**    • **1.5056**
Ancient Indonesian art / by A. J. Bernet Kempers. — Amsterdam: C. P. J. van der Peet, 1959. vi, 124 p., [140] leaves of plates: ill. 1. Art — Indonesia. I. T. N7326.B4 1959   LC 59-4979

**Wagner, Frits A.**    • **1.5057**
Indonesia: the art of an island group / [Translated by Ann E. Keep] New York: McGraw-Hill, [1961, c1959]. 256 p. illus. (part mounted col.) maps 24 cm. (Art of the world; the historical, sociological and religious backgrounds). 1. Art — Indonesia — History. I. T. N7326.W297 1959   LC 62-5072

## N7336–7337 EAST ASIA (GENERAL)

**Lee, Sherman E.**    • **1.5058**
A history of Far Eastern art / Sherman E. Lee. — 4th ed. — New York: H.N. Abrams, 1982. 548 p.: ill. (some col.); 30 cm. Includes index. 1. Art, Far Eastern I. T. N7336.L43 1982   709/.5 19   LC 81-3603   ISBN 0810910802

## N7340–7349 CHINA

**Munsterberg, Hugo, 1916-.**    **1.5059**
Dictionary of Chinese and Japanese art / Hugo Munsterberg. — New York: Hacker Art Books, 1981. vii, 354 p. 1. Art, Chinese — Dictionaries — Englsih 2. Art, Japanese — Dictionaries — English I. T. N7340 M818   LC 79-83856   ISBN 0878172483

**Sickman, L. C. S. (Laurence C. S.)**    • **1.5060**
The art and architecture of China [by] Laurence Sickman [and] Alexander Soper. — 3rd ed. — Harmondsworth: Penguin, 1968. xxix, 350 p.: 192 plates, illus. (incl. 1 col.), 2 maps, plans.; 27 cm. — (The Pelican history of art, Z10) 1. Art — China — History. 2. Architecture — China — History. I. Soper, Alexander Coburn, 1904- II. T. III. Series. N7340.S46 1968   709/.51   LC 75-422837   ISBN 0140560106

**Sullivan, Michael, 1916-.**    **1.5061**
The arts of China / Michael Sullivan. — 3rd ed. — Berkeley: University of California Press, c1984. xvii, 278 p.: ill. (some col.); 27 cm. Includes index. 1. Art, Chinese I. T. N7340.S92 1984   709/.51 19   LC 82-16027   ISBN 0520049179

**Watson, William, 1917-.**    **1.5062**
Style in the arts of China / William Watson. — Harmondsworth: Penguin, 1974. 126 p., [127] p. of plates: ill.; 20 cm. (Pelican books) Errata slip inserted. 1. Art, Chinese I. T. N7340.W37   709/.51   LC 74-193821   ISBN 0140218637

**Fontein, Jan.**    **1.5063**
Unearthing China's past [by] Jan Fontein & Tung Wu. Boston, Museum of Fine Arts; distributed by New York Graphic Society, Greenwich, Conn. 1974 [c1973] 239 p. illus. 26 cm. Catalogue of an exhibition held at the Boston Museum of Fine Arts. 1. Art, Chinese — Exhibitions. I. Wu, Tung, joint author. II. Museum of Fine Arts, Boston. III. T. N7342.F66   730/.0951   LC 73-79825   ISBN 0878460764

**Lee, Sherman E.**    **1.5064**
Chinese art under the Mongols: the Yüan dynasty, 1279–1368 [by] Sherman E. Lee [and] Wai-kam Ho. — [Cleveland]: Cleveland Museum of Art; [distributed by the Press of Case Western Reserve University, 1968] viii, 403 p.: ill. (1 col.), maps.; 27 cm. Based on an exhibition sponsored by the Cleveland Museum of Art. 1. Art, Chinese — Exhibitions. 2. China — History — Yüan dynasty, 1260-1368 I. Ho, Wai-kam. II. Cleveland Museum of Art. III. T. N7342.L37   709/.51   LC 68-9276

**Royal Ontario Museum.**    **1.5065**
The Chinese exhibition: the exhibition of archaeological finds of the People's Republic of China held at the Royal Ontario Museum, Toronto, Ontario, Canada, 8 August–16 November 1974 = L'exposition chinoise: l'exposition des découvertes archéologiques de la Republique Populaire de Chine au Musée Royal de l'Ontario, Toronto, Ontario, Canada, 8 sout–16 novembre 1974 / Royal Ontario Museum; [text by William Watson; traduction française de Gérard Bourlier]. — [Toronto: The Museum], 1974,c1973. 23, xii, 43-159, [8] leaves of plates: ill. (some col.), map on lining paper; 24 cm. — 1. Art, Chinese — Exhibitions. 2. China — Antiquities — Exhibitions. 3. China — Antiquities — Exhibitions. I. Watson, William, 1917- II. T. III. Title: L'exposition chinoise. IV. Title: The exhibition of archaeological finds of the People's Republic of China. V. Title: L'exposition des découvertes archéologiques de la République Populaire de Chine. N7342.T67   ISBN 0723001073

**Arts of China.**    **1.5066**
[1st ed.] Tokyo, Palo Alto, Calif., Kodansha International [1968-[1970] 3 v. illus. (part col.), map. 38 cm. Translation of Chūgoku bijutsu with new material added. 1. Art, Chinese 2. China — Antiquities I. Akiyama, Terukazu, 1918- N7343.C5613   709/.51   LC 68-17454

**Davidson, J. Leroy.**    **1.5067**
The Lotus Sutra in Chinese art; a study in Buddhist art to the year 1000. New Haven, Yale University Press, 1954. xvi, 105 p. 41 plates. 28 cm. (Yale studies in the history of art [8]) Title also in Chinese (transliterated: Miâo fâ lien hua ching hsien hsiang) 'Bibliographical note': p. 94-100. 1. Art — China. 2. Art, Buddhist 3. Saddharma-Pundarika. I. T. N7343.D35   709.51   LC 54-5604

**Rawson, Jessica.**    **1.5068**
Ancient China, art and archaeology / Jessica Rawson. — London: Published for the Trustees of the British Museum by British Museum Publications, c1980. 240 p., [4] leaves of plates: ill. (some col.); 24 cm. Includes indexes. 1. Art, Chinese — To 221 B.C. 2. Art, Chinese — Ch'in-Han dynasties, 221 B.C.-220 A.D. I. T. N7343.22.R38   709/.31 19   LC 81-457316   ISBN 0714114154

**Los Angeles County Museum of Art.**    **1.5069**
Art of Tibet: a catalogue of the Los Angeles County Museum of Art collection / by Pratapaditya Pal; with an appendix on inscriptions by H.E. Richardson. — Los Angeles, Calif.: The Museum; Berkeley: In association with University of California Press, 1983. 280 p.: ill. (some col.); 30 cm. Includes index. 1. Los Angeles County Museum of Art — Catalogs. 2. Art, Tibetan — Influence — Catalogs. 3. Art — California — Los Angeles — Catalogs. 4. Art, Tibetan — Catalogs. I. Pal, Pratapaditya. II. Richardson, Hugh Edward, 1905- III. T. N7346.T5 L6 1983   709.51/5074019494 19   LC 83-8194   ISBN 0875871127

**Olschak, Blanche Christine.**    **1.5070**
Mystic art of ancient Tibet / [by] Blanche Christine Olschak, in collaboration with Geshé Thupten Wangyal; [translated from the German]. — New York: McGraw, [c1973]. 224 p.: ill. (some col.); 32 cm. Translation of Mystik und Kunst Alttibets. Ill. on lining papers. Includes indexes. 1. Art, Tibetan 2. Buddhist art and symbolism — Tibet. I. Thupten Wangyal. joint author. II. T. N7346.T5 O4513   704.948/9/4392309515   709.515

## N7350–7359 JAPAN

**The Heibonsha survey of Japanese art.**    **1.5071**
New York: Weatherhill, 1973-. v.: ill (some col.); 24 cm. 1. Art, Japanese N7350.H45

**Katō, Shūichi, 1919-.**    **1.5072**
Form, style, tradition; reflections on Japanese art and society. Translated from the Japanese by John Bester. Berkeley, University of California Press 1972, [c1971] 216 p. illus., ports. 23 cm. 1. Art, Japanese — History. 2. Art and society — Japan. I. T. N7350.K3513   709/.52   LC 79-129612   ISBN 0520018095

**Lee, Sherman E.** • 1.5073
Japanese decorative style / [by] Sherman E. Lee. — [Cleveland]: Cleveland Museum of Art; distributed by H. N. Abrams, 1961. ix, 161 p.: ill.; 24 cm. 'A by-product of the exhibition ... organized by the Cleveland Museum of Art and co-sponsored by the Art Institute of Chicago.' 1. Art, Japanese — History. 2. Decoration and ornament — Japan I. Cleveland Museum of Art. II. T.
N7350.L43      709/.52      LC 61-9910

**Noma, Seiroku.** 1.5074
The arts of Japan / by Seiroku Noma; translated and adapted by John Rosenfield; photos. by Takahashi Bin. — Popular ed. — Tokyo: Kodansha International; New York: Kodansha International/USA; distributors, U.S., Harper & Row, 1978. 2 v.: ill. (some col.), maps. Translation of Nihon bijutsu. Vol. 2 translated and adapted by Glenn T. Webb. 1. Art, Japanese 2. Art — Japan. I. Takahashi, Bin. II. T.
N7350.N63913 1978      709/.52      LC 78-18531      ISBN 0870113356

**Paine, Robert Treat, 1900-.** • 1.5075
The art and architecture of Japan [by] Robert Treat Paine [and] Alexander Soper. — [Baltimore]: Penguin Books, [1955] xviii, 316 p.: illus., plates, maps, plans, tables.; 27 cm. — (Pelican history of art. Z8) 1. Art — Japan — History. 2. Architecture — Japan — History. I. Soper, Alexander Coburn, 1904- II. T. III. Series.
N7350.P3      709.52      LC 55-12839

**Lee, Sherman E.** 1.5076
Reflections of reality in Japanese art / text by Sherman E. Lee; catalogue by Michael R. Cunningham with James T. Ulak. — Cleveland, Ohio: Cleveland Museum of Art; Bloomington, Ind.: Distributed by Indiana University Press, c1983. xii, 292 p., [16] p. of plates: ill. (some col.); 27 cm. 'Exhibition ... organized jointly by the Cleveland Museum of Art, the Agency for Cultural Affairs of the Japanese Government, the Japan Foundation'—T.p. verso. 'Index' and 'Errata'([8] p.) inserted. 1. Art, Japanese — Exhibitions. 2. Realism in art — Japan — Exhibitions. I. Cunningham, Michael R. II. Ulak, James T. III. Cleveland Museum of Art. IV. Japan. Bunkachō. V. Kokusai Kōryū Kikin. VI. T.
N7352.L43 1983      709/.52/074017132 19      LC 82-45940      ISBN 0910386706

**Rosenfield, John M.** 1.5077
Traditions of Japanese art; selections from the Kimiko and John Powers Collection [by] John M. Rosenfield [and] Shūjirō Shimada. [Cambridge, Mass.] Fogg Art Museum, Harvard University, 1970. 393 p. illus. (part col.), facsims., maps. 29 cm. Exhibition catalog. 1. Powers, Kimiko — Art collections. 2. Powers, John — Art collections. 3. Art, Japanese — Exhibitions. I. Shimada, Shūjirō, 1907- joint author. II. Fogg Art Museum. III. T.
N7352.R67      709.52      LC 76-133788      ISBN 0674901258

**Roberts, Laurance P.** 1.5078
A dictionary of Japanese artists: painting, sculpture, ceramics, prints, lacquer / Laurance P. Roberts; with a foreword by John M. Rosenfield. 1st ed. — Tokyo; New York: Weatherhill, 1976. xi, 299 p.; 27 cm. Title on spine: Japanese artists. Includes indexes. 1. Artists — Japan — Biography. I. T.
N7358.R6      709/.2/2 B      LC 76-885      ISBN 0834801132

**Hillier, Jack Ronald.** 1.5079
Hokusai: paintings, drawings, and woodcuts / J. Hillier. — 3d ed. — Oxford: Phaidon; New York: Dutton, 1978. 136 p.: ill. (some col.); 29 cm. 1. Katsushika, Hokusai, 1700-1849.
N7359.K37 H54 1978      760/.092/4      LC 78-50628      ISBN 071481833X

**Kim, Chewŏn, 1909-.** 1.5080
Arts of Korea / Chewŏn Kim, Lena Kim Lee; photos. by Masakatsu Yamamoto. — 1st ed. — Tokyo; New York: Kodansha International; New York: distributed by Harper & Row, 1974. 365 p.: chiefly ill. (some col.); 35 cm. Includes index. 1. Art, Korean — To 1900 I. Lee, Lena Kim, joint author. II. T.
N7360.K44      709/.519      LC 73-79768      ISBN 0870112066

**The Arts of Korea.** 1.5081
Seoul: Dong Hwa Pub. Co., c1979. 6 v.: ill. (some col.); 31 cm. Based on the series Han'guk misul. 1. Art, Korean 2. Art objects, Korean I. Tonghwa Ch'ulp'ansa. II. Han'guk misul chŏnjip.
N7363.A79      709/.519      LC 79-124447

## N7380–7399 Africa

**Leuzinger, Elsy.** • 1.5082
[Afrika. English] Africa; the art of the Negro peoples. [Translated by Ann E. Keep] New York, McGraw-Hill [1960] 247 p. illus. (part mounted col.) 4 col. maps (3 on fold. 1) 24 cm. (Art of the world) 1. Art, Black — Africa — History. I. T. I. Series.
N7380.L363      709.67      LC 60-13819

**Willett, Frank.** • 1.5083
African art, an introduction. — [New York]: Praeger, [1971] 288 p.: illus. (part col.), maps, plan.; 22 cm. — ([Praeger world of art series]) 1. Art, African I. T.
N7380.W5 1971b      709/.01/1096 19      LC 76-117394

**Badawy, Alexander.** 1.5084
Coptic art and archaeology: the art of the Christian Egyptians from the late antique to the Middle Ages / Alexander Badawy. — Cambridge, Mass.: MIT Press, c1978. xii, 387 p.: ill.; 29 cm. Includes index. 1. Art, Coptic 2. Christian antiquities — Egypt. I. T.
N7382.B3      704.948/2/0962      LC 77-25101      ISBN 0262020254

**African art & leadership. Edited by Douglas Fraser and Herbert M. Cole.** 1.5085
Madison, University of Wisconsin Press [1972] xvii, 332 p. illus. 24 cm. Fourteen papers, 6 of which were presented at a symposium entitled The aristocratic traditions in African art, held at Columbia University, May 1965. 1. Art — Africa, West — Addresses, essays, lectures. 2. Art, Primitive — Africa, West — Addresses, essays, lectures. 3. Africa — Kings and rulers — Religious aspects — Addresses, essays, lectures. I. Fraser, Douglas. ed. II. Cole, Herbert M. ed.
N7398.A35      709/.66      LC 72-157391      ISBN 0299058204

**Bravmann, René A.** 1.5086
Islam and tribal art in West Africa [by] René A. Bravmann. — [London; New York]: Cambridge University Press, [1974] xii, 189 p.: illus.; 23 cm. — (African studies series. no. 11) 1. Art — Africa, West. 2. Art, Primitive — Africa, West. 3. Islam and art I. T. II. Series.
N7398.B72      732/.2/0967      LC 73-77262      ISBN 0521201926

**Cornet, Joseph.** • 1.5087
[Art de l'Afrique noire au pays du fleuve Zaire. English] Art of Africa; treasures from the Congo. [Translated by Barbara Thompson] [London] Phaidon [distributed by Praeger Publishers, New York 1971] 365 p. illus. (part col.) 30 cm. Translation of Art de l'Afrique noire au pays du fleuve Zaire. 1. Art, Black — Zaire. 2. Art, Zairian I. T.
N7399.C6 C613      732.2      LC 77-158096      ISBN 0714814962

**Eyo, Ekpo.** 1.5088
Treasures of ancient Nigeria / text by Ekpo Eyo and Frank Willett [editor, Rollyn O. Krichbaum; photographer, Dirk Bakker; designer, Betty Binns]. — 1st ed. — New York: Knopf: distributed by Random House, 1980. xiii, 161, [1] p.: ill. (some col.); 28 cm. The exhibition held at the Detroit Institute of Arts, Jan. 17-Mar. 16, 1980, the California Palace of the Legion of Honor, San Francisco, Apr. 28-June 29, 1980, the Metropolitan Museum of Art, New York, Aug. 11-Oct. 12, 1980. 1. Art, Nigerian — Exhibitions. 2. Art, Primitive — Nigeria — Exhibitions. I. Willett, Frank. joint author. II. Krichbaum, Rollyn O. III. California Palace of the Legion of Honor. IV. Metropolitan Museum of Art (New York, N.Y.) V. T.
N7399.N5 E94 1980      730/.09669      LC 79-3497      ISBN 0394509757

**Ben-Amos, Paula.** 1.5089
The art of Benin / Paula Ben-Amos. — New York, N.Y.: Thames and Hudson, c1980. 93, [1]: ill. (some col.); 25 cm. — (Tribal art.) Includes index. 1. Art, Primitive — Nigeria — Benin. 2. Art, Bini (African people) 3. Rites and rituals — Nigeria — Benin. I. T. II. Series.
N7399.N52 B453 1980      709/.01/1096693 19      LC 80-50794      ISBN 0500060096

**Thompson, Robert Farris.** 1.5090
Black gods and kings: Yoruba art at UCLA / by Robert Farris Thompson. Bloomington: Indiana University Press, 1976. 94 p. in various pagings: ill. (some col.); 29 cm. 1. Art, Yoruba I. T.
N7399.N52 Y66 1976      732/.2      LC 75-10719      ISBN 0253312043

## N7400–7411 Oceania

**Te Maori: Maori art from New Zealand collections / edited by Sidney Moko Mead; text by Sidney Moko Mead ... [et al.]; photographs by Athol McCredie.** 1.5091
New York: Abrams in association with the American Federation of Arts, c1984. 244 p.: ill. (some col.); 29 cm. 1. Art, Maori — Exhibitions. 2. Art, Primitive — New Zealand — Exhibitions. 3. Art — Collectors and collecting — New Zealand — Exhibitions. I. Mead, Sidney M. II. American Federation of Arts.
N7407.M36 T4 1984      709/.01/109931074013 19      LC 83-25725      ISBN 0810913445

**The Art of the Pacific Islands / Peter Gathercole, Adrienne L. Kaeppler, Douglas Newton.** 1.5092
Washington: National Gallery of Art, 1979. 365 p.: ill. (some col.) 28 cm. Catalogue of an exhibition held at the National Gallery of Art, July 1-October 14, 1979. 1. Art, Primitive — Islands of the Pacific — Exhibitions. 2. Art — Islands of the Pacific — Exhibitions. I. Gathercole, P. W. II. Kaeppler,

Adrienne Lois. III. Newton, Douglas, 1920- IV. National Gallery of Art (U.S.)
N7410.A74     730/.099/0740153     *LC* 79-16114

**Exploring the visual art of Oceania: Australia, Melanesia,**     **1.5093**
**Micronesia, and Polynesia / edited by Sidney M. Mead;**
**assisted by Isabelle Brymer and Susan Martich.**
Honolulu: University Press of Hawaii, c1979. xviii, 455 p.: ill.; 25 cm. Includes index. 1. Art — Oceanica. 2. Art, Primitive — Oceanica. I. Mead, Sidney M.
N7410.E95     709/.01/1099     *LC* 79-12707     *ISBN* 0824805984

**Smith, Bernard William.**     • **1.5094**
European vision and the South Pacific, 1768–1850; a study in history of art and ideas. Oxford, Clarendon Press, 1960. xviii, 287 p. plates. 1. Art — Oceanica 2. Art — Australia 3. Art, European 4. Art and science 5. Oceania — Description and travel — Views I. T.
N7410 S6     *LC* 60-2082

**Newton, Douglas.**     • **1.5095**
Art styles of the Papuan Gulf. — New York, Museum of Primitive Art; distributed by University Publishers, 1961. 100 p. illus., maps (1 fold.) 29 cm. 'Prepared in conjunction with an exhibition at the Museum of Primitive Art.' 1. Art — Papua. 2. Art, Primitive I. T.
N7411.N4 N43     709.95     *LC* 61-16108

**Barrow, Terence, 1923-.**     **1.5096**
The art of Tahiti and the neighbouring Society, Austral and Cook Islands / Terence Barrow. — London: Thames and Hudson, 1979. 96 p.: ill.; 25 cm. Includes index. 1. Art — Polynesia. 2. Art, Primitive — Polynesia. 3. Polynesia — Social life and customs. I. T.
N7411.T3 B37     *LC* 79-63810

## N7415–7418 Jewish Art

**Blatter, Janet.**     **1.5097**
Art of the Holocaust / by Janet Blatter and Sybil Milton; historical introduction by Henry Friedlander; preface by Irving Howe. — New York: Rutledge Press, c1981. 272 p.: ill. (some col.); 31 cm. 'A Layla Productions book.' 1. Holocaust, Jewish (1939-1945), in art 2. Art, Jewish I. Milton, Sybil. II. T.
N7417.6.B59 1981     741.94 19     *LC* 81-5895     *ISBN* 0831704187

## N7420–7438 Art: General Works. Technique. Criticism

**Alberti, Leon Battista, 1404-1472.**     **1.5098**
[De pictura. English] On painting and On sculpture. The Latin texts of De pictura and De statua [by] Leon Battista Alberti. Edited with translations, introduction and notes by Cecil Grayson. [London] Phaidon [1972] viii, 159 p. illus. 26 cm. 1. Painting — Early works to 1800. 2. Sculpture — Early works to 1800. I. Grayson, Cecil, ed. II. Alberti, Leon Battista, 1404-1472. De statua. English. 1972. III. T. IV. Title: On sculpture.
N7420.A413 1972     750/.1     *LC* 75-190598     *ISBN* 0714815527

**Theophilus, Presbyter.**     • **1.5099**
The various arts. Translated from the Latin with introd. and notes by C.R. Dodwell. London, T. Nelson [1961] lxxvii, 171, 171, 175-178 p. (Medieval texts) Oppostie pages numbered in duplicate. English and Latin; added t.p.: De diuersis artibus. The title 'normally used in past publications has been the Diuersarum artium schedula.' 1. Art — Early works to 1800. 2. Christian art and symbolism 3. Technology — Early works to 1800 I. Dodwell, Charles Reginald. II. T. III. Title: De diuersis artibus
N7420 T413 1961     *LC* 61-66685

**Vasari, Giorgio.**     • **1.5100**
Vasari on technique: being an introduction to the three arts of design, architecture, sculpture and painting, prefixed to the lives of the most excellent painters, scuptors and architects / by Giorgio Vasari; translated into English by Louisa S. Maclehose; edited with introduction and notes by G. Baldwin Brown. — New York: Dover Publications, 1960. xxiv, 328 p.,[15] leaves of plates: ill., maps. 1. Architecture — Early works to 1800. 2. Sculpture — Early works to 1800. 3. Painting — Early works to 1800. 4. Art — Technique I. Maclehose, Louisa S. II. Brown, Gerard Baldwin, 1849-1932. III. Vasari, Giorgio, 1511-1574. Le vite de' piu eccellenti pittori, scultorie architetti. IV. Brown, G. Baldwin. V. Vasari, Giorgio. Le vite de piu eccellenti pittori, scultorie architetti. VI. T.
N7420.V3     702.8     *ISBN* 048620717X

**Art and education / by John Dewey, Albert C. Barnes,**     • **1.5101**
**Laurence Buermeyer [and others].**
[Merion, Pa.]: The Barnes Foundation Press, [c1929]. x, 349 p.; 21 cm. 'A conspectus of the work done [by the Barnes foundation]'. I. Dewey, John, 1859-1952. II. Barnes, Albert C. (Albert Coombs), 1872-1951.
N742.A7     *LC* 29-12687

**Friedländer, Max J., 1867-1958.**     • **1.5102**
On art and connoisseurship / by Max J. Friedländer; [translated from the author's manuscript by Tancred Borenius]. — Boston: Beacon Press, 1960. 284 p., [20] leaves of plates: ill., ports.; 20 cm. 1. Art 2. Art — Philosophy 3. Art — Expertising I. T.
N7425.F72 1960     *LC* 60-2000

**Muehsam, Gerd, 1913-.**     **1.5103**
Guide to basic information sources in the visual arts / by Gerd Muehsam. — Santa Barbara, Calif.: J. Norton Publishers/ABC-Clio, c1978. x, 266 p.; 22 cm. — (Information resources series) Includes index. 1. Art — Sources. I. T.
N7425.M88     707     *LC* 77-17430     *ISBN* 0874362784

**Munro, Thomas, 1897-.**     • **1.5104**
The arts and their interrelations. — [Rev. and enl. ed.]. — Cleveland: Press of Western Reserve University, [1967] xvi, 587 p.: illus.; 24 cm. 1. Art 2. Aesthetics I. T.
N7425.M9 1967     700     *LC* 67-11482

**Read, Herbert Edward, Sir, 1893-1968.**     • **1.5105**
The meaning of art. New York, Pitman Pub. Corp. [1951] 262 p. illus. 20 cm. Published in 1932 under title: The anatomy of art. 1. Art 2. Art — History 3. Aesthetics I. T.
N7425.R4 1951     704     *LC* 51-12743

**Kepes, Gyorgy, 1906- ed.**     • **1.5106**
The man–made object. — New York: G. Braziller, [1966] 230 p.: illus.; 29 cm. — (Vision + value series) 1. Creation (Literary, artistic, etc.) 2. Art — Philosophy 3. Art — Technique I. T.
N7428.K4     701     *LC* 66-13046

**Rowland, Benjamin, 1904-1972.**     • **1.5107**
Art in East and West: an introduction through comparisons / Benjamin Rowland, Jr. — Boston: Beacon, 1954. xiii, 144 p.: ill. 1. Art I. T.
N7428.R65 1954     *ISBN* 0807066850

**Ettinghausen, Richard.**     **1.5108**
From Byzantium to Sasanian Iran and the Islamic world; three modes of artistic influence. — Leiden: Brill, 1972. viii, 69 p.: illus.; 28 cm. — (The L. A. Mayor memorial studies in Islamic art and archaeology, v. 3) 1. Art, Sassanid — Byzantine influences 2. Art, Islamic — Byzantine influences 3. Art, Islamic — Sassanid influences. I. T. II. Series.
N7429.E88     709/.02     *LC* 74-174223     *ISBN* 9004035095

**Impey, O. R. (Oliver R.)**     **1.5109**
Chinoiserie: the impact of oriental styles on Western art and decoration / Oliver Impey. New York: Scribner; 1977. 208 p., [8] leaves of plates: ill (some col.); 25 cm. Includes index. 1. Art — Chinese influences. I. T.
N7429.I4 1977     709     *LC* 75-46100     *ISBN* 0684146797

**Sullivan, Michael, 1916-.**     **1.5110**
The meeting of Eastern and Western art from the sixteenth century to the present day. — [Greenwich, Conn.]: New York Graphic Society, [1973] 296 p.: illus. (part col.); 26 cm. 1. Art — Chinese influences. 2. Art — Japanese influences. 3. Art, Chinese — Occidental influences. 4. Art, Japanese — Occidental influences. I. T.
N7429.S93 1973b     709     *LC* 73-77665     *ISBN* 0821205439

**Arnheim, Rudolf.**     **1.5111**
The power of the center: a study of composition in the visual arts / Rudolf Arnheim. — Berkeley: University of California Press, c1982. xii, 227 p.: ill.; 24 cm. Includes index. 1. Composition (Art) I. T.
N7430.A69 1982     701/.8 19     *LC* 81-10332     *ISBN* 0520044266

**Gilson, Etienne, 1884-1978.**     • **1.5112**
[Matieres et formes. English] Forms and substances in the arts [by] Étienne Gilson. Translated from the French by Salvator Attanasio. New York, Scribner [1966] 282 p. 22 cm. Translation of Matières et formes. 1. Art — Technique 2. Composition (Art) 3. Form (Aesthetics) I. T.
N7430.G513     701.8     *LC* 66-24495

**Kepes, Gyorgy, 1906- ed.**     • **1.5113**
Sign, image, symbol. — New York: G. Braziller, [1966] 281 p.: illus.; 29 cm. — (Vision [plus sign] value series) 1. Art — Technique 2. Composition (Art) 3. Symbolism in art I. T.
N7430.K47     701.8     *LC* 66-13045

**Moholy-Nagy, László, 1895-1946.**      • **1.5114**
The New vision, 1928: and, Abstract of an artist. — 4th rev. ed. 1947. — New York: Wittenborn, reprinted 1967. 92 p.: ill. — (The Documents of modern art: director, Robert Motherwell) 1. Art — Technique 2. Architecture 3. Sculpture I. T. II. Title: Abstract of an artist.
N7430.M6 1967      *LC* 48-6384

**Moholy-Nagy, László, 1895-1946.**      • **1.5115**
Vision in motion. — Chicago: P. Theobald, [1947] 371 p.: illus. (part col.: incl. plans, facsims.) diagrs.; 29 cm. — (ID book, Institute of design [Chicago]) At head of title: L. Moholy-Nagy. 'An extension of my previous book, 'The new vision' ... [It] concentrates on the work of the Institute of design, Chicago,'— Foreword. 1. Art — Technique 2. Art and society I. T.
N7430.M62     701     *LC* 47-4349

**Ways of seeing; a book made by John Berger [and others].**    **1.5116**
New York: Viking Press, [1973, c1972] 160 p.: illus.; 21 cm. 'A Richard Seaver Book.' 'Based on the television series with John Berger.' 1. Visual perception 2. Art — Technique I. Berger, John.
N7430.5.W39 1973    759.94    *LC* 73-3502    *ISBN* 0670752738

**Wright, Lawrence, 1906-.**      **1.5117**
Perspective in perspective / Lawrence Wright. — London; Boston: Routledge & K. Paul, 1983. xiii, 386 p.: ill.; 25 cm. Includes index. 1. Visual perception 2. Perspective I. T.
N7430.5.W7 1983    701/.8 19    *LC* 82-21450    *ISBN* 0710007914

**Artist and computer / edited by Ruth Leavitt.**      **1.5118**
New York: Harmony Books, c1976. ix, 121 p.: ill. (some col.); 28 cm. 1. Computer art 2. Art, Modern — 20th century I. Leavitt, Ruth.
N7433.8.A77 1976    702/.8/54    *LC* 76-440    *ISBN* 0517527359

**Prueitt, Melvin L.**      **1.5119**
Art and the computer / Melvin L. Prueitt. — New York: McGraw-Hill, c1984. ix, 246 p.: chiefly ill. (some col.); 21 x 26 cm. Includes index. 1. Computer art I. T.
N7433.8.P7 1984    760 19    *LC* 83-24818    *ISBN* 0070508941

**Venturi, Lionello, 1885-1961.**      • **1.5120**
History of art criticism / Lionello Venturi; translated from the Italian by Charles Marriott. — New York: E. P. Dutton, c1936. xv, 345 p. 1. Art criticism — History I. T.
N7435.V42    701.18    *LC* 36-30920

**Ozenfant, Amédée, 1886-1966.**      • **1.5121**
Foundations of modern art. Translation by John Rodker. — [New American ed., augm.]. — New York: Dover Publications, [1952] xviii, 348 p.: illus.; 25 cm. Translation of Art. 1. Art 2. Art, Modern — 20th century — History I. T.
N7438.O82 1952    701.17    *LC* 52-14596

# N7442–7470 Collected Writings

**Kleinbauer, W. Eugene, 1937- comp.**      • **1.5122**
Modern perspectives in Western art history; an anthology of 20th-century writings on the visual arts [by] W. Eugene Kleinbauer. — New York: Holt, Rinehart and Winston, [1971] xiii, 528 p.: illus., plans, ports.; 24 cm. 1. Art — Addresses, essays, lectures. I. T.
N7443.2.K57    704.92    *LC* 73-153955    *ISBN* 0030782201

**Ackerman, James S.**      • **1.5123**
Art and archaeology [by] James S. Ackerman [and] Rhys Carpenter. — Englewood Cliffs, N.J.: Prentice-Hall, [1963] xi, 241 p.; 22 cm. — (The Princeton studies; humanistic scholarship in America) 1. Art — Addresses, essays, lectures. 2. Archaeology — Addresses, essays, lectures. I. Carpenter, Rhys, 1889- II. T. III. Series.
N7445.A26 1963    701    *LC* 63-12267

**Bell, Clive, 1881-1964.**      • **1.5124**
Art. — New York: Capricorn Books, [1958] 190 p.; 19 cm. — (A Putnam Capricorn book; CAP4) 1. Art — Addresses, essays, lectures. 2. Art — History 3. Aesthetics I. T.
N7445.B53 1958    704    *LC* 58-59755

**Bell, Clive, 1881-1964.**      • **1.5125**
Since Cézanne. — Freeport, N.Y.: Books for Libraries Press, [1969] 229 p.: illus.; 22 cm. — (Essay index reprint series) Reprint of the 1922 ed. 1. Art — Addresses, essays, lectures. 2. Post-impressionism (Art) I. T.
N7445.B54 1969    709.04    *LC* 68-22902

**Berenson, Bernard, 1865-1959.**      • **1.5126**
Seeing and knowing. New York, Macmillan, 1953. 48 p. 88 plates. 22 cm. 1. Art — Addresses, essays, lectures. I. T.
N7445.B546 1953a    701.1    *LC* 54-2143

**Coomaraswamy, Ananda Kentish, 1877-1947.**      • **1.5127**
[Why exhibit works of art?] Christian and Oriental philosophy of art. New York, Dover Publications [1956] 146 p. illus. 21 cm. First published in 1943 under title: Why exhibit works of art? 1. Art — Addresses, essays, lectures. I. T.
N7445.C78x    704.91    *LC* 57-3496

**Fry, Roger Eliot, 1866-1934.**      • **1.5128**
Last lectures. With an introd. by Kenneth Clark. Boston, Beacon Press [1962] xxix, 370 p. plates. 21 cm. (Beacon paperback, no. 131) 1. Art — Addresses, essays, lectures. 2. Art criticism I. T.
N7445.F73 1962    701.18    *LC* 63-6053

**Gabo, Naum, 1890-.**      • **1.5129**
Of divers arts. [New York] Pantheon Books [1962] xviii, 205 p. illus. (part col.) 26 cm. (Bollingen series, 35. The A.W. Mellon lectures in the fine arts, 8) 1. Art — Addresses, essays, lectures. I. T.
N7445.G19    704.9/2    *LC* 62-9369

**Giedion, S. (Sigfried), 1888-1968.**      • **1.5130**
Architecture, you and me; the diary of a development. Cambridge, Harvard University Press, 1958. 221 p. ill. 1. Architecture — Addresses, essays, lectures 2. Art — Addresses, essays, lectures 3. Art and society I. T.
N7445 G433    *LC* 58-6578

**Gombrich, Ernst Hans Josef, 1909-.**      • **1.5131**
Meditations on a hobby horse, and other essays on the theory of art. With 140 illus. London, Phaidon Press [1963] xii, 184 p. ill., ports., diagrs. 1. Art — Addresses, essays, lectures 2. Art — Philosophy I. T.
N7445 G63    *LC* 64-1059

**Panofsky, Erwin, 1892-1968.**      • **1.5132**
Meaning in the visual arts: papers in and on art history. — [1st ed.]. — Garden City, N.Y.: Doubleday, 1955. xviii, 362 p.: illus.; 18 cm. — (Doubleday anchor books, A59) 1. Art — Addresses, essays, lectures. I. T.
N7445.P22    704.91    *LC* 55-9754

**Reynolds, Joshua, Sir, 1723-1792.**      **1.5133**
Discourses on art. Edited by Robert R. Wark. San Marino, Calif., Huntington Library, 1959. xxxv, 321 p. 24 plates. (Huntington Library publications) 1. Art — Addresses, essays, lectures I. T.
N7445 R3 1959    *LC* 59-10148

**Rodin, Auguste, 1840-1917.**      • **1.5134**
On art and artists / translated by Mrs. Romilly Fedden; with an introduction by Alfred Werner. — New York: Philosophical Library, 1957. — 252 p.: ill., ports. 1. Art 2. Sculpture I. T.
N7445.R566    701    *LC* 57-59574

**Ruskin, John, 1819-1900.**      **1.5135**
The art criticism of John Ruskin. Selected, edited, and with an introd. by Robert L. Herbert. Garden City, N.Y., Anchor Books, 1964. xliii, 430 p. 1. Art 2. Aesthetics I. Herbert, Robert L., 1929- II. T.
N7445 R73    *LC* 64-16241

**Ruskin, John, 1819-1900.**      • **1.5136**
The lamp of beauty: writings on art / selected and edited by Joan Evans. — London: Phaidon: distributed by Doubleday, Garden City, N.Y., [1959]. 344 p.; ill. (incl. port., part col.); 26 cm. — (Ruskin's writings on art) 1. Art I. Evans, Joan, 1893- ed. II. T.
N7445.R835    700    *LC* 60-382

**Shahn, Ben, 1898-1969.**      • **1.5137**
The shape of content. — Cambridge: Harvard University Press, 1957. 131 p.: illus.; 24 cm. — (The Charles Eliot Norton lectures, 1956-1957) 1. Art — Addresses, essays, lectures. I. T.
N7445.S516    704.91    *LC* 57-12968

**Soby, James Thrall, 1906-.**      • **1.5138**
Modern art and the new past / James Thrall Soby; with an introd. by Paul J. Sachs. — 1st ed. — Norman: University of Oklahoma Press, 1957. vii, 217 p. 1. Art — Addresses, essays, lectures. 2. Art, Modern — 20th century — Addresses, essays, lectures. I. T.
N7445.S562    704.91    *LC* 57-5959

**Gombrich, Ernst Hans Josef, 1909-.**      **1.5139**
The image and the eye: further studies in the psychology of pictorial representation / E.H. Gombrich. — Ithaca, N.Y.: Cornell University Press, c1982. 320 p.: ill. 'Cornell/Phaidon books.' 1. Art — Philosophy I. T.
N7445.2.G62    *LC* 81-68788    *ISBN* 0801414849

**Janson, H. W. (Horst Woldemar), 1913-.**    **1.5140**
16 studies, by H. W. Janson. New York, H. N. Abrams [1974?] xi, 338 p. illus. 27 cm. 'A collection of essays published in periodicals between 1937 and 1970.' 1. Art — Addresses, essays, lectures. I. T.
N7445.2.J36     704.9/2     LC 73-4757     ISBN 0810901307

**Rosenberg, Harold.**    **1.5141**
Art & other serious matters / Harold Rosenberg. — Chicago: University of Chicago Press, 1985. vi, 332 p.; 22 cm. Includes index. 1. Art — Addresses, essays, lectures. 2. Art, Modern — 20th century — Addresses, essays, lectures. 3. Artists — United States — Addresses, essays, lectures. 4. Art and society — Addresses, essays, lectures. I. T. II. Title: Art and other serious matters.
N7445.2.R66 1985     709/.04 19     LC 84-8781     ISBN 0226726940

**Smithson, Robert.**    **1.5142**
The writings of Robert Smithson: essays with illustrations / edited by Nancy Holt; introd. by Philip Leider; designed by Sol LeWitt. — New York: New York University Press, 1979. vii, 221 p.: ill.; 29 cm. 1. Art — Addresses, essays, lectures. I. Holt, Nancy, 1938- II. T.
N7445.2.S62     700     LC 78-15693     ISBN 0814733948

**Winckelmann, Johann Joachim, 1717-1768.**    **1.5143**
[Selections. English. 1972] Writings on art. Selected and edited by David Irwin. [London] Phaidon [1972] x, 166 p. illus. 26 cm. Distributed in the United States of America by Praeger Publishers, New York. 1. Art — Addresses, essays, lectures. I. Irwin, David G. ed. II. T.
N7445.4.W56     709     LC 78-172993     ISBN 071481508X

**Kandinsky, Wassily, 1866-1944.**    **1.5144**
Kandinsky, complete writings on art / edited by Kenneth C. Lindsay and Peter Vergo. — Boston, Mass.: G.K. Hall, c1982. 2 v. (xi, 924 p.): ill.; 24 cm. — (The Documents of twentieth century art) Includes index. 1. Art — Addresses, essays, lectures. I. Lindsay, Kenneth Clement, 1919- II. Vergo, Peter. III. T.
N7454.K3 1982     700 19     LC 81-12798     ISBN 0805799508

**Picasso, Pablo, 1881-1973.**    **1.5145**
Picasso on art: a selection of views. [Compiled by] Dore Ashton. New York, Viking Press [1972] xxvii, 187 p. illus. 22 cm. (The Documents of 20th-century art) 1. Art — Addresses, essays, lectures. I. T. II. Series.
N7454.P52 1972     701     LC 73-184538     ISBN 0670553271 ISBN 0670019437

**Lippard, Lucy R.**    **1.5146**
Changing: essays in art criticism [by] Lucy R. Lippard. — [1st ed.]. — New York: Dutton, 1971. 320 p.: illus.; 22 cm. — (Documents in modern art criticism, 2) 1. Art criticism — History — 20th century — Addresses, essays, lectures. 2. Art, Modern — 20th century — Addresses, essays, lectures. I. T.
N7476.L56 1971     709.04/6     LC 71-87187     ISBN 0525079424

**Pepper, Stephen Coburn, 1891-.**    • **1.5147**
Principles of art appreciation [by] Stephen C. Pepper. — Westport, Conn.: Greenwood Press, [1970, c1949] vii, 326 p.: illus., 20 plates.; 23 cm. 1. Art appreciation. I. T.
N7477.P44 1970     701.18     LC 70-98238     ISBN 0837136903

# N7480 Historiography. Criticism

**Hauser, Arnold, 1892-1978.**    • **1.5148**
The philosophy of art history / Arnold Hauser. — 1st American ed. — New York: Knopf, 1959, c1958. 4, 410, xvi p.; 22 cm. 1. Art — Historiography 2. Art — Philosophy 3. Art — Psychology 4. Art and society I. T.
N7480.H3413 1959     LC 58-10966

**Brookner, Anita.**    **1.5149**
The genius of the future; studies in French art criticism: Diderot, Stendhal, Baudelaire, Zola, the brothers Goncourt, Huysmans. — London, New York, Phaidon, 1971. viii, 172 p., 16 plates. illus., ports. 26 cm. index. Distributed in the U.S.A. by Praeger, New York. 1. Art criticism — France. I. T.
N7482.B76 1971     701.18/0944     LC 75-156471     ISBN 0714814970

**Samuels, Ernest, 1903-.**    **1.5150**
Bernard Berenson: the making of a connoisseur / Ernest Samuels. — Cambridge, Mass.: Belknap Press of Harvard University Press, 1979. xvi, 477 p., [10] leaves of plates: ill.; 24 cm. Includes index. 1. Berenson, Bernard, 1865-1959. 2. Art critics — United States — Biography. I. T.
N7483.B4 S25     709/.2/4 B     LC 78-26748     ISBN 0674067754

**Woolf, Virginia, 1882-1941.**    **1.5151**
Roger Fry: a biography / Virginia Woolf. — New York: Harcourt Brace Jovanovich, 1976, c1940. 303 p., [8] leaves of plates: ill.; 21 cm. (A Harvest book; HB338) Includes index. 1. Fry, Roger Eliot, 1866-1934. I. T.
N7483.F79 W66 1976     709/.2/4 B     LC 75-34023     ISBN 015678520X

**Holly, Michael Ann.**    **1.5152**
Panofsky and the foundations of art history / Michael Ann Holly. — Ithaca, N.Y.: Cornell University Press, 1984. 267 p.; 23 cm. Includes index. 1. Panofsky, Erwin, 1892-1968. 2. Art — Historiography I. T.
N7483.P3 H64 1984     709/.2/4 19     LC 84-45143     ISBN 0801416140

**Ruskin, the critical heritage / edited by J.L. Bradley.**    **1.5153**
London; Boston: Routledge & K. Paul, 1984. xiii, 436 p.; 23 cm. — (Critical heritage series.) 1. Ruskin, John, 1819-1900. 2. Art criticism — Great Britain — History — 19th century. I. Bradley, J. L. II. Series.
N7483.R8 R87 1984     709 19     LC 83-11102     ISBN 0710092865

# N7525 Indexes to Illustrations

**Korwin, Yala H., 1923-.**    **1.5154**
Index to two–dimensional art works / by Yala H. Korwin. — Metuchen, N.J.: Scarecrow Press, 1981. 2 v.; 22 cm. 1. Art — Indexes. I. T.
N7525.K67     701/.6 19     LC 80-25002     ISBN 0810813815

**Vance, Lucile E.**    • **1.5155**
Illustration index, by Lucile E. Vance and Esther M. Tracey. — 2d ed. — New York: Scarecrow Press, 1966. 527 p.; 22 cm. 'Books and periodicals indexed': p. vii. 1. Pictures — Indexes. I. Tracey, Esther M., joint author. II. T.
N7525.V3 1966     011     LC 65-13558

# N7560–8266 Special Subjects of Art

**Hall, James, 1917-.**    **1.5156**
Dictionary of subjects and symbols in art / James Hall; introd. by Kenneth Clark. — 1st U.S. ed. — New York: Harper & Row, c1974. xxix, 345 p.: ill.; 23 cm. (Icon editions) 1. Art — Themes, motives — Dictionaries. 2. Symbolism in art — Dictionaries. I. T.
N7560.H34 1974b     704.94/094     LC 74-6578     ISBN 0064333159

## N7570–7649 HUMAN FIGURES. PORTRAITS

**Selz, Peter Howard, 1919-.**    • **1.5157**
New images of man. With statements by the artists. [New York, Published for the Museum of Modern Art by Arno Press, 1969] 159 p. illus. 25 cm. Reprint of the 1959 ed. 'Errata': p. [2] 1. Men in art 2. Art, Modern — 20th century I. Museum of Modern Art (New York, N.Y.) II. T.
N7570.S38 1969     704.94/2     LC 76-86447

**Clark, Kenneth, 1903-.**    • **1.5158**
Nude: a study in ideal form. Garden City, N.Y.: Doubleday, [1956] 575p.: ill. (Bollingen series. 35.) (A.W. Mellon lectures in the fine arts. 2.) 1. Nude in art I. T. II. Series. III. Series: A.W. Mellon lectures in the fine arts. 2.
N7572.C55     704.942     LC 56-10423

**Gerdts, William H.**    **1.5159**
The great American nude; a history in art [by] William H. Gerdts. — New York: Praeger, [1974] 224 p.: illus. (part col.); 29 cm. — (American art & artists) 1. Nude in art 2. Art, American — History. I. T. II. Series.
N7574.4.G47     704.94/21/0973     LC 72-88496     ISBN 0275435105

**L'Orange, Hans Peter, 1903-.**    **1.5160**
Apotheosis in ancient portraiture. Oslo: H. Aschehoug, 1947. 156 p.: ill., ports.; 30 cm. (Instituttet for sammenlignende kulturforskning. Serie B: Skrifter, 44) 1. Portraits 2. Art, Ancient 3. History, Ancient — Portraits. 4. Apotheosis I. T.
N 7580 L86 E5 1947     LC 49-2322

**Richter, Gisela Marie Augusta, 1882-1972.**                    **1.5161**
The portraits of the Greeks / by Gisela M.A. Richter. — London: Phaidon Press, 1965. 3 v. (xiii, 337 p.): ill. 1. Portraits, Greek. 2. History, Ancient — Portraits. 3. Greece — History — Portraits. I. T.
N7586.R5        LC 66-4110

**A.L.A. portrait index; index to portraits contained in printed**          **• 1.5162**
**books and periodicals. Edited by William Coolidge Lane and Nina E. Browne.**
New York: B. Franklin, [196-?] 3 v. (1601 p.); 27 cm. — (Burt Franklin bibliography and reference series, #68) Reprint of the 1906 ed. 1. Portraits — Catalogs. I. Lane, William Coolidge, 1859-1931, ed. II. Browne, Nina Eliza, ed. III. American Library Association.
N7620.A2 1960z        016.757        LC 77-6494

**Wenig, Steffen.**                              **• 1.5163**
[Frau im alten Ägypten. English] The woman in Egyptian art. [Translated from the German by B. Fischer] New York, McGraw-Hill [c1969] 59 p., 112 p. of illus. (part col.), map. 28 cm. (The Image of woman) Translation of Die Frau im alten Ägypten. 1. Art, Egyptian 2. Women — Portraits 3. Women in art I. T.
N7638.E35 W43 1969b        709/.32        LC 70-87839

# N7660–7668 ANIMALS

**Klingender, Francis Donald.**                        **1.5164**
Animals in art and thought to the end of the Middle Ages. Edited by Evelyn Antal and John Harthan. — Cambridge, Mass.: M.I.T. Press, [1971] xxviii, 580 p.: illus.; 29 cm. 1. Animals in art 2. Animals in literature I. T.
N7660.K55 1971        704.94/32        LC 77-123254        ISBN 0262110407

# N7690–7760 DEVICES. SYMBOLISM. MYTHOLOGY

**Ripa, Cesare, fl. 1600.**                          **1.5165**
[Iconologia. English, German & Latin] Baroque and Rococo pictorial imagery. The 1758–60 Hertel edition of Ripa's 'Iconologia.' Introd., translations, and 200 commentaries by Edward A. Maser. New York, Dover Publications [1971] xxi, 200 (i.e. 400) p. 200 illus. 24 cm. (The Dover pictorial archives series) 1. Emblems 2. Allegories I. Maser, Edward Andrew, 1923- II. T.
N7740.R515 1971        704.94/6        LC 78-100544        ISBN 0486227480

**Trendall, A. D. (Arthur Dale), 1909-.**                    **1.5166**
Illustrations of Greek drama, by A. D. Trendall and T. B. L. Webster. [London] Phaidon; [New York, Distributed by Praeger Publishers, 1971] x, 159 p. illus. (part col.) 31 cm. 1. Greek drama (Satyr play) — Illustrations. 2. Greek drama (Tragedy) — Illustrations. 3. Greek drama (Comedy) — Illustrations. I. Webster, T. B. L. (Thomas Bertram Lonsdale), 1905-1974. joint author. II. T.
N7760.T7        792/.0938        LC 78-158099        ISBN 071481492X

# N7790–8199 RELIGIOUS ART

**Schiller, Gertrud.**                              **1.5167**
Iconography of Christian art / Gertrud Schiller; translated by Janel Seligman. Greenwich, Conn.: New York Graphic Society, 1971-1972. 2 v. . ill., facsims. Includes index in v.2. Translated from the 2nd German ed. of Ikonographie der Christlichen Kunst. Gutersloh, Gutersloher Veragshaus Gerd Mohn, 1969. 1. Jesus Christ — Art I. T.
N7830.S3513        LC 76-132965        ISBN 0821203657 v.1

**Beckwith, John, 1918-.**                            **• 1.5168**
Early Christian and Byzantine art. — Harmondsworth: Penguin, 1970. xxv, 211 p., 193 plates.: illus. (incl. 1 col.), facsims., map.; 27 cm. — (The Pelican history of art) 1. Art, Early Christian 2. Art, Byzantine I. T. II. Series.
N7832.B3        709.02        LC 79-23592        ISBN 0140560335

**Gough, Michael.**                              **1.5169**
The origins of Christian art. — New York: Praeger, [1974, c1973] 216 p.: illus. (part col.); 22 cm. — (Praeger world of art series) 1. Art, Early Christian 2. Art, Byzantine I. T.
N7832.G62 1974        709/.01/5        LC 73-8233

**Hubert, Jean.**                              **• 1.5170**
[Europe des invasions. English] Europe of the invasions [by] J. Hubert, J. Porcher [and] W. F. Volbach. [Translated by Stuart Gilbert and James Emmons] New York, G. Braziller [1969] xv, 387 p. illus. (part fold. col.), facsims. (part col.), col. maps (3 fold.), plans (part col.) 29 cm. (The Arts of

mankind) Translation of L'Europe des invasions. 1. Art, Early Christian 2. Art, Medieval 3. Rome — History — Germanic Invasions, 3d-6th centuries I. Porcher, Jean. II. Volbach, Wolfgang Friedrich, 1892- III. T. IV. Series.
N7832.H813 1969        709.01/5        LC 75-81858

**Schapiro, Meyer, 1904-.**                        **1.5171**
Late antique, early Christian and mediaeval art / Meyer Schapiro. — New York: G. Braziller, 1979. xvi, 414 p.: ill.; 24 cm. — (His Selected papers; v. 3) 1. Art, Early Christian 2. Art, Medieval I. T. II. Series.
N7832.S26        709/.02        LC 79-13333        ISBN 0807609277

**Volbach, Wolfgang Friedrich, 1892-.**                    **• 1.5172**
[Frühchristliche kunst. English] Early Christian art. Photography by Max Hirmer. [Translated by Christopher Ligota] New York, Abrams [1962] 363 p. illus., 258 plates (part col.) plans. 32 cm. 1. Art, Early Christian 2. Church architecture — Europe. I. Hirmer, Max, 1893- II. T.
N7832.V63        709.02        LC 61-8333

**Mâle, Emile, 1862-1954.**                          **1.5173**
[Art religieux de la fin du Moyen Age en France. English] The late Middle Ages: a study of medieval iconography and its sources / Emile Mâle; edited by Harry Bober; translated by Marthiel Mathews. — Princeton, N.J.: Princeton University Press, c1986. p. cm. — (Bollingen series. 90:3) (Studies in religious iconography) Translation of: L'art religieux de la fin du Moyen Age en France. 5th ed. Includes index. 1. Art, French 2. Art, Medieval — France. 3. Christian art and symbolism — Medieval, 500-1500 — France. I. Bober, Harry, 1915- II. T. III. Series.
N7949.A1 M3313 1986        704.9/482/0944 19        LC 84-26359        ISBN 0691099146

**Mâle, Emile, 1862-1954.**                          **1.5174**
[Art religieux du XIIe siècle en France. English] Religious art in France, the twelfth century: a study of the origins of medieval iconography / Émile Mâle. — Princeton, N.J.: Princeton University Press, c1978. xxxi, 575 p.; 28 cm. — (Bollingen series. 90:1) (His Studies in religious iconography) Translation of L'art religieux du XIIe siècle en France. Includes index. 1. Christian art and symbolism 2. Art, Romanesque — France. 3. Art, French I. T. II. Series.
N7949.A1 M3413        709/.44        LC 72-14029        ISBN 069109912X

**Mâle, Emile, 1862-1954.**                          **1.5175**
[Art religieux du XIIIe siècle en France. English] Religious art in France, the thirteenth century: a study of medieval iconography and its sources / Emile Male. — Princeton, N.J.: Princeton University Press, c1984. xv, 564 p.: ill.; 28 cm. — (Bollingen series. 90:2) (Studies in religious iconography / by Emile Mâle) Translation of 9th ed.: L'art religieux du XIIIe siècle en France. Includes index. 1. Christian art and symbolism — Medieval, 500-1500 — France. 2. Art, French 3. Art, Gothic — High Gothic — France. I. T. II. Series.
N7949.A1 M3513 1984        704.9/482/0944 19        LC 82-11210        ISBN 0691099138

**Christensen, Carl C., 1935-.**                        **1.5176**
Art and the Reformation in Germany / Carl C. Christensen. — Athens: Ohio University Press, 1979. 269 p.: ill.; 24 cm. (Studies in the Reformation; v. 2) Includes index. 1. Art, German 2. Art, Renaissance — Germany. 3. Reformation and art — Germany. 4. Christian art and symbolism — Modern period, 1500- — Germany. I. T. II. Series.
N7950.A1 C47        704.948/2/0943        LC 79-16006        ISBN 0821403885

**Onasch, Konrad.**                              **1.5177**
Icons / [translated from the German by Marianne von Herzfeld; revised by Talbot Rice]. — London, Faber and Faber [c1963] 423 p. illus., col. plates. 34 cm. 1. Icons, Russian I. T.
N7956.O513 (fol)        LC 67-6469

**Schapiro, Meyer, 1904-.**                          **1.5178**
Words and pictures. On the literal and the symbolic in the illustration of a text. The Hague, Mouton, 1973. 74 p., 34 p. of photos. 23 cm. (Approaches to semiotics. Paperback series, 11) 'The substance of this book was presented at a symposium, 'Language, Symbol, Reality', held at St. Mary's College, Notre Dame, Indiana, on November 7, 1969.' 1. Bible — Illustrations 2. Christian art and symbolism 3. Artists — Psychology I. T. II. Series.
N8020.S32        704.948/4        LC 73-176481

**Steinberg, Leo, 1920-.**                          **1.5179**
The sexuality of Christ in Renaissance art and in modern oblivion / Leo Steinberg. — 1st ed. — New York: Pantheon Books, c1983. 222 p.: 246 ill.; 24 cm. 'Present essay was originally delivered as a Lionel Trilling seminar at Columbia University, New York, on November 19, 1981'–P. [ix] 'The entire work first appeared in the summer 1983 issue of October'—T.p. verso. 'A Pantheon/October book.' Includes index. 1. Jesus Christ — Art 2. Jesus Christ — Humanity 3. Jesus Christ — Physical appearance 4. Art, Renaissance 5. Art, Modern I. T.
N8050.S74 1983        704.9/4853/094 19        LC 83-19520        ISBN 0394722671

**Weitzmann, Kurt, 1904-.** 1.5180
The icon: holy images—sixth to fourteenth century / Kurt Weitzmann. — New York: G. Braziller, 1978. 134 p.: ill. (some col.); 29 cm. 1. Icons 2. Icon painting 3. Votive offerings in art 4. Christian art and symbolism I. T.
N8187.W44 1978     704.948/2     LC 78-6495     ISBN 0807608920

**Rice, David Talbot, 1903-1972.** 1.5181
Icons and their dating: a comprehensive study of their chronology and provenance / [by] David and Tamara Talbot Rice. — London: Thames and Hudson, 1974. 192 p., [8] p. of plates: ill. (some col.); 29 cm. Includes index. 1. Icons — Chronology. 2. Icons — History. I. Rice, Tamara Abelson Talbot. joint author. II. T.
N8187.5.R52     755/.2     LC 74-196199     ISBN 0500231826

**Weitzmann, Kurt, 1904-.** 1.5182
The Monastery of Saint Catherine at Mount Sinai, the icons / with photos. by John Galey. — Princeton, N.J.: Princeton University Press, c1976-. v.     : ill.; 36 cm. Includes index. 1. Saint Catherine (Monastery: Mount Sinai). 2. Icons, Byzantine — Egypt — Sinai — Catalogs. 3. Icons — Sinai — Catalogs. I. Galey, John. II. T.
N8189.E32 S558     755/.2     LC 75-3482     ISBN 0691035431

**Seckel, Dietrich, 1910-.** 1.5183
The art of Buddhism / [Translated by Ann E. Keep] London: Methuen, [1964] (Art of the world, non-European cultures; the historical, sociological and religious backgrounds) 1. Art, Buddhist — History. I. T.
N8190.S413     709.5     LC 64-23800

**Buddhism, art and faith / edited by W. Zwalf.** 1.5184
London: British Museum Publications for the Trustees of the British Museum and the British Library Board, c1985. 300 p.: ill. (some col.), facsims., maps; 28 cm. Includes index. 1. Art, Buddhist — History. 2. Buddhist art and symbolism — History. I. Zwalf, W. II. British Museum. Trustees. III. British Library. Board.
N8193.A5 B83     704.9/48943/09 19     ISBN 0714114324

**Härtel, Herbert.** 1.5185
Along the ancient silk routes: Central Asian art from the West Berlin State Museums: an exhibition lent by the Museum für Indische Kunst, Staatliche Museen Preussischer Kulturbesitz, Berlin, Federal Republic of Germany. — New York: Metropolitan Museum of Art, [1982?] 223 p.: ill. (some col.); 28 cm. Catalog by Herbert Härtel and Marianne Yaldiz, with contributions by Raoul Birnbaum, Martin Lerner and Willibald Veit. Published in conjunction with the exhibition at the Metropolitan Museum of Art, Apr. 3-June 30, 1982. 1. Museum für Indische Kunst (Germany) — Exhibitions. 2. Art, Buddhist — Asia, Central — Exhibitions. 3. Art, Ancient — Asia, Central — Exhibitions. 4. Art — Asia, Central — Exhibitions. I. Yaldiz, Marianne. II. Museum für Indische Kunst (Germany) III. Metropolitan Museum of Art (New York, N.Y.) IV. T.
N8193.A7515 H37 1982     709/.58/07401471 19     LC 82-80801     ISBN 0870993003

**Light of Asia: Buddha Sakyamuni in Asian art / organized by** 1.5186
**Pratapaditya Pal; with essays by Robert L. Brown ... [et al.].**
Los Angeles, Calif.: Los Angeles County Museum of Art, c1984. 331 p.: ill. (some col.); 28 cm. Catalog of an exhibition held at Los Angeles County Museum of Art, Mar. 4-May 20, 1984, the Art Institute of Chicago, June 30-Aug. 26, 1984, and the Brooklyn Museum, Nov. 1, 1984-Feb. 10, 1985. Includes index. 1. Gautama Buddha — Art — Exhibitions. 2. Art, Asian — Exhibitions. I. Pal, Pratapaditya. II. Los Angeles County Museum of Art. III. Art Institute of Chicago. IV. Brooklyn Museum.
N8193.2.A3 C44 1984     704.9/4894363 19     LC 84-788     ISBN 087587116X

**The Image of the Buddha / general editor, David L. Snellgrove;** 1.5187
**[contributors] Jean Boisselier...[et al.].**
1st ed. — Tokyo: Kodansha International/Unesco, 1978. 482 p.: ill., maps. 1. Buddhist art and symbolism — History. 2. Buddhism I. Snelgrove, David L. II. Boisselier, Jean.
N8193.2 A4145 1978     704.94894     LC 77-75964     ISBN 087011302X

**Lauf, Detlef Ingo.** 1.5188
[Erbe Tibets. English] Tibetan sacred art: the heritage of Tantra / by Detlef Ingo Lauf; [translated into English by Ewald Osers]. — Berkeley, Calif.: Shambhala: [New York]: distributed by Random House, 1976. 228 p.: ill. (some col.); 31 cm. Translation of Das Erbe Tibets. Includes index. 1. Art, Tibetan 2. Art, Tantric-Buddhist — Tibet. I. T.
N8193.3.T35 L3813     704.948/9/4392309515     LC 76-14204

**Kramrisch, Stella, 1898-.** 1.5189
Exploring India's sacred art: selected writings of Stella Kramrisch / edited and with a biographical essay by Barbara Stoler Miller. — Philadelphia: University of Pennsylvania Press, 1983. xviii, 356 p.: ill.; 27 cm. 1. Kramrisch, Stella, 1898- — Bibliography. 2. Kramrisch, Stella, 1898- 3. Art, Hindu 4. Buddhist

art and symbolism — India. 5. Art historians — United States — Biography. I. Miller, Barbara Stoler. II. T.
N8195.A5 K7 1983     704.9/4894 19     LC 82-60302     ISBN 0812278569

## N8217–8266 SPECIAL SUBJECTS, A-Z

**Hollander, Anne.** 1.5190
Seeing through clothes / Anne Hollander. — New York: Viking Press, 1978. xvi, 504 p.: ill.; 25 cm. Includes index. 1. Costume in art 2. Human figure in art 3. Art — Psychology I. T.
N8217.C63 H64 1978     704.9/42 19     LC 78-15598     ISBN 0670631744

**L'Orange, Hans Peter, 1903-.** 1.5191
Studies on the iconography of cosmic kingship in the ancient world / by H. P. L'Orange. — New York: Caratzas Brothers, 1982. 205 p.: ill. En-tête du titre: Instituttet for sammenlignende kulturforskning 'This work was published in Oslo, Norway, in 1953 by H. Aschehoug & Co. for the Instituttet for Sammenlignende Kulturforskning, series A; Forelesninger publication number XXIII.' 1. Kings and rulers in art 2. Apotheosis 3. Art, Ancient I. Instituttet for sammenlignende kulturforskning, Oslo. II. T.
N8219.K5 L6 1982     ISBN 0892411503

**The Image of the Black in Western art / foreword by Amadou–** 1.5192
**Mahtar M'Bow.**
[Fribourg]: Office du livre, [1976-<79>. v. <1-2> in <3>: ill. (some col.); 29 cm. 1. Blacks in art — Addresses, essays, lectures. 2. Art — Addresses, essays, lectures. I. Vercoutter, Jean, 1911-
N8232.I46     704.94/9/30145196     LC 76-25772     ISBN 0688030866

## N8354 WOMEN AS ARTISTS

**Hess, Thomas B. ed.** 1.5193
Art and sexual politics; women's liberation, women artists, and art history. Edited by Thomas B. Hess and Elizabeth C. Baker. — New York: Macmillan, [1973] ix, 150 p.: illus.; 21 cm. — (Art news series) Consists chiefly of revised essays which originally appeared in Art news, v. 69, no. 9, Jan. 1971. 1. Women artists 2. Women — Social conditions I. Baker, Elizabeth C 1934- ed. II. Art news. III. T.
N8354.A7     704/.042     LC 72-85182

**Parker, Rozsika.** 1.5194
Old mistresses: women, art, and ideology / Rozsika Parker, Griselda Pollock. — 1st American ed. — New York: Pantheon Books, c1981. xxi, 184 p.: ill.; 24 cm. Originally published: London: Routledge and Kegan Paul, 1981. Includes index. 1. Women artists 2. Feminism and art I. Pollock, Griselda. II. T.
N8354.P37 1981     704/.042 19     LC 81-48253     ISBN 0394524306

**Tufts, Eleanor.** 1.5195
Our hidden heritage: five centuries of women artists. — [New York]: Paddington Press, [1974] 256 p. 1. Women artists — Biography. I. T.
N8354.T93     709/.2/2 B     LC 73-20955     ISBN 0913600296

## N8370–8660 Art Collectors. Art Dealers

**Berenson, Bernard, 1865-1959.** • 1.5196
The Bernard Berenson treasury: a selection from the works, unpublished writings, letters, diaries, and journals of the most celebrated humanist and art historian of our times, 1887–1958 / selected and edited by Hanna Kiel; introd. by John Walker. — New York: Simon and Schuster, 1962. 414 p.: ill.; 22 cm. 1. Berenson, Bernard, 1865-1959. I. T.
N8375.B46 A15     706.9     LC 62-14273

**Berenson, Bernard, 1865-1959.** • 1.5197
The selected letters of Bernard Berenson / edited by A. K. McComb; with an epilogue by Nicky Mariano. — Boston: Houghton Mifflin, 1964, c1963. xvi, 310 p., [1] leaf of plates: port. 1. Berenson, Bernard, 1865-1959. 2. Art historians — United States — Correspondence I. McComb, Arthur Kilgore, 1895- II. T.
N8375.B46 A35     N7483B465 Z48 1964.     LC 63-17241

Haskell, Francis, 1928-.　　　　　　　　　　　　　• 1.5198
Patrons and painters; a study in the relations between Italian art and society in the age of the Baroque. New York, Knopf, 1963. xix, 454 p. 64 plates. 1. Art patronage 2. Art and society 3. Art, Italian 4. Art, Baroque I. T.
N8410 H3　　　LC 63-20833

Heydenryk, Henry.　　　　　　　　　　　　　　　• 1.5199
The art and history of frames: an inquiry into the enhancement of paintings / by Henry Heydenryk. — New York: J.H. Heineman, 1963. 119 p. 1. Picture frames and framing I. T.
N8550 H4　　　LC 63-12084

Duveen, James Henry, 1873-.　　　　　　　　　　　• 1.5200
The rise of the house of Duveen / James Henry Duveen. — 1st American ed. — New York: Knopf, c1957. ix, 293, vi p., [8] p. of plates: ill., geneal. table, ports.; 22 cm. Includes index. 1. Duveen Brothers. 2. Art dealers 3. Art — Collectors and collecting I. T.
N8660.D8 D89　　　LC 55-9282

# N8700–8795 Art and State. Government Support of Art. Forgeries

The Forger's art: forgery and the philosophy of art / edited by　　1.5201
Denis Dutton.
Berkeley: University of California Press, c1983. x, 276 p.: ill.; 24 cm. Includes index. 1. Art — Forgeries — Addresses, essays, lectures. 2. Art — Philosophy — Addresses, essays, lectures. I. Dutton, Denis.
N8790.F67 1983　　702/.8/74 19　　LC 82-11029　　ISBN 0520043413

McKinzie, Richard D.　　　　　　　　　　　　　1.5202
The New Deal for artists [by] Richard D. McKinzie. — [Princeton]: Princeton University Press, [1973] xii, 203 p.: illus.; 23 x 27 cm. 1. Federal Art Project. 2. Federal aid to the arts — United States. I. T.
N8838.M32　　338.4/7/70973　　LC 70-39053　　ISBN 0691046131

O'Connor, Francis V. comp.　　　　　　　　　　　1.5203
Art for the millions; essays from the 1930s by artists and administrators of the WPA Federal Art Project, edited, and with an introd., by Francis V. O'Connor. — Greenwich, Conn.: New York Graphic Society, [1973] 317 p.: illus.; 26 cm. 1. Art, American 2. Art, Modern — 20th century — United States 3. Federal aid to the arts — United States. I. Federal Art Project. II. T.
N8838.O25　　338.4/7/70973　　LC 78-181347　　ISBN 0821204394

# NA Architecture

Pevsner, Nikolaus, Sir, 1902-.　　　　　　　　　　1.5204
Some architectural writers of the nineteenth century. — Oxford: Clarendon Press, 1972. xiv, 338 p.: illus.; 25 cm. 'A considerably, enlarged version of the Slade Lectures ... [given] at Oxford in the session 1968-9.' 1. Architecture — Addresses, essays, lectures. I. T.
NA25.P48　　720/.9　　LC 72-170683　　ISBN 0198173156

Pevsner, Nikolaus.　　　　　　　　　　　　　　1.5205
A dictionary of architecture / Nikolaus Pevsner, John Fleming and Hugh Honour. — Rev. and enl. — Woodstock, N.Y.: The Overlook Press, 1976. 556 p.: ill.; 23 cm. 1. Architecture — Dictionaries. I. T.
NA31 F59 1976　　LC 75-27325　　ISBN 087950404

Summerson, John Newenham, Sir, 1904-.　　　　　　1.5206
The classical language of architecture [by] John Summerson. — Cambridge: M.I.T. Press, [1966, c1963] 56 p.: 63 numbered illus.; 19 x 24 cm. 'Scripts of six talks, written for the B.B.C. and delivered in May-July 1963.' 1. Architecture — Terminology. 2. Architecture — Details I. British Broadcasting Corporation. II. T.
NA31.S86 1966　　721　　LC 66-24572

Zevi, Bruno, 1918-.　　　　　　　　　　　　　1.5207
[Linguaggio moderno dell'architettura. English. Selections] The modern language of architecture / by Bruno Zevi. — Seattle: University of Washington Press, 1978, [c1977] xiv, 241 p.: ill.; 21 cm. Translated from the author's Il linguaggio moderno dell'architettura, and Architettura e storiografia. 'The two parts formed the basis of two Walker-Ames lectures delivered at the University of Washington, Seattle, on January 27 and February 1, 1977.' Includes index.

1. Architecture — Terminology. 2. Architecture — Historiography I. Zevi, Bruno, 1918- Architettura e storiografia. English. Selections. 1978. II. T.
NA31.Z48213　　720/.1/4　　LC 77-3829　　ISBN 0295955686

Macmillan encyclopedia of architects / Adolf K. Placzek, editor　　1.5208
in chief.
New York: Free Press; London: Collier Macmillan, c1982. 4 v.: ill.; 29 cm. Includes indexes. 1. Architects — Biography. I. Placzek, Adolf K. II. Title: Encyclopedia of architects.
NA40.M25 1982　　720/.92/2 B 19　　LC 82-17256　　ISBN 0029250005

# NA200–1613 History

Architecture of the Western World / edited and with an introd.　　1.5209
by Michael Raeburn; foreword by Sir Hugh Casson; individual chapters by J. J. Coulton ... [et al.].
New York: Rizzoli, 1980. 304 p.: ill. (some col.); 30 cm. Includes index. 1. Architecture — History. I. Raeburn, Michael.
NA200.A73　　720/.9 19　　LC 80-50659　　ISBN 084780349X

Ball, Victoria Kloss.　　　　　　　　　　　　　1.5210
Architecture and interior design / Victoria Kloss Ball. — New York: Wiley, c1980. — 2 v: ill. (some col.); 29 cm. 'A Wiley-Interscience publication.' 1. Interior decoration — History. 2. Architecture — Europe — History 3. Architecture, Modern — Europe — History. 4. Architecture — United States — History. 5. Architecture, Modern — United States — History. 6. Interior decoration — Europe — History. 7. Interior decoration — United States — History. I. T.
NA200.B15　　720/.9　　LC 79-21371　　ISBN 0471051624

Fletcher, Banister, Sir, 1866-1953.　　　　　　　　1.5211
[History of architecture] Sir Banister Fletcher's A history of architecture. — 18th ed. / rev. by J. C. Palmes. — New York: Scribner, 1975, 1390 p.: ill.; 24 cm. Sixth-16th ed. published under title: A history of architecture on the comparative method, for students, craftsmen, and amateurs; 17th ed. published under title: A history of architecture on the comparative method. 1. Architecture — History. I. Palmes, J. C. (James C.) II. T. III. Title: History of architecture.
NA200.F63 1975b　　720/.9　　LC 74-25545　　ISBN 0684142074

Kostof, Spiro.　　　　　　　　　　　　　　　1.5212
A history of architecture: settings and rituals / Spiro Kostof; original drawings by Richard Tobias. — New York: Oxford University Press, 1985. 788 p.: ill., maps, plans. 1. Architecture — History. I. T.
NA200.K65 1985　　720/.9 19　　LC 84-25375　　ISBN 0195034724

Giedion, S. (Sigfried), 1888-1968.　　　　　　　　• 1.5213
Space, time, and architecture: the growth of a new tradition. 4th ed., enl. Cambridge, Harvard University Press, 1962. xlviii, 778 p. ill., maps, diagrs., plans. (The Charles Eliot Norton lectures for 1938-1939) 1. Architecture — History 2. Cities and towns — Planning — History I. T. II. Series.
NA203 G5 1962　　LC 62-14459

Norberg-Schulz, Christian.　　　　　　　　　　　1.5214
Meaning in Western architecture / Christian Norberg-Schulz. — New York: Praeger, 1975. 445 p.: ill.; 22 cm. Translation of Significato nell' architettura occidentale. Includes index. 1. Architecture — History. 2. Architecture and society — History. I. T.
NA203.N6213　　720/.9　　LC 74-21607　　ISBN 0275496805

# NA210–340 Ancient Architecture

Badawy, Alexander.　　　　　　　　　　　　　• 1.5215
A history of Egyptian architecture. — Giza: Studio Misr, 1954-. v.　: illus. (part col.), map, plans. Vols. 2-3 have imprint: Berkeley, University of California Press. 1. Architecture — Egypt — History. I. T.
NA215.B3　　LC a 55-4746

Smith, E. Baldwin (Earl Baldwin), 1888-1956.　　　• 1.5216
Egyptian architecture as cultural expression, by E. Baldwin Smith ... illustrations by the author. New York, London, D. Appleton-Century company incorporated, 1938. xviii, 264 p. incl. front. (map) illus. (incl. plans) 27.5 cm. 1. Architecture — Egypt I. T.
NA215.S6　　722.2　　LC 38-32148

**Coulton, J. J.**    **1.5217**
Ancient Greek architects at work: problems of structure and design / J. J. Coulton. Ithaca, N.Y.: Cornell University Press, 1977. 196 p., [4] leaves of plates: ill.; 25 cm. Includes index. 1. Architecture — Greece I. T.
NA270.C65 1977    722/.8    LC 76-44117    ISBN 0801410770

**Dinsmoor, William Bell, 1886-.**    • **1.5218**
The architecture of ancient Greece: an account of its historic development / by William Bell Dinsmoor. — [3d] rev. and enl. ed., based on the first part of the Architecture of Greece and Rome / by William J. Anderson and R. Phené Spiers. — London: Batsford, c1950. xxiv, 424 p.: ill., maps (1 fold.) 1. Architecture — Greece I. Anderson, William James, 1864-1900. Architecture of ancient Greece. II. Spiers, Richard Phené, 1838-1916. III. T.
NA270.D5 1950    722/.8    LC 51-6495

**Lawrence, A. W. (Arnold Walter), 1900-.**    • **1.5219**
Greek architecture. [Harmondsworth, Middlesex] Penguin Books [1957] xxxiv, 327 p. illus., 152 plates, maps. 27 cm. (Pelican history of art. Z11) 1. Architecture — Greece — History. I. T. II. Series.
NA270.L36    722.8 722.6*    LC 57-59193

**Berve, Helmut, 1896-.**    • **1.5220**
Greek temples, theatres, and shrines. Texts by Helmut Berve and Gottfried Gruben. Photos. by Max Hirmer. New York, H. N. Abrams [1963] 508 p. illus. (36 mounted col.) 176 plates, maps, plans. 31 cm. Bibliography: p. 495-499. 1. Temples, Greek 2. Theaters — Greece 3. Shrines — Greece. 4. Architecture, Greek I. Gruben, Gottfried. II. Hirmer, Max. III. T.
NA275.B413    722.8    LC 62-19131

**Scully, Vincent Joseph, 1920-.**    • **1.5221**
The earth, the temple, and the gods; Greek sacred architecture [by] Vincent Scully. — Rev. ed. — New York: Praeger, [1969] xxxii, 271, [192] p.: illus., maps, plans.; 26 cm. 'Illustrations': p. [1]-[192] (3d group) 1. Temples, Greek I. T.
NA275.S3 1969    726.1/2/08    LC 69-15754

**Graham, James Walter, 1906-.**    **1.5222**
The palaces of Crete. — Princeton, N.J.: Princeton University Press, 1962. xii, 269 p.: illus., maps, plans.; 25 cm. 1. Palaces — Crete. 2. Architecture, Domestic — Crete. I. T.
NA279.C7 G7    722.61    LC 62-7039

**Traulos, Iōannēs N., 1908-.**    **1.5223**
Pictorial dictionary of ancient Athens [by] John Travlos. [Prepared in collaboration with the] German Archaeological Institute. — New York: Praeger, [1971] xvi, 590 p.: illus., maps, plans.; 30 cm. 1. Architecture — Athens. 2. Architecture, Greek — Athens. I. Deutsches Archäologisches Institut. II. T.
NA280.T68    913.38/5    LC 70-89608

**Boëthius, Axel, 1889-1969.**    • **1.5224**
Etruscan and early Roman architecture / Axel Boëthius. — 2d integrated ed., rev. / by Roger Ling and Tom Rasmussen. — Harmondsworth, Eng.; New York: Penguin Books, 1978. 264 p.: ill.; 21 cm. — (Pelican history of art.) Earlier ed. published in 1970 under title: Etruscan and Roman architecture. Includes index. 1. Architecture — Italy — Etruria. 2. Architecture — Rome I. Ling, Roger. II. Rasmussen, Tom. III. T. IV. Series.
NA300.B63 1978    722/.7    LC 78-1875    ISBN 0140561447

**Brown, Frank Edward, 1908-.**    • **1.5225**
Roman architecture. — New York: G. Braziller, 1961. 125 p.: 100 illus.; 26 cm. — (The Great ages of world architecture) 1. Architecture, Roman I. T. II. Series.
NA310.B75    722.7    LC 61-13688

**MacDonald, William Lloyd.**    • **1.5226**
The architecture of the Roman Empire [by] William L. MacDonald. New Haven, Yale University Press, 1965-. ill. (part fold.) plans. (Yale publications in the history of art. 17) 1. Architecture, Roman — History I. T. II. Series.
NA310 M24    LC 65-22333

**Nash, Ernest.**    • **1.5227**
Pictorial dictionary of ancient Rome / by Ernest Nash. — New York: Hacker Art Books, 1981. 2 v.: illus., plans.; 30 cm. 1. Architecture, Roman — Pictorial works. 2. Architecture — Rome I. T.
NA310.N28 1981    722/.7    LC 79-91827    ISBN 0878172653

**Smith, E. Baldwin (Earl Baldwin), 1888-1956.**    **1.5228**
Architectural symbolism of imperial Rome and the Middle Ages / by E. Baldwin Smith. — Princeton, Princeton University Press, 1956. ix, 219 p., [15] leaves of plates: ill.; 30 cm. (Princeton monographs in art and archaeology. 30) 1. Architecture, Roman 2. Architecture, Medieval 3. Symbolism in art I. T. II. Series.
NA310 S6    LC 56-7636

**Ward-Perkins, J. B. (John Bryan), 1912-.**    **1.5229**
Roman architecture / John B. Ward–Perkins. — New York: H. N. Abrams, 1977, c1974. 360 p.: ill.; 29 cm. (History of world architecture) Includes index. 1. Architecture, Roman I. T.
NA310.W32 1977    722/.7    LC 75-29475    ISBN 0810910225

**Ward-Perkins, J. B. (John Bryan), 1912-.**    • **1.5230**
Roman imperial architecture / J. B. Ward–Perkins. — Harmondsworth, Eng.; New York: Penguin Books, c1981. 532 p.: ill.; 21 cm. (The Pelican history of art) Includes index. 1. Architecture, Roman I. T.
NA310.W34    722/.7    LC 79-26799    ISBN 0140560459

## NA350–497 Medieval Architecture

**Harvey, John Hooper.**    **1.5231**
The mediaeval architect [by] John Harvey. — New York: St. Martin's Press, [1972] 296 p.: illus.; 25 cm. 1. Architecture, Medieval 2. Architecture — Vocational guidance I. T.
NA350.H26 1972b    723    LC 79-190103

**Conant, Kenneth John, 1894-.**    **1.5232**
Carolingian and Romanesque architecture, 800 to 1200 / Kenneth John Conant. — 3rd ed. — Harmondsworth; Baltimore [etc.]: Penguin, 1973. xxxix, 345 p., leaf of plate, [184] p. of plates: ill. (incl. 1 col.), maps (some col.), plans; 27 cm. (Pelican history of art.) Includes index. 1. Architecture, Carlovingian 2. Architecture, Romanesque I. T. II. Series.
NA365.C6 1973    723/.4    LC 76-354254    ISBN 0140560130

**Mango, Cyril A.**    **1.5233**
Byzantine architecture / Cyril Mango. — New York: H. N. Abrams, 1976. 383 p.: ill.; 29 cm. (History of world architecture) 1. Architecture, Byzantine — History. I. T.
NA370.M36 1976    723/.2    LC 75-4805    ISBN 0810910047

**Architecture of the Islamic world: its history and social**    **1.5234**
**meaning: with a complete survey of key monuments and 758 illustrations, 112 in color / texts by Ernst J. Grube ... [et al.]; edited by George Michell.**
New York, N.Y.: Thames and Hudson, 1984, c1978. 288 p.: ill. (some col.); 28 cm. Includes index. 1. Architecture, Islamic — Addresses, essays, lectures. I. Grube, Ernst J. II. Michell, George.
NA380.A78 1984    720/.917/671 19    LC 84-50341    ISBN 0500340765

**Hoag, John D.**    **1.5235**
Islamic architecture / John D. Hoag. New York: H. N. Abrams, 1977, c1975. 424 p.: ill.; 29 cm. (History of world architecture) Includes index. 1. Architecture, Islamic I. T.
NA380.H58 1977    720/.917/671    LC 76-41805    ISBN 0810910101

**Creswell, K. A. C. (Keppel Archibald Cameron), Sir, b. 1879.**    **1.5236**
Early Muslim architecture, by K. A. C. Creswell; with a contribution by Marguerite Guatier-van Berchem. 2nd ed. Oxford, Clarendon P., 1969-. v. in illus. (some col.), facsims., plans. 45 cm. 1. Architecture, Islamic I. Gautier-van Berchem, Marguerite. II. T.
NA381.C72    723/.3    LC 75-877456    ISBN 0198171544

**Kubach, Hans Erich, 1909-.**    **1.5237**
Romanesque architecture. Translated by Robert Erich Wolf. Abrams [c1975] 431p. ill., plans. (History of world architecture) Translation of Architettura romanica. 1. Architecture, Romanesque I. T.
NA390.K7913    LC 73-21549    ISBN 0810910241

**Fitchen, John.**    **1.5238**
The construction of Gothic cathedrals: a study of medieval vault erection / by John Fitchen. — Phoenix ed. — Chicago: University of Chicago Press, 1981, c1961. xix, 344 p., [3] leaves of plates: ill.; 23 cm. Includes indexes. 1. Architecture, Gothic 2. Vaults (Architecture) 3. Cathedrals I. T.
NA440.F5 1981    726/.5143 19    LC 80-26291    ISBN 0226252035

**Frankl, Paul, 1878-1962.**    • **1.5239**
The Gothic: literary sources and interpretations through eight centuries / by Paul Frankl. — Princeton, N.J.: Princeton University Press, 1960. — x, 916 p., [16] leaves of plates: ill.; 25 cm. 1. Architecture, Gothic 2. Art, Gothic I. T.
NA440.F7    LC 57-5471

**Frankl, Paul, 1878-1962.**    **1.5240**
Gothic architecture. [Translated from the German by Dieter Pevsner] Baltimore, Penguin Books [1962] xxii, 315 p. ill., 192 plates, maps, plans. (Pelican history of art. Z19) 1. Architecture, Gothic — History I. T. II. Series.
NA440 F733    LC 63-2733

Grodecki, Louis, 1910-.                                    1.5241
[Architecture gothique. English] Gothic architecture / Louis Grodecki, in collaboration with Anne Prache and Roland Recht; translated from the French by I. Mark Paris. — New York: H. N. Abrams, 1977, c1976. 442 p.: ill.; 29 cm. — (History of world architecture series) Translation of L'architecture gothique. Includes index. 1. Architecture, Gothic I. Prache, Anne. joint author. II. Recht, Roland. joint author. III. T.
NA480.G7613 1977        723/.5        LC 77-4853        ISBN 081091008X


# NA500–680 Modern Architecture

Collins, Peter.                                    1.5242
Changing ideals in modern architecture, 1750–1950 / Peter Collins. — London: Faber and Faber, 1965. 308 p., [8] leaves of plates: ill.; 23 cm. Includes indexes. 1. Architecture, Modern — History. I. T.
NA500.C6 1977        724        LC 65-89350

Frampton, Kenneth.                                    1.5243
Modern architecture: a critical history / Kenneth Frampton. — New York: Oxford University Press, 1980. 324 p.: ill.; 22 cm. — (World of art.) Includes index. 1. Architecture, Modern — History. I. T. II. Series.
NA500.F75        724        LC 79-21554        ISBN 0195201787

Murray, Peter, 1920-.                                    1.5244
Architecture of the Renaissance. New York, H. N. Abrams [1972, c1971] 401 p. illus. 29 cm. (History of world architecture) 1. Architecture, Renaissance — History. I. T.
NA510.M87        724/.1        LC 70-149850        ISBN 0810910004

Baroque & rococo: architecture & decoration / Anthony Blunt        1.5245
... [et al.]; edited by Anthony Blunt; photographs by Wim Swaan.
1st U.S. ed. — New York: Harper & Row, c1978. 352 p.: chiefly ill. (some col.) 1. Architecture, Baroque 2. Architecture, Rococo 3. Decoration and ornament, Baroque 4. Decoration and ornament, Rococo I. Blunt, Anthony, Sir, 1907-
NA590.B37        NA590 B37.        ISBN 0060104171

Kaufmann, Emil, 1891-1953.                                    • 1.5246
Architecture in the Age of Reason; baroque and post–baroque in England, Italy, and France. [Hamden, Conn.] Archon Books, 1966 [c1955] xxvi, 293 p. illus. 24 cm. 1. Architecture, Baroque I. T.
NA590.K3 1966        724.19        LC 66-18643

Norberg-Schulz, Christian.                                    1.5247
Baroque architecture. — New York: H. N. Abrams, [1972, c1971] 407 p.: illus.; 29 cm. — (History of world architecture) 1. Architecture, Baroque — History. I. T.
NA590.N6        724/.19        LC 74-149851        ISBN 0810910020

Norberg-Schulz, Christian.                                    1.5248
Late Baroque and Rococo architecture. — New York: H. N. Abrams, 1975, [c1974] 415 p.: illus.; 29 cm. — (History of world architecture) 1. Architecture, Baroque 2. Architecture, Rococo I. T.
NA590.N63        724/.19        LC 73-980        ISBN 0810910128

Rykwert, Joseph, 1926-.                                    1.5249
The first moderns: the architects of the eighteenth century / Joseph Rykwert. — Cambridge, Mass.: MIT Press, c1980. viii, 585 p.: ill.; 27 cm. Includes index. 1. Neoclassicism (Architecture) 2. Architecture, Modern — 17th-18th centuries I. T.
NA600.R94        724/.1        LC 79-22123        ISBN 0262180901

Clark, Kenneth, 1903-.                                    1.5250
The Gothic revival: an essay in the history of taste. / [by] Kenneth Clark. — New York: Harper & Row, 1974, c1962. xii, 236 p.: ill.; 21 cm. — (Icon editions.) 1. Gothic revival (Architecture) 2. Architecture — England I. T.
NA610.C5 1974        720/.942        LC 73-21308        ISBN 006430048X

Garrigan, Kristine Ottesen, 1939-.                                    1.5251
Ruskin on architecture: his thought and influence. — [Madison]: University of Wisconsin Press, [1973] xv, 220 p.: illus.; 25 cm. 1. Ruskin, John, 1819-1900 — Influence. 2. Gothic revival (Architecture) 3. Architecture, Victorian I. T.
NA610.G37        720/.9        LC 73-2045        ISBN 0299064603

Germann, Georg.                                    1.5252
[Neugotik. English] Gothic revival in Europe and Britain: sources, influences, and ideas. Translated by Gerald Onn. [1st American ed.] Cambridge, Mass., MIT Press [1973, c1972] 263 p. illus. 28 cm. Translation of: Neugotik. 1. Gothic revival (Architecture) — History. I. T.
NA610.G4713 1973        724/.3/094        LC 72-9999        ISBN 0262070596

Girouard, Mark, 1931-.                                    1.5253
Sweetness and light: the Queen Anne movement, 1860–1900 / Mark Girouard. — Oxford [Eng.]: Clarendon Press, 1977. xvi, 250 p., [4] leaves of plates: ill. (some col.); 29 cm. 1. Architecture, Queen Anne 2. Eclecticism in architecture 3. Architecture, Modern — 19th century I. T.
NA630.G57        724        LC 77-30113        ISBN 019817330X

Benevolo, Leonardo.                                    1.5254
[Storia dell'architettura moderna. English] History of modern architecture. Cambridge, Mass., M.I.T. Press [1971] 2 v. (xxxiv, 868 p.) illus. 25 cm. Translation of Storia dell'architettura moderna. 1. Architecture, Modern — 19th century 2. Architecture, Modern — 20th century I. T.
NA642.B413 1971b        724        LC 77-157667        ISBN 0262020815

Frampton, Kenneth.                                    1.5255
Modern architecture, 1851–1945 / Kenneth Frampton, Yukio Futagawa. — New York: Rizzoli, 1984 [c1983]. 465 p.: ill. (some col.); 31 cm. 1. Architecture, Modern — 19th century 2. Architecture, Modern — 20th century I. Futagawa, Yukio, 1932- II. T.
NA642.F7 1983        724 19        LC 83-61363        ISBN 0847805069

Hitchcock, Henry Russell, 1903-.                                    • 1.5256
Modern architecture: romanticism and reintegration. — New York: Hacker Art Books, 1970. xvii, 252 p.: illus.; 29 cm. 'First published ... 1929.' 1. Architecture, Modern — 19th century 2. Architecture, Modern — 20th century I. T.
NA642.H57        724        LC 73-116356        ISBN 0878170448

Risebero, Bill, 1938-.                                    1.5257
Modern architecture and design: an alternative history / Bill Risebero. — 1st MIT Press ed. — Cambridge, Mass.: MIT Press, 1983, c1982. 256 p.: ill.; 26 cm. Includes index. 1. Architecture, Modern — 19th century 2. Architecture, Modern — 20th century I. T.
NA642.R57 1983        724 19        LC 82-61310        ISBN 0262181088

Hitchcock, Henry Russell, 1903-.                                    • 1.5258
Architecture: nineteenth and twentieth centuries. — [2d ed.]. — Baltimore: Penguin Books, [1963, c1958] xxix, 510 p.: illus., 192 plates, plans.; 27 cm. — (Pelican history of art. Z15) 1. Architecture, Modern — 19th century 2. Architecture, Modern — 20th century I. T. II. Series.
NA645.H55 1963        724.9        LC 63-5619

Art nouveau architecture / edited by Frank Russell.                                    1.5259
New York: Rizzoli, 1979. 332 p.: ill. (some col.); 32 cm. Bibliography: p. 316-321. Includes index. 1. Art nouveau (Architecture) — Addresses, essays, lectures. 2. Architecture, Modern — 19th century — Addresses, essays, lectures. I. Russell, Frank, 1949-
NA645.5.A7 A77 1979        724.9/1        LC 78-58703        ISBN 0847801861

Watkin, David, 1941-.                                    1.5260
Morality and architecture: the development of a theme in architectural history and theory from the Gothic revival to the modern movement / by David Watkin. — Oxford [Eng.]: Clarendon Press, 1977. viii, 126 p.; 23 cm. 1. Eclecticism in architecture 2. Architecture, Modern — 19th century 3. Architecture, Modern — 20th century I. T.
NA645.5.E25 W37        724        LC 77-6815        ISBN 0198173504


# NA680 20th Century

Banham, Reyner.                                    1.5261
Megastructure: urban futures of the recent past / Reyner Banham. — 1st U.S. ed. — New York: Harper & Row, c1976. 224 p.: ill., plans; 26 cm. 'Icon editions.' 1. Architecture, Modern — 20th century I. T.
NA680.B249 1976        LC 76-12061        ISBN 0064303713

Banham, Reyner.                                    1.5262
Theory and design in the first machine age / Reyner Banham. — 1st MIT Press paperback ed. — Cambridge, Mass.: MIT Press, 1980, c1960. 338 p.: ill.; 21 cm. '2d ed.' Reprint of the ed. published by the Architectural Press, London. Includes index. 1. Architecture, Modern — 20th century I. T.
NA680.B25 1980        724.9/1        LC 80-14        ISBN 0262520583

Behrendt, Walter Curt, 1884-1945.                                    • 1.5263
Modern building: its nature, problems, and forms / by Walter Curt Behrendt. — New York: Harcourt, Brace, c1937. — 241 p., [16] leaves of plates: ill.; 24 cm. The author's lectures on modern building given at Dartmouth college in the winter of 1934-35 form the nucleus of this book. cf. Acknowledgment. 'First edition.' Bibliography: p. 227-230. 1. Architecture, Modern — 20th century I. T.
NA680.B45        720.904        LC 37-27251

Benton, Tim. comp.                                    1.5264
Architecture and design, 1890–1939: an international anthology of original articles / edited by Tim and Charlotte Benton, with Dennis Sharp. — New

York: Whitney Library of Design, 1975. xxiii, 252 p., [6] leaves of plates: ill.; 25 cm. 1. Architecture, Modern — 20th century — Addresses, essays, lectures. 2. Architectural design — Addresses, essays, lectures. I. Benton, Charlotte, joint comp. II. Sharp, Dennis. III. T.
NA680.B48 1975     724.9/1 19     *LC* 74-30215     *ISBN* 082307045X

**Contemporary architects / editor, Muriel Emanuel; architectural**    **1.5265**
**consultant, Dennis Sharp; assistant editors, Colin Naylor, Craig**
**Lerner.**
New York: St. Martin's Press, 1980. ix, 933 p.: ill.; 31 cm. 1. Architecture, Modern — 20th century 2. Architects — Biography. I. Emanuel, Muriel. II. Sharp, Dennis.
NA680.C625     720/.92/2 B 19     *LC* 79-67803     *ISBN* 0312166354

**Curtis, William J. R.**                **1.5266**
Modern architecture since 1900 / William J.R. Curtis. — Englewood Cliffs, N.J.: Prentice-Hall, 1983, c1982. 416 p.: ill. (some col.); 25 cm. Includes index. 1. Architecture, Modern — 20th century I. T.
NA680.C87 1983     724.9/1 19     *LC* 82-12289     *ISBN* 0135866774

**Gropius, Walter, 1883-1969.**          • **1.5267**
[Neue Architektur und das Bauhaus. English] The new architecture and the Bauhaus. Translated from the German by P. Morton Shand, with an introd. by Frank Pick. Cambridge, Mass., M.I.T. Press [1965] 112 p. illus. 21 cm. (The M.I.T. paperback series, MIT21) 1. Bauhaus. 2. Architecture, Modern — 20th century 3. Industrial arts — Study and teaching — Germany. I. T.
NA680.G7 1965     724.9     *LC* 65-10279

**Gropius, Walter, 1883-1969.**          • **1.5268**
Scope of total architecture / by Walter Gropius; planned and edited by Ruth Nanda Anshen. — [1st ed.] New York, Harper 1955. — xxii, 185 p., [4] leaves of plates: ill.; 20 cm. — (World perspectives. v. 3) 1. Architecture, Modern — 20th century I. T. II. Series.
NA680.G766     720     *LC* 54-12179

**Hamlin, Talbot Faulkner, 1889-, ed.**      • **1.5269**
Forms and functions of twentieth-century architecture; with an introd. by Leopold Arnaud. New York, Columbia University Press, 1952. 4 v. ill., plans. 1. Architecture, Modern — 20th century I. T.
NA680 H3     *LC* 52-1511

**Hitchcock, Henry Russell, 1903-.**      • **1.5270**
The international style [by] Henry-Russell Hitchcock and Philip Johnson. With a new foreword and appendix by Henry-Russell Hitchcock. New York, Norton [1966] xiii, 260 p. ill., plans. (The Norton library, N311) 1. Architecture 2. Architecture — Designs and plans I. Johnson, Philip, 1906- joint author II. T.
NA680 H5 1966     *LC* 66-15312

**Jencks, Charles.**                  **1.5271**
The language of post-modern architecture / Charles A. Jencks. New York: Rizzoli, 1977. 104 p.: ill. (some col.); 31 cm. 1. Architecture, Modern — 20th century 2. Communication in architectural design I. T.
NA680.J457     724.9     *LC* 76-62545     *ISBN* 0847800717

**Johnson, Philip, 1906-.**            **1.5272**
Writings / Philip Johnson; foreword by Vincent Scully; introd. by Peter Eisenman; commentary by Robert A. M. Stern. — New York: Oxford University Press, 1979. 291 p.: ill.; 26 cm. Includes index. 1. Architecture, Modern — 20th century — Collected works. 2. Architecture — Collected works. I. T.
NA680.J63     724.9     *LC* 77-17482     *ISBN* 0195023781

**Scully, Vincent Joseph, 1920-.**      • **1.5273**
Modern architecture; the architecture of democracy, by Vincent Scully, Jr. — Rev. ed. — New York: G. Braziller, [1974] ix, 158 p.: illus.; 26 cm. — (The Great ages of world architecture) 1. Architecture, Modern — 20th century I. T. II. Series.
NA680.S395 1974     724.9     *LC* 74-157053     *ISBN* 0807601594

**Sharp, Dennis.**                   **1.5274**
A visual history of twentieth-century architecture. — [Greenwich, Conn.]: New York Graphic Society, [1972] 304 p.: illus. (part col.); 32 cm. 1. Architecture, Modern — 20th century I. T. II. Title: Twentieth-century architecture.
NA680.S52 1972b     724.9     *LC* 78-177906     *ISBN* 0821204254

**Tafuri, Manfredo.**               **1.5275**
[Architettura contemporanea. English] Modern architecture / Manfredo Tafuri and Francesco Dal Co; translated from the Italian by Robert Erich Wolf. — New York: H. N. Abrams, 1979. 448 p.: ill.; 29 cm. — (History of world architecture) Translation of Architettura contemporanea. Includes index. 1. Architecture, Modern — 19th century 2. Architecture, Modern — 20th century 3. City planning I. Dal Co, Francesco, 1945- joint author. II. T.
NA680.T2513     724.9     *LC* 79-10202     *ISBN* 0810910063

**Wright, Frank Lloyd, 1867-1959.**      • **1.5276**
The future of architecture / Frank Lloyd Wright. — New York: Horizon Press, c1953. 326 p.: ill. 1. Architecture, Modern — 20th century I. T.
NA680.W7     724.91     *LC* 53-3814     *ISBN* 0818000031

**Portoghesi, Paolo.**             **1.5277**
[Dopo l'architettura moderna. English] After modern architecture / Paolo Portoghesi; [translated from the Italian by Meg Shore]. — New York: Rizzoli, 1982, c1980. xv, 150 p.: ill. (some col.); 24 cm. Translation of: Dopo l'architettura moderna. 1. Architecture, Postmodern 2. Architecture, Modern — 20th century I. T.
NA682.P67 P6713 1982     724.9/1 19     *LC* 81-51379     *ISBN* 0847804089

## NA701–1613 MEDIEVAL AND MODERN ARCHITECTURE, BY COUNTRY

## NA702 Latin America

**Damaz, Paul F.**               • **1.5278**
Art in Latin American architecture. Pref. by Oscar Niemeyer. New York, Reinhold Pub. Corp. [1963] 232 p. ill. 1. Architecture — Latin America 2. Art, Latin American 3. Art, Modern — 20th century I. T.
NA702 D3     *LC* 63-11424

**Hitchcock, Henry Russell, 1903-.**      • **1.5279**
Latin American architecture since 1945. New York, Museum of Modern Art [1955] 203 p. ill., plans. 'Biographies of architects': p. 198-200. 1. Architecture — Latin America 2. Architecture, Modern — 20th century 3. Architecture — Designs and plans I. New York. Museum of Modern Art II. T.
NA702 H5     *LC* 55-12305

## NA703–738 North America. United States

**Noble, Allen George, 1930-.**        **1.5280**
Wood, brick, and stone: the North American settlement landscape / Allen G. Noble; drawings by M. Margaret Geib. — Amherst: University of Massachusetts Press, 1984. 2 v.: ill.; 26 cm. Spine title: Wood, brick, & stone. 1. Vernacular architecture — North America. I. Geib, M. Margaret. II. T. III. Title: Wood, brick, & stone.
NA703.N6 1984     728/.097 19     *LC* 83-24110     *ISBN* 0870234102

**Andrews, Wayne.**             **1.5281**
Architecture, ambition, and Americans: a social history of American architecture / Wayne Andrews. — Rev. ed. — New York: Free Press, c1978. xxx, 332 p.: ill.; 25 cm. Includes index. 1. Architecture — United States — History. I. T.
NA705.A5 1978     720/.973     *LC* 78-50786     *ISBN* 0029007704

**Burchard, John Ely, 1898-.**        • **1.5282**
The architecture of America; a social and cultural history, by John Burchard and Albert Bush-Brown. [1st ed.] Boston, Little, Brown [1961] 595 p. ill. 1. Architecture — United States — History I. Bush-Brown, Albert. joint author II. T.
NA705 B8     *LC* 61-5736

**Fitch, James Marston.**          **1.5283**
American building: 2, the environmental forces that shape it / by James Marston Fitch. — 2d ed., rev. and enl. — Boston: Houghton, 1966-1972. 2 v.: ill., plates. 1. Architecture and society — United States. I. T.
NA705.F512     720/.973     *LC* 65-10689

**Historic America: buildings, structures, and sites / recorded by**    **1.5284**
**the Historic American Buildings Survey and the Historic**
**American Engineering Record; checklist compiled by Alicia**
**Stamm; essays edited by C. Ford Peatross.**
Washington: Library of Congress: For sale by Supt. of Docs., U.S. G.P.O., 1983. xvi, 708 p.: ill.; 29 cm. 1. Architecture — United States 2. Historic buildings — United States. 3. Historic sites — United States. I. Stamm, Alicia. II. Peatross, C. Ford. III. Historic American Buildings Survey. IV. Historic American Engineering Record. V. Library of Congress.
NA705.H53 1983     973 19     *LC* 83-14422     *ISBN* 0844404314

**Mumford, Lewis, 1895-.**          • **1.5285**
The South in architecture. New York, Da Capo Press, 1967. 147 p. 21 cm. (Da Capo Press series in architecture and decorative art, v. 6) (The Dancy lectures, 1941.) Reprint of the 1941 ed. 1. Jefferson, Thomas, 1743-1826. 2. Richardson,

H. H. (Henry Hobson), 1838-1886. 3. Architecture — United States
4. Architecture — Southern States. I. T.
NA705.M78 1967    720/.975    *LC* 67-27462

**Mumford, Lewis, 1895-.**                                    • **1.5286**
Sticks and stones; a study of American architecture and civilization. — [2d rev.
ed.]. — New York: Dover Publications, [1955] 238 p.: illus.; 21 cm.
1. Architecture — United States I. T.
NA705.M8 1955    720.973    *LC* 55-14852

**Pierson, William Harvey, 1911-.**                                    • **1.5287**
American buildings and their architects [by] William H. Pierson, Jr. — [1st
ed.]. — Garden City, N.Y.: Doubleday, 1970-1980. 5 v.: illus., plans.; 24 cm.
Vols. 3-4 by W. H. Jordy. 1. Architecture — United States — History.
2. Architects — United States I. Jordy, William H. II. T.
NA705.P5    720/.973    *LC* 79-84361

**Scully, Vincent Joseph, 1920-.**                                    • **1.5288**
American architecture and urbanism [by] Vincent Scully. New York, Praeger
[1969] 275 p. illus., maps, plans. 26 cm. 1. Architecture — United States —
History. 2. City planning — United States — History. I. T.
NA705.S36    720/.973    *LC* 70-76793

**Whiffen, Marcus.**                                    • **1.5289**
American architecture since 1780: guide to the styles. — Cambridge, Mass.:
M.I.T. Press, [1969] x, 313 p.: illus.; 20 cm. 1. Architecture — U.S. I. T.
NA705.W47    720/.973    *LC* 69-10376

**Whiffen, Marcus.**                                    **1.5290**
American architecture, 1607–1976 / Marcus Whiffen and Frederick Koeper. —
Cambridge, Mass.: MIT Press, c1981. xv, 495 p.: ill.; 26 cm. Includes index.
1. Architecture — United States I. Koeper, Frederick. joint author. II. T.
NA705.W473    720/.973 19    *LC* 80-23251    *ISBN* 0262231050

## NA707–712 By Period

**Hamlin, Talbot Faulkner, 1889-1956.**                                    • **1.5291**
Greek revival architecture in America: being an account of important trends in
American architecture and American life prior to the war between the states /
by Talbot Hamlin; together with a list of articles on architecture in some
American periodicals prior to 1850 by Sarah Hull Jenkins Simpson Hamlin
(1887–1930) and an introduction by Leopold Arnaud. — London: Oxford
University Press, 1944. xl, 439 p., xciv p. de planches: ill. I. Hamlin, Sarah Hull
Jenkins Simpson, 1887-1930. II. T.
NA707.H32    *LC* 44-865

**Morrison, Hugh Sinclair, 1905-**                                    • **1.5292**
Early American architecture, from the first colonial settlements to the national
period / Hugh S. Morrison. — New York: Oxford University Press, 1952. xiv,
619 p.: ill., maps, plans. 1. Architecture — United States I. T.
NA707.M63    *LC* 52-7831

**Eaton, Leonard K.**                                    **1.5293**
American architecture comes of age; European reaction to H. H. Richardson
and Louis Sullivan [by] Leonard K. Eaton. Cambridge, Mass., MIT Press
[1972] xiii, 256 p. illus. 27 cm. 1. Richardson, H. H. (Henry Hobson),
1838-1886. 2. Sullivan, Louis H., 1856-1924. 3. Architecture — United States
4. Architecture, Modern — 19th century — United States I. T.
NA710.E24    720/.973    *LC* 76-171556    *ISBN* 0262050102

**Maass, John, 1918-.**                                    • **1.5294**
The gingerbread age; a view of Victorian America. New York, Rinehart [1957]
212 p. ill. 1. Architecture — United States — History I. T.
NA710 M3    *LC* 57-7370

**Mumford, Lewis, 1895- ed.**                                    • **1.5295**
Roots of contemporary American architecture; a series of thirty–seven essays
dating from the mid–nineteenth century to the present. Contains an
introductory essay and biographies of the twenty–nine writers whose work
appears herein. — New York: Reinhold, [1952] vii, 454 p.; 24 cm.
1. Architecture — United States — Addresses, essays, lectures.
2. Architecture, Modern — 19th century — United States — Addresses,
essays, lectures. 3. Architecture, Modern — 20th century — United States —
Addresses, essays, lectures. I. T.
NA710.M8    720.973    *LC* 52-10519

**The Rise of an American architecture [by] Henry–Russell**                                    • **1.5296**
**Hitchcock [and others] Edited with an introd. and exhibition**
**notes by Edgar Kaufmann, Jr.**
New York: Published in association with the Metropolitan Museum of Art by
Praeger, [1970] x, 241 p.: illus., maps, plans, ports.; 25 cm. 'This book was
conceived as counterpart to an exhibition opening under the same name ... at
the Metropolitan Museum of Art in May of 1970.' 1. Architecture — U.S. —
Addresses, essays, lectures. 2. Architecture, Modern — 19th century — U.S.
— Addresses, essays, lectures. 3. Architecture, Modern — 20th century —

Addresses, essays, lectures. I. Hitchcock, Henry Russell, 1903- II. Kaufmann,
Edgar, 1910- ed. III. New York. Metropolitan Museum of Art.
NA710.R5    720/.973    *LC* 70-116442

**Schuyler, Montgomery, 1843-1914.**                                    • **1.5297**
American architecture, and other writings. Edited by William H. Jordy and
Ralph Coe. Cambridge, Belknap Press of Harvard University Press, 1961. 2 v.
(xvi, 664 p.) ill., plans. (John Harvard library.) 1. Architecture — United
States I. T. II. Series.
NA710 S42    *LC* 61-13743

**The Critical edge: controversy in recent American architecture /**                                    **1.5298**
**edited by Tod A. Marder.**
[New Brunswick, N.J.]: Jane Voorhees Zimmerli Art Museum, Rutgers, State
University of New Jersey; Cambridge, Mass.: MIT Press, c1985. 203 p.: ill.
(some col.); 31 cm. Based on an exhibition of the same title sponsored by and
held at the Jane Voorhees Zimmerli Art Museum from Mar. 24 to June 9, 1985
and at other museums. 1. Architecture, Postmodern — United States —
Addresses, essays, lectures. 2. Architecture, Modern — 20th century — United
States — Addresses, essays, lectures. I. Marder, Tod A. II. Jane Voorhees
Zimmerli Art Museum.
NA712.5.P67 C74 1985    720/.973 19    *LC* 84-63027    *ISBN*
0262132079

## NA715–735 Regions. Cities

**Brooks, H. Allen (Harold Allen), 1925-.**                                    **1.5299**
The prairie school; Frank Lloyd Wright and his midwest contemporaries [by]
H. Allen Brooks. [Toronto, University of Toronto Press, 1972] xxiii, 373 p.
illus. 23 cm. 1. Wright, Frank Lloyd, 1867-1959. 2. Prairie school
(Architecture) 3. Architecture — Middle West 4. Architecture, Modern —
20th century — Middle West I. T.
NA722.B7 1972    720/.977    *LC* 72-151363    *ISBN* 0802052517
*ISBN* 0802000398

**Cummings, Abbott Lowell, 1923-.**                                    **1.5300**
The framed houses of Massachusetts Bay, 1625–1725 / Abbott Lowell
Cummings. — Cambridge, Mass.; London: Harvard University Press, c1979.
xiv, 261 p.: ill., maps, 1 coat of arms, plans; 27 x31 cm. 1. Wooden-frame
houses — Massachusetts — Massachusetts Bay region. 2. Architecture,
Colonial — Massachusetts — Massachusetts Bay region. I. T.
NA730.M4    728.3 18    728.3 19    *LC* 78-8390    *ISBN* 0674316800

**Condit, Carl W.**                                    • **1.5301**
The Chicago school of architecture; a history of commercial and public building
in the Chicago area, 1875–1925 [by] Carl W. Condit. Chicago, University of
Chicago Press [1964] xviii, 238 p. 196 ill. 'Revised and enlarged from 'The rise
of the skyscraper ... 1952.' 1. Architecture — Chicago — History
2. Architecture — United States — History I. T.
NA735 C4 C6    *LC* 64-13287

**Stern, Robert A. M.**                                    **1.5302**
New York 1900: metropolitan architecture and urbanism, 1890–1915 / by
Robert A.M. Stern, Gregory Gilmartin, John Montague Massengale. — New
York: Rizzoli, 1983. 502 p.: ill.; 29 cm. 1. Architecture, Modern — 19th
century — New York (N.Y.) 2. Architecture, Modern — 20th century — New
York (N.Y.) 3. City planning — New York (N.Y.) 4. Buildings — New York
(N.Y.) 5. New York (N.Y.) — Buildings, structures, etc. I. Gilmartin,
Gregory. II. Massengale, John Montague. III. T.
NA735.N5 S73 1983    720/.9747/1 19    *LC* 83-42995    *ISBN*
0847805115

**Downing, Antoinette Forrester.**                                    • **1.5303**
The architectural heritage of Newport, Rhode Island, 1640–1915, by
Antoinette F. Downing and Vincent J. Scully, Jr. — 2d ed., rev. — New York:
C. N. Potter, [1967] xvi, 526 p.: illus., maps, plans.; 29 cm. 1. Architecture —
Newport, R.I. I. Scully, Vincent Joseph, 1920- joint author. II. T.
NA735.N54 D6 1967    720/.9745/7    *LC* 67-24838

**Whiffen, Marcus, 1916-.**                                    • **1.5304**
The eighteenth–century houses of Williamsburg; a study of architecture and
building in the colonial capital of Virginia. Williamsburg, Va., Published by
Colonial Williamsburg; distributed by Holt, Rinehart, and Winston, New York
[1960] xx, 223 p. ill., map (on lining papers) disgrs., facsim., plans.
(Williamsburg architectural studies. [v.2]) 1. Architecture, Domestic —
Williamsburg, Va. 2. Architecture, Colonial I. T. II. Series.
NA735 W5 W45    *LC* 60-13174

## NA737 ARCHITECTS, A–Z

**Breuer, Marcel, 1902-.** • **1.5305**
Buildings and projects, 1921–1961. Captions and introd. by Cranston Jones. New York, Praeger [1963, c1962] 262 p. illus. (part col.) port., plans. 23 x 29 cm. (Books that matter) I. T.
NA737.B68 A45 1963      720.973      *LC* 62-21001

**Breuer, Marcel, 1902-.** • **1.5306**
Sun and shadow, the philosophy of an architect. Editing and notes by Peter Blake; book design and cover by Alexey Brodovitch. New York, Dodd, Mead [1955] 205 p. ill., port. 1. Architecture, Modern — 20th century I. Blake, Peter, 1920- II. T.
NA737 B68 B56      *LC* 55-9928

**Place, Charles Alpheus, 1866-.** • **1.5307**
Charles Bulfinch, architect and citizen, by Charles A. Place. New York, Da Capo Press, 1968 [c1925] xiv, 294 p. illus., maps, plans, ports. 26 cm. (Da Capo Press series in architecture and decorative art, v. 16) (A Da Capo Press reprint edition) 1. Bulfinch, Charles, 1763-1844. I. T.
NA737.B8 P5 1968      720/.924 B      *LC* 68-27717

**Hines, Thomas S.** **1.5308**
Burnham of Chicago, architect and planner / Thomas S. Hines. — New York: Oxford University Press, 1974. xxiii, 445 p.: ill.; 24 cm. Includes index. 1. Burnham, Daniel Hudson, 1846-1912. I. T.
NA737.B85 H56      720/.92/4 B      *LC* 74-79625      *ISBN* 0195018362

**Makinson, Randell L., 1932-.** **1.5309**
Greene & Greene / Randell L. Makinson; with new photos. by Marvin Rand; and an introd. by Reyner Banham. — Salt Lake City: Peregrine Smith, c1977-1979. 2 v.: ill. (some col.); 24 cm. Vol. 2 published in Santa Barbara, Calif. Includes indexes. 1. Greene & Greene. 2. Architecture — California. 3. Architecture, Modern — 20th century — California. 4. Furniture — California — History — 20th century. 5. Design — California — History — 20th century. I. T.
NA737.G73 M33      728.3/092/2      *LC* 76-57792      *ISBN* 0879050233

**Bridenbaugh, Carl.** • **1.5310**
Peter Harrison, first American architect. Chapel Hill, Univ. of North Carolina Press, 1949. xvi, 195 p. ill., ports., maps. 'Published for the Institute of Early American History and Culture at Williamsburg, Virginia.' 1. Harrison, Peter, 1716-1775. I. Institute of Early American History and Culture (Williamsburg, Va.) II. T.
NA737 H3 B7      *LC* 49-9109

**Stern, Robert A. M.** **1.5311**
George Howe: toward a modern American architecture / Robert A. M. Stern. — New Haven: Yale University Press, 1975. xiii, 273 p., [40] leaves of plates: ill.; 26 cm. 'Writings by George Howe': p. 253-259. 1. Howe, George, 1886-1955. I. T.
NA737.H65 S83      720/.92/4      *LC* 73-86918      *ISBN* 0300016425

**Baker, Paul R.** **1.5312**
Richard Morris Hunt / Paul R. Baker. — Cambridge, Mass.: MIT Press, c1980. xvi, 588 p.: ill.; 26 cm. Includes index. 1. Hunt, Richard Morris, 1828-1895. 2. Architects — United States — Biography. I. T.
NA737.H86 B34      720/.92/4 B      *LC* 79-25008      *ISBN* 0262021390

**Ronner, Heinz.** **1.5313**
Louis I. Kahn: complete works, 1935–74 / Heinz Ronner, Sharad Jhaveri, Alessandro Vasella. Boulder, Colo.: Westview Press, 1977. 455 p.: chiefly ill.; 25 x 43 cm. 1. Kahn, Louis I., 1901-1974. I. Jhaveri, Sharad, joint author. II. Vasella, Alessandro, joint author. III. T.
NA737.K32 R66      720/.92/4      *LC* 76-41392      *ISBN* 0891586482

**Hamlin, Talbot, 1889-1956.** • **1.5314**
Benjamin Henry Latrobe / Talbot Hamlin. — New York, Oxford University Press, 1955. xxxvi, 633 p. illus., ports., facsims., plans. 24 cm. 1. Latrobe, Benjamin Henry, 1764-1820. I. T.
NA737.L34H3      NA737L3 H36.      927.2      *LC* 55-8117

**Kimball, Fiske, 1888-1955.** • **1.5315**
Mr. Samuel McIntire, carver, the architect of Salem. [Salem, Mass.] Essex Institute of Salem, 1940. Gloucester, Mass., P. Smith, 1966. xiii, 157 p. illus., fold. map, plans, ports. 28 cm. 1. McIntire, Samuel, 1757-1811. I. Essex Institute. II. T. III. Title: The architect of Salem.
NA737.M25 K5 1966      720.97445 B      *LC* 67-297

**McKim, Mead & White.** **1.5316**
A monograph of the works of McKim, Mead & White, 1879–1915. With an essay by Leland Roth. — New ed. — New York: B. Blom, 1973. 73 p., 408 p. of illus.; 34 cm. 1. McKim, Mead & White. 2. Architecture, Modern — 19th century — United States 3. Architecture, Modern — 20th century — United States I. T.
NA737.M4 A5 1973      720/.6/57471      *LC* 72-152624

**Roth, Leland M.** **1.5317**
McKim, Mead & White, architects / Leland M. Roth. — 1st ed. — New York: Harper & Row, c1983. xxi, 441 p.: ill.; 28 cm. — (Icon editions) Includes index. 1. McKim, Mead & White. 2. Architecture, Modern — 19th century — United States I. T. II. Title: McKim, Mead, and White.
NA737.M4 R65 1983      720/.92/2 19      *LC* 83-47559      *ISBN* 0064384918

**Cardwell, Kenneth H., 1920-.** **1.5318**
Bernard Maybeck: artisan, architect, artist / Kenneth H. Cardwell. — Santa Barbara: Peregrine Smith, 1977. 255 p.: ill.; 24 cm. Includes index. 1. Maybeck, Bernard R. 2. Architects — California — Biography. I. T.
NA737.M435 C37      720/.92/4 B      *LC* 77-13773      *ISBN* 0879050225

**Meier, Richard, 1934-.** **1.5319**
Richard Meier, architect, 1964/1984 / introduction by Joseph Rykwert. — New York: Rizzoli, c1984. 411 p.: ill. (some col.); 27 cm. 1. Meier, Richard, 1934- 2. Architecture, Modern — 20th century — United States I. T.
NA737.M44 A4 1984      720/.92/4 19      *LC* 83-42911      *ISBN* 0847804968

**Gallagher, Helen Mar (Pierce) d. 1942.** • **1.5320**
Robert Mills, architect of the Washington Monument, 1781–1855. — New York: AMS Press, 1966 [c1935] xxv, 233 p.: illus.; 24 cm. 1. Mills, Robert, 1781-1855. I. T.
NA737.M5 G3 1966      720/.92/4 B      *LC* 72-183878

**Drexler, Arthur.** **1.5321**
The architecture of Richard Neutra: from international style to California modern / Arthur Drexler and Thomas S. Hines. — New York: Museum of Modern Art, c1982. 114 p.: ill. (some col.); 26 cm. Catalog of an exhibition which opened July 14, 1982 at the Museum of Modern Art, New York. 1. Neutra, Richard Joseph, 1892-1970 — Exhibitions. 2. Architecture, Modern — 20th century — United States — Exhibitions. I. Hines, Thomas S. II. Neutra, Richard Joseph, 1892-1970. III. Museum of Modern Art (New York, N.Y.) IV. T.
NA737.N4 A4 1982      720/.92/4 19      *LC* 82-81426      *ISBN* 0870705067

**Hines, Thomas S.** **1.5322**
Richard Neutra and the search for modern architecture: a biography and history / Thomas S. Hines. — New York: Oxford University Press, 1982. 356 p.: ill.; 26 cm. 1. Neutra, Richard Joseph, 1892-1970. 2. Architects — United States — Biography. I. T.
NA737.N4 H5 1982      720/.92/4 B      *LC* 81-22530      *ISBN* 0195030281

**Ochsner, Jeffrey Karl.** **1.5323**
H.H. Richardson, complete architectural works / Jeffrey Karl Ochsner. — [Cambridge, MA: MIT Press], c1982. xiii, 466 p.: ill.; 29 cm. 1. Richardson, H. H. (Henry Hobson), 1838-1886 — Catalogs. I. T.
NA737.R5 A4 1982      720/.92/4 19      *LC* 82-6603      *ISBN* 0262150239

**Hitchcock, Henry Russell, 1903-.** • **1.5324**
The architecture of H.H. Richardson and his times. [Rev. ed.] Hamden, Conn., Archon Books, 1961. xxvi, 343 p. ill., plans. 1. Richardson, H. H. (Henry Hobson), 1838-1886. 2. Architecture — History I. T.
NA737 R5 H5 1961      *LC* 61-4984

**O'Gorman, James F.** **1.5325**
H. H. Richardson and his office, a centennial of his move to Boston, 1874: selected drawings: [exhibition organized by the Department of Printing and Graphic Arts, Harvard College Library, Fogg Art Museum, Harvard University, October 23–December 8, 1974, Albany Institute of History and Art, January 7–February 23, 1975, Renwick Gallery, Washington, D.C., The National Collection of Fine Arts, Smithsonian Institution, March 21–June 22, 1975: catalogue] — / [James F. O'Gorman]. — [Cambridge, Mass.]: Dept. of Printing and Graphic Arts, Harvard College Library, 1974. xii, 220 p., [8] leaves of plates: ill. (some col.); 22 x 28 cm. 1. Richardson, H. H. (Henry Hobson), 1838-1886. 2. Artists' preparatory studies I. Richardson, H. H. (Henry Hobson), 1838-1886. II. Harvard College Library. Dept. of Printing and Graphic Arts. III. Fogg Art Museum. IV. Albany Institute of History and Art. V. Renwick Gallery. VI. T.
NA737.R5 O35      720/.92/4      *LC* 74-80839      *ISBN* 0914630008

**Hoffmann, Donald.** **1.5326**
The architecture of John Wellborn Root. — Baltimore: Johns Hopkins University Press, [1973] xviii, 263 p.: illus.; 24 cm. — (The Johns Hopkins studies in nineteenth-century architecture) 1. Root, John Wellborn, 1850-1891. I. T. II. Series.
NA737.R6 H6      720/.92/4      *LC* 72-4008      *ISBN* 0801813719

**Gebhard, David.** 1.5327
Schindler. Pref. by Henry–Russell Hitchcock. New York, Viking Press [1972, c1971] 216 p. illus., plans. 22 cm. (A Studio book) 1. Schindler, R. M. (Rudolph M.), 1887-1953. 2. Architects — United States — Biography. I. T.
NA737.S5 G37 1972     720/.924     LC 71-172899     ISBN 0670620637
ISBN 0670020222

**Gilchrist, Agnes Eleanor (Addison) 1907-.** • 1.5328
William Strickland, architect and engineer, 1788–1854, by Agnes Addison Gilchrist. — Enl. ed. — New York: Da Capo Press, 1969. 1 v. (various pagings): illus., plans, ports.; 29 cm. — (A Da Capo Press reprint edition) 'An unabridged republication of the first edition, published in ... 1950 ... It includes as a supplement three articles about Strickland prepared by Mrs. Gilchrist [and first published in 1953-54]' 1. Strickland, William, 1787-1854. 2. Architecture — U.S. I. T.
NA737.S68 G5 1969     720/.924 B     LC 69-13714

### NA737.S9 Sullivan

**Sullivan, Louis H., 1856-1924.** • 1.5329
The autobiography of an idea. Foreword by Claude Bragdon. With a new introd. by Ralph Marlowe Line, and 35 illus. of Sullivan's works selected and photographed by Ralph Marlowe Line for this ed. — New York: Dover Publications, 1956. 329 p.: illus.; 21 cm. 1. Sullivan, Louis H., 1856-1924. 2. Architects — United States — Biography. I. T.
NA737.S9 A2 1956     927.2     LC 57-2899

**Morrison, Hugh Sinclair, 1905-.** • 1.5330
Louis Sullivan, prophet of modern architecture. — 1st. ed. New York: Museum of Modern Art and W.W. Norton, c1935. xxi, 23-391 p. illus. 20 cm. — (Norton library, N116) 'Dankmar Adler, a biographical sketch': p. 283-293. Includes bibliographies. 1. Sullivan, Louis Henry, 1856-1924. 2. Adler, Dankmar, 1844-1900. 3. Architecture — U.S. I. T.
NA737.S9M6 1962     927.2     LC 36-27013

**Szarkowski, John.** • 1.5331
The idea of Louis Sullivan. Minneapolis, University of Minnesota Press [1956] 161 p. ill., ports. 1. Sullivan, Louis Henry, 1856-1924 I. T.
NA737 S9 S9     LC 56-11616

**Wright, Frank Lloyd, 1867-1959.** • 1.5332
Genius and the mobocracy. [Enl. ed.] New York, Horizon Press [1971] 247 p. illus., plan. 26 cm. 1. Sullivan, Louis H., 1856-1924. I. T.
NA737.S9 W7 1971     720/.924     LC 79-132328     ISBN 0818000228

### NA737.W7 Wright

**Wright, Frank Lloyd, 1867-1959.** 1.5333
An autobiography / Frank Lloyd Wright. New York: Horizon Press, c1977. 620 p., [20] leaves of plates: ill.; 24 cm. Includes index. 1. Wright, Frank Lloyd, 1867-1959. 2. Architects — United States — Biography. I. T.
NA737.W7 A3 1977     720/.92/4 B     LC 72-86739     ISBN 0818002220

**Wright, Frank Lloyd, 1867-1959.** 1.5334
Letters to apprentices / Frank Lloyd Wright; selected and with commentary by Bruce Brooks Pfeiffer. — [Fresno]: Press at California State University, Fresno, c1982. x, 211 p.: ill.; 23 cm. Includes index. 1. Wright, Frank Lloyd, 1867-1959. 2. Architects — In-service training — United States. 3. Architects — United States — Correspondence. I. Pfeiffer, Bruce Brooks. II. T.
NA737.W7 A3 1982     720/.92/4 B 19     LC 83-115910

**Wright, Frank Lloyd, 1867-1959.** • 1.5335
A testament. — New York: Horizon Press, [1957] 256 p.: illus., plans.; 31 cm. — I. T.
NA737.W7 A33     927.2     LC 57-14545

**Wright, Frank Lloyd, 1867-1959.** 1.5336
[Ausgeführte Bauten und Entwürfe. English & German] Studies and executed buildings = Ausgeführte Bauten und Entwürfe / by Frank Lloyd Wright. — Palos Park, Ill.: Prairie School Press, 1975. [32] p., 64 [i.e. 100] leaves of plates: ill., plans; 23 x 37 cm. Reduced photoreprint of the 1910 Berlin ed., published with German introd. under title: Ausgeführte Bauten und Entwürfe. Includes also the English version of the introd. printed at Chicago for inclusion in sets of the original plates distributed in America. 'Comment' (p. [32]) signed: Wilbert R. Hasbrouck. 1. Wright, Frank Lloyd, 1867-1959 — Contributions in organic architecture. I. T. II. Title: Ausgeführte Bauten und Entwürfe.
NA737.W7 A4 1975     720/.22/2     LC 75-27623     ISBN 0873700015

**Storrer, William Allin.** 1.5337
The architecture of Frank Lloyd Wright: a complete catalog / William Allin Storrer. — 2d ed. — Cambridge, Mass.: MIT Press, 1978. ca. 500 p.: ill.; 21 cm.

Includes indexes. 1. Wright, Frank Lloyd, 1867-1959 — Catalogs. I. Wright, Frank Lloyd, 1867-1959. II. T.
NA737.W7 A4 1978     720/.92/4     LC 78-1306     ISBN 0262191717

**Wright, Frank Lloyd, 1867-1959.** 1.5338
[Ausgeführte Bauten. English] The early work of Frank Lloyd Wright = The 'Ausgeführte Bauten' of 1911 / with a new introduction by Grant Carpenter Manson. — Dover ed. — New York: Dover Publications, 1982. 141 p.: chiefly ill.; 29 cm. Originally published: Ausgeführte Bauten. Berlin: Wasmuth, 1911. With translations of captions and a glossary of German words on floor plans. 1. Wright, Frank Lloyd, 1867-1959. I. T. II. Title: 'Ausgeführte Bauten' of 1911.
NA737.W7 A4 1982a     720/.92/4 19     LC 82-9437     ISBN 0486243818

**Wright, Frank Lloyd, 1869-1959.** • 1.5339
Writings and buildings. Selected by Edgar Kaufmann and Ben Raeburn. [New York] Horizon Press [1960] 346 p. illus. 22 cm. 1. Architecture I. Kaufmann, Edgar, 1910- comp. II. T.
NA737.W7A48 1960a     720.973     LC 60-8166

**Hitchcock, Henry Russell, 1903-.** • 1.5340
In the nature of materials, 1887–1941; the buildings of Frank Lloyd Wright. New foreword and bibliography by the author. — New York: Da Capo Press, 1973 [c1942] xlix, 143 p.: illus.; 22 cm. — (Da Capo Press series in architecture and decorative art, v. 28) 1. Wright, Frank Lloyd, 1867-1959. I. T.
NA737.W7 H5 1973     720/.92/4     LC 72-75322     ISBN 0306712830

**Scully, Vincent Joseph, 1920-.** • 1.5341
Frank Lloyd Wright. — New York: G. Braziller, 1960. 125 p.: plates, port., plans.; 26 cm. — (The Masters of world architecture series) 1. Wright, Frank Lloyd, 1867-1959. I. T. II. Series.
NA737.W7 S3     720.973     LC 60-6075

## NA740–939 Canada. Latin America

**Clerk, Nathalie.** 1.5342
Palladian style in Canadian architecture / Nathalie Clerk. — Ottawa, Ont.: National Historic Parks and Sites Branch, Parks Canada: Environment Canada; Hull, Quebec, Canada: Canadian Govt. Pub. Centre, Supply and Services Canada [distributor], 1984. 154 p.: ill.; 25 cm. (Studies in archaeology, architecture, and history. 0821-1027) 1. Palladio, Andrea, 1508-1580 — Influence. 2. Architecture, Colonial — Canada. 3. Vernacular architecture — Canada. 4. Neoclassicism (Architecture) — Influence. I. T. II. Series.
NA743.C55 1984     720/.9713 19     LC 84-211146     ISBN 0660115301

**Cameron, Christina.** 1.5343
Second empire style in Canadian architecture / by Christina Cameron and Janet Wright. — Ottawa: National Historic Parks and Sites Branch, Parks Canada, 1980. 247 p.: ill. — (Canadian historic sites. no. 24) 1. Architecture, Modern — 19th century — Canada. I. Wright, Janet. II. T. III. Series.
NA744.C3     NA744 C3.     ISBN 0660104466

**Brosseau, Mathilde.** 1.5344
Gothic revival in Canadian architecture / by Mathilde Brosseau. — Ottawa: Minister of Supply and Services Canada, [1980] 208 p.: ill.; 22 cm. — (Canadian historic sites: occasional papers in archaeology and history; 25) Cover title. 1. Gothic revival (Architecture) — Canada. 2. Architecture — Canada. 3. Architecture, Modern — 19th century — Canada. I. T.
NA744.5.G67 B76 1980     720/.971 19     LC 82-109114     ISBN 0660104474

**Maitland, Leslie.** 1.5345
Neoclassical architecture in Canada / Leslie Maitland. — [Ottawa]: National Historic Parks and Sites Branch, Parks Canada, Environment Canada; Hull, Quebec, Canada: Canadian Govt. Pub. Centre, [distributor], 1984. 150 p.: ill.; 24 cm. (Studies in archaeology, architecture, and history. 0821-1027) 1. Neoclassicism (Architecture) — Canada. 2. Architecture, Modern — 19th century — Canada. I. T. II. Series.
NA744.5.N45 M35 1984     720/.971 19     LC 84-221137     ISBN 0660115298

**Ede, Carol Moore, 1944-.** 1.5346
Canadian architecture, 1960/70. Photography and text: Carol Moore Ede. — Toronto: Burns and MacEachern, [c1971] 264 p.: illus., ports.; 27 cm. 1. Architecture — Canada. 2. Architecture, Modern — 20th century — Canada. I. T.
NA745.E3     720/.9/71     LC 70-158488     ISBN 0887680216

**Shapiro, Barbara E.** 1.5347
Arthur Erickson: selected projects 1971–1985: an exhibition organized by the Center for Inter–American Relations, New York, an affiliate of the Americas Society / curator, Barbara E. Shapiro; [authors, Barbara E. Shapiro, Rhodri W. Liscombe]. — New York (680 Park Ave., New York 10021): The Center,

c1985. 48 p.: ill. (some col.); 28 cm. Exhibition held at the Center for Inter-American Relations, New York City, and at other galleries from Mar. 27, 1985 to Aug. 13, 1986. 1. Erickson, Arthur, 1924- — Exhibitions. 2. Architecture, Modern — 20th century — Canada — Exhibitions. I. Erickson, Arthur, 1924- II. Liscombe, R. W., 1946- III. Center for Inter-American Relations. IV. T.
NA749.E74 A4 1985     720/.92/4 19     *LC* 85-71480

**Iglauer, Edith.**       **1.5348**
Seven stones: a portrait of Arthur Erickson, architect / by Edith Iglauer. — [Vancouver] B.C.: Harbour Pub.; Seattle: University of Washington Press, 1981. 117 p.: ill. (some col.); 23 x 27 cm. Includes index. 1. Erickson, Arthur, 1924- I. T.
NA749.E74 I34     720/.92/4 19     *LC* 81-13154     *ISBN* 0295958820

**Wagg, Susan W.**       **1.5349**
Percy Erskine Nobbs: architecte, artiste, artisan / Susan Wagg; [traduction, Cécile Grenier et Suzie Toutant] = Percy Erskine Nobbs: architect, artist, craftsman / Susan Wagg; [translation, Cécile Grenier and Suzie Toutant]. — Kingston [Ont.]: Publié pour le Musée McCord, Université McGill par McGill-Queen's University Presss = Published for the McCord Museum, McGill University by McGill-Queen's University Press, c1982. xii, 99 p.: ill.; 21 x 26 cm. Text in French and English on parallel columns. Exhibition held at the McCord Museum, McGill University, Montreal, Quebec, Apr. 21-July 18, 1982, and other museums. 1. Nobbs, Percy E. (Percy Erskine), 1875-1966 — Exhibitions. 2. Architects — Quebec (Province) — Biography. I. Nobbs, Percy E. (Percy Erskine), 1875-1966. II. McCord Museum. III. T.
NA749.N62 A4 1982     720/.92/4 19     *ISBN* 0773503951

**James, Ellen, 1940-.**       **1.5350**
John Ostell, architecte, arpenteur = John Ostell, architect, surveyor / Ellen James; [traduction, Cécile Grenier et Jocelyne Marquis..., Sarah L. Dawbarn]. — Montreal: McCord Museum, McGill University, 1985. xxi, 112 p.: ill. (some col.), facsim..; 21 x 26 cm. Text in English and French on opposite columns. 1. Ostell, John, 1813-1892. 2. Montréal (Québec) — Buildings. I. McCord Museum. II. T. III. Title: John Ostell, architect, surveyor.
NA749.O88 J34 1985     *ISBN* 0771701063

**Barrett, Anthony, 1941-.**       **1.5351**
Francis Rattenbury and British Columbia: architecture and challenge in the Imperial Age / Anthony A. Barrett & Rhodri Windsor Liscombe. — Vancouver: University of British Columbia Press, 1983. xii, 391 p.: ill.; 24 cm. Includes index. 1. Rattenbury, Francis, 1867-1935. 2. Architects — British Columbia — Biography. 3. Eclecticism in architecture — British Columbia. I. Liscombe, R. W., 1946- II. T.
NA749.R37 B37 1983     720/.92/4 B 19     *LC* 84-146737     *ISBN* 0774801786

**Kubler, George, 1912-.**       • **1.5352**
Mexican architecture of the sixteenth century. — New Haven: Yale University Press, 1948. 2 v. (xxv, 574 p.): ill., ports., maps (part fold.) diagrs., facsims., plans.; 28 cm. — (Yale historical publications. History of art; 5) I. T. II. Series.
NA753.K8

**Goodwin, Philip Lippincott, 1885-.**       • **1.5353**
Brazil builds; architecture new and old, 1652-1942, by Philip L. Goodwin; photographs by G. E. Kidder Smith. New York, The Museum of Modern Art, 1943. 198 p. ill. (some col.) 29 cm. English and Portuguese; added t.-p. in Portuguese. 1. Architecture — Brazil I. Smith, G. E. Kidder (George Everard Kidder), 1913- II. Museum of Modern Art (New York, N.Y.) III. T.
NA 850 G65 1943     *LC* 43-51045

**Papadaki, Stamo.**       • **1.5354**
Oscar Niemeyer. New York, G. Braziller, 1960. 127 p. plates, plans. 26 cm. (The Masters of world architecture series) 1. Niemeyer, Oscar, 1907- I. T. II. Series.
NA859.N5 P27     720.981     *LC* 60-13307

# NA950–1455 Europe

**Pevsner, Nikolaus, Sir, 1902-.**       • **1.5355**
An outline of European architecture / Nikolaus Pevsner. — 7th ed. reprinted (with rev. bibliography). — Harmondsworth, Eng.; Baltimore: Penguin Books, 1963, 1974 printing, c1943. 496 p.: ill.; 20 cm. (Pelican books; A109) Includes index. 1. Architecture — Europe — History. I. T.
NA950.P4 1974     720/.94     *LC* 75-306293     *ISBN* 0140201092

**Pérez Gómez, Alberto, 1949-.**       **1.5356**
[Génesis y superación del funcionalismo en arquitectura. English] Architecture and the crisis of modern science / Alberto Pérez-Gómez. — Cambridge, Mass.: MIT Press, c1983. x, 400 p.: ill.; 24 cm. Revised translation of: Le génesis y superación del funcionalismo en arquitectura. Includes index. 1. Architecture, Modern — 17th-18th centuries — Europe. 2. Functionalism (Architecture) — Europe. 3. Architecture — Philosophy. I. T.
NA956.P413 1983     720/.1 19     *LC* 82-18010     *ISBN* 0262160919

**Mignot, Claude.**       **1.5357**
[Architecture au 19e siècle. English] Architecture of the nineteenth century in Europe / by Claude Mignot; [translated by D.Q. Stephenson]. — New York: Rizzoli, 1984. 322 p.: ill. (some col.); 31 cm. Translation of: L'architecture au 19e siècle. Includes indexes. 1. Architecture, Modern — 19th century — Europe. 2. Architecture — Europe I. T.
NA957.M5313 1984     724 19     *LC* 83-43266     *ISBN* 0847805301

## NA961–997 Britain. Ireland

**Colvin, Howard Montagu.**       **1.5358**
The history of king's works. London, H.M. Stationery Off., 1963. 2 v. This work was commissioned in 1951 by the Ministry of Public Building and Works under its earlier name: Ministry of Works. 1. Architecture — Great Britain 2. Great Britain — Kings and rulers I. Great Britain. Ministry of Public Building and Works. II. T.
NA961.C64     720/.942 19     *LC* 64-1679

**Vitruvius Britannicus: or, The British architect / introd. by John Harris.**       **1.5359**
New York: B. Blom, 1967-1972. 4 v.: ill. map. I. Title: The British architect. NA 961.V52     NA961 V5.     *LC* 67-18052

**Watkin, David, 1941-.**       **1.5360**
English architecture: a concise history / David Watkin. — New York: Oxford University Press, 1979. 216 p.: ill.; 22 cm. Includes index. 1. Architecture — England — History. I. T.
NA961.W37 1979     720/.942     *LC* 79-4409     *ISBN* 0195201477

**Bony, Jean.**       **1.5361**
The English decorated style: Gothic architecture transformed, 1250–1350 / Jean Bony. — Ithaca, N.Y.: Cornell University Press, 1979. 315 p.: ill.; 27 cm. — (The Wrightsman lecture; 10th) Includes index. 1. Architecture — England 2. Architecture, Gothic — England I. T.
NA963.B66     720/.942     *LC* 78-74211     *ISBN* 0801412439

**Fernie, E. C.**       **1.5362**
The architecture of the Anglo–Saxons / Eric Fernie. — New York: Holmes & Meier, c1983. 192 p.: ill.; 26 cm. Includes index. 1. Architecture, Anglo-Saxon I. T.
NA963.F4 1983     720/.941 19     *LC* 83-12915     *ISBN* 0841909121

**Taylor, Harold McCarter, 1907-.**       • **1.5363**
Anglo–Saxon architecture, by H. M. Taylor and Joan Taylor. — Cambridge [Eng.]: University Press, 1965-78. 3 v. (1118 p.): illus.; 29 cm. 1. Architecture, Anglo-Saxon I. Taylor, Joan Sills, joint author. II. T.
NA963.T3     726/.5/0942     *LC* 65-3244     *ISBN* 0521216931

**Webb, Geoffrey Fairbank, 1898-.**       • **1.5364**
Architecture in Britain: the middle Ages / Geoffrey Webb. — Harmondsworth, Middlesex: Penguin Books, 1956. xxi, 234 p., [97] leaves of plates: ill. (some col.); 27 cm. (Pelican history of art. Z12) 1. Architecture — Great Britain — History. 2. Architecture, Medieval I. T. II. Series.
NA963.W4 1965     726/.0941     *LC* 57-927

**Jenkins, Frank.**       • **1.5365**
Architect and patron; a survey of professional relations and practice in England from the sixteenth century to the present day. London, Oxford University Press, 1961. xvi, 254 p. plates. (University of Durham publications) 'An earlier form of this book as submitted in ... 1953 as a dissertation for the degree of master of arts in the University of Durham.' 1. Architects, British 2. Art partonage 3. Architecture — England — History I. T.
NA964 J4 1961     *LC* 61-19793

**Summerson, John Newenham, Sir, 1904-.**       • **1.5366**
Architecture in Britain, 1530 to 1830 / [by] John Summerson. — 6th revised ed. — Harmondsworth; New York [etc.]: Penguin, 1977. 611 p.: ill., maps, plans; 21 cm. — (Pelican history of art. PZ3) Includes index. 1. Architecture — Great Britain 2. Architecture, Renaissance — Great Britain. 3. Architecture, Baroque — Great Britain. 4. Neoclassicism (Architecture) — Great Britain. I. T. II. Series.
NA964.S85 1977     720/.941     *LC* 79-307193     *ISBN* 014056103X

**Davey, Peter.**       **1.5367**
Architecture of the arts and crafts movement / Peter Davey. — New York: Rizzoli, 1980. 224 p.: ill.; 26 cm. Includes index. 1. Gothic revival (Architecture) — Great Britain. 2. Gothic revival (Architecture) — Influence. 3. Arts and crafts movement — Influence. I. T.
NA966.D37 1980     724/.3 19     *LC* 80-51623     *ISBN* 0847803538

**Downes, Kerry.**       **1.5368**
English baroque architecture / Kerry Downes. — London: A. Zwemmer, 1966. — xvi, 135 p., [100] leaves of plates: ill., plans. 1. Architecture, Baroque — Great Britain. I. T.
NA 966.D6     720.942     *LC* 66-71053

**Macaulay, James.**                                    1.5369
The Gothic revival, 1745–1845 / [by] James Macaulay. — Glasgow: Blackie, 1975. xx, 451 p.: ill., plans; 29 cm. Includes index. 1. Gothic revival (Architecture) — Great Britain. 2. Architecture — Great Britain 3. Architecture, Modern — 17th-18th centuries — Great Britain. 4. Architecture, Modern — 19th century — Great Britain I. T.
NA966.M32        720/.9411        LC 76-364822        ISBN 0216898927

**Crook, J. Mordaunt (Joseph Mordaunt), 1937-.**        1.5370
The Greek revival; neo–classical attitudes in British architecture, 1760–1870 [by] J. Mordaunt Crook. [London] J. Murray [1972] xi, 204 p. illus. 24 cm. 1. Neoclassicism (Architecture) — Great Britain. I. T.
NA966.5.N4 C76        720/.942        LC 73-154133        ISBN 0719527244

**Dixon, Roger, 1935-.**                                1.5371
Victorian architecture / Roger Dixon, Stefan Muthesius. — New York: Oxford University Press, 1978. 288 p.: ill. (World of art.) Includes index. 1. Architecture, Victorian — Great Britain. 2. Architecture — Great Britain I. Muthesius, Stefan. II. T. III. Series.
NA967.D59        720/.941        LC 77-26262        ISBN 0195200489

**Hitchcock, Henry Russell, 1903-.**                  • 1.5372
Early Victorian architecture in Britain. New Haven: Yale University Press, 1954. 2 v.: illus., maps, plans; 28 cm. (Yale historical publications. History of art; 9) 1. Architecture — Great Britain I. T.
NA967 H55        LC 54-5085

**Muthesius, Stefan.**                                  1.5373
The High Victorian movement in architecture, 1850–1870. London, Boston, Routledge & K. Paul, 1972. xvii, 252 p. illus., plans. 26 cm. 1. Architecture, Victorian — Great Britain. I. T.
NA967.M83        720/.942        LC 72-193291        ISBN 0710070713

**Watkin, David, 1941-.**                               1.5374
Regency: a guide and gazetteer / David Watkin. — London: Barrie & Jenkins, 1982. 192 p.: ill., maps, plans. — (Buildings of Britain) 1. Architecture, Regency — Great Britain — Guide-books I. T. II. Series.
NA967 W37        ISBN 0091479916

**Summerson, John Newenham, Sir, 1904-.**               1.5375
Georgian London / John Summerson. — 3d ed. — Cambridge, Mass.: MIT Press, 1978. 348 p., [24] leaves of plates: ill.; 22 cm. '1st MIT Press ed.' Includes index. 1. Architecture — England — London. 2. Architecture, Georgian — England — London. I. T.
NA970.S8 1978        720/.9421        LC 78-53798        ISBN 0262191733

**Craig, Maurice James.**                               1.5376
The architecture of Ireland: from the earliest times to 1880 / Maurice Craig. — London: Batsford distributed by David & Charles, 1983, [c1982] 358 p.: ill.; 26 cm. Includes index. 1. Architecture — Ireland. I. T.
NA982.C72 1983        720/.9415 19        LC 83-200312        ISBN 0713425865

**Eastlake, Charles L. (Charles Locke), 1836-1906.**   • 1.5377
A history of the Gothic revival [by] Charles L. Eastlake; edited with an introduction by J. Mordaunt Crook. Leicester, Leicester U.P., New York, Humanities P., 1970. xviii, 372, 209 p., 35 plates. illus. 25 cm. (The Victorian library) Facsimile reprint of 1st ed., London, Longmans, 1872. 1. Architecture — England — History. 2. Gothic revival (Architecture) I. Crook, J. Mordaunt (Joseph Mordaunt), 1937- ed. II. T. III. Title: Gothic revival.
NA988.E17 1872a        720/.942        LC 70-17391        ISBN 0718550056

**Colvin, Howard Montagu.**                            • 1.5378
A biographical dictionary of British architects, 1600–1840 / Howard Colvin. — London: J. Murray, 1978. 1080 p.: geneal. tabs.; 25 cm. Rev. and enl. ed. of the author's A biographical dictionary of English architects, 1600-1840. Includes indexes. 1. Architects — Great Britain — Biography. I. T.
NA996.C6 1978        720/.92/2 B        LC 78-313391        ISBN 0719533287

## NA997 Architects, A–Z

**Adam, Robert, 1728-1792.**                            1.5379
The works in architecture of Robert & James Adam / with a new introduction by Henry Hope Reed. — New York: Dover Publications, 1980. 131 p.: ill. Reprint. Originally published: London, 1778-1822. 1. Adam, Robert, 1728-1792. 2. Adam, James, d. 1794. 3. Neoclassicism (Architecture) — Great Britain. I. Adam, James, d. 1794. II. T.
NA997.A4 A4 1980        720/.92/4 19        LC 78-62405        ISBN 0486238105

**Fleming, John, 1919-.**                              • 1.5380
Robert Adam and his circle in Edinburgh and Rome / John Fleming. — Cambridge, Mass.: Harvard University Press, 1962. xii, 393 p., [22] leaves of plates: ill., facsims., ports.; 23 cm. 1. Adam, Robert, 1728-1792 — Biography. 2. Adams family 3. Architects — Great Britain — Biography. I. T.
NA997.A4 F55        LC 62-2399

**Lees-Milne, James.**                                 • 1.5381
The age of Adam / by James Lees–Milne. — London: B.T. Batsford, 1947. — viii, 184 p., [46] leaves of plates: ill.; 22 cm. Includes index. 1. Adam, Robert, 1728-1792. 2. Adam, James, d. 1794. 3. Architecture — Great Britain 4. Decoration and ornament, Architectural — Great Britain. I. T.
NA997.A4 L4        720/.92/4 B        LC 48-3247

**Rykwert, Joseph, 1926-.**                             1.5382
Robert and James Adam: the men and the style / Joseph and Anne Rykwert. — Milano: Electa; New York: Rizzoli, 1985. 223 p.: ill. (some col.); 25 cm. (Architectural documents.) Includes index. 1. Adam, Robert, 1728-1792 — Criticism and interpretation. 2. Adam, James, d. 1794 — Criticism and interpretation. 3. Neoclassicism (Architecture) — Great Britain. 4. Decoration and ornament — Great Britain — Neoclassicism. I. Rykwert, Anne. II. T. III. Series.
NA997.A4 R95 1985        720/.92/4 19        LC 84-43099        ISBN 0847805891

**Thompson, Paul Richard, 1935-.**                     1.5383
William Butterfield / Paul Thompson. — Cambridge, Mass.: M.I.T. Press, 1971. xxix, 526 p., [6] f. de planches: ill. (certaines en coul.) plans, portr., table; 26 cm. 1. Butterfield, William, 1814-1900. I. T.
NA997B988 T471 1971        720/.924        LC 79-169976        ISBN 0262200201

**Harris, John, 1931-.**                                1.5384
Sir William Chambers, Knight of the Polar Star. With contributions by J. Mordaunt Crook and Eileen Harris. — University Park: Pennsylvania State University Press, [c1970] xvi, 397 p.: illus., plans, ports.; 31 cm. — (Studies in architecture, v. 9) 1. Chambers, William, Sir, 1726-1796. I. T.
NA997.C5 H3 1970        720/.924        LC 70-113198

**Cantacuzino, Sherban.**                              1.5385   — ∂ —
Wells Coates, a monograph / Sherban Cantacuzino. — London: G. Fraser, 1978. 119 p.: ill.; 31 cm. 1. Coates, Wells, 1895-1958. I. T.
NA997.C59 C36        720/.91/4 B        LC 79-307584        ISBN 0900406593

**Watkin, David, 1941-.**                              1.5386
The life and work of C. R. Cockerell / [by] David Watkin. — London: Zwemmer, 1974. xxiii, 272 p., [2] leaves, [94] p. of plates, leaf of plate: ill., facsims., plans, ports; 26 cm. (Studies in architecture; v. 14) Includes index. 1. Cockerell, Charles Robert, 1788-1863. I. T.
NA997.C6 W38        720/.92/4 B        LC 75-324386        ISBN 0302025715

**Friedman, Terry.**                                    1.5387
James Gibbs / Terry Friedman. — New Haven, Conn.: Published for the Paul Mellon Centre for Studies in British Art by Yale University Press, 1984. vi, 362 p.: ill. (some col.); 29 cm. 'Gibbs's fine art library': p. [327]-330. Includes index. 1. Gibbs, James, 1682-1754. 2. Architecture, Modern — 17th-18th centuries — Great Britain. I. T.
NA997.G5 F73 1984        720/.92/4 19        LC 84-40184        ISBN 0300031726

**Downes, Kerry.**                                      1.5388
Hawksmoor / Kerry Downes. — 2d ed., 1st MIT Press ed. — Cambridge, Mass.: MIT Press, 1980, c1979. xvi, 298 p., [48] leaves of plates: ill.; 26 cm. Includes index. 1. Hawksmoor, Nicholas, 1661-1736. I. T.
NA997.H3 D6 1980        720/.92/4 B 19        LC 79-90962        ISBN 0262040603

**Harris, John, 1931-.**                                1.5389
The King's Arcadia—Inigo Jones and the Stuart court: a quatercentenary exhibition held at the Banqueting House, Whitehall, from July 12th to September 2nd, 1973, catalogue by John Harris, Stephen Orgel and Roy Strong. — [London]: Arts Council of Great Britain, 1973. 232 p.: illus., facsims., plans, ports.; 24 cm. Includes index. 1. Jones, Inigo, 1573-1652. I. Jones, Inigo, 1573-1652. II. Orgel, Stephen. joint author. III. Strong, Roy C. joint author. IV. Whitehall Palace. V. T.
NA997.J7 H37        720/.92/4        LC 73-177808        ISBN 0900085894

**Lees-Milne, James.**                                 • 1.5390
The age of Inigo Jones. London, Batsford [1953] 242 p. ill., ports. 1. Jones, Inigo, 1573-1652. 2. Architecture — England 3. Decoration and ornament, Architectural I. T.
NA997 J7 L4        LC A 54-777

**Summerson, John Newenham, Sir, 1904-.**             • 1.5391
Inigo Jones, by John Summerson. — Harmondsworth: Penguin, 1966. 149 p.: illus. (incl. port.) plans.; 20 cm. — (The Architect and society) Pelican book A839. 1. Jones, Inigo, 1573-1652. I. T.
NA997.J7 S8 1966        720.924 B        LC 67-76465

**Irving, Robert Grant, 1940-.**                       1.5392
Indian summer: Lutyens, Baker, and Imperial Delhi / Robert Grant Irving. — New Haven: Yale University Press, 1981. x, 406 p.: ill. (some col.); 27 cm. Includes index. 1. Lutyens, Edwin Landseer, Sir, 1869-1944. 2. Baker,

Herbert, Sir, 1862-1946. 3. Architecture — India — New Delhi — British influences 4. Buildings — India — New Delhi. 5. New Delhi (India) — Buildings, structures, etc. I. T.
NA997.L8 I7 1981     722/.44/56 19     *LC* 81-14648     *ISBN* 0300024223

**Mackintosh, Charles Rennie, 1868-1928.**        **1.5393**
Mackintosh architecture: the complete buildings and selected projects / edited by Jackie Cooper; foreword by David Dunster; introd. by Barbara Bernard. — New York: Rizzoli, 1980. 111 p., [8] leaves of plates: chiefly ill.; 29 cm. Includes index. 1. Mackintosh, Charles Rennie, 1868-1928. 2. Eclecticism in architecture — Great Britain. I. Cooper, Jackie. II. T.
NA997.M3 A4 1980     720/.92/4 19     *LC* 80-51133     *ISBN* 0847803309

**Howarth, Thomas, 1914-.**        • **1.5394**
Charles Rennie Mackintosh and the modern movement / by Thomas Howarth. — New York: Wittenborn, 1953. xxviii, 329 p., [48] leaves of plates: ill., ports.; 26 cm. 1. Mackintosh, Charles Rennie, 1868-1928. I. T.
NA997.M3 H6 1953     *LC* 53-13143

**Summerson, John Newenham, Sir, 1904-.**        **1.5395**
The life and work of John Nash, architect / John Summerson. — 1st MIT Press ed. — Cambridge, Mass.: MIT Press, 1980. 217 p., [24] leaves of plates: ill.; 26 cm. 1. Nash, John, 1752-1835. 2. Architects — England — Biography. I. T.
NA997.N3 S85 1980     720/.92/4 B     *LC* 80-14011     *ISBN* 0262191903

**Quiney, Anthony, 1935-.**        **1.5396**
John Loughborough Pearson / Anthony Quiney. — New Haven: Published for the Paul Mellon Centre for Studies in British Art by Yale University Press, 1979. 306 p.: ill.; 27 cm. — (Studies in British art.) Includes index. 1. Pearson, John Loughborough, 1817-1897. 2. Architects — England — Biography. I. T. II. Series.
NA997.P39 Q56 1979     720/.92/4 B     *LC* 79-9832     *ISBN* 0300022530

**Stanton, Phoebe B.**        **1.5397**
Pugin [by] Phoebe Stanton. Pref. by Nikolaus Pevsner. — New York: Viking Press, [1972, c1971] 216 p.: illus.; 22 cm. — (A Studio book) 1. Pugin, Augustus Welby Northmore, 1812-1852. I. T.
NA997.P9 S7 1972     720.9/24     *LC* 78-172898     *ISBN* 0670582166

**Curl, James Stevens, 1937-.**        **1.5398**
The life and work of Henry Roberts, 1803–1876: the evangelical conscience and the campaign for model housing and healthy nations / James Stevens Curl. — Chichester, Sussex: Phillimore, 1983. xxii, 273 p., [64] p. of plates: ill.; 26 cm. Includes index. 1. Roberts, Henry, 1803-1876. 2. Architects — England — Biography. 3. Architecture, Victorian — England. I. T.
NA997.R6 C87 1983     720/.92/4 B 19     *LC* 84-123966     *ISBN* 0850334462

**Saint, Andrew.**        **1.5399**
Richard Norman Shaw / Andrew Saint. New Haven: Published for the Paul Mellon Centre for Studies in British Art (London) by Yale University Press, 1976. xx, 487 p.: ill.; 26 cm. (Studies in British art.) Includes index. 1. Shaw, Richard Norman, 1831-1912. 2. Architects — Great Britain — Biography. I. Paul Mellon Centre for Studies in British Art. II. T. III. Series.
NA997.S5 S35     720/.92/4     *LC* 75-4333     *ISBN* 0300019556

**Girouard, Mark, 1931-.**        **1.5400**
Robert Smythson & the Elizabethan country house / Mark Girouard. — New Haven: Yale University Press, 1983. viii, 328 p.: ill. (some col.); 27 cm. Updated ed. of: Robert Smythson and the architecture of the Elizabethan era. 1967. Facims. on lining papers. 1. Smythson, Robert, 1534 or 5-1614. 2. Architecture, Elizabethan — England. 3. Country homes — England I. Girouard, Mark, 1931- Robert Smythson and the architecture of the Elizabethan era. II. T. III. Title: Robert Smythson and the Elizabethan country house.
NA997.S6 G5 1983     720/.92/4 19     *LC* 83-50004     *ISBN* 0300031343

**Du Prey, Pierre de la Ruffinière.**        **1.5401**
John Soane, the making of an architect / Pierre de la Ruffinière du Prey. — Chicago: University of Chicago Press, 1982. xxiv, 408 p., [8] p. of plates: ill. (some col.); 23 cm. Includes index. 1. Soane, John, Sir, 1753-1837. 2. Architects — England — Biography. 3. Neoclassicism (Architecture) — England. I. T.
NA997.S7 D85 1982     720/.92/4 B 19     *LC* 81-16453     *ISBN* 0226172988

**John Soane.**        **1.5402**
London: Academy Editions; New York: St. Martin's Press, 1983. 123 p., [6] folded leaves of plates: ill. (some col.); 30 cm. — (Architectural monographs) Summaries in French, German, Italian, and Spanish. 1. Soane, John, Sir,

1753-1837 — Addresses, essays, lectures. 2. Neoclassicism (Architecture) — England — Addresses, essays, lectures.
NA997.S7 J6 1983     720/.92/4 19     *LC* 82-62490     *ISBN* 0312048114

**Stroud, Dorothy.**        • **1.5403**
Sir John Soane, architect / Dorothy Stroud. — London; Boston: Faber & Faber, 1984. 300 p.: ill.; 26 cm. Includes index. 1. Soane, John, Sir, 1753-1837. I. Soane, John, Sir, 1753-1837. II. T.
NA997.S7 S76 1984     720/.92/4 19     *LC* 83-11488     *ISBN* 057113050X

**Bingham, Madeleine, Baroness Clanmorris.**        **1.5404**
Masks and façades: Sir John Vanbrugh: the man in his setting / Madeleine Bingham. — London: Allen & Unwin, 1974. 376 p., [12] leaves of plates: ill.; 22 cm. Includes index. 1. Vanbrugh, John, Sir, 1664-1726. I. T.
NA997.V3 B56     822/.4 B     *LC* 74-194545     *ISBN* 0049280295

**Downes, Kerry.**        **1.5405**
Vanbrugh / by Kerry Downes. — London: A. Zwemmer, c1977. xiv, 291 p., [48] leaves of plates: ill.; 30 cm. — (Studies in architecture; v. 16) Includes indexes. 1. Vanbrugh, John, Sir, 1664-1726. 2. Architects — England — Biography. 3. Architecture, Baroque — England. I. T.
NA997.V3 D68     720/.92/4 B     *LC* 78-354492     *ISBN* 0839002076

**Liscombe, R. W., 1946-.**        **1.5406**
William Wilkins, 1778–1839 / R. W. Liscombe. — Cambridge [Eng.]; New York: Cambridge University Press, 1980. xv, 297 p., [48] leaves of plates: ill.; 24 cm. Includes index. 1. Wilkins, William, 1778-1839. 2. Architects — England — Biography. 3. Architecture, Regency — England. I. T.
NA997.W48 L57     720/.92/4 B     *LC* 78-73247     *ISBN* 0521225280

**Downes, Kerry.**        **1.5407**
The architecture of Wren / Kerry Downes. — New York: Universe Books, 1982. xviii, 139 p., [96] p. of plates: ill.; 26 cm. 1. Wren, Christopher, Sir, 1632-1723. 2. Architects — England — Biography. I. T.
NA997.W8 D59 1982     720/.92/4 B 19     *LC* 82-8425     *ISBN* 0876633955

**Summerson, John Newenham, Sir, 1904-.**        • **1.5408**
Sir Christopher Wren / by John Summerson. — Hamden: Archon Books, 1965. 159 p.: ill., plans, port.; 21cm. — (Makers of history) 1. Wren, Christopher, Sir, 1632-1723. I. T.
NA997.W8 S8 1965a     *LC* 65-19160

**Linstrum, Derek.**        **1.5409**
Sir Jeffry Wyatville: architect to the king. — Oxford: Clarendon Press, 1972. xvi, 279 p., [3] fold. leaves.: illus., geneal. table, plans, ports.; 30 cm. — (Oxford studies in the history of art and architecture.) 1. Wyatville, Jeffry, Sir, 1776-1840. I. T. II. Series.
NA997.W95 L56     720/.92/4     *LC* 73-154086     *ISBN* 0198171900

## NA1001–1011.5 AUSTRIA

**Aurenhammer, Hans.**        **1.5410**
J. B. Fischer von Erlach. — Cambridge, Mass.: Harvard University Press, 1973. 193 p.: illus.; 26 cm. 1. Fischer von Erlach, Johann Bernhard, 1656-1723. I. Fischer von Erlach, Johann Bernhard, 1656-1723. II. T.
NA1011.5.F57 A94 1973b     720/.92/4     *LC* 73-83421     *ISBN* 0674469887

**Gravagnuolo, Benedetto.**        **1.5411**
Adolf Loos, theory and works / Benedetto Gravagnuolo; preface by Aldo Rossi; photography, Roberto Schezen; [English translation by C. H. Evans]. — New York: Rizzoli, 1982. 228 p.: ill. (some col.); 28 cm. — (Idea Books architectural series.) 1. Loos, Adolf, 1870-1933. 2. Architecture, Modern — 20th century — Austria. I. Evans, C. H. II. T. III. Series.
NA1011.5.L6 G7 1982     720/.92/4 19     *LC* 81-51716     *ISBN* 0847804143

**Geretsegger, Heinz.**        **1.5412**
Otto Wagner 1841–1918: the expanding city, the beginning of modern architecture / by Heinz Geretsegger and Max Peintner; associate author Walter Pichler; introd. by Richard Neutra; translated by Gerald Onn. — English language ed. — New York: Rizzoli, 1979. 272 p.: ill; 28 cm. Includes index. 1. Wagner, Otto, 1841-1918. I. Peintner, Max. joint author. II. Pichler, Walter, 1936- joint author. III. T.
NA1011.5.W3 G413 1979     720/.92/4 B     *LC* 78-68493     *ISBN* 0847802175

## NA1041–1053 FRANCE

**Braham, Allan.**  **1.5413**
The architecture of the French Enlightenment / Allan Braham. — Berkeley: University of California Press, c1980. 288 p.: ill.; 28 cm. Includes index. 1. Neoclassicism (Architecture) — France. 2. Architecture — France. 3. Architecture, Modern — 17th-18th centuries — France. I. T.
NA1046.B75  720/.944  *LC* 79-3606  *ISBN* 0520041178

**Boullée, Etienne Louis, 1728-1799.**  • **1.5414**
Treatise on architecture: a complete presentation of the Architecture, essai sur l'art, which forms part of the Boullée papers (Ms. 9153) in the Bibliothèque nationale, Paris / edite by Helen Rosenau. — London: A. Tiranti, 1953. ix, 131 p.: ill., plans.; 22 cm. Text in French, introd. and notes in English. I. Rosenau, Helen. ed II. T.
NA1053.B6x  *LC* 55-2103

**Tadgell, Christopher, 1939-.**  **1.5415**
Ange–Jacques Gabriel / by Christopher Tadgell. — London: A. Zwemmer, c1978. xxv, 215 p., [75] leaves of plates: ill. (some col.); 31 cm. — (Studies in architecture; v. 19) Includes index. 1. Gabriel, Jacques Ange, 1698-1782. 2. Architecture, Modern — 17th-18th centuries — France. I. T.
NA1053.G3 T33  720/.92/4  *LC* 79-305320  *ISBN* 0302027815

**Blake, Peter, 1920-.**  • **1.5416**
The master builders. — [1st ed.]. — New York: Knopf, 1960. 399 p.: illus.; 25 cm. 1. Le Corbusier, 1887-1965. 2. Mies van der Rohe, Ludwig, 1886-1969. 3. Wright, Frank Lloyd, 1867-1959. 4. Architecture, Modern — 20th century I. T.
NA1053.J4 B55  724.9  *LC* 60-10276

**Moos, Stanislaus von.**  **1.5417**
[Corbusier, Elemente einer Synthese. English] Le Corbusier, elements of a synthesis / Stanislaus von Moos. — Cambridge, Mass.: MIT Press, c1979. viii, 379 p.: ill.; 24 cm. Translation of Le Corbusier, Elemente einer Synthese. 1. Le Corbusier, 1887-1965. I. T.
NA1053.J4 M613  720/.92/4  *LC* 78-25940  *ISBN* 0262220237

**Sekler, Eduard F. (Eduard Franz)**  **1.5418**
Le Corbusier at work: the genesis of the Carpenter Center for the Visual Arts / Eduard F. Sekler, William Curtis; with contributions by Rudolph Arnheim, Barbara Norfleet. — Cambridge: Harvard University Press, 1978. ix, 357 p.: ill.; 29 cm. Includes index. 1. Le Corbusier, 1887-1965. 2. Carpenter Center for Visual Arts. I. Curtis, William, 1948- joint author. II. T.
NA1053.J4 S44  727/.4/7  *LC* 77-7315  *ISBN* 0674520599

**Braham, Allan.**  **1.5419**
François Mansart [by] Allan Braham and Peter Smith. — London: A. Zwemmer, 1974 [c1973] 2 v.: illus.; 31 cm. — (Studies in architecture, v. 13) 'Partly based on two theses submitted at the Courtauld Institute—François Mansart as a designer of hotels (1965) by Peter Smith, and François Mansart's drawings for the Louvre (1967) by Allan Braham.' 1. Mansart, François, 1598-1666. 2. Architecture, Baroque — France. I. Smith, Peter R. II. T.
NA1053.M25 B72  720/.92/4  *LC* 74-169454  *ISBN* 0302022511

**Villard, de Honnecourt, 13th cent.**  • **1.5420**
[Album de Villard de Honnecourt. English] The sketchbook of Villard de Honnecourt. Edited by Theodore Bowie. Bloomington, Indiana University Press [196-,c1959] 144 p. facsims. 21 cm. 1. Architecture, Medieval 2. Architecture — Early works to 1800. I. T.
NA1053.V6 A423  *LC* 68-14615

**Eugène Emmanuel Viollet–le–Duc, 1814–1879.**  • **1.5421**
[New York, N.Y.]: Rizzoli, [c1980] 96 p.: ill. (some col.); 28 cm. (Architectural design profile.) Cover title: Viollet-le-Duc. Publisher taken from label on p. 3. 1. Viollet-le-Duc, Eugène-Emmanuel, 1814-1879. I. Title: Viollet-le-Duc. II. Series.
NA1053.V7 E9  720/.92/4 19  *LC* 81-110823  *ISBN* 0847853136

## NA1061–1088 GERMANY

**Hitchcock, Henry Russell, 1903-.**  **1.5422**
German Renaissance architecture / Henry–Russell Hitchcock. — Princeton, N.J.: Princeton University Press, c1981. xxxiv, 379 p., [131] leaves of plates: ill.; 29 cm. 1. Architecture, Renaissance — Germany. 2. Architecture — Germany. I. T.
NA1065.H57  720/.943  *LC* 80-16399  *ISBN* 0691039593

**Lane, Barbara Miller.**  • **1.5423**
Architecture and politics in Germany, 1918–1945. — Cambridge, Mass.: Harvard University Press, 1968. 278 p.: illus.; 25 cm. 1. National socialism and architecture. 2. Architecture — Germany. I. T.
NA1068.L3  720/.943  *LC* 67-22867

**Von Eckardt, Wolf.**  • **1.5424**
Eric Mendelsohn. — New York: G. Braziller, 1960. 128 p.: illus., plates.; 26 cm. — (The Masters of world architecture series) 'Selected bibliography of books and articles written by Eric Mendelsohn': p. 119. 'Selected bibliography on Eric Mendelsohn': p. 121. 1. Mendelsohn, Erich, 1887-1953. I. T. II. Series.
NA1088.M57 V6  720.943  *LC* 60-14514

**Museum of Modern Art (New York, N.Y.)**  • **1.5425**
Mies van der Rohe / by Philip C. Johnson. — 2d ed., rev. — New York: The Museum, c1953. — 215 p.: ill., plans; 26 cm. 1. Mies van der Rohe, Ludwig, 1886-1969. I. Johnson, Philip, 1906- II. T.
NA1088.M65 N4 1953  *LC* 54-7774

**Schulze, Franz, 1927-.**  **1.5426**
Mies van der Rohe: a critical biography / Franz Schulze in association with the Mies van der Rohe Archive of the Museum of Modern Art. — Chicago: University of Chicago Press, 1985. xxiii, 355 p.: ill.; 27 cm. Includes index. 1. Mies van der Rohe, Ludwig, 1886-1969. 2. Architects — Germany — Biography. 3. Architects — United States — Biography. I. Mies van der Rohe Archive. II. T.
NA1088.M65 S38 1985  720/.92/4 B 19  *LC* 85-8488  *ISBN* 0226740595

**Spaeth, David A.**  **1.5427**
Mies van der Rohe / David Spaeth; pref. by Kenneth Frampton. — New York: Rizzoli, c1985. 205 p.: ill.; 26 cm. Includes index. 1. Mies van der Rohe, Ludwig, 1886-1969. 2. Architecture, Modern — 20th century — Germany. 3. Architecture, Modern — 20th century — United States I. T.
NA1088.M65 S54 1985  720/.92/4 19  *LC* 84-42768  *ISBN* 0847805638

**Otto, Christian F.**  **1.5428**
Space into light: the churches of Balthasar Neumann / Christian F. Otto. — New York: Architectural History Foundation, c1979. 296 p.: ill. (some col.); 26 cm. — (The Architectural History Foundation/MIT Press series; 2) Includes index. 1. Neumann, Balthasar, 1687-1754. 2. Church architecture — Germany. 3. Architecture, Modern — 17th-18th centuries — Germany. 4. Light in architecture 5. Space (Architecture) I. T.
NA1088.N4 O87  726/.5/0924 19  *LC* 78-27782  *ISBN* 0262150190

**Whyte, Iain Boyd, 1947-.**  **1.5429**
Bruno Taut and the architecture of activism / Iain Boyd Whyte. — Cambridge [Cambridgeshire]; New York: Cambridge University Press, 1982. xiii, 280 p.: ill.; 26 cm. (Cambridge urban and architectural studies. no. 6) Based on the author's thesis (doctoral—University of Cambridge) 1978. Includes index. 1. Taut, Bruno, 1880-1938 — Influence. 2. Functionalism (Architecture) — Germany. I. T. II. Series.
NA1088.T33 W47 1982  720/.92/4 19  *LC* 81-12301  *ISBN* 052123655X

## NA1111–1123 ITALY

**Burckhardt, Jacob, 1818-1897.**  **1.5430**
[Geschichte der Renaissance. English] The architecture of the Italian Renaissance / Jacob Burckhardt; revised and edited by Peter Murray; translated by James Palmes. — Chicago: University of Chicago Press, c1985. xxxv, 283 p.: ill.; 29 cm. Translation of: Die Geschichte der Renaissance. Includes indexes. 1. Architecture, Renaissance — Italy. 2. Architecture — Italy I. Murray, Peter, 1920- II. Palmes, J. C. (James C.) III. T.
NA1115.B813 1985  720/.945 19  *LC* 83-18113  *ISBN* 0226080471

**Heydenreich, Ludwig Heinrich, 1903-.**  **1.5431**
Architecture in Italy, 1400 to 1600 [by] Ludwig H. Heydenreich and Wolfgang Lotz. Translated by Mary Hottinger. — [Harmondsworth, Eng.]: Penguin Books, [1974] xxvii, 432 p., [112] leaves of plates: illus.; 27 cm. — (The Pelican history of Art) 1. Architecture — Italy 2. Architecture, Renaissance — Italy. 3. Mannerism (Architecture) — Italy. I. Lotz, Wolfgang, 1912- II. T.
NA1115.H4913  720/.945  *LC* 74-179842  *ISBN* 0140560386

**Murray, Peter.**  • **1.5432**
The architecture of the Italian renaissance / Peter Murray. — New York: Schocken Books, [1964,c1963]. xviii, 268 p.: ill., plans; 21 cm. 1. Architecture — Italy 2. Architecture, Renaissance I. T.
NA1115.M8  720.945  *LC* 64-11469  *ISBN* 0805201343

**Wölfflin, Heinrich, 1864-1945.**  • **1.5433**
[Renaissance und Barock. English] Renaissance and baroque. Translated by Kathrin Simon. With an introd. by Peter Murray. Ithaca, N.Y., Cornell University Press [1966] 183 p. illus., plans. 23 cm. 1. Architecture, Renaissance — Italy. 2. Architecture, Baroque — Italy 3. Architecture, Italian I. T.
NA1115.W613 1966  724.19  *LC* 65-22724

**Blunt, Anthony, Sir, 1907-.**    **1.5434**
Guide to Baroque Rome / Anthony Blunt. — 1st. U.S. ed. — New York: Harper & Row, c1982. xviii, 317 p.: ill., facsims., plans. (Icon editions) 1. Architecture, Baroque — Italy — Rome (City). 2. Rome (Italy) — Buildings — Guide-books I. T.
NA1120.B55    *LC* 82-47546    *ISBN* 0064303950

**Goldthwaite, Richard A.**    **1.5435**
The building of Renaissance Florence: an economic and social history / Richard A. Goldthwaite. — Baltimore: Johns Hopkins University Press, 1981 (c1980). xviii, 459 p.: ill.; 24 cm. 1. Construction industry — Italy — Florence — History. 2. Architecture — Italy — Florence — History. 3. Florence (Italy) — Economic conditions. 4. Florence (Italy) — Social conditions. 5. Florence (Italy) — History I. T.
NA1121.F5 G6x    338.4/7624/094551    *LC* 80-7995    *ISBN* 0801823420

**Lieberman, Ralph.**    **1.5436**
Renaissance architecture in Venice 1450–1540 / Ralph Lieberman. — New York: Abbeville Press, c1982. 144 p.: ill. (some col.); 25 x 30 cm. Includes index. 1. Architecture, Renaissance — Italy — Venice. I. T.
NA1121.V4 L53    *ISBN* 089639310X

**McAndrew, John.**    **1.5437**
Venetian architecture of the early Renaissance / John McAndrew. — Cambridge, Mass.: MIT Press, c1980. xiii, 599 p.: ill.; 29 cm. Includes index. 1. Architecture, Renaissance — Italy — Venice. 2. Architecture — Italy — Venice. 3. Buildings — Italy — Venice. 4. Venice (Italy) — Buildings, structures, etc. I. T.
NA1121.V4 M32    720/.945/31    *LC* 80-17045    *ISBN* 0262131579

**Blunt, Anthony, 1907-1983.**    **1.5438**
Borromini / by Anthony Blunt. — Cambridge, Mass.: Harvard University Press, [1979] 240 p.: ill., plans; 24 cm. Includes index. 1. Borromini, Francesco, 1599-1667. 2. Architects — Italy — Biography. 3. Architecture, Baroque — Italy I. T.
NA1123.B6 B56    720/.92/4    *LC* 78-11320    *ISBN* 0674079256

**Battisti, Eugenio.**    **1.5439**
[Filippo Brunelleschi. English] Filippo Brunelleschi: the complete work / Eugenio Battisti; [translated from Italian, Filippo Brunelleschi by Robert Erich Wolf; text revised by Eugenio Battisti and Emily Lane]. — New York: Rizzoli, 1982. 400 p.: ill.; 30 cm. Includes index. 1. Brunelleschi, Filippo, 1377-1446. 2. Architects — Italy — Biography. I. Brunelleschi, Filippo, 1377-1446. II. T.
NA1123.B8 B3613 1981    720/.92/4 19    *LC* 78-68509    *ISBN* 0847850153

**Manetti, Antonio, 1423-1497.**    **1.5440**
[Vita di Filippo di Ser Brunelleschi. English & Italian] The life of Brunelleschi, by Antonio di Tuccio Manetti. Introd., notes, and critical text ed. by Howard Saalman. English translation of the Italian text by Catherine Enggass. University Park, Pennsylvania State University Press [1970] vii, 176 p. illus., facsims. 24 cm. English and Italian. Translation of Vita di Filippo di Ser Brunelleschi. 1. Brunelleschi, Filippo, 1377-1446. I. T.
NA1123.B8 M33    720/.924 B    *LC* 68-8183    *ISBN* 0271000759

**Ackerman, James S.**    • **1.5441**
The architecture of Michelangelo: catalogue / James S. Ackermann. — Rev. ed. — London: A. Zwemmer, 1964, c1961. vii, 152 p. — (Studies in architecture; v. 5) 1. Michelangelo Buonarroti, 1475-1564. I. Michelangelo Buonarroti, 1475-1564. II. T.
NA1123.B9 A63 1964    *LC* 67-46321

**Hibbard, Howard, 1928-.**    **1.5442**
Carlo Maderno and Roman architecture, 1580–1630. University Park, Pennsylvania State University Press 1972, [cc1971] xvi, 404 p. illus. 31 cm. (Studies in architecture, v. 10) English or Italian. 'Catalogue': p. 107-234. 1. Maderno, Carlo, 1556-1629. 2. Architecture — Rome (City) I. T.
NA1123.M3 H5    720/.92/4 B    *LC* 73-37774

## NA1125–1455 Other European Countries

**Collins, George Roseborough, 1917-.**    **1.5443**
The designs and drawings of Antonio Gaudí / George R. Collins, Juan Bassegoda Nonell. — Princeton, N.J.: Princeton University Press, c1983. 326 p. 1. Gaudí, Antoni, 1852-1926. I. Bassegoda Nonell, Juan. II. T.
NA1313.G3 C63 1983    720/.92/4 19    *LC* 81-8596    *ISBN* 0691039852

**Martinell, César, 1888-1973.**    **1.5444**
[Gaudí: su vida, su teoría, su obra. English] Gaudí: his life, his theories, his work / César Martinell; translated from the Spanish by Judith Rohrer; edited by George R. Collins. — Cambridge, Mass.: MIT Press, [1975] 486 p.: ill. (some col.); 28 cm. Translation of Gaudí: su vida, su teoría, su obra. Includes indexes. 1. Gaudí, Antoni, 1852-1926. 2. Architects — Spain — Biography. I. T.
NA1313.G3 M2813 1975    720/.92/4 B    *LC* 74-109    *ISBN* 0262130726

**Pearson, Paul David, 1936-.**    **1.5445**
Alvar Aalto and the international style / by Paul David Pearson. — New York: Whitney Library of Design, 1978. 240 p.: ill.; 29 cm. Includes index. 1. Aalto, Alvar, 1898-1976. 2. International style (Architecture) I. T.
NA1455.F53 A255    720/.92/4 B    *LC* 77-20029    *ISBN* 0823070239

## NA1460–1605 Asia. Africa. Australia

**Fergusson, James, 1808-1886.**    • **1.5446**
History of Indian and eastern architecture. Rev. and edited, with additions [on] Indian architecture, by James Burgess, and Eastern architecture, by R. Phene Spiers. Delhi, Munshiram Manoharlal [1967] 2 v. illus., maps (part fold.), plans, plates, port. 22 cm. First published in 1876. 'This edition is reprinted from the revised edition of 1910.' 'Select bibliography of Fergusson's works': v. 1, p. vii-ix. Bibliographical footnotes. 1. Architecture — India 2. Architecture, Oriental I. Burgess, James, 1832-1916. ed. II. Spiers, Richard Phené, 1838-1916. ed. III. T.
NA1460.F3 1967    720/.954    *LC* SA 67-6740

**Brown, Percy, 1872-1955.**    • **1.5447**
Indian architecture. — [5th ed.]. — Bombay: D. B. Taraporevala, [1965-68] 2 v.: illus. maps., plans.; 29 cm. 1. Architecture — India — History. I. T.
NA1501.B724    *LC* sa 68-12828

**Liang, Ssu-ch'eng, 1901-.**    **1.5448**
A pictorial history of Chinese architecture: a study of the development of its structural system and the evolution of its types / Liang Ssu-ch'eng; edited by Wilma Fairbank. — Cambridge, Mass.: MIT Press, c1984. xxiv, 200 p., [1] leaf of plates: ill.; 29 x 32 cm. Includes index. 1. Architecture — China I. Fairbank, Wilma. II. T.
NA1540.L536 1984    720/.951 19    *LC* 83-25607    *ISBN* 0262121034

**Pirazzoli-t'Serstevens, Michèle.**    **1.5449**
[Chine. English] Living architecture: Chinese. Research by Nicholas Bouvier, assisted by Denise Blum. English translation: Robert Allen. New York, Grosset & Dunlap [c1971] 191 p. illus. 22 cm. (Living architecture) Translation of Chine. 1. Architecture — China I. T.
NA1540.P513    722/.1    *LC* 75-170730

**Wu, Nelson Ikon, 1919-.**    • **1.5450**
Chinese and Indian architecture; the city of man, the Mountain of God, and the realm of the immortals, by Nelson I. Wu (Wu No-sun). — New York: G. Braziller, 1963. 128 p.: illus., map, plans.; 26 cm. — (The Great ages of world architecture) 1. Architecture — China 2. Architecture — India I. T. II. Series.
NA1543.W8    720.95    *LC* 63-7513

**Alex, William, fl. 1963-.**    • **1.5451**
Japanese architecture. — New York: G. Braziller, 1963. 127 p.: illus., map, plans.; 26 cm. — (The Great ages of world architecture) 1. Architecture — Japan I. T. II. Series.
NA1550.A75 1963    722/.1    *LC* 63-7516

**New York. Museum of Modern Art.**    • **1.5452**
The architecture of Japan, by Arthur Drexler. — New York, [1955] 286 p.: illus., map.; 27 cm. 'Supplement: Japanese exhibition house': p. 262-286. 1. Architecture — Japan I. Drexler, Arthur. II. T.
NA1550.N4    720.952    *LC* 55-5987

**Soper, Alexander Coburn, 1904-.**    • **1.5453**
The evolution of Buddhist architecture in Japan / [by] Alexander Coburn Soper, III. — Princeton: Princeton University, 1942. 330 p.: ill.; 30 cm. 1. Architecture — Japan — History 2. Architecture, Buddhist 3. Temples, Buddhist 4. Temples — Japan. I. T.
NA1550.S6 1978    722.1    *LC* 42-24943

**Ishimoto, Yasuhiro, 1921-.**    • **1.5454**
Katsura: tradition and creation in Japanese architecture.Architecture in Japan / by Walter Gropius.Tradition and creation in Japanese architecture,by Kenzo Tange. New Haven: Yale U.P., 1960. vi, 36 p.: illus., plans.; 29 cm. 1. Architecture — Japan 2. Kyoto. Katsura Rikyu I. Gropius, Walter, 1883-1969. II. Tange, Kenzō, 1913- III. T.
NA1557.K9 I83 1960    720.952    *LC* 60-51016

**Creswell, Keppel Archibald Cameron, 1879-.**    • **1.5455**
The Muslim architecture of Egypt. Oxford: Clarendon Press 1952-59. 2v. I. T.
NA1581.C7

**Taylor, Jennifer.** 1.5456
John Andrews: architecture, a performing art / Jennifer Taylor & John Andrews. — New York: Oxford University Press, 1982. 176 p.: ill.; 23 x 26 cm. 1. Andrews, John, 1933- I. Andrews, John, 1933- joint author. II. T.
NA1605.A5 A4 1982 720/.92/4 LC 78-13466 ISBN 0195505573

# NA1995–1997 Architecture as a Profession

**The Architect: chapters in the history of the profession** / edited 1.5457
by Spiro Kostof.
New York: Oxford University Press, 1977. x, 371 p.: ill.; 24 cm. 1. Architecture — Vocational guidance — Addresses, essays, lectures. I. Kostof, Spiro.
NA1995.A73 720/.23 LC 75-46368 ISBN 0195020677

**Saint, Andrew.** 1.5458
The image of the architect / Andrew Saint. — New Haven: Yale University Press, 1983. xi, 180 p.: ill.; 27 cm. 1. Architecture — Vocational guidance 2. Architectural practice I. T.
NA1995.S27 1983 720/.68 19 LC 82-48909 ISBN 0300030134

**Women in American architecture: a historic and contemporary** 1.5459
perspective: a publication and exhibition organized by the Architectural League of New York through its Archive of Women in Architecture / edited by Susana Torre.
New York: Whitney Library of Design, 1977. 224 p.: ill.; 29 cm. Includes index. 1. Women architects — United States — Addresses, essays, lectures. I. Torre, Susana, 1944- II. Architectural League of New York.
NA1997.W65 720/.973 LC 76-54960 ISBN 0823074854

**The Beaux–arts and nineteenth–century French architecture** / 1.5460
edited by Robin Middleton.
1st MIT Press ed. — Cambridge, Mass.: MIT Press, 1982. 280 p.: ill. (some col.); 26 cm. 1. Ecole nationale supérieure des beaux-arts (France) 2. Architecture — Study and teaching — France. 3. Architecture — France. 4. Architecture, Modern — 19th century — France. I. Middleton, Robin.
NA2310.F8 E33 1982 720/.7/1144361 19 LC 81-82327 ISBN 0262131730

**Rudofsky, Bernard, 1905-.** 1.5461
Architecture without architects, an introduction to nonpedigreed architecture. New York, Museum of Modern Art; distributed by Doubleday, Garden City, N.Y. [1964] 1 v. (unpaged) illus. 25 cm. 1. Architecture — Exhibitions. 2. Architecture, Primitive I. T.
NA2430.R8 720.9 LC 64-8755

# NA2500–4050 Architecture: General Works. Details. Decoration

**Alexander, Christopher.** 1.5462
A pattern language: towns, buildings, construction / Christopher Alexander, Sara Ishikawa, Murray Silverstein, with Max Jacobson, Ingrid Fiksdahl–King, Shlomo Angel. — New York: Oxford University Press, 1977. xliv, 1171 p.: ill.; 21 cm. Companion volume to The timeless way of building and The Oregon experiment. 1. Signs and symbols in architecture 2. Semiotics I. Ishikawa, Sara, joint author. II. Silverstein, Murray, joint author. III. T.
NA2500.A445 720/.1 LC 74-22874 ISBN 0195019199

**Scruton, Roger.** 1.5463
The aesthetics of architecture / Roger Scruton. — Princeton, N.J.: Princeton University Press, c1979. x, 302 p.: ill.; 24 cm. — (Princeton essays on the arts; 8) Includes indexes. 1. Architecture I. T.
NA2500.S43 720/.1 LC 79-84026 ISBN 0691039488

**Steadman, Philip, 1942-.** 1.5464
The evolution of designs: biological analogy in architecture and the applied arts / Philip Steadman. — Cambridge; New York: Cambridge University Press, 1979. x, 276 p.: ill.; 24 cm. (Cambridge urban and architectural studies. 5) 1. Architecture — Philosophy. 2. Architectural design 3. Nature (Aesthetics) I. T. II. Series.
NA2500.S74 720/.1 LC 78-18255 ISBN 0521223034

**Zevi, Bruno, 1918-.** • 1.5465
[Saper vedere l'architettura. English] Architecture as space; how to look at architecture. Edited by Joseph A. Barry; translated by Milton Gendel. New York, Horizon Press [1957] 288 p. illus., diagrs., plans. 26 cm. Translation of Saper vedere l'architettura. 1. Space (Architecture) I. T.
NA2500.Z413 720 LC 57-7362

**Alberti, Leon Battista, 1404-1472.** • 1.5466
Ten books on architecture. Translated into Italian by Cosimo Bartoli and into English by James Leoni; edited by Joseph Rykwert. London, A. Tiranti, 1955. viii p., reprint (ix-xx, 240 p.) 241-256 p. 68 ill. ([Tiranti library, v. 5]) 1. Architecture — Early works to 1800 I. T.
NA2515 A32 1955 LC 55-12712

**Filarete, ca. 1400-ca. 1469.** • 1.5467
Treatise on architecture; being the treatise by Antonio di Piero Averlino, known as Filarete. Translated with an introd. and notes by John R. Spencer. — New Haven, Yale University Press, 1965. 2 v. illus. 37 cm. — (Yale publications in the history of art. 16) Includes facsim of the Magliabecchiana MS. in Florence (Bib. Naz., Magl. II, I. 140) 1. Architecture 2. Drawing — Study and teaching 3. Medici, House of. I. Spencer, John Richard, ed. and tr. II. T. III. Series.
NA2515.F493 720 LC 65-12547

**Palladio, Andrea, 1508-1580.** 1.5468
The four books of architecture. With a new introd. by Adolf K. Placzek. New York, Dover Publications [1965] vii, 110 p. 212 plates. 1. Architecture — Early works to 1800 2. Rome — Antiquities I. T.
NA2515 P253 1965 LC 64-18862

**Vitruvius Pollio.** • 1.5469
[De architectura. English] Vitruvius: the ten books on architecture. Translated by Morris Hicky Morgan. With illus. and original designs prepared under the direction of Herbert Langford Warren. New York, Dover Publications [1960] 331 p. illus. 21 cm. 'An unabridged and unaltered republication of the first edition of the English translation by Morris Hicky Morgan, originally published ... in 1914.' 1. Architecture — Early works to 1800. I. Morgan, Morris Hicky, 1859-1910, tr. II. T.
NA2515.V73 1960 720 LC 60-50037 *(NA 2515 V84 1960)*

**Serlio, Sebastiano, 1475-1554.** • 1.5470
[Tutte l'opere d'architettura] The book of architecture by Sebastiano Serlio, London, 1611. Introd. by A. E. Santaniello. New York, B. Blom, 1970. 1 v. (unpaged) illus., plans. 37 cm. A facsim. of the 1611 ed., with a new introd., bibliography, and publisher's note, published under title: The first[-fift] booke of architecture. 1. Architecture — Early works to 1800. I. Santaniello, A. E. II. T.
NA2517.S5 1970 720 LC 68-56509

**Le Corbusier, 1887-1965.** • 1.5471
Towards a new architecture, by Le Corbusier. Translated from the French by Frederick Etchells. New York, Praeger [1970] 269 p. illus., plans. 22 cm. Reprint of the 1927 ed. Translation of Vers une architecture. 1. Architecture I. T.
NA2520.J4 1970 720 LC 76-92371

**Viollet-le-Duc, Eugène-Emmanuel, 1814-1879.** • 1.5472
Discourses on architecture. Translated from the French by Benjamin Bucknall. New York, Grove Press [1959] 2 v. illus. 29 cm. 1. Architecture I. T.
NA2520.V7 1959 LC 59-6254

**Wright, Frank Lloyd, 1867-1959.** • 1.5473
Frank Lloyd Wright on architecture: selected writings 1894–1940. / Edited with an introd., by Frederick Gutheim. New York: Grosset and Dunlap, [1959, c1941] 275p. (The Universal library; UL-70) "Published writings of Frank Lloyd Wright":p.267-269. 1. Architecture — Addresses, essays, lectures. I. Gutheim,Frederick Albert, ed. II. T.
NA2520.W85 1959 LC 60-90

**Cook, John Wesley, 1933-.** 1.5474
Conversations with architects: Philip Johnson, Kevin Roche, Paul Rudolph, Bertrand Goldberg, Morris Lapidus, Louis Kahn, Charles Moore, Robert Venturi & Denise Scott Brown, by John W. Cook and Heinrich Klotz. Foreword by Vincent Scully. New York, Praeger [1973] 272 p. illus. 25 cm. 1. Architecture 2. Architects, American — Interviews. I. Klotz, Heinrich. joint author. II. Johnson, Philip, 1906- III. T.
NA2540.C63 720/.92/2 LC 72-85972

**Wright, David, 1941-.** 1.5475
Natural solar architecture: a passive primer / by David Wright; technical advice, Jeffrey Cook; ill., Dennis A. Andrejko. — New York: Van Nostrand Reinhold Co., c1978. 245 p.: ill.; 22 x 38 cm. Includes index. 1. Architecture and solar radiation I. T.
NA2542.S6 W74 728 LC 77-28541 ISBN 0442295855 *(NA 2542 S6 W74)*

**Buildings and society: essays on the social development of the**    **1.5476**
**built environment / edited by Anthony D. King.**
London; Boston: Routledge & Kegan Paul, 1980. ix, 318 p.: ill.; 26 cm.
1. Architecture and society — Addresses, essays, lectures. 2. Architecture —
Environmental aspects — Addresses, essays, lectures. I. King, Anthony D.
NA2543.S6 B76    720/.1/03 19    *LC* 80-40938    *ISBN* 0710006160

**Raskin, Eugene.**       **1.5477**
Architecture and people. — Englewood Cliffs, N.J.: Prentice-Hall, [1974] xiii,
191 p.: illus.; 24 cm. — (Prentice-Hall international series in architecture)
1. Architecture and society I. T.
NA2543.S6 R37    720    *LC* 73-9832    *ISBN* 0130445940

**Tafuri, Manfredo.**       **1.5478**
[Progetto e utopia. English] Architecture and utopia: design and capitalist
development / Manfredo Tafuri; translated from the Italian by Barbara Luigia
La Penta. — Cambridge, Mass.: MIT Press, c1976. xi, 184 p.: ill.; 19 cm.
Translation of Progetto e utopia. 1. Architecture — Environmental aspects
2. City planning 3. Form (Aesthetics) I. T.
NA2543.S6 T3313    720    *LC* 75-33128    *ISBN* 0262200333

**Rasmussen, Steen Eiler, 1898-.**       • **1.5479**
Experiencing architecture. [Translation from Danish by Eve Wendt. — 2d
United States ed.]. — Cambridge [Mass.]: M.I.T. Press, Massachusetts Institute
of Technology, 1962. 245 p.: illus.; 25 cm. 1. Architecture I. T.
NA2550.R313 1962    720    *LC* 62-21637

**Ruskin, John, 1819-1900.**       • **1.5480**
The poetry of architecture: or, The architecture of the nations of Europe
considered in its association with natural scenery and national character / by
John Ruskin; with illustrations by the author. — Sunnyside: G. Allen, 1893. xii,
261 p.: illus.; 24 cm. 1. Architecture I. T.
NA2550.R7

**Ruskin, John, 1819-1900.**       • **1.5481**
The seven lamps of architecture / Ruskin; introduction by Sir Arnold Lunn. —
London: Dent; New York: Dutton, [1963] xxvi, 228 p., [14] f. de planches: ill.
— (Everyman's library; no. 207) I. Lunn, Arnold Henry Moore, Sir,
1888-1974. II. T.
NA2550 R956 1963

**Le Corbusier, 1887-1965.**       **1.5482**
The ideas of Le Corbusier on architecture and urban planning / texts edited and
presented by Jacques Guiton; translation by Margaret Guiton. — New York:
G. Braziller, 1981. 127 p.: ill.; 26 cm. Chronological list of the author's
works: p. 15-16. Includes index. 1. Architecture — Addresses, essays, lectures.
2. City planning — Addresses, essays, lectures. I. Guiton, Jacques. II. T.
NA2560.L413 1981    720 19    *LC* 80-70993    *ISBN* 0807610046

**Mumford, Lewis, 1895-.**       • **1.5483**
From the ground up; observations on contemporary architecture, housing,
highway building, and civic design. — New York: Harcourt, Brace, [c1956]
243 p.; 19 cm. — (A Harvest book, 13) 1. Architecture, Modern — 20th
century — Addresses, essays, lectures. 2. Cities and towns — Planning —
1945- — Addresses, essays, lectures. 3. Cities and towns — Planning — New
York (City) 4. Housing 5. Traffic engineering I. T.
NA2560.M8    720.4    *LC* 56-13736

**Sullivan, Louis H., 1856-1924.**       • **1.5484**
Kindergarten chats (revised 1918) and other writings. — New York:
Wittenborn, Schultz, 1947. 252 p.: illus., ports.; 26 cm. — (The documents of
modern art) Kindergarten chats was first published serially in 1901-02, in
Interstate architect & builder. cf. Editorial note, signed: Isabella Athey.
1. Architecture — Addresses, essays, lectures. I. Athey, Isabella, ed. II. T.
III. Series.
NA2560.S82    720.4    *LC* 47-4782

**Huxtable, Ada Louise.**       **1.5485**
Kicked a building lately? / Ada Louise Huxtable. New York: Quadrangle/The
New York Times Book Co., c1976. xvi, 304 p.: ill.; 24 cm. Includes index.
1. Architecture — Addresses, essays, lectures. 2. Architecture, Modern —
20th century — Addresses, essays, lectures. I. T.
NA2563.H88 1976    720    *LC* 75-36276    *ISBN* 0812906306

**Summerson, John Newenham, Sir, 1904-.**       • **1.5486**
Heavenly mansions, and other essays on architecture. — [London]: Cresset,
[1949]. — ix, 253 p.: illus. 22 cm. — (Books that live.) Includes index.
1. Architecture — Addresses, essays, lectures. I. T.
NA2563.S8 1949    720.4

**Bonta, Juan Pablo.**       **1.5487**
[Sistemas de significación en arquitectura y diseño. English] Architecture and
its interpretation: a study of expressive systems in architecture / Juan Pablo
Bonta. — New York: Rizzoli, 1979. 271 p.: ill.; 21 cm. Translation of Sistemas

de significación en arquitectura y diseño. Includes index. 1. Architectural
criticism I. T.
NA2599.5.B6613 1979b    720/.01    *LC* 79-64574    *ISBN*
084780237X

## NA2700–3070 ARCHITECTURAL DRAWING. DESIGN. DETAILS

**Masterpieces of architectural drawing / edited by Helen Powell**    **1.5488**
**and David Leatherbarrow.**
New York: Abbeville Press, 1983, c1982. 192 p.: ill.; 28 cm. Includes index.
1. Architectural drawing I. Powell, Helen. II. Leatherbarrow, David.
NA2700.M38 1983    720/.22/2 19    *LC* 82-22643    *ISBN*
0896593266

**Nelson, George, 1908-.**       **1.5489**
George Nelson on design. — New York: Whitney Library of Design, 1979.
191 p.: ill.; 27 cm. 1. Architectural design I. T. II. Title: On design.
NA2750.N34 1979    745.4    *LC* 78-32097    *ISBN* 0823072045

**Arnheim, Rudolf.**       **1.5490**
The dynamics of architectural form: based on the 1975 Mary Duke Biddle
lectures at the Cooper Union / Rudolf Arnheim. — Berkeley: University of
California Press, c1977. vi, 289 p.: ill.; 25 cm. Includes index. 1. Architecture
— Composition, proportion, etc. 2. Architecture — Psychological aspects
3. Visual perception I. T.
NA2760.A74    729    *LC* 76-19955    *ISBN* 0520033051

**Venturi, Robert.**       **1.5491**
Complexity and contradiction in architecture / Robert Venturi; with an introd.
by Vincent Scully. — 2d ed. — New York: Museum of Modern Art; Boston:
distributed by New York Graphic Society, 1977. 132 p.: ill.; 23 x 29 cm. (The
Museum of Modern Art papers on architecture) 1. Architecture —
Composition, proportion, etc. I. Museum of Modern Art (New York, N.Y.)
II. T.
NA2760.V46 1977    720/.1    *LC* 77-77289    *ISBN* 0870702815

**Moore, Charles Willard, 1925-.**       **1.5492**
Dimensions: space, shape & scale in architecture / Charles Moore, Gerald
Allen. New York: Architectural Record Books, c1976. viii, 183 p.: ill.; 24 cm.
1. Space (Architecture) 2. Architecture — Composition, proportion, etc.
3. Visual perception 4. Harmony (Aesthetics) I. Allen, Gerald. joint author.
II. T.
NA2765.M66    729    *LC* 76-28406    *ISBN* 0070023360

**Architectural acoustics / edited by Thomas D. Northwood.**    **1.5493**
Stroudsburg, Pa.: Dowden, Hutchinson & Ross; New York: exclusive
distributor, Halsted Press, c1977. xv, 428 p.: ill.; 26 cm. (Benchmark papers in
acoustics; 10) Articles chiefly in English, some in French or German, with
English summaries. 1. Architectural acoustics — Addresses, essays, lectures.
I. Northwood, Thomas D.
NA2800.A68    729/.29    *LC* 76-54182    *ISBN* 0879332573

**Beranek, Leo Leroy, 1914-.**       **1.5494**
Music, acoustics & architecture. — New York: Wiley, [1962] 586 p.: illus.; 28
cm. 1. Architectural acoustics 2. Music — Acoustics and physics 3. Music-
halls I. T.
NA2800.B4 1962    729.2    *LC* 62-19866

**Cremer, Lothar, 1905-.**       **1.5495**
[Wissenschaftlichen Grundlagen der Raumakustik. English] Principles and
applications of room acoustics / Lothar Cremer and Helmut A. Müller;
translated by Theodore J. Schultz. — London; New York: Applied Science;
New York, NY, USA: Sole distributor in the USA and Canada, Elsevier Science
Pub. Co., c1982. 2 v.: ill.; 23 cm. Translation of: Die wissenschaftlichen
Grundlagen der Raumakustik. Includes indexes. 1. Architectural acoustics
I. Müller, Helmut A. II. T.
NA2800.C713 1982    729/.29 19    *LC* 84-119658    *ISBN* 0853341133

**Roberts, Howard C.**       **1.5496**
Acousticks: an introductory lecture series on acoustics for architects / by
Howard C. Roberts. — [Denver, Co: The Author], 1984. ii, 141 leaves: ill; 28
cm. 1. Architectural acoustics I. T.
NA2800.R6x

**Sabine, Wallace Clement, 1868-1919.**       **1.5497**
Collected papers on acoustics / by Wallace Clement Sabine; with a new
introduction by Frederick V. Hunt. — New York: Dover Publications, 1964.
xix, 279 p.: ill., port. 1. Architectural acoustics I. T.
NA2800.S3 1964    729.2    *LC* 64-18864    *ISBN* 0486611965

**Normand, Charles Pierre Joseph, 1765-1840.** • **1.5498**
Parallel of the orders of architecture, Greek, Roman, and Renaissance. / Edited by R.A. Cordingley. — Chicago: Quadrangle Books [1959] 16 p.: ill., 80 plates; 29 cm. — 1. Architecture — Orders I. Cordingley, Reginald Annandale, 1896- II. T.
NA2812 N6 1959     *LC* 59-15548

**Smith, E. Baldwin (Earl Baldwin), 1888-1956.** • **1.5499**
The dome, a study in the history of ideas. Princeton, Princeton University Press, 1950. ix, 164 p. 228 ill. (Princeton monographs in art and archaeology. 25) 1. Domes I. T. II. Series.
NA2890 S6     *LC* 50-8444

## NA3310–4050 ARCHITECTURAL DECORATION

**Southworth, Susan.**     **1.5500**
Ornamental ironwork: an illustrated guide to its design, history & use in American architecture / by Susan and Michael Southworth; photos. by Charles C. Withers. — Boston: D. R. Godine, 1978. 202 p.: ill.; 24 cm. Includes index. 1. Architectural ironwork — United States. 2. Decoration and ornament, Architectural — United States. I. Southworth, Michael. joint author. II. Withers, Charles C. III. T.
NA3503.S68     739/.4773     *LC* 77-94111     *ISBN* 0879232331

**Badger, Daniel D.**     **1.5501**
[Illustrations of iron architecture, made by the Architectural Iron Works of the city of New York] Badger's Illustrated catalogue of cast–iron architecture / by Daniel D. Badger; with a new introduction by Margot Gayle. — New York: Dover Publications, c1981. xvii, 35 p., 102 p. of plates: ill.; 31 cm. Reprint. Originally published: Illustrations of iron architecture, made by the Architectural Iron Works of the city of New York. New York: Baker & Godwin, 1865. 1. Architectural Iron Works (Firm) — Catalogs. 2. Architectural ironwork — United States — History — 19th century — Catalogs. 3. Cast-iron fronts (Architecture) — United States — Catalogs. I. Architectural Iron Works (Firm) II. T. III. Title: Illustrated catalogue of cast-iron architecture. IV. Title: Cast-iron architecture.
NA3503.7.B32 1981     721/.0447141 19     *LC* 81-68875     *ISBN* 0486242234

**Beard, Geoffrey W.**     **1.5502**
Stucco and decorative plasterwork in Europe / Geoffrey Beard. — 1st U.S. ed. — New York: Harper & Row, c1983. 224 p.: ill. (some col.); 28 cm. — (Icon editions) Includes indexes. 1. Stucco — Europe. 2. Plasterwork, Decorative — Europe. I. T.
NA3542.B4 1983     729/.5 19     *LC* 82-49006     *ISBN* 0064303837

**Borg, Alan.**     **1.5503**
Architectural sculpture in Romanesque Provence. — Oxford: Clarendon Press, 1972. x, 144 p.: illus.; 30 cm. — (Oxford studies in the history of art and architecture.) 1. Decoration and ornament, Architectural — Provence. 2. Sculpture, Romanesque — Provence. I. T. II. Series.
NA3549.A3 P762     729/.5     *LC* 73-152045     *ISBN* 0198171927

**Beard, Geoffrey W.**     **1.5504**
Decorative plasterwork in Great Britain / Geoffrey Beard. — London: Phaidon, 1976, [c1975]. ix, 262 p., [2] leaves of plates: ill. (some col.); 26 cm. Includes indexes. 1. Plasterwork, Decorative — Great Britain. I. T.
NA3690.B4     729/.5     *LC* 76-360825     *ISBN* 0714816868

## NA3750–3860 Mosaics

**Rossi, Ferdinando.** • **1.5505**
[Mosaico. English] Mosaics, a survey of their history and techniques [by] Ferdinando Rossi. [Translated from the Italian by David Ross] New York, Praeger [1970] 200 p. illus. (part col.) 30 cm. Translation of Il mosaico. 1. Mosaics 2. Marquetry 3. Carving (Art industries) I. T.
NA3750.R6713 1970     729/.7     *LC* 72-89606

**Bovini, Giuseppe.** • **1.5506**
Ravenna mosaics: the so–called Mausoleum of Galla Placidia, the Baptistery of the Cathedral, the Archiepiscopal Chapel, the Baptistery of the Arians, the Basilica San Apollinare nuovo, the Church of San Vitale, the Basilica of San Apollinare in Classe / Giuseppe Bovini; [Translated by Gustina Scaglia]. — Greenwich, Conn.: New York Graphic Society, [1956]. –. 55, [2] p.: ill., 46 plates (part col.); 39 cm. — (The Great masters of the past: 4) 1. Mosaics 2. Art — Ravenna. 3. Christian art and symbolism I. T. II. Series.
NA3780.B663     738.52     *LC* 57-1067

**Demus, Otto.** • **1.5507**
The mosaics of Norman Sicily / Otto Demus. — London: Routledge & K. Paul, [1950] xx, 478 p., [61] leaves of plates: ill.; 26 cm. 1. Mosaics 2. Art — Sicily. 3. Christian art and symbolism I. T.
NA3780.D4 1950a

**Demus, Otto.**     **1.5508**
The mosaics of San Marco in Venice / Otto Demus. — Chicago: University of Chicago Press, 1984. 2 v. in 4: ill. (some col.); 32 cm. 'Published for Dumbarton Oaks, Washington, D.C.' Issued in a case. Pts. 2 of v. 1 and 2 contains plates. 1. Basilica di San Marco (Venice, Italy) 2. Mosaics — Italy — Venice. 3. Mosaics, Medieval — Italy — Venice. I. T.
NA3788.D45 1984     729/.7/094531 19     *LC* 82-2787     *ISBN* 0226142892

**Oakeshott, Walter Fraser, 1903-.**     **1.5509**
The mosaics of Rome, from the third to the fourteenth centuries [by] Walter Oakeshott. — Greenwich, Conn.: New York Graphic Society, [1967] 388 p.: illus. (part col.); 31 cm. 1. Mosaics — Rome (City) 2. Mosaics, Early Christian — Rome (City) 3. Mosaics, Medieval — Rome (City) I. T.
NA3850.R6 O15 1967b     729/.7/0945632     *LC* 67-25494

## NA3950 Ironwork

**Geerlings, Gerald K. (Gerald Kenneth), 1897-.**     **1.5510**
Wrought iron in architecture ... [by] Gerald K. Geerlings. New York, Scribner [1972, c1929] v, 202 p. illus. 29 cm. 1. Architectural ironwork 2. Wrought-iron 3. Decoration and ornament, Architectural I. T.
NA3950.G4 1972     729     *LC* 72-183895     *ISBN* 068412842X

# NA4100–8480 Special Classes of Buildings

## NA4100–4160 BY MATERIAL OR FORM

**Hix, John, 1938-.**     **1.5511**
The glass house. — Cambridge, Mass.: MIT Press, [1974] 208 p.: illus.; 26 cm. 1. Glass construction 2. Greenhouses I. T.
NA4140.H59 1974     721/.044     *LC* 74-5201     *ISBN* 0262080761

**Drew, Philip, 1943-.**     **1.5512**
Tensile architecture / Philip Drew. — Boulder, Colo.: Westview Press, 1979. xxii, 237 p.: ill.; 26 cm. Includes index. 1. Tensile architecture I. T.
NA4160.D73 1979     720 19     *LC* 79-7357     *ISBN* 0891585508

## NA4170–7010 PUBLIC BUILDINGS

**Pevsner, Nikolaus, Sir, 1902-.**     **1.5513**
A history of building types / Nikolaus Pevsner. — Princeton, N.J.: Princeton University Press, c1976. 352 p.: ill.; 30 cm. (A.W. Mellon lectures in the fine arts. 19) (Bollingen series. 35) Includes index. 1. Public buildings I. T. II. Series. III. Series: Bollingen series. 35
NA4170.P48     725/.09     *LC* 75-4459     *ISBN* 0691099049

**Craig, Lois A.**     **1.5514**
The Federal presence: architecture, politics, and symbols in United States government building / Lois Craig and the staff of the Federal Architecture Project. — Cambridge, Mass.: MIT Press, c1978. xv, 580 p.: ill.; 29 cm. Includes index. 1. Architecture and state — United States. 2. Public buildings — United States I. Federal Architecture Project (U.S.) II. T.
NA4205.C7     725/.1/0973     *LC* 78-15366     *ISBN* 0262030578

**The Houses of Parliament / edited by M. H. Port.**     **1.5515**
New Haven: Published for the Paul Mellon Centre for Studies in British Art (London) by Yale University Press, 1976. xxi, 347 p., [1] leaf of plates: ill. (some col.); 31 cm. — (Studies in British art.) 1. Great Britain. Parliament (The buildings) 2. Gothic revival (Architecture) — England — London. I. Port, Michael Harry. II. Paul Mellon Centre for Studies in British Art. III. Series.
NA4415.G72 L664     725/.11/0942132     *LC* 76-3374     *ISBN* 0300020228

**Lebovich, William L.**    **1.5516**
America's city halls / William L. Lebovich; Historic American Buildings Survey. — Washington, D.C.: Preservation Press, c1984. 223 p.: ill.; 27 cm. Includes indexes. 1. City halls — United States. 2. Historic buildings — United States. I. Historic American Buildings Survey. II. T.
NA4431.A47 1984    725/.13/0973 19    *LC* 83-21310    *ISBN* 0891331158

**Court house, a photographic document / edited by Richard**    **1.5517**
**Pare; conceived and directed by Phyllis Lambert; the writers of Court house, Phyllis Lambert ... [et al.]; the photographers of Court house, Harold Allen ... [et al.].**
New York: Horizon Press, c1978. 255 p.: ill.; 34 cm. Includes index. 1. Courthouses — United States — Addresses, essays, lectures. I. Pare, Richard. II. Lambert, Phyllis. III. Allen, Harold, 1912-
NA4475.U6 C68    725/.15    *LC* 77-94016    *ISBN* 0818000287

# NA4590–6113 Religious Buildings

**Krautheimer, Richard, 1897-.**    ● **1.5518**
Early Christian and Byzantine architecture / Richard Krautheimer. — 3d. ed. — Harmondsworth, Eng.; Baltimore: Penguin Books, 1979. 583 p.: ill.; 21 cm. (Pelican history of art. PZ24) Includes index. 1. Architecture, Early Christian 2. Architecture, Byzantine 3. Church architecture — History. I. T. II. Series.
NA4817.K7 1979    726

**Gimpel, Jean.**    **1.5519**
[Bâtisseurs de cathédrales. English] The cathedral builders / by Jean Gimpel; translated by Teresa Waugh. — 1st ed. — New York: Grove Press, 1983. 127 p.: ill. (some col.); 29 cm. Translation of: Les bâtisseurs de cathédrales. Includes index. 1. Cathedrals 2. Architecture, Medieval 3. Christian art and symbolism — Medieval, 500-1500 I. T.
NA4830.G5313 1983    726/.6/094 19    *LC* 82-48042    *ISBN* 039452893X

**Simson, Otto Georg von, 1912-.**    ● **1.5520**
The Gothic cathedral: origins of Gothic architecture and the medieval concept of order / Otto von Simson. — 2d ed., rev. with additions. — New York: Pantheon Books, 1962. xxiii, 278 p., [22] leaves of plates: ill., plans. — (Bollingen series. v.48) 1. Cathédrale de Chartres. 2. Cathedrals 3. Architecture, Gothic I. T. II. Series.
NA4830.S5 1962    *LC* 63-2039

**Braunfels, Wolfgang.**    **1.5521**
[Abendländische Klosterbaukunst. English] Monasteries of Western Europe; the architecture of the orders. [3d ed. Princeton, N.J.] Princeton University Press [1973, c1972] 263 p. illus. 30 cm. Includes 'Selections from documentary sources' with parallel Latin text and English translation. Translation of Abendländische Klosterbaukunst. 1. Monasteries I. T.
NA4850.B713 1973    726/.7/094    *LC* 73-2472    *ISBN* 0691038961

**Gowans, Alan.**    **1.5522**
Church architecture in New France. — Toronto, University of Toronto Press, 1955. xii, 162 p. illus., maps. 27 cm. Bibliographical footnotes. 1. Church architecture — Quebec (Province) I. T.
NA5246.Q4G6    726.5    *LC* 54-6839

**Baird, Joseph Armstrong.**    ● **1.5523**
The churches of Mexico, 1530–1810. Photos. by Hugo Rudinger. — Berkeley: University of California Press, 1962. xxii, 126 p.: illus., 163 plates (part col.) maps, plans.; 29 cm. 1. Church architecture — Mexico — History. 2. Churches — Mexico. I. Rudinger, Hugo, illus. II. T.
NA5253.B3    726.50972    *LC* 62-13073

**McAndrew, John.**    ● **1.5524**
The open-air churches of sixteenth-century Mexico: atrios, posas, open chapels, and other studies. Cambridge, Mass., Harvard University Press, 1965. xxxi, 755 p. ill., maps, plans. 1. Church architecture — Mexico 2. Indians of Mexico — Missions 3. Mexico — Religion 4. Mexico — History — To 1810 I. T.
NA5253 M23    *LC* 63-17205

**Buxton, David Roden, 1910-.**    **1.5525**
The wooden churches of Eastern Europe: an introductory survey / David Buxton. — Cambridge [Cambridgeshire]; New York: Cambridge University Press, 1981. 405 p.: ill.; 29 cm. Includes index. 1. Church architecture — Europe, Eastern. 2. Building, Wooden — Europe, Eastern. 3. Stave churches — Europe, Eastern. I. T.
NA5450.B89 1981    726/.5/0947 19    *LC* 80-41517    *ISBN* 0521237866

**Pevsner, Nikolaus, Sir, 1902-.**    **1.5526**
The cathedrals of England / by Nikolaus Pevsner and Priscilla Metcalf, with contributions by various hands. — Harmondsworth, Middlesex, England; New York, N.Y., U.S.A.: Viking, 1985. 2 v.: ill.; 25 cm. 1. Cathedrals — England. 2. Church decoration and ornament — England. I. Metcalf, Priscilla. II. T.
NA5461.P48 1985    726/.6/0942 19    *LC* 84-51886    *ISBN* 0670801259

**Randall, Gerald.**    **1.5527**
The English parish church / Gerald Randall. — New York: Holmes & Meier, 1982. 192 p.: ill.; 26 cm. Includes index. 1. Church architecture — England 2. Churches — England. I. T.
NA5461.R38 1982    726/.5/0942 19    *LC* 82-232477    *ISBN* 071343404X

**Fergusson, Peter, 1934-.**    **1.5528**
Architecture of solitude: Cistercian abbeys in twelfth-century England / Peter Fergusson. — Princeton, N.J.: Princeton University Press, c1984. xxv, 188 p., [100] p. of plates: ill.; 29 cm. Includes index. 1. Architecture, Cistercian — England. 2. Abbeys — England 3. Architecture, Medieval — England. I. T.
NA5463.F4 1984    726/.7/0942 19    *LC* 83-43072    *ISBN* 0691040249

**Harvey, John Hooper.**    **1.5529**
The perpendicular style, 1330–1485 / [by] John Harvey. — London: Batsford, 1978. 308 p.: ill., maps; 26 cm. Includes indexes. 1. Architecture, Gothic — Great Britain. 2. Church architecture — Great Britain. I. T.
NA5463.H3    720/.942    *LC* 78-326626    *ISBN* 0713416106

**Whiffen, Marcus, 1916-.**    ● **1.5530**
Stuart and Georgian churches: the architecture of the church of England outside London, 1603–1837 / by Marcus Whiffen. — London; New York: B.T. Batsford, 1948. viii, 118 p., : ill., plans. 1. Church architecture — England I. T.
NA5466 W45    726.538    *LC* 49-2966

**Bony, Jean.**    **1.5531**
French Gothic architecture of the 12th and 13th centuries / Jean Bony. — Berkeley: University of California Press, c1983. xliii, 623 p.: ill.; 29 cm. — (California studies in the history of art. 20) Includes index. 1. Architecture, Gothic — France. 2. Church architecture — France. I. T. II. Series.
NA5543.B66 1983    726/.5/0944 19    *LC* 74-82842    *ISBN* 0520028317

**Katzenellenbogen, Adolf Edmund Max, 1901-.**    **1.5532**
The sculptural programs of Chartres Cathedral: Christ, Mary, Ecclesia / Adolf Katzenellenbogen. — Baltimore: Johns Hopkins Press, [1959]. –. xiv, 149 p.: plates; 29 cm. — 1. Cathédrale de Chartres. 2. Sculpture — France — Chartres. I. T.
NA5551.C5 K3    726.64094451    *LC* 59-14894

**Harries, Karsten.**    **1.5533**
The Bavarian rococo church: between faith and aestheticism / Karsten Harries. — New Haven [Conn.]: Yale University Press, c1983. xv, 282 p., [16] p. of plates: ill.; 29 cm. 1. Church architecture — Germany (West) — Bavaria. 2. Architecture, Rococo — Germany (West) — Bavaria. I. T.
NA5573.H37 1983    726/.5/09433 19    *LC* 82-11168    *ISBN* 0300027206

**Connors, Joseph.**    **1.5534**
Borromini and the Roman oratory: style and society / Joseph Connors. — New York: Architectural History Foundation; Cambridge, Mass.: MIT Press, c1980. xiv, 375 p.: ill.; 26 cm. — (Architectural History Foundation/MIT Press series. 3) Includes index. 1. Borromini, Francesco, 1599-1667. 2. Oratorio dei Filippini, Rome. 3. Architecture, Baroque — Italy — Rome (City) 4. Oratorians. I. T. II. Series.
NA5620.O7 C66 1980    726/.4    *LC* 80-16111    *ISBN* 0262030713

**Hartt, Frederick.**    **1.5535**
The Chapel of the Cardinal of Portugal, 1434–1459, at San Miniato in Florence [by] Frederick Hartt, Gino Corti [and] Clarence Kennedy. Philadelphia, University of Pennsylvania Press [1964] 192 p. 158 plates (part col.) (The Haney Foundation series of studies in English, American and foreign literature; modern history, sociology, and economics; music and art, v. 1) 1. Florence. San Miniato al-Monte (Church) 2. Jaime de Portugal, Cardinal, 1434?-1459 I. T. II. Series.
NA5621 F8 H3    *LC* 62-17064

**Mathews, Thomas F.**    **1.5536**
The Byzantine churches of Istanbul: a photographic survey / Thomas F. Mathews. — University Park: Pennsylvania State University Press, c1976. xx, 405 p.: chiefly ill.; 29 cm. 1. Churches — Turkey — Istanbul — Pictorial works. 2. Architecture, Byzantine — Turkey — Istanbul. 3. Church architecture — Turkey — Istanbul. I. T.
NA5870.A1 M37    726/.5/094961    *LC* 75-27173    *ISBN* 0271012102

**Mathews, Thomas F.**     **1.5537**
The early churches of Constantinople: architecture and liturgy [by] Thomas F. Mathews. — University Park: Pennsylvania State University Press, [1971] xviii, 194, [60] p.: illus.; 27 cm. A revision of the author's thesis, New York University. 1. Architecture, Byzantine — Turkey — Istanbul. 2. Church architecture — Istanbul. 3. Liturgy and architecture I. T.
NA5870.I7 M3    726/.5/094961    *LC* 78-111972    *ISBN* 0271001089

**Underwood, Paul Atkins.**     **1.5538**
The Kariye Djami, Vol.4: Studies in the art of the Kariye Djami and its intellectual background / Paul A. Underwood, editor .. Princeton: [s.n.] 1975. xvii, 371 p., [103] p. of plates, fold leaf of plate: ill., plans, ports.; 33 cm. (Bollinger series,; 70) 1. Underwood, Paul Atkins. 2. Mosaics — Istanbul. 3. Mural painting and decoration — Istanbul. I. T. II. Series.
NA5870.K3 U5    729/.7/094961 759.496/1    *LC* 65-10404    *ISBN* 069199778X

**Kramrisch, Stella, 1898-.**     **1.5539**
The Hindu temple / by Stella Kramrisch; photographs by Raymond Burnier. — Delhi: Motilal Banarsidass, 1976. 2 v. (xi, 466 p., lxxx leaves of plates): ill.; 29 cm. Reprint of the 1946 ed. published by the University of Calcutta, Calcutta. Includes index. 1. Temples, Hindu I. Burnier, Raymond. II. T.
NA6002.K72 1976    726/.1/45    *LC* 77-911201

**Williams, Joanna Gottfried, 1939-.**     **1.5540**
The art of Gupta India: empire and province / Joanna Gottfried Williams. — Princeton, N.J.: Princeton University Press, c1982. xxvi, 209 p., [143] p. of plates: ill.; 22 x 26 cm. Includes index. 1. Architecture, Gupta 2. Temples, Hindu 3. Sculpture, Gupta 4. Sculpture, Hindu I. T.
NA6002.W5 1982    722/.44 19    *LC* 81-13783    *ISBN* 0691039887

**Galey, John.**     **1.5541**
Sinai and the Monastery of St. Catherine / John Galey; introductions by Kurt Weitzmann and George Forsyth. — Garden City, N.Y.: Doubleday, 1980. 191 p.: col. ill.; 32 cm. 1. Saint Catherine (Monastery: Mount Sinai). I. T.
NA6084.S5 G34 1980    726/.7/09531 19    *LC* 80-951    *ISBN* 0385171102

## NA6210–7010 Other Public Buildings

**Geist, Johann Friedrich, 1936-.**     **1.5542**
[Passagen, ein Bautyp des 19. Jahrhunderts. English] Arcades, the history of a building type / Johann Friedrich Geist. — Cambridge, Mass.: MIT Press, c1983. viii, 596 p.: ill.; 29 cm. 'Based on a translation by Jane O. Newman and John H. Smith'—T.p. verso. 1. Arcades 2. Architecture, Modern — 19th century I. T.
NA6218.G4313 1983    725/.21 19    *LC* 82-10014    *ISBN* 0262070820

**Huxtable, Ada Louise.**     **1.5543**
The tall building artistically reconsidered: the search for a skyscraper style / Ada Louise Huxtable. — 1st ed. — New York: Pantheon Books, c1984. 128 p.: ill.; 27 cm. Includes index. 1. Skyscrapers I. T.
NA6230.H89 1984    725/.2 19    *LC* 84-42664    *ISBN* 0394537734

**Grand Central Terminal: city within the city / Deborah Nevins, general editor; with a foreword by Jacqueline Kennedy Onassis; essays by Deborah Nevins ... [et al.].**     **1.5544**
[New York]: Municipal Art Society of New York, c1982. 145 p.: ill. (some col.); 32 cm. 'Originally published as the catalog of an exhibition presented by the Municipal Art Society'—Verso of t.p. Grand Central model kit on 7 sheets in pocket. 1. Grand Central Terminal (New York, N.Y.) 2. New York (N.Y.) — Public buildings — Conservation and restoration. I. Nevins, Deborah, 1947- II. Municipal Art Society of New York.
NA6313.N4 G72 1982    725/.31/097471 19    *LC* 82-81177    *ISBN* 0960689222

**Richards, James Maude.**     **1.5545**
The functional tradition in early industrial buildings. With photos. by Eric de Maré. London, Architectural Press [1958] 200 p. (chiefly ill.) 1. Industrial buildings 2. Architecture — England I. T.
NA6400 R5    *LC* 59-25979

**Burris-Meyer, Harold, 1902-.**     • **1.5546**
Theatres and auditoriums, by Harold Burris–Meyer and Edward C. Cole. — 2d ed. — New York: Reinhold Pub. Corp., [1964] vii, 376 p.: illus., plans.; 27 cm. 1. Theaters — Construction 2. Auditoriums I. Cole, Edward Cyrus. joint autho. II. T.
NA6821.B8 1964    25.82    *LC* 64-8896

**Izenour, George C.**     **1.5547**
Theater design / by George C. Izenour; with two essays on the room acoustics of multiple–use by Vern O. Knudsen and Robert B. Newman; foreword by Alois M. Nagler. — New York: McGraw-Hill, c1977. xxxiii, 631: ill.

1. Theaters — Construction I. Knudsen, Vern Oliver, 1893-1974. joint author. II. Newman, Robert B., joint author. III. T.
NA6821.I94    NA6821 I94.    725/.822    *LC* 76-56258    *ISBN* 0070320861

**Mullin, Donald C.**     • **1.5548**
The development of the playhouse; a survey of theatre architecture from the Renaissance to the present [by] Donald C. Mullin. — Berkeley: University of California Press, 1970. xvi, 197 p.: illus., plans.; 29 cm. 1. Theaters — Construction — History. I. T.
NA6821.M83    725/.822    *LC* 77-84532    *ISBN* 0520013913

**McNamara, Brooks.**     **1.5549**
The American playhouse in the eighteenth century. — Cambridge, Mass.: Harvard University Press, 1969. xviii, 174 p.: illus. (part col.), map.; 21 cm. 1. Theaters — United States — Construction. 2. Theater — United States — History. I. T.
NA6830.M3    725/.822    *LC* 68-54021

**Leacroft, Richard.**     **1.5550**
The development of the English playhouse. — Ithaca, N.Y.: Cornell University Press, [1973] xiii, 354 p.: illus.; 29 cm. 1. Theaters — England — Construction. 2. Theater — England. I. T.
NA6840.G7 L4    725/.822/0942    *LC* 72-6713    *ISBN* 0801407508

**Hodges, C. Walter (Cyril Walter), 1909-.**     **1.5551**
Shakespeare's Second Globe; the missing monument [by] C. Walter Hodges. London, Oxford University Press, 1973. 99 p. illus. 30 cm. 1. Shakespeare, William, 1564-1616 — Stage history — To 1625 2. Globe Theatre (Southwark, London, England) I. T.
NA6840.G72 S6874    792./09421/64    *LC* 74-185794    *ISBN* 0192129627

**Allen, John Jay, 1932-.**     **1.5552**
The reconstruction of a Spanish Golden Age playhouse: El Corral del Príncipe, 1583–1744 / John J. Allen. — Gainesville: University Presses of Florida, c1983. xii, 129 p., [2] folded p. of plates: ill.; 27 cm. 'A University of Florida book.' English and Spanish. Includes index. 1. Corral del Príncipe. 2. Madrid (Spain) — Buildings, structures, etc. I. T.
NA6840.S72 M3233 1983    725/.822/094641 19    *LC* 83-1241    *ISBN* 0813007550

## NA7100–8480 Domestic Architecture. Dwellings

**Serlio, Sebastiano.**     **1.5553**
On domestic architecture: different dwellings from the nearest hovel to the most ornate palace: the sixteenth–century manuscript of book VI in the Avery Library of Columbia University / [by] Sebastiano Serlio; foreword by Adolf K. Placzek; introduction by James S. Ackerman; text by Myra Nan Rosenfeld. — New York: Architectural History Foundation; Cambridge, Mass.; London: M.I.T. Press, 1978. 89, [15] p.: ill., facsims., plans, port.; 36 cm. — (Architectural History Foundation/MIT Press series. no.1) Italian text, English commentary. 1. Architecture, Domestic 2. Architecture — Early works to 1800. I. Rosenfeld, Myra Nan. II. Avery Library. MSS. III. T. IV. Series.
NA7109.S4x    728    *LC* 78-16112    *ISBN* 0262191741

**Neutra, Richard Joseph, 1892-1970.**     • **1.5554**
Life and human habitat= Mensch und Wohnen. — Stuttgart: A. Koch, 1956. — 317 p.: ill., ports., plans. Text in English:ill. have descriptive legends in English and German. I. T.
NA7110.N38    728    *LC* 56-2606

**Rowe, Colin.**     **1.5555**
The mathematics of the ideal villa, and other essays / Colin Rowe. — Cambridge, Mass.: MIT Press, c1976. 223 p.: ill.; 26 cm. 1. Architecture, Domestic — Addresses, essays, lectures. I. T.
NA7110.R68    720/.8    *LC* 75-33908    *ISBN* 0262180774

**Sherwood, Roger.**     **1.5556**
Modern housing prototypes / Roger Sherwood. — Cambridge, Mass.: Harvard University Press, c1978. x, 167 p.: ill. (some col.); 28 cm. 1. Architecture, Domestic — Designs and plans 2. Architecture, Modern — 20th century — Designs and plans. I. T.
NA7126.S48    728.3/1/0222    *LC* 78-15508    *ISBN* 0674579410

**McAlester, Virginia, 1943-.**     **1.5557**
A field guide to American houses / by Virginia and Lee McAlester; with drawings by Lauren Jarrett, and model house drawings by Juan Rodriguez-Arnaiz. — New York: Knopf, 1984. xv, 525 p.: ill. (some col.); 24 cm. Includes index. 1. Architecture, Domestic — United States — Guide-books. 2. United

States — Description and travel — Guide-books I. McAlester, A. Lee (Arcie Lee), 1933- II. T.
NA7205.M35 1984    917.3/04927 19    *LC* 82-48740    *ISBN* 0394739698

**Handlin, David P.**     **1.5558**
The American home: architecture and society, 1815–1915 / David P. Handlin. — 1st ed. — Boston: Little, Brown, c1979. xii, 545 p.: ill.; 24 cm. 1. Architecture, Domestic — United States 2. Architecture, Modern — 19th century — United States 3. Architecture, Modern — 20th century — United States 4. Architecture and society — United States. I. T.
NA7207.H32    728.3    *LC* 79-14894    *ISBN* 0316343005

**Scully, Vincent Joseph, 1920-.**     • **1.5559**
The shingle style; architectural theory and design from Richardson to the origins of Wright. New Haven, Yale University Press, 1955. 181 p. ill. (Yale historical publications. History of art, 10) 1. Architecture, Domestic — United States I. T.
NA7207 S38    *LC* 55-5988

**Woodward, George Evertson.**     **1.5560**
Woodward's Victorian architecture and rural art: a facsimile of volume one (1867) and volume two (1868). — [Watkins GLen, N. Y.]: American Life Foundation, 1978. 144, 132 p.: ill., plans. — (Library of Victorian culture) 1. Architecture, Domestic — United States 2. Architecture, Modern — 19th century — United States 3. Architecture, American 4. Architecture, Domestic — Designs and plans I. Woodward, George Evertson. Woodward's architecture and rural art. II. T. III. Title: Woodward's architecture and rural art. IV. Title: Victorian architecture and rural art. V. Title: Architecture and rural art.
NA7207.W67 1978    728.0973    *ISBN* 089257044X

**Wright, Frank Lloyd, 1867-1959.**     • **1.5561**
The natural house. New York: Horizon Press, 1954. 223 p.: illus., port., plans.; 26 cm. 1. Architecture, Domestic — United States 2. Architecture, Modern — 20th century — United States 3. Architecture, Domestic — Designs and plans I. T.
NA7208.W68    728.081    *LC* 54-12278

**Bay area houses / edited by Sally Woodbridge; introd. by David Gebhard; photos. by Morley Baer, Roger Sturtevant, and others; architectural drawings by Randolph Meadors and Floyd Campbell.**     **1.5562**
New York: Oxford University Press, 1976. 329 p.: ill.; 29 cm. 1. Architecture, Domestic — California — San Francisco Bay Area. 2. Dwellings — California — San Francisco Bay Area. I. Woodbridge, Sally Byrne. II. Baer, Morley. III. Sturtevant, Roger.
NA7235.C22 S353    728.3    *LC* 76-9261    *ISBN* 0195020847

**Wright, Janet B.**     **1.5563**
Architecture of the picturesque in Canada / Janet Wright. — Ottawa, Ont.: National Historic Parks and Sites Branch, Parks Canada, Environment Canada; Hull, Quebec, Canada: Canadian Govt. Pub. Centre, Supply and Services Canada [distributor], 1984. 183 p.: ill.; 25 cm. (Studies in archaeology, architecture, and history. 0821-1027) 1. Architecture, Domestic — Canada. 2. Architecture, English — Canada. 3. Picturesque, The, in architecture — Canada. I. T. II. Series.
NA7241.W75 1984    728.3/7/09713 19    *LC* 84-235109    *ISBN* 0660116413

**Brunskill, R. W.**     • **1.5564**
Illustrated handbook of vernacular architecture [by] R. W. Brunskill. — New York: Universe Books, [1971, c1970] 229 p.: illus., maps, plans.; 22 cm. 1. Vernacular architecture — Great Britain. I. T.
NA7328.B83 1971    728/.0942    *LC* 71-134757    *ISBN* 0876631383

**Hill, Oliver, 1887-.**     **1.5565**
English country houses: Caroline, 1625–1685 [by] Oliver Hill and John Cornforth. London, Country Life, 1966. 255 p. front., ill. (incl. ports.) plans. 1. Architecture, Domestic — England 2. England — Historic houses, etc. I. Cornforth, John, 1937- joint author II. T.
NA7328 H5    *LC* 66-76657

**Muthesius, Hermann, 1861-1927.**     **1.5566**
[Englische Haus. English] The English house / by Hermann Muthesius; edited with an introd. by Dennis Sharp; and a pref. by Julius Posener; translated by Janet Seligman. — New York: Rizzoli, 1979. xxii, 246 p.: ill.; 30 cm. Translation of Das englische Haus. Includes index. 1. Architecture, Domestic — England 2. Architecture, Modern — 19th century — England. 3. Dwellings — England I. Sharp, Dennis. II. T.
NA7328.M8713    728/.0942    *LC* 78-68490    *ISBN* 0847802191

**Downing, A. J. (Andrew Jackson), 1815-1852.**     **1.5567**
The architecture of country houses; including designs for cottages, and farmhouses, and villas, with remarks on interiors, furniture, and the best modes of warming and ventilating. [1st ed.] New York, Dover Publications [1969]

xxiv, 484 p. illus., plans. 22 cm. Reprint of the 1850 ed., with a new introd. by J. Stewart Johnson. 1. Country homes I. T.
NA7561.D75 1969    728.6    *LC* 69-17702    *ISBN* 0486220036

**Girouard, Mark, 1931-.**     **1.5568**
The Victorian country house / Mark Girouard. — Rev. and enl. ed. — New Haven: Yale University Press, 1979. vii, 467 p.: ill., facsims. (on lining papers); 27 cm. 1. Country homes — Great Britain. 2. Architecture, Victorian — Great Britain. I. T.
NA7562.G5 1979    728.8/3/0942    *LC* 79-64077    *ISBN* 0300023901

**King, Anthony D.**     **1.5569**
The bungalow: the production of a global culture / Anthony D. King. — London; Boston: Routledge & Kegan Paul, 1984. 310 p.: ill. Includes index. 1. Bungalows I. T.
NA7570.K56 1984    728.3/73 19    *LC* 83-13778    *ISBN* 0710095384

**Coffin, David R.**     • **1.5570**
The Villa d'Este at Tivoli. Princeton, N.J. [Published for the Dept. of Art and Archaeology, Princeton University by] Princeton University Press, 1960. xvi, 186 p. 137 ill. (incl. map, plans) (Princeton monographs in art and archaeology. 34) 1. Tivoli, Italy. Villa d'Este I. T. II. Series.
NA7595 E73 C6    *LC* 60-5744

**Lewis, Arnold.**     **1.5571**
American country houses of the Gilded Age (Sheldon's 'Artistic country-seats') / new text by Arnold Lewis. — New York: Dover Publications, [1982] xxii, [100] p.: ill. Consists primarily of pictorial material from Artistic country-seats, edited by George William Sheldon. Includes index. 1. Country homes — United States — Pictorial works. 2. Country homes — United States — Designs and plans. 3. Architecture, Modern — 19th century — United States — Pictorial works. I. Sheldon, George William, 1843-1914. II. Artistic country-seats. III. T.
NA7610.A58    *LC* 81-17384    *ISBN* 048624301X

**Cook, Olive.**     **1.5572**
The English country house: an art and a way of life / Olive Cook; photos. by A. F. Kersting. — New York: Putnam, [1974] 240 p.: ill. (some col.); 27 cm. Includes index. 1. Manors — England — History. 2. Country homes — England — History. 3. England — Social life and customs — History. I. T.
NA7620.C58 1974b    942    *LC* 74-80029    *ISBN* 0399114041

**Hussey, Christopher, 1899-.**     • **1.5573**
English country houses / Christopher Hussey. — London: Country Life, 1955 [v.1 1966] .— v.: ill.; 32 cm. 1. Architecture, Domestic — England 2. Historic buildings — England. I. Hill, Oliver. II. Cornforth, John, 1937- III. T.
NA7620 H87

**Lees-Milne, James.**     **1.5574**
English country houses: Baroque, 1685–1715. — Feltham: Country Life Books, 1970. 303 p.; ill., plans.; 32 cm. 1. Country homes — England 2. Architecture, Baroque — England. I. T.
NA7620.L4    728.8/3/0942    *LC* 76-871167    *ISBN* 0600431231

**Gébelin, François, 1884-.**     • **1.5575**
Les châteaux de France. [1. éd.] Paris, Presses universitaires de France, 1962. 184 p. illus. 21 cm. ('Le Lys d'or'; histoire de l'art français) 1. Castles — France — History. I. T.
NA7735.G37    *LC* 63-32045

**Renn, Derek Frank.**     **1.5576**
Norman castles in Britain [by] D. F. Renn. — London: Baker; New York: Humanities P., 1968. xiii, 364 p.: 49 plates, illus. (incl. col.), 6 maps, 76 plans.; 26 cm. 1. Architecture, Norman — Great Britain. 2. Castles — Great Britain. I. T.
NA7745.R4 1968    728.8/1/0942    *LC* 68-118549    £6/6/-

**Coffin, David R.**     **1.5577**
The villa in the life of Renaissance Rome / David R. Coffin. — Princeton, N.J.: Princeton University Press, c1979. xx, 385 p.: ill.; 29 cm. (Princeton monographs in art and archaeology. 43) Includes index. 1. Palaces — Italy — Rome. 2. Architecture, Renaissance — Italy — Rome. 3. Palaces — Italy — Rome Region. 4. Architecture, Renaissance — Italy — Rome Region. 5. Rome (Italy) — Social life and customs 6. Rome Region (Italy) — Social life and customs. 7. Rome (Italy) — Buildings, structures, etc. I. T. II. Series.
NA7755.C6    945/.632/05    *LC* 78-9049    *ISBN* 0691039429

# NA9000–9425 Cities. City Planning

(see also HT)

**Le Corbusier, 1887-1965.**    **1.5578**
The Athens charter. With an introd. by Jean Giraudoux. Translated from the French by Anthony Eardley. With a new foreword by Josep Lluis Sert. — New York: Grossman Publishers, 1973. xix, 111 p.: illus.; 22 cm. At head of title: Le Corbusier. Le Corbusier's commentary on the Athens charter drawn up at the 4th International Congress for Modern Architecture held in Athens 1933; includes the text of the charter and introductory material. 1. International Congress for Modern Architecture. 4th, Athens, 1933. La Charte d'Athènes. 2. Cities and towns — Planning — Congresses. I. International Congress for Modern Architecture. 4th, Athens, 1933. La Charte d'Athènes. English. 1973. II. T. III. Title: La Charte d'Athènes.
NA9010.I53 1933zf    309.2/62    LC 70-188311    ISBN 067013970X

**Geddes, Patrick, Sir, 1854-1932.**    • **1.5579**
Cities in evolution; an introduction to the town planning movement and to the study of civics. With a new introd. by Percy Johnson–Marshall. New York, H. Fertig, 1968. xxxv, 409 p. illus., maps, plans. 23 cm. Reprint of the 1915 ed. 1. City planning — History. I. T.
NA9030.G4 1968    711/.4/09    LC 68-54893

**Goodman, Percival.**    • **1.5580**
Communitas; means of livelihood and ways of life [by] Percival and Paul Goodman. [2d ed., rev.] New York, Vintage Books [1960] 248 p. illus. 19 cm. 1. City planning I. Goodman, Paul, 1911-1972. joint author. II. T.
NA9030.G6 1960    711.4    LC 60-6381

**Hegemann, Werner, 1881-1936.**    **1.5581**
The American Vitruvius: an architects' handbook of civic art, by Werner Hegemann and Elbert Peets. New York, B. Blom [1972] vi, 298 p. illus. 34 cm. Half title: Civic art. Reprint of the 1922 ed. published by the Architectural Book Pub. Co., New York. 1. Art, Municipal 2. City planning I. Peets, Elbert, 1886-1968, joint author. II. T. III. Title: Civic art.
NA9030.H4 1972    711/.4    LC 68-57189

**Barnett, Jonathan.**    **1.5582**
An introduction to urban design / by Jonathan Barnett. — 1st ed. — New York: Harper & Row, c1982. vii, 260 p.: ill.; 24 cm. — (Icon editions) 1. City planning 2. Architecture 3. Architecture and society I. T.
NA9031.B33 1982    711/.4 19    LC 81-47792    ISBN 0064303764

**Benevolo, Leonardo.**    **1.5583**
[Origini dell'urbanistica moderna. English] The origins of modern town planning. Translated by Judith Landry. Cambridge, Mass., M.I.T. Press [1967] xiv, 154 p. illus., facsims., maps, plans. 23 cm. Translation of Le origini dell'urbanistica moderna. 1. City planning — History. I. T.
NA9031.B4x    711/.4/09    LC 67-17494

**De Chiara, Joseph, 1929-.**    **1.5584**
Urban planning and design criteria / [by] Joseph De Chiara [and] Lee Koppelman. — 2d ed. — New York: Van Nostrand Reinhold, [1975] 646 p.: ill.; 23 x 31 cm. First published in 1969 under title: Planning design criteria. 1. Cities and towns — Planning — 1945- — Handbooks, manuals, etc. I. Koppelman, Lee. joint author. II. T.
NA9031.D4 1975    711/.4/0973 19    LC 74-16413    ISBN 0442220553

**Wright, Frank Lloyd, 1867-1959.**    • **1.5585**
The living city. — New York: Horizon Press, 1958. 222 p.: illus., port., plans. 27 cm. 1. City planning I. T.
NA9031.W7    711.4    LC 58-13550

**Sitte, Camillo, 1843-1903.**    **1.5586**
[Städte-Bau nach seinen künstlerischen Grundsätzen. English] The art of building cities: city building according to its artistic fundamentals / by Camillo Sitte; translated by Charles T. Stewart. — Westport, Conn.: Hyperion Press, 1979, c1945. xi, 128 p.: ill.; 26 cm. Translation of Der Städte-Bau. Reprint of the ed. published by Reinhold Pub. Corp., New York. Includes index. 1. Urban beautification 2. Art, Municipal I. T.
NA9052.S5813 1979    711/.4    LC 78-14144    ISBN 0883558173

**Rudofsky, Bernard, 1905-.**    • **1.5587**
Streets for people; a primer for Americans. Photos. by the author. — [1st ed.]. — Garden City, N.Y.: Doubleday, [1969] 351 p.: illus. (part col.), music.; 27 cm. 1. Urban beautification 2. Streets I. T.
NA9053.S7 R8    711/.74    LC 76-78735

**Zucker, Paul, 1889-1971.**    • **1.5588**
Town and square, from the agora to the village green. — [1st M.I.T. Press paperback ed.]. — Cambridge: M.I.T. Press, [1970, c1959] xxiii, 287 p.: illus., plans.; 26 cm. 'MIT 152. Architecture.' 1. Plazas 2. City planning — History. I. T.
NA9070.Z8 1970    711/.5    LC 78-123257    ISBN 0262740052

**Caro, Robert A.**    **1.5589**
The power broker: Robert Moses and the fall of New York, by Robert A. Caro. [1st ed.] New York, Knopf, 1974. ix, 1246, xxxiv p. illus. 25 cm. 1. Moses, Robert, 1888-1981. I. T.
NA9085.M68 C37 1974    974.7/04/0924 B    LC 73-20751    ISBN 0394480767

## NA9090–9095 HISTORY

**Le Corbusier, 1887-1965.**    **1.5590**
[Urbanisme. English] The city of to–morrow and its planning, by Le Corbusier. Translated from the 8th French ed. of Urbanisme by Frederick Etchells. Cambridge, Mass.: MIT Press, 1972, c1971. xv, 301 p. illus. 22 cm. 'Facsimile ... edition.' Originally published by Harcourt, 1929. 1. City planning I. T.
NA9090.J413 1929a    711/.4    LC 78-148855    ISBN 0262120410

**Lavedan, Pierre, 1885-.**    • **1.5591**
Histoire de l'urbanisme. Paris, H. Laurens, 1926-52. 3 v. ill., maps, plans. 1. Cities and towns — Planning — History I. T.
NA9090 L38

**Moholy-Nagy, Sibyl, 1905-.**    • **1.5592**
Matrix of man; an illustrated history of urban environment [by] Sibyl Moholy–Nagy. New York, Praeger [1968] 317 p. illus., maps, plans. 27 cm. 1. City planning — History. I. T.
NA9090.M58    711/.4/09    LC 68-11320

**Rosenau, Helen.**    **1.5593**
The ideal city, its architectural evolution / Helen Rosenau. — Rev. ed. — New York: Harper & Row, [1975] c1972. 176 p.: ill.; 26 cm. — (Icon editions) Published in 1959 under title: The ideal city in its architectural evolution. Includes index. 1. City planning — History. I. T.
NA9090.R6 1975    711/.4/094    LC 74-188931    ISBN 0064384616

**Argan, Giulio Carlo.**    • **1.5594**
The Renaissance city [by] Giulio C. Argan. [Translated by Susan Edna Bassnett]. — New York: G. Braziller, [1970, c1969] 128 p.: illus., maps, plans.; 25 cm. — (Planning and cities) 1. City planning 2. Architecture, Renaissance I. T.
NA9094.A713    711/.4    LC 70-90409

**Loyer, François.**    **1.5595**
[Siècle de l'industrie. English] Architecture of the industrial age, 1789–1914 / François Loyer; [translated from the French by R.F.M. Dexter]. — Geneva, Switzerland: Skira, c1983. 319 p.: ill. (some col.); 33 cm. Translation of: Le siècle de l'industrie. Includes index. 1. City planning — History — 19th century. 2. Urbanization — History. 3. Industrialization — History. I. T.
NA9094.8.L6913 1983    711/.4/094 19    LC 83-42959    ISBN 0847805018

## NA9101–9284 BY COUNTRY

**Reps, John William.**    • **1.5596**
The making of urban America: a history of city planning in the United States / by John W. Reps. — Princeton, N.J.: Princeton University Press, 1965. xv, 574 p.: ill., maps. 1. City planning — United States. I. T.
NA9105.R45    LC 63-23414

**Jacobs, Jane, 1916-.**    • **1.5597**
The death and life of great American cities. [New York] Random House [1961] 458 p. 24 cm. 1. City planning — United States. I. T.
NA9108.J3    711.40973    LC 61-6262

**Lynch, Kevin, 1918-.**    • **1.5598**
The image of the city. Cambridge [Mass.] Technology Press, 1960. 194 p. illus. 22 cm. (Publications of the Joint Center for Urban Studies) 1. City planning — United States. I. T.
NA9108.L9    711.40973    LC 60-7362

**Stein, Clarence S.**     • **1.5599**
Toward new towns for America. With an introd. by Lewis Mumford. [Rev. ed.]
New York, Reinhold Pub. Corp. [1957] 263 p. illus., plans (part col.) tables. 27
cm. 1. City planning — United States. 2. Garden cities — United States. I. T.
NA9108.S8 1957     711.0973     *LC* 57-6538

**Tunnard, Christopher.**     • **1.5600**
Man–made America: chaos or control? An inquiry into selected problems of
design in the urbanized landscape, by Christopher Tunnard and Boris
Pushkarev in association with Geoffrey Baker [and others] With drawings by
Philip Lin and Vladimir Pozharsky and photos. by John Reed and Charles R.
Schulze. New Haven, Yale University Press, 1963. xii, 479 p. illus., maps. 29
cm. 1. Architecture — Environmental aspects — United States. 2. Urban
beautification — United States. 3. Architecture — United States —
Conservation and restoration. 4. Regional planning — United States.
I. Pushkarev, Boris. joint author. II. T.
NA9108.T82     711.30973     *LC* 62-16243

**Whyte, William Hollingsworth.**     • **1.5601**
Cluster development, by William H. Whyte. Foreword by Laurance S.
Rockefeller. — [1st ed.]. — New York: American Conservation Association,
1964. 130 p.: illus., plans (part col.); 28 cm. 1. Cluster housing — Planning —
United States. I. T.
NA9108.W5     711.58     *LC* 64-18592

**Ashworth, William.**     **1.5602**
The genesis of modern British town planning; a study in economic and social
history of the nineteenth and twentieth centuries. London, Routledge & Paul
[1954] xii, 259 p. (International library of sociology and social reconstruction)
1. Cities and towns — Planning — Great Britain I. T. II. Series.
NA9185 A795     *LC* 54-1614

**Wycherley, R. E. (Richard Ernest)**     **1.5603**
How the Greeks built cities / by R.E. Wycherley. — 2d ed. — New York:
Norton, 1976, c1962. xxi, 235 p., [8] leaves of plates: ill.; 19 cm. (The Norton
library) Reprint of the ed. published by Macmillan, London. 1. Cities and
towns — Planning — Greece. 2. Architecture — Greece I. T.
NA9201.W85 1976     711/.4/0938     *LC* 76-10762     *ISBN* 0393008142

**Westfall, Carroll William.**     **1.5604**
In this most perfect paradise; Alberti, Nicholas V, and the invention of
conscious urban planning in Rome, 1447–55. University Park, Pennsylvania
State University Press [1974] xvi, 228 p. illus. 28 cm. 1. Alberti, Leon Battista,
1404-1472. 2. Nicolaus V, Pope, d. 1455. 3. City planning — Italy — Rome —
History. 4. Rome (Italy) — History — 1420-1798 I. T.
NA9204.R7 W47     711/.4/0945632     *LC* 73-3352     *ISBN*
0271011750

**Burke, Gerald L.**     **1.5605**
The making of Dutch towns; a study in urban development from the tenth to
the seventeenth centuries. Foreword by Sir William Holford. London, Cleaver-
Hume Press [1956] 176 p. ill. (part col.) maps. 1. Cities and towns — Planning
— Netherlands I. T.
NA9207 B8     *LC* 57-389

**Lampl, Paul.**     • **1.5606**
Cities and planning in the ancient Near East. New York, Braziller [1968] 128 p.
illus., maps, plans. 25 cm. (Planning and cities) 1. City planning — Near East.
I. T.
NA9245.N4 L3     711/.4/093     *LC* 68-24699

**Kutcher, Arthur.**     **1.5607**
The new Jerusalem, planning and politics / Arthur Kutcher; foreword by
Vincent Scully. — 1st American ed. — Cambridge: M.I.T. Press, 1975, c1973.
128 p.: ill.; 23 x 24 cm. 1. City planning — Jerusalem. 2. Architecture —
Jerusalem. I. T.
NA9246.6.J4 K87 1975     711/.4/0956944     *LC* 74-10483     *ISBN*
026211058X. *ISBN* 0262610205 pbk

**Sharon, Aryeh, 1900-.**     **1.5608**
Planning Jerusalem: the master plan for the old city of Jerusalem and its
environs, by Arieh Sharon. Planning team of the outline townplanning scheme:
Arieh Sharon, David Anatol Brutzkus [and] Eldar Sharon. Art editor and
design: Chava Mordohovich. New York, McGraw-Hill [1974, c1973] 211 p.
illus. 28 cm. 'Sponsors: the Ministry of the Interior of the State of Israel and the
Municipality of Jerusalem.' 1. City planning — Jerusalem. I. Brutzkus, David
Anatol. II. Sharon, Eldar. III. Israel. Miśrad ha-penim. IV. Jerusalem. V. T.
NA9246.6.J4 S46 1974     309.2/62/0956944     *LC* 73-8521     *ISBN*
0070564507

# NB Sculpture

**Clapp, Jane.**     **1.5609**
Sculpture index. — Metuchen, N.J.: Scarecrow Press, 1970 [c1970-71] 2 v. in 3.;
22 cm. 1. Sculpture — Indexes. I. T.
NB36.C55     730/.16     *LC* 79-9538     *ISBN* 081080249X

**New dictionary of modern sculpture. General editor: Robert**     • **1.5610**
**Maillard. [Translated from the French by Bettina Wadia].**
New York: Tudor Pub. Co., [1971] 328 p.: illus.; 24 cm. Translation of Nouveau
dictionnaire de la sculpture moderne, first published in 1960 under title:
Dictionnaire de la sculpture moderne. 1. Sculptors — Dictionaries.
I. Maillard, Robert. ed.
NB50.N6813     730/.922     *LC* 70-153118     *ISBN* 0814804799

# NB60–1113 History

**Butler, Ruth, 1931-.**     **1.5611**
Western sculpture: definitions of man / Ruth Butler. — Boston: New York
Graphic Society, c1975. xv, 304 p.: ill.; 28 cm. Includes index. 1. Sculpture —
History I. T.
NB60.B88     730/.9     *LC* 74-21497     *ISBN* 0821204297

**Chase, George Henry, 1874-1952.**     • **1.5612**
A history of sculpture, by George Henry Chase and Chandler Rathfon Post. —
Westport, Conn.: Greenwood Press, [1971, c1925] 582 p.: illus.; 23 cm.
Originally issued in the series: Harper's fine arts series. 1. Sculpture — History
I. Post, Chandler Rathfon, 1881-1959. joint author. II. T.
NB60.C5 1971     730/.9     *LC* 72-138105     *ISBN* 0837156815

## NB69–169 Ancient Sculpture

**Murray, Margaret Alice.**     • **1.5613**
Egyptian sculpture. With a pref. by Ernest A. Gardner. — Westport, Conn.:
Greenwood Press, [1970] xxiv, 207 p.: illus.; 23 cm. Reprint of the 1930 ed.
1. Sculpture, Egyptian I. T.
NB75.M8 1970     732/.8     *LC* 74-109802     *ISBN* 0837142938

**Barnett, Richard David, 1909-.**     **1.5614**
Assyrian sculpture in the British Museum / text by R. D. Barnett; photography
by Amleto Lorenzini. — Toronto: McClelland and Stewart, c1975. 39, 179 p.:
chiefly ill.; 31 cm. 1. British Museum. 2. Sculpture, Assyro-Babylonian —
Catalogs. 3. Sculpture — London — Catalogs. I. Lorenzine, Amleto.
II. British Museum. III. T.
NB80.B3185     NB80 B3185.     732/.5     *LC* 76-353580     *ISBN*
0771053452

**British Museum. Dept. of Western Asiatic Antiquities.**     **1.5615**
Assyrian palace reliefs in the British Museum; text by R. D. Barnett;
photography by W. Forman. London, British Museum, 1970. 47 p., 20 plates.
20 illus., maps. 25 cm. Shortened ed. of Barnett and Forman's Assyrian palace
reliefs and their influence on the sculptures of Babylonia and Persia; now
retitled and adapted to serve as a guide to the British Museum collection.
1. Sculpture, Assyro-Babylonian 2. Bas-relief — Iraq. I. Barnett, Richard
David, 1909- Assyrian palace reliefs and their influence on the sculptures of
Babylonia and Persia. 1970. II. Forman, W. (Werner) illus. III. T.
NB80.B772     732/.5     *LC* 78-587015     *ISBN* 0714110744

**Gadd, Cyril John.**     • **1.5616**
The stones of Assyria; the surviving remains of Assyrian sculpture, their
recovery and their original positions. London, Chatto and Windus, 1936. 252,
14 p. ill. 1. Sculpture, Assyro-Babylonian 2. Nineveh 3. Assyria —
Antiquities I. T.
NB80 G3

**Lawrence, A. W. (Arnold Walter), 1900-.**     **1.5617**
Greek and Roman sculpture. [Rev. ed.] New York: Harper & Row, 1972.
369 p., 96 plates: ill. (Icon editions) Previous ed. published as: Classical
sculpture, 1929. 1. Sculpture — Greece 2. Sculpture — Rome. I. Lawrence,
A. W. (Arnold Walter), 1900- Classical sculpture II. T. III. Title: Classical
sculpture
NB85 L3 1972     *LC* 72-82943     *ISBN* 0064352609

**Vermeule, Cornelius Clarkson, 1925-.**                    **1.5618**
Greek and Roman sculpture in America: masterpieces in public collections in
the United States and Canada / Cornelius C. Vermeule. — Malibu, Calif.: The
J. Paul Getty Museum; Berkeley: University of California Press, 1982, c1981.
ix, 406 p., [30] p. of plates: ill.; 29 cm. Includes indexes. 1. Sculpture, Classical
— United States. I. T.
NB86.V47 1981        733/.074/013 19       *LC* 81-3057        *ISBN* 0520043243

**Payne, Humfry, 1902-1936.**                              • **1.5619**
Archaic marble sculpture from the Acropolis; a photographic catalogue, by the
late Humfry Payne and Gerard Mackworth–Young, with an introd. by Humfry
Payne. [2d ed.] New York, W. Morrow [1951] xiii, 79 p. plates. 34 cm. 'A
descriptive catalogue of the Acropolis Museum, the work of students of the
Brititsh School at Athens, was published some years ago—the first volume in
1912, the second in 1921. The first of these by the late Guy Dickins, deals with
the archaic sculpture, and the present photographic catalogue is
complementary to it.'—Pref. 1. Sculpture, Greek 2. Athens (Greece)
Mouseion tēs Akropoleōs. I. Young, Gerard Mackworth, 1884- II. T.
NB87.A8 P3x        *LC* a 52-7032

**Museum of Fine Arts, Boston.**                           **1.5620**
Sculpture in stone: the Greek, Roman and Etruscan collections of the Museum
of Fine Arts, Boston / Mary B. Comstock and Cornelius C. Vermeule. —
Boston: The Museum; distributed by C. E. Tuttle, Rutland, Vt., c1976. xxxi,
296 p.: ill.; 29 cm. 1. Sculpture, Greek — Catalogs. 2. Sculpture, Etruscan —
Catalogs. 3. Sculpture, Roman — Catalogs. 4. Sculpture — Massachusetts —
Boston — Catalogs. I. Comstock, Mary. II. Vermeule, Cornelius Clarkson,
1925- III. T.
NB87.B6 B6        *LC* 70-40711        *ISBN* 0878461035

**Bieber, Margarete, 1879-.**                              • **1.5621**
The sculpture of the Hellenistic Age. Rev. ed. New York, Columbia University
Press [1961] xi, 259 p. ill., plates. 1. Sculpture, Greek I. T.
NB90 B48 1961        *LC* 61-66470

**Bluemel, Carl, 1893-.**                                  • **1.5622**
[Griechische Bildhauerarbeit. English] Greek sculptors at work; [translated
from the German by Lydia Holland]. 2nd English ed.; [revised by Betty Ross].
London, Phaidon, 1969. viii, 86 p. illus. 28 cm. Translation of Griechische
Bildhauerarbeit. 1. Sculpture, Greek I. T.
NB90.B552 1969        733/.3        *LC* 77-81234        *ISBN* 0714813591

**Casson, Stanley, 1889-1944.**                            • **1.5623**
The technique of early Greek sculpture. — New York: Hacker Art Books, 1970.
xiii p., [1] l., 246 p.: illus.; 25 cm. Reprint of the 1933 ed. 1. Sculpture, Greek
2. Sculpture — Technique I. T.
NB90.C3 1970        733/.3        *LC* 72-116353        *ISBN* 0878170413

**Lullies, Reinhard, 1907-.**                              • **1.5624**
Greek sculpture. Text and notes by Reinhard Lullies. Photos. by Max Hirmer.
[Translated from the German by Michael Bullock. Rev. and enl. ed.] New
York, H.N. Abrams [1960] 115 p. illus., 292 plates (part col.) 31 cm.
1. Sculpture, Greek I. Hirmer, Max, 1893- II. T.
NB90.L813 1960        733.3        *LC* 60-10887

**New York. Metropolitan Museum of Art.**                  • **1.5625**
Catalogue of Greek sculptures / by Gisela M.A. Richter. — Cambridge:
Published for the Museum by Havard University Press, 1954. xviii, 123 p.: ill.,
164 plates; 29 cm. I. Richter, Gisela Marie Augusta, 1882-1972. II. T.
NB90.N4        *LC* 54-10056

**Richter, Gisela Marie Augusta, 1882-1972.**              • **1.5626**
The sculpture and sculptors of the Greeks, by Gisela M. A. Richter. — 4th ed,
newly rev. — New Haven: Yale University Press, 1970. xvi, 317, [345] p.: illus.,
maps.; 29 cm. At head of title: The Metropolitan Museum of Art. 1. Sculpture,
Greek 2. Sculptors — Greece. I. T.
NB90.R54 1970        733/.3        *LC* 70-99838        *ISBN* 0300012810

**Ridgway, Brunilde Sismondo, 1929-.**                     **1.5627**
The archaic style in Greek sculpture / by Brunilde Sismondo Ridgway. —
Princeton, N.J.: Princeton University Press, c1977. xix, 336 p., [24] leaves of
plates: ill.; 29 cm. 1. Sculpture, Greek I. T.
NB90.R56        733/.3        *LC* 76-19655        *ISBN* 0691039208

**Ridgway, Brunilde Sismondo, 1929-.**                     **1.5628**
Fifth century styles in Greek sculpture / by Brunilde Sismondo Ridgway. —
Princeton, N.J.: Princeton University Press, c1981. xxiv, 256 p., [37] leaves of
plates: ill.; 29 cm. 1. Sculpture, Greek 2. Classicism in art — Greece. I. T.
NB90.R564        733/.3 19        *LC* 80-8574        *ISBN* 0691039658

**Ridgway, Brunilde Sismondo, 1929-.**                     • **1.5629**
The severe style in Greek sculpture. — Princeton, N.J.: Princeton University
Press, 1970. xviii, 155, [67] p.: plates; 29 cm. 1. Sculpture, Greek I. T.
NB90.R57        733/.3        *LC* 77-113008        *ISBN* 0691038694

**Brommer, Frank.**                                        **1.5630**
The sculptures of the Parthenon: metopes, frieze, pediments, cult–statue /
Frank Brommer; foreword by John Boardman; with 220 illustrations. —
London: Thames and Hudson, 1979. 74 p. of text: 220 ill.; 32 cm. 1. Athens.
Parthenon. Sculpture. 2. Sculpture, Greek I. T.
NB91.A782 1979        *LC* 79-63883        *ISBN* 0500232962

**Langlotz, Ernst, 1895-.**                                • **1.5631**
Ancient Greek sculpture of South Italy and Sicily / by Ernst Langlotz; photos.
by Max Hirmer; [translated by Audrey Hicks] New York, H. N. Abrams [1965]
312 p. illus., col. plates, maps, plans. 30 cm. Translation of Die Kunst der
Westgriechen in Sizilien und Unteritalien. Bibliographical references included
in 'Notes to the text' (p. 71-72) English edition published under title: The art of
Magna Graecia; Greek art in Southern Italy and Sicily. 1. Sculpture, Greek
2. Sculpture — Italy, Southern. 3. Sculpture — Italy — Sicily. I. Hirmer, M.
illus. II. T.
NB91.I8L33        *LC* 65-19227

**Ashmole, Bernard, 1894-.**                               • **1.5632**
Olympia: the sculptures of the temple of Zeus, by Bernard Ashmole and
Nicholas Yalouris; with new photographs by Alison Frantz. London, Phaidon
[1967] [3], 188 p. front., illus., 7 plates, map, plan. 31 cm. 1. Olympia. Temple
of Zeus. 2. Sculpture, Greek 3. Olympia (Greece: Ancient sanctuary)
I. Gialourēs, Nikolaos, 1917- joint author. II. Frantz, Alison. III. T.
NB91.O6 A78        733/.3        *LC* 67-98066

**Gialourēs, Nikolaos, 1917-.**                            • **1.5633**
Classical Greece; the Elgin marbles of the Parthenon / by Nicholas Yalouris.
Photographed by F.L. Kenett. Greenwich, Conn., New York Graphic Society
[c1960] xv p.: ill., 33 plates.; 38 cm. (The Acanthus history of sculpture)
1. Athens. Parthenon. 2. Sculpture, Greek 3. Elgin marbles I. Kenett, F. L.
II. T.
NB92.G5        *LC* 60-10477

**Ashmole, Bernard, 1894-.**                               **1.5634**
Architect and sculptor in classical Greece. — New York: New York University
Press, 1972. 218p.: ill. maps. (Wrightsman lectures; 6th) 1. Parthenon (Athens,
Greece) 2. Sculpture, Greek 3. Olympia. Temple of Zeus 4. Hallcarnassus.
Mausoleum I. T. II. Series.
NB94.A83 1972        *LC* 72-76019        *ISBN* 0814705537

**Richter, Gisela Marie Augusta, 1882-1972.**              **1.5635**
Korai: archaic Greek maidens; a study of the development of the Kore type in
Greek sculpture, by G. M. A. Richter; with 800 illustrations, including 400
from photographs by Alison Frantz. — London: Phaidon, 1968. xi, 327 p.:
illus., plates.; 32 cm. 1. Sculpture, Greek 2. Women in art I. T.
NB94.R52        733/.3        *LC* 68-18904        *ISBN* 0714813281

**Richter, Gisela Marie Augusta, 1882-1972.**              • **1.5636**
Kouroi: archaic Greek youths: a study of the development of the Kouros type in
Greek sculpture, by Gisela M. A. Richter; in collaboration with Irma A.
Richter; photographs by Gerard Mackworth–Young. — 3rd ed. — London;
New York: Phaidon, 1970. xvii, 365 p.: illus.; 32 cm. Revision of Kouroi, a
study of the development of the Greek kouros from the late seventh to the early
fifth century B.C., published in 1942. Distributed in the U.S. by Praeger
Publishers. 1. Sculpture, Greek 2. Human figure in art I. Richter, Irma Anne.
II. T.
NB94.R53 1970        733/.3        *LC* 75-118660        *ISBN* 0714814598

**Goldscheider, Ludwig, 1896-.**                           • **1.5637**
Etruscan sculpture ... New York, Oxford university press [1941] 159, [1] p. incl.
illus., 120 pl. on 60 l. 36 cm. Half-title: Etruscan sculptre, by Ludwig
Goldscheider. 'Phaiden edition.' 1. Sculpture, Etruscan I. Lengyel, Frau Ilse
(Schneider) II. T.
NB110.G6        732        *LC* 42-13241

**Strong, Eugénie Sellers.**                               • **1.5638**
Roman sculpture from Augustus to Constantine. — New York: Arno Press,
1969. xvi, 408 p.: 130 plates.; 23 cm. Reprint of the 1907 ed. 'Based upon a series
of lectures.' 1. Sculpture, Roman 2. Sculpture, Greco-Roman I. T.
NB115.S8 1969        733/.5        *LC* 79-88825

**Toynbee, J. M. C. (Jocelyn M. C.), d. 1985.**            **1.5639**
The Hadrianic school, a chapter in the history of Greek art. by Jocelyn M. C.
Toynbee... Cambridge, Eng., The University Press, 1934. xxxi, 254 p. iix pl. on
30 l. 22 cm. 'Presented as a thesis for the degee of D. Phil. at Oxford university.'-
Pref. 1. Sculpture, Roman 2. Sculpture, Greek 3. Numismatics — Rome.
I. T.
NB115.T6        *LC* 34-19714

**Charbonneaux, Jean, 1895-1969.**                         • **1.5640**
Greek bronzes. Translated by Katherine Watson. New York, Viking Press,
1962. 163 p. illus. 22 cm. (A Studio book) 1. Bronzes, Greek I. T.
NB140.C413        *LC* 61-5482

## NB170–180 Medieval Sculpture

**Hibbard, Howard, 1928-.**                                                    **1.5641**
Masterpieces of Western sculpture: from medieval to modern / Howard
Hibbard. — New York: Harper & Row, [1977?] 239 p.: 205 ill. (148 col.) bibl.
(An Alexis Gregory book.) 1. Sculpture, Medieval 2. Sculpture, Modern
3. Sculpture — History I. T.
NB170 H52    NB170 H52.    *LC* 77-2416    *ISBN* 0060118784

**Salvini, Roberto.**                                                        • **1.5642**
Medieval sculpture. — Greenwich, Conn.: New York Graphic Society, [1970,
c1969] 368 p.: illus., col. plates.; 25 cm. — (A History of Western sculpture)
Translation from the Italian. 1. Sculpture, Medieval I. T. II. Series.
NB170.S213    734    *LC* 68-12365

**Hearn, M. F. (Millard Fillmore), 1938-.**                                  **1.5643**
Romanesque sculpture: the revival of monumental stone sculpture in the
eleventh and twelfth centuries / M. F. Hearn. — Ithaca, N.Y.: Cornell
University Press, 1981. 240 p.: ill.; 29 cm. Includes index. 1. Sculpture,
Romanesque I. T.
NB175.H39    734/.24    *LC* 80-14383    *ISBN* 0801412870

**Schapiro, Meyer, 1904-.**                                                  **1.5644**
Romanesque art / Meyer Schapiro. — New York: G. Braziller, 1977. ix, 368 p.,
[34] leaves of plates: ill.; 24 cm. (His Selected papers; 1) 1. Sculpture,
Romanesque — Addresses, essays, lectures. 2. Art, Romanesque — Addresses,
essays, lectures. I. T. II. Series.
NB175.S28 1977b    709/.02/1    *LC* 76-11842    *ISBN* 080760853X

**Müller, Theodor, 1905-.**                                                  **1.5645**
Sculpture in the Netherlands, Germany, France, and Spain: 1400 to 1500;
translated from the German by Elaine and William Robson Scott. —
Harmondsworth, Penguin, 1966. xxiv, 262 p. col. front., 192 plates, maps. 27
cm. — (The Pelican history of art) I. T.
NB180.M82    735.21    *LC* 66-68067

## NB185–198 Modern Sculpture

**Elsen, Albert Edward, 1927-.**                                             **1.5646**
Origins of modern sculpture: pioneers and premises [by] Albert E. Elsen. —
New York: G. Braziller, [1974] ix, 179 p.: illus.; 27 cm. An enl. and altered
version of the introd. to the author's Pioneers of modern sculpture originally
published in 1973. 1. Sculpture, Modern — 19th century 2. Sculpture, Modern
— 20th century I. T.
NB197.E44 1974    735/.29    *LC* 73-90927    *ISBN* 0807607363

**Janson, H. W. (Horst Woldemar), 1913-.**                                   **1.5647**
19th–century sculpture / H.W. Janson; [editor, Phyllis Freeman; designer Bob
McKee]. — New York: Abrams, 1985. 288 p.: ill.; 30 cm. Includes index.
1. Sculpture, Modern — 19th century I. Freeman, Phyllis. II. McKee, Bob.
III. T. IV. Title: Nineteenth-century sculpture.
NB197.3.J36 1985    735/.22 19    *LC* 84-12508    *ISBN* 0810913690

**Metamorphoses in nineteenth–century sculpture: [exhibition,**             **1.5648**
**November 19, 1975–January 7, 1976, Fogg Art Museum,**
**Harvard University: catalogue] / edited by Jeanne L.**
**Wasserman.**
[Cambridge, Mass.]: The Museum: distributed by Harvard University Press,
1975. xvi, 267 p.: ill.; 28 cm. 1. Sculpture, Modern — 19th century —
Exhibitions. I. Wasserman, Jeanne L. II. Fogg Art Museum.
NB197.3.M48    735/.22/07401444    *LC* 75-31618    *ISBN*
0674570804

**Burnham, Jack, 1931-.**                                                    • **1.5649**
Beyond modern sculpture; the effects of science and technology on the sculpture
of this century. — New York: G. Braziller, [1968] x, 402 p.: illus.; 25 cm.
1. Sculpture, Modern — 20th century 2. Sculpture — Technique I. T.
NB198.B84    735/.29    *LC* 68-16106

**Giedion-Welcker, Carola.**                                                 • **1.5650**
Contemporary sculpture, an evolution in volume and space. Rev. and enl. ed.
New York, G. Wittenborn [1961, c1960] xxxi, 400 p. illus., ports. 26 cm. —
(Documents of modern art, 12) Translation of Moderne Plastik. 'Modern art and
sculpture, a selective bibliography by Bernard Karpel': p. 355-394.
1. Sculpture, Modern — 20th century — History 2. Sculptors I. T. II. Series.
NB198.G513 1961    730.904    *LC* 60-15444

**Kelly, James J.**                                                          **1.5651**
The sculptural idea / James J. Kelly. — 3rd ed. — Minneapolis, Minn.: Burgess
Pub. Co., c1981. xii, 219 p.: ill.; 26 cm. Includes index. 1. Sculpture, Modern —
20th century 2. Sculpture — Technique I. T.
NB198.K4 1981    735/.23 19    *LC* 80-68099    *ISBN* 0808711423

**Krauss, Rosalind E.**                                                      **1.5652**
Passages in modern sculpture / Rosalind E. Krauss. — New York: Viking
Press, 1977. ix, 308 p.: ill.; 24 cm. Includes index. 1. Sculpture, Modern — 20th
century I. T.
NB198.K69    735/.29    *LC* 76-41914    *ISBN* 0670541338

**Kultermann, Udo.**                                                         **1.5653**
[Neue Dimensionen der Plastik. English] The new sculpture; environments and
assemblages. New York, F. A. Praeger [1968] 236 p. illus. (part col.), ports. 28
cm. Translation of Neue Dimensionen der Plastik. 1. Sculpture, Modern —
20th century I. T.
NB198.K813 1968    735/.29    *LC* 68-17366

**Read, Herbert Edward, Sir, 1893-1968.**                                    • **1.5654**
A concise history of modern sculpture [by] Herbert Read. — New York:
Praeger, [1964] 310 p.: illus. (part col.); 22 cm. — (Praeger world of art series)
1. Sculpture, Modern — 20th century I. T. II. Title: Modern sculpture.
NB198.R4    735.29    *LC* 64-19789

## NB201–1113 Sculpture, by Country

## NB205–237 United States

**Craven, Wayne.**                                                           • **1.5655**
Sculpture in America / Wayne Craven. — New and rev. ed. — Newark:
University of Delaware Press; New York: Cornwall Books, c1984. xxi, 782 p.:
ill.; 26 cm. — (American art journal/Kennedy Galleries book.) Includes index.
1. Sculpture, American I. T. II. Series.
NB205.C7 1984    730/.973 19    *LC* 82-40439    *ISBN* 0874132258

**Taft, Lorado, 1860-1936.**                                                 • **1.5656**
The history of American sculpture, by Lorado Taft. New ed., rev. with new
matter. New York, The Macmillan company, 1924. vii, xi-xiii, 604 p. incl. illus.,
plates. 26 cm. 1. Sculpture — United States — History. 2. Sculpture,
American. I. T.
NB205.T3 1924    *LC* 24-3172

**200 years of American sculpture / Tom Armstrong ... [et al.].**           **1.5657**
[Boston]: D. R. Godine, c1976. 350 p.: ill. (part col.), ports.; 30 cm. 'A
Bicentennial exhibition organized by the Whitney Museum of American Art,
New York, shown from March 16 to September 26, 1976.' 1. Sculpture,
American — Exhibitions. 2. Neoclassicism (Art) — United States —
Exhibitions. 3. Sculpture, Modern — 19th century — United States —
Exhibitions. 4. Sculpture, Modern — 20th century — United States —
Exhibitions. I. Armstrong, Tom, 1932- II. Whitney Museum of American
Art.
NB205.T86    NB205 T86.    730/.973/07401471    *LC* 76-1762
    *ISBN* 0879231858

**Gardner, Albert Ten Eyck.**                                                • **1.5658**
Yankee stonecutters; the first American school of sculpture, 1800–1850.
Freeport, N.Y., Books for Libraries Press [1968, c1945] 84 p. illus. 32 cm.
(Essay index reprint series) 'Early nineteenth-century American sculpture in
the collection of the Metropolitan Museum of Art': p. [75] 1. Sculpture,
American — History. 2. Sculpture, Modern — 19th century — United States.
3. Sculptors, American. I. Metropolitan Museum of Art (New York, N.Y.)
II. T.
NB210.G3 1968    730/.922    *LC* 68-58790

**Andersen, Wayne V.**                                                       **1.5659**
American sculpture in process, 1930–1970 / Wayne Andersen. — Boston: New
York Graphic Society, c1975. ix, 278 p., [2] leaves of plates: ill. (some col.); 28
cm. 1. Sculpture, American 2. Sculpture, Modern — 20th century — United
States I. T.
NB212.A43 1975    730/.973    *LC* 74-21498    *ISBN* 0316036811

**Ashton, Dore.**                                                            • **1.5660**
Modern American sculpture. — New York, H. N. Abrams [1968?] 54, [78] p.
illus. (part col.) 37 cm. 1. Sculpture, American 2. Sculpture, Modern — 20th
century — United States I. T.
NB212.A8    730/.973    *LC* 68-23168

**Wye, Deborah.**                                                            **1.5661**
Louise Bourgeois / Deborah Wye. — New York: Museum of Modern Art,
c1982. 123 p.: ill. (some col.), ports.; 26 cm. 'Published on the occasion of a
retrospective at the Museum of Modern Art, New York, November 3,
1982-February 8, 1983'—T.p. verso. 1. Bourgeois, Louise, 1911- —
Exhibitions. I. Bourgeois, Louise, 1911- II. Museum of Modern Art (New
York, N.Y.) III. T.
NB237.B65 A4 1982    709/.2/4 19    *LC* 82-60847    *ISBN*
0870702572

**Calder, Alexander, 1898-1976.**       • **1.5662**
Calder; an autobiography with pictures. — New York: Pantheon Books, [1966] 285 p.: illus. (part col.) ports.; 28 cm. 1. Calder, Alexander, 1898-1976. 2. Sculptors — United States — Biography. I. T.
NB237.C28 A2    730.924    *LC* 66-23203

**Calder, Alexander, 1898-1976.**       • **1.5663**
Calder. Photos. and design by Ugo Mulas. Introd. by H. Harvard Arnason. With comments by Alexander Calder. — New York: Viking Press, [1971] 216 p.: illus., ports.; 32 cm. — (A Studio book) I. Mulas, Ugo. II. Arnason, H. Harvard. III. T.
NB237.C28 M8 1971    730/.924    *LC* 71-125244    *ISBN* 0670112194

**Sweeney, James Johnson, 1900-.**       • **1.5664**
Alexander Calder / James Johnson Sweeney. — New York: Museum of Modern Art, [1951] 80 p.: ill., ports.; 26 cm. 1. Calder, Alexander, 1898-1976. I. Museum of Modern Art (New York, N.Y.) II. T.
NB237.C28 S9 1951    730.973    *LC* 51-8022

**Richman, Michael.**       **1.5665**
Daniel Chester French, an American sculptor / Michael Richman; postscript by Paul W. Ivory. — New York: Metropolitan Museum of Art for the National Trust for Historic Preservation, c1976. xi, 208 p.: ill.; 26 cm. Catalog of the exhibition to be held at the Metropolitan Museum of Art, Nov. 4, 1976-Jan. 10, 1977; the National Collection of Fine Arts, Smithsonian Institution, Feb. 11-Apr. 17, 1977; the Detroit Institute of Arts, June 15-Aug. 28, 1977; Fogg Art Museum, Harvard University, Sept. 30-Nov. 30, 1977. 1. French, Daniel Chester, 1850-1931. I. French, Daniel Chester, 1850-1931. II. Metropolitan Museum of Art (New York, N.Y.) III. National Trust for Historic Preservation in the United States. IV. T.
NB237.F7 R49    730/.92/4    *LC* 76-40897    *ISBN* 0870991531 pbk

**Greenough, Horatio, 1805-1852.**       • **1.5666**
Form and function: remarks on art, design, and architecture. Edited by Harold A. Small. With an introd. by Erle Loran. [1st paper-bound ed.] Berkeley, University of California Press, 1957. 136 p. 19 cm. 1. Art — Addresses, essays, lectures. I. T.
NB237.G8F6x    701.17    *LC* 57-13996

**Wright, Nathalia.**       • **1.5667**
Horatio Greenough, the first American sculptor. Philadelphia, University of Pennsylvania Press [1963] 382 p. ill., ports. 1. Greenough, Horatio, 1805-1852. I. T.
NB237 G8 W75    *LC* 62-11261

**Hoffman, Malvina, 1887-1966.**       • **1.5668**
Malvina Hoffman. New York, W.W. Norton, under the auspices of the National Sculpture Society, [1948] 64 p. (p. 6-60 plates) port. 17 cm. (American sculptors series; 5) 1. Hoffman, Malvina, 1887-1966. I. T. II. Series.
NB237.H55 A55    *LC* 42-2587

**Glimcher, Arnold B.**       **1.5669**
Louise Nevelson [by] Arnold B. Glimcher. New York: Praeger, [1972] 172 p.: illus.; 29 cm. 1. Nevelson, Louise, 1900- 2. Sculptors — United States — Biography. I. T.
NB237.N43 G55    730/.92/4 B    *LC* 70-145946

**Hunter, Sam, 1923-.**       **1.5670**
Isamu Noguchi / text by Sam Hunter. — New York: Abbeville Press, [1978] 334 p.; ill. (some col.); 34 cm. Includes index. 1. Noguchi, Isamu, 1904- 2. Sculptors — United States — Biography. I. T.
NB237.N6 H86    730/.92/4    *LC* 78-5288    *ISBN* 0896590038

**Rickey, George.**       **1.5671**
George Rickey / Nan Rosenthal. New York: H. N. Abrams, 1977. 220 p.: chiefly ill. (some col.); 28 x 30 cm. 'Films and taped interviews': p. 216-217. Includes index. 1. Rickey, George. I. Rosenthal, Nan. II. T.
NB237.R5 R67    730/.92/4    *LC* 76-20569    *ISBN* 0810904330

**Dryfhout, John, 1940-.**       **1.5672**
The work of Augustus Saint–Gaudens / John H. Dryfhout. — Hanover, NH: University Press of New England, 1982. xii, 356 p.: ill.; 32 cm. Includes indexes. 1. Saint-Gaudens, Augustus, 1848-1907 — Catalogs. I. Saint-Gaudens, Augustus, 1848-1907. II. T.
NB237.S2 A4 1982    730/.92/4 19    *LC* 82-7095    *ISBN* 0874512433

**Hunter, Sam, 1923-.**       **1.5673**
George Segal / Sam Hunter, Don Hawthorne. — New York: Rizzoli, 1984. 379 p.: ill. (some col.); 30 cm. Includes index. 1. Segal, George, 1924- 2. Photo-realism — United States. I. Hawthorne, Don. II. Segal, George, 1924- III. T.
NB237.S44 H86 1984    730/.92/4 B 19    *LC* 84-2095    *ISBN* 0847805417

**Smith, David, 1906-1965.**       • **1.5674**
David Smith. Text and photos. by the author. Edited by Cleve Gray. — New York: Holt, Rinehart, and Winston, [1968] 176 p.: illus., (part col.), facsims., port.; 29 cm. 1. Smith, David, 1906-1965. I. Gray, Cleve. ed. II. T.
NB237.S567 G7    730/.924    *LC* 68-18582

**Marcus, Stanley E., 1926-.**       **1.5675**
David Smith, the sculptor and his work / Stanley E. Marcus. — Ithaca, N.Y.: Cornell University Press, 1983. 207 p.: ill.; 27 cm. Includes index. 1. Smith, David, 1906-1965. I. T.
NB237.S567 M27 1983    730/.92/4 19    *LC* 83-45148    *ISBN* 0801415101

**Hobbs, Robert Carleton, 1946-.**       **1.5676**
Robert Smithson—sculpture / Robert Hobbs; with contributions by Lawrence Alloway, John Coplans, Lucy R. Lippard. — Ithaca: Cornell University Press, 1981. 261 p.: ill. (some col.); 29 cm. Includes index. 1. Smithson, Robert. I. T.
NB237.S5694 H6    709/.2/4 19    *LC* 80-69989    *ISBN* 0801413249

**James, Henry, 1843-1916.**       • **1.5677**
William Wetmore Story and his friends; from letters, diaries, and recollections. — New York: Kennedy Galleries, 1969. 2 v. in 1.: ports.; 24 cm. — (Library of American art) Reprint of the 1903 ed. 1. Story, William Wetmore, 1819-1895. I. T.
NB237.S7 J3 1969    709/.24 B    *LC* 69-18460

**Zorach, William, 1887-1966.**       **1.5678**
Art is my life; the autobiography of William Zorach. Cleveland, World Pub. Co. [1967] ix, 205 p. illus., ports. 26 cm. 1. Artists — Biography. 2. Art — United States. I. T.
NB237.Z6 A2    730/.924    *LC* 67-12900

**Baur, John I. H. (John Ireland Howe), 1909-1987.**     • **1.5679** *IN COLLECTION*
William Zorach. New York, Published for the Whitney Museum of American *NO call #* Art by Praeger, 1959. 116 p.: illus., plates (part col.) port. 30 cm. (Books that *in OPAC* matter) Bibliography: p. 112-114. 1. Zorach, William, 1887-1966. I. Whitney Museum of American Art. II. T.
NB237.Z6B3    730.973    *LC* 59-10500

## NB250–439 Latin America

**Weismann, Elizabeth Wilder, 1908-.**       • **1.5680**
Mexico in sculpture, 1521–1821. — Westport, Conn.: Greenwood Press, [1971, c1950] 226 p. — ill.; 27 cm. Reprint ed. includes additions to the bibliography. 1. Sculpture — Mexico. I. T.
NB253.W4 1971    730/.972    *LC* 75-95137    *ISBN* 0837125308

## NB450–955 Europe

**Elsen, Albert Edward, 1927-.**       **1.5681**
Modern European sculpture, 1918–1945: unknown beings and other realities / Albert E. Elsen. — New York: G. Braziller, c1979. 192 p.: ill.; 26 cm. 1. Sculpture, European 2. Sculpture, Modern — 20th century — Europe. 3. Avant-garde (Aesthetics) — Europe. I. T.
NB458.E45    NB458 E45.    735/.29    *LC* 78-27519    *ISBN* 080760920X

### NB461–497 GREAT BRITAIN

**Gardner, Arthur, 1878-.**       • **1.5682**
English medieval sculpture. The original handbook rev. and enl. — Cambridge [Eng.] University Press, 1951. viii, 351 p. illus. 28 cm. First ed. published in 1935 under title: A handbook of English medieval sculpture. Bibliography: p. 345-346. 1. Sculpture — Gt. Brit. 2. Sculpture, Medieval I. T.
NB463.G27 1951    734.42    *LC* 51-14711

**Stone, Lawrence.**       • **1.5683**
Sculpture in Britain: the Middle Ages. [Baltimore] Penguin Books, [1955] 297p.,illus. (Pelican history of art. Z9.) 1. Sculpture — Great Britain. 2. Sculpture, Medieval I. T. II. Series.
NB463.S8    735.42    *LC* 55-3485

**Zarnecki, George.**       • **1.5684**
English romanesque sculpture, 1066–1140 / by George Zarnecki. — London: A. Tiranti, 1951. — 40 p., [64] p. of plates: ill.; 19 cm. 1. Sculpture — Great Britain 2. Sculpture, Romanesque I. T.
NB463 Z37    *LC* 52-9346

### Zarnecki, George.                                                    • 1.5685
Later English Romanesque sculpture, 1140–1210. London, A Tiranti, 1953. 67 p. ill., map. (Chapters in art series, v. 22) 1. Sculpture — Great Britain 2. Sculpture, Romanesque I. T.
NB463 Z38    *LC* 53-11104

### Whinney, Margaret Dickens.                                          1.5686
Sculpture in Britain, 1530–1830 [by] Margaret Whinney. [Harmondsworth, Mddx.] Penguin Books [1964] xxii, 314 p. 192 plates. (Pelican history of art.) 1. Sculpture, British I. T. II. Series.
NB464 W5    *LC* 64-56858

### Read, Benedict.                                                      1.5687
Victorian sculpture / Benedict Read. — New Haven: Published for Paul Mellon Centre for Studies in British Art by Yale University Press, 1982. x, 414 p.: ill.; 29 cm. Includes index. 1. Sculpture, British 2. Sculpture, Victorian — Great Britain 3. Sculpture, Modern — 19th century — Great Britain I. T.
NB467.R4 1982    730/.941 19    *LC* 81-70483    *ISBN* 0300025068

### Beattie, Susan.                                                      1.5688
The new sculpture / Susan Beattie. — New Haven: Published for the Paul Mellon Centre for Studies in British Art by Yale University Press, 1983. 272 p.: ill.; 29 cm. — (Studies in British art.) Includes index. 1. New sculpture (Art movement) — Great Britain. 2. Sculpture, British 3. Sculpture, Modern — 19th century — Great Britain 4. Sculpture, Modern — 20th century — Great Britain I. Paul Mellon Centre for Studies in British Art. II. T. III. Series.
NB467.5.N48 B42 1983    730/.942 19    *LC* 83-42876    *ISBN* 0300028601

### Gunnis, Rupert.                                                      • 1.5689
Dictionary of British sculptors, 1660–1851. — New revised ed. — London: [Murrays Book Sales], 1968. 515 p.: 32 plates, illus., ports.; 25 cm. — (The Abbey library) ([Abbey arts series]) 1. Sculptors — Great Britain — Biography. I. T.
NB496.G85 1968    730/.922    *LC* 78-381295

### Rubin, William Stanley.                                             1.5690
Anthony Caro / William Rubin. — New York: Museum of Modern Art; Boston: distributed by New York Graphic Society, [1975] 196 p.: ill. (some col.); 29 cm. 'Published on the occasion of a retrospective exhibition of Anthony Caro's work presented by the Museum of Modern Art, New York, and the Museum of Fine Arts, Boston.' 1. Caro, Anthony, 1924- I. Caro, Anthony, 1924- II. Museum of Modern Art (New York, N.Y.) III. Museum of Fine Arts, Boston. IV. T.
NB497.C35 R82    730/.92/4    *LC* 74-21725    *ISBN* 0870702750

### Waldman, Diane.                                                      1.5691
Anthony Caro / by Diane Waldman. — New York: Abbeville Press, c1982. 232 p.: ill. (some col.); 30 cm. 1. Caro, Anthony, 1924- 2. Sculptors — Great Britain — Biography. I. Caro, Anthony, 1924- II. T.
NB497.C35 W3 1982    730/.92/4 B 19    *LC* 81-67311    *ISBN* 0896592308

### Epstein, Jacob, Sir, 1880-1959.                                     • 1.5692
Epstein: an autobiography. — 2d ed. with an introd / by Richard Buckle. — London: Vista Books, 1963. — xvii, 294 p., [53] leaves of plates: ill. Includes index. 1. Epstein, Jacob, Sir, 1880-1959. 2. Sculpture 3. Artists — Biography. 4. Sculptors — Biography. I. T.
NB497.E6 A2 1963    *LC* 64-113

### Gill, Eric, 1882-1940.                                              • 1.5693
Autobiography. — New York: Biblo and Tannen, 1968 [c1941] xv, 300, [33] p.: illus., ports.; 22 cm. 'Illustrations': p. [301]-[333] 1. Gill, Eric, 1882-1940. I. T.
NB497.G55 A3 1968    709/.24 B    *LC* 68-54231

### Hepworth, Barbara, Dame, 1903-1975.                                 • 1.5694
The sculpture of Barbara Hepworth, 1960–69. Edited by Alan Bowness. — New York: Praeger Publishers, [1971] 222 p.: illus., plates (part col.), port.; 31 cm. I. Bowness, Alan. ed. II. T.
NB497.H4 B6    730/.924    *LC* 79-150452

### Moore, Henry, 1898-.                                                • 1.5695
Henry Moore on sculpture; a collection of the sculptor's writings and spoken words edited, with an introd., by Philip James. — New York: Viking Press, [1967] 293 p.: illus. (part col.), facsim. (on lining paper); 29 cm. — (A Studio book) I. James, Philip Brutton, 1901- ed. II. T.
NB497.M6 A35 1967    730    *LC* 66-20426

### Moore, Henry, 1898-.                                                1.5696
Henry Moore: sculpture and environment / photos. and text by David Finn; foreword by Kenneth Clark; commentaries by Henry Moore. — New York: H. N. Abrams, 1976. 490 p.: ill. (some col.); 31 cm. 1. Moore, Henry, 1898- I. Finn, David, 1921- II. T.
NB497.M6 F52    730/.92/4    *LC* 76-12588    *ISBN* 0810913135

### Neumann, Erich.                                                     • 1.5697
The archetypal world of Henry Moore. Translated from the German by R. F. C. Hull. — [New York] Pantheon Books [1959] 138 p. illus. 27 cm. — (Bollingen series, 68) Includes bibliography. 1. Moore, Henry, 1898- I. T.
NB497.M6N43    730.942    *LC* 58-8988

### Moore, Henry, 1898-.                                                1.5698
Henry Moore, sculpture and drawings / edited by David Sylvester; with an introduction by Herbert Read. — 4th ed., rev. — London: Lund Humphries, 1957-1983. 5 v.: chiefly ill. (some col.); 30 cm. 1. Moore, Henry, 1898- I. Sylvester, David. II. Bowness, Alan. III. T. IV. Title: Sculpture and drawings.
NB497.M6 S9    NB497.M6 S94 1957.

## NB541–553 FRANCE

### Aubert, Marcel, 1884-1962.                                          1.5699
French sculpture at the beginning of the Gothic period, 1140–1225. — New York: Hacker Art Books, 1972. xiii, 119 p.: 88 plates.; 32 cm. Reprint of the 1929 ed. 1. Sculpture, French 2. Sculpture, Gothic — France. I. T.
NB543.A8 1972    730/.944    *LC* 75-143337    *ISBN* 087817057X

### Sauerländer, Willibald.                                             1.5700
Gothic sculpture in France, 1140–1270. Translated by Janet Sondheimer. Photos. by Max Hirmer. — New York: H. N. Abrams, [1973, c1970] 527 p.: illus. (part col.); 32 cm. 1. Sculpture, Gothic — France. 2. Sculpture, French I. Hirmer, Max, 1893- illus. II. T.
NB543.S31413 1973    731/.88/20944    *LC* 76-160223    *ISBN* 0810901471

### Stoddard, Whitney S.                                                1.5701
The façade of Saint–Gilles–du–Gard; its influence on French sculpture, by Whitney S. Stoddard. — [1st ed.]. — Middletown, Conn.: Wesleyan University Press, [1973] xxiv, 340 p.: illus.; 29 cm. 1. Saint-Gilles, France (Gard). Church. 2. Sculpture, Romanesque — Saint Gilles, France (Gard) 3. Sculpture — Saint-Gilles, France (Gard) I. T.
NB543.S79    731/.54    *LC* 72-3696    *ISBN* 0819540560

### Arp, Jean, 1887-1966.                                               • 1.5702
Jean Arp [by] Carola Giedion–Welcker. Documentation: Marguerite Hagenbach. [Translation by Norbert Guterman] New York, H.N. Abrams [c1957] xliii, 122 p. (p. 1-101 plates (part fold.)) ill. ([An Abrahams art book]) I. Giedion-Welcker, Carola. II. T.
NB553 A7 G5    *LC* 58-3464

### New York. Museum of Modern Art.                                     • 1.5703
Arp. Edited with an introd. by James Thrall Soby. Articles by Jean Hans Arp [and others] Garden City, N.Y., Distributed by Doubleday [1958] 126 p. ill. 1. Arp, Jean, 1887-1966. I. Soby, James Thrall, 1906- II. T.
NB553 A7 N4    *LC* 58-13761

### Millard, Charles W.                                                 1.5704
The sculpture of Edgar Degas / Charles W. Millard. — Princeton, N.J.: Princeton University Press, 1977, [c1976]. xxiv, 141 p., [40] leaves of plates: ill.; 26 cm. 1. Degas, Edgar, 1834-1917. 2. Sculpture, French 3. Sculpture, Modern — 19th century — France I. Degas, Edgar, 1834-1917. II. T.
NB553.D4 M44    730/.92/4    *LC* 73-2485    *ISBN* 0691038988

### Hohl, Reinhold.                                                     1.5705
[Alberto Giacometti. English] Alberto Giacometti. New York, H. N. Abrams [1972, c1971] 328 p. illus. (part col.) 31 cm. Translated from German. 1. Giacometti, Alberto, 1901-1966. I. T.
NB553.G4 H613 1972    730/.92/4 B    *LC* 70-160216    *ISBN* 0810901390

### Goldwater, Robert John.                                             • 1.5706
Lipchitz. — New York: Universe Books, [c1959] 32 p.: ill. — (Universe sculpture series) 1. Lipchitz, Jacques. 2. Sculpture I. T.
NB553.L55G63    730.9475

### Lipchitz, Jacques, 1891-.                                           1.5707
Jacques Lipchitz. [Text] by A. M. Hammacher, translated by James Brockway. — New York: Abrams, [1975] 223 p.: illus.; 31 cm. 1. Lipchitz, Jacques, 1891- I. Hammacher, Abraham Marie, 1897- II. T.
NB553.L55 H297    730/.92/4 B    *LC* 74-11331    *ISBN* 0810902389

### Hammacher, Abraham Marie, 1897-.                                    • 1.5708
Jacques Lipchitz: his sculpture. With an introductory statement by Jacques Lipchitz. New York, H.N. Abrams [1961] 176 p. illus., ports., facsims. 31 cm. 1. Lipchitz, Jacques, 1891- I. T.
NB553.L55 H3    730.947    *LC* 60-10889

### Rewald, John, 1912-.                                                • 1.5709
Maillol, by John Rewald. New York [etc.] Hyperion Press, 1939. 2 p. l., 7-167, [1] p. incl. illus., plates (part col. mounted) plates. 33 x 25 cm. 'Edited by André

Gloeckner.' 'Bibliographie': p. 29-30. 1. Maillol, Aristide, 1861-1944.
I. Gloeckner, André, ed. II. T.
NB553.M3R45      927.3      *LC* 39-27914

**Elsen, Albert Edward, 1927-.**                                                    **1.5710**
The sculpture of Henri Matisse [by] Albert E. Elsen. — New York: Abrams,
[1972?] 223 p.: illus.; 31 cm. 1. Matisse, Henri, 1869-1954. I. Matisse, Henri,
1869-1954. II. T.
NB553.M39 E47      730/.92/4      *LC* 72-135915      *ISBN* 0810902826

**Penrose, Roland, Sir.**                                                        • **1.5711**
The sculpture of Picasso. Chronology by Alicia Legg. New York, Museum of
Modern Art [1967] 231 p. illus., port. 31 cm. Issued in conjunction with the
exhibition at the Museum of Modern Art, Oct. 11, 1967 to Jan. 1, 1968.
1. Picasso, Pablo, 1881-1973. I. Museum of Modern Art (New York, N.Y.)
II. T.
NB553.P45 P42      730/.924      *LC* 67-29395

**Tancock, John L.**                                                              **1.5712**
Sculpture of Auguste Rodin: the collection of the Rodin Museum, Philadelphia.
John L. Tancock;special photography by Murray Weiss.— Boston: David R.
Godine in association with the Philadelphia Museum of Art, c1976. 664 p.: ill.
(some col.), ports. 1. Rodin, Auguste, 1840-1917. I. Weiss, Murray II. Rodin
Museum, Philadelphia. III. Philadelphia Museum of Art. IV. T.
NB553R7 T34      *LC* 75-5211      *ISBN* 0879231572

**Hammacher, Abraham Marie.**                                                    • **1.5713**
Zadkine. — New York: Universe books, [c1959] [15] p.: ill., 32 plates. —
(Universe sculpture series) 1. Zadkine, Ossip. 2. Sculpture, Russian I. T.
NB553.Z3H33      730.947

## NB560–588 GERMANY

**Liebmann, M. J. (Michael J.), 1920-.**                                          **1.5714**
Die deutsche Plastik 1350–1550 / M.J. Liebmann; [Übersetzung aus dem
Russischen von Hans Störel]. — Leipzig: Seemann, 1982. 546 p.: ill.; 25 cm.
1. Sculpture, German 2. Sculpture, Medieval — Germany. 3. Sculture,
Renaissance — Germany. I. T.
NB563.L54 1982      730/.943 19      *LC* 84-175709      *ISBN* 3570092321

**German expressionist sculpture / organized by Stephanie**                      **1.5715**
**Barron.**
Los Angeles, CA: Los Angeles County Museum of Art, [1983] 224 p.: ill.; 30
cm. Catalog of an exhibit organized by the Los Angeles County Museum of Art
and also held at the Hirshhorn Museum and Sculpture Garden and at Josef-
Haubrich Kunsthalle Köln. Includes index. 1. Sculpture, German —
Exhibitions. 2. Expressionism (Art) — Germany — Exhibitions. 3. Sculpture,
Modern — 20th century — Germany — Exhibitions. I. Barron, Stephanie.
II. Los Angeles County Museum of Art. III. Hirshhorn Museum and
Sculpture Garden. IV. Josef-Haubrich-Kunsthalle Köln.
NB568.5.E9 G47 1983      730/.943/074 19      *LC* 83-13552      *ISBN*
0875871151

**Carls, Carl Dietrich, 1905-.**                                                 • **1.5716**
[Ernst Barlach. English] Ernst Barlach; [translated from the German]. [New
ed.] London, Pall Mall P., 1969. 216 p. illus. 28 cm. Originally published as
Ernst Barlach: das plastische, graphische und dichterische Werk. Berlin,
Rembrandt-Verlag, 1931. 1. Barlach, Ernst, 1870-1938. I. T.
NB588.B35 C313 1969b      730/.924      *LC* 70-498863      *ISBN*
0269671293

**Lehmbruck, Wilhelm, 1881-1919.**                                               **1.5717**
The art of Wilhelm Lehmbruck [By] Reinhold Heller. Washington, National
Gallery of Art, 1972. 200 p. illus. 29 cm. Held from May 20, 1972 to Mar. 15,
1973, at the National Gallery of Art, Washington [and others] I. Heller,
Reinhold. II. National Gallery of Art (U.S.) III. T.
NB588.L45 H4      730/.92/4      *LC* 72-76727

**Bier, Justus, 1899-.**                                                         **1.5718**
Tilmann Riemenschneider, his life and work / Justus Bier. — Lexington, KY:
University Press of Kentucky, c1982. xiii, 128 p., [128] p. of plates: ill.; 24 cm.
1. Riemenschneider, Tilman, d. 1531. 2. Sculptors — Germany — Biography.
I. Riemenschneider, Tilman, d. 1531. II. T.
NB588.R5 B55      730/.92/4 B 19      *LC* 80-5171      *ISBN* 0813114284

**Lehmbruck, Wilhelm, 1881-1919.**                                               • **1.5719**
Wilhelm Lehmbruck / by Werner Hofmann. — New York: Universe Books,
[1959]. [20] p.: 32 plates, port.; 22 cm. — (Universe sculpture series) Captions
in French, English, German, and Dutch. Errata slip inserted. I. Hofmann,
Werner, 1928- II. T.
NB588.L45 H63      *LC* 59-10158

## NB611–623 ITALY

**Crichton, George Henderson, 1885-.**                                           • **1.5720**
Romanesque sculpture in Italy. [London] Routledge and Paul [1954] 172p.
1. Sculpture — Italy 2. Sculpture, Romanesque I. T.
NB613 C7

**Pope-Hennessy, John Wyndham, Sir, 1913-.**                                      **1.5721**
Italian Gothic sculpture / John Pope-Hennessy. — 1st Vintage Books ed. —
New York: Vintage Books, c1985. 295 p.: ill. Reprint of v. 1 of Introduction to
Italian sculpture. Originally published: 2nd ed. London; New York: Phaidon,
1970-1972. 1. Sculpture, Italian 2. Sculpture, Gothic — Italy. I. T.
NB613.P59 1985      730/.945 19      *LC* 84-43004      *ISBN* 0394729322

**Pope-Hennessy, John Wyndham, Sir, 1913-.**                                      **1.5722**
Italian Renaissance sculpture / John Pope-Hennessy. — 1st Vintage Books ed.
— New York: Vintage Books, 1985. 388 p.: ill.; 28 cm. (An Introduction to
Italian sculpture / by John Pope-Hennessy; pt. 2) 'Third edition'—Foreword.
Includes indexes. 1. Sculpture, Italian 2. Sculpture, Renaissance — Italy I. T.
II. Series.
NB614.P6 1985 pt. 2 NB615      730/.945 s 730/.945 19      *LC* 84-43007
*ISBN* 0394729331

**Pope-Hennessy, John Wyndham, Sir, 1913-.**                                      **1.5723**
Italian High Renaissance and Baroque sculpture / John Pope-Hennessy. — 1st
Vintage Books ed. — New York: Vintage Books, 1985. 486 p.: ill.; 28 cm. (An
Introduction to Italian sculpture / by John Pope-Hennessy; pt. 3) 'Third
edition'—Foreword. Includes indexes. 1. Sculpture, Italian 2. Sculpture,
Renaissance — Italy 3. Sculpture, Baroque — Italy. I. T.
NB614.P6 1985 pt. 3 NB615      730/.945 s 730/.945 19      *LC* 84-43008
*ISBN* 039472934X

**Seymour, Charles, 1912-.**                                                     **1.5724**
Sculpture in Italy, 1400–1500 / Charles Seymour. — Harmondsworth, Eng.:
Penguin Books, 1966. xxvi, 295 p., 160 p. of plates: ill., map. — (Pelican history
of art.) 1. Sculpture, Italian — History. I. T. II. Series.
NB615.S45      *LC* 66-73887      *ISBN* 0140560262

**Montagu, Jennifer.**                                                           **1.5725**
Alessandro Algardi / Jennifer Montagu. — New Haven: Published in
association with the J. Paul Getty Trust by Yale University Press, 1985. 2 v. (xv,
487 p., [200] p. of plates): ill. (some col.); 29 cm. Vol. 2 is the complete and fully
illustrated catalogue raisonné. Includes index. 1. Algardi, Alessandro,
1598-1654 — Criticism and interpretation. 2. Algardi, Alessandro, 1598-1654
— Catalogs. I. Algardi, Alessandro, 1598-1654. II. T.
NB623.A44 M66 1985      730/.92/4 19      *LC* 84-52244      *ISBN*
0300031734

**Wittkower, Rudolf.**                                                           • **1.5726**
Gian Lorenzo Bernini: the sculptor of the Roman baroque / Rudolf Wittkower.
— 3rd ed. / revised by Howard Hibbard, Thomas Martin, and Margot
Wittkower. — Oxford: Phaidon, 1981. xii, 290 p.: ill.; 31 cm. Includes indexes.
1. Bernini, Gian Lorenzo, 1598-1680. 2. Sculpture, Baroque — Italy — Rome.
I. Hibbard, Howard, 1928- II. Martin, Thomas. III. Wittkower, Margot.
IV. T.
NB623.B5 W55 1981      730/.92/4 19      *LC* 81-190249      *ISBN*
0714821934

**Finn, David, 1921-.**                                                          **1.5727**
Canova / photographs by David Finn; text by Fred Licht. — 1st ed. — New
York: Abbeville Press, c1983. 280 p.: ill.; 34 cm. Includes index. 1. Canova,
Antonio, 1757-1822. 2. Neoclassicism (Art) — Italy. I. Licht, Fred, 1928-
II. T.
NB623.C2 F56 1983      730/.92/4 19      *LC* 82-16309      *ISBN*
0896593274

**Cellini, Benvenuto, 1500-1571.**                                               • **1.5728**
The autobiography of Benvenuto Cellini / Benvenuto Cellini; translated by
Robert Hobart Cust, with 8 full-page ill., and an introd. by Raimondo Legame.
— New York: Dodd, Mead, 1961. xv, 547 p.; plates: ill. — (Great illustrated
classics: Titan editions) 1. Cellini, Benvenuto, 1500-1571. 2. Cellini,
Benvenuto, 1500-1571. I. Cust, Robert Henry Hobart, 1861- II. T.
NB623.C3C8 1961

**Janson, H. W. (Horst Woldemar), 1913-.**                                       **1.5729**
The sculpture of Donatello / by H. W. Janson; incorporating the notes and
photos. of the late Jenö Lányi. — Princeton: Princeton University Press, 1957. 2
v.: ill. 1. Donatello, 1386?-1466. I. Donatello, 1386?-1466. II. Lányi, Jenö.
III. T.
NB623.D7 J3      *LC* 57-5473

**Krautheimer, Richard, 1897-.**                                                 • **1.5730**
Lorenzo Ghiberti / by Richard Krautheimer in collaboration with Trude
Krautheimer–Hess. — 2d printing, with corrections and new pref. —
Princeton: Princeton University Press, 1970. 2 v. (xxiii, 457 p.): ill., plates. —
(Princeton monographs in art and archaeology. 31) 'Sources [documents]': p.

359-421. 1. Ghiberti, Lorenzo, 1378-1455. I. Krautheimer, Trude Hess. II. T. III. Series.
NB623.G45 K7 1970     [734.45] 927.3     *LC* 56-8383     *ISBN* 0691038201

**Manzù, Giacomo, 1908-.**         • **1.5731**
[Giacomo Manzù. English] Giacomo Manzù [by] John Rewald. Greenwich, Conn., New York Graphic Society [1967, c1966] 327 p. illus. (part col.), plates (part col.) 31 cm. I. Rewald, John, 1912- II. T.
NB623.M24 R413 1967b     730.92/4     *LC* 67-19374

**Marini, Marino, 1904-.**         • **1.5732**
Marino Marini / by Ém. Langui. — New York: Universe Books, [1959] [16] p. 3: 32 plates, port.; 22 cm. — (Universe sculpture series) Captions in French, English, German, and Dutch. I. Langui, Emile. II. T.
NB623.M32 L3     *LC* 59-10153

**Martini, Arturo, 1889-1947.**         • **1.5733**
Martini / by G. Argan. — New York: Universe Books, [1959]. [20] p.: 32 plates, port.; 22 cm. — (Universe sculpture series) Captions in French, English, German, and Dutch. I. Argan, Giulio Carlo. II. T.
NB623.M38 A83     *LC* 59-10161

**Baldini, Umberto.**         **1.5734**
[Michelangelo scultore. English] The sculpture of Michelangelo / Umberto Baldini; photographs by Liberto Perugi; [translated by Clare Coope]. — New York: Rizzoli, 1982, c1981. 299 p.: ill.; 31 cm. Translation of: Michelangelo scultore. 1. Michelangelo Buonarroti, 1475-1564. I. Michelangelo Buonarroti, 1475-1564. II. Perugi, Liberto. III. T.
NB623.M515 B3 1982     730/.92/4 19     *LC* 82-60032     *ISBN* 084780447X

**Michelangelo Buonarroti, 1475-1564.**         • **1.5735**
The sculptures of Michelangelo ... New York, Oxford University Press [1940] 33 p., 3 l. incl. front. (port.) illus., VIII pl. on 4 l. 128 pl. on 64 l. 36 cm. 'Foreword' signed: Ludwig Goldscheider. 'Made in Great Britain.' 'Phaidon edition.' Half-title: Michelangelo's sculptures; complete edition. 'Photographs by J. Schneider-Lengyel.'-p. [35] I. Goldscheider, Ludwig, 1896- II. Lengyel, Ilse (Schneider) III. T.
NB623.M515 G6x     735.0945     *LC* 40-27849

**Crichton, George Henderson, 1885-.**         • **1.5736**
Nicola Pisano and the revival of sculpture in Italy / by G.H. & E.R. Crichton. — Cambridge: The University Press, 1938. xiii, 126 p., [112] p. of plates: ill.; 22 cm. 1. Pisano, Niccolò, 1206?-1280? 2. Sculpture — Italy. I. Crichton, Elsie Robertson, 1885- joint author. II. T.
NB623.P5 C7     *LC* 39-14956

**Seymour, Charles, 1912-.**         **1.5737**
Jacopo della Quercia, sculptor. New Haven, Yale University Press, 1973. xxviii, 146 p., [172] p. of illus. 29 cm. (Yale publications in the history of art. 23) 1. Jacopo, della Quercia, 1372?-1436. I. T. II. Series.
NB623.Q4 S49     730/.92/4     *LC* 72-75208     *ISBN* 0300015291

**Marquand, Allan, 1853-1924.**         **1.5738**
Luca della Robbia. — New York: Hacker Art Books, 1972. xxxix, 286 p.: illus.; 27 cm. Reprint of the ed. published by Princeton University Press, which was issued as v. 3 of Princeton monographs in art and archaeology. 1. Robbia, Luca della, 1400?-1482. I. T.
NB623.R72 M3 1972     730/.92/4     *LC* 73-164572     *ISBN* 0878171037

**Pope-Hennessy, John Wyndham, Sir, 1913-.**         **1.5739**
Luca della Robbia / John Pope-Hennessy. — Ithaca, N.Y.: Cornell University Press, 1980. 288 p.; [32] leaves of plates: ill. (some col.); 29 cm. Errata slip inserted. Includes index. 1. Robbia, Luca della, 1400?-1482. I. T.
NB623.R72 P66 1980     730/.92/4     *LC* 79-13566     *ISBN* 0801412560

**Seymour, Charles, 1912-.**         **1.5740**
The sculpture of Verrocchio. — Greenwich, Conn.: New York Graphic Society, 1972. 192 p.: illus.; 26 cm. 1. Verrocchio, Andrea del, 1435?-1488. I. T.
NB623.V5 S48 1971b     730/.92/4     *LC* 77-154326     *ISBN* 0821203754

### NB625–955 OTHER EUROPEAN COUNTRIES

**Withers, Josephine.**         **1.5741**
Julio Gonzalez: sculpture in iron / Josephine Withers. — New York: New York University Press, c1978. xv, 181 p.; 29 cm. Includes index. 1. González, Julio, 1876-1942. 2. Sculptors — Spain — Biography. I. T.
NB813.G6 W57     730/.92/4 B     *LC* 76-26798     *ISBN* 0814791719

**Christo, 1935-.**         **1.5742**
Christo. Text by David Bourdon. — New York: H. N. Abrams, [1972] 321 p.: illus.; 28 x 30 cm. I. Bourdon, David. II. T.
NB893.C5 B6     730/.92/4     *LC* 70-165543     *ISBN* 0810900513

**Geist, Sidney.**         **1.5743**
Brancusi: the sculpture and drawings. — New York: H. N. Abrams, [1975] 200 p.: illus. (part col.); 28 x 30 cm. 'Catalogue of the sculpture': p. [171]-193. 1. Brancusi, Constantin, 1876-1957. I. Brancusi, Constantin, 1876-1957. II. T.
NB933.B7 G43     730/.92/4     *LC* 74-17450     *ISBN* 0810901242

**Brancusi, Constantin, 1876-1957.**         • **1.5744**
Constantin Brancusi / Carola Giedion-Welcker; translated by Maria Jolas and Anne Leory. — New York: G. Braziller, 1959. 240 p.: ill. (some col.), ports.; 31 cm. 1. Brancusi, Constantin, 1876-1957. I. Giedion-Welcker, Carola. II. T.
NB933.B7G5x     *LC* 59-9867

**Meštrović, Ivan, 1883-1962.**         • **1.5745**
Ivan Meštrović: sculptor and patriot / [prepared by] Laurence Schmeckebier. — [Syracuse]: Syracuse University Press, 1959. vi, 66 p., [180] p. of plates: 200 ill.; 23 cm. Published to commemorate the sculptor's 75th year. I. Schmeckebier, Laurence Eli, 1906- II. T.
NB953.M4 S3     *LC* 59-7951

## NB960–1113 Asia. Africa. Oceania

**Barasch, Moshe.**         **1.5746**
[De imaginatione. English and Latin] Crusader figural sculpture in the Holy Land; twelfth century examples from Acre, Nazareth and Belvoir Castle. New Brunswick, N.J., Rutgers University Press [1971] 237 p. illus. 29 cm. 1. Sculpture, Romanesque — Latin Orient. 2. Sculpture — Latin Orient. I. T.
NB977.B3     734/.24     *LC* 74-129513     *ISBN* 0813506808

**Pal, Pratapaditya.**         **1.5747**
The sensuous immortals: a selection of sculptures from the Pan-Asian collection / Pratapaditya Pal. — Los Angeles: Los Angeles County Museum of Art; Cambridge, Mass.: distributed by the MIT Press, [1977]. 264 p.: ill. (some col.); 28 cm. Catalog of an exhibition shown at Los Angeles County Museum of Art, October 25, 1977-January 15, 1978 and other places. 1. Sculpture — South Asia — Exhibitions. 2. Sculpture — Asia, Southeastern — Exhibitions. I. Los Angeles County Museum of Art. II. T.
NB1000.P34     732/.4/074019494     *LC* 77-2619     *ISBN* 0875870791

**Bachhofer, Ludwig, 1894-.**         **1.5748**
Early Indian sculpture. — New York: Hacker Art Books, 1972. 2 v. in 1.: 161 plates.; 32 cm. Reprint of the 1929 ed. 1. Sculpture, Indic 2. Sculpture, Buddhist — India. I. T.
NB1002.B3 1972     732/.4     *LC* 79-143338     *ISBN* 0878170588

**Chandra, Pramod.**         **1.5749**
The sculpture of India, 3000 B.C.–1300 A.D. / Pramod Chandra. — Washington: National Gallery of Art, c1985. 224 p.: ill. (some col.); 30 cm. 'Exhibition dates: National Gallery of Art, 5 May-2 September 1985'—T.p. verso. 1. Sculpture, Indic — Exhibitions. I. National Gallery of Art (U.S.) II. T.
NB1002.C535 1985     732/.44/0740153 19     *LC* 85-4832     *ISBN* 089468082X

**Harle, James C.**         **1.5750**
Gupta sculpture: Indian sculpture of the fourth to the sixth centuries A.D. / J. C. Harle. — Oxford [Eng.]: Clarendon Press, 1974. xii, 57 p., [40] leaves of plates: ill.; 29 cm. 1. Gupta dynasty 2. Sculpture, Hindu I. T.
NB1002.H33     732/.4     *LC* 75-306296     *ISBN* 0198173229

**Lippe, Aschwin.**         **1.5751**
Indian mediaeval sculpture / Aschwin de Lippe. — Amsterdam; New York: North-Holland Pub. Co.; New York: distributors for the U.S.A. and Canada, Elsevier-Holland, 1978. xxiii, 411 p.: chiefly ill.; 31 cm. Includes index. 1. Sculpture, Medieval — India. 2. Sculpture, Indic I. T.
NB1002.L565     732/.4     *LC* 77-18869     *ISBN* 0444850864

**Pal, Pratapaditya.**         **1.5752**
The ideal image: the Gupta sculptural tradition and its influence / by Pratapaditya Pal. — [New York]: Asia Society in association with J. Weatherhill, c1978. 144 p.: ill. (some col.); 25 x 27 cm. 'Catalogue of an exhibition shown in Asia House Gallery in the fall of 1978.' 1. Sculpture, Gupta — Exhibitions. 2. Sculpture, Gupta — Influence. 3. Sculpture, Nepali — Exhibitions. 4. Sculpture — Asia, Southeastern — Exhibitions. 5. Sculpture, Chinese — Exhibitions. I. Asia Society. II. Asia House Gallery. III. T.
NB1002.P27     732/.4     *LC* 78-14901     *ISBN* 0878480528

**Asher, Frederick M.** 1.5753
The art of Eastern India, 300–800 / Frederick M. Asher. — Minneapolis: University of Minnesota Press, c1980. 255 p.: ill., maps. Includes index. 1. Sculpture, Hindu — India — Bihar (State) 2. Sculpture — India — Bihar (State) 3. Sculpture, Hindu — Bengal. 4. Sculpture — Bengal. 5. Sculpture, Hindu — Bangladesh. 6. Sculpture, Bangladeshi I. T.
NB1007.B55 A84   732/.44/1   LC 80-10352   ISBN 0816609756

**Kramrisch, Stella, 1898-.** 1.5754
The presence of Śiva / Stella Kramrisch; photography by Praful C. Patel. — Princeton, N.J.: Princeton University Press, c1981. x, 514 p., 32 leaves of plates: ill.; 24 cm. Includes index. 1. Śiva (Hindu deity) — Art. 2. Sculpture, Hindu — India — Elephanta Island. 3. Cave temples — India — Elephanta Island. 4. Sculpture, Hindu — India — Ellora. 5. Cave temples — India — Ellora. I. T.
NB1007.S67 K7   704.9/48945211 19   LC 80-8558   0691031304

**Giteau, Madeleine.** 1.5755
Khmer sculpture and the Angkor civilization. [Translated by Diana Imber] New York, H. N. Abrams, [1966, c1965] 301 p.: illus., map, plans, 24 col. plates.; 30 cm. Translation of Les Khmers. 1. Sculpture, Khmer. 2. Khmers I. T.
NB1015.G5413   730.9596   LC 66-10991

**Boisselier, Jean.** 1.5756
[Sculpture en Thailande. English] The heritage of Thai sculpture / by Jean Boisselier; with commentaries by Jean–Michel Beurdeley and photos. by Hans Hinz. — 1st English language ed. — New York: Weatherhill, 1975. 269 p.: ill. (some col.); 30 cm. Translation of La sculpture en Thailande. Includes index. 1. Sculpture, Thai — History. 2. Sculpture, Buddhist — Thailand — History. I. Beurdeley, Jean Michel. joint author. II. T.
NB1021.B5713   732/.4   LC 75-7515   ISBN 0834801094

**Rudolph, Richard C.** • 1.5757
Han tomb art of West China; a collection of first– and secnd–century reliefs [by] Richard C. Rudolph in collaboration with Wen Yu. Berkeley, University of California Press, 1951. vii, 67, [81] p. plates, map, plans. Erratum slip inserted. 1. Sculpture, Chinese 2. Relief (Sculpture) 3. Szechwan Province (China) I. Wen, Yu, 1901- II. T.
NB1043.R8 1951

**Sullivan, Michael, 1916-.** 1.5758
The cave temples of Maichishan. Photos. by Dominique Darbois. With an account of the 1958 expedition to Maichishan by Anil de Silva. — Berkeley: University of California Press, 1969. xiv, 77 p.: illus., map. 104 plates (part col.); 29 cm. 1. Art, Buddhist — Kansu (Province) 2. Sculpture — Kansu (Province) 3. Mai-chi Shan Caves. I. De Silva, Anil. II. T.
NB1043.S77   731.8/8/943095145   LC 69-15829

**Yün–kang shih k'u / Shan–hsi sheng wen wu kung tso wei yüan hui, Shan–hsi yün–kang shih k'u wen wu pao kuan so pien.** 1.5759
Pei-ching: Wen wu ch'u pan she, 1977. [140] p.: ill.; 27 cm. 'The Yunkang caves' in English, published as suppl. (29 p.) and inserted at end. 1. Sculpture, Buddhist — China — Yün-kang chen. 2. Sculpture, Chinese — Three kingdoms-Sui dynasty, 220-618 3. Relief (Sculpture) — China — Yün-kang chen. 4. Yün-kang shih k'u (Temple) I. Shansi, China. Wen wu kung tso wei yüan hui. II. Shan-hsi Yün-kang shih k'u wen wu pao kuan so. III. Title: Yunkang caves.
NB1047.Y86 S46 1977   LC 78-840786

**Nishikawa, Kyōtarō.** 1.5760
The great age of Japanese Buddhist sculpture, AD 600–1300 / Nishikawa Kyōtarō, Emily J. Sano. — Fort Worth: Kimbell Art Museum; New York: Japan Society, [1982] 151 p.: ill. (some col.); 31 cm. Cover title: Japanese Buddhist sculpture. Exhibition held at Kimbell Art Museum, Sept. 8-Oct. 31, 1982 and at Japan House Gallery, Nov. 23, 1982-Jan. 16, 1983. 'Catalogue': p. [55]-146. Includes index. 1. Sculpture, Japanese — To 794 — Exhibitions. 2. Sculpture, Japanese — Heian period, 794-1185 — Exhibitions. 3. Sculpture, Japanese — Kamakura-Momoyama periods, 1185-1600 — Ehibitions. 4. Sculpture, Buddhist — Japan — Exhibitions. I. Sano, Emily J. II. Kimbell Art Museum. III. Japan House Gallery. IV. T. V. Title: Japanese Buddhist sculpture.
NB1053.N54 1982   732/.72/07401645315 19   LC 82-82805   ISBN 0912804076

**Warner, Langdon, 1881-1955.** • 1.5761
Japanese sculpture of the Tempyo period; masterpieces of the eighth century. Edited and arr. by James Marshall Plumer. [One-volume ed.] Cambridge, Mass., Harvard University Press [1964] xix, 165 p., A-B, 217 p. of ill., maps, ports. 1. Sculpture, Japanese 2. Art, Buddhist I. T.
NB1053 W32 1964   LC 64-23111

**Watson, William, 1917-.** • 1.5762
The sculpture of Japan, from the fifth to the fifteenth century. New York, Viking [1960] 216 p. plates. 38 cm. (A Studio book) 1. Sculpture, Japanese 2. Art, Buddhist I. T.
NB1053.W34   730.952   LC 60-910

**Sugiyama, Jirō, 1928-.** 1.5763
[Tempyō chōkoku. English] Classic Buddhist sculpture: the Tempyō period / Jirō Sugiyama; translated and adapted by Samuel Crowell Morse. — 1st ed. — Tokyo; New York: Kodansha International: Shibundo; New York: Distributed by Kodansha International/USA through Harper & Row, 1982. 230 p.: ill. (some col.); 27 cm. (Japanese arts library. 11) Translation of: Tempyō chōkoku. Includes index. 1. Sculpture, Buddhist — Japan. 2. Sculpture, Japanese — To 794 I. Morse, Samuel Crowell. II. T. III. Series.
NB1053.2.S913 1982   732/.72 19   LC 82-80738   ISBN 0870115294

**Elisofon, Eliot.** • 1.5764
The sculpture of Africa; 405 photographs. Text by William Fagg. Pref. by Ralph Linton. Design by Bernard Quint. New York: Praeger, [1958] 256 p. illus., map (on lining papers) 36 cm. (Books that matter) 'Bibliographical notes': p. 252-254. 1. Sculpture — Africa. I. Fagg, William Buller. II. T.
NB1080.E57   730.96   LC 58-8971

**Fagg, William Buller.** • 1.5765
African tribal images; the Katherine White Reswick Collection [by] William Fagg. — [Cleveland]: Cleveland Museum of Art, [1968] 1 v. (unpaged): illus., maps.; 24 cm. 1. Reswick, Katherine White — Art collections. 2. Sculpture, African — Catalogs. I. Cleveland Museum of Art. II. T.
NB1080.F312   730/.967   LC 68-31762

**Wingert, Paul S. (Paul Stover), 1900-1974.** • 1.5766
The sculpture of Negro Africa. New York, Columbia University Press, 1950. vii, 96 p. ill., plates, map. 1. Sculpture — Africa 2. Negro art I. T.
NB1080 W5   LC 50-11001

**Fagg, William Buller.** • 1.5767
Nigerian images: the splendor of African sculpture / Photos. by Herbert List. New York: Praeger, [1963] 124 p. 144 plates, map. 30 cm. 1. Sculpture — Nigeria. 2. Sculpture, Primitive I. T.
NB1097.N5F2   730.9669   LC 63-20393

**Willett, Frank.** • 1.5768
Ife in the history of West African sculpture. New York, McGraw-Hill [1967] 232 p. illus. (part col.), maps. 26 cm. (New aspects of archaeology) 1. Sculpture — Nigeria — Ife. 2. Sculpture, Primitive I. T.
NB1097.W4 W5 1967b   732/.2/096692   LC 67-14151

**For spirits and kings: African art from the Paul and Ruth Tishman Collection / edited by Susan Vogel; translations and additional research by Kate Ezra; photographs by Jerry L. Thompson.** 1.5769
New York: Metropolitan Museum of Art: Distributed by H.N. Abrams, c1981. 256 p.: ill. (some col); 27 cm. Includes index. 1. Tishman, Paul — Art collections — Exhibitions. 2. Tishman, Ruth — Art collections — Exhibitions. 3. Sculpture, Black — Africa, West — Exhibitions. 4. Sculpture, Primitive — Africa, West — Exhibitions. I. Vogel, Susan Mullin. II. Thompson, Jerry L. III. Metropolitan Museum of Art (New York, N.Y.)
NB1098.F67   730/.967/07401471 19   LC 81-4368   ISBN 0870992678

**Barrow, Terence, 1923-.** • 1.5770
Maori wood sculpture of New Zealand [by] T. Barrow. Rutland Vt., C.E. Tuttle [1970, c1969] 162 p. 234 illus. (39 col.), ports. 30 cm. 1. Wood-carving, Maori I. T.
NB1106.B3x   736/.4/09931   LC 79-109412   ISBN 0804808600

**Schmitz, Carl August.** • 1.5771
Oceanic sculpture: sculpture of Melanesia. Photographed by F. L. Kenett. Greenwich, Conn., New York Graphic Society [1962] xv p. 33 plates, map. 38 cm. (The Acanthus history of sculpture) 1. Sculpture, Melanesian. I. Kenett, F. L. II. T. III. Series.
NB1111.M4S3   730.993   LC 62-7574

# NB1135–1170 SCULPTURE: GENERAL WORKS. TECHNIQUE

**Martin, F. David, 1920-.** 1.5772
Sculpture and enlivened space: aesthetics and history / F. David Martin. — Lexington, Conn.: University Press of Kentucky, c1981. 276 p., [32] leaves of plates: ill.; 24 cm. 1. Sculpture — Philosophy. 2. Painting — Philosophy. I. T.
NB1137.M37   730/.1   LC 79-4006   ISBN 0813113865

**Hoffman, Malvina, 1887-.**                                                    • **1.5773**
Sculpture inside and out [by] Malvina Hoffman. — New York: W. W. Norton & company, [c1939] 330 p.: incl. illus., plates, diagrs.; 26 cm. 'First edition.' 1. Sculpture 2. Sculpture — Technique I. T.
NB1140.H6        730        LC 39-27322

**Meyer. Frederick Robert.**                                                     **1.5774**
Sculpture in ceramic, by Fred Meyer. — New York: Watson-Guptill Publications, [1971] 156 p.: illus.; 29 cm. 1. Sculpture I. T.
NB1140.M4        738        LC 79-152753        *ISBN* 082304694X

**Read, Herbert Edward, Sir, 1893-1968.**                                        • **1.5775**
The art of sculpture / Herbert Read. — New York: Pantheon, 1956. xxxi, 152 p., [224] p. of plates. (A.W. Mellon lectures in the fine arts. 3) (Bollingen series. 35) 1. Sculpture I. T. II. Series. III. Series: Bollingen series. 35
NB1140.R4        LC 56-10426

**Verhelst, Wilbert, 1923-.**                                                    **1.5776**
Sculpture: tools, materials, and techniques. — Englewood Cliffs, N.J.: Prentice-Hall, [1973] xiii, 287 p.: illus.; 28 cm. 1. Sculpture I. T.
NB1140.V47       731.4       LC 72-10335        *ISBN* 0137966156

**Wittkower, Rudolf.**                                                           **1.5777**
Sculpture: processes and principles / Rudolf Wittkower. — New York: Harper & Row, c1977. 288 p.: ill.; 24 cm. — (Icon editions) Lectures given at Cambridge University during 1970-71. Includes index. 1. Sculpture I. T.
NB1140.W57 1977b        730        LC 77-258        *ISBN* 0064300919

**Andrews, Oliver.**                                                             **1.5778**
Living materials: a sculptor's handbook / Oliver Andrews. — Berkeley: University of California Press, c1983. xii, 348 p.: ill.; 27 cm. 1. Sculpture — Technique 2. Modeling I. T.
NB1170.A63 1983        731/.2 19        LC 77-71057        *ISBN* 0520034473

**Clarke, Carl Dame, 1904-.**                                                    **1.5779**
Metal casting of sculpture. Butler, Md., Standard Arts Press [1948] xi, 170 p. illus. 29 cm. 1. Precision casting 2. Sculpture — Technique I. T.
NB1170.C5        731.45       LC 48-6434 *

**Mills, John W.**                                                               **1.5780**
The technique of sculpture / John W. Mills. — New York: Watson-Guptill Publications, 1976. 168 p.: ill.; 26 cm. Includes index. 1. Sculpture — Technique I. T.
NB1170.M53 1976        731.4        LC 75-19461        *ISBN* 0823052109

**Rich, Jack C., 1914-.**                                                        • **1.5781**
The materials and methods of sculpture. New York: Oxford Univ. Press, 1947. xxi, 416 p.: illus.; 25 cm. 1. Sculpture — Technique I. T.
NB1170.R5        731        LC 47-11263

**Forsyth, Ilene H.**                                                            **1.5782**
The Throne of Wisdom; wood sculptures of the madonna in Romanesque France [by] Ilene H. Forsyth. — Princeton, N.J.: Princeton University Press, [1972] xviii, 226, [64] p.: illus.; 29 cm. A revision of the author's thesis, Columbia, 1960. 1. Mary, Blessed Virgin, Saint — Art 2. Sculpture, Romanesque — France. 3. Sculpture, French 4. Wood-carving — France. I. T.
NB1255.F8 F67 1972        731/.88/550944        LC 72-166372        *ISBN* 0691038376

**Baxandall, Michael.**                                                          **1.5783**
The limewood sculptors of Renaissance Germany / Michael Baxandall. — New Haven: Yale University Press, 1980. xx, 420 p.: ill. (some col.); 28 cm. Includes index. 1. Sculpture, Renaissance — Germany. 2. Sculpture, German 3. Wood-carving, Renaissance — Germany. 4. Wood-carving — Germany I. T.
NB1255.G3 B39        730/.943        LC 79-23258        *ISBN* 0300024231

**Cox, J. Halley, 1910-.**                                                       **1.5784**
Hawaiian sculpture / J. Halley Cox with William H. Davenport. — Honolulu: University Press of Hawaii, [1974] ix, 198 p.: ill.; 29 cm. 1. Sculpture, Hawaiian. 2. Wood-carving — Hawaii. I. Davenport, William H., 1922- joint author. II. T.
NB1255.U6 C68        732/.2/09969        LC 73-151453        *ISBN* 0824802810

**Newman, Thelma R.**                                                            **1.5785**
Plastics as sculpture [by] Thelma R. Newman. — [1st ed.]. — Radnor, Pa.: Chilton Book Co., [1974] 223 p.: illus.; 26 cm. 1. Plastic sculpture I. T.
NB1270.P5 N48        731.4        LC 74-691        *ISBN* 0801957672

## NB1282–1950 SPECIAL FORMS

**Finn, David, 1921-.**                                                          **1.5786**
The Florence Baptistery doors / photos. by David Finn; introd. by Kenneth Clark; commentaries by George Robinson. — New York: Viking Press, 1980. 328 p.: ill. (some col.); 31 cm. — (A Studio book) Includes index. 1. Ghiberti, Lorenzo, 1378-1455. 2. Florence. San Giovanni (Baptistery). Porte di bronzo. I. Clark, Kenneth, 1903- II. Robinson, George, 1931- III. T.
NB1287.F6 F56 1980        730/.92/4        LC 80-14120        *ISBN* 067031997X

**Toynbee, J. M. C. (Jocelyn M. C.), d. 1985.**                                  **1.5787**
Roman historical portraits / J. M. C. Toynbee. — Ithaca, N.Y.: Cornell University Press, 1978. 208 p.: ill.; 26 cm. — (Aspects of Greek and Roman life) 1. Portrait sculpture, Roman 2. History, Ancient — Portraits. 3. Rome — Biography — Portraits. I. T. II. Series.
NB1296.3.T69 1978b        730/.0937        LC 75-38428        *ISBN* 0801410118

**Richter, Gisela Marie Augusta, 1882-1972.**                                    • **1.5788**
The archaic gravestones of Attica. With 216 illus., including 108 from photos. by Alison Frantz, and an appendix with epigraphical notes by Margherita Guarducci. — London, Phaidon Press, 1961. viii, 184 p. illus.; 31 cm. Bibliography: p. 57-58. I. T.
NB1370.R5

**Ludwig, Allan I.**                                                             **1.5789**
Graven images; New England stonecarving and its symbols, 1650–1815, by Allan I. Ludwig. [1st ed.] Middletown, Conn., Wesleyan University Press [1966] xxxi, 482 p. illus., maps. 29 cm. Includes bibliographical references. 1. Sepulchral monuments — New England. 2. Sculpture, American I. T.
NB1856.N4L8        731.76        LC 66-14665

**Feininger, Andreas, 1906-.**                                                   • **1.5790**
Maids, madonnas & witches; women in sculpture from prehistoric times to Picasso. Photos. by Andreas Feininger. Introd. by Henry Miller. Text by J. Bon. [Translated from the German by Joan Bradley] New York: Abrams, [1961] 194 p.: plates.; 33 cm. Translation of Frauen und Göttinnen von der Steinzeit bis zu Picasso. 1. Sculpture 2. Women in art I. Bon, J. II. T.
NB1930.F413        731.824        LC 61-13859

# NC GRAPHIC ARTS. DRAWING. DESIGN

**Who's who in graphic art.**                                                    • **1.5791**
1st ed.-       . — Zurich: Amstutz & Herdeg Graphis Press, 1962-. v.: ill., ports.; 30 cm. Vol. 2- published: Dübendorf, Switzerland: De Clivo Press, 1982- Beginning with edition published in 1982, vols. are numbered v. 2- 1. Artists — Dictionaries. 2. Graphic arts I. Amstutz, Walter.
NC45.W5        LC 62-51802

# NC50–376 History

**Pignatti, Terisio, 1920-.**                                                    **1.5792**
[Disegno. English] Master drawings: from cave art to Picasso / Terisio Pignatti; captions by Maria Agnese Chiari. — New York: Abrams, 1982. 397 p.: ill. (some col.); 32 cm. Translation of: Il disegno. Includes index. 1. Drawing I. Chiari, Maria Agnese. II. T.
NC52.P513 1982        741/.09 19        LC 82-4048        *ISBN* 0810916630

**Marks, Claude.**                                                               **1.5793**
From the sketchbooks of the great artists. New York, Crowell [1972] 480 p. illus. 29 cm. 1. Drawing — Themes, motives 2. Drawing 3. Art — Psychology I. T.
NC53.M37 1972        741.9        LC 74-170998        *ISBN* 0690319991

## NC101–376 BY COUNTRY

**Chernow, Burt.**                                                               **1.5794**
The drawings of Milton Avery / Burt Chernow; with a foreword by Sally Avery. — New York: Taplinger Pub. Co., 1984. 136 p.: ill. 1. Avery, Milton, 1885-1965. I. Avery, Milton, 1885-1965. II. T.
NC139.A93 A4 1984        741.973 19        LC 83-9245        *ISBN* 0800822986

**De Kooning, Willem, 1904-.**                                **1.5795**
Willem de Kooning drawings. [Text by] Thomas B. Hess. — Greenwich, Conn.: New York Graphic Society, 1973, [c1972] 296 p.: illus. (part col.); 32 cm. — (A Paul Bianchini book) 1. De Kooning, Willem, 1904- I. Hess, Thomas B. II. T. NC139.D45 H47 1972b   741.9/73   *LC* 70-181345   *ISBN* 0821204181

**Shapiro, David, 1947-.**                                   **1.5796**
Jasper Johns drawings, 1954–1984 / text by David Shapiro; project director, David Whitney; editor, Christopher Sweet. — New York: Abrams, 1984. 211 p.: ill. (some col.); 31 cm. Includes index. 1. Johns, Jasper, 1930- I. Johns, Jasper, 1930- II. T. NC139.J58 S5 1984      741/.092/4 19   *LC* 83-25775   *ISBN* 0810911566

**Rivers, Larry, 1923-.**                                    **1.5797**
Drawings and digressions / by Larry Rivers with Carol Brightman. — New York: C.N. Potter: Distributed by Crown, 1979. 263 p.: chiefly ill. (some col.); 29 cm. 1. Rivers, Larry, 1923- 2. New York School. I. Brightman, Carol. joint author. II. T. NC139.R56 A4 1979      741.9/73   *LC* 79-4614   *ISBN* 0517534304

**McLaren, Norman, 1914-.**                                  **1.5798**
The drawings of Norman McLaren = Les dessins de Norman McLaren / text by Norman McLaren, edited from taped interviews by Michael White; [French translation by René Chicoine]. — Montreal: Tundra Books, c1975. 192 p.: ill. 1. McLaren, Norman, 1914- I. White, Michael. II. T. III. Title: Les dessins de Norman McLaren. NC143.M32 W45   NC143M32 W45.   *ISBN* 091276628X

**Pierpont Morgan Library.**                                 **1.5799**
European drawings, 1375–1825: catalogue / compiled by Cara D. Denison & Helen B. Mules, with the assistance of Jane V. Shoaf. — New York: Pierpont Morgan Library: Dover Publications, 1981. 291 p.: ill.; 30 cm. 1. Pierpont Morgan Library — Catalogs. 2. Drawing, European — Catalogs. 3. Drawing — New York (City) — Catalogs. I. Denison, Cara D. II. Mules, Helen B., 1948- III. Shoaf, Jane V. IV. T. NC225.P5 1981   741.94/074/01471 19   *LC* 80-27913   *ISBN* 0486241599

**Brophy, Brigid, 1929-.**                                   **1.5800**
Beardsley and his world / Brigid Brophy. — London: Thames and Hudson, c1976. 128 p.: ill.; 24 cm. Includes index. 1. Beardsley, Aubrey, 1872-1898. I. T. NC242.B3 B68 1976b      741/.092/4 B   *LC* 76-366635   *ISBN* 0500130574

**Hayes, John T.**                                           **1.5801**
The drawings of Thomas Gainsborough / John Hayes. — New Haven: Published for the Paul Mellon Centre for Studies in British Art (London) by Yale University Press, 1971, c1970. 2 v. (x, 368 p., [143] leaves of plates): ill.; 30 cm. Includes index. 1. Gainsborough, Thomas, 1727-1788 — Catalogs. I. Gainsborough, Thomas, 1727-1788. II. T. NC242.G3 A4 1970   741/.092/4   *LC* 78-140108   *ISBN* 0300014252

**Jones, Inigo, 1573-1652.**                                 **1.5802**
The theatre of the Stuart Court; including the complete designs for productions at court, for the most part in the Collection of the Duke of Devonshire, together with their texts and historical documentation [by] Stephen Orgel and Roy Strong. — [London]: Sotheby Parke Bernet; [Berkeley]: University of California Press, 1973. 2 v. (843 p.): illus. (part col.); 35 cm. 1. Jones, Inigo, 1573-1652. 2. Devonshire, Victor Christian William Cavendish, 9th Duke of, 1868-1938 — Art collections. 3. Theaters — Stage-setting and scenery — Catalogs. 4. Costume — Catalogs. I. Orgel, Stephen. II. Strong, Roy C. III. T. NC242.J65 O73 1973   792/.026   *LC* 73-78548   *ISBN* 0520024699

**Blunt, Anthony, 1907-1983.**                               **1.5803**
The drawings of Poussin / Anthony Blunt. — New Haven: Yale University Press, 1979. xiii, 209 p.: ill.; 27 cm. Includes index. 1. Poussin, Nicolas, 1594?-1665. I. T. NC248.P64 B55      741/.092/4   *LC* 75-43304   *ISBN* 0300019718

**Schilling, Edmund, 1888-.**                                **1.5804**
The German drawings in the collection of Her Majesty the Queen at Windsor Castle, by Edmund Schilling; and, Supplements to the catalogues of Italian and French drawings, with a history of the Royal Collection of Drawings, by Anthony Blunt. London, New York, Phaidon [1971] viii, 239 p. illus., facsims. 31 cm. (The Drawings at Windsor Castle) 'Distributors in the United States: Praeger Publishers Inc.' 1. Windsor, House of — Art collections. 2. Drawing, German — Catalogs. 3. Windsor Castle. I. Blunt, Anthony, 1907-1983. II. T. NC249.S3   741.9/4/0740229   *LC* 73-111053   *ISBN* 0714814466

**Weber, Nicholas Fox, 1947-.**                              **1.5805**
The drawings of Josef Albers / Nicholas Fox Weber. — New Haven: Yale University Press, c1984. xiv, 61 p., [106] p. of plates: ill. (some col.); 28 cm. 1. Albers, Josef. I. Albers, Josef. II. T. NC251.A36 W4 1984   741.973 19   *LC* 83-23459   *ISBN* 0300031688

**Koschatzky, Walter.**                                      **1.5806**
Dürer drawings in the Albertina [by] Walter Koschatzky [and] Alice Strobl. Translated from the German by Heide and Alastair Grieve. Greenwich, Conn., New York Graphic Society, 1972. 365 p. illus. (part col.) 22 cm. Translation of Die Dürerzeichnungen der Albertina. 1. Dürer, Albrecht, 1471-1528. I. Dürer, Albrecht, 1471-1528. II. Strobl, Alice. III. Graphische Sammlung Albertina. IV. T. V. Title: Die Dürerzeichnungen der Albertina. NC 251 D8 V66 E5 1972   *LC* 74-186456   *ISBN* 0821204378

**White, Christopher.**                                      **1.5807**
Dürer: the artist and his drawings. New York, Watson-Guptill [1971] 231 p. illus. (part col.) 29 cm. 1. Dürer, Albrecht, 1471-1528. I. T. NC 251 D8 W58 1971   *LC* 72-159562   *ISBN* 0823015343

**Kollwitz, Käthe, 1867-1945.**                          • **1.5808**
The diary and letters of Kaethe Kollwitz / edited by Hans Kollwitz; translated by Richard and Clara Winston. — Chicago: Regency, 1955. — 200 p.: ill. 1. Kollwitz, Käthe, 1867-1945. 2. Artists — Germany — Correspondence. I. T. NC251.K6 A312      B   *LC* 55-9336

**Nagel, Otto, 1894-1967.**                                  **1.5809**
[Käthe Kollwitz. English] Käthe Kollwitz. [Translated by Stella Humphries] Greenwich, Conn., New York Graphic Society [1971] 261, [1] p. illus. 28 cm. 1. Kollwitz, Käthe, 1867-1945. I. T. NC251.K6 N213      769/.924   *LC* 79-137655   *ISBN* 0821204017

**Szabó, George.**                                           **1.5810**
Masterpieces of Italian drawing in the Robert Lehman Collection, the Metropolitan Museum of Art / by George Szabó. — 1st American ed. — New York: Hudson Hills Press: Distributed in the U.S. by Viking Penguin, c1983. xii, 243 p.: ill. (some col.); 32 cm. 1. Lehman, Robert, 1892-1969 — Art collections. 2. Metropolitan Museum of Art (New York, N.Y.) 3. Drawing, Italian I. Metropolitan Museum of Art (New York, N.Y.) II. T. NC255.S97 1983   741.945/074/01471 19   *LC* 82-25849   *ISBN* 0933920350

**Graphische Sammlung Albertina.**                           **1.5811**
Italian drawings in the Albertina. Edited by Walter Koschatzky, Konrad Oberhuber [and] Eckhart Knab. Greenwich, Conn., New York Graphic Society 1972 [c1971] 321 p. illus. (part col.) 32 cm. 1. Drawing, Italian — Catalogs. 2. Drawing — Austria — Vienna — Catalogs. I. Koschatzky, Walter. II. Oberhuber, Konrad. III. Knab, Eckhart. IV. T. NC255.V53   741.9/45/07403613   *LC* 72-80899   *ISBN* 0821204734

**DeGrazia, Diane, 1943-.**                                  **1.5812**
Correggio and his legacy: sixteenth–century Emilian drawings / Diane DeGrazia; with an essay by Eugenio Riccòmini. — Washington: National Gallery of Art, 1985, c1984. 415 p.: ill. (some col.); 28 cm. Catalog of an exhibition held at the National Gallery of Art, Washington, D.C., March 11-May 13, 1984 and at the Galleria nazionale, Parma, June 3-July 15, 1984. Includes index. 1. Correggio, 1489?-1534 — Influence — Exhibitions. 2. Drawing — 16th century — Italy — Reggio Emilia (Province) — Exhibitions. 3. Drawing, Italian — Italy — Reggio Emilia (Province) — Exhibitions. I. National Gallery of Art (U.S.) II. Italy. Galleria nazionale (Parma, Italy) III. T. NC256.R4 D43 1984   741.945/4/0740153 19   *LC* 83-24943   *ISBN* 0894680722

**Tietze, Hans, 1880-1954.**                                 **1.5813**
The drawings of the Venetian painters in the 15th and 16th centuries / by Hans Tietze and E. Tietze–Conrat. — New York: Hacker Art Books, 1979. xvi, 398 p., [100] leaves of plates: ill. Reprint of the 1944 ed. 1. Drawing, Italian — Italy — Venice — Catalogs. 2. Drawing, Renaissance — Italy — Venice. I. Tietze-Conrat, Erika, 1883-1958 II. T. NC256.V4 T5 1979   741.9/45   *LC* 79-84535   *ISBN* 0878172548

**Smyth, Craig Hugh.**                                       **1.5814**
Bronzino as draughtsman; an introduction, with notes on his portraiture and tapestries. Locust Valley, N.Y., J. J. Augustin [1971] x, 104, [38] p. illus. 26 cm. 1. Bronzino, Agnolo, 1503-1572. I. T. NC257.B7 S6   741/.092/4   *LC* 74-178089

**Joannides, Paul.**                                         **1.5815**
The drawings of Raphael: with a complete catalogue / Paul Joannides. — Berkeley: University of California Press, c1983. 271 p.: ill. (some col.); 32 cm. Includes index. 1. Raphael, 1483-1520. 2. Raphael, 1483-1520 — Catalogs. I. Raphael, 1483-1520. II. T. NC257.R3 J6 1983   741.945 19   *LC* 83-47658   *ISBN* 0520050878

**Knox, George.**            **1.5816**
Giambattista and Domenico Tiepolo: a study and catalogue raisonné of the chalk drawings / George Knox. — Oxford: Clarendon Press; New York: Oxford University Press, 1980. 2v.; 29 cm. Includes indexes. 1. Tiepolo, Giovanni Battista, 1696-1770 — Catalogs. 2. Tiepolo, Giovanni Domenico, 1726?-1804 — Catalogs. I. Tiepolo, Giovanni Battista, 1696-1770. II. Tiepolo, Giovanni Domenico, 1726?-1804. III. T.
NC257.T5 A4 1980     741.945 19     *LC* 79-42916     *ISBN* 019817313X

**Goya, Francisco, 1746-1828.**          **1.5817**
[Dessins de Goya: les albums. English] Drawings; the complete albums. [Reconstruction] by Pierre Gassier. [Translated by James Emmóns and Robert Allen] New York, Praeger [1973] 656 p. illus. 31 cm. Translation of Les dessins de Goya: les albums. 1. Goya, Francisco, 1746-1828. I. Gassier, Pierre. II. T.
NC287.G65 G37     741.9/46     *LC* 72-81582

# NC703–757 Drawing: General Works. Design. Technique. Perspective

**Klee, Paul, 1879-1940.**        • **1.5818**
Pedagogical sketchbook / [Introd. and translation by Sibyl Moholy–Nagy]. — New York: Praeger, 1953. 60 p.: ill.; 21 cm. — (Books that matter.) 1. Composition (Art) 2. Design I. T. II. Series.
NC703 K58 1952     745.42     *LC* 52-13103

**Meder, Joseph, 1857-1934.**          **1.5819**
[Handzeichnung. English] The mastery of drawing / Joseph Meder; translated and revised by Winslow Ames. — New York, N.Y.: Abaris Books, 1978. 2 v.: ill.; 31 cm. Translation of: Die Handzeichnung. Includes indexes. 1. Drawing I. Ames, Winslow. II. T.
NC710.M413     741 19     *LC* 76-22300     *ISBN* 0913870161

**Watrous, James.**         • **1.5820**
The craft of old–master drawings. Madison, University of Wisconsin Press, 1957. 170 p. illus. 27 cm. 1. Drawing — Study and teaching 2. Drawing — History. 3. Drawing I. T.
NC735.W36     741     *LC* 56-9307

**Franke, Herbert W., 1927-.**         **1.5821**
[Computergraphik, Computerkunst. English] Computer graphics, computer art [by] Herbert W. Franke. [London, New York] Phaidon [1971] 133 p. illus. 25 cm. Translation of Computergraphik-Computerkunst. Distributed in the U.S.A. by Praeger Publishers, 111 Fourth Ave., New York, N.Y. 1. Computer drawing I. T.
NC740.F713     702/.8/5443 19     *LC* 72-162314     *ISBN* 0714815039

**White, John, 1924 Mar. 5-.**        • **1.5822**
The birth and rebirth of pictorial space. Boston, Boston Book and Art Shop [1970, c1967] 289 p. illus. 26 cm. 1. Perspective 2. Painting, Italian 3. Painting, Renaissance — Italy I. T.
NC750.W48 1970     759.5     *LC* 73-12070

# NC760–780 Anatomy

**Schider, Fritz, 1846-1907.**        • **1.5823**
[Plastisch-anatomischer Handatlas. English] An atlas of anatomy for artists. Rev. by M. Auerbach and translated by Bernard Wolf. New bibliography by Adolf Placzek. Additional illus. from the old masters and historical sources. With a new section on hands selected by Heidi Lenssen. 3d American ed. [New York] Dover Publications [c1957] 1 v. (chiefly illus., part col.) 29 cm. Translation of Plastisch-anatomischer Handatlas. 1. Anatomy, Artistic 2. Anatomy, Human — Atlases I. Auerbach, Max, 1879- II. T.
NC760.S32 1957     743.4     *LC* 58-3622

**Kramer, Jack.**          **1.5824**
Human anatomy & figure drawing; the integration of structure and form. — New York: Van Nostrand Reinhold Co., [1972] 143 p.: illus.; 29 cm. 1. Figure drawing 2. Anatomy, Artistic I. T.
NC765.K7 1972     743/.4     *LC* 73-162680

# NC800–825 Landscape Studies

**Baer, Curtis O.**          **1.5825**
Landscape drawings [by] Curtis O. Baer. — New York: H. N. Abrams, [1973] 360 p.: illus. (part col.); 28 x 34 cm. 'Published in association with the Drawing Society.' 1. Landscape drawing — Exhibitions. I. T.
NC800.B29     743/.9/36     *LC* 72-135655     *ISBN* 0810902559

# NC950–1003 Illustration. Commercial Art

**Bland, David.**        • **1.5826**
A history of book illustration; the illuminated manuscript and the printed book. — [2d rev. ed.]. — Berkeley: University of California Press, 1969. 459 p.: facsims. (part col.); 29 cm. 1. Illustration of books — History. 2. Illumination of books and manuscripts — History. I. T.
NC960.B62 1969b     745.6/7     *LC* 69-12472

**Museum of Fine Arts, Boston.**        • **1.5827**
The artist and the book, 1860–1960, in western Europe and the United States. — [Cambridge, Mass.] Harvard College Library, Dept. of Printing and Graphic Arts [1961] 232 p. illus. (part col.); 29 cm. 'Exhibition held at the Museum of Fine Arts, Boston, May 4-July 16, 1961.' Bibliography: p. 222-227. I. Harvard University. Library. Dept. of Graphic Arts II. T.
NC960.B7     *LC* 61-13493

**Hofer, Philip.**        • **1.5828**
Baroque book illustration: a short survey from the collection in the Department of Graphic Arts, Harvard College Library. — Cambridge: Harvard U.P. 1951, 1970 printing. 43p.: 149 illus. 1. Illustration of books 2. Engraving — History. 3. Illustrated books — 17th century I. Harvard University. Library. Dept. of Graphic Arts. II. T.
NC960.H6     *LC* 51-14003     *ISBN* 0674061756

**Bader, Barbara.**          **1.5829**
American picturebooks from Noah's ark to the Beast within. — New York: Macmillan, c1976. 615 p.: ill.; 28 cm. Includes index. 1. Illustrated books, Children's — History and criticism. 2. Illustrators — United States. 3. Picture-books for children 4. Children's literature, American — History and criticism. 5. Illustrated books — United States. I. T.
NC965.B32     741.6/42     *LC* 72-93304     *ISBN* 0027080803

**Science fiction art** / compiled & introduced by Brian Aldiss.          **1.5830**
New York: Bounty Books, c1975. 128 p.: ill. (some col.); 38 cm. Includes index. 1. Science fiction in art. 2. Science fiction — Illustrations. 3. Magazine illustration — Great Britain. I. Aldiss, Brian Wilson, 1925-
NC968.S33     741.65     *LC* 75-13823     *ISBN* 0517524325

**Kery, Patricia Frantz.**          **1.5831**
Great magazine covers of the world / Patricia Frantz Kery. — New York: Abbeville Press, c1982. 384 p.: ill. (some col.); 32 cm. Includes index. 1. Magazine covers I. T.
NC974.K47 1982     741.65/2 19     *LC* 81-19066     *ISBN* 0896592251

**Reed, Walt.**          **1.5832**
The illustrator in America, 1880–1980: a century of illustration / Walt and Roger Reed; design by Art Weithas. — New York: Published for the Society of Illustrators by Madison Square Press: Distributed by R. Silver Associates, c1984. 355 p.: ill. (some col.); 31 cm. Rev. ed. of: The illustrator in America, 1900-1960's. 1967, c1966. Includes index. 1. Illustrators — United States — Biography. 2. Illustration of books — 19th century — United States. 3. Illustration of books — 20th century — United States. I. Reed, Roger. II. Reed, Walt. The illustrator in America, 1900-1960's. III. Society of Illustrators (New York, N.Y.) IV. T.
NC975.R4 1984     741.6/092/2 B 19     *LC* 85-124243     *ISBN* 0942604032

**Ludwig, Coy, 1939-.**          **1.5833**
Maxfield Parrish. — [New York: Watson-Guptill Publications, [1973] 223 p.: illus. (part col.); 32 cm. 1. Parrish, Maxfield, 1870-1966. I. T.
NC975.5.P37 L82     741/.092/4     *LC* 73-5691     *ISBN* 0823038971

**Rand, Paul, 1914-.**    **1.5834**
Thoughts on design. — Revised ed. — London: Studio Vista; New York: Van Nostrand Reinhold, 1971. 95 p.: illus., facsims.; 21 cm. — (A Studio Vista Van Nostrand Reinhold art paperback) 1. Design 2. Commercial art I. T. NC997.R3 1970    659.13/24    LC 72-126307    ISBN 0289798361

**History of graphic design and communication: a source book /**    **1.5835**
**compiled by Clive Ashwin.**
London: Pembridge, 1983. x, 279 p.: ill., facsims., ports.; 23 cm. — (Pembridge history of design series.) 1. Commercial art — History. I. Ashwin, Cliv. II. Series.
NC998    NC998.H584 1983.    741.6/09/034 19    ISBN 0862060052 0826060052

**Kince, Eli, 1953-.**    **1.5836**
Visual puns in design: the pun used as a communications tool / by Eli Kince. — New York: Watson-Guptill, 1982. 168 p.: ill. (some col.); 29 cm. Includes index. 1. Graphic arts — History — 20th century. 2. Communication in design 3. Signs and symbols in art. 4. Puns and punning 5. Visual perception I. T. NC998.4.K56 1982    741.6 19    LC 82-16065    ISBN 0823074900

**Glaser, Milton.**    **1.5837**
Graphic design. — Woodstock, N.Y.: Overlook Press, [1973]. — 242 p.: ill. (some col.); 27 cm. Pref. by J. M. Folon. 1. Graphic arts, American. I. T. NC999.4.G55    741.6/094/4    LC 73-79228    ISBN 0879510137

**Snyder, Gertrude.**    **1.5838**
Herb Lubalin: art director, graphic designer, and typographer / by Gertrude Snyder & Alan Peckolick. — New York: American Showcase: U.S. & Canadian distribution, R. Silver Associates, c1985. 184 p.: ill. (some col.); 31 cm. Includes index. 1. Lubalin, Herb, 1918- — Criticism and interpretation. I. Lubalin, Herb, 1918- II. Peckolick, Alan. III. T. NC999.4.L8 S69 1985    741.6/092/4 19    LC 84-72129    ISBN 0931144280

# NC1005–1890 Collections of Drawings. Caricatures. Cartoons. Posters

**Berenson, Bernard, 1865-1959.**    • **1.5839**
The drawings of the Florentine painters, by Bernard Berenson. Amplified ed. New York, Greenwood Press [1969] 3 v. illus. 32 cm. (University of Chicago publications in art) 'Originally published in 1938.' 1. Drawing, Florentine — History. 2. Painters, Italian — Florence. I. T. NC1045.B5 1969    741.9/45    LC 69-13822

**De Tolnay, Charles, 1899-.**    • **1.5840**
The drawings of Pieter Bruegel the elder: with a critical catalogue / [translated by Charles R. Sleeth from the German]. — New York: Twin Editions, [1953?] 92, xcvi p.: ill.; 31 cm. 1. Brueghel, Peeter, the elder, d. 1569. I. T. NC1055.B85D4x    LC a 53-8625

**Leonardo, da Vinci, 1452-1519.**    • **1.5841**
Selected drawings from Windsor Castle: Leonardo da Vinci / by Kenneth Clark. — London: Phaidon Press, 1954. [8] p., [28] leaves of plates: front., ill., ports.; 31 cm. 'This book reproduces 57 out of the 600 drawings by Leonardo da Vinci which are preserved in the Royal Library at Windsor Castle.' -Preface. Half title: Selected drawings from the collection of Her Majesty the Queen at Windsor Castle. 1. Leonardo, da Vinci, 1452-1519. I. Clark, Kenneth, 1903- comp. II. Windsor Castle. Royal Library. III. T. IV. Title: Leonardo da Vinci. V. Title: Selected drawings from the collection of Her Majesty the Queen at Windsor Castle.
NC1055.L5 C63    LC 55-14295

**Beardsley, Aubrey, 1872-1898.**    **1.5842**
Beardsley [by] Brian Reade. Introduction by John Rothenstein. London, Studio Vista [1967]. 2-372 p. front., 502 illus. (incl. 9 col.). 31 cm. I. Reade, Brian. II. T.
NC1115.B314 1967b    LC 68-109775    ISBN 0289278902

**French master drawings of the nineteenth century / selected and**    • **1.5843**
**edited by Klaus Berger; translated by Robert Allen.**
London: Allen and Unwin; Basel: Holbein, 1950. 90 p.: ill.; 25 cm. (The Holbein art books) 1. Drawings, French. I. Berger, Klaus, 1901- II. Series. NC1130.B4 1950    741.944

**Fuchs, Wolfgang J., 1945-.**    **1.5844**
[Comics. English] Comics; anatomy of a mass medium [by] Reinhold Reitberger [and] Wolfgang Fuchs. [Translated from the German by Nadia Fowler. 1st American ed.] Boston, Little, Brown [1972] 264 p. illus. 30 cm. On the original German ed. Fuchs' name appeared first. 1. Comic books, strips, etc — History and criticism. I. Reitberger, Reinhold C., 1946- joint author. II. T. NC1320.F8    741.5/973    LC 72-1826

**The World encyclopedia of cartoons / Maurice Horn, editor,**    **1.5845**
**Richard Marschall, assistant editor.**
Detroit: Gale Research Co., 1980. 2 v.: ill. (some col.); 31 cm. 1. Caricatures and cartoons 2. Comic books, strips, etc. 3. Wit and humor, Pictorial I. Horn, Maurice. II. Marschall, Richard. III. Title: Encyclopedia of cartoons. NC1325.W67 1980b    741.5/03 19    LC 79-21953    0877540977

**A History of the comic strip, by Pierre Couperie [and others]**    • **1.5846**
**Translated from the French by Eilleen B. Hennessy.**
New York: Crown Publishers, [1968] 256 p.: illus.; 28 cm. Translation of Bande dessinée et figuration narrative. 'Created in conjunction with the exhibition of comic-strip art at Musée des arts décoratifs, Palais du Louvre.' 1. Comic books, strips, etc — History and criticism. I. Couperie, Pierre. NC1355.B28513    741.5/09    LC 68-20471

**Becker, Stephen D., 1927-.**    **1.5847**
Comic art in America; a social history of the funnies, the political cartoons, magazine humor, sporting cartoons, and animated cartoons. With an introd. by Rube Goldberg. — New York: Simon and Schuster, 1959. xi, 387 p.: illus.; 29 cm. 1. American wit and humor, Pictorial — History. 2. Caricature and cartoons — Social aspects — United States. I. T. NC1420.B4    741.5973 19    LC 59-13140

**The New Yorker twenty–fifth anniversary album, 1925–1950.**    • **1.5848**
New York: Harper, [1951] 1 v. (chiefly illus.); 32 cm. 1. American wit and humor, Pictorial I. The New Yorker (New York, 1925- ) NC1428.N427    741.5    LC 51-13315

**Steranko, 1938-.**    **1.5849**
The Steranko history of comics. [Reading, Pa., Supergraphics, 1970-. v. illus. 36 cm. (A Supergraphics publication) I. T. II. Title: History of comics. NC1429.S62 A56    741.5    LC 72-20236

**Thurber, James, 1894-1961.**    • **1.5850**
Thurber's men, women and dogs, a book of drawings, with a preface by Dorothy Parker. New York, Harcourt, Brace and company [1943] x, [2], 211 p. of illus. 24 cm. 'First edition.' I. T. II. Title: Men, women and dogs. NC1429.T48    741.5    LC 43-17507

**George, M. Dorothy (Mary Dorothy)**    **1.5851**
English political caricature; a study of opinion and propaganda. Oxford, Clarendon Press, 1959. 2 v. ill. 1. Caricature — Great Britain — History I. T. NC1470 G4    LC 60-1102

**George, M. Dorothy (Mary Dorothy)**    **1.5852**
Hogarth to Cruikshank: social change in graphic satire [by] M. Dorothy George. New York, Walker [1967] 224 p. illus. (part col.) 31 cm. 1. Caricatures and cartoons — Great Britain. 2. Great Britain — Social life and customs — Pictorial works. I. T. NC1470.G4x    914.2/03    LC 67-13227

**Wardroper, John.**    **1.5853**
The caricatures of George Cruikshank / John Wardroper. — 1st U.S. ed. — Boston: D. R. Godine, 1978. 144 p.: ill. (some col.); 24 x 26 cm. Includes index. 1. Cruikshank, George, 1792-1878. 2. English wit and humor, Pictorial I. T. NC1479.C9 A4 1978    741/.092/4    LC 77-94112    ISBN 0879232315

**Wechsler, Judith, 1940-.**    **1.5854**
A human comedy: physiognomy and caricature in 19th century Paris / Judith Wechsler; foreword by Richard Sennett. — Chicago: University of Chicago Press, 1982. 208 p.: 161 ill., facsims., ports.; 27 cm. Includes index. 1. Gesture — Caricatures and cartoons. 2. French wit and humor, Pictorial 3. Paris (France) — Social life and customs — Caricatures and cartoons. 4. France — Social life and customs — 19th century — Caricatures and cartoons. 5. Paris (France) — Population — Caricatures and cartoons. I. T. NC1495.W4 1982    741.5/0944/361 19    LC 82-70647    ISBN 0226877701

**Finch, Christopher.**    **1.5855**
The art of Walt Disney: from Mickey Mouse to the Magic Kingdoms. New concise ed. New York, H. N. Abrams [1975] 160 p. illus. (part col.) 29 cm. 1. Disney, Walt, 1901-1966. 2. Walt Disney Productions. I. T. NC1766.U52 D533 1975    791/.092/4    LC 74-8435    ISBN 0810903210

**Thomas, Frank, 1912-.**    **1.5856**
Disney animation: the illusion of life / Frank Thomas and Ollie Johnston. — 1st ed. — New York: Abbeville Press, c1981. 575 p.: ill. (some col.); 29 cm.

Includes index. 1. Walt Disney Productions. 2. Animated films — United States. I. Johnston, Ollie, 1912- II. T.
NC1766.U52 D58 1981     741.5/8/0979494 19     *LC* 81-12699     *ISBN* 0896592324

**Ades, Dawn.**            1.5857
The 20th–century poster: design of the avant–garde / by Dawn Ades with contributions by Robert Brown ... [et al.]; Mildred Friedman, editor. — New York: Abbeville Press, 1984. 215 p.: ill. (some col.); 26 cm. At head of title: Posters. Produced in conjunction with an exhibition first shown at the Walker Art Center, Minneapolis, May 12-August 12, 1984. Includes index. 1. Posters — History — 20th century — Themes, motives. I. Brown, Robert K. II. Friedman, Mildred S. III. Walker Art Center. IV. T. V. Title: Twentieth-century poster.
NC1815.A33 1984     741.67/4/0904 19     *LC* 83-73420     *ISBN* 0896594335

**Rennert, Jack.**            1.5858
Alphonse Mucha: the complete posters and panels / Jack Rennert and Alain Weill. — Boston, Mass.: G.K. Hall, c1984. 405 p.: ill. (some col.); 33 cm. (A Hjert & Hjert book) English, French, and German. Includes index. 1. Mucha, Alphonse Marie, 1860-1939 — Catalogs. 2. Decoration and ornament — Art nouveau — Catalogs. I. Weill, Alain, 1946- II. Mucha, Alphonse Marie, 1860-1939. III. T.
NC1850.M8 A4 1984     741.6/092/4 19     *LC* 84-9022     *ISBN* 0816187193

# ND PAINTING

**Greer, Germaine, 1939-.**            1.5859
The obstacle race: the fortunes of women painters and their work / Germaine Greer. — 1st ed. — New York: Farrar, Straus, Giroux, 1979. 373 p., [16] leaves of plates: ill. (some col.); 26 cm. Includes index. 1. Women painters — Biography. 2. Painting — History I. T.
ND38.G73 1979     759 B     *LC* 79-17026     *ISBN* 0374224129

**Sparrow, Walter Shaw, 1862- ed.**            1.5860
Women painters of the world: from the time of Caterina Vigri, 1413–1463, to Rosa Bonheur and the present day / edited by Walter Shaw Sparrow. New York: Hacker Art Books, 1976. 332 p.: ill.; 29 cm. Reprint of the 1905 ed. published by F. A. Stokes, New York, which was issued as v. 3 of the Art and life library. Includes index. 1. Women painters — Biography. 2. Painting — History I. T.
ND38.S7 1976     759     *LC* 75-10526     *ISBN* 0878171843

**Monro, Isabel Stevenson.**            • 1.5861
Index to reproductions of European paintings; a guide to pictures in more than three hundred books, by Isabel Stevenson Monro and Kate M. Monro. New York, Wilson, 1956. 668 p. 1. Painting — Indexes I. Monro, Kate M., joint author II. T.
ND45 M6     *LC* 55-6803

# ND49–1113 History

## ND55–196 BY PERIOD

**Dodwell, C. R. (Charles Reginald)**            1.5862
Painting in Europe, 800 to 1200 [by] C. R. Dodwell. [Harmondsworth, Eng.] Penguin Books [1971] xxviii, 261 p. illus., 4 maps, 240 plates. 27 cm. (Pelican history of art.) 1. Painting, Medieval I. T. II. Series.
ND140.D63     759.02     *LC* 70-851354     *ISBN* 0140560343

**Cutler, Anthony, 1934-.**            1.5863
Transfigurations: studies in the dynamics of Byzantine iconography / Anthony Cutler. — University Park: Pennsylvania State University, c1975. xvi, 158 p., [22] leaves of plates: ill.; 26 cm. Includes index. 1. Painting, Byzantine 2. Icon painting — Byzantine Empire. 3. Christian art and symbolism I. T.
ND142.C87     755/.2     *LC* 75-1482     *ISBN* 0271011947

**Meiss, Millard.**            1.5864
The painter's choice: problems in the interpretation of Renaissance art / Millard Meiss. 1st ed. — New York: Harper & Row, 1977. x, 374 p.: ill.; 25 cm. (Icon editions) 1. Painting, Renaissance — Addresses, essays, lectures. I. T.
ND170.M4 1976     759.03     *LC* 75-12290     *ISBN* 0064356574

**Levey, Michael.**            1.5865
Rococo to Revolution; major trends in eighteenth–century painting. New York, Praeger [1966] 252 p. ill. (part col.) ports. (part col.) (Praeger world of art series) 1. Painting, Modern — 17th-18th centuries — History I. T.
ND180 L4     *LC* 66-21785

**Norman, Geraldine.**            1.5866
Nineteenth–century painters and painting: a dictionary / Geraldine Norman. — Berkeley: University of California Press, 1977. 240 p.: ill. (some col.); 28 cm. 1. Painters — Biography. 2. Painting, Modern — 19th century I. T.
ND190.N57 1977b     759.05     *LC* 76-24594     *ISBN* 0520033280

**Rosenblum, Robert.**            1.5867
Modern painting and the northern romantic tradition: Friedrich to Rothko / Robert Rosenblum. — 1st. U.S. ed. — New York: Harper & Row, c1975. 240 p.: ill.; 26 cm. (Icon editions) 1. Romanticism in art 2. Painting, Modern — 19th century 3. Painting, Modern — 20th century I. T.
ND192.R6 R67 1975     759.05     *LC* 74-6579     *ISBN* 0064384500

**Haftmann, Werner.**            • 1.5868
[Malerei im 20. Jahrhundert. English] Painting in the twentieth century. [Newly designed and expanded ed.] New York, Praeger [1965] 2 v. illus. (part col.) 24 cm. 1. Painting, Modern — 20th century 2. Painters I. T.
ND195.H323 1965     759.06     *LC* 65-25066

**Hess, Thomas B.**            • 1.5869
Abstract painting; background and American phase. New York, Viking Press, 1951. 164 p. ill. (some col.) 29 cm. (A Lee Ault edition.) 1. Painting 2. Painting, American 3. Art, Abstract I. T.
ND 195 H58 1951     *LC* 51-14481

**Kultermann, Udo.**            1.5870
[Neue Formen des Bildes. English] The new painting / Udo Kultermann; [translated from the German Neue Formen des Bildes by Wesley V. Blomster]. — Rev. and updated ed. — Boulder, Colo.: Westview Press, 1978, [c1977]. 73, 195 p., 48 leaves of plates: ill. (some col.); 28 cm. Includes index. 1. Painting, Modern — 20th century I. T.
ND195.K8413 1977     759.06     *LC* 76-26656     *ISBN* 0891586229

**Malevich, Kazimir Severinovich, 1878-1935.**            • 1.5871
The non–objective world. [Translated from the German by Howard Dearstyne] Chicago, P. Theobald [c1959] 102 p. ill. 1. Art, Modern — 20th century 2. Painting I. T.
ND195 M333     *LC* 60-21761

**Read, Herbert Edward, Sir, 1893-1968.**            • 1.5872
A concise history of modern painting. — [Rev. and enl. ed.]. — New York: Praeger, [1969, c1968] 380 p.: illus. (part col.); 22 cm. — (Praeger world of art series) 1. Painting, Modern — 20th century I. T. II. Title: Modern painting.
ND195.R4 1969     759.06     *LC* 70-5526

**Soby, James Thrall, 1906-.**            • 1.5873
Contemporary painters. Reprint ed. New York, Published for the Museum of Modern Art by Arno Press, 1966 [c1948] 151 p. illus. 27 cm. 1. Painting, Modern — 20th century I. Museum of Modern Art (New York, N.Y.) II. T.
ND195.S63 1966     *LC* 66-26119

**Waddington, Conrad Hal, 1905-.**            • 1.5874
Behind appearance; a study of the relations between painting and the natural sciences in this century [by] C. H. Waddington. — [1st ed.]. — Cambridge, Mass.: MIT Press, [1970, c1969] x, 256 p.: illus., col. plates; 31 cm. 1. Painting, Modern — 20th century 2. Art and science I. T.
ND195.W27 1970     759.06     *LC* 77-97772     *ISBN* 0262230437

**Wolfe, Tom.**            1.5875
The painted word / Tom Wolfe. — New York: Farrar, Straus and Giroux, 1975. 121 p.: ill.; 21 cm. 1. Painting, Modern — 20th century 2. Painting — Psychological aspects. I. T.
ND195.W64 1975     759/.06     *LC* 75-8978     *ISBN* 0374228787

**Daix, Pierre.**            1.5876
[Journal du cubisme. English] Cubists and cubism / Pierre Daix. — Geneva: Skira; New York: Rizzoli, c1982. 170 p.: ill. (some col.); 35 cm. Translation of: Journal du cubisme. Includes index. 1. Cubism 2. Painting, Modern — 20th century 3. Cubism — France. 4. Painting, Modern — 20th century — France. I. T.
ND196.C8 D34 1982     759.06/32 19     *LC* 82-60070     *ISBN* 0847804577

**Golding, John.** • 1.5877
Cubism: a history and an analysis, 1907–1914. — 2nd ed. — London: Faber, 1968. 208 p.: 99 plates, illus. (incl. 3 col.).; 26 cm. 1. Cubism 2. Art, Modern — 20th century I. T.
ND196.C8 G6 1968    759.06    LC 76-368417

**Vogt, Paul, 1926-.** 1.5878
[Expressionismus. English] Expressionism: German painting, 1905–1920 / by Paul Vogt; text translated by Antony Vivis; color plate commentary translated by Robert Erich Wolf. — New York: H. N. Abrams, 1980, c1978. 136 p.: ill. (some col.); 33 cm. Includes index. 1. Expressionism (Art) 2. Painting, Modern — 20th century 3. Prints — 20th century I. T.
ND196.E9 V6313 1980   759.3   LC 79-18049   ISBN 0810908522

**Diehl, Gaston.** 1.5879
[Fauves. English] The fauves / Gaston Diehl. — New York: H. N. Abrams, 1975. 168 p.: ill. (some col.); 34 cm. — (The Library of great art movements) Includes index. 1. Fauvism — History. 2. Painting, Modern — 20th century I. T.
ND196.F3 D5313   759.06   LC 72-5650   ISBN 0810901145

**Breton, André, 1896-1966.** 1.5880
[Surréalisme et la peinture. English] Surrealism and painting / André Breton; translated from the French by Simon Watson Taylor. — 1st U.S. ed. — New York: Harper & Row, 1972. 415 p.: ill.; 26 cm. — (Icon editions; IN-24) Translation of Le surréalisme et la peinture. 1. Surrealism 2. Painting, Modern — 20th century I. T.
ND196.S8 B7313 1972b   759.06   LC 70-188930   ISBN 0064304078. ISBN 0064300242 pbk

## ND197–198 ZEN PAINTING. ISLAMIC PAINTING

**Fontein, Jan.** 1.5881
Zen painting & calligraphy; an exhibition of works of art lent by temples, private collectors, and public and private museums in Japan, organized in collaboration with the Agency for Cultural Affairs of the Japanese government [by] Jan Fontein & Money L. Hickman. Boston, Museum of Fine Arts; distributed by New York Graphic Society, Greenwich, Conn. [1971, c1970] liv, 173 p. illus. (part col.) 29 cm. Catalog of the exhibition held Nov. 5-Dec. 20, 1970, at the Boston Museum of Fine Arts. 1. Painting, Zen — Exhibitions. 2. Calligraphy, Zen — Exhibitions. I. Hickman, Money L., joint author. II. Japan. Bunkachō. III. Museum of Fine Arts, Boston. IV. T.
ND197.F6 1971   759.952/074/014461   LC 76-127853   ISBN 0878460004

**Ettinghausen, Richard.** • 1.5882
Arab painting / text by Richard Ettinghausen. — Geneva: Skira; New York: Rizzoli, 1977. 208 p.: col. ill., map; 28 cm. — (Treasures of Asia) 1. Painting, Islamic 2. Illumination of books and manuscripts, Islamic I. T.
ND198.E8 1977   759.956   LC 76-62898   ISBN 0847800814

## ND200 PAINTING, BY COUNTRY

**Museum of Fine Arts, Boston.** • 1.5883
M. and M. Karolik collection of American paintings, 1815 to 1865. Cambridge, Published for Museum of Fine Arts, Boston [by] Harvard University Press, 1949 [i. e. 1951] lx, 544 p. 233 illus. 32 cm. Errata leaf inserted. 1. Painting — Boston — Catalogs. 2. Paintings, American. 3. Painters, American. I. Karolik, Maxim. II. Karolik, Martha Catherine Codman. III. T.
ND200.B73   759.135   LC 51-8136

## ND205–238 United States

**Barker, Virgil, 1890-.** • 1.5884
American painting, history and interpretation. — New York: Macmillan, 1950. xxvii, 717 p.: illus.; 26 cm. 1. Painting — United States — History. I. T.
ND205.B29   750.973   LC 50-10368

**Burroughs, Alan, 1897-1965.** • 1.5885
Limners and likenesses; three centuries of American paintings. New York, Russell & Russell, 1965 [c1936] ix, 246 p. plates. 26 cm. (Harvard-Radcliffe fine arts series) 1. Painting, American — History. I. T.
ND205.B8 1965   759.13   LC 65-18793

**Monro, Isabel Stevenson.** • 1.5886
Index to reproductions of American paintings; a guide to pictures occuring in more than eight hundred books, by Isabel Stevenson Monro and Kate M.

Monro. New York, H.W. Wilson Co., 1948. 731 p. 1. Paintings, American 2. Painters, American I. Monro, Kate M., joint author II. T.
ND205 M57   LC 48-9663

**Metropolitan Museum of Art (New York, N.Y.)** 1.5887
American paintings in the Metropolitan Museum of Art / edited by Kathleen Luhrs. — New York: The Museum in association with Princeton University Press, 1980-. v.: ill.; 28 cm. 1. Metropolitan Museum of Art (New York, N.Y.) — Catalogs. 2. Painting, American — Catalogs. 3. Painting — New York (City) — Catalogs. I. Luhrs, Kathleen, 1941- II. Burke, Doreen Bolger, 1949- III. T.
ND205.N373 1980   759.13/074/01471   LC 80-81074   ISBN 0870992449

**Prown, Jules David.** 1.5888
American painting: from the Colonial Period to the present / introd. by John Walker; text by Jules David Prown and Barbara Rose. — New updated ed. — New York: Rizzoli, 1977. 276 p.: ill. (col.) 1. Painting, American 2. Painters — United States I. Rose, Barbara. II. T.
ND205.P74   ND205 P74 1977.   759.13   LC 70-80455   ISBN 0847800490

**Richardson, Edgar Preston, 1902-.** • 1.5889
American romantic painting / Edgar P. Richardson; with 236 illustrations; edited by Robert Freund. — New York: E. Weyhe, c1944. 50 p., [170] p. of plates: ill.; 31 cm. 1. Painting — United States — History. 2. Painting, American I. Freund, Robert. II. T.
ND205.R5   LC 45-878

**Richardson, Edgar Preston, 1902-.** • 1.5890
Painting in America, from 1502 to the present [by] E. P. Richardson. — New York: Crowell, [1965] xiii, 456 p.: illus. (part col.) ports.; 26 cm. 1. Painting, American — History. I. T.
ND205.R53 1965   759.13   LC 65-23777

**American folk painters of three centuries / Jean Lipman, Tom Armstrong, editors.** 1.5891
1st ed. New York, Hudson Hills Press in association with the Whitney Museum of American Art; New York, trade distribution by Simon & Schuster, c1980. 233 p. ill. 28 cm. 'Exhibition organized by the Whitney Museum of American Art, New York, February 26-May 13, 1980.' 1. Painting, American — Exhibitions. 2. Primitivism in art — United States — Exhibitions. I. Lipman, Jean (Herzberg) 1909- II. Armstrong, Tom, 1932-
ND205.5.P74 A43   759.13/074/01471   LC 79-21212   ISBN 0933920059

**Flexner, James Thomas, 1908-.** • 1.5892
America's old masters. — Rev. [i. e. 2d] ed. — New York, Dover Publications [1967] 365 p. illus., ports. 22 cm. 1. West, Benjamin, 1738-1820. 2. Copley, John Singleton, 1737-1815. 3. Peale, Charles Willson, 1741-1827. 4. Stuart, Gilbert, 1755-1828. 5. Painters, American. I. T.
ND207.F55 1967   759.13   LC 67-16702

**Flexner, James Thomas, 1908-.** • 1.5893
First flowers of our wilderness; American painting, the colonial period. New York: Dover Publications, [1969, c1947] xxix, 369 p.: illus.; 22 cm. 1. Painting, American — History. 2. Painting, American I. T.
ND207.F57 1969   759.13   LC 68-8811   ISBN 0486221806

**Flexner, James Thomas, 1908-.** • 1.5894
That wilder image; the painting of America's native school from Thomas Cole to Winslow Homer. — New York: Dover Publications, [1970] xxii, 110 illus.; 22 cm. 'An unabridged republication of the work orginally published in 1962.' 1. Painting, American — History. 2. Painting, Modern — 19th century — U.S. I. T.
ND210.F6 1970   759.13   LC 76-125911   ISBN 0486225801

**Mather, Frank Jewett, 1868-1953.** • 1.5895
Estimates in art. Series II. Sixteen essays on American painters of the nineteenth century. — Freeport, N.Y.: Books for Libraries Press, [1970, c1931] xii, 337 p.: illus., ports.; 23 cm. — (Essay index reprint series) 1. Painters — United States 2. Painting, Modern — 19th century — United States. I. T.
ND210.M3   759.13   LC 70-93356   ISBN 0836915275

**Novak, Barbara.** • 1.5896
American painting of the nineteenth century; realism, idealism, and the American experience. — New York: Praeger, [1969] 350 p.: illus. (part col.); 26 cm. 1. Painting, American — History. 2. Painting, Modern — 19th century — U.S. I. T.
ND210.N68 1969   759.13   LC 77-76792

**Perlman, Bennard B.** • 1.5897
The immortal eight: American painting from Eakins to the Armory show (1870–1913) / by Bennard B. Perlman; introd. by Mrs. John Sloan. — New

York: Exposition Press, c1962. 226 p.: ill. 1. Painting, American — History. I. T.
ND210.P4    *LC* 62-21058

**Gerdts, William H.**      **1.5898**
American impressionism / William H. Gerdts. — 1st ed. — New York: Abbeville Press, c1984. 336 p.: ill. (some col.); 34 cm. Includes index. 1. Impressionism (Art) — United States. 2. Painting, American 3. Painting, Modern — 19th century — United States. I. T.
ND210.5.I4 G474 1984    759.13 19    *LC* 84-6365    *ISBN* 0896594513

**Lipman, Jean, 1909-.**      • **1.5899**
American primitive painting. — London; New York: Oxford Univ. Press, 1942. 158 p.: illus., plates (part col.); 31 cm. 1. Primitivism in art — United States 2. Painting, American 3. Painting, Modern — 19th century — United States. I. T.
ND210.5.P7 L56 1942    759.13 19    *LC* 42-14277

## ND212 20TH CENTURY

**Baur, John I. H. (John Ireland Howe), 1909-1987. ed.**   • **1.5900**
New art in America: fifty painters of the 20th century, by John I.H. Baur, editor [and others] Greenwich, Conn., New York Graphic Society in cooperation with Praeger, New York [1957] 280 p. ill. (part col.) 1. Painters, American 2. Paintings, American I. T.
ND212 B38    *LC* 57-9100

**Brown, Milton Wolf, 1911-.**      • **1.5901**
American painting: from the Armory Show to the depression / by Milton W. Brown. — Princeton: Princeton University Press, c1955. xii, 243 p.: ill. 1. Painting, American I. T.
ND212.B74    *LC* 53-10147    *ISBN* 0691038686

**Fried, Michael.**      **1.5902**
Three American painters, Kenneth Noland, Jules Olitski, Frank Stella: Fogg Art Museum, 21 April–30 May 1965. — New York: Garland Pub. Co., [1978] c1965. 59 p., [10] leaves of plates: ill.; 22 cm. Exhibition held also at the Pasadena Art Museum, 6 July-3 Aug. 1965. 1. Noland, Kenneth, 1924- 2. Olitski, Jules, 1922- 3. Stella, Frank. 4. Painting, Modern — 20th century — United States — Exhibitions. I. Fogg Art Museum. II. Pasadena Art Museum. III. T.
ND212.F67 1978    759.13/074/01444    *LC* 77-2760    *ISBN* 0824019571

**Geldzahler, Henry.**      • **1.5903**
American painting in the twentieth century. — New York: Metropolitan Museum of Art; distributed by New York Graphic Society, Greenwich, Conn., [1965] 236 p.: illus.; 25 cm. 1. Painting, American 2. Painting, Modern — 20th century — United States I. New York. Metropolitan Museum of Art. II. T.
ND212.G36    759.13    *LC* 65-16668

**Goodrich, Lloyd, 1897-.**      • **1.5904**
Pioneers of modern art in America; the decade of the Armory show, 1910–1920. — New York, Praeger, 1963. 94 p. illus. 24 cm. 1. Painting, American 2. Painters — United States I. T.
ND 212 G65

**Janis, Sidney, 1897-.**      • **1.5905**
They taught themselves: American primitive painters of the 20th century / by Sidney Janis; foreword by Alfred H. Barr, Jr. — New York: Dial Press, 1942. xx, 236 p.: ill. (some col.): ports.; 24 cm. 1. Painters — United States 2. Painting — United States. I. T.
ND212.J3    *LC* 42-36065

**Museum of Modern Art (New York, N.Y.)**      • **1.5906**
Abstract painting and sculpture in America, by Andrew Carnduff Ritchie. Reprint ed. [New York] Published for the Museum of Modern Art by Arno Press, 1969 [c1951] 159 p. illus. 27 cm. Catalogue of the exhibition held Jan. 23-Mar. 25, 1951, by Margaret Miller: p. 148-156. 1. Art, Abstract — Exhibitions. 2. Art, Modern — 20th century — United States I. Ritchie, Andrew Carnduff. II. T.
ND212.N395 1969    709/.73    *LC* 70-86432

**Rose, Barbara.**      • **1.5907**
American painting: the 20th century. — [Lausanne]: SKIRA, [1969] 125 p.: col. plates.; 35 cm. — (Painting, color, history) Distributed in the U.S. by: The World Publishing Company, Cleveland. 1. Painting, American 2. Painting, Modern — 20th century — United States I. T.
ND212.R62    759.13    *LC* 79-87059

**Whitney Museum of American Art.**      • **1.5908**
The new decade; 35 American painters and sculptors. [Edited by John I. H. Baur, curator. Research by Rosalind Irvine, associate curator] New York, Macmillan, 1955. 96 p. illus. 28 cm. 'The result of an exhibition held at the

Whitney Museum of American Art in the spring of 1955.' 'Catalogue of the exhibition': p. 92-96. 1. Painters, American. 2. Sculptors, American. I. Baur, John I. H. (John Ireland Howe), 1909-1987. ed. II. T.
ND212.W45    *LC* 55-3046

**Cox, Annette.**      **1.5909**
Art–as–politics: the abstract expressionist avant–garde and society / by Annette Cox. — Ann Arbor, Mich.: UMI Research Press, c1982. x, 206 p.: ill.; 24 cm. — (Studies in fine arts. The avant-garde; no. 26) A revision of the author's thesis (Ph.D.)—University of North Carolina at Chapel Hill, 1977. Includes index. 1. Abstract expressionism — United States. 2. Avant-garde (Aesthetics) — United States — History — 20th century. 3. Painting, Modern — 20th century — United States 4. Politics in art — United States. I. T.
ND212.5.A25 C69 1982    759.13 19    *LC* 82-4760    *ISBN* 0835713180

**Hobbs, Robert Carleton, 1946-.**      **1.5910**
Abstract expressionism, the formative years / by Robert Carleton Hobbs and Gail Levin. — Ithaca: Cornell University Press, 1981, c1978. 140 p.: ill. (some col.); 29 cm. 'Published in conjunction with a traveling exhibition organized in 1978 by the Herbert F. Johnson Museum of Art and the Whitney Museum of American Art.' Reissue. Originally published: Ithaca, N.Y.: Herbert F. Johnson Museum of Art, Cornell University, 1978. 1. Abstract expressionism — United States — Exhibitions. 2. Painting, American — Exhibitions. 3. Painting, Modern — 20th century — United States — Exhibitions. 4. Painters — United States — Biography. I. Levin, Gail, 1948- II. Herbert F. Johnson Museum of Art. III. Whitney Museum of American Art. IV. T.
ND212.5.A25 H63 1981    759.13 19    *LC* 80-69992    *ISBN* 0801413656

**Sandler, Irving, 1925-.**      • **1.5911**
The triumph of American painting; a history of abstract expressionism. — New York: Praeger Publishers, [1970] xv, 301 p.: illus. (part col.); 32 cm. 1. Abstract expressionism — U.S. — History. I. T.
ND212.5.A25 S2 1970    759.13    *LC* 75-124607

**Tsujimoto, Karen.**      **1.5912**
Images of America: precisionist painting and modern photography / Karen Tsujimoto. — Seattle: Published for the San Francisco Museum of Modern Art by University of Washington Press, c1982. 248 p.: ill. (some col.); 29 cm. Catalogue of an exhibition scheduled to be held at the San Francisco Museum of Modern Art and other institutions, Sept. 9, 1982-Oct. 9, 1983. Includes index. 1. San Francisco Museum of Modern Art — Exhibitions. 2. Painting, Modern — 20th century — United States — Exhibitions. 3. Photography — United States — Exhibitions. 4. United States in art — Exhibitions. 5. Precisionism — United States — Exhibitions. I. San Francisco Museum of Modern Art. II. T.
ND212.5.P67 T83 1982    759.13/074/013 19    *LC* 82-2586    *ISBN* 0295959355

**Levin, Gail, 1948-.**      **1.5913**
Synchromism and American color abstraction, 1910–1925 / Gail Levin. — 1st ed. — New York: G. Braziller, c1978. 144 p.: ill. (some col.); 28 cm. Issued in conjunction with an exhibition of the same name organized by the Whitney Museum of American Art. 1. Synchromism (Art) — United States. 2. Painting, American 3. Painting, Abstract — United States I. Whitney Museum of American Art. II. T.
ND212.5.S9 L48 1978    759.13    *LC* 77-21051    *ISBN* 0807608823

## ND236 COLLECTIVE BIOGRAPHY

**Three American modernist painters: Max Weber, with an introd.**  • **1.5914**
**by Alfred H. Barr, Jr.; Maurice Sterne, by H. M. Kallen, with a note by the artist; Stuart Davis, by James Johnson Sweeney.**
Reprint ed. — New York: Published for the Museum of Modern Art by Arno Press, 1969. 1 v. (various pagings): illus., ports.; 29 cm. Reprint of 3 catalogs of exhibitions at the Museum of Modern Art, originally issued separately, 1930-1945. 1. Weber, Max, 1881-1961. 2. Sterne, Maurice, 1878-1957. 3. Davis, Stuart, 1894-1964. I. Sweeney, James Johnson, 1900- Stuart Davis. 1969. II. Museum of Modern Art (New York, N.Y.) Max Weber, retrospective exhibition, 1907-1930. 1969. III. Museum of Modern Art (New York, N.Y.) Maurice Sterne retrospective exhibition, 1902-1932. 1969.
ND236.T44    759.13/074/01471    *LC* 70-86440

**Three painters of America: Charles Demuth, by Andrew**  • **1.5915**
**Carnduff Ritchie. Charles Sheeler, with an introduction by William Carlos Williams. Edward Hopper, with texts by Alfred H. Barr, Jr. and Charles Burchfield, and notes by the artist.**
Reprint ed. — [New York]: Published for the Museum of Modern Art by Arno Press, 1969. 96, 53, 83 p.: illus., ports.; 27 cm. The three exhibition catalogs were originally published separately, 1933-1950. 1. Demuth, Charles, 1883-1935. 2. Sheeler, Charles, 1883-1965. 3. Hopper, Edward, 1882-1967. I. Museum of Modern Art (New York, N.Y.) Charles Demuth. 1970. II. Museum of Modern Art (New York, N.Y.) Edward Hooper, retrospective exhibition. 1970.
ND236.T447 1969    759.13/074/01471    *LC* 78-86442

## ND237 Painters, A–Z

### ND237.A–.C

**Gerdts, William H.**                                      **1.5916**
'A man of genius': the art of Washington Allston (1779–1843) / by William H. Gerdts & Theodore E. Stebbins, Jr. — Boston: Museum of fine Arts, c1979. 255 p.: ill. (some col.); 27 cm. Catalog of an exhibition held at the Museum of Fine Arts, Boston, Dec. 12, 1979-Feb. 3, 1980, and the Pennsylvania Academy of the Fine Arts, Feb. 28-Apr. 27, 1980. Includes index. 1. Allston, Washington, 1779-1843 — Exhibitions. I. Allston, Washington, 1779-1843 II. Stebbins, Theodore E. joint author. III. Museum of Fine Arts, Boston. IV. Pennsylvania Academy of the Fine Arts. V. T.
ND237.A4 A4 1979     759.13     LC 79-56222     ISBN 0878461469

**Braider, Donald, 1923-.**                                • **1.5917**
George Bellows and the ashcan school of painting. [1st ed.] Garden City, N.Y., Doubleday [1971] xi, 153 p. illus., ports. 25 cm. 1. Bellows, George, 1882-1925. I. T.
ND237.B45 B7     759.13     LC 70-144251

**Benton, Thomas Hart, 1889-1975.**                        • **1.5918**
An artist in America. 3d [rev. ed.] Columbia, University of Missouri Press [1968] xxii, 369 p. illus. 24 cm. 1. Benton, Thomas Hart, 1889-1975. 2. Artists — Biography. 3. United States — Description and travel — 1920-1940 I. T.
ND237.B47 A3 1968     759.13 B     LC 68-20096

**Hendricks, Gordon.**                                     **1.5919**
Albert Bierstadt: painter of the American West. [Text by] Gordon Hendricks. New York, H. N. Abrams [1974] 360 p. illus. (part col.) 28 cm. Published in association with the Amon Carter Museum of Western Art. 1. Bierstadt, Albert, 1830-1902. 2. United States in art. 3. Landscape in art I. Amon Carter Museum of Western Art. II. T.
ND237.B585 H42     759.13     LC 73-14954     ISBN 081090151X

**Bloch, E. Maurice.**                                     • **1.5920**
George Caleb Bingham, by E. Maurice Bloch. Berkeley, University of California Press, 1967. 2 v. illus. (part col.), ports. (part col.) 28 cm. (California studies in the history of art. 7) 1. Bingham, George Caleb, 1811-1879. I. T. II. Series.
ND237.B59 B4     759.13     LC 65-10714

**Agee, William C.**                                       **1.5921**
Patrick Henry Bruce, American modernist: a catalogue raisonne / William C. Agee & Barbara Rose. — New York: Museum of Modern Art, c1979. vii, 225 p.: ill. (some col.); 23 x 25 cm. Catalogue to accompany exhibitions held: May 1979 at the Museum of Fine Arts, Houston; August 1979 at the Museum of Modern Art, New York; November 1979 at the Virginia Museum, Richmond. 1. Bruce, Patrick Henry, 1881-1936 — Exhibitions. I. Rose, Barbara. joint author. II. Museum of Fine Arts, Houston. III. Museum of Modern Art (New York, N.Y.) IV. Virginia Museum of Fine Arts. V. T.
ND237.B876 A4 1979a     759.13     LC 79-64632     ISBN 0870702599

**Breeskin, Adelyn Dohme, 1896-.**                         • **1.5922**
Mary Cassatt; a catalogue raisonné of the oils, pastels, watercolors, and drawings. — Washington: Smithsonian Institution Press, 1970. vi, 322 p.: illus. (part col.), ports.; 34 cm. 1. Cassatt, Mary, 1844-1926. I. T.
ND237.C3 B68     759.13     LC 73-104775     ISBN 0874741009

**Bullard, Edgar John, 1942-.**                            **1.5923**
Mary Cassatt: oils and pastels, by E. John Bullard. — New York: Watson-Guptill Publications, [1972] 87 p.: col. illus.; 29 cm. 1. Cassatt, Mary, 1844-1926. I. T.
ND237.C3 B8     759.13     LC 70-190524     ISBN 0823005690

**Sweet, Frederick Arnold, 1903-.**                        • **1.5924**
Miss Mary Cassatt, impressionist from Pennsylvania, by Frederick A. Sweet. Norman, University of Oklahoma Press [1966] xx, 242 p. ill. (part col.) 1. Cassatt, Mary, 1844-1926. I. T.
ND237 C3 S9     LC 66-13423

**McCracken, Harold, 1894-.**                              • **1.5925**
George Catlin and the old frontier. New York, Dial Press, 1959. 216 p. illus. (part col.), ports. (part col.) 32 cm. 1. Catlin, George, 1796-1872. 2. Indians of North America — West (U.S.) — Pictorial works. I. T.
ND237.C35 M3 1959     759.13     LC 59-9434

**Truettner, William H.**                                  **1.5926**
The natural man observed: a study of Catlin's Indian gallery / William H. Truettner. — 1st ed. — Washington: Smithsonian Institution Press, 1979. 323 p.: ill. (some col.); 30 cm. 'Published in cooperation with the Amon Carter Museum of Western Art, Fort Worth, and the National Collection of Fine Arts, Smithsonian Institution.' Includes indexes. 1. Catlin, George, 1796-1872.

2. Painters — United States — Biography. 3. Indians of North America — Pictorial works 4. West (U.S.) in art. I. T.
ND237.C35 T78 1979     759.13 B     LC 78-15152     ISBN 0874749182

**Chicago, Judy, 1939-.**                                  **1.5927**
Through the flower: my struggle as a woman artist / by Judy Chicago; with an introd. by Anais Nin. — 1st ed. — Garden City, N.Y.: Doubleday, 1975. xi, 226 p., [24] leaves of plates: ill.; 22 cm. Autobiographical. 1. Chicago, Judy, 1939- I. T.
ND237.C492 A28     759.13     LC 74-12680     ISBN 0385097824

**Huntington, David C.**                                   **1.5928**
The landscapes of Frederic Edwin Church; vision of an American era, by David C. Huntington. New York, G. Braziller [1966] xii, 210 p. illus. (part col.) 21 x 23 cm. Bibliographical references included in 'Notes' (p. [197]-204) 1. Church, Frederick Edwin, 1826-1900. I. T.
ND237.C52H8     759.13     LC 66-16675

**Flexner, James Thomas, 1908-.**                          • **1.5929**
John Singleton Copley. Boston, Houghton Mifflin Co., 1948. xv, 139 p. [33] plates. 29 cm. 'A completely revised and ... enlarged version of the biography of John Singleton Copley originally published ... as part of [the author's] ... America's old masters.' 1. Copley, John Singleton, 1737-1815. I. T.
ND237.C7 F6     927.5     LC 48-10262

**Prown, Jules David.**                                    • **1.5930**
John Singleton Copley. Cambridge, Published for the National Gallery of Art, Washington [by] Harvard University Press, 1966. 2 v. (xxiv, 491 p.) illus., geneal. tables, ports. 29 cm. (The Ailsa Mellon Bruce studies in American art, 1) 1. Copley, John Singleton, 1737-1815. I. National Gallery of Art (U.S.) II. T.
ND237.C7 P7     759.13     LC 66-13183

**Schmeckebier, Laurence Eli, 1906-.**                     • **1.5931**
John Steuart Curry's pageant of America / by Laurence E. Schmeckebier. — New York: American Artists Group, 1943. xviii, 363 p., [1] leaf of plate: ill. (part col.); 24 cm. 1. Curry, John Steuart, 1897-1946. I. American Artist Group, New York. II. T.
ND237.C88.S35     LC 43-16938

### ND237.D–.G

**Davis, Stuart, 1894-1964.**                              **1.5932**
Stuart Davis. Edited by Diane Kelder. — New York: Praeger, [1971] xi, 212 p.: illus. (part col.); 23 cm. — (Documentary monographs in modern art) 1. Davis, Stuart, 1894-1964. I. T.
ND237.D333 K4     759.13     LC 70-122089

**De Kooning, Willem, 1904-.**                             • **1.5933**
Willem de Kooning, by Thomas B. Hess. New York, Museum of Modern Art; distributed by New York Graphic Society. Greenwich, Conn. [1969, c1968] 170 p. illus. (part col.), port. 26 cm. Catalog of an exhibition held at the Museum of Modern Art, New York, Mar. 6-Apr. 27, 1969, and at 4 other museums. 1. De Kooning, Willem, 1904- I. Hess, Thomas B. II. Museum of Modern Art (New York, N.Y.) III. T.
ND237.D334 H42     759.13     LC 68-54925

**Hendricks, Gordon.**                                     **1.5934**
The life and work of Thomas Eakins / Gordon Hendricks. — New York: Grossman Publishers, 1974. xxx, 367 p., [25] leaves of plates: 306 ill. (some col.); 31 cm. Includes index. 1. Eakins, Thomas, 1844-1916. I. Eakins, Thomas, 1844-1916. II. T.
ND237.E15 H46 1974     759.13 B     LC 73-4174     ISBN 0670427950

**Porter, Fairfield.**                                     • **1.5935**
Thomas Eakins. — New York: G. Braziller, 1959. 127 p.: illus. (part col.), port.; 26 cm. — (The Great American artist series) 1. Eakins, Thomas, 1844-1916. I. T.
ND237.E15 P6     759.13     LC 59-12225

**Ernst, Jimmy, 1920-.**                                   **1.5936**
A not–so–still life: a memoir / by Jimmy Ernst. — 1st ed. — New York: St. Martin's/Marek, c1984. xi, 272 p., [16] p. of plates: ill.; 25 cm. Includes index. 1. Ernst, Jimmy, 1920- 2. Painters — United States — Biography. 3. Avant-garde (Aesthetics) — Europe — History — 20th century. I. T.
ND237.E7 A2 1984     759.13 B 19     LC 83-21088     ISBN 0312579551

**Estes, Richard, 1932-.**                                 **1.5936a**
Richard Estes: the urban landscape / essay by John Canaday; catalogue and interview by John Arthur. — Boston: Museum of Fine Arts: New York Graphic Society, 1979, [c1978]. 69 p.: ill. (some col.); 23 x 31 cm. Catalogue of an exhibition held May 31-Aug. 6, 1978 at the Museum of Fine Arts, Boston, and other museums. 1. Estes, Richard, 1932- — Exhibitions. 2. Cities and towns in art — Exhibitions. 3. Painters — United States — Interviews.

I. Canaday, John, 1907- II. Arthur, John, 1939- III. Museum of Fine Arts, Boston. IV. T.
ND237.E75 A4 1978　　759.13　　LC 78-59702　　ISBN 0878461264

**Evergood, Philip, 1901-1973.**　　　　　　　　　　**1.5937**
Philip Evergood. Text by John I. H. Baur. — New York: H. N. Abrams, [1975] 215 p.: illus. (part col.); 28 x 30 cm. 1. Evergood, Philip, 1901-1973. I. Baur, John I. H. (John Ireland Howe), 1909-1987. II. T.
ND237.E8 B32　　759.13　　LC 72-11790　　ISBN 0810901048

**Foote, Henry Wilder, 1875-1964.**　　　　　　　　● **1.5938**
Robert Feke, colonial portrait painter. — New York: Kennedy Galleries, 1969 [c1930] xix, 223 p.: illus., geneal. table.; 27 cm. — (Library of American art) 1. Feke, Robert, 1705 (ca.)-1750. I. T.
ND237.F35 F6 1969　　759.13 B　　LC 72-75357

**Glackens, Ira, 1907-.**　　　　　　　　　　　● **1.5939**
William Glackens and the Ashcan group: the emergence of realism in American art / Ira Glackens. — New York: Crown Publishers, c1957. 267 p., [37] p. of plates: ill. (some col.), ports. 1. Glackens, William J., 1870-1938. 2. Painters, American — Biography. 3. Realism in art I. T.
ND237.G5G55　　LC 57-8771

## ND237.H–.R

**Frankenstein, Alfred Victor, 1906-.**　　　　　● **1.5940**
After the hunt; William Harnett and other American still life painters, 1870–1900 [by] Alfred Frankenstein. — Rev. ed. — Berkeley: University of California Press, 1969. xix, 200 p.: illus., col. front.; 29 cm. — (California studies in the history of art. 12) 1. Harnett, William Michael, 1848-1892. 2. Painters — United States 3. Still-life painting, American. I. T. II. Series.
ND237.H315 F7 1969　　759.13　　LC 68-31417

**Haskell, Barbara.**　　　　　　　　　　　　**1.5941**
Marsden Hartley / Barbara Haskell. — New York: Whitney Museum of American Art, in association with New York University Press, c1980. 224 p.: ill. (some col.); 30 cm. Catalogue of an exhibition held at the Whitney Museum of American Art, New York, Mar. 4-May 25, 1980, and at other museums, June 10, 1980-Mar. 15, 1981. 1. Hartley, Marsden, 1877-1943 — Exhibitions. I. Hartley, Marsden, 1877-1943. II. Whitney Museum of American Art. III. T.
ND237.H3435 A4 1980　　759.13 19　　LC 79-25117　　ISBN 0874270278

**Hofmann, Hans, 1880-1966.**　　　　　　　　● **1.5942**
Hans Hofmann. With an introd. by Sam Hunter and five essays by Hans Hofmann. 2d ed. New York, H.N. Abrams [1963?] 227 p. ill. (part mounted col.) group port. I. Hunter, Sam, 1923- II. T.
ND237 H667 H8 1963　　LC 63-12457

**Gardner, Albert Ten Eyck.**　　　　　　　　● **1.5943**
Winslow Homer, American artist: his world and his work. — [1st ed.]. — New York: C. N. Potter, [c1961] 262 p.: illus., col. plates, port.; 32 cm. 1. Homer, Winslow, 1836-1910. I. T.
ND237.H7 G3　　759.13　　LC 61-11762

**Goodrich, Lloyd, 1897-.**　　　　　　　　　● **1.5944**
Winslow Homer. — New York: G. Braziller, 1959. 127 p.: illus. (part col.) port.; 26 cm. — (The Great American artists series) 1. Homer, Winslow, 1836-1910. I. T.
ND237.H7 G58　　759.13　　LC 59-12226

**Hendricks, Gordon.**　　　　　　　　　　　**1.5945**
The life and work of Winslow Homer / Gordon Hendricks. — New York: H. N. Abrams, 1979. 345 p.: ill. (some col.); 31 x 35 cm. Includes index. 1. Homer, Winslow, 1836-1910. 2. Painters — United States — Biography. I. T.
ND237.H7 H46　　759.13 B　　LC 79-210　　ISBN 0810910632

**Hopper, Edward, 1882-1967.**　　　　　　　　**1.5946**
Edward Hopper: the art and the artist / Gail Levin. — 1st ed. — New York: Norton: Whitney Museum of American Art, 1980. xv, 299 p.: ill. (some col.); 28 cm. Accompanies the exhibition organized by the Whitney Museum and sponsored by Philip Morris Incorporated and the National Endowment for the Arts; to be held at Hayward Gallery, London, Feb. 11-Mar. 29, 1981, and four other museums, Apr. 22, 1981-Feb. 10, 1982. Includes index. 1. Hopper, Edward, 1882-1967 — Exhibitions. I. Levin, Gail, 1948- II. Whitney Museum of American Art. III. Philip Morris Incorporated. IV. National Endowment for the Arts. V. Hayward Gallery. VI. T.
ND237.H75 A4 1980　　759.13　　LC 79-27958　　ISBN 039301374X

**Inness, George, 1825-1894.**　　　　　　　　**1.5947**
George Inness / Nicolai Cikovsky, Jr., Michael Quick; organized by Michael Quick. — Los Angeles, Calif.: Los Angeles County Museum of Art; New York: Harper & Row, 1985. 213 p.: ill. (some col.); 32 cm. Catalogue of an exhibition organized by the Los Angeles County Museum of Art, and held at the

Metropolitan Museum of Art, New York, Apr. 1-June 9, 1985, and at other museums. 1. Inness, George, 1825-1894 — Exhibitions. I. Cikovsky, Nicolai. II. Quick, Michael. III. Los Angeles County Museum of Art. IV. Metropolitan Museum of Art (New York, N.Y.) V. T.
ND237.I5 A4 1985　　759.13 19　　LC 84-28836　　ISBN 0064307107

**Inness, George, 1854-1926.**　　　　　　　　● **1.5948**
Life, art, and letters of George Inness. Introd. by Elliott Daingerfield. — New York: Kennedy Galleries [and] Da Capo Press, 1969. xxviii, 290 p.: illus., ports.; 24 cm. — (Library of American art) Reprint of the 1917 ed. 1. Inness, George, 1825-1894. I. T.
ND237.I5 I6 1969　　759.13 B　　LC 76-87444

**McCausland, Elizabeth, 1899-1966.**　　　　　● **1.5949**
George Inness: an American landscape painter, 1825–1894 / by Elizabeth McCausland. — New York: American artists group, inc., 1946. xvi, 87 p.: ill.; 24 cm. 1. Inness, George, 1825-1894 — Exhibitions. I. T.
ND237.I5 M3　　759.13　　LC 46-3370

**Rose, Barbara.**　　　　　　　　　　　　　**1.5950**
Lee Krasner: a retrospective / Barbara Rose; Museum of Modern Art, New York. — New York: The Museum, 1983. 184 p.: ill. (some col.); 26 cm. 1. Krasner, Lee, 1908- I. Krasner, Lee, 1908- II. Museum of Modern Art (New York, N.Y.) III. T.
ND237.K68 R6　　LC 83-62554　　ISBN 087070415X

**Wilmerding, John.**　　　　　　　　　　　**1.5951**
Fitz Hugh Lane. — New York: Praeger, [1971] 203 p.: illus. (part col.), ports.; 27 cm. — (American art & artists) 1. Lane, Fitz Hugh, 1804-1865. I. T. II. Series.
ND237.L27 W48　　759.13　　LC 75-159501

**Louis, Morris, 1912-1962.**　　　　　　　　● **1.5952**
Morris Louis, 1912–1962. — Boston: Museum of Fine Arts, 1967. 82 p.: chiefly ill. (some col.); 22 cm. Exhibition held at Los Angeles County Museum of Art, February 15-March 26, 1967; Museum of Fine Arts, Boston, April 13-May 24, 1967 [and] City Art Museum of St. Louis, June 16-August 6, 1967. 'Introduction by Michael Fried': p. 7-24. I. Fried, Michael. II. Los Angeles County Museum of Art. III. Museum of Fine Arts, Boston. IV. City Art Museum of St. Louis. V. T.
ND237.L75 F7　　LC 67-17663

**Marin, John, 1870-1953.**　　　　　　　　　● **1.5953**
Selected writings of John Marin / edited with an introduction by Dorothy Norman. —. — New York: Pellegrini & Cudahy, c1949. xv, 241 p.: ill., ports.; 25 cm. Includes material from the Letters of John Marin published in 1931. I. Norman, Dorothy, 1905- II. T.
ND237.M24A2

**Helm, MacKinley, 1896-.**　　　　　　　　　● **1.5954**
John Marin. — New York: Kennedy Graphics, 1970 [c1948] 239 p.: illus., col. plates, port.; 26 cm. — (Library of American art) 1. Marin, John, 1870-1953. I. T.
ND237.M24 H4 1970　　759.13　　LC 75-87484　　ISBN 0306714892

**Rothschild, Lincoln, 1902-.**　　　　　　　　**1.5955**
To keep art alive; the effort of Kenneth Hayes Miller, American painter (1876–1952). — Philadelphia: Art Alliance Press, [1974] 104 p., [100] p. of illus. (part col.); 29 cm. 1. Miller, Kenneth Hayes, 1876-1952. I. Miller, Kenneth Hayes, 1876-1952, illus. II. T.
ND237.M48 R67　　759.13 B　　LC 73-9301　　ISBN 0879820128

**Larkin, Oliver W.**　　　　　　　　　　　● **1.5956**
Samuel F. B. Morse and American democratic art. [1st ed.] Boston, Little, Brown, 1954. viii, 215 p. illus., ports. 21 cm. (Library of American biography.) 1. Morse, Samuel Finley Breese, 1791-1872. 2. Art — United States. — History. I. T. II. Series.
ND237.M75 L3　　927.5 926.2　　LC 54-8284

**Kallir, Otto, 1894-.**　　　　　　　　　　　**1.5957**
Grandma Moses. — New York: Abrams, [1973] 357 p.: illus. (part col.); 31 x 35 cm. 1. Moses, Grandma, 1860-1961. I. Moses, Grandma, 1860-1961. II. T.
ND237.M78 K32　　759.13　　LC 73-6930　　ISBN 0810901668

**Arnason, H. Harvard.**　　　　　　　　　　**1.5958**
Robert Motherwell / text by H.H. Arnason; introduction by Dore Ashton; interview with Robert Motherwell by Barbaralee Diamonstein. — 2nd ed., new and rev. — New York: Abrams, 1982. 250 p.: ill. (some col.); 30 cm. Includes index. 1. Motherwell, Robert. I. Ashton, Dore. II. Diamonstein, Barbaralee. III. Motherwell, Robert. IV. T.
ND237.M852 A89 1982　　759.13 19　　LC 81-3492　　ISBN 081091333X

**Cowdrey, Bartlett.**　　　　　　　　　　　● **1.5959**
William Sidney Mount, 1807–1868; with a foreword by Harry B. Wehle. New York, Columbia Univ. Press, 1944. xiii, 54 p. front. (port.) pl. Pub. for the

Metropolitan Museum of Art. 1. Mount, William Sidney, 1807-1868. 2. Metropolitan Museum of Art, New York I. Williams, Hermann Warner, jt. author II. T.
ND237.M855C7

**O'Keeffe, Georgia, 1887-.** • **1.5960**
Georgia O'Keeffe. New York: Viking Press, 1976. ca. 200 p.: col. ill.; 42 cm. (A Studio book) 1. O'Keeffe, Georgia, 1887- I. T.
ND237.O5 A46 1976      759.13 B      *LC* 76-23452      *ISBN* 0670337080

**Peale, Charles Willson, 1741-1827.** **1.5961**
Charles Willson Peale and his world / Edgar P. Richardson, Brooke Hindle, Lillian B. Miller; with a foreword by Charles Coleman Sellers. — 1st ed. — New York: H.N. Abrams, 1983. 272 p.: ill. (some col.); 30 cm. 'A Barra Foundation book.' Includes index. 1. Peale, Charles Willson, 1741-1827. 2. Painters — United States — Biography. I. Richardson, Edgar Preston, 1902- II. Hindle, Brooke. III. Miller, Lillian B. IV. T.
ND237.P27 A4 1983      759.13 B 19      *LC* 82-8838      *ISBN* 0810914786

**Sellers, Charles Coleman, 1903-.** • **1.5962**
Charles Willson Peale. — New York: Scribner, [1969] xiv, 510 p.: illus., facsims. (music), ports.; 29 cm. Based on the author's Charles Willson Peale, published in 1947 as v. 23, pts. 1-2 of the Memoirs of the American Philosophical Society. 1. Peale, Charles Willson, 1741-1827. I. T.
ND237.P27 S44      759.13 B      *LC* 68-17345

**Rhys, Hedley Howell.** • **1.5963**
Maurice Prendergast, 1859–1924. Cambridge, Harvard University Press, 1960. 156 p. mounted col. illus., plates, ports. 19 cm. At head of title: Museum of Fine Arts, Boston. 'Catalogue of the exhibition [Oct. 26-Dec. 4, 1960] prepared by Peter A. Wick': p. [65]-108. Bibliography: p. 64. 1. Prendergast, Maurice Brazil, 1859-1924. I. Museum of Fine Arts, Boston. II. T.
ND237.P85R5      759.13      *LC* 60-16756

**Amon Carter Museum of Western Art.** **1.5965**
Charles M. Russell; paintings, drawings, and sculpture in the Amon Carter Museum [by] Frederic G. Renner. [Rev. ed.] New York, H. N. Abrams [1974] 296 p. illus. (part col.) 31 x 35 cm. 1. Russell, Charles M. (Charles Marion), 1864-1926 — Catalogs. 2. Amon Carter Museum of Western Art — Catalogs. 3. West (U.S.) in art — Catalogs. 4. Indians of North America — Pictorial works — Catalogs. I. Renner, Frederic Gordon, 1897- II. T.
ND237.R75 A72 1974      709/.2/4      *LC* 74-5114      *ISBN* 0810904667

**Goodrich, Lloyd, 1897-.** • **1.5966**
Albert P. Ryder. — New York: G. Braziller, 1959. 128 p.: illus. (part col.) port.; 26 cm. — (The Great American artists series) 1. Ryder, Albert Pinkham, 1847-1917. I. T.
ND237.R8 G6      759.13      *LC* 59-12227

## ND237.S–.Z

**Ormond, Richard.** • **1.5967**
John Singer Sargent: paintings, drawings, watercolors. — [1st U.S. ed.]. — New York: Harper & Row, [1970] 264 p.: plates (part col.), ports. (part col.); 32 cm. 1. Sargent, John Singer, 1856-1925. I. T.
ND237.S3 O7 1970b      759.13      *LC* 76-114743

**Ratcliff, Carter.** **1.5968**
John Singer Sargent / by Carter Ratcliff. — 1st ed. — New York: Abbeville Press, 1982. 256 p.: ill. (some col.); 34 cm. Includes index. 1. Sargent, John Singer, 1856-1925. I. T.
ND237.S3 R3 1982      759.13 B 19      *LC* 82-6779      *ISBN* 089659307X

**Rodman, Selden, 1909-.** • **1.5969**
Portrait of the artist as an American; Ben Shahn: a biography with pictures. [1st ed.] New York, Harper [1951] xiv, 180 p. illus. (part col.) ports. 26 cm. I. Shahn, Ben, 1898-1969. II. T.
ND237.S465R6      *LC* 51-13491

**Sheeler, Charles, 1883-1965.** • **1.5970**
Charles Sheeler. Essays by Martin Friedman, Bartlett Hayes [and] Charles Millard. Washington, Published for the National Collection of Fine Arts by the Smithsonian Institution Press, 1968. 156 p. illus. (part col.) 21 x 27 cm. (Smithsonian publication 4746) Catalog of an exhibition held Oct. 10 to Nov. 24, 1968, at the National Collection of Fine Arts, Jan. 10 to Feb. 16, 1969, at the Philadelphia Museum of Art, Mar. 11 to Apr. 27, 1969, at the Whitney Museum of American Art. I. National Collection of Fine Arts (U.S.) II. Philadelphia Museum of Art. III. Whitney Museum of American Art. IV. T.
ND237.S47 A43      760/.0924      *LC* 68-57069

**Rourke, Constance, 1885-1941.** • **1.5971**
Charles Sheeler, artist in the American tradition. New York, Kennedy Galleries, 1969 [c1938] 203 p. illus. 26 cm. (Library of American art) 1. Sheeler, Charles, 1883-1965. I. T.
ND237.S47 R6 1969      709/.24 B      *LC* 70-87603

**Sloan, John, 1871-1951.** • **1.5972**
John Sloan's New York scene; from the diaries, notes, and correspondence, 1906–1913. Edited by Bruce St. John, with an introd. by Helen Farr Sloan. New York, Harper & Row [1965] xxvi, 658 p. ill. 24 cm. 1. New York (N.Y.) — Social life and customs I. T. II. Title: New York scene.
ND237.S57 A2      *LC* 64-25122 rev.

**Sloan, John, 1871-1951.** • **1.5973**
John Sloan, 1871–1951; his life and paintings [by] David W. Scott; his graphics [by] E. John Bullard. Washington, National Gallery of Art, 1971. 215 p. illus. (part col.), ports. 27 cm. Exhibition held at National Gallery of Art, Sept. 18 - Oct. 31, 1971; Georgia Museum of Art, Athens, Nov. 20, 1971 - Jan. 16, 1972; etc. I. National Gallery of Art (U.S.) II. T.
ND237.S57 U5      759.13      *LC* 76-158452      *ISBN* 0843520264

**Jaffe, Irma B.** • **1.5974**
Joseph Stella [by] Irma B. Jaffe. Cambridge, Mass., Harvard University Press, 1970. xviii, 262, 114 p. illus. (part col.), facsim., ports. 27 cm. 1. Stella, Joseph, 1877-1946. I. T.
ND237.S685 J3      759.13      *LC* 71-82294      *ISBN* 0674483650

**Flexner, James Thomas, 1908-.** • **1.5975**
Gilbert Stuart; a great life in brief. — [1st ed.] — New York: Knopf, 1955. 197 p.; 20 cm. — (Great lives in brief; a new series of biographies) 1. Stuart, Gilbert, 1775-1828. I. T.
ND237.S8 F5      759.13 927.5      *LC* 55-6218

**Morgan, John Hill, 1870-1945.** • **1.5976**
Gilbert Stuart and his pupils. Together with the complete notes on painting, by Matthew Harris Jouett, from conversations with Gilbert Stuart in 1816. — New York: Kennedy Galleries, 1969 [c1939] 102 p.: illus., ports.; 24 cm. — (Library of American art) 1. Stuart, Gilbert, 1755-1828. 2. Portrait-painters — United States. 3. Portraits, American 4. Portraits, Colonial — United States. I. Jouett, Matthew Harris, 1788-1827. II. T.
ND237.S8 M6 1969      759.13      *LC* 72-96440

**Whitley, William Thomas, 1858-1942.** • **1.5977**
Gilbert Stuart. — New York: Kennedy Galleries, 1969. xiv, 240 p.: illus., port.; 27 cm. — (Library of American art) Reprint of the 1932 ed. 1. Stuart, Gilbert, 1755-1828. I. T.
ND237.S8 W5 1969      759.13 B      *LC* 77-87680

**Trumbull, John, 1756-1843.** • **1.5978**
The autobiography of Colonel John Trumbull, patriot–artist, 1756-1843. Edited by Theodore Sizer. — New York: Kennedy Graphics, 1970 [c1953] xxiii, 404 p.: ports.; 24 cm. — (Library of American art) Contains a supplement to the editor's The works of Colonel John Trumbull. 1. Trumbull, John, 1756-1843. I. Sizer, Theodore, 1892-1967. The works of Colonel John Trumbull. II. T.
ND237.T8 A32 1970      759.13      *LC* 79-116912      *ISBN* 0306712423

**Cooper, Helen A.** **1.5979**
John Trumbull: the hand and spirit of a painter / Helen A. Cooper; with essays by Patricia Mullan Burnham ... [et al.]. — New Haven: Yale University Art Gallery; Distributed by Yale University Press, c1982. xv, 292 p.: ill. (some col.); 31 cm. Catalogue of an exhibition held Oct. 28, 1982-Jan. 16, 1983. 1. Trumbull, John, 1756-1843 — Exhibitions. I. Yale University. Art Gallery. II. T.
ND237.T8 A4 1982      759.13 19      *LC* 82-50609      *ISBN* 0894670247

**Jaffe, Irma B.** **1.5980**
John Trumbull, patriot–artist of the American Revolution / Irma B. Jaffe. — Boston: New York Graphic Society, c1975. 4, 346 p., [8] leaves of plates: ill.; 29 cm. Includes index. 1. Trumbull, John, 1756-1843. I. T.
ND237.T8 J33      759.13 B      *LC* 74-22504      *ISBN* 0821204599

**Sizer, Theodore, 1892-.** • **1.5981**
The works of Colonel John Trumbull, artist of the American Revolution. New Haven, Yale University Press, 1950. xviii, 117 p. illus., ports. 1. Trumbull, John, 1756-1843. I. T.
ND237.T8S5

**Alberts, Robert C.** **1.5982**
Benjamin West: a biography / Robert C. Alberts. — Boston: Houghton Mifflin, 1978. xvi, 525 p., [24] leaves of plates: ill.; 24 cm. Includes index. 1. West, Benjamin, 1738-1820. 2. Painters — United States — Biography. I. T.
ND237.W45 A86      759.13 B      *LC* 78-17241      *ISBN* 0395262895

**Evans, Grose.**     • **1.5983**
Benjamin West and the taste of his times. Carbondale, Southern Illinois University Press, 1959. 144 p. 73 ill., col. plate. 1. West, Benjamin, 1738-1820. I. T.
ND237 W45 E85     *LC* 58-12322

**Young, Andrew McLaren.**     **1.5984**
The paintings of James McNeill Whistler / Andrew McLaren Young, Margaret MacDonald, Robin Spencer, with the assistance of Hamish Miles. — New Haven: Published for the Paul Mellon Centre for Studies in British Art by Yale University Press, 1980. 2 v.: ill.; 31 cm. — (Studies in British art.) Includes index. 1. Whistler, James McNeill, 1834-1903 — Catalogs. I. MacDonald, Margaret F. II. Spencer, Robin. III. Paul Mellon Centre for Studies in British Art. IV. T. V. Series.
ND237.W6 A4 1980     759.13     *LC* 80-5214     *ISBN* 0300023847

**Cary, Elisabeth Luther, 1867-1936.**     • **1.5985**
The works of James McNeill Whistler, a study. With a tentative list of the artist's works. Freeport, N.Y., Books for Libraries Press [1971] 302 p. illus., ports. 23 cm. Reprint of the 1907 ed. 1. Whistler, James McNeill, 1834-1903. I. T.
ND237.W6 C3 1971     760/.092/4     *LC* 77-157328     *ISBN* 0836957881

**Laver, James, 1899-.**     • **1.5986**
Whistler. [2d ed.] London, Faber and Faber [1951] 256 p. illus. 23 cm. 1. Whistler, James McNeill, 1834-1903. I. T.
ND237.W6L3 1951     927.5     *LC* 52-27870

**Sutton, Denys.**     • **1.5987**
James McNeill Whistler; paintings, etchings, pastels & watercolours. [London] Phaidon Press [1966] 197 p. illus. (part col.) 32 cm. 1. Whistler, James McNeill, 1834-1903. I. T.
ND237.W6 S83     759.13     *LC* 66-8772

**Sutton, Denys.**     • **1.5988**
Nocturne: the art of James McNeill Whistler. Philadelphia: Lippincott, 1964, c1963. 153 p.: illus.(part col.) ports. 1. Whistler, James McNeill, 1834-1903. I. T.
ND237.W6 S84 1963     759.13     *LC* 64-22181

**Dennis, James M.**     **1.5989**
Grant Wood: a study in American art and culture / James M. Dennis. — New York: Viking Press, 1975. 256 p.: ill. (some col.); 27 x 29 cm. (A Studio book) 1. Wood, Grant, 1892-1942. I. T.
ND237.W795 D46 1975     759.13 B     *LC* 75-23108     *ISBN* 0670347841

**Wyeth, Andrew, 1917-.**     **1.5990**
Two worlds of Andrew Wyeth: a conversation with Andrew Wyeth / by Thomas Hoving. — Boston: Houghton Mifflin, 1978, c1976. 170 p., [9] leaves of plates: ill. (some col.); 28 cm. Originally published as the catalog of an exhibition held at the Metropolitan Museum of Art, New York. 1. Wyeth, Andrew, 1917- — Exhibitions. I. Hoving, Thomas, 1931- II. Metropolitan Museum of Art (New York, N.Y.) III. T.
ND237.W93 A4 1978     759.13     *LC* 78-16545     *ISBN* 0395270898

**Wyeth, Andrew, 1917-.**     • **1.5991**
Andrew Wyeth. Introd. by David McCord. Selection by Frederick A. Sweet. Boston, Museum of Fine Arts [1970] 224 p. illus. (part col.) 22 x 28 cm. Centennial exhibition of the Museum of Fine Arts. I. Sweet, Frederick Arnold, 1903- ed. II. Museum of Fine Arts, Boston. III. T.
ND237.W93 S95     759.13     *LC* 76-127419

**Highwater, Jamake.**     **1.5992**
Song from the earth: American Indian painting / Jamake Highwater. 1st ed. — Boston: New York Graphic Society: published by Little, Brown, c1976. viii, 212 p.: ill. (some col.); 29 cm. Includes index. 1. Painting, Indian — North America. I. T.
ND238.A4 H53     759.13     *LC* 75-37201     *ISBN* 0821206982

## ND240–249 Canada

**Harper, J. Russell.**     **1.5993**
Painting in Canada: a history / J. Russell Harper. — 2d ed. — Toronto; Buffalo: University of Toronto Press, 1977, c1966. vii, 463 p.: ill., ports.; 24 cm. — (Canadian university paperbooks; 198) Includes index. 1. Painting, Canadian I. T.
ND240.H3 1977     759.11     *LC* 78-302907     *ISBN* 0802022715

**Reid, Dennis R.**     **1.5994**
A concise history of Canadian painting [by] Dennis Reid. — Toronto: Oxford University Press, 1973. 319 p.: illus. (part col.); 22 cm. 1. Painting, Canadian — History. I. T.
ND240.R44 1973     759.11     *LC* 74-157032     *ISBN* 0195402073

**Hill, Charles C.**     **1.5995**
Canadian painting in the thirties / Charles C. Hill. Ottawa: National Gallery of Canada, 1975. 223 p.: ill. (some col.); 31 cm. Published to coincide with an exhibition sponsored by the National Gallery of Canada. Includes index. 1. Painting, Canadian 2. Painting, Modern — 20th century — Canada. 3. Painters — Canada. I. National Gallery of Canada. II. T.
ND245.H54     759.11/074/011384     *LC* 75-323857     *ISBN* 0888842856

**Gagnon, François Marc, 1935-.**     **1.5996**
Paul-Émile Borduas, 1905–1960: biographie critique et analyse de l'oeuvre / François–Marc Gagnon. — Montréal: Fides, c1978. xv, 560 p., [40] leaves of plates: ill. (some col.), diagr., port.; 26 cm. Includes indexes. 1. Borduas, Paul Émile. 2. Painters — Canada — Biography. I. T.
ND249.B6 G34     759.11 B     *LC* 79-354370     *ISBN* 0775506982

**Shadbolt, Doris.**     **1.5997**
The art of Emily Carr / Doris Shadbolt. — Seattle: University of Washington Press, 1980, [c1979] 223 p.: ill. (some col.); 33 cm. 1. Carr, Emily, 1871-1945. 2. Painters — Canada — Biography. I. Carr, Emily, 1871-1945. II. T.
ND249.C3 S5     759.11     *LC* 79-4918     *ISBN* 0295956879

**Kane, Paul, 1810-1871.**     **1.5998**
Paul Kane's frontier; including Wanderings of an artist among the Indians of North America, by Paul Kane. Edited with a biographical introd. and a catalogue raisonné by J. Russell Harper. Austin, Published for the Amon Carter Museum, Fort Worth, and the National Gallery of Canada by the University of Texas Press [1971] xviii, 350 p. illus. (part col.), ports. (part col.) 30 cm. 1. Indians of North America — Pictorial works I. Harper, J. Russell. ed. II. Kane, Paul, 1810-1871. Wanderings of an artist among the Indians of North America. 1971. III. Amon Carter Museum of Western Art. IV. Ottawa. National Gallery of Canada. V. T.
ND249.K3 H3     759.11     *LC* 79-146522     *ISBN* 0292701101

**Harper, J. Russell.**     **1.5999**
Krieghoff / J. Russell Harper. — Toronto; Buffalo: University of Toronto Press, 1979. xvi, 204 p.: ill. (some col.); 26 cm. Includes index. 1. Krieghoff, Cornelius, 1815-1872. 2. Painters — Canada — Biography. I. Krieghoff, Cornelius, 1815-1872. II. T.
ND249.K7 H37     759.11 B     *LC* 80-452634     *ISBN* 0802023487

**Porter, John R.**     **1.6000**
[Joseph Légaré, 1795-1855. English] The works of Joseph Légaré, 1795–1855: catalogue raisonné / by John R. Porter, with the collaboration of Nicole Cloutier, Jean Trudel. — Ottawa: National Gallery of Canada, 1978. 160 p.: ill. (some col.); 30 cm. Translation of Joseph Légaré, 1795-1855. Includes catalogue of an exhibition organized by the National Gallery of Canada. Includes indexes. 1. Légaré, Joseph, 1795-1855 — Catalogs. I. Légaré, Joseph, 1795-1855. II. Cloutier, Nicole. joint author. III. Trudel, Jean, 1940- joint author. IV. National Gallery of Canada. V. T.
ND249.L386 A4 1978     759.11     *LC* 80-476898     *ISBN* 0888843585

## ND250–439 Latin America

**Myers, Bernard Samuel, 1908-.**     • **1.6001**
Mexican painting in our time. — New York: Oxford University Press, 1956. xiv, 283 p.: illus.; 29 cm. 1. Painting, Mexican. I. T.
ND255.M9     759.972     *LC* 56-5166

**Orozco, José Clemente, 1883-1949.**     • **1.6002**
An autobiography / José Clemente Orozco; translated by Robert C. Stephenson; introduction by John Palmer Leeper. — Austin, Texas: University of Texas Press, 1962. 171 p., 6 leaves of plates: ill., port. (The Texas Pan-American series) 1. Orozco, José Clemente, 1883-1949 — Biography. 2. Artists — Biography. I. T.
ND259.O7 A213     927.5     *LC* 62-9790

**Orozco, José Clemente, 1883-1949.**     **1.6003**
Orozco!, 1883-1949: an exhibition / organised by the Ministry of Foreign Affairs and the Institute of Fine Arts, Mexico; editor, David Elliott. — Oxford: Museum of Modern Art, 1983, [c1980]. 128 p.: ill.; 29 cm. Catalogue of an exhibition held Nov. 1980-Jan. 1981 at the Museum of Modern Art. 1. Orozco, José Clemente, 1883-1949 — Exhibitions. 2. Mural painting and decoration, Mexican — Exhibitions. I. Elliott, David, 1949- II. Museum of Modern Art (Oxford, Oxfordshire) III. T.
ND259.O7 A4     759.972

**Helm, MacKinley, 1896-.**　　　　　　　　　　　• **1.6004**
Man of fire: J. C. Orozco, an interpretative memoir. — 1st. ed. New York:
Harcourt, Brace, 1953. — ix, 245 p.: ill, port. 1. Orozco, José Clemente,
1883-1949. I. T.
ND259.O7 H43　　　759.972　　*LC* 52-13764

**Wolfe, Bertram David, 1896-1977.**　　　　　　• **1.6005**
The fabulous life of Diego Rivera [by] Bertram D. Wolfe. — London: Barrie &
Rockliff, 1968. xxi, 457 p.: 96 plates, illus., ports.; 24 cm. 1. Rivera, Diego,
1886-1957. I. T.
ND259.R5 W56 1968　　　759.972 B　　*LC* 71-369000

**Tamayo, Rufino, 1899-.**　　　　　　　　　　　**1.6006**
Rufino Tamayo / texts by Octavio Paz, Jacques Lassaigne; [translation by
Kenneth Lyons]. — New York: Rizzoli, 1982. 299 p.: ill. (some col.); 30 cm.
1. Tamayo, Rufino, 1899- I. Paz, Octavio, 1914- II. Lassaigne, Jacques, 1910-
III. T.
ND259.T3 A4 1982　　　759.972 19　　*LC* 82-50504　　*ISBN* 0847804550

**Genauer, Emily, 1910-.**　　　　　　　　　　　**1.6007**
Rufino Tamayo. — New York: Abrams, [1975] 175 p.: illus. (part col.); 28 x 30
cm. 1. Tamayo, Rufino, 1899- I. Tamayo, Rufino, 1899- II. T.
ND259.T3 G4　　　759.972　　*LC* 74-2150　　*ISBN* 0810905000

**Botero, Fernando, 1932-.**　　　　　　　　　　**1.6008**
Fernando Botero: Hirshhorn Museum and Sculpture Garden, Smithsonian
Institution / [compiled by] Cynthia Jaffee McCabe. — Washington:
Smithsonian Institution Press: for sale by the Supt. of Docs., U.S. Govt. Print.
Off., c1979. 119 p.: chiefly ill. (some col.); 20 cm. Catalog of an exhibition held
at the Hirshhorn Museum and Sculpture Garden, Washington, D.C., Dec. 20,
1979-Feb. 10, 1980 and at the Art Museum of South Texas, Corpus Christi,
Mar. 27-May 10, 1980. 1. Botero, Fernando, 1932- — Exhibitions. I. McCabe,
Cynthia Jaffee. II. Hirshhorn Museum and Sculpture Garden. III. Art
Museum of South Texas. IV. T.
ND379.B6 A4 1979　　　709/.2/4　　*LC* 79-607807

# ND450–955 Europe

**Toledo Museum of Art.**　　　　　　　　　　　**1.6009**
European paintings / the Toledo Museum of Art. — Toledo: The Museum;
University Park: distributed by Pennsylvania State University Press, 1976.
396 p.: ill. (some col.); 27 cm. 1. Toledo Museum of Art. 2. Painting, European
— Catalogs. 3. Painting — Ohio — Toledo — Catalogs. I. T.
ND450.T64 1976　　　759.94/074/017113　　*LC* 76-24500　　*ISBN*
0271012498

**Cuttler, Charles D.**　　　　　　　　　　　　**1.6010**
Northern painting from Pucelle to Bruegel: fourteenth, fifteenth, and sixteenth
centuries / Charles D. Cuttler. — New York: Holt, Rinehart and Winston,
1968. xii, 500 p.: ill. (part. col.) 1. Painting, Renaissance — Europe.
2. Painting — Europe. I. T.
ND454.C8　　　*LC* 68-20103　　*ISBN* 003089476X

## ND461–497 GREAT BRITAIN

**Oakeshott, Walter Fraser, 1903-.**　　　　　　• **1.6011**
The sequence of English medieval art, illustrated chiefly from illuminated mss.,
650–1450. — London: Faber, 1950. 55 p. illus., 56 plates (part col.) map. 29 cm.
1. Painting, British 2. Illumination of books and manuscripts 3. Painting,
Medieval I. T.
ND463.O35 1950　　　*LC* 50-4716

**Rickert, Margaret Josephine, 1888-.**　　　　　• **1.6012**
Painting in Britain: the Middle Ages. Baltimore, Penguin Books [1954] xxvi,
253 p. illus., maps. 27 cm. (Pelican history of art.) 1. Painting, Medieval
2. Painting — Great Britain. I. T. II. Series.
ND463.R5 1954　　　*LC* 55-1759

**Redgrave, Richard, 1804-1888.**　　　　　　　• **1.6013**
A century of British painters, by Richard & Samuel Redgrave. New ed. [by
Ruthven Todd] London, Phaidon Press, 1947. viii, 612 p. illus., plates. 19 cm.
1. Painters — Great Britain. 2. Painting, British I. Redgrave, Samuel,
1802-1876. joint author. II. Todd, Ruthven, 1914- ed. III. T.
ND464.R4x　　　*LC* a 49-2836

**Waterhouse, Ellis Kirkham, 1905-.**　　　　　• **1.6014**
Painting in Britain, 1530 to 1790 / Ellis Waterhouse. — 4th ed. —
Harmondsworth, Eng.; New York: Penguin Books, c1978. 387 p.: ill.; 21 cm. —
(Pelican history of art.) Includes index. 1. Painting, British — Great Britain.
2. Painting, Renaissance — Great Britain. 3. Painting, Modern — 17th-18th
centuries — Great Britain. I. T. II. Series.
ND464.W37 1978　　　759.2　　*LC* 77-19107　　*ISBN* 0140561013

**Barrell, John.**　　　　　　　　　　　　　　**1.6015**
The dark side of the landscape: the rural poor in English painting, 1730–1840 /
John Barrell. — Cambridge [Eng.]; New York: Cambridge University Press,
1980. 179 p.: ill.; 26 cm. 1. Gainsborough, Thomas, 1727-1788. 2. Morland,
George, 1763-1804. 3. Constable, John, 1776-1837. 4. Painting, English
5. Painting, Modern — 17th-18th centuries — England. 6. Painting, Modern
— 19th century — England 7. Rural poor in art I. T.
ND466.B28　　　759.2　　*LC* 78-72334　　*ISBN* 0521225094

**Hunt, William Holman, 1827-1910.**　　　　　• **1.6016**
Pre–Raphaelitism and the pre-Raphaelite brotherhood / by William Holman-
Hunt; second ed., rev. from the author's notes by M.E. H.–H. — New York:
E.P. Dutton & Company, 1914. 2 v.: fronts., (ports.), ill.; 26 cm. I. Hunt,
Marion Edith (Waugh) Holman, ed. II. T.
ND467.H9 1914　　　*LC* 14-2978

**Strong, Roy C.**　　　　　　　　　　　　　**1.6017**
Recreating the past: British history and the Victorian painter / Roy Strong. —
[New York]: Thames and Hudson, c1978. 176 p.: ill. (some col.); 24 cm. —
(Franklin Jasper Walls lectures. 1974) 1. Painting, Victorian — Great Britain.
2. Painting, Modern — 19th century — Great Britain. 3. History in art
4. Great Britain — History — Pictorial works. I. T. II. Series.
ND467.S73 1978b　　　759.941　　*LC* 77-92269　　*ISBN* 0500232814

**Wood, Christopher.**　　　　　　　　　　　　**1.6018**
Victorian panorama: paintings of Victorian life / Christopher Wood. London:
Faber, 1977, [c1976]. 260 p., [8] leaves of plates: ill. (some col.); 26 cm. Includes
index. 1. Painting, English 2. Painting, Victorian — England. 3. England in
art. 4. England — Social life and customs — 19th century — Pictorial works.
I. T.
ND467.W66　　　758　　*LC* 77-355487　　*ISBN* 057110780X

## ND496 Collective Biography

**Cecil, David, Lord, 1902-.**　　　　　　　　　• **1.6019**
Visionary and dreamer; two poetic painters: Samuel Palmer and Edward
Burne–Jones. [Princeton, N.J.] Princeton University Press [1970, c1969] xxii,
177 p. illus. (part col.) 27 cm. (Bollingen series, 35. The A. W. Mellon lectures
in the fine arts, 15) 1. Palmer, Samuel, 1805-1881. 2. Burne-Jones, Edward
Coley, Sir, 1833-1898. I. T.
ND496.C4 1970　　　759.2 B　　*LC* 68-57088　　*ISBN* 0691098530

**Reynolds, Graham.**　　　　　　　　　　　　• **1.6020**
Painters of the Victorian scene. London, Batsford [1953] xiv, 112 p. illus. (part
col.) 26 cm. 1. Painters — England. 2. Painting, English I. T.
ND496.R48　　　759.2　　*LC* 53-3195

**Rothenstein, John, Sir, 1901-.**　　　　　　　• **1.6021**
Modern English painters. London, Eyre & Spottiswoode, 1952-1974. 3 v. illus.
23 cm. Volume 3 published 1974 by Macdonald. 1. Painters — Great Britain
— Biography. I. T.
ND496.R65　　　759.941　　*LC* 52-40976

## ND497 Painters, A–Z

### ND497.A–.J

**Alley, Ronald.**　　　　　　　　　　　　　　**1.6022**
Francis Bacon. Intro. by John Rothenstein. Catalogue raisonné and
documentation by Ronald Alley. New York, Viking Press [1964] 292 p. illus.
(part mounted col.) ports. 29 cm. (A Studio book) 1. Bacon, Francis, 1909-
I. T.
ND497.B16 A65　　　759.2　　*LC* 64-15492

**Russell, John, 1919-.**　　　　　　　　　　　**1.6023**
Francis Bacon. — Greenwich, Conn.: New York Graphic Society, [c1971]
242 p.: illus. (part col.); 27 cm. 1. Bacon, Francis, 1909- 2. Painters — Great
Britain — Biography. I. T.
ND497.B16 R8 1971b　　　759.9415　　*LC* 70-162718　　*ISBN*
0821202822

**Spalding, Frances.**　　　　　　　　　　　　**1.6024**
Vanessa Bell / Frances Spalding. — New Haven: Ticknor & Fields, 1983. xvi,
399 p., [30] p. of plates: ill. (some col.); 25 cm. Includes index. 1. Bell, Vanessa,
1879-1961. 2. Painters — England — Biography. I. T.
ND497.B44 S62 1983　　　759.2 B 19　　*LC* 83-4967　　*ISBN*
089919205X

**Blunt, Anthony, 1907-.**　　　　　　　　　　• **1.6025**
The art of William Blake. New York, Columbia University Press, 1959. ix,
122 p. 64 plates (incl. facsims.) (Bampton lectures in America. no. 12) 1. Blake,
William, 1757-1827. I. T. II. Series.
ND497 B6 B42　　　*LC* 59-12399

**Crehan, A. S.** 1.6026
Blake in context / Stewart Crehan. — Dublin: Gill and MacMillan; Atlantic Highlands, N.J.: Humanities Press, c1984. 364 p.: ill. 1. Blake, William, 1757-1827. I. T.
ND497.B6 C74 *ISBN* 0717113132

**Constable, John, 1776-1837.** • 1.6027
Correspondence / edited, with an introd. and notes, by R.B. Beckett. — London: H.M.S.O., 1962-. v.: facsim., maps, ports., geneal. tables. — (Historical Manuscripts Commission; JP3) 1. Constable, John, 1776-1837 — Correspondence. I. Beckett, Ronald Bryner. II. T.
ND497.C7 A47

**Leslie, Charles Robert, 1794-1859.** • 1.6028
Memoirs of the life of John Constable, composed chiefly by his letters [edited by Jonathan Mayne. — 2d ed.]. — London, Phaidon Press, 1951. xv, 434 p. plates (part col.) ports. 19 cm. — ([Phaidon pocket series]) Bibliography: p. 333. 1. Constable, John, 1776-1837. 2. Artists — Correspondence, reminiscences, etc. I. T.
ND497.C7L4 1951 927.5 *LC* 52-2065

**Reynolds, Graham.** 1.6029
Constable, the natural painter. New York, McGraw-Hill [1965] 238 p. plates (part mounted col.) 1. Constable, John, 1776-1837. I. T.
ND497 C7 R4 *LC* 65-25519

**Clifford, Derek Plint.** • 1.6030
John Crome, by Derek Clifford and Timothy Clifford. — Greenwich, Conn.: New York Graphic Society, [1968] 301 p.: illus. (part col.); 26 cm. 1. Crome, John, 1768-1821. I. Clifford, Timothy. joint author. II. T.
ND497.C9 C5 1968b 760/.0924 *LC* 68-25739

**Gainsborough, Thomas, 1727-1788.** 1.6031
Gainsborough: paintings and drawings / [selected by] John Hayes. — London: Phaidon, 1975. 232 p.: ill. (some col.); 29 cm. Includes index. 1. Gainsborough, Thomas, 1727-1788. I. Hayes, John T. II. T.
ND497.G2 H38 759.2 *LC* 75-721 *ISBN* 0714816396

**Hayes, John T.** 1.6032
The landscape paintings of Thomas Gainsborough: a critical text and catalogue raisonné / John Hayes. — Ithaca, N.Y.: Cornell University Press, 1982. 2 v. (xiii, 620 p., [12] p. of plates): ill. (some col.); 31 cm. Includes index. 1. Gainsborough, Thomas, 1727-1788. I. T.
ND497.G2 H383 1982 759.2 19 *LC* 82-70753 *ISBN* 0801415284

**Antal, Frederick, 1887-1954.** • 1.6033
Hogarth and his place in European art. New York Basic Books [c1962] xxi, 270 p. 152 plates. 26 cm. 1. Hogarth, William, 1697-1764. I. T.
ND497.H7 A63 759.2 *LC* 62-13871

**Hogarth, William, 1697-1764.** 1.6034
The art of Hogarth / [text by] Ronald Paulson. — London: Phaidon; New York: distributed by Praeger Publishers, 1975. 206 p.: chiefly ill. (some col.); 29 cm. Includes index. 1. Hogarth, William, 1697-1764. I. Paulson, Ronald. II. T.
ND497.H7 P37 760/.092/4 *LC* 75-52 *ISBN* 071481640X

### ND497.K–.Z

**Lawrence, Thomas, Sir, 1769-1830.** • 1.6035
Sir Thomas Lawrence [by] Kenneth Garlick. [London] Routledge & Kegan Paul [1954] viii, 92 p. ill. (chiefly ports.) (English master painters) I. Garlick, Kenneth, 1916- II. T. III. Series.
ND497 L4 G3

**Noakes, Vivien, 1937-.** 1.6036
Edward Lear; the life of a wanderer. — [1st American ed.]. — Boston: Houghton Mifflin, 1969 [c1968] 359 p.: illus., facsims., map, ports.; 23 cm. 1. Lear, Edward, 1812-1888. 2. Painters — England — Biography. 3. Poets, English — 19th century — Biography. I. T.
ND497.L48 N6 1969 760/.0924 B *LC* 69-15024

**Reynolds, Joshua, Sir, 1723-1792.** 1.6037
Reynolds [by] Ellis Waterhouse. — [New York]: Phaidon; [distributed by Praeger, 1973] 192 p.: 127 plates (part col.); 29 cm. 1. Reynolds, Joshua, Sir, 1723-1792. I. Waterhouse, Ellis Kirkham, 1905- II. T.
ND497.R4 W3 1973 759.2 *LC* 78-158100 *ISBN* 0714815195

**Butlin, Martin.** 1.6038
The paintings of J.M.W. Turner / Martin Butlin and Evelyn Joll. — Rev. ed. — New Haven: Published for the Paul Mellon Centre for Studies in British Art and the Tate Gallery by Yale University Press, 1984. 2 v.: ill. (some col.); 31 cm. (Studies in British art.) Includes indexes. 1. Turner, J. M. W. (Joseph Mallord William), 1775-1851 — Catalogs. I. Turner, J. M. W. (Joseph Mallord William), 1775-1851. II. Joll, Evelyn, 1925- III. Paul Mellon Centre for Studies in British Art. IV. Tate Gallery. V. T. VI. Series.
ND497.T8 A4 1984 759.2 19 *LC* 84-40182 *ISBN* 0300032765

**Finberg, Alexander Joseph, 1866-1939.** • 1.6039
The life of J.M.W. Turner, R.A. 2d ed., rev., and with a supplement, by Hilda F. Finberg. Oxford, Clarendon Press, 1961. xvi, 543 p. ill., ports. 'List of Turner's oil-paintings and water-colours exhibited during his lifetime': p. [456]-516. 1. Turner, J. M. W. (Joseph Mallord William), 1775-1851. I. T.
ND497 T8 F5 1961 *LC* 61-4374

**Gage, John.** 1.6040
Turner: Rain, steam, and speed. [New York, Viking Press, 1972] 99 p. illus. 23 cm. (Art in context) 1. Turner, J. M. W. (Joseph Mallord William), 1775-1851. Rain, steam and speed. I. T.
ND497.T8 G28 1972 759.2 *LC* 72-161061 *ISBN* 0670732893

**Turner, J. M. W. (Joseph Mallord William), 1775-1851.** 1.6041
Turner: paintings, watercolors, prints & drawings / [text by] Luke Herrmann. — Boston: New York Graphic Society, 1975. 240 p.: chiefly ill. (some col.); 29 cm. Includes index. 1. Turner, J. M. W. (Joseph Mallord William), 1775-1851. I. Herrmann, Luke. II. T.
ND497.T8 H42 1975b 759.2 *LC* 75-9101 *ISBN* 0821206575

**Reynolds, Graham.** 1.6042
Turner. London, Thames & Hudson, 1969. 216 p. 175 illus. (33 col.), col. port. 22 cm. ([World of art library: artists]) 1. Turner, J. M. W. (Joseph Mallord William), 1775-1851. I. T.
ND497.T8 R4 760/.0924 *LC* 70-407278 *ISBN* 0500180911

**Wilson, Richard, 1713-1782.** • 1.6043
Richard Wilson / W.G. Constable. — London: Routledge & Paul, 1953. xiii, 306 p.: ill. — (English master painters) I. Constable, W. G. (William George), 1887- II. T. III. Series.
ND497.W7 C6 1953 *LC* 53-12173

**Nicolson, Benedict.** • 1.6044
Joseph Wright of Derby: painter of light. — London: Paul Mellon Foundation for British Art; Routledge and K. Paul; New York: Pantheon Books, 1968. 2 v.: illus. (some col.), facsims., ports.; 33 cm. — (Studies in British art.) 1. Wright, Joseph, 1734-1797. I. Paul Mellon Foundation for British Art. II. T. III. Series.
ND497.W8 N5 759.2 *LC* 68-28393 *ISBN* 0710062842

### ND501–538 AUSTRIA. HUNGARY. CZECHOSLOVAKIA

**Klimt, Gustav, 1862-1918.** 1.6045
Gustav Klimt / Alessandra Comini. — New York: G. Braziller, 1975. 29, 80 p.: ill. (some col.); 28 cm. 1. Klimt, Gustav, 1862-1918. I. Comini, Alessandra. II. T.
ND511.5.K55 C65 759.36 *LC* 75-10965 *ISBN* 080760805X

**Kokoschka, Oskar, 1886-.** 1.6046
[Mein Leben. English] My life / Oskar Kokoschka; translated by David Britt. — 1st American ed. — New York: Macmillan, 1974. 240 p., [8] leaves of plates: ill.; 24 cm. Translation of Mein Leben. Includes index. 1. Kokoschka, Oskar, 1886- 2. Painters — Austria — Correspondence, reminiscences, etc. I. T.
ND511.5.K6 A213 1974 759.2 B *LC* 74-2645

### ND541–553 FRANCE

**Wilenski, Reginald Howard, 1887-.** • 1.6047
French painting. [Rev. ed.] Boston, C. T. Branford Co. [1949] xv, 310 p. plates (part col.) ports. 24 cm. 1. Painting — France — History. 2. Painters, French I. T.
ND541.W5 1949 *LC* A 51-8975

**Ring, Grete.** • 1.6048
A century of French painting, 1400–1500. London, Phaidon Press [distributed in U.S.A. by Oxford University Press, New York, 1949] 251 p. illus. (part mounted col.) plates, map. 31 cm. 'Biographical notes on the painters': p. 244-246. 1. Painting, French I. T.
ND545.R5 759.4 *LC* 50-7280

**Conisbee, Philip.** 1.6049
Painting in eighteenth–century France / Philip Conisbee. — Ithaca, N.Y.: Cornell University Press, 1981. 223 p.: ill. (some col.); 29 cm. 'Cornell/Phaidon books.' Includes index. 1. Painting, French 2. Painting, Modern — 17th-18th centuries — France. I. T.
ND546.C66 759.4 19 *LC* 81-66151 *ISBN* 0801414245

**Founders Society.**                                    **1.6050**
French painting 1774–1830: the age of revolution / Exhibition sponsored by
Founders Society, the Detroit Institute of Arts, the Metropolitan Museum of
Art and the Réunion des Musées Nationaux, Paris. — Detroit: Wayne State
University Press , 1975. 712 p.: ill. (some col.); 22 cm. 1. Paintings, French —
Exhibitions. 2. Paintings, Modern — 17th-18th centuries — France.
3. Painting, Modern — 19th century — France I. Metropolitan Museum of
Art (New York, N.Y.) II. Réunion des musées nationaux (France) III. T.
ND546.D4

**Fried, Michael.**                                    **1.6051**
Absorption and theatricality: painting and beholder in the age of Diderot /
Michael Fried. — Berkeley: University of California Press, c1980. xvii, 249 p.:
ill.; 26 cm. 1. Painting, French 2. Painting, Modern — 17th-18th centuries —
France. I. T.
ND546.F73        759.4        LC 78-62843        ISBN 0520037588

**Goncourt, Edmond de, 1822-1896.**                    • **1.6052**
[Art du dix-huitième siècle. English] French eighteenth–century painters:
Watteau, Boucher, Chardin, La Tour, Greuze, Fragonard / Edmond and Jules
de Goncourt; [translated with an introduction by Robin Ironside; illustrations
selected by Ludwig Goldscheider]. — Ithaca, N.Y.: Cornell University Press,
1981. xiii, 418 p., [5] p. of plates: ill.; 21 cm. — (Landmarks in art history.)
(Cornell paperbacks) Translation of: L'art du dix-huitième siècle. Reprint.
Originally published: London: Phaidon Press, 1948. 'A Phaidon book.'
1. Painting, French 2. Painting, Modern — 17th-18th centuries — France.
3. Painters — France — Biography. I. Goncourt, Jules de, 1830-1870. II. T.
III. Series.
ND546.G613 1981        759.4 19        LC 80-69739        ISBN 0801492181

**Rosenberg, Pierre.**                                    **1.6053**
[Peinture française du XVIIe siècle dans les collections américaines. English]
France in the golden age: seventeenth–century French paintings in American
collections / Pierre Rosenberg. — New York: Metropolitan Museum of Art,
[1982] xviii, 397 p.: ill. (some col.); 24 cm. Consists mainly of a catalog of an
exhibition organized by the Réunion des musées nationaux, Paris, and the
Metropolitan Museum of Art, New York, with the cooperation of the Musée du
Louvre and the Galeries nationales du Grand Palais, and held at the Galeries
nationales du Grand Palais, Paris, Jan. 29-Apr. 26, the Metropolitan Museum
of Art, New York, May 26-Aug. 22, and the Art Institute of Chicago, Sept.
18-Nov. 28, 1982. Translation of: La peinture française du XVIIe siècle dans les
collections américaines. Includes indexes. 1. Painting, French —
2. Painting, Baroque — France — Exhibitions. 3. Classicism in art — France
— Exhibitions. 4. Painting, French — United States — Exhibitions.
I. Réunion des musées nationaux (France) II. Metropolitan Museum of Art
(New York, N.Y.) III. Musée du Louvre. IV. Galeries nationales du Grand
Palais (France) V. Art Institute of Chicago. VI. T.
ND546.R6713 1982        759.4/074 19        LC 81-86011        ISBN
0870992953

**French painting 1774–1830, the Age of Revolution: Grand**        **1.6054**
**Palais, Paris, 16 November 1974–3 February 1975, the Detroit**
**Institute of Arts, 5 March–4 May 1975, the Metropolitan**
**Museum of Art, New York, 12 June–7 September 1975:**
**exhibition sponsored by Founders Society the Detroit Institute**
**of Arts, the Metropolitan Museum of Art, and the Réunion des**
**Musées Nationaux, Paris....**
English language ed. — Detroit: distributed by Wayne State University Press,
[1975] 712 p.: ill. (some col.); 22 cm. French translation has title: De David à
Delacroix: la peinture française de 1774 à 1830. Includes index. 1. Painting,
French — Exhibitions. 2. Neoclassicism (Art) — France — Exhibitions.
3. Romanticism in art — France — Exhibitions. I. Galeries nationales du
Grand Palais (France) II. Detroit Institute of Arts. III. Metropolitan Museum
of Art (New York, N.Y.) IV. Founders Society. V. Réunion des musées
nationaux (France)
ND546.5.N4 D43        759.4/074        LC 75-322567

**Friedlaender, Walter F., 1873-1966.**                    • **1.6055**
[Von David bis Delacroix. English] David to Delacroix. Translated by Robert
Goldwater. New York, Schocken Books [1968, c1952] xii, 136 p. 83 illus. 21
cm. Translation of Von David bis Delacroix. 1. Painting, French I. T.
ND547.F7613 1968        759.4        LC 68-9567

**Herbert, Robert L., 1929-.**                            **1.6056**
Barbizon revisited, essay and catalogue. [Boston, Museum of Fine Arts, 1962]
208 p. ill. (part col.) Exhibition to be held at the California Palace of the Legion
of Honor and other places, from Sept. 1962 to Apr. 1963. 1. Barbizon school
2. Paintings, French — Exhibitions I. California Palace of the Legion of
Honor. II. T.
ND547 H47        LC 62-21297

**Lindsay, Jack, 1900-.**                                • **1.6057**
Death of the hero; French painting from David to Delacroix. London, Studio
[c1960] 185 p. plates (part col.) 1. Painting, French — History I. T.
ND547 L5

**Sloane, Joseph C.**                                    • **1.6058**
French painting between the past and the present; artists, critics, and traditions,
from 1848 to 1870. Princeton, Princeton University Press, 1951. xii, 241 p.
plates. (Princeton monographs in art and archaeology. 27) 1. Painting, French
I. T. II. Series.
ND547 S55        LC 51-13872

**Bouret, Jean.**                                        **1.6059**
[L'école de Barbizon et le paysage français au XIXe siècle. English] The
Barbizon School and 19th century French landscape painting / Jean Bouret. —
Greenwich, Conn.: New York Graphic Society, 1973. 271 p.: illus. (part col.);
29 cm. Translation of L'école de Barbizon et le paysage français au XIXe siècle.
1. Barbizon school 2. Painting, Modern — 19th century — France
3. Landscape painting, French I. T.
ND547.5.B3 B6813        ND547.5B3 B6813 1973b.        758/.1/094437
LC 73-78566        ISBN 0821204955

**Champa, Kermit Swiler.**                                **1.6060**
Studies in early impressionism [by] Kermit Swiler Champa. New Haven, Yale
University Press, 1973. xviii, 106 p. illus. (part col.) 29 cm. (Yale publications in
the history of art. 22) 1. Impressionism (Art) — France. 2. Painting, French
3. Painting, Modern — 19th century — France I. T. II. Series.
ND547.5.I4 C46        759.4        LC 70-151569        ISBN 0300012853

**Roskill, Mark W., 1933-.**                            **1.6061**
Van Gogh, Gauguin, and the Impressionist circle [by] Mark Roskill. —
Greenwich, Conn.: New York Graphic Society, [1970] 310 p.: illus.; 26 cm.
1. Gogh, Vincent van, 1853-1890. 2. Gauguin, Paul, 1848-1903.
3. Impressionism (Art) — France. I. T.
ND547.5.I4 R6 1970b        759.9492        LC 76-110665        ISBN
0821203886

**Roskill, Mark W., 1933-.**                            **1.6062**
The interpretation of cubism / Mark Roskill. — Philadelphia: Art Alliance
Press; London: Associated University Presses, c1985. 301 p., [40] p. of plates:
ill.; 25 cm. Includes index. 1. Cubism — France. 2. Cubism — Philosophy.
3. Painting, Modern — 20th century — France. I. T.
ND548.5.C82 R67 1985        759.4 19        LC 83-45957        ISBN
0879825081

**Giry, Marcel.**                                        **1.6063**
Fauvism: origins and development / Marcel Giry; [translated from the French
by Helga Harrison]. — New York: Alpine Fine Arts Collection, 1982,c1981.
275 p.: ill. (some col.); 29 cm. Translation of Le fauvisme: ses origines, son
evolution. 1. Fauvism — France. 2. Painting, French 3. Painting, Modern —
20th century — France. I. T. II. Title: Le fauvisme.
ND548.5.F3 G513        ISBN 0933516584

**Clark, T. J. (Timothy J.)**                            **1.6064**
The painting of modern life: Paris in the art of Manet and his followers / T.J.
Clark. — 1st ed. — New York: Knopf, 1985, c1984. xv, 338 p., [31] p. of plates:
ill. (some col.); 24 cm. Includes index. 1. Manet, Edouard, 1832-1883 —
Influence. 2. Impressionism (Art) — France — Paris. 3. Painting, French —
France — Paris. 4. Painting, Modern — 19th century — France — Paris.
5. Paris (France) in art. I. T.
ND550.C55 1985        758/.9944361 19        LC 84-5670        ISBN
0394495802

## ND553 Painters, A–Z

### ND553.A–.B

**Ashton, Dore.**                                        **1.6065**
Rosa Bonheur: a life and a legend / text by Dore Ashton; illustrations and
captions by Denise Browne Hare. — New York: Viking, 1981. xiii, 206 p.: ill.;
26 cm. — (A Studio book) Includes index. 1. Bonheur, Rosa, 1822-1899.
2. Painters — France — Biography. I. Hare, Denise Browne. II. T.
ND553.B6 A9        759.4 B        LC 80-36749        ISBN 0670608130

**Rewald, John, 1912-.**                                • **1.6066**
Pierre Bonnard / John Rewald. — New York: The Museum of Modern Art,
New York, in collaboration with the Cleveland Museum of Art, 1948. 151 p.:
ill., col. plates, ports. 1. Bonnard, Pierre, 1867-1947. 2. Paintings, French —
Exhibitions. I. New York. Museum of Modern Art. II. Cleveland Museum of
Art. III. T.
ND553.B65 R4        ND553.B7 R4.        LC 48-3246

**Leymarie, Jean.**                                      • **1.6067**
Braque. Translated by James Emmons. — [New York]: Skira; [distributed by
World Pub. Co., Cleveland, 1961] 133 p.: mounted col. illus.; 19 cm. — (The
Taste of our time, v. 35)-1. Braque, Georges, 1882-1963. I. T.
ND553.B86 L45        759.4        LC 61-10170

**Richardson, John, 1924-.** • **1.6068**
Georges Braque / by John Richardson. — Harmondsworth, Middlesex: Penguin Books, 1959. 31 p., 32 leaves of plates: ill. (part col.). — (The Penguin modern painters; 20) 1. Braque, Georges, 1882-1963. I. T.
ND553.B86 R5 1959   *LC* 59-1581

## *ND553.C*

[Ref] →
ND
553
C33
+23

**Cézanne, Paul, 1839-1906.** • **1.6069**
[Correspondence. English] Paul Cézanne, letters / edited by John Rewald; translated by Seymour Hacker. — Rev. and augm. ed. — New York, N.Y.: Hacker Art Books, 1984. xiv, 339 p.: ill.; 25 cm. 'Letters to Zola...make up more than a third of this volume'—Pref. Includes index. 1. Cézanne, Paul, 1839-1906 — Correspondence. 2. Zola, Emile, 1840-1902. Correspondence 3. Painters — France — Correspondence. 4. Authors, French — 19th century — Correspondence. I. Rewald, John, 1912- II. Hacker, Seymour. III. T.
ND553.C33 A3 1984   759.4 B 19   *LC* 81-81716   *ISBN* 0878172769

**Cézanne: the late work: essays / by Theodore Reff ... [et al.];** **1.6070**
**edited by William Rubin.**
New York: Museum of Modern Art; Boston: distributed by New York Graphic Society, c1977. 416 p.: ill. (some col.); 29 cm. 'Published on the occasion of the exhibition ... organized by the Museum of Modern Art, New York, and the Réunion des musées nationaux, France, and shown also at the Museum of Fine Arts, Houston.' 1. Cézanne, Paul, 1839-1906 — Addresses, essays, lectures. I. Cézanne, Paul, 1839-1906. II. Reff, Theodore. III. Rubin, William Stanley. IV. Museum of Modern Art (New York, N.Y.) V. Réunion des musées nationaux (France) VI. Museum of Fine Arts, Houston.
ND553.C33 A35 1977   759.4   *LC* 77-77287   *ISBN* 0870702785

**Fry, Roger Eliot, 1866-1934.** • **1.6071**
Cézanne: a study of his development / / Roger E. Fry; introd. by Alfred Werner. — New York: Noonday Press [1958] 88 p.: ill.; 21 cm. 1. Cézanne, Paul, 1839-1906. I. T.
ND553.C33F7 1958   759.4   *LC* 58-13196

**Lindsay, Jack, 1900-.** • **1.6072**
Cezanne; his life and art. — [Greenwich, Conn.]: New York Graphic Society, [1969] viii, 360 p.: illus (part col.), ports.; 25 cm. Title on spine: Cezanne; life and art. 1. Cézanne, Paul, 1839-1906. I. T.
ND553.C33 L5 1969b   759.4 B   *LC* 76-77230   *ISBN* 0821203401

**Loran, Erle, 1905-.** • **1.6073**
Cézanne's composition: analysis of his form, with diagrams and photographs of his motifs. — [3d ed.]. — Berkeley, University of California Press, 1963 [c1943] 143 p. illus. (part col.) ports., diagrs. 32 cm. Bibliographical footnotes. 1. Cézanne, Paul, 1839-1906. 2. Composition (Art) I. T.
ND553.C33L6 1963   759.4   *LC* 64-2459

**Schapiro, Meyer.** • **1.6074**
Paul Cézanne / text by Meyer Schapiro. — 2nd ed., with corrections. — New York: Abrams, 1962, c1952. 126 p.: ill. (some col.), ports. (some col.). — (The Library of great painters) I. Cézanne, Paul. II. T.
ND553.C33 S38 1962   759.4   *LC* 63-5318

**Venturi, Lionello, 1885-1961.** **1.6075**
Cézanne / Lionello Venturi; pref. by Giulio Carlo Argan. — New York: Rizzoli, 1978. 175 p.: ill. (some col.); 35 cm. — (Discovering the nineteenth century) Includes index. 1. Cézanne, Paul, 1839-1906. I. Cézanne, Paul, 1839-1906. II. T. III. Series.
— O — ND553.C33 V39 fol   759.4   *LC* 78-58702   *ISBN* 084780187X

**Rosenberg, Pierre.** **1.6076**
[Chardin, 1699-1779. English] Chardin, 1699-1779: a special exhibition organized by the Réunion des Musées Nationaux, Paris, the Cleveland Museum of Art, and Museum of Fine Arts, Boston / Pierre Rosenberg; catalog translated by Emilie P. Kadish and Ursula Korneitchouk; edited by Sally W. Goodfellow. — Cleveland: Cleveland Museum of Art, c1979. 423 p.: ill. (some col.); 25 cm. Held at Grand Palais, Paris, Jan. 29-Apr. 30, 1979; the Cleveland Museum of Art, June 6-Aug. 12, 1979; Museum of Fine Art, Boston, Sept. 11-Nov. 19, 1979. 1. Chardin, Jean Baptiste Siméon, 1699-1779 — Exhibitions. I. Chardin, Jean Baptiste Siméon, 1699-1779. II. Goodfellow, Sally W. III. Réunion des musées nationaux (France) IV. Galeries nationales du Grand Palais (France) V. Cleveland Museum of Art. VI. Museum of Fine Arts, Boston. VII. T.
ND553.C4 A413 1979   759.4   *LC* 78-74107   *ISBN* 091038648X

**Sloane, Joseph C.** • **1.6077**
Paul Marc Joseph Chenavard, artist of 1848. Chapel Hill, University of North Carolina Press [1962] 214 p. illus. 24 cm. Includes bibliography. 1. Chenavard, Paul Marc Joseph, 1807-1895. 2. Paris. Panthéon. 3. France — Intellectual life I. T. II. Title: Artist of 1848.
ND553.C48S55   759.4   *LC* 62-3624

**Hours, Madeleine, 1913-.** **1.6078**
Jean–Baptiste–Camille Corot. — New York: H. N. Abrams, [1972] 167 p.: illus. (part col.); 34 cm. — (The Library of great painters) I. Corot, Jean-Baptiste-Camille, 1796-1875. II. T.
ND553.C8 H77   759.4   *LC* 79-99240   *ISBN* 0810900580

**Leymarie, Jean.** **1.6079**
[Corot. English] Corot / Jean Leymarie; [translated from the French by Stuart Gilbert]. — Geneva: Skira; New York: Rizzoli, 1979. 175 p.: ill. (some col.); 35 cm. — (Discovering the nineteenth century) Includes indexes. 1. Corot, Jean-Baptiste-Camille, 1796-1875. 2. Painters — France — Biography. I. T. II. Series.
ND553.C8 L43 1979   *LC* 79-64710   *ISBN* 0847802388

**Lindsay, Jack, 1900-.** **1.6080**
Gustave Courbet: his life and art / Jack Lindsay.— New York: Harper & Row, 1973. xi, 383 p., [24] feuillets de planches; 25 cm. 1. Courbet, Gustave, 1819-1877. I. T.
ND553C858 L748 1973   759.4   *LC* 73-6422   *ISBN* 0643529020

**Boas, George, 1891- ed.** • **1.6081**
Courbet and the naturalistic movement; essays read at the Baltimore Museum of Art, May 16, 17, 18, 1938. — New York, Russell & Russell [1967, c1938] x, 149 p. illus., ports. 23 cm. Bibliographical footnotes. 1. Courbet, Gustave, 1819-1877. 2. Naturalism in art 3. Naturalism in literature I. T.
ND553.C9B6 1967   700/.1   *LC* 66-27041

**Clark, T. J. (Timothy J.)** **1.6082**
Image of the people: Gustave Courbet and the second French Republic, 1848–1851 / T. J. Clark. — Greenwich, Conn.: New York Graphic Society, c1973. 208 p.: ill., (some col.), ports. Includes index. 1. Courbet, Gustave, 1819-1877. 2. Art and society — France — History. 3. France — History — Second Republic, 1848-1852 — Art I. T.
ND553.C9 C55   759.4   *LC* 72-93941   *ISBN* 0821205196

**Fernier, Robert.** • **1.6083**
Gustave Courbet. With an introd. by Rene Huyghe. [Translated from the French by Marcus Bullock]. — New York: Praeger, [1969] 139 p.: illus. (part col.), facsims., ports.; 28 cm. 1. Courbet, Gustave, 1819-1877. I. T.
ND553.C9 F4153   759.4   *LC* 70-84856

**Boime, Albert.** **1.6084**
Thomas Couture and the eclectic vision / Albert Boime. — New Haven: Yale University Press, 1980. xxii, 683 p.: ill.; 27 cm. Includes index. 1. Couture, Thomas, 1815-1879. 2. Eclecticism in art — France. 3. Painters — France — Biography. I. T.
ND553.C9565 B64   759.4   *LC* 79-23507   *ISBN* 0300021585

## *ND553.D*

**Adhémar, Jean.** • **1.6085**
Honoré Daumier. — Paris, P. Tisné [1954] 147 p. illus., plates.; 29 cm. Bibliography: p. 133-137. I. T.
ND553.D24A65

**Daumier, Honoré, 1808-1879.** • **1.6086**
Honoré Daumier; catalogue raisonné of the paintings, watercolours, and drawings [by] K. E. Maison. — [Greenwich, Conn.] New York Graphic Society [1968] 2 v. illus., port. 29 cm. Includes bibliographies. I. Maison, K. E. II. T.
ND553.D24M3 1968   016.760/0924   *LC* 67-25493

**Brookner, Anita.** **1.6087**
Jacques–Louis David / Anita Brookner. — New York: Harper & Row, 1980. 223 p., [104] p. of plates: ill. (some col.), ports. (some col.); 26 cm. — (Icon editions) 1. David, Jacques Louis, 1748-1825. 2. Painters — France — Biography I. David, Jacques Louis, 1748-1825. II. T.
ND553.D25 B68   759/.4   *LC* 79-3386   *ISBN* 0064305074

**Dowd, David Lloyd.** • **1.6088**
Pageant–master of the Republic; Jacques–Louis David and the French Revolution. — Freeport, N.Y.: Books for Libraries Press, [1969, c1948] xiv, 205 p.: illus., ports.; 24 cm. — (Select bibliographies reprint series) 1. David, Jacques Louis, 1748-1825. 2. France — History — Revolution, 1789-1799 — Pictorial works I. T.
ND553.D25 D6 1969   944.04/0924   *LC* 72-75507

**McMullen, Roy.** **1.6089**
Degas: his life, times, and work / Roy McMullen. — Boston: Houghton Mifflin, 1984. viii, 517 p.: ill.; 24 cm. Includes index. 1. Degas, Edgar, 1834-1917. 2. Painters — France — Biography. I. T.
ND553.D298 M38 1984   709/.2/4 B 19   *LC* 84-677   *ISBN* 0395276039

**Boggs, Jean Sutherland.**    • **1.6090**
Portraits by Degas. Berkeley, University of California Press, 1962. xv, 142 p. plates (part col.) (California studies in the history of art. 2) 1. Degas, Edgar, 1834-1917. I. T. II. Series.
ND553 D3 B6     *LC* 62-11142

**Reff, Theodore.**      **1.6091**
Degas: the artist's mind / Theodore Reff. — [New York]: Metropolitan Museum of Art, c1976. 352 p.: ill. (some col.); 26 cm. Includes index. 1. Degas, Edgar, 1834-1917. I. T.
ND553.D3 R38 1976    759.4    *LC* 75-45190    *ISBN* 0870991469

**Degas, Edgar, 1834-1917.**    • **1.6092**
Edgar Hilaire Germain Degas. Text by Daniel Catton Rich. — [1st ed.]. — New York, H. N. Abrams 1951. 126 p. illus., col. plates. 34 cm. — (The Library of great painters) I. Rich, Daniel Catton, 1904- II. T.
ND553.D3R45    759.4    *LC* 52-6130

**Delacroix, Eugène, 1798-1863.**    • **1.6093**
[Journal. English. Selections] The journal of Eugène Delacroix: a selection / edited with an introd. by Hubert Wellington; translated from the French by Lucy Norton. — Ithaca, N.Y.: Cornell University Press, 1980. xxxiv, 504 p., [8] leaves of plates: ill.; 21 cm. — (Landmarks in art history.) (Cornell paperbacks) 'A Phaidon book.' Reprint of the 1951 ed. published by Phaidon Publishers, New York. 1. Delacroix, Eugène, 1798-1863. 2. Painters — France — Biography. I. Wellington, Hubert. II. T. III. Series.
ND553.D33 A2 1980    759.4 B 19    *LC* 80-66413    *ISBN* 0801491967

**Johnson, Lee, art historian.**    **1.6094**
The paintings of Eugène Delacroix: a critical catalogue, 1816–1831 / Lee Johnson. — Oxford: Clarendon Press, 1981. 2 v.: ill.; 31 cm. Includes indexes. 1. Delacroix, Eugène, 1798-1863 — Catalogs. I. T.
ND553.D33 A4 1981    759.4 19    *LC* 80-40988    *ISBN* 0198173148

**Huyghe, René.**    • **1.6095**
Delacroix. 56 colour plates, 405 black and white illus. [Translated from the French by Jonathan Griffin. New York] H. N. Abrams [1963] 564 p. illus. plates (part col.) ports., facsims. 31 cm. 1. Delacroix, Eugène, 1798-1863. I. T.
ND553.D33 H793    759.4    *LC* 63-19565

**Trapp, Frank.**    **1.6096**
The attainment of Delacroix. Baltimore, Johns Hopkins Press [c1970] xix, 371 p. illus., col. plates, ports. 29 cm. 1. Delacroix, Eugène, 1798-1863. I. T.
ND553.D33 T77    759.4    *LC* 70-79728    *ISBN* 0801810485

**Delaunay, Robert, 1885-1941.**    **1.6097**
[R. Delaunay. English] R. Delaunay / by Michel Hoog; [translated from the French by Alice Sachs]. — New York: Crown Publishers, c1977. 96 p.: ill. (some col.); 29 cm. 1. Delaunay, Robert, 1885-1941. I. Hoog, Michel. II. T.
ND553.D357 H6613    759.4    *LC* 76-41382    *ISBN* 0517528754

**Dunlop, Ian, 1940-.**    **1.6098**
Degas / by Ian Dunlop. — New York: Harper & Row, c1979. 240 p.: ill. (some col.), ports. 1. Degas, Edgar, 1834-1917. 2. Painting, French 3. Painting, Modern — France. 4. Impressionism (Art) — France. I. T.
ND553.D45 D8    759.4/092/4    *LC* 79-1660    *ISBN* 0006111119

**Cabanne, Pierre.**    **1.6099**
[Entretiens avec Marcel Duchamp. English] Dialogues with Marcel Duchamp. Translated from the French by Ron Padgett. New York, Viking Press [1971] 136 p. illus., ports. 22 cm. (The Documents of 20th century art) Translation of Entretiens avec Marcel Duchamp. 1. Duchamp, Marcel, 1887-1968. I. Duchamp, Marcel, 1887-1968. II. T. III. Series.
ND553.D774 C313 1971    759.4    *LC* 77-83255    *ISBN* 0670240176

**Lebel, Robert.**    • **1.6100**
Marcel Duchamp. With chapters by Marcel Duchamp, Andre Breton & H. P. Roche. Translation by George Heard Hamilton. [New York, Paragraphic Books, 1967] 201 p. illus., ports. 28 cm. Translation of Sur Marcel Duchamp. 1. Duchamp, Marcel, 1887-1968. I. T.
ND553.D774 L43 1967    759.4    *LC* 67-21258

**Schwarz, Arturo, 1924-.**    • **1.6101**
The complete works of Marcel Duchamp. — New York: H. N. Abrams, [1969] xxi, 630 p.: illus., plates (part col.); 32 cm. 1. Duchamp, Marcel, 1887-1968. I. T.
ND553.D774 S3    709/.24    *LC* 69-11987

**Duchamp, Marcel, 1887-1968.**    • **1.6102**
Notes and projects for the Large Glass [by] Marcel Duchamp. Selected, ordered and with an introd. by Arturo Schwarz. New York, H. N. Abrams [1969] 217 p. illus. (part col.) 44 cm. English and French. 1. Duchamp, Marcel, 1887-1968. Bride stripped bare by her bachelors, even I. Schwarz, Arturo, 1924- II. T.
ND553.D774 S32    759.4 19    *LC* 69-11986

## ND553.F–.G

**Thuillier, Jacques.**    • **1.6103**
[Fragonard. English] Fragonard; biographical and critical study. Translated from the French by Robert Allen. [Geneva] Skira [distributed in the U.S. by the World Pub. Co., Cleveland, 1967] 156 p. col. plates. 19 cm. (The Taste of our time [v. 46]) 1. Fragonard, Jean Honoré, 1732-1806. I. T.
ND553.F7 T413 1967    759.4    *LC* 66-30307

**Gauguin, Paul, 1848-1903.**    • **1.6104**
The intimate journals of Paul Gauguin / by Paul Gauguin. — London: KPI, 1985. x, 138 p.; 24 cm. (Pacific Basin books.) 1. Painters — France — Biography. I. T. II. Series.
ND553.G27    759.4 19    *ISBN* 0710301057

**Gauguin, Paul, 1848-1903.**    **1.6105**
Paul Gauguin / [text by] Robert Goldwater. — New York: Abrams, 1983. p. cm. Concise ed. of the author's Paul Gauguin originally published: New York: Abrams, 1957. 1. Gauguin, Paul, 1848-1903. I. Goldwater, Robert John, 1907-1973. II. T.
ND553.G27 A4 1983    759.4 19    *LC* 82-18168    *ISBN* 0810953358

**Gauguin, Paul, 1848-1903.**    **1.6106**
[Oviri. English] The writings of a savage / Paul Gauguin; edited by Daniel Guérin; with an introduction by Wayne Andersen; translated by Eleanor Levieux. — New York: Viking Press, 1978. xxxix, 304 p.; 22 cm. Translation of Oviri. Includes index. 1. Gauguin, Paul, 1848-1903. 2. Painters — France — Biography. I. T.
ND553.G27 A4813 1978    759.4 B    *LC* 76-53574    *ISBN* 0670791733

**Andersen, Wayne V.**    **1.6107**
Gauguin's paradise lost [by] Wayne Andersen. With the assistance of Barbara Klein. — New York: Viking Press, [1971] xii, 371 p.: illus.; 25 cm. 1. Gauguin, Paul, 1848-1903. I. Klein, Barbara. II. T.
ND553.G27 A74 1971    759.4 B    *LC* 72-135347    *ISBN* 0670335932

**Berger, Klaus, 1901-.**    • **1.6108**
Géricault and his work. Translated by Winslow Ames. Lawrence, University of Kansas Press, 1955. 92 p. plates (part col.) 1. Géricault, Théodore, 1791-1824. I. T.
ND553 G45 B444    *LC* 55-6524

**Eitner, Lorenz.**    **1.6109**
Géricault, his life and work / Lorenz E.A. Eitner. — London: Orbis Pub., c1983. 376 p.: ill.; 30 cm. Includes index. 1. Géricault, Théodore, 1791-1824. 2. Painters — France — Biography. I. T.
ND553.G45 E317 1983    760/.092/4 B 19    *LC* 81-68742    *ISBN* 0801414687

**Brookner, Anita.**    **1.6110**
Greuze: the rise and fall of an eighteenth–century phenomenon. — Greenwich, Conn.; New York: Graphic Society, [1972] xvi, 176 p.: 121 illus. (part col.); 26 cm. Appendix in English and French. 1. Greuze, Jean-Baptiste, 1725-1805. I. T.
ND553.G8 B76 1972b    759.4    *LC* 72-80422    *ISBN* 0821204831

## ND553.I–.L

**Condon, Patricia.**    **1.6111**
Ingres, in pursuit of perfection: the art of J.–A.–D. Ingres: the J.B. Speed Art Museum, Louisville, Kentucky, December 6, 1983 to January 29, 1984, the Kimbell Art Museum, Fort Worth, Texas, March 3, 1984 to May 6, 1984 / by Patricia Condon with Marjorie B. Cohn, and Agnes Mongan; edited by Debra Edelstein. — Louisville, Ky.: J.B. Speed Art Museum; Bloomington, Ind.: Indiana University Press, c1984. 255 p.: ill. (some col.); 31 cm. Includes indexes. 1. Ingres, Jean-Auguste-Dominique, 1780-1867 — Exhibitions. I. Ingres, Jean-Auguste-Dominique, 1780-1867. II. Cohn, Marjorie B. III. Mongan, Agnes. IV. Edelstein, Debra. V. J.B. Speed Art Museum. VI. Kimbell Art Museum. VII. T.
ND553.I5 A4 1983    759.4 19    *LC* 83-81727    *ISBN* 0961227605

**Pach, Walter, 1883-1958.**    • **1.6112**
Ingres / by Walter Pach; illustrated with reproductions of paintings and drawings by the artist. — New York: Harper, 1939. xii, 290 p., [64] p. of plates: ill., ports.; 26 cm. I. Ingres, Jean-Auguste-Dominique, 1780-1867. II. T.
ND553.I5 P3    *LC* 39-32477

**Ingres, Jean-Auguste-Dominique, 1780-1867.**    • **1.6113**
Jean–Auguste–Dominique Ingres. Text by Robert Rosenblum. New York, H. N. Abrams [1967] 176 p. illus. (part col.) 33 cm. (The Library of great painters) 1. Ingres, Jean-Auguste-Dominique, 1780-1867. I. Rosenblum, Robert. II. T.
ND553.I5 R63    759.4    *LC* 67-21262

**Ingres, Jean-Auguste-Dominique, 1780-1867.** • **1.6114**
Ingres, by Georges Wildenstein. [2d, rev. ed.] London, Phaidon Press [1956]
246 p. (chiefly ill. (part mounted col.)) 'Catalogue': p. [159]-232.
I. Wildenstein, Georges II. T.
ND553 I5 W5 1956    *LC* 57-28089

**De Francia, Peter.** **1.6115**
Fernand Léger / Peter De Francia. — New Haven: Yale University Press, 1983.
viii, 280 p.: ill. (some col.); 32 cm. Includes index. 1. Léger, Fernand,
1881-1955. I. T.
ND553.L58 D35 1983    709/.2/4 19    *LC* 83-42878    *ISBN*
0300030673

## *ND553.M–.N*

**Hamilton, George Heard.** • **1.6116**
Manet and his critics. — New York: Norton, [1969] xii, 295 p.: 39 illus.; 20 cm.
— (The Norton library, N372) 1. Manet, Edouard, 1832-1883. I. T.
ND553.M3 H3 1969    759.4    *LC* 77-17733

**Hanson, Anne Coffin.** **1.6117**
Manet and the modern tradition / Anne Coffin Hanson. — New Haven: Yale
University Press, 1977. xvii, 222 p., [40] leaves of plates: ill. (some col.); 26 cm.
Includes index. 1. Manet, Edouard, 1832-1883. I. T.
ND553.M3 H33    759.4    *LC* 75-43319    *ISBN* 0300019548

*(margin handwritten: ND 553 M3 H33)*

**Sandblad, Nils Gosta.** **1.6118**
Manet: three studies in artistic conception / by Nils Gosta Sandblad; [translated
by Walter Nash]. — Lund: C.W.K. Gleerup, 1954. 183 p.: ill., ports.; 25 cm. —
(Skrifter utgivna av Vetenskapssocieteten i Lund. 46) 1. Manet, Edouard,
1832-1883. I. Nash, Walter. II. Manet, Edouard, 1832-1883. III. T.
IV. Series.
ND 553 M3 S22 E5 1954    *LC* 57-18507

**Barr, Alfred Hamilton, 1902-.** • **1.6119**
Matisse, his art and his public / by Alfred H. Barr, Jr. — New York: Museum
of Modern Art; Boston: distributed by New York Graphic Society, 1974, c1951.
591 p., [5] leaves of plates: ill. (some col.); 25 cm. Includes index. 1. Matisse,
Henri, 1869-1954. I. T.
ND553.M37 B34 1974    759.4 B    *LC* 74-81656    *ISBN* 0870704699

**Matisse, Henri, 1869-1954.** • **1.6120**
Henri Matisse. Exposition du centenaire, Grand Palais, avril–septembre 1970.
[Catalogue rédigé par Pierre Schneider avec la collaboration de Tamara Préaud.
Paris] Ministère d'État, Affaires culturelles [1970] 319 p. illus. (part col.) and 2
portfolios (24 col. plates) 24 cm. 'Exposition ... organisée par la Réunion des
musées nationaux.' I. Schneider, Pierre. II. Préaud, Tamara. III. Grand
Palais (Paris, France) IV. Réunion des musées nationaux (France) V. T.
ND553.M37 S32    *LC* 75-508637

**Fermigier, André.** **1.6121**
Jean–François Millet / by André Fermigier; [translated from the French by
Dinah Harrison]. — Geneva: Skira; New York: Rizzoli, 1977. 158 p.: ill.; 35
cm. — (Discovering the nineteenth century) 1. Millet, Jean François,
1814-1875. 2. Painters — France — Biography I. Millet, Jean François,
1814-1875. II. T. III. Series.
ND553.M6.F4    759.4    *LC* 77-77034    *ISBN* 0847801209

**Monet, Claude, 1840-1926.** **1.6122**
Monet's years at Giverny: beyond impressionism. — New York: Metropolitan
Museum of Art, c1978. 180 p.: ill. (some col.); 26 cm. English or French.
Catalog of an exhibition. 1. Monet, Claude, 1840-1926 — Exhibitions.
2. Monet, Claude, 1840-1926 — Homes and haunts — France — Giverny.
3. Impressionism (Art) — France — Exhibitions. 4. Post-impressionism (Art)
— France — Exhibitions. I. Metropolitan Museum of Art (New York, N.Y.)0
II. T.
ND553.M7 A4 1978    759.4    *LC* 78-328    *ISBN* 0870991744

**Gordon, Robert, 1946-.** **1.6123**
Monet / by Robert Gordon and Andrew Forge. — New York: Abrams, 1983.
304 p.: ill. (some col.); 33 cm. Includes index. 1. Monet, Claude, 1840-1926.
2. Painters — France — Biography. I. Forge, Andrew. II. Monet, Claude,
1840-1926. III. T.
ND553.M7 G67 1983    759.4 B 19    *LC* 83-2717    *ISBN* 0810913127

**Isaacson, Joel.** **1.6124**
Claude Monet, observation and reflection / Joel Isaacson. — Oxford: Phaidon;
New York: Dutton, 1978. 240 p.: ill. (some col.), map (on lining papers); 29 cm.
Includes index. 1. Monet, Claude, 1840-1926. 2. Monet, Claude, 1840-1926.
II. T. III. Title: Observation and reflection, Claude Monet.
ND553.M7 I79    759.4    *LC* 77-93079    *ISBN* 0714817813

**Museum of Modern Art (New York, N.Y.)** • **1.6125**
Claude Monet: seasons and moments, by William C. Seitz. Reprint ed. [New
York] Published for the Museum of Modern Art by Arno Press, 1969. 64 p.

illus. 25 cm. Issued in connection with the exhibition held Mar. 9-May 15, 1960,
in the Museum of Modern Art, New York, and June 14-Aug. 7, 1960, in the Los
Angeles County Museum. 1. Monet, Claude, 1840-1926. I. Seitz, William
Chapin. II. Los Angeles County Museum. III. T.
ND553.M7 N4 1969    759.4    *LC* 72-86446

**Mathieu, Pierre-Louis.** **1.6126**
[Gustave Moreau, sa vie, son o euvre. English] Gustave Moreau: with a
catalogue of the finished paintings, watercolors, and drawings / Pierre–Louis
Mathieu; [translated from the French by James Emmons]. — 1st U.S. ed. —
Boston, Mass.: New York Graphic Society, c1976. 400 p.: ill. (some col.); 29
cm. Translation of: Gustave Moreau, sa vie, son o euvre. Includes indexes.
1. Moreau, Gustave, 1826-1898. 2. Moreau, Gustave, 1826-1898 — Catalogs.
3. Painters — France — Biography. I. Moreau, Gustave, 1826-1898. II. T.
ND553.M8 M3313 1976    759.4 B 19    *LC* 76-21928    *ISBN*
0821207016

## *ND553.P*

**Arnheim, Rudolf.** • **1.6127**
Picasso's Guernica; the genesis of a painting. Berkeley, University of California
Press, 1962. 139 p. ill. (1 fold., 1 col.) 1. Picasso, Pablo, 1881-1973. I. T.
II. Title: Guernica
ND553 P5 A75    *LC* 62-20637

**Cirlot, Juan Eduardo.** **1.6128**
[Nacimiento de un genio. English] Picasso, birth of a genius. Foreword by Juan
Ainaud de Lasarte. New York, Praeger [1972] 288 p. illus. (part col.) 30 cm.
Translation of El nacimiento de un genio. 1. Picasso, Pablo, 1881-1973. I. T.
ND553.P5 C5313    741.944    *LC* 72-186477

**Daix, Pierre.** • **1.6129**
[Picasso, 1900-1906. English] Picasso: the blue and rose periods; a catalogue
raisonné of the paintings, 1900–1906 [by] Pierre Daix and Georges Boudaille.
Catalogue compiled with the collaboration of Joan Rosselet. [Translated from
the French by Phoebe Pool] Greenwich, Conn., New York Graphic Society
[1967, c1966] 348 p. illus., col. plates, ports. 33 cm. 1. Picasso, Pablo,
1881-1973. I. Boudaille, Georges. joint author. II. T.
ND553.P5 D2553    759.6    *LC* 66-19492

**Museum of Modern Art (New York, N.Y.)** **1.6130**
Picasso: fifty years of his art / by Alfred H. Barr, Jr. — New York: The
Museum of Modern Art; Boston: distributed by New York Graphic Society,
1974, c1946. 314 p., [10] leaves of plates: ill. (some col.); 26 cm. Includes index.
1. Picasso, Pablo, 1881-1973. I. Barr, Alfred Hamilton, 1902- II. T.
ND553.P5 N4 1974    759/.4    *LC* 74-81655    *ISBN* 0870705393

**O'Brian, Patrick.** **1.6131**
Picasso: Pablo Ruiz Picasso: a biography / by Patrick O'Brian. New York:
Putnam, c1976. 511 p.; 24 cm. Includes index. 1. Picasso, Pablo, 1881-1973.
2. Painters — France — Biography. I. T.
ND553.P5 O27 1976    759.4 B    *LC* 75-41334    *ISBN* 0399116397

**Picasso in perspective / edited by Gert Schiff.** **1.6132**
Englewood Cliffs, N.J.: Prentice-Hall, c1976. viii, 184 p., [4] leaves of plates: ill.;
24 cm. (The Artists in perspective series) (A Spectrum book) 1. Picasso, Pablo,
1881-1973 — Addresses, essays, lectures. I. Schiff, Gert.
ND553.P5 P477    759.4    *LC* 76-40110    *ISBN* 0136758010

**Picasso, in retrospect. Advisory editors: Sir Roland Penrose** **1.6133**
**[and] John Golding. [Authors] Daniel–Henry Kahnweiler [and**
**others]**
New York, Praeger [1973] 283 p. illus. (part col.) 30 cm. 1. Picasso, Pablo,
1881-1973 — Addresses, essays, lectures. I. Penrose, Roland, Sir. II. Golding,
John.
ND553.P5 P48    759.4    *LC* 71-163098

**Pissarro, Camille, 1830-1903.** • **1.6134**
[Camille Pissarro, lettres à son fils Lucien. English] Camille Pissarro: letters to
his son Lucien, edited with the assistance of Lucien Pissarro by John Rewald.
3d ed., rev. and enl. Mamaroneck, N.Y., P. P. Appel, 1972. 399 p. illus. 26 cm.
Includes the letters of Pissarro to Camille Pissarro published for the first time in
English translation. 1. Pissarro, Camille, 1830-1903. 2. Painters — France —
Biography. I. Rewald, John, 1912- ed. II. Pissarro, Lucien, 1863-1944. III. T.
ND553.P55 P4813 1972    759.4 B    *LC* 77-162499    *ISBN*
0911858229

**Pissarro, Camille, 1830-1903.** • **1.6135**
Camille Pissaro. Text by John Rewald. — [1st ed.]. — New York: H. N.
Abrams, [1963] 158, [2] p.: illus., col. plates, ports.; 34 cm. — (The Library of
great painters) I. Rewald, John, 1912- II. T.
ND553.P55 R39    759.4    *LC* 63-14212

**Shikes, Ralph E.**                                              **1.6136**
Pissarro, his life and work / by Ralph E. Shikes and Paula Harper; [designed by Abe Lerner]. — New York: Horizon Press, c1980. 362 p.: ill.; 27 cm. Includes index. 1. Pissarro, Camille, 1830-1903. 2. Painters — France — Biography. I. Harper, Paula. joint author. II. T.
ND553.P55 S53        759.4 B 19        *LC* 79-56132        *ISBN* 0818001283

**Blunt, Anthony, Sir, 1907-.**                                  • **1.6137**
Nicolas Poussin / Anthony Blunt. — New York: Bollingen Foundation: distributed by Pantheon Books, 1967. 2 v.: ill. — (Bollingen series. 35) (A.W. Mellon lectures in the fine arts. 7) 1. Poussin, Nicolas, 1594?-1665. I. T. II. Series. III. Series: A.W. Mellon lectures in the fine arts. 7
ND553.P8 B64        *LC* 66-16237

**Friedlaender, Walter F., 1873-1966.**                          • **1.6138**
Nicolas Poussin; a new approach [by] Walter Friedlaender. — New York: H. N. Abrams, [1966?] 203, [1] p.: 130 illus., 49 col. plates.; 33 cm. — (The Library of great painters) 1. Poussin, Nicolas, 1594?-1665. I. T.
ND553.P8 F68 1966        759.4        *LC* 64-10763

## *ND553.R–.Z*

**Bacou, Roseline.**                                              • **1.6139**
Odilon Redon. Genève, P. Cailler [1956] 2 v. 13 mounted col. ill., 109 plates. (Peintres et sculpteurs d'hier et d'aujourd'hui, 37) 1. Redon, Odilon, 1840-1916. I. T.
ND553 R35 B3        *LC* A 57-1847

**Hobbs, Richard.**                                               **1.6140**
Odilon Redon / Richard Hobbs. — Boston: New York Graphic Society, c1977. 192 p.: ill. (some col.); 28 cm. 1. Redon, Odilon, 1840-1916. I. T.
ND553.R35.H63        *LC* 76-10035        *ISBN* 0821206745

**New York. Museum of Modern Art.**                              • **1.6141**
Odilon Redon, Gustave Moreau [and] Rodolphe Bresdin. The Museum of Modern Art, New York, in collaboration with the Art Institute of Chicago. — Garden City, N.Y.: Distributed by Doubleday, [1961] 184 p.: illus. (part col.); 24 cm. 'Exhibition dates: the Museum of Modern Art ... December 4, 1961-February 4, 1962; the Art Institute of Chicago, March 2, 1962-April 15, 1962.' 1. Redon, Odilon, 1840-1916. 2. Moreau, Gustave, 1826-1898. 3. Bresdin, Rodolphe, 1825-1885. I. T.
ND553.R35 N4        759.4        *LC* 61-17804

**Renoir, Auguste, 1841-1919.**                                  • **1.6142**
Pierre Auguste Renoir. Introd. by Walter Pach. — New York, Abrams [1960?] 120 p. illus. (part mounted col.) 33 cm. — (The Library of great painters) I. Pach, Walter, 1883-1958. II. T.
ND553.R45 P3 1960        759.4        *LC* 60-10396

**White, Barbara Ehrlich.**                                       **1.6143**
Renoir, his life, art, and letters / Barbara Ehrlich White. — New York: Abrams, 1984. 311 p.: ill. (some col.); 36 cm. Includes index. 1. Renoir, Auguste, 1841-1919. 2. Painters — France — Biography. I. Renoir, Auguste, 1841-1919. II. T.
ND553.R45 W452 1984        759.4 B 19        *LC* 84-406        *ISBN* 0810915553

**Rouault, Georges, 1871-1958.**                                 **1.6144**
[Rouault. English] Georges Rouault / text by Pierre Courthion. — New York: H. N. Abrams, 1977. 160 p.: ill. (some col.); 33 cm. — (The Library of great painters) Translation of Rouault. Includes index. 1. Rouault, Georges, 1871-1958. I. Courthion, Pierre. II. T.
ND553.R66 C6313        759.4        *LC* 76-53575        *ISBN* 0810904594

**Museum of Modern Art (New York, N.Y.)**                        • **1.6145**
Georges Rouault; paintings and prints, by James Thrall Soby. [3d ed. New York, Museum of Modern Art, 1947] 141 p. illus. (part col.) 26 cm. 1. Rouault, Georges, 1871-1958. 2. Painting — France — Exhibitions. 3. Engraving — France — Exhibitions. I. Soby, James Thrall, 1906- II. T.
ND553.R66 N45 1947        759.4        *LC* 48-5601

**Henri Rousseau: essays / by Roger Shattuck ... [et al.;**      **1.6146**
translations from the French by Richard Miller].**
New York: Museum of Modern Art; Boston: Distributed by New York Graphic Society Books, 1985. 269 p.: ill. (some col.); 25 cm. '[Exhibition held at] Galeries nationales du Grand Palais, Paris, September 14, 1984-January 7, 1985; the Museum of Modern Art, New York, February 21-June 4, 1985'—T.p. verso. Includes index. 1. Rousseau, Henri Julien Félix, 1844-1910 — Exhibitions. 2. Primitivism in art — France — Exhibitions. I. Rousseau, Henri Julien Félix, 1844-1910. II. Shattuck, Roger. III. Museum of Modern Art (New York, N.Y.) IV. Galeries nationales du Grand Palais (France)
ND553.R67 A4 1985        759.4 19        *LC* 84-61967        *ISBN* 0870705644

**Vallier, Dora.**                                                • **1.6147**
[Henri Rousseau. English] Henri Rousseau. New York, H. N. Abrams [1964] 327 p. illus. (part mounted, part col.) facsims., music, ports. 31 cm. 1. Rousseau, Henri Julien Félix, 1844-1910. I. T.
ND553.R67 V33        759.4        *LC* 62-16467

**Courthion, Pierre.**                                            • **1.6148**
Georges Seurat. Text by Pierre Courthion. [Translated by Norbert Guterman. 1st ed.] New York, H. N. Abrams [1968] 160 p. illus. (part col.) 33 cm. (The Library of great painters) 1. Seurat, Georges, 1859-1891. I. T.
ND553.S5 C643        759.4        *LC* 68-13066

**Seurat, Georges, 1859-1891.**                                  • **1.6149**
Seurat. With an essay by Roger Fry and a foreword & notes by Sir Anthony Blunt. [London] Phaidon Publishers; distributed by New York Graphic Society Publishers, Greenwich, Conn. [1965] 86 p. illus., 50 col. plates. 31 cm. 1. Seurat, Georges, 1859-1891. I. Fry, Roger Eliot, 1866-1934. II. T.
ND553.S5F7        *LC* 65-6826

**New York. Museum of Modern Art.**                              • **1.6150**
Yves Tanguy; [exhibition and catalogue] by James Thrall Soby. — New York, [1955] 71 p.: illus., plates (part col.) ports.; 25 cm. 1. Tanguy, Yves, 1900-1955. I. Soby, James Thrall, 1906- II. T.
ND553.T26 N4        759.4        *LC* 55-11796

**Wentworth, Michael.**                                           **1.6151**
James Tissot / Michael Wentworth. — Oxford [Oxfordshire]: Clarendon Press; New York: Oxford University Press, 1984. xxii, 227 p., [150] p. of plates: 210 ill. (some col.); 26 cm. — (Oxford studies in the history of art and architecture.) Includes indexes. 1. Tissot, James Jacques Joseph, 1836-1902. I. T. II. Series.
ND553.T6 A4 1984        759.4 19        *LC* 83-12196        *ISBN* 0198173644

**Toulouse-Lautrec, Henri de, 1864-1901.**                       • **1.6152**
[Toulouse-Lautrec. English] Toulouse–Lautrec, by F. Novotny. [Translated from the German by Michael Glenney. New York] Phaidon; [Distributors in the U.S.: Praeger, 1969] 198,[2] p. illus. (part col.) 32 cm. 1. Toulouse-Lautrec, Henri de, 1864-1901. I. Novotny, Fritz, 1902- II. T.
ND553.T7 N613        760/.0924        *LC* 69-19808        *ISBN* 0714813869

**Warnod, Jeanine.**                                              **1.6153**
Suzanne Valadon / by Jeanine Warnod. — 1st ed. — New York: Crown, c1981. 96 p.: ill. (some col.); 28 cm. 1. Valadon, Suzanne, 1865-1938. 2. Painters — France — Biography. I. T.
ND553.V3 W3 1981        759.4 B 19        *LC* 81-5412        *ISBN* 0517544997

**Vasarely, Victor, 1908-.**                                     **1.6154**
Vasarely [by] Werner Spies. [Translated from the German by Leonard Mins]. — New York: H. N. Abrams, 1971. 76 p.: illus., plates (part col.); 21 x 23 cm. — (Modern artists) I. Spies, Werner, fl. 1965- II. T.
ND553.V35 S613 1969        759.4        *LC* 69-12796        *ISBN* 0810902443

**Baillio, Joseph.**                                              **1.6155**
Elisabeth Louise Vigée Le Brun, 1755–1842 / by Joseph Baillio; with a preface by David M. Robb, Jr. — Fort Worth: Kimbell Art Museum, 1982. 143 p.: ill. (some col.); 28 cm. Catalogue of an exhibition held at the Kimbell Art Museum, Fort Worth, June 5-Aug. 8, 1982. 1. Vigée-Lebrun, Louise-Elisabeth, 1755-1842 — Exhibitions. I. Vigée-Lebrun, Louise-Elisabeth, 1755-1842. II. Kimbell Art Museum. III. T.
ND553.V5x        759.4 19        *LC* 82-81554        *ISBN* 0912804068

**Russell, John, 1919- comp.**                                   **1.6156**
Vuillard. — Greenwich, Conn.: New York Graphic Society, [1971] 238 p.: illus., plates (part col.); 25 cm. 1. Vuillard, Edouard, 1868-1940. I. T.
ND553.V9 R87        759.4        *LC* 71-159807        *ISBN* 0821202812

**Posner, Donald.**                                               **1.6157**
Antoine Watteau / Donald Posner. — Ithaca, N.Y.: Cornell University Press, 1984. 300 p.: ill. (some col.); 30 cm. Includes index. 1. Watteau, Antoine, 1684-1721. 2. Painters — France — Biography. 3. Genre painting — 18th century — France. I. T.
ND553.W3 P66 1984b        759.4 B 19        *LC* 83-45154        *ISBN* 0801415713

## ND561–588 GERMANY

**Landolt, Hanspeter.**                                           • **1.6158**
[Deutsche Malerei: das Spätmittelalter (1350-1500) English] German painting; the late Middle Ages (1350-1500). Translated by Heinz Norden. [Geneva] Skira [1968] 167 p. 89 illus. (72 col.) 35 cm. (Painting, color, history) 'Distributed in the United States by the World Publishing Company ... Cleveland.' Translation of Die deutsche Malerei: das Spätmittelalter (1350-1500). 1. Painting, German — History. 2. Painting, Medieval — Germany. I. T.
ND563.L313        759.3        *LC* 68-54210

**Benesch, Otto, 1896-1964.** • 1.6159
German painting, from Dürer to Holbein. Text by Otto Benesch [translated from the German by H. S. B. Harrison. Geneva] Skira; [distributed in the U.S. by the World Pub. Co., Cleveland, 1966] 197 p. mounted col. illus. 35 cm. (Painting, color, history) 1. Painting, German — History. 2. Painting, Renaissance — Germany. I. T.
ND565.B413  759.3  *LC* 66-22489

**Andrews, Keith.** • 1.6160
The Nazarenes; a brotherhood of German painters in Rome. Oxford, Clarendon Press, 1964. xvii, 148 p. 81 plates (part col.) 1. Nazarenes (German painters) I. T.
ND567 A5  *LC* 64-6050

**Champa, Kermit Swiler.** 1.6161
German painting of the 19th century. Introd. and catalogue by Kermit S. Champa with Kate H. Champa. New Haven, Conn., Yale University Art Gallery [1970] 239 p. illus. (part col.) 26 cm. Exhibition: Yale University Art Gallery, Oct. 15-Nov. 22, 1970; The Cleveland Museum of Art, Dec. 9, 1970-Jan. 24, 1971; The Art Institute of Chicago, Feb. 27-Mar. 28, 1971. 1. Painting, German — Exhibitions. 2. Painting — 19th century — Germany I. Champa, Kate H. II. Yale University. Art Gallery. III. Cleveland Museum of Art. IV. Art Institute of Chicago. V. T.
ND567.C45  759.3/074/013  *LC* 78-137506

**Finke, Ulrich.** 1.6162
German painting from romanticism to expressionism / Ulrich Finke. — Boulder, Colo.: Westview Press, 1975, c1974. 256 p.: ill. (some col.); 25 cm. Includes index. 1. Painting, German 2. Painting, Modern — 19th century — Germany 3. Painting, Modern — 20th century — Germany. I. T.
ND567.F56 1975  759.3  *LC* 75-19426  *ISBN* 0891585036

**Vaughan, William, 1943 Mar. 7-.** 1.6163
German romantic painting / William Vaughan. — New Haven, Conn.: Yale University Press, [1980] p. cm. Includes index. 1. Romanticism in art — Germany. 2. Painting, German 3. Painting, Modern — 19th century — Germany I. T.
ND567.5.R6 V38 1980  759.3  *LC* 80-13170  *ISBN* 0300023871

**Selz, Peter Howard, 1919-.** • 1.6164
German expressionist painting. Berkeley, University of California Press, 1957. xx, 379 p. 37 illus., 180 plates (part col.) 29 cm. 1. Expressionism (Art) — Germany. 2. Painting, Modern — 20th century — Germany. 3. Painting, German I. T.
ND568.5.E9 S45  759.915  *LC* 57-10501

## ND588 Painters, A–Z

**Lackner, Stephan.** 1.6165
Max Beckmann / text by Stephan Lackner. — New York: H. N. Abrams, 1977. 175 p.: ill. (some col.); 34 cm. — (The Library of great painters) Includes index. 1. Beckmann, Max, 1884-1950. 2. Painters — Germany, West — Biography. I. T.
ND588.B37 L297   ND588B37 L297.   759.3   *LC* 74-22446
*ISBN* 0810902699

**Selz, Peter Howard, 1919-.** 1.6166
Max Beckmann. With contributions by Harold Joachim and Perry T. Rathbone. — New York: Museum of Modern Art, Distributed by Doubleday, Garden City, N.Y., [1964] 160 p.: illus. (part col.); 24 cm. 'Catalogue of the exhibition, prepared by Alicia Legg': p. 150-154. 1. Beckmann, Max, 1884-1950. I. T.
ND588.B37 S4   759.3   *LC* 64-18334

**Schade, Werner.** 1.6167
[Malerfamilie Cranach. English] Cranach, a family of master painters / Werner Schade; translated by Helen Sebba. — 1st American ed. — New York: Putnam, 1980. 476 p.: ill. (some col.); 31 cm. Translation of Die Malerfamilie Cranach. Includes reproductions of works chiefly by Lucas Cranach, Lucas Cranach the Younger, and Hans Cranach. Includes index. 1. Cranach family I. Cranach, Lucas, 1472-1553. II. Cranach, Lucas, 1515-1586. III. Cranach, Hans, d. 1537. IV. T.
ND588.C78 S3313 1980   759.3 B 19   *LC* 76-17503   *ISBN* 0399118314

**Friedländer, Max J., 1867-1958.** 1.6168
[Gemälde von Lucas Cranach. English] The paintings of Lucas Cranach / Max J. Friedländer & Jakob Rosenberg; [catalogue translated by Heinz Norden; introd. translated by Ronald Taylor]. — Rev. ed. — Ithaca, N.Y.: Cornell University Press, c1978. 202 p., [180] leaves of plates: ill.; 29 cm. Translation of Die Gemälde von Lucas Cranach. Includes indexes. 1. Cranach, Lucas, 1472-1553 — Catalogs. I. Rosenberg, Jakob, 1893- joint author. II. Cranach, Lucas, 1472-1553. III. T.
ND588.C8 A4 1978   759.3   *LC* 77-18410   *ISBN* 0801410164

**Panofsky, Erwin, 1892-1968.** • 1.6169
The life and art of Albrecht Dürer. [4th ed.] Princeton, N.J., Princeton University Press, 1955. xxxii, 317 p. ill. 1. Dürer, Albrecht, 1471-1528. I. T.
ND588 D9 P28 1955   *LC* 55-6248

**Vaughan, William, 1943 Mar. 7-.** 1.6170
Caspar David Friedrich, 1774-1840: romantic landscape painting in Dresden: [catalogue of an exhibition held at the Tate Gallery, London, 6 September–16 October, 1972, by] William Vaughan, Helmut Börsch–Supan [and] Hans Joachim Neidhardt. London, Tate Gallery, 1972. 112 p. illus. (some col.), facsims., port. 29 cm. 1. Friedrich, Caspar David, 1774-1840 — Exhibitions. I. Friedrich, Caspar David, 1774-1840. II. Börsch-Supan, Helmut. III. Neidhardt, Hans Joachim. IV. Tate Gallery. V. T.
ND588.F75 A4 1972   759.3   *LC* 73-156250   *ISBN* 090087435X
*ISBN* 0900874368

**Börsch-Supan, Helmut.** 1.6171
[Caspar David Friedrich. English] Caspar David Friedrich / Helmut Börsch-Supan; [translated from the German by Sarah Twohig]. — New York: G. Braziller, 1974. 184 p.: ill. (some col.); 30 cm. Includes index. 1. Friedrich, Caspar David, 1774-1840. I. Friedrich, Caspar David, 1774-1840. II. T.
ND588.F75 B6213   759.3   *LC* 73-93687   *ISBN* 0807607479

**Grünewald, Matthias, 16th cent.** 1.6172
[Grünewald, Zeichnungen. English] Grünewald: drawings; complete edition by Eberhard Ruhmer [translated from the German Mss. by Anna Rose Cooper] London, Phaidon, 1970. 100 p. illus. 31 cm. Translation of Grünewald, Zeichnungen. I. Ruhmer, Eberhard. II. T.
ND588.G7 R783   741.943   *LC* 69-12791   *ISBN* 0714813729

**Grünewald, Matthias, 16th cent.** • 1.6173
Paintings. Complete ed. With two essays by J.–K. Huysmans and a catalogue by E. Ruhmer. London Phaidon Press [1958] 128p. I. T.
ND588 G7 R83

**Scheja, Georg.** 1.6174
[Isenheimer Altar des Matthias Grünewald. English] The Isenheim Altarpiece. Photos. by Bert Koch. [Translated from German by Robert Erich Wolf] New York, H. N. Abrams [c1969] 80 p. plates (part col.) 30 cm. Translation of Der Isenheimer Altar des Matthias Grünewald. 1. Grünewald, Matthias, 16th cent. Isenheim Altar. I. T.
ND588.G7 S3713   759.3   *LC* 71-125784   *ISBN* 0810901900

**Rowlands, John, 1931-.** 1.6175
Holbein: the paintings of Hans Holbein the younger / John Rowlands. — Complete ed. — Boston: D.R. Godine, c1985. 288 p.: ill. (some col.) 1. Holbein, Hans, 1497-1543. 2. Painters — Germany I. T.
ND588.H7 R68   *LC* 85-70147   *ISBN* 0879235780

**Klee, Paul, 1879-1940.** 1.6176
Notebooks / edited by Jürg Spiller. New York: G. Wittenborn, [1969-73] 2 v. illus. (part col.) 23 cm. (Documents of modern art; 15, 17) 1. Art — Addresses, essays, lectures. I. Spiller, Jürg, ed. II. T. III. Title: The thinking eye. IV. Title: The nature of nature. V. Series.
ND588.K5 Ax   *ISBN* 0815000405

**Grohmann, Will, 1887-1968.** 1.6177
Paul Klee / text by Will Grohmann; [translated by Norbert Gutermann]. — New York: H.N. Abrams, [1967]. 167 p.: ill. (some col.), facsim., ports.; 33 cm. — (The Library of great painters) 1. Klee, Paul, 1879-1940. I. T.
ND588.K5 G763   759.9/494   *LC* 67-14056   *ISBN* 0810902281

## ND611–623 ITALY

**Berenson, Bernard, 1865-1959.** • 1.6178
The study and criticism of Italian art / by Bernhard Berenson. First series. London: Bell, 1920. xiv, 152 p., [43] leaves of plates: ill.; 23 cm. 'First published 1901. 1. Art, Italian I. T.
ND611.B39 1920

**Marle, Raimond van, 1888-1936.** 1.6179
The development of the Italian schools of painting. — New York: Hacker Art Books, 1970. 19 v.: illus.; 25 cm. Reprint of the 1923-38 ed. 1. Painting, Italian — History. I. T.
ND611.M272   759.5   *LC* 70-116366

**Baxandall, Michael.** 1.6180
Painting and experience in fifteenth century Italy; a primer in the social history of pictorial style. — Oxford: Clarendon Press, 1972. viii, 165 p.: illus. (part col.); 21 cm. 1. Painting, Renaissance — Italy 2. Painting, Italian — History. 3. Painting — Psychological aspects. 4. Italy — History — 15th century — Pictorial works I. T.
ND615.B32   759.5   *LC* 73-156125   *ISBN* 0198173210

**Freedberg, S. J. (Sydney Joseph), 1914-.**                • **1.6181**
Painting in Italy, 1500 to 1600 [by] S. J. Freedberg. [Harmondsworth, Middlesex, Baltimore] Penguin Books [1971, c1970] xix, 554 p. 300 illus., col. plate. 27 cm. (Pelican history of art.) 1. Painting, Italian 2. Painting, Renaissance — Italy 3. Mannerism (Art) — Italy. I. T. II. Series.
ND615.F66 1971      759.5      LC 78-27513      ISBN 0140560351

**Freedberg, S. J. (Sydney Joseph), 1914-.**                • **1.6182**
Painting of the high Renaissance in Rome and Florence. — Cambridge, Harvard University Press, 1961. 2 v. plates. 27 cm. Vol. 2: Plates. Bibliographies: v. 1, p. 581-609. 1. Painting — Rome (City) — Hist. 2. Painting, Florentine — Hist. 3. Paintings, Italian. I. T.
ND615.F67      759.5      LC 61-7390

**Friedlaender, Walter F., 1873-1966.**                • **1.6183**
Mannerism and anti–mannerism in Italian painting, two essays. — New York, Columbia University Press, 1957. xiv, 89 p. plates. 24 cm. 'Presented to Walter Friedlaender on the occasion of his eightieth birthday, March 10, 1953, by his friends and former students, with the support of the Warburg Institute, London and the Alumni Association of the Institute of Fine Arts of New York University.' '[Previously] appeared in Repertorium für Kunstwissenschaft, vol. XLVII, 1925, and in Vorträge der Bibliothek, Warburg, XIII, 1929 ... presented here in translations.' 1. Paintings, Italian. 2. Painting — Italy — Hist. 3. Mannerism (Art) I. T.
ND615.F7      759.5      LC 57-8295

**Mahon, Denis.**                • **1.6184**
Studies in seicento art and theory / Denis Mahon. — London: Warburg Institute, University of London, 1947. — ix, 351 p.: ill.; 26 cm. — (Studies of the Warburg Institute. v. 16) 1. Painting, Italian — History. 2. Painting, Modern — 17th-18th centuries — Italy. I. T. II. Series.
ND616.M34 1971      759.5      LC 51-32832

**Waterhouse, Ellis Kirkham, 1905-.**                • **1.6185**
Italian baroque painting, by Ellis Waterhouse. — 2nd ed. — London, Phaidon, 1969. 237 p. 198 illus. 26 cm. — (Phaidon paperback, PH61) Distributed in the U.S.A. by F. A. Praeger, New York. Bibliography: p. 228-229. 1. Painting, Italian 2. Painting, Baroque — Italy. I. T.
ND616.W38 1969      759.5      LC 69-12793      ISBN 714813672

**Taylor, Joshua Charles, 1917-.**                **1.6186**
Futurism. New York, Museum of Modern Art; distributed by Doubleday, Garden City [1961] 153p. 'Biographies and catalogue of the exhibition [May 31-Sept. 5, 1961]': p. 141-[148] 1. Futurism (Art) 2. Painting, Italian — Exhibitions. I. T.
ND618.5 F8 T35      LC 61-11271

**Fremantle, Richard.**                **1.6187**
Florentine Gothic painters from Giotto to Masaccio: a guide to painting in and near Florence, 1300 to 1450 / by Richard Fremantle. — London: Secker & Warburg, 1975. xxv, 665 p.: chiefly ill. (1 col.); 32 cm. 1. Painting, Gothic — Italy — Florence. 2. Painting, Italian — Italy — Florence. I. T.
ND621.F7 F73 1975      759.5/51 B      LC 76-355074      ISBN 043616468X

**Meiss, Millard.**                • **1.6188**
Painting in Florence and Siena after the Black Death. Princeton, Princeton University Press, 1951. xiv, 194 p. 169 illus. 31 cm. 1. Painting, Italian — Italy — Florence. 2. Painting, Italian — Italy — Siena. 3. Paintings, Florentine. 4. Paintings, Sienese. 5. Painting, Renaissance I. T.
ND621.F7 M4      750.945      LC 51-14790

**Levey, Michael.**                **1.6189**
Painting in eighteenth–century Venice / Michael Levey. — Rev. ed., 2d ed. — Ithaca, N.Y.: Cornell University Press, 1980. 256 p.: ill (some col.); 25 cm. 'A Phaidon book.' Includes index. 1. Painting, Italian — Italy — Venice. 2. Painting, Rococo — Italy — Venice. I. T.
ND621.V5 L4 1980      759.5/31 19      LC 80-549      ISBN 0801413311

## ND623 Painters, A–Z

### ND623.A–.B

**Kennedy, Ruth Wedgwood.**                **1.6190**
Alesso Baldovinetti: a critical & historical study / by Ruth Wedgwood Kennedy. — New Haven: Yale University Press, 1938. 253 leaves: ill.; 30 cm. 1. Baldovinetti, Alesso, ca. 1425-1499. I. Baldovinetti, Alesso, ca. 1425-1499. II. T.
ND623.B18 K4

**Lightbown, R. W.**                **1.6191**
Sandro Botticelli / Ronald Lightbown. — Berkeley: University of California Press, c1978. 2 v.: ill. (some col.); 29 cm. On spine: Botticelli. 1. Botticelli,

Sandro, 1444 or 5-1510. 2. Painters — Italy — Biography. I. Botticelli, Sandro, 1444 or 5-1510. II. T.
ND623.B7 L53 1978b      759.5 B      LC 76-46237      ISBN 0520033728

**Seymour, Charles, 1912- comp.**                **1.6192**
Michelangelo, the Sistine Chapel ceiling: illustrations, introductory essays, backgrounds and sources, critical essays. [1st ed.] New York, Norton [1972] xxi, 243 p. illus. 21 cm. (A Norton critical study in art history) 1. Michelangelo Buonarroti, 1475-1564. 2. Vatican Palace (Vatican City). Sistine Chapel I. T.
ND623.B92 S42      759.5      LC 74-90982      ISBN 0393043193 ISBN 0393098893

**Seymour, Charles, 1912-.**                **1.6193**
Michelangelo's David; a search for identity. [Pittsburgh] University of Pittsburgh Press [1967] xxi, 194 p. illus. 21 cm. (A. W. Mellon studies in the humanities) 1. Michelangelo Buonarroti, 1475-1564. David. I. T. II. Series.
ND623.B92 S43      730/.924      LC 67-22277

### ND623.C

**Constable, W. G. (William George), 1887-.**                **1.6194**
Canaletto: Giovanni Antonio Canal 1697–1768 / by W. G. Constable. — 2d ed. / rev. by J. G. Links. — Oxford [Eng.]; New York: Clarendon Press, 1976. 2 v. (x, 723 p., [117] leaves of plates): ill.; 26 cm. Vol. 2: Catalogue raisonné. Includes indexes. 1. Canaletto, 1697-1768. I. Links, J. G. II. T.
ND623.C2 C6 1976      759.5      LC 77-359771      ISBN 0198173245

**Links, J. G.**                **1.6195**
Canaletto / J.G. Links. — Ithaca, N.Y.: Cornell University Press, 1982. 239 p.: ill. (some col.); 32 cm. 'Cornell/Phaidon books.' Includes index. 1. Canaletto, 1697-1768. 2. Painters — Italy — Biography. I. Canaletto, 1697-1768. II. T.
ND623.C2 L49 1982      759.5 B 19      LC 82-70752      ISBN 0801415322

**Friedlaender, Walter F., 1873-1966.**                • **1.6196**
Caravaggio studies. — New York: Schocken Books, [1969, c1955] xxviii, 320 p.: illus., plates, port.; 24 cm. 1. Caravaggio, Michelangelo Merisi da, 1573-1610. I. T.
ND623.C26 F7 1969      759.5 B      LC 72-86848

**Hibbard, Howard, 1928-.**                **1.6197**
Caravaggio / Howard Hibbard. — 1st ed. — New York: Harper & Row, c1983. xii, 404 p.: ill.; 26 cm. — (Icon editions) Includes index. 1. Caravaggio, Michelangelo Merisi da, 1573-1610. I. T.
ND623.C26 H44 1983      759.5 19      LC 78-2145      ISBN 0064333221

**Horster, Marita.**                **1.6198**
Andrea del Castagno: complete edition with a critical catalogue / Marita Horster. — Ithaca, N.Y.: Cornell University Press, 1980. 224 p., [2] leaves of plates: ill. (some col.); 29 cm. 'A Phaidon book.' Includes indexes. 1. Castagno, Andrea del, 1423-1457. 2. Painters — Italy — Biography. I. T.
ND623.C47 H67      759.5 B 19      LC 79-6028      ISBN 0801413168

**Soby, James Thrall, 1906-.**                • **1.6199**
Giorgio de Chirico. New York, Museum of Modern Art [1955] 267 p. illus. (part mounted col.) ports. 25 cm. A revision of The early Chirico, published in 1941. 1. De Chirico, Giorgio, 1888- I. T.
ND623.C56 S6 1955      LC 55-5422

**Stubblebine, James H.**                **1.6200**
Duccio di Buoninsegna and his school / James H. Stubblebine. — Princeton, N.J.: Princeton University Press, 1980 ,c1979. 2 v.: ill.; 29 cm. Includes index. 1. Duccio, di Buoninsegna, d. 1319. 2. Painting, Gothic — Italy. I. T.
ND623.D8 S84      759.5      LC 78-22016      ISBN 0691039445

**White, John, 1924 Mar. 5-.**                **1.6201**
Duccio: Tuscan art and the medieval workshop / John White. — [New York, N.Y.]: Thames and Hudson, c1979. 280 p., [2] leaves of plates: ill. (some col.); 26 cm. Includes index. 1. Duccio, di Buoninsegna, d. 1319. 2. Duccio, di Buoninsegna, d. 1319 — Influence. 3. Artists' studios — Tuscany. I. T.
ND623.D8 W46      759.5      LC 79-63880      ISBN 0500091358

### ND623.F

**Angelico, fra, ca. 1400-1455.**                • **1.6202**
Fra Angelico / John Pope–Hennessy. — 2d ed. — Ithaca, N.Y.: Cornell University Press, 1974. vi, 242 p., [32] leaves of plates: ill. (some col.); 32 cm. 'Catalogue': p. 189-239. Includes index. 1. Angelico, fra, ca. 1400-1455. I. Pope-Hennessy, John Wyndham, Sir, 1913- II. T.
ND623.F5 P65 1974      759.5      LC 74-9200      ISBN 0801408555

**Clark, Kenneth McKenzie, Sir, 1903-.**    • **1.6203**
Piero della Francesca, complete edition [by] Kenneth Clark. [2nd. ed., revised.] London, New York, Phaidon [1969.] 239 p. illus. (part col.), plates (part col.), ports. (part col.) 31 cm. 1. Francesca, Piero della, 1416?-1492. I. T.
ND623.F78 C6 1969     759.5     *LC* 69-19805

**McKillop, Susan Regan.**     **1.6204**
Franciabigio / Susan Regan McKillop. — Berkeley: University of California Press, c1974. xvii, 322 p., [38] leaves of plates: ill.; 32 cm. (California studies in the history of art. 16) Includes indexes. 1. Franciabigio, 1484-1525. I. T. II. Series.
ND623.F783 M32     ND623 F783 M32.     *LC* 76-107661    *ISBN* 0520016882

## ND623.G

**Christiansen, Keith.**     **1.6205**
Gentile da Fabriano / Keith Christiansen. — Ithaca, N.Y.: Cornell University Press, 1982. ix, 193 p., [98] p. of plates: ill. (some col.); 27 cm. Includes index. 1. Gentile, da Fabriano, ca. 1370-1427. 2. Painters — Italy — Biography. I. Gentile, da Fabriano, ca. 1370-1427. II. T.
ND623.G35 C45 1982     759.5 B 19     *LC* 80-70584    *ISBN* 0801413605

**Giorgione, 1477-1511.**    • **1.6206**
All the paintings of Giorgione. Text by Luigi Coletti. Translated by Paul Colacicchi. New York, Hawthorn Books [1962, c1961] 80 p. 124 plates (part col.) 19 cm. (The Complete library of world art, v. 3) I. Coletti, Luigi, 1886- II. T.
ND623.G5 C573     759.5     *LC* 62-10517

**Pignatti, Terisio, 1920-.**    • **1.6207**
[Giorgione. English] Giorgione. Complete ed. [New York] Phaidon; [distributors in the U.S.: Praeger Publishers, 1971] 369 p. illus., col. plates. 29 cm. 1. Giorgione, 1477-1511. I. T.
ND623.G5 P543     759.5     *LC* 70-118659    *ISBN* 0714814571

**Battisti, Eugenio.**    • **1.6208**
Giotto, biographical and critical study. Translated from the Italian by James Emmons. [Lausanne] Skira; Cleveland [distributed in the U. S. by World Pub. Co., 1960. 146 p. mounted col. illus. 19 cm. (The Taste of our time, v. 32.) 1. Giotto, 1266?-1337. I. T.
ND623.G6B33     *LC* 60-8730

**Schneider, Laurie, comp.**    • **1.6209**
Giotto in perspective. Englewood Cliffs, N.J., Prentice-Hall [1974] xii, 172 p. illus. 21 cm. (The Artists in perspective series) (A Spectrum book) 1. Giotto, 1266?-1337. I. T.
ND623.G6 S37 1974     759.5     *LC* 74-8016    *ISBN* 0133567176 *ISBN* 0133567095

**Stubblebine, James H. comp.**    **1.6210**
Giotto: the Arena Chapel frescoes. Edited by James H. Stubblebine. [1st ed.] New York, Norton [1969] xiii, 218 p. 129 illus. 22 cm. (Norton critical studies in art history) Includes an introductory essay, backgrounds and sources, and criticism. 1. Giotto, 1266?-1337. 2. Padua (Italy) Madonna dell'Arena (Chapel) I. T.
ND623.G6 S7     759.5     *LC* 67-17689

**Hartt, Frederick.**    • **1.6211**
Giulio Romano. New Haven, Yale University Press, 1958. 2 v. plates, plans. 29 cm. Bibliography: v. 1, p. 331-[339] 1. Romano, Giulio, 1499-1546. I. T.
ND623.G65H3     N6923.R65 H3 1958.     927     *LC* 58-5460

## ND623.L5 Leonardo

**Leonardo, da Vinci, 1452-1519.**    • **1.6212**
[Literary works of Leonardo da Vinci] The notebooks of Leonardo da Vinci. Compiled and edited from the original manuscripts by Jean Paul Richter. New York, Dover Publications [1970] 2 v. illus., facsims., maps, plans, ports. 28 cm. Text in English and Italian, with introductory material and notes in English. English translations mainly by Mrs. R. C. Bell. 'An unabridged edition of the work first published ... in 1883 ... with the title The literary works of Leonardo da Vinci.' I. Richter, Jean Paul, 1847-1937, ed. II. Bell, R. C., Mrs., tr. III. T.
ND623.L5 A15 1970b     709     *LC* 72-104981    *ISBN* 0486225720

**Clark, Kenneth McKenzie, Saron Clark, 1903-.**    • **1.6213**
Leonardo da Vinci, an account of his development as an artist. — [Rev. ed.]. — Baltimore, Penguin Books [1959] 181 p. plates. 19 cm. — (A Pelican book, A430) Bibliography: p. 165-168. 1. Leonardo, da Vinci, 1452-1519.
ND623.L5C5 1959     759.5     *LC* 59-1638

**Heydenreich, Ludwig Heinrich, 1903-.**    • **1.6214**
Leonardo da Vinci / by Ludwig H. Heydenreich. — New York: Macmillan, 1954. 2 v.: ill. 1. Leonardo, da Vinci, 1452-1519. I. T.
ND623.L5 H445     *LC* 55-3122

**Mantegna, Andrea, 1431-1506.**    **1.6215**
Mantegna: paintings, drawings, engravings / complete ed. by E. Tietze–Conrat. — London: Phaidon, 1955. 258 p., 182 leaves of plates: ill. 1. Mantegna, Andrea, 1431-1506. I. Tietze-Conrat, Erika, 1883- II. T.
ND623.M3 T5     *LC* a 55-8663

**Masaccio, 1401-1428?**    • **1.6216**
[Tutta la pittura di masaccio. English] All the paintings of Masaccio. Text by Ugo Procacci. Translated by Paul Colacicchi. [London] Oldbourne [1969?] 50 p. plates. 18 cm. (The Complete library of world art, v. 6) I. Procacci, Ugo. II. T. III. Series.
ND623.M43 P763 1969     759.5     *LC* 76-409062

**Masolino, 1383-1447?**    • **1.6217**
Masolino a Castighione Olona; testo di Pietro Toesca. Milano, Hoepli [1946] [xiii] p. 1 col. illus., 28 col. pl. (Collezione Silvana) At head of title: Affreschi Italiani. I. Toesca, Pietro, 1877-1962.
ND623.M45T59

**Freedberg, S. J. (Sydney Joseph), 1914-.**    • **1.6218**
Parmigianino: his works in painting [by] Sydney J. Freedberg. Westport, Conn., Greenwood Press [1971, c1950] xx, 265 p. 167 plates. 26 cm. 1. Parmigianino, 1503-1540.
ND623.M55 F68 1971     759.5     *LC* 72-95120    *ISBN* 0837137179

### *ND623.M Michelangelo: see under Buonarroti*

### *ND623.P–.R*

**Fischel, Oskar, 1870-1939.**    • **1.6219**
Raphael / tr. from the German by Bernard Rackham. — London: K. Paul, [1948] — 2 v., 302 plates: ill.; 26 cm. Errata slip inserted in v. 2. 1. Raphael, 1483-1520. I. T.
ND623.R28F55     759.5     *LC* 49-1082

**Ribera, José de, 1588?-1652.**    **1.6220**
Jusepe de Ribera, lo Spagnoletto, 1591–1652 / edited by Craig Felton and William B. Jordan. — Fort Worth: Kimbell Art Museum; Seattle: Distributed by Washington University Press, 1983 (c1982). 241 p.: ill. (some col.); 28 cm. 'Published on the occasion of an exhibition at the Kimbell Art Museum, Fort Worth, December 4, 1982-February 6, 1983'–Verso t.p. 1. Ribera, José de, 1588?-1652 — Exhibitions. I. Felton, Craig. II. Jordan, William B., 1940- III. Kimbell Art Museum. IV. T.
ND623.R618 A4     759.5 19     *LC* 82-84144    *ISBN* 0912804106

### *ND623.S–.Z*

**Freedberg, S. J. (Sydney Joseph), 1914-.**    • **1.6221**
Andrea del Sarto. — Cambridge, Mass., Belknap Press of Harvard University Press, 1963. 2 v. illus. 29 cm. 'Biographical documents and commentary': v. 2, p. 265-278. Bibliography: v. 1, p. 101; v. 2, p. 281-287. 1. Sarto, Andrea del, 1486-1530.
ND623.S2F73     759.5     *LC* 63-17198

**Shearman, John K. G.**    • **1.6222**
Andrea del Sarto / John Shearman. Oxford: Clarendon Press, 1965. 2 v. (xi, 466 p.) : ill. 29 cm. Includes bibliographies. 1. Sarto, Andrea del, 1486-1530. I. T.
ND623.S2S5     *LC* 65-22669

**Pope-Hennessy, John, 1913-.**    • **1.6223**
Sassetta. London, Chatto, 1939. xiii, 239 p. pl. 1. Sassetta, Stefano di Giovanni, known as, 1392-1450
ND623.S3P6

**Morassi, Antonio, 1892-.**    • **1.6224**
A complete catalogue of the paintings of G.B. Tiepolo, including pictures by his pupils and followers wrongly attributed to him. London, Phaidon Press [1962] x, 239 p. 429 illus. 31 cm. 1. Tiepolo, Giovanni Battista, 1696-1770. I. T.
ND623.T5 M77     *LC* 63-2694

**Tintoretto, 1512-1594.**    • **1.6225**
Tintoretto: the paintings and drawings / by Hans Tietze; with 300 illustrations. — London: Phaidon Press: distributed by Oxford Univ. Press, New York, 1948. 383 p.: ill. (some mounted col., some fold.); 27 cm. 1. Tintoretto, 1512-1594. I. Tietze, Hans, 1880-1954. II. T.
ND623.T6 T5     *LC* 49-26856

**Rosand, David.**    **1.6226**
Titian / text by David Rosand. — New York: Abrams, [1978] 158 p.: ill. (some col.); 33 cm. (Library of great painters) Includes index. 1. Titian, ca. 1488-1576. I. T.
ND623.T7 R595    759.5    *LC* 77-11042    *ISBN* 0810916541

**Wethey, Harold E. (Harold Edwin), 1902-1984.**    **1.6227**
The paintings of Titian: v. II; the portraits. — London: Phaidon, 1972, [c1971] 426 p. 1. Titian, ca. 1488-1576. I. T.
ND623.T7 W4    759.5    *LC* 73-81197    *ISBN* 0714814245

**Uccello, Paolo di Dono, known as, 1396 or 7-1475.**    • **1.6228**
The complete work of Paolo Uccello, by John Pope–Hennessy. — London, Phaidon; Distributed by Oxford University Press, New York [1950] 173 p. ill. (part col.); 31 cm. 'Catalogue': p. [141]-173. I. Pope-Hennessy, John Wyndham, 1913- II. T.
ND623.U4P56 1950

## ND625–653 NETHERLANDS

**Mander, Carel van, 1548-1606.**    **1.6229**
Dutch and Flemish painters; translation from the Schilderboeck, and introduction by Constant Van de Wall. New York, McFarlane, Warde, McFarlane, 1936. lxix, 560 p. 25 cm. 1. Painters — Netherlands. I. T. II. Title: Schilderboeck.
ND 625 M27 E5 1936    *LC* 36-25229

**Friedländer, Max J., 1867-1958.**    • **1.6230**
[Altniederländische Malerei. English] Early Netherlandish painting. Pref. by Erwin Panofsky. Comments and notes by Nicole Veronee–Verhaegen. Translation by Heinz Norden. New York, Praeger [1967-. v. illus. 28 cm. Translation of Die Altniederländische Malerei. 1. Painting, Dutch — History. 2. Painting, Dutch 3. Painters, Dutch. I. Veronee-Verhaegen, Nicole, ed. II. T.
ND635.F68132    759.92    *LC* 67-13538

**Friedländer, Max J., 1867-1958.**    • **1.6231**
[Von Eyck bis Bruegel. English] From Van Eyck to Bruegel. Edited and annotated by F. Grossmann. [Translated from the German by Marguerite Kay] [3d ed. London] Phaidon [1969] x, 409 p. illus. (part col.) 24 cm. Distributors in the U.S.: Frederick A. Praeger Inc., New York. Translation of Von Eyck bis Bruegel. 1. Painting, Flemish 2. Painters, Flemish. 3. Painting, Dutch 4. Painters — Netherlands. I. T.
ND635.F713 1969    759.9492    *LC* 69-19803    *ISBN* 0714813753

**Fromentin, Eugène, 1820-1876.**    **1.6232**
[Maîtres d'autrefois, Belgique-Hollande. English] The masters of past time: Dutch and Flemish painting from Van Eyck to Rembrandt / Eugène Fromentin; edited by H. Gerson; [translation by Andrew Boyle]. — Ithaca, N.Y.: Cornell University Press, 1981. xvi, 389 p.: ill.; 21 cm. — (Landmarks in art history.) (Cornell paperbacks) Translation of: Maîtres d'autrefois, Belgique-Hollande. Reprint. London: Phaidon Press, 1948. 'A Phaidon book.' 1. Painting, Flemish 2. Painting, Medieval — Belgium — Flanders. 3. Painting, Modern — Belgium — Flanders. 4. Painting, Dutch 5. Painting, Medieval — Netherlands. 6. Painting, Modern — Netherlands. I. Gerson, H. (Horst) II. Boyle, Andrew. III. T. IV. Series.
ND635.F7513 1981    759.9492 19    *LC* 80-69738    *ISBN* 080149219X

**Lane, Barbara G.**    **1.6233**
The altar and the altarpiece: sacramental themes in early Netherlandish painting / Barbara G. Lane. — 1st ed. — New York: Harper & Row, c1984. 180 p.: ill.; 25 cm. — (Icon editions) Includes index. 1. Altarpieces, Flemish 2. Altarpieces, Gothic — Belgium 3. Altarpieces, Dutch. 4. Altarpieces, Gothic — Netherlands. 5. Mass in art 6. Christian art and symbolism — Medieval, 500-1500 I. T.
ND635.L36 1984    755/.2/09492 19    *LC* 83-48364    *ISBN* 0064350002

**Panofsky, Erwin, 1892-1968.**    • **1.6234**
Early Netherlandish painting, its origins and character. Cambridge, Harvard University Press, 1953. 2 v. plates. 32 cm. 1. Painting — Netherlands — History. 2. Painting, Dutch I. T.
ND635.P35    759.9492    *LC* 52-5402

**Leymarie, Jean.**    • **1.6235**
Dutch painting. [Translated by Stuart Gilbert. — Geneva, New York] Skira [1956] 213 p. mounted col. illus. 34 cm. — (Painting, color, history) Bibliography: p. 201-204. 1. Painting — Netherlands — Hist. 2. Paintings, Dutch.
ND644.L42    759.9492    *LC* 56-9861

**Châtelet, Albert.**    **1.6236**
[Primitifs hollandais. English] Early Dutch painting: painting in the northern Netherlands in the fifteenth century / Albert Châtelet; translated by

Christopher Brown and Anthony Turner. — New York: Rizzoli, 1981. 264 p.: ill. (some col.); 31 cm. Translation of: Les primitifs hollandais. 'First published as Gérard de Saint Jean et la peinture dans les Pays-Bas du Nord au XVe siècle (3 vols.) by the Service de réproduction des thèses of the University of Lille III in 1979, as a private edition of 200 copies. The present book is an up-dated version of the original thesis, which was written in 1973'—p. 247. Includes index. 1. Painting, Dutch 2. Painting, Gothic — Netherlands. I. T.
ND645.C513    759.9492 19    *LC* 80-51169    *ISBN* 0847803694

**Alpers, Svetlana.**    **1.6237**
The art of describing: Dutch art in the seventeenth century / Svetlana Alpers. — Chicago: University of Chicago Press, 1983. xxvii, 273 p., [4] p. of plates: ill. (some col.); 27 cm. 1. Painting, Dutch 2. Painting, Modern — 17th-18th centuries — Netherlands 3. Visual perception I. T.
ND646.A72 1983    759.9492 19    *LC* 82-6969    *ISBN* 0226015122

**Haak, B.**    **1.6238**
The Golden Age: Dutch painters of the seventeenth century / Bob Haak; translated from the Dutch and edited by Elizabeth Willems–Treeman. — New York: H.N. Abrams, 1984. 536 p.: ill. (some col.); 35 cm. Includes index. 1. Painting, Dutch 2. Painting, Modern — 17th-18th centuries — Netherlands I. Willems-Treeman, Elizabeth. II. T.
ND646.H3 1984    759.9492 19    *LC* 83-25657    *ISBN* 0810909561

**The Hague School: Dutch masters of the 19th century / edited**    **1.6239**
**by Ronald de Leeuw, John Sillevis, Charles Dumas.**
London: Royal Academy of Arts, in association with Weidenfeld and Nicolson, 1983. 336 p.: ill. (some col.), 1 map, ports.; 31 cm. Exhibition catalogue. Includes index. 1. Painting, Dutch — Exhibitions. 2. Painting, Modern — 19th century — Netherlands — Exhibitions. I. Leeuw, Ronald de. II. Sillevis, John. III. Dumas, Charles, 1949- IV. Royal Academy of Arts (Great Britain)
ND647.H3x    759.9492/074 19    *ISBN* 0297780697

## ND653 Painters, A–Z

### ND653.A–.G

**Bax, Dirk.**    **1.6240**
[Ontcijfering van Jeroen Bosch. English] Hieronymus Bosch: his picture–writing deciphered / by D. Bax; translated by N. A. Bax–Botha. — Rotterdam: A. A. Balkema; Montclair, N.J.: distributed in North America by Abner Schram, 1979. xvi, 416 p.: ill.; 29 cm. Translation of Ontcijfering van Jeroen Bosch. Includes index. 1. Bosch, Hieronymus, d. 1516. I. T.
ND653.B65 B3813    759.9492    *LC* 79-337271    *ISBN* 906191020X

**De Tolnay, Charles, 1899-.**    • **1.6241**
[Hieronymus Bosch. English] Hieronymus Bosch. [New York] Reynal [1966, c1965] 451 p. illus. (part col.) 33 cm. 'Catalogue Raisonne': p. [331]-377. 1. Bosch, Hieronymus, d. 1516.
ND653.B65 D413 1966a    760/.0924    *LC* 66-23355

**Fraenger, Wilhelm, 1890-1964.**    **1.6242**
Hieronymus Bosch / Wilhelm Fraenger; translated by Helen Sebba. — 1st American ed. — New York: Putnam, 1983. 526 p., 157 p. of plates (2 folded): ill (some col.); 31 cm. Translation of: Hieronymus Bosch. 1. Bosch, Hieronymus, d. 1516. I. Bosch, Hieronymus, d. 1516. II. T.
ND653.B65 F71913 1983    *LC* 81-48072    *ISBN* 0399127135

**Gogh, Vincent van, 1853-1890.**    **1.6243**
The complete letters of Vincent van Gogh: with reproductions of all the drawings in the correspondence. — 2d ed. — Boston: New York Graphic Society, 1978. 3 v.: ill.; 25 cm. Includes index (v. 3) 1. Gogh, Vincent van, 1853-1890. 2. Painters — Netherlands — Correspondence. I. T.
ND653.G7 A3 1978    759.9492 B    *LC* 78-7073    *ISBN* 0821207350

**Hammacher, Abraham Marie, 1897-.**    **1.6244**
Van Gogh, a documentary biography / A.M. Hammacher, Renilde Hammacher. — 1st American ed. — New York: Macmillan, 1982. 240 p.: ill. (some col.); 31 cm. 1. Gogh, Vincent van, 1853-1890. 2. Painters — Netherlands — Biography. I. Hammacher-Van den Brande, Renilde. II. T.
ND653.G7 H255 1982    759.9492 B 19    *LC* 82-7224    *ISBN* 0025477102

**Krauss, André.**    **1.6245**
Vincent van Gogh: studies in the social aspects of his work / André Krauss. — Göteborg: Acta Universitatis Gothoburgensis, 1983. 205 p.: 58 ill.; 22 cm. — (Gothenburg studies in art and architecture. 0348-4114; 2) Includes index. 1. Gogh, Vincent van, 1853-1890. 2. Painting — Social aspect. I. T. II. Series.
ND653.G7 K73 1983    759.9492 19    *LC* 83-229149    *ISBN* 9173461180

**Meier-Graefe, Julius, 1867-1935.**    • **1.6246**
[Vincent van Gogh. English] Vincent van Gogh; a biographical study. Translated by John Holroyd–Reece. Westport, Conn., Greenwood Press [1970]

xvi, 239 p. 61 plates. 23 cm. Reprint of the 1933 ed. 1. Gogh, Vincent van, 1853-1890.
ND653.G7 M5 1970      759.9492      *LC* 76-109788      *ISBN* 0837142784

**Gogh, Vincent van, 1853-1890.**                    • **1.6247**
Vincent van Gogh. Text by Meyer Schapiro. [1st ed.] New York, H.N. Abrams, 1950. 130 p. ill., col. plates. (The Library of great painters) I. Schapiro, Meyer, 1904-
ND653 G7 S38      *LC* 50-12714

## *ND653.H–.Z*

**Slive, Seymour, 1920-.**                    • **1.6248**
Frans Hals. London, Phaidon, 1970-[74] 3 v. illus., facsims., ports. 32 cm. (National Gallery of Art: Kress Foundation studies in the history of European art) 'Distributors in the United States: Praeger Publishers, New York.' Errata slip inserted: v. 3. 1. Hals, Frans, 1584-1666.
ND653.H2 S56      759.9/492      *LC* 71-112414      *ISBN* 071481444X

**Sutton, Peter C.**                    **1.6249**
Pieter de Hooch / Peter C. Sutton. — Complete ed. with a catalogue raisonné. — Ithaca, N.Y.: Cornell University Press, 1980. 168 p., [72] leaves of plates: ill. (some col.); 29 cm. 'A Phaidon book.' Includes index. 1. Hooch, Pieter de 2. Hooch, Pieter de — Catalogs. 3. Painters — Netherlands — Biography. I. T.
ND653.H726 S9      759.9492 B 19      *LC* 80-7667      *ISBN* 0801413397

**Haverkamp Begemann, Egbert.**                    **1.6250**
Rembrandt, the Nightwatch / E. Haverkamp–Begemann. — Princeton, N.J.: Princeton University Press, 1983 (c1982). xv, 138 p., [59] p. of plates: ill. (1 col.); 25 cm. — (Princeton essays on the arts. 12) Includes index. 1. Rembrandt Harmenszoon van Rijn, 1606-1669. Night watch I. T. II. Series.
ND653.R4 A7      759.9492 19      *LC* 81-47921      *ISBN* 0691039917

**Rembrandt Harmenszoon van Rijn, 1606-1669.**                    • **1.6251**
[Rembrandt schilderijen. English] The complete edition of the paintings [of] Rembrandt, by A. Bredius. 3rd ed.; revised by H. Gerson. London, Phaidon, 1969. xvi p. 544 p. of illus., ports., 545-636 p. 28 cm. Translation of Rembrandt schilderijen. 1. Bredius, Abraham, 1855-1946. II. Gerson, H. (Horst) III. T.
ND653.R4 B83 1969      759.9492      *LC* 68-27416      *ISBN* 0714813419

**A Corpus of Rembrandt paintings / Stichting Foundation**      **1.6252**
**Rembrandt Research Project; J. Bruyn ... [et al.]; with the**
**collaboration of L. Peese Binkhorst–Hoffscholte; translated by**
**D. Cook–Radmore.**
The Hague; Boston: M. Nijhoff Publishers; Hingham, MA: Distributor for the U.S. and Canada, Kluwer Boston, 1982-<1986 >. v. <1-2 >: ill.; 35 cm. Includes indexes. Accompanied by 'Annex to 'A corpus of Rembrandt paintings' (<1 plate of ill. > and inserted at end. 1. Rembrandt Harmenszoon van Rijn, 1606-1669 — Addresses, essays, lectures. I. Bruyn, J. II. Rembrandt Harmenszoon van Rijn, 1606-1669. III. Stichting Foundation Rembrandt Research Project.
ND653.R4 C638 1982      759.9492 19      *LC* 82-18790      *ISBN* 902472614X

**Schwartz, Gary, 1940-.**                    **1.6253**
[Rembrandt. English] Rembrandt: his life, his paintings: a new biography with all accessible paintings illustrated in colour / Gary Schwartz. — New York, N.Y., U.S.A.: Viking, 1985. 380 p.: ill. (some col.); 32 cm. Translation of: Rembrandt: zijn leven, zijn schilderijen. Includes index. 1. Rembrandt Harmenszoon van Rijn, 1606-1669. 2. Rembrandt Harmenszoon van Rijn, 1606-1669 — Criticism and interpretation. 3. Painters — Netherlands — Biography. I. T.
ND653.R4 S3813 1985      759.9492 B 19      *LC* 85-40546      *ISBN* 0670808768

**Slive, Seymour, 1920-.**                    • **1.6254**
Rembrandt and his critics, 1630–1730. The Hague M. Nijhoff 1953. 240p. (Utrechtse bijdragen tot de kunstgeschiedenis, 2) 1. Rembrandt Harmenszoon van Rijn, 1606-1669. 2. Rembrandt Harmenszoon van Rijn, 1606-1669 — Criticism and interpretation 3. Art criticism I. T. II. Series.
ND653.R4 S65

**Vries, A. B. de (Ary Bob de), 1905-.**                    **1.6255**
Rembrandt in the Mauritshuis: an interdisciplinary study / by A. B. de Vries, Magdi Tóth–Ubbens, W. Froentjes; with a foreword by H. R. Hoetink; [translated from the Dutch by James Brockway]. — Alphen aan den Rijn: Sijthoff & Noordhoff, 1978. 223 p.: ill. (some col.); 29 cm. 1. Rembrandt Harmenszoon van Rijn, 1606-1669. 2. Mauritshuis (Hague, Netherlands) 3. Painting — Expertising I. Tóth-Ubbens, Magdi. joint author. II. Froentjes, W. joint author. III. T.
ND653.R4 V72      759.9492      *LC* 78-385007      *ISBN* 9028600280

**Blankert, Albert.**                    **1.6256**
Vermeer of Delft: complete edition of the paintings / Albert Blankert, with contributions by Rob Ruurs and Willem L. van de Watering. — Oxford: Phaidon, c1978. 176 p.: ill. (some col.); 29 cm. 1. Vermeer, Johannes, 1632-1675. 2. Painting, Dutch I. T.
ND653.V5 B55      *LC* 77-89295      *ISBN* 0714818194

## ND661–673 FLANDERS. BELGIUM

**Musées royaux des beaux-arts de Belgique.**                    **1.6257**
Le siècle de Bruegel: la peinture en Belgique au xvie siècle / Musées royaux des beaux–arts de Belgique. 2. éd. — Bruxelles: les Musées, 1963. 246 p., [50] leaves of plates: ill. Exhibition held September 27 to November 24, 1963 at the Musées royaux des beaux-arts de Belgique, Brussels. 1. Paintings, Belgian — Exhibitions. I. T.
ND665.B76      *LC* 66-33962

**Lassaigne, Jacques, 1910-.**                    • **1.6258**
Flemish painting. Text by Jacques Lassaigne. [Translated by Stuart Gilbert. New York] A. Skira [1957-. v. mounted col. illus. 35 cm. (Painting, color, history) Vol. 2: Text by Jacques Lassaigne and Robert L. Delevoy. 1. Painting, Flemish
ND665.L33      759.9493      *LC* 57-11640

**Blum, Shirley Neilsen.**                    **1.6259**
Early Netherlandish triptychs; a study in patronage. Berkeley, University of California Press, 1969. xv, 176 p. plates (part col., incl. plans) 32 cm. (California studies in the history of art. 13) 1. Panel painting, Flemish 2. Panel painting, Renaissance — Flanders. 3. Art patrons — Portraits. 4. Triptychs — Belgium — Flanders. I. T. II. Series.
ND669.F5 B55      755/.2/09492      *LC* 69-10902      *ISBN* 0520014448

## ND673 Painters, A–Z

**Gibson, Walter S.**                    **1.6260**
Bruegel / Walter S. Gibson. New York: Oxford University Press, 1977. 216 p.: ill. (some col.); 21 cm. (World of art.) Includes index. 1. Bruegel, Pieter, ca. 1525-1569. I. T. II. Series.
ND673.B73 G47 1977b      760/.092/4      *LC* 76-56922      *ISBN* 0195199537

**Bruegel, Pieter, ca. 1525-1569.**                    **1.6261**
[Bruegel. English] Bruegel [Photos. and picture research by] M. Seidel. [Text, catalog, and notes by] R. H. Marijnissen. [1st American ed.] New York, Putnam [1971] 351 p. illus. (part col.) 31 cm. 1. Bruegel, Pieter, ca. 1525-1569. I. Seidel, Max, 1904- II. Marijnissen, Roger H. III. T.
ND673.B73 S413 1971      759.9493      *LC* 77-150587

**Haesaerts, Paul, 1901-.**                    • **1.6262**
James Ensor. Pref. by Jean Cassou. [Translated from the French by Norbert Guterman]. — New York, Abrams [1959, c1957] 386 p. illus. (part mounted col.) plates, ports. 30 cm. Bibliography: p. 369-[374] 1. Ensor, James, 1860-1949.
ND673.E6H313      759.9493      *LC* 58-9032

**Philip, Lotte Brand.**                    **1.6263**
The Ghent altarpiece and the art of Jan van Eyck. Princeton, N.J., Princeton University Press, 1972, [c1971]. xvii, 255, [106] p. illus. 31 cm. 1. Eyck, Jan van, 1390-1440. Ghent altarpiece I. T.
ND673.E87 P5      *LC* 73-113007      *ISBN* 0691038708

**Purtle, Carol J., 1939-.**                    **1.6263a**
The Marian paintings of Jan van Eyck / Carol J. Purtle. — Princeton, N.J.: Princeton University Press, c1982. xviii, 221 p., [48] P. of plates: ill.; 29 cm. Appendices (p. [175]-201): Little Office of the Blessed Virgin Mary; Matins, Nocturne I — Office of the Assumption: usage of the Church of St. Donatian, Bruges — Fundacie van Missus ... van M. Pieter Cotrel. Includes index. 1. Eyck, Jan van, 1390-1440. 2. Mary, Blessed Virgin, Saint — Art I. T.
ND673.E87 P75 1982      759.9493 19      *LC* 81-47943      *ISBN* 0691039895

**Baldass, Ludwig von, 1887-.**                    • **1.6264**
Jan van Eyck. [London] Phaidon Press [1952] 297 p. (p. [107]-[266] plates (part col.)) ill. (part col.) 1. Eyck, Jan van, 1390-1440. I. T.
ND673 E9 B33      *LC* 52-9471

**Hulst, Roger Adolf d'.**                    **1.6265**
Jacob Jordaens / R.-A. d'Hulst; translated from the Dutch by P.S. Falla. — Ithaca, N.Y.: Cornell University Press, 1982. 374 p.: ill. (some col.); 34 cm. Cover title: Jordaens. 1. Jordaens, Jacob, 1593-1678. 2. Painters — Belgium — Biography. I. Jordaens, Jacob, 1593-1678. II. T. III. Title: Jordaens.
ND673.J8 H8 1982b      759.9493 B 19      *LC* 82-182877      *ISBN* 0801415195

**Gablik, Suzi.**                                                                            • **1.6266**
Magritte. — Greenwich, Conn.: New York Graphic Society, [1970] 208 p.: illus. (part col.), ports.; 26 cm. 1. Magritte, René, 1898-1967. ND673.M35 G3 1970    759.9493    *LC* 77-125894    *ISBN* 0500490031

**Noël, Bernard, 1930-.**                                                                         **1.6267**
[Magritte. English] Magritte / by Bernard Noël; [translated from the French by Jeffrey Arsham]. — New York: Crown Publishers, c1977. 94, [1] p.: ill. (some col.); 29 cm. (Q.L.P. series.) 1. Magritte, René, 1898-1967. I. T. ND673.M35 N613    759.9493    *LC* 76-57235    *ISBN* 0517530090

**Silver, Larry.**                                                                                **1.6268**
The paintings of Quinten Massys with catalogue raisonné / Larry Silver. — Montclair, N.J.: Allanheld & Schram, 1984. xvii, 361 p.: ill.; 29 cm. Includes index. 1. Metsys, Quentin, 1465 or 6-1530 — Catalogs. I. Metsys, Quentin, 1465 or 6-1530. II. T. ND673.M43 A4 1984    759.9493 19    *LC* 84-2939    *ISBN* 0839003226

**McFarlane, K. B. (Kenneth Bruce)**                                                             **1.6269**
Hans Memling. by K. B. McFarlane. Edited by Edgar Wind with the assistance of G. L. Harriss. Oxford [Eng.], Clarendon Press, 1972, [c1971] 74 p., [144] plates. ill. 30 cm. 1. Memling, Hans, 1430?-1494. I. T. ND673.M5 M3    *LC* 72-200900    *ISBN* 019817179X

**Koch, Robert A., 1919-.**                                                                       **1.6270**
Joachim Patinir / by Robert A. Koch. Princeton, N.J., Princeton University Press, 1968. xvi, 98 p. col. illus., 92 plates. 31 cm. (Princeton monographs in art and archaeology. 38) 1. Patinir, Joachim, ca. 1485-1524. I. T. II. Series. ND673.P27 K6    759.9/493    *LC* 68-10392

**Held, Julius Samuel, 1905-.**                                                                   **1.6272**
The oil sketches of Peter Paul Rubens: a critical catalogue / by Julius S. Held. — Princeton, N.J.: published for the National Gallery of Art by Princeton University Press, c1980. 2 v.: ill.; 29 cm. (Kress Foundation studies in the history of European art; no. 7) Includes index. 1. Rubens, Peter Paul, Sir, 1577-1640 — Catalogs. I. Rubens, Peter Paul, Sir, 1577-1640. II. T. ND673.R9 A4 1980    759.9493    *LC* 77-2532    *ISBN* 0691039294

**Rubens, Peter Paul, Sir, 1577-1640.**                                                          • **1.6273**
Letters. Translated and edited by Ruth Saunders Magurn. Cambridge, Harvard University Press, 1955. xiv, 528 p. illus., ports., facsim. 26 cm. I. T. ND673.R9 A43 1941    927.5 [759.9493]    *LC* 55-5223

**Burckhardt, Jacob, 1818-1897.**                                                                • **1.6274**
Recollections of Rubens. [Edited, with an introd., by H. Gerson, Translation of Burckhardt's essay by Mary Hottinger. Translation of the selected letters by R. H. Boothroyd and I. Grafe] New York, Phaidon Publishers; distributed by Oxford University Press [1950] xi, 374, [1] p. 143 plates (part col.) 19 cm. 'Selected letters of Rubens': p. [191]-249. Bibliography: p. [375] 1. Rubens, Peter Paul, Sir, 1577-1640. I. T. ND673.R9B784    927.5    *LC* 50-9158

**Downes, Kerry.**                                                                                **1.6275**
Rubens / by Kerry Downes. — London: Jupiter Books, 1980. vi, 170, 32 p.: ill. (some col.); 30 cm. Includes index. 1. Rubens, Peter Paul, Sir, 1577-1640. I. T. ND673.R9 D68    759.9493 19    *LC* 80-512129    *ISBN* 0906379040

**Vergara, Lisa, 1948-.**                                                                         **1.6276**
Rubens and the poetics of landscape / Lisa Vergara. — New Haven: Yale University Press, c1982. xv, 207 p., [2] leaves of plates: 121 ill. (some col.); 19 x 26 cm. Includes index. 1. Rubens, Peter Paul, Sir, 1577-1640. 2. Landscape in art 3. Ut pictura poesis (Aesthetics) I. T. ND673.R9 V37 1982    759.9493 19    *LC* 81-11385    *ISBN* 0300025084

**Davies, Martin, 1908-.**                                                                        **1.6277**
Rogier van der Weyden; an essay, with a critical catalogue of paintings assigned to him and to Robert Campin. London, Phaidon, 1972. [5] 272, [11] p. illus. (some col.) 31 cm. Distributed in the U.S. by Praeger Publishers, Inc., New York. 1. Weyden, Roiger van der, 1399 or 1400-1464. 2. Campin, Robert, d. 1444. I. T. ND673.W4 D3    759.9493    *LC* 79-173437    *ISBN* 0714815160

## ND681–699 Russia

**Gosudarstvennaia Tret'iakovskaia galereia.**                                                   **1.6278**
The Tretyakov Gallery, Moscow: Russian painting / [introduced by V. Volodarsky; notes by M. Epstein ... et al.; translated by B. Meyerovich]. — New York: H. N. Abrams; Leningrad: Aurora Art Publishers, c1979. 326 p.: ill. (some col.); 31 cm. 1. Gosudarstvennaia Tret'iakovskaia galereia. 2. Painting,

Russian — Catalogs. 3. Painting — Russian Republic — Moscow — Catalogs. I. Volodarskiĭ, V. M. (Vsevolod Matveevich) II. T. ND681.M6 1979a    759.7/074/07312 19    *LC* 79-51258    *ISBN* 0810916576

**Valkenier, Elizabeth Kridl.**                                                                   **1.6279**
Russian realist art: the state and society: the Peredvizhniki and their tradition / by Elizabeth Valkenier. — Ann Arbor: Ardis, c1977. xv, 251 p.: ill.; 24 cm. (Studies of the Russian Institute, Columbia University) Includes index. 1. Realism in art — Russia. 2. Peredvizhniki. 3. Painting, Modern — 19th century — Russia. 4. Socialist realism in art — Russia. 5. Art and state — Russia. I. T. ND687.5.R4 V34    759.7    *LC* 77-151042    *ISBN* 0882332643

**Alexander, Sidney, 1912-.**                                                                     **1.6280**
Marc Chagall: a biography / by Sidney Alexander. — New York: Putnam, c1978. 526 p., [8] leaves of plates: ill.; 24 cm. Includes index. 1. Chagall, Marc, 1887- 2. Painters — Russian Republic — Biography. I. T. ND699.C5 A67 1978    759.7 B    *LC* 77-16526    *ISBN* 0399118942

**Meyer, Franz, writer on art.**                                                                  **1.6281**
[Marc Chagall. English] Marc Chagall. [Translated from the German by Robert Allen] New York, H. N. Abrams [1964] 775 p. illus. (part mounted col.) ports., facsims. 31 cm. Translation of Marc Chagall: Leben und Werk. 1. Chagall, Marc, 1887- I. T. ND699.C5 M43    759.7    *LC* 63-19571

**Long, Rose-Carol Washton.**                                                                     **1.6282**
Kandinsky, the development of an abstract style / Rose–Carol Washton Long. — Oxford: Clarendon Press; New York: Oxford University Press, 1980. xxvi, 201 p., [52] leaves of plates: ill.; 26 cm. — (Oxford studies in the history of art and architecture.) Includes index. 1. Kandinsky, Wassily, 1866-1944. 2. Painting, Abstract I. T. II. Series. ND699.K3 L66    759.7    *LC* 79-41130    *ISBN* 0198173113

**Weiss, Peg.**                                                                                   **1.6283**
Kandinsky in Munich: the formative Jugendstil years / by Peg Weiss. — Princeton, N.J.: Princeton University Press, c1979. xxi, 268 p., [48] leaves of plates: ill. (some col.); 23 cm. Includes index. 1. Kandinsky, Wassily, 1866-1944. 2. Art nouveau — Germany, West — Munich. I. T. ND699.K3 W43    759.7    *LC* 78-51203    *ISBN* 0691039348

## ND701–793 Scandinavia

**Varnedoe, Kirk, 1946-.**                                                                        **1.6284**
Northern light: realism and symbolism in Scandinavian painting, 1880–1910 / Kirk Varnedoe. — Brooklyn, NY: Brooklyn Museum, c1982. 240 p.: ill. (some col.), map, ports.; 28 cm. Exhibition held: Corcoran Gallery of Art, Washington, D.C., Sept. 8-Oct. 17, 1982; Brooklyn Museum, New York, November 10, 1982-Jan. 6, 1983; Minneapolis Institute of Arts, Minnesota February 4-Apr. 19, 1983. Includes index. 1. Painting, Scandinavian — Exhibitions. 2. Realism in art — Scandinavia — Exhibitions. 3. Symbolism in art — Scandinavia — Exhibitions. 4. Painting, Modern — 19th century — Scandinavia — Exhibitions. 5. Painting, Modern — 20th century — Scandinavia — Exhibitions. I. Corcoran Gallery of Art. II. Brooklyn Museum. III. Minneapolis Institute of Arts. IV. T. ND707.5.R43 V37 1982    759.8 19    *LC* 82-71937    *ISBN* 0872730948

**Heller, Reinhold.**                                                                             **1.6285**
Munch: his life and work / Reinhold Heller. — Chicago: University of Chicago Press, 1984. 240 p.: ill. (some col.); 28 cm. Includes index. 1. Munch, Edvard, 1863-1944. 2. Painters — Norway — Biography. I. T. ND773.M8 H43 1984    759.81 B 19    *LC* 83-24098    *ISBN* 0226326438

## ND801–833 Spain. Portugal

**Post, Chandler Rathfon, 1881-1959.**                                                            **1.6286**
A history of Spanish painting, by Chandler Rathfon Post. Cambridge, Mass., Harvard University Press, 1930-66. 14 v. in 20 illus., ports. 25 cm. Vols. 6-14 issued in series: Harvard-Radcliffe fine arts series. Vols. 4, 6-9, 12 issued in two parts paged continuously. Vols. 13-14 edited by H. E. Wethey. 1. Painting, Spanish — History. I. Wethey, Harold E. (Harold Edwin), 1902-1984. II. T. ND801.P6    *LC* 30-7776

**Brown, Jonathan.**                                                                              **1.6287**
Images and ideas in seventeenth–century Spanish painting / Jonathan Brown. — Princeton, N.J.: Princeton University Press, c1979 (c1978). viii, 168 p., [16] leaves of plates: ill.; 24 cm. (Princeton essays on the arts; 6) Based on the author's thesis, Princeton University, 1964. Includes index. 1. Painting, Spanish 2. Painting, Baroque — Spain. 3. Art and society — Spain. 4. Catholic Church in art. I. T. ND806.B76    759.6    *LC* 78-52485    *ISBN* 0691039410

**Moreno Galván, José María.**                                                 **1.6288**
[Última vanguardia. English] The latest avant–garde. Translation by Neville
Hinton. [Madrid] Magius; [Greenwich, Conn., New York Graphic Society,
1972] 273, [2] p. col. illus. 33 cm. (Spanish painting collection) Translation of
La última vanguardia. 1. Painting, Spanish 2. Painting, Modern — 20th
century — Spain I. T.
ND808.M6213          759.6          LC 72-80898          *ISBN* 0821204904

## ND813 Painters, A–Z

**Ades, Dawn.**                                                                **1.6289**
Dali and surrealism / Dawn Ades. — 1st U.S. ed. — New York: Harper &
Row, c1982. 216 p.: ill. (some col.). — (Icon editions) Includes index. 1. Dalí,
Salvador, 1904- 2. Surrealism I. T.
ND813D3 A64 1982          LC 82-47545          *ISBN* 0064302954

**Dalí, Salvador, 1904-.**                                                     **1.6290**
Salvador Dali. Text by Robert Descharnes. Translated by Eleanor R. Morse. —
New York: Abrams, [1976] 175 p.: illus. (part col.); 33 cm. — (The Library of
great painters) 1. Dalí, Salvador, 1904- 2. Painters — Spain — Biography.
I. Descharnes, Robert. II. T.
ND813.D3 D4413          759.6          LC 74-4257          *ISBN* 0810902222

**Gassier, Pierre.**                                                         • **1.6291**
Goya: his life and work, with a catalogue raisonné of the paintings, drawings
and engravings, [by] Pierre Gassier and Juliet Wilson; edited by François
Lachenal; preface by Enrique Lafuente Ferrari. London, Thames and Hudson,
1971. 400 p. illus. (some col., facsim., plans, ports.) 34 cm. Rev. translation of
Vie et oeuvre de Francisco Goya, 1970. 1. Goya, Francisco, 1746-1828.
I. Wilson, Juliet, joint author. II. T.
ND813.G7 G3413 1971          760/.0924          LC 73-887333          *ISBN*
0500090750

**Glendinning, Nigel, 1929-.**                                                 **1.6292**
Goya and his critics / Nigel Glendinning. — New Haven: Yale University
Press, 1977. xii, 340 p.: ill.; 26 cm. 1. Goya, Francisco, 1746-1828. I. T.
ND813.G7 G53          759.6          LC 76-49693          *ISBN* 0300020112

**Goya, Francisco, 1746-1828.**                                              • **1.6293**
Goya / text by José Gudiol; [translated by Priscilla Muller]. — New York: H.
N. Abrams, [1965] 168 p.: ill. (some col.), ports. (some col.) — (The Library of
great painters) I. Gudiol, José. II. T.
ND813.G7 G773          LC 64-10760          *ISBN* 0810901498

**Licht, Fred, 1928- comp.**                                                   **1.6294**
Goya in perspective. Englewood Cliffs, N.J., Prentice-Hall [1973] x, 180 p. illus.
22 cm. (The Artists in perspective series) (A Spectrum book) 1. Goya,
Francisco, 1746-1828. I. T.
ND813.G7 L562 1973          759.6          LC 73-6932          *ISBN* 0133619648
*ISBN* 0133619567

**Licht, Fred, 1928-.**                                                        **1.6295**
Goya, the origins of the modern temper in art / Fred Licht. — 1st Icon ed. —
New York: Harper & Row, 1983, c1979. 288 p.: ill.; 23 cm. — (Icon editions)
Includes index. 1. Goya, Francisco, 1746-1828. I. T.
ND813.G7 L564 1983          759.6 19          LC 82-48152          *ISBN* 0064301230

**Rose, Barbara.**                                                             **1.6296**
Miró in America / Barbara Rose; with essays by Judith McCandless and
Duncan Macmillan. — Houston: Museum of Fine Arts, Houston, c1982. ix,
153 p.: ill. (some col.); 27 cm. To accompany an exhibition held Apr. 21-June
27, 1982, Museum of Fine Arts, Houston. Includes index. 1. Miró, Joan, 1893-
— Exhibitions. I. Miró, Joan, 1893- II. McCandless, Judith. III. Macmillan,
Duncan. IV. Museum of Fine Arts, Houston. V. T.
ND813.M5 A4 1982          709/.2/4 19          LC 82-81357          089090066X

**Soby, James Thrall, 1906-.**                                               • **1.6297**
Joán Miró. — New York: Museum of Modern Art; distributed by Doubleday,
Garden City, N.Y., [1959] 164 p.: illus. (part col.), port.; 25 cm. 1. Miró, Joan,
1893-
ND813.M5 S6          759.6          LC 59-10311

**Murillo, Bartolomé Esteban, 1617-1682.**                                     **1.6298**
Bartolomé Esteban Murillo, 1617–1682: Museo del Prado Madrid, 1982, Royal
Academy of Arts London, 1983. — [S.l.]: Royal Academy of Arts (dist. by
Allenheld & Schram), 1983 (c1982) 239 p.: ill. (some col.); 29 cm. Includes
indexes. 1. Murillo, Bartolomé Esteban, 1617-1682 — Exhibitions. I. Museo
del Prado. II. Royal Academy of Arts (Great Britain) III. T.
ND813.M9 A4          759.6 19          LC 83-168350          *ISBN* 0297781936

**Wethey, Harold E. (Harold Edwin), 1902-1984.**                             • **1.6299**
El Greco and his school. — Princeton, N. J., Princeton University Press, 1962.
2 v. plates. 29 cm. Includes bibliographical references. 1. Greco, 1541?-1614.
2. Artists, Italian.
ND813.T4W4          759.6          LC 61-7427

**Harris, Enriqueta.**                                                         **1.6300**
Velázquez / Enriqueta Harris. — Ithaca, N.Y.: Cornell University Press, 1982.
240 p.: ill. (some col.); 32 cm. Includes index. 1. Velázquez, Diego, 1599-1660.
2. Painters — Spain — Biography. I. Velázquez, Diego, 1599-1660. II. T.
ND813.V4 H37 1982          759.6 B 19          LC 82-70748          *ISBN*
0801415268

**Ortega y Gasset, José, 1883-1955.**                                          **1.6301**
[Selected works. English. 1972] Velazquez, Goya and the dehumanization of
art. Translated by Alexis Brown. With an introd. by Philip Troutman. New
York, W. W. Norton [1972] 142 p. illus. 26 cm. 1. Velázquez, Diego,
1599-1660. 2. Goya, Francisco, 1746-1828. 3. Art — Philosophy I. T.
ND813.V4 O69413 1972          759.6          LC 74-177440          *ISBN* 0393043584

## ND841–953 OTHER EUROPEAN COUNTRIES

**Deuchler, Florens, 1931-.**                                                  **1.6302**
[Schweizer Malerei. English] Swiss painting: from the Middle Ages to the dawn
of the twentieth century / Florens Deuchler, Marcel Roethlisberger, Hans
Lüthy; [English translation by James Emmons]. — Geneva: Skira; New York:
Rizzoli, c1976. 197 p.: ill. (some col.); 35 cm. Translation of Schweizer Malerei.
Includes index. 1. Painting, Swiss — History. 2. Painting, Medieval —
Switzerland — History. 3. Painting, Renaissance — Switzerland — History.
4. Painting, Modern — Switzerland — History. I. Roethlisberger, Marcel,
1929- joint author. II. Lüthy, Hans, joint author. III. T.
ND844.D4813          759.9494          LC 76-15491          *ISBN* 0847800563

**Hirsh, Sharon L.**                                                           **1.6303**
Ferdinand Hodler / by Sharon L. Hirsh. — New York: Braziller, c1982. 144 p.:
ill. (some col.); 30 cm. 1. Hodler, Ferdinand, 1853-1918. I. Hodler, Ferdinand,
1853-1918. II. T.
ND853.H6 H5 1982          759.9494 B 19          LC 81-21622          *ISBN*
080761033X

**Selz, Peter Howard, 1919-.**                                                 **1.6304**
Ferdinand Hodler [by] Peter Selz with contributions by Jura Brüschweiler,
Phyllis Hattis [and] Eva Wyler. [Berkeley, University Art Museum, 1972]
140 p. illus. (part col.) 26 cm. Catalogue of an exhibition held at the University
Art Museum, Berkeley, Nov. 22, 1972-Jan. 7, 1973, at the Solomon R.
Guggenheim Museum, New York, Feb. 2-Apr. 8, 1973, and at the Busch-
Reisinger Museum, Harvard University, May 1-June 22, 1973. 1. Hodler,
Ferdinand, 1853-1918. I. University of California, Berkeley. University Art
Museum. II. Solomon R. Guggenheim Museum. III. Busch-Reisinger
Museum. IV. T.
ND853.H6 S44          759.9494          LC 72-619599

**The Quiet conquest: the Huguenots, 1685–1985: [exhibition**                  **1.6305**
**catalogue] / compiled by Tessa Murdoch.**
London: Museum of London in association with A.H. Jolly Ltd., 1985. 326 p.:
ill. (some col.); 30 cm. A Museum of London exhibition in association with the
Huguenot Society of London 15 May to 31 October 1985. 1. Huguenots 2. Art,
Huguenots — Exhibitions I. Murdoch, Tessa. II. Museum of London.
ND947.H83 Q53          *ISBN* 0904818144

## ND960–1113 Asia. Australia

**Gray, Basil, 1904-.**                                                      • **1.6306**
Persian painting. — [New York]: Skira; [distributed by World Pub. Co.,
Cleveland, 1961] 191 p.: mounted col. illus., map.; 29 cm. — (Treasures of Asia)
1. Illumination of books and manuscripts — Iran. 2. Painting — Iran. I. T.
II. Series.
ND980.G72          759.955          LC 61-10169

**Archer, W. G. (William George), 1907-.**                                   • **1.6307**
Indian painting. Introd. and notes by W. G. Archer. New York, Oxford
University Press, 1957. 22 p. mounted ill., 15 col. plates. 35 cm. (Iris books)
1. Painting — India — History. 2. Paintings, Indic. I. T. II. Series.
ND1002.A7          LC 57-59192

**Barrett, Douglas E.**                                                        **1.6308**
Painting of India, text by Douglas Barrett and Basil Gray. [Geneva?] Skira;
[distributed in the U.S. by World Pub. Co., Cleveland, 1963] 213 p. mounted
col. ill., map. (Treasures of Asia) 1. Painting — India — History I. Gray,
Basil, 1904- joint author II. T. III. Series.
ND1002 B3          LC 63-8982

**Sivaramamurti, C.**                                                          **1.6309**
South Indian paintings [by] C. Sivaramamurti. New Delhi, National Museum
[1968] 174 p. illus., (part col.) 35 cm. 1. Painting — India, South. 2. Mural
painting and decoration — India, South. I. T.
ND1007.S6 S5          759.954/8          LC sa 68-12996

**Unesco.**                                                                          • **1.6310**
Ceylon: paintings from temple, shrine and rock / preface, W. G. Archer; introduction, S. Paranavitana. — [Greenwich, Conn.]: New York Graphic Society, [1957] 29 p., 32 leaves of plates: ill. — (UNESCO world art series; 8) Materials assembled by experts from UNESCO and the New York Graphic Society. 1. Paintings, Sinhalese. 2. Art, Buddhist I. New York Graphic Society. II. T. III. Series.
ND1010.6.U6x N5300.U56 v.8a        *LC* 57-59245

**Boisselier, Jean.**                                                                  **1.6311**
[Peinture en Thaïlande. English] Thai painting / Jean Boisselier; translated by Jeant Seligman. — 1st ed. — Tokyo; New York: Kodansha International; New York: distributor, Harper & Row, 1976. 270 p.: ill. (some col.); 29 cm. Translation of La peinture en Thaïlande. Includes index. 1. Painting, Thai. 2. Painting, Buddhist — Thailand. I. T.
ND1021.B6413      759.9593      *LC* 76-11454      *ISBN* 0870112805

## ND1040–1049 CHINA

**Artists and traditions: uses of the past in Chinese culture /**         **1.6312**
**edited by Christian F. Murck.**
Princeton, N.J.: The Art Museum, Princeton University: distributed by Princeton University Press, 1977, [c1976] xxi, 230 p.: ill.; 27 cm. Based on a colloquium on Chinese art entitled 'Artists and Traditions', jointly sponsored by the Departments of Art and Archaeology and East Asian Studies at Princeton, and held on May 17, 1969 in conjunction with an exhibition of Chinese paintings called 'In Pursuit of Antiquity.' 1. Painting, Chinese — Addresses, essays, lectures. 2. Art and society — China — Addresses, essays, lectures. I. Murck, Christian F. II. Princeton University. Art Museum.
ND1040.A77      759.951      *LC* 74-77300      *ISBN* 0691039097

**Chinese painting / general editor, Torao Miyagawa; translated**         **1.6313**
**and adapted by Alfred Birnbaum; contributing authors, Yoshiko**
**Doi ... [et al.].**
1st English ed. — New York: Weatherhill/Tankosha, 1984, [c1983]. 228 p.: ill. (some col.); 31 cm. — (History of the art of China.) Adapted from: Chūgoku no bijutsu. 3. Kaiga. Includes index. 1. Painting, Chinese I. Miyagawa, Torao, 1908- II. Birnbaum, Alfred. III. Doi, Yoshiko, 1935- IV. Chūgoku no bijutsu. 3. Kaiga. V. Series.
ND1040.C5758 1983      759.951 19      *LC* 83-3505      *ISBN* 0834815273

**Gulik, Robert Hans van, 1910-1967.**                                        **1.6314**
Chinese pictorial art as viewed by the connoisseur; notes on the means and methods of traditional Chinese connoisseurship of pictorial art, based upon a study of the art of mounting scrolls in China and Japan. With 160 plates, and 42 actual samples of Chinese and Japanese paper, in pocket. Roma, Istituto italiano per il Medio ed Estremo Oriente, 1958. xxxvii, 537 p. ill., port., mounted samples. (Serie orientale Roma. 19) Title also in Chinese. 1. Painting, Chinese 2. Penmanship, Chinese 3. Painting, Japanese I. T. II. Series.
ND1040 G8      *LC* 59-31931

**Kuo, Jo-hsü, fl. 1070-1075.**                                                **1.6315**
[T'u hua chien wên chih. English] Experiences in painting (T'u–hua chien–wên chih) An eleventh century history of Chinese painting, together with the Chinese text in facsimile; translated and annotated by Alexander Coburn Soper. Washington, American Council of Learned Societies, 1951. xiii, 216 p., facsim.: [68] p. 26 cm. (American Council of Learned Societies. Studies in Chinese and related civilizations, no. 6) 1. Painting, Chinese 2. Painters — China. I. Soper, Alexander Coburn, tr. II. T.
ND1040.K783      759.951      *LC* 52-190

**Loehr, Max.**                                                                  **1.6316**
The great painters of China / Max Loehr. — 1st U.S. ed. — New York: Harper & Row, 1980. 336 p.: ill. (some col.); 27 cm. 1. Painting, Chinese 2. Landscape painting, Chinese I. T.
ND1040.L58      ND1040 L6.      759.951      *LC* 79-6030      *ISBN* 0064353265

**Silbergeld, Jerome.**                                                          **1.6317**
Chinese painting style: media, methods, and principles of form / Jerome Silbergeld. — Seattle: University of Washington Press, c1982. xi, 68 p., [48] p. of plates: ill.; 29 cm. Added t.p. in Chinese: Chung-kuo hua chih feng ko. Includes index. 1. Painting, Chinese 2. Painting — Technique I. T. II. Title: Chung-kuo hua chih feng ko.
ND1040.S47 1982      751.42/51 19      *LC* 81-21837      *ISBN* 0295958960

**Sirén, Osvald, 1879-.**                                                       **1.6318**
The Chinese on the art of painting: translations and comments / by Osvald Sirén. — New York: Schocken Books, 1963. 261 p.: ill. — (Selected Schocken paperbacks; 0057-6) 1. Painting, Chinese I. T.
ND1040.S48 1963      *LC* 63-20262      *ISBN* 0805200576

**Sirén, Osvald, 1879-.**                                                       **1.6319**
Chinese painting: leading masters and principles / Osvald Sirén. — New York: Hacker Art Books, 1974. 7 v.: ill. 1. Painting — China — History. 2. Painting, Chinese 3. Painters, Chinese. I. T.
ND1040.S49 1973      *LC* 74-182842      *ISBN* 0878171304

**Acker, William Reynolds Beal, 1907- ed. and tr.**                           **1.6320**
Some T'ang and pre-T'ang texts on Chinese painting / translated and annotated by William Reynolds Beal Acker. — Hyperion reprint ed. — Westport, Conn.: Hyperion Press, [1979, c1954] lxii, 414 p.; 22 cm. Chinese and English. Reprint of the ed. published by E. J. Brill, Leiden, which was issued as v. 8 of Sinica Leidensia. Includes index. 1. Painting, Chinese 2. Painting — Early works to 1800. I. T.
ND1043.A26 1979      759.931 19      *LC* 78-20444      *ISBN* 0883558254

**Bush, Susan.**                                                                 **1.6321**
The Chinese literati on painting; Su Shih (1037–1101) to Tung Ch'i–ch'ang (1555–1636). — Cambridge: Harvard University Press, 1971. x, 227 p.: illus.; 25 cm. — (Harvard-Yenching Institute studies, 27) 1. Painting, Chinese I. T. II. Series.
ND1043.B88      759.951      *LC* 78-152698      *ISBN* 0674124251

**Cahill, James Francis, 1926-.**                                             • **1.6322**
Chinese painting. [Geneva?] Skira; [distributed in the U.S. by World Pub. Co., Cleveland, 1960] 211 p. mounted col. illus. 29 cm. (Treasures of Asia) 1. Painting, Chinese I. Series.
ND1043.C28      759.951      *LC* 60-15594

**Cahill, James Francis, 1926-.**                                               **1.6323**
Hills beyond a river: Chinese painting of the Yüan Dynasty, 1279–1368 / James Cahill. — 1st ed. — New York: Weatherhill, 1976. xv, 198 p.: ill.; 31 cm. — ([His A history of later Chinese painting, 1279-1950; v. 1]) Includes index. 1. Painting, Chinese — Sung-Yüan dynasties, 960-1368 I. T.
ND1043.C33 vol. 1 ND1043.4      759.951 s 759.951      *LC* 75-44083      *ISBN* 0834801205

**Cahill, James Francis, 1926-.**                                               **1.6324**
Parting at the shore: Chinese painting of the early and middle Ming dynasty, 1368–1580 / James Cahill. — 1st ed. — New York: Weatherhill, 1978. xiv, 281 p.: ill. (some col.); 31 cm. — (His A history of later Chinese painting, 1279-1950; v. 2) Includes index. 1. Painting, Chinese — Ming-Ch'ing dynasties, 1368-1912 I. T.
ND1043.C33 vol. 2 ND1043.5      759.951      *LC* 77-8682      *ISBN* 0834801280

**Cahill, James Francis, 1926-.**                                               **1.6325**
The distant mountains: Chinese painting of the late Ming Dynasty, 1570–1644 / James Cahill. — 1st ed. — New York: Weatherhill, 1983, [c1982]. xvi, 302 p.: ill. (some col.); 31 cm. — (A History of later Chinese painting, 1279-1950; v. 3) Includes index. 1. Painting, Chinese — Ming-Ch'ing dynasties, 1368-1912 I. T.
ND1043.C33 vol. 3 ND1043.4      759.951 s 759.951 19      *LC* 82-6939      *ISBN* 0834801744

**Sze, Mai-mai.**                                                             • **1.6326**
The tao of painting; a study of the ritual disposition of Chinese painting. With a translation of the Chieh tzŭ yüan chuan; or, Mustard Seed Garden manual of painting, 1679–1701. [2d ed.,] [New York] Pantheon Books [c1963] (Bollingen series. 49) 1. Painting, Chinese I. Wang, Kai, fl. 1677-1705. Chieh tzu yüan hua chuan ed. II. T. III. Title: Mustard Seed Garden manual of painting IV. Series.
ND1043 S9 1963

**William Rockhill Nelson Gallery of Art and Mary Atkins**                    **1.6327**
**Museum of Fine Arts.**
Eight dynasties of Chinese painting: the collections of the Nelson Gallery–Atkins Museum, Kansas City, and the Cleveland Museum of Art / with essays by Wai–kam Ho ... [et al.]. — Cleveland, Ohio: Cleveland Museum of Art in cooperation with Indiana University Press; Bloomington, Ind.: Distributed by Indiana University Press, c1981, [c1980]. lvi, 408 p., [8] p. of plates: ill. (some col.); 32 cm. Exhibition catalog. Includes index. 1. William Rockhill Nelson Gallery of Art and Mary Atkins Museum of Fine Arts — Exhibitions. 2. Cleveland Museum of Art — Exhibitions. 3. Painting, Chinese — Exhibitions. I. Ho, Wai-kam. II. Cleveland Museum of Art. III. T.
ND1043.W54 1980      759.951/074/017132 19      *LC* 80-66110      *ISBN* 0910386536

**Cahill, James Francis, 1926-.**                                               **1.6328**
An index of early Chinese painters and paintings: T'ang, Sung, and Yüan / by James Cahill, incorporating the work of Osvald Sirén and Ellen Johnston Laing. — Berkeley: University of California Press, c1980. x, 391 p.; 27 cm. 1. Painting, Chinese — T'ang-Five dynasties, 618-960 — Indexes 2. Painting, Chinese — Sung-Yüan dynasties, 960-1368 — Indexes. I. T.
ND1043.3.C3      759.951/016 19      *LC* 77-85755      *ISBN* 0520035763

**Cahill, James Francis, 1926–.**     **1.6329**
The compelling image: nature and style in seventeenth–century Chinese painting / James Cahill. — Cambridge, Mass.: Harvard University Press, 1982. 250 p., [14] p. of plates: ill. (some col.); 30 cm. — (Charles Eliot Norton lectures. 1978-1979) 1. Painting, Chinese — Ming-Ch'ing dynasties, 1368-1912 2. Painting, Chinese — Foreign influences. I. T. II. Series.
ND1043.5.C34     759.951 19     *LC* 81-1272     *ISBN* 0674152808

**Fu, Marilyn.**     **1.6330**
Studies in connoisseurship; Chinese paintings from the Arthur M. Sackler Collection in New York and Princeton [by] Marilyn and Shen Fu. [Princeton, N.J.] Distributed by Princeton University Press [c1973] xv, 375 p. illus. (part col.) 36 cm. Catalog of an exhibition held at the Art Museum, Princeton, Dec. 8, 1973-Feb. 3, 1974 [and others] 1. Sackler, Arthur M — Art collections. 2. Painting, Chinese — Exhibitions. 3. Painting, Chinese — Ming-Ch'ing dynasties, 1368-1912 I. Fu, Shen, 1937- joint author. II. Princeton University. Art Museum. III. T.
ND1043.5.F82     759.951     *LC* 73-77442

**Pal, Pratapaditya.**     **1.6331**
Tibetan paintings: a study of Tibetan thankas, eleventh to nineteenth centuries / Pratapaditya Pal. — London: Ravi Kumar, Sotheby Publications, 1984. 223 p.: ill. (some col.); 29 cm. Includes index. 1. Tankas (Tibetan scrolls) 2. Painting — Tibet. 3. Art, Buddhist I. T.
ND1046.T5 P3     *LC* 84-51458     *ISBN* 0856671894

**Coleman, Earle Jerome.**     **1.6332**
Philosophy of painting by Shih–T'ao: a translation and exposition of his Hua–P'u (Treatise on the philosophy of painting) / Earle Jerome Coleman. — The Hague (Noordeinde 41): Mouton, 1978. 147 p.: 21 cm. (Studies in philosophy; 19) Includes an uninterrupted English translation of the Hua p'u. 1. Tao-chi, 1630-1707. 2. Painting — Philosophy. I. Tao-chi, 1630-1707. Hua p'u. English. 1978. II. T.
ND1049.T3 C58     759.951     *LC* 78-391911     *ISBN* 9027977569

## ND1050–1059 JAPAN

[Ref] ND 1051 T33

**Akiyama, Terukazu, 1918–.**     • **1.6333**
Japanese painting. [Geneva?] Skira; [distributed by World Pub. Co., Cleveland, 1961] 216 p. mounted col. ill., maps, tables. (Treasures of Asia) Original text in French. English translation by James Emmons. 1. Painting, Japanese — History 2. Paintings, Japanese I. Series.
ND1050 A413     *LC* 61-15270

**Murase, Miyeko.**     **1.6334**
Emaki, narrative scrolls from Japan / by Miyeko Murase. — [New York, N.Y.]: Asia Society, [1983] 175 p.: ill. (some col.); 27 cm. 'Catalogue of an exhibition organized by the Asia Society in cooperation with the Agency for Cultural Affairs (Bunka-chō), Tokyo, and presented at the Society in the fall of 1983'—T.p. verso. 1. Scrolls, Japanese — Exhibitions. 2. Narrative painting, Japanese — Exhibitions. I. Asia Society. II. Japan. Bunkachō. III. T.
ND1052.M884 1983     745.6/7/0952 19     *LC* 83-9232     *ISBN* 0878480609

**Murase, Miyeko.**     **1.6335**
Iconography of the Tale of Genji: Genji monogatari ekotoba / Miyeko Murase. — 1st ed. — New York: Weatherhill, 1983. xi, 351 p., [8] p. of plates: ill. (some col.); 27 cm. Consists primarily of translation, with illustrations, of the Genji monogatari ekotoba'; p. 35-312. Includes indexes. Errata slip inserted. 1. Murasaki Shikibu, b. 978? Genji monogatari — Illustrations 2. Narrative painting, Japanese — To 1868 3. Narrative painting, Japanese — Technique. I. Genji monogatari ekotoba. English. 1983. II. T.
ND1053.M79 1983     759.952 19     *LC* 83-3452     *ISBN* 0834801884

**Unesco.**     • **1.6336**
Japan: ancient Buddhist paintings / pref.: Serge Elisséeff; introd.: Takaaki Matsushita. — [Greenwich, Conn.]: Published by the New York Graphic Society by arrangement with Unesco, c1959. 21, [4] p.: 37 ill. (chiefly col.). — (UNESCO world art series; 11) Material assembled by experts from UNESCO and the New York Graphic Society. 1. Paintings, Japanese 2. Art, Buddhist I. New York Graphic Society. II. T. III. Series.
ND1053.U5     759.952     *LC* 59-1730

**Cahill, James Francis, 1926–.**     **1.6337**
Scholar painters of Japan: the Nanga school [by] James Cahill. [New York] Asia Society; distributed by New York Graphic Society [1972] 135 p. illus. 31 cm. Catalog of an exhibition held at the Asia House Gallery, New York City, Jan. 12-Feb. 27, 1972; and University Art Museum, University of California, Berkeley, Apr. 3-30, 1972. 1. Painting, Japanese — Exhibitions. 2. Japanese — Edo period, 1600-1868. 3. Nanga I. Asia House Gallery. II. University of California, Berkeley. University Art Museum. III. T.
ND1053.5.C3     759.952/074/013     *LC* 72-182236     *ISBN* 0878480382

# ND1130–1155 Painting: General Works

**Alberti, Leon Battista, 1404-1472.**     **1.6338**
[De pictura. English] On painting / Leon Battista Alberti; translated with introd. and notes by John R. Spencer. — Westport, Conn.: Greenwood Press, 1976. 141 p.: ill.; 23 cm. Translation of De pictura. Reprint of the 1966 rev. ed. published by Yale University Press, New Haven. 1. Painting — Early works to 1800. I. Spencer, John Richard. II. T.
ND1130.A483 1976     750     *LC* 76-22485     *ISBN* 0837189748

ND 1130 C38

**Cennini, Cennino, 15th cent.**     • **1.6339**
The craftsman's handbook; the Italian 'Il libro dell'arte' / Cennino d'Andrea Cennini. Translated by Daniel V. Thompson. — New York: Dover, c1960. xxvii, 142 p.: ill. Imprint on spine: Peter Smith. 1. Painting — Early works to 1800 2. Painting — Technique I. T. II. Title: Il libro dell'arte
ND1130 C3822     ND1130 C3822 1960b.     751     *LC* 54-3194     *ISBN* 048620054X

**Leonardo, da Vinci, 1452-1519.**     • **1.6340**
Treatise on painting = Codex urbinas latinus 1270 / by Leonardo da Vinci; translated and annotated by A. Philip McMahon; with an introd. by Ludwig H. Heydenreich. — Princeton: Princeton University Press, 1956. 2v.: ill.; 23 cm. 1. Painting — Early works to 1800. I. McMahon, Amos Philip, 1890-1947. II. T.
ND1130.L515     *LC* 52-13164

**Venturi, Lionello, 1885-1961.**     • **1.6341**
Painting and painters; how to look at a picture, from Giotto to Chagall. New York, C. Scribner's sons, [1945] xx p., 1 l., 250 p. plates. 24 cm. 1. Painting 2. Painters I. T.
ND1145.V4     759     *LC* 45-35033

**Gilson, Etienne, 1884-1978.**     • **1.6342**
Painting and reality. [New York] Pantheon Books [1957] xxiv, 367 p. illus. 26 cm. (Bollingen series. 35.) (A.W. Mellon lectures in the fine arts. 4, 1955) 1. Painting — Addresses, essays, lectures. 2. Art — Philosophy 3. Reality I. T. II. Series. III. Series: A.W. Mellon lectures in the fine arts. 4, 1955
ND1150.G5 1957     750.4     *LC* 57-11125

# ND1259–1286 Technique. Special Styles. Color

**Doerner, Max, 1870-1939.**     • **1.6343**
The materials of the artist and their use in painting, with notes on the techniques of the old masters; tr. by Eugen Neuhaus. Rev. ed. New York, Harcourt, Brace [1949] xvi, 435 p. illus. 23 cm. Bibliography: p. [415] 1. Painting — Technique 2. Artists' materials I. T.
ND1260.D62 1949     751     *LC* 49-9996 *

**Herberts, Kurt.**     • **1.6344**
[Maltechniken. English] The complete book of artists' techniques. New York, Praeger [1958] 351 p. illus., 80 col. plates. 21 cm. (Books that matter) Translation of Die Maltechniken. 1. Painting — Technique 2. Art — Technique
ND1260.H463 1958     751.4     *LC* 58-12424

**Cheney, Sheldon, 1886–.**     • **1.6345**
Expressionism in art. — Rev. ed. — New York: Liveright Pub. Corp., 1958, c1948. 415 p.: ill.; 25 cm. 1. Expressionism (Art) I. T.
ND1265.C5 1958     *LC* 58-13737

**Fry, Edward F.**     • **1.6346**
Cubism [by] Edward F. Fry. — New York: McGraw-Hill, [1966] 200 p.: illus., facsims., plates (part col.), ports.; 21 cm. — (McGraw-Hill paperbacks) 1. Cubism I. T.
ND1265.F7     759.06     *LC* 66-24888

**Habasque, Guy.**     • **1.6347**
Cubism: biographical and critical study. Translated by Stuart Gilbert. — [New York]: Skira, [1959] 169 p.: mounted col. illus.; 19 cm. — (The Taste of our time, v. 27) 1. Cubism 2. Art, Modern — 20th century
ND1265.H313     759.06     *LC* 59-7254

**Jean, Marcel.**    1.6348
The history of surrealist painting / by Marcel Jean; with the collaboration of Arpad Mezei; translated from the French by Simon Watson Taylor. — New York: Grove Press, 1960. 383 p., 40 leaves of plates: ill., ports. Translation of Histoire de la peinture surréaliste. 1. Surrealism 2. Painting I. T. II. Title: Surrealist painting.
ND1265.J483 1960

**Kahnweiler, Daniel Henry, 1884-.**    • 1.6349
The rise of cubism; tr. by Henry Aronson. New York, Wittenborn, Schultz [1949] xi, 35 p. ill. (The Documents of modern art, 9) 1. Cubism I. T. II. Series.
ND1265 K313      LC 49-8931

**Nochlin, Linda, ed.**    1.6350
Impressionism and post–impressionism, 1874–1904; sources and documents. — Englewood Cliffs, N.J.: Prentice-Hall, [1966] ix, 222 p.: facsim.; 23 cm. — (Sources and documents in the history of art series.) 1. Impressionism (Art) 2. Post-impressionism (Art) 3. Art, Modern — 19th century — Sources. I. T. II. Series.
ND1265.N58      759.05      LC 66-23610

**Rewald, John, 1912-.**    1.6351
Post–impressionism: From Van Gogh to Gauguin. — 3rd ed., rev. — New York: Museum of Modern Art; Boston: distributed by New York Graphic Society, 1978. 590 p.: ill. (some col.), ports.; 26 cm. 1. Post-impressionism (Art) 2. Painters I. T.
ND1265.R43 1978      759.915 759.06*      LC 77-77286      ISBN 0870705326

**Itten, Johannes, 1888-1967.**    • 1.6352
[Kunst der Farbe. English] The art of color; the subjective experience and objective rationale of color. Translated by Ernst van Haagen. New York, Reinhold Pub. Corp. [1961] 155 p. mounted illus. (part col.) 29 x 32 cm. 1. Color — Psychological aspects 2. Painting — Technique 3. Aesthetics I. T.
ND1280.I813      752      LC 61-11190

**Munsell, Albert Henry, 1858-1918.**    • 1.6353
A color notation, by A. H. Munsell. An illustrated system defining all colors and their relations by measured scales of hue, value, and chroma. Introduction by Royal B. Farnum. 10th ed. (edited and rearranged) Baltimore, Md., Munsell color company, inc., 1946. 74 p. front. (port.) illus., III col. pl., diagrs. 20 cm. Preface signed: A. E. O. Munsell, Walter T. Spry, Blanche S. Bellamy. 1. Color I. Munsell, A. E. O. (Alexander Ector Orr) ed. II. T.
ND1280.M9 1946      752      LC 46-1651

# ND1290–1460 Special Subjects: Portraits, Landscapes

**Freer Gallery of Art.**    1.6354
Chinese figure painting, by Thomas Lawton. Washington, Smithsonian Institution, 1973. x, 236 p. illus. (part col.) 31 cm. (Its fiftieth anniversary exhibition, v. 2) Catalogue. 1. Figure painting — Exhibitions. 2. Figure painting — China. I. Lawton, Thomas, 1931- II. T.
ND1293.C6Fx N5020.W52 F733 1973 vol.2      709/.5/0740153 s
757/.0951      LC 73-87219      ISBN 0879230886 ISBN 0879230878

**Strong, Roy C.**    1.6355
The English Renaissance miniature / Roy Strong. — New York, N.Y.: Thames and Hudson, 1983. 208 p.: ill. (some col.); 27 cm. 1. Portrait miniatures, English 2. Portrait miniatures, Renaissance — England. I. T.
ND1337.G7 S85 1983      757/.7/0942 19      LC 83-70147      ISBN 0500233705

**Clark, Kenneth, 1903-.**    • 1.6356
Landscape into art / Kenneth Clark. — 1st U.S. ed. — New York: Harper & Row, c1976. xv, 248 p., [8] leaves of plates: ill. (some col.); 26 cm. 'Based on lectures given ... to the University of Oxford.' Includes index. 1. Landscape painting I. T.
ND1340.C55 1976      758/.1      LC 75-23876      ISBN 0060107812

**American light: the luminist movement, 1850–1875 / [edited by]**    1.6357
**John Wilmerding, with contributions by Lisa Fellows Andrus ... [et al.].**
Washington, D.C.: National Gallery of Art, c1980. 330 p.: ill. (some col.); 23 x 28 cm. An exhibition to be held at the National Gallery of Art, Feb. 10-June 15, 1980. Includes index. 1. Luminism (Art) — Exhibitions. 2. Landscape painting, American — Exhibitions. 3. Landscape painting — 19th century — United States — Exhibitions. 4. Hudson River school of landscape painting — Exhibitions. 5. Drawing — 19th century — United States — Exhibitions.

6. Photography, Artistic — Exhibitions. I. Wilmerding, John. II. Andrus, Lisa Fellows.
ND1351.5.A46      758/.1/09730740153      LC 79-24409

**Novak, Barbara.**    1.6358
Nature and culture: American landscape and painting, 1825–1875 / Barbara Novak. — New York: Oxford University Press, 1980. xi, 323 p.: ill.; 26 cm. Includes index. 1. Landscape painting, American 2. Landscape painting — 19th century — United States I. T.
ND1351.5.N68      758/.1/0973      LC 79-10131      ISBN 0195026063

**Nasgaard, Roald.**    1.6359
The mystic north: symbolist landscape painting in northern Europe and North America, 1890–1940 / Roald Nasgaard. — Toronto; Buffalo: Published in association with the Art Gallery of Ontario by University of Toronto Press, c1984. x, 253 p.: ill. (some col.); 23 cm. Based on an exhibition held at the Art Gallery of Ontario and the Cincinnati Art Museum. Includes index. 1. Landscape painting — Europe, Northern — Exhibitions. 2. Landscape painting — 19th century — Europe, Northern — Exhibitions. 3. Landscape painting — 20th century — Europe, Northern — Exhibitions. 4. Landscape painting, American — Exhibitions. 5. Landscape painting — 20th century — United States — Exhibitions. 6. Landscape painting, Canadian — Exhibitions. 7. Landscape painting — 20th century — Canada — Exhibitions. 8. Symbolism (Art movement) — Exhibitions. I. Art Gallery of Ontario. II. Cincinnati Art Museum. III. T.
ND1353.5.N37 1984      758/.1/09480740113541 19      LC 84-175026
ISBN 0802025307

**Herrmann, Luke.**    1.6360
British landscape painting of the eighteenth century. — New York: Oxford University Press, 1974 [c1973] 151 p.: illus. (part col.); 29 cm. 1. Landscape painting, British I. T.
ND1354.4.H47 1974      758/.1/0942      LC 73-88405      ISBN 0195197577

**Staley, Allen.**    1.6361
The Pre–Raphaelite landscape. — Oxford: Clarendon Press, 1973. xxvi, 193, [108] p.: illus. (some col.); 30 cm. — (Oxford studies in the history of art and architecture.) Based on the author's thesis, Yale University, 1965. 1. Landscape painting, English 2. Preraphaelitism — England. I. T. II. Series.
ND1354.5.S72      758/.1/0942      LC 73-169702      ISBN 0198173075

**A Day in the country: impressionism and the French landscape**    1.6362
**/ Los Angeles County Museum of Art [and] the Art Institute of Chicago [and] Réunion des musées nationaux; [edited by Andrea P.A. Belloli].**
New York: Abrams, 1984. — 375 p.: ill. (some col.); 28 cm. 'Exhibition itinerary: Los Angeles County Museum of Art, June 28-September 16, 1984; the Art Institute of Chicago, October 18, 1984-January 6, 1985; Galeries nationales d'exposition du grand palais, Paris, February 8-April 22, 1985'—T.p. verso. Includes index. 1. Landscape painting, French — Exhibitions. 2. Landscape painting — 19th century — France — Exhibitions. 3. Impressionism (Art) — France — Exhibitions. 4. France in art — Exhibitions. I. Belloli, Andrea P. A. II. Los Angeles County Museum of Art. III. Art Institute of Chicago. IV. Réunion des musées nationaux (France)
ND1356.5.D39 1984      758/.1/0944074 19      LC 84-3885      ISBN 0810908271

**Munsterberg, Hugo, 1916-.**    • 1.6363
The landscape painting of China and Japan. [1st ed.] Rutland, Vt., C.E. Tuttle [1955] xv, 144 p. ill. (1 col.) 1. Landscape painting — China 2. Landscape painting — Japan
ND1366 M8

**Sullivan, Michael, 1916-.**    1.6364
Chinese landscape painting: volume II: the Sui and T'ang dynasties / Michael Sullivan. — Berkeley: University of California Press, c1980. xiv, 191 p., [56] leaves of plates: ill., map. 1. Landscape painting, Chinese 2. Nature (Aesthetics) 3. Symbolism in art I. T.
ND1366.7 S93      LC 77-83111      ISBN 0520035585

**Sullivan, Michael, 1916-.**    1.6365
Symbols of eternity: the art of landscape painting in China / Michael Sullivan. — Stanford, Calif.: Stanford University Press, 1979. xiii, 205 p.: ill. (some col.); 27 cm. Includes index. 1. Landscape painting, Chinese I. T.
ND1366.7.S94      758/.1/0951      LC 78-65393      ISBN 0804710252

**Gerdts, William H.**    1.6366
Painters of the humble truth: masterpieces of American still life, 1801–1939 / William H. Gerdts. — Columbia, Mo.: University of Missouri Press; [Tulsa, Okla.]: Philbrook Art Center, 1982. xiii, 293 p.: ill. (some col.); 31 cm. Based on: American still-life painting. Issued in connection of an exhibition held at the Philbrook Art Center. Includes indexes. 1. Still-life painting, American —

Exhibitions. I. Gerdts, William H. American still-life painting. II. Philbrook Art Center. III. T.
ND1392.G48    758/.4/0973074016686 19    LC 81-11400    ISBN 0826203558

**Friedmann, Herbert, 1900-1987.**      1.6367
A bestiary for Saint Jerome: animal symbolism in European religious art / Herbert Friedmann. — Washington: Smithsonian Institution Press, 1980. 378 p.: ill. (some col.); 29 cm. Includes index. 1. Jerome, Saint, d. 419 or 20 — Art. 2. Painting, European 3. Animals in art 4. Animals — Folklore I. T.
ND1432.E85 F74 1980    704.94/6    LC 79-607804    ISBN 0874474466

**Masters of seventeenth–century Dutch genre painting:**    1.6368
**Philadelphia Museum of Art, March 18 to May 13, 1984, Gemäldegalerie, Staatliche Museen Preussischer Kulturbesitz, Berlin (West), June 8 to August 12, 1984, Royal Academy of Arts, London, September 7 to November 18, 1984 / [edited by Jane Iandola Watkins].**
Philadelphia: Philadelphia Museum of Art, 1984. lxxxviii, 397 p.: ill. (some col.); 28 cm. Exhibition organized by Peter C. Sutton. Includes index. 1. Genre painting, Dutch — Exhibitions. 2. Genre painting — 17th century — Netherlands — Exhibitions. I. Watkins, Jane Iandola. II. Sutton, Peter C. III. Brown, Christopher, 1948- IV. Philadelphia Museum of Art. V. Gemäldegalerie (Berlin, Germany: West) VI. Royal Academy of Arts (Great Britain)
ND1452.N43 M37 1984    754/.09492/074 19    LC 84-5798    ISBN 0812279514

**Fu, Shen, 1937-.**      1.6369
Traces of the brush: studies in Chinese calligraphy / by Shen C. Y. Fu in collaboration with Marilyn W. Fu, Mary G. Neill, Mary Jane Clark. — New Haven, Conn.: Yale University Art Gallery, c1977. xii, 314 p.: ill.; 30 cm. 'This catalogue accompanies an exhibition held at the Yale University Art Gallery, New Haven, Connecticut, between April 6 and June 27, 1977, and at the University Art Museum, Berkeley, California, between September 20 and November 27, 1977.' Includes index. 1. Calligraphy, Chinese — Exhibitions. I. Yale University. Art Gallery. II. University of California, Berkeley. University Art Museum. III. T.
ND1457.C52 N483    745.6/199/51074014967    LC 76-49688    ISBN 089467000X

**Princeton University. Art Museum.**      1.6370
Images of the mind: selections from the Edward L. Elliott family and John B. Elliott collections of Chinese calligraphy and painting at the Art Museum, Princeton University / Wen C. Fong ... [et al.]. — Princeton: Art Museum, Princeton University in association with Princeton University Press, c1984. xvi, 504 p.: ill. (some col.) 'Dates of the exhibition: April 15-June 17, 1984.' 1. Calligraphy, Chinese — Exhibitions 2. Painting, Chinese — Exhibitions I. Fong, Wen C. II. T. III. Title: Selections from the Edward L. Elliott family and John B. Elliott collections of Chinese calligraphy and painting at the Art Museum, Princeton University
ND1457.C52 P744 1984    LC 83-43056    ISBN 0691040273

**Shimizu, Yoshiaki.**      1.6371
Masters of Japanese calligraphy, 8th–9th century / Yoshiaki Shimizu, John M. Rosenfield. — [New York?]: Asia Society Galleries, Japan House Gallery, 1984. 340 p.: ill.; 30 cm. 'This book is published on the occasion of an exhibition of Japanese calligraphy Organized jointly by Japan House Gallery and the Asia Society Galleries ...' 1. Calligraphy, Japanese — History — Exhibitions. 2. Calligraphy, Zen — Japan — Exhibitions. 3. Calligraphy, Buddhist — Japan — Exhibitions. 4. Calligraphers — Japan. I. Rosenfield, John M. II. Japan House Gallery. III. Asia Society. Galleries. IV. T.
ND 1457 J32 R82 1984    LC 84-82053

# ND1500–1660 Painting Materials. Conservation. Forgeries

**Early Chinese texts on painting / compiled and edited by Susan**    1.6372
**Bush and Hsio–yen Shih.**
Cambridge, Mass.: Published for the Harvard-Yenching Institute by Harvard University Press, 1985. xii, 391 p., [8] p. of plates: ill.; 24 cm. Includes index. 1. Painting — Technique 2. Painting, Chinese — Technique. I. Bush, Susan. II. Shih, Hsio-yen, 1933-
ND1500.E25 1985    759.951 19    LC 84-12859    ISBN 0674220250

**Mayer, Ralph, 1895-.**      • 1.6373
The artist's handbook of materials and techniques / by Ralph Mayer. — 1982 ed., rev. and updated. — New York: Viking Press, 1981. xv, 733 p.: ill.; 25 cm. Includes index. 1. Painting — Technique 2. Artists' materials I. T.
ND1500.M3 1982    750/.28 19    LC 81-50514    ISBN 0670136662

**Mayer, Ralph, 1895-.**      1.6374
The painter's craft: an introduction to artists' methods and materials / Ralph Mayer. — 3d ed. — New York: Viking Press, 1975. 200 p.: ill.; 25 cm. (A Studio book) Includes index. 1. Painting — Technique 2. Artists' materials I. T.
ND1500.M32 1975    751    LC 75-1578    ISBN 0670535699

**Thompson, Daniel Varney, 1902-.**      • 1.6375
The materials and techniques of medieval painting. With a foreword by Bernard Berenson. — New York, Dover Publications [1956] 239 p. 21 cm. Unabridged and unaltered republication of the first ed. published in 1936 under title: The materials of medieval painting. 1. Painting — Technique 2. Pigments 3. Painting, Medieval I. T.
ND1500.T5 1956    751    LC 57-4711

**Burroughs, Alan, 1897-1965.**      • 1.6376
Art criticism from a laboratory. Westport, Conn., Greenwood Press [1971, c1938] xxiii, 277 p. illus. 24 cm. 1. Painting — Radiography 2. Painting — Forgeries I. T.
ND1635.B87 1971    751.5/8    LC 70-110267    ISBN 0837144930

**Keck, Caroline (Kohn)**      • 1.6377
A handbook on the care of paintings, by Caroline K. Keck. New York, Published for the American Association for State and Local History by Watson-Guptill Publications 1967, c1965. xii, 136 p. illus., ports. 24 cm. 1. Painting — Conservation and restoration. I. American Association for State and Local History. II. T.
ND1640.K38 1967    751.6    LC 67-13743

# ND1700–2495 Watercolor Painting

**Stebbins, Theodore E.**      1.6378
American master drawings and watercolors: a history of works on paper from colonial times to the present / by Theodore E. Stebbins, Jr., with the assistance of John Caldwell and Carol Troyen. — 1st ed. — New York: Harper & Row, c1976. xv, 464 p.: ill. (some col.); 29 cm. Includes index. 1. Watercolor painting, American 2. Drawing, American I. Caldwell, John, 1941- II. Troyen, Carol. III. T.
ND1805.S73 1976    759.13    LC 75-37156    ISBN 0060140682

**Hoopes, Donelson F.**      1.6379
Eakins watercolors, by Donelson F. Hoopes. — New York: Watson-Guptill, [1971] 87 p.: illus. (part col.); 29 cm. 1. Eakins, Thomas, 1844-1916. I. T.
ND1839.E2 H6    759.13    LC 78-152785    ISBN 0823015904

**Latrobe, Benjamin Henry, 1764-1820.**      1.6380
Latrobe's view of America, 1795-1820: selections from the watercolors and sketches / Edward C. Carter II, John C. Van Horne, and Charles E. Brownell, editors, Tina H. Sheller, associate editor; with the assistance of Stephen F. Lintner, J. Frederick Fausz, and Geraldine S. Vickers. — New Haven: Published for the Maryland Historical Society by Yale University Press, 1985. xxi, 400 p.: ill. (some col.); 23 x 28 cm. (The Papers of Benjamin Henry Latrobe. Series III, The Sketchbooks and miscellaneous drawings) Includes index. 1. Latrobe, Benjamin Henry, 1764-1820. 2. United States in art. I. Carter, Edward Carlos, 1928- II. Van Horne, John C. III. Brownell, Charles E. IV. Maryland Historical Society. V. T.
ND1839.L35 A4 1985    759.13 19    LC 84-7580    ISBN 0300029497

**Lawrence, Jacob, 1917-.**      1.6381
Jacob Lawrence, by Milton W. Brown, with the assistance of Louise A. Parks. New York, Whitney Museum of American Art [1974] 64 p. illus. (part col.), port. 25 cm. 'Compiled for the Jacob Lawrence exhibition held at the Whitney Museum of American Art, May, 1974.' Errata slip inserted. 1. Lawrence, Jacob, 1917- I. Brown, Milton Wolf, 1911- II. Whitney Museum of American Art. III. T.
ND1839.L36 B76    759.13    LC 74-78123

**Clark, Carol, 1947-.**      1.6382
Thomas Moran: watercolors of the American West: text and catalogue raisonné / by Carol Clark. — Austin: Published for the Amon Carter Museum of Western Art by the University of Texas Press, c1980. 180 p., [2] leaves of plates: ill. (some col.); 29 cm. Issued on the occasion of an exhibition to be held May 23-July 13, 1980 at Amon Carter Museum of Western Art, Fort Worth, Tex., Aug. 5-Oct. 5, 1980 at Cleveland Museum of Art, and Oct. 23, 1980-Jan. 4, 1981 at Yale University Art Gallery. 'Catalogue raisonné': p. 121-158. Includes indexes. 1. Moran, Thomas, 1837-1926 — Exhibitions. 2. West (U.S.) in art — Exhibitions. I. Moran, Thomas, 1837-1926. II. Amon Carter Museum of Western Art. III. Cleveland Museum of Art. IV. Yale University. Art Gallery. V. T.
ND1839.M84 A4 1980    759.13    LC 80-13459    ISBN 0292750595

**Bell, Michael. comp.**     **1.6383**
Painters in a new land. [Greenwich, Conn.] New York Graphic Society [1973]
224 p. illus. 32 cm. 1. Canada in art. 2. Watercolor painting, Canadian
3. Drawing, Canadian I. T.
ND1841.B44 1973     758     *LC* 73-79998     *ISBN* 0821205811

**Hardie, Martin, 1875-1952.**     **1.6384**
Water–colour painting in Britain; edited by Dudley Snelgrove with Jonathan
Mayne and Basil Taylor. — [2nd. ed.] London: Batsford, [1967-69. 3v.   : col.
front., plates.; 31 cm. 1. Watercolor painting — Great Britain — History.
I. Snelgrove, Dudley. ed. II. T.
ND1928.H37    ND1928.H37 1967.    759.2    *LC* 66-77981    *ISBN*
0713407166

**Dunbar, Pamela.**     **1.6385**
William Blake's illustrations to the poetry of Milton / Pamela Dunbar. —
Oxford [Eng.]: Clarendon Press; New York: Oxford University Press, 1980.
261 p.: ill. Includes index. 1. Blake, William, 1757-1827. 2. Milton, John,
1608-1674 — Illustrations. I. T.
ND1942.B55 D86    759.2    *LC* 79-41155    *ISBN* 0198173458

**Blake, William, 1757-1827.**     **1.6386**
[William Blake's designs for Gray's poems] Water–colours illustrating the
poems of Thomas Gray. With an introd. and commentary by Sir Geoffrey
Keynes. Chicago, J. P. O'Hara, 1972. xx, 72 p. port. 30 cm. Each water-color
contains the text illustrated. All 116 are reproduced in monochrome, 16 also in
color. Originally published in 1922 under title: William Blake's designs for
Gray's poems. 1. Gray, Thomas, 1716-1771 — Illustrations. I. Gray, Thomas,
1716-1771. II. Keynes, Geoffrey, Sir, 1887- III. T.
ND1942.B55 G72 1972    759.2    *LC* 70-186889    *ISBN* 0879556005

**Hayes, John T.**     **1.6387**
Rowlandson; watercolours and drawings [by] John Hayes. — [London]:
Phaidon [Distributed in U.S.A. by Praeger, New York, 1972] 214 p.: illus. (part
col.); 29 cm. 1. Rowlandson, Thomas, 1756-1827. I. Rowlandson, Thomas,
1756-1827. II. T.
ND1942.R64 H39    759.2    *LC* 79-190599    *ISBN* 0714815551

**Koschatzky, Walter.**     **1.6388**
[Albrecht Dürer: Die Landschaftsaquarelle. English] Albrecht Dürer: the
landscape water–colours. [Translated from the German by Philippa
McDermott] New York, St. Martin's Press [c1973] 111 p. illus. (part col.) 31 x
42 cm. Translation of Albrecht Dürer: Die Landschaftsaquarelle. 1. Dürer,
Albrecht, 1471-1528. 2. Landscape in art I. Dürer, Albrecht, 1471-1528.
II. T.
ND1954.D8 K613 1973    759.3    *LC* 73-85310    *ISBN* 090262086X

**Bodmer, Karl, 1809-1893.**     **1.6389**
Karl Bodmer's America / introduction by William H. Goetzmann; annotations
by David C. Hunt and Marsha V. Gallagher; artist's biography by William J.
Orr. — Lincoln: University of Nebraska Press, 1984. 376 p.: ill., map.
1. Bodmer, Karl, 1809-1893. 2. United States in art. 3. West (U.S.) in art.
4. Watercolorists — Switzerland — Biography. I. Hunt, David C., 1935-
II. Gallagher, Marsha V. III. T.
ND2010.B58 A4 1984    759.9494 19    *LC* 83-27391    *ISBN*
0803211856

**Japanese ink paintings from American collections: the**     **1.6390**
**Muromachi period: an exhibition in honor of Shūjirō Shimada /**
**edited by Yoshiaki Shimizu and Carolyn Wheelwright.**
Princeton, N.J.: Art Museum, Princeton University: distributed by Princeton
University Press, c1976. 300 p.: ill.; 29 cm. Exhibition held Apr. 25-June 13,
1976. Includes index. 1. Shimada, Shūjirō, 1907- 2. Ink painting, Japanese —
Kamakura-Momoyama periods, 1185-1600 — Exhibitions. I. Shimizu,
Yoshiaki, 1936- II. Wheelwright, Carolyn. III. Princeton University. Art
Museum.
ND2071.J36    759.952/074/014967    *LC* 75-33450    *ISBN*
0691039135. *ISBN* 0691039186 pbk

**Miyajima, Shin'ichi.**     **1.6391**
Japanese ink painting / Miyajima Shin'ichi, Satō Yasuhiro; George Kuwayama,
editor; Los Angeles County Museum of Art, Agency for Cultural Affairs,
Government of Japan. — Los Angeles: The Museum, c1985. 191 p.: ill. (some
col.); 32 cm. Catalogue of a loan exhibition of Japanese ink painting, Los
Angeles County Museum of Art, March 10-May 12, 1985. Includes index.
1. Ink painting, Japanese — Kamakura-Momoyama period, 1185-1600 —
Exhibitions. 2. Ink painting, Japanese — Edo period, 1600-1868 —
Exhibitions. I. Sato, Yasuhiro. II. Kuwayama, George. III. Los Angeles
County Museum of Art. IV. Japan. Bunkachō. V. T.
ND2071.M59 1985    759.952/074/019494 19    *LC* 84-26088    *ISBN*
0875871232

**The English miniature / John Murdoch ... [et al.].**     **1.6392**
New Haven: Yale University Press, 1981. vi, 230 p.: ill. (some col.); 27 cm.
1. Portrait miniatures, English — Addresses, essays, lectures. 2. Watercolor
painting, English — Addresses, essays, lectures. I. Murdoch, John, 1945-
ND2202.G7 E5    757/.7/0942 19    *LC* 81-70055    *ISBN* 0300027699

# ND2550–2888 Mural Painting

**Demus, Otto.**     **1.6393**
[Romanische Wandmalerei. English] Romanesque mural painting. Photos. by
Max Hirmer. [Translated from the German by Mary Whittall] New York, H.
N. Abrams [1970] 654 p. maps, plates (part col.) 32 cm. Translation of
Romanische Wandmalerei. 1. Mural painting and decoration, Romanesque
I. T.
ND2580.D413 1970b    751.7/3/094    *LC* 76-82874    *ISBN*
0810904535

**Borsook, Eve.**     **1.6394**
The mural painters of Tuscany: from Cimabue to Andrea del Sarto / by Eve
Borsook. — 2d ed., rev. and enl. — Oxford: Clarendon Press; New York:
Oxford University Press, c1980. 314 p.: ill. (Oxford studies in the history of art
and architecture.) Includes index. 1. Mural painting and decoration, Italian —
Italy — Tuscany. 2. Mural painting and decoration, Gothic — Italy —
Tuscany. 3. Mural painting and decoration, Renaissance — Italy — Tuscany.
I. T. II. Series.
ND2756.T9 B6 1980    751.7/3/09455    *LC* 78-40645    *ISBN*
0198173016

**Stubblebine, James H.**     **1.6395**
Assisi and the rise of vernacular art / James H. Stubblebine. — 1st ed. —
Cambridge: Harper & Row, c1985. xiii, 140 p.: ill.; 24 cm. (Icon editions)
Includes index. 1. Giotto, 1266?-1337. 2. Francis, of Assisi, Saint, 1182-1226
— Art 3. San Francisco (Church: Assisi, Italy) 4. Mural painting and
decoration, Gothic — Italy — Assisi. 5. Mural painting and decoration, Italian
— Italy — Assisi. 6. Mural painting and decoration — Expertising I. T.
ND2757.A8 S88 1985    751.7/3/0945651 19    *LC* 84-43239    *ISBN*
0064385566

**Restle, Marcell, 1932-.**     **1.6396**
[Bysantinische Wandmalerei in Kleinasien. English] Byzantine wall painting in
Asia Minor. Greenwich, Conn., New York Graphic Society [1968, c1967] 3 v.
illus. (part col.), maps, plans. 28 cm. Translation of Die bysantinische
Wandmalerei in Kleinasien. 1. Mural painting and decoration, Byzantine —
Turkey. 2. Mural painting and decoration — Turkey. I. T.
ND2794.R413    751.7/3/09561    *LC* 68-12371

**Singh, Madanjeet.**     **1.6397**
Ajanta; Ajanta painting of the sacred and the secular. New York, Macmillan
[1965] 189 p. illus., plans, 82 plates (part col.) 31 cm. Bibliography: p. 189.
1. Mural painting and decoration — Ajanta. 2. Art, Buddhist 3. Cave temples
I. T. II. Title: Ajanta painting of the sacred and the secular.
ND2827.S48    759.95484    *LC* 65-22616

**Singh, Madanjeet.**     • **1.6398**
India; paintings from Ajanta caves. Introd. by Madanjeet Singh. [New York]
New York Graphic Society [1954] 10 p. ill., 32 col. plates. (UNESCO world art
series, 1) 1. Painting — Ajanta 2. Cave temples 3. Mural painting and
decoration I. T. II. Series.
ND2827.S5    *LC* 54-3144

**Pal, Pratapaditya.**     **1.6399**
A Buddhist paradise: the murals of Alchi, western Himalayas / text by
Pratapaditya Pal; photographs by Lionel Fournier. — Hongkong: Published by
Ravi Kumar for Visual Dharma Publications, 1982. 67 p., [140] leaves of plates:
col. ill.; 29 cm. Includes index. 1. Mural painting and decoration, Tibetan.
2. Painting — Ladakh — Alchi. 3. Art, Tantric-Buddhist — Ladakh.
I. Fournier, Lionel. II. T. III. Title: The Murals of Alchi, Western
Himalayas.
ND2829.A4 P3    *ISBN* 9627049026

# ND2890–3416 Illumination of Books and Manuscripts

**Calkins, Robert G.** 1.6400
Illuminated books of the Middle Ages / Robert G. Calkins. — Ithaca, N.Y.: Cornell University Press, 1983. 341 p., [24] p. of plates: ill. (some col.); 29 cm. Includes index. 1. Illumination of books and manuscripts, Medieval I. T.
ND2920.C28 1983    745.6/7/0902 19    *LC* 83-5208    *ISBN* 0801415063

**Weitzmann, Kurt, 1904-.** 1.6401
Late antique and early Christian book illumination / Kurt Weitzmann. — New York: G. Braziller, 1977. 126 p.: ill.; 29 cm. 1. Illumination of books and manuscripts, Early Christian I. T.
ND2930.W42    745.6/7/09495    *LC* 76-16444    *ISBN* 0807608300

**Weitzmann, Kurt, 1904-.** 1.6402
Studies in classical and Byzantine manuscript illumination. Edited by Herbert L. Kessler. With an introd. by Hugo Buchthal. — Chicago: University of Chicago Press, [1971] xxii, 346 p.: illus.; 27 cm. 1. Illumination of books and manuscripts, Byzantine — History. I. T.
ND2930.W43    745/.6/7    *LC* 77-116381    *ISBN* 0226892468

**Nordenfalk, Carl Adam Johan, 1907-.** 1.6403
Celtic painting and Anglo–Saxon painting: book illumination in the British Isles, 600–800 / Carl Nordenfalk. — New York: G. Braziller, 1977. 124 p.: ill. (some col.); 29 cm. 1. Illumination of books and manuscripts, Celtic I. T.
ND2940.N67    745.6/7/0941    *LC* 76-16443    *ISBN* 0807608254

**Carolingian painting / introduction by Florentine Mutherich;** 1.6404
**commentaries by J. E. Gaehde.**
New York: G. Braziller, 1977. 126 p., 48 leaves of plates: ill. 1. Illumination of books and manuscripts, Carlovingian I. Mütherich, Florentine. II. Gehde, J. E.
ND2950.C37    ND2950 C37.    745.6/7/094    *LC* 76-15908    *ISBN* 0807608513

**Robertson, Donald, 1919-.** 1.6405
Mexican manuscript painting of the early colonial period: the Metropolitan Schools. New Haven, Yale University Press, 1959. xix, 234 p. 88 plates. (Yale historical publications. History of art, 12) 1. Miniature painting — Mexico 2. Illumination of books and manuscripts — Mexico 3. Manuscripts, Mexican I. T.
ND3044 R6    *LC* 59-12700

**Alexander, J. J. G. (Jonathan James Graham)** 1.6406
Insular manuscripts, 6th to the 9th century / by J. J. G. Alexander. — London: H. Miller, c1978. 219 p.: ill. (some col.); 34 cm. — (Survey of manuscripts illuminated in the British Isles. v. 1) 1. Illumination of books and manuscripts, Medieval — Great Britain. 2. Illumination of books and manuscripts, English. 3. Illumination of books and manuscripts, Irish. I. T. II. Series.
ND3128.K35 vol. 1    745.6/7/0942 s 745.6/7/0941    *LC* 78-320143    *ISBN* 0905203011

**Temple, Elżbieta.** 1.6407
Anglo–Saxon manuscripts, 900–1066 / by Elżbieta Temple. — London: Harvey Miller, c1976. 243 p.: ill. (some col.); 34 cm. (Survey of manuscripts illuminated in the British Isles. v. 2) 1. Illumination of books and manuscripts, Anglo-Saxon — Catalogs. I. T. II. Series.
ND3128.K35 vol. 2 ND2940    745.6/7/0942 s 745.6/7/0942    *LC* 76-373399    *ISBN* 0856020168

**Kauffmann, C. M. (Claus Michael), 1931-.** 1.6408
Romanesque manuscripts, 1066–1190 / by C. M. Kauffmann. — London: H. Miller, [1975] 235 p.: ill. (some col.); 34 cm. — (Survey of manuscripts illuminated in the British Isles. v. 3) 1. Illumination of books and manuscripts, Romanesque — England — Catalogs. 2. Illumination of books and manuscripts, English — Catalogs. I. T. II. Series.
ND3128.K35 vol. 3    745.6/7/0942 s 745.6/7/0942    *LC* 75-319256    *ISBN* 0856020176

**Morgan, Nigel J.** 1.6409
Early Gothic manuscripts / by Nigel Morgan. — London: H. Miller; Oxford; New York: Oxford University Press, c1982-. v. < 1 > : ill.; 34 cm. (Survey of manuscripts illuminated in the British Isles. v. 4-) 1. Illumination of books and manuscripts, Gothic — England — Catalogs. 2. Illumination of books and manuscripts, English — Catalogs. I. T. II. Series.
ND3128.K35 vol. 4 ND2980    745.6/7/0942 s 745.6/7/0942 19    *LC* 83-155524    *ISBN* 0199210268

**Morgan, Nigel J.** 1.6410
The golden age of English manuscript painting (1200–1500) / Nigel Morgan and Richard Marks. New York: G. Braziller, 1981. 119 p.: ill. (some col.); 29 cm. (Illuminated manuscript series) 1. Illumination of books and manuscripts, English. 2. Illumination of books and manuscripts, Gothic — England. I. Marks, Richard, 1945- joint author. II. T. III. Series.
ND3128.M67    745.6/7/0942    *LC* 80-12985    *ISBN* 0807609714

**Avril, François.** 1.6411
Manuscript painting at the court of France: the fourteenth century, 1310–1380 / François Avril; [translated from the French by Ursule Molinaro, with the assistance of Bruce Benderson]. — New York: G. Braziller, 1978. 118 p.: ill. (some col.); 29 cm. 1. Illumination of books and manuscripts, French 2. Illumination of books and manuscripts, Gothic — France. I. T.
ND3147.A8813    745.6/7/0944    *LC* 77-78721    *ISBN* 0807608785

**Meiss, Millard.** 1.6412
French painting in the time of Jean De Berry; the late Fourteenth century and the patronage of the Duke. London, Phaidon, 1967. 2 v. illus., plates (1 col.) 31 cm. (National Gallery of Art: Kress Foundation studies in the history of European art no. 2) 'U.S. distributors: F. A. Praeger, New York.' 1. Berry, Jean de France, duc de, 1340-1416. 2. Illumination of books and manuscripts, Medieval — France. 3. Miniature painting, French 4. Miniature painting, Medieval — France. I. T.
ND3147.M37 1967    745.6/7/0944    *LC* 67-29885    *ISBN* 0714813095

**Meiss, Millard.** 1.6413
French painting in the time of Jean de Berry: the Limbourgs and their contemporaries / by Millard Meiss, with the assistance of Sharon Off Dunlap Smith and Elizabeth Home Beatson. — New York: G. Braziller, 1974. 2 v.: ill. (some col.); 32 cm. (Franklin Jasper Walls lectures.) Includes indexes. 1. Limbourg, Pol de, ca. 1385-ca. 1416. 2. Limbourg, Hermann de, ca. 1385-ca. 1416. 3. Limbourg, Hennequin de, ca. 1385-ca. 1416. 4. Berry, Jean de France, duc de, 1340-1416. 5. Illumination of books and manuscripts, French 6. Illumination of books and manuscripts, Gothic — France. 7. Hours, Books of I. Smith, Sharon Off Dunlap, joint author. II. Beatson, Elizabeth Home, joint author. III. T. IV. Title: The Limbourgs and their contemporaries V. Series.
ND3147.M38 1974    ND3147 M38 1974.    745.6/7/0944    *LC* 73-90120    *ISBN* 0807607347

**Porcher, Jean.** 1.6414
Medieval French miniatures. [Translated from the French by Julian Brown] New York, H. N. Abrams [1960?] 275 p. illus. (part col.) col. plates. 31 cm. 'Bibliographical commentary': p. 85-[94] 1. Miniature painting — France. 2. Illumination of books and manuscripts — France. I. T.
ND3147.P643    759.4    *LC* 59-12874

**Meiss, Millard.** 1.6415
French painting in the time of Jean de Berry; the Boucicaut master, by Millard Meiss, with the assistance of Kathleen Morand and Edith W. Kirsch. London, Phaidon, 1968. 384 p. illus. (some col.), facsims., plates, indexes. 31 cm. (National Gallery of Art: Kress Foundation studies in the history of European art, no. 3) 'Distributors in the United States: Frederick A. Praeger Inc.' 1. Boucicaut, Jean Le Maingre de, d. 1421. 2. Berry, Jean de France, duc de, 1340-1416. I. Morand, Kathleen. II. Kirsch, Edith W. III. T.
ND3150.B57 M4    745/.0924    *LC* 70-400305    *ISBN* 071481346X

**Illuminated Greek manuscripts from American collections; an** 1.6416
**exhibition in honor of Kurt Weitzmann. Edited by Gary Vikan.**
[Princeton, N.J.]: Art Museum, Princeton University; distributed by Princeton University Press, [1973] 231 p.: illus. (part col.); 27 cm. Catalog of an exhibition held at the Princeton University Art Museum Apr. 14-May 20, 1973. 1. Illumination of books and manuscripts, Greek — Exhibitions. 2. Illumination of books and manuscripts — United States. I. Weitzmann, Kurt, 1904- II. Vikan, Gary, ed. III. Princeton University. Art Museum.
ND3155.I4 1973    745.6/7/09495074014967    *LC* 72-92151    *ISBN* 0691038899

**Delaissé, L. M. J.** 1.6417
A century of Dutch manuscript illumination, by L. M. J. Delaissé. Berkeley, University of California Press, 1968. xii, 102 p., [79] p. of illus. (part col.) 33 cm. (California studies in the history of art. 6) Includes bibliographical references. 1. Illumination of books and manuscripts, Dutch 2. Illumination of books and manuscripts, Gothic — Netherlands. I. T. II. Series.
ND3167.D4 1968    091    *LC* 65-10577

**Williams, John, 1928 Feb. 25-.** 1.6418
Early Spanish manuscript illumination / John Williams. — New York: G. Braziller, 1977. 117 p.: ill. (some col.); 29 cm. 1. Illumination of books and manuscripts, Spanish. 2. Illumination of books and manuscripts, Medieval — Spain. I. T.
ND3199.W54    745.6/7/0946 19    *LC* 77-4042    *ISBN* 0807608661

**Titley, Norah M.**    1.6419
Persian miniature painting and its influence on the art of Turkey and India: the British Library collections / Norah M. Titley. — 1st University of Texas Press ed. — Austin: University of Texas Press, 1984, c1983. 272 p.: ill. (some col.); 28 cm. 'Published in co-operation with the British Library.' Includes indexes. 1. British Library. 2. Illumination of books and manuscripts, Iranian 3. Illumination of books and manuscripts, Turkish — Iranian influences 4. Illumination of books and manuscripts, Indic — Iranian influences I. British Library. II. T.
ND3241.T58 1984   745.6/7/0955 19   *LC* 83-81752   *ISBN* 0292764847

**The Arts of the book in Central Asia, 14th–16th centuries /**   1.6420
general editor, Basil Gray; Oleg Akimushkin ... [et al.].
Boulder, Colo.: Shambhala; Paris, France: UNESCO; [New York]: distributed in the U.S. by Random House, 1979. xiv, 314 p.: ill. (some col.); 32 cm. Includes index. 1. Miniature painting, Islamic — Asia, Central. 2. Miniature painting — Asia, Central. 3. Illumination of books and manuscripts, Islamic — Asia, Central. 4. Illumination of books and manuscripts — Asia, Central. 5. Calligraphy, Islamic — Asia, Central. 6. Calligraphy — Asia, Central. 7. Bookbinding, Islamic — Asia, Central. 8. Bookbinding — Asia, Central. I. Gray, Basil, 1904- II. Akimushkin, O. F.
ND3244.A77 1979b   745.6/7/0958   *LC* 79-2148   *ISBN* 0877731659

**Beach, Milo Cleveland.**    1.6421
The imperial image: paintings for the Mughal court / Milo Cleveland Beach. — Washington, D.C.: Freer Gallery of Art, Smithsonian Institution, 1981. 237 p.: ill. (some col.), map; 30 cm. 'Published on the occasion of an exhibition held at the Freer Gallery of Art, Washington, D.C., September 25, 1981-January 10, 1982'—T.p. verso. Map on lining papers. Includes index. 1. Illumination of books and manuscripts, Mogul — Exhibitions. 2. Illumination of books and manuscripts, Islamic — India — Exhibitions. 3. Painting, Mogul — Exhibitions. 4. Painting, Islamic — India — Exhibitions. I. Freer Gallery of Art. II. T.
ND3247.B39   745.6/7/09540740153 19   *LC* 81-8762   *ISBN* 0934686386

**Khandalavala, Karl J.**    1.6422
New documents of Indian painting; a reappraisal [by] Karl J. Khandalavala [and] Moti Chandra. — Bombay: Board of Trustees of the Prince of Wales Museum of Western India, 1969. viii, 162 p. (chiefly illus. (part col.)); 29 cm. 1. Miniature painting, Indic I. Chandra, Moti. joint author. II. T.
ND3247.K47   730/.954   *LC* 73-911326   Rs125.00

**Welch, Stuart Cary.**    1.6423
Imperial Mughal painting / Stuart Cary Welch. — 1st ed. — New York: George Braziller, 1978. 119 p.: col. ill.; 29 cm. 1. Illumination of books and manuscripts, Mogul 2. Miniature painting, Mogul. I. T.
ND3247.W44   745.6/7/0954   *LC* 77-4049   *ISBN* 080760870X

**Backhouse, Janet.**    1.6424
The illuminated manuscript / Janet Backhouse. — Oxford: Phaidon, 1979. 80 p.: ill. (some col.); 29 cm. 1. Illumination of books and manuscripts I. T.
ND3310.B32 1979   745.6/7   *LC* 78-73502   *ISBN* 0714819697

**Cahn, Walter.**    1.6425
Romanesque Bible illumination / Walter Cahn. — Ithaca, N.Y.: Cornell University Press, 1982. 304 p.: ill. (some col.); 30 cm. Includes index. 1. Bible — Illustrations 2. Illumination of books and manuscripts, Romanesque I. T.
ND3356.C33 1982   745.6/7/094 19   *LC* 82-71593   *ISBN* 0801414466

**Backhouse, Janet.**    1.6426
The Lindisfarne Gospels / Janet Backhouse. — Ithaca, N.Y.: Cornell University Press, 1981. 96 p.: ill. (some col.); 29 cm. 'A Phaidon book' Includes index. 1. Bible. N.T. Gospels Anglo-Saxon. Lindisfarne Gospels — Illustrations. 2. Illumination of books and manuscripts, Anglo-Saxon I. Bible. N.T. Gospels. Anglo-Saxon. Lindisfarne Gospels. II. Bible. N.T. Gospels. Latin. Lindisfarne Gospels. III. T.
ND3359.L5 B3 1981   745.6/7/0942889 19   *LC* 81-65990   *ISBN* 0801413540

**Harthan, John P.**    1.6427
[Books of hours and their owners] The book of hours / with a historical survey and commentary by John Harthan. — New York: Crowell, c1977. 192 p.: ill. (some col.); 32 cm. Simultaneously published as: Books of hours and their owners. London: Thames & Hudson, c1977. Includes index. 1. Hours, Books of 2. Illumination of books and manuscripts, Medieval I. T.
ND3363.A1 H37 1977b   745.6/7/094   *LC* 77-620   *ISBN* 0690016549

**The Très riches heures of Jean, Duke of Berry. Musée Condé,**   • 1.6428
**Chantilly. Introd. and legends by Jean Longnon and Raymond Cazelles. Pref. by Millard Meiss. [Translated from the French by Victoria Benedict]**
New York, G. Braziller [1969] 26, [2] p., 139 col. plates. 30 cm. Miniatures from MS. 65 in the Bibliothèque du Musée Condé, Chantilly, by the brothers Jean, Herman, and Pol de Limbourg, under the direction of Pol; the work was completed by Jean Colombe. 1. Hours, Books of I. Limbourg, Pol de, ca. 1385-ca. 1416. II. Colombe, Jean, d. 1529. illus. III. Longnon, Jean, 1887- ed. IV. Cazelles, Raymond. ed. V. Berry, Jean de France, duc de, 1340-1416. VI. Très riches heures du duc de Berry. VII. Catholic Church. Book of hours (Ms. Très riches heures du duc de Berry) VIII. Très riches heures du duc de Berry.
ND3363.B5 T713 1969b   745.6/7/0944   *LC* 70-79776

**The Hours of Catherine of Cleves. Introd. and commentaries by**   • 1.6429 ← ND 3363 C3 P73 1966
**John Plummer.**
New York, G. Braziller [1966] 359 p. 160 col. facsims. 21 cm. 'Reproduced from the illuminated manuscript belonging to the Guennol Collection and the Pierpont Morgan Library.' 1. Hours of Catherine of Cleves. 2. Illumination of books and manuscripts, Dutch I. Catherine, of Cleves, Duchess, consort of Arnold, van Egmond, Duke of Gelderland, 1417-1476. II. Plummer, John, 1919-
ND3363.C3 P55 1966   096.1   *LC* 66-23096

# NE PRINT MEDIA

# NE400–800 History

**Eichenberg, Fritz, 1901-.**    1.6430
The art of the print: masterpieces, history, techniques. — New York: H. N. Abrams, [1976] 611 p.: illus. (part col.); 30 cm. 1. Prints — History. 2. Prints — Technique I. T.
NE400.E32   769/.9   *LC* 74-18024   *ISBN* 081090103X

**Hind, Arthur Mayger, 1880-1957.**    • 1.6431
[Short history of engraving & etching] A history of engraving & etching from the 15th century to the year 1914; being the 3d and fully rev. ed. of A short history of engraving and etching. New York, Dover Publications [1963] xviii, 487 p. illus. 22 cm. 'Unabridged and unaltered republication of the third, fully revised edition, as published ... in 1923.' 1. Engraving — History. 2. Etching — History. I. T.
NE400.H66 1963   765.09   *LC* 63-5658

**Hutchison, Jane C.**    1.6432
The Master of the Housebook [by] Jane C. Hutchison. New York, Collectors Editions [1972] ix, 190 p. illus. 30 cm. (Northern European engravers of the fifteenth century) 1. Master of the Housebook, 15th cent. I. T. II. Series.
NE468.A5 H87   769/.92/4   *LC* 74-110442   *ISBN* 0876810415

**Castleman, Riva.**    1.6433
Prints of the twentieth century: a history: with ill. from the collection of The Museum of Modern Art / Riva Castleman. — New York: The Museum: distributed by Oxford University Press, 1976. 216 p.: ill. (some col.); 22 cm. Includes index. 1. Prints — 20th century I. Museum of Modern Art (New York, N.Y.) II. T.
NE490.C39 1976b   769/.904   *LC* 75-34694   *ISBN* 0870705202

**Printed art: a view of two decades / Riva Castleman.**   1.6434
New York, N.Y.: Museum of Modern Art, c1980. 144 p.: ill. (some col.); 24 cm. Published in conjunction with a loan exhibition at the Museum of Modern Art. 1. Prints — 20th century — Exhibitions. I. Castleman, Riva. II. Museum of Modern Art (New York, N.Y.)
NE491.P76   769.9/046/07401471   *LC* 79-56089   *ISBN* 0870705318

**Watrous, James, 1908-.**    1.6435
American printmaking: a century of American printmaking, 1880–1980 / James Watrous. — Madison, Wis.: University of Wisconsin Press, 1984. x, 334 p.: ill. (some col.); 29 cm. Spine title: A century of American printmaking, 1880-1980. Includes index. 1. Prints, American. 2. Prints, Modern — 19th century — United States. 3. Prints, Modern — 20th century — United States. I. T. II. Title: Century of American printmaking, 1880-1980.
NE507.W37 1984   769.973 19   *LC* 83-16956   *ISBN* 0299096807

**Johnson, Una E.**    1.6436
American prints and printmakers: a chronicle of over 400 artists and their prints from 1900 to the present / Una E. Johnson. — 1st ed. — Garden City,

N.Y.: Doubleday, 1980. xviii, 266 p.: ill. (some col.); 29 cm. Includes index. 1. Prints, American 2. Prints — 20th century — United States. 3. Printmakers — United States. I. T.
NE508.J63     769.92/2     *LC* 79-8931     *ISBN* 0385149212

**Fern, Alan Maxwell, 1930-.**       **1.6437**
The complete prints of Leonard Baskin: a catalogue raisonné 1948–1983 / by Alan Fern and Judith O'Sullivan; introduction by Ted Hughes. — 1st ed. — Boston: Little, Brown, c1984. 304 p.: ill. (some col.); 32 cm. 'A New York Graphic Society book.' Includes index. 1. Baskin, Leonard, 1922- — Catalogs. I. Baskin, Leonard, 1922- II. O'Sullivan, Judith. III. T.
NE539.B3 A4 1984     769.92/4 19     *LC* 84-860     *ISBN* 0821215620

**Breeskin, Adelyn Dohme, 1896-.**       **1.6438**
Mary Cassatt: a catalogue raisonné of the graphic work / Adelyn Dohme Breeskin. — 2d ed., rev. — Washington: Smithsonian Institution Press, 1979. 189 p.: ill.; 30 cm. Previous ed. published in 1948 under title: The graphic work of Mary Cassatt. 1. Cassatt, Mary, 1844-1926 — Catalogs. I. T.
NE539.C3 A4 1979     769/.92/4     *LC* 78-22472     *ISBN* 0874742846

**Dine, Jim, 1935-.**       **1.6439**
Jim Dine prints, 1970–1977. — 1st ed. — New York: Published in association with the Williams College artist-in-residence program by Harper & Row, c1977. 134 p.: ill. (some col.); 31 cm. — (Icon editions) Catalogue of an exhibition held Oct. 3-Nov. 5, 1976, at Williams College Museum of Art and at other places. 1. Dine, Jim, 1935- — Exhibitions. I. Williams College. Museum of Art. II. T.
NE539.D5 A4 1977     769/.92/4     *LC* 77-3758     *ISBN* 0064300838

**Feininger, Lyonel, 1871-1956.**       **1.6440**
Lyonel Feininger; a definitive catalogue of his graphic work: etchings, lithographs, woodcuts. Das graphische Werk: Radierungen, Lithographien, Holzschnitte [by] Leona E. Prasse. [German translations by Annegret Janda. Cleveland] Cleveland Museum of Art; [distributed by Press of Case Western Reserve University, 1972] 304 p. illus. 31 cm. On spine: Feininger: his graphic work. Introductory matter in English and German. Errata slip inserted. 1. Feininger, Lyonel, 1871-1956. I. Prasse, Leona E. II. T. III. Title: Feininger: his graphic work.
NE539.F44 P72     760/.092/4     *LC* 74-108899     *ISBN* 0910386188

**Fine, Ruth, 1941-.**       **1.6441**
Gemini G.E.L.: art and collaboration / Ruth E. Fine. — 1st ed. — Washington, D.C.: National Gallery of Art; New York: Abbeville Press, 1985, c1984. 280 p.: ill. (some col.); 31 cm. Catalog of an exhibition to be held at the National Gallery of Art, Nov. 18, 1984-Feb. 24, 1985. Includes index. 1. Gemini G.E.L. (Firm) — Exhibitions. 2. Prints — 20th century — United States — Exhibitions. I. National Gallery of Art (U.S.) II. T. III. Title: Gemini GEL.
NE539.G4 A4 1984     769.973/074/0153 19     *LC* 84-1181     *ISBN* 0896595188

**Hopper, Edward, 1882-1967.**       **1.6442**
Edward Hopper, the complete prints / [compiled by] Gail Levin. — New York: Norton, c1979. 36, [89] p.: ill.; 29 cm. 1. Hopper, Edward, 1882-1967 — Catalogs. I. Levin, Gail, 1948- II. T.
NE539.H65 A4 1979     769/.92/4     *LC* 79-13567     *ISBN* 0393012751

**Field, Richard S.**       **1.6443**
Jasper Johns: prints 1970–1977 / by Richard S. Field. — Middletown, Conn.: Wesleyan University, 1978. 127 p.: ill. (some col.); 28 x 26 cm. Catalog of a traveling exhibition to be held at the Center for the Arts, Wesleyan University and other institutions, Mar. 27, 1978-Nov. 18, 1979. 1. Johns, Jasper, 1930- — Exhibitions. I. Wesleyan University (Middletown, Conn.). Center for the Arts. II. T.
NE539.J57 A4 1978     769/.92/4     *LC* 77-93988     *ISBN* 0931266009

**Marsh, Reginald, 1898-1954.**       **1.6444**
The prints of Reginald Marsh: an essay and definitive catalog of his linoleum cuts, etchings, engravings, and lithographs / Norman Sasowsky. 1st ed. — New York: C. N. Potter; distributed by Crown Publishers, c1976. 287 p.: chiefly ill.; 26 cm. Includes index. 1. Marsh, Reginald, 1898-1954. I. Sasowsky, Norman. II. T.
NE539.M27 S28 1976     769/.92/4     *LC* 75-45374     *ISBN* 0517524937

**Terenzio, Stephanie.**       **1.6445**
The prints of Robert Motherwell / by Stephanie Terenzio; a catalogue raisonné, 1943–1984 by Dorothy C. Belknap. — New York: Hudson Press in association with the American Federation of Arts, c1984. 304 p.: ill. (some col.); 32 cm. Includes index. 1. Motherwell, Robert — Catalogs. I. Belknap, Dorothy C. II. T.
NE539.M67 A4 1984     769.92/4 19     *LC* 84-10737     *ISBN* 0933920482

**Prescott, Kenneth Wade, 1920-.**       **1.6446**
The complete graphic works of Ben Shahn [by] Kenneth W. Prescott. — [New York]: Quadrangle, [1973] xxii, 250 p.: illus. (part col.); 25 x 31 cm. 1. Shahn, Ben, 1898-1969. I. Shahn, Ben, 1898-1969. II. T.
NE539.S4 P73 1973     769/.92/4     *LC* 73-79928     *ISBN* 0812903676

**Axsom, Richard H., 1943-.**       **1.6447**
The prints of Frank Stella: a catalogue raisonné, 1967–1982 / by Richard H. Axsom; with the assistance of Phylis Floyd and Matthew Rohn; foreword by Evan M. Maurer. — 1st ed. — New York: Hudson Hills Press; Ann Arbor: University of Michigan Museum of Art, c1983. 192 p.: ill.; 26 cm. 'Published in conjunction with the exhibition organized by The University of Michigan Museum of Art and The American Federation of Arts with the aid of a grant from the National Endowment for the Arts'-T.p. verso. Includes index. 1. Stella, Frank — Catalogs. I. Stella, Frank. II. Floyd, Phylis. III. Rohn, Matthew. IV. University of Michigan. Museum of Art. V. American Federation of Arts. VI. National Endowment for the Arts. VII. T.
NE539.S72 A4 1983     769.92/4 19     *LC* 82-15729     *ISBN* 0933920407

**Allodi, Mary.**       **1.6448**
Printmaking in Canada: the earliest views and portraits = Les débuts de l'estampe imprimée au Canada: vues et portraits / Mary Allodi; with contributions from Peter Winkworth ... [et al.]. — Toronto: Royal Ontario Museum, c1980. xxviii, 244 p.: ill.; 28 cm. English and French. Catalog of an exhibition held at the Royal Ontario Museum, Toronto, Apr. 18-May 25, McCord Museum, Montreal, June 11-July 13, and the Public Archives of Canada, Ottawa, July 25-Sept. 1, 1980. Includes index. 1. Prints, Canadian — Exhibitions. 2. Prints — 19th century — Canada — Exhibitions. I. Winkworth, Peter S. II. Royal Ontario Museum. III. McCord Museum. IV. Public Archives Canada. V. T. VI. Title: Les débuts de l'estampe imprimée au Canada.
NE541.3.A44     769.971/074/011 19     *LC* 80-507925     *ISBN* 0888542607

**Tovell, Rosemarie L.**       **1.6449**
Reflections in a quiet pool: the prints of David Milne / Rosemarie L. Tovell. — Ottawa: National Gallery of Canada, National Museums of Canada, 1981, [c1980]. xvi, 244 p.: ill. (some col.); 24 x 29 cm. 'Aussi publié sous le titre: Reflets dans un miroir d'eau: estampes de David Milne'—T.p. verso. Includes index. 1. Milne, David, 1882-1953 — Exhibitions. I. National Gallery of Canada. II. T.
NE543.M5 A4 1980     769.92/4 19     *LC* 81-149267     *ISBN* 0888844573

**Posada's Mexico / edited by Ron Tyler.**       **1.6450**
Washington: Library of Congress: for sale by the Supt. of Docs., U.S. Govt. Print. Off., 1979. xii, 315 p.: ill.; 31 cm. Catalog of an exhibition held at the Library of Congress, Washington, D.C., Nov. 1, 1979-Jan. 1, 1980, the Amon Carter Museum of Western Art, Fort Worth, Tex., Jan. 25-Mar. 9, 1980, and the Colorado Springs Fine Arts Center, Colorado Springs, Colo., Apr. 26-June 1, 1980. Includes index. 1. Posada, José Guadalupe, 1852-1913 — Exhibitions. 2. Prints, Mexican — Exhibitions. 3. Mexico in art — Exhibitions. I. Tyler, Ronnie C., 1941- II. Library of Congress. III. Amon Carter Museum of Western Art. IV. Colorado Springs Fine Arts Center.
NE546.P6 A4 1979     769/.92/4     *LC* 79-22460     *ISBN* 0844403156

**Posada, José Guadalupe, 1852-1913.**       **1.6451**
Posada's popular Mexican prints; 273 cuts, by José Guadalupe Posada. Selected and edited, with an introd. and commentary, by Roberto Berdecio and Stanley Appelbaum. — New York: Dover Publications, [1972] xxi, 156 p.: illus.; 29 cm. 1. Posada, José Guadalupe, 1852-1913. 2. Mexico in art. I. Berdecio, Roberto, ed. II. Appelbaum, Stanley. ed. III. T.
NE546.P6 B47 1972     769/.92/4     *LC* 77-178994     *ISBN* 0486228541

**National Gallery of Art (U.S.)**       **1.6452**
Fifteenth century engravings of northern Europe from the National Gallery of Art, Washington, D.C. Catalogue by Alan Shestack. Washington [1967] [unpaged] 1. Engravings — Europe, Northern 2. Engravings — Exhibitions I. Shestack, Alan. II. Rosenwald, Lessing J. (Lessing Julius), 1891-1979. III. T.
NE626 N6 U5

**Bindman, David.**       **1.6453**
The complete graphic works of William Blake / David Bindman, assisted by Deirdre Toomey. — New York: Putnam, c1978. 494 p.: 765 ill.; 34 cm. 1. Blake, William, 1757-1827. I. Toomey, Deirdre. II. T.
NE642.B5 A4 1978b     769/.92/4     *LC* 77-92146     *ISBN* 0399121528

**Bindman, David.**       **1.6454**
William Blake—his art and times / David Bindman. — New York: Thames and Hudson, c1982. 192 p.: ill. (some col.); 29 cm. Catalog of the exhibition held at the Yale Center for British Art 15 Sept.-14 Nov. 1982 and at the Art Gallery of Ontario, Toronto, 3 Dec. 1982-6 Feb. 1983. Includes index. 1. Blake, William,

1757-1827 — Exhibitions. 2. Yale Center for British Art. 3. Art Gallery of Ontario. I. T.
NE642.B5 A4 1982b      760/.092/4 19      *LC* 82-80977      *ISBN* 0500233608

**Essick, Robert N.**      **1.6455**
William Blake, printmaker / by Robert N. Essick. — Princeton, N.J.: Princeton University Press, c1980. 429 p.: ill. Includes index. 1. Blake, William, 1757-1827. I. T.
NE642.B5 E78      769.92/4 19      *LC* 79-3205      *ISBN* 0691039542

**Hogarth, William, 1697-1764.**      • **1.6456**
Hogarth's graphic works / compiled and with a commentary by Ronald Paulson. — Rev. ed. — New Haven: Yale University Press, 1970. 2 v.: 346 ill., map (on lining papers), port.; 26 x 32 cm. 1. Hogarth, William, 1697-1764. I. Paulson, Ronald. II. T.
NE642.H6 A4 1970      769/.92/4      *LC* 79-118892

**Hogarth, William, 1697-1764.**      **1.6457**
Hogarth: the complete engravings, by Joseph Burke and Colin Caldwell. — London: Thames & Hudson, 1968. 30, [35] p. (4 fold.).: 248 plates.; 34 cm. — ([Masters of graphic art series]) I. Burke, Joseph. II. Caldwell, Colin. III. T.
NE642.H6 B8 1968      769/.924      *LC* 68-124534      *ISBN* 0500230854

**Regency to empire: French printmaking, 1715–1814 / organized**      **1.6458**
**by Victor I. Carlson, John W. Ittmann; contributing authors,**
**David Becker ... [et al.].**
[Baltimore]: Baltimore Museum of Art; [Minneapolis]: Minneapolis Institute of Arts, c1984. 371 p.: ill. (some col.); 29 cm. 'Exhibition organized by the Baltimore Museum of Art and the Minneapolis Institute of Arts; [scheduled at] the Baltimore Museum of Art, 10 November 1984-6 January 1985, Museum of Fine Arts, Boston, 6 February 1985-31 March 1985, the Minneapolis Institute of Arts, 27 April 1985-23 June 1985'-T.p. verso. 1. Prints, French — Exhibitions. 2. Prints — 18th century — France — Exhibitions. 3. Prints — 19th century — France — Exhibitions. I. Carlson, Victor I. II. Ittmann, John W. III. Becker, David. IV. Baltimore Museum of Art. V. Museum of Fine Arts, Boston. VI. Minneapolis Institute of Arts.
NE647.2.R44 1984      769.944/074/014 19      *LC* 84-61968      *ISBN* 0912964227

**The Graphic works of the impressionists; Manet, Pissarro,**      **1.6459**
**Renoir, Cezanne, Sisley. [Text by] Jean Leymarie. Catalogue by**
**Michel Melot.**
New York: H.N. Abrams, [1972] 353 p. (chiefly illus. (part col.)); 33 cm. Translation of Les Gravures des impressionistes. 1. Prints, French — Catalogs. 2. Impressionism (Art) — France. I. Leymarie, Jean. II. Melot, Michel.
NE647.6.I4 G713 1972b      769/.944      *LC* 72-160222      *ISBN* 0810901544

**Reed, Sue Welsh.**      **1.6460**
Edgar Degas: the painter as printmaker / Sue Welsh Reed and Barbara Stern Shapiro; with contributions by Clifford S. Ackley and Roy L. Perkinson; essay by Douglas Druick and Peter Zegers. — Boston: New York Graphic Society, 1985, c1984. lxxii, 272 p.: ill. (some col.); 29 cm. Spine title: Degas. Exhibition held at the Museum of Fine Arts, Boston, Nov. 14, 1984- Jan. 13, 1985, Philadelphia Museum of Art, Feb. 17-April 14, 1985, and Arts Council of Great Britain, Hayward Gallery, May 15-July 7, 1985. 1. Degas, Edgar, 1834-1917 — Exhibitions. I. Shapiro, Barbara Stern. II. Museum of Fine Arts, Boston. III. Philadelphia Museum of Art. IV. Hayward Gallery. V. T. VI. Title: Degas.
NE650.D45 A4 1984      769.92/4 19      *LC* 84-61859      *ISBN* 0878462430

**British Museum. Department of Prints and Drawings.**      **1.6461**
The print in Germany, 1880–1933: the age of expressionism: prints from the Department of Prints and Drawings in the British Museum / Frances Carey and Antony Griffiths; with a section of illustrated books from the British Library [by] David Paisey. — New York: Harper & Row, c1984. 272 p.,: ill.; 28 cm. Paperback. 1. British Museum. Dept. of Prints and Drawings — Catalogs. 2. Prints, Modern — 19th century — Germany — Exhibitions. 3. Prints, Modern — 20th century — Germany — Exhibitions. 4. Illustration of books — Germany — Exhibitions. I. Griffiths, Antony. II. Paisey, David. III. Carey, Frances. IV. British Library. V. T.
NE651.6.E9 C37 1984      *LC* 84-48846      *ISBN* 0064301516

**Dürer, Albrecht, 1471-1528.**      **1.6462**
Albrecht Dürer: master printmaker [by] Dept. of Prints & Drawings. — Boston: Museum of Fine Arts, [c1971] xxiv, 295 p.: illus.; 30 cm. Exhibition held Nov. 17, 1971, through Jan. 16, 1972, at the Museum of Fine Arts, Boston. Errata slip inserted. I. Boston. Museum of Fine Arts. Dept. of Prints and Drawings. II. Museum of Fine Arts, Boston. III. T.
NE654.D9 B63      769/.92/4      *LC* 77-183708

**Dürer, Albrecht, 1471-1528.**      **1.6463**
Dürer in America: his graphic work. Charles W. Talbot, editor. Notes by Gaillard F. Ravenel and Jay A. Levenson. Essay by Wolfgang Stechow. New York, Macmillan [1972?] xv, 9-362 p. illus. 29 cm. Catalog of an exhibition held at the National Gallery of Art, Washington, D.C., Apr. 25-June 6, 1971. 1. Dürer, Albrecht, 1471-1528. I. Talbot, Charles W., ed. II. National Gallery of Art (U.S.) III. T.
NE654.D9 T3 1972      769/.92/4      *LC* 74-154251

**Ackley, Clifford S.**      **1.6464**
Printmaking in the age of Rembrandt: [exhibition catalogue] / Clifford S. Ackley. — Boston: Museum of Fine Arts, [c1981] xlviii, 316 p.: ill. (some col.); 22 x 26 cm. 1. Prints, Dutch — Exhibitions. 2. Prints — 17th century — Netherlands — Exhibitions. I. Museum of Fine Arts, Boston. II. T.
NE667.2.A25      769.9492/074/014461 19      *LC* 80-84002      *ISBN* 0878461965

**Goya, Francisco, 1746-1828.**      • **1.6465**
Goya, his complete etchings, aquatints, and lithographs. Text by Enrique Lafuente Ferrari. [Translated from the Spanish by Raymond Rudorff.] New York, Abrams [1962] xxxiv, p., 288 p. of plates. 34 cm. I. Lafuente Ferrari, Enrique. II. T.
NE702.G7 L253      709.46      *LC* 62-11623

**Chibbett, David G.**      **1.6466**
The history of Japanese printing and book illustration / David Chibbett. — 1st ed. — Tokyo; New York: Kodansha International; New York: distributed by Harper & Row, 1977. 264 p.: ill. (some col.); 29 cm. Includes indexes. 1. Prints, Japanese — Japan. 2. Illustration of books — Japan 3. Printing — History — Japan. I. T.
NE771.C48      769/.952      *LC* 76-9362      *ISBN* 0870112880

# NE820–962 General Works. Techniques

**Heller, Jules.**      **1.6467**
Printmaking today, an artist's handbook. — 2d ed. — New York: Holt, Rinehart and Winston, [1972] viii, 344 p.: illus. (part col.); 26 cm. 1. Prints — Technique I. T.
NE850.H45 1972      760/.28 19      *LC* 73-171523      *ISBN* 0030914035

**Ross, John, 1921-.**      **1.6468**
The complete printmaker; the art and technique of the relief print, the intaglio print, the collagraph, the lithograph, the screen print, the dimensional print, photographic prints, children's prints, collecting prints, print workshop [by] John Ross [and] Clare Romano. — New York: Free Press, [1972] xiv, 306 p.: illus. (part col.); 32 cm. 1. Prints — Technique I. Romano, Clare. joint author. II. T.
NE850.R59      760/.28      *LC* 72-77151

**Saff, Donald, 1937-.**      **1.6469**
Printmaking: history and process / Donald Saff, Deli Sacilotto. — New York: Holt, Rinehart and Winston, c1978. xii, 436 p.: ill.; 28 cm. Includes index. 1. Prints — Technique I. Sacilotto, Deli. joint author. II. T.
NE850.S23      760/.2/8      *LC* 76-54995      *ISBN* 0030421063

**Sachs, Paul Joseph, 1878-1965.**      • **1.6470**
Modern prints & drawings; a guide to a better understanding of modern draughtsmanship. Selected and with an explanatory text by Paul J. Sachs. New York, Knopf [1954] 261 p. illus. 27 cm. 1. Prints 2. Drawing I. T.
NE940.S3      769      *LC* 54-6137

**Vitsaxis, Basile.**      **1.6471**
Hindu epics, myths, and legends in popular illustrations / by Vassilis G. Vitsaxis; with a foreword by A. L. Basham. — Delhi: Oxford University Press, 1977. xii, 98 p.: ill. (some col.); 26 cm. 1. Prints — India. 2. Mythology, Hindu — Illustrations. 3. Legends, Hindu — Illustrations. I. T.
NE958.3.I4 V57      769/.4/8945      *LC* 78-106720

# NE1000–1325 Wood Engraving. Woodcuts

**National Gallery of Art (U.S.)**      **1.6472**
Fifteenth century woodcuts and metalcuts from the National Gallery of Art, Washington, D.C. Catalogue prepared by Richard S. Field. Washington Publications Dept., National Galleryy of Art [1965] 1. Wood-engraving — History 2. Wood-engraving — Washington, D.C. — Catalogs 3. Engraving —

History 4. Engravings — Washington, D.C. — Catalogs I. Field, Richard S. II. Rosenwald, Lessing J. (Lessing Julius), 1891-1979. III. T. NE1020 U5

**Hind, Arthur Mayger, 1880-1957.**    • **1.6473**
An introduction to a history of woodcut, with a detailed survey of work done in the fifteenth century. — New York, Dover Publications [1963] 2 v. (xl, 838 p.) illus., facsims. 21 cm. 'T952-T953.' 'An unabridged and unaltered republication of the work first published ... in 1935.' Includes bibliographies. Bibliographical footnotes. 1. Wood-engraving — Hist. 2. Illustrated books — 15th and 16th centuries 3. Illustrated books — 15th and 16th centuries — Bibl. I. T. NE1030.H55 1963   761.209   *LC* 63-5621

**British Museum. Dept. of Prints and Drawings.**    **1.6474**
Catalogue of early German and Flemish woodcuts: preserved in the Department of Prints and Drawings in the British Museum / by Campbell Dodgson. — Liechtenstein: Quarto Press in association with British Museum Publications, 1980. 2 v.: ill. 1. British Museum. Dept. of Prints and Drawings — Catalogs. 2. Wood-engraving — England — London — Catalogs 3. Wood-engraving, German — Catalogs 4. Wood-engraving, Flemish — Catalogs 5. Art museums — England — London — Catalogs I. Dodgson, Campbell, 1867-1948. II. T. NE1050.B7 1980   *ISBN* 3858510092

**Rosand, David.**    **1.6475**
Titian and the Venetian woodcut: a loan exhibition / introduction and catalogue by David Rosand, Michelangelo Muraro; organized and circulated by International Exhibitions Foundation, 1976–1977. — Washington: The Foundation, c1976. 315 p.: ill.; 22 x 26 cm. Held at the National Gallery of Art, the Dallas Museum of Fine Arts, and the Detroit Institute of Arts. 1. Titian, ca. 1488-1576. 2. Wood-engraving, Italian — Italy — Venice — Exhibitions. I. Muraro, Michelangelo. joint author. II. International Exhibitions Foundation. III. National Gallery of Art (U.S.) IV. Dallas Museum of Fine Arts. V. Detroit Institute of Arts. VI. T. NE1152.4.V46 R67   769/.945/31   *LC* 77-351487

**Sander, David M.**    **1.6476**
Wood engraving: an adventure in printmaking / David M. Sander. — New York: Viking Press, 1978. 159 p.: ill.; 19 x 25 cm. — (A Studio book) 1. Wood-engraving — Technique. I. T. NE1227.S27   761/.2   *LC* 78-8097   *ISBN* 0670780839

**Tschichold, Jan, 1902-1974.**    **1.6477**
Chinese color prints from the Ten Bamboo Studio. With 24 reproductions in full–color facsim. of prints from the masterpiece of Chinese color printing from the Ming period. New York, McGraw-Hill [1972] 55 p. illus., 24 col. plates. 32 x 35 cm. 'Some parts of the text ... have been adapted from the writer's previous books: Der frühe chinesische Farbendruck, Basle, 1940; Der Holzschneider und Bilddrucker, Hu Chêng-yen, Basle, 1943; and Chinesisches Gedichtpapier vom Meister der Zehnbambushalle, Basle, 1947.' 1. Color prints, Chinese — Ming-Ch'ing dynasties, 1368-1912 I. Hu, Cheng-yen, ca. 1582-ca. 1672. Shih chu chai chien p'u. II. T. NE1300.8.C6 T72   769/.951   *LC* 76-37748   *ISBN* 0070653909

## NE1310–1325 Japanese Prints. Ukiyoe Prints

**Hillier, Jack Ronald.**    **1.6478**
The Japanese print: a new approach / J. Hillier. — 1st Tuttle ed. — Rutland, Vt.: C. E. Tuttle Co., 1975. xvi, 184 p., [32] leaves of plates: ill.; 19 cm. (Tut books: A) 1. Color prints, Japanese 2. Prints, Japanese I. T. NE1310.H53 1975   769/.952   *LC* 75-332702   *ISBN* 0804811539

**Michener, James A. (James Albert), 1907-.**    • **1.6479**
Japanese prints; from the early masters to the modern, by James A. Michener, with notes on the prints by Richard Lane. With the cooperation of the Honolulu Academy of Arts. Tokyo, Rutland, Vt., C. E. Tuttle Co. [1959] 287 p. illus. (part mounted col.) 32 cm. 1. Color prints, Japanese I. T. NE1310.M48   769.952   *LC* 59-10410

**Narazaki, Muneshige, 1904-.**    **1.6480**
The Japanese print: its evolution and essence. English adaptation by C. H. Mitchell. [1st ed.] Tokyo, Palo Alto, Calif., Kodansha International [1966] 274 p. 107 mounted col. illus. 37 cm. Print identification and artists' names also in Sino-Japanese characters. 1. Color prints, Japanese 2. Ukiyoe — Japan. I. T. NE1310.N3   769.952   *LC* 66-12551

**Freer Gallery of Art.**    **1.6481**
Ukiyo-e painting, by Harold P. Stern. Washington, Smithsonian Institution, 1973. xv,319p. illus.(part col.) 31cm. (Freer Gallery of Art. Fiftieth anniversary exhibition, 1) 'Catalogue of a special exhibition of Ukiyoe paintings in the

collection' - Foreword. Errata slip inserted. 1. Ukiyoe — Exhibitions. 2. Painting, Japanese — Exhibitions. I. Stern, Harold P. II. T. III. Series. NE1314.W3x

**Whitford, Frank.**    **1.6482**
Japanese prints and Western painters / Frank Whitford. 1st American ed. — New York: Macmillan, 1977. 264 p.: ill. (some col.); 28 cm. Includes index. 1. Ukiyoe — History. 2. Color prints, Japanese — History. 3. Prints, European — Japanese influences I. T. NE1321.W47   769/.952   *LC* 76-45182   *ISBN* 002627180X

**Allen Memorial Art Museum.**    **1.6483**
Japanese woodblock prints: a catalogue of the Mary A. Ainsworth Collection / Roger S. Keyes, with contributions by Robert L. Feller, Mary Curran, and Catherine W. Bailie. — Oberlin, Ohio: Allen Memorial Art Museum, Oberlin College; Bloomington, Ind.: Distributed by Indiana University Press, 1984. 269 p.: ill. (some col.); 29 cm. 1. Ainsworth, Mary Andrews, b. 1867 — Art collections. 2. Allen Memorial Art Museum — Catalogs. 3. Color prints, Japanese — Edo period, 1600-1868 — Catalogs. 4. Color prints, Japanese — Meiji period, 1868-1912 — Catalogs. 5. Color prints — Private collections — Ohio — Oberlin — Catalogs. I. Keyes, Roger S. II. T. NE1321.8.A45 1984   769.952/074/017123 19   *LC* 82-61869   *ISBN* 0942946014

**Lane, Richard Douglas, 1926-.**    **1.6484**
Images from the floating world: the Japanese print: including an illustrated dictionary of ukiyo–e / Richard Lane. — New York: Putnam, c1978. 364 p.: ill. (some col.); 29 cm. Includes indexes. 1. Ukiyoe 2. Color prints, Japanese — Edo period, 1600-1868 3. Color prints, Japanese — Meiji period, 1868-1912 4. Ukiyoe — Dictionaries. 5. Japan — Social life and customs — Pictorial works. I. T. NE1321.8.L36 1978   769/.952   *LC* 78-53445   *ISBN* 0399121935

**Hillier, Jack Ronald.**    • **1.6485**
Utamaro: colour prints and paintings / J. Hillier. — 2d ed. — Oxford: Phaidon, 1979. 160 p.: ill. (some col.); 29 cm. 1. Kitagawa, Utamaro, 1753?-1806. I. Kitagawa, Utamaro, 1753?-1806. II. T. NE1325.K5 H5 1979   769/.92/4   *LC* 78-20503   *ISBN* 0714819743

## NE1860 Color Prints: Catalogs

**Unesco.**    • **1.6486**
Catalogue de reproductions en couleurs de peintures antérieures à 1860. Catalogue of colour reproductions prior to 1860. Paris, 1950-. v. plates. 23 cm. Title also in Spanish. 1. Painting — Catalogs. I. Catalogue of colour reproductions prior to 1860. II. T. ND47.U49   NE1860.A2U5.

**Unesco.**    • **1.6487**
Catalogue de reproductions en coleur de peintures. = Catalogue of colour reproductions of paintings. = Catálogo de reproducciones en color de pinturas. 1860/1949-. Paris. v. illus. (United Nations Educational, Scientific and Cultural Organizations. UNESCO publication no.409.) Catalogue for 1949 issued as the Organization's Publication no.409. Title varies slightly. 1. Color prints — Catalogs. I. T. II. Series. NE1860.A2 U52   759.0838   *LC* 58-975

## NE1940–2230 Etching

**Getscher, Robert H.**    **1.6488**
The stamp of Whistler: catalogue / by Robert H. Getscher; introduction by Allen Staley. — [Oberlin, Ohio]: Allen Memorial Art Museum, Oberlin College, c1977. x, 285 p.: ill.; 29 cm. An exhibition held at Allen Memorial Art Museum, Oberlin College, Oct. 2-Nov. 6, 1977, Museum of Fine Arts, Boston, Nov. 22, 1977-Jan. 1, 1978, and the Philadelphia Museum of Art, Jan. 22-Feb. 25, 1978. 1. Whistler, James McNeill, 1834-1903 — Influence — Exhibitions. 2. Etching — 20th century — Exhibitions. 3. Prints — 19th century — Exhibitions. 4. Prints — 20th century — Exhibitions. 5. Etching — 19th century — Exhibitions. I. Allen Memorial Art Museum. II. Museum of Fine Arts, Boston. III. Philadelphia Museum of Art. IV. T. NE1994.G48 1977   769/.074/014 19   *LC* 77-10035

**Lochnan, Katharine Jordan.**    **1.6489**
The etchings of James McNeill Whistler / Katharine A. Lochnan. — New Haven: Published in association with the Art Gallery of Ontario by Yale University Press, 1984. xi, 308 p.: ill.; 27 cm. An accompanying volume of an exhibition held at the Metropolitan Museum of Art, New York, Sept. 14-Nov.

11, 1984; the Art Gallery of Ontario, Toronto, Nov. 24, 1984-Jan. 13, 1985. Includes index. 1. Whistler, James McNeill, 1834-1903. 2. Etchers — United States — Biography. I. Whistler, James McNeill, 1834-1903. II. Metropolitan Museum of Art (New York, N.Y.) III. Art Gallery of Ontario. IV. T.
NE2012.W45 L6 1984   769.92/4 19   *LC* 84-40185   *ISBN* 0300032757

**Hayes, John T.**   **1.6490**
Gainsborough as printmaker / John Hayes. — New Haven: Published for the Paul Mellon Centre for Studies in British Art (London) by Yale University Press, 1972, c1971. xx, 114 p.: ill.; 30 cm. — (Studies in British art.) Includes index. 1. Gainsborough, Thomas, 1727-1788. I. Gainsborough, Thomas, 1727-1788. II. Paul Mellon Centre for Studies in British Art. III. T. IV. Series.
NE2047.6.G34 H39 1972   769/.92/4   *LC* 79-179475   *ISBN* 0300015615

**Rizzi, Aldo. comp.**   **1.6491**
[Opera grafica dei Tiepolo. Le acqueforti. English] The etchings of the Tiepolos [by] Aldo Rizzi. Complete ed. [London] Phaidon [distributed in the USA by Praeger, New York, 1971] 456 p. illus. 29 cm. Translation of L'Opera grafica dei Tiepolo. Le acqueforti. 1. Etching, Italian — Catalogs. I. Tiepolo, Giovanni Battista, 1696-1770. II. Tiepolo, Giovanni Domenico, 1726?-1804. III. Tiepolo, Lorenzo, b. 1736-1776. IV. T.
NE2052.5.T5 R5213   769/.945   *LC* 79-162313   *ISBN* 0714814997

**López-Rey, José.**   • **1.6492**
Goya's Caprichos; beauty, reason & caricature. Westport, Conn., Greenwood Press [1970, c1953] 2 v. 265 illus. 23 cm. 1. Goya, Francisco, 1746-1828. Caprichos I. T.
NE2062.5.G6 L6 1970   760/.0924   *LC* 69-13976   *ISBN* 0837144655(Set)

**Sayre, Eleanor.**   **1.6493**
The changing image: prints by Francisco Goya: [exhibition, Museum of Fine Arts, Boston, October 24–December 29, 1974, The National Gallery of Canada, Ottawa, January 24–March 14, 1975] / Eleanor A. Sayre and the Department of Prints and Drawings. — Boston: Museum of Fine Arts, 1974. xii, 325 p.: ill.; 28 cm. Errata slip inserted. 1. Goya, Francisco, 1746-1828. I. Goya, Francisco, 1746-1828. II. Boston. Museum of Fine Arts. Dept. of Prints and Drawings. III. Museum of Fine Arts, Boston. IV. Ottawa. National Gallery of Canada. V. T.
NE2062.5.G6 S29   760/.092/4   *LC* 74-19964   *ISBN* 0878460853

**White, Christopher.**   • **1.6494**
Rembrandt as an etcher; a study of the artist at work. . — University Park: Pennsylvania State University Press, [1969] 2 v.: illus., ports.; 31 cm. 1. Rembrandt Harmenszoon van Rijn, 1606-1669. I. T.
NE2165.R5 W45 1969   769/.924   *LC* 69-17493

**Goya, Francisco, 1746-1828.**   • **1.6495**
The disasters of war. With a new introd. by Philip Hofer. New York, Dover Publications [1967] 12 p. 83 plates. 21x24 cm. Translation of Los desastres de la guerra. With 3 extra plates and some new material. 1. Spain — History — Napoleonic Conquest, 1808-1813 — Pictorial works. I. T.
NE2195.G78D43 1967   769/.924   *LC* 67-15964

# NE2242–2890 Monotype (Printmaking). Lithography. Printing of Engravings

**The Painterly print: monotypes from the seventeenth to the twentieth century; [exhibition] The Metropolitan Museum of Art, May 1–June 29, 1980, Museum of Fine Arts, Boston, July 29–September 28, 1981.**   **1.6496**
New York: Metropolitan Museum of Art, c1980. xiii, 259 p.: ill. (some col.); 27 cm. Includes index. 1. Monotype (Engraving) — Exhibitions. I. Metropolitan Museum of Art (New York, N.Y.) II. Museum of Fine Arts, Boston.
NE2243.P34   769/.074/014461   *LC* 80-10441   *ISBN* 0870992236

**Currier & Ives: a catalogue raisonné / compiled by Gale Research Company; with an introduction by Bernard F. Reilly.**   **1.6497**
Detroit, MI: Gale Research, c1983. 2 v. (xliii, 1029 p.); ill.; 31 cm. 'A comprehensive catalogue of the lithographs of Nathaniel Currier, James Merritt Ives, and Charles Currier, including ephemera associated with the firms, 1834-1907.' Includes indexes. 1. Currier & Ives — Catalogs. 2. Lithography — 19th century — United States — Catalogs. I. Reilly, Bernard. II. Gale Research Company. III. Title: Currier and Ives.
NE2312.C8 A4 1983a   769.92/4 19   *LC* 83-20844   *ISBN* 0810316382

**Rawls, Walton H.**   **1.6498**
The great book of Currier & Ives' America / by Walton Rawls. — New York: Abbeville Press, c1979. 487 p., [4] leaves of plates: ill. (chiefly col.); 40 cm. Includes index. 1. Currier & Ives. 2. Lithography, American. I. T.
NE2312.C8 R3   764.2   *LC* 79-89549   *ISBN* 0896590704

**Litografia. English.**   **1.6499**
Lithography: 200 years of art, history, & technique / Domenico Porzio, general editor, with the collaboration of Rosalba and Marcello Tabanelli; essays by Jean Adhémar ... [et al.]; translated from the Italian by Geoffrey Culverwell. — New York: H.N. Abrams, 1983. 280 p.: ill. (some col.); 32 cm. Translation of: La litografia. Includes indexes. 1. Lithography I. Porzio, Domenico, 1921- II. Tabanelli, Rosalba. III. Tabanelli, M. R. IV. Adhémar, Jean. V. Culverwell, Geoffrey. VI. T.
NE2425.L5713 1983   763 19   *LC* 83-3691   *ISBN* 0810912821

**Twyman, Michael.**   **1.6500**
Lithography, 1800–1850: the techniques of drawing on stone in England and France and their application in works of topography. — London; New York: Oxford U.P., 1970. xxi, 304 p., 88 plates.: illus., facsims.; 28 cm. 1. Lithography — Technique. I. T.
NE2425.T85   763/.09   *LC* 70-460065   *ISBN* 0192151681

**Daumier, Honoré, 1808-1879.**   • **1.6501**
Honoré Daumier; 240 lithographs. New York, Reynal & Hitchcock [1946] 12 p. l, 240 pl. (2 double) on 120 l., [8] p. illus. 40 cm. 'Introduction by Bernard Lemann.' 'The captions and explanatory notes by Dr. Wilhelm Wartmann were translated by James Galston.'—p. [1] at end. I. Lemann, Bernard. II. Wartmann, Wilhelm, 1882- III. Galston, James Austin, 1881- tr. IV. T.
NE2451.D32   763   *LC* 47-193   [ref] NE 2451 D24 1946

**Toulouse-Lautrec, Henri de, 1864-1901.**   • **1.6502**
Toulouse–Lautrec; his complete lithographs and drypoints [by] Jean Adhémar. New York, H.N. Abrams [1965] xxxviii p. 370 ill. (part col.) I. Adhémar, Jean. II. T.
NE2451 T64   *LC* 65-21831

**Marzio, Peter C.**   **1.6503**
The democratic art: pictures for a 19th–century America: chromolithography, 1840–1900 / Peter C. Marzio. — Boston: D. R. Godine; Fort Worth: Amon Carter Museum of Western Art, 1979. xiv, 357 p.: ill. (some col.); 29 cm. Includes index. 1. Chromolithography — United States. I. T.
NE2505.M38   764/.2/0973   *LC* 79-84494   *ISBN* 0879232900

**Glassman, Elizabeth.**   **1.6504**
Cliché–verre, hand–drawn, light–printed: a survey of the medium from 1839 to the present / Elizabeth Glassman, Marilyn F. Symmes. — Detroit: Detroit Institute of Arts, 1980. 211 p.; 28 cm. Catalog of an exhibition presented at the Detroit Institute of Arts, July 12-Aug. 17, 1980, and at the Museum of Fine Arts, Houston, Sept. 11-Oct. 13, 1980. Includes index. 1. Cliché-verre — Exhibitions. 2. Prints — 19th century — Exhibitions. 3. Prints — 20th century — Exhibitions. I. Symmes, Marilyn F. joint author. II. Detroit Institute of Arts. III. Museum of Fine Arts, Houston. IV. T.
NE2685.G54   769/.074/017434 19   *LC* 80-17402   *ISBN* 0895580810

# NK DECORATIVE ARTS

**Connoisseur (The)**   • **1.6505**
The concise encyclopedia of antiques / L. G. G. Ramsey, ed. — New York: Hawthorn Books, 1955-1961. 4 v.: ill.; 25 cm. 1. Art objects — Dictionaries. 2. Furniture — Dictionaries. 3. Decorative arts — Dictionaries. 4. Collector and collecting. I. Ramsey, L. G. G. ed. II. T.
NK30.C63   745.1   *LC* 55-5162

**Fleming, John.**   **1.6506**
Dictionary of the decorative arts / John Fleming and Hugh Honour. — New York: Harper & Row, 1977. 896 p.: ill.; 24 cm. 1. Decoration and ornament — Dictionaries. 2. Decorative arts — Dictionaries. I. Honour, Hugh. II. T.
NK30 F597 1977   745.03   *ISBN* 0060119365

**The Oxford companion to the decorative arts / edited by Harold Osborne.**   **1.6507**
Oxford: Clarendon Press, 1975. xiv, 865 p.: ill.; 25 cm. 1. Decorative arts — Dictionaries. I. Osborne, Harold, 1905-
NK30.O93   745/.03   *LC* 75-331784   *ISBN* 0198661134

**Pevsner, Nikolaus, Sir, 1902-.**      • **1.6508**
High Victorian design; a study of the exhibits of 1851. London, Architectural
Press [1951] 162 p. illus. 19 cm. 1. Crystal Palace, Hyde Park. 2. Great
Exhibition (1851: London, England) 3. Decorative arts — Exhibitions. I. T.
NK510.L6P4     745.074     LC 51-14251

**Lucie-Smith, Edward.**                           **1.6509**
The story of craft: the craftsman's role in society / Edward Lucie-Smith. —
New York: Van Nostrand Reinhold, 1984, c1981. 288 p.: ill.; 25 cm. Reprint.
Originally published: Ithaca, N.Y.: Cornell University Press, 1981. Includes
index. 1. Decorative arts — History. 2. Decorative arts — Social aspects.
3. Arts and crafts movement — Social aspects. I. T.
NK600.L8 1984     745/.09 19     LC 83-6516     ISBN 0442259107

**Roman crafts / edited by Donald Strong & David Brown.**    **1.6510**
New York: New York University Press, 1977, [c1976]. 256 p., [6] leaves of
plates: ill. (some col.); 29 cm. 1. Decorative arts — Handicraft —
Rome. I. Strong, Donald Emrys. II. Brown, David (P. David C.)
NK680.R65 1976     709/.37     LC 76-28589     ISBN 0814778011

## NK801–1094 By Country

**Folk art of the Americas / general editor, August Panyella;**    **1.6511**
**photographer, Francesc Català Roca.**
New York: Abrams, 1981. 328 p.: ill.; 31 cm. Includes index. 1. Folk art —
America. I. Panyella, Augusto. II. Català Roca, Francesc.
NK801.F64     745/.09181/2 19     LC 80-20602     ISBN 081090912X

## NK805–839 United States

**Comstock, Helen. ed.**                        • **1.6512**
The concise encyclopedia of American antiques. — New York: Hawthorn
Books, [1965] 848 p.: illus., facsims., maps, ports.; 26 cm. 1. Decorative arts —
United States. 2. Art, American 3. Antiques — Dictionaries. 4. Collectors
and collecting I. T. II. Title: Encyclopedia of American antiques.
NK805.C65 1965     745.10973 19     LC 65-9391

**Davidson, Marshall B.**                        **1.6513**
Three centuries of American antiques: American heritage / by the editors of
American heritage; author and editor in charge, Marshall B. Davidson. — New
York: Bonanza Books, 1979. 3 v. in 1: ill.; 29 cm. Originally published in 3 v.
under separate titles, 1967-1969 by the American Heritage Pub. Co., New
York. Includes indexes. 1. Antiques — United States 2. Americana
I. Davidson, Marshall B. The American heritage history of colonial antiques.
1979. II. Davidson, Marshall B. The American heritage history of American
antiques from the Revolution to the Civil War. 1979. III. Davidson, Marshall
B. The American heritage history of antiques from the Civil War to World War
I. 1979. IV. American heritage. V. T.
NK805.D38     745.1/0973     LC 79-15915     ISBN 0517294222

**Dewhurst, C. Kurt.**                          **1.6514**
Artists in aprons: folk art by American women / C. Kurt Dewhurst, Betty
MacDowell, Marsha MacDowell. — 1st ed. — New York: Dutton, c1979. xviii,
202 p., [8] leaves of plates: ill. (some col.); 24 cm. Includes indexes. 1. Folk art
— United States. 2. Women artists — United States I. MacDowell, Betty. joint
author. II. MacDowell, Marsha. joint author. III. T.
NK805.D48 1979     745/.0973     LC 78-55945     ISBN 0525058575

**Hornung, Clarence Pearson.**                  **1.6515**
Treasury of American design; a pictorial survey of popular folk arts based upon
watercolor renderings in the Index of American Design, at the National Gallery
of Art, by Clarence P. Hornung. Foreword by J. Carter Brown. Introd. by
Holger Cahill. New York, H. N. Abrams [1972] 2 v. (xxvii, 846 p.) illus. (part
col.) 31 cm. 1. Decorative arts — United States 2. Decoration and ornament
— United States I. Index of American Design. II. T.
NK805.H67     745.4/0973     LC 76-142742     ISBN 0810905167

**Lipman, Jean, 1909-.**                        • **1.6516**
American folk art in wood, metal and stone. 183 illus., 4 color plates. [New
York] Pantheon [1948] 193 p. illus. (part col.) 29 cm. 1. Decorative arts —
United States 2. Folk art — United States. 3. Sculpture, American I. T.
NK805.L5     730/.0973 19     LC 48-11569

**Stillinger, Elizabeth.**                        **1.6517**
The Antiques guide to decorative arts in America, 1600–1875. With an introd.
by Alice Winchester. Illustrated with 192 drawings by Pauline W. Inman and
434 photos. — [1st ed.]. — New York: Dutton, 1972. xv, 463 p.: illus.; 21 cm.
1. Antiques — United States — History. I. Antiques. II. T.
NK805.S7 1972     745.1/0973     LC 77-158605     ISBN 0525055851

**Antiques.**                             • **1.6518**
The antiques treasury of furniture and other decorative arts: at Winterthur,
Williamsburg, Sturbridge, Ford Museum Cooperstown, Deerfield, Shelburne /
edited by Alice Winchester and the staff of Antiques magazine. — [1st ed.]. —
New York: Dutton, 1959. 320 p.: ill. (some col.); 31 cm. 1. Furniture — United
States 2. Decorative arts — United States. 3. Art — United States.
4. Museums — United States. I. Winchester, Alice. II. T.
NK806.A5     749.213     LC 59-12514     ISBN 0525056130

**Cooper, Wendy A.**                          **1.6519**
In praise of America: American decorative arts, 1650–1830; fifty years of
discovery since the 1929 Girl Scouts loan exhibition / Wendy A. Cooper; with a
foreword by J. Carter Brown; selected photography by Richard Cheek. — 1st
ed. — New York: Knopf: distributed by Random House, 1980. 280 p.: ill. (some
col.); 29 cm. 1. Decorative arts, Early American 2. Decorative arts — United
States — 19th century. 3. Antiques — United States I. T.
NK806.C63 1980     745/.0974     LC 79-3477     ISBN 0394509943

**Lipman, Jean, 1909-.**                        • **1.6520**
American folk decoration. By Jean Lipman, with practical instruction by Eve
Meulendyke. New York, Dover Publications [1972, c1951] xii, 163 p. illus. 29
cm. 1. Decoration and ornament — United States 2. Folk art — United States.
I. Meulendyke, Eve. II. T.
NK806.L5 1972     745.4     LC 77-182096     ISBN 0486222179

**Howe, Katherine S.**                          **1.6521**
The gothic revival style in America, 1830–1870 / by Katherine S. Howe and
David B. Warren, with an introd. by Jane B. Davies. — Houston: Museum of
Fine Arts, 1976. viii, 101 p.: ill. (some col.), facsims., plans. [Catalogue] of 'an
Exhibition of Decorative Arts, April 1 through June 6, 1976, the Museum of
Fine Arts, Houston.' 1. Decoration and ornament — United States —
Exhibitions. 2. Gothic revival (Art) — United States — Exhibitions. 3. Art,
American — Exhibitions. 4. Art, Modern — 19th century — United States —
Exhibitions. I. Warren, David B. II. Museum of Fine Arts, Houston. III. T.
NK807.H69     709.73     LC 76-9009

**Metropolitan Museum of Art (New York, N.Y.)**      **1.6522**
19th-century America: furniture and other decorative arts; an exhibition in
celebration of the hundredth anniversary of the Metropolitan Museum of Art,
April 16 through September 7, 1970. Introd. by Berry B. Tracy. Furniture texts
by Marilynn Johnson. Other decorative arts texts by Marvin D. Schwartz and
Suzanne Boorsch. [New York] Distributed by New York Graphic Society
[1970] 1 v. (unpaged) illus. (part col.) 27 cm. 1. Decorative arts — United
States — Exhibitions. I. Johnson, Marilynn. II. Schwartz, Marvin D.
III. Boorsch, Suzanne. IV. T.
NK807.N4     745.2/0973     LC 77-109965     ISBN 0870990047

**Afro-American folk art and crafts / edited by William Ferris.**    **1.6523**
Boston, Mass.: G.K. Hall, c1983. 436 p.: ill.; 25 cm. (Perspectives on the Black
world.) 1. Afro-American folk art 2. Afro-American decorative arts I. Ferris,
William R. II. Series.
NK839.3.A35 A35 1983     745/.08996073 19     LC 82-11752     ISBN
0816190453

## NK841–1094 Other Countries

**Connoisseur.**                            • **1.6524**
[Connoisseur period guides] The Connoisseur's complete period guides to the
houses, decoration, furnishing and chattels of the classic periods; edited by
Ralph Edwards and L. G. G. Ramsey. London, The Connoisseur, 1968. 1536 p.
illus., facsim., plans, ports. 26 cm. Earlier editions published in 6 vols. under
title: The Connoisseur period guides ... 1. Decorative arts — Great Britain —
History. 2. Art, British — History. 3. Great Britain — Civilization — History.
I. Edwards, Ralph, 1894- ed. II. Ramsey, L. G. G. ed. III. T.
NK928.C63     709/.42     LC 70-369442

**Rococo: art and design in Hogarth's England: 16 May–30**    **1.6525**
**September 1984, the Victoria and Albert Museum.**
[s.l.]: Allanheld & Schram, 1985, [c1984] 333 p., [24] p. of plates: ill. (some
col.); 26 cm. 'Exhibition is sponsored by Trusthouse Forte.' Includes index.
1. Decorative arts, Rococo — England — Exhibitions. 2. Decorative arts —
England — History — 18th century — Exhibitions. 3. Art, Rococo — England
— Exhibitions. 4. Art, English — Exhibitions. 5. Art, Modern — 17th-18th
centuries — England — Exhibitions. I. Victoria and Albert Museum.
NK928.R56 1984     709/.42/07402134 19     LC 85-165949     ISBN
0839003536

**Campbell, Joan, 1929-.**                      **1.6526**
The German Werkbund: the politics of reform in the applied arts / by Joan
Campbell. — Princeton, N.J.: Princeton University Press, c1978. xii, 350 p., [5]
leaves of plates: ill.; 23 cm. Includes index. 1. Deutscher Werkbund.
2. Decorative arts — Germany. I. T.
NK951.C35     745/.06/243     LC 77-71974     ISBN 0691052506

**Bussabarger, Robert F.**                                1.6527
The everyday art of India, by Robert F. Bussabarger and Betty Dashew Robins. Andrew Tau, photographer. New York, Dover Publications [1968] xi, 205 p. illus. (part col.), maps. 28 cm. 1. Decorative arts — India. 2. Folk art — India I. Robins, Betty Dashew, joint author. II. T.
NK1047.B84      709/.54      LC 68-20951

**Lawton, Thomas, 1931-.**                                1.6528
Chinese art of the warring states period: change and continuity, 480–222 B.C. / Thomas Lawton. — Washington, D.C.: Published for the Freer Gallery of Art by the Smithsonian Institution Press: For sale by Supt. of Docs., U.S. G.P.O., 1983, c1982. 202 p.: ill. (some col.), maps; 28 cm. 'Published on the occasion of an exhibition held at the Freer Gallery of Art, Smithsonian Institution, Washington, D.C., October 1, 1982-February 15, 1983'—Verso t.p. Includes index. 1. Art objects, Chinese — To 221 B.C. I. Freer Gallery of Art. II. T.
NK1068.L35 1983      730/.0931/0740153 19      LC 82-600184      ISBN 0934686394

**Kim, Chewŏn, 1909-.**                                ● 1.6529
Treasures of Korean art; 2000 years of ceramics, sculpture, and jeweled arts. Text by Chewon Kim and Won–Yong Kim. — New York: H. N. Abrams, [1966] xv, 283 p.: illus. (part mounted col.) maps.; 30 cm. 1. Art objects, Korean 2. Pottery — Korea. 3. Art, Buddhist — Korea. I. Kim, Wonyong, 1922- joint author. II. T.
NK1073.5.K52      709.519      LC 66-23402

## NK1135–1149 ARTS AND CRAFTS MOVEMENT

**Lambourne, Lionel.**                                1.6530
Utopian craftsmen: the arts and crafts movement from the Cotswolds to Chicago / Lionel Lambourne. — Salt Lake City [Utah]: Peregrine Smith, 1980. vi, 218 p., [4] leaves of plates: ill. (some col.); 25 cm. Includes index. 1. Arts and crafts movement — History. I. T.
NK1140.L35 1980      745/.0941 19      LC 80-17889      ISBN 0879050802

**Naylor, Gillian.**                                1.6531
The arts and crafts movement: a study of its sources, ideals, and influence on design theory / Gillian Naylor. — Cambridge, Mass.: MIT Press, 1980, c1971. 208 p.: ill. (some col.); 25 cm. Includes index. 1. Arts and crafts movement 2. Aesthetic movement (British art) I. T.
NK1140.N3 1980      745.4/4942 19      LC 79-165508      ISBN 026264018X

**Clark, Robert Judson.**                                ● 1.6532
The arts and crafts movement in America, 1876–1916; an exhibition organized by the Art Museum, Princeton University and the Art Institute of Chicago. Edited by Robert Judson Clark. With texts by the editor and others. [Princeton, N.J.] distributed by Princeton University Press [1972] 190 p. illus. 35 cm. Catalog of an exhibition held at the Art Museum, Princeton University, Oct. 21-Dec. 17, 1972; the Art Institute of Chicago, Feb. 24-April 22, 1973; and the Renwick Gallery of the National Collection of Fine Arts, Smithsonian Institution, June 1-Sept. 10, 1973. 1. Decorative arts — United States — Exhibitions. 2. Arts and crafts movement I. Princeton University. Art Museum. II. Art Institute of Chicago. III. Renwick Gallery. IV. T.
NK1141.C55 1972      745/.0973/074013      LC 72-77734      ISBN 069103883X ISBN 0691038848

## NK1160–1590 Decoration and Ornament. Design

**Anscombe, Isabelle.**                                1.6533
A woman's touch: women in design from 1860 to the present day / Isabelle Anscombe. — New York, N.Y.: Viking Penguin, 1984. 216 p., [8] p. of plates: col. ill.; 25 cm. 'Elisabeth Sifton books.' Includes index. 1. Women designers 2. Design — History — 19th century. 3. Design — History — 20th century. I. T.
NK1174.A57 1984      745.4/442/088042 19      LC 84-40262      ISBN 0670778257

**Aslin, Elizabeth.**                                1.6534
The aesthetic movement; prelude to Art nouveau. New York, Praeger [1969] 192 p. illus. (part col.), ports. 29 cm. 1. Arts and crafts movement — Great Britain. 2. Aesthetic movement (British art) I. T.
NK1175.A8      709/.03      LC 76-84860

**Evans, Joan, 1893-.**                                ● 1.6535
Style in ornament. London, Oxford University Press, 1950. 63 p. ill. 1. Decoration and ornament — History I. T.
NK1175 E9      LC 51-10705

**Glazier, Richard, 1851-1918.**                                ● 1.6536
A manual of historic ornament, treating upon the evolution, tradition, and development of architecture & the applied arts; prepared for the use of students and craftsmen by Richard Glazier. 6th ed., rev. and enl., with 700 illustrations by the author and from photos., etc. London, New York, B. T. Batsford [1948] 184 p. illus. (part col.) 25 cm. 1. Decoration and ornament — History. 2. Architecture — Details 3. Decorative arts — History. I. T.
NK1175G5 1948      LC 49-9811

**Hamlin, Alfred Dwight Foster, 1855-1926.**                                ● 1.6537
A history of ornament ... by A. D. F. Hamlin ... New York, The Century co., 1916-23. 2 v. fronts., illus., plates (part col.) 22-23 cm. Contains bibliographies. 1. Decoration and ornament — History. I. T.
NK1175.H3      745      LC 16-23391

**Margaret Woodbury Strong Museum.**                                1.6538
A scene of adornment: decoration in the Victorian home from the collections of the Margaret Woodbury Strong Museum: exhibited at Memorial Art Gallery of the University of Rochester, March 7-April 13, 1975. — [Rochester: s.n.], c1975. 109, [2] p.: ill. (some col.); 27 cm. 1. Decoration and ornament — Victorian style — Exhibitions. 2. Decorative arts, Victorian — Exhibitions. I. University of Rochester. Memorial Art Gallery. II. T.
NK1378.M37 1975      745.1/09/034      LC 76-351727

**The Art nouveau style in jewelry, metalwork, glass, ceramics,**                                1.6539
**textiles, architecture, and furniture / edited by Roberta Waddell.**
New York: Dover Publications, 1977. xi, 288 p.: chiefly ill.; 29 cm. Selections from the Paris journal Art et décoration, 1897-1911. Includes index. 1. Decoration and ornament 2. Decoration and ornament, Architectural I. Waddell, Roberta. II. Art et décoration.
NK1380.A76 1977      745.4/44      LC 77-80034      ISBN 0486235157

**Battersby, Martin.**                                ● 1.6540
The decorative Thirties. New York, Walker [1971] 208 p. illus. 30 cm. 1. Decorative arts 2. Decoration and ornament I. T.
NK1390.B3      740      LC 70-159516      ISBN 0802703534

**Bishop, Robert Charles.**                                1.6541
American decorative arts: 360 years of creative design / Robert Bishop and Patricia Coblentz. — New York: Abrams, 1982. 405 p.: ill. (some col.); 34 cm. Includes index. 1. Decoration and ornament — United States — History. I. Coblentz, Patricia. joint author. II. T.
NK1403.B57 1982      745/.0973 19      LC 80-39631      ISBN 0810906929

**Christensen, Erwin Ottomar, 1890-.**                                ● 1.6542
The Index of American Design / Erwin O. Christensen; introduction by Holger Cahill. — New York: Macmillan, 1950. xviii, 229 p.: ill. (some col.) 1. Index of American Design. I. T.
NK1403.C5      LC 50-10215

**Fowler, John, 1906-.**                                1.6543
English decoration in the 18th century / John Fowler and John Cornforth. — Princeton, [N.J.]: Pyne Press, [1974] 288 p., [16] leaves of plates: ill. (some col.); 31 cm. Includes indexes. 1. Decoration and ornament, English. 2. Decoration and ornament — Neoclassicism I. Cornforth, John, 1937- joint author. II. T.
NK1443.F68      942.07      LC 74-81180      ISBN 0878610758

**Scandinavian modern design, 1880–1980 / Cooper–Hewitt**                                1.6544
**Museum; David Revere McFadden, general editor.**
New York: Abrams, 1982. 287 p.: ill. (some col.); 29 cm. Catalogue of an exhibition at Cooper-Hewitt Museum, New York, Sept. 14, 1982-Jan. 2, 1983; Minnesota Museum of Art, Landmark Center, St. Paul, Feb. 27-Apr. 24, 1983; Renwick Gallery, Washington, D.C., July 8-Oct. 10, 1983. Includes index. 1. Design — Scandinavia — History — 19th century — Exhibitions. 2. Design — Scandinavia — History — 20th century — Exhibitions. I. McFadden, David Revere. II. Cooper-Hewitt Museum. III. Minnesota Museum of Art. IV. Renwick Gallery.
NK1457.S35 1982      745.4/4948 19      LC 82-8899      ISBN 0810916436

**Christie, Archibald H.**                                ● 1.6545
[Traditional methods of pattern designing] Pattern design; an introduction to the study of formal ornament, by Archibald H. Christie. New York, Dover Publications [1969] xii, 313 p. illus. 22 cm. Reprint of the 1929 ed. first published under title: Traditional methods of pattern designing. 1. Design 2. Pattern perception I. T.
NK1510.C5 1969      745.4      LC 72-79234      ISBN 0486222217

**Meyer, Franz Sales, 1849-.**                                ● 1.6546
[Handbuch der Ornamentik. English] Handbook of ornament; a grammar of art, industrial and architectural designing in all its branches for practical as well

as theoretical use. New York, Dover Publications [1957] xiv, 548 p. illus. 21 cm. 'An unabridged and unaltered republication of the English translation of the last revised edition of Handbook of ornament.' 1. Decoration and ornament 2. Decoration and ornament I. T.
NK1510.M6 1957      745      *LC* 57-14417

**Stillman, Damie.**                                                   **1.6547**
The decorative work of Robert Adam / Damie Stillman. — London: Academy Editions; New York: St. Martin's Press, 1973. viii, 119 p., [85] leaves of plates: illus.; 26 cm. Reprint of the 1966 ed. published by A. Tiranti London, which was issued as no. 42 of Chapters in art. Includes index. 1. Adam, Robert, 1728-1792. I. T.
NK1535.A3 S8 1973      745.4/49/24      *LC* 74-187949

**Kühnel, Ernst, 1882-1964.**                                          **1.6548**
[Islamische Kleinkunst. English] The minor arts of Islam. Translated from the German by Katherine Watson. Ithaca, N.Y., Cornell University Press [1971, c1970] viii, 255 p. illus. (part col.), facsims. (part col.) 24 cm. Translation of Islamische Kleinkunst. 1. Art objects, Islamic I. T.
NK1674.K813 1971      709/.176/71      *LC* 75-110331      *ISBN* 0801405637

# NK1700–3505 Interior Decoration. Furniture

**Thornton, Peter.**                                                   **1.6549**
Seventeenth–century interior decoration in England, France, and Holland / Peter Thornton. — New Haven: Published for the Paul Mellon Centre for Studies in British Art by Yale University Press, 1978. xii, 427 p.: ill. (some col.); 27 cm. — (Studies in British art.) 1. Interior decoration — England — History — 17th century. 2. Interior decoration — France — History — 17th century. 3. Interior decoration — Netherlands — History — 17th century. I. Paul Mellon Centre for Studies in British Art. II. T. III. Series.
NK2043.T45      747.2/036 19      *LC* 77-91067      *ISBN* 0300021933

**Wharton, Edith Newbold Jones, 1862-1937.**                           **1.6550**
The decoration of houses / Edith Wharton and Ogden Codman, Jr.; introductory notes by John Barrington Bayley and William A. Coles. — New York: Norton, 1978. xlix, 204 p., [41] leaves of plates: ill.; 24 cm. (Classical America series in art and architecture.) Reprint of the 1902 ed. published by Scribner, New York; with additional material. 1. Interior decoration I. Codman, Ogden. joint author. II. T. III. Series.
NK2110.W5 1978      747/.8/8      *LC* 78-17020      *ISBN* 0393044688. *ISBN* 0393008401 pbk

**Eastlake, Charles L. (Charles Locke), 1836-1906.**                   **1.6551**
Hints on household taste in furniture, upholstery, and other details. — New York: Dover Publications, [1969] xxx, 304 p.: illus. (part col.), front.; 21 cm. Reprint of the 1878 ed., with a new introd. by John Gloag. 1. Interior decoration 2. Furniture I. T. II. Title: Household taste in furniture, upholstery, and other details.
NK2115.E3 1969      749      *LC* 69-16924      *ISBN* 0486223078

**Freeman, John Crosby, comp.**                                        **1.6552**
Furniture for the Victorian home; from A. J. Downing, American: County houses (1850) and J. C. Loudon, English: Encyclopedia (1833) New introd. and index by John C. Freeman. [Watkins Glen, N.Y.] American Life Foundation; [distributed by Century House] 1968. 212 p. illus. 24 cm. (Library of Victorian culture) 1. Interior decoration 2. Furniture design I. Downing, A. J. (Andrew Jackson), 1815-1852. Architecture of country houses. II. Loudon, J. C. (John Claudius), 1783-1843. Encyclopaedia of cottage, farm, and villa architecture and furniture. III. T.
NK2115.F67      749.204      *LC* 68-55040

**Boger, Louise Ade.**                                               • **1.6553**
The complete guide to furniture styles. — Enl. ed. — New York: Scribner, [1969] xii, 500 p.: illus.; 26 cm. 1. Furniture — History. I. T. II. Title: Furniture styles.
NK2270.B63 1969      749.2      *LC* 73-85267

**Hayward, Helena. ed.**                                               **1.6554**
World furniture; an illustrated history [by] Douglas Ash [and others] New York, McGraw-Hill, 1965. 320 p. ill., col. plates. 1. Furniture — History I. Ash, Douglas. II. T.
NK2270 H3      *LC* 65-18175

**Lucie-Smith, Edward.**                                               **1.6555**
Furniture: a concise history Edward Lucie–Smith. — New York: Oxford University Press, 1979. 216 p.: ill. (some col.); 22 cm. Includes index. 1. Furniture — History. I. T.
NK2270.L82 1979      749.2      *LC* 79-4393      *ISBN* 0195201450

**Schmitz, Hermann, 1882-.**                                         • **1.6556**
[Möbelwerk. English] The encyclopedia of furniture; an outline history of furniture design in Egypt, Assyria, Persia, Greece, Rome, Italy, France, the Netherlands, Germany, England, Scandinavia, Spain, Russia, and in the Near and Far East up to the middle of the nineteenth century. Compiled by authorities in various countries under the general direction of Herman Schmitz, and with an introd. by H. P. Shapland. New York, F. A. Praeger [1957] liii p., 320 p. of illus. 30 cm. 1. Furniture — History. I. T.
NK2270.S363 1957      749.09      *LC* 57-9791

**Richter, Gisela Marie Augusta, 1882-1972.**                        • **1.6557**
Ancient furniture: a history of Greek, Etruscan and Roman furniture / by Gisela M. A. Richter; with an appendix by Albert W. Barker. — Oxford: Clarendon Press, 1926. 191 p., 51 leaves of plates: ill. (some col.); 29 cm. 1. Furniture — History I. T.
NK2280.R5      *LC* 26-15818

**Mang, Karl, 1922-.**                                                 **1.6558**
[Geschichte des modernen Mobels. English] The history of modern furniture / Karl Mang; translated by John William Gabriel. — New York: Abrams, c1978. 185 p.: ill.; 29 cm. Translation of Geschichte des modernen Mobels. 1. Furniture — History — 19th century. 2. Furniture — History — 20th century. I. T.
NK2385.M3613      749.2/04      *LC* 79-11551      *ISBN* 0810910667

**Larrabee, Eric.**                                                    **1.6559**
Knoll design / Eric Larrabee, Massimo Vignelli. — New York: H.N. Abrams, c1981. 307 p.: ill. (some col.); 31 cm. Includes index. 1. Knoll International, inc. 2. Interior decoration — History — 20th century. I. Vignelli, Massimo. joint author. II. T.
NK2399.K58 L37 1981      747/.204      *LC* 79-14459      *ISBN* 0810909073

# NK2401–2694 BY COUNTRY

**Andrews, Edward Deming, 1894-1964.**                               • **1.6560**
Shaker furniture; the craftsmanship of an American communal sect, by Edward Deming Andrews and Faith Andrews. Photos. by William F. Winter. — New York: Dover Publications, 1950 [c1937] xi, 133 p.: 48 plates.; 28 cm. 1. Shakers — Industries. 2. Furniture, American. I. Andrews, Faith. joint author. II. T.
NK2405.A7 1950      749.211      *LC* 50-7797

**Fitzgerald, Oscar P.**                                               **1.6561**
Three centuries of American furniture / Oscar P. Fitzgerald. — Englewood Cliffs, N.J.: Prentice-Hall, c1982. xii, 323 p., [4] p. of plates: ill. (some col.); 29 cm. 'A Spectrum book.' Includes index. 1. Furniture — United States — History I. T.
NK2405.F58      749.213 19      *LC* 81-17898      *ISBN* 0139203710

**Comstock, Helen.**                                                 • **1.6562**
American furniture: seventeenth, eighteenth, and nineteenth century styles. New York, Viking Press [1962] 336 p. ill. (A Studio book) 1. Furniture, American — History I. T.
NK2406 C58      *LC* 62-18074

**Downs, Joseph.**                                                     **1.6563**
American furniture in the Henry Francis du Pont Winterthur Museum. Foreword by Henry Francis du Pont. New York, Macmillan, 1952- v. ill. (part col.) 1. Furniture, American — History I. Du Pont, Henry Francis, 1880- II. Henry Francis du Pont Winterthur Museum. III. T.
NK2406 D6      *LC* 52-8567

**Henry Francis du Pont Winterthur Museum.**                           **1.6564**
American furniture, the Federal period, in the Henry Francis du Pont Winterthur Museum, by Charles F. Montgomery. Foreword by Henry Francis du Pont. With photos. by Gilbert Ask. — New York: Viking Press, [1966] 497 p.: illus. (part col.); 32 cm. — (Winterthur book.) 1. Furniture, American — Catalogs. I. Montgomery, Charles F. II. Du Pont, Henry Francis, 1880- III. T. IV. Series.
NK2406.H4      749.213      *LC* 66-19411

**Nutting, Wallace, 1861-1941.**                                     • **1.6565**
Furniture treasury (mostly of American origin): All periods of American furniture with some foreign examples in America also American hardware and household utensils. Five thousand illustrations with descriptions on the same page. Unabridged. New York: Macmillan Publishing Co., inc. 1963[c1928] 2 v. in 1: ill.; 27 cm. 1. Furniture — United States 2. Hardware — United States. 3. Implements, utensils, etc — United States. 4. Clock and watch makers — United States. 5. Clocks and watches I. T.
NK2406.N732 1963      749.21      *LC* a 55-8656

**Sack, Albert.**　　　　　　　　　　　**1.6566**
Fine points of furniture: early American / by Albert Sack; foreword by Israel Sack; introduction by John Meredith Graham. New York: Crown Pub., 1950. xvi, 303 p.: ill.; 26 cm. 1. Furniture, American. 2. Furniture — Collectors and collecting. I. T.
NK2406.S29　　749.21　　*LC* 50-11156　　*ISBN* 0517001489

**Tracy, Berry B.**　　　　　　　　　　　**1.6567**
Federal furniture and decorative arts at Boscobel / text by Berry B. Tracy; with painting documentation by Mary Black. — New York, N.Y.: Boscobel Restoration: Abrams, 1981. 165 p.: col. ill.; 30 x 31 cm. Includes index. 1. Dyckman, States Morris — Homes and haunts — New York (State) 2. Garrison, N.Y. Boscobel. 3. Boscobel Restoration, inc. 4. Furniture — New York (State) — Garrison — History — 19th century. 5. Decoration and ornament — Federal style 6. Art objects — New York (State) — Garrison. I. Black, Mary C. II. T.
NK2406.T7　　749.2147/074/014732 19　　*LC* 80-26062　　*ISBN* 0810909170

**Fales, Dean A.**　　　　　　　　　　　**1.6568**
The furniture of historic Deerfield / Dean A. Fales, Jr. 1st ed. — New York: Dutton, 1976. 294 p.: ill. (some col.), map (on lining paper); 29 cm. Includes index. 1. Furniture, Colonial — New England. 2. Furniture — New England. 3. Furniture — Massachusetts — Deerfield. I. T.
NK2410.F34 1976　　749.2/14/074014422　　*LC* 76-25790　　*ISBN* 0525111018

**Wilk, Christopher.**　　　　　　　　　　**1.6569**
Marcel Breuer, furniture and interiors / by Christopher Wilk; introduction by J. Stewart Johnson. — New York: Museum of Modern Art, c1981. 192 p.: ill.; 27 cm. Published in conjunction with the exhibition presented at the Museum of Modern Art. Errata slip inserted. 1. Breuer, Marcel, 1902- 2. Furniture — History — 20th century. I. Breuer, Marcel, 1902- II. Museum of Modern Art (New York, N.Y.) III. T.
NK2439.B7 W5　　749.213 19　　*LC* 81-81191　　*ISBN* 0870702645

**McClelland, Nancy Vincent, 1876-.**　　　　**1.6570**
Duncan Phyfe and the English Regency, 1795–1830 / by Nancy McClelland; with a foreword by Edward Knoblock. — New York: Dover Publications, 1980. xxix, 364 p.: ill.; 24 cm. Reprint of the 1939 ed. published by W. R. Scott, New York. Includes index. 1. Phyfe, Duncan, 1768-1854. 2. Furniture — United States — History — 19th century 3. Decoration and ornament — Regency style I. T.
NK2439.P5 M25 1980　　749.213 B　　*LC* 79-55747　　*ISBN* 0486239888

**Fastnedge, Ralph, 1913-.**　　　　　　• **1.6571**
English furniture styles from 1500 to 1830 / Ralph Fastnedge. — 1st American ed. — New York: Barnes, 1964, 1962. xxiii, 320 p.: ill. 1. Furniture, English — History. I. T.
NK2529 F25　　749.22

**Fastnedge, Ralph, 1913-.**　　　　　　• **1.6572**
Sheraton furniture. New York: T. Yoseloff [1962] 125 p. 100 plates (4 col.) Bibliography: p. 115. 1. Sheraton, Thomas, 1751-1806. 2. Furniture, English. I. T.
NK2529.F26 1962b　　749.22　　*LC* 62-10187

**Hayward, Charles Harold, 1898-.**　　　　**1.6573**
English period furniture / [by] Charles H. Hayward. — Revised and reset [ed.]. — London: Evans Bros., 1977. 240 p.: ill.; 23 cm. Includes index. 1. Furniture — England I. T.
NK2529.H44 1977　　749.2/2 19　　*LC* 80-490357　　*ISBN* 023744867X

**Ward-Jackson, Peter W.**　　　　　　　**1.6574**
English furniture designs of the eighteenth century / by Peter Ward-Jackson. — London: H. M. Stationery Off., 1958. viii, 68 p., [280] p. of plates: ill.; 28 cm. At head of title: Victoria & Albert Museum. 1. Furniture — England. I. Victoria and Albert Museum. II. T.
NK2529.V47　　NK2528.W3.　　*LC* 59-44906

**Harris, Eileen.**　　　　　　　　　　**1.6575**
The furniture of Robert Adam. — London: Academy Editions; New York: St. Martin's Press, [1973] viii, 110 p.: illus.; 19 cm. Reprint of the 1963 ed. 1. Adam, Robert, 1728-1792. 2. Furniture, English. I. T.
NK2542.A3 H3 1973　　749.2/2　　*LC* 74-168294

**Musgrave, Clifford.**　　　　　　　　**1.6576**
Adam and Hepplewhite and other neo-classical furniture. [1st American ed.] New York, Taplinger Pub. Co. [1966] 223, [96] p. illus. (part col.) 26 cm. Bibliography: 175-178. 1. Adam, Robert, 1728-1792. 2. Hepplewhite, George, d. 1786. 3. Furniture, English. I. T.
NK2542.A3M8 1966　　749.22　　*LC* 66-11302

**Chippendale, Thomas, 1718-1779.**　　　　• **1.6577**
The gentleman & cabinet-maker's director. — New York: Dover Publications, [1966] 1 v. (chiefly illus.); 31 cm. 'Unabridged and unaltered republication of the third ed. published by the author in London in 1762.' 1. Furniture 2. Decoration and ornament — Chippendale style I. T.
NK2542.C5 A3 1762a　　749.22　　*LC* 66-24135

**Chippendale, Thomas, 1718-1779.**　　　　**1.6578**
Thomas Chippendale: an exhibition to mark the bicentenary of Thomas Chippendale's death in November 1779: Leeds Art Galleries at Temple Newsam House, 24 October to 25 November 1979. — [Leeds, West Yorkshire: Temple Newsam House, 1979] 76 p.: ill.; 25 cm. Introd. and catalogue by Christopher Gilbert. 1. Chippendale, Thomas, 1718-1779 — Exhibitions. 2. Furniture — England — History — 18th century — Exhibitions. I. Gilbert, Christopher. II. Temple Newsam House. III. T.
NK2542.C5 A4 1979a　　749.22 19　　*LC* 81-147912

**Duncan, Alastair, 1942-.**　　　　　　**1.6579**
Art deco furniture: the French designers / Alastair Duncan. — 1st American ed. — New York: Holt, Rinehart, and Winston, c1984. 192 p.: ill. (some col.); 28 cm. Includes index. 1. Furniture — France — History — 20th century. 2. Art deco — France. I. T.
NK2549.D86 1984　　749.24 19　　*LC* 84-81003　　*ISBN* 0030000998

**Sieber, Roy, 1923-.**　　　　　　　　**1.6580**
African furniture & household objects / Roy Sieber. — New York: American Federation of Arts, c1980. 279 p.: ill. (some col.); 29 cm. Catalog published in conjunction with an exhibition organized by the American Federation of Arts. 1. Furniture — Africa, Sub-Saharan — Exhibitions. 2. House furnishings — Africa, Sub-Saharan — Exhibitions. I. American Federation of Arts. II. T.
NK2685.75.S53　　749.2/967/074013　　*LC* 79-5340　　*ISBN* 0253119278

## NK2713–2740 SPECIAL ITEMS

**Bishop, Robert Charles.**　　　　　　**1.6581**
Centuries and styles of the American chair, 1640–1970, by Robert Bishop. Foreword by Charles F. Hummel. [1st ed.] New York, Dutton, 1972. 516 p. illus. 29 cm. 1. Chairs — United States. I. T. II. Title: The American chair.
NK2715.B55　　749/.32/0973 19　　*LC* 72-82702　　*ISBN* 0525078266

**A Century of chair design / editor, Frank Russell; introduction,**　**1.6582**
**Philippe Garner; drawings, John Read.**
New York: Rizzoli, 1980. 160 p.: ill. (some col.); 32 cm. Includes index. 1. Chair design — History — 19th century. 2. Chair design — History — 20th century. I. Russell, Frank, 1949- II. Read, John.
NK2715.C4 1980　　749/.32/09032 19　　*LC* 79-64344　　*ISBN* 0847802329

**Kane, Patricia E.**　　　　　　　　　**1.6583**
300 years of American seating furniture: chairs and beds from the Mabel Brady Garvan and other collections at Yale University / Patricia E. Kane. — 1st ed. — Boston: New York Graphic Society, c1976. 319 p., [8] leaves of plates: ill. (some col.); 26 cm. Includes index. 1. Yale University. 2. Chairs — United States — Catalogs. 3. Beds — United States — Catalogs. I. T.
NK2715.K36 1976　　749/.3　　*LC* 78-17892　　*ISBN* 0821206788

## NK2775–3296 RUGS. CARPETS.
### TAPESTRIES

**Dilley, Arthur Urbane, 1873-.**　　　　**1.6584**
Oriental rugs and carpets; a comprehensive study. Rev. by Maurice S. Dimand. [Rev. ed.] Philadelphia, Lippincott [1959] xxi, 289 p. 75 plates (part col.) maps. 1. Rugs, Oriental 2. Carpets I. T.
NK2808 D5 1959　　*LC* 59-13247

**Ford, P. R. J.**　　　　　　　　　　**1.6585**
The oriental carpet: a history and guide to traditional motifs, patterns, and symbols / P. R. J. Ford. — New York: Abrams, 1981. 352 p.: ill. (some col.); 33 cm. Includes indexes. 1. Rugs, Oriental I. T.
NK2808.F65 1981　　746.7/5 19　　*LC* 80-28851　　*ISBN* 0810914050

**Yetkin, Şerare.**　　　　　　　　　　**1.6586**
Early Caucasian carpets in Turkey / [by] Şerare Yetkin; translated from the Turkish MS. by Arlette and Alan Mellaarts. — London: Oguz Press, 1978. 2 v.: ill. (some col.), map; 28 cm. — (Turkish studies on the oriental carpet) English and German text in Vol.1. Leaves printed on both sides. Col. ill. tipped in. Index. 1. Rugs, Caucasian — Turkey. I. Mellaarts, Arlette. II. Mellaarts, Alan. III. T. IV. Series.
NK2809.C3　　746.7/59　　*ISBN* 0905820045

**Rostov, Charles I.**      **1.6587**
Chinese carpets / by Charles I. Rostov and Jia Guanyan, with Li Linpan and Zhang H.Z. — New York: Abrams, 1983. 223 p.: ill. (some col.); 30 cm. Includes index. 1. Rugs — China. I. Jia, Guanyan. II. T.
NK2883.R67 1983    746.7/51 19    *LC* 83-3836    *ISBN* 0810907852

**Ackerman, Phyllis, 1893-.**      • **1.6588**
Tapestry, the mirror of civilization. — New York: AMS Press, [1970] xi, 451 p.: illus.; 23 cm. Reprint of the 1933 ed. 1. Tapestry — History 2. Civilization — History I. T.
NK3000.A25 1970    746.3/9    *LC* 74-108123    *ISBN* 040400279X

**Jarry, Madeleine.**      **1.6589**
[Tapisserie. English] World tapestry, from its origins to the present. New York, Putnam [1969] 358 p. illus. (part col.) 32 cm. Translation of La tapisserie. 1. Tapestry — History I. T.
NK3000.J313    746.3/9    *LC* 68-22257

**Thomson, W. G. (William George), 1865-1942.**      **1.6590**
A history of tapestry from the earliest times until the present day, by W. G. Thomson. 3d ed. with revisions edited by F. P. & E. S. Thomson. East Ardsley, [Eng.] EP Publishing, 1973. xxiv, 596 p. illus. (part col.) 26 cm. 1. Tapestry — History I. Thomson, F. P. (Francis Paul) ed. II. Thomson, Ester Sylvia, ed. III. T.
NK3000.T4 1973    746.3/09    *LC* 74-157028    *ISBN* 0854097686

**Stenton, F. M. (Frank Merry), 1880-1967.**      • **1.6591**
The Bayeux tapestry; a comprehensive survey by Sir Frank Stenton, general editor, Simone Bertrand [and others. 2d ed., rev. and enl. London, Phaidon Press [1965] 194 p. ill. (part mountd, part col.) map. 1. Bayeux tapestry I. T.
NK3049 B3 S73 1965    *LC* 65-28977

**Cloisters (Museum)**      **1.6592**
The unicorn tapestries / Margaret B. Freeman, Curator Emeritus, The Cloisters. — New York: Metropolitan Museum of Art: distributed by Dutton, 1976. 244 p.: ill. (some col.); 32 cm. 1. Cloisters (Museum) 2. Hunt of the unicorn (Tapestries) 3. Tapestry, Gothic — France I. Freeman, Margaret Beam, 1899- II. T.
NK3049.U5 N43 1976    746.3/94    *LC* 76-2466    *ISBN* 0870991477

**Yates, Frances Amelia.**      **1.6593**
The Valois tapestries / Frances A. Yates. — 2d ed. — London: Routledge & K. Paul, 1975. xxvii, 150 p., [28] leaves of plates: ill.; 28 cm. 1. Feasts at the Valois court (Tapestries) 2. Tapestry, Flemish I. T.
NK3055.V3 Y3 1975    746.3/9493/30740551    *LC* 76-359541    *ISBN* 0710082444

**Szablowski, Jerzy.**      **1.6594**
The Flemish tapestries at Wawel castle in Cracow. Treasures of King Sigismund Augustus Jagiello. (Authors: Jerzy Szablowski ... Sophie Schneebalg–Perelman, Adelbrecht L. J. van de Walle). Edited under the direction of Jerzy Szablowski. (Version in English by Haakon Chevalier). Antwerp, Fond Mercator, (under the auspices of the Banque de Paris et des Pays-Bas), 1972. 501 p. col. illus. (part fold.) 35 cm. 1. Zamek Królewski na Wawelu (Kraków, Poland) 2. Tapestry — Poland — Krakow. 3. Tapestry, Flemish — Krakow. I. T.
NK3071.P63 K78    746.3/9493/10740386    *LC* 73-345021

## NK3375–3496 WALLPAPER

**Oman, Charles Chichele, 1901-.**      **1.6595**
Wallpapers: an international history and illustrated survey from the Victoria and Albert Museum / Charles C. Oman and Jean Hamilton; bibliography by E.A. Entwisle. — New York: Abrams, in association with the Victoria and Albert Museum, 1982. 486 p.: ill. (some col.); 29 cm. Includes indexes. 1. Victoria and Albert Museum — Catalogs. 2. Wallpaper — England — London — Catalogs. 3. Wallpaper — History. I. Hamilton, Jean. II. Victoria and Albert Museum. III. T.
NK3386.G7 L666 1982    747/.3 19    *LC* 81-69549    *ISBN* 0810917785

**Teynac, Françoise.**      **1.6596**
[Monde du papier peint. English] Wallpaper, a history / Françoise Teynac, Pierre Nolot, Jean–Denis Vivien; foreword by David Hicks; [translated from the French, Le monde du papier peint, by Conway Lloyd Morgan]. — New York: Rizzoli, 1983, c1982. 251 p.: ill. (some col.); 32 cm. Includes index. 1. Wallpaper — History. I. Nolot, Pierre. II. Vivien, Jean-Denis. III. T.
NK3400.T4913 1982    747/.3 19    *LC* 81-86461    *ISBN* 0847804348

**Lynn, Catherine.**      **1.6597**
Wallpaper in America: from the seventeenth century to World War I / Catherine Lynn; with a foreword by Charles van Ravenswaay. — 1st ed. — New York: W.W. Norton, c1980. 533 p.: ill. (some col.); 27 cm. 'A Barra

Foundation/Cooper-Hewitt Museum book.' Includes index. 1. Wallpaper — United States. I. Cooper-Hewitt Museum. II. T.
NK3412.L9 1980    676/.2848/0973 19    *LC* 81-112123    *ISBN* 0393014487

# NK3600 Other Arts

## NK3600–3640 LETTERING

**Degering, Hermann, 1866-1942.**      **1.6598**
Lettering; modes of writing in western Europe from antiquity to the end of the 18th century. New York, Universe Books [1965] xxxvii, 240 p. illus., facsims. 30 cm. 1. Lettering 2. Writing I. T.
NK3600.D4 1965    745.61    *LC* 65-24561

**Goudy, Frederic W. (Frederic William), 1865-1947.**      • **1.6599**
The Alphabet: and, Elements of lettering. — Rev. and enl., with many full-page plates and other ill. drawn & arranged by the author. — New York: Dover Publications, 1963. 101 p., [4] leaves of plates: ill.; 27 cm. 1. Alphabet — History 2. Lettering I. Goudy, Frederic W. (Frederic William), 1865-1947. Elements of lettering II. T. III. Title: Elements of lettering
NK3600.G6 1963    *LC* 63-23603    *ISBN* 0486207927

**Gray, Nicolete, 1911-.**      **1.6600**
Lettering as drawing / Nicolete Gray. — 1st pbk. ed. — New York: Taplinger Pub. Co., 1982, c1971. 195 p.: ill.; 24 cm. 'A Pentalic book.' 1. Lettering — History. I. T.
NK3600.G819 1982    745.6/197 19    *LC* 81-84750    *ISBN* 0800847296

**Neugebauer, Friedrich.**      **1.6601**
[Kalligraphie als Erlebnis. English] The mystic art of written forms: an illustrated handbook for lettering / by Friedrich Neugebauer; translated by Bruce Kennett. — 1. English ed. — Salzburg; Boston: Neugebauer Press, c1980. 142 p.: ill. (some col.); 25 cm. Translation of: Kalligraphie als Erlebnis. 1. Lettering I. T.
NK3600.N4413 1980    745.6/197 19    *LC* 82-184407    *ISBN* 0907234003

**Svaren, Jacqueline.**      **1.6602**
Written letters: 29 alphabets for calligraphers / written out by Jacqueline Svaren. — Rev. and expanded ed. — New York: Taplinger Pub. Co., 1982. vii, 66, [3] p.: ill. (some col.); 34 cm. 'A Pentalic book.' 1. Calligraphy 2. Alphabets I. T.
NK3600.S95 1982    745.6/197 19    *LC* 81-86266    *ISBN* 0800887344

**Whalley, Joyce Irene.**      **1.6603**
The pen's excellencie: a pictorial history of western calligraphy / Joyce Irene Whalley. — 1st pbk. ed. — New York: Taplinger Pub. Co., 1982, c1980. 400 p.: ill.; 28 cm. 'A Pentalic book.' Includes index. 1. Calligraphy — History. I. T.
NK3603.W48 1982    745.6/197/09 19    *LC* 82-241503    *ISBN* 0800862821

**Dürer, Albrecht, 1471-1528.**      **1.6604**
Of the just shaping of letters, from the Applied geometry of Albrecht Dürer, book III. [Translated by R. T. Nichol from the Latin text of the edition of 1535] New York, Dover Publications [1965] 40 p. illus. 28 cm. 'Unabridged and unaltered republication of the work first published by the Grolier Club in 1917.' 1. Lettering I. T.
NK3615.D733    *LC* 64-18848

**Modern scribes and lettering artists.**      **1.6605**
New York: Taplinger Pub. Co., 1980. 160 p.: all ill.; 29 cm. 'A Pentalic book.' Includes index. 1. Calligraphy 2. Lettering
NK3620.M56 1980    745.6/197/09047 19    *LC* 80-50362    *ISBN* 0800852974

**Chiang, Yee, 1903-.**      • **1.6606**
Chinese calligraphy: an introduction to its aesthetic and technique / by Chinag Lee; with a foreword by Sir Herbert Read. — 2n ed., with an new preface. — Cambridge: Harvard University Press, [1954] xvi, 230 p.: ill., facsims. Half title in Chinese. 1. Calligraphy, Chinese I. T.
NK3634.A2 C465 1973    NK3634A2 C465 1954.    745.6/199/51    *ISBN* 0674122259

**Ecke Tseng, Yu-ho, 1923-.**      **1.6607**
Chinese calligraphy. Co-published by the Philadelphia Museum of Art and Boston Book & Art, Publisher. — [Philadelphia]: [s.n.], 1971. 1 v. (unpaged):

illus.; 31 cm. Catalogue of an exhibition, Philadelphia Museum of Art. 1. Calligraphy, Chinese I. Philadelphia Museum of Art. II. T.
NK3634.A2 E25    745.6/19/951    *LC* 75-161453

**Schimmel, Annemarie.**            **1.6608**
Calligraphy and Islamic culture / Annemarie Schimmel. — New York: New York University Press, 1984. xiv, 264 p., [12] p. of plates: ill. (some col.); 28 cm. — (Hagop Kevorkian series on Near Eastern art and civilization.) Includes indexes. 1. Calligraphy, Islamic 2. Alphabet — Religious aspects — Islam. 3. Civilization, Islamic I. T. II. Series.
NK3636.5.A2 S34 1984    745.6/19927 19    *LC* 83-8115    *ISBN* 0814778305

# NK3700–4695 CERAMICS

**Cooper, Emmanuel.**            **1.6609**
A history of pottery / Emmanuel Cooper. — New York: St. Martin's Press, 1973, [c1972] 276 p., [4] leaves of plates: ill. (some col.); 26 cm. Second ed. published under title: A history of world pottery. Includes index. 1. Pottery — History. I. T.
NK3780.C66 1972    738/.09    *LC* 72-85262

**Cox, Warren Earle, 1895-.**            **1.6610**
The book of pottery and porcelain, by Warren E. Cox. — Rev. ed. — New York: Crown Publishers, [c1970] 2 v. (xvi, 1158 p.): illus.; 24 cm. 1. Pottery — History. 2. Porcelain — History. 3. Pottery — Marks I. T.
NK3780.C7 1970    738/.09    *LC* 75-127511

**Grube, Ernst J.**            **1.6611**
Islamic pottery of the eighth to the fifteenth century in the Keir Collection / Ernst J. Grube. — London: Faber and Faber, 1976. 378 p., [14] col. leaves of plates: ill. (some col.); 29 cm. Includes index. 1. De Unger, Edmund — Art collections. 2. Pottery, Islamic — Catalogs. I. T.
NK3880.G78    738.3/0917/67107402176    *LC* 76-383703    *ISBN* 057109953X

**Lane, Arthur, 1909-1963.**            **1.6612**
Later Islamic pottery: Persia, Syria, Egypt, Turkey. — 2nd ed.; [revised by Ralph Pinder-Wilson]. — London: Faber and Faber Ltd, 1971. xvi, 133, 100 p. [8] l.: illus. (some col.), map.; 26 cm. — (The Faber monographs on pottery and porcelain) 1. Pottery, Islamic I. Pinder-Wilson, Ralph H. II. T.
NK3880.L33 1971    738.3/0917/671    *LC* 72-179330    *ISBN* 057104736X

**Hillier, Bevis, 1940-.**            **1.6613**
Pottery and porcelain, 1700–1914; England, Europe, and North America. — New York: Meredith Press, [1968] 386 p.: illus. (part col.), facsims., ports.; 24 cm. — (The Social history of the decorative arts) 1. Pottery — History. 2. Porcelain — History. I. T.
NK3900.H5 1968b    738/.09    *LC* 68-27001

**Clark, Garth, 1947-.**            **1.6614**
A century of ceramics in the United States, 1878–1978: a study of its development / Garth Clark; foreword by Ronald A. Kuchta; pref. by Margie Hughto. — 1st ed. — New York: E. P. Dutton, c1979. xxv, 371 p., [12] leaves of plates: ill. (some col.); 24 cm. 'Published in conjunction with the exhibition 'A century of ceramics in the United States, 1878-1978' at the Everson Museum of Art, Syracuse, New York, May 5-September 23, 1979 ... also at the Renwick Gallery of the National Collection of Fine Arts ... Washington, D.C., November 9, 1979-January 27, 1980.' Includes index. 1. Pottery, American 2. Pottery — 19th century — United States. 3. Porcelain, American 4. Porcelain — 19th century — United States. 5. Potters — United States — Biography. I. Everson Museum of Art. II. T.
NK4007.C56 1979    738/.0973    *LC* 78-73341    *ISBN* 0525078207

**Ceramic sculpture: six artists / Richard Marshall and Suzanne**    **1.6615**
**Foley.**
New York: Whitney Museum of American Art; Seattle: In association with the University of Washington Press, 1982, [c1981]. 144 p.: ill. (some col.); 28 cm. — Catalog of an exhibition of the same title held at the Whitney Museum of American Art, Dec. 9, 1981-Feb. 7, 1982, and subsequently at the San Francisco Museum of Modern Art. 1. Ceramic sculpture — California — Exhibitions. 2. Pottery — 20th century — California — Exhibitions. I. Foley, Suzanne. II. Marshall, Richard, 1947- III. Whitney Museum of American Art. IV. San Francisco Museum of Modern Art.
NK4008.C47 1981    730/.0973/07401471 19    *LC* 81-14703    *ISBN* 0874270359

**Espejel, Carlos.**            **1.6616**
Mexican folk ceramics / Carlos Espejel; photographer, F. Català Roca; [translated from the Spanish by Diorki]. — Barcelona: Editorial Blume, 1976, [c1975]. 219 p.: ill. (some col.); 28 cm. (Nueva imagen series) Includes index. 1. Pottery, Mexican 2. Folk art — Mexico. I. Català Roca, Francesc. II. T.
NK4031.E8713    738/.0972    *LC* 75-45776    *ISBN* 0876632614

**Medley, Margaret.**            **1.6617**
The Chinese potter: a practical history of Chinese ceramics / Margaret Medley. New York: Scribner, c1976. 288 p., [4] leaves of plates: ill.; 26 cm. Includes index. 1. Pottery, Chinese — History. 2. Porcelain, Chinese — History. I. T.
NK4165.M39 1976b    738/.0951    *LC* 76-6023    *ISBN* 0684146843

**Valenstein, Suzanne G.**            **1.6618**
A handbook of Chinese ceramics / Suzanne G. Valenstein. — New York: Metropolitan Museum of Art; Boston: distributed by New York Graphic Society, [1975] xii, 251 p.: ill.; 26 cm. 1. Pottery, Chinese — History. 2. Porcelain, Chinese — History. I. Metropolitan Museum of Art (New York, N.Y.) II. T.
NK4165.V34    738/.0951    *LC* 75-22208    *ISBN* 0870991310

**Watson, William, 1917-.**            **1.6619**
Tang and Liao ceramics / by William Watson. — New York: Rizzoli, 1984. 283 p.: ill. (some col.); 33 cm. Includes index. 1. Pottery, Chinese — T'ang-Five dynasties, 618-960 2. Pottery, Chinese — Sung-Yuan dynasties, 960-1368 I. T.
NK4165.3.W37 1984    738/.0951 19    *LC* 83-24630    *ISBN* 0847805263

**Tregear, Mary.**            **1.6620**
Song ceramics / Mary Tregear. — English ed. — New York: Rizzoli, 1982. 262 p.: ill. (some col.); 33 cm. Includes index. 1. Pottery, Chinese — Sung-Yuan dynasties, 960-1368 I. T.
NK4165.4.T7 1982    738.2/0951 19    *LC* 81-84083    *ISBN* 0847804240

**Garnsey, Wanda.**            **1.6621**
China, ancient kilns and modern ceramics: a guide to the modern potteries / Wanda Garnsey, with Rewi Alley. — Canberra, Australia; Miami, Fla.: Australian National University Press; Miami, Fla.: Books Australia [distributor], 1984, [c1983]. xiii, 144 p., [16] p. of plates: ill.; 29 cm. Includes index. 1. Pottery, Chinese 2. Pottery, Chinese — 20th century. 3. Porcelain, Chinese 4. Porcelain, Chinese — 20th century. I. Alley, Rewi, 1897- II. T.
NK4165.7.G37 1983    738/.0951 19    *LC* 82-74202    *ISBN* 0708113133

**Mino, Yutaka.**            **1.6622**
Freedom of clay and brush through seven centuries in northern China: Tz'u-chou type wares, 960–1600 A.D.: Indianapolis Museum of Art, November 17, 1980–January 18, 1981, China House Gallery, New York, March 16–May 24, 1981, The Denver Art Museum, June 27–August 9, 1981 / Yutaka Mino; catalogue with the assistance of Katherine R. Tsiang. — Indianapolis: Indianapolis Museum of Art; Bloomington: Indiana University Press, c1980. 264 p.: ill. (some col.); 29 cm. Third exhibition location covered by label which reads: Cleveland Museum of Art, August 5, 1981-September 6, 1981. 1. Tz'u ware — Exhibitions. 2. Pottery, Chinese — Sung-Yüan dynasties, 960-1368 — Exhibitions. 3. Pottery, Chinese — Ming-Ch'ing dynasties, 1368-1912 — Exhibitions. I. Tsiang, Katherine R. II. Indianapolis Museum of Art. III. China House Gallery. IV. Cleveland Museum of Art. V. T.
NK4166.T95 M56    738.3/7 19    *LC* 80-8642    *ISBN* 0253131707

**Cort, Louise Allison, 1944-.**            **1.6623**
Shigaraki, potters' valley / by Louise Allison Cort. — 1st ed. — Tokyo; New York: Kodansha International, 1979. xi, 428 p.: ill. (some col.); 31 cm. Includes index. 1. Shigaraki pottery I. T.
NK4168.S48 C67    738.3/7    *LC* 79-89265    *ISBN* 0870113828

**Leach, Bernard, 1887-.**            **1.6624**
Hamada: potter / Bernard Leach. — 1st ed. — Tokyo; New York: Kodansha International; New York: [distributed by] Harper & Row, 1975. 305 p.: ill. (some col.); 31 cm. Includes index. 1. Hamada, Shōji, 1894-1978. 2. Potters — Japan — Biography. I. Hamada, Shōji, 1894-1978. II. T.
NK4210.H32 L4    738.3/092/4 B    *LC* 75-11394    *ISBN* 087011252X

**Rawson, Philip S.**            **1.6625**
Ceramics / Philip Rawson. — 1st pbk. ed. — Philadelphia: University of Pennsylvania Press, 1984. xv, 223 p.: ill.; 21 cm. Reprint. Originally published: London; New York: Oxford University Press, 1971. (The Appreciation of the arts; 6). Includes index. 1. Pottery 2. Porcelain I. T.
NK4225.R3 1984    738 19    *LC* 83-12480    *ISBN* 0812211561

**Rhodes, Daniel, 1911-.**            ● **1.6626**
Clay and glazes for the potter. All photos. by the author. New York: Greenberg, [1957] 219 p.: illus.; 27 cm. — (Arts and crafts series) 1. Pottery 2. Clay 3. Glazes I. T.
NK4225.R45    738.312    *LC* 57-11905

**Speight, Charlotte F., 1919-.**            **1.6627**
Images in clay sculpture: historical and contemporary techniques / Charlotte F. Speight. — 1st ed. — New York: Harper & Row, c1983. vii, 216 p., [12] p. of plates: ill. (some col.); 29 cm. — (Icon editions) Includes index. 1. Ceramic sculpture — Technique. 2. Modeling I. T.
NK4235.S6 1983    731.4 19    *LC* 83-47560    *ISBN* 0064385256

**Caiger-Smith, Alan.**      **1.6628**
Tin–glaze pottery in Europe and the Islamic world; the tradition of 1000 years in maiolica, faience & delftware [by] Alan Caiger-Smith. [s.l.]: Humanities, 1973. 236 p. illus. 25 cm. 1. Enameled ware — History. I. T.
NK4290.C33    738.3    *LC* 73-181068    *ISBN* 0571093493

**Patterson, Jerry E.**      **1.6629**
Porcelain / Jerry E. Patterson. — [New York]: Cooper-Hewitt Museum, c1979. 132 p.: ill. (some col.); 29 cm. (The Smithsonian illustrated library of antiques) Includes index. 1. Porcelain I. Cooper-Hewitt Museum. II. T.
NK4370.P37    738.2    *LC* 78-62736

**Palmer, Arlene M.**      **1.6630**
A Winterthur guide to Chinese export porcelain / Arlene M. Palmer. New York: Crown, c1976. 144 p.: ill.; 20 cm. 'A Winterthur book/Rutledge books.' 1. Henry Francis du Pont Winterthur Museum. 2. China trade porcelain I. Henry Francis du Pont Winterthur Museum. II. T.
NK4565.5.P34 1976    738.2/0951/07401511    *LC* 76-10848    *ISBN* 0517527847

**Arias, Paolo Enrico.**      • **1.6631**
A history of 1000 years of Greek vase painting. Text and notes by P. E. Arias. Photos. by Max Hirmer. [Translated and rev. by B. Shefton]. — New York, H. N. Abrams [1962] 410 p. mounted col. illus., plates. 32 cm. Includes bibliographical references. 1. Vases, Greek 2. Vase-painting, Greek I. Hirmer, Max. II. T. III. Title: 1000 years of Greek vase painting.
NK4645.A69    738.382    *LC* 61-13857

**Cook, Robert Manuel.**      **1.6632**
Greek painted pottery [by] R. M. Cook. — 2nd ed. — [London]: Methuen, [1972] xxiv, 390 p.: illus.; 24 cm. — ([Methuen's handbooks of archaeology series]) Distributed in the USA by Harper & Row; Barnes & Noble Import Division. 1. Pottery, Greek 2. Vases — Greece 3. Vase-painting, Greek I. T.
NK4645.C6 1972    738.3/0938    *LC* 72-193710    *ISBN* 0416761704

**Noble, Joseph Veach, 1920-.**      • **1.6633**
The techniques of painted Attic pottery. New York, Watson-Guptill Publications [1965] xvi, 217 p. ill. (part col.) Published in cooperation with the Metropolitan Museum of Art. 1. Vase-painting, Greek 2. Vases, Greek I. New York. Metropolitan Museum of Art II. T.
NK4645 N6    *LC* 65 25311

**Beazley, J. D. (John Davidson), 1885-1970.**      • **1.6634**
Attic black–figure vase–painters. Oxford Clarendon Press 1956. 851p. 1. Vase-painting, Greek 2. Vases, Greek I. T.
NK4648 B4

**Beazley, J. D. (John Davidson), 1885-1970.**      • **1.6635**
The development of Attic black–figure. Berkeley, University of California Press, 1951. xiv, 127 p. ill. 49 plates. 27 cm. (Sather classical lectures. v. 24) Bibliographical references included in 'Notes' (p. [101]-119) 1. Vases, Greek I. T. II. Title: Attic black-figure. III. Series.
NK4648.B42    738.38    *LC* 51-61810

**Boardman, John, 1927-.**      **1.6636**
Athenian black figure vases. — New York: Oxford University Press, 1974. 252 p.: illus.; 22 cm. 1. Vases — Greece 2. Vase-painting, Greek I. T.
NK4648.B62 1974    738.3/82/09385    *LC* 73-89034

**Webster, T. B. L. (Thomas Bertram Lonsdale), 1905-1974.**      **1.6637**
Potter and patron in classical Athens / [by] T. B. L. Webster. — London: Methuen, 1972. xvi, 312, 16 p.: ill.; 23 cm. 'Distributed in the USA by Harper & Row Publishers, Inc., Barnes & Noble Import Division.' 1. Vase-painting, Greek — Greece 2. Potters — Greece — Athens. 3. Art patronage — Greece — Athens. I. T.
NK4648.W4 1972    738.3/82/0938    *LC* 73-159352    *ISBN* 0416756301

**Beazley, J. D. (John Davidson), 1885-1970.**      • **1.6638**
Attic red–figure vase–painters. 2d ed. Oxford, Clarendon Press, 1963. 3 v. (lvi, 2036 p.) 1. Vase-painting, Greek 2. Vases, Greek I. T.
NK4649 B44 1963    *LC* 64-714

**Boardman, John, 1927-.**      **1.6639**
Athenian red figure vases: the archaic period: a handbook / John Boardman. — London: Thames and Hudson, c1975. 252 p.: ill.; 22 cm. Includes indexes. 1. Vase-painting, Greek — Greece — Athens. I. T.
NK4649.B62    738.3/82/09385    *LC* 75-522687    *ISBN* 0500181497

**Vollmer, John.**      **1.6640**
In the presence of the Dragon Throne: Ch'ing Dynasty costume (1644–1911) in the Royal Ontario Museum / by John E. Vollmer. — Toronto: Royal Ontario Museum, c1977. 88 p.: ill.; 20 x 23 cm. 1. Costume — China — History — Ming-Ch'ing dynasties, 1368-1912 — Exhibitions. I. Royal Ontario Museum. II. T.
NK4783.A1 V64    746.9/2    *LC* 78-321084    *ISBN* 0888541953

# NK5100–5440 GLASS

**Mehlman, Felice.**      **1.6641**
Phaidon guide to glass / Felice Mehlman. — Englewood Cliffs, N.J.: Prentice-Hall, c1983. 256 p.: ill. (some col.); 22 cm. 'A Spectrum book.' Includes index. 1. Glassware I. T.
NK5104.M42 1983    748.2 19    *LC* 83-3319    *ISBN* 0136620159

**Charleston, R. J. (Robert Jesse), 1916-.**      **1.6642**
Masterpieces of glass: a world history from the Corning Museum of Glass / Robert J. Charleston; [editor, Joan E. Fisher]. — New York: H. N. Abrams, c1980. 239 p.: ill. (some col.); 31 cm. — (A Corning Museum of Glass monograph) Includes index. 1. Corning Museum of Glass. 2. Glassware — History I. Fisher, Joan E. II. Corning Museum of Glass. III. T.
NK5106.C47    748.2/9    *LC* 79-17657    *ISBN* 081091753X

**Arwas, Victor.**      **1.6643**
Glass: art nouveau to art deco / Victor Arwas. — New York: Rizzoli, 1978 [c1977] 256 p.: ill. (some col.); 32 cm. Includes index. 1. Glassware — History — 19th century 2. Decoration and ornament — Art nouveau 3. Glassware — History — 20th century 4. Art deco I. T.
NK5109.85.A7 A78 1977    748.2/904    *LC* 76-62548    *ISBN* 0847801128

**McKearin, George Skinner, 1874-.**      **1.6644**
American glass, by George S. and Helen McKearin. 2000 photos., 1000 drawings by James L. McCreery. New York, Crown Publishers [1948] xvi, 634 p. illus. 28 cm. 1. Glassware — United States 2. Glass manufacture — United States. I. McKearin, Helen, joint author. II. T.
NK5112.M26 1948    748    *LC* 48-2187

**Koch, Robert, 1918-.**      • **1.6645**
Louis C. Tiffany, rebel in glass. New York, Crown Publishers [1964] 246 p. illus. (part col.) facsims., ports. 29 cm. 1. Tiffany, Louis Comfort, 1848-1933. I. T.
NK5198.T5 K6    *LC* 63-21121

**International Colloquium of the Corpus Vitrearum. (11th: 1982: New York)**      **1.6646**
Corpus Vitrearum: selected papers from the XIth International Colloquium of the Corpus Vitrearum, New York, 1–6 June 1982 / Madeline H. Caviness and Timothy Husband, editors. — New York: Metropolitan Museum of Art, 1985. 157 p., [1] leaf of plates: ill. (some col.); 32 cm. (Corpus vitrearum United States occasional papers. 1) 'Studies on medieval stained glass'—Cover. 1. Glass painting and staining, Medieval — Congresses. I. Caviness, Madeline Harrison, 1938- II. Husband, Timothy. III. Metropolitan Museum of Art (New York, N.Y.) IV. T. V. Series.
NK5308.I57 1982    748.59/02 19    *LC* 85-4973    *ISBN* 0870993917

**Sewter, A. C.**      **1.6647**
The stained glass of William Morris and his circle [by] A. Charles Sewter. — New Haven: Published for the Paul Mellon Centre for Studies in British Art by Yale University Press, 1974. xii, 119 p., [324] p. of illus. (part col.); 32 cm. — (Studies in British art.) 1. Morris, William, 1834-1896. 2. Glass painting and staining, Victorian — Great Britain. 3. Glass painters — Great Britain. I. T. II. Series.
NK5343.S48    748.5/92    *LC* 72-91307    *ISBN* 0300014716

**Caviness, Madeline Harrison, 1938-.**      **1.6648**
The early stained glass of Canterbury Cathedral, circa 1175–1220 / Madeline Harrison Caviness. — Princeton, N.J.: Princeton University Press, c1977. xix, 190 p., [52] leaves of plates: ill.; 29 cm. Includes index. 1. Canterbury Cathedral. 2. Glass painting and staining, Romanesque — England — Canterbury. 3. Glass painting and staining, Gothic — England — Canterbury. 4. Glass painting and staining — England — Canterbury. I. T.
NK5344.C3 C38    748.5/922/34    *LC* 77-10419    *ISBN* 0691039275

**Raguin, Virginia Chieffo, 1941-.**      **1.6649**
Stained glass in thirteenth–century Burgundy / Virginia Chieffo Raguin. — Princeton, N.J.: Princeton University Press, c1982. xviii, 182 p., [83] p. of plates: ill. (some col.); 29 cm. Includes index. 1. Glass painting and staining, Gothic — France — Burgundy. 2. Glass painting and staining — France — Burgundy. I. T.
NK5349.A3 B876 1982    748.594/4 19    *LC* 81-47946    *ISBN* 0691039879

**Johnson, James Rosser.**      • **1.6650**
The radiance of Chartres: studies in the early stained glass of the cathedral / James Rosser Johnson. — New York: Random House, [1965] xii, 96 p.: ill. (part col.); 21 cm. — (Columbia University studies in art, history, and archaeology; no. 4) 1. Cathédrale de Chartres. 2. Glass painting and staining — France — Chartres. I. T. II. Series.
NK5349.C5 J6    *LC* 64-15894

**Lillich, Meredith P., 1932-.**    **1.6651**
The stained glass of Saint–Père de Chartres / by Meredith Parsons Lillich. — 1st ed. — Middletown, Conn.: Wesleyan University Press, c1978. xiv, 212 p., [53] leaves of plates (1 fold.): ill. (some col.); 29 cm. Includes indexes. 1. Chartres, France. Saint Père (Church) 2. Glass painting and staining, Gothic — France — Chartres. 3. Glass painting and staining, French — France — Chartres. I. T.
NK5349.C5 L54    748.5/945/1    LC 77-13926    ISBN 081955023X

**Duncan, Alastair, 1942-.**    **1.6652**
Tiffany windows / Alastair Duncan. — New York: Simon and Schuster, c1980. 224 p.: ill. (some col.); 31 cm. 1. Tiffany, Louis Comfort, 1848-1933. 2. Glass painting and staining — United States. I. T.
NK5398.T52 D86    748.5913    LC 80-5352    ISBN 0671249517

# NK5566–8459 Gems. Metals

**Snowman, A. Kenneth (Abraham Kenneth), 1919-.**    **1.6653**
Carl Fabergé: goldsmith to the Imperial Court of Russia / A. Kenneth Snowman. — New York: Viking Press, c1979. 160 p.: ill. (some col.); 28 cm. (A Studio book) Includes index. 1. Faberzhe, Karl Gustavovich, 1846-1920. 2. Faberzhe (Firm) I. T.
NK5698.F3 S66 1979b    739.2/092/4    LC 79-63369    ISBN 0670204862

**Baer, Eva.**    **1.6654**
Metalwork in medieval Islamic art / Eva Baer. — Albany: State University of New York Press, c1983. xxiv, 371 p.: ill.; 24 cm. Includes index. 1. Art metalwork, Islamic 2. Art metal-work, Medieval — Islamic countries. I. T.
NK6408.9.B3 1983    739/.0917/671 19    LC 81-23243    ISBN 0873956028

**Museum of Fine Arts, Boston.**    **1.6655**
American silver, 1655–1825, in the Museum of Fine Arts, Boston, by Kathryn C. Buhler. Boston; distributed by New York Graphic Society, Greenwich, Conn. [1972] 2 v. (xx, 708 p.) illus. 29 cm. 1. Silverwork, American — Catalogs. I. Buhler, Kathryn C. II. T.
NK7112.B577    739.2/3/773074014461    LC 75-190547    ISBN 0878460640

**Fales, Martha Gandy.**    **1.6656**
Early American silver. — Rev. and enl. ed. — New York: Dutton, 1973 [c1970] x, 336 p.: illus.; 26 cm. 1. Silverwork — United States. I. T.
NK7112.F3 1973    739.2/3/773    LC 74-154280    ISBN 0525472991

**Kovel, Ralph M.**    • **1.6657**
A directory of American silver, pewter, and silver plate, by Ralph M. & Terry H. Kovel. New York, Crown Publishers [1961] 352 p. illus. 26 cm. 1. Silversmiths — United States — Directories. 2. Pewter — United States — Directories. 3. Silver-plated ware — United States — Directories. 4. Hallmarks — United States — Directories. I. Kovel, Terry H. joint author. II. T. III. Title: American silver, pewter, and silver plate.
NK7112.K66    739.205873    LC 60-8620

**Silver in American life: selections from the Mabel Brady**    **1.6658**
**Garvan and other collections at Yale University / edited by Barbara McLean Ward & Gerald W. R. Ward.**
Boston, Mass.: D. R. Godine, 1979. xiii, 193 p.: ill. (some col.); 29 cm. 1. Yale University. Art Gallery — Catalogs. 2. Silverwork — United States — Catalogs. 3. Art — Private collections — Catalogs. 4. Silverwork — United States — History. I. Ward, Barbara McLean. II. Ward, Gerald W. R.
NK7112.S45    739.2/3773/07401468    LC 78-74920    ISBN 0879232889

**Hernmarck, Carl, 1901-.**    **1.6659**
The art of the European silversmith, 1430–1830 / [by] Carl Hernmarck. — London; New York: Sotheby Parke Bernet, 1978, [c1977]. 2 v. (411, [19] p., 386 p. of plates): ill.; 31 cm. Includes index. 1. Silverwork — Europe. 2. Silverwork, Renaissance — Europe. 3. Silverwork, Baroque — Europe. 4. Silverwork, Rococo — Europe. 5. Silverwork — Europe — History — 19th century. I. T.
NK7142.H47    739.2/3/74    LC 79-314491    ISBN 0856670340

**Taylor, Gerald, 1923-**    **1.6660**
Silver / Gerald Taylor. — 2nd ed. — Baltimore: Penguin Books, [1963] ill., port.; 19 cm. — (Pelican books) 'A306 Original.' 1. Silverwork — Great Britain — History I. T.
NK7143 T3    NK7143.T3 1963.    739.23    LC 63-25568    ISBN

**Munn, Geoffrey C.**    **1.6661**
[Bijoutiers Castellani et Giuliano. English] Castellani and Giuliano: revivalist jewellers of the 19th century / by Geoffrey C. Munn. — New York: Rizzoli, c1984. 207 p.: ill. (some col.); 26 cm. Translation of: Les bijoutiers Castellani et Giuliano. Includes index. 1. Castellani (Firm) 2. Giuliano (Firm) 3. Jewelers — Italy — Rome. 4. Jewelers — England — London. 5. Jewelry — History — 19th century 6. Eclecticism in art I. T.
NK7198.C36 M8613 1984    739.27/0945/632 19    LC 83-43257    ISBN 0847805271

**Wyler, Seymour B.**    • **1.6662**
The book of old silver: English, American, foreign / by Seymour B. Wyler; with all available hallmarks, including Shef field plate marks. — New York: Crown publishers, c1937. x, 447 p.: ill. 1. Plate 2. Hallmarks 3. Silverwork I. T.
NK7230 W9    NK7230 W9.    LC 37-24775

**Ogden, Jack.**    **1.6663**
Jewellery of the ancient world / Jack Ogden. — New York: Rizzoli, c1982. 185 p., 32 p. of plates: ill. (some col.); 26 cm. 1. Jewelry, Ancient I. T. II. Title: Jewelry of the ancient world.
NK7307.O34 1982    739.27/093 19    LC 82-60069    ISBN 0847804445

**Hinks, Peter.**    **1.6664**
Twentieth century British jewellery, 1900–1980 / Peter Hinks. — London; Boston: Faber and Faber, 1983. 192 p., [24] p. of plates: ill. (some col.); 26 cm. Includes index. 1. Jewelry — Great Britain — History — 20th century. I. T.
NK7343.H56 1983    739.27/0941 19    LC 83-5520    ISBN 0571108016

**Aldred, Cyril.**    **1.6665**
Jewels of the pharaohs; Egyptian jewelry of the dynastic period. Special photography in Cairo by Albert Shoucair. — New York: Praeger, [1971] 256 p.: illus. (part col.); 26 cm. 1. Jewelry, Egyptian. 2. Jewelry, Ancient I. T.
NK7388.A1 A7    739.27/0932    LC 72-108266

**Solodkoff, A. von.**    **1.6666**
Masterpieces from the House of Fabergé / Alexander von Solodkoff; with essays by Roy D.R. Betteley ... [et al.]; edited by Christopher Forbes. — New York: H.N. Abrams, 1984. 192 p.: ill. (some col.); 29 cm. Includes index. 1. Faberzhe (Firm) 2. Easter eggs — Russian S.F.S.R. 3. Goldwork — Russian S.F.S.R. 4. Jewelry — Russian S.F.S.R. I. Forbes, Christopher. II. Faberzhe (Firm) III. T.
NK7398.F33 S65 1984    739.2/092/4 19    LC 84-2779    ISBN 0810909332

**Yale University. Art Gallery.**    **1.6667**
The American clock, 1725–1865; the Mabel Brady Garvan and other collections at Yale University. Essay and technical notes by Edwin A. Battison. Commentary by Patricia E. Kane. Foreword by Charles F. Montgomery. Introd. by Derek de Solla Price. — Greenwich, Conn.: New York Graphic Society, [1973] 207 p.: illus.; 27 cm. 1. Yale University. Mabel Brady Garvan Collection. 2. Clocks and watches — United States. I. Battison, Edwin A. II. Kane, Patricia E. III. T.
NK7492.Y34 1973    681/.113/0973    LC 72-93856    ISBN 0821204939

**Museum of Fine Arts, Boston.**    **1.6668**
Greek, Etruscan, & Roman bronzes in the Museum of Fine Arts, Boston, by Mary Comstock & Cornelius Vermeule. [Boston]; distributed by New York Graphic Society, Greenwich, Conn. [1971] xxvi, 511 p. illus. 24 cm. 1. Bronzes — Greece 2. Bronzes — Italy — Etruria — Catalogs. 3. Bronzes — Rome — Catalogs. 4. Bronzes — Massachusetts — Boston — Catalogs. I. Comstock, Mary, 1934- II. Vermeule, Cornelius Clarkson, 1925- III. T.
NK7907.3.B6    733    LC 75-166291    ISBN 0878460608

**Kilbride-Jones, H. E.**    **1.6669**
Celtic craftsmanship in bronze / H. E. Kilbride–Jones. — New York: St. Martin's Press, 1980. 266 p.: ill.; 25 cm. 1. Bronzes, Celtic — Great Britain. 2. Bronzes — Great Britain. 3. Bronzes, Celtic — Ireland. 4. Bronzes — Ireland. I. T.
NK7943.K54 1980    739/.512/0899160941    LC 80-10520    ISBN 0312126980

**The Chinese bronzes of Yunnan / foreword by Jessica Rawson.**    **1.6670**
London: Sidgwick and Jackson, in association with Cultural Relics Pub. House, Beijing, c1984, [c1983]. 261 p.: col. ill. — (Bowater library of Chinese civilization.) 1. Bronzes, Chinese — China — Yunnan (Province). 2. Yunnan Province (China) — Antiquities. I. Rawson, Jessica. II. Series.
NK7983.A3 Y86    739.512095135    ISBN 0283988924

**The Great Bronze Age of China: a symposium / George**    **1.6671**
**Kuwayama, editor.**
Los Angeles, Calif.: Los Angeles County Museum of Art; Seattle: Distributed by University of Washington Press, c1983. 136 p.: ill.; 28 cm. Held May 23-24, 1981. 1. Bronzes, Chinese — To 221 B.C. — Congresses. 2. China — Antiquities — Congresses. 3. China — History — To 221 B.C. — Congresses. I. Kuwayama, George. II. Los Angeles County Museum of Art.
NK7983.22.G73 1983    730/.0931 19    LC 83-9393    ISBN 0875871135

**Metropolitan Museum of Art (New York, N.Y.)**          **1.6672**
The great bronze age of China: an exhibition from the People's Republic of
China / edited by Wen Fong; introductory essays by Ma Chengyuan ... [et al.];
catalogue edited by Robert W. Bagley, Jenny F. So, Maxwell K. Hearn. — New York:
Metropolitan Museum of Art, c1980. xv, 386 p.: ill. (some col.), fold. map
(inserted); 31 cm. Catalogue of an exhibition to be held at the Metropolitan
Museum of Art, New York, and at four other cities during the period,
1980-1981. 1. Bronzes, Chinese — To 221 B.C. — Exhibitions. 2. Bronzes,
Chinese — Ch'in-Han dynasties, 221 B.C.-220 A.D. — Exhibitions. 3. Terra-
cotta sculpture, Chinese — Ch'in-Han dynasties, 221 B.C.-220 A.D. —
Exhibitions. I. Fong, Wen. II. Bagley, Robert W. III. So, Jenny F.
IV. Hearn, Maxwell K. V. T.
NK7983.22.N48 1980        730/.0951/074013        LC 79-27616        ISBN
0870992260

**Montgomery, Charles F.**          **1.6673**
A history of American pewter / Charles F. Montgomery. — Rev. and enl. ed.
— New York: Dutton, c1978. 307 p.: ill.; 26 cm. — (A Winterthur book)
Includes index. 1. Pewter — United States. I. T.
NK8412.M66 1978        739.533 M.        739/.533/0973        LC 77-77937
ISBN 0525474676

## NK8800–9499 TEXTILES. LACE

**Flemming, Ernst Richard, b. 1866.**          • **1.6674**
An encyclopaedia of textiles from the earliest times to the beginning of the 19th
century / with an introduction by Ernst Flemming. — New York: E. Weyhe,
1927. xxxviii, 320 p.: ill.; 32 x 25 cm. 1. Textile fabrics I. T.
NK8804.F5

**Sieber, Roy, 1923-.**          **1.6675**
African textiles and decorative arts. New York, Museum of Modern Art;
distributed by New York Graphic Society, Greenwich, Conn. [1972] 239 p.
illus. (part col.) 29 cm. Issued in connection with the exhibition to be held at the
Museum of Modern Art, New York, Oct. 11, 1972-Jan. 31, 1973, the Los
Angeles County Museum of Art, March 20-May 31, 1973, the M. H. de Young
Memorial Museum, San Francisco, July 2-Aug. 31, 1973, and the Cleveland
Museum of Art, Oct 3-Dec. 2, 1973. 1. Textile industry and fabrics, African.
2. Decoration and ornament — Africa. I. Museum of Modern Art (New York,
N.Y.) II. T.
NK8887.S53 1972        745/.0967        LC 72-76268        ISBN 0870702289
ISBN 0870702270

**Parry, Linda.**          **1.6676**
William Morris textiles / Linda Parry. — New York: Viking Press, c1983.
192 p.: ill. (some col.); 29 cm. — (A Studio book) 1. Morris, William,
1834-1896. 2. Textile fabrics — England — History — 19th century. I. T.
NK8898.M67 P37 1983        747.22 19        LC 82-70184        ISBN
0670770752

**Geijer, Agnes.**          **1.6677**
A history of textile art / Agnes Geijer. — London: Pasold Research Fund in
association with Sotheby Parke Bernet; Totowa, N.J.: distributed by Biblio
Distribution Center, 1979. xi, 317 p., [48] leaves of plates: ill.; 22 cm. Rev.
translation of the 1972 ed. published under title: Ur textilkonstens historia.
Includes index. 1. Textile fabrics — History. I. T.
NK8906.G413 1979        677/.009        LC 80-453993        ISBN 0856670553

**Noma, Seiroku.**          **1.6678**
[Kosode to Nō ishō. English] Japanese costume and textile arts / by Seiroku
Noma; translated by Armins Nikovskis. — 1st English ed. — New York;
Weatherhill, 1974. 168 p., [1] fold. leaf of plates: ill. (some col.); 24 cm. — (The
Heibonsha survey of Japanese art; v. 16) Translation of Kosode to Nō ishō.
1. Textile fabrics — Japan 2. Costume — Japan I. T. II. Series.
NK8984.A1 N6513        746.9/2        LC 74-76781        ISBN 0834810263

**Levey, Santina M.**          **1.6679**
Lace: a history / Santina M. Levey. — [London]: Victoria & Albert Museum;
Leeds: W.S. Maney, 1983. 140 p., [360] p. of plates: ill.; 34 cm. Includes index.
1. Lace and lace making — History. I. Victoria and Albert Museum. II. T.
NK9406.L48 1983        746.2/2/094 19        LC 84-209711        ISBN
090128615X

# NX THE ARTS IN GENERAL

**The Language of images / edited by W. J. T. Mitchell.**          **1.6680**
Chicago: University of Chicago Press, c1980. 307 p.: ill.; 23 cm. — (A Phoenix
book) 1. Arts — Addresses, essays, lectures. I. Mitchell, W. J. Thomas, 1942-
NX60.L33        700 19        LC 80-5225        ISBN 0226532151

**Barthes, Roland.**          **1.6681**
A Barthes reader / edited, and with an introd. by Susan Sontag. — New York:
Hill and Wang, c1982. xxxviii, 495 p.; 22 cm. 1. Arts — Addresses, essays,
lectures. I. Sontag, Susan, 1933- II. T.
NX65.B37 1982        700 19        LC 80-26762        ISBN 0809028158

**Bronowski, Jacob, 1908-1974.**          **1.6682**
The visionary eye: essays in the arts, literature, and science / J. Bronowski;
selected and edited by Piero E. Ariotti in collaboration with Rita Bronowski. —
Cambridge, Mass.: MIT Press, c1978. x, 185 p.: ill.; 24 cm. Includes index.
1. Arts — Addresses, essays, lectures. 2. Science and the arts — Addresses,
essays, lectures. 3. Imagination — Addresses, essays, lectures. I. Ariotti, Piero
E. II. Bronowski, Rita. III. T.
NX65.B696 1978        700        LC 78-18163        ISBN 0262021293

**Montale, Eugenio, 1896-.**          **1.6683**
The second life of art: selected essays of Eugenio Montale / edited and
translated by Jonathan Galassi. — 1st ed. — New York: Ecco Press, 1982. xxx,
354 p.; 25 cm. Includes index. 1. Arts — Addresses, essays, lectures.
I. Galassi, Jonathan. II. T.
NX65.M65 1982        700 19        LC 81-9861        ISBN 0912946849

**Wackenroder, Wilhelm Heinrich, 1773-1798.**          **1.6684**
Confessions and Fantasies / Wilhelm Heinrich Wackenroder; translated and
annotated with a critical introduction by Mary Hurst Schubert. — University
Park: Pennsylvania State University Press, c1971. 219 p.: ill. Translation of
Herzensergiessungen eines kunstliebenden Klosterbruders and the essays by
W.H. Wackenroder in Phantasien über die Kunst für Freunde der Kunst.
1. The arts — Addresses, essays, lectures. I. Wackenroder, Wilhelm Heinrich,
1773-1798. Phantasien über die Kunst für Freunde der Kunst. English.
Selections, 1971. II. T.
NX65.W213        838.8        LC 73-136958        ISBN 0027111505

**The Arts and cognition / edited by David Perkins and Barbara**          **1.6685**
**Leondar.**
Baltimore: Johns Hopkins University Press, c1977. viii, 341 p.: ill.; 24 cm.
1. Arts — Psychological aspects — Addresses, essays, lectures. 2. Cognition
— Psychology — Addresses, essays, lectures. I. Perkins, David. II. Leondar,
Barbara.
NX165.A79        700/.1        LC 76-17237        ISBN 0801818435

**Jencks, Charles, 1939-.**          **1.6686**
Adhocism: the case for improvisation. 1st ed. Garden City: Anchor Books,
1973, c1972. 216p. 1. Arts — Psychology 2. Creation (Literary, artistic, etc.)
3. Functionalism in art I. Silver, Nathan, 1936- II. T.
NX165.J4 J46        LC 73-331306        ISBN 0385017111

**Vygotskiĭ, L. S. (Lev Semenovich), 1896-1934.**          **1.6687**
[Psikhologiia iskusstva. English] The psychology of art [by] Lev Semenovich
Vygotsky. Introd. by A. N. Leontiev. Commentary by V. V. Ivanov.
[Translated from the Russian by Scripta Technica] Cambridge, Mass., M.I.T.
Press [1971] xi, 305 p. 24 cm. Translation of Psikhologiia iskusstva. 1. Arts —
Psychological aspects. I. T.
NX165.V913        701.15        LC 74-103904        ISBN 026222013X

**Winner, Ellen.**          **1.6688**
Invented worlds: the psychology of the arts / Ellen Winner. — Cambridge,
Mass.: Harvard University Press, 1982. xvi, 431 p.: ill.; 26 cm. Includes index.
1. Arts — Psychological aspects. I. T.
NX165.W5 1982        700/.1/9 19        LC 82-1020        ISBN 0674463609

**Lauter, Estella, 1940-.**          **1.6689**
Women as mythmakers: poetry and visual art by twentieth–century women /
Estella Lauter. — Bloomington: Indiana University Press, c1984. xvii, 267 p.:
ill.; 24 cm. Includes index. 1. Feminism and the arts 2. Women artists
3. Women poets 4. Art and mythology I. T.
NX180.F4 L38 1984        700/.88042 19        LC 83-48636        ISBN
0253366062

**Hauser, Arnold, 1892-1978.**          **1.6690**
[Soziologie der Kunst. English] The sociology of art / Arnold Hauser;
translated by Kenneth J. Northcott. — Chicago: University of Chicago Press,

1982. xxi, 776 p.; 24 cm. Translation of: Soziologie der Kunst. 1. Arts and society I. T.
NX180.S6 H3413 1982      700/.1/03 19      LC 81-13098      ISBN 0226319490

**Hillier, Bevis, 1940-.**                                                        **1.6691**
The style of the century, 1900–1980 / Bevis Hillier. — 1st ed. — New York: Dutton, 1983. 239 p.: ill. (some col.); 26 cm. Includes index. 1. Popular culture — History — 20th century. 2. Arts, Modern — 20th century 3. Civilization, Modern — 20th century I. T.
NX180.S6 H5 1983      700/.9/04 19      LC 83-71008      ISBN 0525933018

**Krueger, Myron W.**                                                             **1.6692**
Artificial reality / Myron W. Krueger. — Reading, Mass.: Addison-Wesley, c1983. xviii, 312 p.: ill.; 24 cm. 1. Technology and the arts 2. Man-machine systems 3. Avant-garde (Aesthetics) I. T.
NX180.T4 K7 1983      700/.1/05 19      LC 82-3897      ISBN 0201047659

**Changing concepts of art / editors, Raphael Stern and Esther**                 **1.6693**
**Robison.**
New York: Haven Publications, c1983. 738 p.: ill.; 25 cm. 1. Photography of art I. Stern, Raphael.
NX200.C432 1983      ISBN 0930586190

**The arts, cognition, and basic skills / Stanley S. Madeja, editor.**           **1.6694**
St. Louis, Mo.: CEMREL, c1978. 263 p.: ill.; 24 cm. — (Yearbook on research in arts and aesthetic education. 2) 'Based on a conference held at Aspen, Colorado, June 19-25, 1977. Co-sponsored by CEMREL, Inc., and The Education Program of the Aspen Institute for Humanistic Studies, with support from The National Institute of Education.' 1. Arts — Study and teaching — Congresses. 2. Cognition — Congresses. 3. Aesthetics — Congresses. I. Madeja, Stanley S. II. Central Midwestern Regional Educational Laboratory. III. Aspen Institute for Humanistic Studies. Education Program. IV. Series.
NX282.A772      LC 78-57674

**Goodlad, John I.**                                                              **1.6695**
Arts and the schools / John I. Goodlad ... [et al.]; Jerome J. Hausman, editor, assisted by Joyce Wright. — New York: McGraw-Hill, c1981. xvii, 332 p.: ill.; 24 cm. — (A Study of schooling in the United States) Includes index. 1. Arts — Study and teaching — United States. 2. Arts and society — United States. I. Hausman, Jerome J. II. T.
NX304.A1 A77      375/.7      LC 80-10208      ISBN 0070272255

# NX440–600 History

**Paxton, John.**                                                                 **1.6696**
Calendar of creative man / John Paxton and Sheila Fairfield. — New York, N.Y.: Facts on File, 1980, c1979. xxviii, 497 p.: ill.; 29 cm. 1. Arts — History — Chronology. I. Fairfield, Sheila. joint author. II. T.
NX447.5.P38      700/.9 19      LC 80-131977      ISBN 0871964708

## NX448–458 BY PERIOD

**Pater, Walter, 1839-1894.**                                                     **1.6697**
The Renaissance: studies in art and poetry: the 1893 text / Walter Pater; edited, with textual and explanatory notes, by Donald L. Hill. — Berkeley: University of California Press, c1980. xxv, 489 p., [8] leaves of plates: ill.; 23 cm. 1. Arts, Renaissance I. Hill, Donald L. II. T.
NX450.5.P37 1980      700/.94 19      LC 76-24582      ISBN 0520033256

**Ashton, Dore.**                                                                 **1.6698**
A fable of modern art / Dore Ashton. — New York: Thames and Hudson, 1980. 128 p., [16] leaves of plates: ill.; 25 cm. Includes index. 1. Balzac, Honoré de, 1799-1850 Le chef-d'oeuvre inconnu — Influence. 2. Arts, Modern — 20th century 3. Nature (Aesthetics) 4. Arts, Modern — 19th century I. T.
NX454.A8 1980      700/.9/04 19      LC 79-66137      ISBN 0500233012

**Greenberg, Clement, 1909-.**                                                  • **1.6699**
Art and culture: critical essays / Clement Greenberg. — Boston: Beacon Press, [1984?], c1961. x, 278 p.; 21 cm. (Beacon paperback; 212) Includes index. 1. Arts, Modern — 19th century — Addresses, essays, lectures. 2. Arts, Modern — 20th century — Addresses, essays, lectures. I. T.
NX454.G73 1984      700/.9/04 19      LC 84-12354      ISBN 0807066818

**Jullian, Philippe.**                                                            **1.6700**
[Esthètes et magiciens. English] Dreamers of decadence; symbolist painters of the 1890s. [Translated by Robert Baldick] New York, Praeger 1974. 272 p. illus. (part col.) 26 cm. Translation of Esthètes et magiciens. 1. Arts 2. Art nouveau I. T.
NX454.J813      759.05      LC 77-147094

**Poggioli, Renato, 1907-1963.**                                                • **1.6701**
[Teoria dell'arte d'avanguardia. English] The theory of the avant–garde. Translated from the Italian by Gerald Fitzgerald. Cambridge, Mass., Belknap Press of Harvard University Press, 1968. xvii, 250 p. 21 cm. Translation of Teoria dell'arte d'avanguardia. 1. Arts — History 2. Avant-garde (Aesthetics) I. T. II. Title: Avant-garde.
NX456.P613      709.04      LC 68-17630

**Art after modernism: rethinking representation / edited and**                   **1.6702**
**with an introduction by Brian Wallis; foreword by Marcia**
**Tucker.**
New York: New Museum of Contemporary Art; Boston: D.R. Godine, 1984. xviii, 461 p.: ill.; 25 cm. (Documentary sources in contemporary art.) Includes index. 1. Postmodernism — Addresses, essays, lectures. 2. Arts, Modern — 20th century — Addresses, essays, lectures. I. Wallis, Brian, 1953- II. Series.
NX456.5.P66 A74 1984      700/.9/04 19      LC 84-22708      ISBN 0879235632

**Butler, Christopher.**                                                          **1.6703**
After the wake: an essay on the contemporary avant–garde / Christopher Butler. — Oxford: Clarendon Press; New York: Oxford University Press, 1980. xi, 177 p., [8] p. of plates: ill.; 23 cm. 1. Avant-garde (Aesthetics) 2. Arts, Modern — 20th century I. T.
NX458.B87      700/.9/04 19      LC 79-41663      ISBN 0198157665

**Davis, Douglas, 1933-.**                                                        **1.6704**
Artculture: essays on the post–modern / Douglas Davis; introd. by Irving Sandler. — 1st ed. — New York: Harper & Row, c1977. xii, 176 p.: ill.; 23 cm. — (Icon editions) 1. Arts, Modern — 20th century 2. Avant-garde (Aesthetics) I. T.
NX458.D38 1977      700/.9/04      LC 76-27504      ISBN 0064310000

## NX501–596 BY COUNTRY

**Kouwenhoven, John Atlee, 1909-.**                                              **1.6705**
Half a truth is better than none: some unsystematic conjectures about art, disorder, and American experience / John A. Kouwenhoven. — Chicago: University of Chicago Press, 1982. xiii, 248 p.: ill.; 24 cm. Errata slip inserted. 1. United States — Popular culture — Addresses, essays, lectures. I. T.
NX503.K67 1982      700/.973 19      LC 81-24051      ISBN 0226451550

**Silverman, Kenneth.**                                                           **1.6706**
A cultural history of the American Revolution: painting, music, literature, and the theatre in the Colonies and the United States from the Treaty of Paris to the Inauguration of George Washington, 1763–1789 / Kenneth Silverman. — New York: T. Y. Crowell, c1976. xvii, 699 p.: ill.; 24 cm. 1. Arts, American 2. Arts, Modern — 18th century — United States. 3. United States — History — Revolution, 1775-1783 — Art and the Revolution. I. T.
NX503.5.S54 1976      700/.974 19      LC 75-35947      ISBN 0690010796

**The Colonial revival in America / edited by Alan Axelrod.**                     **1.6707**
1st ed. — New York: Norton, c1985. x, 377 p.: ill.; 22 cm. 'Published for The Henry Francis du Pont Winterthur Museum. 1. Colonial revival (Art) 2. Arts, Modern — 19th century — United States I. Axelrod, Alan, 1952- II. Henry Francis du Pont Winterthur Museum.
NX503.7.C64 1985      700/.973 19      LC 84-1092      ISBN 039301942X

**Haskell, Barbara.**                                                             **1.6708**
Blam! the explosion of pop, minimalism, and performance, 1958–1964 / Barbara Haskell; with an essay on the American independent cinema by John G. Hanhardt. — New York: Whitney Museum of American Art in association with W.W. Norton & Co., c1984. 160 p.: ill.; 28 cm. Published in connection with an exhibition held at the Whitney Museum, Sept. 20-Dec. 2, 1984. 1. Arts, American — Exhibitions. 2. Avant-garde (Aesthetics) — United States — History — 20th century — Exhibitions. I. Hanhardt, John G. II. Whitney Museum of American Art. III. T.
NX504.H36 1984      700/.973/07401471 19      LC 84-7304      ISBN 0874270006

**The Harlem Renaissance: a historical dictionary for the era /**                 **1.6709**
**edited by Bruce Kellner.**
Westport, Conn.: Greenwood Press, 1984. xliii, 476 p.: ill.; 24 cm. Includes index. 1. Afro-American arts — New York (N.Y.) — Dictionaries. 2. Harlem Renaissance — Dictionaries. I. Kellner, Bruce.
NX511.N4 H37 1984      700/.899607307471 19      LC 83-22687      ISBN 0313232326

**Lewis, David L.**                                                              **1.6710**
When Harlem was in vogue / David Levering Lewis. — 1st ed. — New York:
Knopf: distributed by Random House, 1981. xiv, 381 p., [16] leaves of plates:
ill.; 24 cm. 1. Afro-American arts — New York (N.Y.) 2. Arts, Modern —
20th century — New York (N.Y.) 3. Harlem Renaissance 4. Harlem (New
York, N.Y.). I. T.
NX511.N4 L48 1981     NX511N4 L48 1981.      700/.899607307471 19
    LC 80-2704     ISBN 0394495721

**Locke, Alain LeRoy, 1886-1954.**                                              **1.6711**
The critical temper of Alain Locke: a selection of his essays on art and culture /
[edited by] Jeffrey C. Stewart. — New York: Garland Pub., 1983. xx, 491 p.: ill.;
29 cm. — (Critical studies on Black life and culture. v. 8) Includes index.
1. Afro-American arts — Addresses, essays, lectures. I. Stewart, Jeffrey C.,
1950- II. T. III. Series.
NX512.3.A35 L62 1983     700/.8996073 19      LC 80-9046     ISBN
0824093186

**Butcher, Margaret Just, 1913-.**                                              **1.6712**
The Negro in American culture / based on materials left by Alain Locke. — 2d
ed. New York: Knopf, 1972 [c1971] x, 313, xiv p.; 23 cm. (Borzoi books)
1. Negro arts — U.S. 2. Afro-American arts I. T.
NX512.3 N5 B8 1972     NX512.3.N5 B8 1972.     700/.8996073 19
    LC 74-38321     ISBN 0394479432

**Gayle, Addison, 1932- comp.**                                                 **1.6713**
The Black aesthetic. [1st ed.] Garden City, N.Y., Doubleday, 1971. xxiv, 432 p.
22 cm. 1. Afro-American arts I. T.
NX512.3.N5 G38     709.73     LC 71-123692

**Huggins, Nathan Irvin, 1927-.**                                             • **1.6714**
Harlem renaissance. New York, Oxford University Press, 1971. xi, 343 p. illus.,
ports. 22 cm. 1. Afro-American arts — New York (N.Y.) 2. Arts, Modern —
20th century — New York (N.Y.) 3. Harlem Renaissance I. T.
NX512.3.N5 H8     700/.97471     LC 70-159646     ISBN 0195014561

**The Mind and art of Victorian England / edited by Josef L.**                  **1.6715**
**Altholz.**
Minneapolis: University of Minnesota Press, c1976. vii, 206 p., [18] leaves of
plates: ill. (some col.); 24 cm. Includes index. 1. Arts, Victorian — England —
Addresses, essays, lectures. 2. Arts, English — Addresses, essays, lectures.
I. Altholz, Josef Lewis, 1933-
NX543.A1 M55 1976     700/.942     LC 75-22686     ISBN 0816607729

**Meisel, Martin.**                                                             **1.6716**
Realizations: narrative, pictorial, and theatrical arts in nineteenth–century
England / Martin Meisel. — Princeton, N.J.: Princeton University Press,
c1983. xix, 471 p.: ill.; 29 cm. Includes index. 1. Arts, English — Addresses,
essays, lectures. 2. Arts, Modern — 19th century — England — Addresses,
essays, lectures. I. T.
NX543.M4 1983     700/.942 19     LC 82-12292     ISBN 0691065535

**Pre–Raphaelitism: a collection of critical essays / edited and**             **1.6717**
**with an introd. by James Sambrook.**
Chicago: University of Chicago Press, 1974. 277 p.; 24 cm. — (Patterns of
literary criticism; [12]) Includes index. 1. Preraphaelitism — Great Britain —
Addresses, essays, lectures. 2. Arts, English — Addresses, essays, lectures.
3. Arts, Modern — 19th century — England — Addresses, essays, lectures.
I. Sambrook, James.
NX543.P73     700/.942     LC 73-89790     ISBN 0226734528

**Riede, David G.**                                                             **1.6718**
Dante Gabriel Rossetti and the limits of Victorian vision / David G. Riede. —
Ithaca: Cornell University Press, 1983. 288 p.: ill.; 24 cm. 1. Rossetti, Dante
Gabriel, 1828-1882. 2. Rossetti, Dante Gabriel, 1828-1882 — Criticism and
interpretation. I. T.
NX547.6.R67 R53 1983     821/.8 19     LC 82-22099     ISBN
0801415527

**Jullian, Philippe.**                                                          **1.6719**
The symbolists. [Translated by Mary Anne Stevens. — New York]: Phaidon;
[distributed by Praeger Publishers, 1973] 240 p.: illus. (part col.); 29 cm.
1. Symbolism (Art movement) — France. 2. Arts, Modern — 19th century —
France. 3. Symbolism (Art movement) — Belgium. 4. Arts, Modern — 19th
century — Belgium. I. T.
NX549.A1 J8413     760/.0944     LC 72-89483     ISBN 071481590X

**Goncourt, Edmond de, 1822-1896.**                                             **1.6720**
[Journal des Goncourt. English. Selections] Paris and the arts, 1851–1896; from
the Goncourt Journal. Edited and translated by George J. Becker and Edith
Philips. With an afterword on Japanese art and influence by Hedley H. Rhys.
Ithaca [N.Y.] Cornell University Press [1971] vi, 374 p. illus., ports. 22 cm.
Translation of selections from Journal des Goncourt. 1. Arts — France —

Paris. I. Goncourt, Jules de, 1830-1870. joint author. II. Becker, George
Joseph. ed. III. Philips, Edith, ed. IV. T.
NX549.P3 A2513 1971     709/.4436     LC 72-161309     ISBN
0801406552

**Art and culture in nineteenth–century Russia / edited by**                    **1.6721**
**Theofanis George Stavrou.**
Bloomington: Indiana University Press, c1983. xix, 268 p., [47] p. of plates: ill.;
25 cm. 'Result of two scholarly projects, a lecture series and a symposium,
which were held at the University of Minnesota in the fall of 1978 ... organized
by the University of Minnesota Gallery with the Committee on Institutional
cooperation and the Ministry of Culture of the U.S.S.R.'—Pref. 1. Arts,
Russian — Addresses, essays, lectures. 2. Arts, Modern — 19th century —
Soviet Union — Addresses, essays, lectures. 3. Arts and society — Soviet
Union — History — 19th century — Addresses, essays, lectures.
4. Nationalism and art — Soviet Union — Addresses, essays, lectures.
I. Stavrou, Theofanis George, 1934- II. University of Minnesota. University
Gallery. III. Committee on Institutional Cooperation. IV. Soviet Union.
Ministerstvo kul'tury.
NX556.A1 A74 1983     700/.947 19     LC 81-48634     ISBN
0253310512

**Sheppard, Mubin, Tan Sri Datuk, 1905-.**                                      **1.6722**
Taman indera: a royal pleasure ground; Malay decorative arts and pastimes.
Kuala Lumpur, Oxford University Press, 1972. xvii, 207 p. illus. 29 cm.
1. Arts, Malay. I. T.
NX579.A3 M397     700/.9595/1 19     LC 72-170622

**Chinese literature for the 1980s: the Fourth Congress of Writers**            **1.6723**
**& Artists / edited with an introduction by Howard Goldblatt.**
Armonk, N.Y.: M.E. Sharpe, c1982. xviii, 175 p.: ports.; 24 cm. Compilation of
14 articles on the Fourth Congresses and 2 articles on the Third Congress
translated from various sources by different translators. 1. Arts — China —
Congresses. I. Goldblatt, Howard, 1939- II. Chung-kuo wen hsüeh i shu kung
tso che tai piao ta hui (4th: 1979: Peking, China)
NX583.A1 C4524 1982     700/.951 19     LC 82-744     ISBN
0873322088

**Popular Chinese literature and performing arts in the People's**              **1.6724**
**Republic of China, 1949–1979 / edited by Bonnie S.**
**McDougall; contributors, Paul Clark ... [et al.].**
Berkeley: University of California Press, c1984. xvi, 341 p.: music; 24 cm.
(Studies on China. 2) Based on papers presented at a workshop held at Harvard
University, June 1979. Includes index. 1. Arts, Chinese — 20th century —
Addresses, essays, lectures. I. McDougall, Bonnie S., 1941- II. Clark, Paul,
1949- III. Series.
NX583.A1 P66 1984     790.2/0951 19     LC 82-21942     ISBN
0520048520

**Theories of the arts in China / edited by Susan Bush and**                    **1.6725**
**Christian Murck.**
Princeton, N.J.: Princeton University Press, c1983. xxvi, 447 p.: ill.; 26 cm.
Papers presented at a conference sponsored by the Committee on Studies of
Chinese Civilization of the American Council of Learned Societies held June
6-June 12, 1979, at the Breckinridge Public Affairs Center of Bowdoin College,
York, Maine. 1. Arts, Chinese — Congresses. I. Bush, Susan. II. Murck,
Christian F. III. American Council of Learned Societies. Committee on
Studies of Chinese Civilization.
NX583.A1 T48 1983     700/.1 19     LC 83-42551     ISBN 0691040206

**Hempel, Rose.**                                                               **1.6726**
[Japan zur Heian Zeit. English] The golden age of Japan, 794–1192 / Rose
Hempel; translated by Katherine Watson. — New York: Rizzoli, 1983. 252 p.:
ill. (some col.); 29 cm. Translation of: Japan zur Heian Zeit. Includes index.
1. Arts, Japanese — Heian period, 794-1185 2. Arts, Buddhist — Japan.
3. Japan — History — Heian period, 794-1185 I. T.
NX584.A1 H4513 1983     700/.952 19     LC 83-42924     ISBN
0847804925

**Thompson, Robert Farris.**                                                    **1.6727**
African art in motion; icon and act in the Collection of Katherine Coryton
White. [Catalog of an exhibition] National Gallery of Art, Washington, D.C.;
Frederick S. Wight Art Gallery, University of California, Los Angeles. Los
Angeles, University of California Press [1974] xv, 275 p. illus. (part col.) 28 cm.
1. White, Katherine Coryton — Art collections. 2. Arts, African —
Exhibitions. 3. Arts — Africa, Sub-Saharan. I. National Gallery of Art (U.S.)
II. Frederick S. Wight Art Gallery. III. T.
NX588.75.T47     709/.67     LC 73-91679     ISBN 0520026853 ISBN
0520027035

**The Traditional artist in African societies. Warren L.**                      **1.6728**
**d'Azevedo, editor.**
Bloomington, Indiana University Press [1973] xxi, 454 p. illus. 25 cm. Erratum
slip inserted. 1. Arts, Black — Africa, West. I. D'Azevedo, Warren L. ed.
NX589.T72     700/.966     LC 79-160126     ISBN 0253399017

**Serle, Geoffrey.**      **1.6729**
From deserts the prophets come: the creative spirit in Australia 1788–1972 [by] Geoffrey Serle. — Melbourne: Heinemann, 1973. xii, 274 p.; 23 cm. Index. 1. Arts, Australian — History. I. T.
NX590.A1 S47     700/.994     *LC* 72-97325     *ISBN* 0855610298

## NX600 By Movement, A–Z

**Battcock, Gregory, 1937- comp.**      **1.6730**
Idea art; a critical anthology. — [1st ed.]. — New York: Dutton, 1973. xii, 203 p.: illus.; 19 cm. 1. Conceptual art — Addresses, essays, lectures. I. T.
NX600.C6 B37 1973     709/.04     *LC* 73-174858     *ISBN* 0525473440

**Ball, Hugo, 1886-1927.**      **1.6731**
[Flucht aus der Zeit. English] Flight out of time: a Dada diary / by Hugo Ball; edited with an introd., notes, and bibliography by John Elderfield; translated by Ann Raimes. — New York: Viking Press, 1974. lxiv, 254 p., [6] leaves of plates: ill.; 22 cm. — (The Documents of 20th-century art) Translation of Die Flucht aus der Zeit. Includes index. 1. Dadaism — History — Sources. I. T. II. Series.
NX600.D3 B3413 1974     838/.9/1203 B     *LC* 72-75755     *ISBN* 0670318418

**Bigsby, C. W. E.**      **1.6732**
Dada & Surrealism [by] C. W. E. Bigsby. — [London]: Methuen [Distributed in the U.S.A. by Barnes and Noble, 1972] 91 p.; 20 cm. — (The Critical idiom, 23) 1. Dadaism 2. Surrealism I. T.
NX600.D3 B54     700/.9/04     *LC* 72-188395     *ISBN* 0416081509

**Huelsenbeck, Richard, 1892-1974.**      **1.6733**
Memoirs of a Dada drummer / by Richard Huelsenbeck; edited, with an introd., notes, and bibliography, by Hans J. Kleinschmidt; translated by Joachim Neugroschel. — New York: Viking Press, 1974. L, 202 p., [6] leaves of plates: ill.; 22 cm. (The Documents of 20th-century art) 'The major portion of the text ... is a translation ... of ... Mit Witz, Licht und Grütze.' Includes index. 1. Dadaism — Addresses, essays, lectures. 2. Arts, Modern — 20th century — Addresses, essays, lectures. I. T. II. Series.
NX600.D3 H79 1974     709/.04     *LC* 73-380     *ISBN* 067046791X

**Apollonio, Umbro, 1911- comp.**      **1.6734**
[Futurismo. English] Futurist manifestos / edited and with an introd. by Umbro Apollonio; translations by Robert Brain ... [et al.]. — New York: Viking Press, 1973. 232 p.: ill. (some col.); 22 cm. — (The Documents of 20th-century art) Translation of Futurismo. Includes index. 1. Futurism (Art) — Addresses, essays, lectures. 2. Arts, Modern — 20th century — Addresses, essays, lectures. I. T. II. Series.
NX600.F8 A6513 1973b     700/.9/04     *LC* 72-89124     *ISBN* 0670019666

**Marinetti, Filippo Tommaso, 1876-1944.**      • **1.6735**
Marinetti; selected writings. Edited, and with an introd., by R. W. Flint. Translated by R. W. Flint and Arthur A. Coppotelli. — New York: Farrar, Straus and Giroux, [1972] 366 p.: illus.; 24 cm. Includes selections from the author's Futurist theory and invention, The untamables, and Futurist memoirs. 1. Futurism (Art) — Addresses, essays, lectures. I. Flint, R. W., ed. II. T.
NX600.F8 M37 1972     700/.9/04     *LC* 71-189338     *ISBN* 0374202907

**Clark, Kenneth, 1903-.**      **1.6736**
The romantic rebellion: romantic versus classic art / Kenneth Clark. — 1st U. S. ed. — New York: Harper & Row, c1973. 366 p.: 278 ill. (part col.); 26 cm. 1. Romanticism in art 2. Classicism in art 3. Art, Modern — 19th century — History I. T.
NX600.R6 C5     N6465.R6 C55 1973b.     759.05     *LC* 72-9751     *ISBN* 0060108029

**Honour, Hugh.**      **1.6737**
Romanticism / by Hugh Honour. — 1st U.S. ed. — New York: Harper & Row, c1979. 415 p.: ill.; 24 cm. — (Icon editions) Includes index. 1. Romanticism in art 2. Arts, Modern — 19th century I. T.
NX600.R6 H66 1979     700/.9/034     *LC* 78-2146     *ISBN* 0064333361

**The Autobiography of surrealism / edited by Marcel Jean.**      **1.6738**
New York: Viking Press, 1980. xxiii, 472 p.; ill.; 25 cm. — (The Documents of 20th century art) Includes index. 1. Surrealism — Addresses, essays, lectures.

2. Arts, Modern — 20th century — Addresses, essays, lectures. I. Jean, Marcel.
NX600.S9 A95 1980     700/.9/04     *LC* 76-46637     *ISBN* 0670142352

**Duplessis, Yvonne, 1912-.**      • **1.6739**
[Surréalisme. English] Surrealism, by Yves [sic] Duplessis. Translated by Paul Capon. — New York: Walker, [1963, c1962] 158 p.; 21 cm. — (A Sun book, SB-8. Literature and the arts) 1. Surrealism 2. Arts, Modern — 20th century I. T.
NX600.S9 D8413 1963     700/.9/04     *LC* 62-12752

**Lippard, Lucy R. comp.**      • **1.6740**
Surrealists on art. Edited by Lucy R. Lippard. — Englewood Cliffs, N.J.: Prentice-Hall, [1970] x, 213 p.; 21 cm. — (A Spectrum book) 1. Surrealism I. T.
NX600.S9 L5     709/.04     *LC* 78-104858     *ISBN* 0138780900

## NX650–694 Special Topics

**Webb, Peter, 1941-.**      **1.6741**
The erotic arts / Peter Webb. — Rev. ed. — New York: Farrar, Straus, Giroux, 1983. xxix, 569 p.: ill.; 25 cm. Includes index. 1. Erotica 2. Arts I. T.
NX650.E7 W4 1983     700 19     *LC* 83-8896     *ISBN* 0374148635

**Stanford, William Bedell.**      **1.6742**
The quest for Ulysses [by] W. B. Stanford and J. V. Luce. New York, Praeger [1974] 256 p. illus. 26 cm. 1. Odysseus (Greek mythology) — Art. I. Luce, John Victor, 1920- joint author. II. T.
NX652.O3 S72     704.94/7     *LC* 70-154604     *ISBN* 027546560X

**Cummings, Mary.**      **1.6743**
The lives of the Buddha in the art and literature of Asia / Mary Cummings. — Ann Arbor: University of Michigan, Center for South and Southeast Asian studies, 1982. xiii, 225 p.: ill.; 23 cm. — (Michigan papers on South and Southeast Asia. no. 20) 1. Gautama Buddha — Art. 2. Arts, Buddhist — Asia. 3. Arts, Asian I. T. II. Series.
NX676.2.C86 1982     700/.95 19     *LC* 80-67341     *ISBN* 0891480234

**Krishna, the divine lover: myth and legend through Indian art / [created under the direction of Enrico Isacco, with the editorial supervision of Anna L. Dallapicolla, and contributions by Anna L. Dallapicolla ... [et al.]].**      **1.6744**
London: Serindia Publications; Boston: David R. Godine, c1982. 218 p.: ill. (some col.); 32 cm. Errata inserted. 1. Krishna (Hindu deity) in art — Addresses, essays, lectures. 2. Arts, Indic — Addresses, essays and lectures. 3. Mythology, Hindu — Addresses, essays, lectures. I. Isacco, Enrico. II. Dahmen-Dallapiccola, Anna Liberia.
NX680.3.K75 K75 1982     *LC* 82-83044     *ISBN* 0906026113

## NX700–820 Art Patronage

**Havens, Thomas R. H.**      **1.6745**
Artist and patron in postwar Japan: dance, music, theater, and the visual arts, 1955–1980 / Thomas R.H. Havens. — Princeton, N.J.: Princeton University Press, c1982. ix, 324 p.: ill.; 22 cm. Includes index. 1. Art patronage — Japan. 2. Arts, Japanese 3. Arts — Japan. I. T.
NX705.5.J3 H38 1982     700/.7952 19     *LC* 82-47598     *ISBN* 0691053634

**Guide to corporate giving 3 / edited by Robert A. Porter.**      **1.6746**
New York, NY: American Council for the Arts, c1983. xxiii, 567 p.; 29 cm. Rev. ed. of: Guide to corporate giving in the arts 2 / edited by Robert A. Porter. c1981. Includes indexes. 1. Art patronage — United States. 2. Corporations — United States — Charitable contributions. I. Porter, Robert. II. American Council for the Arts. III. Guide to corporate giving in the arts 2. IV. Title: Corporate giving 3.
NX711.U5 G8 1983     700/.79 19     *LC* 82-20732     *ISBN* 0915400391